CHOISEUL

Volume I

FATHER AND SON

1719–1754

Étienne-François, Duke de Choiseul, formerly
Count de Stainville, in earlier years.

CHOISEUL

Volume I

FATHER AND SON
1719–1754

by

ROHAN BUTLER

CLARENDON PRESS · OXFORD

1980

Oxford University Press, Walton Street, Oxford OX2 6DP

OXFORD LONDON GLASGOW
NEW YORK TORONTO MELBOURNE WELLINGTON
KUALA LUMPUR SINGAPORE JAKARTA HONG KONG TOKYO
DELHI BOMBAY CALCUTTA MADRAS KARACHI
NAIROBI DAR ES SALAAM CAPE TOWN

*Published in the United States
by Oxford University Press New York*

British Libraries Cataloguing Data

Butler, Rohan
Choiseul.
Vol. 1: Father and son, 1719–1754
1. Choiseul, Etienne François, *duc de*
2. Statesmen – France – Biography
944′.034′0924   DC135.C5   79–41033

ISBN 0–19–822509–1

Typeset by CCC, printed and bound in Great Britain
by William Clowes (Beccles) Limited, Beccles and London

TO
LUCY

PREFACE

WHEN I began to consider the political importance of the Duke de Choiseul in its personal and social context I was surprised to notice that the two most recent works covering this full range of biographical interest were a German opuscule from about a century ago and an English prize-essay – a good one – some forty years old. Recent years have indeed produced two shortish and attractive, if not invariably quite exact, studies in French; but I am less surprised than I was that there has hitherto been no comprehensive treatment of so prominent a figure in modern history.

The present volume covers the first half of Choiseul's life. One authority, who worked more than he published upon aspects of this statesman, the late Professor Pierre Muret, wrote a generation ago, 'Sur l'enfance et l'éducation de Choiseul il faut nous résigner à ne savoir presque rien.' Resignation sometimes comes hard and now we may know a little more, at least, about his early and formative years: something, for instance, of what they owed to the then first minister of France, the Cardinal Fleury. The long elusiveness of such circumstances suggests particular archival difficulties. First, though, one may mention some broader considerations.

Even today the writing of political history in France can remain appreciably political. This may be one reason why political history is often less professionally fashionable there than economic or social history, to which modern French historians have made such striking contributions. Political reservations have been especially applicable to Choiseul since the time, at least, of the French Revolution. In that undoing of the reign of Louis XVI it was understandable if its protagonists should tend to blame things off upon those under his predecessor, and pre-eminently upon Choiseul, conveniently just dead after having bestridden the later years of Louis XV. This hostile propaganda was grist to republican revolutionaries and latter-day patriots like Michelet in their Girondin denunciation of Austrian conspiracy against France. Michelet, arguably the worst of the great historians, wrote of Choiseul and his family, 'Le meilleur de leur patrimoine avait été la trahison'.

Any early reassessment of Choiseul was hardly in the interest of any particular faction in France. He remained an outstanding exponent of the old regime without having been one of its devoted apologists. His wife had written proudly of him: 'Ministre d'un Sultan, *il avoit été citoyen comme dans une République, et sujet comme dans une Monarchie.*' The main run of Choiseul's memoirs, written in injured eclipse and in caustic criticism of Louis XV and his evocative court, remained unpublished for over a century after the French Revolution. And for years after their publication, even, royalists figured not least among those seeking to discount the memoirs of Choiseul as largely apocryphal. Whereas, as I was able to verify and as is now generally recognized, the main narrative of the memoirs published in 1904 is in his own horrid hand.

All this may be one way of saying that the history of eighteenth-century France is specially subject to the fallacy lurking in all historical investigation. Historical wisdom is always wise after the event. The historian can only view past events backwards. Distortion, due to the inevitability of his peering at them through the wrong end of the telescope, is liable to be dangerously increased when it comes to considering events precedent to a climacteric such as the French Revolution. The dangers here can be intensified by too resolutely analytic a treatment.

One can but do one's best, and in this volume I have sought to reestablish the context and preconditions of Choiseul's political career, its course unfolding through particulars of time and place, often by that process of indirection which underlies human development and mostly precludes direct attainment to goals only glimpsed. Those ultimately reached are indeed important, but deterministic history nourishes distortion. In this study Choiseul may emerge from the setting of events rather as he did in his lifetime, gradually and with increasing importance.

Men regularly die in a world of difference from that into which they were born. Certainly this was so with Choiseul who died upon the eve of revolution, political and industrial, whereas he was born into a society whose basis still was largely feudal: so much so that, despite the revolutionary outcome, the eighteenth century like others carries warning against the chronological mesmerism of the double nought, with suggestions of an effective turning-point around the middle of the century, at the close of this volume.

The context of Choiseul's career was so deeply embedded that significant aspects of it were obscure both to contemporaries and to historians. This was partly but only partly due to his personality in its rather disconcerting blend of frankness lapsing into indiscretion and of secretiveness at submerged levels. Choiseul's uninhibited memoirs reveal remarkably little when he so chooses, for instance with regard to his private life. Even in an artistic concern of no political consequence he once enjoined the Duke de Nivernais, one of his closest friends, '*Motus*'.

One salient circumstance about this Lorrainer was at least clearer to contemporaries than it always has been since: Choiseul was not born a Frenchman. If his external origin was liable to distance him from some French attitudes, it introduced him even in youth to French society at the high level of diplomacy through his father. The Marquis de Stainville was for years the representative in Paris of one foreign sovereign in threefold transfiguration, lastly as the Emperor Francis I. The marquis, certainly by comparison with his more brilliant son, cut an inconspicuous figure; but by that very token this minor diplomatist positioned in wartime between France and Austria was repeatedly involved in most secret soundings which, hitherto, have mostly remained secret. If such shrouded initiatives through the Marquis de Stainville remained without immediate effect, yet they pointed towards important aspects of the policies of the Duke de Choiseul. More than one might gather from sparse references in his disparaging recollections, the diplomatic background to the statesmanship of Choiseul was one of father and son.

Such hidden origins were long protected by the loyal discretion of the Marquis de Stainville and by archival complications to match his unusual career. Contentious records from Lorraine, which in pursuance of arrangements mounted by himself were privily preserved in Vienna for nearly two centuries, were only in this one returned in part to Nancy, only to be moved west again within twenty years for safety during the Second World War, recalled under orders of the German occupying power, and further restricted in availability for a spell after the war (cf. p. 176, note 23). In the other part of the Lothringisches Hausarchiv of the Habsburg archives, still preserved in Vienna, the later run of dispatches from the Marquis de Stainville presents large and sometimes arbitrary gaps. These can, however, usually be filled since I have been able to verify that the files in Vienna dovetail or overlap with others preserved in the archives of the Segreteria degli Esteri del Granducato di Toscana in Florence.

It has been noticed that the Duke de Choiseul during his ascendancy bestowed 'la plus grande faveur aux travaux d'histoire ... Il invitait ceux qui voulaient traiter les maitières de l'histoire à ne pas suivre les sentiers battus, à fuir la redite des lieux communs, à user des sources non fréquentées jusqu'alors'. If that unhappily has not always been fully possible for me, yet I have tried to write the story of Choiseul in the spirit of Choiseul.

The convenient supposition that the records for the history of one's country are nearly all to be found within it tempts a good many historians, French ones not least; though there have of course been outstanding exceptions such as the masterly Dr. Pierre Boyé, who was partly instrumental in promoting the archival transfer from

Vienna to Nancy. Central for Choiseul, naturally, remain the French archives, whether in the departmental records at Nancy, Bar-le-Duc, and elsewhere or, for his later career especially, in those of the great ministries which he came to direct, such as the Archives des Affaires Étrangères, Archives de la Guerre, Archives de la Marine. Nevertheless any national restriction in archival coverage is particularly inappropriate to Choiseul. Even for his early private life one of the most important sources is Danish. And in his case the position is more difficult in regard to private papers than to public records.

The personal papers of the Duke de Choiseul passed to collateral descendants. These papers were the subject of a lawsuit in the last century and have, with a few partial exceptions years ago, remained inaccessible in a remote and beautiful fastness. I would only say that thanks to past personal kindness I have, perhaps, been able to get rather closer to them than have most others, and that I have been given some grounds for hoping that their unhappy unavailability may not be serious for the earlier part of Choiseul's life. For that period, certainly, a major source is the private correspondence preserved in collections of the Marquis de Stainville's personal papers, which I have been able to use. I also venture to hope that the position as to my use of Choiseul's own papers may, if earlier kindness is resumed, become easier in regard to study of his later career. Meantime the existing position is one reason for my having so far concentrated upon the earlier years and it also has some bearing upon my indication below of current reticences in the interest, I trust, of future enlightenment.

At the heart of Choiseul's personal documentation in history stand his memoirs. These present complications even greater than for other sources. A thorough evaluation of the memoirs would almost require a separate study, which I may perhaps be in a position to provide in due course. Meanwhile I would only give a summary and provisional indication of some salient particulars.

One of the earliest publications of so-called memoirs by Choiseul was the now almost forgotten *Staatsdenkwürdigkeiten des Herzogs von Choiseul*, a rare octavo of 231 pages published in German, as given on the title-page, at Berne in 1790. These memoirs are there described (my translation) as: 'Recorded by himself – Translated from the French.' I have, hitherto at least, traced no French original of this work, of which indeed it is admitted in the anonymous preface that it was 'brought into its present form by a discerning modern author, and has been continued by him into most recent times'. The chief problem would thus seem to be whether these memoirs are apocryphal in part or in whole, with probability inclining to the latter.

The *Staatsdenkwürdigkeiten des Herzogs von Choiseul* present a political survey of European developments since the Peace of Aix-la-Chapelle in 1748 with some emphasis upon eastern affairs concerning Austria, Poland, Russia, and Turkey. The argument tends to be sharply critical of Austria, the Austrian connection of France, the Peace of Paris, and other aspects of Choiseul's own ministry. Choiseul is more than once referred to in the third person and a large part of these implausible memoirs relates to events after his fall from power, notably the First Partition of Poland and the War of the Bavarian Succession.

Quite different from this production in German, and more considerable, was a French one of that same year of 1790, the *Mémoires de M. le duc de Choiseul* in two slight volumes. These memoirs are described on the title-page as *'écrits par lui-même, et imprimés sous ses yeux, dans son Cabinet, à Chanteloup, en 1778'*, when in retirement upon his estate. These Mémoires de Chanteloup, as they are usually known, are a diverse collection of some fifteen occasional pieces and memoranda with some related correspondence. Some eleven of these opuscules were ascribed to Choiseul and four to his wife, depending upon just how one categorizes this miscellany. The pieces by Choiseul range from a financial programme to a comedy in three acts.

Choiseul's family disavowed the Mémoires de Chanteloup upon publication, ascribed to the infidelity of a secretary. In 1829 Choiseul's heir and nephew by marriage qualified this disavowal as having been due to the addition of some frivolous pieces, as indicated above, to the political material likely indeed to have been privately printed at Chanteloup in 1778. The nineteenth-century Duke de Choiseul did not destroy the credentials of any of the opuscules. Their authenticity had been accepted by Horace Walpole, who had known the Choiseuls, and the Mémoires de Chanteloup are now generally considered to be genuine, so far as they go. That was not far according to the apostate Abbé Soulavie, the great plunderer and exploiter of historical manuscripts during the French Revolution, when he published in parts a succession of alleged memoirs, including those ascribed to the Duke de Richelieu and to the Count de Maurepas, from texts which Soulavie was widely, if even to excess, accused of having doctored if not forged. The Mémoires de Chanteloup were indeed ascribed to Soulavie but, in the convincing opinion of Muret and others, wrongly. In 1791 Soulavie had disparaged the *'deux volumes de fragments'* in indicating his own intention to publish in twelve volumes Choiseul's memoirs properly speaking, written in the form of letters to a friend. In the event there was no such publication, which might indeed have proved controversial and, perhaps, undesirably favourable to Choiseul.

More than a century was to elapse before it was fully and publicly confirmed that the primary part of the memoirs of Choiseul, covering his life up to his appointment in 1757 to be ambassador in Vienna, are indeed written by himself in the stylized form of twenty letters to an unnamed correspondent. The manuscript comprises some hundred and fifty sides of foolscap, with a calligraphic suggestion of some break after the fifth letter. From the sixth onwards the manuscript is written down the right-hand half of each page, the left being blank as a wide margin to allow for insertions, relatively few but sometimes substantial.

A collection of original manuscripts, largely from the reigns of Louis XV and Louis XVI, had belonged to Soulavie and had been acquired from his widow by the savant, Feuillet de Conches. By 1875 a manuscript of Choiseul's memoirs had been seen in whole or in part in the collection of Feuillet de Conches by Armand Baschet, who in that year published his *Histoire du dépôt des archives des Affaires Étrangères*. He there included the first two, shortish, extracts to be printed from this then unpublished manuscript, while confirming that these 'Mémoires particuliers' of Choiseul were different from the Mémoires de Chanteloup, were written in the form of letters, did not extend beyond 1756 (actually 1757) and were, from what Baschet had seen, '*tout entières écrites de sa propre main*'.

After the death of Feuillet de Conches in 1887 it was from his family that Étienne Charavay, the expert in manuscripts, bought the manuscript of the twenty letters of Choiseul's memoirs for five hundred francs. Charavay began to edit the manuscript for publication in collaboration with his friend, the historian Jules Flammermont. The latter meantime arranged the publication of six of the twenty letters, from the fourteenth to the nineteenth (minus the last sentence) inclusive, in the *Revue de Paris* for 1899. This publication in three instalments included one of the two extracts which Baschet had printed, from the sixteenth and twentieth letters respectively. During the advance-publication in the *Revue de Paris* Flammermont died, and Charavay two months later. The usual complications besetting the legacy of Choiseul were thus compounded and were described in the preface to the full publication of these memoirs in 1904 by their ultimate editor, Fernand Calmettes.

Calmettes rounded out his publication by the unscholarly device of increasing the number of Choiseul's autobiographical letters to twenty-seven by arbitrarily labelling as letters other fragments, all but one of which had figured in the Mémoires de Chanteloup ('letters' XXI and XXIII–XXVII). Reliance upon the authenticity of the opuscules from the Mémoires de Chanteloup was clinched for Calmettes, and apparently for Charavay and Flammermont before him, by the circumstance that they were nearly all included in an old two-volume manuscript collection, in the single hand of a copyist or secretary, entitled 'Manuscrits de Choiseul'. This collection, available for the editing of the memoirs but not subsequently, evidently did not include copies of the twenty letters in Choiseul's own hand but did include copies of other fragments by him and of some of his correspondence, notably with Louis XV and Voltaire.

Fernand Calmettes helped himself to the further fragments for one of the additional letters, so-called (XXII), and for material in fourteen appendices which he published at the end of the twenty-seven letters. From the available source-material Choiseul's letters to Voltaire had already been creamed off by Pierre Calmettes, son of Fernand Calmettes, and published separately in 1902. They are recognized to be authentic.

The hodgepodge produced by Fernand Calmettes was critically received. In particular it encouraged the admirably cautious Pierre Muret to cast some reasoned doubt upon the authenticity of four of the twenty-one additional opuscules and fragments as embodied in the seven supplementary letters, so-called, and the fourteen appendices. These had all been accepted as genuine by the scrupulous Charavay and Flammermont. Muret raised his limited doubt in an important article, summarizing earlier scholarship, on 'Les mémoires du duc de Choiseul' in the *Revue d'histoire moderne et contemporaine* for 1904. Muret prudently allowed that his reservation was not conclusive, and suggested '*que la publication de M. Calmettes ne représente qu'un stade dans la mise au jour des papiers particuliers de Choiseul, et que si elle accroît considérablement les premiers mémoires de Choiseul parus en 1790, elle est appelée elle-même à s'augmenter dans l'avenir*'.

Others were less cautious than Muret in extending his critique, and a generation later a leading apologist of Louis XV felt able to pronounce: '*Les "mémoires de Choiseul" ... sont un horrible amalgame d'opuscules suspects, presque tous fabriqués par des faussaires professionnels. Les seuls morceaux pour lesquels on hésite sont précisément ceux qui ne contiennent rien.*' Such convenient dismissal may have been encouraged by the circumstance that after publication the manuscript of the original twenty letters of Choiseul's autobiography was also lost to sight. It disappeared into an English collection formed by Mr.

C. H. St. John Hornby, and was bound with an endpaper cryptically inscribed. The title-page was an old one reading: '*Mémoires de la main d'Étienne François de Choiseul-Stainville, Duc de Choiseul. Ecrits dans sa retraite de Chanteloup, après son Ministère.*' The red morocco binding of the manuscript was incribed in gold, 'Duc de Choiseul. Mémoires. 1772. The original holograph manuscript.' The date is plausible if a little earlier than previous supposition. These memoirs were evidently written more or less consecutively after Choiseul's fall from power at the end of 1770 and, Charavay and Flammermont had already concluded, shortly before the death of Louis XV in 1774. When this manuscript reappeared rather more than ten years ago I was myself able to verify its authenticity during the all too brief period in which I held it before it found an appropriate resting-place in the Bibliothèque de Versailles.

I have also been able to uncover some further evidence bearing upon the memoirs of Choiseul. In the choice Bibliothèque de l'Arsenal in Paris I located an untitled manuscript catalogued as 'Essay sur la vie de M. le duc de Choiseul'. This anonymously written manuscript, which seems to have been curiously overlooked hitherto, comprises 126 folio sheets in professional calligraphy from the end of the eighteenth century, with amendments in more than one hand. I have been given to understand that the original provenance is uncertain, though it was evidently included in the great collection formed in the Arsenal by the Marquis de Paulmy (who died in 1787), or in its continuation. I have so far been unable to establish the authorship, while hoping that this may yet prove possible. Meantime I have established from internal evidence that this unpublished work, written after Choiseul's death in 1785, was criticized and corrected by the Duke de Nivernais, who seems in later years rather to have specialized in such tasks of literary supervision. This circumstance dates the manuscript to between 1785 and 1798, and strongly supports its authenticity and factual accuracy.

The essay on the life of Choiseul covers the same period as his twenty autobiographical letters for his memoirs, only up to 1757. The essay is indeed a bland reworking of these memoirs, which it follows closely with more or less judicious omissions, occasional insertions from the information of the author, who had known Choiseul personally, and eulogy of the duke in reply to contemporary criticism.

Perhaps the most interesting of the fresh material in the essay derives from the fact that the author was evidently able to work from a complete text of the memoirs including the now missing eight pages of the lacuna between the second and third letters in both the original manuscript, preserved in the Bibliothèque de Versailles, and the edition printed from it by Fernand Calmettes (*Mémoires*, pp. 5–7). This points towards the use by the author of the essay either of a complete text of the memoirs dating from Choiseul's lifetime or of the originals or copies of the missing pages, possibly as some separate holding for integration in the story of the main manuscript of the twenty letters: because it would appear from their original manuscript that the lacuna was, in whole or in part, of the choosing of Choiseul himself, who very roughly tried to adjust it, possibly with some unfulfilled intention of later bridging it over (cf. p. 417, note 25). A further suggestion now is that the epistolary form of Choiseul's memoirs may have been rather less of a mere convention than might appear, at least to the extent that, perhaps even during his lifetime, these memoirs or a portion of them seem to have been in hands other than his own. In any case it now appears that soon after Choiseul's death, if not before, the twenty autobiographical letters already formed a distinct category of material.

Another large corpus of material concerning Choiseul came to light quite separately when I managed to establish that there are indeed further memoirs, the 'Mémoires inédits du duc de Choiseul'. This collection would appear to be, in its primary composition at least, distinct from all those previously mentioned; though, not very surprisingly, it is partly related to other items and it complements the twenty letters in so far as it chiefly covers the period after they end, namely the later and more important years of office.

I have so far been unable to prove conclusively that the 'Mémoires inédits' are genuine. From study of the internal evidence, however, I now believe that they are, probably as a whole, and in this volume I have occasionally used them accordingly. To reject these further memoirs as spurious, even as Choiseul's earlier memoirs had formerly been wrongly rejected, would require greater allowances for coincidence and inherent improbabilities than I find it easy to make: a consideration, incidentally, which also applies in large measure to the supplementary material published by Fernand Calmettes.

I do not feel, however, that I am yet in a position to discuss with sufficient confidence and comprehensiveness the source-problems in regard to the 'Mémoires inédits'. For the present I find myself only a stage further upon the difficult way into Choiseul's memoirs which Pierre Muret signposted. Scholars will appreciate my deep regret at having to go to press in these conditions but perhaps they may also be able to sense by now some of the reasons. One contributory reason is that this potentially important source for Choiseul mainly relates, as I have indicated, to the period posterior to the present volume so that its provisional privation of full warranty in this respect may not prove too serious. If readers should nevertheless find this position unsatisfactory, and publication of this volume premature, I can only agree with them. I should have preferred to defer publication but unhappily the passage of the years tells upon books as upon persons.

All quotations here from the 'Mémoires inédits du duc de Choiseul' carry footnotes with numerical references which will enable each passage to be located when I have advanced further in working upon this source and in supplying the key. Meantime readers are entitled, at least, to suspend judgement upon such material as may be furnished by these occasional quotations. Though I would hope that even from them others too may begin to appreciate how they cohere in style and content.

The main texts of Choiseul's memoirs are regularly designated in footnote references by abbreviations. These are included in the alphabetical list of Abbreviated Sources and Authorities at the end of the volume. This select list also includes a number of the more important secondary sources which I have used. Such coverage should be clear enough from the numerous footnotes, though they are naturally not comprehensive for sources consulted. But I have already explained elsewhere my distrust of bibliographies. A specialized bibliography is an illiberal compilation. But one that is ample must still be arbitrary and incomplete. The really sound advice for studying any piece of history is to read, or skim, virtually everything likely that you can lay hands on. It is rare indeed that a book, even rather remotely relevant, even considerably bad, will not provide one or two suggestions. It is the penance of historians that they more especially need to read so many second-rate books.

Since this study of the eighteenth century is written in English, I have generally followed eighteenth-century rather than modern fashion in using English forms in preference, for instance, to foreign titles of rank. For one thing, French titles are by no means the only foreign ones in question and I would not wish to emulate Carlyle with his Friedrich, Kaiser Karl, and the rest. I am afraid that any solution to this little difficulty is in certain respects liable to be imperfect but mine at least matches that adopted, evidently for sufficient reasons also, by the British Library in its general catalogue of printed books. I have not, however, followed this English usage with such tiresome consistency as to write, say, the Marchioness de Pompadour. All translations of quotations from the French and other foreign originals are my own unless the contrary is indicated. A footnote reference with an indication such as 'and for the following' signifies that the reference also covers one or more citations directly following.

As to historical fact and presentation, in trying to cover a large canvas in keeping with Choiseul it would be foolish conceit to suppose that no errors of commission and omission can have arisen. Critics particularly familiar with one or other aspect of the whole will, I am sure, be pleased enough to illustrate this point for me. It is said that one of France's leading historians, Alphonse Aulard, in making ready a second edition of his *Histoire politique de la révolution française*, confessed himself dismayed by the number of mistakes he needed to correct. One may hardly expect to do better than Aulard. The consolation may be that in literature, unlike life, one can at least hope for a second rendering in which to make improvements.

It is fashionable for lazy readers to criticize long books as self-indulgent. Ideas of indulgence clearly vary. This book, like any book based upon research, stands rather as the tip of an iceberg – sometimes almost literally as in my recall of the chill upon the leatherbound volumes of records from 1741 of French campaigning out to Prague, appropriately brought up from the Réserve in midwinter; or of the freezing temperatures which rendered the Archives départementales des Vosges a snug resort in Épinal; whereas all the cross-draughts created in the little reading-room on the Ballhausplatz, if they stirred the unbound records of the Habsburgs in the sweltering heat, could not exempt them from its dripping sweat. Climatic conditions, however, only accentuate the solitary stints in archives abroad under pressure, if not of money, then almost always of time, with the critical discovery somehow surfacing usually in the last flurry of departure. Such is the perennial lot of students of foreign history.

Sometimes, as in any investigation, the illumination of an unexpected breakthrough into new truth can make all worth while. And memories are not only of archive-rooms but of consulting one manuscript source while discussing a Langouste Choiseul done with morels in that very Château de Stainville which, years earlier, had been offered to me for a song one wet afternoon; of doubling through a remote landscape under snow with a French sailor back from Indo-China, his pompom bobbing as we ran; of the tommy-gun of a communist sentry eyeing Lucy and myself as we peered at a French plaque still astonishingly visible upon a military depot in Prague in witness of occupation by the invading troops of the Marshal de Belle-Isle; of the battlefield of Groczka bathed in a golden sunset out beyond Belgrade with peasants bearing fruit as in a golden age – eastward, though, lay battlemented Semendria, prolific in poisonous thornapple.

But then the writing of *Choiseul* would really be another book, and one, I hope, not yet finished. One of the pleasures of writing this one has been making or deepening many friendships in France and elsewhere. While taking full responsibility myself for all that I have written, I have received so much kind help from so many people that I cannot hope to thank them all individually but only to have their understanding if they are included in this general acknowledgement of my keen gratitude. This applies especially to the large number of learned archivists who have generously helped a foreigner to obtain otherwise impossible results. If I mention particularly M. Maurice Degros, lately Conservateur en chef des Archives du Ministère des Affaires Etrangères, it is as one of the kindest and earliest of my guides, and in specially important archives. Other particular friends in matters documentary have been the expert M. Michel Castaing and M. Marc Loliée. More broadly, I am deeply indebted to the Comte and Comtesse Philippe de Salverte-Marmier, to the Duc de Mouchy and to the Duchesse douairière de Mouchy, to the Comte F. and the Comte C. de Limburg Stirum, also to Monsieur R. Lacour-Gayet in his generosity. The Duc de Praslin may scarcely recall his erstwhile kindness to me but I do, as also encouragement which I received from the late Duc de La Force and the late Isabelle de Broglie, Marquise de La Moussaye, that rare spirit. I have also received counsel and assistance from the late Professor Paul Vaucher, Madame Philippe Sagnac, and Professor Roland Mousnier, who warned me early what I should be in for. He suggested – it was back in the days of rationing – that the Bon Dieu should really grant historians an extra ration of years, because their work is so slow. This is especially so when, as in my case, it is regularly limited by other calls.

In Paris I was also valuably helped by the late Hon. Mrs. Peter Rodd (Nancy Mitford) and by Sir Patrick Reilly. Among my other particular debts are those to the Countess Waldegrave, Sir John Habakkuk, Sir Francis Watson, Mr. A. R. A. Hobson, Mr. Herman W. Liebert, Librarian of the Beinecke Rare Book Library at Yale, Professor the Revd. J. McManners, Professor A. Goodwin, Dr. John Rogister, and Miss Nicole Jordan. I owe special thanks to the Leverhulme Trustees in connection with research for this book, and to the Oxford University Press for its publication. And for me, as for so many, the London Library has proved almost as great a pleasure as it has been a standby. Indispensable also has been the large amount of typing accomplished by several experts, notably the late Miss M. Wallis, Mrs. J. Fincham, Mrs. Edna Laird, and my old friend, Miss F. L. J. Sturgess.

My warmest thanks are due to the Warden and Fellows of All Souls for generous and patient support without which this book would not have been written. There is also a more personal debt whose magnitude precludes specification. The writing of a big book demands sacrifices, but it is hard when the heaviest fall upon someone other than the author.

White Notley Hall   R. D'O. B.
Whit Sunday 1977

CONTENTS

PART I
BEGINNING. 1719–1740

PART II
CAMPAIGNING. 1740–1743

PART III
COMMANDING. 1744–1748

CHAPTER VI. ROCOUX

CHAPTER VII. INTRIGUE

CHAPTER VIII. ESTATES

CHAPTER IX. EMBASSIES

CHAPTER X. IDEAS

CHAPTER XI. DEPARTURE

ILLUSTRATIONS

MAPS

PART I

BEGINNING
1719–1740

CHAPTER I

PRELUDE

I

'MONSIEUR DE CHOISEUL will figure in history merely as a man who for eleven years governed France by the despotism of fashion, without his name recalling either battles won, or glorious treaties, or useful ordinances or regulations; and he paved the way for great evils experienced down to our own day.'[1]

Such was the verdict upon the Duke de Choiseul passed by a more renowned foreign minister of France than he, by the Prince de Talleyrand. The very completeness of the condemnation, however, may give pause. And, turning back to another judgement delivered by Talleyrand himself something less than twenty years earlier: 'The Duke de Choiseul, one of the men of our century whose spirit most embraced the future, already in 1769 foresaw the separation of America from England and feared the partition of Poland; from this period he sought by negotiations to prepare the cession of Egypt to France so as to be ready, with the same products and a more extensive trade, to replace the [remaining] American colonies on the day on which they should slip from our power.'[2]

Talleyrand was hardly a model of disinterested consistency; but he was a gifted professional who had known Choiseul personally. In the light of his two appreciations of his predecessor's statesmanship it may not seem wholly surprising that the place of Choiseul has not subsequently been very securely fixed in the history of France, of Europe and beyond. Few figures of comparable stature in modern history still feature so ambiguously.

Étienne-François, Duke de Choiseul, was destined to be chief minister of France for twelve years late in the reign of King Louis XV, from December 1758 to December 1770. Choiseul was not born a Frenchman but it was during his ministry that his little homeland of Lorraine was united finally with France; and he endowed her with Corsica, hence with another and more famous overlord from outside

---

[1] Prince de Talleyrand, 'De M. de Choiseul' in *Mémoires du prince de Talleyrand*, ed. duc de Broglie (Paris, 1891–2), v. 590.
[2] Talleyrand, *Essai sur les avantages à retirer des colonies nouvelles dans les circonstances présentes par le citoyen Talleyrand, lu à la séance publique de l'Institut national le 15 messidor an V* (Paris [1797]), p. 14.

whose Napoleonic vision also embraced Egypt, and enemy England.

Although Choiseul attained power, aptly for so ardent an amorist, largely through the influence of the Marquise de Pompadour, yet it was a more considerable woman than she, the Empress Catherine the Great, who called him the Coachman of Europe. Had Choiseul confined his bold policies to the continent of Europe he might perhaps have been more remembered by the country which he served and governed. But his vision was less usual and more extensive, ranging out to new confines, geographical, economic, and even scientific towards the age of steam. Politically this inlander from Lorraine sought to wreck the British empire and to blazon the achievement of France across the world. In this he failed. Choiseul was indeed constrained to yield Canada in the heavy Peace of Paris. Yet it was after this loss that, with his resolute optimism, he wrote: 'I cannot see who can prevent France from becoming a great maritime power.'[3] And the chief preventer hitherto, the Earl of Chatham, is recorded to have told parliament that 'since the late Cardinal de Richelieu France had not had so great a minister as the Duke de Choiseul'.[4] His name is still commemorated across the erstwhile empire of his opponents, annexed from the seas and the oceans, in Saint Lucia among the Windward Islands, in the Falkland Islands of the South Atlantic, and in the Solomon Islands of the far Pacific.

II

'I will not speak to you, Sir, of my birth. They have always told me that I was of a noble descent as ancient as any there be. I am absolutely ignorant of my genealogy which is, like that of everyone, in the books that deal with this subject.' Choiseul's characteristic introduction to his memoirs[5] cut through the dead wood of family trees. Yet despite, or, on rather deeper reading, in accordance with this offhand opening, pride of birth was one impelling force in the career of the future Duke de Choiseul.

It was at Nancy[6] on 28th June 1719 that a first child was born to

[3] Duc de Choiseul, 'Mémoires inédits du duc de Choiseul' (henceforth cited as Choiseul, 'Mémoires inédits'), 2/6/3/180/1.

[4] Horace Walpole to Duchess de Choiseul, 28 Jan. 1771: Mrs. Paget Toynbee, *The Letters of Horace Walpole* (Oxford, 1903f.) viii. 10. (For the dating of this letter cf. *The Yale Edition of Horace Walpole's Correspondence*, ed. W. S. Lewis – London, 1937f: henceforth cited as Walpole Correspondence–v. 18).

[5] Duc de Choiseul, *Mémoires du duc de Choiseul 1719–1785*, ed. Fernand Calmettes (Paris, 1904: henceforth cited as Choiseul, *Mémoires*), p. 2.

[6] Choiseul's birthplace was long obscured by some uncertainty. It was wrongly given as Lunéville, with a query, by Calmettes: Choiseul, *Mémoires*, p. 2. Choiseul's birthplace had been established as Nancy more then forty years earlier by Louis Lallement: 'Quelques notes biographiques: le poëte Gilbert, le littérateur Hoffman et le ministre Choiseul' in *Journal de la*

Françoise-Louise, wife of François-Joseph de Choiseul, Marquis de Stainville, Baron de Beaupré, courtier to the sovereign Duke of Lorraine. Traditionally at least, this infant son was born in a house overlooking the handsome Place de la Carrière, formerly the tilting lists where Stainvilles had jousted in the last great tournament in the little ducal capital in 1517. And recently at least quintain was still practised of a Saturday upon this parade-ground for the ducal guards marching 'with hautboys and drums on to the Carrière'.[7] Three days after the birth, in central Nancy in the square-towered church of Saint-Epvre under the Curé Thierrion, the baby was christened Étienne-François, Stephen Francis. This was he who would be known to history as Choiseul. But that was not yet. For the first thirty-nine years of his life, that is for the greater part of it, he went by the narrower name of the Count de Stainville.

The Count de Stainville's godfather at the font was another Count de Stainville, the bachelor Jean-François, lord of Beurey and Mussey, first cousin once removed to the infant and a future contributor to his fortunes. More immediately important, however, was his godmother, his maternal grandmother, the 'high and mighty lady Catherine Diane de Beauvau'.[8] At the time of the christening this lady of forty-eight had already run through a couple of husbands and was on to her third, the Count de Rouerke. The countess was influential from being a Beauvau by birth and in particular the sister-in-law of 'la belle Craon', the lovely, fair-skinned, short-tempered Marquise de Beauvau-Craon, reigning mistress of reigning Duke Leopold. The Countess de Rouerke's third husband was dynastically the least important though historically not the least remarkable. De Rouerke was the local rendering of O'Rourke, and Eugene O'Rourke was one illustration of the Irish and Jacobite influence at the miniature court of Duke Leopold, whose mentor and minister had been staunch Taaffe, third Earl of Carlingford. The earl had enlisted many compatriots from the bodyguards of King James II. Under Leopold the Count de Rouerke served as a major in the ducal guards, of which another company was commanded by a Captain Butler.

société d'archéologie et du comité du musée lorrain (11ème année. Nancy, 1862), pp. 159f.: part ii, 'Où est né Choiseul, le ministre de Louis XV?' This location had been confirmed and specified as the Place de la Carrière by Chr. Pfister, *Histoire de Nancy* (Paris and Nancy, 1902f.), iii. 836: unmentioned, in indicating the Carrière with less certainty than Nancy, by Jacques Levron, *Choiseul: un sceptique au pouvoir* (Paris, 1976), pp. 30–1.

[7] 'Règlement général de S[on] A[ltesse] R[oyale] Léopold] pour son régiment des gardes', Archives départementales de Meurthe-et-Moselle, Série F, Fonds de Vienne (henceforth cited as Arch. M-et-M/Vienne), Affaires militaires: cited, undated, by Zoltan Harsany, *La Cour de Léopold duc de Lorraine et de Bar 1698–1729* (Nancy, 1939), p. 396.

[8] Baptismal register of Choiseul's christening: 'Extrait du livre pour servir d'enregistrement pour les baptesmes, marriages et enterrements de la paroisse Saint-Epvre de Nancy... de 1714 à 1720.' cited, Lallement, op. cit., p. 169.

The Marquise de Stainville, mother of the infant count, was the third daughter of the Countess de Rouerke by her first marriage, dating from 1690, to the Marquis de Bassompierre (Anne-François-Joseph), a descendant of that Marshal of France who, celebrated in war, in diplomacy, in letters, and in love, had for twelve years been kept in the Bastille by the Cardinal de Richelieu. In 1698 the widowed Marquise de Bassompierre had married, secondly, the sixtyish Count de Couvonges, great chamberlain and leading administrator under the youthful Duke Leopold. She thereby became a member of yet another of the great families of Lorraine, the Stainvilles. And the Stainvilles had intermarried in successive generations with the neighbouring Choiseuls.

III

Choiseul did not exaggerate in claiming an ancient descent equal to any. The house of Choiseul was documented way back into the tenth century though just what happened there was matter for learned debate between the Jesuit Father Vignier, who traced the line back to Hugh, Count de Bassigny, floruit 937, and the Abbé Le Laboureur who looked rather to the counts of Langres – by about 1060 their chief vassal was a Choiseul. Modern scholarship inclines to derive the Choiseuls from a cadet branch, indeed, of the house of Bassigny, a region where they were dominant by the thirteenth century.[9] Suffice it that the Choiseuls were a very old family from Champagne, issuing from the same reaches as the river Meuse and specifically from the village of Choiseul, traditionally called after a little hill looking like a cheese (from the Latin *caseolus*, a small cheese). Though another possibility is a watermill (*moulin à choisel*). This strategic siting of their lands upon the disputed confines of Champagne, Lorraine, and Burgundy gave them disproportionate influence. The Choiseuls boasted Capetian blood from a marriage between the head of the clan early in the thirteenth century and Alix de Dreux, granddaughter of King Louis VI of France. Two centuries later, in 1420, a Choiseul heiress, Jeanne, Dame de Choiseul and Montaiguillon, married a chamberlain to King Henry V of England. Her father had been captured by the English and ransomed by the Duke of Burgundy. This Jeanne was the last of the main stem of the Choiseuls, henceforth flourishing in many branches.

The English connection of the Choiseuls is better authenticated than a story of a marital link with Joan of Arc's dubious colleague,

[9] Cf. H. de Faget de Casteljau, 'Recherches sur la maison de Choiseul' in *Les Cahiers haut-marnais* for 1970, no. 102., pp. 148–9.

fair Alison du May, another young woman of Lorraine working in
the patriotic cause of France by seducing the then Duke of Lorraine.
Certain it is that for centuries already the Choiseuls had been
prominent in the perennial strife along those borderlands of France
and had spilt over towards what became the Duchy of Bar, united to
that of Lorraine in 1473.

It was in the renaissance, however, that the fighting line of Choiseul
blossomed out. Charles de Choiseul so persevered in courage during
the French wars of religion that when he died a Marshal of France
in 1626 he was credited with twenty wounds, forty-seven battles, and
fifty-three successful sieges. He had also taken an almost premonitory
hand at Troyes against the Jesuits. His nephew, Caesar de Choiseul,
a stiff fighter in Piedmont and elsewhere, faithful to the court during
the Fronde, was also created a Marshal of France as well as the first
Duke de Choiseul. In 1670 he accompanied Madame, Duchess of
Orleans, to witness the signature of the secret Treaty of Dover, and
was honoured by Charles II. Five years later Caesar de Choiseul died
'loved by the Great and honoured by everyone'.[10] He had been
predeceased by his three sons upon the field of battle, two of them
killed before his eyes. An old compilation of that time claimed that
'as a delicious garden is agreeable as much by the lively brilliance of
its flowers and fruit as by their sweet fragrance, in the same manner
can one observe in this family of Choiseul (whose happy stem has
produced divers branches) several persons of honour and merit ...
who have made their name shine and will carry it into future
centuries'.[11]

If this lustre was shed primarily by the branch of Choiseul-Praslin,
others by then included Choiseul de Traves, Choiseul-Meuse, and
Choiseul-Beaupré, the one of immediate concern. Chrétien de
Choiseul, Baron de Beaupré, had been killed in May 1593 in
defending the Château de Monteclair in the cause of the still
protestant Henry IV against that catholic League so largely of Guise-
Lorraine inspiration. Such, in the tapestry of high courage and high
deeds among the Choiseuls, was the latitudinarian strand introduced
by the direct forbear of Étienne-François, Duke de Choiseul.

The Château de Beaupré is pleasantly situated by miniature lakes
in rolling country about ten miles from Domrémy where Saint Joan
was born. This was the home of Chrétien de Choiseul's great-
grandson, the first Francis Joseph de Choiseul generally known as
the Count de Choiseul, grandfather of the future duke.

[10] Louis Moreri, *Le Grand Dictionnaire historique* (revised ed., Basel, 1731), ii. 141.
[11] Scaevole and Louis de Saincte-Marthe, 'Généalogie sommaire de l'ancienne et illustre
maison de Choiseul' (manuscript, probably *c.* 1670): Bibliothèque Nationale, Manuscrits
française (henceforth cited as B.N. MS. fr.) no. 32631, fo. 19.

The Count de Choiseul-Beaupré varied the military tradition by
enlisting in the French navy. In the summer of 1683[12] he was serving
as a lieutenant in the squadron of Du Quesne and Tourville during
one of their bombardments of Algiers in the war waged by Louis
XIV against the Barbary pirates. They were exacerbated by the
havoc wrought by a new French weapon, a naval mortar christened
the Petit Renau after its inventor.

On the night of 29–30 July 1683 the Count de Choiseul was
patrolling in a longboat with five marines and a few seamen when he
was beset by five Algerian vessels. Whereupon 'my sailors', he wrote,
'having all thrown themselves down as though dead, blows and
shouts could not make them raise their heads, they answering only
that they were dead'.[13] Cumbered by the sham corpses of these
'sleepers', as he called them, the count fought on together with a
couple of unwounded marines till, grappling hand to hand with the
boarding pirates, he toppled an assailant into the water and went in
with him. Fished out, captured, and enslaved, Choiseul-Beaupré,
'unable to stand upright, being nearly dead from the buffets which
they had given me', was flung at the feet of the governor of Algiers.
The governor 'told me that, knowing of the death of the consul, I was
a fool to come of purpose to burn his ships'. The acting French
consul, Father Le Vacher, had two days before been strapped naked
to the mouth of an outsize cannon, named Baba Merzoug, which had
discharged shreds of him over the offlying French men-of-war. They
rechristened that cannon La Consulaire. The Arab chief now told
Choiseul-Beaupré that next day this would be his fate. The count
replied: 'Directly, if you wish.' But they did not. It was only after a
week of chains and the bastinado that, reserved to be one of the last
victims, he was lashed to the mouth of the cannon. The Moors were
about to touch it off when in the nick of time 'the captain of the
caravel which the Chevalier de Hery had captured placed himself
upon the cannon saying that he wished to die if I did not receive
mercy, which they granted him'. Choiseul-Beaupré insisted that they
should release his servant, expecting a like fate, before he was himself
unbound.

The count's own account tends to substantiate the story that this
pirate captain, called Ali, acted from gratitude to him for having
earlier secured Ali's release. At other times, certainly, the count
befriended corsairs. This is not to say that his rescuer may not, sooner

[12] This episode in the life of the Count de Choiseul is wrongly dated in several works of
reference.
[13] Count de Choiseul to (?) Marquis de Seignelay, Algiers, 19 Dec. 1683: B.N. MS. fr., no.
12763, vol. ii., fo. 117–18 for the following.

or later, have touched some of the four hundred Spanish pieces of eight which the count managed to borrow from Benjamin Zacuto, a locally established Jewish merchant from Leghorn, 'for his subsistence and for the expenditures which he was obliged to make in order to protect himself from the cruelty of the authorities of this [Barbary] republic, who wished to put him to death at the mouth of a cannon'.[14]

Even after his adventure-story rescue the Count de Choiseul, still threatened with execution, was 'for two months spouting blood due to blows'.[15] All this he related, while yet in captivity, in a long letter apparently addressed to the French Minister of Marine, Colbert's adept son, who was asked by the intrepid lieutenant to assure his father 'that he should in no wise grieve himself, that under whatever colour they paint death to me, it is nowise capable of making me falsify my religion or bring shame upon his house'.

Choiseul-Beaupré also asked his correspondent for help, mentioning that 'the Chevalier de Tourville has sent me fifteen louis and some linen'. So the count was in the debt as well as in the school of the future Marshal de Tourville, one of the great sailors of his age, long versed in operations against the corsairs. Tourville incidentally was by no means so rich as he was handsome. However, every little would help the Count de Choiseul, who had to pay twenty-five per cent interest on his borrowing from Zacuto. His pieces of eight may have helped to ensure the count's release when some months later nominal peace was concluded with the chastened corsairs.

The nautical count was less prompt in finance than in war. Ten years later at Toulon he began a letter to Zacuto about the loan of 1683: 'Last year the Marshal de Choiseul told me, Sir, that I ought to think about paying you.'[16] This Marshal of France, Claude de Choiseul, Marquis de Francières with service stretching from Hungary to Crete, was yet another ornament of that military family and in particular of the branch of Beaupré. The marshal, like many of the Choiseuls more a soldier than a courtier, was himself as conspicuously impecunious as he was nobly distinguished, earning an encomium even from Saint-Simon. The likewise straitened circumstances of his younger relation, the Count de Choiseul-Beaupré, came out in the latter's letter to Zacuto: 'The reproaches which you have so often made to me oblige me to say to you that

[14] Benjamin Zacuto, letter of procuration to François Le Prestre (of Paris), Algiers, after mid-Oct. 1693: Archives du consulat de France à Alger, registre X, fo. 99, cited by Albert Devoulx, 'M. de Choiseul-Beaupré et le Turc reconnaissant', in *Revue africaine* (16ème année, Algiers, 1872), p. 163. (Devoulx analysed this episode in ignorance of the Count de Choiseul's own evidence as cited above from the original manuscript.)

[15] Count de Choiseul to (?) Marquis de Seignelay, *u.s.*, fo. 118–19 for the following.

[16] Count de Choiseul to Zacuto, Toulon, 25 Sept. 1693: Archives du consulat de France à Alger, registre X, fo. 98: cited, A. Devoulx, op. cit., pp. 163–4 for the following.

when one is paying twenty-five per cent ... it seems to me that this difference should defray you for so long a wait. In fine, Sir, it is not a question of giving you a full account of our adverse transactions and of the mishaps which have befallen me since I had the honour of seeing you.' The count, however, did have a small pension which he now offered to assign to the Jew till the debt was cleared. Choiseul-Beaupré reckoned that meanwhile he could scrape through since 'I have some property, thank heavens, apart from that ... I am not such a dishonest person as to let myself be buried without paying anyone to whom I owe.'

The Count de Choiseul was not quite on his way to the grave but two years later he did get married. On 2 May 1695, at the ancestral Château de Beaupré, he wed Nicole de Stainville, his cousin, being a Choiseul on her mother's side. This union promptly produced the second Francis Joseph, the future father of the future statesman.

IV

The fighting days of the elder Francis Joseph de Choiseul were not yet over. During the War of the Spanish Succession, in April 1705, he was promoted captain of his own ship. He was also decorated with the coveted red ribbon of the military Order of Saint Louis, recently created to rank second only to the Cordon Bleu of the Order of the Saint-Esprit. Within a year, as commander of the sixtysix-gun *La Bretagne*, the count was participating in a successful French swoop upon British settlements in the disputed West Indian island of Saint Christopher, executed by five ships of the line 'with twenty-three or twenty-four brigantines and sloops'.[17] This stroke heralded another, mounted by a celebrated French-Canadian captain, Lemoyne d'Iberville, against the British stronghold of Nevis in revenge for an earlier raid on Guadeloupe. Such was the latest phase of the internecine struggle between the two foremost interlopers into the Spanish Main and the Spanish preserves of the Caribbean and the Antilles.

After Nevis had been reduced d'Iberville put into Saint Domingo, that western part of the island of Hispaniola which the French had within the last two generations wrested from the Spaniards much as the English had neighbouring Jamaica, the next target for d'Iberville. But he died at the end of that year. Within another year the Count de

[17] Enclosure, Edmund Dummer to Robert Harley, London, 21 May 1706: *The Manuscripts of his Grace the Duke of Portland* (London, 1891f.), viii. 228. (Report of the Historical Manuscripts Commission, Cd. 3475 of 1907.)

Choiseul-Beaupré had been appointed 'Governor for the King of the Islands of Saint Domingo and the Turtle Coast',[18] another piratical part of the world. If one of the earliest haunts of French (and English) buccaneers, since about 1626, had been the fertile fastness of the turtle-island of Tortuga off the northern coast of Saint Domingo, the later Haiti, one of their last and more creditable actions had been the co-operation of over a thousand hard-swearing filibusters, as French buccaneers were more strictly termed, in the descent of 1706 upon Nevis.

In the intervening eighty years luxuriant Saint Domingo had especially nourished French participation in the heyday of the buccaneers in their bloodthirsty adventures after loot. This maritime free-for-all was mainly directed against the Spaniards because they had most booty and were also specially hated for their cruelties by such as Montbars the Exterminator, the avenger from Languedoc. In loose extension of European hostilities French buccaneers (*flibustiers*) claimed as often as not to have from the governor of Saint Domingo letters of marque constituting them privateers in distinction from mere pirates (*forbans*). The notorious Laurent de Graff, a golden-haired filibuster who habitually sailed with an orchestra to entertain his crew, had indeed served under Governor Du Casse in his swoop upon Jamaica in 1694. Three years later the buccaneers sailed again with Du Casse to capture Carthagena: only, the regular French naval commander, to the indignation of Du Casse himself, withheld from the filibusters a part of their claimed share of the fabulous booty. The squabbling freebooters took to pillage and were largely mopped up by the British and Dutch men-of-war, a blow from which they never fully recovered. Though Du Casse could still describe Saint Domingo as 'a place of arms for joining to the French monarchy the important keys of Mexico, Peru and the realm of Santa-Fé'[19] – keys to Eldorado. Earlier that decade a buccaneering pioneer from Bordeaux, Massertie, had already been sweeping the Pacific from Patagonia to the Gulf of California. And from about the turn of the century mariners from Saint-Malo were frequenting what became known as the Îles Malouines, later the Falkland Islands, bleak islands of destiny for the future Duke de Choiseul.

In the event Du Casse had been unable to achieve even his more limited ambition of conquering the whole island of Hispaniola. The scattered French settlements along its western seaboard were in

---

[18] 'Inventaire fait au Château de Beaupré après le décès de Mr. de Choiseul Beaupré et de Madame son épouse', 4–5 Mar. 1712: Archives départementales de la Meuse (henceforth cited as Arch. Meuse), J18²⁹, docket III.
[19] Du Casse, 13 Jan. 1699: Archives du Ministère des Colonies, Correspondance générale, Saint-Domingue, C9, iv, cited, Pierre de Vaissière, *Saint-Domingue* (Paris, 1909), p. 16.

danger of being pinched out between the English from Jamaica and the Spaniards from their two-centuries-old capital of Santo Domingo, the oldest European city in America. Two generations of cruel but indecisive hostilities through the rugged hinterland of the island between the French buccaneers, by origin hunters and crack marksmen with their long guns, and the Spanish lancers or Cinquantaines (they prudently moved in fifties) had christened such features as the Rivière du Massacre, up beyond Limonade almost upon the present frontier, before Spain at last conceded the existence of a French colony upon Hispaniola. That was done in the Peace of Ryswick, ten years before the Count de Choiseul-Beaupré became the governor.

In Saint Domingo the Count de Choiseul held sway over forbidding terrain of thick forest spread across a tangled confusion of rugged hills and low mountains, the *mornes*, cut up by countless streams which storms could make torrents. Mosquitoes swarmed. The sweltering climate was at once scorching and humid, alleviated by breezes but still a deadly promoter of dysentery and Siamese Sickness as they called the yellow fever. Death stalked the savannas bathed in radiant light, lush with palms, mahogany, mangoes, bananas, and incipient gardens hedged with oranges and lemons. Plantations had already been hacked out under the early Right of the Axe (*Droit de Hache*) whereby a settler could acquire valid possession of land by clearing it, a splendid contrast in freedom to the feudal encumbrance, still, of land in Europe.

Buccaneers were tending to settle down as planters, especially since the Bourbon takeover of Spain had left the French Skimmers of the Sea with less to skim. A society which could be if anything crueller, and richer, than that of the pirates themselves had begun to flourish upon a basis of slavery. As in other West Indian islands, negroes were imported in unspeakable conditions from the western coasts of Africa, ranging from Angolans of a notorious stench to combative Senegalese specially inviting the lash. By the beginning of the century there were already over ten thousand negroes just in Léogane, then the capital of Saint Domingo. Their slavery was becoming diversified as the early monoculture of tobacco gave way to indigo, cocoa, above all sugar. In 1701 thirty-five sugar-mills were already crushing cane in Saint Domingo with over a hundred others about to start production. Next year the acting governor, de Gallifet, wrote: 'Most of the [French] inhabitants make their negroes work beyond human strength, all day and the greater part of the night.'[20] The negroes were already rated by their exploiters as 'redoubtable

[20] De Gallifet, Léogane, 20 Apr. 1702: op. cit., p. 166.

domestic enemies'.[21] If constant fear of black revolt inspired exemplary cruelties in the cycle of repression upon that bloodsoaked island, the spirit of revolt was largely endemic in the colonists themselves as against central authority, an illogical overlap which was ultimately to destroy the colony of Saint Domingo. In early days the rebelliousness of settlers was mainly against the Exclusif, which confined their trade to the mother-country through the monopolistic Compagnie des Indes or (after 1698) Compagnie de Saint-Domingue so that the colonists could not profitably dispose of surpluses, were starved of specie and encouraged to restrict production before rising prosperity was confirmed in 1724 by the collapse there of company control.

When the Count de Choiseul became governor in 1707 Saint Domingo was already a long way on from its first phase of buccaneering adventure into the second one of governmental direction in the aftermath of Colbert. In 1685 the absolute authority of the governor as commander-in-chief had been mitigated by local jurisdictions with appeal to a Conseil Supérieur at the then capital of Petit Goave. The Count de Choiseul in 1708 moved his headquarters back from Léogane to Petit Goave, while upon the northern seaboard a second court of appeal had been set up at Le Cap eastward from Tortuga. And a great trial it proved to the subordinate governor of Le Cap, Pierre de Charitte, a formidable figure who had lost one jaw in the wars so that he could take only liquid nourishment out of keeping with his robust disposition, which included a detestation of lawyers. The Count de Choiseul had another lieutenant at Léogane in the person of de Brach, liable to lay about him literally, no respecter of superiors (notably de Gallifet), and apt to maintain that he had never met an intendant or civil commissary who was not a robber ripe for stringing up.

The civil administration of a Commissaire-Ordonnateur or intendant under the governor had only been introduced in Saint Domingo in 1703. Commissary de Mithon helped the Count de Choiseul to sort out his lamentable lot of colonists – 'a collection of rapscallions from every province'[22] of France. In such a society the Countess de Choiseul, who bravely accompanied her husband, found few other white women as yet, unless one counted the periodical consignments from France of waifs and drabs – usually the ugliest, grumbled de Gallifet, who nearly ran into trouble for abducting a negress, 'the most beautiful of four or five who stand guard around him in bed'.[23] He himself had written a little earlier: 'One cannot

---

[21] Governor de Cussy, 18 Oct. 1685: ibid., p. 229.   [22] De Gallifet, 22 July 1699: ibid., p. 48.
[23] Governor Auger, 22 Mar. 1704: ibid., p. 76.

imagine a more licentious country.'[24] Also, as the Count de Choiseul wrote to Charitte, 'there are many heads here worn out with drink and tobacco smoke'.[25] In the preceding year of his governorship about one-sixth of the total official revenue of the colony, nearly ten thousand livres out of nearly sixty, had come from dues from taverns. If wine was expensive one could soak rum of every kind, from strong, tart Guldive to the cheapest Tafia. Tobacco was an early form of currency in the cash-starved island and one is vouchsafed 'a burlesque sight' from these years of a lawcourt in session in Saint Domingo with the judge 'delivering a sentence with a pipe in his mouth'.[26] Ten years earlier the clerk of the court at Léogane had been a seasoned rapist.

It was only in 1704 that Laurent de Graff had ended his days as the predecessor of Charritte in the local governorship of Le Cap. Four years later the Count de Choiseul had to take cognizance of a public set-to between the corsair's formidable widow, born Anne Dieu-le-veut, and one of the Gallifets. There was a buccaneering background too to the Count de Choiseul's confirmation in February 1709 of a huge grant of cattle-raising land to a surgeon called Minguet.[27] He had secured it from Du Casse in recognition of his stalwart conduct as a prisoner of the Spaniards after the raid on Carthagena in 1697, for he was surgeon to the buccaneers. Thus, incidentally, was the Right of the Axe giving way in Saint Domingo to regular, or irregular, concessions authorized by the governor or his intendant. Governor de Choiseul also sought to put in order the administration of the hospital which the buccaneers had established – they tried to provide their men with proper medical attention and with invalid pensions from the common kitty. But now the corsairs, as was their wont, faded away in the face of what seemed to them undue restriction. So that the anchorage of L'Hôpital gradually changed its name to Port-au-Prince, the present capital of Haiti a little to the north of the earlier ones of Léogane and Petit Goave.

Petit Goave, raided by the English so recently as 1697 and 1703, had been the headquarters of the filibusters in the south of Saint Domingo as Turtle Island had been to the north. It was at Petit Goave that the filibusters, in the words of an old compilation, had had 'built a very fine church, which these astonishing men enriched with all the spoils which, in their continual raids, they carried off

[24] De Gallifet, 15 May 1701: ibid., p. 50.
[25] Count de Choiseul to Charritte, 22 May 1710: ibid., p. 71.
[26] Count d'Arquyan, 1 Aug. 1711: ibid., p. 85.
[27] For this concession cf. further Léon Vignols, 'Early French Colonial Policy', *Journal of Economic and Business History* (Cambridge, Mass., 1928f), ii. 107–8.

from other temples to the same God. This church was never called anything but the Church of the Filibusters.'[28] The French buccaneers are said to have been shocked by the irreligion of their British brethren, though even the catholic faith had a somewhat loose and eccentric hold upon a colony where priests could be renegades scarcely better than their flock; yet there were as always devoted fathers, especially the Jesuits to whom the Count de Choiseul and Mithon granted additional lands in 1709. At Petit Goave a calvary stood in the middle of the settlement but in the previous year one inhabitant, Jacques Gagnès, having had a child killed by lightning, shot up the crucifix.

The Count and Countess de Choiseul that same year probably moved not into the old quarters of the governor in the little coastal fortress at Petit Goave but into the pleasanter habitation that became known as the governor's house. This collection of buildings lay above the well-built township, up an avenue amid more or less formal gardens laid out beside what was then known as the Rivière du Kiment. There was good hunting round about (largely wild pigs descended from Spanish strains) and the Choiseuls were establishing themselves in the favourite district of the buccaneers as they settled into agricultural retirement. That may not have been by chance.

The Count de Choiseul, perhaps impressed by the contribution of the corsairs to the raid on Nevis, was keen to reactivate the buccaneers despite his brush with them over their hospital. He had them paid the balance of what they had vainly claimed in booty at Carthagena and by ordinance of 9 September 1709 he offered them bounties for rejoining French service in the hostilities against England. The Count de Choiseul further dispatched an emissary into Spanish parts, whither many filibusters had withdrawn, sometimes in the English interest. An amnesty further encouraged most of these French corsairs to return to their original haunts and allegiance in Saint Domingo. Thus did the count seek to rescue French commerce in those reaches and to prime a comeback against the English who had been picking off 'all the merchant vessels which appeared on our coasts, and they did not miss one. The [French] court much relished the reasoning of the new governor and gave him full powers.'[29] His design was favoured by a lull after 1707 owing to some British withdrawal of naval strength from the West Indies to Europe. By

[28] Moreau de Saint-Méry, *Description topographique, physique, civile, politique et historique de la partie française de l'isle Saint-Domingue* (new ed. by Blanche Maurel and Étienne Taillemite, Paris, 1958), iii. 1170.
[29] P. Pierre-François-Xavier de Charlevoix, *Histoire de l'Isle Espagnole ou de S. Domingue* (Paris, 1730–1), ii. 388.

about 1710 the hope was that it only needed the arrival of French frigates to protect the colony against reprisals before the Count de Choiseul unleashed his corsairs against Jamaica and sought to wrest from the enemy supremacy in local waters.

The vigorous policy of the Count de Choiseul in mounting a naval comeback against England was oddly prefigurative of that pursued upon a vaster scale two generations later by his grandson, the Duke de Choiseul. The grandfather had done much in the war of the Spanish Succession to overcome the first at least of the two main causes discerned by his early historian, good Father de Charlevoix, as having saved 'the English from succumbing beneath the two powers which could easily unite against them in order to drive them out of South America. The first was that a pretty good number of our filibusters took sides with them [the English]; the second, that the Spaniards for their part carried out badly the orders which the two [Bourbon] kings had sent their subjects in the New World, that they should afford each other mutual succour if they were attacked.'[30] The latter consideration lay close to the heart of the future world-strategy of the Duke de Choiseul in his System of the South embracing the two Mediterraneans, that in Europe and in America the Gulf of Mexico with the Caribbean Sea. All this may have been coincidence, or not.

Neither grandfather nor grandson were destined to carry to fruition their manly policies of offensive recoil against British maritime supremacy.

Petit Goave was rated unhealthy even for Saint Domingo, and the Countess de Choiseul died out there. Her children were lucky to have been spared such a country. It may possibly have been in order to see to them, as well as to clinch at court his aggressive design, that the count set sail for France in the earlier part of 1711 aboard a French man-of-war, the *Thétis* commanded by Captain Hennequin. During the voyage he was putting out from Havana when intercepted by two British warships. The *Thétis* fought four hours, losing some seventy casualties before she surrendered, a rich prize in cargo. Among her dead lay the Count de Choiseul. His corpse was sent ashore when the British captain put into Havana[31] to disembark his prisoners. The count had been fated after all for violent death in piratical parts. Thus it came that the grandfather of the Count de Stainville lay buried in the distant island of Cuba, a prefigurative pledge upon Spanish soil of endeavour overseas for France.

---

[30] Ibid., ii. 374–5.

[31] Cf. de Bourival to Voysin, Brest, 22 July 1711: Archives de la Guerre, Archives Historiques (A I: henceforth cited as Arch. Guerre), vol. 2339, no. 10.

It is recorded that this adventurous seaman was the twenty-eighth member of the house of Choiseul to lay down his life in the service of King Louis XIV: an epitome in one family of the kind of sacrifice exacted by the glory of the Roi Soleil.

CHAPTER II

MARQUISATE

I

THE colony of Saint Domingo and not least the island of Tortuga were later to be linked with the governor's grandson, the Duke de Choiseul. And other members of the clan of Choiseul were to move in upon those parts in the course of the eighteenth-century influx of French aristocracy into Saint Domingo in search of quick profits. That development had however hardly begun in the time of their harbinger, the Count de Choiseul-Beaupré, who had honourably failed to make his fortune in Saint Domingo. His heir, the second Francis Joseph, was left an orphan, and not a rich one, when hardly fifteen.

Also, just at that time, on 15 March 1711, the Count de Choiseul's illustrious mentor, the Marshal Claude de Choiseul, died childless. Young Francis Joseph and his two little sisters, Claire-Madeleine and Marie-Anne, could at least turn to a rather formidable-sounding trio of maternal maiden aunts, the countesses Anne, Claude, and Hyacinthe de Stainville. All three ladies were canonesses at the Benedictine convent of Remiremont, one of the richest in Europe with an abbess who was a princess of the Holy Roman Empire. This highly select and snug institution did not impose perpetual vows or a nun's habit but did provide an income, reckoned to be over 2,000 livres per annum, for each lady gracing that noble chapter pending marriage. Entrants needed so many quarterings that the local boast had it that a French royal princess would be ineligible owing to her Medici blood. The youngest of the Stainville sisters, Hyacinthe, was the guardian of the orphaned heir, who would appear to have received a good education: he was an elder schoolmate and lifelong friend of the Count de Sillery, slightly better known as the Marquis de Puysieulx, a future foreign minister of France.

The Countess Hyacinthe de Stainville supervised the legal business of her nephew's inheritance. The necessary documents, obtained in chancery at Paris, were 'registered and ratified at the bailiwick of Chaumont in Bassigny'[1] on 29 September 1711. And upon the spring

---

[1] 'Inventaire fait au Château de Beaupré après de décès de Mr. de Choiseul Beaupré et de Madame son épouse', 4–5 Mar. 1712: Arch. Meuse, J 18²⁹, docket III, for the following.

morning of 4 March 1712 young Francis Joseph de Choiseul began to inventory his inheritance at the Château de Beaupré in company with the family agent, Antoine Molet. The first item was 'two large cast-iron cooking-pots with their lids', jointly valued at two livres five sous, something under two shillings in the currency of that day.[2] There followed a rather pathetic little list including a goffering-iron worth two livres, 'a basin for jam with skimmer' (four livres), 'an old garden watering-can' (two livres ten sous), 'an old copper bucket with an old warming-pan' (one livre). The emphasis upon antiquity confirms the impression of a scrap lot of hardware.

If other household ranges made better showing, it still sounds like a tolerably modest inheritance of effects: 'three small oaken tables whereof two are with two drawers, taken together, nine livres'; only one livre ten sous for two little folding tables of pinewood; a dozen rush-bottomed chairs rated six livres the lot, but twelve times as much for a 'dozen walnut chairs ornamented with cross-stitch and flowers'. A spare set of twelve pieces of floral embroidery in silk to upholster six chairs, back and seat, was assessed at forty-five livres. Other items ranged up from a violet silk bedcover edged with ribbon (twenty livres) to a gilt mirror valued at fifty, to ninety livres in respect of 'wall-hangings for a room in high-warp tapestry with little figures, in five pieces, small and large'. This, one infers, was the stuff left behind when the Count de Choiseul and his wife had sailed for Saint Domingo. There was a noticeable absence of crockery and plate from the 'effects found in the said château'.

More valuable than the household effects of the Château de Beaupré were its landed revenues. These, in accordance with a growing practice in that part of the world, had in January 1707 been leased out for six years to two middlemen, Claude Collet and Étienne Joly, at a yearly rental of 2,150 livres, round about £90, each. But when the younger Francis Joseph de Choiseul entered into his inheritance each rental was in fact reduced by ninety per cent to a mere 210 livres since 'the surplus has been distrained' by two merchants of Paris 'for the sum of three thousand and so many livres principal which they allege to be owing to them beside the interest and costs'. Outside the main lease there were a few small dues in kind owing to the estate, seven bushels of barley valued at five livres five sous, two measures of corn worth three livres, owed by a certain François Brussel – he did pay up. Such offsets, though, evidently did not take one far.

---

[2] Reckoning the French livre at approximately 10d. in the English currency of that time. French £ s. d. units (12 deniers = 1 sou, 20 sous = 1 livre) were also employed in Lorraine. Estimating the livre of Lorraine at a 30 per cent discount against that of France, it was worth approximately 7d. English.

Encumbered Beaupré upon the confines of France illustrated the way in which lordly landowners there were tending to run into debt just then, almost at the bottom of a sharp agricultural depression in accentuation of the long decline that so largely represented the reign of Louis XIV in its economic aspect. That spring of 1712 was but three winters on from the great one of 1709, the classic cold of that Grand Hiver which had congealed the wine in the cellars, had frozen to death the bird in the thicket, the beast in the stall, the traveller by the wayside. Famine had stalked a land ground down by war. The traditionally 'tight season' for subsistence in late spring had squeezed tighter. The aftermath of that frozen calamity is reckoned[3] to have been the most miserable time for rural France, essential France, since the Fronde certainly, perhaps since her Wars of Religion. And the present war continued.

The impoverishment of the inheritance at Beaupré contrasted with the superior title of the Marquis de Choiseul already ascribed to young Francis Joseph, although his seafaring father had never claimed to be better than a count: there was then considerable fluidity in French fashion in all ranks below a 'titled' dukedom. It was apparently about then that the new Marquis de Choiseul began his personal acquaintance with Duke Leopold. The honorific elevation was to be consolidated in Lorraine by a more material one which may have already enabled or obliged the young marquis to let Beaupré go as a French dowry, in principle at least, to his elder sister. In that year of 1712 Claire-Madeleine de Choiseul brought the estate into her generation-skipping marriage with her thirtyfive-year-old cousin Charles Joseph, Baron de Choiseul, a colonel of infantry who was the son by a second marriage of the elder brother of her grandfather. So Beaupré was nicely tied back into the elder branch under the dynastic principles of aristocracy.

II

Apart from marriage the prime concern of aristocracy, of the Marquis de Choiseul in the following year, was still war. Anyone then in eastern France was unlikely to make the mistake of supposing that the signature on 11 April 1713 of the main instruments of the Peace of Utrecht between England, France, Holland, Prussia, Portugal, and Savoy had terminated the War of the Spanish Succession. If the

---

[3] Cf. Pierre Goubert, 'Le "tragique" XVIIᵉ siècle' in F. Braudel and E. Labrousse, *Histoire économique et sociale de la France* (Paris, 1970f.), ii. 362 *et passim* for social and economic data in this and other sections.

terms of Utrecht were of substantial satisfaction both to selfish England, now poised to take off overseas, and to exhausted France, with her Bourbon duly enthroned at Madrid, this Spanish setback to the aggrieved house of Habsburg prevented their signature by the young Emperor Charles VI, kept sharp by his 'nighthawk', Count Rocca Stella, and other Spanish courtiers in Vienna. So the summer of 1713 found the imperial captain, Prince Eugene, fighting on to a finish against the superior forces of Marshal de Villars. The marshal was related by marriage to one branch of the Choiseul clan (Choiseul de Traves), and in the ultimate operations of that campaign upon the Rhine he had serving under him the Marquis Francis Joseph de Choiseul as a young volunteer of about seventeen.

Villars pounced on Landau, then darted across the Rhine to punch through the Austrian lines of Ettlingen on 20 September 1713 and, surprising Eugene yet again, swung against formidable Freiburg-im-Breisgau. By the end of September it was under siege. The French were not only digging trenches and saps against town and citadel but also fortifying their rear against surprise. For Eugene himself still held off strategically to the north. Freiburg, reinforced under the tough command of Lieutenant-Fieldmarshal Baron von Harsch, seemed strong enough to hold through the late season. In the hardy endeavour against it the young Marquis de Choiseul served in the second company of French musketeers to maintain the family tradition of so much service beneath the standards of the Sun King, now towards sunset.

From 5 October 1713 the French bombardment of Freiburg became almost incessant. On the afternoon of 14 October close combat against an Austrian sortie raged for two hours along the earthworks already under snow. Finally the gallant garrison withdrew, leaving corpses littered everywhere – French casualties were nearly two thousand. Soon, even in that cold, 'the stench in the saps was unbearable'.[4] But even Harsch was being worn down with no Eugene to the rescue. On 1 November French troops occupied the town of Freiburg but not the still resistant citadel. The lower town yielded some five thousand Austrian prisoners. Villars informed the Austrian commander that the only food which the captives would get would come from his garrison of the citadel. The chivalry of eighteenth-century warfare could sometimes be exaggerated. On 17 November 1713 the citadel of Freiburg-im-Breisgau capitulated. The Austrians came marching out in honour through the French lines. Though it was only with difficulty that they trudged off through two

4 Marshal de Villars, *Mémoires du Maréchal de Villars*, ed. Marquis de Vogüé (Paris, 1884 f.), iii. 223.

foot of snow. That was the end of the end of the War of the Spanish Succession.

Villars and Eugene met in unfeigned amity and on 7 March 1714 signed the Peace of Rastatt, rounding off that of Utrecht, to be further completed that September in respect of the Holy Roman Empire by the Treaty of Baden. Spain passed away for ever from the Habsburgs. Their pincer against France was broken. This great change looked towards another. At the Congress of Baden the goodwill between Villars and Eugene led into 'the system of Baden',[5] a new and tentative system of Franco-Austrian reconciliation in a catholic union over against the maritime and protestant powers. Louis XIV and his foreign minister, Torcy, sought to promote this in the embassy to Vienna in 1715 of the Count du Luc. It proved abortive after all. Contrary influences, not least Spanish ones in Vienna, for the present remained too strong. Only forty years later was the logic of the System of Baden in a revised balance of power to find fulfilment through the Diplomatic Revolution, after long and secret endeavours for Franco-Austrian rapprochement by the then Marquis de Choiseul.

For the present the end of the war at Freiburg had offered the young Marquis de Choiseul a vivid sample of military hardship, squalor, and glory. He came to hold that 'war is a profession which one cannot begin too early'.[6] That campaign had promoted his acquaintance, if not with the Marshal de Villars himself, yet with the young flower of the French nobility who were to characterize the eighteenth century. The news of the capture of the citadel was carried to Versailles by Villars' stripling aide-de-camp, the seventeen-year-old Duke de Fronsac who had already seen the inside of the Bastille, who was for decades to mark and mar the court of Versailles as the profligate Duke de Richelieu. If the Count de Broglie, a hero of Freiburg in the melee of 14 October, was already a veteran general of forty-two, a close contemporary of young Choiseul was the eighteen-year-old Duke de Luynes, the future chronicler of his age. During the siege Luynes was a comrade of Choiseul in the musketeers and it was he who, years later, recalled with that flat accuracy of his that when campaigning before Freiburg young Choiseul 'then had very little property'.[7]

The pinched background from Beaupré still obtained. A richer

[5] Count du Luc to Count de Bonneval, 9 Mar. 1715: cited, Max Braubach, *Versailles und Wien von Ludwig XIV bis Kaunitz* (Bonn, 1952: henceforth cited as Braubach), p. 81.

[6] Marquis de Stainville to Grand Duke Francis II of Tuscany, Paris, 29 Dec. 1742: Archivio di stato di Firenze: Segreteria degli Esteri del Granducato di Toscana (henceforth cited as Esteri del Granducato di Toscana), vol. 2295/1286, fo. 206.

[7] Duc de Luynes, *Mémoires du duc de Luynes sur la cour de Louis XV*, ed. L. Dussieux and E. Soulié (Paris, 1860-5: henceforth cited as Luynes), x. 389.

inheritance was, however, coming to the Marquis de Choiseul from across the recent divide of war, through his Stainville relations, in particular from the younger brother of his three aunts, Count Stephen de Stainville.

III

Whereas the Choiseuls had remained in French service, the political affinities of Count Stephen de Stainville, like those of his master, Duke Leopold of Lorraine, lay with Austria, whom Stainville served throughout Europe from Poland to Italy: a broad yet compact illustration of the way in which the nobility of Lorraine were then finding outlets of promise with the greater powers on either hand. Stephen de Stainville followed the eagles of Austria out over the plains of Eastern Europe and rose to be an imperial field-marshal and commandant-general of Transylvania and later Wallachia, wrested from the Ottoman Empire by the Peace of Passarowitz which in 1718 clinched the renewed victories of Prince Eugene at Peterwardein and at Belgrade. In this triumph against the Turk Stainville added fresh laurels to his earlier ones from the classic fields of Mohacz and Vienna. This valiant proconsul had hankered, however, after his family domains back in his little homeland. And he could afford to do so since he had been more successful than his brother-in-law in redeeming his straitened circumstances by his shining sword if not also by mining interests in Lorraine.

At the end of the sixteenth century the castle and lands of Stainville, upon the extinction of the elder line of the family, had reverted to the ducal crown. The cadet branch, to which Stephen de Stainville belonged, had retained two smaller seats on either side of Stainville itself, the châteaux of Beurey and of Demange-aux-Eaux. The main Stainville property, then reckoned to be worth 57,500 French livres, had in 1672 been acquired by a certain Daniel Morel, a secretary in the French royal service and member of the Chambre aux Deniers. He sounds a fairly typical representative of the rising bureaucratic and financial class in the carry-through from the capitalist, often bourgeois, thrust which had begun in the sixteenth century. After Morel's death Stephen de Stainville, in June 1704, had secured from Duke Leopold a renunciation in his favour of the ducal right of repurchase against the Morel heir, a canon of Notre-Dame at Paris. In effect this enabled Stainville to exercise something approximating at least to the customary right of pre-emption by kin (*retrait lignager*) whereby relations of an original landowner enjoyed a priority of repurchase on property changing hands from a subsequent owner. Such was the importance in the old order of society of family, of landed inheritance, of the long weight of the past.

Stainville's territorial comeback stands out against the broad tendency then in parts, at least, of northern and eastern France for the old nobility of the sword to be overtaken on the ground by the new one of the robe deriving especially from a middle-class magistracy. If it was true, for instance, that the latter's buying of fiefs in northern Burgundy was irreversible,[8] this was apt to be less so in Lorraine and the Barrois, partly thanks to ducal policy. But it cost to get back. Canon Morel was not selling easily, and the following year of 1705 found the count scraping around, borrowing from his relations, the Count de Couvonges and his wife, the later Countess de Rouerke. This debt of 4,000 livres was subsequently taken over by another lender to the Count de Stainville, the Sieur du Tertre,[9] an official in the administration of Lorraine and future disturber of the Stainville estate. At last on 26 January 1706 its repurchase was concluded. The count had regained possession of the 'ancient patrimony of his ancestors'[10] against payment of 95,000 livres, currency of France. Only, the redeemer, 'feeling no inclination for marriage',[11] had no heir.

Stephen de Stainville did have his sisters and in April 1705, in Vienna, he had invested the eldest of the canonesses, the Countess Anne de Stainville, with a power of attorney over his business interests. She supervised the arrangements for the repurchase of Stainville and thereafter the management of the property. Such was the survival of that antique pattern of feudalism which tended to give women so important a part in running the estates while their menfolk were away at the wars.

The Stainville estates had found a vigorous superintendent, as was suggested, in the year of their repurchase, by another activity of Anne de Stainville. Her convent at Remiremont then had a child for abbess in the person of Duke Leopold's eldest daughter; during this approximation to an interregnum Anne de Stainville was hotly competing with another noble lady for election to the coveted dignity of a Secrète de Remiremont. In a tense election she secured, under disputable conditions, twenty-eight votes against the twenty-nine of her rival, Marguerite de Méchatin. Refusing to concede so marginal

---

[8] Cf. P. de Saint Jacob, *Les Paysans de la Bourgogne du nord au dernier siècle de l'ancien régime* (Paris, 1960), p. 54.

[9] Cf. Arch. Meuse, J 18, dockets II–III.

[10] Letters-patent from the Duke Leopold of Lorraine to Marquis de Choiseul, Lunéville, 20 Oct. 1717: Archives municipales de Stainville, cited O. Toussaint, *Histoire des forêts dans les hautes vallées de l'Ornain et de la Saulx* (Bar-le-Duc, 1898), p. 376.

[11] Ibid.

a defeat, the spirited Anne de Stainville proceeded to Rome, where she obtained a papal provision in her favour to the disputed office, under decree of 5 September 1707 in the pontificate of Clement XI.[12]

In dealing with the Countess Anne de Stainville one evidently had to look sharp, as the family agent, Molet, was reminded ten years later in a brush over the canoness's young nephew, the Marquis de Choiseul. As procurator-fiscal of Stainville, Molet was responsible to her for the estate accountancy. In his account for 1717 much the largest item read: 'Paid on the verbal order of my said Lady the Countess [Anne] de Stainville the sum of nineteen hundred and sixty five francs, ten gros, currency of Bar,[13] to wit, to Sieur Chavot six hundred and seventy francs, ten gros, which he had paid to Sieur Magot, merchant at Bar, for the Marquis de Choiseul in the terms of his receipt of 22 November 1714, and to Sieur Colin twelve hundred and ninety-five francs which he borrowed from the said Sieur Magot for my said sire the Marquis de Choiseul in the terms of his receipt of 21 April 1715.'[14]

This item was struck through by the countess who noted in the margin: 'Deleted seeing that the accountant produces no [written] order, under reserve to him of suing whom he shall judge proper for its recovery, the documents having been returned to him.'[15] As may be imagined, this bleak annotation cast down Molet, who only signed off the account with the countess under specific reserve of non-acceptance of her deletion, and protest on behalf of the reinstatement of the item.

The background to this financial flurry over the indebtedness to local tradesmen of young Francis Joseph de Choiseul was his transition from his French affiliation at impoverished Beaupré to the lusher property of Stainville. It would appear that Count Stephen de Stainville had put his head together with his sovereign, Duke Leopold, and his influential relative, the Countess de Rouerke, to the end that he, a resolute bachelor 'desiring however to perpetuate his name',[16] should constitute his orphaned nephew as heir to all his

[12] Cf. Jean Dyckhoff, 'Notes sur Stainville, son château, ses seigneurs': manuscript in the Château de Stainville; also Arch. M-et-M/Vienne, 3F 491.

[13] The accounts of Stainville were at this period still kept in the old local currency of Bar: 16 deniers = 1 gros, 12 gros = 1 franc. One franc of Bar was worth about $4\frac{1}{2}d.$, that is rather over half a livre of Lorraine and rather under half a livre of France. All three currencies have to be reckoned with in the local accounts of the period.

[14] 'Compte que Rend à l'Ilustre et puissante dame Madame la Comtesse de Stainville, Dame administratisse de la terre et Baronnye de Stainville, Antoine Molet procureur fiscal de la ditte terre et baronnye chargé de la recepte des domains et droits dominiaux deubs à la ditte baronnye en deniers, grains, poulles et chappons pour l'année mil sept cent dix sept': Arch. Meuse, J 18[18].

[15] Ibid.

[16] Letters-patent from Duke Leopold of Lorraine to Marquis de Choiseul, Lunéville, 20 Oct. 1717: Archives municipales de Stainville, cited, O. Toussaint, loc. cit.

estates in Lorraine on condition that young Francis Joseph de
Choiseul took the name and arms of Stainville in proud adherence to
one of the greatest houses, traditionally providing Seneschals of
Lorraine. This was the basis of the handsome and ingenious
marriage-settlement which was worked out during 1717 to promote
the marriage of the young heir to the daughter of the Countess de
Rouerke, Françoise-Louise de Bassompierre, maid of honour to the
Duchess of Lorraine, Elizabeth Charlotte of Orleans, sister to the
Regent Orleans of France.

By this arrangement the Duke of Lorraine for his part renounced
those rights of reversion and repurchase on the Stainville lands which
he would otherwise have enjoyed upon the extinction of the direct
line. In return for this renunciation the duke was to receive 28,420
livres of Lorraine. This figure represented the difference between the
valuation of some 198,000 livres now placed upon the estate by the
ducal Council of Finance and sum of 170,000 livres which they
reckoned that the Count de Stainville had spent on it in buying from
the Morel family and in subsequent improvements. Furthermore the
duke was to be deemed 'quit and discharged as of this present of the
dowry of which the said demoiselle de Bassompierre would have had
expectation in her quality of maid of honour'.[17] In this way Duke
Leopold, a ruler both benevolent and acute, not only avoided the
expense of a dowry for the bride and scooped in a useful little sum
besides, but also, not least important, secured an undertaking from
the orphaned bridegroom that he would adhere to the service of
Lorraine. The marriage-settlement had a wider import as an
illustration of Leopold's policy of consolidating his duchy by
attaching nobles to its service and so far as possible stemming that
dispersal which the Choiseuls and the Stainvilles had themselves
exemplified.

All this was embodied in the ducal letters-patent of 20 October
1717, which formed the charter of the new line of Choiseul-Stainville
now added to the many branches of the famous house of Choiseul.

So everyone, one gathers, was happy: everybody except perhaps
the Countess Anne de Stainville who had for years administered the
family estate and, but for the new arrangement, would have inherited
its usufruct jointly with her sisters. It seems possible that her rejection
of that little matter of the debt to Sieur Magot may have been
something in the nature of a parting shot at her lucky nephew. It
would appear, however, that he nevertheless was, or became, sincerely

---

[17] 'Lettres d'entérinement par la Chambre des comptes du Duché de Bar des lettres patentes
obtenues le 20 octobre 1717 par Joseph-François Marquis de Choiseul', 6 Nov. 1717: Arch.
Meuse, 2F 19. Cf. also O. Toussaint, loc. cit.

fond of his aunt. She did allow another item included in the same account on the strength of her verbal order. This was a special payment of thirty livres of Lorraine to Sieur Heyblot, the family lawyer at Bar-le-Duc, 'for his journeys and extraordinary pieces of work done in connection with business concerning the marriage of the Marquis de Choiseul'.[18] The nuptial benediction of the marriage was performed at the ducal court at Lunéville, in the presence of Leopold, his duchess, and lords and ladies, on 23 November 1717.

One stipulation of the letters-patent had been that, in default of direct male descent by the marriage, the Duke of Lorraine could resume possession of the Stainville inheritance upon payment to the family of the agreed figure of 170,000 livres, roughly some £5,000. So the Marquis and the Marquise de Stainville, as they were now styled, must have been particularly gratified that their first-born of midsummer 1719 should have been a son. All the same £5,000 was not a great capital sum, even allowing for the high purchasing-power of money in those days and especially in Lorraine where prices were notoriously low. Contemporaries considered that the future Duke de Choiseul was born 'in a very mediocre condition of fortune'.[19]

IV

The year of the Count de Stainville's birth was a vintage year for Lorraine. An old chronicler of that region recorded that 'the year 1719 was extremely hot, the earth was as dry as a cinder, the crops burnt as they stood, provisions increased in price, a prodigious quantity of cicadas devoured the meadows: but it afforded great abundance of excellent wines, of which the reputation has long been preserved'[20] to rival the classic vintage of 1622.

The price of burgundy was halved from five years previously whereas corn in that area showed a two-year price-rise of twenty-five per cent or more. That was what would weigh upon peasants mainly living close enough to subsistence-level to perpetuate the primordial equation of an abundant harvest with a good year. The poor, as of yore, were those who lacked bread. For most people in Lorraine, in Europe, what mattered most was the permutation of the natural round, as in the incidence of weather and of sickness, in a society still preponderantly rural. Its ancient patterns of existence, largely deriving from the middle ages, were laboriously unfolded over and over again, year in, year out, in countrysides everywhere under the

---

[18] Stainville accounts for 1717, *u.s.*
[19] Mouffle d'Angerville, *Vie privée de Louis XV* (London, 1781), iii. 181.
[20] Durival, *Description de la Lorraine et du Barrois* (Nancy, 1778–9), i. 116.

28 BEGINNING 1719–1740

sign of the cross, high upon churches, humbly in cottages, carved upon landmarks delineating the scope of local existence. Saints' days and religious ceremonies rotated in an outstanding significance often blended with the elements in the endless and precarious round of agriculture, ploughing, haymaking, harvesting, back to the long grind of flailing through the winter. Life was nourished from the past, by customs legal as well as social, upon precedents traditional from time immemorial.

In this old order, so largely local and hereditary, not all movement remained cyclic. Political initiatives and, often more deeply, obscure undercurrents of economic change came working through with gradual but cumulative effect. At the time that the Count de Stainville was born special circumstances made this particularly true of Lorraine by comparison, even, with France under the Regency, politically revised and economically almost upon the turn after a century, more or less, of agricultural depression, roughly between those two classic vintages. Such a turn for the better was still around the corner and imperceptible as yet, so soon after the affliction and depopulation of the War of the Spanish Succession, the Grand Hiver, the great murrain of 1714, and now the difficult years around 1720, difficult enough even apart from the collapse of John Law's financing through the Mississippi Company. Yet upon the whole there lay ahead a sunnier climate, perhaps even literally as to weather. If the future Choiseul was born under an auspicious sign for the prosperity of the country which he was to govern, in the land of his birth, still more vividly, was the worst of the long reign of the three ancient scourges, war, famine, pestilence, at last drawing to a close; though this again was not yet evidently certain.

The year 1720 was of sinister note in the annals of the little duchy as of France herself. That May there docked at Marseilles a merchantman bringing not only wares from the east but also death from the plague. This was the last great outbreak in western Europe of the black death. Amid agonizing scenes Belzunce, Bishop of Marseilles, proclaimed it to be the wrath of God against the Jansenists, catholic sectaries then active as rigorists hardly better than Calvinists, fit only, according to another outraged priest, to be treated 'as pagans and publicans'.[21] Whether or not such episcopal wrath was wrath divine, from Marseilles the plague went spreading to Toulon, to Arles.

The fear of the time came out in the anxious precautions,

[21] Archbishop de Mailly of Rheims, *Lettre de Mgr l'archevêque-duc de Reims à MMgrs les cardinaux, archevêques et évêques du royaume qui sont soumis à la bulle Unigenitus* (1719): cited, Félix Rocquain, *L'Esprit révolutionnaire avant la révolution* (Paris, 1878), p. 19.

Château de Stainville.
The lowest window in the turret at left is that of the oratory.

contradicting any assumption of invariable indifference then, that Duke Leopold took to protect his subjects against this hateful scourge. He did not indeed persecute those Jansenists who had found shelter across the borders of Lorraine – they included the tutor to his own children, the vehement Abbé de Vence from the Sorbonne, now however become submissive. Rather were fairs, the great carriers of contagion, forbidden throughout the duchy, and the court was largely dispersed, Leopold noting that 'orders must be given . . . to the nobles to withdraw to their estates'. [22] Thus the Stainvilles and their baby probably spent that summer in the country. The hot months nourished a plague. A clamp was imposed upon all foreign trade, which Lorraine could afford since she was almost self-supporting. Traffic from the frontiers was controlled by check-points manned by a militia of harquebusiers. No traveller might leave the roads without authorization. The duke further had medicines stocked up for his subjects to the value of 150,000 livres out of his own pocket and proposed that every town should prepare three hospitals plus one isolation hospital. The local authorities were to make ready against a possible shortage of beds and to supplement them with 'palliasses of good ticking'. [23] The French administration, however, had also been active. The contagion was confined to the south. Leopold's untested precautions at any rate enabled the down-and-outs of the duchy to sleep soft for some years.

Next year the duke, provident but uneconomic, was enjoining his subjects to stock up grain for two years. On this he was gently reminded of practicalities by the Marquis de Stainville, writing from Bar-le-Duc in September 1721: 'Most well off people had already taken their precautions in advance and those who are able will not fail to satisfy Your Royal Highness's wish. . . . For the present there is no dearth in the land. On the contrary provisions have come down a lot since the diminution of specie and from the abundance . . . of corn. Notwithstanding this there is a lot of fever in the countryside but it is not sickly and is attributed to the quantity of plums which the populace has been eating.' [24] If this vague fever in country districts was vaguely disquieting there could be sharper anxieties around then, not least for young mothers.

In Lorraine 'during the summer and autumn of 1723 smallpox carried off nearly all the little children: more than fifteen hundred dead were counted in the town of Nancy alone', [25] then totalling less

---

[22] Memorandum by Duke Leopold of Lorraine: cited, Durival, op. cit., i. 118.
[23] Memorandum by Duke Leopold: ibid., i. 119.
[24] Marquis de Stainville to Duke Leopold, Bar-le-Duc, 19 Sept. 1721: Arch. M-et-M/Vienne, 3F 85, no. 1.
[25] Durival, op. cit., i. 125.

than twenty thousand inhabitants. In June that year Leopold himself thus lost his sixteen-year-old heir, Prince Leopold Clement. And twelve years earlier the Duke and Duchess had within a single week been bereft by smallpox of three of their children including the little Abbess of Remiremont. Queen Anne of England had not been the only royal mother in successive mourning in an age when only massive mortality had made Louis XV the little king of a country wherein, it is estimated overall, it took roughly two children to ensure one adult, with every other infant falling victim to the regular massacre of the innocents. In the eighteenth century it was still necessary to get on to matter-of-fact terms with death.

Luck is one ingredient of fame, certainly in the life of the future Choiseul. He was fortunate to survive the age of four, but survive he did together with his baby sister Charlotte-Eugénie, born that year. They may have owed something to the unusual zeal of their mother for cleanliness and sanitary hygiene. (The Marquise de Stainville was later described as taking pleasure in emptying her own close-stool and scrubbing the pan out by the hour.)[26] The children probably spent much of their time in the sheltering countryside, either at the Château de Stainville itself some miles to the south-west of the little town of Ligny-en-Barrois or, to the south-east across a typical involution of French territory, at the Château de Demange. This Château de l'Ennui, as a friend of the Marquise was to christen it, was another family property inherited from 'this dear uncle'[27] after his death in October 1720. Field-Marshal de Stainville deserved the outlay of eighty-four livres made by his patrimonial estate for his memorial service whereat, in September 1721, the Franciscan Father Gérard pronounced the funeral oration in eulogy of the profitable success-story of this warrior who had himself inherited 'only the examples of a father as illustrious in his virtue as exhausted in his fortune'.[28]

V

The redeemed family seat, the Château de Stainville (from the Latin *septem villae*, seven houses), lay in the wooded hill-country to the

[26] Cf. Madame de Graffigny to François Devaux, Cirey, 29 Dec. 1738: Eugène Asse, *Lettres de Mme de Graffigny* (Paris, 1879), p. 137.

[27] 'Enregistrement des lettres d'érection en marquisat de la baronnie de Stainville au profit de M. de Choiseul, Marquis de Stainville, du 7 Avril 1722', cited Marquis de Marmier, 'Stainville et Choiseul-Stainville', *Bulletin mensuel de la société d'archéologie lorraine et du musée historique lorrain*, 2e série, tom. XI, vol. 60 (Nancy, 1911), p. 252.

[28] Funeral oration by Father Augustin Gérard on Field-Marshal de Stainville, 24 Sept. 1721: Arch. Meuse, B 2923: cited, Henri de La Perrière, *Beurey: ses seigneurs et leur demeures* (Bar-le-Duc, 1928), p. 29.

south of Bar-le-Duc, cupped in a sudden hollow where the little river Saulx crossed what was soon to become the highroad from Nancy to Paris (at that period the main road westward from Ligny was still doglegged, up by Bar). Medieval in origin, the castle survived mainly as a construction of the early sixteenth century retaining the traditional features with renaissance embellishment. A tower-flanked gate, watched at that time by François Didelot the porter, opened into an outer courtyard whence access to the main donjon was over a drawbridge spanning a moat 'of about forty feet in width, partly filled: note, the inhabitants of the villages subject to the said Stainville are obliged to empty it':[29] a seigneural corvée which elsewhere at least was then tending to be particularly resented. The note of enduring feudalism was struck again in the enumeration of a 'tower where are three prisons the one above the other for the service of prisoners, criminal and civil'.[30] A wall five foot thick with a way along the top was part of the perimeter of curtain-walls furnished with the usual posterns and loopholes pierced for guns, probably in accordance with ducal letters-patent of 1516 authorizing the further fortification of Stainville.

Typical, high-pitched slate roofs, complete with gargoyles and ornate dormer windows in the renaissance manner, crowned the residential block of the château, flanked by pepperpot turrets. Internally the main features were 'two chambers one upon the other of fifty feet in length and thirty in breadth: in the lower chamber one hears mass from the chapel which is in the neighbouring tower':[31] a domestic arrangement which is comprehensible when one has seen the diminutive proportions of the circular oratory, ornamented with the cross anchored of the Stainvilles. Other features were the corkscrew staircase, a secret chamber, the vaulted kitchen with admirable cellars, the bakery, butchery, barns, stables, together with such seigneural appendages as the winepress and dovecot.

At just about this period, from 1723 onwards, the Marquis de Stainville was setting in order and embellishing his inheritance. Employing an architect called Boquet, he put in hand repairs and improvements to the château itself, the market, the auditory or seigneurial court-house, and other buildings in the village. This was the next stage in the restoration of the Stainville estate, the outward mark of local participation in the postwar phase of seigneurial reaction. This French reaction, traditionally late, is now coming to be

[29] 'Table du Plan du Chasteau de Stainville': Arch. Meuse, J 18[22]. (This undated schedule would appear to date from the earlier part of the eighteenth century.)
[30] Ibid.
[31] Ibid.

recognized as operative, more or less, from about the middle of the seventeenth century.[32] Which may be coming close to indicating that most forms of self-help or initiative by landowners could be classed as reaction of one kind or another, whether against the sly encroachments of tenacious peasants or the long devaluation of money, of rents over a period only just drawing to a close. The upswing at Stainville in the seventeen-twenties could be closely matched on estates in Burgundy. Nor was it only at Stainville that the impetus of seigneurial restoration after 1715 was reflected in the long neglected reconstruction of châteaux,[33] specially called for in battered Lorraine.

The hammering of builders in Stainville was probably backed by a quickening thud of axes in forests round about. In the forestry returns of the estate, timber-felling in 1723 suddenly jumped up to about twice the norm, and in 1725, still, forty-three oaks and oaklings were felled for building. (Comparative yearly cuttings were: 1721, 67 acres 1 rood; 1722, 54 acres $36\frac{1}{2}$ roods; 1723, 130 acres $19\frac{1}{2}$ roods; 1724, 60 acres $47\frac{3}{4}$ roods; 1725, 59 acres $4\frac{1}{2}$ roods.)[34] Besides this immediate object, the sale of timber, as so often on estates, was in any case the easiest way of raising cash on the Stainville lands in their woodland economy. Timber prices had usually held up better than any in the depression from the seventeeth century, and forestry was the form of cultivation with special appeal to lordly landowners. In 1723 the returns on timber at Stainville touched a peak at 15,362 livres. Thus might one contrive to cover such items of extraordinary expenditure as that in the account for 1725 for payments made 'to the masons, slaters, carpenters, joiners, glaziers, nailmakers, carters, workmen, and others'[35] employed on the restoration-work to a total figure of 3,171 livres. Next year the corresponding figure was 2,988 livres. These were considerable sums even if they reflected the relatively high wages of builders in a low-wage economy.

Within the château reconstruction probably converted the ancestral halls into more comfortable apartments with a good deal of pleasant panelling and, for instance, in one of the main fireplaces, a fine backing wherein heraldic trophies framed a Stainville escutcheon, paired now with one bearing the chevrons of the Bassompierre lineage of the young Marquise de Stainville. It may have been then or some years later that several of the great beams supporting ceilings

---

[32] Cf. in F. Braudel and E. Labrousse, op. cit., ii. 590f.

[33] Cf. Pierre Goubert, *Beauvais et le Beauvaisis de 1600 à 1730* (Paris, 1960), p. 534.

[34] Arch. Meuse, J 18[9] (Gruerie de Stainville: Juridiction: Bois: Arpentages: 1618–an VIII), docket II: Arpentages, rearpentages et recollements. (By Stainville measurement at that period 10 inches = 1 foot, 20 square feet = 1 verge or rood, 100 *verges* = 1 *arpent* or acre.)

[35] Stainville accounts for 1725: Arch. Meuse, J 18[18].

acquired corbels elegantly fashioned in the form of classical heads. One of these, in a room adjoining the oratory, was, if not actually a likeness of the Marquis de Choiseul, at any rate a vivid and ironical approximation to the chubby Choiseul cast of countenance, complete with snub nose and thick lips.

Such was the stir and revival of those years in the château of Stainville and in its little market-town. Featured there were a good many streets, the church with its several chantries and a remarkable frieze of harpies round one door, the market as the centre of activity every Thursday, and the court-house along with numbers of taverns and, even, more than one school. Popular education was relatively advanced in the north-eastern confines of France and it is reckoned that in the eighteenth century, in a belt from Normandy across to Lorraine, eight out of every ten men came to be able to sign their names correctly in their marriage-contracts, roughly twice as many as under Louis XIV. More striking still, Stainville possessed a separate school for girls. This may be associated with Father Claude Varnerot (1648–1734), a native of Stainville who scored a literary success with a book called *Le Bon Paroissien*. A student from the celebrated Collège du Plessis in Paris, Varnerot figured in a circle of Jansenist priests in the diocese of Toul which, in accordance with a feminine strain in Jansenism, helped to put eighteenth-century Lorraine in the forefront of education for women, of primary education devised just for village girls.

If the market-town of Stainville, like the château itself, was considerably larger than today, the provostship (*prévôté*) of Stainville then stretched along the Saulx almost to the level of Mognéville beyond Beurey as one of the ten juridical districts comprised in the bailiwick (*bailliage*) of Bar-le-Duc, itself one of the eighteen bailiwicks of the duchy. Interlocking was the importance of Stainville as the miniature capital of a feudal domain in a system of territorial lordship arguably older than feudalism itself. Stainville was a village enlarged but true to its kind, primarily a community of toil looking up to its master, the lord of his castle. In such a fief tenure still tended to take precedence over property, certainly for the peasants. They would mostly, indeed, own a little land, sometimes more than a little, occasionally even as an allodial holding in full ownership free of any lord. But in general their ownership remained contingent upon the seignory and, most usually, upon the annual payment to the lord of a quitrent (*cens*), often small but signifying territorial obligation. The quitrent, apart from any other rent, was a pretty regular indication that while a peasant could indeed sell his land it was with the consent of the seigneur and generally subject to his right in that event to buy it in (*droit de retenue*), subject in turn, as always then, to almost endless local variations.

Beneath this legalistic involvement there lurked that ancestral antagonism of the soil between the seigneur in his proprietorial primacy, wherein peasant-holdings were in the main concessions in more or less terminable alienation, and the peasants cherishing their long grievance that land surely all theirs by the sweat of their brows should somehow have been filched from their forbears, ages ago. Such was the perennial stuff of peasant revolts and resistance, due within less than a generation to make some stir there at Stainville.

For the present tradition, still vividly etched against a recent background of strife and disorder, kept people huddled into hierarchy, into hierarchy upon hierarchy deep down into the graded masses of the peasantry itself. A rich peasant, owning quite a few acres with a plough to match and having the say in the village assembly, would hardly countenance one of his children marrying into the family of a mere labourer or farmhand. In that clannish society the family counted for much and everybody knew his place, or should do.

If, through the feudal legacy, property was at all levels the palladium of the old regime, at all but the highest it was localized. Small wonder that the peasant horizon was mainly bounded by the massively self-contained, largely self-sufficient lordship with its own customs and, as at Stainville, measurements if not, still, prices locally imposed. Peasants might differ from their lord but they often remained in a real sense solidary, participants in a single community braced against interlopers, the suspect *forains*, against the uncertain world of chance outside, difficult and expensive of access, and risky too what with footpads by the wayside and shady characters lurking in woodlands, isolated crofters who did not fit in and remote shepherds knowing more than was healthy. Peasants were individualists in all conscience in their relentless pursuit of meagre profits but it was individualism sieved, to an extent not always easy to recapture, through the fine mesh of a corporative existence. Even in the eighteenth century a village could profit psychologically as well as economically from the delimited certainty of its surrounding *finage* or confine.

At Stainville the village and the castle stood each in its setting. The garden of the château featured 'alleys of full-grown bushes'[36] interspersed with fruit trees. The flower-garden was laid out in formal French fashion, precisely delineated with a 'parterre composed of six square beds whereof the double borders of box are furnished with platbands round about'. The garden was stocked up and the

[36] 'Table du Plan du Chasteau de Stainville', *u.s.*, and for the following.

gardener, Antoine Francque, was paid the relatively high wage of one hundred livres of Lorraine a year, comparing with thirty to Didelot the porter. In the estate accounts for 1726, however, Francque's wages were 'allowed provisionally subject to rendering account of the fruit and produce of the garden and dovecot'.[37] In that tight economy the garden was expected to pay off no less than the surrounding countryside, in the case of a château as of a cottage. The château and its curtilage were after all the largest manse of the village, that of its first inhabitant. Of primary importance also to a peasant, even in the relation to the fields he tilled, was his own manse comprising his house, courtyard, and immediate surround, nearly always including a bit of garden, his only land exempt from tithe (but not quitrent). So he crammed it with precious stuff, in Lorraine as often as not with cabbages overhung by bullaces (*mirabelles*), the little yellow plums yielding the solace of the local gin.

In springtime Stainville, down in its hollow, acquires a white coronal of blossom. The fruit-trees in the garden of the château matched the orchards upon the surrounding slopes, notably cherry and pear – perry was a standby and pears tended to be an older crop than apples. As for cherrytrees, the estate had, for instance, sold off sixty-three dead ones in 1716. That countryside is rich with fruit and Bar-le-Duc had since the middle ages been famous for its preserves. In the eighteenth century the landscape was also embroidered with vineyards though they may well, there as elsewhere in those latitudes, have been already in retreat before the orchards. When in blossom the fruit-trees of Stainville are undercarpeted with cowslips, while kingcups and cuckooflowers decorate the watermeadows down by the little river Saulx. During the boyhood of the future Duke de Choiseul local landmarks included two peartrees known as Poirier la Géante and Poirier l'Homme Pendu. Huge peartrees were apt to be a feature of the landscape of the old regime in northern France.[38]

If the intimate microcosm of Stainville in the early eighteenth century looked to a giant peartree, it also included a fairy vineyard, the Vigne de Fée. Other spots were La Borne Fourchue and Gratte Loup of the scratching wolf; the fields too were personal, Champ David, Champ du Valet, Champ Godard over towards the Côte Joly carrying more vineyards and another distinctive peartree. Bois Thomas and the Bois du Petit Val lay out by Ménil-sur-Saulx, the most attractive of the dependent villages tucked away on the southern confines of the Stainville estate. These marched with the lands of the Premonstratensian abbey of Jovilliers, rich and old, founded in the twelfth century by a disciple of Saint Norbert. The woods there

[37] Stainville accounts for 1726, *u.s.*   [38] Cf. P. Goubert, op. cit., pp. 98 and 114.

occasioned the usual kind of boundary disputes between two important domains. During 1725 joint parties of surveyors, foresters, and estate-officers from Stainville and Jovilliers were perambulating the Bois Thomas in order to define the limits more exactly and improve the boundary-stones inscribed with the Stainville cross on the northern face and with a crosier upon the southern: more symbols of religion to delimit ancient territories, local horizons. But the abbot subsequently refused to sign the procès-verbal of agreement. More than thirty years later the officers of the future Duke de Choiseul were still at it, drawing up long documents and negotiating with the monks about the woodlands in those parts. Life then was deliberate, and law ever tends to lag behind life.

On the other side of Stainville, to the north, the road led out past the church and the cemetery up on the hill behind the castle along the valley of the Saulx to Lavincourt. Thence the vineyards and woods of Bia stretched up towards Montplonne at the northern extremity of the Stainville lands. There lay the Bois de Ruissart and the Bois de Tuilerie – the tileworks at Montplonne were a feature of the estate and were doubtless helping with the roof of the château. (A tiled roof then was apt to proclaim financial superiority over thatch.) The shortest way from Stainville to Montplonne, however, runs by track across lonely uplands. If these were then even more afforested than today, yet the felling was already considerable so that some stretches of the chalky hills probably presented their open aspect where flocks might graze. Wild strawberries nestle in the sudden coppices of hazel, birch, and hawthorn where larks in springtime sing the season in.

VI

More attractively situated than the Château de Stainville was the subsidiary Château de Demange, the home of the Stainvilles before Count Stephen had bought back the main seat. It looks, however, as though this repurchase and the borrowing to finance it had brought trouble upon Demange. In 1713 Nicolas du Tertre had secured judgement against Count Stephen de Stainville, again represented by the Countess Anne, for a debt of two thousand French livres. The debt remained unpaid and by the summer of 1714 Demange and the dependent Baudignécourt were being put up for public auction to the highest bidder 'upon the bid made by the said Sieur du Tertre in the sum of fifteen thousand livres'.[39] The outcome of this sale is uncertain but Duke Leopold may well have stepped in since on 8 May 1719 he was leasing to Count Stephen de Stainville and his heirs 'the justices, lordships, domains and lordly rights'[40] of Demange at an annual rental of 2,500 francs, currency of Bar. On the count's death in the following year this property too passed to his nephew, the Marquis de Stainville, who on 13 December 1721 secured from his open-handed sovereign letters-patent releasing him from all rent for Demange. Thus did the young marquis enter into free enjoyment of Demange on the other side of the forest of Ligny from Stainville.

Demange-sur-Eaux lies in the delicious little valley of the Ornain, looking through a gap in the low hills over towards the crests of Vaucouleurs marking the river Meuse. The picturesque situation reminded a visitor some years later of the watering-place of Plombières, already patronized.[41] The Château de Demange was publicly described as a 'very fine castle',[42] privately by that same visitor, the carping Madame de Graffigny, as a disorderly hole of a place:[43] which, to a child, can mean a real home. An old mansion with attic-rooms and passages of polished flags, it largely became the country residence of the Marquise de Stainville, who crammed it with furniture till there were writing-tables, and books, dotted everywhere. She was a great one for picking things up at sales, corner-pieces and umpteen closestools.

Externally Demange, like Stainville, had survived complete with drawbridge and moats, noted as being full of water. That quite often applied to most parts of watery Demange, where the church was charmingly if precariously built upon an islet embraced by two arms of the Ornain, twisting into loops above and below the village. So that, as the villagers were to complain some twenty years later, 'they are continually inundated at the least rain, the waters spreading in the locality, in their houses and gardens to such a point that in winter they often ran the risk of perishing along with their cattle'.[44]

In summer, though, the Ornain might seem hardly more than a

---

[39] 'Extrait des registres du gref du bailliage de Bassigny, siège de St. Thiébaut, de vingt juin 1714': Archives Nationales (henceforth cited as Arch. Nat.), 5 AP42 (Fonds Bassompierre), docket 162 (Seigneurie de Demange: titres de propriété et du domaine; procès; droits seigneuriaux, 1529–1786).

[40] 'Chambre des comptes du Duché de Bar, 1723–6', fo. 42: Arch. Meuse, B 282.

[41] Cf. Madame de Graffigny to François Devaux, Demange-aux-Eaux, 7–10 Oct. 1738: Yale University Library (Beinecke Rare Book and Manuscript Library), former collection of Sir Thomas Phillipps/Graffigny 23900 (henceforth cited as Yale/Beinecke: Phillipps/Graffigny 23900), vol. ii, fo. 69.

[42] Durival, op. cit., iii. 108.

[43] Madame de Graffigny to Devaux, Demange-aux-Eaux, 6 Oct. 1738: u.s., vol. ii, fo. 63.

[44] 'Placet pour les habitans et communauté de Demange aux Eaux, office de Gondrecourt', 20 Aug. 1741: Arch. Nat., 5 AP42 (Fonds Bassompierre), docket 162.

rivulet, flowing deliciously clear and famous for its trout. Crayfish, too, were then dirt cheap at Demange. And in season one might get a pot-shot at a woodcock even from the garden of the château. The garden was a pleasance bounded on two sides by the river, winding round it like a ribbon of velvet, one is told, and watering the roots of a peripheral 'alley of hornbeam as high as the eye can reach'.[45] Beneath lay the kitchen-gardens lush with beds of artichokes and asparagus; the Marquise de Stainville was not above taking a personal interest in procuring the seed of some specially choice chicory. Among the beds the hum of hives offset the cooing from the seigneurial dovecots. From the garden one could slip out into pastures like the Gagnage du Potier, Potter's Pasture, along by the water-meadows inlaid with flowers, the river itself blossoming into waterlilies and yellow flags sliced across by the blue of dragonflies darting through long afternoons. The smiling vale dimpled back into mossy hillocks exuberant with bluebells and dogroses, and, behind again, beckoning hills and woodlands abounding in wild life: just the place for a boy to grow up in.

Such was the setting, at Demange and at Stainville, of the childhood of the future Duke de Choiseul, one day to be one of the foremost model farmers in France and the minister whose long government was to set a landmark in the expansion of her agriculture, as of her economic prosperity overall. Choiseul did not, however, inherit his father's love of hunting. It was a pursuit, he confessed, for which 'I have never had much taste'.[46] He hated cruelty. In after years he was keener on indoor sport.

For sociable lads in those parts there was the outstanding attraction of the fairs, held four times a year at Stainville in normal times. Children of the continental aristocracy in the eighteenth century tended to spend much of their time with the servants, and the little count was probably on familiar terms with those at Stainville, the porter, the gardener, and the maid Babette. They likely all had a hard enough life of it under his exacting mother. It is also likely that, at a higher level, there was a fair amount of visiting around the neighbourhood, especially since so many of the local mansions were in the family in one way or another.

Social intercourse developed between Demange-aux-Eaux and the ancestral seat of the Choiseuls less than ten miles to the south at Beaupré, now settled back upon the Count de Stainville's aunt and uncle, the Baron de Choiseul, less smart than the Stainvilles though

---

[45] Madame de Graffigny to Devaux, Demange-aux-Eaux, 6 Oct. 1738: Yale/Beinecke: Phillipps/Graffigny 23900, vol. ii, fo. 64; cf. also fo. 67.
[46] Choiseul, 'Mémoires inédits', 3/18/13/566/1.

seemingly not too badly off after all. Aunt Claire-Madeleine, however, grew into a regular countrywoman, at her distaff from early morn, supervising the baking of bread and the cut of joints, practical and penny-pinching. At the same time, like her brother, the Marquis, she was not wholly stupid, less so perhaps than her husband. The former Colonel de Choiseul became an old buffer who tried to relieve the tedium of their days with scraps of news and awful jokes ('*de bon mot archy sot*').[47]

Individuals were after all subordinate to dynasty. Those depressing relations did represent the persistence of the old line of Choiseil-Beaupré along with the new branch of Choiseul-Stainville through that intricate policy of intermarriage and territorial general-post whereby great families then sought to conserve and extend their reach. The way in which the younger Francis Joseph de Choiseul took over the line of Stainville illustrated what the creation of a new branch of nobility was apt to mean in practical terms in eighteenth-century Europe.

Even after the young Marquis de Stainville had taken over, there remained a last survivor of the direct line of Stainville. This was the godfather of the future duke, the Count Jean-François de Stainville, born in 1668, son of Count George de Stainville (died 1692), elder brother of the beneficent Count Stephen. Jean-François was a cavalry lieutenant in his uncle's company of the ducal bodyguard,[48] a ducal chamberlain (1705), and counsellor of state. His main activity, however, was improving and extending his little estate at Beurey, further up the river Saulx from Stainville. After his father's death he had rebuilt the château at Beurey in the form of an oblong stone box of a house with the usual high chimneys and slate roof. Its completion was recorded on one of the stones in 1704. It made an attractive enough modern residence in its sunny simplicity of line, relieved only by a pillared porch. In order to command a southern aspect the new château was sited askew from the old so that it was set sideways to the Saulx flowing alongside the grounds. This was the Count Jean-François's 'very fine house which he has embellished with gardens and other commodities, and in which he has made his residence',[49] in the terms of the letters-patent of 23 June 1719 whereby Duke Leopold formally erected Beurey and the dependent Mussey into a barony. Five days later was born the future Duke de Choiseul, for whom Beurey was in due course to be the first home of his own.

[47] Madame de Graffigny to Devaux, Demange-aux-Eaux, 26–7 Nov. 1738: *u.s.*, vol. ii, fo. 172; cf. also fos. 182–3.

[48] Cf. Arch. dép. Meurthe-et-Moselle, B 191, fo. 72.

[49] Letters-patent from Duke Leopold to Count Jean-François de Stainville, Lunéville, 23 June 1719: Arch. Meuse, B 279, fo. 129, cited, H de La Perrière, op. cit., p. 34.

The future duke was to benefit, like his father the marquis, from the small enthusiasm for matrimony among the Stainvilles of that day. Count Jean-François de Stainville was then a close and crusty bachelor of over fifty living in seclusion at Beurey with his old mother who scolded and domineered over him. When this lady at last died in 1733 at the age of ninety-eight this mother's son was scarely still of marriageable age. Ten years earlier Duke Leopold, running over his nobles with an eye to escorts to take his eldest son to Prague upon a state occasion, had noted against Count Jean-François, by then a captain of his bodyguard: 'Not suitable because of his temper, his little politeness, and the little company which he keeps.'[50]

Probably more sociable than the Château de Beurey and certainly more impressive was that of Sorcy,[51] the seat of the family of Choiseul-Meuse by the banks of that river a little further to the east. The future Duke de Choiseul described it as 'an ancient and noble castle'.[52] It is uncertain whether, when he was still a boy as the Count de Stainville, Sorcy had yet acquired its striking gateposts surmounted by squatting hounds. But the door displayed a motto which so lastingly impressed him that he adopted it for his own: *A force d'aller mal tout ira bien*, by dint of going badly all shall go well.

VII

The countryside of the Choiseuls and the Stainvilles now acquired a new focus of honour and power. On 7 April 1722 Duke Leopold of Lorraine granted the Marquis de Stainville letters-patent erecting the barony of Stainville into a marquisate. In view of the prevailing elasticity of titles the very existence of such letters-patent is almost

---

[50] 'Mémoire de la main propre du Duc Leopold de Lorraine sur les individus principaux de la Noblesse de son Duché pour en choisir les compagnons de voyage de son fils François à Prague'; undated memorandum of early 1723: Österreichisches Staatsarchiv, Haus-, Hof- und Staatsarchiv, (henceforth cited as Ö.S./H.H.S.), Lothringisches Hausarchiv, cited, Maurice Payard, 'Trois mémoires autographes du duc Léopold' in *Bulletin mensuel de la société d'archéologie lorraine et du musée historique lorrain*, 2e série, tom, XIX, vol. 68 (1924), p. 94.

[51] The Château de Sorcy was, like that of Beurey, burnt down during the Second World War. Of the other châteaux in the Choiseul-Stainville country, that at Demange has also disappeared so that the central building of the Château de Stainville is the only survival. At Stainville, in contrast to Beurey, the château escaped when a large part of the village was destroyed by German formations which ravaged the district during their retreat in 1944. The destruction of the Château de Beurey is recorded by its last owner in the following terms: 'Le 29 août 1944, une bande de S.S. a brûlé les trois villages qui se posent sur la Saulx: Couvonges, Beurey et Robert-Espagne, en y massacrant une centaine de personnes. Le Château de Beurey, assis sur la rivière au bout du village, a été entièrement détruit par obus incendiaires et lance-flammes avec tout ce qu'il contenait.' (Manuscript note by the author inserted facing p. 33 of the copy of Henri de La Perrière, op. cit., in the Bibliothèque de la Ville de Bar-le-Duc, reference B5/I.)

[52] Duke de Choiseul to Voltaire, Versailles, 12 Nov. 1759: Pierre Calmettes, *Choiseul et Voltaire* (Paris, 1902), p. 38.

more striking than the delay in according territorial confirmation to a previously assumed rank – the Count de Rouerke, to take another local instance, waited much longer before securing his patent in 1727. Such letters of ennoblement were, however, part of the policy of the Duke Leopold, who indeed debased their currency by issuing between two and three hundred for his little duchy.

Lorraine, Barrois, Stainville were in their social setting typical of the continent in the early eighteenth century, still basically feudal. Contemporaries called it feudal without bothering too much about subsequent refinements of a seigneurial order. Being the Marquis de Stainville meant even then domination as the lord of 'the borough of Stainville, of the villages of Ménil-sur-Saulx, Lavincourt, and Montplonne, in all rights of high, middle, and low justice: as of having justice administered there by a verderer (*prévost gruyer*) and other ordinary officers, of establishing there notaries, scriveners, and other like prerogatives, which have always caused this barony to be considered one of the principal fiefs of our duchy of Bar.'[53] The attributes of a fief were legal as well as territorial, legal precisely because it was grounded in the soil. If a seignory was largely an economic unit, it was traditionally a juridical one wherein cases were judged in the name of the lord often concerned in them and to the advantage of his officers by way of legal fees and pickings.

In the marquisate of Stainville the verderer or provost and his lieutenant 'have cognizance of all cases, civil and criminal, of the first instance save and excepting the privileged cases which are reserved to the bailiwick of Bar, whither lies the appellate jurisdiction from Stainville'.[54] This was standard practice. Appeals did lie externally, expensively, though seigneurial justice might seek to discourage them; and the bailiwick or *bailliage* was the legal sphere wherein central authority regularly impinged upon the seigneurial system. In the ordinary way lordly justice, often directed by a procurator-fiscal, tended to be busier than is sometimes supposed and perhaps also more equitable – it is seldom easy to get away with much in a country community. The auditory at Stainville was the setting for the usual civil actions, for breaches of contract and so forth, between the litigious peasants. From time to time it had to deal with some local rumpus like the 'affair of cudgels' wherein six drunken villagers beat the place up at the christmastide of 1720. One of these lively lads was Nicolas La Pique from a long-established family at Stainville; and

---

[53] 'Enregistrement des lettres d'érection en marquisat de la baronnie de Stainville au profit de M. de Choiseul, Marquis de Stainville, du 7 Avril 1722'; cited, Marquis de Marmier, op. cit., vol. 60, p. 251.

[54] 'Comptes des domaines et grurie du marquisat de Stainville de l'année 1726', fo. 3: Arch. Meuse, J 18[18].

six years later there was a grim reference to 'the extraordinary case prosecuted in the provostship of Stainville on the demand of the procurator-fiscal against Claude La Pique, who has been condemned to be hung and executed in effigy':[55] in effigy only but close enough to the real thing to suggest that on occasions at Stainville at least the criminal aspect of seigneurial justice then lay rather less in the past than is sometimes supposed. The gibbet was the mark from afar of seigneurial high justice.

Along with the judicial attributions of the marquisate went the local assay of weights and measures and other 'fair rights', fiscal and feudal. The *taille à volonté* was a patrimonial levy, in theory at the good pleasure of the lord in vague redemption of the erstwhile servitude of his vassals. This due was by then stabilized and collectively assessed in the usual way at 200 francs a year for the borough of Stainville, payable on the widely traditional day of Saint Rémi, 1 October. (At nearby Beurey this levy, assessed there at 63 francs, was known as the *taille Saint Rémi*.) Then there were the seigneurial corvées of work for the lord, three days a year without payment except for small subsistence-grants. This meant ploughing in the case of the *corvée de charrue* but at Stainville and Ménil-sur-Saulx this servitude had been commuted for annual cash payments at the rate of one franc six gros per plough. At Lavincourt and Montplonne, though, the ploughing still had to be done: an illustration of how conditions varied even within a single fief under this late feudalism in transition. And at Stainville itself there was no commutation of the imposition upon the poorer peasants of the *corvée de bras* whereby those not owning or contributing to a ploughteam similarly gave a hand twice yearly (thrice at Lowincourt), at haymaking and at harvest-tide.

All those parts remained subject also to such clamps as formarriage and the right of pursuit (*droit de poursuite*) or retention (*droit de retenue*). Formarriage meant that no inhabitant of Stainville could marry anybody from outside the marquisate without their lord's permission and payment to him of a small due on pain of confiscation of a third of the goods of the transgressor. By the right of pursuit or retention, if an inhabitant went to live locally outside the jurisdiction of the marquis he was still bound to pay his local dues to him, 'and if it is a woman she owes a due of one chicken [a year] to witness that the children are subject'.[56] A chicken was the customary acknowledgment in those parts that local ties still meant something more than sentiment.

Such antique survivals were, however, probably less aggravating

[55] Ibid., fo. 29.   [56] Ibid., fo. 3.

than the two feudal rights which appear to have borne most heavily upon the peasants of Stainville in everyday existence. These were the rights of the forest and the banal utilities.

The seigneurial rights of the chase and the forest were of prime interest to the woodlanders of Stainville, and to so keen a hunter as the young marquis. Aristocratic huntsmen were mostly also country-men and, despite the propaganda against them, it would seem that on the whole they did not too often abuse their privileges. Certainly, it was like the Marquis de Stainville to do the decent thing when occasion arose. In 1723, for instance, 31 livres, 14 sous, 6 deniers were 'given by order of the Marquis to an individual of Maulan for a foal eaten by his hounds'.[57] By and large, however, it was that familiar pattern of the countryside: something of a running war between the chief huntsman and rangers of the marquisate, more or less uniformed, on the one hand and on the other the local poachers and pilferers for their illicit snaring, fishing, and snitching of fuel and the like from lordly forests, which were economically exploited down to the right of pannage (*glandée*) or mast for swine. Peasants, too, could damage the timber, stripping oaklings for tan or supplying sly carpenters and coopers, not to mention the occasional ferocity of interlopers. The keepers were kept keen against their fellow-villagers by a cut of one-third of the fine imposed by the seigneurial court upon anybody whom they caught. The fines were indeed mostly so small that their collection was farmed out to two local inhabitants on a three-year lease as from 1 January 1715 for only 70 francs per annum, representing another petty squeeze delegated down from the seigneurial level. The two farmers of the fines, who were peasants like the poachers themselves, may have been the immediate targets for the disproportionate resentment which such sanctions often arouse, since the poor are apt to regard scrounging as their legitimate levy upon the rich.

A legitimate levy of the rich upon the poor at Stainville as elsewhere were the banal mills, ovens, and presses to which the peasants had to bring their produce for processing to the profit of the marquis under pain of confiscation of any goods in question and a fine of three francs. Just because of their heavy incidence, however, these rights were by then, there as elsewhere, in active process of commutation and modified exploitation in a significant variety of arrangements.

At Lavincourt the Countess Anne de Stainville had by deed of April 1714 commuted the rights of the banal oven in consideration of an annual payment by each full household of a sum, including receipt

[57] 'Comptes des domaines et grurie du marquisat de Stainville de 1723': *u.s.*

duty, of 3 francs, 11 gros, 1 blanc, 'widows half and bachelors and spinsters a quarter'.[58] A full household or fiscal 'hearth' there in the Barrois may not have differed so much from one in the Beauvaisis where it is reckoned from just about that date to have averaged four or four and a half persons.[59] At Lavincourt at all events the yield from this payment in 1717 was 135 francs, 6 gros, based on a census 'according to the roll extracted from that of the subvention',[60] the main impost levied by the central government of Lorraine, comparable in importance to the royal *taille* or tax on persons or property in France. In both countries the peasant was traditionally taxed by all three of the authorities exercising the principal power, nationally by his sovereign, locally by his lord, and of course ecclesiastically by his church through tithes apt to be specially resented in so far as they accrued not to the local priest but to rich absentees such as cathedral chapters. One begins to sense the burden on agriculture even though the villagers on the Stainville estate with its profitable woodland, in favoured Lorraine, were liable to be considerably better off than that poor little village of Semontier which complained in Burgundy that the accumulation of imposts meant in effect that an inhabitant could work but one day a week wholly for his own profit.[61] That was an extreme case.

The commutation of the rights of the banal oven at Lavincourt was matched at Montplonne as at nearby Beurey where, after years of litigation, Count Jean-François had given way in 1710. On the other hand at Ménil-sur-Saulx and at Stainville itself the lord at that time still retained the banal utilities but leased them out to local peasants and tradesfolk. The bakehouse at Stainville had been let for three or six years as from 1 January 1713 to Claude Abraham and a partner at an annual rental of 350 francs. The Abrahams were another prominent clan at Stainville and appear to have acquired a leading interest in the bakery business there. In order, incidentally, to set up as a baker and build one's commercial oven at Stainville, it was necessary not only to be received into the guild but also, as usual, to secure seigneurial permission.

More remunerative than the banal oven at Stainville were the two banal watermills, which were similarly leased to one Nicolas Chauvry for 1,040 francs a year. This was much the largest single receipt from a seigneurial title at Stainville. Comparable receipts for 1717 were: rentals from meadows, 365 francs, 6 gros; banal oven, 350 francs;

[58] Stainville accounts for 1717: ibid.
[59] Cf. P. Goubert, op. cit., p. 25, n. 1.
[60] Stainville accounts for 1717: *u.s.*
[61] Cf. P. de Saint Jacob, *Les Paysans de la Bourgogne du nord au dernier siècle de l'ancien régime*, p. 139.

rental from lease of the domainal registry-office (*greffe*), the focus of
seigneurial justice, 280 francs; lease of fines, 70 francs. The high yield
of the meadows suggests that Stainville conformed to the pattern
then widespread in France where the peasants very often had to rent,
rather rarely owned, precious pasture of high quality for their beasts,
the very sinews of arable and other agriculture. In general the profits
of leased utilities and of local legalism at Stainville were thus
conspiciously greater than those of the often more emphasized levies,
with the *taille à volonté* bringing in its 200 francs and the *corvée de
charrue* only 30 francs, 9 gros. Similar but usually smaller incomes
were derived from the other villages of the fief. And there were still
ancillary rents in kind to swell 'the receipt of the domains and
domainal rights due ... in cash, grain, chickens, and capons'[62], plus
a couple of pounds of wax.

Such was the heavy incidence of enduring feudalism upon the
landscape of Stainville and, with regional modification, upon the
continent of Europe in the early part of the eighteenth century. Yet
it was not merely the feudalism of the middle ages, even in Lorraine
where change tended to be slow and survivals manifold. (Thus banal
presses for liquor, such as existed at Stainville in cellars underneath
the market-place, appear to have been becoming rare by then in
France.) In eastern Lorraine remnants of serfdom were in 1712 done
away with by the Duke Leopold, who in general particularly
protected the peasants. Their relations with their lords were
increasingly modified, sometimes by the expanding activity of central
government and usually by current economic development.

If the peasants of Stainville were subject to a rich variety of petty
dues and imposts, one also derives the impression that even so early
as about 1715 a good number of them were by no means badly off. In
1716 Claude La Pique of Lavincourt – quite likely he who was ten
years later to be executed in effigy – was buying from his lord's estate
the brushwood off 15 acres, 29 roods for 640 francs, 6 gros, while
Nicolas La Pique bought half a dozen oaks for 106 francs. A dozen
oaks went to Toussaint Labreche, also of Lavincourt, for 280, and 27
acres, 57¾ roods of brushwood cost Pierre Champion of Stainville
1,228 francs, 4 gros. Such purchases were indeed among the large
ones but on a lesser scale the examples could be multiplied many
times, and one often finds groups of peasants clubbing together in
order to buy, almost as a syndicate of merchants. And of course
almost every peasant, by and large, was incidentally more or less of an
agricultural dealer. At Stainville numbers of the leading locals appear
to have been actively participating in the sharply rising profits on

[62] Stainville accounts for 1717: *u.s.*

timber. And even further down the scale the wages of woodcutters correspondingly tended then to be well above most others.

In that year of 1716 the total seigneurial income of the Stainville estate from sales of timber amounted to 10,181 francs as compared with 8,291 francs from all the traditional lordly rights and revenues. Both these figures, however, included a significantly large backlog of debts owing, respectively, 3,709 and 2,180 francs. Agriculture is apt at the best of times to rely considerably upon credit, upon active debt in then French terminology. But, especially in a bad year, active debt could so easily slide into passive debt, that is, into debt pure and simple. Peasant agriculture, anyway short of specie, was then riddled with arrears often only cleared at death even though a good part of peasant toil might represent uphopeful attempts to reduce them.

As for that indebtedness on the seigneurial dues at Stainville, it speaks for itself in relation to the extent to which the peasants were currently securing their commutation for cash or else, in a number of cases, themselves renting the exploitation of dues to their own profit as against their fellows. A leading element of the local population thus acquired vested interests corresponding to those of their lord. This factor of peasant mulcting peasant represented a significant modification of the crude relationship between lord and vassal. Now, however, at the time when the future Marquis de Stainville was taking over the estate from his aunt, this policy of leasing seigneurial rights received a large revision and extension symptomatic of another suggestive shift in the society of that time.

The high proportion of debts outstanding in the figure for 1716 included such items as 787 francs, 6 gros due from 'Sieur Renault' (thus better than a peasant) for the tilekiln at Montplonne, leased to him for 700 francs a year. Rather more than a year's rental, in this case 393 francs, 9 gros, was similarly owing from Claude Abraham and his partner for the banal oven. Gabriel Labreche, too, was 115 francs, 5 gros behind on his rent for the banal winepress. Next year Nicolas Chauvry was 956 francs, 5 gros, 8 deniers down in respect of the watermills, and the collective payment of the 200 francs for the *taille à volonté* was only raked in after undue delay. One derives the impression of a tough, tight peasant community, full of enterprise indeed but also, as usual, full of pressures and of debts.

The advantage to the newly incoming Marquis de Stainville was self-evident when all these little leases were called in and consolidated in one lease for six or nine years as from 1 January 1719 to Sieur Claude Vautier of Ligny of all the 'domains and revenues of the estate and lordship of the said Stainville consisting of grain, meadows, pastures, banal mills, ovens and presses, a tilekiln, quitrents, revenues, and seigneurial dues'[63] for an annual rent, payable quarterly, of 4,500 livres of Lorraine (the accountancy was switched from francs to livres) plus two hundred bushels of corn, as many measures of oats, and six tons of hay. The directly agricultural emphasis was reflected not only in this form of payment but also in the term of the lease, adjusted as usual to the traditionally triennial rotation of crops. Excluded from the new lease and reserved to the marquis were the château itself, the vineyards and forests, all forest fines and other fines over five francs. In 1722 the marquis further removed the tilekiln of Montplonne, and Vautier's rent was reduced to 4,100 livres.

By introducing at Stainville the system already in force at Beaupré the young marquis at a stroke assured himself of a large slice of regular income in ready cash, unloading on to Vautier both the worry of debts overdue from the peasants and much of the odium of enforcing seigneurial rights and dues. And Vautier was no peasant but a townsman from Ligny, more or less of a middleclass middleman, of a bourgeois entrepreneur taking over the running of a feudal estate for profit as a business proposition. Such was the rise, already, in Lorraine as pretty widely in north-eastern France, of what has been termed a rural bourgeoisie,[64] tending, in another sociological quantification, to move into a kind of social complicity[65] with the large, often noble landowners for whom it provided the financial agents. That was indeed to be the tendency at Stainville where this middleclass modernization of feudalism was to mould the peasant way of life for the next two generations. The examples of Stainville and Beaupré point to local involvement in the earlier stages of this basic shift in the agrarian society of the old regime, a shift promoted by the difficult times around the turn of the seventeenth century wherein a rising bourgeoisie began to come forward as farmers-general on a seigneurial level rather as it did also, more conspicuously, on the national level of tax-farming in the French development of the *fermes générales* since Colbert.

The interest of the Marquis de Stainville in this changeover was doubtless of a more immediate kind. For him, at first at any rate, it paid off handsomely. On the Stainville estate the surplus of income over expenditure and receipts overdue, which had stood in 1716 at 1,845 francs or some 1,000 livres, had risen five years later to 8,826 livres. In 1723 the net profit was reckoned at no less than 26,347 livres, 5 sous, 7 deniers on a total income of something over thirty thousand deriving from three main items, Vautier's lease plus two

[63] 'Comptes des domaines et grurie du marquisat de Stainville de l'année 1726': *u.s.*
[64] Cf. Georges Lefebvre, *Les Paysans du nord pendant la révolution française* (Bari, 1959), pp. 321f.
[65] Cf. F. Braudel and E. Labrousse, op. cit., ii. 145.

exceptionally large incomings totalling 15,362 livres from sale of timber and other woodland profits, and, significantly, a surplus of 12,025 livres carried forward from the preceding year. By 1725, however, the accounts are not wholly clear, probably because they already registered a heavy wobble before the bleak deficit of 1,134 livres, 19 sous, 6 deniers in 1726.

The background to this sharp dip in the profits of the marquisate was, in general, an economically uneasy spell towards the middle twenties, still in the aftermath of Law's financial collapse and also, in Lorraine, a particularly bad year. There in 1725 'on the eve of the harvest a rain began which, during six weeks, was scarcely interrupted by moments of sunshine . . . The corn yielded only a glutinous black bread without substance, although they had it dried in the oven and employed all means inspired by necessity.'[66] (The chronicler went on to relate how Duke Leopold, 'afflicted at seeing his peoples suffering from want in a country ordinarily abundant in corn', proceeded to take measures against cornering in wheat and established twenty-two compulsory granaries.) Even in the preceding year of 1724, however, the Marquis de Stainville had been touching the French envoy to Lorraine, d'Audiffret, for a matter of 23,000 livres 'in a pressing need':[67] which sum the diplomat obligingly lent him without interest over a term of two years. The pressing need may have related, in part at least, to the building operations then in hand at Stainville. But it would probably pay the local contractors to be amenable, and at that period the young marquis was also launching out in other directions.

VIII

When the beneficent Duke Leopold had elevated the barony of Stainville to a marquisate in 1722 he had further enriched the marquis by the grant to him of the separate village of Bazincourt 'situated a bare league from Stainville'[68] in a hairpin bend of the Saulx as it wound its way down towards Beurey and Couvonges. Leopold had himself bought the overlordship of Bazincourt only the year before from his brother-in-law, the Regent Orleans, in his capacity as Baron of Ancerville, an inheritance which had come to him through the Guises. Leopold's personal acquisition of the barony

[66] Durival, op. cit., i. 127 for the following.
[67] D'Audiffret to Count de Morville, Nancy, 9 Apr. 1726: Archives des Affaires Étrangères, Correspondance Politique (henceforth cited as Arch. Aff. Étr. C.P.): Lorraine, vol. 115, fo. 110.
[68] 'Mémoire sur la terre de Bazincourt' (undated: after 1785): Arch. Meuse, J 18[29] (Seigneuries de Bazincourt-sur-Saulx, de Couvonge, de Beaupré – Chassey-Beaupré – et d'Illoud, Haute-Marne, 1598–1793).

of Ancerville in 1721, as of Ligny the year before, had carried forward the territorial tidying up which the duke, profiting from his French marriage, had put in hand in 1718 through the Franco-Lorraine Treaty of Paris. Equally characteristic, however, was his prompt alienation of ducal domains in favour of his nobility.

The snag about the gift now to the lucky Marquis de Stainville of the village of Bazincourt (it included the ducal hunting and fishing rights but not the judicial ones, reserved to the provostship of Ancerville) was that, on a lower but more practical level, Bazincourt had in 1718 been sold for 25,000 French livres by the sitting proprietors to Sieur Charles du Tertre, counsellor in the Chambre des Comptes of Bar-le-Duc. The Marquis de Stainville was probably justified in claiming that Bazincourt had been pledged in 1599 for 5,333 écus 'under perpetual option of repurchase by the barons of Ancerville or their assigns and has passed to Sieur du Tertre only upon the condition of this option ... Sieur du Tertre has not only refused this repayment [offered by the marquis], but he has further opposed entry into possession by the Marquis de Stainville',[69] promptly securing a legal injunction against it (arrêt de défense) on 10 June 1722. The dispute ground on for years and was to spread in circles high and wide.

It looks as though the du Tertre interest was being squeezed out by the clan of Stainville in the wake of Leopold's own territorial policy, and princely subvention. Around that time one of his financial officials anonymously revealed: 'Several persons in favour made pretence of buying estates ... but they paid in bills to bearer which they drew upon His Royal Highness ... The Marquis de Stainville in four years [drew] 118,616 livres.'[70] That roughly matched outgoings to two of the duke's older, Italian, favourites – 256,300 livres over ten years to the winning Marquis de Spada, a polyglot Roman whose French wife had briefly rivalled the infuriated Marquise de Beauvau-Craon as ducal mistress: 297,500 in ten years to the Milanese Marquis de Lunati-Visconti, Lunati the Wag (Badin), an early adherent, advanced to be colonel of the duke's Swiss Guard, and the pitied husband of another French beauty who had once divided the little court against La Craon by becoming the mistress of Leopold's brother, Prince Charles, Bishop of Osnabrück. The total amounts may well have been larger, for the same source remarked of the chief beneficiary, the husband of the duke's mistress and his chief

---

[69] 'Mémoire à Monseigneur le Procureur Général de la part du Sr. Comte de Choiseul Marquis de Stainville contre le Sr. du Tertre demeurant à Bar le Duc', undated: Ö.S./H.H.S., Lothringisches Hausarchiv 178/655, no. 4.

[70] Memorandum, after 1721, on finances of Lorraine: Arch. M-et-M/Vienne, Finances; cited, Z. Harsany, op. cit., p. 536, and for the following.

adviser, that the recently created 'Prince de Craon in twelve years has drawn 628,250 livres on known bills without counting the unknown and current cash'. If that put the Marquis de Stainville in the shade, he was evidently to be numbered among those denounced to Leopold in 1722 as 'all the bloodsuckers who surround you'.[71] The description came from his chancellor, the bourgeois Le Bègue, himself understandably described by Craon to Stainville as 'such a declared enemy'.[72]

For the unrepentant Duke of Lorraine 'there cannot be greater happiness in the world than making a number of people happy'.[73] Thus might the relatively needy continental aristocracy of the eighteenth century still sometimes lever their way back territorially against the rising legal and financial classes. Although it was precisely the bourgeoisie which often primed an early seigneurial reaction, it could yet be truly aristocratic, against not only peasants but the middle class itself. What the uncle had begun against the Morels, the Marquis de Stainville was pursuing against the du Tertres, Charles at Bazincourt, Nicolas at Demange.

At Demange the Marquis de Stainville, having unloaded the previous rent, in 1724 secured from his ever-liberal sovereign its erection into a barony with grant of lordly rights, saving only the high justice of adjacent Houdelaincourt and Baudignécourt. The immediate financial benefit was perhaps doubtful in view of an unspecified 'contract granted by the marquis to the profit of Madame de Stainville of Demange',[74] possibly the Countess Anne de Stainville. At all events a Countess de Stainville was in 1728 in enjoyment not only of the marquis's three-eighths share of dues at Demange but also of a cut of one-half from the ducal five-eighths accruing to Leopold, once more perhaps a generous promoter.

Demange was not the only addition to the Marquis de Stainville's property through part-ownership. His wife had brought him a half-share of the marquisate of Removille, the other half belonging to his sister-in-law and her husband, Francis Emmanuel, Marquis de Ligny. The two neighbouring and related marquises were thus joint lords of the third marquisate of Removille. Their kinship may have spared it the worst effects often produced by co-proprietorship through weakened estate-management and fragmentation. The Bassompierre inheritance of Removille, which included the barony

---

[71] La Bègue to Duke Leopold, Paris, 29 Apr. 1722: ibid., p. 543.

[72] Prince de Craon to Marquis de Stainville, Lunéville, 2 Feb. 1730: Arch. M-et-M/Vienne, 3F 370, no. 219.

[73] Duke Leopold, memorandum: Arch. M-et-M/Vienne, Finances, cited, Z. Harsany, op. cit., p. 541.

[74] 'Compte des domaines et grurie du marquisat de Stainville de 1723': u.s.

of Châtelet, brought the Marquis de Stainville into seigneurial relation to a considerable number of villages to the south of the main Stainville estates. It was both Choiseul and Bassompierre country: one case in which the two marquises were involved in 1730 was against a widowed Marquise de Bassompierre over the surveying of sixty-two acres of brushwood which she had an annual right to cut within the confines of their high justice.

Woodcutting had become a vexed issue in those parts, and in 1731 the peasants in neighbouring Franche-Comté were already rising in revolt against forest depredations by industrialists. In Burgundy the price of timber had by 1725 trebled within twenty years. This boom was tending to promote resentment against just such proprietors as the Marquis de Stainville. For the most interesting thing about the Removille estate was that it included 'the forges of Châtelet, the slitting-mill of Fruze and furnaces of Attignéville',[75] let by the two co-proprietors to a Sieur Nicolas Gilbert in August 1727 at a basic rent, apparently, of some 8,500 livres. The Marquis de Stainville was thus directly interested in those iron-workings of Lorraine which looked back to the Iron Age itself and forward to the new iron age of the nineteenth century.

The industrial income of the Marquis de Stainville was, directly, moderate compared with that from feudal and agricultural sources. Indirectly, though, the industrial demand was largely capitalizing that timber which by then bulked so much larger in the Stainville budget than the production of corn. Stainville's creditor, d'Audiffret, in a monumental report on Lorraine running into 573 pages of elegant manuscript, explained that the river valleys in the Barrois were 'fertile in grain, and as they produce much more than is needed for the subsistence of the inhabitants, it is nearly always low in price and the other provisions in proportion'. Neither the Meuse nor the Moselle, however, were then navigable in the Barrois so that 'the revenues are moderate, because a sale or issue is there lacking, which affords the landowners the means of leading an easy life there with less expense'.[76] Granted the low cost of living in Bar, as in Lorraine generally, one sees, more broadly, the limitations there as also in France of what remained primarily subsistence-farming based upon modest holdings and often trading by barter; and, more broadly again, how the feudal system, traditionally so often meshed in with

---

[75] Announcement of forthcoming reletting of these properties at Châtelet, Fruze, and Attignéville; Nancy, 3 Sept. 1735: Archives départementales des Vosges (henceforth cited as Arch. Vosges), E 115.

[76] 'Mémoire sur le Duché de Lorraine par M. d'Audiffret', 1732: Arch. Aff. Étr. C.P., Lorraine, vol. 124, fos. 216–17.

subsistence-farming, was being, not superseded indeed, but economically overlaid. In his revenues, feudally derived, industrially
expanding, the Marquis de Stainville was of his age.

By the middle seventeen-twenties the father of the future Duke de
Choiseul was a considerable landowner by the little standards of
Lorraine. That he was a popular one is suggested by the tale of the
bell of Montplonne.

In 1727–8 the villagers of Montplonne on the northern edge of the
Stainville estate were raising funds for a church bell, usually the
summoner also to village meetings, real organs of popular action at
the base of the old regime. Often, too, an alarm would be pealed
against bad weather, critical for the community. A bell signalled a
parish.

To provide their bell the men of Montplonne imitated their lord in
raising ready cash, by selling timber, in this case from the communal
woods which would appertain to a village while yielding the lord
one-third of any profits (his *tiers denier*): the marquis's rangers
protected the communal woods as well as his own. Montplonne was
lucky to possess such woods, and such a seigneur. Towards the cost
of the bell 'the Marquis de Stainville their lord had contributed a
large part and had remitted . . . the third penny due to him'.[77] Bells,
like cannon, were then apt to enjoy a personalized prestige, and the
grateful villagers asked their priest, Master Claude Souttain, to ask
the marquis to stand 'godfather' to the bell, to be inscribed accordingly.

Master Souttain, however, had his own ideas and, evidently,
friends. The bell was engraved: 'I have been blessed by Master
Souttain, Curé of Montplonne, and I have been named Jeanne by M.
Garodel, merchant at Bar, and by D.elle Jeanne Marguerite Payen de
Courcelles.'

Montplonne was was in a commotion of indignation at Souttain's
flouting of its loyal desire. On the morrow of Pentecost 1728 the
stubborn priest himself had to help to knock up a cart to convey the
bell to the church in the presence of Garodel and his wife. And for
the little procession Souttain ordered the lads of the village to stand
to arms in a rustic version of military honours. (Peasants then pretty
commonly had guns.) Jean Martin, a labourer of Montplonne,
snatched the guns out of the hands of two of the youths, impounded
the weapons in the registry-office of the provostship of Stainville,
and, acting as the representative (*député*) of the community of

---

[77] 'Cloche de Monplonne', procès-verbal of 16 May 1728 in 'Inventaire général des titres,
papiers, documents et enseignements de la terre, seigneurie, haute, moyenne et basse justice de
Monplonne dépendante et faisant partie du marquisat de Stainville appartenant à haut et
puissant seigneur Messire François Joseph, Marquis de Choiseul Stainville', fo. 61: Arch.
Meuse, 5 E 62.

Montplonne, brought proceedings, with likely success, in the seigneurial court claiming satisfaction against Souttain and permission to recast the bell and inscribe it duly to the marquis. Such was the legalistic vigour often displayed then by village communities, which could likewise contract collective agreements, and debts.

Thus reversed at Montplonne was the eighteenth-century stereotype of the village-priest as the champion of his flock, with the aristocrat as its oppressor. Nor is this the only suggestion that in patriarchal Lorraine, perhaps even more than in France, peasants still retained social affiliations which could be at least as strong vertically, up to their lord, as horizontally, towards others of their own class beyond the confines of their everyday existence. Nor yet, in the earlier eighteenth century, was the protective function of seigneurs always exhausted, whether in trying to protect their peasants influentially against excessive taxation by central authority or even in affording them the physical protection of their châteaux for communal refuge, still, in time of trouble.

The bell of Montplonne was no isolated example of the benevolent generosity of the Marquis of Stainville, who followed his master, Duke Leopold, in bestowing benefits upon adherents. (Profiteers are not invariably mean.) The villagers of Montplonne had been following a precedent of the year before from Ménil-sur-Saulx when the marquis had granted a petition 'signed by all the inhabitants who know how to sign'[78] for the remission of the third penny in the interests of the reroofing of their church. The upkeep of village churches tended then to fall not so much upon local lords or even upon the religious establishment as upon the village communities of peasants, already burdened by tithes. However, the classical façade of the church of sunny Ménil bears witness to this day, together with several bridges, pumps, and other structures upon the lands of Stainville, to the fact that their time of prominent prosperity was then, as a marquisate.

[78] Concession to inhabitants of Ménil-sur-Saulx by Marquis de Stainville, Paris, 2 Jan. 1727: ibid., fo. 441.

CHAPTER III

DUCHY

I

THE Marquis de Stainville was popular not only upon his estates but also at court. In recognition of his 'fine and laudable qualities'[1] he was appointed a ducal chamberlain in April 1721. He also became a lieutenant in the ducal bodyguard, brilliantly uniformed in scarlet and yellow. The Duchess of Lorraine, a very honest woman, described him as a very honest man. Beauvau-Craon, created a prince of the Holy Roman Empire by Charles VI in November 1722, once assured Stainville: 'You are the only person of my acquaintance, and a very close acquaintance, from whom I have not yet sustained anything queer (*bizarrerie*) or unjust. So, my dear nephew, you are every day inheriting feelings of my friendship and attachment which I am obliged to discard as regards the others; and that amounts to a lot.'[2]

Very different from the Prince de Craon was the disinterested Baron von Pfütschner, tutor to the princes of Lorraine. Learned, frugal, benevolently dry, Pfütschner once described the Marquis de Stainville as 'liberal, all heart and all honour'.[3] It would seem that the future Duke de Choiseul took more after his father than he subsequently chose to admit. The inheritance was physical also, even if the chubby countenance and thick lips of the Choiseuls were rather more handsomely featured in the marquis than in his son.

Representations of the Marquis de Stainville are rare but it looks as though one may occur in a painting of a group of mounted courtiers around Duke Leopold and his heir, Prince Leopold Clement, brilliant, virtuous, perfect, the Wonder Child (*das Wunderkind*). They are being received by the Marquis and Marquise de Lunati-Visconti before their château de Frouard set back in a landscape of, probably, 1722, the year in which Stainville was erected into a marquisate, nine years after Frouard. Immediately in the rear of the

---

[1] Duke Leopold of Lorraine, letters-patent in favour of Marquis de Stainville, Nancy, 27 Apr. 1721: Arch. dép. Meurthe-et-Moselle, B 153 (Registrata au Grand Scel de l'année 1721), fo. 50.
[2] Prince de Craon to Marquis de Stainville, Lunéville, 29 Dec. 1727: Arch. M-et-M/Vienne, 3F 370, no. 89.
[3] Baron von Pfütschner to Marquis de Stainville, Lunéville, 22 Mar. 1731: ibid., 3F 372, no. 23.

central figure of the fifteen-year-old prince upon his white palfrey a bareheaded young horseman, fashionably turned out and with his hat under his arm, presents a striking likeness to the Choiseul cast of feature. It contrasts with those of the other participants, who probably include the clean-cut Marquis de Beauvau-Craon on the other side of Duke Leopold.

This charming evocation of a moment of country pleasure might seem to epitomize the brief brilliance of the golden age for Lorraine under Duke Leopold when that young hopeful, the Marquis de Stainville, was riding high. A year later the Wonder Child would be already dead, dead within three years the Marquise de Lunati-Visconti, her beauty here tantalizingly turned away, dead within seven Duke Leopold himself.

Also, probably, from 1722 comes a social glimpse of the Marquise de Stainville, who had graduated from maid of honour to lady in waiting and lasting friend of the duchess, sensible, kindly Elizabeth Charlotte of Orleans. So early as 1718 the newly married Marquise had been carrying letters and gossip between the duchess and her relations in Paris – in after years Madame de Stainville was full of stories about the Regent and his mistresses. Madame Royale, as the duchess was called, had moderated her looks in producing fourteen children so that her own mother noted that she had acquired 'an ugly flat nose; her eyes have become hollow'.[4] Whereas the beauty of La Craon was aggravatingly unabated by bearing twenty children. Her lasting ascendancy over Leopold (in 1718, still, 'it is comical to see')[5] was an interested one in combination with her deft husband. They remained a fondly united couple in eighteenth-century fashion. The Marquis de Beauvau-Craon wrote to a friend after one of his wife's accouchements: 'In our house we already have a goodly little company consisting of Mesdames Rouerke and de Stainville and Messieurs de Ligniville and de Beauvau.'[6]

The Stainvilles and the Craons were apt to be close neighbours at both Nancy and Lunéville. The Craons boasted a particularly handsome residence at one corner of the Place de la Carrière while at Lunéville they built themselves a large house conveniently backing upon the palace gardens. Less lushly the Stainvilles rented an apartment in a large block recently built further down the same street near the entrance to the palace. Their landlord was a well-to-do bourgeois, Nicolas Devaux, surgeon-major in Lunati-Visconti's Swiss

---

[4] Duchess of Orleans to Countess Palatine Louise, Saint-Cloud, 6 May 1718: G. Brunet, *Correspondance complète de Madame duchesse d'Orléans* (Paris [1857]), i. 400.
[5] Ibid., Paris, 19 Apr. 1718: p. 395.
[6] Marquis de Beauvau-Craon to Prince de Vaudémont, probably 1722: B. N. Coll. Lorraine, v. 582, cited, Z. Harsany, op. cit., p. 166.

Guard and father of a boy who was to cut a literary figure. This establishment reflected class-relationships then in Lorraine where the aristocracy tended to be at once more and less exclusive than that of France.

Ligniville, Lénoncourt, Châtelet, and Haraucourt were the only four families to qualify as the so-called Grands Chevaux of Lorraine. The heads of the houses of Ligniville and of Lenoncourt were said to have drawn respectively upon Duke Leopold for 92,000 livres in eight years, for 125,640 in nine. Next in exclusivity came some dozen Petits Chevaux including the Stainvilles. (Hence the claim of Lorraine to have originated the phrase 'to mount one's high horse', *monter sur ses grands chevaux*.) Under Leopold these lofty families scarcely needed to marry middle-class money, as was by then not so very uncommon in France. On the other hand the duke, that progressive paternalist, would ennoble such as merchant-bankers (the brothers Fromanteau in 1719) and held that it was the third estate of the commons which validated society 'by its work and trade; it is it alone which bears the weight of all the burdens; it is the body and soul of a state'.[7] This vision inspired Leopold's acts of winning familiarity – asking one of his middle-class administrators to dine privately or inviting to court balls and plays even bourgeois who were not carriage-folk, fetching them in ducal coaches.

Duke Leopold and the Prince de Craon also figured aptly at the apex of a court where, as the latter remarked, 'they assume that everybody has a stomach of iron'.[8] If the Marquis de Menuessaire was their champion gourmet, it was to be said of the Marquis de Stainville that the pleasures of the table were 'his dominating passion'.[9] Stainville's divergence, however, from Craon in another predilection appears in the prince's teasing confession to him of 'a great passion for gambling and a horrible aversion from another passion which, I know not how, has slipped into society under the name of hunting. I will say no more on this score for fear of falling out with you.'[10] Craon's earlier letter featuring the Marquise de Stainville in their houseparty had continued: 'Every evening we have news of the court where lansquenet was re-established five or six days ago. The English are shining at it and gold is flying like chaff.'[11]

[7] Duke Leopold of Lorraine, 'Mémoire sur le gouvernement des Etats d'un duc de Lorraine': cited, H. Baumont, *Études sur le règne de Léopold duc de Lorraine et de Bar, 1697–1729* (Paris and Nancy, 1894), p. 461.

[8] Prince de Craon to Marquis de Stainville, Lunéville, 5 Dec. 1726: Arch. M-et-M/Vienne, 3F 370, no. 62.

[9] J. N. Dufort, comte de Cheverny, *Mémoires sur les règnes de Louis XV et Louis XVI et sur la révolution*, ed. Robert de Crèvecoeur (Paris, 1886), i. 137.

[10] Prince de Craon to Marquis de Stainville, Lunéville, 6 June 1726: *u.s.*, no. 11.

[11] Marquis de Beauvau-Craon to Prince de Vaudémont, probably 1722: B. N. Coll. Lorraine, v. 582, cited, Z. Harsany, op. cit., p. 166.

Leopold and Craon led the gambling at Lunéville, where Englishmen upon the grand tour might conveniently polish their French outside France. A reverse of Craon's sketch came from one recommended to him by Sir Robert Walpole some years later, scholarly George Lyttelton, subsequently the poetical politician, Lord Lyttelton: 'I am weary of losing money at cards; but it is no less certain, that without them I shall soon be weary of Lorrain ... This Court is fond of strangers, but with a proviso that strangers love quadrille ... In summer, one may contrive to pass a day without quadrille; but in the winter you are reduced to play at it, or sleep like a fly till the return of spring ... My only improvement here is in the company of the duke [Leopold] and prince Craon, and in the exercise of the academy.'[12]

The academy for young gentlemen founded by Duke Leopold in 1699, under the direction of a baron rather than a priest, had achieved international reputation, and imitation. The military emphasis embraced riding, mathematics and history with provision also for dancing, law and languages so that fees were 650 livres per annum for dayboys and nearly 3,000 for boarders. The lads from this expensive establishment had a standing invitation to Leopold's court, which celebrated so many festivals as to 'occasion a much larger expense in fine cloaths, than is necessary in other Academies'.[13] And since 'Lunéville is but a small place, a young Gentleman cannot be guilty of the least slip, but it is immediately known at Court, where he is sure to meet with a severe Raillery from the Ladies'.[14] This finishing school attracted especially German pupils (criticized for ganging up) and English. It had been justly hoped that such a catch as the young Duke of Norfolk, 'the chief and richest of all the lords of his country ... could help to make the reputation of the academy'.[15] In 1726 the Prince de Craon mentioned to the Marquis de Stainville that 'there are twelve Englishmen at the academy but no more Milord Hopp'.[16]

Lord Hope, then keen on astronomy and the layout of the orangery at Lunéville, was to become well acquainted with Stainville, who had acquired quite an English connection. A real measure of cosmopolitan fellowship could cement the aristocracy of the eighteenth century. Other visitors to the court of Lorraine included a son of Sir Robert Walpole, a Lord Lovelace, and Viscount Bury. Stainville was to

---

[12] George Lyttelton to Sir Thomas Lyttelton, Lunéville, 21 July 1728: Lord Lyttelton, *The Works of George Lord Lyttelton*, ed. J. E. Ayscough (London, 1775), pp. 644–5.
[13] John George Keysler, *Travels through Germany, Hungary, Bohemia, Switzerland, Italy and Lorrain* (trans. from the German; London, 1758), iv. 344.
[14] Ibid.
[15] Baron de Sauter, cited, Z. Harsany, op. cit., p. 409.
[16] Prince de Craon to Marquis de Stainville, Lunéville, 3 Dec. 1726: Arch. M-et-M/Vienne, 3F 370, no. 61.

recall his early acquaintance with Bury when 'he was at the academy of Lunéville in 1717'.[17] This son of the Dutch favourite of William III of England was shortly to succeed as the second Earl of Albemarle. When he came into diplomatic rapport with the Marquis de Stainville a generation later he was warmly to evoke the kindness which he had received in youth from Duke Leopold.

If Stainville was early orientated rather towards England, the duke's international interests first afforded him an initiation to the east.

II

Duke Leopold, in that catalogue of his nobles who might escort his eldest son to the Austrian court in 1723, noted against the Marquis de Stainville in contrast to his curmudgeonly relative at Beurey: 'The young M. de Stainville. Is indeed a little young to be an envoy and yet might be suitable for it with an aide.'[18] Thus, reviving the eastward impulse of his illustrious uncle, Stainville in the company of another chamberlain, Baron Gehlen, drove into Prague on 5 August 1723.

The early background for Duke Leopold was the Austrian court, where his father had found asylum in the bad times. Himself born at Innsbruck in 1679, Leopold was related to the imperial house through his mother, the astute Duchess Eleanor who had largely ensured his return to Lorraine. If Leopold was teased as a Tyrolean by his devoted French wife, that marriage had importantly balanced his policy of cultivating relations with the embracing power of France even though he had 'sucked in with his milk a decided inclination for the whole germanic body-politic'.[19] After the Regent Orleans had, as may appear, failed around 1718 to promote aspirations already cherished by Leopold towards Tuscany – or anywhere else in lieu (Luxemburg, or the emancipation of the Barrois Mouvant), the duke's cousin and boyhood friend, the Emperor Charles VI, had assuaged him with Teschen and the lure of a dynastic union more brilliant, even, than any French one. If this became Leopold's 'great affair', the emperor was personally almost as keen, if politically more circumspect, about closer family ties, in the first instance through Prince Leopold Clement. By 1723 he was due to begin a sojourn at

[17] Marquis de Stainville to Emperor Francis I, Paris, 3 Aug. 1749: Esteri del Granducato di Toscana, vol. 2295/1286, fo. 717.
[18] 'Mémoire de la main propre du Duc Léopold de Lorraine sur les individus principaux de la Noblesse de son Duché, pour en choisir les compagnons de voyage de son fils François à Prague', 1723: Ö.S./H.H.S., Lothringisches Hausarchiv, cited, M. Payard, op. cit., p. 94.
[19] Baron Bourcier de Montureux, 'Réflexions sur l'élection de l'Empereur François Ier, aujourd'hui régnant': cited, Pierre Boyé, Stanislas Leszczynski et le troisième traité de Vienne (Nancy, 1898), p. 326.

the Austrian court in residence in Prague for the coronation of the emperor as King of Bohemia that September. But on 4 June the Wonder Child had met a lonely death at Lunéville, victim of that epidemic of smallpox in Lorraine that year.

Princes die but politics persist. After an anxious interim the emperor graciously accepted as a prompt substitute the younger and more doubtful brother, fifteen-year-old Prince Francis Stephen, disconcertingly lively, taking more after his French mother. If he rather literally stepped into his brother's shoes, the princely wardrobe for the Austrian court now had to be nearly doubled because of mourning, while still including a gross of pairs of white gloves. His ample provision of choice French vintages was supplemented by some four thousand litres of the finest Rhenish to soften up the imperial court. There were also seventy-four schoolbooks. All this went trundling across Germany in advance together with crates of china and silver, of the renowned preserves of the Barrois. In that summer season a passenger-coach from Lunéville to Prague took about ten days. Some four days ahead of Prince Francis had travelled the Marquis de Stainville.

Promptly upon arrival in Prague the Marquis de Stainville went to pay his respects to the imperial chancellor, venal Count von Sinzendorf. 'He', reported Stainville, 'took me with him in a carriage, saying that he wanted to take a little promenade, and he brought me to where I am lodging',[20] probably out in the New Town in or near the mansion rented for Prince Francis from Countess von Werschowitz, who made the classic move of Austrian widows into the attics. From the chancellor's residence it was, explained Stainville, 'certainly a good half an hour away. When I was at my house he proposed that we should return to his, saying that he was very happy for us to take our promenade together.'[21] It was not for the young envoy to refuse so flattering an advertisement of his arrival, made as likely as not in a coach and six complete with running footmen. This was common through the relatively broad streets of the Bohemian capital, where the Austrian nobility made more lavish display even than in Vienna. 'Everybody here lives grand'[22] remarked a traveller to Prague six years later.

Such was the panoramic introduction of the Marquis de Stainville to Prague, sweeping up from the curve of the Moldau, already described as the Queen of Cities in the fifteenth century, as the heart

---

[20] Marquis de Stainville to Duke Leopold of Lorraine, Prague, 7 Aug. 1723: Arch. M-et-M/Vienne, 3F, bobine 193.
[21] Ibid.
[22] Baron von Pöllnitz, *The Memoirs of Charles-Lewis, Baron de Pollnitz* (English trans., 2nd. ed. London, 1738–9), i. 216.

of Europe in the sixteenth. Now this gothic gem, in the aftermath of
the counter-reformation, was just emerging new-made as a triumph
of catholic baroque and imperial ascendancy. The Schwarzenberg
palace echoing the Florentine renaissance, the Waldstein palace built
for great Wallenstein by Marini of Milan had been joined less than
twenty years earlier by the Lobkowitz palace with its lovely flowing
lines probably all the more seductive in low elevation as yet. The
massive serenity of the Czernin palace was at last approaching
completion and the previous year had witnessed the dazzling
achievement of the library of the Clementinum, bastion of Jesuit
culture. In 1723 one was but ten years on from the plague already
eloquent in the column nearly opposite the Schwarzenberg palace up
by the Hradcin, the triumphant citadel, both castle and cathedral,
looking out across the so-called Little Town (*Kleinseite*) over the
graceful Charles Bridge with 'Room for three Carriages to pass
abreast'[23] to the Old Town and on to the New, away towards
Vysherad. The previous year had also brought the death of the elder
Dientzenhofer but not before he had set his stamp in the Little Town
upon the Church of Saint Nicholas, then blossoming as perhaps the
most brilliant expression in Central Europe of the excitement of
ecclesiastical baroque.

Architecture could not claim Stainville's undivided attention on
that first drive, which enabled him to pepper Sinzendorf with
questions about the programme and protocol planned for Prince
Francis. The Lorrainer was assured that the emperor, who would
largely be out hunting, considerately intended a quiet reception with
appropriate incognito and attention to lessons. When the chancellor,
however, threw out that Francis would know the form when he
lodged at court, Stainville anxiously asked Sinzendorf 'if he thought
that he [Francis] would be lodging at court. "I do not know at all" he
said in a laughing manner "but I am talking of it, supposing it should
happen."'[24] Happen it did, for long years to come.

On the morning of 7 August 1723 the Marquis de Stainville had an
audience of the Emperor Charles VI to whom he handed a letter
from Duke Leopold. The emperor, related the marquis, 'said to me in
his own words, "You can inform the Duke of Lorraine of the lively
pleasure which I am giving myself in embracing the Prince of
Lorraine." This remark surprised me but he said it with a kindness
which charmed ... He is shewing much impatience to see him
[Francis]. This assures us many bows and attentions from all the
nobility.'[25]

[23] J. G. Keysler, op. cit., iv. 243-4.
[24] Marquis de Stainville to Duke Leopold, Prague, 7 Aug. 1723: *u.s.*   [25] Ibid.

Duke Leopold of Lorraine received by the Marquis de Lunati-Visconti before the
Château de Frouard. *c.* 1722.

Duke Leopold figures behind the head of the white palfrey bearing Prince Leopold
Clement. The rider immediately to the right of the duke is probably the Marquis de
Beauvau-Craon, later Prince de Craon. The bareheaded figure to the left of the duke
is probably the Marquis de Stainville.

François-Joseph de Choiseul, Marquis de Stainville.

Stainville saw the ingratiating Sinzendorf every day and he handed a letter from Duke Leopold to Prince Eugene of Savoy with whom the young prince was to dine one evening in Prague. Eugene asked Stainville to call again about some business concerning that Ligniville in the Craon-Stainville circle; and indeed Stainville himself, in connection with his inheritance from his uncle, had been in correspondence with Prince Eugene, who had liberally conceded that 'it is not just that the cost of maintaining the Prince of Wallachia during his imprisonment should remain a charge upon the estate of the late Marshal Count de Stainville'.[26]

On 10 August the Prince of Lorraine, accompanied by the inevitable Prince de Craon, arrived in Prague. Stainville informed Francis that the emperor was awaiting him out east again in hunting country near Brandeis. Amid a flurry of changing and unpacking Baron Gehlen coached Francis in imperial ceremonial. He came through with credit. That evening the emperor jotted in his diary: 'Prince of Lorraine is handsome, well grown, speaks polite German.'[27] Next day they went hunting together on the first of so many occasions. On 14 August they returned to Prague and that evening Francis of Lorraine first met the six-year-old Archduchess Theresa. Their meeting up in the Hradcin heralded a new dynasty, a new chapter in European history. That night the imperial annotation ran: 'Will speak to court chancellor about Prince of Lorraine, marriage daughter, yes, in time.'[28]

Next day up in the citadel Charles VI invested Francis with the Golden Fleece at a ceremonial service in All Saints draped in red, forerunner of festivities for the Bohemian coronation. Thereafter Charles returned to the castle of Brandeis while Francis polished up his German and Latin at Winache, a delicious country-seat of Count Czernin. Francis, however, consolidated the imperial favour by his assiduity in the hunting field so that his confessor surmised 'that they want to extirpate the whole republic of wild boars'.[29] Father Günther along with Pfütschner and Craon escorted Francis when the time came on 22 November 1723 for him to quit Prague and follow the emperor to Vienna. Such was the conclusion of the ceremonial mission to Prague of the Marquis de Stainville less than twenty years before his son, the future Choiseul then four, was to enter that city in circumstances grimly different.

[26] Prince Eugene of Savoy to Marquis de Stainville, Vienna, 18 Jan. 1721: Arch. M-et-M/Vienne, 3F 371, no. 1.

[27] Emperor Charles VI, diary for 10 Aug. 1723: Ö.S./H.H.S, Familien Archiv. Sammelbände, Karton 2; 'Tagebuch des K. Karl VI. 1722, 1723, 1724', fo. 41: cited Fred Hennings, *Und sitzet zur linken Hand* (Vienna, 1961), p. 61.

[28] Emperor Charles VI, diary for 14 Aug. 1723: ibid., p. 62.

[29] Father Günther, cited ibid., p. 71.

The new year of 1724 found the Marquis de Stainville retained in Vienna not least by personal affairs probably inherited from his illustrious uncle. It appears that the marquis was to pursue them in Vienna in formidable litigation before a military jurisdiction, the General-Feld-Kriegs-Auditoriat, for the next twenty years and more.[30] This pace allowed him time now to assure Duke Leopold that Francis, lodged in the Hofburg, 'is enjoying the finest health in the world ... They have had placed in his apartment a billiard-table'[31] for his amusement after lessons, or hunting.

Prince Francis became the emperor's chosen companion in his invariable battues, hawking for herons out at Laxenburg each spring, summer staghunting from the Favorita, then the pheasant-season, and in winter boar. Leopold was to correspond anxiously with the lad's tutor who failed to conceal that academic progress was but mediocre. The duke urged upon Baron von Pfütschner that 'to know something of the law would be infinitely necessary for him ... The way in which he writes is frightful; I have already been tempted several times to send him back one of his letters, and to write properly between each line the words, a part of which he often omits; he truncates others, in fine no construction.' Leopold, however, forbore for fear of putting Francis off 'from writing the little which he does, for his letters are the most succinct in the world',[32] as the Marquis de Stainville was unhappily to experience over long years.

Stainville unlike Pfütschner did not stay on in Vienna. At the beginning of 1724 the marquis was hoping to be back in Lorraine by February, when Leopold erected Demange into a barony in his desire 'to give him new marks of our esteem for his person and ... to engage him to continue his services to us with the same zeal, fidelity and attachment which he has shewn up to the present'.[33] The Marquis de Stainville was indeed acquiring the reputation of being 'very attached to the Duke of Lorraine'.[34]

---

[30] Cf. dossier on 'Succession du comte Étienne de Stainville. Procès devant le "General-Feld-Kriegs-Auditoriat", à Vienne, 1701–1747': Arch. Meuse, J 18².

[31] Marquis de Stainville to Duke Leopold, Vienna, 15 Jan. 1724: Arch. M-et-M/Vienne, 3F, bobine 193.

[32] Duke Leopold to Baron von Pfütschner, 23 Mar. 1727: Ö.S./H.H.S., Lothringisches Hausarchiv, 108/425, fo. 41.

[33] 'Lettres de cession faites par Son Altesse Royale au Sr. Joseph Marquis de Choiseul et de Stainville ... du 8 février 1724 ... et érigé en baronnie de Demange-aux-Eaux': Arch. Meuse, B 282 (Chambre des Comptes du Duché de Bar, 1723–1726), fo. 43.

[34] Duke de Bourbon to Count de Broglie, Versailles, 15 Mar. 1725: Arch. Aff. Étr. C.P., Angleterre, vol. 350, fo. 183.

III

The fit introduction to the career of the Duke de Choiseul lies less in the detail of childhood than in the background of politics. It was a family introduction. In 1725, a year after return from Vienna, the Marquis de Stainville, just turning thirty, really entered upon that sphere of diplomacy wherein he was to make his career and his son was to make history. Henceforth the Marquis de Stainville, true to his undertaking to remain in the ducal service, was one of the chief diplomatic representatives of Lorraine. His career had a direct bearing upon that of his son since the final union of Lorraine with France was to be an outstanding event in the ministry of the Duke de Choiseul. Nor was this the only or indeed the most important link between the diplomacies of father and son. For the Marquis de Stainville was destined to become a subordinate but significant contact between the policies of France and Austria even in the decades of hostility before their notorious rapprochement with his more brilliant son in the ascendant. This paternal background in international politics has been little remembered but was present to Choiseul himself. And the background was based on Lorraine.

The duchy of Lorraine still figured for the eighteenth century as 'part of Belgic Gaul ... about fifty French leagues in length and forty in breadth'.[35] This was the central remnant of that middle kingdom of Lothair cast up in the wreck of Charlemagne's empire. The dynasty of Lorraine reached right back to Gerard of Alsace, usually taken as the founder of the hereditary duchy in 1048. And it was the pride of the dukes that they were sovereign in Lorraine. This sovereignty, though, was constricted. To the east the independence of Lorraine had indeed been recognized by the Emperor Charles V in the Treaty of Nuremberg of 1543; but at the same time the duchy had been placed under the safeguard of the Holy Roman Empire and obliged to contribute two-thirds of an electoral quota to the Landfried, the levy against the Turks.

In the eighteenth century twenty-seven villages of Lorraine were wholly or partly enclaves within German territories while nearly as many in the districts of Mertzig and Saargau came under a juridical regime alternating between the Duke of Lorraine and the Archbishop-Elector of Trier. Furthermore he still held the bulk of the duchy of Lorraine within his ecclesiastical province. It included in another national overlap the Three Bishoprics of Metz, Toul, and

---

[35] Quinquet, 'Mémoire sommaire sur les Duchés de Lorraine et de Bar; dressé par ordre de Monsigneur le controler général des finances', Mar. 1746, fo. 1: Arch. Nat. K 1184.

Verdun, since 1648 three French enclaves directing the spiritual life of Lorraine left without a bishopric but with sixteen legal codes. And, to the west, the dukes of Lorraine still – Leopold in 1718 – did homage to the kings of France for that part of the duchy of Bar on the left bank of the Meuse, known as the Barrois Mouvant, under the Treaty of Bruges imposed by King Philip the Fair in 1301. The rub there in practice was that appellate jurisdiction lay to the Parliament of Paris. Already one sees that, so late as the eighteenth century, an attempt to draw the map of Europe on strictly national lines must soon break down. National feeling was indeed strongly developed by then in Western Europe but even there international relations, like local institutions, were still tangled in the legacy of feudalism. Dynasties overtopped nations. Europe was successively torn by the War of the Spanish Succession, the War of the Polish Succession, the War of the Austrian Succession.

The eastward expansion of France under Richelieu and then Louis XIV had borne heavily upon Lorraine during the seventeenth century, the most miserable in her history. 'Misères de la Guerre' was the title of a grim series of engravings by Jacques Callot of Nancy, in this the precursor of Goya. For more than half the century the duchy lay under French occupation, from 1633 to 1661 and, with but brief respite, from 1670 till 1697. Meantime, by the Peace of Westphalia, France, the real winner in the Thirty Years War, had not only legalized her century-old domination of the Three Bishoprics but had secured the bulk of Alsace, though minus Strasburg, on the eastern side of Lorraine. In the local setting France henceforth had Lorraine gripped in a vice; and, in the international, had attained a frontier on the Rhine together with that challenging ascendancy over against the German lands which was to constitute the mainspring of European conflict for three centuries to come. Thus did the last great war of religion issue in the first of those great political settlements which have determined the face of modern Europe.

Fifty years later the Treaty of Ryswick in 1697 confirmed the French grab of Strasburg and accorded her Longwy and Saarlouis at the expense of Lorraine. France indeed accepted the right of innocent passage for her troops (*transitus innoxius*) pending Leopold's cession in the settlement of 1718 of territorial corridors to her strategic bishoprics. The duchy itself had at last been restored to independence so that Ryswick became the palladium of the later liberty of Lorraine. This was one measure of the extent to which France was worn down by the War of the League of Augsburg, which has been described as one of the most exhausting and most uninteresting wars in history.

Thus was the ruling family of Lorraine released from its long sojourn in Austria where Duke Charles V had rendered exile glorious. In 1683 he had shared with John Sobieski the triumphant rout of the Turkish army under the walls of Vienna, and had gone on to hammer the Turks out of Hungary and echo his renown across Europe:

> Hark how the Duke of Lorraine comes,
> The brave victorious soul of war,
> With trumpets and with kettle-drums,
> Like thunder rolling from afar.
> (Thomas Shadwell, *The Victory in Hungary*, 1688.)

The son of Charles V, the young Duke Leopold, was likewise strong against the Turks, charging them with such headlong intrepidity in the luckless battle of Temesvar (1696) that he had to be restrained by Carlingford. The Earl of Carlingford, Eugene O'Rourke, and Stephen de Stainville were among the faithful followers in adversity who in May 1698 accompanied Leopold upon his triumphal return to Lorraine, his cavalcade made brilliant with booty from the east including Arab prisoners in charge of decked-out camels.

Such was the picturesque inauguration of the last forty years of full independence for Lorraine in a final brilliance. Seldom has the initial setting of a golden age been so grimly precarious.

Duke Leopold returned to find the countryside of his fertile duchy scarcely more than a depopulated wasteland. In 1697 the French intendant in Lorraine had reported that its population was barely one-third of what it had been before the Thirty Years War. And in the last year of their occupation the French forces had stripped down the stricken country before handing it over. Peasants were driven from their cottages, and one is told that when winter came they put their children into dungheaps to prevent them from freezing to death. In the rugged Vosges they became marauding partisans, the Schenapans. Several of those caught by the French were agonizingly broken on the wheel. All this on top of the inherited ravages of the Thirty Years War meant that in some districts of Lorraine 'there remained ... only brambles in the midst of which there appeared the hovels and remains of several villages'.[36]

With the return of the duke 'the dispersed Lorrainers swarmed back like bees'[37] and worked like bees to reconstruct their country. It was largely a planned operation. Quite often the contours of ruined

---

[36] D'Audiffret, 'Mémoire sur le Duché de Lorraine par M. d'Audiffret', 1732: Arch. Aff. Étr. C.P., Lorraine, vol. 124, fo. 153.
[37] Durival, op. cit., i. 90.

villages were levelled and superseded by rationalized layouts wherein each cottage was apt to be grouped with its garden and home-field in a regular strip while the confines of the new villages were redrawn with almost geometrical simplicity. Where ruined buildings were left, their repair was compulsory. As frequently after great wars, it was the devastated areas which chiefly benefited from a modernized infrastructure. Thus was the agricultural basis of Lorraine renovated to an extent rare under the old regime.

Duke Leopold topped up this renewal by helping to set peasants on their feet again with allocations of seed-corn and cattle. He distributed among them Hungarian and Arab steeds which had formed part of his triumphal train, and he purchased many more in Germany. By 1711 not only was Leopold assembling one of the finest stables in Europe but his duchy boasted just on 125,000 horses; comparable figures were 511,170 oxen, 153,852 cows, 345,768 sheep, 148,403 pigs. To make good the pitiful depopulation foreign immigration was encouraged by such devices as waiving rules of apprenticeship, and tax-remissions. There was an influx from France, especially Picardy, and the French government favoured this strengthening of the French element in a population which climbed up to 400,000 in 1711 and, it appears, had by 1737 nearly redoubled, reaching some 760,000. This population was four-fifths agricultural and by the end of Leopold's reign the French envoy was able to update his waste of brambles: 'The land is at present so well cultivated everywhere that there are few dominions where Agriculture is in better state; the peasants there are industrious and at their ease, which renders them insolent, mutinous, and pleading against their lords on the least difficulty; the late Duke [Leopold] of Lorraine had it as his maxim to support them in the cases which were brought to his Council of State.'[38]

A somewhat later survey explained that Lorraine 'produces everything that one can wish for as necessary to human life and contains fields fertile in corn, slopes covered with vineyards, mountains full of mines of copper, silver, lead and above all iron, with salt-pits, all sorts of game and rivers abounding in fish, quantities of ponds and considerable forests'.[39] At the same time as agriculture went ahead so did the iron-workings and the activity of blast-furnaces like those which contributed to the fortune of the Marquis de Stainville. Early in Leopold's reign there were fourteen iron-foundries in Lorraine and the Barrois; by the end of it there were fifty-four. Landowners with iron deposits on their property were obliged to

---

[38] D'Audiffret, u.s., vol. 124, fos. 153–4.
[39] Quinquet, 'Mémoire sommaire', Mar. 1746: loc. cit.

exploit them on demand of any local ironmaster or to assign the exploitation to him at a rental of one sol per barrel of ore: compulsory economic development by private owners was a regular feature of Leopoldine policy. Around 1730, however, iron exports from Lorraine still averaged only about half the value of its annual export of either grain or timber, each worth some two million livres. Besides her iron, Lorraine was one of the richest countries in salt, and under Leopold production nearly doubled, with exports up to an annual 650,000 livres.

The duke further stimulated manufactures of all kinds, often by an enlightened and practical generosity. In reviving the cloth industry around Nancy, Leopold in 1719 brought in a manufacturer called Prudhomme from Amiens and helped him to set up business with an advance of 12,000–13,000 livres. A similar sum from the ducal exchequer went five years later to promote a cloth and dyeing works at Lunéville. In eastern Lorraine glassblowing was successfully revived. Papermills and potteries got going. As was to be expected, not everything succeeded, notably an optimistic attempt to found a silk-industry. But by and large the upswing in Lorraine was remarkable, stimulated as it was by a large removal of guild-restrictions and by the abolition in 1721 of zonal dues (rights of *haut-conduit*) within the duchy: though every cart crossing into the interlocked bishoprics still had to pay the small due of the *foraine*.

Externally, with exports running at rather over eight million livres a year by the end of the reign, Lorraine enjoyed a favourable balance of trade, which owed a good deal also to an entrepôt trade. This was indeed often a polite name for smuggling at the expense of France. As the French envoy observed, 'it is not difficult to introduce into a town a sack full of contraband goods as though it were a sack of linen coming from the laundry; a sack of Dutch coffee for a sack of beans; a bale of English cloth for a bale of French cloth . . . To which one can attribute in a state so limited as Lorraine the large fortunes which have been made these twenty years by merchants of Nancy, of Bar, of Pont-à-Mousson and Neufchâteau whom one has seen as shopboys! It is not that the stuffs of foreign manufacturers are more perfect than those of France . . . It is only because they are foreign, and one always wants what one has not got, for neither in England nor in Holland are there made cloths more perfect than ours.'[40] And vice versa, as one English mercantilist was to lament: 'Nothing that is mere English goes down with our modern ladies . . . They must be equipped from dear Paris.'[41]

[40] D'Audiffret, *u.s.* vol. 124, fos. 245–6.
[41] R. Campbell, *The London Tradesman* (London, 1747), p. 197: cited E. Lipson, *The Economic History of England* (London, 1915f.), 3rd ed., ii. 101.

Patriotic d'Audiffret's analysis of Lorraine's economy and balance of trade may serve in passing to correct too ready an assumption that an eighteenth-century diplomatist in a petty principality necessarily confined his attention to court intrigues and diplomatic minutiae. Quite often, indeed, the smuggling of which he complained was intellectual as well as economic. Jansenist books were smuggled into Lorraine in bales of clothes and the interest expressed by a Benedictine at Metz in receiving consignments of 'china and 10 handkerchiefs'[42] might in fact relate to such works as the letters of the Jansenist champion, Arnauld. On the economic side proper, d'Audiffret perceived that Lorraine was, potentially at least, 'an entrepôt very useful to commerce . . . But what renders her situation much more important is the facility one might find there of making the junction of the Ocean and of the Mediterranean Sea without engaging in too great an expense.'[43]

This significant opportunity had not escaped Duke Leopold who had noted in Tacitus a Roman plan to connect the Moselle to the Saône. Towards 1720 Leopold projected a cheaper Saône-Meuse canal and initiated negotiations with both France and Austria for their participation in what would be for them an enormous enterprise as an international utility. Leopold represented the wartime advantage to France of such a link between the Mediterranean and the North Sea to cut out the hazardous passage of the Straits of Gibraltar. France and Austria both gave conditional support but the rub came, as so often, when they got down to apportioning costs, and the scheme died with the Regent Orleans in 1723.

If Lorraine had to wait for her great canals, Duke Leopold was at least able to emulate the Romans in endowing it with an admirable road-network. In less than three years, between 1724 and 1727, some five hundred miles of new roads went radiating out from Nancy and over four hundred bridges of all kinds were built. This remarkable achievement was a model for all Europe and, in particular, for the great French road-building of the seventeen-thirties under controller-general Orry. Even d'Audiffret, slow to praise anything achieved by the 'rough and inhospitable'[44] Lorrainers – he was always applying for a transfer that never came, waxed enthusiastic over a system which embraced not only highways but also country roads leading 'even from one village to another, which is of an incredible utility:

---

[42] Dom Colomban Cambon to Nicolas Thibault, Metz, Apr. 1727: Archives of the Chapter of the Old Catholic Church of Utrecht; Archives of Port-Royal at Seminary of Amersfoort, dossier 3934: cited, René Taveneaux, Le Jansenisme en Lorraine 1640–1789 (Paris, 1960), p. 581.

[43] D'Audiffret, u.s., vol. 124, fo. 167.

[44] D'Audiffret to Count de Morville, Nancy, 25 Sept. 1725: Arch. Aff. Étr. C.P., Lorraine, vol. 114, fo. 226.

eternal witnesses of the love of this Prince for the utility of his subjects, very different from the princes who have thought only of building palaces and other monuments of their vanity and of their self-esteem':[45] a nasty one for Louis XIV whom d'Audiffret had served so long.

Leopold's policies of benevolence and expansion, together with his personal extravagance, cost a lot of money. In 1706 he had the economic resources of the duchy comprehensively catalogued in the Pied-Certain, somewhat in line with the English Domesday Book; within a year the yield of the chief tax, the subvention, jumped up from 823,000 to 1,113,000 livres – by 1721 it was standing at 1,606,000. Similarly the general farm of the ducal domains and salt monopoly was yielding 1,300,000 livres in 1716 as against 884,000 at the beginning of the reign. Most often, however, the duke's Council of Finance (instituted in 1703) set its face rigidly against increases in taxation, and the amiable sovereign usually followed such advice. This aggravated his chronic insolvency, and finance was the weak element in his administration.

The pay of ducal officers and pensioners was regularly far in arrear. They came to be paid in notes of credit called *billets de liquidation*, and in 1718 Leopold was doing some monetary juggling so as to meet them at a discount. Almost every other dodge of the times was employed in hand-to-mouth expedients. In 1706 anticipatory instalments of the subvention were demanded. Five years later those exempt from that tax, notably nobles and courtiers (from ecclesiastics voluntary grants were expected), were subjected to an income-tax which afforded an interesting example of a progressive exception to that regressive taxation – the poor paying most in proportion – that was one of the worst features of the old regime. Under Leopold's system the great officers of state, ladies-in-waiting, and university professors paid one-eighth of their salaries, ranging down to one-twentyfourth on those of the ducal gardeners and chaise-porters; but unearned income in the form of pensions paid a quarter.

Most of Leopold's fiscal shifts were, however, of a less enlightened order. There was the usual multiplication and sale of municipal and legal offices, then further imposts to render them hereditary, then in 1720 revocation of their heredity. This chopping and changing was typical, often, of the duke's benevolence. Whenever he tried to mulct any section of the community, barbers in 1710 or in 1716 those recently ennobled, they would raise an outcry and remissions would usually follow. State loans were successful for a time, stamp duties were slapped on, the currency arbitrarily manipulated in accordance

[45] D'Audiffret, 'Mémoire sur le Duché de Lorraine par M. d'Audiffret': ibid., vol. 124, fo. 299.

with French example, the Jews squeezed as usual, although they fared on the whole better in Lorraine than elsewhere. This ceaseless scrabble for cash seldom caught up with the expenditure of a sovereign who laid out a hundred thousand livres on a preserve for partridges and lavishly subsidized a nobility led by the financial combine of the Craons. Leopold let the prince win thousands off him at billiards and gambling, and in 1709 La Craon's pardon of the duke's fancy for a visiting Duchess of Mantua had cost him a pretty penny. By the end of his reign the public finances were a 'chaos of debts'.[46]

Irregularity in the state finances was, however, nothing peculiar to Lorraine. At the end of the War of the Spanish Succession every government in Europe was insolvent. It was no accident that that was when governments became embroiled in such speculations as the South Sea Bubble and Law's Mississippi scheme. Leopold, incidentally, is credited with having refused a bribe of nine million livres if he would lend himself to this scheme, but he subsequently burnt his fingers locally over similar projects, which landed a Swiss promoter called the Sieur d'Aubonne in the Bastille. Leopold's financial failure also reflected his unusual reluctance to make his subjects pay for his extravagance. Leopold's eudemonic economics were no doubt an impractical attempt to get the best of both worlds but they brought out, as it were in caricature, an important factor in eighteenth-century irregularities in government finance. Often, as in previous centuries, they largely reflected the inadequacy of the fiscal machinery. One could apply to little Lorraine what has been said of its great French neighbour of that period: it was a poor state in a rich country.

Under the old regime the grip of enlightened despotism upon the mercantile economy was often apt to be far from despotic in terms of financial power. The venerable conundrum of how to mulct trade without depressing it still obtained while property-taxes were traditionally difficult to assess and usually hollowed out by exemptions. Such devices as tax-farming and sale of offices approximated dangerously towards state borrowing. Of course there were exceptions such as Prussia under King Frederick-William I whose grim and economical administration contrasted strikingly with that of his contemporary, Duke Leopold. The very impressiveness of this achievement, however, suggests how, upon the whole, states in their sphere, as landlords in theirs, were finding it increasingly difficult to make the old system pay.

[46] D'Audiffret to Chauvelin, Nancy, 12 Apr. 1729: Arch. Aff. Étr. C.P., Lorraine, vol. *supplément* 18, fo. 301.

IV

If the financial basis of Leopold's achievement for Lorraine was precarious, the political was not less so. The resurrection of Lorraine stands out the more remarkably in the light of the fact that the duke was quite shrewd enough to perceive that her remaining days of independence were strictly numbered. In the words of one of his chief administrators, Leopold after his restoration to Lorraine 'soon perceived that his lot was infinitely to be pitied, and that in Europe there was not a sovereign worse placed than he'.[47] Louis XIV for his part had already written off the reconstituted duchy, observing to his ambassador in London that 'the acquisition of Lorraine would be a small addition to my power, that state being so enclosed in my dominions that it is impossible for a duke of Lorraine ever to take any other part than such as shall please me'.[48] This argument was for use with William III of England during those negotiations relative to the ill-fated Spanish Succession which culminated in the Second Treaty of Partition of March 1700 and an arrangement whereby Lorraine should go to France, Leopold (not consulted in advance) being shunted off to Milan. This combination soon fell through when, upon the long-awaited death of the imbecile Charles II of Spain, Louis XIV accepted the bequest to a French prince of the Spanish heritage. Europe was plunged into another decade of grand-scale war while the loyal Lorrainers celebrated the fact that their duke would now be living for a hundred thousand years (*cent mille ans – sans Milan*).

The rejoicings in Lorraine were but for a spell. By the end of 1702 French troops, true to form, were back in occupation of Nancy after an absence of less than five years. In bitterness of heart Duke Leopold, acknowledging the folly of resistance, withdrew with his court eastwards to little Lunéville where he lodged in a dilapidated old castle until such time as his architect, Boffrand, had erected there the elegant palace which, with its celebrated gardens by Yves Desours, became his permanent residence. Leopold, who had prudently married his French princess four years earlier, was able to remain in his duchy and considerably protect his people from rigours comparable to those which they had so recently endured. Despite the

---

[47] Baron Bourcier de Montureux, 'Réflexions sur l'élection de l'Empereur François Ier, aujourd'hui régnant': cited, Comte d'Haussonville, *Histoire de la réunion de la Lorraine à la France* (Paris, 1854–9), iv. 137, n. 1. (For the attribution of authorship, there questioned, cf. P. Boyé, op. cit., p. 326, n. 3.)

[48] King Louis XIV to Count de Tallard, Versailles, 13 Feb. 1699: translation in Paul Grimblot, *Letters of William III and Louis XIV and of their ministers* (London, 1848), ii. 265.

French occupation the duke got his neutrality so respected that Lorraine became an oasis prospering amid war. Nor did the ducal policy stop there, for if Leopold had another extravagance after his mistress and his gambling it was his diplomacy. He spent large sums, for instance, on 'magnificent presents'[49] for the Duke of Marlborough, notoriously partial to such douceurs. He was one of Leopold's chief hopes for the realization of his ambitious designs for the aggrandizement of Lorraine, represented to the powers of the Grand Alliance as the desirable creation of a substantial buffer-state, matching Flanders, between the French and German territories. The fall of Marlborough was a blow for Leopold and at the negotiations for the peace settlement of Utrecht nobody bothered much about his more modest request for recognition by the powers of the perpetual neutrality of Lorraine in a Europe still under the influence of war.

The War of the Spanish Succession had been the first of those great wars which have ushered in each of the last three centuries and left the powers of Europe exhausted at their outset. The price of glory had been heavy both in cash and in lives. This accentuated the picture of a western civilization which was, in general, still cohesive in social structure but sparse in human resources. The Europe of 1715 counted between seventy and eighty million inhabitants, about a quarter of them living in towns. Roughly three-quarters of the royal revenues of France were derived from her rural heritage, parcelled into some forty or fifty thousand seignories. If corn-prices in France were then a barometer for prices of textiles, her main manufacture, that relationship was in turn a gauge of agricultural preponderance still in Europe.

Duke Leopold revived Lorraine at a time when France, the Austrian Netherlands, the Iberian Peninsula, Ireland, many states of Germany, Sweden, Poland, and Russia were all less populous and, by and large, less prosperous than in years gone by. Nor had the settlement of Utrecht set a final term to war in either the northern or the southern extremities of Europe. It was not till 1718 that the meteor of the north, King Charles XII of Sweden, was extinguished in the Norwegian wastes in the course of that Northern War which terminated only three years later with the Treaty of Nystädt. Sweden was not alone in her decline from wider dominion. In the Mediterranean the years from 1717 to 1720 saw war revived by Spain, resentful at being ousted from Italy by Austria, herself unreconciled to losing the hispanic inheritance. But the battle of Cape Passaro, outstanding in that war, mattered less to Austria, to Europe, than the Peace of Passarowitz concluded three weeks earlier

<hr>

[49] D'Audiffret, 6 Apr. 1713: cited, Comte d'Haussonville, op. cit., iv. 237.

with the Ottoman Empire. Throughout the eighteenth century the pattern in Eastern Europe was to be Austria as a bastion against Turkey, and Poland against Russia, and both bastions weak. If the Turkish Empire was to decline, the Russian was rising as a new portent over the eastern horizon. Peter the Great, the winner at Nystädt, swung Russia into Europe with heavy and permanent effect upon the continental balance of power. French pressures ensured that the historic body-politic of Europe was usually on the defensive in the east; in the west, however, new opportunities were opening out to the maritime powers and especially to England, the other outlying newcomer among the greatest nations. The future of European expansion lay out across the oceans, whither Choiseul was to direct his policies. Commerce increasingly superseded religion in another drive which paradoxically promoted war but flourished in peace. Religion, though, still loomed larger than is always allowed. The Constitution Unigenitus of the same year as the Utrecht settlement was to plague French politics for more than a generation. The Emperor Charles VI still cherished the aspiration of reuniting the Holy Roman Empire in the Roman Catholic Church even while joining in the maritime and commercial swim in 1722 by founding the Ostend Company for trading to the Indies.

In 1719 France, England, and Holland between them enjoyed a circulation of currency that was almost half that of all Europe, on estimated figures of forty-six million pounds out of a total of some hundred million. Their Triple Alliance of 1717 expanded next year into the Quadruple Alliance with Austria. Hence came it that the British fleet, which under Admiral Byng had scattered the Spanish ships off Cape Passaro, subsequently found itself supporting the attack on Bourbon Spain by a French army under her erstwhile champion, the Duke of Berwick, illegitimate son of James II of England by Arabella Churchill. From this involved conflict in the Mediterranean the Duke of Lorraine hoped to extract an exchange whereby, as he wrote to the Regent Orleans, 'the state of Tuscany should be assured to me'.[50] This prefigurative Tuscan aspiration partly related to a complicated claim for compensation in lieu of succession to the duchy of Montferrat, with which Leopold had been badgering the courts of Europe ever since the death in 1708 of the Duke of Mantua, whose attractive young widow had briefly competed with La Craon. Such a Tuscan exchange, however, had to wait, for the best part of twenty years. Meanwhile the nimble Leopold thought

---

[50] Duke Leopold to Regent Orleans, 18 Jan. 1718: Arch. Aff. Étr. C.P., Lorraine, cited, Comte d'Haussonville, op. cit. iv. 614, document xl; cf. also d'Audiffret to Regent Orleans, 25 Apr. 1719: Arch Aff. Étr. C.P., Lorraine, vol. 103, fo. 212, cited, H. Baumont, op. cit., p. 327.

he saw another opportunity in that alliance which squashed Spanish bellicosity till Spain herself swung into line to constitute the Quintuple Alliance of 1720. Alliance for peace had significantly spread in widening circles from the decisive combination of the rich nations of the west.

The question of the international status of Lorraine in the first half of the eighteenth century was not wholly dissimilar from the case of Belgium in the first half of the nineteenth. For both those small middle-lands between the French and German antagonists the basic choice lay between an international guarantee of neutrality and participation in a system of collective security. Having failed to obtain the former, Duke Leopold now looked to the latter, though only as a second-best. Naturally a believer in Franco-Austrian reconciliation, Leopold strove for years to secure admittance to the Quadruple Alliance in its successive stages. As he saw it, the purpose of this impressive combination 'was not only to render general the tranquillity of Europe, but even to render it durable for always by Quadruple Alliance between these Powers, and they declared that all the Princes and States of Europe could accede, if they requested it, on obtaining the consent of the Powers'.[51] They all agreed generally that Lorraine should come in and King George I of England, in particular, assured Duke Leopold in a letter of 26 February 1721: 'I agree myself very willingly to your accession to the Quadruple Alliance, and I will have it supported for my part in the said Congress'[52] of Cambrai, then preparing with the primary object of assuaging Spanish discontent – it was still in preparation a year later when enlivened by a visit from Voltaire and a performance of his first play *Œdipe*. The congress finally did open in 1724, only to become proverbial for its tedium (a typical issue was whether Spain or Austria should confer the Golden Fleece), contriving to do very little very slowly so that on 19 February 1725 Leopold was writing to draw the attention of George I to the fact that the British representatives at Cambrai had 'given those of the Emperor to understand at the time that they received their [Austrian] Postulata in which there is an article inserted concerning my accession to the quadruple alliance, that they had in this respect neither order nor instruction on the part of Your

---

[51] Undated memorandum reviewing the foreign policy of Lorraine, communicated to the French government by the Marquis de Stainville in late (probably early Dec.) 1726: Arch. Aff. Étr. C.P., Lorraine, vol. 116, fo. 68.

[52] King George I to Duke Leopold, St. James's, 15 Feb. 1721 (O.S.): Public Record Office, State Papers, Foreign (henceforth cited as P.R.O./S.P.F.), Foreign Entry Book No. 59, F.O. Kings' Letters 19, fo. 113.

Majesty for consenting thereto and sustaining my interests in this assembly.'[53]

On 29 March 1725 this letter was handed to the King of England by the Marquis de Stainville.

[53] Duke Leopold to King George I, Lunéville, 19 Feb. 1725: P.R.O./S.P.F., Royal Letters, vol. 39, fo. 159.

CHAPTER IV

ENVOY

I

THE Duke of Lorraine did not run to a permanent representative at the English court. And he would probably have been prevented from maintaining one by his French neighbours, who kept a sharp eye upon his representation abroad. So, though, did Austria. She promoted the special mission to England which, by November 1724, had been entrusted to the Marquis de Stainville, 'a young man', remarked d'Audiffret, 'very new to the profession which he is going to exercise'.[1] He made a false start that December, the month in which his third child, Leopold Charles, was born. Thereafter Stainville, it appears, was delayed by 'lack of money for the expenses of his voyage, which is very common at this court'.[2] At last he was off on 22 February 1725, equipped with a reminder that the Emperor Charles VI 'has wished ... that ... [he] should assume no official quality'[3] at the Court of Saint James. During the seventeen-twenties Duke Leopold's westward diplomacy, to become Stainville's sphere of action, was validated by the eastern affiliation to Vienna.

The Marquis de Stainville stopped off some three weeks in Paris, where he had the usual shopping commissions from the Duchess of Lorraine. Her particular friend there was the Marquise d'Aulède whose husband was happily lord of Margaux so that Stainville was soon sending the duke half a dozen of that vintage, rated 'excellent for the stomach'.[4] Political initiatives were not expected of the visit, for, as d'Audiffret informed his minister for foreign affairs, the Count de Morville, 'the Duke of Lorraine appears to be persuaded that he has nothing to hope for from Monseigneur the Duke [de Bourbon] or from you on the subject of the neutrality he claims ... One cannot be more stubborn than he is about it and, imagining that he has been unjustly treated in being refused it, he flatters himself that the King of England having given his consent in writing for his accession to

[1] D'Audiffret to King Louis XV, Nancy, 7 Nov. 1724: Arch. Aff. Étr. C.P., Lorraine, vol. 112, fo. 280.
[2] D'Audiffret to Count de Morville, Nancy, 22 Feb. 1725: ibid., vol. 114, fo. 44.
[3] 'Instruction pour Mʳ. le Mqˢ. de Stainville que S[on] A[ltesse] [Royale] envoye en Angleterre', Lunéville, 19 Feb. 1725: Arch. M-et-M/Vienne, 3F 7, no. 31.
[4] Marquis de Stainville to Duke Leopold, Paris, 2 Mar. 1725: Arch. M-et-M/Vienne, 3F 85, no. 3.

the Quadruple Alliance, he will easily secure the application of this consent to the neutrality which he desires, being above all supported by the emperor who has given very positive orders about it to the Count de Starhemberg',[5] the Austrian ambassador in London, whom Stainville was 'to consult on everything'.[6] D'Audiffret, however, judged 'that the constant opposition of His Majesty [Louis XV] will render these démarches and these solicitations useless'.[7]

Behind this judgement lay a recent shift in French policy towards Lorraine from the friendliness of the Regent Orleans to the hostility of the Duke de Bourbon who, having cleared a fortune from the schemes of Law, had succeeded Orleans as prime minister in 1723. The alarmingly ugly young Duke de Bourbon was a mediocrity of limited vision – he had only one eye as the result of a hunting accident – but one of the constants in his policy was to do down the rival branch of Orleans and its associates. This preoccupation was reflected in his personal instructions of 15 March 1725 to the Count de Broglie, French ambassador in London, to keep a sharp eye out for the Marquis de Stainville, wrongly if understandably suspected of leaving Paris 'with some secret commission of M. and Mde. d'Orleans on the affairs of the present conjuncture'.[8]

The reference was almost certainly to the question of the marriage of the fifteen-year-old Louis XV, then in an acute phase since he had the month before fallen seriously ill after over-exertion out hunting, for which the Duke de Bourbon had lately inspired him with a lifelong passion. If Louis died his throne would pass to the young Duke of Orleans, with whose matrimonial affairs Stainville was indeed soon to be concerned. One hears of the prime minister pacing the passages of Versailles by night, in his dressing-gown, muttering: 'What will become of me? . . . I won't be caught like that again . . . If he recovers, he must be married.'[9]

Bourbon, supported indeed by considered opinion at court, had accordingly just infuriated proud Spain by packing back to Madrid the seven-year-old Infanta Maria Anna Victoria, who had come to France as her future queen but, Stainville was assured, had incurred 'the hatred of the king'.[10] The question of the marriage, of consuming interest to the dynasties of Europe, was reopened, and among those

---

[5] D'Audiffret to Count de Morville, Nancy, 22 Feb. 1725: u.s., vol. 114, fos. 44–5.
[6] Duke Leopold to Marquis de Stainville, Lunéville, 24 Mar. 1725: Arch. M-et-M/Vienne, 3F 85, no. 128, fo. 6.
[7] D'Audiffret to Count de Morville: u.s., fo. 45.
[8] Duke de Bourbon to Count de Broglie, Versailles, 15 Mar. 1725: Arch. Aff. Étr. C.P., Angleterre, vol. 350, fo. 183.
[9] Duclos, Mémoires secrets sur les règnes de Louis XIV et de Louis XV (Paris, 1791), ii. 299.
[10] Marquis de Stainville to Duke Leopold, Paris, 2 Mar. 1725: Arch. M-et-M/Vienne, 3F 85, no. 2.

short-listed out of the hundred possible brides was blonde Elisabeth-Thérèse, elder daughter of Duke Leopold. A more likely choice was Bourbon's nineteen-year-old sister, Mademoiselle de Sens. Another front-runner was a daughter of the Princess of Wales, Princess Anne, prudently withheld by George I. Marriage, however, was in the air in late March 1725 when the Marquis de Stainville drove in over what struck him as 'the badly paved streets of London'.[11] Being on temporary mission, he had travelled without his family, with a personal staff comprising a secretary, Joseph Toussaint, a couple of interpreters, a valet, three lackeys, the coachman, and a chef[12] in precaution, for such a gourmet, against English cooking.

II

'I hope that when we are separated by the Channel our correspondence will be more regular.'[13] Duke Leopold's recent dig at the Marquis de Stainville already set his reputation as a bad correspondent. Perhaps, though, that owed almost as much to eagerness for news at the monotonous little court of Lunéville as to the marquis's deficiencies. Certainly he could write in vivid detail, as in his subsequent account of a confidential exchange with the winning Princess of Wales, the future Queen Caroline. When she tipped the Princess of Lorraine as future Queen of France the marquis replied 'that I very much doubted it ... She said to me that apparently that was because of Original Sin, wishing to convey to me that they would avoid choosing a queen who is attached to the House of Orleans.'[14]

For the Duke of Lorraine if not the duchess the dubious chance of a French marriage would hardly have bulked large beside his international scoop in planting his heir in the court of Vienna. In London the Marquis de Stainville was closely questioned about this. For there was already general recognition of the French feeling that, in the words of a British diplomatist a year earlier, 'if the Prince of Lorraine should succeed to the Emperor's hereditary dominions he might succeed to the dignity of Emperor, be a too potent neighbour and hem them in too close, being master of the Netherlands, Flanders,

---

[11] Marquis de Stainville to Duke Leopold, London, 4 June 1725: ibid., no. 16.

[12] Cf. 'Liste des gens que Monsieur le Marquis de Stainville, Chargé d'Affaires de S.A.R de Lorraine, en cette cour, a à sa suite' (list communicated to the sheriffs of London and Middlesex in connection with rights of diplomatic privilege, May 1725): P.R.O./S.P.F., Foreign Ministers in England, no. 68.

[13] Duke Leopold to Marquis de Stainville, Lunéville, 18 Mar. 1725: Arch. M-et-M/Vienne, 3F 85, no. 128, fo. 2.

[14] Marquis de Stainville to Duke Leopold, London, 18 May 1725: Arch. M-et-M/Vienne, 3F 85, no. 14, fo. 2.

Brabant, Luxembourg, Lorraine, and in a manner quite round from the sea to Switzerland'.[15] Against this background the question of the international position of Lorraine remained the chief theme of Stainville's mission.

In London on 26 March 1725 Starhemberg warned Stainville not to count upon securing British support for the adhesion of Lorraine to the Quadruple Alliance. This was borne out three days later when the Austrian introduced the Lorrainer to the Duke of Newcastle whom he described as 'the secretary of state for our department,'[16] the Southern Department under the system then whereby the conduct of British foreign policy was divided between two secretaries of state. Stainville had already met Newcastle's northern colleague, Lord Townshend, Turnip Townshend, brother-in-law to the prime minister, Sir Robert Walpole. They had lately combined to insert the industrious Duke of Newcastle in place of their potential rival, the brilliant and indiscreet Lord Carteret, compromised via Versailles: weakened by the passing of the Regent and Dubois, Carteret had yet embroiled himself there in an intrigue on behalf of the two supplementary favourites of George I, his half-sister, the portly Countess of Darlington, and her more personable sister-in-law, Countess von Platen.

Now Newcastle told Stainville to be at the palace at one o'clock that day, 29 March 1725, when he had an audience of King George I in the presence of both secretaries of state. It was, however, a private audience since the Marquis de Stainville was not so fully accredited as he had apparently made out to the suspicious Count de Broglie, his fellow veteran in London from the rigours of the siege of Freiburg back in 1713. That evening Broglie pumped the two English ministers, asking them if Stainville 'had spoken well to the King of England. They answered ... that the compliment had been very short, that he had handed him a letter on behalf of his master and that he repeated two or three times in the little he had said to him [the king] that the estates of his master were as if invested by France.'[17] King George replied to Stainville in a generally negative sense in accordance with what Newcastle had already said to Stainville and now repeated before his sovereign as to the desire of Duke Leopold to join the Quadruple Alliance. In particular, reported Stainville, the

[15] Lord Polwarth, 'Journal of Lord Polwarth's visit to Paris', 28 May 1724: *Report on the Manuscripts on Lord Polwarth* (London, 1911f.) iv. 84–5. (Report of the Historical Manuscripts Commission, 1940.)
[16] Marquis de Stainville to Duke Leopold, London, 30 Mar. 1725: Arch. M-et-M/Vienne, 3F 85, no. 5.
[17] Count de Broglie to Duke de Bourbon, London, 26 [sic] March 1725: Arch. Aff. Étr. C.P., Angleterre, vol. 350, fo. 258. (The Count de Broglie's dating seems somewhat confused in relation to the first-hand account of the Marquis de Stainville, which I have preferred.)

king 'answered me that one should address oneself to France with whom, I had told him previously, there were many difficulties to surmount. I had the honour to reply to him that it was precisely these same difficulties which obliged Your Royal Highness to have recourse to him.'[18] George thought it not the moment. Stainville thought he should not press further at his first audience.

After Stainville had withdrawn, recounted Newcastle and Townshend, 'His Brittanic Majesty without reading the letter handed it to the Duke of Newcastle and said to him, You have only to make him the same answer as that which you have already made him every time that he has written to me concerning it, and [say] that I cannot alone without the concert of France do anything in the matter, that it could lead to large consequences, the King of Portugal asking the same thing and several other princes also ... The King of England said to his ministers that he had found this envoy well powdered and frizzed in French fashion. [Cypher begins.] They have also told me that they know not wherefore but that their master was not well disposed towards this Duke.'[19] Though probably all present could have made a good guess why. For one way not to ingratiate oneself with the Hanoverian dynasty was to harbour the Old Pretender as Duke Leopold had done for some years after he had been expelled from France under the terms of the Treaty of Utrecht. It had been from a dreary residence in Bar-le-Duc that the Chevalier de Saint Georges, disguised as a servant, had set out upon the forlorn adventure of the Fifteen. Nor were the Jacobite connections of the court of Lorraine at an end.

The Count de Broglie repaid the communicativeness of the English ministers by purloining a letter from Duke Leopold which Lord Townshend shewed him, and carrying it off in his hat. He was hardly one to make much of the mission of the Marquis de Stainville whom he considered ill advised to lean upon Count von Starhemberg, 'having had difficulties, he and Madame de Starhemberg, with the King of England, the Prince and Princess of Wales, and having fallen out with all the ministers'.[20] Starhemberg now suggested that Stainville should at any rate seek from the British government a letter to its ambassador in Paris, Sir Robert's brother, Horatio Walpole, to get him to sound the French government as to their intentions towards Lorraine. 'We know them only too well',[21] replied

[18] Marquis de Stainville to Duke Leopold, London, 30 Mar. 1725: Arch. M-et-M/Vienne, 3F 85, no. 5.

[19] Count de Broglie to Duke de Bourbon, London, 26 March 1725: Arch. Aff. Étr. C.P., Angleterre, vol. 350, fo. 258.

[20] Count de Broglie to Count de Morville, London, 2 Apr. 1725: ibid., fo. 279.

[21] Marquis de Stainville to Duke Leopold, London, 30 Mar. 1725: Arch. M-et-M/Vienne, 3F 85, no. 5.

Stainville, who nevertheless went to work in this sense, approved by Duke Leopold.

A fortnight later Stainville was writing: 'I could not be more pleased than I am with the gracious attentions which the King has for me. I am trying to pay my court to him as much as I can, especially at the opera where, being within range of his box, I thus find myself within reach for talking often to him.'[22] On 4 May 1725 Stainville, after conferring with Newcastle, had another audience of George I. And the king did remit to the young envoy the desired letter to Horatio Walpole, observing, however, 'that he was persuaded that it was useless at present to solicit accession to the Quadruple Alliance, and that his letter would produce absolutely no effect'.[23] The king was right, as the marquis knew, as was swiftly to be demonstrated by a startling development in the high diplomacy of Europe. More than ten days earlier Starhemberg had had a premonitory change of mind as to his own suggestion, now implemented by Stainville.

If the beginner from Lorraine had struck up well with the forbidding king and his primary mistress, the lanky, mercenary, teutonic Duchess of Kendal, yet the Prince of Wales had not addressed a word to Stainville upon introduction. This, gloated Broglie, 'causes him to begin here very disagreeably'[24] – and all because Stainville on Starhemberg's advice had been presented to the prince, as earlier to the king himself, by a groom of the chamber rather than by the master of ceremonies. 'I was very happy', he wrote, 'to have the king informed of this by the Duchess of Kendal, who told me that the king had jested about it. At the same time she flattered me that he had seemed pleased with me.'[25] The Prince of Wales came round and the princess had always been charming to Stainville.

The young marquis began in London a lifelong round of dinners with diplomatic colleagues, including Broglie, as also then with the English aristocracy – 'yesterday I dined with a very large company at milord Malpas',[26] a young Member of Parliament and son of the fighting Earl of Cholmondeley. Stainville had been caught up in reunions with English old boys from the academy at Lunéville. They were full of Duke Leopold's kindnesses towards them so that in London, wrote Stainville, 'I have found more acquaintances than I could have hoped.'[27] These came to include the prime minister's son,

[22] Ibid., 12 Apr. 1725: no. 128, fo. 7.
[23] Ibid., 5 May 1725: no. 12.
[24] Count de Broglie to Count de Morville, London, 2 Apr. 1725: Arch. Aff. Étr. C.P., Angelterre, vol. 350, fo. 280.
[25] Marquis de Stainville to Duke Leopold, London, 16 Apr. 1725: Arch. M-et-M/Vienne, 3F 85, no. 8.
[26] Ibid., 5 May 1725: no. 12.   [27] Ibid., 5 Apr. 1725: no. 7.

Lord Walpole, with whom on 28 April 1725 he followed his bent by
going 'staghunting at Windsor ... I was surprised by the beauty and
good behaviour of the pack, charmed by the gentleness of the horses
and very little satisfied with the strength of the stag, which defended
itself very badly.'[28]

Important among Stainville's 'little commissions'[29] from Leopold
through the long-serving ducal secretary, Molitoris, were those for
plenishing the ducal stables and packs. He arranged to buy ten
carriage-horses at twenty-five pounds each plus transport. Toussaint
could look after them from Calais onwards. Only, they had to be paid
for. Stainville had arrived in London to find that the banker upon
whom his letters of credit were drawn had recently gone bankrupt,
specially awkward in view of 'the enormous expenditures which one
is obliged to make in this country'.[30]

Stainville accordingly represented 'the uselessness of the stay that
I am making here',[31] but was ordered to prolong it till George I set
forth to summer as usual in Hanover. This frustration was
prefigurative of Stainville's diplomatic role over the years. He now
filled in with the English news about bills before parliament, the
usual unpleasantness over the king's civil list, his reconstitution of
the Order of the Bath – almost a Walpole benefit, the controversial
return of the Jacobite Lord Bolingbroke – it was only three years
since a star pupil from Lunéville, the Duke of Norfolk, had been
lodged in the Tower of London for Jacobite conspiracy. Bolingbroke
is said to have bribed his way back through the Duchess of Kendal.
Now the death of her associate, the Countess of Darlington, had
affected the king, reported Stainville, who also conveyed some early
medical intelligence: 'They are talking here of nothing but the
prodigious effects of inoculation. The King has several times ordered
me to write to Your Royal Highness about it. It is true that there are
hardly any examples of accidents befalling people who have had
smallpox in this way; but it is still truer that I shall take great care not
to give advice about that, and that it is only in obedience to the King
that I have the honour of writing about it':[32] hardly superfluously
seeing how Leopold had been ravished of his children. And if the
Marquis de Stainville had been less cautiously supercilious about
inoculation the future Duke de Choiseul might have had cause to be
grateful.

In London as elsewhere, however, the big news still centred around
dynastic ambitions and alliances. Thus the Marquis de Stainville on

[28] Ibid., 30 Apr. 1725: no. 11.   [29] Ibid., 13 May 1725: no. 13.
[30] Ibid., 23 Apr. 1725: no. 10.   [31] Ibid.
                        [32] Ibid., 24 May 1725: no. 15.

4 June 1725: 'The declaration of the marriage of the King of France has much astonished the betters, most of whom were for Mademoiselle de Sens.'[33] Whereas the Duke de Bourbon had in the event decided more moderately that the best security for himself and his almond-eyed mistress, Madame de Prie, lay with the physically robust but dynastically and indeed personally insignificant Marie Leszczynska, daughter of Stanislas, the ephemeral King of Poland who for years had been hanging around as an impecunious refugee, selling off jewels and receiving covert assistance from the generous Duke Leopold. The disappointed Duchess of Lorraine had now been venting her scorn upon the French king's 'misalliance' with the daughter of one who she described with some slight exaggeration as having 'been king only for 24 hours'.[34]

This marriage intertwined with that other more keenly pursued by Duke Leopold. In London that May people were putting it to the hedging Marquis de Stainville 'that there be some secret convention which would throw out the views entertained for the prince'[35] of Lorraine in Vienna. For Philip V of Spain, stung by the French insult to his little daughter, had withdrawn his envoys not only from Paris but also from Cambrai, where the do-nothing congress at last broke up. And the Quadruple Alliance itself had been breached when Spain startled Europe by allying herself with Austria in the First Treaty of Vienna on 30 April 1725. Spain was to support the emperor's cherished Ostend Company while he would help Philip V to regain Gibraltar from England and to appease his dominating queen, Elizabeth Farnese, by promoting her heart's desire for an Italian apanage for her elder son, Don Carlos. Already in the winter of 1724 the chief Spanish minister, a Dutch adventurer called Ripperda who has been described as almost a caricature of his predecessor, Alberoni, had visited Vienna with an alluring proposal for linking the fortunes of Spain and Austria once again by marrying Don Carlos to Maria Theresa, and his younger brother, Don Philip, to her younger sister Maria Anna. Duke Leopold was now up against the termagant of Spain in the matrimonial stakes for the greatest heiress in the world of power-politics. He was for years kept on tenterhooks, as he subsequently confessed to his representative in Vienna: 'My anxiety as to Don Carlos will scarcely cease; the character of the Queen of Spain is so given to intrigue, so acute ...

---

[33] Ibid., 4 June 1725: no. 16.

[34] Duchess of Lorraine to Marquise d'Aulède, Lunéville, 14 Apr. 1725: 'Lettres d'Elisabeth-Charlotte d'Orléans, duchesse de Lorraine, à la marquise d'Aulède, 1715–1738', ed. E. Alexandre de Bonneval in *Recueil de documents sur l'histoire de Lorraine*, 10th vol (Nancy, 1865), p. 198.

[35] Marquis de Stainville to Duke Leopold, London, 18 May 1725: Arch. M-et-M/Vienne, 3F 85, no. 14.

that there is nothing which she does not propose, risk and wish to obtain, by whatever means ... But since we cannot remedy that it is useless to speak of it.'[36]

Duke Leopold's philosophical propensity for making the best of things induced him on 7 July 1725 to adhere to the First Treaty of Vienna. He blandly proceeded to represent the treaty to King George I as a projection of the Quadruple Alliance that he himself might care to join. King George replied tartly that he had 'not the intention of acceding to it'.[37] The Marquis de Stainville, back in Paris, had already written on 31 August to inform his master that the Duke de Bourbon had told him that France would never join the Austro-Spanish pact, 'there being articles therein which are too prejudicial to her'.[38] In fact, three days later, France joined England and Prussia in the Treaty of Hanover in opposition to that of Vienna. Europe was once again ranged into two hostile camps.

III

That summer the Marquis de Stainville caught the atmosphere in Paris under the ministry of the Duke de Bourbon: 'Everybody here is utterly dejected and reserved. The only talk is of distress. Bread has however fallen a little but it is not thought that it will be for long if the rain keeps on as it is doing.'[39] By the end of the year the Lorrainer was relaying murmurs from Versailles that the unpopularity of the government had caused young Louis XV to upbraid Bourbon, who thereafter taxed the king's influential tutor, the seventytwo-year-old Bishop of Fréjus, with being the instigator: as Fleury had boldly admitted, representing to the prime minister 'the prayers of the people, who could no longer bear such a harsh domination as that of M. Duverney and Mme. de Prie. They had written him thousands of anonymous letters.'[40] Under the old regime public opinion, even while still muted, was seldom mute.

Suggestive for the future was the bracketing of the reigning mistress with the rising financier, Pâris-Duverney, who, together with his brother Pâris-Monmartel, stood in chequered succession

---

[36] Duke Leopold to Baron de Jaquemin, 20 Mar. 1729: Ö.S./H.H.S., Lothringisches Hausarchiv 108/425 ('Registre des despeches secrettes de Son Altesse Royale commencé le 19ᵐᵉ octobre 1726, No. I').

[37] King George I to Duke Leopold, Herrenhausen, 15 Sept. 1725 (O.S.): P.R.O./S.P.F., Royal Letters, vol. 39, fos. 145–6.

[38] Marquis de Stainville to Duke Leopold, Paris, 31 Aug. 1725: Arch. M-et-M/Vienne 3F 85, no. 17 (copy in Ö.S./H.H.S., Lothringisches Hausarchiv 112/437.)

[39] Ibid.

[40] Ibid., 12 Dec. 1725: no. 23.

along the great line from Samuel Bernard and the Crozats. Though one of the most unpopular aspects of the Duke de Bourbon's ministry in the aftermath of the Mississippi crash was precisely its monetary policy and arbitrary devaluation of the *louis d'or*. Pâris-Duverney, for the second time, suffered exile from court in consequence of that of Bourbon himself on 11 June 1726. The Marquis de Stainville significantly heard the news at a focus of opposition, the Palais Royal, from the ingratiating Marc-Pierre de Voyer, young Count d'Argenson, the Chancellor and Steward to the Duke of Orleans in anticipation of larger things. Four days later a decree promoted by the controller-general, Le Pelletier des Forts, fixed the louis at twenty-four livres, the écu at six: the livre, a unit of account heralding the franc, being worth approximately tenpence upon the contemporary exchange. This measure was one of the most important in the history of eighteenth-century France. The stabilized currency was to remain almost constant till the French Revolution as the basis of the economic upswing of France in the next two generations.[41] For the present it auspiciously inaugurated the long ministry of retrenchment under the incipient Cardinal Fleury, with whom the Marquis de Stainville promptly made contact.

In the past year Stainville had alternated between Paris and Lorraine. In Paris, where he at first put up at the Hôtel de Saint Thomas in the Rue d'Enfer, Faubourg Saint Germain, he had sought to negotiate lesser issues such as the demolition of the fortifications of the old town at Nancy, a question, harking back to Ryswick, wherein the ingenious duke sought to combine municipal with international advantage since the demolitions to further town-planning might also buttress his claim to neutrality by rendering his capital an open city. In Lorraine too Stainville had been temporarily reduced, in October 1725, to a farewell escort from Lunéville for the duchess's niece, the visiting Princess of Modena, miserable to be returning thither to boredom with a heavy cold.

Such Orleanist associations reinforced those in Paris with the Regent's dissimilar successor as Duke of Orleans, shy and pious, and with the princess of Baden whom he had married in 1724. This young Duchess of Orleans was marked to die in that summer of 1726. It would appear that even a little before that Stainville was taking soundings for a remarriage of the duke to Princess Elisabeth-Thérèse of Lorraine. Having failed to become Queen of France the previous year she might thus still arrive since the Duke of Orleans at present

---

[41] Cf. President Valéry Giscard d'Estaing, 'L'économie française au temps de Louis XV' in *Louis XV: un moment de perfection de l'art français*, catalogue by Hôtel de la Monnaie (Paris, 1974), pp. xxxiv–xxxv.

remained heir-presumptive to the throne. A significant intermediary, on very good terms with Stainville, was the ducal chancellor, the Count d'Argenson, younger brother of the blunter marquis. If Stainville was later to do more business with the count as French Minister of War, young d'Argenson was then something of an expert in royal marriages – he was said to have been the promoter of Marie Leszczynska.

The Marquis de Stainville's own intermediary was also destined for higher things. His diligent secretary was regularly referred to by Craon as 'friend Toussaint', significantly suggesting oxymoron. Stainville now had also been joined in Paris by his wife. She had at the end of May left Lunéville where, wrote Craon, he 'took leave of the Little One (*La Petite*) with tears in my eyes'.[42] Next month Craon began another letter to his confidant in Paris: 'My dear nephew, we are leading very different lives from one another. You tell me by your courier that you have not sat down a moment during the day, and I am spending mine upon a chair gambling, virtually without giving myself leisure to take a walk.'[43]

'Great events', proceeded Craon, 'always cause joy and give birth to hopes in every heart, and each flatters himself with regard to his particular interests. Upon my own account I do not doubt that my lawsuit with the Lady d'Armaillé will be judged more favourably than it would have been perhaps under the ministry of the Duke.' A relation of Bourbon's mistress was involved in another case, concerning a priory of Saint Dagobert, which Craon included in his numerous assignments till Stainville might seem to be representing him hardly less than Leopold. The latter, though, perceived more broadly the opportunities for Lorraine opened by the advent of an ecclesiastical septuagenarian of pacific moderation. In September 1726 the Marquis de Stainville received a permanent appointment as minister for Lorraine to the French court, henceforth his diplomatic sphere.

Shortly before his first public audience Stainville called by appointment at nine o'clock one Wednesday morning, 26 October 1726, upon Fleury, not yet dressed. While his attendants helped to attire him the cardinal chatted, asking after the Craons and 'how many children they had. The number surprised him.'[44] ('I am very flattered'[45] commented Craon subsequently.) Talking of children

[42] Prince de Craon to Marquis de Stainville, Lunéville, 29 May 1726: Arch. M-et-M/Vienne, 3F 370, no. 33.
[43] Ibid., 15 June 1726: no. 14, and for the following.
[44] Marquis de Stainville to Duke Leopold, Paris, 29 Oct. 1726: Arch. M-et-M/Vienne, 3F 85, no. 58.
[45] Prince de Craon to Marquis de Stainville, Lunéville, 2 Nov. 1726: Arch. M-et-M/Vienne, 3F 370, no. 50.

Fleury recalled of little Princess Anne-Charlotte of Lorraine 'that he had never seen anything so beautiful as she had been at [the coronation of 1722 at] Rheims. Being dressed at last', continued Stainville, 'he dismissed his domestics. And then ... he said to me, "Let us both strip ourselves of the quality of ministers and speak from the heart. I know your steadiness (*sagesse*) and I hold you in the highest esteem. You will no longer doubt it after the sincerity with which I am going to talk to you." I was surprised at this beginning.'[46]

The cardinal launched into 'current affairs' in the aftermath of the Quadruple Alliance, with Holland joining the League of Hanover that year and, on the other side, Russia reviving the earlier policy of Peter the Great and entering upon her long alliance with Austria. Fleury confessed to the reporting Stainville:

He was in despair at seeing war so to speak inescapable. At that I remonstrated with him. I represented to him the uselessness for the [French] king of the alliance with the English and, on the contrary, the advantage which he would derive from being always united with the Emperor. At that he said to me ... 'Let us just say that a treaty has been made for good or ill, but it is made. They want to uphold it and France will not fail, which obliges me to tell you that unless an angel comes down from Heaven to reunite the powers I do not believe that that can be done.' He appeared to me to say these last words with bitter grief.

Fleury swept Stainville across from unreliable Prussia to Spain whose 'queen, who had immoderate ambition, wanted to make her son emperor. I could not prevent myself smiling at this remark. At that he said to me, "You do not believe that the emperor has promised the archduchess to Don Carlos." I said, No. "Well", said he, "I swear to you on the word of a priest and an honest man that the promise has been given. I do not know if it will be kept, but as to the giving I am sure." He earnestly begged me never to talk of this, not to write anything of it to Your Royal Highness, or at least not to cite him.' Stainville gave no promise.

The chief minister of France had dipped into the penetralia of secret diplomacy, of the shrouded sequel to the First Treaty of Vienna and counter to the Treaty of Hanover. A further Austro-Spanish treaty of 5 November 1725, unpublished for over a century and a half,[47] had threatened to revive centuries of European strife around an Austro-Spanish hegemony based now upon an alliance, notably against France who stood to lose Alsace and the Three Bishoprics as Avulsa Imperii; and it was provided that the Archduchess Maria Theresa should marry Don Carlos in the event of the Emperor

[46] Marquis de Stainville to Duke Leopold, Paris, 29 Oct. 1726: *u.s.*, and for the following.
[47] Till 1894 when Gabriel Syveton published it in the *Revue historique*, liv. 90f.

Charles VI (then a healthy forty) dying before she attained marriageable age: a transparently flimsy stipulation, however, even for that flimsy handiwork of Ripperda – and Sinzendorf. ('You can count upon its being Sinzendorf who is doing all this',[48] added Fleury later in exculpation of the emperor.) So both the confidential interlocutors in the cardinal's chamber could claim justification, Fleury that a promise to Don Carlos had indeed been given, Stainville in his smiling scepticism as to any promise that would effectively queer the sitting suitor, still, in Vienna, where Prince Francis was becoming for the emperor 'my angel'.[49]

Fleury opined to Stainville that Spanish failure to furnish promised subsidies would in any case afford the emperor a let-out. But:

If he wished to hold out for this marriage all Europe would oppose it, that it was in the interest of this same Europe that it should be the prince of Lorraine who was chosen as successor to the emperor because that would change nothing in the situation of the [imperial] state: that her strength would thereby become neither greater nor less great and that perhaps France would find therein a particular advantage, making me sense that Lorraine could in this way come to her one day, something which I pretended not to hear. In short, Sire, our conversation lasted a good hour and he closed it by telling me that it had not bored him and that he wanted us to have similar ones often.[50]

The artful statesman retained the Marquis de Stainville to a little dinner for six including the Prince of Carignan and the Marshal de Villars, a signal distinction since the parsimonious cardinal did not go in for diplomatic entertaining.

Well might Stainville be astonished. Here, at the inception of Fleury's power, was the secret already of his master-plan for Europe in relation to the leading issues which were to distract her through his sixteen years of office and beyond: in the foreground to deflect the restless intrigues of Elizabeth Farnese for Don Carlos, in the event to get Naples at Austrian expense; remarkable support, so early, for the imperial succession of Francis of Lorraine in contrast to the coil of French opposition in which Fleury was reluctantly entangled in the War of the Austrian Succession, before the ultimate achievement of a Franco-Austrian alliance just a generation after its significant suggestion now by the father of the Duke de Choiseul; last but not least the cardinal, by a backhanded stroke more trenchant than any of the Duke de Bourbon against Lorraine, was already scheming to

[48] Marquis de Stainville to Duke Leopold, Paris, 21 May 1727: Arch. M-et-M/Vienne, 3F 85, no. 98.
[49] Emperor Charles VI to Duke Francis III of Lorraine, early Nov. 1729: F. Hennings, op. cit., p. 115.
[50] Marquis de Stainville to Duke Leopold, Paris, 29 Oct. 1726: Arch. M-et-M/Vienne, 3F 85, no. 58.

secure the duchy for France 'one day'. For the present Stainville
might politely pretend not to hear but within ten years Fleury would
have persuaded Europe to listen and to acquiesce in his subtle design
for aggrandizement. And within two months now rumours of some
such possibility were surfacing in the press.

Duke Leopold's own appreciation of his precarious position had
interested him in a Tuscan exchange. Now, though, his promotion of
an Austrian marriage for Francis was cutting across his increasing
inclination to settle down in Lorraine (this was the period of his
spectacular roadbuilding). By the end of 1726 he was authorizing the
Marquis de Stainville to contradict, if necessary, press reports 'of an
exchange of my estates, to which I could never consent; it is not that
I give credence to these gazettes, but the least thing in this respect
revolts me ... There is no fortune for me or my children which could
make me consent to it ... I cannot speak calmly upon this matter.'[51]
Leopold was given to seeking the best of both worlds in politics as in
finance.

For the present the young Minister for Lorraine to France had
made a brilliant start beneath the long shadow already stretching
ahead. Stainville's important winning of Fleury by his personal
'steadiness' may well have owed something to the striking absence, in
that age, of any attribution to him of a mistress. Duke Leopold was
also gratified by the comparable 'position of confidence'[52] which his
envoy established with the Duke of Orleans, from whom he was soon
to extract early information of secret proceedings of the French royal
council, of which Stainville accordingly 'pretended to be ignorant'[53]
in discussion with the foreign minister: a reminder of the political
significance of a prince of the blood and indeed of any other member
of the council.

Ten days after the heart-to-heart with Fleury the Marquis de
Stainville drove out in a spanking equipage to his first public
audience of the young King and Queen of France on 6 November
1726. In his formal address Stainville was held to have 'spoken to the
King admirably well and with all the dignity possible'.[54] Any idea
that such eloquence was automatic in that ceremonious age was
contradicted by the Prince de Craon, that humane wit who afterwards
wrote to Stainville: 'You must be very pleased no longer to have this
day ahead of you. Nothing weighs upon one so as having public

[51] Duke Leopold to Marquis de Stainville, 26 Dec. 1726: Ö.S./H.H.S., Lothringisches
Hausarchiv 108/425.
[52] Prince de Craon to Marquis de Stainville, Lunéville, 15 June 1726: Arch. M-et-M/Vienne,
3F 370, no. 14.
[53] Marquis de Stainville to Duke Leopold, Paris, 4 Dec. 1726: ibid., 3F 85, no. 62.
[54] Prince de Craon to Marquis de Stainville, Lunéville, 23 Nov. 1726: ibid., 3F 370, no. 56.

compliments to make.'[55] Such an audience ranked a minister
plenipotentiary as a presented courtier with the privilege, agreeable
to Stainville, of hunting with the king. Craon continued: 'You
showed the touch of a clever courtier in hunting a second time in the
king's train. I feel that I am incapable of behaving so well.' On 15
November Stainville rounded off his social advent with a worthy
celebration: Craon began his next: 'I had a good nose, my dear
nephew, to want to be at the good dinner which you gave on Saint
Leopold's day.'

IV

The Prince de Craon commented to the Marquis de Stainville in his
next again: 'It seems that the rumours of war are being confirmed
and the idle young (la jeunesse oisive) should be happier about it than
they seem to be.' In that winter of 1726 cold war had gripped 'Europe,
which,' wrote Duke Leopold to the marquis four days later, 'without
being at war seems to me to be in greater agitation, in wanting to
avoid it on all sides, than if war were already declared. I confess to
you that I may seem suspect on every side when it is a question of
peace', which he passionately desired for its own sake as 'a good
citizen of the continent'.[56]

Such an outlook was congenial to old Fleury whom Leopold
deluged with long letters in his own depressingly serried handwriting.
The duke artfully set his local problem within the European
framework, encouraging the cardinal's perception that through
Lorraine he would be approximating to Austria. The charged
atmosphere of Europe in 1726 produced only an Anglo-Spanish war
mainly confined to a siege of Gibraltar by the unhurrying Spaniards.
This short and desultory conflict was politically contained thanks,
largely, to the lukewarmness of the allies of both belligerents. In May
1727 the cardinal told the Marquis de Stainville, back from a visit to
Lorraine, 'that for a fortnight or three weeks Mr. Walpole had
persecuted him to declare war, which he had always firmly resisted'.[57]
A week later Stainville was assuring Fleury that 'he could well be the
arbiter of Europe', priming him with flattery, 'which he does not
dislike'.

Stainville had lost little time in urging the French government to

[55] Ibid., 14 Nov. 1726, no. 54; and no. 55 of 19 Nov., no. 56 of 23 Nov. for the following.
[56] Duke Leopold to Marquis de Stainville, 27 Nov. 1726: O.S./H.H.S., Lothringisches
Hausarchiv 108/425, fos. 2-3.
[57] Marquis de Stainville to Duke Leopold, Paris, 13 May 1727: Arch. M-et-M/Vienne, 3F 85,
no. 92; and no. 98 of 21 May, no. 121 of 28 Aug., respectively, for the following.

accord to Lorraine her standing request for a guarantee of neutrality, now more than ever desirable. That August Fleury, in presenting Stainville to the new French foreign minister, explained to Chauvelin that the Lorrainer 'should not be regarded here as being completely a foreigner'. This backhanded compliment did not prevent Stainville from being 'charmed by the cardinal'.[58] In welcoming this the Prince de Craon expressed 'infinite pleasure in comparing the situation of His Royal Highness [Leopold] with that of Duke Charles IV, who did not stand so well with Cardinal de Richelieu. That was the period of all the misfortunes of the house of Lorraine.'

Duke Leopold, however, harboured few illusions 'as to France ... At bottom I never expect a sincere friendship.'[59] In this situation his minister in Paris was winning his diplomatic spurs, exploiting his friendship with Fleury, little by little winning France from her traditional opposition to any guarantee of neutrality for a territory of such obvious strategic importance to her in the event of war. Finally, on 14 October 1728 at Fontainebleau, Louis XV signed the long-sought declaration:

We say, declare, decree and ordain that in case of rupture, infraction, invasion, war or hostilities of whatever nature and for whatever reason it may be between us and the other powers of Europe, our said brother the Duke of Lorraine and of Bar and his successors shall enjoy a full and entire neutrality, perpetual and irrevocable for all their estates, lands, towns, boroughs, villages, men and subjects without any exception or reserve, and generally all other rights dependent upon a durable and perfect neutrality.[60]

It was a great day for Lorraine. The court at Lunéville went gay.

The significance of the comprehensive declaration was, however, modified by a secret counter-declaration which Stainville signed the same day at Fontainebleau. A favourite device of eighteenth-century diplomacy was the counter-declaration (*contre-lettre*), a secret instrument modifying or annulling a previously authenticated instrument. In the present instance the Marquis de Stainville undertook to communicate to the French government 'immediately the act whereby H.R.H. [the Duke of Lorraine], accepting, such as it is, that [perpetual neutrality] granted by the king, shall declare that he will not claim that it were a derogation to this neutrality on the part of H.M., if, in case of absolute necessity, as happens in nearly all wars

[58] Prince de Craon to Marquis de Stainville, Lunéville, 31 Aug. 1727: Arch. M-et-M/Vienne, 3F 370, no. 97, and for the following.
[59] Duke Leopold to Baron von Pfütschner, 23 Mar. 1727: Ö.S./H.H.S., Lothringisches Hausarchiv 108/425, fo. 45.
[60] 'Déclaration de neutralité perpetuelle pour la Lorraine', 14 Oct. 1728: Arch. Aff. Étr. C.P., Lorraine, cited, Comte d'Haussonville, op. cit., iv. 623.

and as occurred at different times in the last, H.M. were obliged to make other use thereof.'[61] More bluntly, France was accorded the right to station troops in Lorraine if necessary, as she had always done in previous wars. The disheartening involution of two years of negotiation culminating in two documents signed on the same day in contradiction of each other provides a classic instance of the seemingly pointless intricacies of eighteenth-century diplomacy. As so often in history, however, to dismiss the proceeding as stupid would be to stamp the verdict as superficial. The Duke of Lorraine lost little time in bringing out the point according to the subtle canons of that age. Europe received notice that France was publicly committed to the guarantee of the perpetual neutrality of Lorraine, as was friendly Austria, who readily concurred. Duke Leopold hastened to inform England and Holland of the French guarantee and to suggest that they should follow suit. In doing so he omitted any mention of the secret counter-declaration, as he was entitled and indeed bound to do. This manoeuvre, however, over-reached itself as such sharp diplomacy is always liable to do, especially when practised by weak states. All that happened was that England and Holland in some surprise asked the French government what the meaning of the guarantee might be, and the French did not hesitate to break secrecy and to inform their allies of Stainville's counter-declaration.[62]

V

Since the Marquis de Stainville's mission to London in 1725 relations between Lorraine and England had been chequered, largely for reasons to which his wife's stepfather was no stranger. In 1726 a nephew of Eugene O'Rourke had arrived in Lorraine from Ireland and in the following year the Count de Rouerke himself posted off from Lunéville to Vienna, ostensibly with commissions from Duke Leopold. In Vienna O'Rourke apparently received a more significant commission from the Old Pretender despite the recent fact that the Irishman had not concealed his disapproval of his titular sovereign's circularization of his epistolary slanging-match with his Queen Clementina Sobieska 'within the precincts of his own house'[63] in Rome. She retired to a convent while the Old Pretender withdrew to Bologna. Their reconciliation there was delayed by the sudden death

---

[61] 'Contre-déclaration donnée par M. de Stainville', 14 Oct. 1728: ibid., iv. 624.

[62] Cf., more especially, Chauvelin to d'Audiffret, 29 Jan. 1729: Arch. Aff. Étr. C.P., Lorraine, vol. 120, fos. 10–11.

[63] Count de Rouerke, Lunéville, 8 Dec. 1725: cited, David Daiches, *Charles Edward Stuart* (London, 1973), p. 78.

of King George I in his favourite Germany on 11 June 1727. By 22 June the titular James III was in Nancy and, in his own words, 'drawing nearer to England'[64] where the political survival of Sir Robert Walpole at first seemed uncertain. The Spanish court, still at war with England, appeared to be looking to a Jacobite restoration.

At the French court next month Fleury 'appeared extremely surprised'[65] to learn of the Old Pretender's swoop from a letter from Leopold which Stainville handed to the cardinal. After some reflection and under every seal of secrecy Fleury, himself subject to English pressure, gave Stainville his personal opinion that the kind-hearted Duke of Lorraine 'should not hesitate a moment to have the Chevalier de Saint-Georges asked to leave his dominions . . . "Why is the Chevalier de Saint-Georges so badly informed? For there is assuredly no appearance of trouble in England: very far from it since several Jacobites who did not go to court in the time of the late King George have all gone there upon the accession of this one."'

By 9 August 1727 the Duchess of Lorraine was writing to her particular friend in Paris: 'I do not think, Madam, that King James has crossed over to England. This poor prince is so unfortunate that his enterprises never succeed, for which I am very sorry.'[66] He was in fact lying up 'in a state of indecision which nothing can settle'[67] at that country seat of the Marquis de Lunati-Visconti where Duke Leopold and his court had been ceremoniously welcomed five years since. Three days after the duchess wrote the Prince de Craon was apprising the Marquis de Stainville that 'the Chevalier de Saint Georges departed from Frouard yesterday and is returning to Bologna. It went greatly against the grain for His Royal Highness [Leopold] to make him perceive the necessity of his leaving.'[68]

On Fleury's further advice Stainville now told the British Ambassador what had befallen the Old Pretender. Horatio Walpole, in thanking Stainville, added: '"But since you seem to have confidence in me I too will place a lot in you and I will tell you frankly something which is causing much uneasiness. This is that a certain M. de Rouerke, standing very well at your court"'[69] – had made that voyage to Vienna in the interest of James and, as Walpole rubbed in, with the

[64] Prince James Edward to Lockhart of Carnwarth, Nancy, 22 June 1727: ibid., p. 79.

[65] Marquis de Stainville to Duke Leopold, Paris, 22 July 1727: Arch. M-et-M/Vienne, 3F 85, no. 115, and for the following.

[66] Duchess of Lorraine to Marquise d'Aulède, Lunéville, 9 Aug. 1727: 'Lettres d'Elisabeth-Charlotte d'Orléans, duchesse de Lorraine, à la Marquise d'Aulède, 1715–1738', in Recueil de documents sur l'histoire de Lorraine, u.s., x. 245.

[67] Prince de Craon to Marquis de Stainville, Lunéville, 8 Aug. 1727: Arch. M-et-M/Vienne, 3F 370, no. 115.

[68] Ibid., 12 Aug. 1727: no. 96 (i.e. out of order).

[69] Marquis de Stainville to Duke Leopold, Paris, 21 Aug. 1727: ibid., 3F 85, no. 120, and for the following.

express approval of Leopold. 'Although I am well up in this business', reported Stainville, 'I thought I should feign ignorance of it' so as to gain time for instructions. Walpole, however, genially proposed to Stainville that meanwhile 'we could tomorrow have another discussion together ... I am dying of fear that he may speak to me of the relationship with Chevalier O'Brien, for Your Royal Highness can count upon his being well aware of everything that is happening.'

The Prince de Craon was in correspondence with this delicate contact, a colonel who was likely that French-born Irishman, Colonel O'Brien, whom the Old Pretender later made his envoy in Paris, and Earl of Lismore. Craon was as embarrassed as Stainville, to whom he confided that another correspondence between himself and an O'Neil 'was entirely finished ... I only maintained [it] under orders and ... am delighted for a thousand reasons to see it finish, having sensed its consequences.'[70] English pressure, again, probably induced Fleury to induce Leopold reluctantly to arrest in Lunéville a twentyone-year-old Scot called Murray, a son of Viscount Stormont and brother to the Jacobite Earl of Dunbar. Murray had already been employed by the Austrian and Spanish governments: 'You will be astonished', wrote Craon to Stainville, 'upon reading his interrogation.'[71]

Lorraine, significantly in with Austria and Spain in opposition to England, was the hub of the obscure and forlorn Jacobite push of 1727. And the Marquis de Stainville was sufficiently cognizant of those wheels within wheels to make him an equivocal envoy, perhaps, when in May 1728, again accompanied by Toussaint, he paid his second visit to England in order to present Duke Leopold's congratulations to King George II and Queen Caroline upon their accession.

Stainville, however, fared better than his predecessor, the Marquis de Lambertye, upon the accession of George I. The House of Commons had then been so incensed against Leopold for harbouring the Old Pretender that his envoy was refused an audience. De Lambertye, though, had turned his mission to economic advantage by introducing from England into Lorraine a superior variety of potato –Lorraine had a long lead over France in potato-cultivation. Now Turnip Townshend appears to have made himself more particularly agreeable to Stainville,[72] who also carried letters from his master to the Duke of Newcastle, Count von Bothmer, the

---

[70] Prince de Craon to Marquis de Stainville, Lunéville, 14 ? Aug. 1727: ibid., 3F 370, no. 117.

[71] Ibid., 26 ? 1727: no. 127.

[72] See Viscount Townshend to Duke of Lorraine, Whitehall, June 1728, also Duke of Lorraine to Viscount Townshend, Lunéville, 22 Dec. 1728: P.R.O./S.P.F., Royal Letters, vol. 39, nos. 64 and 73 respectively.

Hanoverian agent in London, and Sir Robert Walpole. Leopold
assured the prime minister that Stainville would testify to the duke's
pleasure 'in seeing Milord Walpol [sic], your son, here during the stay
which he has made'.[73]

The continuing stay in Vienna of the eldest son of Duke Leopold
was again a leading topic for Stainville's mission to England, and he
was briefed upon it on lines laid down by Count von Sinzendorf.
Stainville reported, however, that he was asked many fewer questions
than on his earlier visit upon the dynastic prospect, by then more or
less accepted. Queen Caroline and Sir Robert politely assured him
'that my lord Walgraff [Waldegrave, British Ambassador in Vienna]
had written much good of the conduct'[74] of young Francis at a court
where the stiff ceremonial was, they appreciated, liable to be irksome
for a youth. His lessons were now going somewhat better, notably in
law and German.

VI

For the Duke of Lorraine the imperial prospects of his heir remained
the prime preoccupation with regard to the Congress of Soissons,
sequel to Cambrai, which was about to open (June 1728). This
international development was probably the leading diplomatic topic
during Stainville's mission to England, more particularly since he
was appointed to represent Lorraine at Soissons, Leopold's efforts to
have the congress held at Nancy having failed. The Marquis de
Stainville, primed by an urgent remittance from the duke of two
hundred guineas towards his expenses in England, returned via Paris
where he was to concert his directions for Soissons with his old
acquaintance, Sinzendorf. In particular, Stainville was to try to assist
him by using his own confidential relations with Fleury in order to
sound the probable French attitude in regard to the nub of Austrian
policy, namely recognition of the pragmatic sanction in favour of
Maria Theresa. Stainville was already cast in the role which he was
to fill for the next twenty years: the inconspicuous envoy of the house
of Lorraine working in the direction of a rapprochement between the
two great rivals upon the continent, seeking to promote Austrian
interests through his close contacts with French ministers.

Appeasement was the endeavour at Soissons in the aftermath of
the Anglo-Spanish war, terminated shortly before by the Convention

[73] Duke Leopold to Sir Robert Walpole, 12 May 1728: Ö.S./H.H.S., Lothringisches
Hausarchiv 112/437.
[74] Duke Leopold to Baron de Jacquemin, 7 July 1728: Ö.S./H.H.S., Lothringisches
Hausarchiv 108/425.

of the Pardo. Nor was it the envoys at Soissons who conducted the main negotiations which resulted in breaking down the disturbing Austro-Spanish alliance by means of the Treaty of Seville, concluded in 1729 between Britain, France, and Spain, and succeeded in 1731 by the Second Treaty of Vienna whereby Britain, letting down her French ally, went in with Austria, Spain, and Holland. This treaty was to prompt the philosophic Pfütschner to augur to Stainville 'a very peaceful time until some new event – for since this new century began things have often been taking a fresh turn and treaties are in the height of fashion ... I assure you that if a man were well established in Switzerland with an income of twenty thousand florins, informed of what is happening and able to view the affairs of this world with indifference, that would to my mind be the most interesting and happiest position.'[75] Affluent neutrality in Switzerland offers perennial attraction in times of trouble.

Against this kaleidoscopic background of shifting alliances, which render this period one of the most intricate in European diplomacy, the present for the Marquis de Stainville centred upon the prosaic Congress of Soissons, snarled up in trying to wind up the Ostend Company. The congress at any rate stood out as a fixed point, fixed like its predecessor in such conspicuous sterility as to provoke even contemporary criticism.

This static screening of so much secret activity oppressed Duke Leopold the more since Stainville was after all unable to extract much from the canny Cardinal Fleury. 'I will confess to Monsieur the Cardinal', Leopold wrote to him, 'that the silence of Soissons, and the impenetrable secrecy of the environs of Versailles, does not cease to contain, but not to stifle the anxiety of the curious, among the number of whom I unfortunately am.'[76] To Leopold's less diplomatic duchess it seemed that 'they ought to talk of something other, now that the congress has begun at Soissons, than the meals that are given there'.[77] They presumably interested Stainville, stuck, as Craon sympathized, 'at Soissons where you have not too much business'.[78]

The empty congresses of Cambrai and Soissons have always been severely judged, and understandably. They are nevertheless worth focusing in the longer historical outlook. It had been something more than coincidence that it was in the aftermath of the exhausting War of the Spanish Succession, in the year of the death of the glorious

[75] Baron von Pfütschner to Marquis de Stainville, Brussels, 5 July 1731: Arch. M-et-M/Vienne, 3F 372, no. 40.
[76] Duke Leopold to Cardinal Fleury, Lunéville, 5 Aug. 1728: Ö.S./H.H.S., Lothringisches Hausarchiv 196/III. 319, fo. 5.
[77] Duchess of Lorraine to Marquise d'Aulède, Lunéville, 26 June 1728: u.s., p. 263.
[78] Prince de Craon to Marquis de Stainville, Lunéville, 5 July 1728: Arch. M-et-M/Vienne, 3F 370, no. 192.

king who had chiefly provoked it, that the Abbé de Saint-Pierre published his widely discussed *Project de paix perpetuelle.* (It influenced Frederick the Great as a youth, less later.) This project was for the international ordering of a European confederation through a standing congress, with provisions for arbitration within a 'republic' of sovereigns; only, as Fleury remarked to the Abbé, he had omitted to provide for bands of missionaries to convert the hearts of the princes. Yet ideas for a congress or concert of Europe were in the air, in the Quadruple Alliance itself. George I fostered this and, as noticed, Fleury himself, still more Duke Leopold, hoped that the alliance might afford a lasting system of collective security. Pointing towards such a system were the congresses of Cambrai and Soissons.

The congresses were significant in that they were held not in order to terminate great wars, as those of Westphalia and Utrecht had been, but, if possible, to prevent them. Such a technique of peaceful revision within the concert of Europe was largely novel and it is perhaps hardly surprising that practical achievements were insignificant and procedural difficulties intense. Nevertheless the congresses performed a useful function as delaying mechanisms. Relations between the powers were tense and uncertain, with small wars, the sequelae of great ones, often in the offing. In such conditions it was valuable to have representatives of the powers gathered around one table, even if only a dinner-table, as a steadying symbol of common interests. It helped to ease the pressure and to afford the chanceries of Europe latitude in getting ahead with the real negotiations behind the scenes. It may not be too fanciful to see in the Quadruple Alliance and the congresses of Cambrai and Soissons, in the aftermath of the War of the Spanish Succession, the first term in a progression which led through to the Holy Alliance with its notable extension of the congress system after the Napoleonic Wars, and on again, even, after the World Wars to the League of Nations and the United Nations.

CHAPTER V

REVERSAL

I

LIFE, unlike history, is rarely concentrated in a few large issues. The popular conception of diplomacy as continually concerned with grand affairs of state was scarcely truer in the eighteenth century than in others.

In 1727 the Marquis de Stainville often sent to Lunéville three or four dispatches a week, mainly concerning the day-to-day business which he was transacting with the French ministry of foreign affairs about woodcutting in Lorraine for French shipbuilding, tolls at Saarlouis, those fortifications at Nancy, favours for the Prince de Lixin, a worthier scion of the House of Lorraine than the rascally Duke d'Elboeuf who was to give Stainville quite a bit of trouble. Jacques-Henri, Prince de Lixin, was unhappily married to Anne-Marguerite de Beauvau, a beautiful daughter of the Prince de Craon, himself prolific in commissions. Ducal interests, too, might call for considerable research. Stainville had to grapple with documents preserved at the Sainte-Chapelle but, as is apt to happen with archives, 'it is an extremely delicate business. In the papers are several which are advantageous, establishing the rights of Your Royal Highness; but there are also several contrary to them and destroying them.'[1]

Two aspects, ecclesiastical and jurisdictional, of the French overlap into Lorraine were mainly responsible for the bulk of Stainville's work. He wearily began another dispatch that same day: 'I was quite resolved to talk no more about ecclesiastical affairs, and I was forced to talk about them the whole day yesterday.'[2]

Lorraine remained spiritually subject to the three French bishoprics despite all Leopold's efforts with the papacy, notably to have Saint-Dié elevated as a ducal, and ultramontane, see. The sympathetic Pope Benedict XIII had gone so far as to consecrate Leopold's representative in Rome as titular Archbishop of Caesarea *in partibus*, while he also became Grand Provost of Saint-Dié. This provoked

---

[1] Marquis de Stainville to Duke Leopold, Paris, 21 May 1727: Arch. M-et-M/Vienne, 3F 85, no. 97.

[2] Ibid., 21 May 1727: no. 100.

keen controversy centring upon a Father Hugo, abbot of Premonstratensian Etival and champion of the liberties of Lorraine against
the Gallican Church. The nuncio in Paris now warned Stainville
'that Monsieur de Morville was furious'[3] with Hugo. Sure enough,
the foreign minister opened up at the marquis: 'Why does not the
Duke of Lorraine impose silence upon a little scamp like that?'[4]

Even more aggravating to Leopold than the ecclesiastical jurisdiction of the Bishop of Toul was the appellate jurisdiction of the
Parliament of Paris over the Barrois Mouvant. The Parliament of
Paris, deriving from the medieval court (*curia regis*) and still including
by right the peers of France, was much the greatest of the twelve
regional parliaments which, together with three sovereign courts,
represented the old apparatus of higher justice in France. More than
a third of the land came under the jurisdiction of the Parliament of
Paris, reaching out to the Barrois in the east, up to the Channel and
round by the Atlantic seaboard to the confines of Languedoc. The
highest judicial functions of the parliament were vested in the
Grand'Chambre, recruited by seniority from the other chambers,
notably the Chambres des Enquêtes or general courts of appeal and
the Chambre des Requêtes deriving from the adjudication of petitions
to the king. Members of these chambers, the so-called lay counsellors
(in distinction from the exempted clerical ones), served in rotation in
the criminal jurisdiction of the Chambre de la Tournelle. And if the
Chambre des Requêtes had become a specialized jurisdiction for the
civil suits of privileged persons, Maîtres des Requêtes were key
figures retaining special connections with the king's court and
ministers. Maîtres des Requêtes acted as assessors to the highest legal
authority, the chancellor, and largely maintained liaison between the
parliament and the royal council, to which they presented legal
business.

In the Barrois Mouvant, overhung by the French legal apparatus,
the population had stronger French affinities than in the rest of
Lorraine, where the germanic element was still pronounced. Appeals
from the Barrois to the Parliament of Paris, notably for tax-
exemptions, received regular support not only in individual lawsuits
but also, for instance, by general decrees in 1726 'against the taxes of
the Duke in the Barrois Mouvant with prohibitions against executing
them, although the King [of France] imposes nothing at all there [by
way of taxation] and the parliament does not take cognizance of taxes.

---

[3] Ibid.
[4] Ibid., 21 May 1727: cited, H. Baumont, *Études sur le règne de Léopold duc de Lorraine et de Bar, 1697–1729*, p. 372, n. 1.

That is to wish that these peoples should live without laws and without taxes.'[5]

French opportunities for 'various chicaneries'[6] in the Barrois Mouvant were endless, and this intervention makes an instructive study in the protection of an ethnic fringe in the eighteenth century under cover of feudal formulae.

Under Fleury, however, three fair-minded French commissioners were appointed in 1727 to sort out with the Marquis de Stainville the issues in the Barrois. The commissioners included the Marquis d'Angervilliers, with whom Stainville was to have plenty to do as Minister of War, and Rouillé, a Maître des Requêtes with whom Stainville's son was one day to have still more to do as Foreign Minister. Another and more considerable minister with whom Stainville was then in working touch was the young Minister of Marine, the Count de Maurepas. So early was the Marquis de Stainville's personal acquaintance with central figures in the French establishment for the next twenty years and more.

Since the marquisate of Stainville lay in the Barrois Mouvant just across the frontier from France, the marquis was liable to be personally interested, as in his dispute with Du Tertre over Bazincourt. The original litigation concerning the succession there had been exacerbated because 'the Marquis de Stainville in taking possession of the seigniory of Bazincourt had the river [Saulx] fished. This fishing gave offence to the Sieur du Tertre',[7] already at loggerheads with the villagers about it. Du Tertre, not a lawyer for nothing, lodged an appeal to the Parliament of Paris. On 11 June 1725 it had given judgement against Stainville, not only awarding costs against him but questioning his very marquisate by contesting the Duke of Lorraine's prerogative of ennoblement in the Barrois Mouvant. This question of principle had promptly provoked Leopold to write personally to Louis XV in defence of Stainville's rights and of 'my rights in the Barrois',[8] notably under concordats of 1571 and 1575 with France, with precedents earlier still. A neighbour's quarrel, sharpened by the ticklish question of fishing rights, had become a diplomatic issue in international relations.[9]

[5] Undated 'Liste des differens' presented by Marquis de Stainville to Count de Morville in the summer of 1727: Arch. Aff. Étr. C.P., Lorraine, vol. 117, fo. 179.

[6] Marquis de Stainville to Duke Leopold, Paris, 25 Jan. 1727: Arch. M-et-M/Vienne, 3F 85, no. 80.

[7] 'Mémoire sur la terre de Bazincourt': Arch. Meuse, J 18[20].

[8] Duke Leopold to King Louis XV, Lunéville, 23 June 1725: Arch. Aff. Étr. C.P., Lorraine, vol. 114, fo. 128.

[9] A comprehensive documentation of this case calls for the consultation of archives not only locally, at Nancy and Bar-le-Duc (cf. supra), but internationally, at Paris (cf. supra) and Vienna (Ö.S/H.H.S., Lothringisches Hausarchiv 178/655: 'Streit zw. dem Hg. von Lothringen und dem König v. Frankreich betr. die Verleihung des Titels 'Marquis' an Stainville und das Recht d. Nobilisierung durch die Herzogen von Lothringen.')

The French authorities duly referred the dispute to the attorney-general of the Parliament of Paris, who replied somewhat wearily to the foreign minister that as regards 'the opposition of the Sieur de Bazincourt [Du Tertre] to the letters of erection of the marquisate obtained by the Sieur de Stainville: these oppositions are very common in the kingdom and the King erects few estates into marquisates without the grantees incurring oppositions.'[10] The case dragged on for years before Stainville, indubitably a marquis, finally winkled Du Tertre out of Bazincourt early in 1729.

II

For the Stainvilles now and for many years to come Lorraine provided the home background to diplomacy and Paris. In Paris they had by the spring of 1727 acquired a house at 'sixteen Rue du Bac, near the Convalescents',[11] still in the Faubourg Saint-Germain. That May the Marquise de Stainville was presented at Versailles. 'She was charmingly dressed'[12] and received with all favour. Louis XV 'had her told that she was at perfect liberty to see him from eight o'clock in the morning till eight o'clock of the evening': a likely confirmation that, as even her critics allowed, she was a pretty woman. She was also pregnant again. It was upon embracing her then that the Prince de Craon found her 'fresher than the rose that the shopwoman of Rochefort gave her'[13] – a glancing tribute to beauty now passed into oblivion.

So the Marquise de Stainville might hope to replace the loss in infancy a year earlier, on 24 June 1726, of her latest son. He had died of 'a great bowel-relaxion'[14] with vomiting, back in Lorraine in the absence of his parents, who seem to have been less fond of children than the Craons. The princess had taken a special look at the Stainvilles' 'really very pretty'[15] boy only a week before his death, when the prince interrogated the court doctor, Sieur Bagard, about him and saw to it that the Stainville retainers, notably one Grobert, duly arranged the funeral. Not from heartlessness did Craon reflect that the baby 'was at an age at which no remedy could be adopted,

[10] Joly de Fleury to Count de Morville, Paris, 30 June 1725: Arch. Aff. Étr. C.P., Lorraine, vol. 114, fos. 136–7.
[11] Writ served on the Marquis and Marquise de Stainville in connection with the Bassompierre inheritance, 2 June 1729: Arch. Aff. Étr. C.P., Lorraine, vol. 120, fo. 55.
[12] Prince de Craon to Marquis de Stainville, Lunéville, 8 May 1727: u.s., no. 109, and for the following.
[13] Ibid., 26 July 1727: no. 92.
[14] Ibid., 25 June 1726: no. 17.
[15] Ibid., 18 June 1726: no. 15.

and those whom death carries off are so fortunate that one should not be afflicted by it. He is an angel in paradise . . . We have been in a fine alarm which lasted three hours and of which we are quit but a moment since. My little canary had flown away and was lost.'[16] In a truly eighteenth-century scene 'everybody who knows how to play the flageolet was sent into action and he was found again in the orangery. He came to perch upon a flageolet and I am holding him myself.' Each age has its relativities.

Surviving, developing meanwhile was the eldest son of the Marquis and Marquise de Stainville. The future Duke de Choiseul characteristically recalled: 'My childhood and youth were spent like those of everybody.'[17] He was not one for childish confessions. He later held Jean-Jacques Rousseau in poor esteem as a person. Almost nothing has hitherto transpired concerning Choiseul's early childhood. In fact little Stephen de Stainville too was left in Lorraine when his parents moved to Paris.

The future Choiseul's maternal grandfather Anne-François-Joseph, Marquis de Bassompierre, had had a younger brother, Charles-Louis. This latter Marquis de Bassompierre, a cavalry general in Austrian service, Marshal of Lorraine and the Barrois, Governor and Bailli des Vosges, had married Marie-Louise de Beauvau, half-sister to her sister-in-law, the future Countess de Rouerke, and also to the Prince de Craon. Marie-Louise de Bassompierre produced but one faint son, possibly already dead. Whereas it was this lady living in style in Nancy who was now lodging and caring for the future Choiseul.

It does not sound as though the little boy had a specially lively start, living with his great-aunt, though she could produce a splendid meal, seemingly had a way with children and, perhaps most to the point, was also looking after Lolotte. Lolotte was then a common enough diminutive in Lorraine at least but it would appear that this one was the Princess Charlotte de Beauvau-Craon, the eighth Craon daughter, destined for yet another marriage with a Bassompierre. She was some eighteen months older than Stephen de Stainville.

On 24 July 1726, when the little Count de Stainville was just seven, this household in Nancy was all in a bustle. The occasion was the return from Paris of the elder Craon children, probably for the summer holidays. A week earlier the Prince de Craon had been charging the Marquis de Stainville in the French capital with the kind of little parental concern usual to such occasions: 'If you see my eldest son again do not give him a moment's peace about having his

16 Ibid., 25 June 1726: no. 17, and for the following.
17 Choiseul, *Mémoires*, p. 3.

teeth seen to before he leaves. There is something there to come out.'[18]

Now the fond Craons were driving from Lunéville to Nancy so as to advance the reunion a little. The prince wrote to the marquis:

My children arrived at Nancy yesterday, my dear nephew, about eleven o'clock in the morning and I got there at the same time with Madame de Craon and we all dined together at Madame de Bassompierre's. The company was brilliant and Lolotte was its fairest ornament. You would not believe how much she has changed for the better since she has been in my sister's hands. Your son came in after dinner and kept his end up very well (*tint fort bien son coin*) in the assembly, where he found some of his relations. He is in very good health and my sister praises him highly for his gentleness (*douceur*).[19]

This truly French family reunion provides a first personal appearance of the future Duke de Choiseul. Already he figured as a sweet-tempered child, displaying something of that social aptitude which was to carry him far in an age of civilized refinement. So close already were his connections with the princely Craons, the highest subjects in his little land. And it appears that he was being brought up with a pretty little girl rather older than himself. Her younger brother Charles-Just, Prince de Beauvau, was to become a lifelong friend of Choiseul.

The report on the little Count de Stainville's good health was something more than conventional. There are suggestions that he was a delicate child. In May 1727 his father heard from the Prince de Craon: 'Your little boy has had all the symptoms of smallpox but he has got off with some bouts of fever, and my sister with her fright.'[20] A year later, while still in the care of the Marquise de Bassompierre, the boy suffered an almost exact recurrence of such symptoms. Even in after years Stephen de Stainville appears to have been considerably more delicate than might be supposed from his strenuous career.

Meanwhile the Marquise de Stainville's pregnancy early in 1727 had coincided with yet another of the Princess de Craon. Both ladies being out of sorts, Craon wrote to his friend: 'We have got to fear, you and I, that bad temper will be redoubled unless we are unwilling to be accepted as the authors of the ill'[21] – that from him. Craon took them both on, putting up the Marquise de Stainville for her pregnancy and writing of his own wife by 22 July: 'La Signora gave birth to a twelfth daughter on the 17th last and it is not an event worthy of history.'[22]

[18] Prince de Craon to Marquis de Stainville, Lunéville, 16 July 1726: Arch. M-et-M/Vienne, 3F 370, no. 22.
[19] Ibid., 25 July 1726: no. 23.   [20] Ibid., 8 May 1727: no. 109.
[21] Ibid., 4 Feb. 1727: no. 76.   [22] Ibid., 22 July 1727: no. 134.

The Marquise de Stainville had withdrawn from Paris towards the end of June. Getting things clean enough for her was a worry for the Craons, who this time installed a new lavatory for her room. Her excellent health stood up 'wonderfully'[23] to a nasty fall on the street-paving of Lunéville when eight months with child. Her resilient issue was safely delivered on 6 September 1727. This fourth surviving child was called Jacques after his royal godfather, the Prince de Lixin. The godmother was the Princess de Craon.[24] The Stainvilles had arrived.

Early next year the Stainvilles and the Craons again foregathered upon a family occasion. Both figured in the roll-call of the nobility of Lorraine who on 2 February 1728 witnessed the contract of marriage between a twentynine-year-old cousin of the Marquis de Stainville, Brigadier Charles-Marie de Choiseul of the branch of Choiseul-Daillecourt, and a relation of the Marquise, Henriette-Charlotte de Bassompierre, left by her deceased father as the young heiress of the line of Bassompierre-Baudricourt. This legal celebration had a lively background familiar to the Marquis de Stainville.

The heiress's 'uncle and guardian',[25] the Marquis Jean-Claude de Bassompierre-Baudricourt, had been worried that her mother might be constraining her to this marriage, whereas he made out 'that apart from an income of six thousand livres M. de Choiseul had not a penny of property'.[26] For two years the mother had not let the Marquis de Bassompierre talk to his niece alone. So a few days before Christmas 1727 Duke Leopold, after consulting advisers, had granted a petition from the marquis by sending a police-officer with a lady-in-waiting in a ducal coach to Mademoiselle de Bassompierre's seat at the Château de Savigny, whence they drove her off to the Convent of the Visitation at Nancy. Only at the door of the convent, however, did they manage to shake off her mother. Within the convent the Marquis de Bassompierre was at last able to ascertain his ward's own inclinations. She proved to be her mother's daughter, assuring her uncle 'that she had not been constrained to accept M. de Choiseul'. So, had written the Prince de Craon to the Marquis de Stainville, 'it is only a question now of drawing up the [marriage] articles in such

---

[23] Duchess of Lorraine to Marquise d'Aulède, Lunéville, 9 Aug. 1727: *u.s.*, p. 245.

[24] Baptismal certificate of Jacques de Choiseul-Stainville: Lunéville, Archives communales antérieures à 1790, série GG, section 1; cited, Lieut. Ch. Denis, *Jacques de Choiseul* (Saint-Dié, 1901), pp. 15–16.

[25] Arch. Nat., fonds Bassompierre, docket 153: 'État civil de Savigny, Vosges, arr. Mirecourt, cant. Charmes; mariage du 24 février 1728 au château de Savigny', cited by Marquis de Marmier, 'Choiseul-Stainville et Choiseul-La Baume', *Bulletin menseul de la société d'archéologie lorraine et du musée historique lorrain*, 2e. série, tom. XI, vol. 61 (Nancy, 1912), p. 204.

[26] Prince de Craon to Marquis de Stainville, Lunéville, 29 Dec. 1727: Arch. M-et-M/Vienne, 3F 370, no. 89, and for the following.

a way as not to allow the mother to dispose of the property of her daughter' to the advantage of yet another impecunious Choiseul.

The little story supplies a corrective to another old stereotype, of the wicked uncle carrying off his rich niece and forcing her into marriage. As it was, residual tensions were liable to subsist between the participants as they all gathered that candlemas to witness the signature of those circumscribed articles. The Marquis de Stainville was there with his brother-in-law Anne-François-Joseph the younger, another Marquis de Bassompierre. Other relations included the Marquis de Bissy, said to have had a finger in the marriage, and, in respect of both parties, the Marquis du Châtelet. Also listed were the greedy Marquis de Menuessaire and his Choiseul wife, the Count d'Haussonville, the Prince de Chimay and numbers more. From this elegant marriage, celebrated on 24 February 1728 in the chapel at the Château de Savigny, there was to issue yet another branch of the Choiseuls, Choiseul-La Baume.

III

For the high society of Lorraine de Marquis and Marquise de Stainville acted as Parisian lookouts. The Prince de Craon described how he, his wife and his sister, the Countess de Rouerke together with the Countess de Ferrari would mull over the Marquise de Stainville's 'long letters which we read in common and which keep us posted in the new fashions. I already know what a Tirecoeur and a Postillion are.'[27] A fortnight earlier the Princess de Lixin had been 'enchanted by the dress which Madame de Stainville has chosen for her'.[28] Similarly satisfied had been two of the older Craon girls for whom the prince had ordered through the Marquis de Stainville himself 'two lengths of watered silk... The two dresses must be different from each other. The colours do not matter',[29] each length to be sixteen ells reckoned at six livres an ell, rather over four shillings a yard. Two muffs for the same misses got their father into trouble, one gathers, for having 'forgotten for more than three weeks to ask'[30] Stainville for them.

For the Prince and Princess de Craon themselves the marquis had earlier been pressed for 'two dominoes . . . Madame de Stainville will please to see to having Madame de Craon's made, and you mine. Your wife will recall that Madame de Craon is larger than she is, and

[27] Prince de Craon to Marquis de Stainville, Lunéville, 17 Dec. 1726: ibid., no. 67.
[28] Ibid., 3 Dec. 1726: no. 61.
[29] Ibid., 23 May 1726: no. 32.   [30] Ibid., 22 Dec. 1727: no. 167.

you that you are larger than I ... They could not be too gallant for who knows if the fancy will not take us to mask ourselves, one as Venus and the other as Adonis.'[31] This carnival commission rounded off a classic account of the 'tumultuous Twelfth Nights'[32] of 1727 at the court of Lunéville under the black misrule of the King of the Mississippi: the senior maid of honour, Mademoiselle de Ligniville, passed out from too many loyal toasts, whereupon Doctor Bagard himself was found to be in hardly better shape nor indeed anyone else so that 'the poor ladies died of laughing'.[33]

Then pendant earrings needed Parisian adjustment 'as Madame de Stainville should have explained ... Madame de Craon complains that the knob is not close enough to her ear and that it sags. She was obliged to put a little piece of pasteboard between the knob and her ear.'[34] There were also bracelets and other jewels, a precious sword which the Marquise de Stainville maddeningly left behind at Nancy, silver bridle-trappings, stockings for the prince, and his commissions 'to Sieur du Camp, my tailor in the Rue Fosses St. Germain.'[35] The Prince de Craon once described his wife as 'anxious from having given Madame de Stainville many commissions and little money'.[36]

The commandeering Craons did allow the ducal family of Lorraine a look-in with the Stainvilles. The marquis was asked to send Duke Leopold a dozen magnifying-glasses, to arrange for royal portraits by the family painter, Gobert, for miniatures of the Princesses Elizabeth and Charlotte to be concealed in the mounting of a snuffbox which their father wanted to send to Prince Francis in Vienna. His younger brother Charles troubled Stainville, an early friend, for shoebuckles and garters, adding: 'My dear sisters beg you to get them Couperin's books for the harpsichord.'[37]

The Duchess of Lorraine looked to the gourmet Stainville for mackerel, confessing that 'if I were pregnant, which can no longer be, my children would have been marked like mackerel, for I have a terrible longing to eat some, and they can only come by post'.[38] The Marquise d'Aulède had been thanked by the duchess for joining the Marquise de Stainville in choosing for her 'the needlework and lace ... I am waiting ... to send you the measurements and model for making use of what you and Mme de Stainville have chosen, for one year more or less makes a big difference for measurements... But,

[31] Ibid., 14 Jan. 1727: no. 71.   [32] Ibid., cited, Z. Harsany, op. cit., p. 457.
[33] Ibid., no. 71.   [34] Ibid., 8 Aug. 1727: no. 141.
[35] Ibid., 26 Dec. 1726: no. 60.   [36] Ibid., 10 May 1727: no. 80.
[37] Prince Charles of Lorraine to Marquis de Stainville, Lunéville, 28 Nov. 1726: Arch. M-et-M/Vienne, 3F 371, no. 56.
[38] Duchess of Lorraine to Marquise d'Aulède, Lunéville, 26 June 1728: 'Lettres d'Elisabeth-Charlotte d'Orléans, duchesse de Lorraine, à la marquise d'Aulède, 1715-1738', ed. E. Alexandre de Bonneval, u.s., p. 265.

Madam, be very careful that the drapers do not exchange what has been chosen'[39] for inferior goods.

The Duchess of Lorraine had the right agent in the Marquise de Stainville. The mother of the future Choiseul combined a passion for stuffs, even in preference to jewels, with a tight clamp upon the lower orders – she came to suspect her servants of always cheating her and when workmen were around they were accountable to her for every nail. A lady who went shopping for lace with the Marquise might also have to watch out, as Madame Pâris-Monmartel, the wife of the great financier, was to discover on a joint purchasing-mission in connection with the marriage in 1734 of a young Choiseul-Meuse to a niece of Pâris-Monmartel. The two ladies had an argument in a haberdashery as to whether their fashionable cuffs for the occasion should carry two or three rows of fine lace. Madame Pâris-Monmartel imposed two upon the Marquise de Stainville, who had badly wanted three, only to find a week later that the financier's wife herself was, if you please, sporting four rows – well, not exactly four but with tucks in the lace gathered into frills to give that effect, a pure cheat: 'Oh, for that', exclaimed the Marquise, 'I shall never forgive her so long as I live.'[40]

Choiseul's parents were for ever selecting the finest in that age of taste. From them he apparently inherited, at least, his love of beautiful objects and fine discrimination. One also sees how personal purchasing commissions on behalf of sovereigns and their court could bulk large among the duties of a diplomatic envoy in a period requiring display but restricted, still, in the circulation of luxury-goods.

IV

Those commissioned are trusted. Until 1729 the Marquis de Stainville was in the ascendant. In the summer of 1728 he was renting a house in what was then the village of Boulogne, out by the Bois. Already by 1727 d'Audiffret's inexperienced young man of three years earlier had become one of the 'first officers of this court',[41] listed among those who had graced his party in honour of the birth of the twin daughters which the new Queen of France had somewhat disconcertingly produced as her first effort instead of the hoped-for

[39] Ibid., 23 June 1727: pp. 237–8.
[40] Madame de Graffigny to Devaux, Demange-aux-Eaux, 19–20 Oct. 1738: Yale/Beinecke: Phillipps/Graffigny 23900, vol. ii, fo. 96.
[41] D'Audiffret to Count de Morville, Nancy, 16 Sept. 1727: Arch. Aff. Étr. C.P., Lorraine, vol. 117, fo. 240.

Dauphin. (Perhaps d'Audiffret and Stainville had recovered from their mutual coolness following the latter's failure to repay promptly that little loan of 23,000 livres.) Stainville had become a Counsellor of State and in November 1727 he appropriately received the high, and lucrative, office of Grand Huntsman of Lorraine. Nor indeed was it a sinecure under Duke Leopold.

Stainville was promptly involved in amicably easing out the deputy commandant of the chase, Baron de Schack, a Dane from Germany who repaid Leopold's favour by offering himself to d'Audiffret as a French spy. The new Grand Huntsman was to visit Lorraine in the new year of 1728 in order to regulate his responsibilities, involving a good deal of accounting and contact with tribunals. A year later an ordinance was to consolidate the ducal administration of the chase, organized in twelve captaincies (*capitaineries des chasses*). In Lorraine stags and other game of quality were strictly preserved. Nobles whose lands lay within two hours travelling of Nancy or other towns were forbidden to hunt over them and so disturb the duke's 'pleasures' and incur his 'indignation'. One of Stainville's duties was the allocation of dead game in compensation to such unfortunates. Keeping down lynxes and wolves was apparently another of his preoccupations despite the separate, less honorific, office of grand master of wolfhounds.

A year before Stainville took over, a wolf had chased a cat up to the windows of Craon's mansion in Lunéville. Even in midsummer 1728 the prince was complaining to the marquis 'that we are besieged on all sides by wolves. Four people have been bitten and three taken to hospital ... You will be coming to remedy all these disorders when it shall please you and you will have a lot to do to calm the public, which is very alarmed.'[42] Meanwhile, even in Paris, Stainville's hunting avocation could overlap his diplomatic one. A week later Duke Leopold scribbled him a chit asking him to do a certain 'Mr. de Casanova ... the favours which are in your power, above all for making him acquainted with huntsmen.'[43] The marquis, though, was heading higher.

By September 1728 the Duchess of Lorraine was complaining that 'Stainville only writes to M. de Craon and nothing to anyone besides, unless I write to him first... He has become a great politique since he has been at Paris; he was not so much that here.'[44] Within a month Stainville was to sign the counter-declaration on the neutrality of

[42] Prince de Craon to Marquis de Stainville, Lunéville, 22 July 1728: Arch. M-et-M/Vienne, 3F 370, no. 161.
[43] Duke Leopold to Marquis de Stainville, Lunéville, 28 July 1728: Ö.S/H.H.S., Lothringisches Hausarchiv 196/III 319, fo. 3.
[44] Duchess of Lorraine to Marquise d'Aulède, Lunéville, 26 Sept. 1728: *u.s.*, p. 273.

Lorraine, kept secret even from the duchess. The time was soon to come, however, when Stainville would badly need her friendship. Towards the end of March 1729 Duke Leopold went out one day to inspect a spare château which was being run up by the Prince de Craon. Returning on foot the corpulent duke jumped a brook, slipped and injured his chest. A pious prince, he insisted upon attending a service of benediction in his wet clothes. Complications set in and after five days, on 27 March 1729, Leopold died. He was just not fifty.

V

Duke Leopold of Lorraine was among the earliest of those benevolent despots who set their stamp upon the eighteenth century. Despotic he had been in so far as he had abstained, upon his restoration to the duchy, from reviving the ancient estates-general of Lorraine: such institutions had been rather put in the shade by the radiance of the Roi Soleil. Leopold would not have his authority circumscribed and some of his meticulous legislation became oppressive, or would have done if effectively enforced. In 1723, for instance, he was trying to curb the extravagance of wedding jollifications by forbidding burghers and peasants to invite more than twelve guests, or labourers and artisans more than eight. But Leopold's paternalistic legislation mainly certified his benevolence. His social concern found constant expression, as in his fire-precautions of 1721 or his pioneering insistence that surgeons must be highly qualified and that midwives, by decree of 1708, must pass an oral examination. Such trained midwifery was some two generations ahead of France.[45]

'The restorer and Solomon of Lorraine', as Duke Leopold was called,[46] had cared for all the subjects in his keeping, rich and poor alike. In 1717 he instituted in every parish a detailed system of poor relief by voluntary effort. Funds, too, were ingeniously channelled to the eleemosynary hospital of Saint Charles at Nancy. While Leopold had been careful to content and elevate nobles like Stainville – let alone the Craons – he had confided the day-to-day administration of his duchy to esteemed experts from the bourgeoisie like attorney-general Bourcier, Le Bègue the chancellor, and Lefebvre, 'oracle' of the council of state. They directed the overhaul of the whole duchy, measuring up its resources in the Pied-Certain and codifying its institutions in the liberal Code Leopold of 1701. This code, which

---

[45] Cf. P. Goubert, *Beauvais et le Beauvaisis de 1600 à 1730*, p. 69, n. 119, and in F. Braudel and E. Labrousse, *Histoire économique et sociale de la France*, ii. 69.
[46] [J. Henriquez,] *Abrégé chronologique de l'histoire de Lorraine* (Paris, 1775), i. 456.

featured free legal aid for the poor, achieved the distinction of being placed upon the papal index of forbidden literature.

Duke Leopold's fiscal deficiences caused him in the last year of his life to confess 'the shame of my having to admit to being little of an economist and negligent upon this head'; he was, however, grappling personally with the depressing tangle of debts, 'it being just that he who spoils should himself repair'.[47] If Leopold's generosity had helped to deplete his funds, it had otherwise enriched himself and his heritage. In the words of Voltaire, the duke had 'sought out talents even in the shops and in the forests, so as to bring them to light and encourage them'.[48] The university at Pont-à-Mousson flourished while Lunéville acquired a promising theatre and one of those learned academies which radiated the enlightenment. 'In short', continued Voltaire on Leopold, 'during all his reign, he concerned himself only with the care of procuring for his nation tranquillity, riches, learning and pleasures. "I would quit my sovereignty tomorrow", he would say, "if I could not do good." Thus did he taste the happiness of being loved; and I have seen, long after his death, his subjects shed tears in pronouncing his name.'

As yet the grief was still green and the duke unburied. If there was one thing that the Lorrainers knew how to do, it was how to put on a good funeral. According to a saying then the three best shows in Europe were the coronation of a Holy Roman Emperor, the marriage of a king of France, and the funeral of a duke of Lorraine. It just took time.

Heralds led a hundred of the poor, in black bearing torches, at the head of the procession which, on 10 June 1729, wound its way through Nancy to the Church of the Cordeliers, the ducal burying-place. Then came friars, penitents, and hermits (a feature of Lorraine), each with his taper, followed by escutcheons borne from every town in the duchy. Next marched the academic dignitaries from Pont-à-Mousson and judges in a splash of red, then mounted gendarmerie with muffled drum and trumpet, after them again noblemen in mourning robes bearing the insignia of chivalry. At last the clergy and mitred abbots – still no bishop – solemnly preceded the coffin surmounted by the regalia, borne by six stalwart chamberlains with six others to relieve them and pages carrying torches and trestles for the change-over of the bier. And in the place of honour upon the right hand of the coffin strode the grand huntsman, the Marquis de Stainville, carrying the great standard of Lorraine, 'of crimson silk with a large

---

[47] Duke Leopold to Baron von Pfütschner, 18 July 1728: Ö.S./H.H.S., Lothringisches Hausarchiv 108/425.

[48] Voltaire, *Siècle de Louis XIV* (Amsterdam, 1771), ii. 35, and for the following.

cross of yellow satin in the middle; the rest strewn with crosses of Jerusalem and of Lorraine in golden embroidery'.[49] Jerusalem because Duke Leopold had assumed the evocative title of King of Jerusalem, failing somewhere like Prussia or Sardinia. It was then the fashion for princes to become kings.

Stainville may have been a specially appropriate standard-bearer: three years earlier in Paris he had 'consulted an embroiderer about the flags and purses which are to be made here'[50] to a ducal order worth six thousand livres. Now the standard would never again be carried to the burial of a ruler in Lorraine. Her time of independence was nearly up.

VI

Duke Leopold was succeeded by the twenty-year-old Duke Francis III, still absent in Vienna in accordance, indeed, with his father's prescription. Almost as if in premonition of his early death, Leopold had recently enjoined Pfütschner that in that event Francis should not quit the Austrian power-centre since 'a state governed and submissive like ours, being properly but a province, can be governed from afar'.[51] But imperial government from a distance is the most subject to challenge. Such was the outlook for the new duke in waiting still upon his all-important marriage even though it was already being said that the houses of Austria and of Lorraine 'no longer regard themselves as anything but one single family'. [52]

When young Francis had left Lorraine for the Austrian court at Pràgue in the summer of 1723 he had been a winning lad, gay and affable but, to Leopold's concern, flighty and petulant. Now at last Francis returned via Prague once more and with something of his old spirit sped ahead incognito to reach Lunéville in the early morning of 29 November 1729 and surprise his mother, also his sisters whom he joyously flushed out of bed. He, however, disconcerted his subject Lorrainers, who found him a grave and haughty young man, as aloof as his father had been approachable. Indeed he had been reckoned over-reserved (except with ladies) even at the stiff court of Vienna, now personified at that of Lunéville by an

---

[49] 'Pompe funèbre de feu S.A.R. Léopold I, duc de Lorraine': cf. Noel, *Mémoires pour servir à l'histoire de Lorraine* (Nancy, 1838f.), no. 5. (The present text is from an original copy: Arch. Aff. Étr. C.P., Lorraine, vol. 120, fo. 133.)

[50] Marquis de Stainville to Duke Leopold, Paris, 9 May 1726: Arch. M-et-M/Vienne, 3F 85, no. 27.

[51] Duke Leopold to Baron von Pfütschner, 18 July 1728: Ö.S./H.H.S., Lothringrisches Hausarchiv 108/425.

[52] D'Audiffret, 9 April 1726: Arch. Aff. Étr., cited Comte d'Haussonville, op. cit., iv. 334, n. 1.

accompanying officer of the ducal household and imperial favourite, General Count von Neipperg. The teutonic stuffiness of Duke Francis was emphasized by his heavy German wig and long-skirted coats which in France had gone out with Louis XIV.

The duke's arrival had been preceded by an order from Vienna evicting at short notice from the palace at Lunéville those noble families who had been given free lodging by Leopold. The Marquis de Stainville was deprived of his useful little perquisite of stabling four horses free in the ducal stables, took a cut in salary as grand huntsman, and was in danger of losing the fruits of his recent victory over Du Tertre at Bazincourt under a decree of July 1729 cancelling all alienations of ducal lands made during the preceding reign. By a decision of the following January, however, Stainville was continued in his enjoyment of the village of Bazincourt under reservation of the ducal right of revocation upon payment to the marquis or his heirs of the sum of 45,000 livres. In general, though, 'the nobility of Lorraine is no longer in those happy times when the preservation of its privileges formed the delight of the sovereign'.[53]

Economies at court were indeed overdue and the Craons suffered most. The Princess de Craon, bereft of the duke so long devoted to her, fell ill 'from having shut up her grief in her heart and from having felt too keenly the difference.... She desired, without there having been necessity therefor ..., to receive the viaticum the day of Good Friday. She is better, but the bad temper whereby she has always been dominated has increased to such a point that her servants have refused to serve her and I know very certainly that her husband has said to Mme de Rouvarch [Rouerke] his sister that he was the most unhappy man in the world.'[54]

The Prince de Craon had been appointed to the council of regency to which Duke Leopold willed the government in his son's absence. But in the same way that the testament of Louis XIV had been overthrown and the Duke of Orleans instituted regent of France, so now was Leopold's will quashed and his widow, the dissimilar sister of the Duke of Orleans, made regent of Lorraine. This boded no good for the former favourites, and their fortune was raked through. The regent, however, honoured the memory of the husband she had vainly loved by shewing some clemency to the Craons, who were themselves prudently beforehand in making financial restitution. It was creditable to both sides. If, as the new regent's mother had once

---

[53] Pasquier, French Chargé d'Affaires, to Chauvelin, Nancy, 13 Aug. 1729: Arch. Aff. Étr. C.P., Lorraine, vol. 121, fo. 60.
[54] D'Audiffret to Chauvelin, Nancy, 23 Apr. 1729: Arch. Aff. Étr. C.P., Lorraine, vol. 120, fos. 74–5.

exclaimed of La Craon, 'these wretched mistresses spoil everything'[55] at court, they too might display that sacrifice and self-control which not infrequently underlay an aristocratic *douceur de vivre*.

By the beginning of 1730 the Prince de Craon was writing to the Marquis de Stainville: 'Amid all the afflictions by which I am overwhelmed I have the consolation of having nothing more to fear for I am totally stripped of the benefits from his late Royal Highness. But that is to talk to you too much, my dear nephew, of sad things',[56] with even more in fact to come. Craon continued: 'I go into private houses and I see there only sick or discontented people. I penetrate through to the innermost closet of the court, where the centre of joy should be, and I find no more gaiety than elsewhere. I have little access to our ministers . . . but their saddened looks' threw him back upon the countesses de Rouerke and de Ferrari in his own house where 'we laugh at the mistakes which we see being made . . . if [only] our master was not their first victim'.[57]

A less prejudiced witness allowed that the court of Lunéville 'seems only the ghost of what it used to be'.[58] 'One must', added Craon to Stainville, 'content oneself with echoes. They are the delights of solitude and my house is pretty much like that. Madame de Craon is very well.'[59] And another year later: 'The cold is increasing every day and the snow does not diminish . . . The news is frozen.'[60]

That long cold did thaw at last. The philosophic Craons were to be partly restored to a platonic favour. It remained true that 'under the new Regency of Lorraine one sees a new government, other ministers, different plans. Those who have occupied the first ranks under the preceding reign, expelled and forgotten, those who were not thought of then extracted from obscurity, and raised upon the ruins of their predecessors.'[61] Conspicuous among the new men was 'friend Toussaint'. He had nimbly graduated to be secretary to young Francis in Vienna, so he came to be signing off not the Stainville estate-accounts as previously but ducal registers of diplomatic correspondence. An efficient administrator without the instincts of a gentleman, this 'new favourite'[62] was the first to whom the young duke issued a patent of nobility; and Francis III was much more sparing of such grants than Leopold.

[55] Cited, Gaston Maugras, *La Cour de Lunéville au XVIIIe siècle* (Paris, 1904), p. 19.
[56] Prince de Craon to Marquis de Stainville, Lunéville, 25 Jan. 1730: Arch. M-et-M/Vienne, 3F 370, no. 217.
[57] Ibid.
[58] D'Audiffret to Chauvelin, Nancy, 8 Nov. 1729: Arch. Aff. Étr. C.P., Lorraine, vol. 121, fo. 216.
[59] Prince de Craon to Marquis de Stainville, Lunéville, 9 Feb. 1730: *u.s.*, no. 220.
[60] Ibid., 19 Feb. 1731, no. 238.
[61] Pasquier to Chauvelin, Nancy, 1 Aug. 1729: Arch. Aff. Étr. C.P., Lorraine, vol. 121, fo. 4.
[62] Ibid., 15 Aug. 1729: fo. 65.

Later, certainly, little love was to be lost between Baron Toussaint and his former employers. One gathers that the secretary may indeed have had scores to settle with the overweening Marquise de Stainville, and that with the marquis amounted, so Toussaint claimed, to nearly 5,000 livres in back-wages, now urgently demanded, less urgently paid so that he was still making representations four years later. But it may not have been only financially, as Toussaint suggested in dunning Stainville, 'that you do not know how you stand with me'.[63] This tension could have primed the circumstance that Stainville's new 'master has conceived impressions from his time in Vienna which had ill-disposed him concerning him. Intrigues, court jealousies have injured him [Stainville] with the new ministry.'[64] Nearly a decade later the voluble Marquise de Stainville was still regaling her friends for hours on end with 'the history of Toussaint, ... hundredth edition'.[65]

Three days after the death of Duke Leopold the Cardinal Fleury had written in his own hand to the Marquis de Stainville: 'I know, Sir, that in this prince you are losing a friend rather than a master.[66] The sympathy was accurate. A week later Duke Francis did reaccredit the Marquis de Stainville to the French court.[67] But one who had fought for Louis XIV against the Austrians was perhaps understandably suspect at Vienna. Indeed a French diplomatic memorandum later commented on Stainville: 'One cannot doubt that he is, after his duties, wholly of the French inclination, and that his sentiments are entirely disposed thereto.'[68] This hardly suited at a time when 'everything is becoming German in this court to please the prince'.[69]

The Marquis de Stainville was particularly compromised because early in 1729 he had at last been steering home his long endeavour, supported by Cardinal Fleury, to win over the Duke of Orleans, cast down by his early bereavement, from his almost monastic inclinations and hold him to his promise, now, to take for his second wife his

[63] Toussaint to Marquis de Stainville, Luxemburg, 18 June 1729: Arch. M-et-M/Vienne, 3F 372, no. 168.
[64] D'Audiffret to Chauvelin, Nancy, 17 Dec. 1729: Arch. Aff. Étr. C.P., Lorraine, vol. 121, fo. 299.
[65] Madame de Graffigny to Devaux, Demange-aux-Eaux, 7–10 Oct. 1738: Yale/Beinecke: Phillipps/Graffigny 23900, vol. ii, fo. 69.
[66] Cardinal Fleury to Marquis de Stainville, Versailles, 30 Mar. 1729: Arch. M-et-M/Vienne, 3F 372, no. 149.
[67] Cf. Duke Francis III to King Louis XV, Vienna, 6 Apr. 1729: Arch. Aff. Étr. C.P., Lorraine, vol. 120, fo. 60 (copy in Ö.S./H.H.S., Lothringisches Hausarchiv 202/III 502).
[68] French report of 1737 on personalities of Lorraine: 'Mémoire pour les noms de ceux qui composent le conseil de S. A. R. Monsieur le Duc de Lorraine, divisé par classe et numerottés': Arch. Aff. Étr. C.P., Lorraine, vol. 128, fo. 265.
[69] D'Audiffret to Chauvelin, Nancy, 10 Dec. 1729: Arch. Aff. Étr. C.P., Lorraine, vol. 121, fo. 288.

cousin Elisabeth-Thérèse of Lorraine. A year previously he had been writing to his aunt and would-be mother-in-law: 'Far from desiring this marriage, I am extremely frightened of it; thus I have no curiosity to know if I can marry her, but, indeed, if I can not marry her; I well know that I always can [not marry her] by breaking my word, but ... I shall never exempt myself from the rules of honour ... [but] I should find that I could not have any dealings with you after you had married me in spite of myself ... It is infinitely painful to me to write you such letters, but ... however much I may have the misfortune to displease you at this moment, I beg you to consider that you ought to take it much more unkindly against me if, having such sentiments, I hid them from you.'[70]

Once again, young people then could have some say in their marriage, even ones of convenience and state, and such a letter might well have daunted the most determined mother. But that one 'passionately wishes this marriage'[71] to the youth who remained possibly the future King of France till that September when, in the wording of the British ambassador in Paris, Marie Leszczynska was 'brought to bed of a Dolphin'.[72] The Duchess of Lorraine had an ally in the victim's mother, the dowager Duchess of Orleans. Shortly before Leopold died these powerful ladies, largely working through Stainville, had prevailed. Madame de Stainville was entrusted with secret commissions for the trousseau.

Upon his accession Francis lost little time in countering the proposed French marriage, ill viewed in Vienna, with legalistic objections which one Lorrainer there, Bourcier de Villers, told him were 'but a chimera'.[73] Francis was more vehemently subjected to his mother's fear 'that a rupture [of the marriage] ... will greatly prejudice you in France ... It is you who absolutely wish to break the marriage ... I beseech you, my dear son, as a mother who loves you more than life and who only seeks your good, to think well on it before deciding. Stainville will arrive from Paris on Sunday evening; zealous as he is in your service, he envisages as I do the dangers which you will run in France.' After dictating much more in the same strain she concluded in her own hand: 'I only say this to you, my dear son,

---

[70] Duke of Orleans to Duchess of Lorraine, 20 Mar. 1728: Ö.S./H.H.S., Lothringisches Hausarchiv 112/437.

[71] D'Audiffret to Chauvelin, Nancy, 2 June 1729: Arch. Aff. Étr. C.P., Lorraine, vol 120, fo. 147.

[72] Horatio Walpole, 5 Sept. 1729: P.R.O./S.P.F., France, no. 192, cited in *British Diplomatic Instructions, 1689–1789*, vol. vi (*France 1727–1744*), ed. L. G. Wickham Legg: Camden Third Series, vol. xliii (London, 1930) p. xvii.

[73] Bourcier de Villers to Marquis de Stainville, Vienna, 22 June 1729: Arch. M-et-M/Vienne, 3F 372, no. 171.

for the lively tenderness which I have for you and shall have till the last moment of my sad life. Elizabeth Charlotte.'[74]

The French envoy in Lorraine explained: 'The brunt of the displeasure of the Duke of Lorraine concerning the signature of the articles [of the marriage settlement] has fallen upon M. de Stainville, in that the Duchess of Lorraine, in the thick of her affliction on the morrow of the death of the late Duke, charged him to treat upon these articles with M. d'Argenson conjointly with M. le Bègue and M. Bourcier, believing that as he was already acquainted with this affair he would be capable of conducting it well. But this Minister, having rendered himself too easy in the discussion, lightly engaged himself to have them [the articles] signed, without considering the risk of this demarche without the consent of his Master; which he has recognized too late, for having since strongly solicited permission to go to Vienna on the ground that he had very important things to communicate, it has been refused him.'[75] The duchess was reduced to tears by a dispatch from her son disapproving the articles of marriage and, it was said, expressing himself as 'surprised that this negotiation with M. d'Argenson should have been principally conducted by a young scatterbrain (étourdi) who had neither knowledge nor experience'.[76]

Certainly the rebuffed Marquis de Stainville now plunged into the dangerous course of corresponding on behalf of the regent with the sympathetic Bourcier de Villers in Vienna behind the back of the duke and of his envoy there, Baron de Jacquemin. This correspondence was routed through Stainville's Jacobite connection, the conspiratorial Count de Rouerke, still hanging around Vienna. Only, the letters were intercepted and ultimately forwarded to Rouerke by Jacquemin. And Bourcier warned Stainville that at Lunéville the regent was now surrounded by 'several people in whom she should not trust'.[77] These prompt informers were thought to include her younger daughter, the fair Princess Anne-Charlotte. Such was the atmosphere of delation and espionage which, within three months of the accession of Duke Francis III, had succeeded at the court of Lorraine to the debonair days of his open-hearted father.

The regent was now instructed from Vienna 'to do nothing without the counsel of M. le Bègue and not to admit M. de Stainville to knowledge of secret matters'.[78] Le Bègue had earlier seen Austrian

[74] Regent Elizabeth Charlotte of Lorraine to Duke Francis III, Lunéville, 4 May 1729: Ö.S./H.H.S., Lothringisches Hausarchiv 196/III 319, fos. 15–17.
[75] D'Audiffret to Chauvelin, Nancy, 2 June 1729: Arch. Aff. Étr. C.P., Lorraine, vol. 120, fos. 148–9.
[76] Ibid., vol. 120, fo. 145.
[77] Bourcier de Villers to Marquis de Stainville, Vienna, 29 June 1729: Arch. M-et-M/Vienne, 3F 372, no. 173.
[78] D'Audiffret to Chauvelin, Nancy, 23 July 1729: Arch. Aff. Étr. C.P., Lorraine, vol. 120, fos. 197–8.

service and now took his cue from the young Duke's 'intimate confidant',[79] Pfütschner, himself described as being 'entirely dependent upon Count de Sinzendorf who despotically settles the affairs of Lorraine'.[80] Sinzendorf may have been less impressed by Stainville than that young hopeful could have wished. For the present he was rather relegated with the regent at Lunéville while 'this German baron',[81] as Pfütschner was dubbed in Paris, proceeded thither on a special mission with the object of queering an Orleanist marriage.

Shortly before Pfütschner, simplified to Fischner in the annals of Lorraine, reached Paris in July 1729 Stainville had alerted friendly Fleury, in a letter which the cardinal duly burnt, as to how the land lay. Fleury replied that he would not fail to show the emissary 'in what esteem I hold you and for that I shall only need to tell him my real feelings'.[82] At the same time Stainville insisted with characteristic generosity that Pfütschner should put up free in his own residence in Paris. The baron wrote to the marquis: 'By your kindness I find myself in a fine house and served by a carriage which proclaims the minister ... Your servants ... are beforehand in everything that can please me ... Till now, having been invited out, I have only supped at home, which, according to my good custom, is a glass of iced water':[83] shocking to Stainville of all people so that Pfütschner had to promise him to 'give employment from time to time to your butler and your cook'.[84]

The Marquis de Stainville at the same time remained in secret touch with the Count d'Argenson, who assured him: 'I shall above all be very careful that the German does not suspect that we have the slightest communication together.'[85] Three days later the German blandly wrote to Stainville of d'Argenson that 'it would have been better that he had not been rendered so knowledgeable'.[86] Contrariwise the Orleans dowager was to weigh in with Fleury: 'I should be very glad that the German man should know clearly what you think of the renunciation'[87] of the marriage-articles.

To be German was even then hardly a passport to popularity in Paris. But the renunciation stood. The Duke of Orleans escaped. So too, from another quarter, did his intended.

---

[79] Duke Francis III to Cardinal Fleury, Vienna, 25 June 1729: ibid., vol. 119, fo. 183.

[80] D'Audiffret to Chauvelin, Nancy, 7 July 1729: ibid., vol. 120, fo. 184.

[81] Count d'Argenson to Marquis de Stainville, Paris, 15 July 1729: Arch. M-et-M/Vienne, 3F 372, no. 179.

[82] Cardinal Fleury to Marquis de Stainville, Marly, 5 July 1729: ibid., no. 175.

[83] Baron von Pfütschner to Marquis de Stainville, Paris, 7 July 1729: ibid., no. 182.

[84] Ibid., 18 July 1729: no. 181.

[85] Count d'Argenson to Marquis de Stainville, Paris, 15 July 1729: ibid., no. 179.

[86] Baron von Pfütschner to Marquis de Stainville, 18 July 1729: ibid., no. 181.

[87] Dowager Duchess of Orleans to Cardinal Fleury, 29 Sept. 1729: Arch. Aff. Étr. C.P., Lorraine, vol. 121, fo. 160.

Count von Sinzendorf's dynastic design for the house of Lorraine had pointed eastward, rather, in the interest of the Austrian entente with Russia. Already in 1727 his proposal that the younger princess, Anne-Charlotte, should marry the ephemeral young Czar Peter II had proved too much even for Leopold, with whom usually, as he told Pfütschner, the emperor's 'wishes are orders for me'.[88] Leopold had declared that he 'virtually absolutely could not consent to it', citing 'the perhaps too great vivacity of my younger daughter in relation to a country where there still remain so many vestiges of the old government, and – in short all must be said – the excess of debauchery which reigns in this country and from which the first women are not exempt'.[89] This had not prevented Sinzendorf from reopening the question of a Russian marriage, for either daughter, with the Marquis de Stainville in Paris a year later. And now that Leopold was succeeded by the pliant Francis and the Orleans betrothal broken, Austria looked to the elder princess, plain, pious, gentle Elisabeth-Thérèse. But the Regent of Lorraine was adamant, declaring 'she would rather see her daughter . . . than marry the Czar, which, as her mother, she would oppose with all her might.'[90] The omission was due to the delicacy of the decyphering clerk who left in code this specimen of the blunt language which the regent inherited from her mother. This time the Lorraine dowager prevailed.

VII

Still graver concerns came crowding in upon the regent and her ministers. After Leopold's death their injunctions for public prayers to rest him had promptly provoked jurisdictional complaints from the French bishops of Metz, Toul, and Verdun. By the autumn of 1729 the inhabitants of Bar, playing up true to form, were refusing to pay the special levy of the *joyeux avènement* traditionally imposed upon the accession of a sovereign. They appealed to France. The regent's council, inspired from Vienna, drafted troops into the Barrois where 'sixty villages are counted to be in revolt, and among the most obstinate the inhabitants of the little town of Ligny have distinguished themselves. They stubbornly maintain that they will not pay taxes so long as the Duke of Lorraine has not rendered homage to the King [of France].'[91] The soldiery of Lorraine took reprisals and the French

[88] Duke Leopold to Baron von Pfütschner, 28 July 1728: Ö.S./H.H.S., Lothringisches Hausarchiv 108/425.
[89] Duke Leopold to Baron de Jacquemin, 18 Dec. 1727: ibid.
[90] D'Audiffret to Chauvelin, Nancy, 16 July 1729: Arch. Aff. Étr. C.P., Lorraine, vol. 120, fo. 194.
[91] Pasquier to Chauvelin, Nancy, 27 Oct. 1729: Arch. Aff. Étr. C.P., Lorraine, vol. 121, fo. 197.

government in turn threatened military intervention. The agitated Regent of Lorraine consulted her council: 'the Marquis de Stainville began to speak, and told her that she should not be troubled by it, since it was not her fault, but that of her Council. M. le Bègue opined that M. Stainville should be sent to France, but this last replied that as they gave him no agreeable commissions, he did not wish to undertake vexatious ones, unless the Duke of Lorraine commanded him after his [forthcoming] arrival, in which case he would do his best ... The order has been sent to withdraw the troops from Bar.'[92]

A day or two after this lively debate the Marquis de Stainville fell seriously ill. This was not his first illness at about that time. He had been sick after his return from England the year before. Whatever the cause, it may perhaps have been aggravated by his constant journeying. In recent years he seemed to have been continually on the go, posting back and forth in his coach between Lunéville and Paris, which might then take anything from three days upwards, travelling in foul weather,[93] travelling into the night.[94] On top of this he had had a grim year of it. He went down with a violent fever there in Lunéville on 18 November 1729, the same day that his wife was delivered of her fifth and last surviving child, her daughter Beatrix, a name which seems to have been locally fashionable. Such was the troubled birthday of the little sister who was later to play so large a part in the life of her eldest brother.

For about a week Stainville's fever continued fierce, his life in danger. On 24 November the regent reported to her friend: 'Poor Stainville ... is very ill to-day, whereat I am, I assure you, very sorry, for he is a very honest man and well capable of serving my son well.'[95] The son himself, just arrived at Lunéville, was less sure. Stainville's convalescence – for he pulled through – was soured by the duke's publication early in December of the new list of his counsellors. The Marquis de Stainville had been dropped from the council of state. This was the last straw. He felt 'obliged next day to bring his Patent of the Office of Grand Huntsman to Madam the Duchess of Lorraine, and to beg her to remit it to the Duke of Lorraine, being no longer able to serve him after the dishonour which he had just received, but considering that he should withdraw to the country, and never return to court. As she has always been the refuge of malcontents, she spoke of it strongly to the Prince, her son, who had M. de Stainville summoned to him and told him that he had

[92] D'Audiffret to Chauvelin, Nancy, 23 Nov. 1729: Arch. Aff. Étr. C.P., Lorraine, vol. 121, fos. 262–3.

[93] See the Duchess of Lorraine to Marquise d'Aulède, 22 Nov. 1728: op. cit., p. 275.

[94] See d'Audiffret to Count de Morville, Nancy, 25 Feb. 1727: Arch. Aff. Étr. C.P., Lorraine, vol. 117, fo. 70.

[95] Regent of Lorraine to Marquise d'Auléde, Lunéville, 24 Nov. 1729: op. cit., p. 285.

no cause to complain of him; that he had not known that he was a Counsellor of State in the lifetime of his Father; and that he had given order that he should be placed on the list. He [Stainville] has evinced to one of his friends that he did not intend to remain in France so as not to ruin his children and that he wished to come and exercise his office [of Grand Huntsman].'⁹⁶

Whatever his paternal solicitude, the marquis, reported the French envoy, 'senses well that they are preparing tribulations for him',⁹⁷ notably by constituting 'as their tutelary angel in France'⁹⁸ the disreputable Prince d'Elboeuf, who had been making up to Le Bègue. Nevertheless the Marquis de Stainville was off again from Lunéville to Paris soon after the middle of December, though 'still very feeble when he left'.⁹⁹ He planned to stop off at his estates for a few days, but pushed on again before Christmas, disfigured that year in Lorraine by 'a nasty black cold, which is very unhealthy'.¹ Only later was Stainville joined by his wife who tarried a little at Lunéville, supping with the ducal family and on the Twelfth Night of 1730 with the Prince de Craon, telling him that her husband in Paris was back in bed with a feverish cold.

Such was the chilly and precarious return of the Marquis de Stainville to his mission at the court of France, where Louis XV had received him two days after Christmas. Chauvelin suggested that 'motives might supervene which would induce him [Stainville] not to desire to reside long in France. One of the most powerful would be the reflection which he makes that the spirit which reigns at present at this court would not stand to furnish him with negotiations very gracious to follow here.'² That spirit was incorporated in his erstwhile secretary, through whom now he largely had to correspond with Duke Francis. Toussaint was to tell Stainville off because the concluding compliments in his dispatches were not in his own hand. And the baron had the prompt impertinence to tell the Grand Huntsman how to run even that office: 'I repeat, Sir, that you would do well to review all the licences which you have issued.'³

Yet the Marquis de Stainville's mission in Paris was to occupy him still for years to come, and the primary negotiation after his return

---

⁹⁶ D'Audiffret to Chauvelin, Nancy, 12 Dec. 1729: Arch. Aff. Étr. C.P., Lorraine, vol. 121, fo. 292–3.
⁹⁷ D'Audiffret to Chauvelin, Nancy, 17 Dec. 1729: Arch Aff. Étr. C.P., Lorraine, vol. 121, fo. 299.
⁹⁸ Ibid.
⁹⁹ Regent of Lorraine to Marquise d'Aulède, Lunéville, 26 Dec. 1729: op. cit., p. 288.
¹ Ibid.
² Chauvelin to d'Audiffret, Versailles, 27 Dec. 1729: Arch. Aff. Étr. C.P., Lorraine, vol. 119, fo. 246.
³ Baron Toussaint to Marquis de Stainville, Lunéville, 5 Jan. 1730: Arch. M-et-M/Vienne, 3F 372, no. 70.

promoted detente, political with France, personal for Stainville. This lucky break was the advent of Duke Francis at the French court in order to do homage to Louis XV for the recalcitrant duchy of Bar. Stainville had a busy time of it since, as Toussaint rubbed in, Francis 'likes everything to be done without fuss and at the same time with the utmost punctuality'.[4] The young duke himself was writing the same day of the approaching ceremony: 'They tell me that I have to embrace them all, so, not wanting to seem ridiculous',[5] would Stainville brief him precisely.

The visit to France in 1730 of the Duke of Lorraine was a success so far as it went. Although he travelled incognito as the Count de Blamont he could expect entertainment from the highest in the land, the Cardinal Fleury, the Marshal de Villars. Francis put off his cumbersome German gear for his stay in the Palais Royal and recaptured something of his earlier spirits, hunting with the king, doing the sights and 'all the plays'[6] somewhat to the embarrassment of his pious cousin and host, the young Duke of Orleans. Francis was to touch Orleans, perhaps grateful for his marital reprieve, for a loan of 400,000 livres but he fended off his host's enterprising sister, Mademoiselle de Beaujolais.

On 1 February 1730 the ancient ceremony of homage for the duchy of Bar was performed at Versailles for the last time. Louis omitted from the ritual some particulars most likely to disconcert the sensitive Francis. Even so the French courtiers taking part tended to feel embarrassed. Thus did this ceremony, with the duke, one day to be emperor, kneeling bare-headed to the king, symbolize both the long reach of feudalism and its incipient demise. The old order persisted but was passing.

The visit concluded, Baron Toussaint treated the Marquis de Stainville to a farewell backhander, maybe: upon the return journey 'we found frightful roads from St. Dizier to Stainville'.[7] The marquis however plodded on in Paris with the legal substance beneath the ceremony, and that to such effect that by 29 June the Duke of Lorraine, a carefully arranged character, was assuring him 'that the news which you have given me of the justice which has been provisionally done to me concerning my right of *joyeux avènement* in the Barrois Mouvant has caused me real pleasure. I attribute it to the

---

[4] Ibid., 21 Jan. 1730: no. 76.

[5] Duke Francis III to Marquis de Stainville, Lunéville, 21 Jan. 1730: ibid., 3F 362, no. 113.

[6] Barbier, *Chronique de la Régence et du règne de Louis XV: ou, Journal de Barbier* (Paris, 1857; henceforth cited as Barbier), ii. 90.

[7] Baron Toussaint to Marquis de Stainville, Lunéville, 20 Feb. 1730: Arch. M-et-M/Vienne, 3F 372, no. 84.

pains and initiative which you have taken, with which I am fully satisfied.'[8]

The crisis of confidence in the Marquis de Stainville was over. But it cast shadows ahead.

---

[8] Duke Francis III to Marquis de Stainville, Lunéville, 29 June 1730: Arch. M-et-M/Vienne, 3F 362, no. 120.

CHAPTER VI

UPBRINGING

I

AT STAINVILLE on 13 April 1728 a steward, the faithful Mathieu, writing to the Marquise mainly about sales of timber, had added: 'I am reckoning to receive in a day or so the 1,500 livres from the lessee of Stainville . . . I am reckoning to go to Demange in a day or so to see if I can have some money. I should much wish, Madam, if it would please you, to bring your son to you in Paris. Ways would be found to bring him without great expense, so soon as I may have had your orders for it.'[1]

The mother's reply would not appear to have been promptly positive. A month later the future Duke de Choiseul, then eight, was still at his great-aunt's at Nancy, suffering from a recurrence of fever. But removal was in the air and within some months Stephen de Stainville joined his parents in the Faubourg Saint-Germain, then the select district of Paris.

Fashion in the French capital, as in others, was then moving out westward from the medieval city. This urban advance was two-pronged, through the Faubourg Saint-Honoré on the northern bank, on past the Louvre and the Tuileries towards the Champs-Elysées, and on the south bank through the Faubourg Saint-Germain, up the long axes of the Rue Saint-Dominique and the Rue de Grenelle in the direction of the domed and still mainly isolated grandeur of the Invalides, lately erected by the Roi Soleil for his war-veterans in what contemporaries considered the happiest blend 'of piety and of magnificence'.[2]

The Faubourg Saint-Germain, featuring the Hôtels de Saint-Simon, de Richelieu, de Biron, the Hôtel Matignon, and numbers more, was becoming conspicuous 'for the number of magnificent houses which it contains and for the great people who live there. All these advantages render this district alone comparable to several capital towns which are famed in the world . . . The air there is infinitely purer and healthier than elsewhere, most of the houses

[1] Mathieu to Marquise de Stainville, Stainville, 13 Apr. 1728: Arch. M-et-M/Vienne, 3F 371, no. 144.
[2] Germain Brice, *Description de la ville de Paris* (Amsterdam, 1718 ed.), iii. 105.

being separated by gardens which render them agreeable, and being built almost all of them upon new ground ... as though in an asylum remote from the noise and fuss which trade and business people always bring in their wake.'[3] In this garden-suburb of Saint-Germain, in so much of the eighteenth century, the countryside still overhung the town.

In this rural fringe of Parisian elegance the Rue du Bac, where the Stainvilles lived in style, led up from the Pont Royal in replacement of the ferry which still names the street. It crossed the Rue de Varenne and just beyond, on the right-hand side coming up from the river, rose the steeple of the little chapel of the 'hospital of the Convalescents, founded in 1652 by Angélique Faure ... for eight poor sick leaving the hospital of La Charité, who could stay there for eight or ten days to restore themselves and re-establish their strength'.[4] From the back-windows of the Convalescents one could then look clear across gardens with hardly a building to interrupt the view over to the Invalides. At about this level of the Rue du Bac stood 'several houses, newly built by the administrators of the hospital of the Incurables, which produce very large rents'. The Marquis de Stainville, not rising to a mansion of his own, could well have been one of those who swelled the fat rents of the Incurables, larger than the Convalescents.

Against this setting of hospitals the health of little Stephen de Stainville continued anxious. In February 1729 the Prince de Craon was taking the Marquis de Stainville to task for not giving him the latest bulletin upon the delicate condition 'of my great-nephew'[5] in Paris. The little Count de Stainville once again pulled through, against a home background that was select enough if not exactly gay. His mother had strict ideas of rank and propriety, allegedly maintaining that she would not have inside her doors anyone addicted to such diversions as backgammon or chess. While the marquis was acquainted with much of the aristocracy of France and with some few of Austria and England also, he did not greatly consort with smart courtiers at Versailles. He enjoyed, indeed, his diplomatic privilege of hunting with the king, stood especially well with Fleury and the Orleanist interest, and frequented any sojourners in Paris from among the Craons and other easterners such as the Bissys. One gathers, though, that the elder Stainville was specially at home at excellent little dinners with diplomatic colleagues in Paris or in elegant suburbs, amid 'the pleasures of Saint-Cloud'[6] at the Count d'Argenson's or, later at least, in a convivial coterie at Chaillot.

---

[3] Ibid., iii. 2–3.   [4] Ibid., iii. 121–2 for the following.
[5] Prince de Craon to Marquis de Stainville, Lunéville, 17 Feb. 1729: Arch. M-et-M/Vienne, 3F 370, no. 203.
[6] Ibid., 1728: no. 146.

It was expensive, even so, to maintain the standards set by the Marquis and Marquise de Stainville. To eke out his emoluments he had to dip into private income. If his residence in the Rue du Bac became only intermittently home for his 'big boy'[7] thanks to schooling, thanks to financial straits it could well have ceased to be home at all.

In a crisis early in 1731 the marquis turned to his pawky friend, Pfütschner. A year earlier the baron had, a little rashly perhaps, conveyed the hope that his appointment to the ducal council of finances might render him 'fortunate enough to be able to be of use to you'.[8] Now he did try, in a way. Pfütschner wrote to Stainville on 22 March 1731 'in all frankness. It is certain that since you have been at Paris you have not saved anything, but it is also very sure that your emoluments are considerable and that there [are] no envoys, or hardly any, who have as much; and you will very easily be suspected either of being a bad manager, or of falling into excessive expenditure, for having hitherto engaged your own fortune. But when one has once adopted a certain style at a foreign court one can hardly reduce it with honour, especially'[9] – if one possessed Stainville's outgoing liberality.

The mentor warned the marquis:

The longer you remain in this position the more you will injure yourself. A wise paterfamilias does not diminish the position of his children in the service of a sovereign . . . The best course to my mind . . . is to ask for your recall and here restrict . . . your expenditure to your income. The most solid thing that one has in this world is what one has at home. The rest is subject to continual quirks and reversals . . . Do not grandsons often repent rather the effect of favours which their sires may have deserved by the sacrifice of their property and lives for the good of the state? The Bible affords us the story of Mordecai but these examples are not too common and . . . you do not need a preacher.

Negative advice is usually prudent, often suspect. Stainville did not take it. Instead of cash he had got a cautioning. He can hardly have gathered that he was considered indispensable in Paris. His decision to remain there among influential friends may even have been taken partly in the interest of his eldest son, already angled towards France. If the Duke de Choiseul's notorious extravagance was largely hereditary, his subsequent estimate of his father's unhelpfulness, in so far as it was true, related more particularly to a somewhat withdrawn way of life which the Marquis de Stainville

---

[7] Ibid., 19 Feb. 1729: no. 204.
[8] Baron von Pfütschner to Marquis de Stainville, Lunéville, 6 Mar. 1730: Arch. M-et-M/Vienne, 3F 372, no. 90.
[9] Ibid., 22 Mar. 1731: no. 23, and for the following.

may increasingly have adopted in order to suit his purse. He proceeded to scrape along in Paris and in the following year, for instance, was borrowing thirty louis, even, from Bourcier de Villers, who had to jog him for repayment while also sending 'a thousand thanks for all the kindness and friendship which you showed me during my stay in Paris'.[10] The marquis too was to borrow much larger sums from a much richer friend, the famous financier, Pâris-Monmartel.

The spanking days of the Marquis de Stainville's advent in Paris were over, perhaps psychologically also. Under prolonged chill from above most functionaries begin to lose heart. If Stainville hung on for long years yet, there was already some suspicion of a brokenbacked career: some suggestion also of a not specially happy marriage. Even in the high days when his wife had been staying with indulgent Craon, the prince had written to the marquis in terms conceivably veiling rather more than her pregnancy: 'Madame de Stainville loves you at intervals and writes to you as though she still loved you.'[11] A later and less friendly friend described her as guying her husband: 'She imitates him, and says of him a million things worth printing, so original are they.'[12] It may have been an even match, for in an apostrophe to the Marquise de Stainville her husband was described as 'a man who spends his day in unearthing everything that can afflict you, and who comes to tell it you every evening in transports of laughter'.[13]

These glimpses come, indeed, from a few years later and a hostile witness, Madame de Graffigny. Françoise-Paule de Graffigny, born d'Issembourg du Buisson d'Happoncourt, nicknamed La Grosse, was a catty widow-lady with theatrical interests and literary aspirations, clever with her pen indeed, amusing, capable of warm affections but apt to spoil them, a somewhat squalid, complaining, pathetic creature with rarely enough either of money or of luck. Such was the literary lady from Lorraine whom the Prince de Craon had watched performing in a court comedy at Lunéville early in 1729, who was to achieve reputation as the authoress of *Lettres d'une Péruvienne* (1747), sugary derivatives from Montesquieu's stimulating *Lettres Persanes*. More acid was her appreciation of the Marquise de Stainville whose later hospitality to the impecunious Madame de Graffigny was to give full scope to the gossip that she retailed for the amusement of her

[10] Bourcier de Villers to Marquis de Stainville, Lunéville, 29 Nov. 1733: Arch. M-et-M/Vienne, 3F 373, no. 99.
[11] Prince de Craon to Marquis de Stainville, Lunéville, 22 July 1727: Arch. M-et-M/Vienne, 3F 370, no. 134.
[12] Madame de Graffigny to Devaux, Cirey, 29 Dec. 1738: Eugène Asse, *Lettres de Mme de Graffigny*, p. 137.
[13] Madame de Graffigny, 'Portrait de Bélinde', op. cit., p. 140.

dear Panpan, otherwise François Devaux, the indolently literary son
of the Stainvilles' landlord, once, at Lunéville. Madame de Graffigny
also impinged upon the circle of Voltaire though his blue-stocking
mistress from Lorraine, the Marquise du Châtelet, came to detest
her.

Voltaire and his friends laughed at the Marquise de Stainville for
knowing all the dullest people in Paris, though the Stainville
acquaintanceship apparently came to include his own friend, the
charmingly clever Francesco Algarotti, future favourite of Frederick
the Great. The young Venetian was soon to launch his fashionable
rendering of Newtonianism for ladies. The poetical Algarotti's range
of painting, music, and mathematics was also to be that of his junior
by seven years, the Count de Stainville, if not of the count's mother.
The Marquise de Stainville, though not a stupid woman, was no
match for the Marquise du Châtelet. Madame de Stainville is said to
have sung and read aloud badly, jumbling her words. While she
seems to have had plenty of books around, she did not keep up
intellectually. So alien from her was the frivolity of the theatre that
she was said not to know what *Les Précieuses ridicules* was, or by
whom, or even what an act of a play might be. It seemed inconceivable
to Madame de Graffigny, and not to her alone. But then the Marquise
de Stainville held a low opinion of the progressivism of what she
called 'the dreary influence of this Paris of theirs (*la maussade
éducation de ce Paris-ci*)'.[14] She and her cronies took gossiping revenge
upon such as Madame du Châtelet, said to spend six hours at her
toilet if you please, 'to be dressed in Roman fashion every day of her
life and to act comedies every night',[15] not getting to bed till eight in
morning, and so extravagant and whimsical, really the most boring
person in Paris despite her gift of the gab. Madame de Stainville
could get quite red in speaking of the aggravating creature.

Another target was the Pincushion, Beatrix de Choiseul-Meuse,
who gadded around Paris with her sister Bibi, hit off by Madame de
Stainville as a feather-broom (*houssoir*), and married to Cotocco,
otherwise Joseph Eliott of Jacobite stock. The Marquise de Stainville
did have her own sister, the Marquise de Ligny, who visited her in
Paris in the summer of 1730 when she was convalescing upon quinine
from a feverish attack.

The circle of the Marquise de Stainville was not, however,
restricted to friends and relations from Lorraine. If the Prince de
Craon was proud of his 'beautiful little niece',[16] he was not her only

[14] Madame de Graffigny to Devaux, Demange-aux-Eaux, 12–13 Oct. 1738: Yale/Beinecke:
Phillipps/Graffigny 23900, vol. ii, fo. 77.   [15] Ibid., 15–20 Nov. 1738: fo. 149.
[16] Prince de Craon to Marquis de Stainville, Lunéville, 5 Mar. 1729: Arch. M-et-M/Vienne,
3F 370, no. 211.

admirer. She was, one gathers, more inclined to favour a handsome officer than a wit; but with her there were liable to be limits. She discreetly concealed the name of the wicked man who pined for her for four years in Paris. He was evidently an aristocrat, for she was great friends with both his wife and mother-in-law. The unsporting inamorata told them of her guilty adorer. Monks were mobilized to cool his ardour, though with no prompt effect.[17]

One of the admirers of the Marquise de Stainville who can now be named was the less culpable, because unmarried, Louis Charles Caesar Le Tellier, Marquis de Courtenvaux, slightly better known as the later Marshal d'Estrées, victor against the Duke of Cumberland. The then Marquis de Courtenvaux was a grandson of the great minister of war, Louvois, and a close contemporary of the Marquis de Stainville. Courtenvaux, having first served as a cavalry-officer under the Duke of Berwick in his Spanish campaign of 1719, had commanded a guard of honour at Wissembourg, the Alsatian residence of the refugee King Stanislas Leszczynski. The young colonel had so ingratiated himself that he sought the hand of the king's daughter Marie. Stanislas, unpretentious as he was, is said to have consented on condition that his prospective son-in-law should at least acquire a dukedom. But the Regent Orleans, reputedly no friend of the Louvois, had refused to oblige. Courtenvaux had to wait for that elevation for some forty years, till the administration of the Duke de Choiseul. Whereas the prospective bride within a few years found herself Queen of France. She remained loyally favourable towards her luckless lover, who was more particularly affected to her service in his capacity of Captain-Colonel of the Swiss Guard at Versailles. A keen horseman and a good shot, Courtenvaux became a member of the intimate circle of the young Louis XV in some contrast to the aged Fleury, whom Courtenvaux called Nasty Thing (*Vilain Chose*). To have such a dashing courtier for an admirer was quite a conquest by the Marquise de Stainville. Which was probably one reason why Madame de Graffigny tried to smear their relationship.

II

Madame de Graffigny followed literary fashion in working up her impressions of the Marquise de Stainville into a Portrait de Bélinde, the only available full-length study of her and of the atmosphere which she created for her husband and children. The portrait dates

[17] Cf. Madame de Graffigny to Devaux, Demange-aux-Eaux, 1 Nov. 1738: *u.s.*, fo. 116.

from some years later and one certainly needs to set it against the much more favourable assessments of the more considerable Prince de Craon. Madame de Graffigny herself admitted to painting Belinda in a fit of spite, while also maintaining 'there is not half [of what might be said] in it. There is not a word of invention in it.'[18] At all events there is usually something in what one woman says of another, especially when it is unkind.

'Belinda is a woman of quality, and the single aim of all her actions is to prove that she is a woman of quality. Envy, ambition, vanity would be her dominating passions, if it were decent for a woman of her rank to be strongly moved.'[19]

At her well served table Belinda 'would be content if a woman of quality did not need to be disdainful, and would even satisfy her appetite if there were a way of eating distinguished from that of commoners. The first of these inconveniences is easy to remove; by disdaining everything and wrangling about it with one's servants, one re-establishes oneself; but nature has rendered the second insurmountable: the shame which Belinda feels in it [eating] displays itself in her silence; her face is disturbed by it, and her embarrassment communicates itself to her guests so as to make them lose countenance; but how well Belinda indemnifies herself for the rest of the day for this little humiliation! Lying nonchalantly upon twenty cushions of down, the universe is submitted to her criticism, or rather her counsel: she teaches the powers of the earth to govern their empires; she fathoms the characters of ministers, prescribing for them the rules of politics; she takes an equal interest in all the crowned heads, and thus smooths out all the difficulties which divide them: her vast genius does not limit itself to these great objects; social circles seem to her ill assorted; she dissolves them to form others; her pains extend even to individuals. Damon is ill served; she reforms his household and gives him valets unique in their talents.'[20]

The Marquise de Stainville's friends did in fact turn to her for servants: 'Madame de Craon begs you [Stainville] to tell Madame de Stainville that she is so disgusted with chambermaids from Paris that she does not want to take any more of them' unless the Marquise could choose one herself and vouch for her 'in her own name'.[21]

The managing lady would also go on and on, one is told, about the ridiculous arrangement of a brother-in-law's house; and would 'bring

---

[18] Madame de Graffigny to Devaux, Cirey, 29 Dec. 1738: Eugène Asse, *Lettres de Mme de Graffigny*, p. 137.
[19] Madame de Graffigny, 'Portrait de Bélinde': ibid., p. 138.
[20] Ibid., p. 142.
[21] Prince de Craon to Marquis de Stainville, Lunéville, 14 June 1727: Arch. M-et-M/Vienne, 3F 370, no. 94.

the history of Confucius back to her carpenter, to a valet and a cook whom she also hates'.[22] Nor did the upper classes escape. Belinda would explain that 'Cephisa is given to magnificence but without taste; she [Belinda] amasses with infinite circumstance all the useless scraps of cotton stuff, and composes for her a furnishing of rags, in truth, but in very good taste.'[23] (Madame de Stainville evidently did have good taste in fabrics, and was a great one with her needle.) 'She teaches Araminth that it is ridiculous to have a beautiful complexion at the age of fifty, because one should begin to turn sallow at forty; and Emily that she is ill unbecomingly and that there is a decency in being ill in a certain fashion.'

In such judgements Belinda was imperfectly consistent. 'If Cleon is odious to you for having boxed his lackey's ears, do you not approve Ferragus who has killed his coachman?'[24] The Marquise's husband in fact failed to get Craon to dismiss an insolent coachman, Gabriel, who proved to be 'the faithful driver'[25] of the Countess de Rouerke, who soon came it over her brother. Stainville did have a 'wretched postillion'[26] called Michael clapped into gaol for ten days for impertinence, by virtue of a *lettre de cachet* signed by Louis XV himself. They were a maddening crew, and once at Demange, upon hearing that her coachman had been to fetch some hay without orders, the infuriated Madame de Stainville dashed to the ground 'a little bitch, which she idolizes . . . This storm . . . lasted four hours'.[27] It was one of her moods. She also knew how to sulk.

'Is there anything so agreeable as the variety of your sentiments? To what can one compare that of your conversation?' continued the apostrophe to Belinda. 'What surprising interruptions! . . . What an intrepid continuity of words! What an immense complication of false analogies in a story!'[28] She could chatter all day long, and with her, according to Madame de Graffigny, 'the last person about whom you are talking is often two thousand families away from the one who started the subject. One would need to be a fairy to connect it all.'[29] One can still catch the iterated echo of her pet expressions, 'From another angle, I can't tell you, It is nonsense.'[30]

[22] Madame de Graffigny to Devaux, Demange-aux-Eaux, 12–13 Oct. 1738: Yale/Beinecke: Phillipps/Graffigny 23900, vol. ii, fo. 77.
[23] Madame de Graffigny, 'Portrait de Bélinde', *u.s.*, pp. 142–3 and for the following.
[24] Ibid., p. 141.
[25] Prince de Craon to Marquis de Stainville, Lunéville, 5 Nov. 1726: *u.s.*, no. 51.
[26] Marquis de Stainville to Count de Maurepas, Paris, 9 May 1734: Bibliothèque de l'Arsenal, MS. Bastille 11263, fo. 99.
[27] Madame de Graffigny to Devaux, Demange-aux-Eaux, 14–16 Oct. 1738: Yale/Beinecke: Phillipps/Graffigny 23900, vol. ii, fo. 85.
[28] Madame de Graffigny, 'Portrait de Bélinde': Eugène Asse, op. cit., p. 141.
[29] Madame de Graffigny to Devaux, Demange-aux-Eaux, 14–16 Oct. 1738: *u.s.*, vol. ii, fo. 83.
[30] Ibid., 12–13 Oct. 1738: fo. 77.

How can one reconcile all these things with the uniformity of your character, with the modesty, the timidity of your deportment, the indolence of your spirit and the intensity of your heart? Ah, of what a price is a high birth; it alone can combine so many contrasts! Belinda condescends on one point; she is in some respects obliging without ostentation, but also without humanity and without friendship; this name of *friend* for men and women is nevertheless familiar to her. Glycera, her intimate friend, has been dead a week; Belinda knows and relates the least particulars of her life; ... the names of the footmen and of the dogs are even not forgotten therein; ... she comes back at last to the death of this dear friend; she has not had the time to see her during an illness of three months; she has learnt of her death unexpectedly by public report; they have taken no precaution over informing her of it; ... well, she is as touched by it as she has been by her illness.[31]

The Marquise de Stainville further displayed, in this portrait, the reverse aspect of a snob. 'Whither does not her generous care extend! The people, situated so far from her, would surely resent its effects if they could hear with what economy she prescribes for them the rules of misery; how much they should increase their work and diminish their wages in order to render themselves more agreeable and less sullen! ... Her servants do not at all like her despite the care which she ceaselessly takes to instruct them.' She was capable, if only in passing petulance, of accusing her maid of 'putting arsenic in her coffee'.[32]

'Belinda is the most unhappy woman in the world: she is of the first rank but she is not titled;[33] she is rich, but she has not got a million to put in her stocking; she is pretty but other women are more attractive than she.'[34] She did not seem to know what the words Gaity and Pleasure meant, though that in itself prevented her from being really bored. For Belinda 'plays are acted by nobodies: one exposes oneself, at a ball at the Opera, to sitting beside a washerwoman; at those at court, to blushing to see women of quality lose their air of dignity in dancing. Books are written by every kind of person; it is true that the doctors of the Church are authors of dignity, but one could not always be reading them. Magnificence in dress puts you on a level with a financier's wife; gaming on that of lackeys; softness on that of the voluptuous philosophs, who are execrable people. Cleanliness would be a perfect pleasure if some atom were not always circulating in the guise of dust.' The Marquise was depicted as 'getting seriously angry if, while sewing, one lets fall an atom of thread ... She spends her life picking them up.'[35] The recipient of

---

[31] Madame de Graffigny, 'Portrait de Bélinde': *u.s.*, pp. 141–4 for the following.
[32] Madame de Graffigny to Devaux, Demange-aux-Eaux, 22 Oct. 1738: Yale/Beinecke: Phillipps/Graffigny 23900, vol. ii, fo. 101.
[33] i.e. not a duchess: cf. p. 20.
[34] Madame de Graffigny, 'Portrait de Bélinde': *u.s.*, pp. 143–4 for the following.
[35] Madame de Graffigny to Devaux, Cirey, 29 Dec. 1738: ibid., p. 137.

this sketch, François Devaux, had himself commented earlier that she 'carries tidiness and cleanliness to the point of absurdity.'[36]

The Marquise de Stainville's unusual distaste for gallic grub and her houseproud hegemony resting upon her insipid yet overweening pride of rank might seem to match the remotely German origins of the Bassompierres. Except that she entertained a low opinion of the dreary Germans: one of the respects in which the future Choiseul was to take after her rather than react against her, as he did in so much else.

One evidently has to take the rendering of Madame de Graffigny with a pinch of salt, or drop of vinegar. She was not best placed to criticize Belinda as ungrateful, as she did in rounding off her portrait, one of the minor classics of feminine invective: 'Take good care they say, not to render a service to Belinda; she will not fail to accuse you of roguery, even to suspect you of baseness, and to overwhelm you with ridicule.'[37] If the ridicule embraced her husband, he could chuckle with a friend over an unfortunate slip of his wife's tongue which might seem to compromise her in regard to Courtenvaux. The easy-going marquis knew all about her 'gallant'.[38] In general he is described as leaving his wife the 'mistress of his property, of his expenditure, even of his conduct, but he rarely follows her advice'.[39]

The Marquise de Stainville has been noticed so early as 1728 as busy with sales of timber and with running the estates of Stainville and Demange, as also of subsidiary Illoud. Three years later she was visiting the Craons at Haroué but all too briefly for them from 'the necessity of going to Demange-aux-Eaux',[40] her future base. In Paris the marquis sought consolation in that eating which so embarrassed his wife rather than in the more conventional mistresses.

Madame de Graffigny concluded her portrait by exclaiming: 'O Belinda! How unhappy are you! Why were you born?'[41] Apart from the obvious answer, the ultimate reason is not yet known. Perhaps, though, it was intended that Choiseul should exist. Not that the Marquise de Stainville strikes one as a very fond mother even if one subtracts something from the assurance that her idea of bringing up children was 'to dress them magnificently and to hate them'.[42] To love them would be bourgeois. One of her maxims was: 'One should

[36] Devaux to Madame de Graffigny, Lunéville, autumn 1738: Yale/Beinecke: Phillipps/Graffigny 23900, vol. i, fo. 172.

[37] Madame de Graffigny, 'Portrait de Bélinde', u.s., p. 140.

[38] Madame de Graffigny to Devaux, Demange-aux-Eaux, 6 Oct. 1738: Yale/Beinecke: Phillipps/Graffigny 23900, vol. ii, fo. 66.

[39] Madame de Graffigny 'Portrait de Bélinde', u.s., p. 143.

[40] Prince de Craon to Marquis de Stainville, Haroué, 11 July 1731: Arch. M-et-M/Vienne, 3F 370, no. 248.

[41] Madame de Graffigny, 'Portrait de Bélinde', u.s., p. 144.

[42] Ibid., p. 143.

not be anxious for news of anybody.'[43] In his memoirs Choiseul did not mention his mother.

Such was the background for Stephen Francis. From his childhood there was once, at least, a supposed glimpse of him framed in a celebrated picture, the delicious *Un Jeune Élève* by François-Hubert Drouais, who specialized in painting children. The traditional identification of this roguish schoolboy, carrying an artist's portfolio, with the future Duke de Choiseul is, however, disallowed by modern scholarship on good if not comprehensively conclusive grounds.[44] Still ahead, too, lay an artistic association through Nicolas Robert, a valet of the Marquis de Stainville. Now at all events the count did become a young pupil.

III

The education of the Count de Stainville was the best to be had in France, perhaps in Europe. He was sent to school in Paris, further up the left bank from the Rue du Bac, at the famous Collège Louis-le-Grand in the Rue Saint-Jacques hard by the regularly hostile Sorbonne. Louis-le-Grand was a showpiece of the Jesuits. Founded in 1563 as the Collège de Clermont, it had primed their thrust in the counter-reformation towards reconciling religion with the new humanism of the renaissance. In 1682 the college had been refounded under its new title of royal patronage. Henceforth the golden inscription *Ludovici Magni* over its portal might seem to betoken for many of its pupils that that was indeed their entrance upon careers of high distinction in the realm of France. Louis XIV encouraged his

[43] Madame de Graffigny to Devaux, Demange-aux-Eaux, 12–13 Oct. 1738: *u.s.*, vol. ii, fo. 77.
[44] This painting by F.-H. Drouais (1727–75) was exhibited in the Paris Salon of 1761 and bore relation to that artist's *Le Petit Polisson* of 1755. In 1802 identification with Choiseul was recorded in respect of a reproduction by Pierre-François Cozette in Gobelins tapestry derived from Choiseul's seat at Chanteloup by the Musée de Tours, where it was so catalogued. This identification long prevailed, notably in Dr. Ulrich Thieme and Dr. Felix Becker, *Allgemeines Lexikon der bildenden Künstler von der Antike bis zur Gegenwert* (Leipzig, 1907f.), ix. 578; but it has been rejected by modern scholarship on obvious grounds of dating. An evaluation of this picture, known in a number of copies, and of its identification is, however, complicated by some uncertain considerations, and even a select list of sources would include: *Catalogue des tableaux anciens et modernes composant la collection de feu M. Raymond Sabatier* (Paris, 1883); Charles de Grandmaison, 'Origines du musée de Tours – provenances des tableaux' in *Réunion des Sociétés des Beaux-Arts des Départements*, 21ème session (Paris, 1897); [L.-A. Bosseboeuf] *La Touraine historique et monumentale: Amboise, le château, la ville et le canton* (Mémoires de la société archéologique de Tours. Tours, 1897); *Catalogue des tableaux anciens et modernes, objets d'art et d'ameublement composant la collection Mame de Tours* (Paris, 1904); Prosper Dorbec, 'Les Drouais' in *La Revue de l'art ancien et moderne*, vols. xvi–xvii (Paris, 1904–5); C. Gabillot, 'Les Trois Drouais' in *Gazette des beaux-arts*, 3ème période, vol. xxxiv (Paris, 1905); Diderot, *Salons*, ed. Jean Seznec and Jean Adhémar (Oxford, 1957–67), vol. i; Georges Wildenstein, 'A propos des portraits peints par François-Hubert Drouais' in *Gazette des beaux-arts*, 6ème période, vol. li (Paris, 1958); Boris Lossky, 'Les Tapisseries du Musée de Tours' in *Tours – France*, no. 35 (Tours, 1958); B. Lossky, preface to *L'Art ancien dans les collections privées de Touraine* (Tours, 1959).

courtiers to send their sons to his chosen academy, and eighty years after its renewal it could be maintained with perhaps pardonable exaggeration that 'everybody who bears a name in France dates his earliest youth from Louis-le-Grand'.[45]

The Jesuit fathers took their pupils young, sometimes as early as five. But a boy was more usually about eight or, as with little Stainville, nine years old when he first penetrated the forbidding walls of Louis-le-Grand, looming up five or six storeys high so as to capitalize a constricted site, in a condition of grimed dilapidation since money was rarely spared for repairs or cleaning even though the college was the richest in France: by 1746 its income stood at rather over 44,000 livres. A new pupil had to be conducted to the college by a parent or other responsible person, and to produce birth-certificate and references before sitting a preliminary examination to determine whether he rated higher than the lowest form, the eighth. Then he had to find his feet in classes which might range to a hundred, two hundred, three hundred boys. In the eighteenth century the whole school numbered anything up to three thousand pupils.

In this huge bear-garden there was a minority of boarders, the Convictores. These convictors or messmates ate in the first-floor refectory behind windows grilled against breakages by balls, under the eye of the headmaster, the rector, and of Our Lady of Pity as represented by Annibale Carraci, offset by a horribly repainted crucifixion. They lived, most of them, fifteen or twenty to a room: except for the élite Chambristes, rich and glorious youths each of whom enjoyed a room to himself with his own furniture, valet, and tutor.

Rich pupils were encouraged to subsidize poor ones. For though tuition was free, board and lodging were not, except for scholars, of whom there were only some thirty or forty. The impecunious scholars seem to have enjoyed a tolerably meagre existence, receiving, traditionally at least, reduced helpings at mealtimes; though the poorest, the Boursiers de Clermont, possessed scavenging rights to broken meats, candle-ends, and lost property. There were also king's scholars on a royal foundation, and the Boursiers Molony, half a dozen or more Irish scholars endowed in 1701 by John Molony, Bishop of Limerick. Thanks to the broadminded bishop they, unlike most other scholars, were not bound to study for the church but could read law or medicine. Another secular outlet for scholars had been opened up by far-sighted Colbert and his king in instituting at Louis-

---

[45] Archbishop of Paris, in 1762: cited, Gustave Dupont-Ferrier, *Du Collège de Clermont au Lycée Louis-le-Grand* (Paris, 1921–5), i. 79.

le-Grand the so-called Jeunes de Langues, young linguists, originally
Levantines, later French boys holding bursaries for Turkish and
Arabic studies to qualify them as dragomans in the French consular
and diplomatic service in the Near East. The Jeunes de Langues
were in practice chosen by the Minister of Marine, responsible for
oversea establishments, and he handsomely added a *louis d'or* to any
prize they won.

At Louis-le-Grand the Jeunes de Langues boarded in the so-called
Bâtiment des Arméniens. Boarders were under a senior master called
the Principal, but three-quarters and more of all the pupils at the
school were Externi or dayboys. Many lived nearby in cheap lodgings
supervised by another senior, the Prefect of Studies, who both
directed all the teaching and had care of dayboys. He kept in touch
over homework with the parents of the boys who lived at home, as
might seem an economical arrangement for the Count de Stainville,
coming from so close; though there is some contrary suggestion from
his start at school, when his parents were away from Paris.

Soon after young Stainville arrived in the capital he had been
entered at Louis-le-Grand. In the bad year of 1729, when his parents
were confronting adversity in Lorraine and their house in the Rue
du Bac was occupied by Baron von Pfütschner, the latter had taken
a little time off from his diplomatic mission. Pfütschner, formerly a
tutor and the son of a schoolmaster at Würzburg, began a letter to the
Marquis de Stainville on 5 September 1729: 'I have been to see your
son at the college. I found him in fairly good health apart from a
cough, which deserves attention and care. He told me that he was
going on holiday, which is no small thing for young people who are
shut up the rest of the year.'[46]

Once again in the boyhood of the future Choiseul one has an
impression of delicate health causing his parents rather less concern
than others. A summer cough sounds a little ominous at Louis-le-
Grand. The freezing cold there in winter, with classrooms and chapel
innocent of any heating, seems to have been among the poignant
recollections of its pupils even in that robust age, even though lucky
Chambristes, for instance, might fit double windows. Little Stainville
may have been one of them for that summer at least, when his parents
had left him behind at school. The boy was served by a faithful valet
who was to be a sad loss two years later. From a few years earlier one
is assured that 'Brother du Soleil, apothecary of the college, has a
perfect knowledge of the illnesses of children'.[47] This matched the

---

[46] Baron von Pfütschner to Marquis de Stainville, Paris, 5 Sept. 1729: Arch. M-et-M/Vienne,
3F 372, no. 194.
[47] Germain Brice, op. cit., ii. 295.

mainly admirable pedagogy of Father de Jouvancy's *De ratione discendi et docendi*, which enjoined teachers to remember in dealing with pupils that 'the blood of Christ is consecrated, beneath a human form, in these little bodies'.[48]

Stephen de Stainville now found himself almost in a masculine microcosm of his time. Most of the pupils naturally came from Paris but there were plenty of others, provincial lads including southerners who, one is told, tried to shed their accents there. Colonials came from Canada and, in particular, the rich West Indies. Among the cosmopolitan connections there was a good number of English-speaking boys, especially from Ireland and London, especially catholics no doubt, although the proselytizing Jesuits did not exclude protestants – or Jansenists. Louis-le-Grand maintained an active interest in Jesuit missions from Peking to Ecuador. Father Charlevoix, the historian of young Stainville's grandfather in Saint Domingo, had gone from Louis-le-Grand to become professor in Quebec. The worldwide outlook at Stainville's school was reinforced by an occasional pupil from Russia or China. This mixture was not only national but also social.

The Jesuits traditionally worked through the upper crust of society and Louis-le-Grand was not short of the right names, Conti, La Rochefoucauld, Luxembourg, Richelieu, Broglie, shading off into the administrative nobility, Amelot de Chaillou, Machault d'Arnouville, with the Marquis de Stainville's friend, the Count d'Argenson and his elder brother, the marquis, also René-Nicolas de Maupeou, who was largely to bring the future Choiseul down. The school reflected the hierarchic structure of that age of privilege including the occasional anomaly of one boy of fourteen who was Grand Prior of Malta, or an eleven-year-old Bishop of Metz.

Louis-le-Grand also encompassed another, broader tradition. It had produced Molière. If Cardinal Fleury was an old boy, so was Voltaire. Even then there was a considerable amount of social interplay in French education. In any social study of the French aristocracy in the eighteenth century the youthful connections formed at Louis-le-Grand are apt to repay attention not only as cementing individuals into the aristocratic establishment but also as indicating the extent, perhaps not always appreciated, to which the more intelligent young aristocrats at any rate formed personal contacts with quite different classes of society. This was certainly the case with the Count de Stainville, so different from his mother. One is assured that from his boyhood, while proudly aware of his quality,

---

[48] Father de Jouvancy, *De ratione discendi et docendi*, part II, chap. iii, art. 3: cited, G. Dupont-Ferrier, op. cit. i. 59.

he yet displayed 'that gentle and kind simplicity which is only concerned to make those of inferior rank forget that imposing and awkward effect which higher rank may sometimes produce in society'.[49]

Stephen de Stainville was at school with numbers of other young noblemen whose careers were subsequently to be interwoven, more or less, with his own. He overlapped at Louis-le-Grand with one destined to be his immediate predecessor as foreign minister, the later Cardinal de Bernis, then a star pupil with his quick facility. Stainville also coincided with a future prime antagonist of his foreign ministry, the headstrong Count de Broglie, younger son of that ambassador in London who had disparaged the mission of the Marquis de Stainville. Yet at Louis-le-Grand at that period at least three-quarters of the pupils from Paris were drawn from bourgeois, or poorer, families. Nor were the provincials all from châteaux. One of the Count de Stainville's schoolfriends was the son of a goldsmith at Quimper; young Élie Fréron was a year and a half older than Stainville and a novice in the Jesuit order. In after years Choiseul defended to prickly Voltaire his literary patronage of Fréron 'with whom I was at college without any extreme familiarity (he was however a Jesuit and I a schoolboy without having had smallpox)'.[50] The precise significance of the parenthesis remains equivocal; in later life Choiseul the ladykiller did not escape some suggestion of effeminacy. Sodomy at Louis-le-Grand had been alleged in 1708[51] but Voltaire himself, who specialized in such accusations, looked back to his education there 'for seven years among men who take gratuitous and indefatigable pains to form the minds and morals of youth'.[52]

Intellectually the twenty or so teachers at Louis-le-Grand were the élite of an élite. Few in proportion to pupils, they might be helped out by the Étudiants Scolastiques, senior graduates usually in their later twenties. From their number had emerged Bourdaloue, the great preacher (a professor at Louis-le-Grand at twenty-four), and Belzunce, that bishop of Marseilles, soon to be joined by a religious renegade, the poet Gresset, another literary name to be linked with that of Stainville.

Teaching and research went together at Louis-le-Grand, as at a university. Father de Jouvancy had warned against teachers going

---

[49] 'Essay sur la vie de M. le duc de Choiseul': Bibliothèque de l'Arsenal, MS. 5808 (henceforth cited as Essai/Arsenal 5808), fo. 8.

[50] Duke de Choiseul to Voltaire, Versailles, 16 June 1760: P. Calmettes, op. cit., p. 98.

[51] Cf. René Pomeau, *La Religion de Voltaire* (Paris, 1956), p. 41.

[52] Voltaire to Father de La Tour, c. 1 April 1746: *Voltaire's Correspondence*, ed. Theodore Besterman (Geneva, 1953f.), xv. 37.

stale and at Louis-le-Grand they could enjoy sabbatical spells with
the research side, the Scriptores Librorum whom pupils could also
consult. Specialization was still happily relative. Of the then masters
Father Bougeant was a theologian, physician, and poet besides
holding the chair of history, wherein he was a particular authority on
the Peace of Westphalia. Father Brumoy was a mathematician, a
hellenist noted for his translations of Greek plays, and a poet in his
own right. Hailing himself from Quimper, it was probably Brumoy
who brought in young Fréron, already heading towards a literary
career. The boy 'was passionately fond of poetry, and Father Brumoy
did but inflame this ardour'.[53] Louis-le-Grand was famous for its
library of nearly fifty thousand volumes deriving from the benefaction
of Nicholas Fouquet, the sumptuous Superintendent of Finances
under Louis XIV. Books are not everything with most schoolboys
and the Count de Stainville may well have been already laying the
foundation of his later reputation according to which 'he read little,
but never forgot anything that he had read'.[54] His lively intelligence
and personality were already bringing him to notice. An early
authority wrote of the Count de Stainville in boyhood: 'Gayer, more
amiable, wittier than the others, these happy qualities procured him
the little successes of his age; from that time simplicity accompanied
all his actions; he was not vainer of these advantages than he was
subsequently dazzled by the brilliance of his [political] favour.'[55]

Throughout life Stainville carried off his superiority with gay
insouciance; and, especially, with what his contemporaries called
simplicity, with naturalness. He was acute yet open, artful without
affectation, always an aristocrat, never a snob. He was intensely
himself.

Such a character, exempt from any profundity of religious belief,
might not take kindly to all aspects of Jesuit discipline at Louis-le-
Grand with its emphasis upon Christian observance including
frequent communion. The chill classrooms were decorated with
religious pictures. In after years the Count de Stainville generally
avoided them, especially cruel crucifixions, in forming his own art-
collection, of which he was to write to a friend: 'You know ... how
strong is my aversion from holy subjects. There are sometimes some
agreeable ones which might find favour with me, but they are rare.'[56]

The alienation from the Jesuits of the future Duke de Choiseul was

[53] Élie Fréron, Paris, 10 Jan. 1774, in Fréron, L'Année littéraire (Paris, 1774), i. 7.
[54] Baron von Gleichen, Denkwürdigkeiten des Barons Carl Heinrich von Gleichen (Leipzig,
1847: henceforth cited as Gleichen), p. 65.
[55] Essai/Arsenal 5808, fo. 9.
[56] Count de Stainville to Duke de Nivernais, 21-2 Sept. 1749: White Notley Archives
(henceforth cited as W.N.A.), docket V/1, fo. 12.

not only artistic. If he was later to evince contemptuous disgust for the underhand intrigue of the court of Louis XV, he already had to reckon with schoolmates distinguished as Syndics, licensed sneaks who reported to the Jesuits whatever was afoot among their classmates. But if discipline was in principle severe, including corporal punishment, it was largely lax in practice in the style of much of the old regime in France. Courtiers were trained under Jesuit emphasis upon emulation, upon competition spiced with judicious flattery of success. And, more deeply, the religious teaching itself tended to acknowledge if not actually strengthen the human spirit of the age.

The catechism in use at Louis-le-Grand was an adaptation of the best-selling one by the Jesuit Father Canisius. This limpid formulary played down original sin, the fall and the redemption, hellfire and that divine strictness preached by gloomy Jansenists. This open faith of rational optimism under an all-loving God already looked towards the eighteenth-century deism of Voltaire and inferentially of Choiseul in his ethic of pleasured happiness. The benign Jesuits, in compromising with an ascendent humanism, were training up not friends alone but also future enemies of their religion. Such is the logic of the law of let go.

The emphasis at Louis-le-Grand was not only upon book-learning and constant Latin (to the considerable neglect of Greek) but also upon that general intelligence, style and accomplishment which befits an educated gentleman. A central figure here, with his strong nose and wavy hair, was the winning professor of rhetoric, Father Porée, probably the best teacher of them all for his 'dearest boys (*pueri amantissimi*)'.[57] Porée was beloved and admired even by Voltaire, which few Jesuits were. One of Porée's later pupils was the Count de Stainville. Another, two years Stainville's junior, was Malesherbes, who was to do much to liberalize French literature and to earn the Duke de Choiseul's subsequent encomium: 'He has the simplicity of an honest man.'[58]

Porée encouraged his pupils to debate, often upon practical subjects of current controversy such as the merits of scientific careers or the most equitable way to bequeath one's fortune. Father Porée actually approved of the light touch of the French in light matters, of their predilection for the fine arts, for comfort and subtle cooking. There was a tendency at Louis-le-Grand to make fun of learned German dry-as-dusts with latinized names like Goetzius or Opitius with his solomonic candlestick. Such a tone was congenial to young Stainville.

[57] Cited, R. Pomeau, loc. cit.
[58] Choiseul, 'Mémoires inédits', 3/30/16/950/1.

Father Porée was central to the climax of the year at Louis-le-Grand, the Latin play performed at prize-giving about the beginning of every August. He was a relentless rehearser for the lavish performance, which was one of the social events in the Parisian calendar. Porée urged that by encouraging boys to act 'you transport your pupils from the dust of the schools to the brilliant school of the theatre, to instruct in good time those youths who are one day to play important roles in the state'.[59] Porée himself composed many of the Latin tragedies performed by his pupils, but he could not feel quite happy about the frivolity of their performing the ballets, including recitations in French, which interspersed the Latin plays in the manner of the time: more particularly since the school habitually secured some of the leading actors from the Opera to coach the boys and even appear with them. But these ballets at Louis-le-Grand had appealed to its monarchical patron and remained much more of a popular attraction than the Latin plays, even, one gathers, to some pious parents who, like the Marquise de Stainville, did not hold with the Opera. Propaganda was, after all, a word of catholic origin. So came it that on 1 August 1731 Count Stephen de Stainville was dancing in the ballet *L'Empire de la mode*.[60]

The empire of fashion was an appropriate medium for what was possibly the first public appearance of the future Duke de Choiseul, to be described by Talleyrand as governing France by the despotism of fashion.[61] The ballet sounds like a lively piece in the tradition of Louis-le-Grand. Six years earlier had been the stir of that ballet, Theseus and Hippolytus, calling for no less than fourteen female parts, classical ladies though they were. Then there was that other, *Le Monde malade*, wherein the world had appeared splendidly arrayed in maps with Italy for a leg, Germany the belly, France the heart, and his bottom boldly inscribed *Terra australis incognita*.

The performers in these spectacles received an early experience of publicity since they were regularly written up in the *Mercure de France*, written down in the Jansenist *Nouvelles ecclésiastiques*, which deplored the 'excess to which pomp, tumult, immodesties, dissipation'[62] were carried in the ballets. But the highest in the land came to watch in the elaborate theatre erected in the main quadrangle with tenting strung over the auditorium as a protection against sun but not rain so that it was said that for days before the performance all

[59] Charles Porée, *Caroli Porée e Societate Jesu sacerdotis orationes* (Paris, 1735), iii. 145: cited, J. de la Servière, *Le Père Charles Porée S.J.* (Paris, 1899), p. 94.
[60] Cf. reference Choiseul-Stainville in Fiches Dupont-Ferrier: Archives du Lycée Louis-le-Grand.
[61] Cf. p. 3 above.
[62] Review in *Nouvelles ecclésiastiques*, cited, J. de la Servière, op. cit., p. 92.

noses at Louis-le-Grand were in the air, snuffing the weather. On the day the Chambristes, whose windows were often the boxes, laid on elegant collations while others tucked in to the buffet provided by the good fathers, complete with cold drinks, burgundy, and champagne. It is on record that when the Latin play came on after the ballet the ruder part of the audience used to signify their boredom by noisily swigging their liquid refreshment and other unseemly demonstrations.

The Count de Stainville may well have made the most of his early theatrical contacts, like others. The Jesuits could largely have been to blame for any note of criticism in Madame de Graffigny's observation some years later that young Stainville was addicted to the light theatre. Jesuit education primed the great vogue in eighteenth-century France for private theatricals, which were then beginning to include sketches in a rabelaisian form of farce or satirical anti-theatre called Parades.[63] The Marquise de Stainville most likely disapproved of her son's penchant as she would also of his association with such a one as Fréron – as for Gresset, she dismissed him as a 'little fool (*petit sot*)'.[64] But then Stephen was to deviate from his mother's ideas of propriety in quite a number of respects. To perform, however, in the ballet at Louis-le-Grand was, one gathers, a distinction usually reserved for boys marked out by high birth or superior attainment. Possibly young Stainville qualified on both counts.

IV

The fathers of Louis-le-Grand are said to have perceived the quick intelligence of the Count de Stainville and to have taken special pains with him. Certainly he later displayed that subtle and penetrating turn of mind associated with Jesuit tuition. We are told that the Jesuits wanted to keep Stainville, like Voltaire before him, for their own order, holding out prospects of speedy ecclesiastical preferment, which with them spelt power. A life of religious pacifism and celibacy was not, however, quite in Stainville's line. He left that to his younger brother Leopold Charles, who succeeded him at Louis-le-Grand and was probably the Stainville, rather than Stephen, mentioned as dancing in the *Ballet de Mars* in August 1735, the year that the Jesuits packed the house out by engaging the great tenor from the Opera, Pierre Jélyotte.

Stephen de Stainville's own career was to run not so much with the

63 Cf. Jacques Scherer, *Théâtre et anti-théâtre au XVIIIᵉ siècle* (Oxford, 1975), pp. 19f.
64 Madame de Graffigny to Devaux, Demange-aux-Eaux, 1 Nov. 1738: Yale/Beinecke: Phillipps/Graffigny 23900, vol. ii, fo. 116.

Jesuits as against them. He was to be the power in the land when they were evicted from his old school. Whereas the present prime authority, another former pupil, was its protector. Cardinal Fleury kept well in touch. On the teaching he was to pronounce that Father Brumoy possessed 'more solidity and less frivolity'[65] than Father Bougeant. The cardinal likely kept an eye upon promising pupils also. He was quickly aware that little Stephen de Stainville was in fact orientated in the tradition of a nobleman's eldest son towards the call of arms.

On 26 June 1730 the Marquis de Stainville began a letter in his own hand to Duke Francis of Lorraine:

Monseigneur, As I find myself saddled with a large family I ought to think about providing for them, but I do not want to take any step without having previously obtained the approval of Your Royal Highness. I have a son here at the College who is eleven years old. Some time ago the Cardinal de Fleury spoke to me of this and asked me whether I was not thinking of placing him in the service of the King [of France], to which I replied that he had the honour to be a subject of Your Royal Highness: that it was consequently for you to dispose of him.

At this [continued Stainville], the cardinal told me that if I had a mind to have him serve in this country it was time to think of it, and that he would be delighted to shew his friendship for me by getting him a position forthwith in the train of a foreign regiment [in the French army], so that on leaving College he would have enough seniority to obtain the satisfaction of purchasing [a regimental commission]. He said that he had even thought of placing him as a lieutenant in the train of Royal Allemand.[66]

The marquis thanked the benevolent cardinal and now put it to the duke: 'If it were incompatible for him to serve the king and Your Royal Highness, I should take good care not to think of it, but what I shall be doing will only serve to place my son in a better position to render his very humble services to Your Royal Highness, who will always be the master to dispose of him as of myself and all my family.' Stainville further asked that, if Francis agreed, he should 'write a line of recommendation' to Fleury since the marquis wished 'to owe only to my master the favour which may be granted me here'.

The Marquis de Stainville for once received a prompt reply, in a postscript to that despatch of 29 June 1730 wherein Duke Francis thanked him for his successful exertions over levies in the Barrois:[67] 'P.S. I have seen from the one which was delivered to me by Grobert,

---

[65] Cardinal Fleury to Cardinal de Tencin, 5 Jan. 1740: in *Mémoires du Président Hénault*, ed. Baron de Vigan (Paris, 1855: henceforth cited as Hénault), p. 292.

[66] Marquis de Stainville to Duke Francis III, Paris, 26 June 1730: Arch. M-et-M/Vienne, 3F 86, no. 95, and for the following.

[67] Cf. p. 122 above: Duke Francis III to Marquis de Stainville, Lunéville, 29 June 1730: Arch. M-et-M/Vienne, 3F 362, no. 120.

who arrived last night, that Cardinal de Fleury is shewing himself well disposed towards you and in particular towards your eldest son. I wish you at the first opportunity to notify him [Fleury] that I have learnt of it with pleasure and that, in the interest that I take in what concerns you, I shall be very obliged to him for what he will kindly be doing to oblige you.'

If Francis characteristically avoided writing himself to Fleury, the reply was fully gracious. No time was lost in acting upon it. Five days later, on 4 July 1730, the Count de Stainville was gazetted a 'Lieutenant on half pay in the train of the Royal Allemand Regiment of Cavalry'[68] appropriate to a Lorrainer.

In the long reign of King Louis XV the two leading statesmen, in eminence and in tenure of office, were the Cardinal Fleury and the Duke de Choiseul. It now transpires that the first personally recruited the second for the service of France. Ultimately, this was not the least significant of the cardinal's stealthy acts of policy. It was validated by that postscript from a future Holy Roman Emperor, clearing the way for Choiseul to serve France rather than Austria.

The hinges of history are often countersunk. For the present the little lieutenant was too young to serve in what he called 'the war of 1733'.[69]

[68] Pinard, *Chronologie historique-militaire* (Paris, 1760f.), v. 685.
[69] Choiseul, *Mémoires*, p. 3.

CHAPTER VII

ABDICATION

I

THE War of the Polish Succession, chiefly France supported by Spain against Austria backed by Russia, was a war of old men, certainly in the west where the main operations were cautiously dragged out. In the Rhineland this was deliberate French policy, some said,[1] so as not to provoke the intervention of Holland and, especially, England, uneasily neutral after all, to Austrian indignation. Part of this pattern was picked out for the Marquis de Stainville by a friend, Count Frederick Harrach; he had lately succeeded a Visconti as prime minister of the Austrian Netherlands, 'where we are enjoying a false neutrality which France has concluded only with a view to gobbling us up last. It is to be hoped, however, that the Maritime Powers will finally open their eyes.'[2]

In the field delimited, Prince Eugene, seventy now and past his victorious prime, failed with his 100,000 imperial troops to prevent Philippsburg from falling to the French. During the protracted siege the French lost their sixtythree-year-old commander, the Duke of Berwick. He was succeeded by old d'Asfeld, another tired general. Five days after Berwick's death came that of the other chief French commander, the octogenarian Marshal-General de Villars (June 1734), who had been operating in the second main theatre of the western warfare, in Italy. There an array of French, Spanish and Sardinian forces bore witness to Chauvelin's deftness in whipping up a coalition to further his favourite designs against Austria in Italy. It was, however, a lopsided combination since nothing would induce Spain and Sardinia, both separately allied to France, to come together. Both, in particular, coveted strategic Mantua. Nevertheless the jealous Latin armies, especially the Spaniards under Don Carlos, did well against the thinly spread Austrians. Elizabeth Farnese having for years badgered Europe for Italian principalities for her sons, Charles and Philip, the elder, baulked of marriage to Maria Theresa, now conquered from Austria for himself the Kingdom of the Two

---

[1] Cf. Lord Harvey, *Some Materials towards Memoirs of the Reign of George II*, ed. R. Sedgwick (London, 1931), ii. 333 and 338.

[2] Count Frederick Harrach to Marquis de Stainville, Brussels, 9 Jan. 1734: Arch. M-et-M/Vienne, 3F 373, no. 108.

Sicilies. There Don Carlos founded that Bourbon dynasty which was to endure till Italy united more than a century later. Such were the rich firstfruits for the house of Bourbon of that Treaty of the Escurial, provoked by the Polish war, wherein France and Spain had on 7 November 1733, in terms unpublished for over a century, concluded 'a perpetual and irrevocable family compact',[3] destined to figure as the First Family Compact. The tilt against Austria of the balance of power in Italy was the most notable event of the warfare in the west: that and, for the first time in history, the appearance upon the Rhine of Russian forces. They symbolized the significance of the Austro-Russian alliance in furthering the emergence of Russia as a new and heavy factor in European politics.

In the east the Austro-Russian combination dominated the situation in Poland itself, permanently the geopolitical flaw in Europe. The trouble there had started this time with the death in February 1733 of King Augustus the Strong, strong especially in amorous prowess so that reputedly his last words were, 'My whole life was an unceasing sin, God have mercy on me.'[4] The year before, secret Russian negotiations with France had broken down owing to French reluctance to buy Russian alliance and support for the succession in Poland of Stanislas, the French king's father-in-law, at the price of rectifying the eastern frontiers of Poland to the advantage of Russia and of recognizing her sovereignty in the Baltic regions of Courland. (If this was the first time that such a situation arose between Russia and the west, it was not to be the last.) Russia resumed her germanic orientation under Ostermann and Münnich (veteran of Oudenarde and Malplaquet), the able advisers in foreign and military affairs of the sadistic Empress Anne (1730–40), herself from Courland like her smooth favourite, Biren. By 1733 she was at one with Austria in supporting Frederick Augustus of Saxony to succeed his father as King of Poland in opposition to Stanislas, re-elected king in Warsaw with Polish national backing that September. Stanislas cut down his stay there to a fortnight since the Russians under the Irish General Lacy were already marching into Poland and next month imposed his Saxon rival as King Augustus III, who had to concede Courland to Biren as a fief. Stanislas was chased to Danzig, besieged and later blockaded by a Russian fleet commanded by the Jacobite Admiral Gordon. The weakness of France in those eastern parts was more emphasized than masked by the personal initiative of the valiant Count de Plélo, French Minister at

---

[3] Article 14 of the Treaty of the Escurial, 7 Nov. 1733: Don Alejandro del Cantillo, *Tratados, convenios y declaraciones de paz y de commercio* (Madrid, 1843), p. 281.

[4] Cited Prof. W. Konopczyński in *The Cambridge History of Poland 1697–1935* (Cambridge, 1941), p. 24.

Copenhagen, in landing a diminutive French contingent at Danzig where he fell at the head of his troops in a hopeless assault against the lines of Field-Marshal Münnich in May 1734. This romantic incident, one of the few from that flattish stretch of European history, marked the first occasion upon which French troops fought Russians.

Almost throughout the war, however, there was much more going on at hidden levels of diplomacy than met the eye upon the military surface. In this the War of the Polish Succession was typical of the eighteenth century and in particular of those limited conflicts which marked the period between the wars of the Spanish and of the Austrian successions. While ancient generals were manoeuvring in the classic theatres of western warfare, the octogenarian Cardinal Fleury was conducting a diplomatic campaign of subtlety and scope. In this high diplomacy the duchy of Lorraine was a pawn of central significance in pursuance, still, of his opening gambit of seven years ago to the Marquis de Stainville.

II

Kehl and Philippsburg, the French captures in the Rhineland, lie directly east of Lorraine. It went almost without saying that in the War of the Polish Succession French forces as usual overran the neutral duchy. Indeed during the summer of impending hostilities the Count de Belle-Isle, the French military commandant of the three bishoprics, had reported of a visit to Lunéville that the Regent of Lorraine told him that 'she quite expected'[5] as much. Nevertheless when friendly Verneuil, a French royal secretary, was subsequently sent to prepare her for the occupation, he reported: 'She said to me, crying, *Well, Verneuil, so you have come to deceive me.* This beginning of the conversation was followed by the liveliest and longest succession of reproaches, complaints and tears that I have ever heard.'[6] The position of the unhappy Verneuil was not improved by the fact that the regent had not been informed of the Marquis de Stainville's secret counter-declaration to the French guarantee of neutrality in 1728.

In the words of the chronicler:

The war continued and the winters were employed only in preparations for the spring. Lorraine, always crossed or occupied by troops, was again constrained to divers services; the least delays were attributed to ill will. Madam the Regent had no respite; she had at Paris the Marquis de Stainville ... They demanded a million

[5] Count (later Marshal) de Belle-Isle to Chauvelin, 20 June 1733. Cited, P. Boyé, op. cit., p. 335.
[6] Verneuil to Chauvelin, Nancy, 15 Oct. 1733: Arch. Aff. Étr. C.P., Lorraine, vol. 125, fo. 105.

rations of hay for conveyance to Landau and Neustadt. During the time that the convoys and wagons of Lorraine were in full march and ready to arrive at their destination, the French troops made a movement which compelled a reversal of the wagons so as to direct them upon the Saar. Our labourers thereby lost a good part of their horses, their carts and harness, which caused a great evil to agriculture.[7]

In these straits the spirited French princess who had Lorraine in her protection did her utmost to defend the little duchy against French exactions. It was the Marquis de Stainville who, as his friend Bourcier foresaw, had to present 'the frequent complaints which Madam Her Royal Highness will be obliged to have conveyed'[8] to the French ministers ranged against them in some graduation of hostility.

If Stainville was friendly enough with Fleury, aloof at the top, so was he also with his most immediate interlocutor as Minister of War, the decent Marquis d'Angervilliers. In months of stubborn argument Stainville whittled down the million rations of fodder to 600,000, to 500,000, to 171,550 and, by April 1735, to only half that number. But so soon as one demand was successfully resisted another was liable to be raised upon a different basis or for other supplies. While fodder was the sinew of land-warfare in that age, timber for shipbuilding was of special interest to the Count de Maurepas. Or it was props for siegeworks and the like.

'On Thursday', reported the Marquis de Stainville on 20 February 1734, 'I had a fairly long interview with M. d'Angervilliers whereat we disputed the matter of the palisades. Our conversation was very lively and I repeated to him several times that never would Your Royal Highness consent to the exorbitant supply demanded from your estates; that you would rather suffer that the king should resort to violence, but that it was impossible for you to consent, during your regency, to their ruining your country.'[9] Stainville, however, had been warned by Belle-Isle that utter obduracy would be useless:

Finally it was agreed that Lorraine will be asked only for the seventy thousand palisades which was asked for in the first place without there being any question either of others or of firs ... During our conference M. Duverney, apparently informed by the minister, arrived and asked to join in our conversation; he said that in a little while he would need many carts in Lorraine for the transport of provisions ... I went yesterday to see the keeper of the seals who, with much more liveliness than the other [d'Angervilliers], complained that, by the refusal which Your Royal

---

[7] Durival, op. cit., ii. 143–4.
[8] Bourcier de Villers to Marquis de Stainville, Lunéville, 29 Nov. 1733: Arch. M-et-M/Vienne, 3F 373, no. 99.
[9] Marquis de Stainville to Regent of Lorraine, 20 Feb. 1734: Ö.S./H.H.S., Lothringisches Hausarchiv 202/III 503 (Nachlass Stainville), cited, P. Boyé, op. cit., p. 284, n. 1.

Highness had made to the supply of wood and palisades, the service of the king had suffered.[10]

The Keeper of the Seals of France was Chauvelin, also foreign minister and, largely, director of her war-effort. A month earlier the Marquis de Stainville had explained: 'The keeper of the seals has taken in one of the clerks of the war office and, at the same time, has secured cognizance of all military matters, which causes M. d'Angervilliers very great discontent. It is even believed that he might well quit.'[11]

Chauvelin was a clever, hostile man, apt to be an unpleasant person to do business with: not one to lighten Stainville's ungrateful task of continually arguing against the law of the strongest: in Lorraine 'the hay has almost all failed this year, and the little which remains is nearly rotted by the continual rain ... If the peasant is deprived of the possibility of feeding the horses it will not be possible for him, in case of need, to perform the convoys which will be demanded of him for the king's service, and he could not even cultivate his land.'[12] Perhaps, though, that would even be in accordance with French policy. For behind Chauvelin again there stood an even grimmer enemy of Lorraine.

A rather rare glimpse into the penetralia of French policy at the outbreak of the War of the Polish Succession is afforded by a letter which had been addressed to Chauvelin by the rough and honest Orry, French controller-general since 1730:

Pay attention to my representations. Do not think that I am talking to you only as controller-general, but as a good citizen and a man concerned for your glory ... Can you indeed flatter yourself as to engaging the Duke of Lorraine in a perfect neutrality by all kinds of regards. Of course not and I am fully persuaded that you do not think so ... He would dishonour himself and would be of all men the most ungrateful; but I am dying for fear lest, if we spare him, ... he may spice the real help in cash which he will be giving the Emperor with stinging jests against us, and that the whole of Europe will find them well founded. In God's name think about your decision. Otherwise you will no longer be in time to take it.[13]

Orry explained the urgency in an enclosed memorandum pointing out that taxation in Lorraine was concentrated in the subvention levied soon after martinmas 'so that here we are on the eve of seeing perhaps two or three millions brought into the coffers of the Duke of Lorraine ... We have a great interest in weakening him and depriving him of resources ... So let us put it beyond his power to subsidize

---

[10] Ibid., partly cited *u.s.*
[11] Marquis de Stainville to Duke Francis III, 25 Jan. 1734: ibid., cited, *u.s.*, p. 200.
[12] Marquis de Stainville to Chauvelin, Paris, 7 July 1734: ibid.
[13] Orry to Chauvelin, Paris, 3 Nov. 1733: Arch. Nat. K 1185 (Monuments historiques), no. 8.

men, and in the name of the Emperor to buy those of Prussia or any other power.'[14] To this end the enterprising Orry even proposed that, after providing for the regular expenses of the household of the Regent of Lorraine, 'all the surplus of the revenues should be placed in the hands of a treasurer chosen and nominated by the King, and that tomorrow if possible, so that it be put as though under sequestration'. If this radical takeover was in the event eschewed, one perceives the purposeful policy now behind Orry's further proposals for quartering French cavalry upon Lorraine, requisitioning forage at a low price, commandeering local transport – all the exactions against which the Marquis de Stainville had to struggle. And if he denounced them as exorbitant, that was because they were meant to be.

This was the very face, to landward, of economic warfare in the eighteenth century, less ostentatious but hardly less grim that the cruel battlefields of martial panoply. To strip a little neutral down and cripple it financially – such were the realities behind an ornate façade. 'But, it will be said, we did not behave like that towards Lorraine in the last war. To which I reply', proceeded the relentless Orry, 'that ... that time the Duke of Lorraine stayed quietly in his possessions. This one is at the court of the Emperor ... Has not his marriage with a daughter of the Emperor been announced?' Meanwhile Francis was actually filling in time at Pressburg in Habsburg service as 'Lieutenant-General of Hungary, an office or dignity created and invented for him'[15] upon his return from a grand tour, explained Toussaint to Stainville.

It was all very well for Duke Francis to express to his mother, as he did, his astonishment 'that the ministers in France are always throwing in Stainville's face the fact that I am outside my possessions, and that from this they draw a pretext for maltreating Lorraine, for I have no intention of doing anything contrary to my neutrality ... It is the fable of the wolf and the lamb. It suffices that I should give no cause for such conduct.'[16] His afflicted subjects may have thought otherwise. His mother certainly did.

The Regent of Lorraine bombarded Cardinal Fleury with expostulations in her own vile handwriting and worse spelling: 'Shall it be said in the world that a Granddaughter of France ...'[17] etcetera

[14] Orry, memorandum of 3 Nov. 1733, 'Reflexions de M^r. Orry sur les subsides levées en Lorraine par l'empereur': ibid., no. 9, and for the following.
[15] Baron Toussaint to Marquis de Stainville, Holy Mount near Olmütz, 12 Apr. 1732: Arch. M-et-M/Vienne, 3F 373, no. 15.
[16] Duke Francis III to Regent of Lorraine, Pressburg, 28 Mar. 1734: ibid., no. 225.
[17] Regent of Lorraine to Cardinal Fleury, Lunéville, 8 Sept. 1735: Arch. Aff. Étr. C.P., Lorraine, vol. 126, fo. 136.

in an indignant flow of rhetorical questioning. Sometimes that staunch lady might indeed muddle Stainville's complex negotiations, impatiently goading him into explaining that he was but striving diplomatically to spare Lorraine still worse. In dealing with the French it was not, he assured her, 'that in my reiterated remonstrances I have not used the term Impossibility, but unhappily all my remonstances have been useless . . . The worst is that when one does not succeed, the fault is indubitably imputed to us.'[18] Stainville meant, imputed by Duke Francis, the baneful absentee.

The Marquis de Stainville kept arguing away, with appreciable success, in his obstinate efforts to alleviate his stricken homeland, haggling for instance with the brothers Pâris over exacted transport: 'I felt that it was better worth to accept three sols [per cart], currency of Lorraine, ready cash, than to await payment for the carts in French currency for ten years and perhaps more.'[19] Though such accounts were in any case to remain outstanding for more like twenty years in the dilatatory diplomacy of that age. For the present it was the most gruelling and most creditable phase of Stainville's diplomatic career.

III

If Stainville disputed supplies with French functionaries he also discussed policy with Fleury, who largely left the dirty work to others, expecially aggressive Chauvelin. While the lesser ministers, however, were vexing Lorraine with their exactions the cardinal himself was softly exploiting the fortunes of war so as to call in question the very existence of the duchy in accordance with that minatory hint which Stainville had pretended not to hear, years ago.

In the earlier part of 1732 Stainville had further reported a delicate discussion with the cardinal about the balance of power in Europe prospectively to an imperial marriage for Francis. Stainville, almost in echo of Duke Leopold's representations to Fleury, sought to assure the latter that 'all the Emperor's views are only directed towards maintaining this balance in order to allow a perpetual peace to reign. "But", the cardinal finally answered me, "it is impossible that your master should hold on to Lorraine." "What then", I said to him, "do you want him to do with it?" After a slight pause he replied to me: "That he should relinquish it to his brother"',[20] Prince Charles. That

---

[18] Marquis de Stainville to Regent of Lorraine, 20 Aug. 1735: Ö.S./H.H.S., Lothringisches Hausarchiv 202/III 503 (Nachlass Stainville).

[19] Ibid., 3 Dec. 1734.

[20] Marquis de Stainville to Duke Francis III, spring 1732: cited, F. Hennings, *Und sitzet zur linken Hand*, p. 155.

was the course favoured at Lunéville where, reported the Count de Belle-Isle in the following year, 'they quite anticipate that the Duke of Lorraine cannot keep Lorraine when he shall have become son-in-law to the Emperor'.[21] Fleury, however, had not discarded his earlier, starker suggestion of French acquisition.

The British government was already hinting that France might obtain Lorraine in return for guaranteeing the Pragmatic Sanction. It was all very well for Queen Caroline to send Francis friendly assurance that 'I wish passionately that ... all your troubles may vanish, that stout Lorraine may be fully prosperous.'[22] At the beginning of 1733 Chauvelin had assured the French Minister in London with compact emphasis: 'We shall never suffer Lorraine and the Imperial Crown in the same House.'[23]

For the present Lorraine preserved her fragile independence. And during large wars the diplomatic missions of small neutrals generally assume increased importance. During those hostilities there was of course no Austrian embassy in Paris but the minister there for nominally neutral Lorraine was free to correspond with the duke at the court of Vienna or its dull annex at Pressburg where 'the hunting ... is in Hungarian fashion, very badly regulated'.[24]

Fleury, always preferring peace to war, did not neglect such a channel through his friend. The cardinal made occasions to meet Stainville and render himself agreeable, inviting him to dinner and asking him to stay on after the other guests for talks in his study. In these private conversations at the beginning of 1735 Fleury made to Stainville significant overtures towards peace with Austria.

The Marquis de Stainville reported on 10 March 1735 that Fleury had said to him: 'You know how much I have resisted this war; ... with what pleasure I should see it finish, and it would be a matter soon concluded if I could have the honour of talking for two hours with the Emperor, whose uprightness I know.'[25] Stainville duly offered to act as intermediary, observing that 'Your Royal Highness had only to permit me to take a turn in Lorraine, and, when I was there, to order me to go as far as Vienna under pretext of rendering you account of your own affairs and that then I could tell you all that I knew of the Cardinal's way of thinking. This minister has approved of my idea.'

[21] Count de Belle-Isle to Chauvelin, 20 June 1733: cited, P. Boyé, op. cit., p. 335.
[22] Queen Caroline of England to Duke Francis III, Richmond, 14 May 1734: Arch. M-et-M/Vienne, 3F 373, no. 116.
[23] Chauvelin to Chavigny, 28 Jan. 1733: Arch. Aff. Étr. C.P., Angleterre, vol. 379, fo. 75: cited, P. Vaucher, *Robert Walpole et la politique de Fleury 1731–1742* (Paris, 1924), pp. 78–9.
[24] Baron Toussaint to Marquis de Stainville, Pressburg, 28 July 1732: Arch. M-et-M/Vienne, 3F 373, no. 28.
[25] Marquis de Stainville to Duke Francis III, Paris, 10 Mar. 1735: Ö.S./H.H.S., Lothringisches Hausarchiv 202/III 503, cited, P. Boyé, op. cit., p. 282, and for the following.

Stainville had omitted to relate this overture earlier because, as he rather naively explained to the Duke of Lorraine, Fleury had asked him to make no use of his confidence till he could talk to Francis. This imperfect diplomatist, having first delayed to report, was now pushing ahead in proposing the line which Fleury wanted, before securing instructions from the duke who, even apart from Habsburg tutelage, would probably not have chosen Stainville as an intermediary. Francis simply kept silent, leaving his unfortunate envoy out on a limb with Fleury pressing him for the reply that never came. This silence on policy was premonitory for Stainville, who was for years to undergo the cold treatment from Vienna. But if this was the first time that Fleury extended secret peace-feelers to Stainville in time of war, it was not to be the last: if this early French approach to Stainville remained unproductive in itself, yet it prefaced another phase of Franco-Austrian rapprochement.

For the present, as usual during hostilities, would-be peace-intermediaries abounded. In the event the one utilized by Austria that summer was a Rhenish busybody, the Count of Wied. These secret negotiations were at Austrian instance inaugurated by Fleury behind the back of Chauvelin and resulted on 3 October 1735 in the Preliminaries of Vienna. By the terms of this compact France was at last to support the Pragmatic Sanction in favour of Maria Theresa, who was to marry Duke Francis III, who was, upon the expected death of the heirless Grand Duke John Gaston of Tuscany, to receive that principality in exchange for Lorraine. The Duchy of Bar was to be ceded forthwith to the unsuccessful Stanislas of Poland; on the death of the Grand Duke John Gaston he would receive Lorraine also, both duchies to be held by Stanislas during his lifetime and thereafter to be annexed to France. Cardinal Fleury was achieving that grand design which he had sketched out to the Marquis de Stainville nine years earlier.

Neither Stanislas nor Francis was informed beforehand of these arrangements.

IV

If Francis, like Stanislas, was indignant, drafting a protest against the Preliminaries of Vienna, still more so was his mother. 'I am not', she wrote, 'like my son, who prefers to be a simple subject of the Emperor to being a sovereign . . . I should have thought he had more firmness . . . I am very fond of Lorraine and the Lorrainers . . . I shall stay with them till the end of my days; but, as for the Emperor, I would rather die forthwith then be under his domination.'[26]

For Francis, though, it was more difficult. The heavy considerations of policy were presented to him in the form of the blonde of eighteen who was to be his bride and one day, one might hope, his imperial consort. The Austrian secretary of state, up-and-coming Bartenstein, was alleged to have put it to him with crude concision: 'Monseigneur, no cession, no archduchess.'[27] To complicate matters the archduchess 'sighs and pines all night for her duke of Lorraine. If she sleeps it is only to dream of him, if she wakes it is but to talk of him to the lady in waiting.'[28] Francis was her little mouse – she closed one of her letters to him: '*Adieu Mäusl, je vous embrasse de tout mon coeur, ménagez vous bien, adieu caro viso.*'[29] Four days after that was written, on the evening of 12 February 1736, Duke Francis all in white and silver was married to the Archduchess Maria Theresa, glittering with diamonds in the Augustinerkirche in Vienna.

This long-awaited marriage, so compounded of policy and love, was one of dynasty and destiny in the history of modern Europe. It founded that house of Habsburg-Lorraine which was to endure into the twentieth century. Back at Lunéville, where the celebrations centred around a soaring temple of hymen surmounted by an imperial eagle, allegorical personifications of the little duchy of Lorraine were jubilating:

> *Les plus écartés rivages*
> *Retentiront de nos voix.*[30]

The paean was their swansong. If the celebrations of the Regent of Lorraine at Lunéville gilded grief, so did those of the Marquis de Stainville at Paris. He, however, had been supplied with commemorative medals in gold and silver for distribution and he made the most of the big splash of his little mission. Francis for once had done the handsome thing by Stainville, sending him 24,000 livres, half as much as his annual salary, to cover the rejoicing which would normally have fallen to the Austrian ambassador. The marquis celebrated the day of the marriage, a Sunday, by the congenial

[26] Regent of Lorraine to Marquise d'Aulède, Lunéville, 11 June 1736: 'Lettres d'Elisabeth-Charlotte d'Orléans, duchesse de Lorraine, à la marquise d'Aulède, 1715–1738', *u.s.*, p. 316.

[27] Thomas Robinson, British Ambassador at Vienna, to Lord Harrington, 31 Dec. 1738: cited, William Coxe, *History of the House of Austria* (London, 1807), ii. 162.

[28] Robinson to Lord Harrington, 5 July 1735: ibid., ii. 154.

[29] Archduchess Maria Theresa to Duke Francis III, Vienna, 8 Feb. 1736 (the letter was addressed: '*Dem durchleuchtigsten Fürsten Francisco Hertzogen zu lothringen meinem villgeliebten brautigamb*'): Ö.S./H.H.S., cited, Alfred Ritter von Arneth, *Geschichte Maria Theresia's* (*Maria Theresia's erste Regierungsjahre*) (Vienna, 1863f.: henceforth cited as Arneth), i. 356, n. 30.

[30] Cited, H. Baumont, op. cit., p. 386.

festivity of a superb dinner. As he explained, he had restricted the
invitations to 'the princes of the blood, the French ministers and the
foreign ones and the great officers of the crown so as not to cause
jealousy among the dukes and bring the nobility down upon my
back'.[31] The only notable absentee was the aged cardinal himself
who, when Stainville had visited Fleury two days before at his house
at Issy, had graciously excused himself on grounds of health and
'because he has made himself a law not to go to dine anywhere in
Paris'. Everybody who did attend seemed to Stainville 'extremely
pleased with the order . . . and, I dare to assert, with the magnificence
of the repast'. The press echoed: 'This repast was served with all
imaginable order, delicacy and profusion. The room was exceptionally decorated and lit by more than five thousand candles placed both
in chandeliers and upon the tables.'[32] Fanfares of trumpets and the
roll of kettledrums accompanied the drinking of the healths 'of all the
crowned heads of Europe'. It would of course have been a serious
breach of protocol to omit one. Madame du Châtelet commented
with some feminist spleen to Algarotti, perhaps a participant in 'this
dreary party of Mr. de Stainville: they tell me that there was copious
drinking there in German fashion. There are no elegant parties
without women.'[33]

The bumper celebration by the Marquis de Stainville was not
restricted to the immediate guests. 'The whole of the exterior of the
mansion was illuminated by an infinity of [lights in] pots and lanterns
artistically arranged. Two fountains of wine were flowing for the
public throughout the whole festivity, which ended with a fine
firework-display and the noise of a large number of [ceremonial]
discharges.'[34] The future Duke de Choiseul did not have far to look
in his later addiction to official magnificence.

'In short Monseigneur', reported Stainville to Francis in the
euphoria of the day after, 'I have been fortunate enough to succeed in
the finest day of my life, since it is that of the happiness of Your Royal
Highness.'[35] Francis, however, refused to reimburse Stainville the
over-expenditure which he had incurred on his allocation since, as he
explained, 'I thought that on such occasions one should not shew any
desire to save.'[36] The financial hangover from this triumphant party
was aggravated shortly afterwards by Stainville's going to the expense

[31] Marquis de Stainville to Duke Francis III, Paris, 13 Feb. 1736: Ö.S./H.H.S., Lothringisches
Hausarchiv 203/III 542, and for the following.
[32] Mercure de France, Feb. 1736, pp. 369–70 for the following.
[33] Marquise du Châtelet to Algarotti, Cirey, 20 Apr. 1736: Les Lettres de la Marquise du
Châtelet, ed. Theodore Besterman (Geneva, 1958), i. 113.
[34] Mercure de France, u.s.
[35] Marquis de Stainville to Duke Francis III, Paris, 13 Feb. 1736: u.s.
[36] Ibid., 10 Mar. 1736 (dated 1735 in error in original).

of full mourning for the empress's mother, who in fact, as Francis did not fail to tell him subsequently, 'is keeping very well'.[37] By another piece of bad luck just then he sprained himself. These were but minor worries, though, in the shadow of the grave uncertainties, personal for Stainville as well as political, attendant upon the demise of that ducal regime which he represented.

At the time of his marriage of happiness and sorrow Duke Francis III had still not signed away his patrimony so that Maria Theresa was, briefly, the last duchess of the long line. In allowing 'the august ceremony'[38] in the Augustinerkirche to precede the cession the Emperor Charles VI had shrewdly obligated the young duke while avoiding the appearance of too crass a bargain and at the same time ensuring that henceforth he would be subjected to the most effective and intimate form of pressure. Bourcier de Montureux, son of the former attorney-general, was one of the Lorrainers then in Vienna in connection with the cession, and he depicted the duke after his marriage as being 'delivered up to domestic vexations ... and ... being beside a justly alarmed bride, even the repose of the night did not exempt him therefrom'.[39] Bourcier himself, backed by the regent, by her younger son, Prince Charles, by almost all Lorraine, entreated the unhappy duke to resist this marital influence, and described an audience with Francis in May 1736 whereat the duke's 'speech was so broken by sobs that, being unable to continue, he withdrew precipitately".[40] Even that cold absentee could not escape emotion at the prospect of severing the ties of nearly seven centuries.

By now the demise of the little duchy as an independent state was almost a foregone conclusion in Europe. The surprise if anything was that it had lasted so long. Two months after Francis had married, France and Austria on 11 April 1736, again without consulting him, concluded a further convention, the Synallagmatic Act. France had got Austria to agree therein that Stanislas should receive Lorraine as well as Bar without awaiting the death of the Grand Duke of Tuscany. The price paid by France was an interim subsidy to Francis and a substantial bribe to venal Bartenstein. (Even so a French representative later indicated from Vienna that Bartenstein's wife was 'piqued at not having had anything. Some diamonds would accommodate the matter.')[41] On 22 April, Francis sent the emperor

---

[37] Duke Francis III to Marquis de Stainville, Vienna, 21 Mar. 1736: Arch. M-et-M/Vienne, 3F 362, no. 162.

[38] Count de Richecourt to Marquis de Stainville, Vienna, 10 Jan. 1736: ibid., 3F 373, no. 122.

[39] Baron Bourcier de Montureux, 'Réflections sur l'élection de l'empereur François premier'. Cited, P. Boyé, op. cit., p. 409.

[40] Baron Bourcier de Montureux, ibid., p. 417.

[41] L'Estang-Laville to Amelot de Chaillou, Vienna, 12 June 1737: Arch. Aff. Étr. C.P., Autriche, vol. 207, fo. 87.

a protest against the new agreement, only to be answered six days later by a further Franco-Austrian accord in elaboration of the preceding one. Already in Lorraine the dismal report was circulating: 'They say that we are ceded.'[42] As the Marquis de Stainville observed to his duke: 'Here is a furious moment for your unhappy subjects.'[43]

The hapless Lorrainers are recorded to have addressed to Duke Francis a passionate petition invoking a constitutional contract even in that age:

> Sovereigns are not dispensed from observing the laws and . . . the possession of great Kingdoms is not exempt from crime when it is not founded upon the justice of the Laws and when it lacks paternal affection towards the Peoples. Upon this principle the lustre of the richer and more extensive throne is not a sufficient motive for Your Royal Highness to abandon that of his ancestors, still less to nullify the oath which you swore in favour of your subjects at the time of your *joyeux avènement* . . . Without plumbing the mysteries of politics, they comprise means other than that of sacrificing innocent victims in order to conciliate the friendship of a warlike nation.[44]

V

For Stainville this political crux was personally precarious. His diplomatic career would be conditioned, perhaps terminated, by the disposal of Lorraine, and that at a time when his financial fortunes were considerably compromised.

In the marquisate at the beginning of the seventeen-thirties there had indeed been some suggestion still of territorial expansion. Toussaint, who apparently retained a local lookout, had written then in his abrasive solicitude for the marquis: 'The poor Du Ménils would like to sell their twelfth in this village. I would think, Sir, that this would suit you in cleaning up (*nettoyer*) all these little gentlefolk on your estate.'[45] The inference was, though, that this socially suggestive transaction would have meant borrowing. And in the impact upon Lorraine of the War of the Polish Succession it is scarcely to be supposed that the Stainville estate escaped scatheless. The outlying lands at Bazincourt were to be mortgaged for part of the debts into which the marquis was running. Yet it would appear that, in his part of the Barrois at least, land-values continued to

[42] Madame de Graffigny to Devaux, early 1736: cited, G. Noël, *Madame de Graffigny 1695–1758* (Paris, 1913), p. 59.
[43] Marquis de Stainville to Duke Francis III, 23 Apr. 1736: Ö.S./H.H.S., Lothringisches Hausarchiv 203/III 542, no. 5: cited, P. Boyé, op. cit., p. 415, n. 3.
[44] 'Requeste des Lorrains à S.A.R. Monseigneur le Duc de Lorraine' in François-Vincent Toussaint, *Anecdotes curieuses de la cour de France sous le règne de Louis XV*, ed. Paul Fould (Paris, 1908), pp. 108–9.
[45] Baron Toussaint to Marquis de Stainville, Lunéville, 10 June 1730: Arch. M-et-M/Vienne, 3F 372, no. 100.

appreciate, and markedly, even during the war. In March 1736 a new general lease of the Stainville estate was granted to the postmaster of Ligny, Sieur Brigeat, as farmer-general for six thousand livres a year as compared with the rental of four thousand five hundred or less in the twenties: roughly a thirty-three per cent increase in little over a decade.

The rise of rent at Stainville was if anything ahead of comparable increases in France while generally matching the beginnings there of that long rise in agricultural rents which was to double them and more within two generations from about 1730. That period marked a turning-point at last away from the long depression of the seventeenth century in France. By and large the seventeen-thirties there were agriculturally, and climatically, benign. On the whole, though, the initial momentum upward gathered slowly, and there were special drags in Lorraine. 'This country which is covered with woods', observed a French survey for the period, 'was nothing but a refuge for robbers, vagrants and other such vagabonds',[46] owing to inadequate policing. The suggestion may be none the less that the Stainville estate was being keenly run, as also that at Demange-aux-Eaux. A change there roughly coincided with one in the family.

In February 1733 the Marquis de Stainville's redoubtable aunt, Secrète of Remiremont, had died. Next month he wrote from Paris, probably to his brother-in-law, the Marquis de Ligny: 'Although I was expecting the misfortune which had just happened to me, Sir, I confess that it is with great difficulty that I bear it. You have taken all imaginable measures for surety and order, but I am a little astonished that the will should not have been sought for first of all . . . Is it known what my sisters wish to do about the will of Madame la Secrète? Since it is in favour of minors I feel obliged to uphold it.'[47] If granted the leave he had asked for 'I shall at once proceed to Ligny where we will see together what is best to be done. Adieu, Sir, I embrace you with all my heart and finish without compliment, Choiseul de Stainville.'[48]

In September that year, at any rate, the Marquis de Stainville was at Ligny, approving the new contracts negotiated for him that summer by Jacques Lescaille, now the verderer of the marquisate of Stainville, in order to extend the policy of a consolidated lease of

---

[46] Quinquet, 'Mémoire Sommaire sur les Duchés de Lorraine et de Bar dressé par ordre de Monseigneur le Contrôleur général des finances', memorandum of March 1746, fo. 32: Arch. Nat., K 1184.

[47] Marquis de Stainville to ?Marquis de Ligny, Paris, 9 Mar. 1733: Arch. Meuse, J 18[6] (Duché de Stainville, Titres généraux. Formariage. Corporations. 1365–an III), docket 1, no. 48.

[48] Ibid.

feudal rights and revenues to the subsidiary holding of Demange-aux-Eaux, henceforth actively exploited through two leases. That in favour of a merchant of Ligny, Antoine Baillet, and his wife Anne was essentially a gardening and home-farming lease of a type common upon the continent. The Baillets paid no rent but were entitled to one room in the château or offices plus all the produce of the grounds including the seigneurial dovecots, dairy, sheepfold, and beehives in return for undertaking their entire upkeep. This included clipping all the hornbeam hedges, seeing to the beds of artichokes and asparagus, and keeping the dovecots 'well populated'.[49]

This arrangement was an exception from the main farm of the domain and domainal rights of Demange 'for the quarter and a half of them which belong to my said lord'[50] the marquis. This lease was in favour of one Louis Lapanne, described as a labourer of that village, and his wife Marianne. (She could not read but had to have the lease read to her.) The rent was two thousand livres a year upon the same kind of terms as for the Stainville estate. One of the labourers at least in those parts was thus a recruit to that rural bourgeoisie which was likewise developing in France, even if his wife lagged behind Stainville standards of feminine literacy.

The Marquis de Stainville approved both leases at Ligny on 15 September 1733. Lapanne's lease was heavily backdated so that by the following year Lescaille was already collecting better bids for its renewal. It went bumping up and Lapanne had to match the highest bid of 2,510 livres in order to prolong his lease. He finally signed the agreement to this effect, in the château of Demange on 25 September 1735, with the managing Marquise de Stainville. She signed 'Bassompierre Stainville'.

Specifically excepted from Lapanne's original lease were the rights of the chase, as befitted a grant from a Grand Huntsman. This function of the Marquis de Stainville had remained operative from Paris, certainly for the ladies of powerful Remiremont, who grumbled that hazelhen were being inadequately protected, that his ducal lieutenants of the chase were 'causing mischievous difficulties'[51] for the abbatial officers and depriving them of fines due. Shortly afterwards, in February 1732, a ducal decree prolonged for two years a previous prohibition against hunting roe-deer and forbade

[49] Lease by Lescaille to Antoine and Anne Baillet, Ligny, 17 Aug 1733: Arch. Nat., 5 AP 42 (Fonds Bassompierre), docket 162 (Seigneurie de Demange).
[50] Lease by Lescaille to Louis and Marianne Lapanne, Gondrecourt, 29 June 1733: ibid.
[51] 'Mémoire du chapitre [de Remiremont] à l'abbesse à Paris, pour obtenir de M. de Stainville, grand veneur de Lorraine, que défenses soient faites aux officiers des chasses à Mircourt et à Charmes d'empêcher que le chapitre ne nomme, en la tenure des plaids, des gardes-chasses dans les forêts indivises', undated (late 1731 or early 1732): Arch. Vosges, G 893, docket N, no. 59.

partridge-shooting for three because most of the birds had perished in 'the severity of the previous winter'.[52] Three days later Toussaint's earlier prod at Stainville for issuing too many special permits was driven home, through the same factotum, in an order to send Duke Francis 'a return of all the hunting licences which you have given in Lorraine'.[53]

This pointed instruction was issued upon the duke's grand tour while he was laid up at Magdeburg by a chill caught returning from England. There incognito, late in 1731, Francis had gone racing at Newmarket, had received seven fine horses from George II, and had himself bought forty more and as many hounds, for which Stainville had to procure a French passport. And four years later, for instance, the Grand Huntsman was broaching for his master a presentation by 'Mr. de Magdanel [?MacDonell], who is attached to the Duke de Bourbon . . . [of] a great Irish wolfhound . . . the finest dog that I have ever seen in my life, . . . 36 inches high.'[54] Hunting figured proportionately larger again in the correspondence of the duke's friendlier brother, Prince Charles, with 'My dear Stainville . . . We are having some very fine hunting but very strenuous. I have never seen the stags so strong as this year.'[55] The marquis kept in close touch and a local ruling upon the chase evoked the protest: 'I am not so foreign from home that they could not have referred it to me myself.'[56] For himself he could manage, for instance, 'two or three days hunting with the king [Louis XV] at Petit Bourg'.[57]

The Grand Huntsman of Lorraine was yet something of a harbinger among the aristocracy of an incipient social shift of the continental eighteenth-century from late feudalism to early industrialism. If he already looked for his income partly to the iron-workings of the Châtelet–Fruze–Attignéville complex, before long the Prince de Croÿ and other magnates would increasingly be moving into mining and heavy industry, where they tended to regard company-direction as but an extension of their seigneurial management of lordly property. At present, though, the Marquis de Stainville's

---

[52] 'Declaration de Son Altesse Royale au sujet des chasses' Lunéville, 14 Feb. 1732: Arch. Nat., K 1187, no. 54.

[53] Baron Toussaint to Marquis de Stainville, Magdeburg, 17 Feb. 1732: Arch. M-et-M/Vienne, 3F 373, No. 9.

[54] Marquis de Stainville to Duke Francis III, Paris, 25 Nov. 1735: Ö.S./H.H.S., Lothringisches Hausarchiv 202/III 503 (Nachlass Stainville).

[55] Prince Charles of Lorraine to Marquis de Stainville, ?Lunéville, 12 Nov. 1733: Arch. M-et-M/Vienne, 3F 373, No. 93.

[56] Marquis de Stainville to Regent of Lorraine, Paris, 26 Aug. 1734: Ö.S./H.H.S., Lothringisches Hausarchiv 202/III 503 (Nachlass Stainville).

[57] Marquis de Stainville to Duke Francis III, Paris, 14 Sept. 1736: Ö.S./H.H.S., Lothringisches Hausarchiv 202/III 542, no. 11.

interest at Châtelet was badly compromised by its entrepreneur, Nicolas Gilbert.

Gilbert's rent to the joint-owning marquises of Stainville and Ligny was heavily in arrear, as were his stipulated deliveries of wood for fuel. By the summer of 1735 he had let the forges run down, to a stop. Gilbert by then owed his landlords a principal sum of 14,559 livres, 18 sous, 4 deniers plus a range of subsidiary debts, as 1,541 livres, 6 sous, 2 deniers 'for half the repairs and enlargements made to the flue of the furnace of Attignéville' and 226 livres, 6 sous 'for other repairs to the conduit for the retention of water at Châtelet and to the coalyards'.[58] The two marquises sued Gilbert who was ordered by the Chambre des Requêtes at Nancy on 5 August 1735 to face up to his obligations and restart the forges within a fortnight on pain of bankruptcy and forfeiture of his lease. Gilbert could not rise to it. Handbills were printed announcing the auction of the lease of the whole works on 7 September following.

Instability in industry was more the rule than the exception in such early enterprises, whose capital tended to be as light as the machinery, whose operation was clogged both by chemical ignorance and by the persistence of an agricultural preponderance. In a foundry in those days the hammers were likely to be striking, when they did, at no more than 120 to 130 beats a minute. If Réaumur in 1722 had stimulated French research into steel, technology was still fancifully caught up with phlogiston. Production too was apt to be regularly interrupted when labour was diverted into haymaking or the harvest, still the priorities and quite likely a factor in Gilbert's failure that summer. Another may have been the fact that industrial profits overall were tending to rise considerably less than agricultural – in neighbouring Burgundy, certainly, prices of iron had slumped during the seventeen-twenties.

Within a few years at any rate the exploitation of the Châtelet and subsidiary workings passed to another middle-class entrepreneur of the district, a merchant from Neufchâteau called Nicolas Cochois, who was to give Stainville hardly less trouble than Nicolas Gilbert, was indeed already doing so in another, feudal context. The two marquises were involved against Cochois that same year over *lods et ventes*, the sizeable due payable to the local lord by the purchaser of leased property on his estate. In regard to Cochois 'the matter', claimed Stainville and Ligny in their pleading, 'is to be explained in two words'.[59] They ran to twenty-one pages.

[58] Judgement of the Chambre des Requêtes *in re* Marquises de Stainville and de Ligny *vs.* Nicolas Gilbert, 5 Aug. 1735: Arch. Vosges, E 115.
[59] 'Inventaire de production' of Marquises de Stainville and de Ligny *vs.* Noels, Thouvenins and Nicolas Cochois before the Chambre des Requêtes, 16 Apr. 1734: ibid.

Briefly, then, Cochois was held to owe this due, in respect of purchase of property for 14,500 livres at Vouxey, to 'Noel and wife, lessees-general (*admodiateurs*) of the said Vouxey ... Cochois has wriggled (*tortillé*) ... Finally the lessees-general took out a summons against him in the provostship of Removille, which ordered that the lords should be cited. The lessees-general have to this effect requested a *pareatis* from the officers of the bailiwick of the Vosges.'[60] This typical lawsuit went lumbering up to the sovereign court of Lorraine and the Barrois. A year later the two marquises were coming to grips with the case, arguing on appeal that 'if the Custom of Lorraine does not speak of *lods et ventes*, the right is nevertheless established there in a large part of the localities within its jurisdiction, as also in the Barrois, and in almost all the neighbouring kingdom ... If the contract of the twenty-sixth February fifteen hundred and forty-four' was not in itself conclusive 'it is beating the air to contradict, as Cochois does, such respectable and authentic titles'[61] as the 'five large registers of accounts'[62] for 1612 to 1636.

This troubled background lay behind an enquiry some years later as to whether the property of Châtelet was for sale, an enquiry directed to the Marquise de Stainville from the conceivably jealous Marquise du Châtelet herself. She made the approach discreetly through Madame de Graffigny. But the Stainvilles were not selling. Nevertheless feudal litigation and industrial failure had been liable to sharpen the Marquis de Stainville's perennial scrabble for resources. In April 1736 the good Regent Elizabeth Charlotte was warning him that 'my son will make no gratification in money, and he ... has only restored estates which had been remitted [to the crown], witness M. de Craon and Mme de Rouerke, your mother-in-law'.[63] This was a painful instance. For Francis, now that sovereignty in Lorraine was slipping from him, had just restored to Craon, subject to a life-interest to the Countess de Rouerke, a property at Morley which Stainville was claiming as his own. The inevitable Toussaint told him it was no go, and Craon himself began a letter to him: 'I was not expecting, my dear nephew, the letter which I received from you two days ago. You formally accuse me of depriving you of Morlaix [*sic*] which you say is a property which comes originally from your family.'[64] But, explained Craon, Duke Leopold had given him

[60] Ibid.
[61] Pleading of the Marquises de Stainville and de Ligny before the Cour Souveraine de Lorraine et Barrois, 12 May 1735: ibid.
[62] 'Inventaire de production', 16 Apr. 1734: *u.s.*
[63] Regent of Lorraine to Marquis de Stainville, Lunéville, 26 Apr. 1736: Arch. Nat., K 1185, no. 19.
[64] Prince de Craon to Marquis de Stainville, Lunéville, 14 May 1736: Arch. M-et-M/Vienne, 3F 370, no. 258, and for the following.

Morley 'about thirty years ago, that is to say five or six years before you were known to him. This property does not come originally from the house of Choiseul to which you belong nor from that of Stainville to which you do not.' Craon could only regard Stainville's letter 'as a mistake of your mind and heart which cannot last' since Stainville would recollect his past benefits from Craon: 'I would not recall them if I were not forced to by the pain I am in at seeing that you have forgotten them.' The firm but feeling rebuke in this rare difference between them opened no lasting rift.

VI

The handsome remuneration of the Marquis de Stainville's services in Paris braced his ramshackle budget. All that is usually remembered of his mission, if remembered at all, is that, besides giving him the right to have his stick carried behind him by a servant, it represented, as a contemporary unkindly said, 'an office of favour which was worth thirty thousand francs to him, obliging him to nothing'.[65] This gloss, it may now seem, represented some slight exaggeration even though Stainville may not ordinarily have been the busiest of ministers. The thirty thousand did roughly match his annual salary then of 48,000 livres of Lorraine, by far the largest single item in the diplomatic budget of the little duchy. Stainville's chargé d'affaires, listed as 'Mr. de Nay',[66] received six thousand livres a year and his secretary Grobert twelve hundred. One gathers, incidentally, that Stainville's secretaries and their wives had a good deal to put up with from the Marquise. According to Madame de Graffigny 'la Grosbert' was one of those classical ladies mentioned as suffering under Belinda, and was treated by her 'at present like Toussaint'.[67]

Now Toussaint, at that turning-point for Lorraine, was in on the personal preoccupations which caused Fleury to greet the marquis upon his entering the cardinal's study one day towards the end of 1735 with the surmise that Stainville 'was troubled in spirit'. This he denied, explaining, as relayed to Duke Francis, 'that I had to deal with a good master ... The minister said to me that whatever should happen, I could never be anything but standing well. I answered him that I knew only one condition for myself which was to follow Your Royal Highness wherever you were, that neither my attachment for

[65] J.N. Dufort, comte de Cheverny, op. cit., p. 137.

[66] Memorandum: 'État des appointements et des dépenses des envoyés, residens et agents de S.A.R. [François III] en differentes cours pour l'année 1736': Arch. Aff. Étr. C.P., Lorraine, vol. 128, fo. 120.

[67] Madame de Graffigny to Devaux, Cirey, 29 Dec. 1738: Eugène Asse, op. cit., p. 137.

my family not the property which I had in Lorraine could distract
me from this resolution if my services were agreeable to Your Royal
Highness.'[68]

Loyalty was traditional with the Choiseuls, but Francis was slower
than Fleury to salute it. More than six months later Stainville was
beseeching the silent duke to resolve 'my cruel situation ... My
affairs are totally deranged; burdened with a large family, whereof
the eldest is ready to enter into the world, my youth past, and being
no longer in condition to restart another service, wishing however to
receive nothing from anybody except through the graces of Your
Royal Highness: there is my state.'[69] Aristocrat as he was, the
marquis assumed that he needed to follow a profession in order to
earn a sufficient living for himself and his family.

Thus anxious was the uncertain start in life of the future Duke de
Choiseul. His father had earlier mentioned to Francis his 'son ready
to enter society, and of whom I nowise wish to dispose without the
orders of Your Royal Highness'.[70] However loyal the father to Duke
Francis, for the eldest son, the heir to the Stainville estates, King
Stanislas and, behind him, King Louis XV were already looming
over Lorraine. Fleury's placing of the Count de Stainville in the
French army may well have been clinched in allegiance now by
Fleury's subtle take-over of the duchy. Such was the background to
Toussaint's observation from Vienna to the marquis in October 1736:
'If your son who is at the academy is the eldest, it seems to me that he
cannot follow any cause other than that of the prince whose vassal he
will become. If it is a younger son, the matter is different.'[71] There
might incidentally be a suggestion that the emergence of the Count
de Stainville from Louis-le-Grand was via one of those finishing
academies for young gentlemen.

With the Marquis de Stainville divided allegiances, for others at
least, was nothing new. He had just been helping to secure an
Austrian commission for a certain Captain Butler 'who has served
[France] for thirty years with every imaginable distinction in the
Irish Route Regiment ... The small justice which has been done to
his merit obliges him to leave the service of France.'[72] It is unclear
just which Jacobite officer this might be, for the French army

[68] Marquis de Stainville to Duke Francis III, 17 Nov. 1735: Ö.S./H.H.S., Lothringisches
Hausarchiv 202/III 503 (Nachlass Stainville).
[69] Marquis de Stainville to Duke Francis III, Paris, 2 July 1736: O.S./H.H.S., Lothringisches
Hausarchiv 203/III 542, no. 9.
[70] Ibid., 23 Apr. 1736: no. 5.
[71] Baron Toussaint to Marquis de Stainville, Vienna, 27 Oct. 1736: Arch. M-et-M/Vienne,
3F 373, no. 142.
[72] Marquis de Stainville to Count Johann von Harrach, Paris, 16 June 1735: Ö.S./H.H.S.,
Lothringisches Hausarchiv 202/III 503 (Nachlass Stainville).

abounded in impecunious Butlers – Lord Galmoy, a French lieutenant-general, had four nephews, James, Richard, Edward, and Peter
Butler, who each served as a French officer for more than thirty
years.[73]

If the Marquis de Stainville busied himself with personal matters
his political involvement in negotiating the cession of Lorraine was
mostly subordinate. Fleury asked him one day 'Does not your master
tell you anything of his affairs? . . . I am astonished.'[74] Three months
after this broad hint Stainville was writing to Francis of a report 'that
the cession of Lorraine will not take place . . . I scarcely dare believe
it, but since everything is being negotiated at Vienna nothing can be
known here save by conjecture.'[75]

Stainville's scepticism was justified. The pressure to cede was too
strong. Duke Francis III first disposed of Bar and finally, on 13
February 1737, a year and a day after his marriage, signed away
Lorraine itself. It was finished.

'H.R.H Madame [the Regent] is as though stunned by it',[76] the
secretary of the cabinet in Lorraine had written earlier in connection
with the cession. Recalling to Stainville its completion, Francis
himself referred to 'the prostration (*accablement*) in which I found
myself'.[77] Such was the emotion of an event most often barely
remembered, if at all, as a minor move in the intricate game of
general-post which rounded off the War of the Polish Succession in
the style of the time: what Choiseul later termed 'these ridiculous
removals'.[78] History has on the whole endorsed his contempt.
Nevertheless it is sometimes not a bad plan to take a look at
diplomatic history from the underside, as from the viewpoint of a
small community. It tends to correct that judgement from on high to
which history is inevitably prone.

VII

In the broad perspective of international relations the transfer of
Lorraine from Francis under Austrian tutelage to Stanislas under
French was yet a large achievement by Fleury in rounding out the
eastward expansion of France. It was ten years now since he had
raised some such possibility with the Marquis de Stainville. It has

[73] Cf. petition from Lord Galmoy to King Louis XV, 10 Sept. 1740: Arch. Guerre, Archives
Administratives, Dossiers Butler.
[74] Marquis de Stainville to Duke Francis III, Paris, 31 May 1736: Ö.S./H.H.S., Lothringisches
Hausarchiv 203/III 542, no. 8.
[75] Ibid., 8 Sept. 1736: no. 10 (partially and imperfectly cited by P. Boyé, op. cit., p. 427).
[76] Poirot to Duke Francis III, Lunéville, 7 May 1736: Ö.S./H.H.S., cited, op. cit., p. 416.
[77] Prince Francis to Marquis de Stainville, Vienna, 15 Apr. 1737: Arch. M-et-M/Vienne, 3F
362, no. 175.
[78] Duke de Choiseul to Voltaire, 14 Jan. 1760: P. Calmettes, *Choiseul et Voltaire*, p. 57.

even been suggested[79] that Fleury's limp support of Stanislas in Poland reflected a subtle wish that he should not prosper there with a view to claiming Lorraine for him in compensation. It remains rather difficult to suppose, though, that in an age exalting dynastic prestige any French statesman, even a pacific cardinal, even for Lorraine, would deliberately promote the humilation in the eyes of all Europe of having his king's father-in-law chased out of those Polish regions once ruled by King Henry III of France: even apart from the great sums which the French government had spent in buying Polish support for Stanislas. Fleury was hardly a spendthrift and there was usually a commonsense limit to his craft.

This is not to say that when things went awry for Stanislas in Poland, as they so swiftly did, Fleury did not cut his losses in the east, concentrating upon the smaller, nearer, more solid objective, extracting diplomatic from military successes in the west. If the transfer of Lorraine matched victories in the Rhineland, those in Italy validated the cession of Novara and Tortona to Sardinia, and of the kingdom of Naples to the Spanish interest of Don Carlos. He in turn relinquished Parma and Piacenza to Austria while Tuscany was taken under the wing of her double eagle as the counterpart to Lorraine in the ingenious swap. This just measured the extent to which Austrian power in Italy had been set back so that henceforth the balance there between the Habsburgs and the Bourbons was almost even. All these adjustments and a good deal more besides, notably the long-sought French guarantee of the Pragmatic Sanction, were finally embodied in the Third Treaty of Vienna concluded on 18 November 1738.

The future Duke de Choiseul was to recall:

After the peace of 1738, on the advice of M. de Bartenstein, an Alsatian in whom the Emperor [Charles VI] had every confidence in political matters, the Emperor had entered into correspondence with the Cardinal de Fleury to find means of linking France with the court of Vienna by a defensive treaty. I have read the letters of Cardinal de Fleury and the Emperor upon this subject. This fairly active correspondence lasted till the death of the Emperor.[80]

In revealing this secret concert Choiseul was in essentials notably accurate even if the correspondence had in fact begun earlier and was pursued in the interest not so much of alliance as of an entente, an entente indeed with important reservations upon either side. Fleury

---

[79] Cf. Arthur McCandless Wilson, *French Foreign Policy during the Administration of Cardinal Fleury 1726–1743* (Cambridge, Mass., 1936), p. 252. (Professor Wilson did not adduce clinching evidence and had himself referred to Fleury – p. 246 – as 'above all else a diplomat, with a diplomat's love of prestige'.)

[80] Choiseul, *Mémoires*, p. 152.

did not lose overnight his suspicion of the pretensions of Austria or his special dislike of her alliance with feared Russia; and the cardinal was adept at pursuing apparently contradictory policies in double harness, as in his rapprochement in 1739 with Prussia over the Jülich-Berg succession. Nevertheless Fleury's 'new system'[81] of 'union' with Austria after the War of the Polish Succession marked the next stage ahead from the System of Baden after the War of the Spanish Succession, and its significant recall by Choiseul was to be in the context of the Diplomatic Revolution after the War of the Austrian Succession.

Such a political evolution for Europe took time. So indeed did treaties themselves about then. The Third Treaty of Vienna was concluded rather more than three years after the signature of the preliminaries of peace.

The protracted precision of so much of the delicate diplomacy of that age was an index to its deeper inspiration. Whereas the medieval ideal of supranational christendom was virtually gone, the stature of every man as an individual was not yet accorded full recognition. After the reformation defection from the single church under the authority of the pope was stabilized for the time at the state and its princely ruler. For a relatively short period between the close of the wars of religion in the seventeenth century and the rise of democratic nationalism in the nineteenth continental statecraft could operate, so to speak, in its pure form, little constricted either from above by confessional zeal or from below by popular demand: seldom indeed by the latter, as was demonstrated by the disposal of Lorraine. The population of the duchy was notorious for its loyalty to the ruling house and, if consulted, would almost certainly have produced a large majority against any change of sovereignty. Difficulties such as the size of the unit selected for self-determination belonged, however, to another age than that of the Third Treaty of Vienna.

Already two years before the treaty, on 30 September 1736, France had tied up Lorraine in an exchange of documents with Stanislas Leszczynski. This was the so-called Declaration of Meudon, that being the royal residence to which he had eventually returned after his adventurous escape from Danzig disguised as a peasant. The declaration demonstrated that the French government of that day did not have much to learn about the technique of coordinating small states while maintaining an outward semblance of their independence.

Under the Declaration of Meudon King Stanislas – he was allowed

[81] La Porte du Theil, French representative in Vienna, 17 Feb. 1737: Braubach, p. 311, n. 111.

to keep the title without the kingdom – was not to touch a penny of
the revenue of his duchy. These revenues, reckoned to have more
than quadrupled in the last forty years, from rather less than a million
and a half livres in 1698 to over six million in 1738,[82] were all to go to
France. In return Louis XV pensioned off Stanislas with an annual
1,500,000 livres, rising to two million. It had been reckoned that
during the reign of Stanislas (1737–66) France extracted from
Lorraine a net profit of at least one hundred million livres.

Stanislas could make judicial and military appointments only with
the concurrence of the French government and, under article 7 of the
declaration, 'will nominate an intendant of justice, police and finance
in the Duchy of Lorraine and Bar, or other person under such title
and denomination as shall be deemed appropriate, who shall be
chosen in concert with H[is] M[ost] C[hristian] M[ajesty]. The said
intendant or other shall exercise in our name the same power and the
same functions as the provincial intendants exercise in France.'[83]
Louis XV further received the right to station, in concert with
Stanislas, French troops in Lorraine and to construct fortifications
there. 'Finally, at the same time as we shall receive the actual oath of
allegiance from our new subjects, we will have it sworn contingently
in the name of H. M. C. M.'[84] Thus was the Count de Stainville, as
heir to that feudal holding, set to become the French king's vassal, as
Toussaint suggested a month later.

The Declaration of Meudon has been described as an abdication
in advance. It was completed by an ordinance of 1738 granting
French subjects the same rights as Lorrainers in the duchy, where
Frenchmen might hold offices and privileges without having to take
out letters of naturalization. Lorrainers in France were accorded
reciprocal treatment: a further significant provision in regard to the
career of the future Duke de Choiseul. Meanwhile villagers of the
duchy along the French frontier might work off their feelings in
pitched fights against their new fellow-citizens, but the process of
assimilation went forward.

The new oaths of allegiance were received in February 1737 for
Bar and in the following month for Lorraine by the official appointed
under the Declaration of Meudon to act as French intendant of
Lorraine, though with the special title of chancellor. This was
Antoine-Martin de Chaumont de La Galaizière, brother-in-law of
controller-general Orry and a rising star of the French administrative

[82] Memorandum: 'Revenus des Duchez de Lorraine et de Bar en 1609 comparé avec ceux de
1698 et 1738': Arch. Aff. Étr. C.P., Lorraine, vol. 128, fo. 361.
[83] Article 7, Declaration by King Stanislas (Declaration of Meudon), 30 Sept. 1736: cited,
Comte d'Haussonville, op. cit., iv. 646 (there dated in error 30 Sept. 1537).
[84] Article 11, ibid.

service wherein he had started at the age of fourteen in the ministry
of war. La Galaizière had already distinguished himself as a hard
administrator in Picardy. Appointed chancellor in despite of the
amiable Stanislas, he skilfully concentrated all effective power in
himself while leaving its trappings to the ducal figurehead. The
people of Lorraine soon twigged and began to sing their sprightly
'Lamentations des Lorrains':

> *Oh! grands dieux! quelle culbute!*
> *Après nos Ducs quelle chute!*
> *Monseigneur de La Galaizière,*
> *Laire, laire, laire, lanlaire,*
> *Laire, laire, laire, lanla.*

> *Que ne laissais-tu à Meudon*
> *Ce roi qui ne l'est de nom,*
> *Monseigneur de La Galaizière!*[85]

Stanislas himself was not at all anxious to be left at Meudon where
he now received offhand treatment from the French. A few days after
the declaration the Marquis de Stainville had a long audience of
Stanislas who 'indicated to me the extreme desire he had to leave
Meudon to go into Lorraine'.[86] The trouble was the determination of
the dowager duchess to remain there while at the same time assuring
Stainville: 'I would rather be in a convent at Paris than resign myself
to being subject to this King Stanislas ... Nothing shall ever make
me consent to obey a person like him.'[87]

Elizabeth Charlotte's defiance issued already from her future
retreat in Lorraine, the delightful Château de Commercy where once,
in more intellectual retirement, the Cardinal de Retz had written his
memoirs and assembled a sunny circle of ecclesiastics to blend the
new insights of Jansen and of Descartes. Now Stainville safeguarded
the duchess against 'this accursed accession of King Stanislas'[88] in
petty but complicated negotiations for the convention which he
signed with Chauvelin at Versailles on 1 December 1736. Thereby
she was to receive the 'principality of Commercy in sovereignty by
usufruct'.[89] By Christmas Francis had ratified under counter-

---

[85] Cited, P. Boyé, op. cit., p. 494.

[86] Marquis de Stainville to Duke Francis III, Paris, 7 Oct. 1736: Ö.S./H.H.S., Lothringisches
Hausarchiv 203/III 543, no. 14: cited, ibid., p. 470, n. 2.

[87] Dowager Duchess of Lorraine to Marquis de Stainville, Commercy, 23 Nov. 1737:
Ö.S./H.H.S., ibid., p. 473.

[88] Ibid., p. 483.

[89] Convention for the cession of the principality of Commercy, Versailles, 1 Dec. 1736:
Comte de Garden, *Histoire générale des traités de paix et autres transactions principales entre
toutes les puissances de l'Europe depuis la paix de Westphalie* (Paris, n.d.), iii. 416.

signature of the inevitable Toussaint; but in the new year the duke
was once again reprimanding the marquis for precipitancy in signing
a subsidiary convention with Chauvelin and, now, the Austrian
envoy, Schmerling.

Stainville waxed indignant. ('I well imagined that Your Royal
Highness would not give me your approval.')[90] There can be times
when one feels that a superior has such an unfair down upon oneself
that one hardly has the heart to go on trying to win his full approval.
The unlucky diplomatist was just then in more trouble over another
negotiation, wherein he had recently assured Francis 'that I shall do
nothing giddy (*point d'étourderie*)'[91] in trying a second time to marry
off his elder sister, Elisabeth-Thérèse. Here Francis still differed
from Fleury, from whom Stainville had gathered that he much
wished that the Orleans marriage 'could be renewed'.[92]

The gentle and generous Elisabeth-Thérèse had stood with her
younger brother Charles behind their mother in her championship
of the interests of Lorraine. Whereas an Austrian faction at the
residual court at Lunéville in the middle thirties had been headed by
the livelier sister, Anne-Charlotte. Favourite with Francis and his
alleged intelligencer, she was said to have promoted dissension with
their mother. In Austrian interests both princesses were now
designated for a nuptial clinch of the new settlement in Italy. The
idea was for Anne-Charlotte to marry Don Carlos, now set up as
King of Naples, and for Elisabeth-Thérèse to be taken by twice
widowed Charles Emmanuel, King of Sardinia. As things turned
out, Don Carlos was matched instead with Princess Maria Amalia of
Saxony so as to form what the British envoy at Naples called the
ugliest couple in the world. If Stainville in Paris could thus relax his
contacts with the Neapolitan minister, he continued in close
collaboration with the Sardinian, Commander de Solar, in seeing to
the French aspects of the matchmaking between Elisabeth-Thérèse
and Charles Emmanuel.

In recognition of the French ties of the house of Lorraine Duke
Francis decided towards the end of 1736 that the honour of
conducting his sister to the Sardinian court should fall to the Princess
of Armagnac, wife of Prince Charles of Armagnac, head of the
Armagnac branch. Its relations with the elder line of Lorraine were
habitually bad and Francis now failed to improve them since this
Prince Charles, French Master of the Horse, had for years been

[90] Marquis de Stainville to Duke Francis III, Paris, 27 Jan. 1737: Ö.S./H.H.S., Lotheringisches
Hausarchiv 123.
[91] Ibid., 14 Sept. 1736: 203/III 542.
[92] Ibid., 8 Dec. 1735: 202/III 503 (Nachlass Stainville).

legally separated from his childless wife, Françoise-Adélaïde. She
was important in her own right as the eldest child of the Marshal de
Noailles by his marriage to the niece and heiress of Madame de
Maintenon. This marshal spanned two reigns on intimate terms
with both Louis XIV and Louis XV, was to exercise a formative
influence upon the career of the future Duke de Choiseul, and was
then in touch with the Marquis de Stainville in the wake of the fury
of Prince Charles d'Armagnac at the distinction proposed for his wife
without his having been consulted. Stainville did not conceal his
'sincere attachment for this prince',[93] drawn together perhaps by
common experience of equestrian pursuits and matrimonial discord.
In the thick of this family squabble the luckless diplomat incurred
blame from every quarter, even from his old friend, the Regent of
Lorraine. At least, though, her daughter Elisabeth-Thérèse did write
in her large, girlish hand from Lunéville to thank Stainville 'for the
interest which you are taking in my marriage'.[94]

From Vienna Francis might refuse 'to enter into the little quarrels
which may exist between Prince Charles and his wife'.[95] At Versailles
Louis XV himself had to impose the ducal commission to the
Princess d'Armagnac. She left for the expiring court at Lunéville,
stirred into a final activity by the wedding-preparations. There the
regent had represented that 'all the liveries . . . are in rags'[96] and must
be renewed; but, correspondingly lamented the Count de Richecourt
in Vienna, 'there is neither red cloth nor galloons for the livery'.[97]
Francis, however, could rise to an occasion. He stepped up his sister's
dowry to 300,000 livres and equipped her with magnificent silks from
Lyons despite black intelligence from the chief minister of Sardinia,
the celebrated Marquis D'Ormea, upon the sober court of Turin.
Court-dresses were something of a problem too for the Princess
d'Armagnac, who had not been presented at Versailles owing to her
marital separation; still, on a ruling from Fleury, she prevailed over
the Princess de Craon for a seat in the bridal carriage.

On 5 March 1737 the Princess Elisabeth-Thérèse was married at
Lunéville to the King of Sardinia in the person of the Prince de
Carignan. It was an ultimate and mournful celebration. Next day the
Regent of Lorraine and her two daughters left Lunéville for ever.

[93] Marquis de Stainville, memorandum enclosed by him to Prince Francis, Paris, 16 Feb.
1737: Ö.S./H.H.S., Lothringisches Hausarchiv 123.
[94] Princess Elisabeth-Thérèse of Lorraine to Marquis de Stainville, Lunéville, 31 Jan. 1737:
Arch. M-et-M/Vienne, 3F 373, no. 163.
[95] Duke Francis III to Marquis de Stainville, Vienna, 16 Jan. 1737: Ö.S./H.H.S.,
Lothringisches Hausarchiv 200, fo. 83.
[96] Regent of Lorraine, undated memorandum (probably late 1736), 'Mémoire de ce que mon
fils s'est chargé pour ce qui regarde le mariage de sa soeur': ibid., fo. 87.
[97] Count de Richecourt, undated memorandum (probably late 1736), 'Une notte du comte de
Richecourt au sujet du mariage de cette princesse avec le Roy de Sardaigne': ibid., fo. 73.

After long centuries the dynasty of Lorraine was taking leave of its people. All were in tears and the assembled crowds gave way to extraordinary transports of affectionate grief, lamenting, imploring, impeding departure so that the startled Sardinian envoy was reminded of some agony from Dante's Inferno.

At last the conclusive cavalcade won through grief to Haroué – the Craons indispensable to the end. Thence the displaced family of Lorraine finally divided upon its several ways, the mother to finish her days at Commercy, the bride in fact to predecease her in Turin.

The Prince de Craon, who saw out the old dynasty of Lorraine, was prevailed upon to usher in the new. It was an uncomfortable position for the landowning aristocracy of Lorraine, with loyalty pointing towards Vienna, prudence to Versailles. In neither court were they popular, the Austrians suspecting them of French sympathies and vice versa. The Lorrainers tried, with appreciable success, to make the best of a bad job and both worlds. Stanislas, an unpretentious person of genuine kindliness, sought to help them and several held office as chamberlains both to him and to Francis. In April 1737 Craon arrived in Paris in order to notify the French court formally of the arrival in Lorraine of Stanislas Leszczynski. Nimble courtier as he was, Craon 'found himself very embarrassed'.[98] As for Francis, he confided to the Marquis de Stainville that Craon's mission 'affects me keenly . . . I was not at all expecting it'[99] from the prince whom he had just appointed to be his master of the horse and harbinger in Tuscany.

At the same time Francis appointed Stainville his great chamberlain in acceptance of his continued services, as had been urged upon their master by Richecourt and Pfütschner. Toussaint, however, assured Stainville that Francis's decision 'was his own. He said with a certain something in speaking that since the fatal moment of the revolution you had shewn him an extreme desire to follow and remain attached to him . . . He would like to be able to do more.'[1] It was enough to cause the marquis to assure Francis that 'it restores me to life, which I should only have dragged out miserably if I had been obliged to pass into another's service'.[2] He now declined that of Stanislas, who characteristically described this refusal as 'increasing my esteem for you . . . So follow your laudable resolve, wishing you all the happiness which you deserve.'[3]

---

[98] Durival, op. cit., i. 156.
[99] Prince Francis to Marquis de Stainville, Vienna, 15 Apr. 1737: Arch. M-et-M/Vienne, 3F 362, no. 175.
[1] Baron Toussaint to Marquis de Stainville, Vienna, 15 May 1737: ibid., 3F 373, no. 186.
[2] Marquis de Stainville to Prince Francis, Paris, 29 Apr. 1737: ibid., 3F 88, No. 126.
[3] King Stanislas to Marquis de Stainville, Lunéville, 7 May 1737: ibid., 3F 373, no. 182.

In thanking Francis the Marquis de Stainville had promptly mentioned 'another interest arising from my heart, namely that of my son. He still needs another year before he is fit to be left behind where the unhappy position of his property forces him to remain' in the proffered French service:'otherwise I should certainly have taken the liberty of offering Your Royal Highness his services like my own'.[4] As it was, the marquis put it to Francis on his son's behalf that 'a bare recommendation to the cardinal [Fleury] could lay the foundation of his fortune'. Francis replied: 'If the opportunity presents itself of recommending your eldest, I will willingly do so, having seen with satisfaction that you accept the position of Great Chamberlain which I offered you.'[5]

This gracious message was couched in the hand of Toussaint, who three days earlier had stuck his own oar in with Stainville:

I think, Sir, that one must now form a system for your family. You will first of all say to me, what am I meddling in, and I shall have the honour to reply that Toussaint is still the same, and after he has said what he thinks, you will at any rate be at perfect liberty to do what you wish. This system should be formed at your end but not at first put to the Master. It must be done imperceptibly. Your eldest can but remain in France. I cannot say anything as to the arrangements to be made with regard to him. The younger ones or the next one could come over here.[6]

At the age of seventeen the destiny of the future Duke de Choiseul was already orientated towards France. If Fleury prospectively endowed her with Lorraine, so too with Choiseul who was to clinch the legacy. For the present it was understood in that April of 1737 that his father would be bridging the family divide by going as great chamberlain 'to maintain the table of the Duke [Francis] of Lorraine at Brussels, with 12,000 florins pension'.[7] Toussaint was soon warning Stainville that he would have to live within his means at Brussels: Brussels because for a while after signing away the duchy of Lorraine in February 1737, Francis was left a prince without a principality as the last of the Medici lingered on in promised Tuscany. So, as a suitable stopgap, the emperor had appointed his son-in-law governor-general of the Austrian Netherlands till Tuscany should fall in. It quickly did.

[4] Marquis de Stainville to Prince Francis, Paris, 29 Apr. 1737: u.s., and for the following.
[5] Prince Francis to Marquis de Stainville, Laxenburg, 18 May 1737: ibid., 3F 362, no. 177.
[6] Baron Toussaint to Marquis de Stainville, Vienna, 15 May 1737: ibid., 3F 373, no. 186.
[7] Luynes, i. 233.

VIII

On 15 June 1737 the British Ambassador in Paris, the Earl Waldegrave, reported that the Marquis de Stainville had told him 'in great confidence that he received the day before yesterday advice from P. de Craon that the Gran Duc is in a very ill way having lost his stomach entirely, and not likely to hold out long'.[8] On 9 July John Gaston of Tuscany opportunely died. For years indeed this degenerate but canny recluse had been rumoured already dead or dying. In contradiction of such reports he had made his last public appearance at the festival of Saint John the Baptist in 1729, when he had driven drunk through the crowds of Florence, vomiting out of the carriage-window and slobbering obscenities till he could be got back to the Pitti palace. There the Grand Duke remained for the last eight years of his reign, almost permanently 'snug in his Bed, not that he was sick, but out of pure indulgence',[9] ministered to by his horrid Ruspanti, a privileged gang of roughs and drabs, largely curly-locked Germans. They would sometimes impersonate the grand duke's chief nobles and their ladies to open the orgies which he had them perform in his stinking bed-chamber: on occasion, 'to stifle the disagreeable smells of the bed, the room was covered entirely... with new gathered roses'.[10] Such was the last representative of that long line of Medici which had done more, perhaps, than any other reigning house to promote the civilization of Europe.

Now Tuscany was back in the European kitty after only a few months of waiting for Francis with nowhere to rule. The Senate and Council of Florence swore fealty to Grand Duke Francis II in the person of his representative, the ubiquitous Prince de Craon. He had arrived with his wife a month before the Medici demise, after a crossing of the Mont Cenis which cost him fifty louis. They found Florence baking in 'excessive heat. We are deprived of appetite and sleep, but one does without them':[11] that to Stainville four days before the demise of John Gaston who, shrewd to the last, had rated Craon more of a gentleman than a genius.[12]

Francis now held the grand duchy as a fief from the emperor. If the days of Guelph and Ghibelline were over, now began that Austrian

[8] Earl Waldegrave to Duke of Newcastle, Paris, 15 June 1737: Waldegrave Papers.
[9] Baron von Pöllnitz, op. cit., ii. 132.
[10] Mark Noble, *Memoirs of the Illustrious House of Medici* (London, 1797), p. 444.
[11] Prince de Craon to Marquis de Stainville, Florence, 5 July 1737: Arch. M-et-M/Vienne, 3F 370, no. 262.
[12] Cf. Alfredo Reumont, 'Il Principe e la Principessa di Craon e i primi tempi della regenza lorena in Toscana' in *Archivo Storico Italiano*, 3rd series, xxv (Florence, 1877), 228.

ascendancy in Tuscany which was to render it a show-piece of enlightened despotism, was to endure till the unification of Italy.

From the Palazzo della Crocetta, once owned by Lorenzo the Magnificent, the Prince de Craon as President of the Provisional Council of Regency inaugurated the new regime and was soon congratulating himself that he had 'reduced the ceremonial by half'.[13] He had settled in and was keen to lure the Stainvilles to Florence, wishing that he could give the marquis 'a foretaste of the wines of this country. I drink no other although I have some excellent burgundy, rhenish and champagne. The fruit is delicious, the game admirable and in a month we are having abundant sea-fish. Tell all this to my little niece and leave everything to come here and enjoy the delights which abound.' A week later Craon was 'counting upon your being here for All Saints. None of the citrons in my garden shall come off before then and I am reserving for Madame de Stainville the pleasure of picking them herself.'[14]

This choice reunion in Florence was to be postponed since Francis was unable to take prompt possession of his principality. He was then in further Serbia in pursuance of hostilities against the Turk which were soon to engage the Count de Stainville also.

In the Eastern War Austria was fighting as the ally of Russia against the Ottoman Empire and a complex background. A Russo-Turkish treaty of 1724 had provided for the dismemberment of Persia, only to be frustrated by the unexpected rise of the Persian patriot, Nadir Shah. During the ensuing Turco-Persian war of 1730–1736 the Turks had found on at least one occasion, after defeating the Persians under the walls of Baghdad in 1733, that numbers of Russian troops and technicians were disguised as Persians in the enemy service. In the same year that the war against the Persians had ended open war with the Russians had begun. In 1736 the Russians had descended upon Turkish Tartary, capturing disputed Azov and overrunning the Crimea. In 1737, while the implausible Russo-Austro-Turkish congress at Nemirov was getting nowhere, the Russians further captured Ochakov by something of a fluke and held it against Turkish counter-attack. In general, however, the Porte followed the French renegade Bonneval's advice to concentrate against Austria, now entering the fray and thrusting out from her great bastion at Belgrade to the traditional accompaniment once again of the Türkenglocken, the bells summoning the faithful throughout the Habsburg dominions to morning prayer against the infidel.

[13] Prince de Craon to Marquis de Stainville, Florence, 17 Aug. 1737: *u.s.*, no. 260, and for the following.
[14] Ibid., 24 Aug. 1737: no. 259.

Francis of Lorraine, separated for the first time from his bride, was participating along with his brother Charles as a volunteer in this Balkan campaign under the command of the protestant Field-Marshal Count Seckendorff, at odds with the controlling Hofkriegsrat in Vienna and subjected in the field to military intrigues to which Francis is said to have lent himself. In this unhopeful set-up Seckendorff in July 1737 thrust southwards from Belgrade across the Turkish frontier in the direction of Nish. It was a gruelling march through sparsely populated country in intense heat. Half the Austrian bread was bad and water ran short. Sweating it out in thick uniforms with cumbersome muskets, many men had to be beaten forward by their officers.[15] However, things were probably not too bad for Francis who went to war along with three personal doctors, eight cooks, and a baggage-train including a tankwagon of sweet water, two of wine and two dozen armchairs.

The day after Francis left for the front, his logistic support down the Danube had been explained by the ever-involved Toussaint to the Marquis de Stainville: 'The equipage consists of 360 persons, 124 tents, 230 horses, 29 mules, 40 convertible carts, 190 oxen, which have left on 31 large boats and 5 rafts. 3 open tables will be kept [for officers] ... All that calls for a tremendous equipage in a country where one has to bring everything. I have been in sole charge of it. I am leaving in four days to join His Royal Highness.'[16] The secretary had qualified as staff-officer even if he was to lament upon campaign, 'I am not a soldier.'[17]

It was in camp before Nish that Francis learnt that he had become Grand Duke of Tuscany. Thence on 26 July 1737 he wrote to Stainville in Paris enclosing formal letters of notification to Louis XV and his court. In private, though, Francis was to observe bitterly that Louis 'has made an Italian of me. He has forced me to cede my dominions.'[18] The new grand duke refused to mourn more than six weeks for his predecessor and cracked down upon the 'malicious trick'[19] whereby illwishers at Vienna were urging him to take up residence forthwith in his new principality, nicely remote from the imperial seat of power.

Upon receiving the grand-ducal notification Fleury assured

---

[15] For this march and campaign cf. Lavender Cassels, *The Struggle for the Ottoman Empire 1717–1740* (London, 1966), pp. 126 *et passim*.

[16] Baron Toussaint to Marquis de Stainville, Vienna, 12 June 1737: Arch. M-et-M/Vienne, 3F 373, no. 154.

[17] Baron Toussaint to Marquis de Stainville, camp at Jagodin, 9 July 1737: ibid., no. 193.

[18] Grand Duke Francis II of Tuscany to Hegherti, cited, Hegherti to Cardinal Fleury, Venice, 16 Mar. 1742: Arch. Aff. Étr. C.P., Autriche, vol. 232, fo. 127.

[19] Grand Duke Francis II to Bartenstein, Nish, 3 Aug. 1737: cited, F. Hennings, op. cit., p. 191.

Stainville 'that all the liquidation would be finished in Lorraine immediately (*incessament*)'.[20] This immediacy was in practice to extend over the next fifteen years and more, for the whole of the rest of the Marquis de Stainville's working life, largely devoted to trying to unravel from remorseless procrastination and prevarication the dreary tangle of financial claims and debts left by Francis's relinquishment of Lorraine, in effect in favour of France, so soon after that power had contracted large obligations to him in his erstwhile capacity of duke in respect of the military contributions levied in Lorraine during the War of the Polish Succession.

That autumn the Marquis de Stainville secured permission to take a turn in Lorraine, where he saw to his own affairs as well as those of his master. The latter plunged him further into prolonged unpleasantness. Stainville grumbled over the inadequacy of his instructions concerning, for instance, the four and a half million livres owing to Francis from the French government in respect of the period when he had been a prince without a principality. The Lorrainers did well, at least, over the division of archives. Here the new French foreign minister, Amelot de Chaillou, had asked Stainville to specify 'those which you consider to be family papers, which should stay with the Duke [Francis] of Lorraine'.[21] Under this agreement the detailed work was done by one of Francis's private secretaries, Molitoris,[22] who stretched the private papers to include nearly everything concerning the foreign affairs of Lorraine. Off they went to constitute what became the Lothringisches Hausarchiv in Vienna; but this contentious division of the papers, handled by Stainville, long remembered, largely reversed, in effect put them into hotchpot for over two hundred years and compromised their contribution to history.[23]

[20] Marquis de Stainville to Grand Duke Francis II, Paris, 26 Aug. 1737: Esteri del Granducato di Toscana, vol. 2295/1286, fo. 1.

[21] Amelot de Chaillou to Marquis de Stainville, Versailles, 10 May 1737: Arch. M-et-M/Vienne, 3F 373, no. 183.

[22] Cf. memorandum of 18 Oct. 1736, 'Titres et autres pièces tirées du Trésor des Chartes de Nancy par les Sieurs Roezen et Molitoris' – Arch. Nat., K 1185, no. 61; and, generally, for the subsequent French inventorying, Paul Marichal, *Catalogue des manuscrits conservés à la Bibliothèque Nationale sous les Nos 1 à 725 de la Collection de Lorraine* (Nancy, 1896), pp. vif.

[23] Cf. Pierre Marot, 'Le "Fonds Lorrain" de Vienne' in *Inventaire-sommaire des archives départementales antérieures à 1790: Meurthe-et-Moselle. Série 3F – Fonds dit de Vienne*, ed. Pierre Marot, Mme P. Marot, Étienne Delcambre, and Marie-Thérèse Aubry (Nancy, 1956), pp. 1f. (In response to some feeling in Lorraine after the First World War the division of the archives of Lorraine made in 1737 was revised in 1923 and ratified in 1926. The Austrian government then surrendered to the French government much but not all of the Lothringisches Hausarchiv prior to 1737. Thus the returned Fonds de Vienne mostly carry archival stamps of both the Habsburg Empire and the French Department. In 1939 the Fonds de Vienne were sent for safety to the Gironde. In 1942 they were returned to Nancy by order of the German occupying power. For about a decade thereafter these by then disordered archives seem in practice to have been in the main inaccessible.)

Molitoris had the enormous task of inventorying for Francis not only his papers but all his movable possessions, which he had the right to remove from Lorraine. Francis, fond of pictures and a future benefactor of the Uffizi, was not too overawed by his Florentine inheritance, and had transported from Lorraine living artists also. Molitoris had to sort out his choicest subjects as well as possessions. Designated to Florence, besides a team of administrators, was the architect Jadot, who was to endow it with a lasting memorial to his master and himself; also the landscape-gardener Gervais and the artist Saint-Urbain. Artists can be prickly people and the harassed secretary was also beset by other loyal Lorrainers begging not to be left under an alien prince. Stainville too, visiting Stanislas at Lunéville that October, put in a word with the economical Francis on behalf of his 'old servants ... who desire nothing so much as to be re-employed'[24] by him. The chosen were concentrated by Molitoris at Brussels and next month he shipped his contingent of four hundred and fifty persons from Ostend to Leghorn. He reported wryly: 'Noah, in order to embark all his animals, did not need so much patience as I.'[25] The argosy included an erstwhile shepherd-lad discovered by Pfütschner, now the librarian Jamerai Duval who rejoiced that his master's library 'arrived as though by a miracle at Leghorn after having more than once been nearly sunk'.[26]

Molitoris also had to organize convoys overland, and estimated that in all at least seven hundred Lorrainers participated in this somewhat unusual migration, comprising as it did the prosperous and well in rather than the poor and the persecuted.

This bustle was towards the arrival in Florence of Francis, who quickly quit the Balkan campaign that was evidently being bungled by Seckendorff. Ottoman forces recaptured Nish and disappointed Austrian hopes of retrieving some of the military prestige lost during the Polish war by cheap successes against the decadent Turks in a sequel to the triumphs of Prince Eugene. This disappointment was visited upon Seckendorff in the form of house-arrest.

Meanwhile the Marquis de Stainville returned to Paris, where he had moved a little up the left bank to the Rue des Saints-Pères, in anticipation of waiting upon Francis in Florence. The prospect sweetened the grand duke's disagreeable decision that Stainville, instead of converting his representation of Lorraine in Paris into a Tuscan mission, should hand over to the former representative there

---

[24] Marquis de Stainville to Grand Duke Francis II, Lunéville, 19 Oct. 1737: Esteri del Granducato di Toscana, vol. 2295/1286, fo. 8.
[25] Molitoris to Grand Duke Francis II, November 1737: cited, F. Hennings, op. cit., p. 190.
[26] Jamerai Duval, cited, Henry Poulet, 'Les Lorrains à Florence' in *Revue lorraine illustrée*, iv (1909), 41.

of the Medici, the Abbé Franquini. In November 1737 it was understood at Versailles that Stainville would bask in honorific attendance upon Francis and 'follow him everywhere. They [Stainville and Franquini] seem very pleased, both of them.'[27] Perhaps Stainville was putting a good face on things. He often had to, as when Francis now postponed his visit to Tuscany for over a year.

On Christmas Eve of 1737 Stainville 'had his leavetaking audience of the King and Queen'[28] in public with ceremonial adieus to the Dauphin and princesses. The queen received 'in her large closet before her room. M. de Nangis was behind the Queen's armchair with M. Dubourdet, brigadier. M. de Stainville at the same time presented his eldest son; but what was odd was that he also presented the Abbé de Franquini, who is staying here in his place ... I have heard it said to the Abbé Franquini himself that ambassadors sometimes presented their successors, but that this was not even the usual custom: but for envoys, it is not thought that there is an example. This same day, the 24th, Milord Waldegrave had a private audience to inform the King and Queen of the death of the Queen of England.'

The death of Queen Caroline and the intriguing diplomatic precedent overshadowed the formal presentation to the court of Versailles of him who would one day dominate it as Duke de Choiseul. He would have participated, however, in the convivial sequel.

'Since', explained the Marquis de Stainville, 'it is the custom on that day for the king to give a large dinner to the representative minister, I invited to it all the ambassadors, who in their first reaction all promised me to come to it.'[29] Then disobliging Delci, the nuncio and so doyen of the diplomatic corps, persuaded all the ambassadors but one to cry off from a farewell to a mere minister. 'Milord Walgrave [sic]', wrote Stainville, 'came to my dinner, saying that friendship took precedence over dignity. The Cardinal [Fleury] sent his nephew to it, and I had at it all the ministers of foreign courts.' Fleury strongly disapproved Delci's slap at the cardinal's old friend.

Thus did a British ambassador lend lustre to the rather modest launching at the French court of the youth destined to become the prime antagonist of England in that age. If the Marquis de Stainville omitted his son's presentation from his report to Francis, the latter's entourage even in the depth of the Serbian campaign had shewn an almost premonitory concern with the future of the future Choiseul

[27] Luynes, i. 403.
[28] Ibid., i. 427, and for the following.
[29] Marquis de Stainville to Grand Duke Francis II, Paris, 30 Dec. 1737: Esteri del Granducato di Toscana, vol. 2295/1286, fo. 9, and for the following.

and of his brothers. 'From the camp of Jagodin near the Morava four leagues from Parachin'[30] Toussaint had written to Stainville on 9 July 1737: 'I have always understood the necessity of leaving the eldest of your sons in France, but with the younger ones I think that, assuming their inclination, one could put one of them into the army and leave him the name of Stainville as in this country, and the other into the church since His Royal Highness will be able to set up this last in the Netherlands where there are good benefices and bishoprics which will be at his disposal.' It may, however, have been on behalf of his ecclesiastically inclined son that the marquis was already in touch with Stanislas Leszczynski.[31]

Baron Toussaint's projection for the divergent sons of the Marquis de Stainville was to be realized in remarkable measure. The Austrian affiliation favoured by the father was indeed to be that of his youngest son, Jacques, who was duly to retain the name of Stainville, was to become a page to Francis and later an officer of dragoons in the imperial forces; whereas the heritage of the eldest, Stephen Francis, was already earmarked to France and, under the patronage of Fleury, he himself was down for the French army; the second son, Leopold Charles, was to enter the French church. By a curious convolution of fortune the eldest brother in the French army was to see his first active service with the Austrian, while it was the youngest brother in the Austrian army who was to become a Marshal of France. For the eldest there were ultimately other things in store.

---

[30] Baron Toussaint to Marquis de Stainville, camp at Jagodin, 9 July 1737: Arch. M-et-M/Vienne, 3F 373, no. 193, and for the following.
[31] Cf. King Stanislas to Marquis de Stainville, Lunéville, 7 May 1737: ibid., no. 182.

CHAPTER VIII

PASTORAL

I

YOUNG Stephen Francis, Count de Stainville, was, in eighteenth-century parlance, 'moved early by an active ambition. Tormented by the noble desire to cover with a new glory a name already illustrious, he had entered upon the career of arms'.[1] The aspiration towards fame, *la gloire,* close to the heart of any true aristocracy, still largely prevailed with the continental nobility of the eighteenth century. The spirited young Stainville perceived that there was more glory for a soldier in fighting than in hanging around on the reserve. And the hostilities of the Polish Succession were hardly over before the Russians and their Austrian allies conveniently went into their attack on Turkey.

Stephen de Stainville only had to overcome the disadvantage of France's not being a belligerent. It is related that 'the young Count de Stainville, with difficulty bearing the idea that his extreme youth had been an obstacle to his serving in the campaigns of 1733 and 1734, desired, asked and obtained permission to go to the army of the emperor till the conclusion of peace. The Marquis de Stainville ... fell in with this desire with all the more compliant ease in that, happy as a father to discover in his son this ardour for instruction, this manly élan, he further hopefully saw therein the means of soon settling him in the service of the emperor: a course which young Stainville rejected despite the advantages which were presented to him, and despite the certainty of the obstacles which he would find in the service of France owing to the attachment of his father for the emperor',[2] the then Grand Duke Francis.

Set now, however, upon the immediate opportunity, the Count de Stainville secured leave of absence from the French army in order to serve with the Austrian on the campaign of 1738. This was the more convenient since the Austrian command for the coming year was nominally attributed to the Grand Duke Francis. While the eighteen-year-old Stainville was intent upon setting out via Vienna, cool

---

[1] Mouffle d'Angerville, *Vie privée de Louis XV,* iii.181.
[2] Essai/Arsenal 5808, fos. 10–11.

treatment from Francis once again spelt 'cruel uncertainty'[3] for the father, lingering on in Paris, settling up his affairs.

On 28 January 1738 the Marquis de Stainville granted a legal power of attorney to his wife to manage all his business and financial affairs, in the way of running the estates, granting leases, and so forth. While it may well have been some relief to unload on to his managing wife, the background was the adherence to the grand duke of the marquis, whose lands were passing under French tutelage. The new arrangement may have looked already towards the early takeover by the Count de Stainville which was in fact to occur. And here, certainly, was another instance of the important part which women could play then in business as in society: evident enough to the Stainville tenantry, who were now going to have to look lively. Later that year extensive work was in hand to renovate the Château de Demange, which the Marquise de Stainville made her principal seat.

Two days after shifting the burden of his patrimony the Marquis de Stainville was to be found playing cards with Fleury – picquet and quadrille were his games – as the cardinal recovered from an upset, sipping broth. Soon, though, sickness was to strike a Stainville.

It could be unhealthy that year to be in Vienna, a city for which vital statistics were already being compiled from official sources in some detail and published promptly in the press, within a fortnight of the close of each year. Recorded causes of death in 1738 ranged from the usual one a year run over by a carriage, two unfortunates 'stifled by coaldust',[4] up to six hundred deaths from consumption, the worst killer in 1737 (589 deaths), but now surpassed. In the early months of 1738 figures for fatal cases of smallpox were hovering upwards (those for 1737 in brackets): in April 15 (9), in May 26 (10), 32 (12) in June, edging up again to 40 (13) that July. That was the background to the terse recollection of the Duke de Choiseul: 'Smallpox, which I caught on the eve of my departure from Vienna to the [imperial] army [in the Banat], prevented me from taking part in this campaign.'[5]

In that summer of 1738 the scourge became epidemic in Vienna. Deaths from smallpox jumped up to 97 in August, 120 in September, to a peak of 132 in October. (Figures for 1737 had been 12, 26, 20.) Over a hundred more succumbed that November, as also in December still. On 12 December 1738 the Emperor Charles VI issued a sanitary ordinance for his capital deploring the poor observance of previous regulations of 1708 and 1732. Each householder was now

[3] Marquis de Stainville to Grand Duke Francis II, Paris, 23 Jan. 1738: Esteri del Granducato di Toscana, vol. 2295/1286, fo. 11.

[4] *Wienerisches Diarium*, 10 Jan. 1739, supplement to no. 3, p.34.

[5] Choiseul, *Mémoires*, p.3.

held responsible, under pain of paying twelve Reichstalers (some £3 on the contemporary exchange) into the official poorbox (Cassa Pauperum), for collecting his refuse into a heap for removal, at 8 a.m. in winter and six in summer, by the municipal refuse-carts operated by the Gemeines-Stadt-Unter-Kammer-Amt. (They were merciful with hyphens then.) But the grim year was already at its close.

Deaths from smallpox in the city and suburbs of Vienna in 1738 totalled 720 compared with 199 the year before. These figures were included in those for deaths there from all causes, 7,363 in 1738 (3,873 male, 3,490 female) compared with 6,735 in 1737. The comparable figures for births as registered by baptism in those two years were respectively 5,622 and 5,704, suggesting the fragility there as elsewhere of the demographic equilibrium; but before assuming a decline in population one needs to reckon that Vienna most likely compared with towns in France which continued to grow, despite a regular excess of deaths over births, owing to an influx, already, from the countryside. In Vienna furthermore the figures in the 'Todten-Protocoll' excluded deaths of 'those children who had not reached one full year of age'.[6] (Regular omissions of infant mortality were apt to be frequent in death-registers about then.)[7] This sinister omission prefaced tables for Vienna of annual deaths by age-groups wherein considerably the largest group was the first – in 1738 (1737), 575 (578) deaths at the age of one, tapering down to a striking low-point of four (two) deaths at the happy age of eleven: whence the figures rose again to an ominously early peak of around a hundred deaths each year by the age of forty as compared with twenty-nine (twenty in 1737) at nineteen, the age of the Count de Stainville. He did survive but might have benefited had his father been less indifferent to that earlier advocacy of inoculation by King George I.

The unpleasant and then so prevalent affliction of smallpox apparently did not much impair the already unhandsome appearance of the Count de Stainville. He was an ugly little fellow, 'repellent even',[8] short and chubby to look at, with a snub nose, thick, sensual lips, fair, reddish hair and the green eyes that often go with it, one of them with a slight cast. Of a build 'more robust than svelte',[9] he was yet 'fairly well proportioned',[10] his best features being his well turned

---

[6] *Wienerisches Diarium*, 11 Jan. 1738, supplement to no. 4, p. 46.

[7] Cf. the recent discussion of 'ce vice majeur' in regard to French parochial registers in the demographic study by Pierre Goubert, *Beauvais et le Beauvaisis de 1600 à 1730*, pp. 27–8. He there cites L.-E. Duvillard du Léman, *Analyse et tableaux de l'influence de la petite vérole sur la mortalité à chaque âge* (Paris, 1806). The present statistics from Vienna antedate the period elucidated by Duvillard.

[8] Prince de Montbarey, *Mémoires autographes de M. le prince de Montbarey* (Paris, 1826–7), i. 200.   [9] Gleichen, p. 61.

[10] Prince de Tallyrand, 'De M. le duc de Choiseul' in *Mémoires du prince de Talleyrand*, v. 584, and for the following.

legs and his hands, those pointers to breeding. Talleyrand tells that Stainville 'derived great advantage from the beauty of his hands which were small, slender, white and adorned with beautiful fingernails'. Nearly all agreed, besides, that overall his was an ugliness which was 'very agreeable, his little eyes sparkled with wit, his tip-tilted nose gave him an amiable air, and thick laughing lips foretold the gaiety of his remarks'.[11] This vivid young subaltern was described in the year of 1738 by Madame de Graffigny as being 'good hearted but he likes balls and the comedy'.[12] These tastes contrasted with those of his father and were not the kind approved by his mother. But then her eldest son seemed to have a double dose of that vivacity and sparkle which she herself so conspicuously lacked.

Young Stainville was one to make the most of his enforced sojourn in sumptuous Vienna, where the aristocratic mansions 'are indeed generally hid, as it were, in narrow streets, but in Stateliness and Extent, they very far surpass those at Paris'.[13] Architecturally Vienna then was just blossoming into that baroque triumph of the Habsburgs which, with its counterpart in Prague, celebrated their empire more splendidly than any other in modern Europe. Only the year before, Fischer von Erlach the younger had rounded off the magnificence of the imperial library in the Hofburg (reputed the best in Europe for printed books) in accordance with designs by his inspired father, who had also planned the brilliant palace at Schönbrunn, as yet unfinished.

Contacts with the Austrian court would have been open to the Count de Stainville through friends of his parents like the Harrachs and Pfütschner, perhaps even through such a prickly intimate as Toussaint. Of Stainville's age-group, though, a German contemporary remarked: 'Nothing is more vain nor more insupportable than a young Austrian, whose Father is in any Rank at Court. They are intoxicated with Pride and Presumption; and ... they think they may despise all the World'.[14] In a later context Stainville was to instance 'a hare-brained fop who, without wit, delivers gross insults; faugh, it makes one sick and reeks of Germanic bad upbringing (*la mauvaise éducation germanique*)'.[15] Stainville's distaste may for once have owed something to his mother, or perhaps to the Jesuits of Louis-le-Grand.

In Viennese society then gambling was 'carried to a very great Height'.[16] The later Choiseul was to be at times a fashionably heavy

[11] Gleichen, loc. cit.
[12] Madame de Graffigny, 'Portrait de Bélinde' in Eugène Asse, op. cit., pp. 143–4.
[13] J. G. Keysler, op. cit., iv. 222.
[14] Baron von Pöllnitz, op. cit., i. 254.
[15] Duke de Choiseul to Voltaire, Versailles, 6 July 1759: P. Calmettes, op. cit., p. 32.
[16] J. G. Keysler, loc. cit.

though not a compulsive gambler. And at that period of his youth he was liable to have other interests, other acquaintance. Stainville was familiar already with the French embassy in Vienna which he was himself to direct within twenty years in a resumption of that 'new system' of entente with Austria, then being cultivated as ambassador by the Marquis de Mirepoix, who had a brother in Austrian service.

Thirtysix-year-old Pierre-Louis de Lévis, Marquis de Mirepoix, came of old stock from Languedoc, where an ancestor's crusading zeal against the Albigensians had earned him and his heirs the title of French Hereditary Marshal of the Faith. For the diminished faith of the eighteenth century the joke was that the Mirepoix 'call cousins with the Virgin Mary'.[17] A chilly carapace of consequence invested the Marquis de Mirepoix, more honest than brilliant. He was glimpsed a few years later 'talking with his elbows, arguing with his chin, ... a decent fellow, hard, polite, dry, civil, etcetera'.[18] More congenial to Stainville, perhaps, was the circumstance that Mirepoix with his military bearing was particularly fond of dancing. And for the ambassador just then that meant mobilizing ladies since he was a widower.

Five years earlier the Marquis de Mirepoix had married little Anne-Gabrielle-Henriette Bernard, eleven-year-old granddaughter of the great banker Samuel Bernard. If the unaristocratic child was 'as pretty as an angel',[19] yet more to the point, perhaps, was her dowry of 800,000 livres. At fifteen she had died after a stillbirth. This marriage was strikingly prefigurative of that which the Count de Stainville was later to contract with a slip of a girl from another great financial family friendly with the Mirepoix.

While the convalescent Count de Stainville was sampling the court of Vienna in that autumn of 1738 his mother was unwell at the opposed court of Commercy, if court was still the term for the sadly reduced establishment of the erstwhile Regent of Lorraine. Faithfully waiting upon her former sovereign, the Marquise de Stainville would scarcely displease in holding forth, as she did, against the Germans. She was more than usually out of sorts just then because an incision for bleeding her right arm had been chafed by her tight sleeves, had formed an abscess and brought fever. She was looked after by her disloyal friend, Madame de Graffigny, who now wrote the Marquise's letters for her and relished the opportunity to pry. For Madame de

---

[17] Horace Walpole to Horace Mann, Strawberry Hill, 17 Aug. 1749 (O.S.): Walpole Correspondence, xx. 88.
[18] President Hénault to Marquise du Deffand, 17 July 1742: Madame du Deffand, Correspondance inédite de Mme du Deffand (Paris, 1809), ii. 121.
[19] Marais to President Bouhier, Paris, 12 Mar. 1733: Journal et mémoires de Mathieu Marais, ed. de Lescure (Paris, 1863 f.), iv. 470.

Graffigny was bored stiff by residual existence at the charming
Château de Commercy.[20] There they relieved the tedium by recalling
tales of its most celebrated inmate, how good old Cardinal de Retz
used to piss upon the hot firedogs for the simple pleasure of the hiss.[21]
Madame de Graffigny was less amused when a careless chambermaid
at an upper window emptied a chamberpot upon her head, only the
dress she was wearing 'was luckily an old one'.[22]

It was at Commercy that the hygienic Marquise de Stainville
admonished the lazy Madame de Graffigny that it was well worth
climbing thirty steps to one's bedroom 'in order to piss cleanly'.[23]
Madame de Graffigny, it was now arranged, should accompany her
upon an autumnal visit to Demange despite the fact that it was still
overrun by workmen so that the Marquise had previously been
camping there in an attic. The jaunt just suited Madame de Graffigny
since one of the trivial but typical effects of the recent change of
dynasty in Lorraine had been the stoppage of her modest state-
pension. The poor thing faced stark poverty. She had indeed
mobilized the indispensable Toussaint and something (a hundred
écus per annum) was eventually sorted out for her, after a resented
hiatus.[24] Meanwhile her strategy for the coming winter was, bluntly,
to live off her friends. For Madame de Graffigny, Demange was
usefully on the way to Cirey where she looked forward to livelier
lodging with Madame du Châtelet and Voltaire, sheltering there
upon the borders of Lorraine from any backlash from his recent
writings then circulating either in manuscript like the rude *Pucelle
d'Orléans* or in print like the *Lettres philosophiques*, which were giving
many French readers their first taste of the more liberal atmosphere
of England.

II

Madame de Graffigny's literary Little Saint, young Saint-Lambert,
was apparently there with the Marquis de Stainville to see the two
ladies off from Commercy on Sunday the 5th October 1738. It was
then that the amused Stainville confided to Madame de Graffigny
that the Marquis de Courtenvaux was no stranger to Demange,
where he made himself less popular with the servants than with their
mistress.

[20] The miniature palace of Commercy was gutted during the German retreat of 1944.
[21] Cf. Madame de Graffigny to Devaux, Commercy, autumn 1738: Yale/Beinecke:
Phillipps/Graffigny 23900, vol. ii, fo. 30.
[22] Ibid, 4 Oct. 1738: fo. 57.
[23] Madame de Graffigny to Devaux, Demange-aux-Eaux, 6 Oct. 1738: ibid., fo. 63.
[24] Cf. Devaux to Madame de Graffigny, Lunéville, 7–9 Oct. 1738, and Madame de Graffigny
to Devaux, Demange-aux-Eaux, 22 Oct. 1738: *u.s.*, respectively vol. i, fos. 211f., vol. ii, fo. 98.

The two ladies took coach for Demange with Madame de Graffigny cherishing an unread letter from Panpan throughout that long day. The distance was only some fifteen miles as the crow flies but their horses were exhausted by the upland country. They gave out in a wood where the party feared they would be spending the night. The lady travellers, then hardy perforce, got out to lighten the load and began to trudge it. Thus, with lifts in the coach off and on, they limped into the Château de Demange at half past one in the morning.

The exertions of the portly Madame de Graffigny were not quite over. She was disconcerted to find herself 'ushered up a stairway like a ladder'[25] and through a trapdoor into the attic previously inhabited by Madame de Stainville who explained that it was the quietest room in the house. That reconciled La Grosse no more than did its fine turkey carpet dotted with little tables and pretty Indian screens concealing a choice 'of charming chamberpots'. She spent next day moving down a floor to a bedroom near that, now, of her hostess.

Madame de Graffigny's new room at Demange was not quite finished. They had not plastered the mantelpiece nor varnished the panelling, a feature of the room which concealed a built-in cupboard, soon to be filled by Madame de Graffigny with books. But you could almost see yourself in the polish of the new parquet-floor. 'The room is cheerful although it has only one window, but it reaches nearly to the floor and the panes are very large', an attractive feature of the period. The furniture comprised a superior bed hung with green damask, armchairs, a commode, and an elegant table. Madame de Stainville always provided plenty of cushions and her guest stocked her room with some downy beauties 'as big as beds and not weighing half a pound'.[26] Even the censorious Madame de Graffigny admitted a little pathetically, 'I am enjoying my comforts, above all the good fire which is always burning in my room whether I am in it or not, and burning candles without it costing me anything, without fear of creditors.'[27] Her description to Panpan of the incidentals of autumnal existence there at Demange enables one to join him over two centuries in picturing her snug retreat: 'I see you in a very clean little room stretched out upon good cushions.'[28]

Madame de Graffigny's rather vinegary maid, Dubois (fond of a nip of something), slept in the adjacent closet, which their hostess had equipped with 'bidets and chamberpots as though for herself – no more to be said'.[29] The Marquise de Stainville's own bedroom, not

[25] Madame de Graffigny to Devaux, Demange-aux-Eaux, 6 Oct. 1738: u.s., vol. ii, fos. 63–4 for the following.
[26] Ibid., 14–16 Oct. 1738: fo. 81.   [27] Ibid., 12–13 Oct. 1738: fo. 79.
[28] Devaux to Madame de Graffigny, Lunéville, 7–9 Oct. 1738: u.s., vol. i, fo. 217.
[29] Madame de Graffigny to Devaux, Demange-aux-Eaux, 6 Oct. 1738: u.s., vol. ii, fo. 64.

specially large, contained a great big bed with a night-table, a
dressing-table, two occasional tables and a couple of embroidery-
frames, a small desk – very narrow, it is true — an Indian corner-
cupboard as large as a wardrobe, a capacious Indian chest, half a
dozen assorted armchairs including two wicker ones, a footstool and
two embroidered tuffets, a delicately worked folding-screen, and then
dotted around four little stands with caskets to match plus a pair of
outsize jars of potpourri. 'You will maintain', Madame de Graffigny
appreciated, 'that that is not true. It is. It is true that we do not wear
any panniers and that we cannot reach our seats without moving
some of the pieces of furniture in order to get through ... The chest,
the chests of drawers and the corner-pieces are surmounted by a
hundred Chinese [lacquered] boxes, workbaskets and small pots of
potpourri. If she could stack them up to the ceiling she would find
her doghole much handsomer.'[30] The spare elegance of much
eighteenth-century furnishing was not for the Marquise de Stainville.
Her visitor found it odd that anyone with such a passion for
cleanliness should live in such a clutter. Madame de Stainville merely
'says that it is her taste and good taste'.[31]

Unfinished as yet was the special attraction for Madame de
Graffigny, the library, due to accommodate some 'very good books
and a good five or six hundred volumes'[32], a decent provision then for
a little château stuck away in Lorraine. While the house was being
done up the attractive garden, as so often in French parts, had been
badly kept. But a lush garden running rather to seed in autumn has
its own attractions tinged with melancholy.

Such was the setting of existence for the two ladies in that distant
fall of 1738. It was a placid existence rippled only by those tensions
and intensities of feeling which imbue even the calm stretches of
human lives, being human.

For Madame de Graffigny mornings at Demange could be what
mornings in country-houses should be, quiet. She could luxuriate in
her own room if Madame de Stainville were busy with her chiding
supervision of her household and its renovation. Subsequently,
indeed, the guest was likely treated to the 'story of all the nails that
have been driven in here and of everything that she said to the
workmen at each hammer-blow'.[33] Sometimes, though, she could
read till noon in bed snugly close to the fire. Or else she would be
writing the latest instalment of her serial letters to Devaux as on one
Sunday, 19 October, when she was mercifully left alone to mind the
house since the weather was too bad for the usual arrangement

[30] Ibid., 22 Oct. 1738: fo. 102.   [31] Ibid: fo. 101.
[32] Ibid., 12–13 Oct. 1738: fo. 78.   [33] Ibid., 7–10 Oct. 1738: fo. 69.

whereby one of the maids went to mass in another village at a
different time from that at Demange attended by the rest of the
household. A fortnight later, though, the visitor did go to mass for
fear of scandal.

Madame de Graffigny's letters to Panpan were really the best kind
between friends, largely all about nothing, as Madame de Graffigny
was keenly aware. In sending him the inventory of her hostess's
bedroom she wrote that it might just as well be a blank sheet of
paper – only, not quite. A week after her arrival she explained to
Devaux, 'I cannot tell you my thoughts for I do not think at all
here.'[34] Reading, however, rescued her from a vegetative existence.

Demange provided atlases, dictionaries, an admirable edition
(presumably the 1734 translation from the Latin) of De Thou's great
history of the French wars of religion, a sumptuous 'Molière in
quarto, ah what prints, what an edition. I kissed it.'[35] In it she was
struck by a vignette of a swarm of cupids, one dressed as a doctor and
holding another down by giving him an enema. But, she grumbled,
there was little elegant literature. Madame de Stainville had given
her some hope of *Triomphe de l'harmonie*, a recent theatrical piece by
the Marquis Lefranc de Pompignan; only it turned out to be older
stuff. There were indeed more solid things by Father Renaud and by
Lok, otherwise John Locke. Madame de Graffigny honed up on him
for her next stopping-point at Cirey where, as she was rather
apprehensively aware, Madame du Châtelet and Voltaire had
Newton awaiting her. Some months earlier Voltaire had published
his greatly successful and controversial *Éléments de la philosophie de
Newton*, which was beginning to wean France from Cartesian
orthodoxy.

Cirey, however, was perhaps a little less of an isolated oasis than
might be supposed, seeing now that intellectual currents from
England had already reached even neighbouring Demange. One
does not know how far the future Choiseul, an admirer of the British
constitution resulting from the Glorious Revolution of 1688, may
have looked at the English philosophy in his father's library. One can
tell that, in later life at least, Choiseul's idea of happiness in a country-
house in winter depended not only upon a few real friends but also
upon 'a good library ... With that there is no longer any loneliness
nor, consequently, any boredom.'[36]

At Demange Madame de Graffigny used to read Locke in bed in
the mornings, mostly in small doses. Even so she found his
abstractions stiffish going, liable to give her headaches though not to

[34] Ibid., 14–16 Oct. 1738: fo. 81.
[35] Ibid., 12–13 Oct. 1738: fo. 78.
[36] Choiseul, 'Mémoires inédits', 3/18/13/566/3.

dull her critical faculty: 'Speaking of Locke, you will surely say that
I am being impertinent, but it is nonetheless true that he positively
has the effect upon me of M. Jourdain's philosophy-teacher,'[37] who in
Le Bourgeois Gentilhomme taught his pupil admirably what he already
knew. Madame de Graffigny would not have believed that Locke
'would have stayed in my head so exactly and at the same time so
incognito. He seems to me to have but a vague idea of it [philosophy]
and I find that he teaches me nearly nothing. In fine, there being no
longer the taste of novelty in it, I need to look for the beauty and
accuracy of his arguments in order not to treat him as a chatterbox
(bavard).' Such was Madame de Graffigny's delicately pointed
critique of the philosopher whom Voltaire revered. As she penned it
one Wednesday morning at Demange, on 19 November 1738, she
was aware that outside, through her large window, it had begun to
snow.

The gentle critic, though, availed herself at Demange of one or two
things which, unlike books, she thought she might not find at Cirey,
notably a wheel-operated lute, the original hurdy-gurdy. She
practised on it the whole morning of 14 October. Then sometimes if
she were lucky, as she had been a week earlier, Madame de Graffigny
could slip out for a solitary walk, before or after dinner in the middle
day, leaving the garden 'by a little door which opens on to a meadow,
my Panpichon . . . There is not a molehill in it. The grass there is like
velvet. The little river surrounds it, this river whose name I do not
know . . . It was more beautiful than a picture and it seems to me that
you entered into it. I have nearly always taken my walks with you.'[38]

Less congenial, often inescapable, was the company of the Marquise
de Stainville. After dinner next day, 8 October, the two ladies climbed
a hill to gain a pretty little wood looking out to more distant crests:
'When one is surrounded by mountains one sees that one sees
nothing. However I should have much enjoyed it if I had been alone.
For one was walking on velvet upon the sward. The woods are still
green. To the devil with people who feel nothing of the beauties of
nature and who chatter without cease.' The disjoint couple still
promenaded through the deteriorating weather of the advancing
season. When, after that November snowfall, frost hardened the
ground they were habitually to be seen between twelve and one
o'clock, walking 'along the meadows like two sad shepherdesses.'[39]

It probably gave them an appetite. The dinner-bell at Demange
usually rang at one o'clock, that for supper sometimes, apparently, at

[37] Madame de Graffigny to Devaux, Demange-aux-Eaux, 15–20 Nov. 1738: u.s., vol. ii, fo.
153, and for the following.
[38] Ibid., 7–10 Oct. 1738: fos. 67–9 for the following.
[39] Ibid., 22 Nov. 1738: fo. 166.

five, perhaps sometimes later. The chef was up to Stainville standards and he made use, for instance, of the local crayfish. It was, one feels, rather tiresome of Madame de Graffigny to make out, as she did, that she would really be happier with her bubble-and-squeak. The embarrassment felt by Madame de Stainville over the vulgar necessity of eating was concentrated one day upon how she should elegantly tackle a pear. 'I asked her', wrote Madame de Graffigny, 'why she did not have a golden knife, and why I saw no jewelry on her. Here is her reply: "Well, what is the use? All these silly women wear it without knowing why. It is good for nothing. From another angle it is intolerable nonsense. For my part I prefer to put my money into a certain quantity of pretty coverlets. From one moment to the next, if one marries off one's son, one at least has a pretty present to give his wife."'[40] The future Choiseul's bride had them coming to her.

For the most part, though, the Marquise de Stainville's constraint at mealtimes afforded an oasis of rest from chatter. Almost the only topic then was apt to be their third companion, an outsize dog only a year old and 'even lazier than Roi. He is always lying on his back and he eats in this position . . . If one throws him a bone two foot from him he does not get up to fetch it.'[41]

The rest of the day was mostly Madame de Stainville's sounding-board. On that afternoon of 8 October 1738 when she particularly spoilt her guest's walk this was because 'the story of Toussaint and the [Stainville] establishment in Paris was treated in detail, in the hundredth edition.'[42] The next evening, would you credit it, she started in again on 'the story of Toussaint at half past nine and made it last till a quarter past one' when Madame de Graffigny pointed to her hostess's watch. (Bedtime for that lady was usually around one.) 'I am lost', commented the visitor, 'if her memory is suffering from tertian fever.' For Panpan need not think that his confidante exactly opened up with 'my fine friend Mole [Taupe ma mie, i.e. Mme de Stainville] . . . about Newton or Boileau.'[43] The mother of the future Choiseul took a dim view of ladies like her neighbour Madame du Châtelet, who made intellectual conversation. In the feminine logic of the Marquise de Stainville it was boring to talk of history with 'people who know history; it does not do for them to hear it talked about since they know it [already], and it does not do either for those who do not know it because it bores them.'[44] Perhaps she had a point.

[40] Ibid., 22 Oct. 1738: fo. 101.
[41] Ibid., 12–13 Oct.: fo. 80.
[42] Ibid., 7–10 Oct.: fos. 69–70 for the following.
[43] Ibid., 9 Nov.: fo. 132.
[44] Ibid., 15–20 Nov.: fo. 160.

III

Gossip, then, was the iterative background to the ploys wherein the two ladies passed that autumn at Demange. The redecoration of the house afforded plenty of scope for rearrangement of furniture, new hangings and more talk: particularly since the mere fact that a conversation had not taken place did not inhibit Madame de Stainville from recounting it. With her 'it constitutes a project to tell an upholsterer to put a curtain in a window. It takes an hour to relate what he will say, what he will reply and think.'[45] Sometimes the two ladies themselves 'pottered around arranging furniture',[46] as after dinner on 14 October. In the process Madame de Graffigny managed to improve her own room with a mirror to go over the mantelpiece and a charming Indian screen which, she felt, afforded her a new landscape with a perspective of little figures. Even she conceded that you only had to say a word to be supplied with whatever you wanted, for Madame de Stainville really cared for her guests' comfort and enjoyment; 'but she would not give away a pin'. That same afternoon they turned out a large Chinese chest full of 'lengths of cotton print, fine, medium and thick, all in unusual and charming taste. It was a tradesman's shop. There are lengths in it which cost only two *louis*. Would she be any the worse for it if she had given me one? It did not enter her head.' Madame de Graffigny was treated only to more gossip, tolerably amusing for once since it was of Paris. One might sympathize with her more did it not appear that she was not above pilfering. ('Do not be afraid that they will hang me for my thefts. Nobody has seen them, not even my hostess.') Madame de Graffigny belonged to that class of person who is not so much nasty as not quite nice enough. It is a large class.

After supper the same day the two of them were up till one sorting through, this time, old family papers. According to Madame de Graffigny her hostess put them into new files without so much as reading the labels. She was also unresponsive about opening the bundle which interested her guest most, a manuscript collection of songs and poems. Such collections could be a feature of private libraries at a time when the diffusion of literature was still apt to be restricted by a limited public, by censorship, by aristocratic reserve. Subsequently one such collection in the circle of Madame de Graffigny was possibly to provide an early poetic sidelight upon the future Choiseul.

[45] Ibid., 22 Oct.: fo. 101.
[46] Ibid., 14–16 Oct.: fos. 81–3 for the following.

A few evenings later Madame de Graffigny did wheedle the Prude (*Bégueule* – another of her shafts) into opening the poetical packet, only to find it disappointing, though there was still hope of a fat notebook of Saint-Lambert's stuff, which Madame de Stainville vaguely thought unpublished. The pieces already to hand she sang and declaimed, ridiculously thought Madame de Graffigny. One could not laugh because the reader 'is silly enough to be made to believe that it is at the matter and not at her displays of ignorance. So one can only get mad. Well I got mad.'[47]

Dubois, fortified by snuff, did on occasion read to her mistress books ranging from one featuring vortices, fashionably Cartesian, to a current success by the adventurous Thémiseul de Saint-Hyacinthe, the *Histoire du Prince Titi*: 'a fairy story'[48] to Madame de Graffigny, it was one laden, already, with satirical menace. Normand, the Stainville footman, read aloud pretty regularly to the two ladies: he once did a stint of three or four hours on De Thou's history. Any idea that indoor servants then necessarily tended to be illiterate hardly applied to that household. Madame de Graffigny herself gladly took a turn at reading aloud – she aimed to educate her hostess in Molière, even if she did not venture upon a play of her own, *Héraclite*, which she had apparently had with her.[49] One week it was *L'Avare*, but Madame de Stainville's failure to grasp the plot left one speechless. Still, it was a pleasure at other times to watch the comic classic set Madame de Stainville yawning, nodding off to sleep in healing silence.

Till sleep intervened Madame de Stainville could stitch away at her endless patchwork coverlets, or unpick old ones. Madame de Graffigny was sewing a cotton cover for a closet. If she dropped a thread her hostess 'squawks like an eagle . . . because it spoils her room. She suddenly rises from her armchair and with her consolation – that is what she calls a duster which she always keeps in a corner – she sets about polishing all her furniture, and then she says that she is happy.'[50] Panpan was treated to 'another picture . . . of this lady so delicate, so prim, with her dress tucked up into its pockets', wielding a broom wrapped 'in a duster which she spends an hour fastening with pins . . . this in the presence of footmen who are laughing and making fun of her'.[51] Perhaps it was difficult for Madame de Graffigny to avoid being that sly kind of guest who

[47] Ibid., 19–20 Oct.: fo. 92.
[48] Ibid., 26 Oct.: fo. 109.
[49] Cf. English G. Showalter Jnr., 'A Woman of Letters in the French Enlightenment: Madame de Graffigny' in *The British Journal for Eighteenth Century Studies*, i, no. 2 (1978), p. 94.
[50] Madame de Graffigny to Devaux, Demange-aux-Eaux, 22 Oct. 1738: *u.s.*, fo. 101.
[51] Ibid., 9 Nov.: fo. 134.

enjoys being more popular than her own hostess with 'all the maids, who fly at my slightest nod'.[52]

Rural domesticity, however, was not the whole horizon at Demange. The Choiseul-Stainville background was after all one of international politics. After supper on 6 October 1738 the remote château carried a murmur of the first of the royal scandals of the reign of Louis XV. Madame de Stainville confided to her guest under seal of secrecy, promptly broken to Panpan, 'the ins and outs (*les tenants et aboutissants*) of the king's loves. It is true that he has already had little bits and that he is very much in love with Mme de Mailly. She knows this from the fountain-head through M. de Courtenvaux',[53] the smart admirer of Madame de Stainville and a companion of the king at court. The early favour there of the Marquis de Courtenvaux and his hostility to Fleury matched a subsequent but well informed account of these formative developments: how the queen, poor foolish woman, concealed from Louis a miscarriage and medical advice against risking a repetition so that her evasion of his favours increased some previous 'cooling; the King began to sup without the Queen in his Cabinets. There were only men at these parties; they used to drink a lot there, and the King more than the others. It was even spoken of fairly freely. The familiarity which reigned at these suppers displeased the Cardinal; preferring a mistress to a male favourite, he let it appear that while he would declare himself against the latter, he could tolerate the other.'[54] Courtiers took the hint and, by this significant account, it was originally with rather than against Fleury that the licentious Duke de Richelieu had promoted to be the first accredited mistress of Louis XV the Countess de Mailly, not specially young or beautiful but experienced with her shapely legs. Their liaison had transpired the previous year but the sexual breach between king and queen had only become definite in that summer of 1738.

Demange garnered in the latest gossip upon either hand, from Versailles as from Vienna. On the same day of 6 October 1738 Maria Theresa produced another girl, Maria Anna. By the evening of 15 October the Marquise de Stainville was already pronouncing upon this 'ridiculous accouchement of the grand duchess. She [Madame de Stainville]: "Is it not pitiable that this dreary German woman (*cette maussade allemande*) produces nothing but girls. She is quite stupid enough to go on doing it till she is a hundred" ... Afterwards we

[52] Ibid., 12–13 Oct.: fo. 79.
[53] Ibid., 6 Oct.: fo. 66.
[54] Count Kaunitz-Rietberg, 'Mémoire sur la cour de France' (1752), ed. Vicomte du Dresnay in *La Revue de Paris* (11ème année. Paris, 1904), vol. iv (henceforth cited as Kaunitz/Mémoire), p. 827.

passed on to the army and she gave methodical paradigms of the engagements, speeches, and projects.'[55] Then on 3 November Madame de Graffigny's leading item was the receipt by her hostess of a letter from Vienna from Le Petit Stainville, her eldest son.

The Count de Stainville wrote to his mother about a piece of gossip that then had society agog in Vienna, as in Lorraine. The French ambassador in Vienna, the Marquis de Mirepoix, was contemplating remarriage, to none other than Anne-Marguerite Princess de Lixin, widowed during the War of the Polish Succession when her prince had insulted the unappealing Duke de Richelieu, who had killed him in a duel before Philippsburg: specially interesting to the Stainvilles since the Prince de Lixin was the godfather of Stephen's younger brother Jacques. Such was the future Choiseul's background from Lorraine of hostility towards the Duke de Richelieu, a man, indeed, to whom it was good to be hostile.

For the present 'little Stainville reports to his mother that M. de Mirepoix strongly discounts [the idea of] his marriage although it is as public at Vienna as here, and that it is thought to be broken off. It is thought so everywhere by this account. My Lord, what a mess. Where could one turn after such a ridiculous scene?'[56] It was heightened by intriguing complications. If Mirepoix had first married beneath him in scooping the Bernard heiress, it would now be the opposite. By becoming the Marquise de Mirepoix the Lixin relict would forfeit at Versailles her precious *tabouret*, the stool ceremoniously restricted to duchesses and princesses. Nevertheless she did turn to the marquis, whom she was to marry on 2 January 1739. A shy woman of notable charm, inheriting her mother's lovely complexion, the new Marquise de Mirepoix was one in whom still waters ran deep. The Count de Stainville was never to trust her as he did her brother, his future friend the Prince de Beauvau.

When young Stainville's letter reached his mother she was apparently thinking already about arranging a marriage for him, if one can rely upon one obscure reference by Madame de Graffigny to her being asked to write, seemingly in this connection, to a Mademoiselle Lubert, scarcely the novelist, one might think, more likely perhaps some relation of an unidentified friend of Devaux.[57] Whatever the precise initiative, it was not to spell matrimony for the Count de Stainville. What is certain is that his mother was a great one for correspondence, remembering and reciting 'all the letters that she has received and written'.[58] Letters, however, were not the only link

55 Madame de Graffigny to Devaux, Demange-aux-Eaux, 14–16 Oct. 1738: u.s., vol. ii, fo. 86.
56 Ibid., 3 Nov.: fo. 124.
57 Cf. *Voltaire's Correspondence*, ed. Theodore Besterman (Geneva, 1953f.), viii. 57.
58 Madame de Graffigny to Devaux, Demange-aux-Eaux, 7–10 Oct. 1738: u.s., vol. ii, fo. 70.

with the outside world for the ladies at Demange. At the beginning
of November the village was echoing for a while to the 'wretched
trumpets'[59] of a company of so-called 'foreign' troops, uniformed in
deep blue in the French service. More amusing than their Alsatian
officers was the Marquis de Stainville's secretary, Grobert, who came
mainly, however, to talk business. Most intriguing was a more
distinguished visitor. In the early days of that November something
began to happen at Demange.

IV

The Marquise de Stainville was quietly smartening herself up,
curling her hair and taking to panniers. Then early one Saturday
evening (8 November 1738) Madame de Graffigny, as often upset by
some contretemps in her emotional correspondence with Panpan,
was resting in her room in a deep armchair (*bergère*), her poor head
propped up on 'a thousand pillows',[60] when it was assailed by the
horns of postillions. Dubois, who had been sent to the halt of the
mailcoach to collect the precious letter, came in with the news. The
Marquis de Courtenvaux had arrived on a visit. So that was it.
Madame de Stainville had been artfully sprucing up in advance
because 'she did not want it to appear that it was for the gentleman'.
   'I think, "Good, I shall be left in peace."' Madame de Graffigny said
she would sup in bed. 'They said that they would have the table
brought into my room. I was very far from wanting this. Finally I
had to go down to supper.' She quickly decided that the Marquis de
Courtenvaux was, 'in three letters, an ass (*sot*)'. But then 'when he
wants to say that something is worthless, he says, "That is Lorraine."'[61]
   'This ass is very good-looking, well built and tall, a noble air, fine
eyes, fine teeth, a fine countenance though a little brutal. I am not at
all surprised that he should have beaten a workman here on his
former visit. I think that if one failed to applaud when he has made
an alleged witticism, abuse would soon follow.'[62] Madame de
Stainville, 'in fits of laughter as soon as he opens his mouth', ran no
risk. Madame de Graffigny wrote: 'I am no longer surprised at his
attachment to my fine friend Mole. He says nothings just like her.
The anecdotes about dogs never end. I fancied myself in Brittany.'
Another afternoon, she reported, the Marquis de Courtenvaux
'related to us his revenues down to the pennies and farthings. He

[59] Ibid., 3 Nov.: fo. 124.
[60] Ibid., 9 Nov.: fos. 127–34 for the following.
[61] Ibid., 15–20 Nov.: fo. 151.
[62] Ibid., 9 Nov.: fos. 132–3 for the following.

gave us an enumeration of all the trees that he has had planted'[63] on his property at Montmirail in the Champagne. 'He already has two million foot planted, but there is not a branch of which he did not compute the value when they are ready for cutting in a hundred years. It is his foible, he says, to work for his descendants. Thence he walked us through the pastures of Normandy. He evaluated what a blade of grass could yield in fatstock, for he plumes himself upon reckoning. Upon what does he not plume himself?'

The Beau, as Monsieur de Courtenvaux became for Madame de Graffigny, also fancied himself as a handyman. 'The first time he arrived he snatched up a hammer and mended a firescreen and an andiron.'[64] Another time he was trying to repair a bodkin for his hostess and wanted to put it in the fire. Madame de Graffigny told him 'that that would spoil it. He replied to me in an oracular tone, "Madam, I beg you to believe that everything that I do, I do well."'[65] As for 'talent for war, ah what an officer. His regiment trembled at his sight': he maintained that the way to win affection was by kicking people in the stomach. At Demange 'he is detested by the peasants whom he enrages over works which he is conducting in the gardens. The servants would like to send him into the moat head first.' When he persuaded his hostess to invite the Alsatian officers to dinner, 'he played the master. He has decided more trifles today[66] than the French Academy would bring under deliberation in a century.'

Literature was not the Beau's forte though he did once broach Horace and he even read cheap novels (romans des halles). One day after dinner, a week after the advent of Courtenvaux, Madame de Graffigny came into the room to find him and his hostess tearing Madame du Châtelet to pieces along familiar lines. Why had this mondaine neighbour ever left Paris – becoming financially a little hot for the extravagant creature? '"Bah"', exclaimed Madame de Stainville to the recording Madame de Graffigny, '"it is all pitiable". I: "Her husband told me that she arranged her affairs very well, and that she has set up a foundry which brought her in a lot."' Well, anyway, she had to look after her precious Voltaire, teaching her all that useless scientific stuff. This led to bickering as to whether he was at present actually exiled. The Beau was sure of it, explaining: '"The Keeper of the Seals told me myself that he had had him [Voltaire] told that never would he let a certain thing appear ... a piece ... something or other in verse ... that he would never forgive him." M[ole] ... "Yes, yes, I do not know what it is but do not you

---

[63] Ibid., 15–20 Nov.: fo. 151, for the following.
[64] Ibid., 9 Nov.: fos. 132–3.
[65] Ibid., 15–20 Nov.: fos. 149–51 for the following.
[66] 16 Nov. 1738.

know, Madam?"'[67] Madame de Graffigny supplied *La Pucelle d'Orléans*. For Voltaire was already working up his burlesque epic, indebted to Ariosto, of goings-on in the time of Joan of Arc. The Marquise de Stainville was sure that it contained 'horrors'. Her assumption is not wholly easy to contradict in respect of a work which has been ruefully described as a base libel upon both history and religion.

The mock heroics of *La Pucelle d'Orléans* often verge upon the horror-comic. In its ultimately published form this robustly sexual and anticlerical poem retains something of its shock-impact with Joan and her flying donkey who developed a crush on her, the Maid of Orleans scribbling fleurs-de-lys on the bottom of Chandos's page and making off with that warrior's pants, which finished up on Agnes Sorel. And if Chandos stripped Agnes he more rudely surprised Dorothy when piously prostrated in chapel. Also on the religious side was Father Bonnifoux's panoramic vision of heroic copulation, and Joan in the nude rescuing a convent from mass-violation by the English. Several cantos of this purient production end repetitiously with a more or less naked woman in a horrid predicament, awaiting the next instalment. It was perhaps just as well that the respectable Marquis de Courtenvaux did not really know much about it.

When Madame de Graffigny had asked Courtenvaux about new plays in Paris, the reply had been: '"Oh, my Lord, Madam, you have come to the wrong address. It is six years since I set foot in theatres... I have too much to do to bother about that kind of foolishness." And to justify his great preoccupations he shewed me that he knew precisely the number of farts which the cardinal Fleury had let off in the interior of his apartments during his illnesses, and the explanation of each one, for and against the interests of the state and of grandees like himself. He also compiles a register of all the sighs which the king gives while caressing Mme de Mailly, and conjectures very fully upon their influences. There is an hour gone.'[68]

It was apparently Grobert rather than Courtenvaux who regaled Demange with a crisper anecdote about the cardinal and the Dauphin's governor, the Duke de Châtillon. The latter complained one day to Fleury that his royal charge had called him a fool. '"Who told him?" replied the cardinal.'[69] As for Courtenvaux's amatory gossip from court, just then at Fontainebleau, it could be slightly below royal level but perhaps more nearly interesting.

Though Madame de Graffigny had supped reluctantly with her hostess and the Marquis de Courtenvaux on the first evening of his

---

[67] Punctuation as in original.   [68] Ibid., 9 Nov.: fo. 133.   [69] Ibid., 22 Nov.: fo. 165.

visit, she had recouped herself afterwards in the drawing-room. She described herself sitting 'in a good armchair in a corner of the fireplace where the light did not reach. I was as though alone and I had as a play the conversation of the Misanthrope.'[70] Madame de Stainville asked about the Minister of War's only child, the Marquise de Ruffec, to be described by another as having 'married better than she deserves'.[71] The Beau now said that the Count de Biron was as much in love with her as ever in a hangdog sort of way. This lorn lover was to figure prominently in the early career of the Count of Stainville, as his colonel. Biron was then a dashing officer of thirty-seven, a bachelor who was already inspector-general of the French infantry. Courtenvaux himself was to become inspector-general of cavalry in the following year.

Still, continued Courtenvaux that evening, Madame de Ruffec was faithful to Biron '"apparently at least, for she is no longer talking about those with whom she has slept." Mole: "But has she fallen out, then, with the whole court?" The Beau: "Yes. As for me, it is two years since she refused to curtsey to me." Mole: "What will she do if the Count de Biron leaves her?" The Beau: "Oh, she has kept in with the lackeys. She is on very good terms with them."'[72]

Such was the gossip by the fire that evening long ago, darting between two conspicuously good-looking persons reported by a fat, plain, poor one. The listener in the shadows explained that he 'lives on Fontainebleau where the smallest trivialities of our peers are as well known as if they were living in a bottle. I tell you that it surprises me.' Hardly less surprising was the matter for gossip emerging closer to hand.

The Beau cast languishing looks at Madame Honesta, yet another nickname for Madame de Stainville, who hardly took her eyes off him. Though she, unlike Madame de Graffigny, did miss two or three gestures by him as though to kiss her hand, which happened to be lying in his. Some days later when she felt out of sorts Courtenvaux knelt to feel her pulse, speaking very low the while. Another time he chucked her under the chin, and upon another simply took her necklace off, explaining that he preferred her without it. She submitted, as also to the remarkable familiarity with which 'he calls her a crazy liar and a thousand other words so little suitable to the lady that in faith I do not know what to think of it'. Then, after he had been there a week, 'he made a very rude gesture at her'[73] with a screw

[70] Ibid., 9 Nov.: fo. 133.

[71] Marquis d'Argenson, *Journal et mémoires du Marquis d'Argenson* ed. E.J.B. Rathery (Paris, 1859-67: henceforth cited as D'Argenson), ii. 291.

[72] Madame de Graffigny to Devaux, Demange-aux-Eaux, 9 Nov. 1738: *u.s.* vol. ii, fos. 132-4 for the following.   [73] Ibid., 14 Nov.: fo. 142.

of paper; and, when she murmured something to him, he jumped upon her and kissed her good and proper. Only, to all outward appearances, one could hardly say that she led him on. As her admirer became more familiar Madame de Stainville became glacial, not replying a word to his coy advances. Even Madame de Graffigny could hardly believe that there was really anything between them. But then, she asked herself, 'what the deuce is he doing here?',[74] staying stuck away in the country with two ladies. And there were some odd indications.

The Marquise de Stainville, who had grumbled at Madame de Graffigny for going to bed when it was only one in the morning, now could hardly wait for the servants to retire before doing likewise. Courtenvaux for his part made out 'that he goes to bed at ten every night of his life. That', commented Madame de Graffigny to Panpan, 'is as likely as if it were said that you run after the girls.'[75] The Beau's bedroom lay between those of the two ladies. He left his door open at night because, he explained, his fire smoked. The chimneys were indeed liable to smoke abominably 'but at night that makes me suspicious. I do not know what I would not give to know.' The servants maliciously did their best, listening for nocturnal noises. One Sunday, 16 November 1738, Dubois claimed 'to have heard him opening and shutting the door of the lady's room at two o'clock last night. As for me, who did not hear it, I cannot say anything. The fact is that Dubois is even closer to his room than I am.'[76]

There the evidence runs out. Madame de Graffigny herself had to return an open verdict upon the suggestive relations between the Marquise de Stainville and the Marquis de Courtenvaux.

Next day, Monday 17 November, was deliciously sunny. Though she had one of her bad heads Madame de Graffigny, complete with panniers, went for a stroll before dinner. Passing through the garden to the meadow she 'saw the fine gentleman with a gun ... As he was telling me that it was a woodcock [he was after] it got up. He fired at it ... Poor thing ... But ... this man who does everything so well missed it. I went my way.' All the rest of that day and the next were taken up with the sportsman's explanations of 'all the circumstances of this shot so as to prove that the finest marksman in the world, and that is him, could only have missed it. He has killed more than a thousand head of different game for me in order to shew us that he never missed.'

That Tuesday the Marquis de Courtenvaux plunged into

[74] Ibid., 9 Nov.: fo. 134.
[75] Ibid., 14 Nov.: fos. 141–2 for the following.
[76] Ibid., 15–20 Nov.: fos. 151–6 for the following.

needlework, 'winding twenty skeins of silk, all out of obstinacy, for the lady did not want it. But . . . when I arrived for supper the great balls were shewn to me as a trophy as if he had to make up for the woodcock.' Still, it was his last day at Demange. He left at five o'clock in the morning of the Wednesday, passing out of the pitiless range of his fellow visitor, down avenues of history rather more respectful to the future Marshal d'Estrées, whose military career was to culminate at Hastenbeck via Fontenoy and those battles of Rocoux and Lawfeldt which were also to engage the Count de Stainville.

V

In order not to overlap with so interesting a guest a visit by the Stainville in-laws from Beaupré had been held over. They arrived a week later, four of them headed by the old buffer of a Colonel de Choiseul and his wife, Madame de Stainville's sister-in-law Claire-Madeleine, 'a village lady if ever there was one, no panniers, a coarse cotton dress, a hairstyle like Dubois's nightcaps'.[77] Tagging along was their daughter 'who is a great spindleshanks as stiff as a ramrod, with an ignoble air, not saying a word,' poor thing: plus a third female, an ancient Choiseul cousin bundled up in worsted.

Madame de Graffigny had had from her hostess the local story that the gawk of a daughter was in fact the child of the farrier's wife whom the barren Madame de Choiseul had smuggled in from her village. Dubois too heard it from one of the servants from Beaupré almost as soon as they came into the kitchen at Demange. As a precaution for the future, thought Madame de Graffigny, it was being put about that 'this poor girl . . . is in love with one of her father's footmen, who is handsomer than she'. The Marquise de Stainville 'would much like to know the truth of this business for they are rich', and an illegitimacy would open up interesting legal possibilities.

It was a ghastly visit. The sister-in-law plied her distaff from seven in the morning, and her bedroom was above Madame de Graffigny's. Then, she related to Panpan on 27 November 1738, 'this morning the lady in worsted, holding the great goose of a girl by the hand and with a sheet that she is sewing in the other, came in as I was writing to you and said that she had brought her work to keep me company'. The horrified Madame de Graffigny took to locking her door. Only, she in her turn had to leave it open because of the smoke. By now the wind was howling round the castle whereas inside a morose silence descended. Upon one occasion they sat together 'without exaggeration

[77] Ibid., 26–7 Nov.: fo. 172 for the following.

for a good hour and a half without speaking. Finally someone opened their mouth to say that it was very cold. Somebody else said, Well, that was a waste of breath.'[78]

If there was some respite from the chatter of Madame de Stainville, her peevish temper had become vile. She was furious that her bossy sister-in-law seemed to know how to run everything even better than herself, treating them to 'a long dissertation upon ways of eating pigmeat'[79] and saying 'a hundred times before dinner that there was no management [at Demange] because they were paying eight sous to the woman who does the washing', whereas, the only too receptive Madame de Stainville was assured, five was more than enough. It was then that she refused to provide any food for a dressmaker (she had to be fed by the mason's wife) whom Madame de Graffigny had over from Gondrecourt to mend some of her clothes. That lady, however, has also taken delivery at Demange of a new dress from Paris in trimmed 'drugget of a very handsome chestnut brown ... I shall put it on this winter for I certainly shall not be buying another.'[80]

At Demange servants became the dreary topic of the day. And indeed the Choiseul in-laws had thrown them into ferment. 'All the servants want to leave. A footman has already been dismissed today. The cook wants to throw in his apron to Madame de Choiseul, who checks up everything.'[81] The relations from Beaupré were further accused of setting their hostess against Madame de Graffigny and trying to get her evicted: if only they had known how she herself longed to leave. It was just because she felt she never would manage to get away that she found herself crying with misery. Also, she had toothache. And there was no chemist at Demange. If only her wretched dentist 'Mr. La Tour had been willing to stop it for me when I told him, I should not be swearing at him every day.'[82]

During the visits of Courtenvaux and the brood from Beaupré, at last beginning to leave, Madame de Graffigny had tended to spend more time alone in her room, spared her hostess but perversely inclined to feel neglected, as she had earlier when indisposed and Madame de Stainville had made no enquiry how she was, feeling unloved and crying in bed. Then at last, on Wednesday 3 December 1738, there came to dine at Demange a welcome visitor in the person of the Marquise de Lenoncourt, sister to the Princess de Craon and lady-in-waiting to the erstwhile Regent of Lorraine. Some weeks back Madame de Stainville had sharply criticized Lolotte Lenoncourt

[78] Ibid., 29 Nov. – 1 Dec.: fo. 177.   [79] Ibid., 1 Dec.: fos. 182–3 for the following.
[80] Ibid., 29–30 Oct.: fo. 111.   [81] Ibid., 29 Nov. – 1 Dec.: fo. 176.
[82] Ibid., 1 Dec.: fo. 183.

in her absence to Madame de Graffigny, exclaiming: '"Just look at
the silliness of this creature who praises her chambermaid for being
wise. From another angle is not it intolerable nonsense? I can't tell
you . . . A wise chambermaid, what silliness"'[83] – just the sort of thing
one picked up in Paris. Whereas Madame de Graffigny had found
Madame de Lenoncourt charming even before she came to the
rescue.

'The first compliment I pay', wrote the detractor of Demange of
the new arrival, 'is to ask her for her horses; she grants them me; I
tremble for joy; my head bursts.'[84] Hitherto Madame de Graffigny
had 'sulked without saying a word, till the arrival of Madame de
Lenoncourt; then I was so transported with joy at leaving that I
laughed to high heaven the rest of the day and talked as much as I
could. That evening, in parting, I kissed her [Mme de Stainville]
with a smiling face, and we had no explanations. She begged me to
write to her; I shall do so and we shall always remain on the same
terms. She made rather a face against Madame de Lenoncourt's
giving me her horses, because she is only going at Christmas',[85]
probably back to Commercy, as projected earlier. However, she gave
in.

Madame de Graffigny lost no time in quitting the Château de
l'Ennui, as she called it. She was up at dawn next morning and,
escaping past the bedroom-door of her hostess, she 'made a large sign
of the cross on it', which caused Dubois to burst out laughing so that
they were afraid of wakening the Marquise. A wearing journey over
horrid roads brought Madame de Graffigny to Cirey at two o'clock
next morning. There she faced the strain of keeping up with Voltaire,
but could enjoy herself in painting her portrait of Belinda and
applauding Madame du Châtelet's brother, the sprightly Abbé de
Breteuil, who took off the Marquise de Stainville so that 'it made one
die of laughter'.[86]

If the Marquise de Stainville had been deprived of her ungrateful
guest by Madame de Lenoncourt, the latter had at least brought her
just the kind of gossip she throve on: how the Duchess of Modena
had had an epistolary slanging-match with her aunt, Madame
Royale, after giving the former regent the maddeningly casual advice
to visit Tuscany, 'saying that there was nothing so easy, that she had
only to put herself into a good berlin, to post day and night'.[87] This

[83] Ibid., 12–13 Oct.: fol. 77.
[84] Madame de Graffigny to Devaux, Cirey, 4 Dec. 1738: Eugène Asse, op. cit., pp. 1–2.
[85] Madame de Graffigny to Devaux, Cirey, 6 Dec. 1738: ibid., p. 28, and for the following.
[86] Ibid., 14 Dec.: p. 73.
[87] Ibid., 6 Dec.: p. 29.

journey which the Duchess of Modena had so irritatingly suggested
bore reference to another journey, by Francis and Maria Theresa,
which was at that time exercising both the Marquis and the Count de
Stainville in Vienna.

CHAPTER IX

SOUTHWARD

I

FOR the campaign of 1738 Francis had obtained the rank but not the experience of a field-marshal. He was instructed by the emperor to do nothing without the approval of the indolent Field-Marshal König-segg, noted for having been handsomely defeated by the Latin armies at the battle of Guastalla in the Italian campaign of 1734. Nevertheless Francis at first did not disgrace his forbears. He was of the third generation of the house of Lorraine to ride out east against the Turks. On the field of Kornia he routed them. Captured Ottoman standards were sent back to Nancy to hang beside those taken by his illustrious grandfather. This lucky victory, though, was not followed up. The Turks hit back; plague ravaged into Hungary; in the imperial army some four or five score men died every day; the grim campaign ended scarcely better than the one before. It was judged opportune that Francis, as unpopular now as he had been popular a few months earlier, should withdraw for a while, not exactly into exile but to make himself known to his new subjects in Tuscany.

Regardless of the season, on 17 December 1738, the new grand duke and duchess set forth from Vienna for Italy. They were accompanied by Prince Charles of Lorraine and the Prince d'Elboeuf, no special friend of the Marquis de Stainville. The marquis too was of the party. He was now duly the great chamberlain if not also, as he was further described, probably in that month, the grand duke's master of the horse for that occasion at least. At the same time he was depicted as 'too fond of good living and does not understand the affairs of Germany'.[1] Stainville nevertheless secured about then from the Emperor Charles VI the further honorific office of counsellor of state. There were some two hundred of these posts, unpaid and expensive to obtain. The Marquis de Stainville's accumulation of offices, plus his shuttling existence between France and Austria, and now Italy, may have lain behind the somewhat cryptic description of the factotum just then by his former comrade in arms, the Duke de

[1] 'Note sur la Cour de Vienne', probably Dec. 1738 (following Sautai's emendation from Dec. 1736): Arch Aff. Étr., Mémoires et Documents, Autriche, vol. vii; cited, Maurice Sautai, *Les Préliminaires de la Guerre de la Succession d'Autriche* (Paris, 1907; henceforth cited as Sautai/Préliminaires), p. 465.

Luynes, as 'a very expensive and very ubiquitous man (*un homme fort cher and fort multiplié*)'.[2] 'My father', wrote the later Choiseul, 'was attached to him [Francis] and obtained of the Grand Duke and Grand Duchess that I should make the Italian voyage together with them'.[3]

The journey across the Alps in the depth of winter was an extraordinary enterprise, whatever the Duchess of Modena might say. The British envoy in Turin commented: 'I own I could hardly give Credit to the Accounts that came from Vienna on the Great Duke's intended Journey into Tuscany ... The Arch Duchess's undertaking such a journey ... and with no greater preparation being made ... seemed so inconsistent with the affectation of Grandeur, and the formal Stiffness of the Court of Vienna, that I looked upon the whole Report as spread designedly to keep up the hopes and Affections of the People of Tuscany; but ...'[4] he had been wrong.

The grand-ducal party travelled south by Judenburg and Klagenfurt, along the valley of the Drave (Drau) to Spittal where Francis and Maria Theresa lodged magnificently in Prince Porcia's renaissance castle, only their double bed collapsed beneath them. On they went through the Tyrol where, according to a traveller a few years earlier, 'the Common People are very ill-favour'd: Most of the Women are disguis'd by Wens in their Throat, and as if that was not enough they disfigure themselves by their Dress'[5] featuring long stays and high-crowned green hats. At seven o'clock on Christmas Eve the train of four hundred posthorses came winding in through the dark as they made Bolzano (Bozen), 'a pretty Town well inhabited'. There on Christmas Day, in the enthusiastic press-report of a local correspondent, 'their Royal Highnesses betook themselves to our big main church, and that on foot by their own gracious pleasure'.[6]

Such was the stately introduction of the Count de Stainville to winter in the Alps at their easterly crossing, round by the Carnic Alps and the Dolomites. Rather different was to be his renewed acquaintance with winters on high, six years later in a westerly crossing of the Maritime Alps.

On 28 December 1738 the grand-ducal cortege entered Venetian territory at Dolce. They were escorted by the Podesta of Verona, Peter Barbarigo, to the so-called Palazzo Buri in the environs of that

---

[2] Luynes, ii. 321.
[3] Choiseul, *Mémoires*, p. 3.
[4] Arthur Villettes to Horace Mann, Turin, 10 Dec. 1738: P.R.O./S.P.F., Archives of British Legations, vol. 281.
[5] Baron von Pöllnitz, op. cit, i. 392–3 for the following.
[6] Report from Bolzano in *Wienerisches Diarium*, 17 Jan. 1739, no. 5, p. 48.

city, where the Venetian government insisted upon isolating the royal couple together with Prince Charles and but a few attendants for some weeks of strict quarantine under military guard. The rest of the party, including Marquis de Stainville and most likely his son, were, as one of the Lorrainers wryly wrote, cut off and 'confined in a Pest-house'[7] nearby. 'Of all the People in Christendom' commented a contemporary, 'the Venetians seem to be most afraid of the Plague.'[8] Its incidence in Hungary during the Turkish campaign of 1738 had prompted them to impose a stringent quarantine against scatheless Austria, Switzerland, Poland even, 'which seemed to be a sort of Blunder in Geography'. Plague from the east, as earlier from the south at Marseilles, still set Europe in alarm.

Italian villas are apt not to be specially snug in winter. That one was severe. With the usual stone floors and whistling draughts the Palace Buri was freezing despite efforts by the Venetians, who equipped even the pesthouse with German stoves, thought to have been the first seen in those parts. The hostages to health were copiously supplied thrice weekly with fish, meat and the best local wine dumped, however, at the guarded entrance by delivery-men who scampered off as though from lepers. In this predicament young Stainville was likely one of those who recognized 'something in it that is comical; and for the first three or four Days it made us merry; but in truth we begin all to be heartily tired of it',[9] counting the days, eleven to date. When Venetian doctors visited what the elder Stainville was to recall as the 'lazaret of Verona'[10] the inmates assured them that the only medicine they needed was patience. The Marquis de Stainville helped to pass the time profitably by writing and having conveyed to the grand duke a memorandum on future prospects in European politics, drawing upon his decade in Paris. This memorandum is not now to hand but it would appear[11] to have counselled action in regard to the likelihood that the Pragmatic Sanction would in due course afford an opening to French, perhaps also Bavarian, hostility to the house of Habsburg. Whether or not the marquis then initiated his son into such considerations of high policy, they were in the following decade to make a sharp impress upon the youth's career.

Meanwhile, when the Venetian government perhaps maliciously

---

[7] Lorrainer in suite of Grand Duke Francis II to a friend in Geneva, Verona, 7 Jan. 1739: translation in *The Life of His Serene Highness, Charles, Prince of Lorrain* (M. Cooper *et al.*, London, 1746: but the copy in the British Library carries the imprint of James Hodges), p. 109.

[8] Op. cit., p. 107, and for the following.

[9] Lorraine letter from Verona, 7 Jan. 1739: ibid., p. 110.

[10] Marquis de Stainville to Grand Duke Francis II, Paris, 19 Oct. 1741: Esteri del Granducato di Toscana, vol. 2295/1286, fo. 62.

[11] Ibid.

refused to shorten the quarantine, the mettlesome Prince Charles of
Lorraine propagated the idea of a general breakout to terminate 'the
detestable sojourn at the Palace Burÿ'.[12] This was accomplished on
12 January 1739 to the alarmed indignation of Venice. The chilly
episode long rankled with Francis and Maria Theresa. It was
apparently from the Palazzo Buri that she sent word of another
pregnancy to her father, who for his part expressed imperial
displeasure with the Venetian 'point-bearded pantaloons (*Spitzbartel-
Pantalons*)'.[13]

Less drastic and unusual were the ceremonial difficulties which
the grand-ducal party encountered at the related court of Modena
and, more particularly, with the papal authorities at Bologna. The
cardinal legate in control there discreetly withdrew. The civic
authorities, however, were keenly hospitable and gave a ball for the
travellers.

From Bologna the sixty miles and more to Florence presented one
of the hardest stretches in that strenuous progress, up across the
wintry Apennines. Harbingers from Florence had for weeks been
busy along the route. Before Christmas the Marquis Filippo
Guadagni, superintendant of Tuscan highways, had already been
begging the papal authorities to let their roadmenders toil through
the holidays, which they pretty much did. The Bailli Balthazar
Suarez della Conca, grand master of the Tuscan posts, had mobilized
three hundred posthorses, though even they did not fully solve the
problem of transport. Meantime the indispensable Count de
Richecourt was conferring with Dom Paolo Salani about midway
accommodation at his Olivetan abbey of San Michele ad Alpes at
Scaricalasino, the modern Monghidoro. They finally convinced
Francis, eager to press on to home ground, that it was 'morally
impossible for the grand duke and his court to proceed from Pianoro
to Firenzuola in one day's travel'[14] at such a season.

So the remote monastery was in a bustle of preparation for visitors
more welcome than those of three years earlier when, during the War
of the Polish Succession, Abbot Salani and his monks had had to
endure the Spanish troops of the Duke of Montemar marching
through from Leghorn and then back again, chased by still more
formidable Hungarian hussars who had drunk incredible quantities

[12] John Walton (i.e. Baron von Stosch) to Duke of Newcastle, Florence, 19 Jan. 1739
(translation from French of original): P.R.O./S.P.F. Tuscany, vol. 41, fo. 247.

[13] Emperor Charles VI to Grand Duke Francis II, Jan. 1739: cited, F. Hennings, op. cit., p.
196.

[14] Dom Paolo Salani, 'Memorie delle cose accadute sotto il governo del Rev.mo Padre Don
Paolo Salani dal 1735 al 1739' in Claudio Vaioli, *I Granduchi di Toscana Francesco terzo di
Lorena e Maria Teresa d'Austria in viaggio verso il Granducato (1739)* (Bologna, 1952), pp. 42–9
for the following.

of the best wine. More civil now was the advent of the grand-ducal 'harbingers, sent on with various chests of linen to prepare the rooms; and as the chit from the court laid down specific measurements for the tables in length, breadth and height it was necessary to send for several carpenters, who with all care set about putting together trestles and joining planks to make the tables'. Dom Salani, recording his moment in history, further explained that he was required to sleep seventy-two, which left him twenty beds short. These had to be procured from Bologna complete 'with sheets and blankets', most desirable in January at an altitude of about two thousand seven hundred feet. Likewise imported were 'those foodstuffs which could not be drawn from the district', the inevitable veal along with 'butter, pheasants, partridges and other game'. These were consigned to the grand-ducal chefs, sent on two days ahead.

Seventy-two beds were nothing like enough for the whole train of not less than three hundred and fifty persons, even though they were travelling by relays. Many would have to put up at the local inns, the porticoed L'Angelo,[15] the still older Scaletta, and the Corona. Rural hostelries, though, were hardly suitable for fine ladies. But since the cardinal legate had ceremonially withdrawn from Bologna it was impossible for Salani to secure in time his licence for the admission to the monastery of women other than royalty, already privileged to enter. In this predicament the magistracy of Bologna, urging the good abbot to do his best, assured him 'that they would make themselves sureties for the said licence'. Salani suavely took the chance.

Just about the middle of January 1739 there came toiling up to the portico of San Michele ad Alpes the first posse of the grand duke's outriders, in somewhat unorthodox shape. 'First of all', wrote Salani, 'there appeared in a carriage drawn by oxen the Marquis Bartolemei, a Florentine, first counsellor to H.R.H., and Commendatore Ricci, a chamberlain, and the son of the great chamberlain Stainville (e il figlio del gran Ciamberlano Steinvil).' Their master had decided that only cattle, hired locally, would afford his convoys enough traction through 'the mountains clogged with ice'. Thus did the future Duke de Choiseul come riding into history behind lumbering oxen. Still, even at nineteen, he somehow managed to be riding out ahead.

The Count de Stainville and his Italian companions were welcomed by Abbot Salani. He had a clever, kindly face with a double chin and large spectacles perched upon his nose. The son of a leading doctor in Bologna, Salani, then fifty, was for all his remote

---

[15] This building was damaged during the Second World War, in the autumn of 1944. It was subsequently pulled down and replaced.

situation a sophisticated, cultivated cleric and something of a poet. He now granted his three guests the hospitality they asked for and had them served with a meal that they were probably glad of.

'The day after', continued the abbot, 'as it was getting late, the carriages of the first column began to appear. They were twenty-five in number and the passengers were in great straits; an extraordinary wind had for a day been blowing so fiercely that a good part of the carriages had been overturned by it upon the Colle di Lojano so that they had to stay up all night, sending time and again for men and oxen to succour them, and all the more since various things in the carriages were dashed to pieces; but with God's aid they all arrived unharmed at eleven o'clock at night.' Young Stainville was lucky to have got through earlier.

The survivors of this nasty spill had already passed on towards Firenzuola when, at two o'clock in the morning of 19 January 1739, the main column including the grand-ducal pair arrived at San Michele 'preceded by six postillions or outriders who from time to time sounded their horns, much larger than those used in Italy'. Dom Salani and all his monks were drawn up to receive Francis and Maria Theresa. 'Not being preceded by their pages, they took six from the locality, who dressed themselves as nicely as they could and carried the lit torches; and their Royal Highnesses entered the Sala della Foresteria with all the ladies and gentlemen of their court' including Baron Toussaint, the Count de Richecourt, and, one supposes, the Marquis de Stainville. There in the ceremonial hall of the monastery, specially carpeted and hung with damask, the lateness of the hour did not spare the travellers the inevitable addresses of welcome and presentations. Maria Theresa, 'having taken off one glove, put out her hand to be kissed by the Abbot and by all the monks'. Dom Salani had composed a sonnet in honour of Francis, victor of Kornia:

> *In te, Gran duca, io lessi oppresse e dome*
> *L'ire dell'Asia a vindicarle eletto*[16]

Thereafter the distinguished travellers sat down to a table duly provided with 'plate, sweetmeats and dessert . . . And both the high-quality bread and the ordinary wine as served to the monks were accepted with approval'.[17] More than forty bottles were drunk. The court then turned in.

[16] Ibid., p. 52. 'In thee, Grand Duke, I beheld the appointed avenger of the wrath of the oppressed and cowed populations of Asia.' C. Vaioli described this sonnet as 'una breve composizione poetica, conservata nelle pagine, che vedono ora la luce per prima volta' (ibid., p. 15). The poem had in fact been published with slight textural variations almost two centuries earlier on the first page of *Poesie diverse del Padre Abate D. Paolo Salani* (Bologna, 1761).

[17] Dom Paolo Salani, 'Memorie delle cose accadute sotto il governo del Rev.mo Padre Don Paolo Salani dal 1735 al 1739' in C. Vaioli, op. cit., pp. 48–51 for the following.

The grand-ducal couple, perhaps cautious after Spittal, slept upon their own travelling beds in the best guest-chamber while Prince Charles of Lorraine had the abbot's own room. This meant that 'the Abbot and all the monks had to sit up the whole night because they did not have anywhere to sleep either in the monastery or outside' in the inns, also crammed.

It was between eleven and twelve next morning before things were astir in the court, for whom 'their lesser serving-women had prepared chocolate, and coffee made with milk', a favourite drink with Maria Theresa that was afterwards to be blamed for her embonpoint. Mass followed but before it 'Mister Tessin [Toussaint], prime minister and secretary to H.R.H.', presented to the abbot on behalf of his masters 'a case in which was a box in fired Saxon china mounted in gold and richly decorated, within as well as without, with the most beautiful miniatures', worth a tidy sum. Toussaint also gave Salani three hundred ducats to cover the hire of the oxen. The abbot passed them to the authorities in Bologna but there the money stuck to somebody's fingers before ever reaching the owners of the beasts: which was to cause poor Salani a lot of unpleasantness when Maria Theresa later wished to return that way.

The whole monastery gathered to give thanks for the box as their Tuscan majesties came out of mass. They proceeded straight to where all the coaches and chaises were assembled. Previously the Bailli Balthazar Suarez della Conca 'had had the hat of every coachman marked with a very visible number, which number corresponded to that of the coach to which the horses were to be harnessed'. It was a splendid plan. Only, now 'the intermingling of Italian coachmen and forty of the Emperor's postilions' produced utter muddle and an awkward wait. Maria Theresa tactfully filled in with the abbot by enquiring about the tenets of the Olivetan order. 'Finally they left'. Hardly, though, had Prince Charles 'reached the spot below the hospital than both the shafts of his calash broke'. It was not the Bailli Balthazar Suarez della Conca's day.

The Bailli's forethought for the stretch ahead from Scaricalasino had, however, ensured that throughout the preceding night there had been toiling 'about thirty people with masons in order to break the ice up to the Radicosa' pass at well over three thousand feet. Thus the grand-ducal train won through to Tuscan territory and exchanged its Bolognese escort for Tuscan troops under the Count della Ghirardesca. That was up in the mountains by Firenzuola, then a 'very dreary'[18] little town. Next came the Giogo pass, 'the worst part

---

[18] Charles de Brosses to de Blancey, 3 Oct. 1739: *Le Président de Brosses en Italie*, ed. R. Colomb (2nd ed., Paris, 1861), i. 267–8 for the following.

of the road'. At last it dipped into the ambient welcome of the Etruscan plain, across which 'one perceives Florence a great way off'.[19]

Now it seemed 'as though the weather itself had undertaken to make the journey of their Royal Highnesses easier and more agreeable; for the snow which had fallen a few days before, covering the whole mountain-chain, had suddenly and unexpectedly melted under a warm rain, and the air seemed altogether softer and more delicious'.[20] Such was their approach at last to the famous capital exchanged for little Nancy, to that early focus of illumination for Europe in literature, in statecraft, in finance, and in the arts.

II

On Tuesday 20 January 1739 Francis and Maria Theresa lunched at the Marquis Corsi's villa out at Montaghi. There they were received by the surviving representative of the house of Medici, John Gaston's sister, the Electress Palatine, left widowed, and venereally diseased. By half past two to three o'clock began the ceremonial entry into Florence in a dozen or more detachments headed by gendarmery. The Marquis de Stainville was probably included in the coachload of high dignitaries which immediately preceded the carriage of the two princes, Charles and Elboeuf. After them came the grand-ducal bodyguard, then a hundred Switzers 'in their new gala kit' preceding the royal coach itself, all in procession to the Porta di San Gallo.

Immediately before this gateway to Florence lay an oval concourse planted round about with elms and espaliers. In the middle, corinthian columns picked out the triple entrances of a triumphal arch of welcome, not the usual makeshift in wood but a fine glorification in stone by Jadot from Lorraine, interviewed about it by the press and unafraid of leaving his mark even upon Florence.[21] Only, when Francis received the keys of the city beneath it, it was as yet unfinished despite the feverish toil of hundreds of workmen day and night: 'upwards of 60 labourers', reported Horace Mann, the British chargé d'affaires, 'have fallen sick and some few have died of pleurisies.'[22] The Florentine nobility had done their bit by buying

---

[19] Baron von Pöllnitz, op. cit., i. 425.

[20] *Wienerisches Diarium*, 21 Feb. 1739, no. 15, special edition ('Extra-Blat: Ausführlicher Bericht von dem den 20sten Jenner lauffenden Jahrs 1739 zu Florentz beschehenen feyrlichen Einzug Ihrer Königl. Hoheiten Francisci III Hertzogs zu Lothringen und Barr &c. &c. als Gross-Hertzogs von Toscana und der Durchläuch-Gross-Hertzogin von Toscana &c.'), pp. 154–5 for the following.

[21] The arch still stands in the present Piazza della Repubblica.

[22] Horace Mann to Duke of Newcastle, Florence, 5 Jan. 1739: P.R.O./S.P.F., Tuscany, vol. 42, fo. 15.

splendid clothes and equipages for the occasion. It was a distinct success considering that 'the people and the nobility of Florence in the past have shewn very little inclination for their new Sovereign on account of the little regard of some Lorrainers for the nation. It nevertheless seemed the contrary'[23] in the first flush of arrival, through decorated streets to the Pitti Palace dating back to Brunelleschi. One gathers, though, that it struck the young sovereigns as not exactly smart.

That evening the steep slope of the Boboli gardens, almost a natural scaffolding, glittered with lamps in the niches and in translucent pyramids of red. Jadot had competed with another Florentine speciality in also designing the fireworks, a serious concern for connoisseurs of the light touch of that age. The display centred upon a huge setpiece of journey's end. Upon a lofty summit Hercules was resting from his labours, at his feet a centaur and the Erymanthian boar. In a cave below lurked the Lernean hydra, its nine heads grimly strewn around. Suddenly the three-entranced cavern blazed forth, coruscating with multicoloured rockets, catherine-wheels and golden rain to the strains of 'excellent music'[24] in the lively press-report designed to satisfy what it already termed 'the universal longing for news'.[25]

If it provided a classic scene of enchantment for such as the young Count de Stainville, it spelt a round of ceremonial for his father, reunited with the Craons. It was the Marquis de Stainville who presented Horace Mann to the grand duke. Francis, choosing to try, was affability itself. He 'enquired after several People of Quality particularly Your Grace [of Newcastle], the Duke of Grafton, and Sir Robert Walpole from whom he said he had received many civilities'.[26] Francis was recalling his two months in England in 1731 when George II had entertained him at Hampton Court and Robert Walpole at his Norfolk seat, Houghton, where Francis had secretly participated in an early lodge of freemasons. (He was now concerned to abate their persecution in Tuscany.) In England Francis seems really to have enjoyed himself, watching from Somerset House the lord mayor's procession up the Thames, viewing Chelsea, and pursuing his favourite pastimes of hunting and music: one finds him singing a part in a 'practice of the revived opera "Tamerlan"'.[27]

[23] Walton (Baron von Stosch) to Duke of Newcastle, Florence, 26 Jan. 1739: ibid., vol. 41, fo. 249.
[24] *Wienerisches Diarium, u.s.*, p. 165.
[25] Ibid., p. 155.
[26] Mann to Duke of Newcastle, Florence, 26 Jan. 1739: P.R.O./S.P.F., Tuscany, vol. 42, fo. 26.
[27] Viscount Percival, 1 Nov. 1731 (O.S.), 'Diary of the first Viscount Percival, subsequently first Earl of Egmont' in *Manuscripts of the Earl of Egmont: Diary* (London, 1920 f.), i. 207 (Historical Manuscripts Commission, Cmd. 8264 of 1920).

The English commercial community or factory occupied a prominent position in the free port of Leghorn, visited early in March 1739 by the grand duke and duchess, accompanied by the Marquis de Stainville. Francis freed several hundred galley-slaves with the object of redeeming Tuscan subjects from the captivity of the corsairs. This was the first and last time that Maria Theresa saw the sea. Francis aroused criticism by the way in which he fraternized there with the English, dining and sailing around with Captain Peters aboard the merchantman *Tiger* and giving him a gold snuff-box with largesse for the crew. (Local publication of this incident was forbidden.) In this context the French foreign minister sourly noted 'the predilection displayed on so many occasions by the Grand Duke for the English'.[28]

The grand duke, as he told the Duke of Newcastle, took a liking to 'Sieur Männ, who is a very fine man, and pleases me infinitely'.[29] The amiable Mann, next year to begin that lifelong friendship with Horace Walpole whereby he is chiefly remembered, also seems to have got on well with the Marquis de Stainville. The day after the arrival of the court at Florence, Mann, after being presented to Maria Theresa, went with Lord Augustus Fitzroy, one of the Graftons, to dine with the great chamberlain.[30] It seems likely that Mann met his host's young son who was one day to stand out as the antagonist of England.

The Marquis de Stainville obtained for Mann the entrée into Maria Theresa's private apartment, La Retraite, from which foreign envoys were supposed to be excluded. This gave great offence to the French representative, Count Lorenzi, who had tried more or less barging his way in. The question, now mooted, of new regulations for the introduction of diplomatic envoys to the Tuscan court closely affected the office of the great chamberlain: it also involved presiding at dinner over a public table which was maintained for the gentlemen at court, the ladies dining separately at a corresponding table under the chief lady-in-waiting.

At the court of Florence it was almost one round of festivities despite a nominal interlude of mourning for a Bavarian prince. The fireworks to celebrate the grand-ducal arrival had formed part of a plan for illuminating the whole city 'in a most expensive manner for three nights'.[31] There were opera parties, hunting parties, traditional

---

[28] Amelot de Chaillou to Count Lorenzi, 22 June 1739: Arch. Aff. Étr. C.P., Toscane, vol. 90, fo. 296.
[29] Grand Duke Francis II of Tuscany to Duke of Newcastle, Florence, 24 Mar. 1739: P.R.O./S.P.F., Tuscany, carton 84, fo 343.
[30] Mann to Duke of Newcastle, Florence, 26 Jan. 1739: P.R.O./S.P.F., Tuscany, vol. 42, fo. 27.
[31] Mann to Duke of Newcastle, Florence, 12 Jan. 1739: P.R.O./S.P.F., Tuscany, vol. 42, fo. 17.

public games, and diversions in the Boboli gardens. On 28 January the grand duke gave a 'very magnificent'[32] masked ball. And so it went on till the festivities merged into the annual saturnalia of Florence, the great carnival before lent. During it, reported Mann, 'the Court and whole Town was taken up with publick diversions which seemed to put a stop to all business'.[33] Horace Walpole, who participated in the carnival of the following year, gave this description: 'I have done nothing but slip out of my domino into bed, and out of bed into my domino. The end of the Carnival is frantic, Bacchanalian; all the morn one makes parties in masque to the shops and coffee-houses, and all the evening to the operas and balls. *Then I have danced, good gods, how I have danced!*'[34] It must have just suited the young Count de Stainville, also perhaps the fact that 'the reputation of the Florentines is not good in the matter of the ladies'.[35]

Already, though, a visit to Florence was not complete without one to the renowned picture-galleries of the Medici despite the fact that according to contemporary taste, of which the coming young lawyer, de Brosses, was probably fairly typical, the 'pictures ... are not much above mediocre. In a word, that which is most curious here in this sort is to see the first monuments of the art which were manufactured by Cimabue, Giotto, Gaddo Gaddi, Lippi, etc., very sorry works for the most part, but which serve nevertheless to demonstrate how the talent has been developed and perfected little by little. But if the painting is weak here, in recompense the sculpture triumphs. It is the town of statues above all: they are scattered there on all sides, in the thoroughfares.'[36] The paintings, however, likely attracted, stimulated the Count de Stainville. Though no indiscriminate admirer of Italian art in subsequently forming his collection, he came to allow that, if no Raphaels or Correggios were to be had, 'I should make do very well with ... Titians, Guidos or Albanos'.[37] We hear of young Stainville, only a few years after his visit to Florence, buying genre pictures; whereas he was to rate studies of heads in the classic tradition as being generally 'a little cold in taste'.[38]

Another enthusiast for pictures was the Grand Duke Francis but the Medici collection of greatest interest was the famous hoard of treasure and jewels. There was the great diamond which nobody had

[32] Count Lorenzi to Amelot de Chaillou, Florence, 31 Jan. 1739: Arch. Aff. Étr. C.P., Toscane, vol. 90, fo. 48.
[33] Mann to Duke of Newcastle, Florence, 16 Feb. 1739: P.R.O,/S.P.F., Tuscany, vol. 42, fo. 36.
[34] Horace Walpole to Richard West, Florence, 27 Feb. 1740: Walpole Correspondence, xiii. 200–1.
[35] De Brosses, op. cit., i. 275.
[36] Ibid. i. 270.
[37] Count de Stainville to Duke de Nivernais, 17 Nov. 1749: W.N.A., docket V/1, fo. 16.
[38] Count de Stainville to Duke de Nivernais, 11 July 1751: ibid., fo. 85.

set eyes on for a generation, a splendid topaz, and 'the celebrated
necklace of 29 Pearls of an extraordinary size and beauty'.[39] John
Gaston's characteristic collection of 'snuffboxes whereon are painted
obscenities'[40] had, however, been sold by his sister and replaced by
the more suitable presentation-gift of a gold basin. The hand-over
was delicately managed, but Maria Theresa was soon wearing the
pearls while the grand duke took the great diamond 'for a button to
his hat'.[41] On 28 January 1739 a special showing of the Medici jewels
was arranged by Francis for the Marquis de Stainville, who had been
having a difficult time persuading the Electress Palatine, in her sad
position, to accept his master's repeated invitations to dinner.
Stainville had to share his private viewing of the jewels with
Toussaint, the favourite adviser still, or at any rate till recently.

Some ten days later the French envoy at Florence suggested:

That what has brought the Grand Duke to diminish the confidence which he has
had up to the present in M. Toussaint were a discourse which M. de Stainville has
made him. I have learnt thereof in a manner which cannot be doubted. I am assured
that M. de Stainville, when he was upon his departure from Vienna, having gone to
take leave of the Count [?Frederick] d'Harrack [sic], the latter said to him that it was
very disagreeable for them to be serving two masters who had placed their greatest
confidence in two persons who did not at all deserve it, the Emperor in M. de
Bartenstein and the Grand Duke in M. Toussaint, but that it was more forgivable in
His Imperial Majesty, who was already at a very advanced age, and who did not
have the designs of His Royal Highness, which might miscarry for lack of People
capable of counselling him well, and that he [M. de Stainville] would render an
essential service to this Prince in warning him thereof. I was told in addition that this
Marquis having returned to this Prince, and excusing himself for being a little late
because the Count d'Harrack had detained him till then, the Grand Duke asked him
what this Minister had said to him, whereupon M. de Stainville gave him the
account of what is above.[42]

If the Marquis de Stainville, by quoting his old friend Harrach,
had temporarily shaken Toussaint's position, he certainly had not
destroyed it. Toussaint was present, and Stainville was not, at the
secret council on 28 February 1739 which decided to reduce the
interest on the public funds, the Luoghi di Monti, from three and a
half to three per cent. This decree was, together with a prohibition
against the import of woollen goods in the interests of home
manufacture, the most important measure which marked the grand-
ducal visit. On 9 March Mann reported that 'Prince Craon told me

[39] Walton (Baron von Stosch) to Duke of Newcastle, Florence, 12 Jan. 1739: P.R.O./S.P.F.,
Tuscany, vol. 41, fo. 245.
[40] Count Lorenzi to Amelot de Chaillou, Florence, 3 Jan. 1739: Arch. Aff. Étr. C.P., Toscane,
vol. 90, fo. 12.
[41] Mann to Duke of Newcastle, Florence, 2 Feb. 1739: P.R.O./S.P.F., Tuscany, vol. 42, fo. 31.
[42] Count Lorenzi to Amelot de Chaillou, Florence, 7 Feb. 1739: Arch. Aff. Étr. C.P., Toscane,
vol. 90, fo. 62.

yesterday that Mons. Toussaint contrary to the opinion of most of his Ministers had induced the Great Duke to take this step'[43] of reducing the rate of interest, calculated to ease the burden of taxation upon the poorer classes; 'by this means He has disobliged the whole Nobility', who tended to follow the Medici model and were rather despised by aristocrats elsewhere for their bourgeois concern with business. Francis did, however, found at Florence an academy for her noble youth on the model of Lunéville.

For all classes of Florentines the gilt was already beginning to wear off the gingerbread. A fortnight later Mann was commenting on 'the great change which has of late been observed in the affections of the People towards the present Government which dayly increases to the greatest height, so as to make it necessary to give orders to the Fiscal to get people in all the Coffee-Houses and publick places to observe most narrowly the discourses which are held there, notwithstanding which a most infamous Satyr [sic] is lately come out'.[44] Nor were Italian tempers improved a few days later by a measure suspending the payment of all official salaries.

III

The Lorrainers afforded further talking-points to discontent by packing off to Austria quantities of the Medici plate and valuables. And not those alone: 'thirty loads of wines, eatables etc. were sent from hence to Germany for the Service of the Prince Charles of Lorrain for the Campaign in Hungary: other Provisions and Eatables are preparing for that purpose for the Great Duke',[45] eager to retrieve his military reputation in the third campaign against the Turks, then preparing against the eastern background of plague. The emperor, however, had other ideas for his son-in-law. On 25 April 'a Courier arrived from Vienna whose dispatches were carried to the Great Duke whilst he was at the opera, in which was a letter from the Emperor absolutely to forbid His Highness's moving from Tuscany, which letter he gave to the Duchess to read saying notwithstanding he would positively go, at which the Great Duchess was seen publickly to cry; the court on this immediately retired from the

---

[43] Mann to Duke of Newcastle, Florence, 9 Mar. 1739: P.R.O./S.P.F., Tuscany, vol. 42, fo. 58, and for the following.

[44] Mann to Duke of Newcastle, Florence, 23 Mar. 1739: P.R.O./S.P.F., Tuscany, vol. 42, fo. 64.

[45] Newsletter enclosed in Mann to Duke of Newcastle, Florence, 9 Mar. 1739: P.R.O./S.P.F., Tuscany, vol. 42, fo. 62.

Opera: the next day the Great Duchess told Princess Craon what I have mentioned.'[46] The grand duke was as good as his word. A generation later Maria Theresa was to write of that troubled farewell to Florence, 'I cried from chagrin at returning; it is true that it was in order to go on campaign against the Turks, plague and famine.'[47]

No later than 27 April 1739 did Francis and the court leave his capital. That was the last that the Florentines were to see of their sovereign, whose brilliant and expensive visit had not reconciled them to alien rule. Later that year de Brosses wrote that the Tuscans so regretted the departed and indigenous glories of the Medici 'that there are scarcely any who would not give a third of their goods to see them come to life again, and another third so as not to have the Lorrainers; I do not believe that anything equals the contempt that they have for them, unless it is the hatred which the people of Milan bear against the Piedmontese.'[48] The Florentines, however, were to have ten years under the Prince de Craon as president of the Tuscan Council of Regency – the princess continued almost as beautiful as ever: 'although', remarked de Brosses that year, 'she is long since a grandmother, in truth I believe that in case of need I could still quite well play the little Duke of Lorraine with her'.[49] Nor, apparently, was he alone in this inclination.

Under Craon the vice-president was Richecourt, further dignified as the Marquis di Treschietto and strengthened by becoming head of the Council of Finance which Francis while in Florence constituted along with a military council to mesh in with the Council of Regency in a triple articulation of his Tuscan government. Thereafter, noted Horace Walpole succinctly, the Craons in Florence 'were extremely ill treated and mortified by the Count de Richecourt, a low Lorrainer, who being a creature of the Great Duke's favourite minister [Toussaint], had the chief ascendant and power there.'[50] Perhaps one should add that the low Lorrainer became the lover of Horace Walpole's unappealing and intellectually pretentious sister-in-law, Lady Walpole, wife of the lord with whom the Marquis de Stainville had once gone hunting at Windsor.

For the present Francis was prevented by heavy seas from executing his plan of proceeding by galley from Leghorn to Genoa where he designed, it was said, 'to make Proposal to the Republick for

[46] Mann to Duke of Newcastle, Florence, 18 May 1739: P.R.O./S.P.F. Tuscany, vol. 42, fo. 125.
[47] Empress Maria Theresa to Archduchess Maria Christina, 11 Jan. 1776: *Briefe der Kaiserin Maria Theresia an ihre Kinder and Freunde*, ed. Alfred Ritter von Arneth (Vienna, 1881), ii. 383.
[48] De Brosses to de Neuilly, 8 Oct. 1739: op. cit., i. 305.   [49] Ibid., i. 309.
[50] Note by Horace Walpole to his letter of 2 Nov. 1741 (O.S.) to Mann: Walpole Correspondence, xvii. 189, n. 53.

the Purchase of Corsica',[51] then the focus of an international imbroglio remarkable even in that intricate age.

The Marquis de Maillebois had just assumed command of a French force then engaged in the Genoese dominion of Corsica in suppressing rebels who still looked to a prudently departed German adventurer, Baron von Neuhoff, lately proclaimed King Theodore I of Corsica upon landing from an English ship with some Tunisian, and subsequent Dutch, commercial backing. This swindler out of an implausible novelette had by 1730 already been passing himself off as an agent of Francis of Lorraine before impersonating an English lord in Genoa while investigating the first phase of the eighteenth-century Corsican rebellion against that debile republic which, that time, had called in an Austrian force under Prince Lewis of Würtemberg to suppress revolt within the shadowy context of imperial suzerainty, still, in Italy. Francis, a secretively ambitious prince, had an eye on Corsica and to schemes like those of Neuhoff, who is said to have known Duke Leopold and to have made a nice sum gambling with him at Lunéville. Like Lorraine itself, Corsica was caught between the ambitions of Austria, friendly with maritime England, and of France, the scheming friend of Genoa. If Fleury here was indeed acting in concert with Austria and had in 1738 prudently eluded a Corsican offer of adhesion to France, yet French military intervention in the insurgent island already signalled a forward policy which was to be driven to success a generation later under the Duke de Choiseul. By then King Theodore had died a bankrupt starveling in London. ('Fate poured its lessons on his living head, Bestowed a Kingdom and denied him Bread.')[52] Theodore's only lasting legacy to Corsica was his flag with the negro's head. For the present the Count de Stainville was liable to be introduced early to those Corsican affairs which were in 1739 a leading topic of interest in Florence and Leghorn.

Young Stainville's fortunes were now to be linked with those of Prince Charles of Lorraine, who accompanied his elder brother on the return journey to Vienna. They avoided Venetian territory this time in travelling to Turin, where their elder sister was queen, then on via Milan and Innsbruck. In the Tyrolean capital where their father had been born the princes spent a week with their mother, who had consented to come that far, accompanied by their younger sister Charlotte, in order to make the acquaintance of her Austrian daughter-in-law whose marriage had occasioned her such grief. From that family reunion the Dowager Duchess of Lorraine and her

[51] Mann to Duke of Newcastle, Florence, 19 Apr. 1739: P.R.O./S.P.F., Tuscany, vol. 42, fo. 95.
[52] Epitaph by Horace Walpole on King Theodore in Saint Anne's, Soho: Horace Walpole to Sir Horace Mann, Strawberry Hill, 29 Sept. 1757: Walpole Correspondence, xxi. 140.

unmarried daughter returned to Commercy while Francis, Charles,
and Maria Theresa boated down the Inn and then on down the
Danube all the way to Vienna: 'which' observed a contemporary,
'shews how convenient a country Germany is for Water Carriage,
and how much their Inland Trade might be thereby improved, if the
country were not divided into so many Principalities'.[53] As it was, the
boating party had to endure copious Bavarian civilities during their
hook through the electorate. The Count de Stainville was in the suite
of the grand duke and duchess upon their return to Vienna where
they made the White Lamb in the Rossau quarter on 30 May 1739.
They drove on to the Laxenburg palace and, hoped the men, to the
eastern campaign.

[53] *The Life of His Serene Highness, Charles, Prince of Lorrain*, p. 124.

CHAPTER X

EASTWARD

I

FRANCIS found upon return that the emperor still forbade him that year's campaign against the Turks and had entrusted it to his enemy, Field-Marshal Count Wallis, described by Frederick the Great as taking pride 'in hating and being hated by everybody'.[1] The imperial prohibition did not include the younger brother, of whom Francis was already inclined to be jealous. Charles, his mother's favourite from his lively boyhood, was the taller, handsomer, more winning, the more affable, certainly, with the Marquis de Stainville. Their friendship extended beyond the hunting-field, as Prince Charles himself had observed in beginning a letter back in 1735: 'I have seen, my dear Stainville, from your handsome presentation to me of the life of M. de Turenne that you take an interest not only in my pleasures but equally in essentials. The portrait of the hero is frank and a little difficult to imitate, especially for those who lack opportunity to train.'[2]

Prince Charles had since worked himself through the Austrian army and the Marquis de Stainville had been assured that on his first campaign against the Turks in 1737 'at the name of Charles of Lorraine they laid down their arms. They thought it useless to defend themselves against the grandson of [Duke] Charles V, the terror of the Ottoman Empire.'[3] Already acclaimed in Austria as the Delight of the Army, this dashing lieutenant-general for the Hungarian campaign of 1739 now took as aide-de-camp his friend's son, the Count de Stainville. They were well matched. Young Stainville may have found the debonair Charles the more congenial since the prince's early sympathies, unlike those of Francis, had lain towards France.

The Count de Stainville did not lose touch with the French army and had in fact just become, on 24 February 1739, an active second lieutenant in the regiment Roi-Infanterie. Now, though, military

[1] King Frederick II of Prussia, *Histoire de mon temps* in *Œuvres de Frédéric le Grand* (Berlin, 1846f: henceforth cited as Frederick), ii. 6.
[2] Prince Charles of Lorraine to Marquis de Stainville, 25 June 1735: Arch. M-et-M/Vienne, 3F 373, no. 119.
[3] Count de Richcourt to Marquis de Stainville, Vienna, 24 July 1737: ibid., no. 196.

opportunity was beckoning from the east, and was liable to be facilitated by the Franco-Austrian rapprochement. Hardly more than a few days after his return from Italy to Vienna young Stainville was riding out over the cruel plains of Hungary, away across the *pusta* to the Banat over against those Transylvanian and Wallachian marches once governed by the family benefactor whose name he bore and whose feats against the Turk he was now to emulate in his first campaign. It was a characteristic army of the time, the fifty thousand and more imperial troops being accompanied by four thousand female auxiliaries. These enterprising women were evidently unde-terred by the fact that in the campaign of two years before the Turks had captured and carried off a thousand of their kind – 'sort of canteen-women disguised as amazons, whereof the imperial camps were full'.[4] The Turks of the 'avid sabre' were yet an intimidating enemy. In victory one of their habits at that time was to erect upon the battlefield a pyramid of chopped-off Austrian heads. Now another battle loomed.

Monday 20 July 1739 found Prince Charles of Lorraine thrusting out from the southern bank of the Danube eastwards of Belgrade. For the occasion he was leading a company as a volunteer in a reconnaissance in strength under Major-General Bernklau. The adventurous Count de Stainville was attached to the right person in a prince who was 'always ready to expose himself to the most hazardous Enterprizes'.[5] Bernklau's reconnaissance-group discov-ered that the bulk of the Ottoman army was already across the river Morava running up to join the Danube roughly at right-angles eastward of the battlemented stronghold of Semendria (Smederevo). The Turks provided confirmation in three strong attacks against the Austrian reconnaisance, threatened with envelopment. Skilful Bernk-lau, however, extricated his force for only twelve killed, and reported back to Field-Marshal Wallis, subsequently criticized for not having been beforehand over against the Morava. As it was, the 'very sharp Skirmish'[6] may well have been the Count de Stainville's baptism of fire.

From the north came the booming of guns upon the Danube. For this was a combined operation. The Count Pallavicini, 'General of the Imperial Ships and Vessels on the Danube' in his two-decked flagship the *Triton* (built in Vienna in 1737), was running up against

<hr/>

[4] Report of 1737 on military operations by Marquis de Villeneuve, French Ambassador at Constantinople: Arch. Aff. Étr. C.P., Turquie; cited, Albert Vandal, *Une Ambassade française en Orient sous Louis XV* (2nd ed., Paris, 1887), p. 303.
[5] *The Life of His Serene Highness, Charles, Prince of Lorrain*, p. 135.
[6] Original translation of Austrian communiqué of 21 July 1739 'from the Imperial Camp near Zweybrook', cited, ibid., p. 134.

a Turkish flotilla of forty caiques in the reaches of Groczka, a village lying between Semendria and the main Austrian advance from Wischnitza (Vrchin). By bombardment that same Monday Pallavicini cleared the slopes round Groczka of four thousand horse in the Turkish van. The admiral too had urgent intelligence for Field-Marshal Oliver Wallis.

During 21 July tension mounted. The Turk was known to be occupying Semendria in strength and reinforcing out to Groczka. That Tuesday Wallis held council of war. It was decided to lose no time in pushing the Turkish van out of Groczka before it could fortify that advantageously hilly position – even as it was, in the night of 21–2 July the enemy artfully constructed two shore-batteries among thick trees to hold Pallavicini in check. Present at the Austrian council of war was General of Artillery Count von Neipperg, the old mentor of the Grand Duke Francis. He had reached Wallis's camp that morning, ahead of the rearward contingent which he was now commanding. The bold but questionable decision was to attack without awaiting its arrival so that Neipperg's force should nourish an engagement already under way.

II

In the undulating country eastward from Belgrade the road to Groczka sloped gently upward to a wooded defile of something more than a mile through broken terrain rich in vineyards and other fruit. Though that was then largely in the form of blackberry-bushes through which the advancing Austrians had to hack their way. Before dawn on 22 July 1739 the van under Field-Marshal Wallis himself was debouching from the defile. Suddenly bullets were whistling all around. The Austrian hussars turned tail, leaving the Johann Palffy cuirassiers and other forward elements to confront a surge of Turks springing from cover among the vineyards. They were newly skilled troops unexpectedly supported already by the main Turkish army. The Austrian van battled almost alone, was torn to shreds. Severely wounded in leading a charge was the twentieth Earl of Crawford, serving on secondment like young Stainville, whom he probably met since the earl was an intimate of Prince Charles of Lorraine. So also had been a young Irish nobleman who now, killing several Turks with his own hands, recaptured an imperial standard and tied it round his waist as a sash so that in the mêlée the enemy could not remove it after he was slain, as he was. Whereas Crawford was to live to fight on the opposite side to Stainville at Dettingen.

The gallant stand afforded time to the main elements of the
Austrian army to issue from the defile and deploy. Then their turn
came. 'The Turks', said an Austrian citation, 'fought upon this
occasion like Disperradoes ... with ... the most hideous outcries.'[7]
From five in the morning till after sundown, fifteen times that day
did the Austrians face the terrible charge of the screaming Janizaries;
and fifteen times did they withstand it. 'Prince Charles of Lorrain',
the account continued, 'gave great proof of his Bravery in this
Engagement, not only charging the Turks intrepidly at the Head of
his own Regiment but rallying and encouraging the others, and by
his own Example animating the Men'. For a commander then to
rally wavering troops amid the din of battle the assistance of one or
more aides-de-camp was almost indispensable; it seems a fair
presumption that the Count de Stainville was creditably active.

As the Austrian troops were wilting into disorder in one phase of
'this obstinate and bloody battle' they were succoured by the arrival
of General Neipperg's thirteen thousand men, marching in at all
speed sans baggage, sans even their coats in that Balkan summer.
Field-Marshal Wallis thereupon renewed the action against the
background all that day of the boom of cannonading upon the
Danube. There Pallavicini, wryly observing the Austrian army
fighting uphill, being bent back from Groczka, was himself beginning
to retire when he rounded upon pursuing Turkish galleys, sank one
and so bruised four more that their rowers abandoned ship and left
them adrift. In that combined operation Wallis too was giving a good
account of himself. Only, he failed to bring his full strength to bear.
Like many bad battles it was lopsided. Some stood idle while others
were locked in that conflict which 'lasted near nineteen Hours, which
was very extraordinary, especially in the Germans, who fought all
that Time against superior Numbers, with great Disadvantages of
ground, and without any Refreshment either for Man or Horse'.
Terser was the Count de Stainville's own recall of 'a celebrated battle
at Kroczka, which the Imperials lost'.[8]

By nightfall the Austrian forces considered themselves almost
victorious, masters not indeed of Groczka village but of the grim
battlefield with good hope of the morrow. When Wallis, dismayed by
the massacre of his advance-guard and the loss of over seven thousand
men, as despondent as he had previously been rash, gave orders to
disengage under cover of darkness. Next day his now disheartened
men did indeed beat off the enemy but night found them once more

[7] Original translation of communiqué from the army of Field-Marshal Wallis, July 1739,
cited, ibid., pp. 137-9 for the following.
[8] Choiseul, *Mémoires*, p. 3.

falling back. Nocturnal retreat, notoriously one of the most difficult operations, imparted momentum to what had begun as an orderly withdrawal till the Austrians were almost in flight, sweeping on through Belgrade itself, left with only a garrison as the main army put the breadth of the Danube behind it. On 27 July Turkish forces began to besiege the strategic bastion of Belgrade rather less than twenty miles to the north-west of the grisly field of Groczka, so strewn with corpses that even a year later one could not walk there for more than ten paces without coming upon a heap of them.[9]

On 30 July 1739, on the marshy north bank of the Danube, Wallis did somewhat revive his men, breasting their way through high grass, by winning a small engagement at Panczova. This combat was, however, strictly beside the point: except perhaps for the Turkish commander in it, the courageous Seraskier of Widin, who subsequently paid for it with his head. The point was that Austria proceeded to treat for peace under French mediation and through the rival of the now distrusted Wallis, who had already put out a feeler to the Turks through his own emissary, Count Gross, henceforth superseded.

On the hot afternoon of 18 August there entered the Turkish camp before Belgrade the Austrian plenipotentiary in the slim person of Count Neipperg, dirty and dispirited. This sarcastic second-rater was recommended for his critical assignment by erstwhile participation in the brilliant peace of Passarowitz, by his command of French, by association with the Grand Duke Francis in the imperial favour. Neipperg, having disregarded an instruction against his entering the Turkish camp, compounded this by presenting his unrestricted full powers to the Turks without demanding hostages to guarantee his free sojourn there. He was left to cool his heels for a week under some threat of constraint, living out of a few valises in a tent hard by the Grand Vizier's own till the humiliated Austrian took shelter under the diplomatic immunity of the tent of the French ambassador to the Porte, the ugly little Marquis de Villeneuve. This expert diplomatist's long campaign for enhancing the position of France in the east now culminated in his personal mediation and domination of the negotiations in the Turkish camp before Belgrade.

The optimum objective of the Cardinal Fleury was the Austrian cession of Belgrade to the Porte. Neipperg was no match for the Franco-Turkish combination and Villeneuve put the wind up him over the military position. This was facilitated by another crass error by Neipperg, afraid of irritating the Turks; he had actually left instructions that Austrian communications should not be maintained

[9] Cf. Lavender Cassels, op. cit., p. 166.

with him in their camp: instructions which jealous Wallis was careful
to observe so that Neipperg remained in ignorance not only of letters
to him from Charles VI in favour of a stiffening stance but also of the
local circumstances behind them. Four days after Neipperg had
crossed the Turkish lines a new general, Baron von Schmettau, had
assumed command of the garrison holding Belgrade behind those
splendid Austrian fortifications which still command the confluence
of the Save and the Danube. The horizon was dominated by this
proud citadel designed to render impregnable the conquest of Prince
Eugene, to constitute the Germanic outpost and 'Principal bulwark
of Christendom'[10] in the Balkans. As Neipperg represented to
Villeneuve, the mother-church of Rome had contributed heavily
towards the fortification of those ramparts to be held by the Holy
Roman Emperor against the Sultan. This duty was now boldly
discharged by Samuel von Schmettau, who was already galvanizing
the Austrian garrison into offensive activity against the inadequate
Turkish siegeworks against Belgrade.

Schmettau gave Neipperg a piece of his mind when the latter re-
entered the city after signing peace-preliminaries on 1 September
1739. He had undone that Treaty of Passarowitz which, with his own
participation, had in 1718 set the seal upon Eugene's defeat of the
Turks at Belgrade. That was over now. The Banat of Temesvar was
the only acquisition substantially left to Austria. Wallachia, once the
province of Stephen de Stainville, was lost to her. Her conquests in
Bosnia and Serbia were gone. Orsova was to revert to the Ottomans
along with the prize of Belgrade itself, where the Turks were to take
prompt possession of one gate as surety. The frustrated Austrian
garrison had to watch Turkish officers prancing around on horses
with saddlecloths that were imperial standards captured upon the
day of Groczka.[11]

The Count de Stainville, amid this collapse of what his ancestor
had helped to secure for the Habsburgs, was eager to obtain a closer
view of the victorious Turkish host. He related that 'as a French
officer, although attached to Prince Charles, I was several days on
end in the Turkish camp with M. de Villeneuve'.[12] There Stainville
could consort with clever Delaria, first dragoman of the French
embassy, with Peyssonnel who had matched Neipperg's Mommartz
in drafting the peace-preliminaries through the night of 31 August,
and with other young Frenchmen in Villeneuve's train, now

[10] Cardinal Kollonitz, memorandum of 1739 to Emperor Charles VI: P.R.O./S.P.F., Vienna
80/136, cited in the present text ibid., p. 199.
[11] Cf. Field-Marshal Count von Schmettau, *Mémoires de la guerre d'Hongrie* (revised ed.,
Frankfurt, 1772), p. 264.
[12] Choiseul, *Mémoires*, p. 4.

increased by a splendid saluki presented to him by the Grand Vizier. Villeneuve's tents formed a little christian oasis in that teeming camp of Islam with its gaudy standards and marquees – the smell of the Turks on campaign, said a later observer at Belgrade, was compounded of ferocity and luxury, of 'death, burning and essence of roses'.[13] (When the Grand Vizier's regular supply of ice had once failed to arrive from Nish during the negotiations with Neipperg, one of the latter's few messages to the Austrian command in Belgrade had been to ask it to remedy the deficiency.)

In the Ottoman encampment young Stainville could appraise the Turkish army and the traditional Turkish factor in French foreign policy, presented as a youth's dream of diplomacy personified in a triumphant ambassador holding great armies in check and whole provinces of contending empires almost at descretion, imposing peace in the very camps of war. It was a diplomatic introduction which the vaulting spirit of the future Choiseul was unlikely to let slip.

III

Villeneuve's work was only completed on 18 September 1739 when, in the open air amid the bustle of breaking camp, he affixed his seals to articles of peace between Turkey and Austria and between Turkey and Russia. For the preliminaries of 1 September had been a separate peace by Austria in desertion of her Russian ally whose very successes in the Balkans were calculated to cause misgivings in Vienna, not for the last time in history.

Early that September two separate pieces of intelligence had reached Vienna within twenty-four hours. First that Neipperg had signed the preliminaries of peace (for which he, like Wallis, was imprisoned till the death of heartbroken Charles VI); secondly, as if to rub in the ignominy of Austria's defection, that the Russians under the enterprising if strict Field-Marshal Münnich – he had once threatened to bury alive any man of his who reported sick – had broken right through into Moldavia, capturing Choczim, entering Jassy and pushing out advance-guards to the Danube and into Wallachia to make contact with the Austrians. On hearing of their negotiations at Belgrade, Münnich wrote to Prince Lobkowitz: 'On the part of the Russians fortresses are being taken; on the part of the Imperial [Austrian] troops, they are being demolished and ceded to the enemy. The Russians acquire principalities, the Imperials render

---

[13] Prince de Ligne, Belgrade, 18 Oct. 1789, in his *Mélanges militaires, littéraires et sentimentaires* (Leopoldsberg, 1795f.), vii. 219.

whole kingdoms to the Turks. The Russians reduce the enemy to extremities, the Imperials grant him everything he wishes and everything that can flatter and increase his pride.'[14]

Such was the Russian repetition of the indignation which Peter the Great had felt, with rather less justification, at the Austro-Turkish Peace of Karlowitz some forty years before, at the time of the first Austro-Russian alliance. Nevertheless Russia had her own reasons now for considering peace. Despite the manoeuvres against Villeneuve's mediation by the Neapolitan representative of Russia at Belgrade, remote Cagnoni, she finally came round and concluded a treaty under Villeneuve's auspices whereby she yielded all her conquests except Azov, and that even was to be dismantled, with no Russian fleet allowed on the Black Sea. The Turks still kept their maritime preserves 'as a pure and immaculate virgin'.[15]

The grim and inglorious Eastern War which terminated thus has not been much remembered since. Yet it was a conflict of some significance since, typical of its time, it marks a watershed between the old order and the new. One way it appears as the last of the long series of campaigns waged in the old style by christendom against the Ottoman menace overhanging Eastern Europe. Pope Clement XII endeavoured to infuse a crusading spirit into the Eastern War, hinged upon the christian bastion of Belgrade; the Austrian army was supported by other contingents, notably Saxon and Bavarian, from the Holy Roman Empire and the flotilla on the Danube was manned, if partly by galley-slaves, partly also by Maltese knights and seamen furnished by their ruler, the Grand Master of the Order of Saint John of Jerusalem, in one of the last expeditions made by that medieval order of crusading chivalry. Looked at another way, the Eastern War might also be taken as the inception of the Eastern Question in that modern form wherein it was to emerge as a leading issue of European diplomacy for nearly two centuries to come. Already one finds the two great empires of Austria and Russia having to reckon with each other in their attempts to reap profit in the Balkans from the weakness of the third, the Ottoman: and already the powers of the west, notably France, felt that the question was one to which they could not afford to remain indifferent. England, though, was then preoccupied with her next maritime conflict with Spain, the War of Jenkins' Ear, which began in 1739.

---

[14] Marshal Münnich to Prince Lobkowitz, 25 Sept. 1739: cited, Général de Manstein, *Mémoires historiques, politiques et militaires sur la Russie depuis l'année MDCCXXVII jusqu'à MDCCXLIV* (Paris, 1860), ii. 66.

[15] Ukraintsev, Russian envoy in Constantinople, 18 July 1700: Ustryalov, *Istoriya tsarstvovaniya Petra Velikago* (Saint Petersburg, 1853), iii. 551; translation as in citation by B. H. Sumner, *Peter the Great and the Ottoman Empire* (Oxford, 1949), p. 23.

The ambivalent aspect of the Eastern War was curiously reflected in the schemes for post-war settlement which it had produced among publicists, including an unemployed elder statesman. The gifted Cardinal Alberoni, having embroiled European diplomacy by his forward policy when guiding the destinies of Spain twenty years before, spent some of the long leisure of retirement in reviving the old call for European unity in subduing the Turk. In 1736 he had published German and English editions of his plan for an international combination of christian powers, catholic and protestant on an equal footing, to conquer the Ottoman Empire and divide the spoils. Alberoni proposed that the subjection of Islam should promote a new Europe united by a single customs tariff and by 'a Perpetual Diet of the Christian Powers, vested with authority to determine all disputes and controversies amicably',[16] and disposing in case of need of an international force wherewith to proceed against any power which persisted for six months in refusing to submit to a decision of the diet. The scheme reflected that interest in projects for perpetual peace which the Abbé de Saint-Pierre had lately stimulated. Nor did Alberoni's project stand alone. The Marquis d'Argenson was a disciple of the Abbé de Saint-Pierre and an imaginative intellectual in politics; he now proposed a chimerical scheme for reviving and confederating the crusading kingdoms of Jerusalem, Antioch, Cyprus and so forth – one new crown to each ruling house of Europe – but also suggested 'making a fine communication canal from the Sea of the Levant to the Red Sea'. This canal was to 'belong in common to all the christian world'.[17]

The eighteenth-century horizon of continental statesmen was not so invariably confined as is sometimes supposed to the wearisome complications of dynastic disputes. Indeed their wider vision, when it occurred, was apt to be too wide for practical accomplishment; and, in this case, too optimistic. The world had to wait more than a century for the Suez Canal since, apart from all else, the Eastern War ended so differently from European expectation. There was general astonishment at the way in which the supposedly effete Turks had hit back and given the Austrians such a drubbing. It was a lesson which they long remembered so that Habsburg ambitions were diverted from the Balkans and did not dent them seriously until the nineteenth century. Russia had done better, indeed, and was to

[16] Cardinal Alberoni, *Cardinal Alberoni's Scheme for reducing the Turkish Empire to the Obedience of Christian Princes; and for a partition of the Conquest. Together with a Scheme of Perpetual Dyet for establishing the publick tranquillity* (London, 1736): cited, W. Evans Darby, 'Cardinal Alberoni's Proposed European Alliance for the Subjugation and Settlement of the Turkish Empire, 1735' in *Transactions of the Grotius Society*, v (London, 1920), 79.
[17] D'Argenson, i. 366.

resume her push against the Ottoman dominions during the reign of Catherine the Great. Nevertheless the Russian advance was checked by the Peace of Belgrade. It also checked the Turkish decline, checked but did not arrest it. Henceforth the Ottoman Empire was on the defensive. The true victor at Belgrade was non-belligerent France, and it was with some reason that Louis XV ordered the peace to be celebrated like a battle won, striking a medal in commemoration. The ascendancy of France was demonstrated by the favourable capitulations which she now secured from Turkey where her influence attained its zenith, and by advances from Russia, though French rapprochement with Austria was correspondingly cooled.

At the end of the seventeen-thirties French diplomacy had to all appearance achieved striking success, and options. By the Third Treaty of Vienna it had extracted Lorraine from the circumstance of Russian and Austrian success in Poland, and now next year it had by the Treaty of Belgrade reduced Austria and contained the Russian advance against Turkey, the traditional friend of France. If she still stood closer to the Habsburgs than of yore, yet French secret diplomacy was already on its way towards mobilizing Germany against Austria in case of need. In 1738 France whetted the appetite of her Bavarian client for Austrian pickings by a secret treaty, and hidden subsidies from Louis XV were assisting the regenerated Prussia of Frederick-William I – 100,000 livres in 1737, twice that amount in 1738, next year another hundred thousand.[18] French cash further secured notable success in 1738 in Sweden where wholesale bribery by the French ambassador, the Italian Count de Saint Séverin, promoted the francophil party of the Hats, eager to reverse the Treaty of Nystädt against Russia. Thus ended the sleepy policy of the opposing Nightcaps or Caps under the long ascendancy of Count Arvid Horn, who had maintained peace with Russia and friendship with an England pursuing a foreign policy under Walpole which was a fair match to his own. The new Swedish government underlined the success of French diplomacy by concluding an alliance with France and making proposals for a league with Turkey, her opposite number on the southern flank of Europe. The threatening possibilities of such a combination helped to incline Russia towards peace. Whether, upon the longer calculation, the French government was wholly wise so to set itself against the new power of Russia is a deeper question of subsequent significance.

[18] Cf. French treasury memorandum of 1750, 'Mémoire concernant les affaires étrangères depuis l'année 1724 jusques et compris 1750: Affaires Secrètes Étrangères, 1716–1750', Trinity College Library (Dublin) MS K.2.6.896; cited, Lawrence Henry Gipson, The British Empire before the American Revolution (Caldwell and New York, 1936f.), vi. 380, n. 27.

IV

The Treaty of Belgrade, like the Third Treaty of Vienna, occupied a special place in the background of the Count de Stainville. Upon its signature he was tempted to accompany the triumphant Villeneuve on his departure from the Turkish camp and 'to return thence by Constantinople to Paris. I have always had some regret at having had the prudence, which was not my dominant quality at that time, not to pursue the project of this voyage.'[19] There may possibly have been hindrances, also, from his position as a princely aide-de-camp and the undesirability of his being assimilated to the young officers who did accompany Villeneuve back to Constantinople as hostages for the Austrian execution of the peace-terms. These included a Lieutenant Verrières and Count Gross, a guarantor of the terms he had been prevented from negotiating. The hostages received slap-up treatment from the Grand Vizier who supplied them with meals of fifteen hot dishes, invited them to hunt during the journey with his two friendly sons, and at Adrianople had them shewn over the empty seraglio, capable of accommodating over three thousand people and equipped with hot and cold baths. Constantinople reached, the officers were caught up in a round of embassy-parties and were given special seats to watch the Grand Vizier's gorgeous victory-parade, wherein his sons particularly saluted the vanquished spectators. Young Stainville seemingly had something to regret. 'However that may be,' he later wrote, 'I derived from my taste for the Turkish army only the satisfaction which my curiosity made me seek out, and a sort of pestilential fever, whereof I was very ill until my return to Vienna, and I still felt it upon my arrival in Paris in the month of January 1740.'

Vienna was then less gay than Constantinople. Mirepoix had to protest against the Viennese execration of Villeneuve and his mediation. The church anathematized the loss of its heavy investment in Belgrade. The outraged mob went for the houses of the defeated and now recriminating generals including that of the protestant Schmettau whose wife was in childbed, was terrified and died. The emperor for his part remarked, without evident exaggeration, 'this year is taking many years off my life.'[20] The unpopularity of Neipperg tended to rub off upon the already unpopular Grand Duke Francis, in whose interest the Marquis de Stainville continued loyally active in Vienna, as with Thomas Robinson. The British minister was on friendly enough terms with the great chamberlain to

---

[19] Choiseul, *Mémoires*, p. 4 for the following.
[20] Emperor Charles VI in late 1739: cited, F. Hennings, op. cit., p. 206.

judge from the way in which Stainville then closed a note to him about an audience of the grand duke by taking the opportunity 'to have the honour to wish you good evening'.[21] The anglophile Francis was later to act as proxy for George II in dubbing Robinson a Knight of the Bath.

Another diplomatic friend of the Marquis de Stainville was Baron (later Count) Henry Hyacinth de Richecourt of that legal family de Nay who were neighbours in the Barrois from Richecourt near Saint Mihiel, had intermarried with the Bourciers and had risen in favour and rank under Dukes Leopold and Francis till the head of the family, Henry's perhaps trickier brother, Count Emmanuel de Richecourt, had attained his eminence of vice-president in the government of Tuscany. It appears that the Baron Henry had helped Stainville out in Paris as chargé d'affaires during the War of the Polish Succession, and he was probably the 'Mr. de Nay' who had been listed as receiving one-eighth as much as Stainville's own salary.[22] They both belonged to the little band of international diplomatists who were to represent three different states on behalf of Francis of Lorraine, and indeed the assignments of Henry de Richecourt were to be the more varied and responsible. He was now posted on a Tuscan mission to the Hague, and the Marquis de Stainville had just previously written to him from Vienna: 'I am leaving here as soon as Madam the Grand Duchess shall be delivered and I am going to take a turn at home and to Paris; so I beg you to address your letters to me to Commercy':[23] he was evidently, on his way through, to bring to the dowager duchess news of the birth of her latest grandchild.

The news proved glum. On 12 January 1740 Maria Theresa produced her third daughter running, Maria Caroline, instead of the son eagerly awaited by the adherents of the unpopular grand duke, by the emperor himself. It seemed as though the Marquise de Stainville's prediction of endless archduchesses might yet prove correct. Another girl much depressed the depressed Emperor.

Young Lieutenant de Stainville may well have travelled with his father upon his return to France even if he was disinclined to associate him with his search for fortune at the opening of a new decade:

I found myself only a sub-lieutenant in the Régiment du Roi and for support a father, who, by his quite peculiar manner of seeing things and of living, could be of

---

[21] Marquis de Stainville to Robinson, Vienna, evening of 7 Nov. 1739: Robinson Papers, vol. xxv: British Library, Add. MSS. 23804, fo. 248.

[22] Cf. p. 162.

[23] Marquis de Stainville to Baron de Richecourt, Vienna, 30 Dec. 1739 (wrongly headed as November): Ö.S./H.H.S., Lothringisches Hausarchiv 189/III 126, fo. 255.

no aid to me in obtaining preferments, and all the less so since, besides the fact that he concerned himself not at all with my advancement, it was not possible for him, in view of his taste for the table and for a very private society, to make me acquainted with good company.[24]

Behind those words lay the circumstance that the Count de Stainville, during his youthful sojourn at Vienna, 'had been treated in a distinguished and seductive manner. His only friends in France were companions of pleasure, that is to say mere acquaintances, [whereas] he was greatly wanted at the court of the emperor.'[25] It was probably, still, of his eldest son, just twenty-one, that the Marquis de Stainville wrote to his master that summer: 'I am sensible as I should be of the kindness with which your Royal Highness is interesting himself in the establishment of my son. I am working at it.'[26] But the family property remained in Lorraine and the inclination of the young count was also oriented towards France, excessively idealized though this probably was by his earliest biographer into a selfless French patriotism.

The Count de Stainville proceeded to try his luck at the court of Versailles. He joined with the French nobles of his own age in applying there for the colonelcy of a regiment. This was refused him and 'the court did not even give him a forthcoming hope of one'.[27] Such a rebuff was perhaps almost to be expected by a young officer just back from Austrian service; at the same time, as Choiseul later emphasized, his father's 'attachment to the Duke of Lorraine . . . was then a blot'[28] in France. This was doubtless true: also, most likely, that the father in his restricted sociability could not launch his eldest son with sufficient éclat despite his many acquaintances in French ruling circles, from Fleury downwards. Choiseul's assertion that his father concerned himself not at all with his advancement is demonstrably untrue. Towards the end of the year the Marquis de Stainville was assuring the Grand Duke Francis that while in Paris 'I am doing my best to finish the establishment proposed for my son, the sole object of my journey'.[29] The marquis, who had earlier tried to help on the military career of his nephew, young Ligny, now applied to friendly Fleury for a French regiment for the future Choiseul, and did not just take No for an answer even though his reiterated efforts this time proved unavailing.

[24] Choiseul, Mémoires, p. 4.
[25] Essai/Arsenal 5808, fo. 13.
[26] Marquis de Stainville to Grand Duke Francis II, 10 July 1740: Esteri del Granducato di Toscana, vol. 2295/1286, fo. 25.
[27] Essai/Arsenal 5808, fo. 12.
[28] Choiseul, Mémoires, p. 4.
[29] Marquis de Stainville to Grand Duke Francis II, Paris, 1 Dec. 1740: Esteri del Granducato di Toscana, vol. 2295/1286, fo. 46.

It would thus appear that there was some exaggeration, and some truth, in the assurance of Choiseul's eulogist that the Marquis de Stainville was without credit at the French court:

His repugnance for any step [thus amended by Nivernais from 'his natural disposition to take no pains'] was, besides, insurmountable even by his attachment for his son . . . The young Stainville . . . [was] more stricken by a kind of shame and chagrin at seeing his father attached to a foreign prince, than by anxiety as to the disadvantages which result therefrom for himself; he had resolved to remain in France and to serve there all his life in a subordinate condition rather than to attach himself to another power. The noblest course was always to be that which the Count de Stainville would take. His courage alone gave him the means to bear its trials, but his extreme gaiety and his happy character moreover made him see under the most favourable and most smiling aspect the resolutions which he adopted, whatever their consequences might be.[30]

This eulogy made no mention of territorial interest in a Lorraine under French tutelage, and the picture of Stainville's modest abnegation calls for some caution in the case of so stout a careerist. Yet a noble courage was truly his. And his resolute optimism was a key to his whole career. The indication of political friction between father and son is of likely significance and may elucidate the latter's somewhat cryptic allusion to his parent and his peculiar outlook. In later life Choiseul was commonly regarded as the spoilt favourite of fortune so that in looking back he may have tended to exaggerate, at his father's expense, the extent to which he had had to stand on his own feet.

The promotion of the eldest son upon his coming of age may well have contributed towards the considerable debts to acquaintances and relations which the Marquis de Stainville had contracted by the close of the difficult thirties. In 1740 he was paying to the famous financier Pâris-Monmartel eleven hundred French livres as the interest at five per cent on a loan of twenty-two thousand. The same rate of interest earmarked one thousand livres of Lorraine to none other than Du Tertre, the old opponent at Bazincourt who had still got his claws in there since he was now to be found lending Stainville twenty thousand on a mortgage of the Bazincourt property. The marquis had further touched his countrified sister, now styled the Countess de Choiseul-Beaupré, for twelve thousand livres of Lorraine, also at the regular five per cent. And in July 1740 he took off her husband, and repaid, an incidental 107 livres 10 sous French. Some months later the Marquis de Stainville was writing wryly to the Baron de Richecourt of 'the dissipation caused by my affairs'[31] and

---

[30] Essai/Arsenal 5808, fos. 12–14.
[31] Marquis de Stainville to Baron de Richecourt, Paris, 11 Nov. 1740: Ö.S./H.H.S., Lothringisches Hausarchiv 189/III 126, fo. 247.

responsible, he pleaded, for his failure (here again) as a correspondent.

The sizeable payments to Stainville's creditors were all made from the Stainville estate so that it was perhaps not too bad that in its accounts for that harsh year of 1740 receipts and expenditure should be balanced at something above 18,000 livres each, to shew an overall deficit of just over 400 livres of Lorraine. The accounts also confirm that, while the Marquis de Stainville was largely in Paris, the estate was now being run by his wife from Demange. Income from sale of timber was now paid to her direct and she in turn paid the wages, ranging from 150 livres to Morel the gardener to 19 livres 12 sous 'to Vadet, Madam's young servant'.[32] The transfer of management incidentally involved that of a cask of brandy from the cellars of Stainville to those of Demange, where there had been none, as Madame de Graffigny noted during her visit. Now a dozen jars of brandy to fill the cask cost twenty-four livres as compared with twenty-nine for seven bushels of broad beans plus two of lentils 'sent to Demange by Madam's cart'. For supplies of meat, however, she paid Simon the butcher as much as 310 livres. A village butcher, incidentally, was then a mark of a village doing well.

The economies of Stainville and Demange were then operating within a darkening context for French agriculture. A chillier climatic cycle or intercycle was setting in. And locally in Lorraine there was gathering trouble which was to involve even the Marquis de Stainville at his distance.

V

The Lorrainers, remembering the mild and generous rule of Duke Leopold, were finding La Galaizière a very different master. Even the tax-dodgers of Bar discovered, as is usual in such cases, that it is one thing to be an allegedly oppressed minority looking to the benevolent protection of a great power and another to be the reclaimed subjects of that power. From the other side of Lorraine, the German east, there was fairly extensive emigration to Germany, Hungary and Tuscany. This loss of manpower was ill viewed by the French government and one finds La Galazière reporting characteristically of the emigration:

I have not discontinued my pains, up to the present, to stop the progress of the evil by having executed in their rigour the regulations which forbid the sale of goods and

---

[32] Stainville accounts for 1740 (wrongly endorsed as for 1748): Arch. Meuse, J 18[19], and for the following.

land by suspected people, whose proceedings I am also having spied on daily by the officers of the localities ... I have verified that the subjects who have thus left the State were all poor and did not find means of gaining their livelihood in their canton, but it is none the less a loss.[33]

This economic distress reflected France's economic squeeze upon Lorraine, accompanied by the burdensome French system of the *corvée*, by spying and by rigorous penalties hitherto unknown there, such as condemnation to the galleys, though in practice the supreme court of Lorraine long ignored that hated punishment. The local poet, Saint-Lambert, wrote of La Galaizière:

> *J'ai vu le magistrat qui régit ma*[34] *province,*
> *L'esclave de la Cour et l'ennemi du prince,*
> *Commander la corvée à de tristes cantons.*[35]

The Lorrainers, though, were sturdy folk not yet trained to submit. They did not confine their protests to elegiacs but embodied them in an anonymous open letter thought to have been drafted by one of the leading nobles of Lorraine, the Marquis de Raigecourt. This notable was in direct correspondence with Fleury, being confidentially charged by the latter 'to render him account of the situation of things and of dispositions in this country and of what is thought of the conduct of the persons charged with the administration and of the effects produced upon the public by the new ordinances and the new taxes and establishments'.[36] This function, incidentally illustrating the way in which the French government frequently counterchecked upon the activities of the agents, was discharged by Raigecourt with a vigorous candour by no means to the liking of La Galazière. The marquis was constituted the spokesman of public opinion in Lorraine and in September 1740 he was assuring Fleury: 'I am acknowledged, Monseigneur, and all the nation speaks through my mouth.'[37] Some weeks later the remarkable open letter ascribed to him claimed to speak on behalf of 'the principal members of the Clergy, the Nobility and the Third Estate of the duchy of Bar and Lorraine.'[38]

The grand remonstrance from Lorraine was addressed to the Marquis de Stainville as follows:

[33] La Galaizière to Amelot de Chaillou, Lunéville, 19 Sept. 1740: Arch. Aff. Étr. C.P., Lorraine, vol. 138, fo. 335.
[34] Later prudently altered to *la*.
[35] Saint-Lambert, *Les Saisons* (inspired by Thomson's *Seasons*): cited, Robert Parisot, *Histoire de Lorraine* (2nd ed., Paris, 1922f.), ii. 244 (reprinted ed.).
[36] Marquis de Raigecourt to Cardinal Fleury, Nancy, 27 Sept. 1740: Arch. Aff. Étr. C.P., Lorraine, vol. 138, fo. 339.
[37] Marquis de Raigecourt to Cardinal Fleury, Nancy, 17 Sept. 1740: ibid., fo. 333.
[38] Letter to the Marquis de Stainville, 5 Nov. 1740: cited, Comte d'Haussonville, op. cit., iv. 658, doc. lxiii, *et passim* for the following.

Your birth, your probity and the place which you occupy today induce us to address ourselves to you; your mother-country will confide her griefs to you. Lorraine is no longer recognizable; she groans under oppression, and it is in the name of all the ranks of the State that we earnestly beg you to bring our complaints to the foot of the throne. You have the honour, Sir, to have access to the Grand Duke of Tuscany; doubtless his heart speaks to him still in favour of a people who adore all who bear his name. If by the protection of His Royal Highness we could procure the mediation of the Emperor with France, we should have occasion to hope therefrom for more humane treatment.

It was explained that this course had been taken as a last resort since previous complaints to the authorities had been met by fair promises never kept: 'all representation is henceforth forbidden us, and our most secret groans already begin, almost, to pass for seditious cries... God forbid that we should ever do anything that could shake the fidelity of peoples; we would wish on the contrary to be able to stifle their murmurs.'

The remonstrance, perhaps rather tactlessly, contrasted the benevolent government of 'those princes who have successively reigned over us for more than 700 years, whom we have always regarded as our fathers, who indeed treated us like their children, whom we shall love and regret always', with the administration of La Galaizière:

(I have heard him say to himself: I hold nothing of the King [Stanislas] of Poland. I am a minister of France, and I am to take orders only from the minister.) A mere executant, or rather the faithful clerk of Sieur Orry, his brother-in-law, while on the one hand M. de Chaumont [de La Galaizière] obeys France like a slave, on the other he commands in Lorraine like a master ... We unhappily have experience that the intrigue of an individual has more credit wherewith to do us harm than the authority of a king has power to do us good. Low and venal souls soon forget themselves; favour puffs them up; issuing from the dregs of the people, unexpected greatness dazzles them, but sooner or later the truth strikes through.

Taxation was denounced as oppressive: 'The increase in the *tailles* has risen by half as much again in three years. They compel payment of kinds of contributions like those in time of war.'

The gaols of Lorraine were crowded with 'unfortunate families who hazard their lives in order to have bread and who prefer hard captivity to extreme misery'. The roads and bridges were no longer properly kept up despite the fact that 'the people have met all the expenses therefor by continual *corvées* which ruin them and their horses ... Thus one sees these poor country folk, their strength exhausted, overburdened with taxes, without resource in the way of trade, abandoned by the Court, leaving their land uncultivated, quitting their cottages, abandoning their homeland, dragging their misery everywhere, and carrying to happier climates, with their regrets and their curses, their industry and their service.'

The nobility also had grievances in plenty. The Marquis de Stainville was assured:

You would scarcely believe it, things have come to a point where one can almost say that there are no more lords with high justice in Lorraine ... One can no longer enjoy in peace the inheritance of one's ancestors. The patrimony of one's fathers is no longer in safety. Estates have become burdensome to those who possess them. One has to buy one's wood in one's own forests. If a winepress happens suddenly to break at the height of the vintage, or if a storm shakes a house; if the lord's château threatens to fall into ruin, in order to obtain permission to cut a tree in his park he has to have recourse to the intendant, to have the officers to the royal forestry assembled, to wait till they shall have nominated commissioners, till the latter shall have arrived on the spot, shall have drawn up their minutes, shall then have made their report, till the matter shall have been discussed and decided and confirmed by M. de Chaumont; and while by applications, by base means and for the price of money, one thus buys the power to enjoy possession of one's property, the vintage perishes and the château collapses.

This spirited denunciation incidentally brings out the comparative novelty of bureaucratic centralization and detailed supervision as it had been developed in France by the great ministers of Louis XIV. It was this administrative clamp, dating from about a century before the French Revolution, which marked a large departure from the old order of feudal society in France.

The remonstrance of the Lorrainers against the heavy hand of France concluded:

What have we done to France? What advantage does she derive from our misfortunates? What glory accrues to her therefrom in the eyes of Europe?... What have we done to the Cardinal de Fleury?... What have we done to M. Chaumont? Does he think to dazzle us by the letters from the Cardinal minister which he shews as his justification, or to intimidate us by the threats which he dares to make to us? ... The haughtiness and the cruelty of the Duke of Alba cost Spain the loss of seventeen provinces. One cannot foresee what the intrigues and the indiscretions of an intendant will perhaps cost France ...

After all what are we asking? We do not at all aspire to independence: quite on the contrary, we are ready to sacrifice the little property that is left to us, and even to shed our blood in the service of our King. But we shall never submit to the most shameful slavery. At the price of all that we have that is most dear, at the risk even of our lives, we shall shake off the unbearable yoke and the odious tyranny of an individual who makes his credit and his administration serve only towards public oppression and desolation, and we shall obtain the revocation of those secret orders and of those public declarations which annihilate our privileges, overturn our rights and ruin our fortunes. Languedoc, Brittany, Franche-Comté, Alsace and Flanders have been maintained in their customs and still enjoy their privileges. It has been solemnly sworn that we shall keep ours. Is it too much for a nation newly acquired on these conditions to ask for their fulfilment? In a word, we ask for the execution of the

Treaty of Vienna . . . This treaty being the basis of our present engagement, and the sole foundation on which rests the oath of loyalty which we have sworn, in asking for its execution according to its form and tenor, we are asking only what humanity, justice and right solicit for us, what France has promised to the contracting powers and guarantors of the exchange made of Lorraine against the grand duchy of Tuscany, what she owes to herself, to her word, to her glory and to public faith.

This impressive and defiant document sounded a note which, if in accord with the previous petition to Francis against his abandonment of Lorraine, was one not often heard in France at that time. Even the rational attack of the philosophs against the old order was then in its early stages; and this remonstrance was in any case something rather different, at once more limited and more immediate. Even allowing for some rhetorical exaggeration and for the limitations made clear in the letter itself, one yet distinguishes the authentic voice of free-minded men in indignant revolt against a crippling bureaucracy, against venality, bad faith and oppression. And, again granting that the circumstances were obviously far from being fully typical of France in general, yet one cannot help wondering whether things might not have gone rather differently if, in the decades before the French Revolution, there had been more instances of this kind of local collaboration between the nobility and the common people in seeking to secure redress against arbitrary action by the central government.

Few things more than this letter addressed to the Marquis de Stainville could bring out at once the similarities to and the differences from France which had hitherto distinguished the little duchy of Lorraine. France was to be the setting of Choiseul's career, but for a full understanding of his direction of her administration one needs to recognize his complex and distinctive background of larger freedom. The Lorraine of his boyhood was indeed in may ways old-fashioned, notably feudal in its society, still paternal in its government, but socially more cohesive than France, and more cosmopolitan in setting. Despite the French upbringing of the Count de Stainville he returned to France in 1740 from outside, with a background comprising not Lunéville alone but Florence, Vienna, Belgrade, and those not just places visited upon a grand tour. Young Stainville was acquiring early that aristocratic attribute of cosmopolitanism which stamped the eighteenth century.

The international nobility of Lorraine also afforded an especial illustration of one main reason why the continental aristocracy then laid such stress upon all questions affecting their personal honour, precedence, and prestige. The concept of a closely compact national state was, as noticed, incomplete even on the west of the continent before the French Revolution. It was the dynasties which stood out, and nobles, though not sovereign, thought of themselves in like terms of dynasty. Not only did many of them seek their fortunes abroad, as was conspicuous in the age of Ripperda and Bonneval, of Carlingford and Neuhoff, but even the others tended to follow their medieval ancestors in feeling that they had to make their way in the world as its principals, employing devices of dignity and protocol which were later increasingly confined to states and their rulers.

Such, then, were the salient circumstances of the Count de Stainville when he came of age in 1740. And such was the embarrassing position of his father, doubly handicapped in helping on his son by having become a focus of sedition even in his diplomatic withdrawal while remaining, even in that retirement, loyally concerned with the interests of the Grand Duke Francis and of his subjects both new and old. At the end of 1739 the Marquis de Stainville's secretary Grobert had been in Florence, still concerned with clearing up one of the grand duke's claims outstanding in France, this time in respect of some Parisian municipal stock, and in active touch with the Abbé Franquini about it. Next spring the Count de Richecourt was writing from Florence both to Franquini and to Stainville about 'a little difficulty beween this [country's] postal service and that of France'[39] wherein the postmaster at Genoa was allegedly making a nice thing, to Tuscan detriment, out of letters in transit from France. Franquini, though, was beginning to fade from the Parisian scene. By July 1740 Fleury was grumbling to Stainville about the resultant void, especially inconvenient in regard to a state including so important a port as Leghorn. That same month it was to Stainville that Messrs. Franco, merchants there, applied for support with the French ministry over a seized cargo of hides and tin from London. Stainville promptly did his best even though it had to be, as he put it, only as a faithful subject.

The Marquis de Stainville's Tuscan preoccupation doubled with his earlier loyalties: that April he had recommended to Francis a farmer-general from Lorraine. Despite Stainville's attachment to his homeland, however, there was probably not very much that he could now do to give effect to the grand remonstrance of his countrymen. The Austrian government had written off Lorraine for the present and as for the French government, the language of the remonstrance was not what it was accustomed to or appreciated. It seized copies of the letter which were circulating in Nancy and had them publicly destroyed by the executioner: perhaps not the best way to damp

---

[39] Count de Richecourt to Marquis de Stainville, Florence, 30 Apr. 1740: Esteri del Granducato di Toscana, vol. 2295/1286, fo. 20.

publicity. In the words of Amelot de Chaillou, the stammering successor to Chauvelin at the French ministry of foreign affairs, the letter to the Marquis de Stainville 'is the most seditious work that has ever been composed'.[40] Yet one wonders what might have become of La Galaizière but for a new conjunction of circumstances which was to cause the French government, so far from restraining him, to urge an intensification of his fiscal efforts, and to garrison Lorraine.

VI

The administration of Lorraine by Chancellor de La Galaizière was still scarcely so severe as that, for example, of Prussia by King Frederick-William I, who died on 31 May 1740, leaving a grim and lasting impress upon his welded dominions, efficiently solvent. On 16 June the Marquis de Stainville was writing to his friend at the Hague: 'The death of the king of Prussia causes much reasoning among the speculators in these parts, as do the five thousand men of the imperial [Austrian] troops who are going over to Corsica',[41] still a soft trouble-spot in Europe, inviting intervention by the powers. Two days earlier Lord Waldegrave had written from Paris to Horace Mann in Florence with regard to Frederick-William's death: 'People seem very intent upon the first steps of his successor, who during his Father's life, had not many opportunities of shewing himself.'[42] There would now be rather more opportunities for the future Frederick the Great to shew himself.

Even in diplomatic eclipse international affairs continue to supply the staple of the Marquis de Stainville's correspondence with the Baron de Richecourt and, after some encouragement that summer, once more with the grand duke. To him Stainville wryly reported on 10 August 1740: 'There is more talk than ever of an accommodation between Spain and England, but the public, when it is a question of an arrangement in Europe, always transplants H.R.H the Grand Duke and the things said about it are so much beyond the bounds of probability that one dare not repeat them, still less write them down.'[43] Francis seemed in some danger of becoming the shuttlecock

[40] Amelot de Chaillou to Count Lorenzi, 22 Nov. 1740: Arch. Aff. Étr., C.P., Toscane, vol. 92, fo. 208.
[41] Marquis de Stainville to Baron de Richecourt, Paris, 16 June 1740: Ö.S./H.H.S., Lothringisches Hausarchiv 189/III 126, fo. 253.
[42] Earl Waldegrave to Mann, Paris, 14 June 1740: P.R.O./S.P.F., Archives of British Legations, vol. 281.
[43] Marquis de Stainville, Paris newsletter of 10 Aug. 1740 enclosed in Marquis de Stainville to Grand Duke Francis II, Paris, 10 Aug. 1740: Esteri del Granducato di Toscana, vol. 2295/1286, fo. 32. (There is evidence from fo. 40, ibid., that at that period the Marquis de Stainville dictated such newsletters.)

of Europe. Perhaps there were compensations for his loyal adherent in Paris in 'being here only for my [own] affairs'.[44] Consequently, he explained to Baron de Richecourt, he spent all that autumn visiting country houses outside Paris.

In the same letter of 11 November 1740 Stainville proceeded: 'The terrible misfortune which has just happened to us is a thunderbolt for me.' This 'cruel catastrophe',[45] as he had described it a week earlier to Francis, was the death on 20 October of the fiftyfive-year-old Emperor Charles VI, never recovered from the humiliation of the Eastern War. On hearing of it Stainville's first impulse had been to rush to join his master in Vienna. But Prince Liechtenstein, the Austrian Ambassador in Paris, and his secretary, Wasner, advised Stainville to await orders since, in the absence now of any formal Tuscan representation, his presence in Paris might prove useful. Their advice was better than any of them could know. For the deaths of the Austrian emperor and of the Prussian king were, in their intertwined effect, to usher in a new war, a new decade, a new period. At this turning-point the Marquis de Stainville himself had some good and prompt advice for Francis, 'that time is precious and that your enemies, enviers or competitors will not lose any'.

Death claimed a third illustrious victim that year. The Emperor Charles VI had been predeceased three days earlier by the Empress Anne of Russia. She was succeeded by her great-nephew, the two-month-old Czar Ivan VI, with favourite Biren as regent, but not for long. On 13 December 1740 the Marquis de Stainville was writing from the French capital:

They are no longer talking of anything here, Sir, but the arrest of M. de Courland [Biren]; that makes a horrible stir; it is M. de Münnich himself who has arrested him and led him into the fort built by Peter I for prisoners of state. They at once declared regent the Princess of Brunswick, mother of the little Czar. For the rest, our affairs seem to be taking a good turn. The letters of notification [of the death of Charles VI and accession of Maria Theresa] have arrived in the desired form and I think that they will go into mourning for the emperor immediately after that for the Czarina, which is being worn at present.[46]

One of the differences between history books and real life is that in the former the sequence of events usually leads up neatly to the outcome. Whereas, in living out their lives and the events of their time, men can never quite know what the morrow may bring.

[44] Marquis de Stainville to Baron de Richecourt, Paris, 11 Nov. 1740: Ö.S./H.H.S., Lothringisches Hausarchiv 189/III 126, fo. 247 for the following.
[45] Marquis de Stainville to Grand Duke Francis II, Paris, 3 Nov. 1740: Esteri del Granducato di Toscana, vol. 2295/1286, fos. 44–5 for the following.
[46] Marquis de Stainville to Baron de Richecourt, Paris, 13 Dec. 1740: Ö.S./H.H.S., Lothringisches Hausarchiv 189/III 126, fo. 245.

Three days after the Marquis de Stainville wrote that letter the Prussian army of King Frederick II suddenly invaded the Austrian province of Silesia. Stainville's warning to his master in Vienna had after all been swiftly justified. Now indeed would there be mourning, not only by court ceremonial but in stricken homes across the continent. Twentyeight-year-old Frederick had plunged Europe into that great war which gripped it for the next eight years in a convulsion that was to shape the careeer of the youthful Count de Stainville.

PART II

CAMPAIGNING
1740–1743

CHAPTER I

MOBILIZATION

I

CHOISEUL wrote:

The motive of the war which finished by the treaty of Aix-la-Chapelle was the succession of the Emperor Charles VI. This prince, last scion of the house of Austria, had fought, in the war of 1700, against Philip V for the throne of Spain. He passed to the imperial throne on the death of his brother, the Emperor Joseph, in 1712 [*sic*]. He had had of his marriage with a princess of Wolfenbüttel a prince and two princesses; the prince died at an early age, and the Emperor, having no further hope of having children, made a Pragmatic Sanction, whereby he assured to his elder daughter and to her descendants all the states over which he reigned, and, in default of his elder daughter and of her descendants, he called his younger daughter to the same succession. It was very natural that the Emperor should have had this wish; it was even just enough in the order of ordinary inheritances, and certainly the best manner of assuring this disposition was to make of it an act which should be agreed to by the Empire, by the different states which composed the Austrian monarchy and by all the catholic princes who could have opposed themselves to the Pragmatic Sanction.

The Emperor Charles VI worked more than twenty years for the success of this Pragmatic. He encountered an infinity of difficulties. The Emperor Joseph, his brother, had left two daughters, of whom one had married the Elector of Bavaria and the second the Elector of Saxony. These two princes found it unjust that the daughters of the elder son should be deprived of their father's succession in order to make it pass to the daughters of the younger son. There had, besides, been some transactions between the house of Austria and that of Bavaria which favoured the pretensions of this latter, so that in the electoral college [of the Holy Roman Empire] there were at first only the Elector of Hanover, that of Brandenburg, those of Mainz, of Trier and the Elector Palatine who consented to the Pragmatic. That of Saxony adhered to it at the beginning of the war of 1733 for the crown of Poland; those of Bavaria and of Cologne remained the only princes in the Empire who refused their consent to this order of succession. Among the sovereigns of Europe, the King of England, the Empress of Russia, the Pope, the King of Sardinia, the Republic of Holland, Denmark and Spain even, in 1725, guaranteed the Pragmatic Sanction. There remained but France, who solemnly guaranteed it by the treaty of peace signed at Vienna in 1738.

The Emperor, furnished with all the guarantees which had successively cost him many sacrifices, believed his succession assured upon the head of his daughter; he was not disquieted by the resistance of the Elector of Bavaria, too weak alone to sustain pretensions with advantage. He [Charles VI] had married his elder daughter to the Duke of Lorraine, who, by the treaty of 1738, had ceded his estates to France in exchange for the eventual succession of Tuscany and still more for the assurance which France gave him to sustain the Pragmatic Sanction. Without this assurance, the Duke of Lorraine, who had no part in the war which had terminated in 1738, would not have made the sacrifice of his hereditary estates for the succession, which was not open and which might be uncertain, of the grand duchy of Tuscany. The Emperor, after the peace of 1738, had an unfortunate war against the Ottoman Porte, which was terminated under the mediation of France. This prince died in the month of October 1740.

The archduchess grand duchess [Maria Theresa], his elder daughter, was first declared sovereign of all the states of the late Emperor, her father. In all the Courts [of Europe] she demanded the guarantee of the Pragmatic Sanction; she even offered France advantages such as the duchy of Luxemburg and confines in Flanders at the will of the King. These cessions would have been very useful; Cardinal Fleury was strongly inclined to accept them and to maintain the word and the signature of the King upon the guarantee of the Pragmatic Sanction; but he was not the master. The King had for mistress the Countess de Mailly. This lady had for sister the Marquise de Vintimille, who, horrible though she was in feature and in character, had acquired a marked ascendancy over the King, who divided his favours between the two sisters. The Marshal de Belle-Isle, in order to make his fortune, had adopted a project for dismembering the states of the house of Austria. Mme. de Vintimille, assisted by the counsels of the young courtiers, adopted the project of Marshal de Belle-Isle, had it adopted by the King. The cardinal felt that he had to yield and they decided upon the most ruinous and one may say the most unjust war without reflecting that the acquisition of a province and the maintenance of peace were much more advantageous to France than the division of the states of the house of Austria. They abandoned themselves to the extravagant projects of Marshal de Belle-Isle, whom they made at the same time general and ambassador [to the imperial diet at Frankfurt]. The Elector of Bavaria was the prince to whom they designated the imperial crown with the two Austrias[1] and a part of Bohemia. The Elector of Saxony, who at first entered into the league, had also portions of Bohemia. The King of Prussia, who was the first to attack the Queen of Hungary, was to have Silesia. Spain claimed Italy and sent into those parts an army with the Infant Don Philip, son of Philip V and the Farnese Queen.

They did not think, in this vast project, of any acquisition for France. There is a very extraordinary blindness in all the great projects which are made at Versailles, which consists in making the Realm run the dangers of war and pay all its costs without stipulating any advantages for the Crown. That is very noble, but it is neither politic nor wise; for two such projects, which do not succeed, so weaken the Monarchy that it loses its consistency, its means and its consideration.[2]

Choiseul's retrospect can be amended on certain points. It was the Emperor Joseph's elder daughter who married the future Elector of Saxony; and, as noticed, the Emperor Charles VI, unlike the then Count de Stainville himself, did not wait till 1738 before turning against the Turks; the King of Sardinia had not guaranteed the Pragmatic Sanction; and the almost incidental mention of Frederick the Great's swoop on Silesia scarcely did justice to its importance. Yet Choiseul's presentation stands out in its lucid grasp, in the incisive

[1] Upper and Lower Austria.
[2] Choiseul, *Mémoires*, pp. 49–52.

authority with which he cut through the horrid tangle of the Pragmatic Sanction. Choiseul particularly brought out the economic bearing upon France of the War of the Austrian Succession. In that great conflict as in others the sinews of war derived from the national economies.

II

In the eighteenth century it was war upon war. The establishment of peace after the War of the Polish Succession had been formally proclaimed in France only at the beginning of June 1739. On 3 June at Versailles the First President of the Cour des Aides, Le Camus, leading a legal deputation of congratulation, had addressed Louis XV:

Sire, the sound of trumpets announces peace to your people, to this people which groans in misery without bread and without money, obliged to dispute its food with the beasts that are in the fields while the immoderate luxury of interested parties and of the business folk seems further to insult the public calamity. One single favourable look from Your Majesty will dissipate all these misfortunes and will render the peace the object of universal joy.[3]

Four days after listening to this succinct allocution the king set out upon one of his hunting excursions to La Meuthe where he supped with the Countess de Mailly and, for the first time, with the future Marquise de Vintimille. A courtier who had found Le Camus's address 'very indiscreet, not to say more',[4] now noted that on this journey about seven hundred people needed to be fed by over two hundred royal provisioning officers 'without counting sixty porters to carry the dishes'.

Even if another chronicler, the more exciting and excitable Marquis d'Argenson, exaggerated in broadly depicting Frenchmen as 'dying as thick as flies, of poverty, and in browsing upon grass',[5] yet, after essential allowances for local and regional variation, it was all too true that the French countryside then was largely a landscape of misery. The preceding harvest had mainly failed. The price of coarse bread sometimes doubled up to five sous a pound in country districts where that might represent the better part of the daily wage of an agricultural labourer, if he still drew wages. For where a peasant

---

[3] Traditional text as cited by Barbier, iii. 180–1. (Cf. D'Argenson, ii. 176, n. 1.)
[4] Luynes, ii. 441–6 for the following.
[5] D'Argenson, ii. 149.

managed to feed his own family he might need to lay off hands or sell off livestock cheap, sending the stringency spiralling down.

It seemed as if the very elements had declared war. Several provinces of France were swept by hail that summer and 1739 produced another bad harvest. By October an exceptionally hard winter was already setting in. The Seine and other great rivers of Western Europe froze up. Right through to March 1740 there were days of piercing cold recalling that Great Winter thirty years before. Woodmerchants did splendidly but others were less cheerful. On 1 July 1740 d'Argenson wrote: 'They affirm that the ecliptic has inclined more towards the equator, and, continuing to turn thus, in a few years we shall have in France the same climate as in Sweden.'[6] They were pessimists. Yet recent climatic research in France[7] has concluded that 1739 did usher in a phase of some twenty years of averagely cooler springs and summers.

'Here we are in full summer', continued d'Argenson that July, 'and fires are going everywhere... All our ministry is ill at once', all except eightyseven-year-old Cardinal Fleury whose persistent health he described as a 'miracle in reverse'.[8] Next month, August 1740, the Marquis de Stainville reported that 'it is more than a century since so many persons of note died in the same year, from which one can judge how great has been the mortality among the populace'.[9] Moved by 'the excessive misery which prevails',[10] he was writing a month later of a general 'dearth of corn in the kingdom, which is alarming the ministry'.[11] It had alarmed Fleury driving through Paris three days earlier, on 23 September 1740, when some two hundred women had surrounded his coach and wrenched open the door, screaming: 'Bread! Bread! We are dying of hunger.'[12]

The miseries of 1740 were not exhausted. That autumn it rained for more than two months until France was flooded. By Christmas Paris was awash from the Invalides to the Palais-Royal with boats the only transport. On Boxing Day the municipal authorities stepped in to curb profiteering in their hire. The minister in charge of the affairs of the capital, Count de Maurepas, congratulated the harassed

---

[6] Ibid., iii. 118, and for the following.

[7] Cf. the work of E. Le Roy-Ladurie in articles summarized in F. Braudel and E. Labrousse, *Histoire économique et sociale de la France*, ii. 391 f.

[8] D'Argenson, ii. 76.

[9] Marquis de Stainville, Paris newsletter of 24 Aug. 1740 enclosed in Marquis de Stainville to Grand Duke Francis II, Paris, 24 Aug. 1740: Esteri del Granducato di Toscana, vol. 2295/1286, fo. 42.

[10] Marquis de Stainville to Grand Duke Francis II, Paris, 24 Aug. 1740: ibid., fo. 40.

[11] Marquis de Stainville to Baron de Richecourt, Paris, 26 Sept. 1740: Ö.S./H.H.S., Lothringisches Hausarchiv 189/III 126, fo. 249.

[12] D'Argenson, iii. 172.

Marville, lieutenant-general of police, for, so far as possible, 'courageously providing for everything'.[13]

For months past the authorities had been taking measures to mitigate distress, trying to bring grain on to the markets and organizing various forms of direct relief. At Châtellerault, for example, every bourgeois had been compelled to feed one poor person. Such alleviation was apt, however, to be too little and too late. Already in May 1740 d'Argenson had written: 'More Frenchmen have died of want in the last two years, than there were killed by all the wars of Louis XIV.'[14] Such a suggestion, even, remains sobering enough. And want as ever bred disease. In 1741 impoverished Brittany is said to have lost over 80,000 souls in epidemics. It seemed a return of the ancient scourges, famine, pestilence, and war – war too at the outset of those forties which, in the eighteenth century as in most modern ones, were to provide a grim decade.

Over now were the good years from around 1730, significantly those of Fleury. A sign, incidentally, of the closeness of most Frenchmen then to subsistence level was the correlation of good years with cheap bread, which peasants themselves mostly had to buy, rather than with dear bread to benefit those with any grain to sell; though of course there were those, too, on the other side of a critical divide across the peasantry. The great dearth in the years around 1740 extended to the other staple, wine, and even depressed French textile-manufacture, still closely related to subsistence. That mysterious periodicity of a generation in economic evolution which has seemed to some analysts, in France certainly, to span the centuries, might appear to be moving ahead again, from around 1709–10 to 1739–40 as it was to do again, to some extent at least, to 1769–70, the time when the Duke de Choiseul was to fall.

Only, it was in fact an economic progression of diminishing severity. So much so that the crisis beginning in 1739 is now seen as the last in the old line, an ultimate demonstration of the rigours of that antique economy that was already upon the turn towards something newer, less regularly precarious or periodically cata-strophic. The great dearth of 1740 in France was a last lacerating spasm from ancient ills rather in the way of that ultimate visitation of the plague in 1720. The suggestion now is that economically and demographically the French seventeenth century truly ended somewhere between these two dates, around 1730; if not somewhere

[13] Count de Maurepas to Marville, Versailles, 29 Dec. 1740: Arch. du dép. de la Seine et de la ville de Paris, D.3. AZ 10².
[14] D'Argenson, iii. 92.

between 1730 and 1750 with the index of change hovering around 1740. Even the climatic reversion beginning about then is seen only as one of those intercycles which so often seem the necessary undertow of cyclic movement. The dearth itself, rather quickly mastered, proved this time but an interruption in that economic ascent which came working through the expanses of political immobility and intellectual ferment in the long and rich reign of King Louis XV.

Men in some danger of starvation are not primarily interested in longterm economic trends. Nor is it surprising that even well-to-do diarists and correspondents should have emphasized the immediate misery to present an unduly sombre picture overall. Numbers of Frenchmen might indeed face economic or even physical ruin, but certainly not France herself in an age still massively compartmentalized economically as elsewise. Despite all local particularism and provincial barriers the land of France yet stood out as an impressive block of fair territory, greater and more coherent than any other country then upon the European mainland. Nations were then at once less uniform internally and less differentiated externally than they later became, but it is with some fitness that eighteenth-century France has been compared to a fine-wrought statue chiselled out from the less worked land-mass of the continent.

The greatness of France resided not least in the fact that the fertility of her soil was matched by that, relatively, of her people. The French population, back at something perhaps under twenty millions after the ravages of the wars of Louis XIV, was about thrice the English and stood comparison with that of Germany in her aftermath, still, from the Thirty Years War and its successors. The rewarding but sluggish French countryside was distributed in all its regional variety in some forty or fifty thousand seigneuries, in turn cut up to an exceptional extent into peasant smallholdings. There was relatively little in France to compare with either the great and efficiently exploited estates that the English nobility had accumulated after the demise of feudalism and catholicism, or with those expanses of lordly domain which in Central and Eastern Europe symbolized, on the contrary, the persistence of feudalism in its more primitive and exacting forms. France was exceptional in Europe in that relatively few Frenchmen owned either very great lands or none at all.

This territorial mean in France was apt to spell comparative indigence for the nobility, perhaps numbering in all something up to four hundred thousand: many more than in England and, contrary to legend, more socially diversified even if the traditional contrast between the old *noblesse d'épée* and the quite often richer *noblesse de*

robe from legal families can be overdone.[15] The proportion of the
French aristocrats who enjoyed the honours of the court has been put
at hardly more than five per cent.[16] The mass of the provincial
nobility further presented large variations. The modest ease of the
nobility around Toulouse,[17] for instance, might contrast with stark
poverty in Brittany. At a time when wealth was already jostling birth
for entry into the ruling few, Les Grands, even so rich a family as the
Contis, princes of the blood and industrially enterprising too, could
only scratch along with royal pensions and the sale of slices of capital.

If the eighteenth-century nobility owned about forty per cent of all
the land in the Orleanais and thirty-five in Burgundy, in the Haute-
Auvergne and Dauphiny it was more like eleven or twelve, to yield
a national average, perhaps, of only about twenty or twenty-five per
cent of noble landholding in France. The corresponding figure for
the French church, comprising about a hundred thousand clerics in
all, was not more than some ten per cent of all land; for ecclesiastical
wealth derived largely from urban property and from tithes.
Furthermore much of the noble and ecclesiastical holdings was in
smallish parcels of woodland unsuitable for an intensive agriculture.

While the peasantry of France possessed some thirty-five to forty
per cent of the land, their share was much smaller in the relatively
rare woodland and in precious pasture. Hence the old cycle of
deficiency: too little pasture producing insufficient cattle producing
not enough manure to produce abundant harvests. And France was
then above all a countryside of cornlands, the provider of bread, the
safeguard against haunting hunger. The peasants tilled the acres of
their lords much as they cultivated their own little holdings, with
tools and methods both old-fashioned, tending to plough too shallow,
to dung too little, to sow too late. France experienced no agricultural
revolution to compare with that in England. A backward agriculture
was the price France paid for the conservation of her peasant
freeholds in the persistence of the old regime of lengthening
precedent and hierarchic tradition.

The triple obligation of the French peasantry to lord, church, and
king may have forced it about then to pay up something, at the
roughest estimate, of the order of 200 to 250 million livres per annum:
that from peasant families whose annual income, equally roughly,
might on the whole be creeping up from a necessarily vague average

[15] Cf. Franklin L. Ford, *Robe and Sword* (Cambridge, Mass., 1953), pp. 202 f.; François
Bluche, *Les Magistrats du parlement de Paris au XVIIIe siècle: 1715–1771* (Paris, 1960), pp.
303 f.; also, however, Jean Egret in *Revue historique*, ccxxviii (1962), 485–6.

[16] Cf. F. Bluche, op. cit., p. 314.

[17] Cf. Robert Forster, *The Nobility of Toulouse in the Eighteenth Century* (Baltimore, 1960), pp.
176 *et passim*.

of 200 to 300 livres at the opening of the century. For peasants between a fifth and a half of their gross incomes would go out again in dues such as seigneurial quitrents and champarts, in tithes and in taxes. In the reverse perspective anything up to three-quarters of the national budget might be drawn from agricultural sources. Royal taxation called for cash payments in an age when even copper coin was still relatively scarce, was all that many labourers ordinarily saw. And such national levies as the *taille* on persons or property, the *capitation* or polltax and – not least – the *gabelle* on salt would be supplemented in time of war, soon now, notably by a reimposition of the *dixième* or ten per cent tax on all revenues. Even when the peasants were prosperous it might be fiscally dangerous to seem so.

From those at the top, however, in the privileged orders of clergy and nobility, ostentation was rather expected, at court certainly. They were notoriously exempt from the *taille*, by origin a levy upon lay noncombatants and particularly resented for its servile implication as also because of its solidary collection by parishes, with arbitrary effects. As usual, though, in the old regime things were not really so simple:[18] a noble's exemption from the *taille* was in fact limited (to four carucates), and leases or prudential calculation might in effect saddle him with the *tailles* of others; in economic reality the privileged exemptions of the nobility were much exceeded by those enjoyed, notably in privileged boroughs (*villes franches*), by that bourgeoisie whose wealth was mounting up; whereas, as is rather little allowed, the original logic of exemption was still far from exhausted for the many noble families who, like the Stainvilles now, fulfilled their military vocation at the high cost of purchasing and quite often subventing companies and regiments under the system of that time. Such was the counterpart, in some measure at least, to the traditional representation of cushy aristocrats profiting from the peasants twice over, directly as feudal lords and through royal grants from the national revenue.

The French nobility, furthermore, paid other taxes and were to do so increasingly till they were paying proportionately as much if not more than their English peers, certainly in direct taxation. The polltax upon the nobility might indeed be disproportionately scaled down and they were apt to command means of evasion, if not always more effectively than the cocks of the walk at village level (*coqs de village*). The bases of assessment were far from self-evidently equitable, a dangerous defect when in practice, after all, the great

---

[18] Cf. in particular Betty Behrens, 'Nobles, privileges and taxes in France at the end of the Ancien Régime' in *The Economic History Review*, 2nd series, xv (Utrecht, 1962–3), 451 f.

burden of taxation, together with the forced labour of the *corvées* bore upon the poorest section of the community.

Bureaucratic centralization under Louis XIV, so far from relieving the feudal pressure upon the peasantry, had added a new and heavier administrative pressure of its own. It was this severe squeeze from the national level, rather than feudal dues, which differentiated France from, for instance, Lorraine, as the incorporated Lorrainers had swiftly discovered to their dismay. In France, in transition from a feudal society to a national state, the peasant got the worst of both worlds.

This system of regressive taxation, with the poor paying most in proportion, tended to produce an amalgam of social stress and fiscal inefficiency. This was a critical weakness for eighteenth-century France even if there has been some exaggeration of the abuses latent in the farming out of indirect taxation to rich farmers-general. In the crisis of 1740 the system itself was more to blame than its administrator, the controller-general denounced by d'Argenson as the 'imbecile and brutal M. Orry'.[19]

Lorraine had already experienced the rather rough approach of Orry, whose functions (1730–45) in 'that ticklish Employment of Comptroller General in France'[20] approximated to those of a minister of finance if not also of the interior owing to his say with the provincial intendants, the linchpins of the French administration and of its direct taxation. Orry once said in reply to a reproach: 'How should I not display ill-humour? Out of twenty people who make requests of me there are nineteen who take me for a fool or a rascal.'[21] Whereas he was neither. He has been more accurately described as a Colbertist who exaggerated Colbertism. Under Orry centralized control and mercantilist direction of the national economy attained their zenith in France. Foreign imports were subjected to stringently protectionist tariffs or were altogether prohibited. Internal trade was regulated with equal determination, and the restrictions upon the circulation of grain between provinces, originally devised largely in the interests of local consumers, were increasingly blamed for aggravating distress in lean years such as 1740. Industry likewise came under the administrative clamp of the powerful Bureau de Commerce, instituted in 1722. This body regularly intervened in every sphere and in detail as regards the raw materials and processes employed, the quality of finished goods, conditions of work and wages. The latter were

---

[19] D'Argenson, ii. 149.
[20] Baron von Pöllnitz, op. cit., ii. 239.
[21] Cited, H. Carré, *Le Règne de Louis XV (1715–1774)* (Paris, 1909; part ii of vol. viii of Ernest Lavisse, *Histoire de France depuis les origines jusqu'à la Révolution*: henceforth cited as Carré/Lavisse), p. 97.

generally kept low so that to earn a livelihood needed long hours: a sixteen-hour day was usual for craftsmen in Paris. Colbert's corporative mobilization of industry was carried forward through an expanding system of guilds, often in restriction of commercial enterprise. Thus Orry fixed the hierarchy of *grand teint* and *petit teint* in the dyeing industry, though he annoyed it by allowing drapers and hatters to dye their own goods; in 1735 the government overhauled the glass industry, in 1739 the paper industry. Amid this all-embracing regimentation some considerable elements of free enterprise, always tugging towards profits, were discernible only in such newer fields as cotton-manufacture. (By 1730 the vigilant Orry had already noticed that even peasants' wives were taking to prints and calico.) The idea of trying to subject an entire state-economy to the planned administration of an overriding bureaucracy is, like most ideas, older than is often supposed.

The clamp on industry was duplicated in agriculture so far as the aggravating insubordination of nature would allow. Orry's tidy attempt to standardize the yield of French wool by ordaining the feast of St. John for sheepshearing throughout the country was defeated by the circumstance that the growth of fleeces varies according to breed and climate. What agricultural Lorrainers thought of Orry's administration as applied by his brother-in-law, La Galaizière, has already appeared. And their complaints, for instance, about bureaucratic control of timber-felling can be amply set against licensing records, even some twenty years later, in the registers of the French royal council.[22] Orry, too, systematically extended the *corvée* as an obligation upon the peasants to perform their stint in maintaining the highroads. Here the rigorous controller-general, resisting the lure of cash-commutation, saw to it that in France, on the model of Lorraine, the roads were actually built so as to become the admiration of eighteenth-century Europe and an appreciable factor in lowering the formidable cost of transport, in reducing local crises, and in the general expansion of commerce.

For France an even more important piece of economic underpinning in this period was the stabilization of the currency within a polity stabilized against civil strife. The monetary decree of 1726 and another of 1738 promoted a steady currency as an index to a striking increase in French agricultural prices between 1726 and 1789 of the order of sixty per cent or more. Whereas it is estimated[23] that between the advent of Louis XV and the revolution French foreign trade as

[22] Cf. for instance Arch. Nat., Séries anciennes, E. 2702 ('Arrets. 22 Novembre 1757 au 8 Juillet 1759'), fo. 178 *passim*; E. 3102 ('Lorraine. Conseil des finances commencé le 1er juillet et fini le 30 Xbre 1758'), nos. 23, 55.
[23] Cf. F. Braudel and E. Labrousse, op. cit., ii. 503 *et passim*.

a whole quintupled while colonial trade alone did twice as well again. And for France, unlike England, the long-distance winner, the rate of growth was greatest in the first half of the eighteenth century. By 1740 this extraordinary expansion of French commerce was lapping ahead.

Voltaire with his quick perception wrote in 1738: 'In the past twenty years they have come to understand trade better in France than it has been understood from Pharamond to Louis XIV.'[24] Significantly, although the System of John Law, a keen financial brain, had failed, his great Compagnie des Indes was by no means wound up. Its shares rose from 680 livres in 1725 to 2,316 livres in 1740. French supremacy in the Levant trade was confirmed by Villeneuve's diplomatic triumph, whereas the number of English trading establishments at Smyrna, for instance, declined from twenty in 1715 to three in 1735. This was partly, also, a reflection of the way in which French woollens were now competing with British in price and quality despite Daniel Defoe's somewhat defensive assurance that 'the French Cloth, with all its superficial French Gloss upon it, is fine, but thin and spungy, and will do the Wearer neither Credit or Service, while the English Cloth wears to the last like a Board, firm and strong, and has a kind of Beauty even in its Rags.'[25]

Already by 1724 another English writer was complaining that the French had almost entirely engrossed the fur-trade of North America, and French beaver-hats were reckoned superior to the British in the Spanish and Spanish American markets. Spain was in general the most important single market for France, and Horatio Walpole, the British ambassador in Paris (1724–30), estimated that the French share in the cargoes freighted by galleons between Cadiz and the Spanish Indies was two-thirds of the whole. The port of Bordeaux was crammed with merchantmen plying, above all, to the rich French Antilles, carrying out manufactures of all kinds along with wine, brandy, slaves, bringing back sugar, coffee, cocoa, indigo, camphor, tobacco, precious woods and others of those products of the new world which were improving the living of the old, to an important extent through re-export from France. Between 1717 and 1741 the maritime traffic of Bordeaux more than quadrupled in value from some twelve million livres to fifty-three.[26]

French navigation and industry naturally participated in this commercial upswing. Between 1732 and 1742 the production of

[24] Carré/Lavisse, p. 106.
[25] Daniel Defoe, *A Plan of the English Commerce* (London, 1728), p. 178: cited, A. McC. Wilson, op. cit., p. 296.
[26] Cf. *Bordeaux au XVIIIe siècle*, ed. François-Georges Pariset (Bordeaux, 1968), p. 195 *et passim*.

cotton stuffs at Rouen more than doubled. In 1739 a French observer of English economic conditions, the shadowy Marquis de Silhouette, reported from London that Pulteney and Wyndham were filled with admiration for Fleury's administration and that 'the increase of our maritime trade is what strikes them most'.[27]

Fleury and Orry formed a close pair of careful administrators, and by 1740 the latter achieved the outstanding feat of balancing the French budget, at rather over 200 million livres, without resort to borrowing. It was the last time in that century that this phenomenon occurred. This picture of national solvency and commercial expansion is the necessary counterpart to the records of agrarian misery in the France of that time. That the two contemporary aspects should contrast so vividly may serve as a warning against too confident generalization in terms of modern economics about a society so different in structure from anything that might supersede it. It is possible, for instance, that on the large view the crude contrast between peasant and seigneur, however socially significant despite such subtler gradations as those noticed at Stainville, was hardly more so economically than the fact that, while Law's Compagnie des Indes survived the smash, his plans for a national bank did not. French banking facilities could not compare with those of England or Holland even though French commercial expansion greatly stimulated the circulation of bills of exchange and the scope of merchant-bankers, who might often enough help to finance the French crown with loyal skill. Wealth, however, tended to silt up among leading financiers such as Bernard, the Crozats, and the brothers Pâris, rich farmers-general like the 'Grand Bouret',[28] and merchants in thriving ports, as with the fortune-making Bonnaffés and Gradis of Bordeaux. Numbers of the bourgeoisie, especially in the north, did indeed own land – perhaps up to twenty or even thirty per cent of the national acreage. And the takeover by middle-class middlemen of the farm of revenues on such feudal estates as that of Stainville has already suggested a shift of capital, and capitalist, importance for the French society as a whole. Even at its rural base the long increase in bourgeois wealth was now accelerating to rival if not surpass or encompass that of the nobility in the great social flow of the French eighteenth century.

France nevertheless could hardly compare with England either in the crossfertilization of commerce and agriculture or in the commer-

---

[27] Marquis de Silhouette to Amelot de Chaillou, London, 26 Nov. 1739: Arch. Aff. Étr. C.P., Angleterre, vol. 405, fo. 286: cited, P. Vaucher, op. cit., p. 302.
[28] For relationships in eighteenth-century France between finance and commerce cf. Yves Durand, *Les Fermiers généraux au XVIIIe siècle* (Paris, 1971), p. 47 *passim*.

cial yield of revenue. A capital defect of the French fiscal system arguably lay less even in its tenderness towards noble privilege than in its relative failure to tap new wealth precisely from bourgeois enterprise in the direction of revolutionary change in a state still dominated by the juridical concept of the three estates, the clergy, the nobles, the third, and of the two castes, the privileged and unprivileged. Perhaps it was towards some such realization that the Marquis d'Argenson was awkwardly groping when he wrote some years later of the English:

Their avarice is an avidity which leads them to extract large profits from foreigners and little from their own citizens; whereas the avidity of our rich people in France leads them only to profit as citizens from citizens, the king from the people, the stockholders and pensioners from the king, the courtiers from rule and order. The order of the financiers is in France what that of the merchants is in England, and these tax-gatherers are but the bloodsuckers of the people. That is not so in England, or not much.[29]

The bloodsuckers, however, had done good work for Orry for whom, as a strict mercantilist, the welfare of the state in its power took precedence over that of individuals in the distress of 1740. He had extracted signal economic benefit from Fleury's pacific policy, which exemplified the mercantilist maxim coined at the time of the Third Treaty of Vienna by the French economist Du Tot: 'To make peace in order to procure for ourselves all the advantages of a large trade is to make war upon our enemies.'[30] This shrewd policy, though, was now jeopardized by its very success.

III

By 1740 the economic expansion of France was matched by her political ascendancy. Her stake in the Spanish trade could not leave her indifferent to the Anglo-Spanish War of Jenkins' Ear, and as Anglo-French tension mounted Horatio Walpole was writing to a colleague: 'I think all is at stake; the whole power of France employed jointly with that of Spain against England without a special Providence will prevail; nothing but a diversion upon the Continent can save us.'[31] Britain was now paying the price of her abstention

---

[29] D'Argenson, v. 90.

[30] Ferrare du Tot, *Réflexions politiques sur les finances et le commerce* (1738): cited, P. Vaucher, op. cit., p. 302. (This citation is from the extract which Pulteney reproduced in the *Craftsman* for 26 Dec. 1739. An English translation of Du Tot's book appeared that year.)

[31] Horatio Walpole to R. Trevor, London, 23 Sept. 1740 (O.S.): *The Manuscripts of the Earl of Buckinghamshire, the Earl of Lindsey, the Earl of Onslow, Lord Ernly, Theodore J. Hare Esq. and James Round Esq, M.P.* (London, 1895), p. 54. (14th Report of the Historical Manuscripts Commission, Appendix, Part IX. C.7882 of 1895.)

from the War of the Polish Succession, finding herself isolated and the continent, as it were, immobilized by French diplomacy, victorious at Belgrade. The French ascendancy in Turkey was matched in Sweden. The position of France over against Russia and Austria in the east was enhanced by the equilibrium of the divided middle-lands of Italy and Germany, which obtruded no power of sufficient strength to alarm their western neighbours. Frederick the Great considered that at the time of his accession France 'since the year 1672 . . . had not found herself in a more brilliant situation'.[32]

When the death of the Emperor Charles VI fulfilled, within the month, Horatio Walpole's hope of a diversion, France remained most enviably situated. She was, it is true, pledged to acknowledge Maria Theresa's succession to her father's hereditary estates but the Pragmatic Sanction itself was, in its territorial aspect, a tacit recognition of that French ascendancy in Europe implicit in the peace settlements of Westphalia and, even, of Utrecht. Furthermore Choiseul was correct in stating that Maria Theresa would have been prepared to clinch French support in Fleury's 'new system' with Austria by such a desirable offer as Luxemburg, more particularly since France still occupied a strong bargaining position. For while Fleury was committed to the succession of Maria Theresa to the Habsburg lands, he was not committed to the election of her husband to be Holy Roman Emperor – these two intertwined but separate threads, the hereditary Habsburg succession and the elective imperial succession, ran right through the tangled diplomacy of the Pragmatic Sanction. The cardinal at first hoped to exploit this dichotomy with his habitual finesse while pacifically maintaining a commanding position in reserve in German affairs and meanwhile assuring the Austrian ambassador that 'the King [Louis XV] will faithfully observe all the engagements which he has undertaken with your Court'.[33]

Mourning the dead emperor in Paris, the Marquis de Stainville perceived 'one subject of consolation in this country, for it seems to me, and I am even sure of it, that at this court they have decided to follow their engagements [to Austria] . . . I know that . . . our adorable queen is doing wonders, that her pregnancy is going very well'.[34] While Maria Theresa was earning such encomiums, Louis XV was incurring criticism for his support of Fleury's prudent policy. Louis

---

[32] Frederick, ii. 7–8.

[33] Cardinal Fleury to Prince Liechtenstein, Fontainebleau, 1 Nov. 1740: Arneth, i. 371, n. 20.

[34] Marquis de Stainville to Baron de Richecourt, Paris, 11 Nov. 1740: Ö.S./H.H.S., Lothringisches Hausarchiv 189/III 126, fo. 247.

is reported to have told the young Marquis de Souvré that he would, characteristically, remain upon Mount Pagnote, implying a prudential isolation above the mêlée: only to be reminded that the king's ancestors had never built upon that mountain.

The serious employment of such young courtiers at Versailles was liable to be war, traditionally war against Austria. They resented the seemingly endless domination of old Fleury, whose rule had been too long, too mild, too successful. Then on 16 December 1740, when the vanguards of the King of Prussia marched into Silesia and 'crossed the Rubicon with flags flying and drums beating',[35] martial ardour might seem to chime with political expediency for France. The unprovoked, unchecked Prussian onslaught against Austria appeared to afford a unique opportunity for France, from her diplomatic power-position, to scrap Fleury's finessing with Austria, to weigh in and deal the hereditary antagonist a knock-out blow. And potential allies such as Bavaria and Spain were only too eager to profit from Austria's isolation, emphasized as it was by factional strife in Russia after the death of the Empress Anne. Hope brightened for the youthful partisans of Belle-Isle.

Charles-Louis-Auguste Fouquet, Count de Belle-Isle, already fifty-six in 1740, was a tall, lean figure with clean-cut features of a mettlesome cast – large nose and keen blue eyes. This grandson of the sumptuous Nicolas Fouquet, under Louis XIV the overmighty superintendent of finances till struck down, had won through from inherited adversity to such military effect as to become a brigadier at twenty-four. Under the Regency he had supplemented intrepidity by intrigue and shared with the minister of war, Le Blanc, the same mistress in Madame de Pléneuf, beautiful mother of the beautiful Marquise de Prie. A violent jealousy between mother and daughter meant that when the latter had her day as the mistress of the Duke de Bourbon, Le Blanc and Belle-Isle both spent a year in the Bastille (1724–5) on financial charges. Subsequently Belle-Isle secured the military command of Metz and the Three Bishoprics, where he did excellent work on the fortifications; he largely replanned Metz, established special relations with the duchy of Lorraine and maintained an extensive reconnaissance in the Rhineland. This keen and popular officer had distinguished himself in peacetime training-camps and as the forward-looking advocate of much needed reforms. Inheriting his grandfather's administrative capacity, Belle-Isle had

---

[35] King Frederick II to Count Podewils, Schweinitz, 16 Dec. 1740: King Frederick II, *Politische Correspondenz Friedrich's des Grossen* (ed. J. G. Droysen, M. Duncker, H. von Sybel: Berlin, 1879 f. Henceforth cited as *Politische Correspondenz*), i. 147.

set himself to master every branch of warfare and especially that of supply, which he considered 'the first and the principal'.[36]

The Count de Belle-Isle, methodical and brilliant, was old friends with Chavigny, the leading expert on German affairs in the French diplomatic service. Now in 1740 this circumstance together with Belle-Isle's particular knowledge of the Rhineland and his relationship by marriage to the Elector Charles-Albert of Bavaria set him in the way of that politico-military intervention in Germany which he so strongly advocated. Belle-Isle fortified his influence by gaining the co-operation of Blondel, the experienced French minister to the Elector Palatine, whom Fleury was then consulting on the German situation. (Blondel was a cousin of Du Theil, the chief civil servant in the French Ministry for Foreign Affairs.) And there was Belle-Isle's ambitious magnetism. In the words of Voltaire, 'Belle-Isle, without having done great things, had a great reputation. He had been neither minister nor general,[37] and passed for the most capable man to lead a state and an army.'[38]

On the day that the King of Prussia launched into Silesia the King of France announced, as the Marquis de Stainville reported, that he had appointed 'M. de Belle-Isle as his ambassador to Frankfurt. It is thought that he will be made a Marshal of France before his departure.'[39] He was. Stainville added: 'If Your Royal Highness is sending thither a great officer of your household, I offer myself. When all is said, may you do something with me or at least may I have the satisfaction of returning to your presence at such an interesting juncture.' In that case he would, he subsequently explained, arrange for his wife to join him in Vienna. In the event an embassy to the imperial diet was certainly not for him. He was kept hanging around as usual, filling in with visits to Versailles. There over Christmas, he related, Fleury 'spoke to me much of the démarche of the King of Prussia. He seemed to me astonished by it but not enough for one to be able to hope that he disapproves of it',[40] not diplomatically at all events. Yet to a considerable extent the issues of war and peace for France were henceforth as though embodied in the splendid marshal and the emaciated cardinal.

Already in December 1740 Belle-Isle, going further than the prudent Blondel, was urging upon Fleury military intervention in

[36] Cited Maurice Sautai, *Les Débuts de la Guerre de la Succession d'Autriche* (Paris, 1909: henceforth cited as Sautai/Débuts), i. 125.

[37] Probably meant loosely for a general officer commanding-in-chief in the field. Belle-Isle had been a lieutenant-general for ten years.

[38] Voltaire, *Précis du siècle de Louis XV* (Garnier edition, Paris), p. 54.

[39] Marquis de Stainville to Grand Duke Francis II, Paris, 19 Dec. 1740: Esteri del Granducato di Toscana, vol. 2295/1286, fos. 48–9 for the following.

[40] u.s. 30 Dec. 1740: ibid., fos. 50–1.

Germany. One of their early interviews that month found the
cardinal moaning at the commander's pitiless tabulation of what
such a campaign would probably require in supplies of all kinds.
Fleury, crestfallen, acquiesced in Belle-Isle's scornful elimination of
what he described as the do-nothing alternative, to 'observe the
Pragmatic and dismiss the King of Prussia',[41] who was already
proposing a defensive alliance with France, insidiously represented
by Frederick, through the French minister in Berlin, as an
opportunity for Fleury 'to arise as the moderator'.[42]

Four days after the Marquis de Valory reported this, Fleury was
being warned of Frederick's 'vast designs' by the special French
envoy sent to congratulate him upon his accession. This nephew of
the Prince de Craon, a young Marquis de Beauvau, wrote personally
to Fleury of Frederick:

His views are so remote from the ordinary course of things that I am not astonished
at the incredulity of Your Eminence up to the present. But there can no longer be
any doubt today. There he is entered into Silesia ... I know beyond doubt that he
[Frederick] detests France at the bottom of his heart and that the true object of his
ambition and of his glory would be to be able to humiliate us and to diminish our
power ... The King of Prussia is a dangerous prince. His conduct resembles a
romance rather than a history, but this romance could have the most real
consequences, and the half of it is already there, in the immense establishment of
troops that he has on foot. It is likely that he will thereby ruin himself, but he has
money; he will spend to his last farthing and will stake all for all.[43]

That appreciation was written the day after Frederick had
embarked upon his first great exploit. The author, a keen cavalry
officer, was in some sort the military mentor of Craon's son Charles-
Juste, who was to figure as the handsome Prince de Beauvau and a
special friend of the Count de Stainville, one year the elder. Certainly
this specimen of what was then known as the Esprit des Beauvau
approximated towards the outlook of the future Choiseul in regard to
the German rivalry, critical for France, between Prussia and Austria.
For the present, however, the lonely warning of the prescient
Marquis de Beauvau was lost among the exhortations of Belle-Isle
and the flatteries of Frederick, and, if Fleury himself is to be believed,
not only flatteries but threats as well. At a later period the cardinal

---

[41] Marshal de Belle-Isle, 'Mémoires': cited, Duc de Broglie, *Frédéric II et Marie-Thérèse*
(Paris, 1883: henceforth cited as Broglie/Fréd-MT), i. 184. (Of these unpublished memoirs one
copy is preserved in the Bibliothèque Nationale and another, incomplete, in the French
Ministry for Foreign Affairs. For the restricted scope and value of these memoirs cf. op. cit., i.
180, n. 1, also Sautai/Préliminaires, p. 153, n. 1.)
[42] Marquis de Valory to Amelot de Chaillou, Berlin, 13 Dec. 1740: Arch. Aff. Étr. C.P.,
Prusse, vol. 112, cited, Sautai/Préliminaires, p. 185.
[43] Marquis de Beauvau to Cardinal Fleury, Berlin, 17 Dec. 1740: ibid., pp. 186–8.

one day unburdened himself remarkably to his old friend, the Marquis de Stainville:

I could let you see that, to conquer the repugnance which I had against allying myself with him [Frederick], he wrote me letters by which he threatened me that he would ally himself with the Queen of Hungary and the Maritime Powers in order to wage an eternal war against France. All imaginable means were employed to embark me, against my will, upon this alliance, and I repeat to you, again, that I have not for a moment ceased to desire to get out of it... On that the Cardinal told me that he had just made his confession to me, that he had never said so much about it to anybody, not even to the minister [? ministry] of the King [Louis XV].[44]

Fleury was speaking from interested motives but his reluctance to follow Frederick towards war had been real, and his significant confession has the ring of some little truth. At the time, however, the old cardinal was pushed along.

The Marquis de Stainville related that on 10 January 1741 Louis XV himself had assured the new Austrian chargé d'affaires, the expert Wasner, that he would keep all his engagements to Maria Theresa 'and the Cardinal added that he would sustain her pragmatic towards and against all'.[45] Amelot said the same and authorized Wasner to report it in writing. 'That is a little consoling', commented Stainville. He did not know that a week earlier Fleury had had the draft of a defensive Franco-Prussian treaty sent to Frederick for his observations. The King of Prussia, having strengthened his hand by jockeying France into treating with him, proceeded to raise his terms, now demanding that France should guarantee him Silesia, should furnish military support, should engage Bavaria against Austria, and Sweden against Russia. The royal author of the *Anti-Machiavel* skilfully played off the French and British envoys, and was already confiding to his minister of state, Count Podewils: 'Although I have thought it necessary to conciliate the favour of France and of her allies towards us, by the perspective of their interests, I have always regarded a liaison with these powers as a last resort.'[46]

Within a month or two Frederick, from being almost an outcast prince, had become the most courted sovereign in Europe: such is apt to be the political precedence of expediency over morality. Frederick

---

[44] Marquis de Stainville to Grand Duke Francis II, Paris, 28 July 1742: Esteri del Granducato di Toscana, vol. 2295/1286, fo. 141. (A copy of this dispatch is in Ö.S./H.H.S., Lothringisches Hausarchiv 77/177A, fos. 7–8. Cf. Dr. Jacob Strieder, *Kritische Forschungen zur österreichischen Politik vom Aachener Frieden bis zum Beginne des Siebenjährigen Krieges* – Leipzig, 1906 – p. 35, n. 3.)

[45] Marquis de Stainville to Baron de Richecourt, 11 Jan. 1741: Ö.S./H.H.S., Lothringisches Hausarchiv 189/III. 126, fo. 244, and for the following.

[46] King Frederick II to Count Podewils, Ottmachau, 14 Jan. 1741: *Politische Correspondenz*, i. 179.

was not to be hustled even by the visit which Belle-Isle payed him in
his camp at Mollwitz a fortnight after the battle there on 10 April
wherein the Prussians had defeated the Austrians under Neipperg,
and Frederick had, as the wits said, emerged from his first action
covered with glory and flour – in the face of an Austrian cavalry
charge he had sought precipitate refuge in a windmill. Only after
Maria Theresa, obdurate in adversity, had refused to cede Silesia was
the Franco-Prussian Treaty of Breslau concluded on 5 June. France
thereby accorded Frederick his increased terms while he on his side
renounced the Prussian claim to Berg and Jülich in favour of the
Elector Palatine and agreed to support the imperial candidature of
the Elector of Bavaria. The Treaty of Breslau cemented that German
master-plan whereby the Marshal de Belle-Isle was seeking to ensure
that the Elector Charles-Albert of Bavaria, and not the Grand Duke
Francis of Tuscany, should be elected emperor at Frankfurt so as to
'break this colossus of Austrian greatness'.[47]

For a century it had been traditional French policy to play off
Bavaria against Austria. Richelieu, Mazarin, Louis XIV had all
cherished the hope of one day transferring the imperial crown from
the Habsburgs to the Wittelsbachs, next greatest of the catholic
princes of Germany. In 1714 France had concluded a secret treaty
with her Bavarian client, just restored to his dominions, whereby
France pledged herself to support, if necessary by arms, the Bavarian
candidature to the empire in default of Austrian male issue. This
compact was confirmed by others in 1727 and 1733 whereby France
further undertook to support Bavarian claims to hereditary lands of
the Habsburgs. On any plain construction Fleury's subsequent
guarantee of the Pragmatic Sanction was a betrayal of Bavaria just as
the secret Franco-Bavarian agreement of 16 May 1738, confirming
and extending that of 1727, was a betrayal of Austria. But Fleury's
constructions were seldom plain. His devices for reconciling his
contradictory undertakings, invoking international law and Germanic custom, setting off the tacit reservation of the rights of third
parties against the specific guarantee *contra quoscumque*, had pushed
finesse to the point of deceit.

On 4 March 1741 the Marshal de Belle-Isle had set out from Paris
upon his German mission, first paying a courtesy visit to the dowager
Duchess of Lorraine in her mournful retirement at Commercy.
Thence he proceeded down the *Pfaffengasse*, that priest's alley of the
ecclesiastical electors of the Rhineland, torn between their obligations
to Austria, by whom they were usually pensioned, and their fear of
neighbouring France. The fat little Elector of Trier, the first visited,

<hr/>
[47] D'Argenson, iii. 303.

streamed with sweat as he received Belle-Isle. Another embarrassment was that, owing to a hunting accident, this electoral hypochon-
driac had to relieve himself every quarter of an hour or so. Just as
Belle-Isle was pressing him hard in favour of the Bavarian
candidature, his diplomatic host would make an urgent exit. Next
after this cunning representative of the up-and-coming Schönborn
family came the Archbishop-Elector of Cologne who was the younger
brother of the Elector of Bavaria himself. Unhappily, though, the
brothers had fallen out – not least over the division of their mother's
diamonds. This titular Archchancellor of Italy subsequently up-
braided the French resident at Cologne, the Count de Sade, the
entertaining father of the sinister marquis, for having 'made M. de
Belle-Isle come to scold me like a child'.[48] For Belle-Isle the third
elector, at Mainz, was the most important since he would preside
over the electoral diet as imperial archchancellor. The way to get at
him was through his venal nephew, Count Hugo von Elz. Belle-Isle
was tough with Elz, bouncing him into accepting a million livres.
When Elz requested complete secrecy Belle-Isle replied: 'Rest
assured, I shall be quite as discreet as [the Austrian] Count Colloredo
has been about the hundred thousand francs which he has given
you.'[49]

Belle-Isle had begun to line up the three electors in the right
direction, and he even achieved something at his next stopping-point,
the much more important and difficult court of Saxony, beholden as
it was to Austria for her support in the War of the Polish Succession.
Augustus III of Saxony was described at that time as 'a soft prince,
lazy, spending his life in his room with the electress and some
gossiping tradeswomen'.[50] He was run by two advisers, first his
sumptuous minister, the Count von Brühl: 'he has the two qualities
which are said to be essential to a courtier, which are to be without ill-
humour and without honour ... The least of his suits is a gala apparel.
The smallest of his suppers is a great feast ... He has more gems and
snuffboxes than one could find among all the jewellers of Paris put
together.'[51] Frederick the Great once observed, not quite fairly, that
Brühl possessed more hats than brains. The other power at the court
of Dresden was the royal confessor, Father Guarini, almost the
caricature of a Jesuit: 'He feelingly clasps his hands when he does not

---

[48] Count de Sade to Amelot de Chaillou, 18 Apr. 1741: Arch. Aff. Étr. C.P., Cologne;
Broglie/Fréd-MT, i. 290.
[49] Marshal de Belle-Isle to Amelot de Chaillou, 8 Apr. 1741: Arch. Aff. Étr. C.P.,
Correspondance de l'ambassade à la diète de Francfort: ibid., p. 298.
[50] Blondel, memorandum of 2 Dec. 1740 in 'Remarques et anecdotes politiques':
Sautai/Préliminaires, p. 478.
[51] Des Alleurs, French envoy to Saxony, to Amelot de Chaillou, Dresden, 27 July 1741:
Arch. Aff. Étr. C.P., Saxe, vol. 23: op. cit., p. 522.

wish to say anything, and laughs when he does not wish to listen to what one has to say to him'.[52] This Neapolitan strongly inclined to the Austrian interest, and the prevailing note at Dresden was a resentful fear of Prussia.

Belle-Isle could yet report from Dresden that Guarini had secured from his relative, Cardinal Albani in Rome, the comforting assurance that the elector could 'in all surety of conscience, assert his rights [against Austria], notwithstanding the guarantee of the Pragmatic'.[53] Neither Guarini nor Brühl had fundamentally abandoned their preference for Austria but that did not prevent them that May from discussing with Belle-Isle alternative plans for partitioning her dominions when the marshal was on his way back through the Saxon court from his visit to the Prussian camp.

On 18 May 1741 the Marshal de Belle-Isle, having ranged across Germany from the Palatinate to Silesia (acquiring crateloads of Dresden china on the way), entered Munich, the focus of his diplomacy. There, at the court reputed to maintain the strictest etiquette in Europe, he was received with extraordinary honours by the tall, aquiline Elector Charles-Albert of Bavaria, more gentlemanly than effective, an authentic Wittelsbach with his dreamy blue eyes, melancholic indecision and taste for sumptuous architecture. Belle-Isle then really set to work.

If Bavaria was the centre of Belle-Isle's combinations in Germany, Germany was but the centre of his grand design for Europe. For him 'Italy, or the South, is what I call the right. Sweden and the negotiations in Denmark to oppose the Russians and the troops of Hanover is what I call the North and left.'[54] The memorandum containing this continental sweep had been communicated back in January to Cardinal Fleury, who was dismayed by what he, like Choiseul later, regarded as Belle-Isle's extravagant projects. For the present, however, the projects were coming true. The marshal's labours steered home a treaty between Bavaria and Spain, signed at ten o'clock on the night of 28 May 1741 in the palace of Nymphenburg, in a setting as delicious as the name. A Spanish subsidy was added to the French to enable the Elector of Bavaria to raise six thousand additional troops. When the Marquis de Stainville later learnt, albeit in garbled and exaggerated form,[55] that the Franco-Bavarian combination in Nymphenburg had lined up Spain, ever impending

[52] Ibid., p. 524.

[53] Marshal de Belle-Isle to Amelot de Chaillou, Dresden, 20 Apr. 1741: Arch. Aff. Étr. C.P., Allemagne, vol. 398: ibid., p. 234.

[54] Count de Belle-Isle, memorandum communicated to Cardinal Fleury on 27 Jan. 1741: Arch. Aff. Étr., Mémoires et documents, Autriche, vol. 31: ibid., p. 516.

[55] Cf. p. 291 below.

upon Italy, he burst out against 'the designs of aggrandizement entertained by France and her ambition to be the sole arbiter of the world. The whole of Europe at this moment supports her. Either from panic terror or from momentary interest everybody is contributing towards doing what she wants and so is abandoning the good cause.'[56]

Within ten days of the Treaty of Nymphenburg came the Treaty of Breslau. At last Prussia had joined the Franco-Bavarian combination in pursuit of her momentary interest, in Stainville's shrewd phrase, though Frederick himself preferred to assure Charles-Albert of 'engagements which shall have for limit but the course of my life'.[57]

IV

The diplomatic effort was but one half of the intensive activity which Belle-Isle directed from the palace of Nymphenburg, where he regretfully denied himself even a stroll in the gardens with their enchanting pavilions. For he was not merely ambassador but marshal too. His was the commanding intelligence of the mobilization and co-ordination of the French and Bavarian forces. The military difficulties which he had to overcome were scarcely less than the diplomatic and if anything even more exasperating since they largely arose from ill-will at home. Belle-Isle had from the beginning urged a swift and crushing military intervention. Granting that there was to be one at all, this was doubtless operationally correct. But Fleury, overborne by the war-party, yet clung to office and characteristically pursued the middle, worst, course of impeding military preparations. Breteuil, the upright, uninfluential successor to d'Angervilliers as minister of war, complained to Belle-Isle on 15 March 1741, 'I still have my hands tied'[58] by Fleury, whereas he would need three months of full-scale preparation.

That same day the foreign minister, Amelot de Chaillou, handed to the Bavarian representative in Paris a military questionnaire. It enquired what total effectives, by categories, the Elector of Bavaria would raise and by when, what French forces he envisaged, what order of march should be followed, what about the crossings of the Neckar, about supplies and prices of forage, of packhorses, of wagons,

---

[56] Marquis de Stainville to Grand Duke Francis II, Paris, 20 Oct. 1741: Esteri del Granducato di Toscana, vol. 2295/1286, fos. 64–5.

[57] King Frederick II to Elector Charles-Albert of Bavaria, Strehlen, 22 June 1741: *Politische Correspondenz*, i. 264.

[58] Marquis de Breteuil to Marshal de Belle-Isle, Versailles, 15 Mar. 1741: Arch. Guerre C., vol. 2914: Sautai/Préliminaires, pp. 292–3.

about commissariat arrangements, biscuit, meat, the price of corn and of sacks and their probable availability, about the width of any material there might be for tents, for uniforms, whether shoes were to be had and for how much, and cooking utensils, concerning the calibre of shot, optimum axle-adjustment for vehicles on German roads, about Bavarian scales of pay, about facilities for pontoon-construction, for hospitals, and so on and on. This formidable document would, Fleury doubtless reckoned, give the Bavarians quite a lot to think about, and until a reply was received he would not allow preliminary preparations to proceed in France. Belle-Isle complained, 'time is strangling us',[59] and much of his labour at Nymphenburg was devoted to gingering up the Bavarian bureaucrats about their replies to the questionnaire. He himself composed copious memoranda of elucidation – Belle-Isle was a great general for paper-work. At last, on 6 June, he was able to load a courier with the wad of information that constituted the complete reply.[60] Louis XV commented at about that time: 'I have received dispatches from M. de Belle-Isle four inches thick; however their style is concise and there is nothing useless in them; I am not too accustomed to receiving such.'[61]

Fleury, however, was dismayed by Belle-Isle's pitilessly precise replies: depots and hospitals would be established at Donauwörth and Ingolstadt; tenting material for officers would cost 34½ kreutzers an ell (Paris measurement), for soldiers, 21 kreutzers; 6,000 pairs of shoes could be supplied in two months at 3 livres 10 sols the pair; axle-specifications were subjoined; and so it went on, page after page. All this dry data added up to bloody war. Fleury could no longer evade it. But he twisted. He agreed to send the Marquis de Beauvau to Bavaria to co-ordinate supply arrangements. Frederick was already turning nasty about French delay in giving effect to the Treaty of Breslau, whereas Fleury, following Beauvau, was vainly representing the King of Prussia to Belle-Isle as 'false in everything . . . He would govern and have his head without any concert with us.'[62] The cardinal was specially reluctant to sanction a build-up of the expensive cavalry – an economy which was to cost France dear – and now actually proposed to halve, or nearly, the marshal's proposal for a French contingent of 40,000 men. It was too much. At about four o'clock on the afternoon of 10 July 1741 the Marshal de Belle-Isle drove into the forecourt at Versailles.

[59] Marshal de Belle-Isle to Hocquard (official in French Ministry of War), Mainz, 5 Apr. 1741: Arch. Guerre C., vol. 2924: op. cit., p. 296.
[60] Printed op. cit., pp. 560–604, i.e. over forty large pages of small print.
[61] Luynes, iii. 427.
[62] Cardinal Fleury to Marshal de Belle-Isle, Issy, 17 June 1741: Arch. Aff. Étr. C.P., Allemagne, vol. 400: Sautai/Préliminaires, p. 327.

On the day after his arrival the marshal was in ministerial conclave for nine hours on end, 'for at least seven of which I was talking'.[63] In a fortnight he galvanized the whole French war-machine. When he left Versailles on 24 July it was all arranged. French troops would advance into Germany without delay and in force, in two separate armies according to Belle-Isle's plan of campaign.

In the diplomatic sphere Belle-Isle's main stroke at Versailles was to secure the despatch on 16 July of a strong intimation to the subsidized Swedish government that it was high time that it moved against Russia. There was no point upon which Frederick the Great was so insistent. He had inherited from his father a healthy respect for Russian might, and the extent to which Russian considerations already influenced Frederick's thinking is most noticeable. At the beginning of August 1741 the trumpets sounded in Stockholm and Sweden duly declared war upon Russia. Belle-Isle's north and left was covered.

Only on his right, to the south, was there a check. There Fleury was reaping the reward of his duplicity towards Spain and Sardinia in the War of the Polish Succession, was running into severe difficulties in his attempt to repeat Chauvelin's feat of combining those powers, however loosely. This combination was urgently to be desired since Elizabeth Farnese, for ever on the go, was intent upon exploiting the Austrian succession to renew that Spanish drive in Italy unleased by the Polish succession. She advanced a cooked-up claim to nothing less than a revival in Bourbon favour of the huge domination of the Emperor Charles V, alleging that her husband, Philip V, had received, along with the crown of Spain and the Indies, the reversionary right of the Spanish Habsburgs to succeed to the Austrian branch upon the extinction of its male line. This extravagant pretension was generally understood to be the handle to the more practical ambition of fitting up Don Philip with an Italian principality now that Don Carlos had been provided with Naples. That meant more war in Italy, and Spain's real attitude towards the Austrian succession was accordingly to support any candidate whose nuisance-value was sufficient to attract Austrian forces away from Lombardy. Hence the Treaty of Nymphenburg. Belle-Isle's determination to exploit the Austrian succession in favour of French intervention in Germany was matched by Elizabeth Farnese's in favour of Spanish intervention in Italy. In this she counted the more confidently upon French support since the amiably spineless Don Philip, a foppish youth who was his mother's pet, had in 1739 been married at the age

[63] Marshal de Belle-Isle to his brother, the Chevalier de Belle-Isle, Versailles, 12 July 1741: Arch. Guerre C., vol. 2914: op. cit., p. 342.

of eighteen to twelve-year-old Marie-Louise-Elisabeth, the eldest and favourite daughter of Louis XV, and, astonishingly, the only one to marry. At the same time the Dauphin had been promised an Infanta. Fleury, though, was specially intent upon holding Spain off from Tuscany, the equivalent for precious Lorraine.

If Fleury had to resign himself to an attack upon the Habsburgs elsewhere in Italy as well as in Germany, he was sure, as Chauvelin had been, that this demanded the co-operation of Sardinia: more so than ever now that England was hostile instead of neutral. For Spain there was nothing doing with Sardinia except through France. But, while Spain was politically and economically closer to France than was Sardinia, Fleury could not abide the maternal activism of the dominating Queen of Spain, who, he considered, 'is born to ruin France, and one can say without exaggeration that she has convulsed all Europe':[64] whereas Fleury felt sympathetic respect for the cautious acumen of Charles Emmanuel of Sardinia. However, that monarch and his outstanding minister, the Marquis D'Ormea, among the foremost Italian diplomatists of his century, only played with Fleury, regularly retailing the cardinal's conversations with Solar, the Sardinian minister in Paris, to verbose Villettes, the English representative in Turin, for transmission to London and Vienna. Nothing came of French attempts to resolve the Sardinian difference with Spain about prospective pickings in northern Italy, especially Mantua: as may be gathered from the following two conversations held at that time on either side of the Gulf of Lions.

First. The Marquis D'Ormea was telling the Marquis de Senneterre, the French envoy, 'that they should try not to cloister him [King Charles Emmanuel], that he had a natural aversion for cloisters, that it was a piece of architecture which he could not abide.'

Marquis de Senneterre. 'Neither can I, when they are closed, but, when they are open on all sides, one can but regard them as colonnades or galleries.'

Marquis D'Ormea. 'Mantua cloisters us furiously.'[65]

Second. The Queen of Spain (interrupting the French ambassador's reading of proposals) 'No, sir.'

The King of Spain. 'I shall not make war for the King of Sardinia.'

The Queen of Spain. 'You hear what the King says to you? I think just like him. We are going to leave. We can talk at Saint Ildefonso.'[66]

[64] Cardinal Fleury to Cardinal de Tencin, 5 June 1741: Hénault, p. 360.

[65] De Saint-Rémy (secretary to Marquis de Senneterre), 'Relation de l'ambassade de M. le Marquis de Senecterre': Arch. Aff. Étr., Mémoires et documents, Sardaigne, vol. 13: Sautai/Préliminaires, p. 400.

[66] Bishop of Rennes to Amelot de Chaillou, Balsin, 29 July 1741: Arch. Aff. Étr. C.P., Espagne, vol. 466: op. cit., p. 401.

And talk she did, and cry as well. Fleury, fed up, finally exclaimed: 'I wash my hands of it.'[67]

If, however, Spain was as yet unforthcoming in the Mediterranean, she struck a resounding blow in the Caribbean in unexpectedly beating off a British attack under Admiral Vernon against the port of Carthagena. So British admirals were not invincible after all. That July the news reverberated through the continent, which tended to endorse the maxim of the merchants of Amsterdam: 'He who is master of Carthagena is master of America.' This British reverse further depressed the low stock of her old friend, Austria. Such was the rosy backcloth to Belle-Isle's triumphant return from Versailles to Frankfurt. The certainty spread in widening rings: France would intervene in Germany.

Belle-Isle's success was as dazzling as his display. For his was among the classic embassies, largely thanks to the organization of the indefatigable Blondel. In vain did Fleury plead for 'economy within a most brilliant exterior'.[68] His parsimony, no less than his pacifism, was overcome. Contemporaries estimated the cost of this brilliant mission at about six million livres or a quarter of a million pounds, a lot of money in those days. The marshal's train included some fifty postilions and grooms along with guards, pages, trumpeters, musi-musicians, and chefs. The table-linen alone cost more than 150,000 livres and set off plate and china of equivalent magnificence, though Belle-Isle's friends helped him out by lending services. His household at Frankfurt bought, it is said, a thousand to twelve hundred pounds of meat a day, not counting game and poultry, and Belle-Isle's butler did nicely out of his wine.

This magnificence attained its apogee at the feast of Saint Louis, the king's feast, with fireworks, a nautical joust on the Main, and fountains playing wine. On the evening of 27 August a supper 'of the utmost delicacy'[69] ushered in a brilliant all-night ball. While the ball was in full swing Belle-Isle had another conversation, lasting two hours, with the Count von Elz. The marshal gave him ten days in which to produce results with his uncle. On 4 September 1741 the Elector of Mainz pledged himself in writing 'to the King of France to give his vote, as the fifth, to the Elector of Bavaria for the forthcoming election of an Emperor'.[70] This critical fifth vote added

---

[67] Cardinal Fleury to Cardinal de Tencin, 5 Feb. 1742: Hénault, p. 380.
[68] Cited by Vicomte Fleury, *Le Secret du maréchal de Belle-Isle* (Paris, 1934), p. 39.
[69] 'Relation des réjouissances faites par Mgr. le maréchal de Belle-Isle a l'occasion de la Saint-Louis, fête du Roi, à Frankfort, 1741': Arch. Aff. Étr. C.P., Allemagne, vol. 402: Sautai/Débuts, i. 275.
[70] Article 1 of the treaty of guarantee of 4 Sept. 1741 between France and Mainz: Arch. Aff. Étr. C.P., Mayence, vol. 42: op. cit., i. 277.

to those already secured, of Bavaria, Cologne, the Palatinate, and Brandenburg-Prussia, gave Charles-Albert the necessary majority in in the electorial diet of nine. Three days later Belle-Isle learnt that another conversation which he had had at the same ball had also taken effect: the Elector of Trier had swung into line. Belle-Isle had scarcely exaggerated in saying of his festivity: 'What would at other times be but a simple ceremony of propriety is today one of policy.'[71]

Within another fortnight, after much haggling and pressure, Saxony was also in. On 19 September, under Belle-Isle's compelling supervision, the Electors of Saxony and Bavaria concluded a defensive and offensive alliance for the partition of the Habsburg inheritance. The future emperor was to extend his direct rule from Bavaria to include Bohemia, Upper Austria and the Tyrol; the Elector of Saxony, dignified as King of Moravia, was to receive that province along with Upper Silesia and also a slice of Lower Austria in compensation for leaving contested Neisse to Prussia; a duty-free highway was to span the gap for Saxony between Upper Lusatia and Upper Silesia. This radical agreement, in the words of the French foreign minister, 'crowns the perfection of the handiwork'.[72] Well might he exult. France had at last achieved, on paper, her new ordering of the German lands. The transfer of imperial power from Austria to Bavaria was to be confirmed by lopping off the Habsburg dominions. Their age-old ascendancy was, under French aegis, to be dissolved into four medium-sized competitors, a truncated Austria–Hungary, and an expanded Bavaria, Saxony, and Prussia.

With Spain keeping England in play upon the one hand and Sweden Russia on the other, the isolated and disjointed territories of the twentyfour-year-old Austrian queen were beset by a formidable and greedy German coalition of Prussia, Saxony, and Bavaria backed by the military weight of France. It was a black crisis in the long history of the Habsburgs. The embassy of the Marshal de Belle-Isle had rivalled in splendour and surpassed in success the great embassy of the Marshal de Gramont in 1658. As the martial ambassador wrote to King Louis XV: 'Your Majesty executes what none of his glorious predecessors has been able to do. Master and depositary of the votes which decide the election ... Your Majesty will place him [the future emperor] in possession of the best part of the States of a house always enemy to yours, which all your predecessors since Francis I have never been able to abase and contain, and against which Henry IV, Louis XIII, and Louis the Great have without intermission employed

[71] Marshal de Belle-Isle, 'Mémoires': op. cit., i. 274.
[72] Amelot de Chaillou to Marshal de Belle-Isle, Versailles, 22 Sept. 1741: Arch. Aff. Étr. C.P., Allemagne, vol. 403: op. cit., i. 327.

all their forces.'[73] On the same day Fleury himself was addressing Belle-Isle as 'at the same time the inventor and the actor of this glorious scene'.[74] Fleury's private opinion was, however, somewhat cooler. 'One must admit', he wrote, 'that our situation is very brilliant and that it seems fairly well consolidated; but *even as it has the lustre of glass, it has its fragility.* The least check is capable, between ourselves, of upsetting it.'[75] The fragile equipoise depended upon that brilliant marshal who, as the Duke de Saint-Simon observed, was 'the single soul of everything, the only one whereby the machine is controlled, and all our eggs in one basket'.[76]

Later historians have almost unanimously agreed with Choiseul in condemning Belle-Isle for thus plunging France into a superfluous and unjust war. One modern authority goes so far as to maintain that there have been few errors in French history more calamitous.[77] That, though, was later. For the present Belle-Isle crested a surge of enthusiasm such as is liable from time to time to sweep over sceptical Frenchmen, especially in favour of striking generals. The enthusiasm for Belle-Isle's German system was comparable to that aroused earlier by Law's financial system. The magnetic marshal stood forth as a veritable crusader – one of his close friends, President Hénault, said that Belle-Isle could have founded a religion. The grandson was truly redeeming the ambitious motto of his too brilliant forebear: *Quo non ascendet.* Whither indeed might he not ascend, seeming, as he did, about 'to scale the skies'.[78] Valade portrayed Belle-Isle framed by figures of fame and victory, surmounted by a floating female pointing upwards with a banner bearing the device, *Sic itur ad astra*, thus the way to the stars.

The way to the stars is proverbially arduous. The ball at Frankfurt was not the only occasion upon which Belle-Isle worked into the night. He had cut his sleep to a bare four hours, a stiff regime for a man permanently delicate from an old chest-wound from the War of the Spanish Succession. Belle-Isle still had to co-ordinate all the military preparations no less than the diplomatic.

The signal to the French administrative services to get going on supply had at last gone out on 22 June 1741. Ten days later timber-felling began for the construction of a thousand military supply-

---

[73] Marshal de Belle-Isle to King Louis XV, Frankfurt am Main, 6 Sept. 1741: Arch. Aff. Étr. C.P., Allemagne, vol. 403: op. cit., i. 278–9.

[74] Cardinal Fleury to Marshal de Belle-Isle, Versailles, 6 Sept. 1741: Arch. Aff. Étr. C.P., Allemagne, vol. 403: Sautai/Préliminaires, p. 423.

[75] Cardinal Fleury to Cardinal de Tencin, 10 Oct. 1741: Hénault, p. 370.

[76] Duke de Saint-Simon to Count de Laval, La Fère, 20 Dec. 1741: Arch. Aff. Étr. Mémoires et documents, France, vol. 1324: Sautai/Préliminaires, p. 354.

[77] Cf. Walter L. Dorn, *Competition for Empire 1740–1763* (New York, 1940), p. 142.

[78] Duke de Saint-Simon, *u.s.*: Sautai/Préliminaires, p. 355.

wagons. They had to be knocked up there and then from the still-green wood, for Fleury's parsimonious procrastination meant that the work, when it did begin, was hectic, and expensive; bonuses had to be paid to expedite output. Then four thousand stout horses had to be procured, no easy job at a time when the peasants were busy on the land and the officers who would be campaigning were bidding up for mounts for their own use. The harassed commissioner for supply, Pavée, besides purchasing in Switzerland, had to scour 'the hamlets and in the mountain farmsteads'.[79] At Strasburg meanwhile more than two thousand kegs had to be manufactured for the conveyance of the 540,000 rations of biscuit that were baking in that district. Even an eighteenth-century army had problems of supply which, relatively simple in themselves, were formidable in terms of the resources of that age. Belle-Isle, though, did not overlook it. There is a story, dating from some years before, of one of Belle-Isle's old soldiers saying to a new recruit who came in lugging a truss of straw for his bed: 'Throw your straw there. With Father Belle-Isle you will find everything you need. It is he who thinks of everything, and one should not worry with this general.'[80]

Belle-Isle's difficulties were multiplied by the Bavarians. Coordination had to be particularly close since France would not be formally declaring war against Austria on her own account but would, by a recognized convention of the time, be technically supplying Bavaria with an auxiliary corps to serve under Bavarian command. This assistance was most necessary since the Bavarians had lost a high proportion of their best troops in supporting Austria in the unlucky Eastern War; what was left – they aimed at putting about twenty thousand men into the field by August – was a pretty scratch lot with no heavy artillery, not much ammunition and practically no logistic backing whatsoever, as Belle-Isle ascertained with exasperation and dismay. The Bavarians and in particular Belle-Isle's friend, the chief minister, Count Törring, like himself created a marshal for the occasion, maintained that they just had not the money to supply their army themselves. The French marshal complained that the Bavarian marshal 'finishes nothing'.[81]

Belle-Isle's righthand man on the staff, the Marquis de Beauvau, wrote to him:

I am frightened when I wake up in the mornings and think that I am older by a

[79] Pavée to Pâris–Duverney, 24 July 1741: Arch. Guerre C., vol. 2924: Sautai/Débuts, i. 81.

[80] Countess de Bonneval to Count de Belle-Isle, Paris, 23 Nov. 1734: Arch. Guerre C., vol. 2771: Sautai/Préliminaires, p. 149. (The Countess de Bonneval, wife of Bonneval Pasha, was a friend of the Count de Belle-Isle.)

[81] Marshal de Belle-Isle to Count de Mortaigne, Frankfurt am Main, 28 Aug. 1741: Arch. Guerre C., vol. 2915: Sautai/Débuts, i. 121, n. 1.

day ... I had the honour to inform you that we should have 15,000 pairs of shoes by the 1st September. Not at all; I learn yesterday evening from M. de Terring, that one should no longer count upon anything as to the time within which they will be done, that the cobblers are short of material, that they could not be compelled to work to a fixed date. Upon what is one to depend? It is the same in everything; it is for the tenth time at least that I am asking that, if forage cannot be bought without our making the advances, at least they should give me a note of the places whence one can draw it and of the quantity that one can hope for ... They only answer me on all this that, provided that the money does not lack, nothing will lack; that they have made war previously and without entering into such great detail ... I was hoping to remedy a part of these delays by means of the [Bavarian] commissioner whom they have granted me to work with him [sic], but he is an old fellow who has the quartan fever and who will not live eight days if they leave him in my hands.[82]

Whether or no at the cost of the Bavarian commissioner's life, the delays were remedied by unremitting effort and by making Orry disburse ever larger sums from the financial cushion which he had so painstakingly provided. Within a week of his heartcry of 14 August Beauvau was writing to Belle-Isle: 'You will see, Monseigneur, by the subjoined return, that our magazines have doubled since my letter of the 14th.'[83] Bread and forage for the French forces were secure up to the 1st November. Sandbags were coming in up to 50,000 and artillery supplies were shaping up at last. On 16 August the French commissioner for artillery, de Rostaing, described by Beauvau as 'seething like myself'[84] at Bavarian backwardness, discovered a furnace at Sulzbach capable of a weekly production of six to seven hundred pieces of shot for the heavy twenty-four pounders. At the same time he was stocking up the arsenal at Munich with 25,000 pounds of lead and another 80,000 pounds to follow. Other French experts were, under Belle-Isle's direction, looking to the Bavarian roads and bridges, and the marshal himself wrote more than fifty letters solely in connection with securing for the French forces rights of free passage through the various neutral principalities of the Rhineland which they must traverse: an application of that principle of *transitus innoxius* through German lands stipulated by the Treaty of Westphalia. Belle-Isle's administrative achievement was scarcely less impressive than his diplomatic.

In all this logistic activity Belle-Isle relied especially upon two intimate collaborators: first, his devoted younger brother, the Chevalier de Belle-Isle, as frigid and reserved as the other was

[82] Marquis de Beauvau to Marshal de Belle-Isle, 14 Aug. 1741: Arch. Aff. Étr. C.P., Bavière, vol. 95: op. cit., i. 122–3.
[83] Marquis de Beauvau to Marshal de Belle-Isle, Munich, 20 Aug. 1741: ibid., op. cit., i. 140.
[84] Marquis de Beauvau to Marshal de Belle-Isle, Munich, midnight, 17 Aug. 1741: ibid., op. cit., i. 149.

expansive and brilliant, but scarcely less ambitious or able, some said abler. The marshal referred to his brother as 'another myself'.[85] The Marquis d'Argenson said that the pair of them operated a 'well adjusted machine'.[86] Belle-Isle's other close collaborator was his old friend de Sechelles, who, like the Chevalier de Belle-Isle, had shared his imprisonment in the Bastille in 1724. Since then de Sechelles had made his mark as intendant of Hainault, and he was now appointed intendant to the Army of Bavaria in accordance with the advanced French practice at that time of attaching to each army a civilian intendant with wide powers in all matters of supply and civil administration of occupied territory. No friend of Belle-Isle's, on the other hand, was the director of supply at the French Ministry of War, Pâris-Duverney. This brilliant and wealthy administrator had been the brain behind the Duke de Bourbon when the Count de Belle-Isle and his friends were cooling in the Bastille. At present the ascendancy of Pâris-Duverney over Breteuil at the Ministry of War was as great as that of his brother, Pâris-Monmartel, over Orry at the treasury. The two brothers constituted a most important and effective power-centre within the French administration. Pâris-Duverney and Belle-Isle were both clever enough to perceive that at this juncture they needed each other, and their reconciliation through their mutual friend Chavigny, now French minister in Portugal, was facilitated by the confidence which Belle-Isle had come to place 'in the activity of M. de Monmartel and in the foresight of M. du Verney'.[87]

The French Ministry of War was in fact 'extremely well equipped'[88] with an outstanding team of senior officials. The degree of efficiency with which, despite all handicaps, they pushed through their logistic mobilization at the double in 1741 is another small pointer towards the broad conclusion that if the seventeenth century had established the great English contribution to western government, parliamentary control, the eighteenth century was consolidating the great continental contribution, administrative control. In the administration of military supply, the stuff of war, France at that time could still stand comparison with Prussia. The same was not quite so true of the French organization of military force, the spearhead of war.

[85] Count de Belle-Isle to Marquis d'Angervilliers, Trier, 25 Oct. 1735: Arch. Guerre C., vol. 2804: Sautai/Préliminaires, p. 135.
[86] D'Argenson, iii. 334.
[87] Marshal de Belle-Isle to Marquis de Breteuil, Frankfurt am Main, 28 Aug. 1741: Arch. Guerre C., vol. 2915: Sautai/Débuts, i. 160.
[88] Barbier, iii. 405.

V

In 1715 Louis XIV had had some 120 regiments of infantry. In 1740 Louis XV had just about the same, though Royal-Corse had been raised during the Corsican campaign of the preceding year. This establishment plus some 22,000 cavalry and such special formations as the royal bodyguard (*Maison du Roi*) and the gendarmerie gave the French army an effective of some 150,000 men, increased by militia and others to a total strength of about 190,000. This was the largest army in the world at a time when an army of over a hundred thousand was the symbol of the greatest continental powers. Besides France only Russia qualified with 130,000 and Austria with some 108,000. The Prussian army was about 83,000 strong, the British, 28,000.[89]

The Age of Reason took a rational view of war. Of few epochs is it so true that war was an extension of diplomacy by other means: hostilities were often not so much an abrupt break with diplomacy as a running commentary upon it. Hence frequent, limited wars for limited objectives, matching the delicate operation of statecraft during the century between the close of fanatical wars of religious faith and the opening of passionate wars of popular nationalism. In keeping with such a situation was the neat practice of old, rather gradually modified, whereby armies were quite largely recruited from the two least productive sections of the community, nobles and vagabonds.

The French army was raised by voluntary enlistment and by the hire of foreign mercenaries – Swiss, Germans, Irish, and Italians – backed by militia drawn by lot. To enrol oneself as a common soldier against the initial gratuity could figure traditionally as an act of desperation, and shady characters could mask their identity behind those picturesque pseudonyms – La Tulipe, La Rose – under which they were enlisted. Thus the soldier of that age was often an object of contemptuous aversion rather than of patriotic respect. Hence also the fact that there was a good deal of indifferent, or worse, fighting material in among the sturdy stock of artisans and peasantry enrolled, not least, by seigneurial recruitment upon a local basis, sometimes to the accompaniment of wives and children.[90]

For a French ranker lieutenancy was ordinarily the summit of possible ambition. If a sprinkling of such 'officers of fortune' was by

---

[89] Cf. *Oesterreichischer Erbfolge-Krieg 1740–1748* (K. und k. Kriegs-Archiv. Vienna, 1896–1914: henceforth cited as *Erbfolge-Krieg*), i. 372 *et seq.*; Dorn, op. cit., p. 84; André Corvisier, *L'Armée française de la fin du XVIIᵉ siècle au ministère de Choiseul: le soldat* (Paris, 1964), i. 55, 154.

[90] Cf. A. Corvisier, op. cit., i. 91–2, 142–3, ii. 749 *et passim* for balancing factors.

no means unusual, yet in the army as in other spheres rank was predominantly assimilated to the hierarchic privilege of aristocracy. And, as usual again, one might buy one's way in. The sale of companies and regiments corresponded to that sale of legal and administrative offices which was one of the most hampering features of the old regime. In the army even when captains and colonels were honest in their administration of those units which were their property, they were most often hard pressed by the rising cost of living so that a good deal of the time which should have been devoted to military application was humiliatingly spent upon financial shifts. If one were rich and noble enough, however, one might become a colonel in one's teens and so join the select band of 'colonels in bibs' (*colonels à la bavette*). In that case, and indeed in a large number of others, the real administration of the regiment fell to the lieutenant-colonel who was most often an experienced officer from the lesser nobility, not rich enough to buy a regiment. One lieutenant-colonel in a thousand might, it was reckoned, ultimately become a brigadier.

If colonelcies could be bought in the flush of youth, subsequent promotion was slow and, in general, according to that seniority which then as at other times commanded particular prestige in the French army, as it emphatically did with eightyeight-year-old Cardinal Fleury. The outstanding Belle-Isle, the youngest French marshal at fifty-six, had had to wait ten years for that rank and another thirteen before that for its immediate inferior, the lieutenant-generalship. At the same time, however, the French army was top-heavy with generals and colonels, or would have been if so many had not been lightweights. A memorandum of 1736 remarked that colonels who in peace time spent a fortnight with their troops 'think that they have given an example of the greatest goodwill'.[91]

Junior officers largely aped their seniors in frivolity. According to one witness, 'the lieutenant-colonels and the majors give all their attention to making the soldiers march well, but not one examines the officers who are at the head of the divisions; they, instead of applying themselves to leading them well and to observing their own marching, play about with their spontoons and guns and prevent the soldiers from marching in order'.[92]

When Belle-Isle visited Frederick the Great in camp at Mollwitz the king put on an impressive parade in a snowstorm and made the marshal keen to emulate in the French army the way in which, in the

[91] Memorandum of the Bureau de Guerre, Mar. 1736: Arch. Aff. Étr., Mémoires et documents, France, vol. 1297: Sautai/Débuts, i. 27.
[92] De la Garrigue (commander of the second battalion of the Régiment de Gondrin), 'Mémoire sur la nécessité d'appliquer les officiers à s'instruire et étudier l'art militaire', 1736: Arch. Guerre, Cartons, Organisation générale: op. cit., i. 31.

Prussian, 'there is not a single officer in each battalion who is not compelled to do, in the course of the drill, all the same movements that the soldier does or which are relevant'.[93]

Belle-Isle, a disciplinarian, had for years been trying without much success to overcome not only the indiscipline within regiments but also the incoherence among them. After commanding a training camp in 1727 he had complained that it had been impossible 'to make several regiments drill together, there being not one who does it in a uniform manner'[94] since each colonel imposed his own drill and words of command. Regiments preferred to step out on their own so that 'in one army, all at the same time one hears drummers beating so fast that one thinks that they are marionettes, and, on another side, steadily like the French Guards and in accordance with the order'.[95]

French drill was antiquated and troops usually lacked firing-practice. This reflected prevalent French tactical theory wherein musketry was a rather despised auxiliary to the infantry charge and close combat with cold steel, supposedly in keeping with French élan in battle. The French army in 1741 was only just being issued with iron ramrods in place of wooden ones. Iron ramrods had long been adopted by the Prussian army, as had the three-rank line of battle. The French, however, kept the old four-rank formation while regretting the still more cumbersome five.

The French infantry, by comparison with the French cavalry, was good. In general the cavalry, besides displaying organizational and tactical defects at least as serious as those in the infantry, suffered from such basic handicaps as that the sabres were too heavy, the musketoons too long, and that, according to an account of 1736, 'the horses are heavy and . . . the horsemen are no more than grooms who are embarrassed when they are mounted on a pig as clumsy as themselves'.[96] That applied, rather surprisingly, not least to the officers, who in time of peace had to provide their own horses and fodder; and those who could afford to do so were exceptional – a sidelight upon the economic position of the lesser French nobility. It was reckoned in 1733 that three-quarters of the French cavalry officers had either no mounts or such bad ones as to be 'not tolerable'.[97] During the Italian campaign in the War of the Polish Succession

[93] Marshal de Belle-Isle to Marquis de Breteuil, camp before Brieg, 28 Apr. 1741: Arch. Guerre C., vol. 3074: Sautai/Préliminaires, p. 258.
[94] Count de Belle-Isle, 'Journal de ce qui s'est passé de plus considérable dans le camp de Richemont sur la Moselle, dont j'ai été honoré du commandement': Arch. Guerre, Cartons, Camp de Richemont 1727: Sautai/Débuts, i. 32.
[95] French infantry captain to Marquis d'Angervilliers, camp at Offenbourg, 8 Sept. 1734: Arch. Guerre C., vol. 2736: op. cit., i. 39.
[96] 'Mémoire sur le abus introduits dans le militaire', 31 July 1736: Arch. Aff. Étr., Mémoires et documents, France, vol. 1305: op. cit., i. 47.
[97] Count de Mortaigne, memorandum of 1733: Arch. Guerre, Carton I, Cavalerie: ibid.

numbers of the ill-equipped, incompetent French officers wobbling about on their horses had rendered themselves the laughing-stock even of the Italian troops.

In the War of the Polish Succession the French army in general probably reached a nadir of inefficiency, whereas only thirty years previously it had been accounted the most formidable in the world. Yet it was the same army: that was just the trouble – too much the same. In 1740 the army of Louis XV was the army of Louis XIV in decay. During the seventeen-twenties and thirties, while Frederick-William I had been remorselessly drilling the Prussian army into existence, the French army had struck one of those periodic patches of unimaginative stagnation to which it appears to be particularly prone in between its heroic phases. Such was the military price of Fleury's pacific economy.

By modern standards the French army of 1740 might seem remarkably inefficient. But for contemporaries the perspective was only the beginning of truly modern warfare in the seventeenth century, the still largely ramshackle armies of the renaissance, the crude levies of feudalism. In the military as in other spheres of French life the feudal carrythrough had not yet wholly expired in the first half of the eighteenth century. For example, desertion, the standing drain of all armies in that age, was apt to be least in French companies of the antique pattern wherein the captain was some country squire who went to war with his wife, his village priest, his relations, their tenantry and peasantry, the social unit making up the military. So too the qualities generally held in highest esteem in the French army at that time were the ancient qualities of bravery and beauty. The innate aesthetic sense of that age – still, on the deeper view, one of its most mysterious aspects – by no means stopped short of armies in the splendid elegance of their uniforms. To look fine upon full-dress parades and to fight finely in close-quarter combat was probably still the simple, knightly tradition for the main run of aristocratic French officers. However otherwise frivolous or incompetent, they habitually displayed high valour upon the field of battle, still the place for personal feats of prowess and renown.

In the military field as in others the antique age of aristocratic chivalry persisted, but was passing. That was the ultimate implication of the detailed planning, the complex staffwork, the logistical preoccupation, the bureaucratic administration of the Marshal de Belle-Isle and his team. They required a different, modern type of officer. The new administrative mould was profoundly modifying the feudal survival in its military, as in its civil, aspects. In the very sphere of war itself the new run of administrative nobility, the *noblesse de robe*, was beginning to jostle the ancient order of combatant nobility, the *noblesse d'épée*. The grandson of Nicolas Fouquet was a fitting sponsor for this process.

Such was the panorama of France going to war in 1741, the setting, the factors, the forces. And the French forces were closer to the continental average of that time than were the Prussian. In estimating eighteenth-century militarism as a whole there has been a rather natural tendency to look too much to the Prussian model just because it was exceptionally modern, exceptionally the best. Whereas a glance at the then Austrian army, for instance, is sufficient to dispel any idea that its French counterpart was very exceptional. The principal defects in the armed forces of the Bourbons were almost duplicated in those of the Habsburgs – the same regimental idiosyncrasies in drill, the same frivolous absenteeism among those aristocratic young colonels who had secured their commissions over the heads of experienced officers. In the military sphere as in others the Ancien Régime was more than merely French.

The very rigour and extent of the quoted criticisms of the French armed forces from the inside would suggest, as the War of the Austrian Succession was to demonstrate, that they contained numbers of keen and capable officers who, even during the bad times, had managed to maintain a high standard in their units. Of no regiment was this more true than that in which the Count de Stainville was then serving as a second lieutenant, the Régiment du Roi, Roi-Infanterie. It was, in fact, the crack regiment of French infantry.

Roi-Infanterie had been raised by Louis XIV in 1663. Six years later it had absorbed the remnants and the renown of the Regiment of Lorraine, cut to pieces in the Cretan campaign of that year. It was thus an appropriate regiment for young Stainville, one of whose ancestors indeed, Antoine de Stainville, Count de Couvonges, had commanded the Regiment of Lorraine with high distinction during the famous siege of Turin in 1640.

Louis XIV had regarded Roi-Infanterie as his personal regiment, and was its colonel. In 1671 he had purchased for it the precedence formerly enjoyed by one of the oldest regiments, Artois. For in the French army the code of privileged seniority applied to regiments no less than to individuals. The king himself had to buy position and precedence for his own creation so that it became the twelfth regiment in the army-list, the junior of the so-called Vieux Corps. This elite comprised the twelve oldest regiments in the army – Champagne, Navarre, Picardy, Piedmont, Normandy, and others raised in the sixteenth or early seventeenth centuries. These regiments were further classified as *vieux* or *petits vieux*, six of each, and Roi-Infanterie thus became the last of the *petits vieux*, though raised so much later than the others. Such seniority conferred very tangible benefits upon the regiment, such as special allowances to its officers above their regular pay, prior choice of position in battle and of billets behind the line, and the prized privilege of *prévôté*, that is, of having regimental delinquents tried by regimental court-martial rather than by summary jurisdiction at army level.

Louis XIV had created his regiment to provide the best training for the sons of the best families. They had been put through it by the first regimental lieutenant-colonel, humbly born de Martinet, still the designation of military strictness. Both at Steenkirk (1692) and at Neerwinden (1693) the Roi largely saved the day. They did less well at Ramillies but more than redeemed regimental honour, even if they could not secure French victory, at Oudenarde, where they fought for five hours surrounded but unbroken, and in the fearful carnage of Malplaquet.

Such was the tradition of the Regiment Roi-Infanterie, now mobilizing with the rest, at the double quick, in the summer of 1741. In this mobilization, in accordance with its training tradition, the king's own regiment of infantry was constituted as the largest in the French army, comprising four battalions with a total effective of 3,080 men.[98] It must have been a busy and expensive time for the young Count de Stainville: 'all the officers have orders to be with their regiments by 10 August. They are in astonishing straits for all the equipages; horses and mules are beyond price, and these gentlemen have even greater difficulty in finding money.'[99] At that time even an infantry subaltern, especially in such an elite as the Roi, was expected to maintain a small equipage at his own expense. Nor was young Stainville ever behindhand in matters of personal presentation.

VI

The gay young Count de Stainville, who was to prove adept at spending money, had that year been concerning himself with the family source of it, helping his father in Paris with correspondence about the Stainville estate. In particular, he had replied for the marquis to the agent, Mathieu, about an estimate by a certain Sieur Pitois for oak-trees for the repair of the mill at Ménil: the trees were

[98] An ordinance of 7 Sept. 1741 laid down that Roi-Infanterie should maintain five supernumerary men in each of its sixty-eight companies: op. cit., i. 84, n. 2.
[99] Barbier, iii. 299.

to be valued and Pitois allowed to have them at half-price. The snag, though, was that bureaucratic clamp on timber which had particularly exasperated the Lorrainers in their manifesto to the Marquis de Stainville, whose own estates now demonstrated how it was in practice evaded. Nobody, explained Mathieu, was permitted 'to sell or deliver any oak, or even windfallen trees, without having obtained ... permission therefor from the council [of Lorraine], but if there were urgent necessity for building or works [one might] deliver on condition of justifying its use. It was agreed' therefore by the estate administration at Stainville 'that it would only indite the procès-verbal of delivery without valuation, or sale or publication, in order to avoid the entanglements and going to the court in this matter since it was works of Monsieur the Marquis ... This is why I did not render it in my accounts':[1] a slim suppression which was later to recoil upon the unhappy agent. What happened if one did go through the proper motions with the authorities was illustrated just then in another case upon the Stainville lands. On 20 August 1741 the inhabitants of watery Demange, liable to have suffered particularly in the floods of the preceding winter, petitioned La Galaizière for permission to canalize the Ornain there, involving the use of some crown land – the marquis had already agreed for his part; it was not till 4 December following that the administration appointed an engineer to investigate the project on the spot, nor till 26 February 1742 that, upon his report, La Galaizière in person finally sanctioned it,[2] after all the wetness of another winter.

If the Count de Stainville in his French orientation was already moving into the affairs of the family estate, his father in his Austrian affiliation was making a formal return to diplomacy. On 5 August 1741 the elder Stainville was appointed to represent Tuscany in Paris, not indeed at his former elevation of minister plenipotentiary but, in keeping with those dark times, in the less conspicuous role of minister acting as chargé d'affaires. He was taking over from Wasner, to whom the Grand Duke Francis had temporarily entrusted his interests early that year, after the Abbé Franquini had left Paris. By August imminent French hostilities were overtaking those false French assurances to Wasner, now due to leave Paris after a last attempt at accommodation. He was preparing to remit to the Marquis de Stainville his charge not only of Tuscan affairs but also of Austrian. The surge of events was significantly widening the scope of that withdrawn diplomatist even if he no longer rated a royal audience at the French court, as he wistfully reminded his master.

[1] N. Mathieu to (?) Carré, Blainville, 30 Sept. 1752: Arch. Meuse, J 18[19].
[2] Cf. Arch. Nat. 5AP 42 (Fonds Bassompierre).

Still, on 29 August 1741, Stainville made his diplomatic reappearance at 'Versailles, where I was extremely well received by everybody and the [French] ministers seemed to me very glad'[3] to see him back. Fleury certainly was. At the same time the son and heir of the Marquis de Stainville was marching out for France in the cause of the grand duke's rival for the imperial throne.

The Régiment du Roi was now ranged at the centre of the French strategic outlay. Among the chief results secured by the Marshal de Belle-Isle during his visit to Versailles in July had been the decision to intervene in Germany not with one army but with two, the Army of Bavaria and the Army of Westphalia, each some 40,000 strong.

The Army of Westphalia was commanded by the Marshal de Maillebois. This descendant of the famous Colbert had, somewhat to the chagrin of Belle-Isle, lately distinguished himself in the Corsican campaign. Maillebois was a real fighting soldier and, in contrast to Belle-Isle, 'a bad politician, a hard and sullen courtier, a great hunter, an excellent father to his family'.[4] Such was the undiplomatic commander of an army whose primary purpose was political. For the Army of Westphalia was ingeniously designed as a menacing power-potential of multiple effect. It was in contemporary parlance an army of observation intended at once to sustain and overawe the vacillating electors of the Rhineland who, in the event, contributed 10,000 auxiliary troops; to stand over against the Austrian Netherlands while imposing respect upon the Dutch on the one hand and the Saxons on the other; and, above all, to bring direct aid to Prussia by holding Hanover in check.

This last was a desirable precaution. On 24 June 1741 George II had concluded with Austria three complementary agreements, one in his capacity of King of England and two as Elector of Hanover. George II thereby undertook to pay Maria Theresa the subsidy of £300,000 lately voted by the British parliament and to intervene against Prussia with an army of 25,000 men not later than 22 July. But his broader aim, to revive against France a great coalition like that of the War of the Spanish Succession, melted away almost before it had materialized. Russia remained remote, Denmark and Hesse began to raise difficulties, the black news from Carthagena had a discouraging effect and still more so that of the military concert between France, Prussia, and Bavaria with her Spanish support: a combination subsequently joined, as noticed, even by Saxony, to

---

[3] Marquis de Stainville to Grand Duke Francis II, Paris, 31 Aug. 1741: Esteri del Granducato di Toscana, vol. 2295/1286, fo. 58.

[4] D'Argenson, iv. 210. The Marquis d'Argenson had particular knowledge of the Marshal de Maillebois, especially under the last head since d'Argenson's daughter married Maillebois's son.

whom George II had also been looking. On 22 July 1741 the King of England, instead of marching out for Maria Theresa, announced his refusal to ratify the two agreements which, a month before, he had concluded as Elector of Hanover. This important consequence of the Marshal de Belle-Isle's diplomatic activity was clinched by the military pressure of the Marshal de Maillebois.

At the end of August 1741 the massive Army of Westphalia moved out from Sedan and Givet, and was by mid-September ranged along the lower Rhine. George II was thrown into alarm for his precious Hanover, threatened now by a Franco-Prussian pincer. Not only, therefore, did he contract with France as to his neutrality (Declaration of Neustadt, 12 October 1741) but he personally promised the Elector of Bavaria to support his imperial candidacy. Well might Belle-Isle crow: 'Hanover is out flat (*ventre à terre*).'[5]

Maillebois's army of observation could snug into winter-quarters after having so swiftly achieved its objective without firing a shot, all in the best eighteenth-century style. This signal success went a good way towards confirming the correctness of a remark which Frederick the Great's lieutenant, the old Prince of Anhalt-Dessau, had earlier made to the French ambassador in Berlin: 'Believe me that an army of 30,000 to 40,000 men, in position to enter into Germany in the quarter of Berg and Jülich, will do more to be in condition to uphold the credit of France among most of the princes of Germany than all the promenades which the Marshal de Belle-Isle will take.'[6] The promenades were to be taken by Belle-Isle's Army of Bavaria, and they were to be long.

On 15 August 1741 advance elements of the Army of Bavaria, concentrated between Strasburg and Landau, began to move out eastward across the Rhine upon newly constructed pontoons. France, impelled by Belle-Isle, had entered upon her unjust and ambitious war.

[5] Marshal de Belle-Isle to Séchelles, Frankfurt am Main: Sautai/Débuts, i. 306.
[6] Marquis de Valory to Amelot de Chaillou, Berlin, 28 Mar. 1741: Sautai/Préliminaires, p. 344, n. 1.

CHAPTER II

PRAGUE

I

THE Marshal de Belle-Isle, diplomatically retained in Frankfurt, had to delegate the immediate command of the Army of Bavaria to the seventytwo-year-old Marquis de Leuville. This correctly senior general with a fine command of Caesar's Commentaries confessed, a little late perhaps, that he 'was as fond of obeying as of commanding'.[1] This, however, rather suited his technical position as the military subordinate of the Elector of Bavaria, seeing that the French force ranked as an auxiliary corps. The French troops, as they marched yet again on to German soil, wore in their hats blue and white ribbons in the Bavarian colours.

Roi-Infanterie did not figure among the twenty-five battalions of the infantry now advancing together with fifty-four squadrons of cavalry under Leuville's personal command. For the French Army of Bavaria was divided into two corps and the Count de Stainville's regiment was reserved in the second for the central thrust in Belle-Isle's spacious strategy.

Belle-Isle's prime objective was Prague. He reckoned that a thrust right through to the heart of Central Europe would effectively link up with the Saxons and with the Prussians in Silesia, would impose upon the enemy a central menace between the Austrian homeland and outlying Silesia, and – an important consideration with so political a commander – would ensure the coronation of the Elector Charles Albert as King of Bohemia and clinch that neutralization of the traditionally Habsburg vote of Bohemia which was one of Belle-Isle's chief objectives in his intricate manoeuvring for the imperial election. At Nymphenburg he had won the elector round from his original preference for going for the still greater prize of Vienna and so, as Frederick the Great urged upon Charles Albert, cutting 'the root of the Austrian Tree':[2] a master-stroke also nicely calculated to draw the army of Neipperg, back in military circulation, down from

[1] Séchelles to Marshal de Belle-Isle, Munich, 4 Sept. 1741: Arch. Guerre C., vol. 2916: Sautai/Débuts, i. 263.
[2] Memorandum by King Frederick II, 'Raisons qui doivent engager l'électeur de Bavière d'agir le plus tôt possible en Autriche', enclosed in King Frederick II to the Elector Charles Albert, Strehlen, 30 June 1741: *Politische Correspondenz*, i. 267.

Silesia and to abandon that province to Prussian rapacity. Belle-Isle, however, considered so great an enterprise too risky in that comparatively late season.

This strategic tug of opinion was to some extent reflected in the plan now pursued. On 31 July 1741 the long and heavy hostilities which were to range across Western Europe in the War of the Austrian Succession were opened by the seizure of the independent bishopric of Passau by Bavarian forces. In their wake Leuville's first contingent came boating down the Danube and easily overran Upper Austria. On 14 September they entered her capital at Linz, where the Bavarian Elector held high court, nourished by eighty cooks, and received the homage of the Upper Austrian Estates. The local Austrian nobility rallied to him to an extent indicative not merely of their selfish subservience but also perhaps, more deeply, of the extent to which national feeling still lagged politically in German lands. Strategically, meanwhile, the occupation of Upper Austria provided not only a buffer for Bavaria but also a diversion from Bohemia and Silesia. From Linz, however, the electoral army advanced not northwards down to Moldau to swell the planned assault on Prague, but eastwards down the Danube, against Vienna after all.

Charles Albert, exhilarated by his walk-over, had been swayed back by a special emissary from the King of Prussia in the person of Field-Marshal Baron von Schmettau, last noticed as the Austrian commander in Belgrade at loggerheads with Neipperg. Schmettau, an expert in both fortification and peculation, was of Silesian origin. Though transfers of allegiance were apt to be liberally regarded in that cosmopolitan age, Schmettau's defection to Prussian service ranked as treachery. This Austrian renegade now assured Austria's enemies that Vienna would fall within a fortnight. They had wasted precious time at Linz but resumed their advance on 4 October 1741. The light covering forces of Count Palffy fell back before the French and Bavarian invaders. On 21 October they camped in strength at Saint Polten whence French cavalry went probing out to within four leagues of Vienna.

This onset against the capital of the Habsburgs had thrown it into initial confusion. In the narrow streets the traffic jammed, what with wagons laden with stones and earth to patch up the inadequate defences, incoming streams of refugees seeking shelter behind them and contrary streams of timid citizens with their belongings heading eastward again towards Pressburg where Maria Theresa and her government were already established. However, the commandant of Vienna, Field-Marshal Count Khevenhüller, got thousands toiling on the fortifications night and day, drilled the students to arms, and

before long scratched up a reasonable semblance of defensive order.
He rejected a summons from the Elector of Bavaria to surrender.

So early as 28 September 1741 the Marquis de Stainville had been
writing from Paris: 'We are threatened in the heart of our states and
they are preparing to sustain the siege of Vienna, which I do not
think will be made. They are assembling [Austrian] troops in
sufficiently considerable force to prevent entry into Bohemia, and the
justice of our cause is so authentic that one must hope that if we are
abandoned by men, heaven will protect us.'[3]

Whether or not by heavenly intervention, the Army of Bavaria
stayed put at Saint Polten. As Belle-Isle had foreseen, its autumnal
excursion to the outskirts of Vienna proved a flimsy venture. Not
only might Charles Albert's extended lines of communication be cut
but he faced the almost equally depressing possibility that Saxony
and Prussia might grab all the takings in Bohemia if their Bavarian
ally was not on the spot. The Elector of Bavaria, having frittered
away a month, decided to retreat and revert to the original plan of
striking into Bohemia. The Marshal de Belle-Isle commented: 'For
two months the Elector has done nothing but float from one opinion
to the other, and has never acted consequently for two days on
end . . . He has sinned against all the true principles, and has
adopted false ones.'[4]

Scarcely, indeed, had the elector arrived at Saint Polten before
elements of his army had, during the last week of October, begun a
turning movement northward from the Danube through the
highland forests in the general direction Budweis–Wesely–Tabor, in
the direction of the second corps of the French Army of Bavaria.

When in mid-August 1741 the Marquis de Leuville had led his
first contingent out from Alsace, he had left the second corps forming
under the efficient Marquis de Gassion. From this force a contingent
under Lieutenant-General de Polastron, a superior commander, was
detached in order to concentrate on the Danube in the rear of the
elector's forces. Simultaneously, on 23 September 1741, Gassion's
main body of fourteen battalions and thirty-two squadrons headed
out from Spires. It was the last and central thrust in the great French
advance into Germany.

The Marquis de Gassion himself commanded the first division of

---

[3] Marquis de Stainville to Baron de Richecourt, Paris, 28 Sept. 1741: Ö.S./H.H.S.,
Lothringisches Hausarchiv 189/III 126, fo. 242.

[4] Marshal de Belle-Isle to Marquis de Breteuil, Frankfurt am Main, 21 Oct. 1741: *Campagne
de Messieurs les Maréchaux de Broglie et de Belle-Isle en Bohème et en Bavière* [ed. P.F. Du
Moulin] (Amsterdam, 1772–3: printed as vols. ii–ix to vol. i, *Campagne de Monsieur le Maréchal
de Maillebois en Westphalie l'an MDCCXLI & II*: henceforth cited as *Campagne*), ii. 90–1.

his force of three. The second division marched out under Lieutenant-General Count de Clermont-Tonnerre, the third under Lieutenant-General du Chayla. The most important infantry of this third formation was the Régiment du Roi whose colonel, the Duke de Biron, served as *maréchal-de-camp* to du Chayla. – *Maréchal-de-camp*, not to be confused with the exalted rank of marshal, was approximately equivalent to the modern major-general. The rank was a relic from that older hierarchy, *maréchal-de-camp, mestre-de-camp, aide-de-camp*, of which only the last has survived.

Louis-Antoine de Gontaut, now Duke de Biron, had distinguished himself in the Italian campaign of the War of the Polish Succession, at those battles of Parma and Guastalla which the Roi had added to its long honours. Biron's other gallantry had contributed to a story[5] of a double mock-marriage wherein he had been ceremonially put to bed with the lively Countess de Rottembourg, also to that gossip involving the Marquise de Ruffec which had caught the attention of the mother of the Count de Stainville. Now he was setting out under a colonel yet to be described as 'noble in character, in birth and in mien'.[6]

The blue and white Bavarian ribbons matched the elegant uniforms of Roi-Infanterie. These, as was usual in the French infantry, were white, in this case faced with royal blue, with blue and white lanyards. The regimental standards flew a white cross studded with golden fleurs-de-lis, quartering two quarters flame-red, symbolic of the Roi Soleil, and two pale green, the old colour of the parent regiment of Lorraine. Such was the regimental aspect of Roi-Infanterie marching out for Bohemia.

Eastwards from Spires they advanced with exemplary discipline through an exceptionally fine autumn. By the middle of October Gassion's corps entered Amberg in the Upper Palatinate of Bavaria. The French left at Amberg was some two hundred miles distant from the right at Saint Polten. It was necessary to get ahead without delay.

In the Upper Palatinate General de Gassion joined forces with Bavarian troops under General von Minutzi. These latter now formed the advance-guard and on 21 October 1741 crossed the border into Bohemia. Six days later the Régiment du Roi, as part of the rearguard under du Chayla, left Amberg and by 6 November the whole army-corps was concentrated at Pilsen, occupied without opposition. On the same day forward elements of Charles Albert's force under the command of Törring entered Wesely from Budweis.

[5] Cf. D'Argenson, ii. 201.
[6] Duc de Lévis, *Souvenirs et portraits, 1780–1789* (Paris, 1813), p. 48.

The military outcome of this great convergence into Bohemia from west and south was, however, now imperilled by the issue of remarkable events in the field of diplomacy.

II

The position in which Maria Theresa had found herself in the summer of 1741 seemed desperate. She fell back upon her innate courage and resolve to fight for her rights, also upon diplomatic attempts to disrupt the great coalition which had come looming up against her. The Austrian government tried to bribe and detach each member separately. In July and August Bavaria was sounded out by roundabout channels, through the Jewish banker Wolf Werthheimber and the widow of Joseph I, the former Empress Amalie, who occupied a mediate position as the mother-in-law of Charles Albert and aunt of Maria Theresa: on 26 August the two ladies had a curious and unproductive meeting. Having failed to detach Bavaria, Austrian efforts were mainly concentrated upon France, again through two separate channels. The first lay through Wasner, previously practised in secret negotiation in connection with the Third Treaty of Vienna and at that time still tarrying in Paris before handing over to the Marquis de Stainville. Already on 24 August 1741 Wasner was authorized to tempt Fleury with that cession of Luxemburg which Choiseul regretfully emphasized in his survey. Shortly afterwards a second, parallel Austro-French contact was promoted at Frankfurt through the intermediary of Maria Theresa's secretary, Ignaz von Koch, and of the Count of Wied, another veteran from the secret soundings at the close of the War of the Polish Succession. In the event France remained faithful to her new alliances, as Fleury himself indicated in a letter of 15 October 1741 to Maria Theresa. But before the Austrian initiatives towards France had petered out Frederick the Great got wind of them, or something like them. And that king tended to judge the loyalty of his allies by his own. On 17 September he directed that Chambrier, his minister in Paris, should keep a specially sharp eye on 'the intrigues of Wasner and of Stainville'.[7]

Austrian diplomacy, having in fact drawn blank with both Bavaria and France, was once more concentrated upon their shifty Prussian partner. Here at last it was better going. A private letter of 23 September from Vienna was already assuring the Marquis de

[7] Minute by King Frederick II to Count Podewils, Neisse, 17 Sept. 1741: *Politische Correspondenz*, i. 339.

Stainville, prematurely as he suspected, that peace was made between Austria and Prussia. It was on 9 October 1741, in the castle of the Starhembergs in Silesia, that there was concluded the most secret, most notorious Austro-Prussian Convention of Kleinschnellendorf. Frederick's betrayal of his allies was to be masked by the typically eighteenth-century device of a sham siege of Neisse for the stipulated period of fifteen days at the end of which the Austrian garrison should surrender to the Prussians (article 2 of the Convention of Kleinschnellendorf). A definitive peace-treaty was foreseen for the end of December, when Austria would buy off Prussia with Lower Silesia together with Neisse. This compact was concluded in the presence of four persons only, King Frederick, Field-Marshal Neipperg and his favourite aide, the German-Swiss Major-General Lentulus (his family claimed descent from the Roman Scipios), plus Lord Hyndford, British minister to Prussia. This intermediary alone signed the instrument in the interests of both parties since the Prussian king refused to affix his signature. Another of his artful devices was to insist upon a particular stipulation (article 18) as to the inviolable secrecy of this hidden agreement.

On the same day that Frederick concluded the Convention of Kleinschnellendorf with Neipperg he wrote to Belle-Isle that he had just dispatched full powers to the Prussian envoy to sign the treaty whereby Prussia adhered to the Bavaro-Saxon partition of the Austrian domains: 'It was reserved for Louis XV to be the arbiter of kings, and to M. de Belle-Isle to be the organ of his power and of his wisdom. I am with all the esteem and friendship imaginable, my dear marshal, your very faithful friend Frederick. [P.S.] M. de Valory will inform you of our operations. I still have the enemy before me, and 6,000 hussars behind.'[8]

Frederick the Great later sought to justify his repellent treachery towards France by adducing her contacts with Austria: 'Let us add, for the greater justification of the King [of Prussia], that he had discovered the secret connections which the Cardinal de Fleury maintained with M. de Stainville, minister of the Grand Duke of Tuscany at Vienna: he knew that the Cardinal was quite disposed to sacrifice the allies of France, if the court of Vienna offered him Luxemburg and a part of Brabant.'[9] Frederick was wrong as to Fleury's disposition just then but so too was the cardinal's old friend whom Frederick had sniffed out. Five days after Fleury's negative communication to Maria Theresa, Stainville advised that her husband 'could have a negotiation broached with the Cardinal who,

[8] King Frederick II to Marshal de Belle-Isle, Friedland, 9 Oct. 1741: ibid., i. 374.
[9] Frederick, ii. 94.

I believe, would be charmed to make a general arrangement. In short I dare to beg you to get the Queen to make up her mind.'[10] (Stainville recalled his advice from that uncomfortable lazaret in Verona.)[11] For those not in the know nothing is more agreeable than to urge greater activity upon those who are and who are as likely as not already doing their restricted best.

A week later the Marquis de Stainville suggested in a flimsy follow-up that if Prince Charles of Lorraine were now being sent to assume 'his government of Flanders it would be appropriate to have him pass incognito through here, where in four days he would advance matters further than others would in a year.'[12] Four days later King Frederick had the acumen, and the effrontery, to tell Valory that it was desirable 'for our common interest that the [French] resolve be taken to dismiss Messrs. Wasner and Stainville, in order to deprive the court of Vienna of all hope of ever succeeding in its artifices.'[13]

Wasner had in fact recently restrained Stainville from his inclination to upbraid Fleury 'for his injustice'[14] over an artfully apocryphal Franco–Bavaro–Spanish Treaty of Nymphenburg of 18–22 May 1741,[15] long credited in some confusion with the veritable Bavaro–Spanish treaty of 28 May. Whereas the marquis, ignorant as he may have been of the extent of Wasner's soundings, described them truly enough as 'useless remonstrances'[16] to the French government. All in all, in relation to Kleinschnellendorf, Frederick was on stronger ground in admitting: 'This matter is delicate; the proceeding of the King of Prussia was scabrous.'[17]

In the insincere Convention of Kleinschnellendorf the one object which both the Prussian and the Austrian negotiators had at heart and were genuinely agreed upon was that expressed in article 9: 'That, on the 16th of this current month, the said Marshal Count de Neipperg shall withdraw with all his army, towards Moravia, and thence whither he will.'[18] Frederick wanted Neipperg's army

---

[10] Marquis de Stainville to Grand Duke Francis II, Paris, 20 Oct. 1741 : Esteri del Granducato di Toscana, vol. 2295/1286, fo. 65.

[11] Cf. p. 206 above.

[12] Marquis de Stainville to Grand Duke Francis II, Paris, 27 Oct. 1741 : u.s., fo. 70.

[13] King Frederick II to Marquis de Valory, Neunz, 31 Oct. 1741 : Politische Correspondenz, i. 395.

[14] Marquis de Stainville to Grand Duke Francis II, Paris, 20 Oct. 1741 : u.s., fo. 64.

[15] A text of this alleged Treaty of Nymphenburg was printed as being genuine by the Austro-Hungarian general staff in the generally scholarly Erbfolge-Krieg, iv. 29–33. The authenticity of this treaty was however rejected in Sautai/Préliminaires, pp. 558–60, citing a specific disclaimer of late October 1741 by the Marshal de Belle-Isle to the French foreign minister.

[16] Marquis de Stainville to Grand Duke Francis II, Paris, 19 Oct. 1741 : u.s., fo. 63.

[17] Frederick, ii. 93.

[18] Convention of Kleinschnellendorf of 9 Oct. 1741, article 9 : Count de Garden, Histoire générale des traités de paix (Paris, n.d.), iii. 263.

withdrawn from Silesia so that he might get Neisse cheap and clamp down Prussian supremacy, while Maria Theresa wanted to switch that army against those western invaders who threatened the citadels of her rule in Vienna and in Prague. This prospect after Kleinschnellendorf caused the Marquis de Stainville to rejoice: 'Perhaps the Bavarian and French allies will not be so much at their ease as they were hoping.'[19] Meantime Frederick remained with a foot in either camp. As the days passed it became increasingly probable that he would step down on the side of whoever held Prague.

III

On the stipulated day, 16 October 1741, Neipperg began his march from the eastern river Neisse towards the Franco–Bavarian spearhead at Saint Polten. Despite imperative instructions to make all speed, Neipperg adhered to the leisurely tradition of Austrian generalship, jogging down by way of Olmütz and Eibenschitz so that it was not till 7 November that he effected his junction at Znaim with the army which had been marching up from Pressburg under the personal command of the Grand Duke Francis of Tuscany.

At Pressburg the unpopular Francis had been forced to watch as a private individual the coronation of Maria Theresa with the crown of Saint Stephen as Queen of Hungary on 25 June 1741. 'The antiquated crown received new graces from her head',[20] reported the British minister, and in traditional conclusion the young girl upon a black charger brandished the sword of state to the four quarters of the globe in apt typification of her aggressive Magyars. Now the Magyar and Slavonic levies commanded by her husband were the tangible result of her patriotic triumph in seeking the special protection of the turbulent Hungarian estates for herself and her six-month son Joseph. – At last she had achieved her prince, who looked to a Hungarian observer 'like a little squirrel'.[21] – Famous in European history is the scene at Pressburg on 11 September 1741 when, in response to Maria Theresa's tearful appeal, the chivalry of Hungary thundered out their pledge, *Vitam nostram et sanguinem consecramus*, we dedicate our life and blood.

The passionate vow reverberated across Europe with a moral impact greater in some ways than in Hungary itself. The same

---

[19] Marquis de Stainville to Baron de Richecourt, Paris, 10 Nov. 1741: Ö.S./H.H.S., Lothringisches Hausarchiv 189/III 126, fo. 237.
[20] Robinson to Lord Harrington, 28 June 1741: W. Coxe, *History of the House of Austria*, ii. 263.
[21] Kolinovics, *Nova Ungariae Periodus*, p. 530: cited, Arneth, i. 305.

meeting of the Hungarian estates had clamoured to see their queen's German ministers strung up. Difficulty and delay clogged the raising of the necessary contingents, often largely undisciplined. However, a Hungarian force was scraped together for the Grand Duke Francis who had on 21 September at last been accepted as co-regent of Hungary: perhaps the greatest proof of Maria Theresa's triumph. Francis cherished the honourable if unlucky belief that it behoved a prince to lead his subjects out to war as the King of Prussia and the Elector of Bavaria were doing. For Francis the opportunity to redeem his military reputation from the Turkish campaigns was at hand.

At Znaim the grand duke assumed supreme command of the Austrian army combined in a fourfold junction of forces from Silesia, Hungary, Austria, and from Bohemia itself elements under Field-Marshal Prince Lobkowitz, in all some forty thousand men. Against them the Elector of Bavaria, seventy-five miles to the west at Budweis, could muster but thirteen to eighteen thousand, even reckoning in his rearguard under Leuville, then only crossing the Danube northwards to Budweis. Whereas Charles Albert had had to detach a French force under the Count de Ségur, injured by a fall from a horse, in order to secure his lines of communication to Linz and his hold upon Upper Austria.

The elector sent orders to Gassion, then marching on from Pilsen against Prague, to deflect south with all speed, putting his infantry on to wheeled transport, so as to join him at Budweis, a strategic middle-point on the axis Linz–Prague. No bad plan in itself, it stretched the Franco–Bavarian tug of opinion almost to breaking-point. Gassion deliberated these orders, received on 10 November 1741, in camp at Zebrak, in council of war with Lieutenant-Generals de Clermont-Tonnerre and de Polastron, the latter joined up from the Danube. They decided to adhere to the French directive to drive for Prague. The rugged terrain prohibited a quick switch by carts to Budweis and, explained Clermont-Tonnerre, had they made that 'step backwards, the Saxons ... would have turned back ... and the Prussians, who are also within reach of Prague, would have done the same thing'.[22]

It only remained for the Elector of Bavaria to effect the junction the other way on, by pressing north. Correspondingly, the strategy for the grand duke was at soonest to interpose his large army between the two invading forces and so prevent their junction against the Bohemian capital. It was a race for Prague.

On 12 November 1741, out east from Budweis, a troop of Austrian

[22] Lieutenant-General de Clermont-Tonnerre to Marquis de Breteuil, Beraun, 13 Nov. 1741: *Campagne*, ii. 279.

hussars rode without reconnaissance into Neuhaus and suddenly encountered French advanced elements. These were pinched out. Four days later Neuhaus was entered by the Grand Duke of Tuscany, who pushed on to the plain of Kardas–Razeschitz on the road to Tabor. This sent the incompetent Marshal Törring scuttling back thence through that broken region of rock and bog which had once afforded Ziska and his Hussites their stronghold. Now Törring imposed retreat also upon Leuville, forced to abandon Budweis itself. Such was the outcome of that faulty strategy wherein the French and Bavarians had got themselves into the position of having their lines of communication with Linz running across the front against the enemy instead of up to it. An Austrian corps mopped up Budweis, Protiwin, Pisek. They captured large supplies and cut off some enemy rearguards who had to retreat south on to the Count de Ségur in Upper Austria. Franco–Bavarian communications thither were severed.

The main Franco–Bavarian retreat, however, was at least northwards, joining in the race for Prague. It rolled forward up the left bank of the Moldau while the Austrians pressed on in parallel march up the right bank. That at least is what the Austrians were expected to do. Only, the Grand Duke Francis found the plain of Kardas–Razeschitz abounding in game and, keen huntsman that he was, saw no harm in knocking off for four days while his troops rested out. Not until 23 November did he enter Tabor, where he spent another day. Thence at last Francis sent on a flying column under Lieutenant-Fieldmarshal Count Kolowrat to drive ahead to Prague and reinforce the garrison. Up there, though, events had been moving.

While the Grand Duke of Tuscany was out hunting, the Elector of Bavaria, on 19 November 1741 in the area Königsaal-Horselitz, had effected his junction with Gassion. The former Army of Bavaria was reunited into the Army of Bohemia. Among the first elements of the Elector's force to establish contact with Gassion's was the cavalry under Count Maurice de Saxe. This fortyfive-year-old lieutenant-general in the French army was the illegitimate brother of King Augustus III of Saxony, being an early product of the expansive amours of Augustus the Strong, his child by the lovely Aurora Königsmark, and his favourite son. The Count de Saxe was now in for quite a family reunion. Next day, 20 November, outposts of Gassion's corps further established contact with advance-guards of the Saxon army, some 20,000 strong, which had come bearing down on Prague from Pirna: and the Saxons were commanded by Count von Rutowski, a younger half-brother of the Count de Saxe by the fair Fatima, a Turkish slave; the Saxon cavalry was under a third

brother, the Chevalier de Saxe, and yet another was also serving. On
23 November, on the day that the Grand Duke of Tuscany entered
Tabor, the Elector of Bavaria at the head of his enlarged army pitched
his tents upon the White Mountain over against the battlements of
Prague.

Prague was become the focus of European tension and was felt to
be so by watchers in far-distant capitals. On that same day, 23
November, the Marquis d'Argenson in Paris noted in his diary:

Yesterday I saw the two ministers of the Queen of Hungary, MM. de Stainville and
Wassenaer [sic]: they said that a battle would decide the affair wherein they [the
Austrians] are, that they are resolved to deliver it and to stake all for all ... The
general rendezvous is at Prague ... Our M. de Belle-Isle has left Frankfurt to go to
place himself at the head of our army, and so we shall see if the great speculation has
suddenly passed into practice, and if his ability in action is equal to his high
reputation so well rewarded in advance.[23]

The Marshal de Belle-Isle, at last exchanging diplomacy for war,
set out from Frankfurt to Prague by way of Dresden on 12 November
1741. But he was not destined yet awhile to satisfy d'Argenson's
critical curiosity. His labours of the past year brought him down with
sciatica, which the journey worsened. On arrival at the Saxon court
Belle-Isle was greeted by Valory, come from Prussia, in pained
surprise. He beheld a cripple disfigured also by an inflammation of
the eye. Next day the stricken marshal was pinned to his bed in
tormenting inactivity just at the hazardous crux of the great campaign
which he had instigated.

On 24 November the Chevalier de Belle-Isle, sent as harbinger to
the armies before Prague, wrote back to his brother: 'The more I see
of the state of things, the more I am confirmed as to the indispensable
necessity that there is of your presence to prevent the most terrible
disasters and catastrophes.'[24] The marshal replied that dark November: 'Your letter crowns my despair ...'[25]

One French officer before Prague dryly observed: 'We need ... a
general for this task, and we have none although the Elector is here
in person'[26] – he had incidentally left behind in Bavaria the engineer
whom Belle-Isle had got to draw up detailed plans of Prague. The
senior French commander, Leuville, was still only plodding up from
Budweis as the whole Austrian army approached Prague, hastening

[23] D'Argenson, iii. 425.
[24] Chevalier de Belle-Isle to Marshal de Belle-Isle, camp before Prague, 24 Nov. 1741: Arch.
Guerre: Broglie/Fréd-MT, ii. 127–8.
[25] Marshal de Belle-Isle to Chevalier de Belle-Isle, Nov. 1741: ibid., ii. 128–9. (Broglie's
dating of this letter as 2 Nov. 1741 is evidently a misprint.)
[26] De Thiers to Marquis de Breteuil, camp before Prague, 22 Nov. 1741: Arch. Guerre C.,
vol. 2919, no. 109.

at last to get to grips with the invaders from the west. The French
and their allies were out on a limb, their Prussian associate fallen
away to the east, their southern communications cut, standing way
out in hostile territory before a great fortified city while they were
quite without siege-artillery. (This item was to be supplied by the
Saxons but had got stuck at Budin for want of horses.) In any case,
though, there was no time to mount a full-scale siege before the grand
duke's army would be upon them. With Prague uncaptured, the
bleak alternatives were an ignominious retreat or the risk of being
pinched out between the onset of the main Austrian army and a
sortie by the garrison of Prague. And the inclement season was at
hand. The continental cold of Central Europe was already clamping
down in rigour. Winter was upon them. There was no time left.
Belle-Isle did not exaggerate in writing feverishly from his sickbed in
Dresden: 'The days and the hours are precious.'[27]

IV

On 24 November 1741 the commandant of Prague, the Jacobite
Count Ogilvy, rejected a summons to surrender. The garrison had
been depleted to reinforce Lobkowitz, so that Ogilvy was in command
of barely 2,500 men, backed, however, by civic militia and volunteers.
The fortifications of Prague were by no means modern and the
surrounding moat was dry. Nevertheless the bastioned ramparts
formed a continuous circuit some thirty foot high and in good enough
repair: a discouraging prospect for an army without siege artillery or
tackle.

At a glum council of war in the elector's camp the Saxon
commander, Count von Rutowski, now headed those who, like
Schmettau, urged that the prompt capture of Prague by hook or by
crook was imperative; that in their predicament they should cut out
the whole apparatus of an eighteenth-century siege, the saps, parallels,
bombardment, and breaching, should go all out for a surprise scaling
attack to carry the city by steel and by storm. To most of the French
generals this seemed a crack-brained project, flouting the classic
teaching of Vauban. One of them was the Count de Stainville's old
acquaintance from Vienna, the Marquis de Mirepoix, who wrote:
'This means [of escalade], little in use with us, was contested by the
soundest and largest part of our general officers, but the Count de
Rutofsky ... settled the uncertainties of the Elector by having him
informed, on the 24th, that he would attack alone with the troops of

[27] Marshal de Belle-Isle to Marquis de Breteuil, Dresden, 22 Nov. 1741: *Campagne*, ii. 307.

the King his Master, even if, on our side, we lent him no assistance.'[28]
The French were constrained to agree to put in a feint attack in
support of an exploit which might in truth seem to belong rather to
medieval deeds of derring-do than to the formalized warfare of the
age of reason. (A recent Prussian precedent in storming Glogau
against the unlucky Wallis was hardly to be counted.) However, the
French generals included Count Maurice de Saxe, not one to rest
content with putting in a feint or two in tame support of his younger
brothers in their enterprise of hazard and of valour.

The moonlit night of 25–6 November 1741 was bitterly cold for the
allied army camped around many-spired Prague, or, more exactly,
round the Hradcin citadel and the Little Town on the left, west bank
of the Moldau. The Régiment du Roi wherein young Stainville
served was posted over against the citadel close in to the walls, behind
a disused, trenched camp which came in very useful. During the day
of 25 November the French had been ostentatiously digging in on
that sector.

Now, at about one o'clock[29] on the morning of 26 November,
Lieutenant-Colonel de La Serre, commanding a battalion of Roi-
Infanterie, fired a shot into the cold air. The report rang out as a
signal. Instantly the French forces all along the line were loosing off
at the ramparts everything they had, not indeed that that was very
big guns. The small-arms fire was intense, but they had only been
able to mock up 'a battery of six little pieces of cannon, three or four-
pounders, not having any [heavy guns] for making a siege'.[30] The
French gunners, however, kept their light field-pieces firing at the
quick, stabbing into the darkness with nearly eight hundred rounds
of shot.[31] The French infantry feinted as though to attack, keeping
the garrison of Prague upon the stretch. The defenders replied in
kind, with gathering vigour, to the cannonade.

After some time, away to the left of the French feint under Gassion

[28] Marquis de Mirepoix, 'Détail de la Prise de Prague, dressé par Mr. de Mirepoix': op. cit.,
iii. 18.
[29] The exact time varies in different accounts, not surprisingly with regard to a night-
operation of this kind. In one version (dated at Prague, 27 Nov. 1741: Arch. Guerre C., vol. 2919,
no. 171) that attack was said to have begun at 12.30 a.m., but the writer was not personally
present and was most probably mistaken. Another account states that La Serre only fired his
opening shot 'at half past one' (Arch. Guerre C., vol. 2920, no. 17). The attack was, however,
timed to begin at one o'clock (cf. Count von Rutowski to King Augustus III: cited, Comte Pajol,
Les Guerres sous Lous XV – Paris, 1881f.: henceforth cited as Pajol – ii. 112) and the consensus
of evidence indicates that it did begin then or soon after. Thus according to the Marquis de
Mirepoix, engaged upon another sector, the gunfire of this attack became audible 'between one
o'clock and half past one' (Campagne, iii. 20).
[30] Count of Bavaria, probably to de Vassé, Prague, 26 Nov. 1741: Arch. Guerre C., vol. 2919,
no. 156.
[31] Campagne, ii. 330; according to one participant, the Count of Bavaria (cf. preceding note),
legitimized brother of the Elector and a French lieutenant-general, they discharged over 1,000
rounds.

and Polastron, further guns came blazing into action. This was the Saxons opening up with their field-artillery on the admired Swedish model as introduced by Charles XII. These quick-firers gave an impressive display, each gun discharging 'nine to ten shots a minute'.[32] After this initial softening-up, at four in the morning, the Saxons went into their main attack with twenty scaling-ladders. Up went the ladders, down came the climbers. For the French feint had not deceived Ogilvy and his garrison as to where the brunt was likely to fall. The defenders were ready, the attackers repulsed. The Saxons rallied and came swarming up again. Furious and stubborn in-fighting raged along the walls in darkness.

Meanwhile a second Saxon attack over by the islands of the Moldau towards the New Town had also run into difficulties. Other events, however, had, in the course of that active night, been afoot on the eastern bank of the Moldau. After nightfall Count Maurice de Saxe, in command of a picked body of French cavalry and infantry, had begun a circuitous march from the village of Kundratitz, having that morning crossed the Moldau down by Königsaal. He was just across when he had received intelligence that the Austrian vanguard of 14,000 men was approaching by forced marches with the intention of entering Prague upon the morrow, the 26th. Such was the urgency of the allied assault, in support of which Saxe was now to mount a further diversion, this time against the New Town on the eastern bank. The race for Prague was coming in to a close finish.

Saxe's force arrived by stealth under the town-walls at about three o'clock on the morning of the 26th. The noise of their arrival was probably blanketed by that of the cannonading on the western bank, booming across the river. Saxe himself went ahead to reconnoitre together with Lieutenant-Colonel de Chevert, an expert officer who had drilled his regiment, Beauce, into a model, and who was now in command of the pick of Saxe's infantry, the leading grenadiers. (French regiments included élite companies of grenadiers, though grenades were no longer their primary weapon.) In preparation for its circular sweep upon Prague Saxe's force had gathered up all the local ladders, ropes, and axes on which it could lay hands. Now it was found that only two of the ladders would measure up to the lofty battlements of Prague. Those two were quietly placed in position. For Saxe intended a rather active kind of diversion.

The French grenadiers went scaling up 'with their usual ease'.[33]

[32] 'Relation de la prise de Prague', Prague, 27 Nov. 1741: Arch. Guerre C., vol. 2919, no. 171.
[33] Marquis de Mirepoix, 'Détail de la Prise de Prague, dressé par Mr. de Mirepoix': *Campagne*, iii. 21. Mirepoix, who was in command of Saxe's reserve, gives, in his official report, what is on the whole the most circumstantial and consecutive account of this phase of the operation. His account is to be compared with that of Saxe himself (Count de Saxe to Chevalier

Some ten of them, including Chevert himself, had gained the battlements when their main ladder broke beneath the weight of too many climbers. The Austrian sentries raised the alarm. As the defenders opened fire from the bastions, Chevert's grenadiers on the parapet, ordered to stab not shoot, flung themselves face downwards while Maurice de Saxe, down in the ditch below, shouted 'To me, dragoons!' His dismounted dragoons started blazing away and thus, at this critical moment, diverted the confused enemy fire against themselves. Meanwhile the broken ladder was hastily patched up and others that were too short were lashed together with bits of harness. More ladders smashed indeed, but the desperate escalade continued with a French drummer-boy upon the battlements drumming the attack.[34]

The weight and attention of the garrison as a whole had been mainly directed away to the other side of the river, and this eastern circuit of the walls was but thinly held. After a mêlée on the ramparts had secured the lodgement of Chevert's men, they pressed on down to the sandbagged postern beside the nearby New Gate. The guard there was overwhelmed, the postern hacked open. Saxe himself entered at the head of more troops on foot. The main gate was flung wide. Down went the drawbridge. A thousand French cavalry came charging across, fanning out at full gallop down the three main streets from the gate, triumphantly shouting '*Vive le roi!*' Resistance melted away before them, the civilian defenders and student volunteers of Prague dispersing discreetly into the darkness and confusion. Arrived at the bridge linking the Old Town with the Little across the Moldau, Saxe parleyed with the guard and gradually edged his way across, having sent his aide-de-camp on ahead to Ogilvy to demand his surrender and an immediate cessation of resistance against the Saxons, still hacking their way through, over by the Hradcin. Then, in Saxe's own words, 'the governor [Ogilvy] came to meet me; I extended my hand to him and peace was soon made, we being known to one another in the wars in Flanders. I betook myself to his house and, after having begged him to give me something to drink (for I was dying of thirst), I requested of him an order that the commandant of the citadel should deliver it to my

---

de Folard, 28 Nov. 1741: Pajol, ii. 113–24). The two versions differ in certain particulars, as is not surprising with regard to such confusing night-fighting, but are both consistent in their support of the narrative here given. Another, shorter account is given by the Duke de Chevreuse, a young officer serving under the Count de Saxe: Duke de Chevreuse to his father, the Duke de Luynes: Luynes, iv. 47–9.

[34] This circumstance was subsequently verified personally by Belle-Isle with a view to rewarding the drummer-boy, who came from the dragoons (Régiment de Mestre-de-Camp-Général): see Marshal de Belle-Isle to Marquis de Breteuil, 28 Dec. 1741: *Campagne*, iii. 93.

troops, which was executed on the spot. An instant afterwards the Saxons entered the town; my three brothers being come to the governor's, I said to them: "Ruffians, I shall always make you see that I am your elder."[35]

The family satisfaction was completed for Saxe by his sense of carrying on from the Thirty Years War the good old Saxon tradition of capturing Prague. The other source of pride for Saxe and other French officers was, creditably, the fact that Prague was taken with practically no pillage, a rare circumstance in a city carried by force of arms, especially by night. Saxe had ordered his dragoons to cut down any French troops caught marauding and in return the grateful magistrates of Prague presented him with a fine diamond. By eight o'clock in the morning, after that strenuous night, traffic was circulating freely in Prague and the city was almost restored to normal.

The Austrian van under Kolowrat turned back to bring to the grand duke at Beneschau the heavy tidings of the city's fall. They had been one day too late. Austria had lost the race to Prague. On 27 November the troops of Leuville and Törring made Königsaal and established contact with the main army of the allies. As Choiseul later wrote of those French operations against Prague: 'Very luckily the division of Bohemia had carried this town by assault, on the eve of the arrival of the troops chased out of Austria.'[36] One gathers that Gassion's captors of Prague, including the Count de Stainville, took a cool view of Leuville's abortive operations against Vienna.

Young Stainville is said to have been wounded during the assault on Prague, but the authority for this is doubtful and inadequate.[37] If Stainville was indeed wounded he must have been exceptionally unlucky since the French losses were astonishingly light: those in Saxe's assault were two lightly wounded and no killed. On the other hand it is conceivable that a wound or sickness might have afforded a stronger argument than Stainville's natural love of pleasure for his spending the winter of 1741-2 in Prague, as he did, instead of marching out with his regiment further east again.

Prague now struck the French as 'immense, being as large again as Lille and extremely populous'.[38] Another first impression: 'This

[35] Count de Saxe to Chevalier de Folard, 28 Nov. 1741: Pajol, ii. 123.
[36] Choiseul, Mémoires, p. 53.
[37] Kurd von Schlözer, Choiseul und seine Zeit (Berlin, 1848), p. 28. Schlözer further stated that because of his wound Stainville returned to Paris, with rather the implication that he remained there during the rest of the Bohemian campaign. This, however, is contradicted by contemporary and other early sources: cf. Marquis de Stainville's dispatch of 8 Sept. 1742 (p. 342 below); Pinard, Chronologie historique-militaire, v. 605, and corroboratively, by implication, in Essai/Arsenal 5808, fos. 21–3.
[38] Séchelles to Marquis de Breteuil, Prague, 4 Dec. 1741: Campagne, iii. 9.

town has magnificent mansions: since the peasants of Bohemia are serfs, the nobles there are extremely rich'[39] – a simple but pertinent social analysis. Against this sumptuous background, however, the stay in Prague of the Count de Stainville was grimly different from that of his father less than twenty years earlier as a participant in the Habsburg pageantry of Bohemian coronation. Another attendant then from Lorraine now also had a likely son in Prague.

Among the brother-officers, including the Marquis de Mirepoix, with whom the Count de Stainville probably consorted, was one who was to be a lifelong friend, Charles-Juste de Beauvau, fourth and within a few months eldest surviving son of the Prince and Princess de Craon. The princess was a devoted mother, worrying in distant Florence. Her son, then a young staff-officer with a fluent command of German, wrote to her from Prague that winter: 'The kind of war which we are waging this year is dangerous only from the rigour of the season, and the fatigue of the continual marches. Moreover one does not see the enemy at all and so far I am only running the risk of dying of cold . . . Moreover everybody believes that this winter will be employed in negotiations for peace, and that everything will be calm in the spring. The best advantage which I could draw from that would be to go to see you in Tuscany.'[40] Such was the international background which he largely shared with Stephen de Stainville, a year older than himself.

Beauvau's fondly rosy reassurance contrasted with the snowy reality of still more marching. Midwinter campaigning was imposed by the strategic situation after the capture of the Bohemian capital.

V

'The capture of Prague', wrote Louis XV, 'has been a decisive stroke and one which, I truly believe, we owe to the approach of Belle-Isle.'[41] The marshal himself was not behindhand in promoting this belief concerning that success which, when the news reached him, swiftly began his recovery. Throughout Europe the brilliant capture of Prague exalted French prestige. Decisive, though, it was not. It has been observed that for the French that capture settled nothing, facilitated everything. On 29 November 1741 the Marshal de Belle-Isle entered Prague.

Next day Belle-Isle 'expressed strong disapproval of the Elector's

---

[39] Chevalier d'Espagnac to Marquis de Breteuil, Prague, 29 Nov. 1741: Arch. Guerre C., vol. 2919, no. 184.
[40] Count de Beauvau to Princess de Craon, Prague, 7 Jan. 1742: Archives de Mouchy.
[41] King Louis XV to Duke de Luxembourg, Dec. 1741: Arch. Guerre C., vol. 2921, no. 12.

having let the Marshal de Törring and M. de Leuville continue their march [up from Budweis], saying that he should have countermanded them from the moment that he became master of Prague, have sent them back with all speed upon Pisek and Budweis to capture this post and forestall the enemy there, should have had them followed by the larger part of the army in order to re-establish communications with Linz.'[42]

On 3–4 December 1741 the military exploitation of the capture of Prague began with French columns fanning out in three directions. A light force of some 900 cavalry struck back west to help eliminate the threat to rearward communications from the continued Austrian hold upon Eger. This flying column was commanded by Colonel the Count d'Estrées, last encountered as the Marquis de Courtenvaux, the admirer of the Marquise de Stainville. (Some months after his visit to Demange he had found it significantly acceptable to take a rather nominal reduction in rank in order to assume the maternally inherited and socially superior appellation of d'Estrées.) The second and main French detachment of some 15,000 men under d'Aubigné was to return south against Pisek and Budweis. A third column under Polastron had assigned to it the crack regiment Roi-Infanterie and the toughest objective: to brace the Saxons, reverting from their outburst of tactical intrepidity to their strategic timidity, in a combined force of some 20,000 bearing south-eastwards down the valley of the Sazawa to Deutsch Brod, thence to hook round by Iglau so as to match up with d'Aubingé's corps in a wide pincer-movement to pinch right out of Bohemia the supposedly demoralized Austrians. Neipperg was wishfully rumoured to have gone off his head.

Maria Theresa, already pregnant again, had indeed burst into tears at Pressburg upon learning of the fall of Prague. Silesia was lost and now, it seemed, Bohemia too. In after years Maria Theresa would look back upon those black days at Pressburg as the bitterest of her life.

The equation of tears with weakness can be superficial. Maria Theresa wrote off to her headstrong confidant, Count Philip Kinsky, High Chancellor of the Kingdom of Bohemia:

Well, Kinsky, here is the time when one must have courage . . . Everything must be risked and lost to sustain Bohemia, and upon this system you can work and make your dispositions. I do not say that I may [?not] have ruined it and that in twenty years it will not recover, but I want to have ground and footing[43] and for that all my

---

[42] 'Mémoire du Mal. de Belle-Isle sur la conduite du Mal. de Broglie' (this memorandum is dated 17 Dec. 1741 but was evidently written or completed later): Arch. Guerre C., vol. 2921, no. 13.

[43] In original, 'mais je veux avoir Grund und Boden'.

armies, all the Hungarians must be killed before I shall yield a thing even ... Do not spare the country; it must be sustained ... Help my poor husband who grieves himself as much for the troops as for the country ... You will say that I am cruel; that is true, but ... at this hour I close my heart to pity. I trust in you ... I am a little cast down, and everything ... moves me much and too much for my present state. I pity the lot of you others whom I render unhappy ... but you will always have and find a grateful heart and I am, Theresa.[44]

It was the letter of a woman, and a brave one. War was settling in in long severity.

Kinsky attended the council of war which the Grand Duke of Tuscany now held at Beneschau together with Neipperg, Lobkowitz, Prince Charles of Lorraine, closest perhaps to his sister-in-law in offensive temper, and cautious General Count Daun who advised withdrawal – more or less what the French were hoping. Whereas it was decided to secure the main Austrian success so far, the severance of enemy communications with Linz by Budweis. Austrian forces began moving into cantonments along the line Tabor–Pisek–Strakonitz so as to screen off to the north the pivotal positions at Budweis and at Neuhaus, constituted as Austrian winter-headquarters.

On the east of this strategic nub, Neipperg stood out towards Chrudim to mask Moravia. Against him General de Polastron together with the Duke de Biron and his men swept the valley of the Sazawa, out to Janowitz and Goltzjenikau, and captured Willimow on 13 December, the day that the Saxons took Czaslau. Their convergence against Neipperg in Chrudim was swelled by Prussian elements in from Prelauc. For Prussia was back in the ring.

The French having captured Prague and the Prussians Neisse, their immediate prize from the two-months-old Convention of Kleinschnellendorf, Frederick mounted yet another of his faithless defections, this time by reverting, against Austria, to those French and German allies with whom, indeed, he had never ostensibly broken. Frederick could sharply adduce Austria's having predictably broken the stipulated secrecy of Kleinschnellendorf. By 9 December 1741 Frederick was maintaining that nobody 'will be more faithfully attached than I am'[45] to the cause of the Elector of Bavaria, proclaimed King of Bohemia in Prague two days earlier in such contrast to the coronation there once attended by the Count de Stainville's father.

The day before the new King of Bohemia had been proclaimed, on

[44] Queen Maria Theresa to Count Philip Kinsky, late 1741: Josef Erwin Folkmann, Die gefürstete Linie des uralten und edlen Geschlechtes Kinsky (Prague, 1861), pp. 59–60, n.
[45] King Frederick II to King of Bohemia, Berlin, 9 Dec. 1741: Politische Correspondenz, i. 426.

6 December, the little Czar Ivan VI of Russia had been deposed. Trends at Saint Petersburg may well have clinched the inclination towards France of the King of Prussia, always sensitive to Russia. There the German regime of the Regent Anne of Mecklenburg and Marshal Münnich was swept away by a palace revolution in favour of Peter the Great's younger daughter Elizabeth. She plucked little Ivan from his cot and packed him off to languish in prison till he was murdered in 1764. Münnich was for Siberia, and Russia was for Elizabeth. The prime agents in this bloodless revolution were Elizabeth's two French favourites, an indifferent doctor called Lestocq and the French ambassador, the Marquis de La Chétardie, by common report her lover. The twenty-year reign of the Empress Elizabeth began under French auspices and brought an attempted though eventually unsuccessful pacification with Sweden, whose General Wrangel had been routed by the Russians at Vilmanstrand. For the present, however, French diplomacy appeared to have redressed the balance in the north. The Marquis de Stainville, unwell from anxiety, commented to Richecourt: 'All the misfortunes are happening to us at the same time. I do not count at all upon the Dutch gentlemen and I perceive more and more that they [the Austrians] have attached themselves to useless allies.'[46] England would not or could not reinsure Maria Theresa against faithless Frederick.

Twenty thousand Prussians under Marshal Schwerin were massing in Silesia for a drive on Olmütz, laying open the whole Austrian flank in Moravia. With this backing allied forces in mid-December 1741 dislodged Neipperg and captured Chrudim. There Polastron's hungry troops rested out a few days. It was freezing cold and for all Belle-Isle's administrative drive the French winter-equipment was cruelly deficient as compared with German. Roi-Infanterie had pushed through to the area of Chrudim by 'cross-country roads from one village to another, whereof we are very tired',[47] tired especially from running warfare in crescendo against the new arm which tactically distinguished the Bohemian campaign.

Maria Theresa's call to arms in Hungary had produced, especially, a swarm of Magyar and Slavonic light horse, hussars, free companies, Croats, Pandours in their white smocks and red capes, bristling with weapons, barbaric with Turkish music. These ferocious irregulars were led by such capable ruffians as the swaggering Menzel and Baron Trenck, lately courtmartialled for insubordination by Neip-

[46] Marquis de Stainville to Baron de Richecourt, Paris, 28 Dec. 1741: Ö.S./H.H.S., Lothringisches Hausarchiv 189/III 126, fol. 233.

[47] Count de Polastron to Marshal de Belle-Isle, Goltzjenikau, noon, 16 Dec. 1741: Arch. Guerre C., vol. 2921, no. 9.

perg, who had been vainly besought by Kinsky to spare Bohemia 'these cursed pandours'.[48] For they spread a trail of terror not least among Maria Theresa's own peasantry, exposed to robbery, rape, and lawless cruelties. The pandours imparted a prematurely cutting edge to a formerly formalized and circumscribed fieldwarfare, imposing their own style of mobile hostilities, persistently harrying enemy columns of march, mercilessly cutting down stragglers and isolated detachments, swooping in sudden raids only to scatter away again so that it was almost useless to send French cavalry lumbering in pursuit of 'these handfuls of fleas'.[49] As is generally the case with any new arm, it produced an exaggerated moral effect.

Geographically no less than tactically this was something to which French troops were unused. For long years their classic campaigning grounds had been the adjacent Low Countries and the Rhineland, the regions of the bordering Alps and Pyrenees. They represented something very different from marching slap through to the eastern fastnesses of Bohemia, hundreds of miles due east of Paris. Those bivouacs way out by Chrudim marked the most easterly advance in strength from the frontiers of France made by any French troops between the time of the Emperor Charlemagne and that of the Emperor Napoleon. To contemporaries it was a portentous operation.

Down the western arm of the French pincer the Count d'Aubigné's vanguards had driven down the Moldau to dent into the Austrian forward elements before they could consolidate their line Tabor–Pisek–Strakonitz. On 6 December the Austrian hussars were barged out of Pisek, back through Protiwin before the bulk of the grand duke's army, entrenching in the quadrilateral Teyn–Tabor–Wesely–Budweis, imposed the price of the delay castigated by Belle-Isle. On 17 December 1741 d'Aubigné resigned himself to winter-quarters in the area of Pisek and Strakonitz with his tip out to captured Frauenberg, a strategic castle a bare two leagues from Budweis. There the heavy pendulum of war came hovering uneasily to rest while, west again, d'Estrées, frustrated in his attempt to rush Eger, had to settle down to protracted investment.

Every prong of the triple thrust outwards from Prague had run up against stiff opposition. 15,000 Saxon reinforcements were slowly heading out to Chrudim and up to 10,000 French reserves were switched to Pisek. In that area there was under way a large momentum which involved the personal direction of the commanders-in-chief on either side. But the French command was in transition.

[48] Count Philip Kinsky to Field-Marshal von Neipperg, 22 Sept. 1741: Ö.S./H.H.S., cited Arneth, i. 406, n. 31.
[49] De Baye to Marquis de Breteuil, 3 Nov. 1741: Pajol, ii. 97, n. 1.

VI

The Marshal de Belle-Isle's strategic stimulus in exploiting the capture of Prague contrasted with his confession while incapacitated at Dresden, in a letter to Amelot de Chaillou, of his mistake in trying to accomplish the superhuman by combining his diplomatic campaign with the military command, whereof he would gladly be relieved. Fleury was not one to neglect such an opening. The ailing marshal soon experienced 'the excess of the cardinal's tenderness'.[50] Into Prague at midnight on 19 December 1741 drove a coach bringing Marshal de Belle-Isle's operational successor, the Marshal de Broglie.

Strictly within that context of 1741 Choiseul subsequently exaggerated, at the least, in making out in his memoirs that Belle-Isle sought to duck out from his stalled campaign:

He had obtained at Frankfurt the dignity of duke and peer[51] and an immensity of money and belongings; the Emperor had created him a prince of the Empire; Spain had sent him the Fleece. He was not unaware that the Cardinal de Fleury took an ill view of this foreign war, which had been begun against his advice. He was sensible from experience that, though the cardinal might have been obliged to acquiesce in his design, he had remained the master of the [financial] means, and that these means were absolutely lacking to the army. The Marshal de Belle-Isle made a very just calculation; he said: 'I have launched the realm upon a great enterprise ... I will leave the misfortunes to my successor while presenting to the public, in my favour, the election of the Emperor and the conquest of Bohemia.' The Marshal de Belle-Isle reasoned wonderfully well, and those who, at the time, disapproved of his having wished to leave the army had not understood his reasoning.[52]

Choiseul's analysis suggests his grip upon economic essentials and he did not exaggerate the financial tension between the parsimonious prelate and the magnificent marshal. Choiseul's malicious probe of Belle-Isle's motives gains in accuracy if the context is expanded to cover, roughly, the ensuing year: as it quite likely should be in the light, for instance, of the allusions to the Bavarian Emperor and of the writer's specific reserve as to chronology: 'I shall try to subject myself to the exactness of dates; however I do not promise it you. This is not a work, nor regular memoirs which I claim to offer you; they are my past ideas as my memory shall present them to me.'[53]

---

[50] Blondel to Marshal de Belle-Isle, cited, Vicomte Fleury, op. cit., p. 313.

[51] Under the Ancien Régime the dignity of *duc et pair* signified that the dukedom was territorially based upon a fief that was a *pairie*, carrying with it such privileges as a seat in the *parlement*. Such attributes did not appertain to the less honorific dignity of *duc à brevet*.

[52] Choiseul, *Mémoires*, pp. 53-4.

[53] Ibid., p. 1.

Certainly within the context of that December 1741 was the persuasive analysis of the then Count de Stainville's father:

The departure of the Marshal de Broglie to go to command the French troops in Bavaria [sic] has caused much astonishment in this part of the world. The partisans of M. de Belle-Isle are saying that it is he who requested it ... Others, and they are the greater number, are saying that it is a trick which his enemies have played on him, and all the ministers of state are his enemies, whom he has brought down upon himself by his haughtiness during the last visit which he paid here [in July]. What makes one believe these last is that, knowing the unmeasured ambition of M. de Belle-Isle, it is easy to judge that he would always have preferred the command of the army to the embassy.[54]

Within a week Fleury was blandly assuring Belle-Isle that 'the Marshal de Broglie will involve himself solely in the military and daily operations. He will resolve nothing of importance except in consent with you ... You will continue to be the soul of our counsels.'[55] Broglie later described his take-over to Fleury thus: 'When I arrived at Prague I found the Marshal de Belle-Isle there all luminous with the honours and dignities wherewith he was loaded, regarding me, despite my powers to command the army, rather as his inferior than as he who [should] always command when we find ourselves together, I being his senior, [Belle-Isle] giving orders to everybody and drunk with glory.'[56] hardly an auspicious prospect for collaboration. On 27 December 1741 Belle-Isle left Prague for renewed diplomacy at Frankfurt.

Broglie had been a resolute critic not only of Belle-Isle's strategy but also of his diplomacy, a field wherein he rather fancied himself from that embassy in London when, back in 1725, he had disparaged the diplomatic debut of the Marquis de Stainville, his erstwhile comrade-in-arms from the siege of Freiburg. Since then Broglie's aristocratic straddle of diplomacy and war had included victories in the Italian campaigns of the War of the Polish Succession, notably over old Königsegg at Guastalla in redemption of the way in which Broglie had let the Austrians surprise him in camp upon the Secchia so that he had himself had to gallop for safety with only one boot on, popularly improved to without his breeches. Now this corpulent and choleric successor to the lanky and ailing Belle-Isle was turning

[54] Marquis de Stainville to Grand Duke Francis II, Paris, 18 Dec. 1741: Esteri del Granducato di Toscana, vol. 2295/1286, fo. 75.
[55] Cardinal Fleury to Marshal de Belle-Isle, Versailles, 23 Dec. 1741: Arch. Guerre C., vol. 2921, no. 84.
[56] Marshal de Broglie to Cardinal Fleury, Frauenberg, 4 June 1742: Arch. Guerre C., vol. 2955, no. 15. Compare, however, the earlier and more friendly account in Marshal de Broglie to Cardinal Fleury, Pisek, 4 Jan. 1742: Campagne, iii. 144–5.

seventy, venerable with his white hair, italianate with his unfashionable grey beard. In the preceding summer he had suffered something of a stroke.

On the day that the Marshal de Belle-Isle left Prague his successor entered Pisek. Within twenty-four hours the French in Pisek, on the night of 28 December 1741, beat back an Austrian irruption right into the little town. But the French garrison of Frauenberg was cut off as the Grand Duke Francis edged forward to grip Protiwin. The aggressiveness of the superior enemy kept Broglie's forces on the stretch and concentrated under canvas outside Pisek in bitter weather. About 10–11 January 1742 it deteriorated further with heavy snowfall. Broglie clung on, unwilling to relax the strategic threat to Budweis. Even old campaigners could recall nothing to match such hardship. For years afterwards, when the sufferings of war were being debated in French messes, the proverbial exemplar was Broglie's bivouac at Pisek.

Broglie's strategic partner Polastron on 3 January 1742 did capture Deutsch Brod with precious stores. The Austrians under Lobkowitz fell back on Iglau. For a while warfare slowed almost to a standstill among the pines upon the snowmantled heights of Bohemia and Moravia. That farthest detachment of Roi-Infanterie had not enjoyed Prussian co-operation south of Chrudim. Whereas, eastward again, a Prussian army under Field-Marshal Schwerin had moved out from Silesia against Moravia and easily marched into Olmütz on Boxing Day.

Frederick the Great followed through from an allied council of war held in Dresden on the afternoon of 19 January 1742. He proposed that, instead of his reinforcing the French and Saxons in Bohemia, maximum allied forces should be diverted thence for an outflanking advance under his personal command through Moravia, directly against Vienna. The western threat of the preceding autumn against the Austrian capital, always advocated by Frederick and Schmettau, would be more formidably reconstituted from the north. This should compel the enemy to thin out in those more westerly theatres of prime concern to the Saxons, Bavarians and French.

It was precisely the evident value of Frederick's strategy that so embarrassed his Saxon listeners. Brühl objected to committing Saxon forces in outlying theatres, and under the untrustworthy Frederick (who depicted Brühl as subject to Austrian blackmail). For the French, such was the scope of their campaigning that the most pressing concern in Dresden for their representatives, Saxe and Valory, related to the forces neither of Broglie nor of Polastron but of Ségur back at Linz where the fears of Charles Albert were coming about in consequence of the critical French failure to restore their communications by Budweis.

Maria Theresa, back in Vienna since 11 December, had not allowed Prussian penetration into Moravia to frighten her out of a long-projected counterstroke in the opposite direction. On 20 December 1741 Vienna had given her former deliverer, Field-Marshal Khevenhüller, a tumultuous send-off to his new army, 16,000 strong. By the new year Khevenhüller had crossed the Enns. Menzel's pandours backed by elements under Bernklau, a superior general, were sent driving through to Schärding and beyond. War was rebounding into Bavaria. Ségur was cut off in Linz.

The French command wanted to plug that central power-vacuum which was beginning to threaten in Bohemia owing to the tendency of each German prince to concentrate upon his own sector of the perimeter. In Dresden the Count de Saxe did his best to win Frederick over from Moravia to Bohemia by stressing the critical position there, not least in shortage of supplies despite all the efforts of intendant Séchelles. Frederick replied that he would himself look into that with Séchelles: not quite what Saxe had wanted. A few days earlier Frederick had confessed to Valory: 'I want the command because your Marshal de Broglie does not suit me.'[57] It was an understatement. When Broglie had succeeded Belle-Isle a chorus of protest from France's allies had been led by Frederick. For him there was a personal background from August 1740 when Frederick had paid the only visit of his life to France. Uninvited, with a false passport, Frederick had arrived incognito in Strasburg as a sightseer, a faintly ridiculous figure, to be confronted by Broglie as Governor of Alsace, described by the young king to Voltaire as 'drunk with his grandeur ... prating of his immense power'.[58]

Broglie was conspicuously absent from that council of war in Dresden which Frederick clinched with Augustus of Saxony in person. When that king entered the council-chamber Brühl hastily folded up the map of Moravia, only to have to produce it again. To the plan of King Frederick, in his own words, 'Augustus III replied Yes to everything, with an air of conviction which was mingled with something in his look which denoted ennui'.[59] Brühl interrupted to announce 'that the opera was going to begin. Ten kingdoms to conquer would not have retained the King of Poland a minute more.' Musical Frederick yielded himself to the cascading harmonies of La

---

[57] Marquis de Valory to Marshal de Belle-Isle, 16 January 1742: Arch. Aff. Étr. C.P., Prusse: Broglie/Fréd-MT, ii. 188.
[58] King Frederick II, 'Description poétique d'un voyage à Strasbourg' enclosed in a letter from him to Voltaire, Wesel, 2 Sept. 1740: Frederick, xiv. 160–1.
[59] Frederick, ii. 108, and for the following.

Faustine, duly disguised himself for the ensuing masked ball, early next morning flattered Father Guarini, 'a kind of favourite, minister, jester and confessor' into clinching Augustus in favour of Moravia.

At eight o'clock on the night of 21 January 1742 the King of Prussia entered Prague to settle up with Séchelles. He was persuaded to agree that for the Moravian campaign he would supply the Saxon forces from French stocks, thus facilitating Frederick's design of reserving to the Prussians whatever might be going in Moravia, enabling him to live off the country: a compact illustration of eighteenth-century development in the technique of military supply. Frederick here was partially adhering to the old doctrine of living off occupied territory, which had largely rendered seventeenth-century warfare so destructive, as back in Lorraine. Whereas Séchelles was a crack exponent of the newer, more complex system, illustrated in the French mobilization of the preceding year, of mainly supplying armies from prepared depots and magazines. This method, if restrictive of mobility yet on balance more efficient, certainly more humane, was, in fact, a military aspect of the centralizing bureaucracy of benevolent despotism. But when Séchelles represented to Frederick the danger of excessive pressure upon conquered peoples, the latter replied: 'It is the kingdom of heaven which is won by gentleness; those of this world belong to force.'[60] In the age of reason the Prussian creed of ruthless might was already coming to the fore.

Frederick the Great, however, recognized an efficient man when he met one. He recounts that Séchelles promised: '"I shall make the impossible possible", a sentence which should be written in letters of gold on the desk of all army intendants.'[61] And Séchelles was as good as his word, noted Frederick in some contrast to his opinion of 'the pitiable generals of the French'.[62]

Such of the pitiable generals as were in Prague, notably Gassion and the illegitimate Count of Bavaria, the town-commandant, did their best to put on a smart show for Frederick as he toured the town the day after his arrival. It is possible, but uncertain, that this occasion may have afforded the young Count de Stainville, wintering in the Bohemian capital, his only personal glimpse of that Prussian ruler against whom he was later to be outstandingly matched in the statecraft of Europe.

While King Frederick was clinching his deflection of French strategy in Bohemia, Marshal de Belle-Isle was achieving his consummation of French diplomacy in Germany. On 24 January

[60] Séchelles to Marshal de Broglie, Prague, 21 Jan. 1742: Arch. Guerre C.: Broglie/Fréd-MT, ii. 198-9.
[61] Frederick, ii. 109.   [62] Ibid., ii. 115.

1742 Charles Albert of Bavaria was elected King of the Romans. For the first time for more than three hundred years there was to be a Holy Roman Emperor who was not a Habsburg. The secular dream of French diplomacy was at long last accomplished. Well might Belle-Isle suppose that he would be for ever numbered among the great men of his nation. The election, however, was made under contrary influence. Choiseul later noted that Belle-Isle's 'political labours were successful as to the election ... but the military operations were not so successful. Ten [French] battalions ... and one or two regiments of dragoons were captured in Linz',[63] precipitately surrendered by Ségur so that on that same 24 January the Grand Duke of Tuscany, nominal successor now to Khevenhüller, made his triumphal entry into the town. Ségur's men marched out indeed with honours of war but his surrender of Linz came as a moral shock and shame to France.

To Bavaria these events spelt invasion and terror, with Menzel threatening that any Bavarian franc-tireur captured would lose nose and ears. By 12 February 1742 Munich was reduced. On the same day the Elector of Bavaria was by a second unlucky coincidence crowned emperor as Charles VII. Back in Paris 'they have put into the Bastille some imprudent fellows who have said before a whole café that the Emperor was John Lackland, and that they would soon have to furnish an appartment for him at Vincennes.'[64]

A week before the fall of Munich the Moravian campaign had opened another grim perspective. Lobkowitz was swiftly prized out of Iglau, back on Neuhaus, but instead of hooking west in pursuit Frederick drove his own plan ahead in the direction of Brünn, Znaim, Vienna. That was the signal for Polastron, under orders from Broglie, to part company in reluctant retreat away from an ally in the field. Polastron assured Frederick that his French troops 'would in your company prefer the huts of Moravia to the palaces of Prague'.[65] But Prague it was for them at last. After a retreat wrapped in a snowstorm the weary soldiers of the Roi-Infanterie regained the Bohemian capital on 28 February 1742.

Frederick, infuriated, wrote off Polastron as a general 'who seemed born more to tell his beads than to go to war',[66] while those 'fucking Saxons'[67] were only too eager to follow the French. On the Prussian front Ziethen's hussars pushed right out to Stockerau, but one

[63] Choiseul, *Mémoires*, pp. 52–3.
[64] Barbier, iii. 337.
[65] Count de Polastron to King Frederick II, Wollein, 16 Feb. 1742: *Campagne*, iii. 378.
[66] Frederick, ii. 109.
[67] King Frederick II to Marquis de Valory (postscript), camp at Czaslau, 19 May 1742: *Mémoires des négociations du marquis de Valori*, ed. Comte H. de Valori (Paris, 1820), ii. 264.

posting-stage from Vienna. But they achieved no more lasting effect than the French had done from Saint Polten the previous autumn, indeed appreciably less. For by this time the Austrians were a different proposition. In Bohemia Prince Charles has assumed the command from his brother and proceeded to exploit his advantage of interior lines eastwards against Moravia. There the Prussians and Saxons had been unsuccessful against Brünn, Frederick of course blaming his allies. Their campaign was folding up. It had been distinguished by deliberate devastation and terror. 'Making war in that style', wrote Valory, 'has never been seen since the Goths.'[68] This Prussian policy of frightfulness was already inspired from above, by Frederick.

One of the chief concerns, however, of the Austrian government was the extent to which the French, by their moderation in Prague and Bohemia generally, had secured local collaboration. Out at Goltzjenikau, for instance, Polastron had had a whip-round from the officers of Roi-Infanterie for the relief of those rendered homeless by an accidental fire. By contrast the tormented peasantry of Moravia now took to arms against the Prussians, become as usual ever more vindictive in retreat. On 25 April 1742 they evacuated Olmütz and soon all Moravia, leaving it a shambles. Such was the cruel correction administered by the Prussians in Moravia, the Austrians in Bavaria, to any generalization from the conduct of officers in western Europe as to the humane gentility of eighteenth-century warfare. Similarly the idea that in winter it was always a conventional affair of snug quarters might have won limited assent from Broglie's men grimly bivouacked at Pisek or from Polastron's in their distant campaigning in the snow.

VII

If the Moravian campaign had laid bare allied disunity, it was reflected in France internally between factions. The personal rivalry between Belle-Isle and Broglie was widening into a political dispute over the equivocal Prussian alliance and its strategic implications. Belle-Isle, Valory, Séchelles, d'Aubigné, Polastron, most of the young officers argued that Frederick, whatever his moral shortcomings, remained a valuable ally with whom to concert an efficient war-effort. Whereas Broglie, Maurice de Saxe, and Des Alleurs, French minister at Dresden, stressed the risk and impropriety of relying

[68] Marquis de Valory to Amelot de Chaillou, 14 Apr. 1742: Arch. Aff. Étr. C.P., Prusse: Broglie/Fréd-MT, ii. 210.

upon such proven faithfulness. This French dilemma and disagreement at the front were as usual duplicated, in rather transmuted terms, at the court.

At Versailles the burning question was who should succeed upon the overdue death of Fleury now that Belle-Isle's rapid splendour was dimmed. All the ministers noted by the Marquis de Stainville as that marshal's enemies found in old Broglie just the required figurehead. Broglie's name was mobilized along with those of the fancied rivals for Fleury's succession, notably the Cardinal de Tencin – a prelate alleged to be catholic especially in his peccadilloes, ranging from simony to incest – and Chauvelin, the fallen foreign minister said to have been intriguing from his country banishment against Fleury through the king's valet, Bachelier, and a dubious banker, Baron Hogguer. This characteristic ascendancy of valets under autocratic rule extended beyond the royal-liveried servants, the Boys in Blue, to Fleury's 'little Barjac',[69] then receiving letters from Broglie's headquarters at Pisek. Broglie further enjoyed the support at court of all the young ladies who looked tenderly upon his dashing protagonist, Count Maurice de Saxe.

Saxe's epistolary propaganda against Belle-Isle was strongly countered by Frederick the Great's against Broglie. Belle-Isle, still attracting the critics and young hopefuls, was well in with both of the king's chief intimates, his valet and his mistress, now the Countess de Mailly, 'a real little goose'[70] given to overdressing. She had, as Choiseul noted, been doubling the royal delight with her less attractive sister, the Marquise de Vintimille – her husband used to say that she stank like a goat – before the Marquise died after childbirth the preceding September. Associated with the Countess de Mailly in favour of Belle-Isle and in the favour of Louis was the Countess de Toulouse, virtuous but accommodating widow of one of Louis XIV's legitimized bastards, influential as such elderly French noblewomen often were in that age of family interests; and her own were those of the important Noailles faction, incidentally hostile to Bachelier.

With this nice equation of forces at court each of the rival marshals, in another illustration of family interests, was nursing his own there through his brother. The Chevalier de Belle-Isle, recently arrived from Frankfurt, did not, however, hit it off with Bachelier and was matched against a formidable rival. The Abbé de Broglie was 'an intriguer without ambition ... indecent without his morals being impugned'.[71] These subtle qualities distinguished him as the Grand

[69] D'Argenson, i. 268.   [70] Ibid., iii. 430.   [71] Hénault, p. 70.

Abbé. He surpassed his brother, the marshal, at strategic retreats, from Versailles to his nearby abbey of Vaux en Cernay, and at outflanking and enfilading manoeuvres. Belle-Isle, however, was good at countering them.

On the evening of Saturday, 3 March 1742, the Marshal de Belle-Isle arrived at Versailles. On 15 March he was created Duke de Gisors, while continuing to be commonly known as Belle-Isle. 'It has been the finest possible *coup de théâtre*', noted d'Argenson, 'when suddenly M. de Belle-Isle . . . has been created a hereditary duke. Only the Bastille was talked of for him.'[72]

In another of Fleury's wan compromises Broglie was now to be transferred to command French forces in devastated Bavaria, where a new army under the Duke d'Harcourt was arriving to replace that of the Count de Ségur. Belle-Isle, scorning the Army of Bavaria 'formed by baroque general officers'[73] (so much, already, for the term *baroque*), was to be re-appointed to command his 'real and first army' in Bohemia. He represented, however, in a long and important memorandum of 21 March 1742 that he could not proceed at once. First he needed to revisit the kings of Prussia and Poland to concert a new plan of campaign and then to report to the emperor at Frankfurt, 'give the first pushes to the opening of the [imperial] diet'[74] in May and conduct in person 'the rest of the negotiations'.

If, historically, Belle-Isle's memorandum of 21 March 1742 seems to have been somewhat neglected that is truer still of another document suggesting its secret context. And the immediate introduction to this arcane diplomacy lay through the personal affairs of the young Count de Stainville, again being pushed by his father. Two days after the Marshal de Belle-Isle composed his memorandum the Marquis de Stainville began a despatch:

Monseigneur, In the last few days, having several times sought the Marshal de Belle-Isle in vain at his house in order to ask him to interest himself in favour of my son, he sent me word to expect him at eight o'clock in the evening at my house, where he presented himself exactly at the time indicated. After the first compliments and after I had asked him to be good enough to ask for a regiment for my son, he suddenly embarked upon present affairs, and he told me 'that he had been extraordinarily grieved to be the instrument which they had used to do all that had happened; but that as a subject and a citizen he could not refuse to serve the king and the state, that I knew his respectful attachment to his late Royal Highness [Duke Leopold] and to his august house'.[75]

[72] D'Argenson, iv. 7.
[73] Marshal de Belle-Isle, 'Mémoires': Broglie/Fréd-MT, ii. 234–5, and for the following.
[74] Memorandum by Marshal de Belle-Isle, Versailles, 21 Mar. 1742: Arch. Guerre C., vol. 2951, no. 126, and for the following. (Not printed in *Campagne* nor cited in Broglie/Fréd-MT.)
[75] Marquis de Stainville to Grand Duke Francis II, Paris, 23 Mar. 1742: Esteri del Granducato di Toscana, vol. 2295/1286, fos. 90–2 for the following.

The implausibly plausible marshal lamented to Stainville that after the death of Charles VI his daughter had been badly advised and, instead of trusting wholly to Fleury, had refused any pickings in Germany to the Elector of Bavaria, then France's only ally. That, he explained, was what had nullified the secret soundings on behalf of Maria Theresa which Koch had conducted with him, Belle-Isle, in Frankfurt. Whereas now France naturally had to have regard also to the claims of the King of Prussia and of the Elector of Saxony. The Marquis de Stainville retorted that on the contrary:

The Queen had in the beginning trusted too blindly in the Cardinal, that for a long while she had been unwilling to believe us, we who were warning her of the preparations being made against her. She ... was relying upon the verbal and written assurances which she had been given that the [French] King would keep all the undertakings which he had contracted with the late Emperor ... Upon that M. de Belle-Isle replied to me 'that the King his master has not been able to excuse himself from profiting from the opportunity to diminish a little the power of the house of Austria'.

Such was the secret moment of truth with the chief French antagonist of Austria. Stainville continued:

But as I wished to know if the Marshal had in view any means of pacification, I said to him that, knowing as I did the Cardinal's wish to make peace, it was useless to recall all that had happened, but that we had to start from where we were at the present moment ... He replied that nobody in the world wished more for peace than the cardinal unless it were himself. 'And indeed', he continued, ... 'what could I wish for more than a solid peace? The public has attributed everything that I have done to my ambition, but even supposing that that was so, has it not every reason to be satisfied, and what more glorious could befall me than to contribute towards the general pacification which everybody and we ourselves so badly need?

So far did Belle-Isle's contemporary factorization of his self-interest during the Bohemian campaign stand comparison with Choiseul's subsequent one.[76] Belle-Isle, however, predictably warned 'that the Queen must make no mistake about it, we shall make the utmost efforts to sustain what we have begun.' For the present she might still conclude a peace to safeguard the greater part of her possessions and, the marshal somewhat obscurely hinted, 'especially by making an Electorate which would place her in a position again to make the imperial crown return to her house'. It would be too late, though, for such accommodation once the armies of France and her allies, at least 150,000 strong, had started out 'in the month of May' – again that term at the outset of the campaigning season.

[76] Cf. p. 306 above.

Belle-Isle suggested that the Dutch would take good care not to provoke a joint drive against them by a Prussian army and that of Maillebois, while 'the King of England is too afraid for his Hanoverian possessions to dare to infringe the neutrality which he has so much wanted'. Whereas Belle-Isle's more candid opinion was in fact that 'anything may be feared from England',[77] although she could not put more than 15,000 British troops in the field; his further fear, even now, of Russia also appears to have been unmentioned to Stainville. He reported that Belle-Isle concluded his minatory survey

'I shall be told in reply that we shall ruin the [French] kingdom in men and money That may be true, but the kingdom remains ours, whereas the Queen is ruining herself in men and money, and is running the risk of losing all her states.' After nearly two hours M. de Belle-Isle finished our conversation by telling me that in seven or eight days he was leaving for Frankfurt and that there he would listen with great pleasure to what the Queen might wish to convey to him; but that there was not a moment to lose if one were to enter upon a negotiation.[78]

The possibility of a Franco-Austrian negotiation for peace was not substantially furthered in a second conversation which Stainville had with Belle-Isle on 10 April 1742, two days before the marshal in fact left for Germany. On this Stainville reported only that Belle-Isle 'seemed to me extremely harassed. He even went so far as to say to me, "Judge, Sir, whether I should not wish for peace, I who feel that I shall perish in torment if this continues, for I am overburdened with work and my health is becoming worse every day." '[79]

If these conversations between the Marshal de Belle-Isle and the Marquis de Stainville have hitherto evaded the attention of historians, the talks did not escape the notice, or speculation, of contemporaries. Stainville was soon complaining, with special reference to the Dutch sounding-board for European intelligence, that 'ill-intentioned people have wanted ... to cause umbrage to the allies of the Queen'.[80] Whereas in fact unforeseen blows, first against Austria with repercussion against France, were to render those political soundings as unfruitful as the request to the marshal for a regiment for the young Count de Stainville.

Belle-Isle had explained in his programmatic memorandum of 21 March 1742 that 'the excessive injustice which I have just experienced through calumnious gossip'[81] obliged him to disclaim in writing any

[77] Memorandum by Marshal de Belle-Isle, Versailles, 21 Mar. 1742: *u.s.*
[78] Marquis de Stainville to Grand Duke Francis II, Paris, 23 Mar. 1742: *u.s.*, fo. 92.
[79] Marquis de Stainville to Grand Duke Francis II, Paris, 13 Apr. 1742: *u.s.*, fo. 102.
[80] Marquis de Stainville to Baron de Richecourt, Paris, 1 May 1742: Ö.S./H.H.S. Lothringisches Hausarchiv 189/III 126, fo. 231.
[81] Memorandum by Marshal de Belle-Isle, Versailles, 21 Mar. 1742: Arch. Guerre C., vol 2951, no. 126.

responsibility for military developments in Bohemia pending his deferred resumption of the French command there. In fact, the distracting pull between his military and political preoccupations was for the present to continue almost as before, with the effective command still resting with 'M. de Broglie, who was at Pisek with a dozen dukes' (Frederick the Great).[82] The rival marshals continued to play box and cox. In the French Ministry of War it was bleakly minuted: 'It results from everything that so long as M. de Broglie, who should command the Army of Bavaria, shall remain in Bohemia, and as M. de Belle-Isle, who should command the Army of Bohemia, shall remain at Frankfurt, nothing of what should properly be done on the one hand and on the other can be done.'[83]

VIII

Almost the only thing done by Broglie was to secure the capitulation to Saxe and others on 19 April 1742 of pivotal Eger, more than ever important for French communications now that those by Linz were gone, with the enemy spread over Bavaria. It was on the march to Eger that old General Leuville died, to be followed early in May by the 'very upright'[84] General de Polastron, killed off medicinally by 'a super-purge (*une superpurgation*)'.[85] Suffering was combing out the French army, especially in the stubborn bivouac at Pisek where whole regiments foundered 'and there are virtually no sick who recover ... The stoves but constantly affect their health, because the prompt passage of the soldiers from their rooms, where it is very hot, into the cold air gives them inflammations of the chest.'[86]

Discipline also was wasting away in Broglie's army. The old marshal, whose initial vigour and resolution had probably saved the day at Pisek, had lapsed back into obstinate immobility. 'The French were dozing at Pisek'[87] rasped Frederick the Great. He himself was kept lively by his eager young rival, Charles of Lorraine, harnessed though that prince was to slow old Königsegg in another duplication of command. On 17 May Charles forced a reckoning in the fierce and even battle of Chotusitz, carried off with honours by the King of Prussia.

[82] Frederick, ii. 117.
[83] 'Observation sur une lettre de M. le Maréchal de Broglie du 3 Mai 1742 et sur les lettres y jointes', unsigned, 18 May 1742: Arch. Guerre C., vol. 2954, no. 119.
[84] Cardinal Fleury to Marshal de Belle-Isle, Issy, 20 May 1742: Arch. Guerre C., vol. 2954, no. 132.
[85] Luynes, iv. 142.
[86] Chevalier d'Espagnac to Marquis de Breteuil, Pilsen, 19 Mar. 1742: *Campagne*, iv. 96.
[87] Frederick, ii. 114.

On the night of Chotusitz the Prince Lobkowitz began a holding-attack against the battered castle of Frauenberg, which incidentally belonged to his nephew for whom he confessed to Broglie 'a rather natural pity'.[88] Broglie reacted true to Austrian anticipation by moving south from Pisek, away from now threatened Prague, to relieve Frauenberg. At Protiwin Broglie was joined by Belle-Isle, interrupting his journey to confer with Frederick. Another addition, of humbler rank, to Broglie's army was the Count de Stainville, out on campaign again after his winter in Prague.

Stainville's earliest biographer wrote of his soldiering in Bohemia:

The French army was then, as French armies always had been hitherto, and as it is to be wished that they should not always be in future, divided into two factions. Messrs. de Broglie were in opposition to Marshal de Belle-Isle; the Count de Stainville, too young, and too gay, to enter into any of the intrigues of these generals, or of their sectaries, attached to his duties, fulfilling them well, had not introduced any politics into his connections, had allowed himself to follow his taste for gaiety, pleasures and good company, and had found wherewith to satisfy it rather among the friends of M. de Belle-Isle than in what was called the faction of Messrs. de Broglie.[89]

Now, however, merrymaking yielded to marching, and with the two marshals for once almost in step. At dawn on 25 May 1742 the French army began its tedious march in two columns southward from Protiwin through a boggy country of sloughs and ditches. By about four o'clock that afternoon the leading French elements debouched from a defile leading to the village of Sahay where Lobkowitz had camped, a league from Frauenberg. The Austrians were pulling out but now their rearguards turned at bay and concentrated upon a wood behind the village. The French forces were not all arrived but contingents successively piled into the fight that was engaged about five o'clock. French cavalry boldly charged the superior Austrian cuirassiers and drove them back into the wood. The hero of the day was the son of the Duke de Luynes, the Duke de Chevreuse, wounded along with his horse, Conquérant. Also wounded was the Count de Broglie, the marshal's eldest son. The morale of the French cavalry was revived by this success over their formidable Austrian counterpart, suffering from the loss of many of its best officers upon the fields of Groczka and of Mollwitz.

While Broglie's cavalry was distinguishing itself in the open field, infantry elements under the personal command of the Marshal de Belle-Isle were attacking Sahay itself. Young Stainville went into

[88] Prince Lobkowitz to Marshal de Broglie, Sahay, 20 May 1742: *Campagne*, v. 78.
[89] Essai/Arsenal 5808, fos. 21-2.

action and, as an infantry officer, probably in this attack, though his precise location in the combat is uncertain since his regiment, the Roi, was not engaged as a unit. But two regiments which did see action that day were later to be successively commanded by him. These were the then Régiment d'Auroy and the famous regiment of Navarre. The latter bore the brunt of the hot fighting against the pandours in the streets of the burning village. Thrice did they surge to the attack. The third time Belle-Isle dismounted and led his troops, sword in hand. The pandours broke. The village fell.

Not having enough cavalry for immediate exploitation of the victory, the French cannonaded the enemy in the wood till nightfall and prepared to storm it in the morning. But when morning came the enemy had gone. Such was the only pitched battle fought by the French in all that Bohemian campaign, and the first engagement in the field wherein the Count de Stainville fought for France.

The Count de Stainville's father, for whom dynastic loyalty so curiously crossed family feeling, consoled himself for the Austrian discomfiture at Sahay with reports that 'the French have lost a lot of people on this occasion. The carabineers and two regiments of dragoons have been entirely undone.'[90] Actual French casualties were about a hundred and fifty killed and as many wounded. The Count de Stainville survived together with his old acquaintance, the Marquis de Mirepoix, who had been hotly engaged. Within a fortnight young Stainville's father, paying one of his visits to Fleury out at Issy, was surprised to encounter Mirepoix there so that 'I had the disagreeable experience of hearing him exalt very high the little affair which occurred near Frauenberg'.[91] For once the Marquis de Stainville might have agreed with King Frederick: 'The battle of Pharsalia did not make more stir at Rome than this little fight did at Paris.'[92] The rearguard action at Sahay did, however, have one immediate result and in this connection the Count de Stainville earned particular mention as having 'contributed to the raising of the siege of Frauenberg by the enemy'.[93]

It was in camp before Frauenberg that Belle-Isle reported his failure to persuade Broglie to nourish success promptly and 'march to Budweis'.[94] But then Broglie was in a vile temper at being transferred to Bavaria, whither he proposed to remove the ten

[90] Marquis de Stainville to Baron de Richecourt, Paris, 4 June 1742: Ö.S./H.H.S., Lothringisches Hausarchiv 189/III 126, fo. 229.

[91] Marquis de Stainville to Grand Duke Francis II, Paris, 9 June 1742: Esteri del Granducato di Toscana, vol. 2295/1286, fo. 116.

[92] Frederick, ii. 127.

[93] Pinard, *Chronologie historique-militaire*, v. 685.

[94] Marshal de Belle-Isle to Marquis de Breteuil, camp before Frauenberg, 27 May 1742: Arch. Guerre C., vol. 2954, no. 178.

battalions of reinforcements which he had recently received for the Army of Bohemia. When Belle-Isle asked Broglie if he thought he could really act so, Broglie was depicted as replying: 'Yes, Sir, without difficulty.'[95] That sparked a blazing row.

Belle-Isle quickly parted company under a patched up arrangement whereby Broglie would temporarily retain the operational command in Bohemia for yet a further spell while Belle-Isle proceeded with his mission to the King of Prussia. Before he left, Belle-Isle urged upon Broglie that failing a prompt follow-through from Sahay against Budweis, the only prudent alternative for him was to withdraw. King Frederick tendered similar advice but Broglie, unmoved, 'stayed placidly at Frauenberg scarcely knowing why'.[96]

A resounding French defeat just then would not suit Frederick's book. That book had for some months past, as often, been set in double columns, military and diplomatic. On the morning before Frederick had set out upon the Moravian campaign, 4 February 1742, he had conferred at Olmütz with a secret envoy from Austria, none other than the grand duke's old confidant, Baron von Pfütschner. (Nobody seemed quite able to master this name sounding like a sneeze: Fischner to the Lorrainers, he was Fitzner to Frederick.) Maria Theresa, less inclined than her husband towards pacific compromise with his Prussian contemporary, took a stiff view of Pfütschner's sounding, though he maintained secret contact with Frederick through a Tuscan ecclesiastic on friendly terms with the grand duke, Canon Count Giannini of Brünn.

It seems to have been almost the rule then for secret negotiations to be conducted at least in duplicate. Prussian diplomacy was also pursuing possible conditions of peace through the veteran team of British mediators, Robinson and Hyndford. England exerted steady pressure upon Austria to come to terms with Prussia, hoping to concentrate them both against her traditional enemy, France. Frederick for his part jolted Maria Theresa towards peace at Chotusitz, also a move in Frederick's diplomatic campaign. An all-out military campaign was not at all what he intended and, deaf to Belle-Isle's exhortations to him to follow through, he sent his troops into peaceable cantonments along the Sazawa, almost inviting the Austrians to swing against the French.

Belle-Isle, exasperated against Broglie and suffering from 'continuing fever with a violent headache and a dry cough',[97] nursing himself upon toastwater, won through to Prussian headquarters at

[95] Marshal de Belle-Isle to Marquis de Breteul, Prague, 31 May 1742: *Campagne*, v. 125.
[96] Frederick, ii. 128–9.
[97] Marshal de Belle-Isle to Marquis de Breteuil, camp before Frauenberg, 27 May 1742: Arch Guerre C., vol. 2954, no. 178.

Kuttenberg on 2 June 1742. Frederick received him with open arms and pressed upon him his own cloak. It was stormy weather.

Belle-Isle, explained Frederick subsequently, 'had chosen his time badly: the king [of Prussia] was far indeed from entering into his views'[98] for vigorous co-operation against the enemy. The marshal, frustrated, was taking his leave at Kuttenberg when Frederick gave him intelligence that Prince Charles of Lorraine at the head of twenty thousand men was marching straight to join Prince Lobkowitz. Upon this grim text Frederick preached peace. With Prussia and Saxony withdrawing from hostilities, the whole weight of the combined Austrian army, some sixty thousand strong, was at last bearing down upon Broglie's debilitated force of not more than twenty-five thousand stuck out by Frauenberg. In that vortex of misfortune Belle-Isle fainted. They revived him with spirits and smelling-salts.[99]

Belle-Isle sent urgent warning to Broglie and made all speed to return by way of Dresden. Even before Belle-Isle had parted from King Frederick, however, Prince Charles had joined Prince Lobkowitz and by about 5 June 1742 was already beginning to bundle French advanced elements backwards. Broglie, abandoning the whole eastern bank of the Moldau, pressed on up towards Beraun. A residual and demoralized French garrison quickly caved in at Pisek, where the pandours and Croats ravaged the ghetto – the Jewry of Bohemia was said to have shewn itself specially sympathetic to the enlightenment of the invading French.

From Pisek Prince Charles carried through to Pilsen, sealing the earlier loss to the French of Budweis and any convenient communication with the Danube. Their only line to the west ran up by Eger. Broglie at Pisek had repeated Ségur's mistake at Linz of standing too far out with too few men. The reckoning had come for those under Broglie, who included the Count de Stainville, as they struggled, straggled back to Beraun.

Broglie's precipitate retreat saved his army, indeed, from envelopment but demoralization set in. And in that central-continental climate, after the icy bivouac of the French at Pisek, their retreat was executed in blazing heat. For stragglers the dreaded haze of Slavonic light cavalry was always in the offing. The peasantry of Bohemia, too, rounded upon the retreating French and began to serve them as the peasantry of Moravia had treated the Prussians. At last, on 13 June 1742, the Army of Bohemia arrived in jumbled haste beneath the

---

[98] Frederick, ii. 127.
[99] Belle-Isle omitted this episode from his reports. It was recorded in a note made by Ledran, chief clerk in the French Foreign Ministry, in the margin of a memorandum submitted by Belle-Isle upon his return to France in 1742: see Broglie/Fréd-MT, ii. 407, n. 1.

walls of Prague where they huddled into camp 'as though in a box'.[1]

In this retreat only better than a rout the place of danger in the rearguard had been assigned to the disciplined Régiment du Roi, wherein young Stainville marched. By the time they reached Prague, where they were posted out to guard the bridges of the Moldau, the four battalions of Roi-Infanterie numbered no more than 1,230 men. Yet they fared much better than most, losing only twenty-seven missing along the road: comparable figures for the regiment of Alsace were 380 arrived, 287 missing, for Navarre 158 arrived, 197 missing; and these figures excluded the sick and dead left in hospitals along the line of retreat.[2] The missing and prisoners totalled over two thousand with corresponding loss of baggage and supplies. Belle-Isle deplored such a 'humiliation' in the face of Frederick, adding: 'I should prefer in all respects that we had lost a complete battle; our destruction would not be greater; we should at least have made the enemy buy it dearly.'[3]

IX

The humiliation forecast by Belle-Isle was already costing France dear. On 11 June 1742 the Marquis de Valory had two rasping audiences of Frederick. At the second, there in the royal tent at the camp at Kuttenberg, the King of Prussia at last let the mask fall, telling Valory: 'I declare to you that peace must be made; as for me, I am going to consider it and to extricate myself from the mess as best I can; I am warned that peace is being negotiated [by France]; I do not want to be the dupe, and I again repeat to you that I am working at mine.'[4]

Frederick himself reported of the same interview: 'No puppet can imitate the contortions of Valory; his eyebrows made zigzags, his mouth widened, he fluttered in a strange way and all this without having anything sound to say to me.'[5] The king apparently enjoyed watching the effect of his treachery. For treachery it was. Frederick had in fact been telling, not warning, Valory of the event. On that same day, 11 June 1742, Prussia and Austria concluded preliminaries of peace at Breslau.

[1] Marshal de Broglie to King Louis XV, Prague, 8 July 1742: Pajol, ii. 218.
[2] 'État de la force dont sont les régiments de cette Armée, et de ce qui manque depuis qu'ils sont partis de Frauenberg' (June 1742): *Campagne*, v. 182.
[3] Marshal de Belle-Isle to Marquis de Breteuil, Aussig, 13 June 1742: Arch. Guerre C., vol. 2955, no. 66.
[4] Marquis de Valory to Marquis de Breteuil, Kuttenberg, 13 June 1742: Arch. Guerre C., vol. 2955, no. 62. (Valory had reported this audience to Amelot de Chaillou on 11 June: Arch. Étr. C.P., Prusse: Broglie/Fréd-MT, ii. 302f.).
[5] King Frederick II to Count Podewils, Kuttenberg, 19 June 1742: *Politische Correspondenz*, ii. 210.

Lord Hyndford's long mediation was steered home. For Hyndford this meant the Order of the Thistle and the right to blazon his arms with the Prussian eagle. For Frederick it meant Prussian sovereignty over Lower Silesia, Upper Silesia (except, notably, Teschen and Troppau), and the county of Glatz. For Maria Theresa it meant bitter immediate humiliation – Bartenstein called Breslau the second edition of Belgrade – with a view to subsequent recuperation and, meantime, to concentrated revenge against that oldest enemy, France. For Belle-Isle and his grand alliance against Austria it meant the imminent prospect of military defeat, the accomplished fact of political collapse, the unjust triumph of him whom Belle-Isle now described as 'the faithless prince who has just betrayed his allies'.[6]

Frederick himself expostulated to Valory: 'But that is not deceiving; it is extricating oneself from the mess.'[7] Prussia was indeed running very low in funds. Frederick tried to justify his breach of faith at Breslau by the same inadequate device as over Kleinschnellendorf, alleging that he had merely beaten pacific Fleury to it in coming to terms with Austria, in this case through a supposed secret emissary to Vienna, vaguely featured as Farget or Farey or Fargis or Dufargis. Fleury denied that any such commission had been entrusted to 'the alleged Fargis, a commissary of war who was indeed employed in 1735 in some affairs relative to the last peace, but of whom no use is since being made'.[8] Fleury had earlier suggested a possible confusion with Hegherti, itself another continental corruption of the name of one of those Irishmen in the employ of the Grand Duke Francis, as a fiscal agent for Tuscany. Fleury knew that Hegherti had earlier travelled from France through Vienna, where he had arrived that February and had been in touch with Francis and Toussaint; Hegherti had himself alluded to a danger lest 'the King of Prussia, who passes at Vienna for a real Butterfly, should seize upon so frivolous a pretext to break with the King [of France] and make it up with the Queen of Hungary'.[9]

For once, perhaps, Anglo-Austrian political warfare, aiming to compromise Franco-Prussian relations, may have matched Frederick in cunning. Belle-Isle for his part seems to have kept as quiet as might have been expected about his own overture in March to the reliably

---

[6] Marshal de Belle-Isle to Cardinal Fleury, Prague, 23 June 1742: Arch. Guerre C., vol. 2955, no. 114.

[7] Marquis de Valory, June 1742: Arch. Aff. Étr. C.P., Prusse; Broglie/Fréd-MT, ii. 310.

[8] Cardinal Fleury to Marshal de Belle-Isle, 21 June 1742: Arch. Aff. Étr. C.P., Correspondance de l'ambassade auprès de la Diète: op. cit., ii. 340.

[9] Hegherti to Cardinal Fleury, Venice, 16 March 1742: Arch. Aff. Étr. C.P., Autriche, vol. 232, fo. 128. (This letter is printed, in part only and in a somewhat inaccurate text, in Broglie/Fréd-MT, ii. 393. Cf. ibid., pp. 337ff. *passim* for refutation of an older story that King Frederick confronted an outraged Belle-Isle with written proofs of Fleury's duplicity.)

discreet Marquis de Stainville; though indeed Belle-Isle had then safeguarded France's commitment to Prussia, never congenial to Fleury. Belle-Isle's protagonists almost fell into line with Frederick in diverting on to the pacific cardinal the odium for France's let-down by the King of Prussia. In a rare outburst Fleury protested to Belle-Isle against this campaign featuring the story that 'I had sent a man secretly to Vienna to negotiate our own [peace]. I forgive the King of Prussia for having adopted this falsehood to justify his change-over, but that a Frenchman in the service of the King should dare to spread such a black calumny, without having the slightest proof, I confess that this conduct surprises me more than it wounds me.'[10]

A tricky person is apt to feel it specially hard to have pinned upon him a trickery of which for once he is innocent.

Thus did the Prussian peacemaking at Breslau spread discord and disaster to French statecraft. It was Prussian policy which emerged triumphant, in getting out quick with the spoils of the smash-and-grab raid on Silesia while leaving the two great catholic antagonists, Austria and France, to bleed each other in protracted conflict. So would they promote the longer Prussian ambition, already, of standing forth as the arbiter and champion of Germany against France. If the Turkish war of 1736–9 had prefigured the Eastern Question of the nineteenth century, the Silesian war of 1740–2 set a landmark pointing towards the later German Question. And, by the same token, it foreshadowed the failure of French hegemony in Germany. Belle-Isle's plan for the aggrandizement of the lesser German states as French satellites over against Austria was crumpling up even more swiftly than Napoleon's was destined to do seventy years later. Belle-Isle's success in placing the empire under a Bavarian prince was to prove even more insubstantial than Napoleon's ephemeral creation of the Confederation of the Rhine. Instead of finishing Austria off for good, Belle-Isle had only helped to conjure up, in the form of an expanding Prussia, a new and more terrible German menace to the ultimate fortunes and felicity of France. Instead of disposing of the destinies of Germany upon the grand scale, Belle-Isle was now intent upon trying to save that battered remnant of his army which was in imminent danger, cut off at Prague.

The shrinkage of French policy was epitomized in a farewell interview at Kuttenberg between Frederick and his stout butt,

---

[10] Cardinal Fleury to Marshal de Belle-Isle, Issy, 5 July 1742: Arch. Guerre C., vol. 2955, no. 181: cited, Duc de Broglie, *Frédéric II et Louis XV* (Paris, 1885: henceforth cited as Broglie/Fréd-LXV), i. 25–6.

Valory. For once, the Marquis de Valory rose to the occasion, remarking that he would be going to Prague so as to contribute 'one more man in case the enemy chose to attack us there'.[11] They did choose.

[11] Marquis de Valory, June 1742: Arch. Aff. Étr. C.P., Prusse: Broglie/Fréd-MT, ii. 309.

CHAPTER III

BESIEGED

I

AT THREE O'CLOCK on the afternoon of 15 June 1742 the Marshal de Belle-Isle drove into Prague. After conferring with Séchelles the marshal and his officers made for Broglie's camp without the walls. They arrived, wrote Broglie, 'all telling me unanimously that everything was lost, adding that the King of Prussia sent me word of it, carrying fear with them by their talk and by their physiognomy'.[1] Whereas Belle-Isle criticized Broglie's 'disposition ... of his army. I find it every day both worse and more dangerous'.[2]

Against Belle-Isle's widely supported criticisms Broglie stood out, stupid, obstinate, conceited. Cooped up together at Prague, the two marshals consumed reams of best-quality foolscap in denouncing each other to the ministers at court, which as usual reflected the divisions in the field. At Versailles the stock of the prussophil Belle-Isle had slumped and Broglie was confirmed in the superior command. On the spot, however, the more accommodating Belle-Isle gradually wheedled Broglie into rectifying the worst dispositions of his encampment. Belle-Isle assumed command inside the city itself and began to put its neglected fortifications into condition for urgent defence.

The Austrian armies under Charles of Lorraine and the Hungarian General Festetics came closing in upon the demoralized and disputing French, and were by 24 June within sight of Prague. On 6 July the Grand Duke of Tuscany, hoping to repeat his fortunate role at Linz, arrived at headquarters at Königsaal to command the confident besiegers, getting on for seventy thousand strong, more than double the French, weakening day by day. Belle-Isle and Séchelles reckoned that on average they were losing forty men a day, half in desertions from Broglie's camp and half in deadly hospitals in Prague.

In the face of such wasting inaction the Marshal de Belle-Isle devised a plan. He proposed that the reduced and supposedly

[1] Marshal de Broglie to Cardinal Fleury, Prague, 16 June 1742: Arch. Guerre C., vol. 2946, no. 275. Cf. *Campagne*, v. 184 f.
[2] Marshal de Belle-Isle to Marquis de Breteuil, Prague, 20 June 1742: Arch. Guerre C., vol. 2946, no. 284.

demoralized French army, stranded on the defensive out there at Prague, should secretly gather itself together and suddenly launch an all-out, full-scale attack upon the superior and unsuspecting Austrians who, taken off balance, should hardly have time to line out for the running battle that would be upon them. Thus were the French to drive slap through the enemy, unfavourably positioned for rearward deployment, and to march out whole in victory and in honour. Belle-Isle wrote of such intrepid unorthodoxy: 'In war it is precisely the things which are thought impossible which most often succeed, when they are well conducted, ... and precautions have not been taken against such an idea [as mine], which would not enter one's mind in an ordinary situation; but, in truth, ours is not so ... I have fruitlessly made proposal of it to M. de Broglie.'[3]

Precious opportunity was lost to the negativism of Broglie, over-sanguine as to relief by the small Army of Bavaria under the Duke d'Harcourt, in fact worsted at Hilkersberg and now held in check by Khevenhüller at Pleinting. If Bavaria was mainly overrun, only she remained of Belle-Isle's great German coalition. To the north of Prague the retreating Saxons were washed along in the Prussian wake, into peace preliminaries with Austria on 23 July 1742. In the west the ecclesiastical principalities of the Rhineland similarly sagged and fell away. That month in Paris it was rumoured that Maria Theresa was 'demanding Bavaria [as indemnity] for expenses of war, [and] the restitution of Lorraine and of Alsace ... that the city of Prague was taken by the Austrians, that Marshal de Belle-Isle was a prisoner and Marshal de Broglie wounded'.[4] What was true was that the residual French strongpoint south of Prague, contested Frauen-berg, had surrendered.

Broglie buoyed himself up with hopes of Belle-Isle's negotiations. For that marshal seemed fated to be pursuing political objectives along with the military. Early that July the erstwhile disposer of the destinies of Germany came 'crawling'[5] for peace to Field-Marshal Königsegg goutridden in the castle of Komorzan near Austrian headquarters at Königsaal. Belle-Isle proposed that, if the French were permitted to march out unmolested from Bohemia, Austria should recover that kingdom entire and should reciprocally withdraw from Bavaria. Königsegg took note. Maria Theresa, gloating too, was in no hurry to vouchsafe a reply to Belle-Isle just as he was becoming even more hated in Vienna for the part ascribed to him over an edict issued by the Emperor Charles VII.

[3] Marshal de Belle-Isle to Marquis de Breteuil, Prague, 26 July 1742: *Campagne*, v. 296.
[4] Barbier, iii. 362–4.
[5] Count Ulfeld to Grand Duke Francis II, c. July 1742: Arneth, ii. 489, n. 35.

In all remnants of Bohemia still under French authority an imperial edict of 5 July 1742 called, in German and Czech, upon the peasantry to take up arms against the Austrians under promise of free booty, three-year tax-exemption and, above all, abolition of their serfdom. After paying all taxes and dues the Bohemian serf just about then was left with barely more than a quarter of his meagre income.[6] One observer had recently spelt this out in human terms: 'As I have told you that the Nobility of Bohemia are the richest in the Empire, I must also acquaint you that the Peasants there are miserable to the last degree; their Persons, and all they have, are at the command of their Lord. The poor Wretches have often not a Bit of Bread to eat; in a Country which is one of the most plentiful in Europe for all sorts of Provisions... So much Subjection keeps the poor Creatures always trembling and humble, so that if you do but speak to 'em they are ready to lick the Dust off your Feet. The Severity with which these people are used is really terrible, but 'tis as true on the other hand, that gentle Usage has no Effect upon 'em.'[7] Such 'harsh Treatment from Generation to Generation'[8] stamped the Teutonic domination of the Slav. To challenge it now by imperial patents was to pile on the stakes almost to desperation. The patents were nothing short of a call to national insurrection, the emperor's social insurrection of Bohemia pitted against the queen's patriotic insurrection of Hungary. Even that early, French intervention in German lands tended to have social consequences. Here too Belle-Isle stands forth as a distant precursor of Bonaparte.

To resort to such social warfare was, by the canons of that time, to sin against the comity of nations, against that dynastic and aristocratic principle which held Europe together and transcended the military incidentals of a war. Austrian fury was vented upon those few villages which dared to reach for freedom. A captured bearer of the edict was quartered, each quarter hung upon a separate gibbet inscribed 'Guilty of the Patents of the Elector of Bavaria'.[9]

French attempts to follow up Belle-Isle's interview with Königsegg received the reply that the sovereigns of Austria and of France were in direct and more appropriate negotiation at their courts. This was true, for these French overtures for peace afford yet another example of eighteenth-century negotiations in duplicate.

Cardinal Fleury was said to have burst into tears upon hearing that Frederick had concluded a separate peace and left 'our whole

---

[6] Cf. Robert Joseph Kerner, *Bohemia in the Eighteenth Century* (New York, 1932), p. 45, citing Joseph Pekař, *Kniha o Kosti* (Prague, 1909–11), ii. 195 f.
[7] Baron von Pöllnitz, *The Memoirs of Charles-Lewis, Baron de Pollnitz*, ed. cit., i. 221.
[8] Ibid.
[9] Capello (Venetian envoy to Vienna), Penzing, 28 July 1742: Arneth, ii. 489, n. 43.

edifice destroyed to its foundations'.[10] Amelot de Chaillou remarked that 'this prince is not perfidious by halves',[11] and lamented to the Marquis de Stainville that France's 'allies have dragged us down the precipice and then they left us there'.[12] The French ministers had, however, quickly pulled themselves together. On 26 June Amelot was presenting the Prussian peace to Stainville (apparently standing higher in relation to the Austrian chargé d'affaires, Gundel, than he had to Wasner) as a welcome step towards that general pacification always dear to Fleury, who would now pursue it if Austria would listen. That evening Fleury himself, at his country seat at Issy, confirmed to Stainville his eagerness to conclude not only peace but even an alliance with Austria. These French overtures were disloyally concealed from allied Bavaria, and Fleury suggested that Austria serve England likewise. When Stainville as usual stressed that Maria Theresa would do nothing behind the back of her ally, Fleury replied 'that that was very just, but that one did not commit oneself by listening';[13] England could be brought in later.

Once again had the chances of war rendered so subordinate a diplomatist as the Marquis de Stainville the channel of critical negotiations between the two greatest powers upon the continent of Europe. He himself may have fostered this with a suggestion to the only too receptive cardinal that Belle-Isle was not an agreeable go-between for Austria.

On Monday, 16 July 1742, at Issy, the Tuscan minister read out to Fleury the Austrian answer 'very slowly and very distinctly, word for word . . . , and in the place wherein it is said "that the Cardinal should know better than anybody the pacific sentiments of the Queen [of Hungary, who had secretly offered Luxemburg]", he cried, "God is my witness that I desire no other thing but peace"; and then in the other place wherein it is said "that the 'Queen has to hand authentic proofs of all the harm which they wished to do her, even to losing sight of christianity [i.e. by inciting the Turks]", "That is not true", said the cardinal, "and nothing of the kind can be imputed to us." He listened quietly to the rest of the memorandum.'[14]

This memorandum recalled that no weight had been attached to the queen's pacific sentiments when it had appeared possible totally

[10] Cardinal Fleury to Emperor Charles VII, 27 June 1742: in F.-V. Toussaint, *Anecdotes curieuses de la cour de France sous le règne de Louis XV*, p. 283.

[11] Amelot de Chaillou to Marshal de Belle-Isle, 15 July 1742: Arch. Aff. Étr. C.P., Allemagne: Broglie/Fréd-LXV, i. 30.

[12] Marquis de Stainville to Grand Duke Francis II, Paris, 14 July 1742: Esteri del Granducato di Toscana, vol. 2295/1286, fo. 134.

[13] Marquis de Stainville to Grand Duke Francis II, Paris, 27 June 1742: ibid, fo. 128. (A copy of this dispatch is in Ö.S./H.H.S., Lothringisches Hausarchiv 77/177A, fos. 1–2.)

[14] Marquis de Stainville to Grand Duke Francis II, Paris 21 July 1742: ibid., fo. 135 (copy u.s., fos. 4–6.)

to lay her low. Her states had been overrun and devastated. Nor was it thanks to France that the house of Austria, whose existence she had presumed to attack, had not ceased to exist. Indeed France had boasted of dictating peace from the ramparts of the Austrian capital. Her aim had been nothing less than to subject to the French yoke all Germany and indeed all Europe. Thus was the cause of the Queen of Hungary that not only of all German princes holding to their fatherland but also of all powers prizing their tranquillity and independence. Only with their concurrence could there be procured that general pacification whereby the queen should receive due recompense for those severe losses to which she had been subjected.

It was a heavy answer. Fleury's pained interjections might almost seem to mock and echo those cries of distress which he had uttered twenty months before when Belle-Isle had first read out to him his catalogue for aggression in Germany.

The cardinal's discomfiture now was liable to be compounded by a letter which he had sent only five days earlier to Königsegg. Fleury had pled for peace in almost fawning accents, and had written:

Many people know how opposed I have been to the resolutions which we have taken, and that I have been in some sort forced to consent to them . . . and Your Excellency is too well informed of what occurs not to guess easily who was the one who employed every means to determine the King to enter into a path which was so contrary to my taste and to my principles.[15]

In such unworthy and disloyal terms had Fleury tried to pin the war-guilt on to Belle-Isle, the fallen idol of the fickle Parisians. The cardinal sought, in line with Stainville's hint, to transfer to Broglie the conduct of local negotiations at Prague. This did not prevent Amelot from adducing Austrian unresponsiveness to Belle-Isle as an excuse for the absence of any French reply to Stainville's communication. Such shuffling between the dual soundings for peace prompted Stainville to cut through again to Fleury. On 25 July 1742 he drove out to Issy 'upon the pretext of going to remind the cardinal of the request which I had made to him so long since for a regiment for my son'.[16] The career of the young Count de Stainville was already embedded, as it were, in international issues of war or peace, in relation to that campaign wherein he was serving.

Fleury now discounted Amelot, remarking of Belle-Isle that 'all the démarches which he has made have been without my knowledge, and to speak frankly to you he must be too odious to everybody who

[15] Cardinal Fleury to Field-Marshal von Königsegg, Versailles, 11 July 1742: Luynes, iv. 322: cf. Braubach, p. 357.
[16] Marquis de Stainville to Grand Duke Francis II, Paris, 28 July 1742: u.s., fo. 140 (copy u.s., fos. 7–8), and for the following.

calls himself Austrian for them to reply to propositions which emanate from him'. Such was the variation now upon Fleury's observation to the Marquis de Stainville on 16th July that Belle-Isle's propositions 'have not been listened to, and I quite predicted it, so I was not of the opinion that they should be made'.[17] Fleury explained to Stainville on 25 July that he was in fact awaiting a reply to his own letter to Königsegg, adding:

I am going to appear before God. I swear and protest to you that I never desired anything other than an immutable alliance between the Queen of Hungary and the King [of France], that I still desire it, and if I have acted contrary to my views, be sure that I was not the master therein ... Everything which they have done has been against my advice. The King of Prussia is the cause of all the ill that is happening.[18]

Thereupon the aged cardinal, who was indeed liable to appear before his god within a sixmonth, launched into his revealing denunciation, already noticed,[19] of the threats wherewith Frederick had pushed him into war. 'I am just', continued the cardinal, 'and I appreciate that the Queen of Hungary must be fully compensated for what she has suffered.' In Vienna this admission was filed for use.

In his next dispatch Stainville described Fleury, still unanswered by Königsegg, as 'very downcast'. The marquis told the cardinal that he was sorry, 'knowing his good intentions. "Ah" he replied to me, "it is no longer the time in which my good intentions can be useful; they can do no more, and I am not listened to."'[20] Such language seemed to Stainville rather to confirm 'the public opinion that his credit with the king has considerably diminished, and I should not be at all astonished if from one day to the other he did not totally quit the ministry. God alone knows in that case who would fill this place. Everything is faction at court ... I think that if the cardinal, in quitting, still has enough power over the mind of the king to present him with a person to replace himself, it will be Cardinal Tencin, but if the party of the women carry it, it will indubitably be Mr. de Belle-Isle, and in that case I hold France for lost.'

A fortnight later the Tuscan envoy was indeed revising his opinion of Fleury's decline to the extent that 'I can well imagine that he no longer has the power to get everything that he wants done, but he still has that of preventing what he does not want'.[21] In the conversation

[17] Marquis de Stainville to Grand Duke Francis II, Paris, 21 July 1742: ibid., fo. 135.
[18] Marquis de Stainville to Grand Duke Francis II, Paris, 28 July 1742: ibid., fos. 140–1 for the following. (Copy u.s. Cf. J. Strieder, op. cit., p. 35, n. 3.)
[19] Cf. p. 262.
[20] Marquis de Stainville to Grand Duke Francis II, Paris, 4 Aug. 1742: ibid., fo. 143, and for the following. (Copy u.s., fos. 11–12. Cited in part in Arneth, ii. 489, n. 47.)
[21] Marquis de Stainville to Grand Duke Francis II, Paris, 18 Aug. 1742: Ö.S./H.H.S., Lothringisches Hausarchiv 77/177A, fo. 15–16, and for the following.

which inspired this reassessment Fleury had complained 'very bitterly' to Stainville of the answer which his letter to Königsegg had at length received. It was reply of merited contempt. The cardinal's craven communication was published, probably through the instrumentality of the Austrian government,[22] in the Dutch press, then the European clearing-house for news. Maria Theresa no longer cared too much for Fleury's feelings. And even apart from her own predilection for revenge, any softening towards France would have had grave repercussions upon her association with Britain, now more than ever important to her by reason of recent developments in that island.

II

February 1742 had marked the end of Sir Robert Walpole's twenty years of power, a sign of the times for Cardinal Fleury whose long and pacific administration had in a number of respects matched that of his counterpart across the Channel. Both ministers had been jockeyed into war against their personal will and judgement, and their carry-over as wartime ministers was neither long nor brilliant.

When Walpole resigned he had been succeeded in form by a nonentity, the Earl of Wilmington, in fact by a driving-force, Lord Carteret, who became Secretary of State for the Northern Department in the so-called Drunken Administration. If Carteret contributed to that, this authoritative aristocrat, a Cornishman rather outside the main English tradition, was credited with the maxim, 'Give any man the Crown on his side, and he can defy everything.'[23] This outdated notion went with Lord Chesterfield's verdict upon Lord Carteret: 'He would have been a great first minister of France, little inferior, perhaps, to Richelieu; in this government, which is yet free, he would have been a dangerous one, little less so, perhaps, than Lord Strafford.'[24]

Kings are apt to like those who like kings. George II found in Carteret an English minister of diplomatic experience, exceptional in his command of German and in his knowledge of the intricacies of the Holy Roman Empire. The chancelleries of Europe soon sensed the brilliant Carteret's return to office. English policy, from being

[22] Arneth (ii. 490, n. 48) supports the contemporary denial that the disclosure was made with Austrian authorization or approval; but cf. *Preussische Staatsschriften aus der Regierungszeit König Freidrichs II*, ed. J. G. Droysen, M. Duncker et al. (Berlin, 1877–92), i. 332. Modern opinion inclines to the view that the Austrian authorities were implicated: see A. McC. Wilson, op. cit. p. 343, n. 49; Braubach, p. 358, n. 263.

[23] Horace Walpole to Mann, London, 26 Nov. 1744: Walpole Correspondence, xviii. 535.

[24] Earl of Chesterfield, 'Lord Chesterfield's Characters': Lord Mahon, *The Letters of Philip Dormer Stanhope, Earl of Chesterfield* (London, 1845–53), ii. 456.

insular under Walpole, became continental under Carteret. He promply assured Maria Theresa of full support and raised her subsidy from £300,000 to £500,000. 'This haughty minister (*diesen hautainen Minister*)',[25] as Frederick called Carteret, had exerted an impelling force towards the Austro–Prussian peacemaking at Breslau, incidentally causing the Prussian foreign minister to grumble that Carteret was tending to treat the continental powers, except France, 'like little boys'.[26] Count Podewils had been reading a communicated report by de Bussy, French envoy in London, that Carteret 'was not at all minded to treat France with the little artifices of the preceding ministry: that between two great powers like France and England one must nobly make peace or war'.[27]

One day when the French foreign minister was kindly warning Maria Theresa, through the Marquis de Stainville, 'that she should beware of the impetuous dash of the English, which is tending to nothing less than to want to destroy France', the marquis drily replied 'that I was astonished at this remark, since I knew beyond doubt that he had made proposals in England for an accommodation through Mr. de Bussy; upon which he replied to me that it was true that in a conversation Lord Carteret had said to M. de Bussy that if France and England wished to reach an understanding they could find means of conciliation'. But Bussy, assured Amelot, had, on instructions, merely 'returned politeness for politeness'.[28] And in truth Carteret was by that time less intent upon conciliation than on war with France.

Lord Carteret induced King George II to abandon the neutrality of his precious Hanover, and when that monarch made out that, as elector, he was too poor to pay his Hanoverian forces, Carteret took 16,000 of them, together with a contingent of Hessian hirelings, on the English payroll. Thus was he to incur the prejudiced invectives of William Pitt against him as the 'Hanover troop-minister', as 'an execrable, a sole minister, who had renounced the British nation and seemed to have drunk the potion ... which made men forget their country'.[29]

Carteret might be whipping up Hanoverian, Hessian, and if possible Dutch troops into a so-called Pragmatic Army, but its nucleus was British. From the early spring of 1742 camps were sprouting upon Lexden Heath and on others, reviews were being

[25] Eichel to Count Podewils, Chrudim, 12 May 1742: *Politische Correspondenz*, ii. 159.
[26] Count Podewils to King Frederick II, Breslau, 14 May 1742: ibid., ii. 160, n. 2.
[27] De Bussy to Cardinal Fleury, London, 23 Mar. 1742: ibid.
[28] Marquis de Stainville to Grand Duke Francis II, Paris, 28 July 1742: Esteri del Granducato di Toscana, vol. 2295/1286, fos. 139–40.
[29] Cited, Basil Williams, *The Whig Supremacy 1714–1760* (2nd ed., Oxford, 1962), p. 246.

held in Hyde Park, troop-movements were converging upon the Kentish coast. Howard's Regiment, Ponsonby's Regiment were on the march, the Royal Scots Greys were quartering at Southwark on their way to Dover. Ligonier's Dragoons, with their kettledrums going, came riding through Bromley to take ship at Gravesend. On 20 May 1742 two British regiments of foot, the precursors, landed at Ostend in the Austrian Netherlands. On 26 September there landed there the final complement of the British park of siege and field artillery. All through the summer forces from England had come ferrying across till now a British expeditionary force, totalling something over 16,000 men, was once again standing to action-stations in the Low Countries, its secular place of arms upon the continent of Europe. Counting in the Hanoverians and Hessians, Carteret's Pragmatic Army numbered nearly forty thousand. The War of the Austrian Succession was spreading. England was coming in. Fleury complained to the British envoy: 'You are treating us like negroes.'[30]

The Pragmatic Army was under the command of the Earl of Stair, nearly seventy: one of Marlborough's outstanding captains, this Scot had thereafter distinguished himself as the sumptuous and authoritative British ambassador at Paris just before and during the regency of Orleans. Stair may have enjoyed Madame de Prie before she passed on to Bourbon but in general he cherished an antipathy against France – his youth had been largely spent in Holland, in disgrace for having accidentally shot his elder brother.

Now the Earl of Stair, sharing Lord Carteret's hostility both to Walpole and to France, became the right-hand man of the new minister in his grandiose designs against the French monarchy. If Walpole had in some respects stood as a counterpart to the pacific Fleury, Field-Marshal Stair now showed that Marshal de Belle-Isle was not the only commanding diplomat with large designs. Just as Belle-Isle's army had nominally intervened only as an auxiliary corps in support of Bavarian forces, so now did Stair's army take the field as an auxiliary in support of Austrian forces. England no more declared war against France than France had done against Austria. And even as Belle-Isle had intended to carve up Germany anew, so now did Stair propose like treatment for France.

On 16 July 1742, the day upon which the Marquis de Stainville delivered Austria's severe rejoinder to Cardinal Fleury at Issy, Field-Marshal Stair at the Hague was writing to Field-Marshal

---

[30] Rev. Anthony Thompson to Duke of Newcastle, Paris, 11 Sept. 1742: P.R.O./S.P.F. France, vol. 227B, fo. 374.

Königsegg to propose that the southern frontier of the Austrian Netherlands should be brought down to the Somme and that this enlarged province, plus Alsace, Lorraine, and Burgundy should be attributed to the Emperor Charles VII. In return he should cede to Maria Theresa nothing less than his Bavarian homeland. Thus, with the ingenious resurrection of something approaching that middle kingdom of Lothair, a truncated France would be called upon to foot the bill for the luxury of having created an emperor who was not a Habsburg. The whole balance of Europe would be swung against France in the Britannic and Germanic interest. Amelot had scarcely exaggerated to Stainville in saying that England wanted to destroy France.

The designs of Carteret and Stair, like those of Belle-Isle upon the other side, suggest that Frederick the Great's radical example in Silesia was proving contagious. Certainly was this the case at Vienna where advisers like Bartensten and Starhemberg, 'whose Austrian inveteracy against France was petrified through the course of four-score years',[31] were eager to make France pay for their bitter loss of Silesia. Not that Austrian and British interests agreed on every point. Maria Theresa was too independent to conform entirely to British diplomacy, more particularly to its grand design of promoting a comprehensive coalition to include Prussia and Sardinia. It seemed to the Austrian government, with long foresight, that England was sponsoring the ultimate supremacy of Sardinia in Italy and of Prussia in Germany. But joint hostility to France remained the effective tie. The ambitious and stringent design against French territory which Stair proposed to Königsegg was almost an elaboration and extension of certain 'secret reflections'[32] which Königsegg himself had committed to paper a month earlier, just after Broglie's army had tumbled back into Prague. Such Anglo–Austrian schemes were indeed encouraged by the pitiable performance which the French forces had latterly put up in the Bohemian campaign. In his secret memorandum Königsegg had observed that for the attainment of such high designs against the French in the west it was indispensable that the French army at Prague should first be totally rubbed out in the east. It was scarcely surprising that the overtures made by Belle-Isle and Fleury to Königsegg met with negative response. In all the panorama of Europe at war it was still from over the spires and battlements of Prague that conflict loomed up immediate.

---

[31] Robinson in a dispatch from Vienna; cited, Coxe, op. cit., ii. 282.
[32] Field-Marshal von Königsegg, 'Réflexions secrètes', memorandum of 17 June 1742: Ö.S./H.H.S.: Arneth, ii. 114–15 and 490.

III

For the Marshal de Belle-Isle in Prague the term of his diplomatic activity had at last run out. Argument was exhausted. War now claimed him wholly and it remained only for cannon to speak.

Belle-Isle, having failed to persuade Broglie to launch a full-scale attack against the Austrians before they could complete their build-up against Prague, likewise failed to induce him at least to keep on harassing and hampering that concentration. Broglie uselessly diverted to Eger half of a precious reinforcement of militia from France but clung to his cavalry, potentially valuable for speeding relief operations, even though it was condemned to early extinction at Prague for lack of fodder, once again the limiting factor in eighteenth-century warfare. It was becoming daily plainer, except to such enemies of Belle-Isle as Fleury, 'that M. de Broglie is in no wise capable of details but that he is very good on horseback at the head of an army'.[33] The old type of fighting soldier like the Marshal de Broglie was becoming increasingly inadequate in high command, which more and more demanded the resource and application of such as the Marshal de Belle-Isle.

Strategically balked, Belle-Isle had to fall back upon his tactical duties as town-commandant of Prague. They afforded scope for his frustrated energies. For the French in Prague were menaced from within as well as from without, were as though trying to defend themselves on a powder-barrel. The Austrian drive right up to the walls of the Bohemian capital had heartened its citizens against the French invaders, and in so large a population Austrian espionage could flourish. Belle-Isle and the indefatigable Séchelles stringently sought to protect the rear of the French forces in their desperate stand. The twenty thousand Jews of the Prague ghetto were forbidden to leave their houses, though it was hoped to extrude the poorer sort from the city in the wake of the hostile students.[34] Remaining citizens were forbidden to walk or assemble in groups of more than three under pain of being shot on the spot; they were forbidden in the streets after curfew at eight in the evening; at night all windows must be lit and anyone appearing at a window before eight in the morning would be shot at. By French military ordinance of 31 July 1742 the municipal contribution to the army of occupation for the month of August was fixed at five thousand florins a day; troops would be billeted on any citizen refusing to contribute his quota, and in any house where nobody could be found to pay, the furniture would be

[33] Luynes (Nov. 1742), iv. 272.
[34] Cf. Marshal de Broglie to Séchelles, camp beneath Prague, 13 Aug. 1742: in F.-V. Toussaint, op. cit., pp. 295-6.

sold up. By further military ordinance of even date every householder
without exception, including ecclesiastics, must on 3 August present
to the municipal authorities an exact list of all inmates in his house,
including children and servants, together with detailed returns of all
stores of food and drink in his possession; the penalty for failure to
comply or for false returns would be summary shooting without trial.

While Belle-Isle and his staff were grimly clamping down upon
the interior of the city, they were also toiling to stiffen its defensive
crust. Belle-Isle, with his experience in fortification at Metz, was
much better at that too than Broglie, who made difficulties about
supplying the military labour. But Belle-Isle inspired the workers
both by example and by gratuities for good work quickly done. The
exceptional circumstance that Prague was being defended not merely
by a garrison but by an entire army further brought within the
bounds of possibility a bold conception: all the fortifications were
mined in order that, in an extremity in any sector, an enemy
lodgement could be blown sky-high and the defending French,
instead of being bottle-necked at the gates, could charge out over the
smoking ruins and engage the shaken enemy hand to hand.

In the words of a French officer: 'The Marshal de Belle-Isle has
worked without respite; despite the infirmity of a very painful
rheumatism, he went two or three times a day to visit the works ...
Everything passed through his hands. Nobody could refuse him his
admiration ... What was his colleague [Broglie] doing all this time?
... By his fireside, whence he scarcely moved, chagrined ... he had
the weakness to display it; he ... declaimed out loud against
everything which the other did; he even had it put in orders – a thing
unheard of – that the troops were too exposed in the works made by
M. de Belle-Isle ... No temper enters into what I have said. I know
the Marshal de Broglie little or not at all; but I know that his greatest
partisans cannot deny that he is no longer the same man. Lack of
memory, fits of passion, ill humour, three former attacks of apoplexy,
whereof there yet remain fairly frequent traces which are called
vapours with him, an extraordinarily short sight and considerable
deafness constitute the general.'[35]

No wonder the young Count de Stainville was in with the followers
of Belle-Isle rather than of Broglie, under whom he was then
encamped outside Prague; it was only in a later context, though, that
he confessed: 'I do not like the Broglies ... So far nothing has come
out of this family that is not entirely mediocre.'[36] Their marshal now

[35] De Montreuil (following the attribution of Dussieux and Soulié), Prague, 11 Oct. 1742:
Luynes, iv. 358–9.
[36] Choiseul, 'Mémoires inédits', 3/23/14/726/1.

waited 'with arms folded'[37] while the investing Austrians came closing in upon him. By 25 July the troops of the Grand Duke Francis completed their encirclement of the French round Prague and four days later beat back with heavy loss an ill-conceived foray mounted by Broglie. It was to be the last time that summer that the French cavalry would be operating in strength. Already by 12 August Belle-Isle was pointing his neglected moral: 'It would be difficult, Sir, to depict to you the despair wherein all this army is; for although it has long since envisaged the loss of the horses, and of its equipages, the fatal moment of the reality has come, with its suffering, to its full extent. The last distributions [of fodder] have ceased ... You could not picture to yourself what it is [like], the spectacle of 15 or 16,000 horses, which are gnawing their halters, the ground, and everything that presents itself . . . The loss which every officer is making casts consternation and discouragement, which is increased by the progress over us which the enemy is making every day.'[38]

The Austrians came continually closing in. The Grand Duke of Tuscany commanded against the Little Town, his brother Charles upon the other, eastern bank of the Moldau. At eleven o'clock on the morning of 9 August the first Austrian battery had begun to play upon an outlying French post in the sector of the Karlstor.[39]

At last, it seemed, was there to be an end to that heavy lull which had endured through nearly two months of fruitless negotiation with neither side quite believing that the other would persist in its military resolve. For neither Broglie nor Belle-Isle could suppose that the Austrians really contemplated the exceptional feat of besieging a city held by an entire army of some thirty thousand so that they would have to attack not so much walls defended by a garrison as an army defended by walls, a very different proposition. But the Austrians, encouraged by the example of Linz and the performance of Broglie, were inclined to write off the French. For some days towards the middle of August the tension was punctuated by intermittent bursts of cannon-shot falling like those first heavy raindrops which give warning that the still and sultry atmosphere is about to crack open into thunderstorm. At first light on 15 August it broke. From the heights which flank the Bohemian capital the whole Austrian artillery, more than a hundred heavy cannon, blazed forth battery by battery in concerted cannonade and kept on firing all day long. The siege of Prague, one of the great sieges of that century, had begun.

[37] Marshal de Belle-Isle to Marquis de Breteuil, Prague, 26 July 1742: *Campagne*, v. 301.
[38] Marshal de Belle-Isle to Marquis de Breteuil, Prague, 12 Aug. 1742: ibid., v. 344–5.
[39] Prince of Zweibrücken, *An Exact Relation of Siege of Prague* (London, 1743 – English translation from the French), p. 4. The date of 9 August is some days earlier than those given, for another sector, by Pajol, ii. 228.

The morale of the French had slumped as Belle-Isle had indicated. With their cavalry had gone their last hope of breaking out to freedom. They were trapped and cut off. As one of them put it, the troops 'acquiring no news from France, we regarded ourselves as people abandoned by reason of our remoteness from all succour; each man studied even the least gesture of our generals, seeking to draw therefrom some favourable conjecture: they said nothing and this silence seemed to us to augur a still more fatal future'.[40]

Even as Belle-Isle was writing to the French Minister of War on 12 August of the extinction of the cavalry, there was delivered to the marshal a smuggled despatch of 29 July from the minister. Belle-Isle lost no time in acting upon its contents. The whole French army was paraded and treated to a rare spectacle of the Marshals de Broglie and de Belle-Isle riding out together, both wreathed in smiles. They rode to the head of each regiment and announced that the Army of Westphalia, forty thousand strong under the Marshal de Maillebois, was marching to the relief of Prague. They were not abandoned after all. 'At that the soldiers threw their hats into the air and shouted *Vive le Roi.*'

All the preceding winter and spring the Marshal de Maillebois in Westphalia had continued to fulfil his strategic assignment of observing the north-western corner of the continent and, by the potential menace of his large army, holding the enemy in check in Hanover, Holland, and the Austrian Netherlands. This function had been rendered increasingly critical by the menacing activity of Carteret, his bringing in of Hanover and assembly of the Pragmatic Army in the Low Countries. The French government, however, refused to be mesmerized by this activity. They calculated coolly and accurately that England would not dare to embark upon a continental offensive without first having secured the adhesion of Holland in the rear; and France, importantly reassured from Berlin, was doing her utmost to see that the Dutch, grown fat and cautious, should abide by their neutrality. 'As for Holland', the Marquis de Stainville had written earlier from Paris, 'I regard her as a dead power who will be the victim of her drowsiness.'[41] She was not yet to be aroused by pressure from Stair or even Carteret's own intervention with the States-General that September.

Meanwhile the French authorities had been scraping up every available soldier. While some had, as noticed, been sent straight through to Bohemia and Bavaria, the bulk had been drafted up to

[40] Le Besgue de Nonsart, 'Relation de ce qui s'est passé au blocus et siège de Prague': Arch. Guerre C., vol. 2957, no. 121, and for the following.

[41] Marquis de Stainville to Baron de Richecourt, Paris, 10 Nov. 1741: Ö.S./H.H.S., Lothringisches Hausarchiv 189/III 126, fo. 237.

Flanders to constitute a fresh force under the veteran Duke de Noailles, to keep watch and ward against the gathering Pragmatic Army. This eased Maillebois of that assignment. Noailles and Orry too were said to have stiffened the French government against the pennypinching negativism of Fleury so as to adopt the bold and correct decision to switch the precious Army of Westphalia right across Europe, marching it behind the backs of the enemy in the Low Countries, six hundred miles through to Prague. At this time of high peril the reserve piece in Belle-Isle's original strategy was being brought into play. After waiting so long the Westphalian army of observation marched into prominence as 'the army of redemption'.

Thus was it that by the beginning of the siege of Prague the morale of the mercurial French had gone rocketing up. The Austrian delay of about a month in mounting the siege might prove expensive.

Under bombardment the Marshal de Broglie at last had to abandon the camp which he had obstinately maintained outside the city walls, and to seek shelter behind them. Among the outlying units effecting this withdrawal on 15 August was the Régiment du Roi, which retired from the Kaisergarten, the imperial pleasure-gardens where it had been posted on the outer rim of the Hirschgraten on the northern face of the Hradcin. This withdrawal brought all troops within the orbit of Belle-Isle's inspiration, and work upon the fortifications proceeded with redoubled vigour. That spirited commander determined, however, that passive resistance was not enough. Now was an opportunity to exploit the exceptional size of the defending force and to impose upon the enemy an offensive defence.

In the dark hours of the night of 18–19 August three of the city gates of Prague quietly opened and some five to six thousand French troops 'proceeded in very great silence'[42] to within striking distance of the enemy entrenchments. There they flattened to the ground and lay awaiting the dawn and the signal, three bombs discharged from Prague. The alerted Austrians, though, greeted the French deployment with concentrated fire. The attack looked like wilting when on the left flank the Duke de Biron, Colonel of Roi-Infanterie, charged ahead and was the first to leap into the enemy trenches, followed now by his grenadiers shouting *Vive le Roi*. They fired no shot but plied their bayonets in that grim in-fighting wherein the French excelled. In the words of an attacker of those Austrians, 'we mixed pell-mell with them in their trenches, where the slaughter at first was very great; but soon after the soldiers' fury being allayed, we took near four hundred prisoners'. For two hours the French spoilt the enemy siegeworks before withdrawing into the city.

[42] Prince of Zweibrücken, op. cit., pp. 9–11 for the following.

This satisfactory outing, organized by Belle-Isle, determined
Broglie not to be outdone. Ignoring Belle-Isle's arguments in favour
of sorties at night or at dawn, Broglie plumped for a full-scale attack
in broad daylight, while keeping his dispositions counter-produc-
tively concealed from Belle-Isle, who lamented that 'the Marshal de
Broglie, who understands nothing about the defence of a town, has
hampered me here as much as the enemy'.[43]

Generals may quarrel but soldiers must fight. On 22 August the
pick of the French garrison, again headed by Roi-Infanterie, marched
out across the ravine of the Hirschgraten, advancing straight into a
withering fire without replying to it. The Roi fell once more upon the
Austrian trenches but pressed their advantage home too far. The
Austrians punched them back and inflicted severe casualties. In the
course of the difficult retreat under fire about a hundred of the Roi-
Infanterie got left behind in the ravine; whereupon the bulk of the
regiment coolly charged yet again into the carnage to disengage their
comrades, an action characterized by the Marshal de Belle-Isle as 'a
monument of courage'.[44]

The military results achieved by this gallant action were incom-
mensurate with the loss of life. Enemy casualties were indeed
estimated at eleven to twelve hundred dead and wounded besides
two hundred prisoners, but the French could ill-afford their loss of
210 dead and 608 wounded. The Régiment du Roi headed the
regimental casualty lists with 53 dead and 163 wounded.[45] The latter
included the gallant Biron himself, twice wounded in the head so
that they had to saw into it and trepan. As they began the agonizing
operation Biron is said to have said, 'I little care what happens. I am
content. My regiment has maintained its reputation.'[46]

The Duke de Biron pulled through from these effects of the
hazardous sortie mounted by his old comrade-in-arms, enthusiastic
over Biron's contribution, 'as much by his courage as by his vigilance
and intelligence, and joined to that his living magnificently, not in
his room but with the troops'.[47] With such an example the young
officers of Roi-Infanterie on that 22 August returned two captains

[43] Marshal de Belle-Isle to Marquis de Breteuil, Prague, 13 Sept. 1742: Arch. Guerre C., vol.
2957, no. 55: *Campagne*, vi. 14.
[44] Marshal de Belle-Isle to Marquis de Breteuil, Prague, 23 Aug. 1742: Arch. Guerre C., vol.
2956, no. 151. (This cyphered dispatch is of exceptionally small format, doubtless due to the
necessity of smuggling it through the Austrian lines. It was one of the few dispatches from
Prague at that period which evaded enemy vigilance and reached its destination: cf. Marquis
de Breteuil to Marshal de Belle-Isle, Versailles, 29 Sept. 1742: Arch. Guerre C., vol. 2947, no.
218.)
[45] 'État des tués, et des Blessés de l'Infanterie à la sortie du 22 aoust 1742 de Prague': Arch.
Guerre C., vol. 2956, no. 146.
[46] Cited, General Susane, *Histoire de l'infanterie française* (Paris, 1876), iii. 221.
[47] Marshal de Broglie to Marquis de Breteuil, Prague, 17 Sept. 1742: Arch. Guerre C., vol.
2947, no. 212: *Campagne*, vi. 22.

killed and ten wounded, two lieutenants killed and eleven wounded. The Count de Stainville was not among the wounded but he was among the brave and distinguished if one may judge from the bald citation that he 'assisted in the defence of Prague, was present at several sorties, and rendered important services during this siege'.[48]

It was an anxious time for young Stainville's father in Paris. While wishing success to the arms of the Grand Duke Francis, the Marquis de Stainville wrote to him on 8 September 1742: 'I have a son in Prague, by the misfortune of his destiny, and I flatter myself that if he falls into the hands of Your Royal Highness you will kindly consent to honour him with your favours.'[49] But at ten o'clock that same night a courier from Count von Harrach brought Stainville not only diplomatic instructions but also letters of 1 September from Prague with first intelligence of that sortie of 22 August wherein his son's regiment had borne itself so finely. Next morning, a Sunday, the marquis was spreading it around Versailles together with loyal assurances that the Austrian 'siege went on with great success; that they had dismounted all the enemy's cannon [in Prague] except one'.[50]

What with his correspondence with Vienna and with the Grand Duke of Tuscany, commanding against Prague, Stainville was an important source for the French court, starved of tidings from its isolated army. This also applied the other way on. The French Minister of War himself corresponded with Belle-Isle by way of Stainville's courier, and one finds that diplomatist writing to his master: 'I am sending to Mr. Toussaint, as I have done previously, several unsealed letters for [French] individuals who are in Prague. If Your Royal Highness saw the distraught families in these parts you would be touched with compassion. This is what makes them hope that you in your generosity will be willing to allow their letters to be delivered to their relations.'[51] A week later one hears of several French generals in Prague receiving letters 'in the packet of M. de Stainville',[52] courteously transmitted by a herald from the grand duke.

The couriers of the Marquis de Stainville were primarily diplomatic since the French government lost no time trying to draw benefit from their threat of checkmate by the Army of Westphalia. On 11 August Stainville had reported that Amelot had assured him

48 Pinard, op. cit., v. 685–6.

49 Marquis de Stainville to Grand Duke Francis II, Paris, 8 Sept. 1742: Esteri del Granducato di Toscana, vol. 2295/1286, fo. 157.

50 Rev. Anthony Thompson to Duke of Newcastle, Paris, 15 Sept. 1742: P.R.O./S.P.F. France, vol. 227B, fo. 377.

51 Marquis de Stainville to Grand Duke Francis II, Paris, 22 Sept. 1742: u.s., fo. 164.

52 Marshal de Broglie to Marquis de Breteuil, Prague, 30 Sept. 1742: Campagne, vi. 77.

that 'if the queen [of Hungary] would consent that the troops from
France should return home [from Prague], he gave me his word of
honour that they would at once send a counter-order to M. de
Maillebois'.[53] News of the ambitious march of the Marshal de
Maillebois, which Stainville had promptly had relayed, had indeed
spelt dismay to the Austrian commanders, especially the Grand Duke
Francis. Though he knew the course was little to the liking of his
high-spirited wife, he authorized Königsegg, on the basis of
Stainville's information, to resume his interrupted parleys with Belle-
Isle who, despite Fleury, continued to conduct the negotiations at
Prague.

The two marshals met on 29 August and some correspondence
ensued. But Belle-Isle, merely from Königsegg's initiative in resuming
negotiations, perceived how much the approach of Maillebois was
improving the complexion of their fortunes. He declared himself
ready to agree to the French evacuation of Prague, but no longer to
that of all Bohemia, explaining that his instructions had altered. So
the siege continued, and with increasing violence.

On 28–9 August the siege-guns opened an intensified phase of
heavy cannonading. One of the French garrison noted: 'Their cannon
and their [mortar] bombs are killing or wounding forty or fifty of our
men a day, sometimes more, sometimes less.'[54] The four crack
regiments, Roi, Auvergne, Piedmont, Orleans took daily turns in
manning exposed positions in the outer defences.

Protracted danger, provided it be not too intense, tends to breed
protective indifference. Among the defenders of Prague 'the soldiers
were so accustomed to the firing that they used to play cards in the
most dangerous places'.[55] It was an index to their 'security of spirit
which verged upon gaiety'. High spirits are nourished by good food,
in that case by the unspectacular and ever successful labour of
Séchelles who had seen to it that the troops had 'bread, wine, beer and
vegetables in abundance; mutton, poultry and pork were not lacking;
it was only beef which was so scarce that we were obliged to eat horse,
to which the troops adapted themselves very well. They even made
jokes by saying to riders who were worrying their horses: "Gentlemen,
spare our Oxen."' This shortage of beef was blamed, as nearly
everything was blamed, upon old Broglie, who, however, set the
example of having only horseflesh served at his open table for officers.

[53] Marquis de Stainville to Grand Duke Francis II, Paris, 11 Aug. 1742: u.s., fo. 148. (Copy
in Ö.S./H.H.S., Lothringisches Hausarchiv 77/177A, fos. 13–14.)
[54] Memorandum: 'Siège de Prague par les Autrichiens contre les François, depuis le
commencement de juillet, jusqu' au 12 octobre [septembre] 1742, jour où ce siège fut levé par les
Autrichiens': Arch. Guerre C., vol. 2858, no. 80.
[55] De Montreuil (following Dussieux and Soulié), 'Exposé simple mais vrai de quelques
essentiels arrivés avant, pendant et après le siège de Prague': Luynes, iv. 360–1, for the following.

Besides a daily pound of horseflesh, even junior officers like young Stainville could count every day upon white bread and a bottle of wine provided by the municipal authorities. But if the provisioning in Prague was good enough, the limited supply of powder and shot caused serious concern. Logistics as well as tactics lay behind the French bayoneting attacks. And these continued.

The defenders of Prague never, indeed, repeated their costly daylight tactics of 22 August or even their large-scale night-attack, but night-fighting sorties on a still considerable scale became routine. They retarded the siege-operations and established a moral ascendancy so that the Austrians 'have never left their trenches and have allowed themselves to have their throats slit like poltroons'.[56]

By daylight, despite the stringency of ammunition, a special company of fifty French snipers kept things lively, and at one point the French and Austrian posts were so close that the rival occupants used to chuck stones and grenades at each other. On the larger scale the French artillery did its imperfect best to reply to the continual pounding of the Austrian heavies. Against this barrage Belle-Isle's fortifications still held out, till at last a new and significant entry occurred in the French journal of the siege: 'Today the eleventh [September] and yesterday the tenth our [artillery] fire has been superior.'

It was true. But as the Austrian fire slackened in intensity it spread in extent: 'The 11th their cannon and mortars fired still more indiscriminately, and only 20 pieces, and as if they intended rather to burn and demolish the Town, than to besiege us; they threw into it all sorts of bombs, balls, and artificial fires. At length, towards the evening, we perceived a great motion in the enemy's army.'[57] It lasted through the twelfth. Between two and three o'clock on the morning of 13 September 1742 the Austrians abandoned their trenches and made the night-sky brilliant by setting light to their camp. In the glow the army of the Grand Duke Francis began to march away in two columns, upon the road to Beraun. They were in retreat.

Reduced in numbers but not in spirit, the French Army of Bohemia had won through. The siege of Prague was over.

IV

'No more bombs, no more cannon, perfect tranquillity ... ' ran an exultant French entry in Prague for 14 September 1742. 'You cannot

[56] Siège de Prague par les Autrichiens' etc.: Arch. Guerre C., vol. 2958, no. 80, and for the following.

[57] Prince of Zweibrücken, op. cit., p. 26.

picture to yourself the excess of jubilation ... on the 13th ...; at daybreak we had two thousand [of our] men outside [the walls] despite everything we could do; the open air had tempted them.'[58] In those days a besieged city stank. Outside, besides, was now the sweet air of liberty regained.

Such was the simple and spontaneous rejoicing which terminated the siege of Prague instead of the sumptuous celebrations confidently planned by the Austrians for the coronation there of Maria Theresa as Queen of Bohemia. Toussaint's preparations for a firework display with which Francis had planned to greet her there now gave 'occasion for much satiric discourse'.[59] The Viennese were 'furious against the Grand Duke'.[60]

French publicity from Prague naturally attributed deliverance mainly to the offensive valour of the defence. But it was the wider danger of the advance of the Army of Westphalia under the Marshal de Maillebois which had caused Maria Theresa's council of war on 27 August to reject the lone advice of unlucky Wallis in favour of storming Prague promptly, and instead to decide to quit. Prague was still invested more loosely, in the first line by General Festetics with nine thousand hussars and light troops. The isolated Army of Bohemia remained the chief Austrian bargaining counter, as the advancing Army of Westphalia was the chief French one.

With the military forces thus balanced, Austro–French diplomatic soundings continued through Stainville in pourparlers now formally authorized by the grand duke in a letter from Königsegg, whose own contacts with Belle-Isle had run out. These instructions reached Stainville, along with news of that French sortie of 22 August, late in the evening of 8 September 1742. Early the next morning the marquis drove out to Versailles where a flurry of activity ensued. Two days later at two o'clock, Fleury's dinner-time, the British chargé d'affaires, ahead in the regular queue for diplomatic audiences of a Tuesday, told Stainville that 'I fancied he would come too late. He said that it did not signify for he must absolutely speak to the cardinal, if he stayed till midnight'.[61] He had let Fleury show Königsegg's letter to Louis XV, but a report that 'the cardinal replied that things were no longer in the same position'[62] came close to the truth. On 14 September 1742 Amelot de Chaillou communicated to Stainville a

---

[58] Memorandum on the siege of Prague, 1742: Arch. Guerre C., vol. 2957, no. 68.
[59] Vincent to Amelot de Chaillou, Vienna, 29 Sept. 1742: Arch. Aff. Étr. C.P., Autriche, vol. 233, fo. 295.
[60] Ibid., 15 Sept. 1742, fo. 248.
[61] Rev. Anthony Thompson to Duke of Newcastle, Paris, 15 Sept. 1742: P.R.O./S.P.F. France, vol. 227B, fos. 376–7.
[62] Barbier, ii. 385.

memorandum signifying French willingness to reach agreement and halt the march of the Army of Westphalia upon two conditions in particular: the Army of Bohemia to withdraw freely from that kingdom but not, as earlier, from Germany also; and even that withdrawal to be dependent upon Austrian evacuation of all Bavaria and of Passau. Such terms seemed to the Marquis de Stainville 'in no way acceptable, being totally contradictory'[63] to what Amelot had earlier proposed to him. The marquis promptly told the latter as much, while hastening to inform the grand duke. Stainville's despatch was accompanied by French correspondence, notably, as Amelot had explained, some for Belle-Isle with 'ampler instructions and full powers to treat on the spot without having recourse here because that loses too much time'.[64] Too much, indeed, for the instructions never reached Belle-Isle. Stainville's courier and his French companion were turned back outside Prague by General Festetics, back to the Grand Duke of Tuscany in camp at Hayd, a strategic defile by the Böhmerwald due west of Pilsen.

Not only had time been lost but secrecy too. It was one of the few occasions, but a particularly important one, upon which anything leaked from the Marquis de Stainville's multifarious soundings in secret. Gossip filtered out not only from one of Stainville's servants to one employed by the chronicling Barbier but also from French ministers so that the Bavarian minister in Paris, the Prince von Grimberghen, played it up for political warfare. The Russian and British envoys expressed concern to Stainville who thereupon, with only the concurrence of Gundel, sent copies of his secret correspondence with the French government to the Duke von Arenberg and to Wasner, who were then dealing with the British, for use as they saw fit: another instance of the elder Stainville's precipitancy. However, by the time that the grand duke received Stainville's despatch of 15 September, Francis was already less immediately concerned with negotiations than with operations.

The Marshal de Maillebois had come marching down by way of Frankfurt am Main, making all speed and losing scarcely a deserter in the keenness to come to the rescue at Prague. By mid-September Maillebois had made Amberg. Thence his vanguard was the smaller Army of Bavaria, up from the south to effect junction and bring the total French relief force to over sixty thousand men. The command of the Army of Bavaria had recently been transferrred from the

[63] Marquis de Stainville to Grand Duke Francis II, Paris, 6 Oct. 1742: Esteri del Granducato di Toscana, vol. 2295/1286, fo. 168 (copy in Ö.S./H.H.S., Lothringisches Hausarchiv 77/177A, fos. 26–7).
[64] Marquis de Stainville to Grand Duke Francis II, Paris, 15 Sept. 1742: Ö.S./H.H.S., Lothringisches Hausarchiv 77/177A, fo. 23.

passive Duke d'Harcourt to Count Maurice de Saxe, back from the coronation of the Empress Elizabeth in Russia.

Saxe's antagonist, Khevenhüller, after a march disgraced by a massacre at Cham by Trenck's pandours (it 'seems to have been a little cruel' observed the Reverend Thompson),[65] joined Francis at Hayd on 27 September 1742. If they had failed to prevent the French unction, they had won the race for the key to the Böhmerwald. And they exploited their advantage of interior lines to counter Maillebois's successive probes over towards Bohemia. The French marshal was hobbled by ill-judged orders of 11 September forbidding him to engage a battle whereof the issue might be doubtful. Only rescinded too late, these instructions were reinforced by a warning from the influential Marshal de Noailles against activating the war in Germany by winning a victory there. So Maillebois only swerved up north to enter Eger, still in French hands, on 7 October. He pushed on painfully, through hostile territory now, through Karlsbad to Schlackenwerth on the road to Kaaden, held by Austrian elements which had blocked the defiles there. Maillebois, already severely short of supplies, was put out by limp support from Prague, where Broglie had once again rejected courses of vigour proposed by Belle-Isle. Still, on 10 October French elements from Prague under the Count de Danois occupied Leitmeritz, less than sixty miles east of Schlackenwerth. So little now separated the Armies of Westphalia and of Bohemia.

Upon entering the Bohemian theatre, however, the Marshal de Maillebois, almost at the end of his supply-line, had been sucked into the miserable feud which crippled the French command. Maillebois was on terms of good trust with Belle-Isle but under Maillebois the Count de Saxe, prominent for Broglie, was complaining to Fleury against Maillebois, much as Belle-Isle disparaged Broglie. And Belle-Isle wrote to warn Maillebois 'that the Count de Saxe has informed M. de Broglie that it was your fault',[66] etcetera, etcetera, round and round. Ten days earlier, on 16 October 1742, Maillebois had written from Schlackenwerth: 'I have ... knocked at all the doors, or rather at all the gorges, which lead into Bohemia; I have everywhere found the grand duke well established before me, with all the greater facility in that he was always describing the cord and that I was always doing the arc.'[67]

Five days later the discomfited Army of Westphalia limped back

[65] Rev. Anthony Thompson to Duke of Newcastle, Paris, 26 Sept. 1742: P.R.O./S.P.F. France, vol. 227B, fo. 384.

[66] Marshal de Belle-Isle to Marshal de Maillebois, Prague, 26 Oct. 1742: Arch. Guerre C., vol. 2958, no. 144.

[67] Marshal de Maillebois, Schlackenwerth, 16 Oct. 1742: Luynes, iv. 362.

into Eger. Leaving a garrison there, Maillebois fell back upon the Upper Palatinate and on 27 October pitched at Neustadt on the Naab. The army of redemption had not got through.

If the disappointing Army of Westphalia had not relieved Prague, still cut off, it had at least raised the siege there. Maillebois's march had also dislodged the Austrians, if not from Bohemia, at all events from Bavaria. Khevenhüller, in swinging north against Maillebois, had left in Bavaria barely five thousand Austrian troops under Lieutenant-Fieldmarshal von Bernklau. The new Bavarian Field-Marshal Seckendorff, another Austrian renegade like Schmettau, hit back to such effect that Bernklau finally held only Schärding and Passau of all Khevenhüller's conquests earlier that year.

This was a heavy blow against Austrian grand strategy. The mistake of trying to do too much with too few troops, of denuding strategic Bavaria was not immediately retrievable. Perhaps, though, it might not be too late to repair to some extent the now widely regretted rejection of Belle-Isle's original offer of the total French evacuation of Bohemia. Field-Marshals Prince Charles of Lorraine, Königsegg, and Khevenhüller advised the Grand Duke Francis that an attempt be made to settle for the French evacuation of Bohemia roughly upon the terms transmitted by Stainville on 15 September, notably that Austrian evacuation of Bavaria and Passau which was by now so largely an accomplished fact. This accorded not only with the moderate inclination of the grand duke but also with the insinuations which the French government continued to make during October to his envoy in Paris – to such an extent that the name of the Marquis de Stainville came to echo through the chancelleries of Europe.

V

On 2 October 1742 the French foreign minister told Stainville, indeed, that in view of the Austrian attitude he regarded negotiations concerning the French proposals of 14 September as terminated; but Amelot now also told the marquis, to the latter's understandable vexation, that the abortive diplomatic instructions to Belle-Isle had authorized him to derogate from the French terms offered through Stainville. This was pushed a stage further a week later by the Cardinal de Tencin, recently appointed a French minister without portfolio, a keen Jacobite who nevertheless shared the pacific proclivities of Cardinal Fleury. The marquis had paid a courtesy visit with Gundel in order to introduce him to Tencin, an old acquaintance of Stainville. To Stainville's surprise Tencin opened up. The marquis told him of his recent negotiation, complaining of 'the little goodwill which I had found in the French ministry'[68] in its 'revolting' proposition embodying the two new conditions concerning Austrian evacuation of Bavaria and French non-evacuation of Germany. To which Tencin replied that he was 'morally persuaded' that the French government would not insist upon the latter condition.

The French cardinal could well afford his moral persuasion since the Bavarian emperor on 22 September 1742 had issued a rescript envisaging French evacuation of his imperial lands in return for Austrian evacuation of his hereditary electorate. And the emperor was in this connection apparently putting out feelers to Vienna through the busy Bishop of Würzburg, while he himself at Frankfurt was beginning to debate propositions with Carteret at the Hague. There was talk of a Bavarian kingdom, Passau to Austria, the Bishop of Passau to get Alsace and the Grand Duke of Tuscany to be elected King of the Romans.

Against such a background of secret soundings and diplomatic intrigue Cardinal de Tencin in that conversation of 9 October assured the grand duke's minister of his belief that 'perfect harmony ... between the house of Bourbon and that of Austria ... was the only means of preserving the [catholic] religion in Europe'. Upon Tencin's expressing his fear of 'the impetuous mettle of the English', Stainville once again dwelt upon Maria Theresa's loyalty to her engagements with her allies. 'The minister replied', he reported, 'that there was engagement and engagement', concluding: 'I have no commission ... to say all that to you, but it is the sincere desire which I have to see the troubles finish, and to respond to the confidence which you have shewn me and of which I hope to prove to you hereafter that I am not unworthy.' Their secret confidences were indeed to continue.

Tencin's pious insinuations to Stainville were rather in keeping with the reports from Italy which were then worrying Frederick the Great, to the effect that Tencin had assured his particular friend, Pope Benedict XIV, that at the peacemaking France would see to it that Silesia did not remain in heretical hands. A further step was taken in that direction by the next French feeler put out to Stainville, through yet another intermediary, the Portuguese ambassador in Paris.

'Since Don Louis d'Acunha, the ambassador of Portugal', explained

---

[68] Marquis de Stainville to Grand Duke Francis II, Paris, 13 Oct. 1742: Esteri del Granducato di Toscana, vol. 2295/1286, fos. 171–3, and for the following. (Copy in Ö.S./H.H.S., Lothringisches Hausarchiv 77/177A, fos. 28–9.)

Stainville subsequently, 'is very advanced in years and can pay scarcely any visits, all the foreign ministers [i.e. envoys], in order to oblige him, meet at his house every week on Wednesday and Sunday and there retail the news which they know, and often even that which they do not know. It is submitted to the reflections of the good ambassador, who really is respectable in all points.'[69] Don Louis, as da Cunha was called in Paris where 'all the foreign ministers regard him as their father',[70] was said to have been abroad since leaving Portugal in 1688 to congratulate King William III of England upon his accession. The clearing-system for diplomatic gossip presided over by this patriarchal expatriate was well suited to a diplomatic corps in fact rather isolated from the French court, seldom visited apart from special occasions and their weekly visits to Versailles every Tuesday, when envoys could pick up items to swap next day at their session in Paris. This remoteness suited the French government well enough, as also, probably, the Marquis de Stainville, liable to be less at home amid the exalted loose-living at Versailles than in those snug confabulations with the 'foreign ministers, my comrades',[71] as he called them. The special position of the Portuguese embassy in Paris was enhanced by the circumstance that d'Acunha's subordinate, the Portuguese resident, Mendez, was a favourite with Fleury.

When Stainville entered the diplomatic gossipshop on Sunday, 21 October 1742, old d'Acunha, he reported, 'said to me out loud that he prayed me not to leave without his having a word with me in private'.[72] The marquis waited till he was taken into another room and treated to 'a great preamble' upon Don Louis's attachment to Maria Theresa: 'although I know, in parenthesis, that he has always had a marked partiality for this court here and that, having nothing to negotiate directly for his master, he has only sought to please the [French] ministers by always approving their conduct.' Don Louis proceeded to explain 'that somebody who was on intimate terms with the Cardinal [Fleury] had told him that this minister desired nothing so much as to be able to cement an alliance between the King his master and the Queen [Maria Theresa], that, solely animated against the King of Prussia, the basis of this alliance would be the guarantee of having Silesia restored to her in entirety'.

Don Louis would not name his informant to the Marquis de

---

[69] Marquis de Stainville to Emperor Francis I, Paris, 10 Dec. 1747: Ö.S./H.H.S., Lothringisches Hausarchiv 77/177A.

[70] Luynes, x. 12.

[71] Marquis de Stainville to Emperor Francis I, Paris, 14 Nov. 1745: Ö.S./H.H.S., Lothringisches Hausarchiv 77/177B.

[72] Marquis de Stainville to Grand Duke Francis II, Paris, 27 Oct. 1742: Esteri del Granducato di Toscana, vol. 2295/1286, fo. 176, and for the following. (The copy in Ö.S./H.H.S., Lothringisches Hausarchiv 77/177A, fos. 30–1 is wrongly dated 28 October.)

Stainville, who, however, knew that it was Mendez, understandably described by the Prussian minister in Paris, Baron de Chambrier, as 'an intriguing and crafty man if ever there was one'.[73]

Stainville was asked to make no use of what he had been told pending further consultation with Fleury. The Tuscan minister promised discretion but said that he expected of the upright queen 'that all the propositions which went against the solemn engagements which she had undertaken [at Breslau], would revolt her ... and that she would never follow the bad example which the other powers, and notably this one [France], could have given her ... I dare flatter myself that you will find nothing rash in my reply.'[74] It was prudent if honest to the point of bluntness on such a delicate démarche. Perhaps it was scarcely surprising that, whatever Stainville's discretion, it should dribble out into difficulties.

On 30 October 1742, out at Versailles, Don Louis stalled Stainville since, on examining his informant 'more closely, he had not found enough solidity in his proposals to go ahead with what he had told me'.[75] The marquis noted, however, that d'Acunha and Mendez had been confabulating with Fleury for about an hour. By 12 November Valory in Berlin was informing Podewils that the French government had heard of the Portuguese approach to Stainville, which Fleury disavowed and considered an Anglo–Austrian manoeuvre to alienate Prussia from France. Stainville had earlier sniffed Prussian intrigue at Versailles but had discounted it against 'the animosity which they feel here'[76] against Frederick, in fact invited through Valory on 20 October to mediate with Austria. Frederick had refused a request so calculated to divide him from England, and now Podewils commented to him upon Fleury's disavowal of the contrary feeler through the Portuguese: 'Perhaps the old fox has observed that his game is discovered and now wants to get in beforehand.'[77] Frederick the Great replied next day:

My dear Podewils, the news which you send me by your letter of yesterday has astonished me, although I fear nothing from it. It seems to me that the intrigue has really existed and that it has perhaps been woven by the Cardinal Tencin, to get France out of her embarrassment, to let the emperor have some morsel, and to revenge herself at the same time for my treaty of peace. It may be that the proposal therefore has been made to the Marquis de Stainville, that the latter, surprised by a proposal upon which he was not instructed at all, may have confided it to some

[73] Dispatch of Baron de Chambrier, 7 Dec. 1742: cited, Joh. Gust. Droysen, *Geschichte der preussischen Politik* (Leipzig, 1868f.: henceforth cited as Droysen), part V, ii. 34, n. 1.
[74] *u.s.*, fo. 177.
[75] Marquis de Stainville to Grand Duke Francis II, Paris 3 Nov. 1742: *u.s.*, fo. 182.
[76] *u.s.*, 13 Oct. 1742, fo. 174.
[77] Count Podewils to King Frederick II, 12 Nov. 1742: Droysen, part V, ii. 34.

English friend, and that thereby the mine was divulged; that the Duke of Lorraine, after having been informed by Stainville, may have gone into the intrigue and that this be the reason why the court of London has taken offence against him ... I fear nothing ... since, even if France, united with Austria, wished to set upon me, she is not in a state to do it without England's continuing the subsidies to the Austrians which England however would then take good care not to.[78]

If Frederick's conjectures, like most, rather outran the truth, yet they were not so far out, and his deft analysis of the deeper forces not at all. Money remained the great mobilizer of war, and here money mostly meant England. Also, England was, within a week, on 18 November 1742, to conclude with Prussia the defensive Treaty of Westminster.

Despite rumours just then around a visit by the Earl of Essex to Paris, Lord Carteret was set against accommodation with France and had warned the Prussian minister in London against the soundings of the Grand Duke Francis, whence the allusions by Frederick. The French government on its side was only too conscious, in its diplomatic endeavours to save the military situation at Prague, that, as Amelot put it to Stainville, 'the English gentlemen only want fire and flame'.[79]

In Anglo-Austrian grand strategy Bohemia was balanced against Bavaria, designated in turn to afford the equivalent for lost Silesia. Maria Theresa minuted at about that time: 'If we once let the equivalent out of our hands, it is done.'[80] That put paid to the French feelers for reciprocal evacuation at a time when Maria Theresa had been taking a leaf out of Frederick's book and issuing proclamations to stimulate the nascent patriotism of all those of 'noble teutonic blood'[81] against the hated French invaders: as Fleury complained to Stainville 'with extreme liveliness'.[82] The Queen of Hungary, keen on pickings from Bavaria and help through the Netherlands, held to England, as Stainville was sure she would. She let the British government know that she had sent a sharpish reprimand to her husband's headquarters, forbidding further negotiations with France and declaring that there was not room for two administrations, one at the army and the other at Vienna. Her 'little mouse' must keep his place.

The high spirit and bold judgement of Queen Maria Theresa rendered more academic than ever the prohibited soundings which

---

[78] King Frederick II to Count Podewils, Potsdam, 13 Nov. 1742: *Politische Correspondenz,* ii. 291.
[79] Marquis de Stainville to Grand Duke Francis II, Paris 6 Oct. 1742: *u.s.,* fo. 168.
[80] Minute by Queen Maria Theresa on a memorandum by Koch: Arneth, ii. 492, n. 78.
[81] Rescript of Queen Maria Theresa: Arch. Aff. Étr. C.P.: Broglie/Fréd-LXV, i. 87.
[82] Marquis de Stainville to Grand Duke Francis II, Paris, 10 Nov. 1742: Esteri del Granducato di Toscana, vol. 2295/1286, fo. 186 (following incorrect pagination).

had yet lingered on and even deepened between the Marquis de
Stainville and his friend, Cardinal Fleury. Twisting and turning,
the old fox on 6 November 1742, even before Valory's disavowal of
the feeler through d'Acunha, had not scrupled to go back on Amelot
as he had on Belle-Isle, and to assure Stainville positively and
indignantly that the French reservation of 14 September against
evacuating Germany has been put forward without his knowledge.
Wishing to clinch this disavowal, Stainville next day wrote to ask
Fleury to authorize him in writing to remit, accordingly, a revised
proposal for French evacuation of all Germany against the practically
accomplished Austrian evacuation of Bavaria. This Fleury did that
same day of 7 November, concluding: 'As I count upon absolute
secrecy on your part I promise you the like without exception of
anybody.'[83]

This last sounding, which has indeed remained secret hitherto –
for over two hundred years, outdistanced not only the political
intention of the Queen of Hungary but also the military predicament
of the Army of Bohemia. For the central fact remained: Maillebois
had failed to relieve Prague. In Paris that autumn this little Austro–
Hungarian conversation-piece made a hit:

> Voici les François qui viennent,
> Hongrois, sauvons-nous!
> Oh! nenny dà, dit la Reine,
> C'est Maillebois qui les mène,
> Et je m'en fous.[84]

VI

By commission of 13 October 1742 Broglie was designated to replace
Maillebois in command of the disheartened Army of Westphalia.
The command of the Army of Bohemia was restored to Belle-Isle. On
27 October Broglie at last left Prague, proceeded in disguise to
Dresden, whence slowly on to join the Army of Westphalia on 19
November. So much for any determined attempt to better Maillebois
in pushing through to Prague. After a diversionary march into
Bavaria old Broglie went into winter cantonments between the Inn
and the Isar.

Before Broglie had left Prague things between him and Belle-Isle
had been going from bad to worse, with the latter nearly in despair at

---

[83] Cardinal Fleury to Marquis de Stainville, Versailles, 7 Nov. 1742: ibid., fo. 191. (Copy in
Ö.S./H.H.S., Lothringisches Hausarchiv 77/177A, fo. 63.)
[84] Barbier, iii. 392. (A slightly variant version is given in Broglie/Fréd-LXV, i. 99.)

Broglie's 'excess of incapacity and drivel'.[85] In their army morale
sagged again as hope of rescue faded. 'All the troops', wrote Belle-Isle,
'are going to the devil'.[86] One of their officers wrote home at about
that time: 'Everything that has happened to us is like enough to a
dream, but a bad dream, rather like the story of the Mississippi
[under Law's system] ... The favourite system of inaction still
persists. Why should one change it since honours, rewards and
praises are its reward? Since the enchanter Merlin there has not been
a man like M. de Broglie. We rub our eyes like Sancho Panza, and we
see only windmills instead of giants. We are apparently too close to
the picture, which needs to be seen from a distance.'[87]

Withdrawal to a distance was just what the French at Prague were
unable to achieve; though a partial reconstitution of the cavalry, from
officers' private mounts and by local purchase, enabled them to forage
the surrounding countryside again. By now, however, there was not
much left to get. The demoralized French troops resorted to
marauding, and from Prague, a gay city since the middle ages, Belle-
Isle reported that 'debauches, libertinism engender many illnesses; I
am not talking of the regular deficiency in the distribution of bread
and meat'.[88]

At this low point Belle-Isle sent dispatch after dispatch pleading to
be recalled on grounds of health, representing himself as 'absolutely
incapable of worthily filling the command' again: 'I experience an
almost continual insomnia, with lively pains from my rheumatism in
my hips and loins, which has obliged me to keep to my room for the
past three weeks; and I believe that if my life depended on it, I could
not remain on horseback for a full quarter of an hour ... The least
sensation of cold would finally cripple me.'[89] Belle-Isle's afflictions
were scarcely mortal, and his eagerness to shed an unenviable
command goes some little way towards justifying Choiseul's criticism
of him, noticed earlier, for trying to leave the army in the lurch in
Bohemia, whither he had first dispatched it.

'You will not be surprised, Sir,' wrote Fleury to Belle-Isle, 'that the
King refuses you permission to come here at the so delicate juncture
wherein we find ourselves ... I beg you also to reconcile me with
Madame de Belle-Isle.'[90] She had been giving ministers some pieces
of her mind as to their indifference to her husband's health. Many in

[85] Marshal de Belle-Isle to Marquis de Breteuil, Prague, 22 Sept. 1742: *Campagne*, vi. 38.
[86] Ibid., vi. 45.
[87] De Montreuil, Prague, 11 Oct. 1742: Luynes, iv. 357-8.
[88] Marshal de Belle-Isle to Marquis de Breteuil, Prague, 27 Oct. 1742: Pajol, ii. 239.
[89] Marshal de Belle-Isle to Marquis de Breteuil, Prague, 25 Oct. 1742: *Campagne*, vi. 125-6.
[90] Cardinal Fleury to Marshal de Belle-Isle, Versailles, 16 Oct. 1742: Arch. Guerre C., vol.
2950, no. 99.

the court and government did not conceal their glee at the predicament of the brilliant Marshal de Belle-Isle.

There being nothing else for it, Belle-Isle sought 'to disentangle this chaos'[91] left by Broglie, who had 'lost five irreparable weeks'.[92] Feuding, however, had not been confined to the French high-command. Differences of opinion flourished at Austrian headquarters, bristling with field-marshals, the Grand Duke of Tuscany, Prince Charles of Lorraine, Königsegg, Khevenhüller, and Lobkowitz. In this pass the grand duke arranged that he with the bulk of his army should encamp near Waidhaus so as to block any fresh move against Bohemia by the Army of Westphalia while at the same time asserting Austrian arms within the Bavarian orbit; Prince Lobkowitz, who had quarrelled with Prince Charles, was detached with twelve thousand men to reinforce General Festetics and finish off the dwindling French army round Prague. They were to have no respite.

On 27 October 1742, the day that Broglie left Prague, Lobkowitz began his return march thither. His force combined with that of Festetics totalled something under twenty thousand or approximately the same as Belle-Isle's. The Austrians, however, enjoyed a great preponderance not only strategically but also tactically, in essential cavalry. Lobkowitz did not aim at repeating the expensive siege of Prague, for which in any case he lacked the heavy artillery, but at closing in the encirclement and starving out the exhausted Army of Bohemia through the winter. It was, as Belle-Isle's dispatches about acute shortages testified, a plan only too likely to succeed. And under instruction of 6 November from Maria Theresa herself Prince Lobkowitz was to grant to the Army of Bohemia no free withdrawal this time, no terms except entire surrender.

Lobkowitz began by closing the ring and smashing the tenuous French communications with Saxony up the Elbe by Leitmeritz, captured by the Austrians on 26 November. The other French outposts along the Elbe were also eliminated. Prague was once again encircled and cut off as another Bohemian winter came clamping down upon the French, still forlornly there with the hope at best of somehow just holding out till the brighter days of spring might at long last bring relief.

The Marshal de Belle-Isle, however, knew the extent of his provision-stocks. They did not flatter hope. Nevertheless he firmly proclaimed his intention of seeing the winter through in Prague and made all the dispositions of 'someone who wants to make a solid

[91] Marshal de Belle-Isle to Marquis de Breteuil, Prague, 27 Oct. 1742: Pajol, ii. 240.
[92] Marshal de Belle-Isle to Marquis de Breteuil, Prague, 25 Oct. 1742: *Campagne*, vi. 139.

establishment'.[93] Isolated as they were, they would hold out to the end. Belle-Isle and Séchelles did a remarkable job on supply, stocking up against time, bringing in convoys of provisions and organizing foraging sorties. Day after day squadrons of French cavalry went jingling down the roads out of Prague, extending their sweeps for sustenance since 'all the environs of Prague, for three leagues round about, were totally devasted and foraged'.[94] The further they went, the more they had to reckon with the attentions of the Austrian hussars and pandours whom Lobkowitz kept in the vicinity to the number of some four thousand while holding his main reserve some miles back. Precisely in order to secure fodder the French had to have horses, which consumed it. That was the vicious circle. French officers, however, helped to keep up the precious cavalry by buying and feeding remounts for themselves. The Count de Stainville and his fellow officers were at least serving now under a general who maintained a confident bearing towards his troops, as he did towards his wife.

On 5 December 1742 the Marshal de Belle-Isle sent to his wife a little slip of paper, about an inch and a quarter by two and a half to three inches and oddly curved to facilitate concealment by the person smuggling it through the enemy lines. The slip bore this message: 'My health is as I have informed you, but my hip is still painful. I am observing the most severe diet, for I should reproach myself more than ever[95] for doing the least thing which could cause me the least harm, so you should be very easy in this respect. I would I could be the same as to you, for I tremble always lest V[ersai]lles should give you a cold. I cannot sufficiently enjoin you earnestly to take good care of yourself; you know how essential that is for your chest. You could not give me a greater mark of affection and one whereof I should be more sensible. My brother charges me with hundreds of compliments to you. I beg you to say as much to all those of our friends whom you shall judge proper. I ever charge you with Bizy[96] and to order M. de La Chèze to have the planting, ploughing and work done there just as if I were there and to spare nothing at all therein. I believe that you will find the form of this letter very extraordinary. He who has undertaken to carry it to Dresden wished it to be thus.'[97] Hitherto the writing had been that of a secretary, a masterpiece of elegant and legible minuscule. Then Belle-Isle concluded, squashing the words

[93] Marshal de Belle-Isle to Chevalier de Folard, Amberg, 13 Jan. 1743: Arch. Guerre C., vol. 3006, no. 72.
[94] Marshal de Belle-Isle, Amberg, 6 Jan. 1743: *Campagne*, vii. 2.
[95] i.e. now that he must retain the command of the Army of Bohemia.
[96] The country estate of the Belle-Isles.
[97] Marshal de Belle-Isle to Duchess de Belle-Isle, Prague, 5 Dec. 1742: Arch. Guerre C., vol. 2960, no. 20, and for the following.

n in his own hand: 'I embrace my dear little master with all my heart
and think of her more keenly than I have ever done, and for always.'

To suppose that no French aristocrat of the eighteenth century
ever loved his wife is inexact.

Belle-Isle's miniature message to his wife got through, but a good
many did not. A little earlier a woman employed by the French to
slip through the Austrian lines had been caught by hussars, but had
had the presence of mind to swallow her missive. And about the
middle of December the Austrians captured a French courier coming
through from Dresden with a dispatch of 2 December from Amelot
to Belle-Isle. He was therein instructed to winter out at Prague. (Also
found on the courier was a separate little slip of paper in a dense
cypher which had to be referred to Vienna for decoding.) This
instruction probably only confirmed for Austrian headquarters what
it already knew, since the citizens of Prague were glumly aware of
Belle-Isle's proclaimed intention of holding on there. So the Austrians
continued to add weight to their investment.

Prince Lobkowitz was, indeed, slack in making his dispositions
immediately around Prague; but he was strengthening his longer
grip upon the surrounding country by bringing up reinforcements of
some six thousand Moravian militia and raising local levies of sturdy
woodsmen and mountaineers. The French invaders were brought to
bay at last and the hostile countryside was closing in for the kill. The
very elements seemingly concurred. Snow fell. 'The weather is
terrible', wrote Belle-Isle on 12 December 1742. 'It is snowing and not
freezing, which never happens at this season in this country.'[98] But
it did then. The soggy weather messed up the roads with heavy slush.
The French foraging-parties, however, kept on at it. The 16th
December brought a temporary frost with a thin coating of ice on the
roads so that 'the horses could not stand up'.[99] Nevertheless a
particularly large body of French cavalry went riding out that day
and, as usual, the advanced elements met up with some Austrian
hussars, with whom, indeed, they were on almost amicable terms: as
is apt to happen in war during periods of inaction when the
comradeship of danger shared, even if from opposite sides, is liable to
overcome prescribed hostility. The Austrians asked the French
horsemen 'if they were coming to forage again, to which ours had
answered them, Yes, upon which they [the Austrians] told them to
make haste and then to leave them in peace'. The French cavalry did
as it was bidden and remained quietly in the plain of Jentsch some

[98] Marshal de Belle-Isle to Marquis de Breteuil, Prague, 12 Dec. 1742: Arch. Guerre C., vol. 2948, no. 186.
[99] Marshal de Belle-Isle, 'Retraite de Prague', Dec. 1742: Arch. Guerre C, Vol. 2960, no. 72, and for the following.

ten or twelve miles west of Prague. They were still there at the early nightfall of that December evening.

After dark that 16 December, between five and six o'clock, almost all the French infantry in Prague was paraded to arms. Forthwith it began to march quietly out of the city, through the Karlstor across 'the big stone bridge'[1] to assembly-points about a mile outside, designated by torch signals. The Brigade of Roi-Infanterie, wherein Stainville marched, assembled with those of Navarre and La Marine 'between the chapel and the town in column by battalion, the head facing the chapel', with three flags per battalion. Meantime the baggage-trains were moving out by the Saint Margaret Gate and assembling 'beyond the burnt inn'. At eleven o'clock that night Belle-Isle himself, unable to mount a horse, drove out in a coach to the head of the column of infantry. At dawn he joined the cavalry, still waiting out by Jentsch.

The French retreat from Prague had begun.

---

[1] 'Ordre pour le 16 decembre 1742': Arch. Guerre C., vol. 2960, no. 58, and for the following.

CHAPTER IV

RETREAT

I

RETREAT was what the Marshal de Belle-Isle had all along intended. All his preceding actions and dispositions now assumed another aspect, like the reverse side of a coin suddenly spun round. The constant foraging had indeed been to build up stocks but stocks for a march – even the trussing of the hay into portable bales had been done in secret. More, though, the foraging parties had been designed to exercise the reconstituted cavalry into some sort of trim again and, above all, to accustom the enemy to seeing French horse constantly on the roads so as to lull their watchfulness. This essential element in Belle-Isle's complex design had met with complete initial success. The whole plan had depended upon secrecy so that the French commander had felt it necessary to keep most of his officers in the dark. The government at Versailles had actively collaborated with the marshal at Prague in his strategic deception. The Austrian capture of the courier with Amelot's instruction to Belle-Isle to sit tight spelt the success of an elaborate French ruse. When the extra little slip was finally decyphered in Vienna it proved to be a message from the French Minister in Dresden explaining the deception to Belle-Isle. For the Austrians, though, it was by then too late.

The secrecy demanded by this masterly plan of strategic deception had been, as Belle-Isle said, 'not the least difficult part since I had to work to two contraries at once so that my true object should be hidden in seeking to persuade people of the other'.[1] For the true plan was intrepid to, and beyond, the point of rashness.

For more than a year the French Army of Bohemia had been campaigning almost continuously under gruelling conditions. Only a weary remnant had survived the siege of Prague and that remnant, unrelieved and still blockaded, had been eaten into by sickness. Such was the force of eleven thousand infantry, three thousand scratch cavalry, and three thousand officers (listed separately in significant disproportion) wherewith the Marshal de Belle-Isle began his retreat at the worst season of the year, in the snowy depths of winter. To

[1] Marshal de Belle-Isle to Chevalier de Folard, Amberg, 13 Jan. 1743: Arch. Guerre C., vol. 3006, no. 72.

crown all, this retreat lay not away from the superior enemy but right into them, slap through hostile territory held by the encircling Austrian army of Prince Lobkowitz with its thirteen rested regiments of infantry and eight regiments of heavy cuirassiers and dragoons over and above the mounted swarm of pandours and Croats together with the fresh irregulars in from Moravia – just the troops to deal with columns toiling in retreat. Those French columns, chiefly guarded by the three thousand horse which Belle-Isle had scraped together, had to reckon above all with eight thousand Austrian cavalry riding light. Whereas the French were travelling anything but light. Belle-Isle had rejected the tempting and much simpler course of slipping through a compact contingent of quick-riding cavalry, who might fairly easily have made it and so created a moral effect to blanket, partially at any rate, the then inevitable surrender of the main body left behind in Prague. Instead the audacious marshal had determined to march out entire and batter his way through or perish in the attempt. The grim choice before him for his army had been certain starvation and surrender on the one hand and, upon the other, terrible risk and hardship. He had chosen the latter, conscious of its implications. On the day he set out from Prague, Belle-Isle wrote, 'Never has an operation been so perilous'.[2]

In accordance with the resolute intention of its commander the French line of march included thirty pieces of artillery and what he himself described as an 'immense quantity of baggage'.[3] Between five and six thousand sumpter-beasts dragged the stuff along. Besides the ammunition and supply-wagons there were carts of tools and engineering equipment, a coal-cart, a mobile smithy, the treasury, hospital wagons, mule-trains, and droves of oxen, Belle-Isle having calculated that an ample meat-ration was essential for so gruelling a march and that it would be most economical to convey it on the hoof. Then there were the travelling-coaches of Belle-Isle himself, of Séchelles, and of a severely limited number of headquarters staff: ordinary officers were strictly ordered to ride at the head of their troops and were forbidden to clutter the retreat with their private carriages upon pain of having them deliberately pillaged and burnt. More coaches, however, were provided for the hostages, over twenty of them, whom Belle-Isle was carrying off. These were leading representatives of a nicely calculated cross-section of the population of Prague, starting with Count Philip Kolowrat and including the rector of the Jesuits along with prominent lawyers, university

[2] Marshal de Belle-Isle to Marquis de Breteuil, Prague, 16 Dec. 1742: Arch. Guerre C., vol. 2948, no. 211.
[3] Marshal de Belle-Isle to Marshal de Broglie, Eger, 27 Dec. 1742: Arch. Guerre C., vol. 2960, no. 111.

authorities, burghers, and members of the Jewish community. These unfortunates were hostages for the good treatment of those residual troops which Belle-Isle had left behind in Prague not merely from necessity but as a component part of his strategic plan.

The French garrison left at Prague comprised four thousand malingerers and invalids who were not up to the march. They were commanded by the stalwart Chevert, almost the first to enter Prague and almost the last to leave. Chevert could be relied upon to brace his crocks and maintain an impression of active defence in order to keep the enemy guessing as to the size of the garrison and, if possible, induce him to retain a disproportionately large force outside Prague, thus facilitating Belle-Isle's getaway. Chevert was to put it about that the marshal was merely engaged on a large foray and would be returning. Even more important was the garrison's task of holding down the citizens of Prague, who would otherwise have lost no time in alerting the Austrians as to Belle-Isle's march. Whereas his whole plan hinged upon his getting off to a good start before the surrounding enemy fully realized what was up.

II

Tensely exasperating was the initial delay which wasted the whole morning of 17 December 1742, clogged by a thaw to mess up the roads and a thick fog to obscure them – vile weather in which to start a march. The French artillery, moving out from Prague, had gone astray in the plain in the fog, 'which lost more than four hours, which were then very precious; which was the reason why the army only resumed its march at midday, in a fog which meant that one could not see from one rank to the next'.[4] Thus did the survivors of the Army of Bohemia begin their perilous march into the mists of the unknown.

If the fog slowed and hampered the march it also, even more important, shrouded it from enemy observation. The first forty miles or more westwards from Prague were flat plain, just the terrain for the Austrian cavalry. It was a great gain to Belle-Isle that on the seventeenth he accomplished his first day's march undetected. Entering Tachlowitz at five o'clock that evening he surprised a troop of Austrian cuirassiers; a score were killed and others captured but in the dark the bulk of them got away and spread the alarm to General Saint-Ignon hard by at Schlau with four regiments of Austrian cuirassiers, to General Festetics out ahead at Beraun, alerted that

[4] 'Retraite de Prague par le Mal. de Belleisle', Dec. 1742: Arch. Guerre C., vol. 2960, no. 72.

same night, to Prince Lobkowitz at Lissa on the Elbe, on the wrong side of Prague, whither the startling intelligence came through next day. Generals Saint-Ignon and Festetics reacted promptly, concentrating all the cavalry they had. Now the hue and cry was out against the French.

The Marshal de Belle-Isle experienced the drawbacks as well as the protection of the fog. His rearguard was very late in reaching Tachlowitz and the underfed draught-horses, in particular, were 'half exhausted'.[5] They had to be rested before the next lap, and Belle-Isle decided 'with great regret'[6] to squat at Tachlowitz for the day of 18 December. It was a tense sojourn, Belle-Isle writing that day: 'The enemy are at present assembling from all quarters; our outposts have sighted them on all sides; I quite expected it ... The greatest ill, as I have always told you, Sir, is that of finding myself crippled whilst I should be everywhere; I am making up for it by perpetual work. It is nearly fifty hours since I closed an eye.'[7]

The most usual glimpse of the Marshal de Belle-Isle upon the stage of European history is that, dating from a year or more back, of himself gorgeously bedizened with decorations, holding high court for German princelings at the imperial city of Frankfurt amid a pomp whereof the political shallowness was swiftly to be revealed. Less often noticed is the reverse picture of him as at present, sick and sleepless in the remote township of Tachlowitz, toiling through the winter night to preserve his little army from the enemy closing in on all hands for the kill.

And behind the enemy came the elements. Belle-Isle wrote from Tachlowitz: 'Besides the roads being impracticable, the ground is covered with partly melted snow, and that which is falling is coating it with thin ice; it is all as bad as it could be.'[8] It was bitterly cold now in the frost, at night especially. On the night of the 18th the snowbound countryside of Bohemia lay pale beneath the frigid moon. For Belle-Isle had timed his desperate retreat for when the moon was high. At eleven o'clock that night the French advance-guards headed out from Tachlowitz in the general direction of Lischau, lying to the north-west. They were to march by night.

Belle-Isle had appreciated that the retreat across the open plain from Tachlowitz would be critical, and had determined to attempt it largely in accordance with the theoretical prescriptions which he had recently received from the Chevalier de Folard, a cross-grained

---

[5] Marshal de Belle-Isle to Marquis de Breteuil, Tachlowitz, 18 Dec. 1742: Arch. Guerre C. vol. 2948, no. 218.
[6] 'Retraite de Prague par le Mal. de Belleisle', Dec. 1742: Arch. Guerre C., vol. 2960, no. 72.
[7] Marshal de Belle-Isle to Marquis de Breteuil, Tachlowitz, 18 Dec. 1742: u.s.
[8] Ibid.

military commentator and eminent authority. Back in Paris this student of Caesar and Polybius had been pondering upon the Anabasis of the Ten Thousand and had worked out those unorthodox dispositions for retreat which were now, to an extent rare in military history, put to prompt test in practice. Belle-Isle had marshalled his column of march in five divisions plus rearguards and, following Folard, a double advance-guard. Each division was an unusual and mixed formation comprising a brigade of over two thousand infantry, a brigade of about five hundred cavalry, and a six-cannon brigade of artillery plus baggage and supply-trains. This meant of course that the pace of the cavalry was scaled down to that of the slowest limber, which was one reason why it was an unusual disposition to adopt. Belle-Isle, however, endorsed Folard's calculation that exceptional circumstances demanded exceptional solutions. In accordance with his overall design of bringing back his army as a whole, the marshal coolly sacrificed swift mobility – so tempting to a general in that position – to that compact strength which, he grimly reckoned, his force would need in order to batter its way through. In each division the cavalry formed a protective crust with the baggage and artillery in the middle. Under the French master-gunner, La Vallière, this involved one of the earliest uses of horse-artillery. Each division thus constituted a self-supporting battle-unit for all-round defence, ready to deploy, complete with artillery, against attack from whatever quarter. The special peril of the French retreat through enemy Bohemia produced an order of march unlike anything which Europe was then used to, but strikingly similar to those convoys of covered waggons through Red Indian territories which the colonial warfare in America was to render increasingly familiar in years to come.

The dispositions of the Chevalier de Folard and the Marshal de Belle-Isle were soon to be put to the test.

Whereas the van of the Army of Bohemia had moved off from Tachlowitz at eleven o'clock on the night of 18 December, the rearguard did not leave till the following dawn. The enemy then launched their first attack.

A swarm of Austrian hussars supported by twelve squadrons of heavy cuirassiers came wheeling in upon the retreating rearguard. The French troops adhered to the exact instructions which Belle-Isle had issued in advance. The whole column of march swung straight into order of battle. The field-guns were swivelled into action and sent volley after volley whizzing into the attacking cavalry while the French grenadiers snapped to action-stations, crouching behind waggons and limbers whence they poured a withering fire into the enemy. This was not the reception the Austrians had counted on.

They withdrew. The French retreat continued. But so did the Austrian attack.

Another body of Austrian hussars, riding up from Beraun, came in to hit the third division, commanded by the Count of Bavaria, at about the centre of the line of march. The marchers with their cannon responded as before, and this time they rounded upon the enemy and charged them. There, too, the Austrians fell back discomfited. The French toiled on. Meantime their vanguards had reached Lischau, to peg out the camp there, when they were subjected to the third Austrian attack. This fared even worse than the others, with the French charging their assailants off the field. 'All that', wrote Belle-Isle, 'slowed the march a little and caused the rearguard to arrive only a little after midnight; the ground was covered with snow with a thin coating of ice and an unbearable cold; that day the army nevertheless did six good leagues'.[9] And the way ahead remained open, for Belle-Isle's hook up to Lischau had skilfully avoided the more obvious Rakonitz, where a vital bridge was already down.

The exhausting march of 19 December with its day-long running fight against the Austrians was of critical significance. It shewed the latter that this retreating remnant of the Army of Bohemia was a much tougher proposition than expected. Sporadic cavalry attacks hastily thrown in with the troops locally available were proving inadequate to disrupt the French retreat. General Festetics had been active enough within his immediate orbit but it now looked as though Prince Lobkowitz, who at first tended to underestimate the gravity of Belle-Isle's break-out, would need to concentrate the full strength of those forces which had slackly dispersed. That might, indeed, be effected but it would need time and certain measures to head the French off.

Marshal de Belle-Isle rested his troops till after midday on 20 December when off they set again from Lischau, marching to the west. The fog had closed in once more and so had the enemy hussars who, under its cover, were 'surrounding us from all sides within pistol-range'. They did not, however, venture to repeat their head-on tactics of the day before. Only intermittent skirmishing broke the plodding progress of the march. It must have been tense going, marching in the fog with the enemy swarming all around, in that incessant cold.

The exhausting march at least did something to counteract the freezing temperatures, so that it was almost worse when columns had to halt by the way when waggons got stuck or for whatever other

---

[9] Marshal de Belle-Isle to Chevalier de Folard, Amberg, 13 Jan. 1743: Arch. Guerre C., vol. 3006, no. 72, and for the following.

reason. 'The indispensable halts, above all at night, have inflicted such unbearable cold upon the troops and batmen that there are plenty of them who have died of cold where they stood and others who have had their feet and limbs frozen.'[10] The natural impulse was to try to huddle out of the gripping frost. In his order of march for 20 December, from Lischau, Belle-Isle stated: 'Yesterday notwithstanding the [previous] prohibition there was an infinity of soldiers who stopped in all the houses along the road, others who lit fires, which occasioned all those who passed to stop at them.'[11] Such tempting solace was too dangerous for the men themselves since the enemy pandours and hussars had a grim way with stragglers. That fear, more even than Belle-Isle's orders, probably helped to keep their numbers down. The Army of Bohemia had to keep on going.

The foggy march of 20 December brought the French retreat to the strategic area Jechnitz–Steben. There the plain ended in the eastern foothills of the Tepler Mountains, the craggy hinge in the right-angle formed by the Bohemian Forest and the Harz Mountains. The first phase of the march across the flat now completed, more difficult country lay ahead. The French had reached the strategic junction of the highroads forking south-west to Pilsen and north-west to Eger round by Karlsbad. Steben lay at the beginning of the road to Eger while Jechnitz pointed the way to Pilsen.

The road to Pilsen was considerably the shorter and easier of the two and Prince Lobkowitz, now organizing the pursuit, ordered all his available troops to concentrate upon that artery so as to block the defiles through which it passed, and blow the bridges. Thus the Army of Bohemia's successful sortie over the plain would all the same only lead into a trap wherein the Austrian advanced elements could keep on whittling the frustrated French away till Lobkowitz himself came up with his main force to finish them off in accordance with the resolve of his queen.

On the evening of the 20th the Army of Bohemia marched into Jechnitz on the road to Pilsen.

There was to be little let-up, though, for most of them that night. Leaving his artillery with some covering troops to rest at Jechnitz and mislead the enemy, the indomitable Marshal de Belle-Isle marched the bulk of his weary force off again under cover of darkness and switched them to Steben on the road to Eger. What with fatigue, the darkness, and the heavy weather, the French rearguard was late in making Steben. So Belle-Isle stood there next day, 21 December, and allowed his men a little of the rest which they so sorely needed.

[10] 'Retraite de Prague par le Mal. de Belleisle', Dec. 1742: Arch. Guerre C., vol. 2960, no. 72.
[11] 'Ordre de marche du 20 Xbre' (1742), Lischau: Arch. Guerre C., vol. 2960, no. 82.

As Belle-Isle wrote from Steben: 'I am obliged to march eighteen hours a day in the snow and fog; it is easy to understand the excessive fatigue.'[12]

The night switch of the French from Jechnitz to Steben was a skilful tactic of deception but it could but postpone the evil day a little for them to attempt the evident alternative of pushing up the post-road to Eger. For that last French stronghold in Bohemia, garrisoned by rather under two thousand effectives left there by Maillebois, lay right on the other side of the Tepler Mountains. The highroad thither skirted around them by way of Karlsbad and Elbogen, both commanding strategic bridges over the Eger river. Both towns were in Austrian hands and both bridges would almost certainly be down before ever Belle-Isle reached them. The long way round would give the enemy plenty of time in which to prepare and concentrate.

After moonrise on the night of 21 December, between eleven and one o'clock, the Army of Bohemia marched out from Steben, along the highroad leading to Karlsbad.

III

Suddenly, some three miles out from Steben, the whole column of march began wheeling sharp left, clean off the road and away up into the hills by what was scarcely more than a track. Now came the crux of Belle-Isle's whole plan of retreat.

For weeks in advance, while still bottled up in Prague, the Marshal de Belle-Isle had had spies out reconnoitring all the likely, and unlikely, countryside, bringing in detailed reports of roads and terrain for sifting at headquarters. In the light of this intelligence Belle-Isle, though unable himself to check it on the ground, had decided to stake everything upon his being able to bring the army through by a steep and lonely track, 'which had never been frequented in years',[13] leading right through the heart of the Tepler Mountains. Now his audacious decision was to be put to the test.

Thus did the dawn of 22 December find the Army of Bohemia toiling up into the snowy highlands. There they emerged at last from the mists of the plain into bright sunshine which might seem to smile upon their hardy struggle to dominate adversity. But the sun could not thaw the biting cold, intensified as it was by 'an unbearable north wind'[14] which came whipping over the crests and beating up the snow upon the pineclad slopes.

[12] Marshal de Belle-Isle to Marquis de Breteuil, Steben, 21 Dec. 1742: *Campagne*, vi. 281.
[13] 'Retraite de Prague par le Mal. de Belleisle', Dec. 1742: Arch. Guerre C., vol. 2960, no. 72.
[14] Marshal de Belle-Isle, Amberg, 6 Jan. 1743: *Campagne*, vii. 9.

Adapting his dispositions to the terrain with characteristic flexibility, Belle-Isle had correctly calculated that the remote and hilly country would now protect his army from running cavalry-attack, and he had accordingly recast his cumbersome mixed divisions into more usual and mobile formations. He now further divided his force and sent his heavy cavalry riding on ahead by a different route from that which he himself intended to follow with the main body. By this diversion the marshal aimed at confusing still further an enemy intelligence already hard put to it by the twisting and turning of their agile adversary who seemed, each morning, to be somewhere quite different from what one would have expected from his dispositions of the preceding day.

In the van of the infantry marched the Regiment of Piedmont followed by Auvergne, then came a Bavarian contingent which had remained with the French army, followed again, in the centre of the column, by headquarters staffs with some grenadiers and dragoons; after them marched Stainville's regiment, Roi-Infanterie, with Maine and Navarre bringing up the rear. Such was the column which at midnight entered Luditz. This was a strategic point 'where it would have been very easy with five hundred men to halt the whole army if this march had been foreseen by the enemy'.[15] But they had not foreseen it. The Austrians were absent and the French came through.

This capital advantage had been bought by gruelling exertion. On the lap from Steben the Army of Bohemia had handsomely exceeded its eighteen-hour average. The retreating French had been on the road or, almost more accurately, off the road for twenty-four hours, marching night and day. The harder going, however, brought them greater rest.

At Luditz the Marshal de Belle-Isle for the first time felt able to relax the strict regulations whereby he had previously camped his troops in line of battle, always on the alert against attack. Now he billeted them around the little township of Luditz and had them provided with every comfort he could muster. No longer need he reprimand officers for leaving their troops in camp while they themselves snugged down in local billets, as had happened for instance at Tachlowitz. At Luditz the refreshment, though, was brief.

During the dark hours of bitter cold, while the weary campaigners were resting out a little, the night mists froze upon the steep sides of the mountain which they must next cross after Luditz. It was clear to Belle-Isle the following day that he could never haul his artillery up such icy obstacles. To abandon it, though, would be a heavy loss: a

[15] 'Retraite de Prague par le Mal. de Belleisle', Dec. 1742: Arch. Guerre C., vol. 2960, no. 72, and for the following.

loss not only in protection, as had been so recently emphasized in the running engagements across the plain, but also in pride and honour. For in those days guns were second only to standards as symbolic trophies. Each cannon was embossed with the royal arms and was of personal concern to its crew, as may be gathered from the names which the guns bore and under which they were officially entered in the artillery returns of the French army – names which still stand out vividly from the lists of about that time: Le Lunatique, Le Piéton, Agamemnon, L'Expéditive, Tintamarre, La Ravissante, Daphné, Le Rêveur, L'Absolu, L'Académicien, L'Outrageur, Le Rhinocéros.

Belle-Isle did not intend to abandon his artillery. Instead he detected a silver lining in the frost which, while it had iced the mountain ahead, had also frozen some marshland to one side of it. The marshal, exploiting his terrain all the way, switched his artillery roundabout over the frozen marshes, which held, while the main column clambered on to Theusing. The Roi marched in the same position of line as before, only having, this time, Auvergne and Piedmont in their rear. From Luditz onwards a few stray hussars were all that the French saw of the enemy. At Theusing intelligence reached the Marshal de Belle-Isle that all the bridges on the road to Pilsen were now down and that on the highroad to Eger the Austrians had broken and burnt the bridge at Karlsbad, just as he had foreseen. The trap was sprung, but empty. As the Austrians scoured and barricaded the valleys on either hand, the little French column of retreat breasted its way through the middle 'in the midst of the woods and the mountains'.

On Christmas Eve the Army of Bohemia entered Einsiedel where Belle-Isle rested his men throughout Christmas Day, allowing stragglers to catch up and the artillery to work its way round to the head of the column in accordance with his dispositions for the lap ahead. Over Christmas the marshal had large rations distributed, and indeed his army would never have got so far nor stood so much had it not been consistently well fed thanks to the foresight of Belle-Isle and Séchelles. The troops each received a pound of fresh beef every day and frequent distributions of bread, biscuit, bacon, and rice, which they generally boiled up into a thick broth. Their commander 'also had them given brandy which he had had brought expressly'. As the supply-waggons were emptied they were set alight so that the path of the French retreat was marked by burnt carts – and by frozen corpses. Besides those frozen to death others, too, died of sheer exhaustion. Among these, there at Einsiedel, there succumbed one of the eminent hostages from Prague, Count Pachta. But the living, eminent and humble alike, had to keep going. All moved under the masterly impulsion of the marshal who never let up, seemingly thought of everything, supervised everything, was everywhere, carried round crippled in a litter, 'astonished still to exist'.[16]

'The Marshal de Belle-Isle, having a continual fever with a heavy cold on the chest, set the army on the march [from Einsiedel] on the 25th at midnight.'[17] They trudged on through the darkness into country more difficult than anything hitherto encountered and 'arrived at the break of day at the entrance of the forest which covers the high mountain of Königswart, whence one descends by a way of precipices, which would have been impracticable without the snow which softened its escarpment'.[18] They even lugged the artillery down 'the defiles and mountains of Königswart, which will seem incredible, so rugged, terrible and almost impracticable is this gorge; yet all the cannon and their appendages and all the munitions came through it'.[19] Picturesque mountain scenery was not much in vogue in the first half of the eighteenth century.

After the artillery came the main body of the troops scrambling and slithering down the precipitous slopes, down into the plain below. By that evening, 26 December, the Régiment du Roi was at Ober-Sandau while the marshal's headquarters staff camped at Unter-Sandau. Already advanced elements were attaining the goal and next day, 27 December 1742, the main force of the Army of Bohemia entered Eger. They had come through. Their extraordinary march and hardship had at last brought them back to safety. The enemy had been fooled utterly by the intrepid ingenuity of their retreat. If ever an army owed its survival to its commander it was the Army of Bohemia.

IV

Such was the winter of retreat of the French army from Prague, just seventy years before the winter retreat of the French army from Moscow. The latter was much the greater, more terrible, and more celebrated operation. Whether it was the more brilliant or successful is more doubtful. The retreat of the Grande Armée of Napoleon, very long and afflicting, yet did not lie from the beginning directly through a superior enemy. And the Grande Armée was shattered by retreat whereas the Army of Bohemia came through as a coherent

[16] Marshal de Belle-Isle to Marquis de Breteuil, Steben, 21 Dec. 1742: Arch. Aff. Étr.: Broglie/Fréd-LXV, i. 144.

[17] 'Retraite de Prague par le Mal. de Belleisle', Dec. 1742: Arch. Guerre C., vol. 2960, no. 72.

[18] Marshal de Belle-Isle to Chevalier de Folard, Amberg, 13 Jan. 1743: Arch. Guerre C., vol. 3006, no. 72.

[19] 'Retraite de Prague par le Mal. Belleisle', Dec. 1742: Arch. Guerre C., vol. 2960, no. 72.

fighting formation, battered and exhausted though it was. Belle-Isle was soon asserting, with perhaps pardonable bravado, that his army 'would still be capable of beating all the Austrian infantry'.[20] Another dissimilarity between the two retreats lay in the personal conduct of the commanders towards the close: the then eupeptic Emperor Napoleon, even if for sufficient reasons of state, drove back ahead in disguise after the Beresina, leaving it to his lieutenants to bring in the broken remnants: the different conduct of the ailing Marshal de Belle-Isle was a powerful factor in the execution of one of the most successful winter retreats of any age.

The Marshal de Belle-Isle was not one of the great captains of history, but his retreat from Prague was one of the classic operations. Certainly his contemporaries thought so. Classical parallels of appreciation came pouring in. Marshal von Seckendorff, the Bavarian commander, wrote to Marshal de Belle-Isle comparing his feat 'with the march of Julius Caesar who attempted to cross the Alps; it is true that the elephants caused all the trouble, but your artillery and caissons could not have caused you less. I have read with avidity and with astonishment the account which you have been kind enough to send me.'[21] The Chevalier de Folard of course preferred the Greek parallel and promptly wrote: 'One would say that you have taken for model the Greek general in the retreat of the ten thousand; for if you do not read Greek, I will indicate to you the passages which I find conformable to yours.'[22] Without waiting for confirmation as to the marshal's classical attainments the chevalier plunged into a detailed comparison between the retreats of Xenophon and of Belle-Isle, who incidentally omitted from his dispatches any mention of his debt to Folard. If the retreat from Prague, unlike the Anabasis, is not enshrined in the annals of world literature yet anybody who, like the young Count de Stainville, was a participant, was unlikely to forget it.

On the same day that Marshal de Belle-Isle completed his retreat to Eger, 27 December 1742, Brigadier Chevert and his French remnant at Prague capitulated to Prince Lobkowitz. Their part was at last played out. Chevert had conducted the capitulation of Prague as skilfully as he had earlier led its escalade. He deceived the enemy as to the size of garrison and alarmed him by threatening, in default of honourable terms, to reduce the whole city to ashes, a devastation

[20] Marshal de Belle-Isle to Marshal von Seckendorf, Amberg, 15 Jan. 1743: Arch. Guerre C., vol. 3006, no. 99.
[21] Marshal von Seckendorff to Marshal de Belle-Isle, Landshut, 13 Jan. 1743: Arch. Guerre C., vol. 3006, no. 77.
[22] Chevalier de Folard to Marshal de Belle-Isle, Paris, 28 Jan. 1743: Arch. Guerre C., vol. 3006, no. 219.

which would evidently have included the delicious palace of Lobkowitz himself. That prince knew how to appreciate valour even when exercised at his own expense, and treated Chevert with every consideration, presenting him with two cannon captured from the Bavarians. On 2 January 1743 the French garrison of Prague marched out as free men, with honours of war. They left behind, affixed to the wall of their depot, a plaque poignantly inscribed *L'art de vaincre est perdu sans l'art de subsister. L'an 1742*. This plaque has survived in Prague down to the present day.[23]

Chevert led his invalids back, at Austrian expense, by way of Beraun, Mauth, Pilsen, Mies, Plan, back to Eger. Marching in that company was a young captain from Stainville's regiment, the Marquis de Vauvenargues. This rare and early spirit, soon to be famous for his maxims and his *Introduction à la connaissance de l'esprit humain*, never recovered from the rigours of that campaign. He died four years later at the age of thirty-one.

The losses suffered by the Army of Bohemia were, all things considered, surprisingly light. A week after his arrival at Eger Belle-Isle put his casualties, nearly all from the march rather than from combat, at about 420 cavalry and 1,000 to 1,100 infantry: and stragglers kept on coming in so that the final total may have been less.[24] Among the survivors, however, was 'an infinite number of sick; general officers and others, nobody is exempt, because everything has been in common'.[25] Belle-Isle had to leave behind at Eger 800 sick, half of them cases of frostbite for amputation, when he moved the little army on, early in January 1743, to Amberg. There he rested out his veterans along the Naab and released his hostages from Prague.

The recapture of the Bohemian capital did not console the Queen of Hungary for the escape of the French army. Numbers of the Bohemian nobility who had bowed to the Bavarian as their king now experienced her displeasure. At last, though, she herself could be crowned in Prague and share with her accompanying husband memories of their first meeting at that preceding coronation there just on twenty years before. The magnificent festivities included a classical chariot-race for ladies only. Maria Theresa in person, together with her sister, were star participants in this representation of the triumph of her sex.

[23] The plaque was moved and restored in 1901. It is or recently was to be seen on the wall of a military building on the corner of Kovpakova and Slovenského Povstani streets in Prague.

[24] This would seem to be indicated by the figures given in Marshal de Belle-Isle's letter of 15 Jan. 1743 to Marshal von Seckendorff (Arch. Guerre C., vol. 3006, no. 99). The basis of that computation, however, leaves some room for doubt.

[25] Marshal de Belle-Isle to Marquis de Breteuil, Eger, 2 Jan. 1742: *Campagne*, vii. 18.

'People attached to the Queen', wrote the Marquis de Stainville from Paris on Belle-Isle's retreat, 'cannot conceive how this expedition could have taken place unless M. Lobkowitz had received orders not to present any opposition to it'.[26] At Versailles, indeed, it was rumoured, typically, that Belle-Isle had only accomplished his incredible exploit by means of some base compact with the enemy. Such interpretations were swept away by the ensuing wave of enthusiastic relief. As sometimes happens in war, the news of such a gallant and improbably successful retreat from out of the jaws of destruction evoked a more heartfelt response from the nation than even great victories are apt to do. Governments and headquarters, however, tend to take coolly strategic views. The tactical brilliance of Belle-Isle's retreat from Prague could not repair the strategic failure of the whole of his ambitious campaigning into Bohemia. In this long campaign, wherein the French army had fought not one large pitched battle, its strength had been so terribly frittered away that barely a quarter of the troops came back. In his proportions, at least, the Marquis de Stainville was roughly right here: 'These fourteen thousand men ... are the residue of over fifty thousand who went into Bohemia. They are the most senior units of all the French troops and they are, so to say, reduced to nothing.' Although, among them, that did not apply to his own son.

For the French government it remained to draw the necessary consequences, and it was decided that Belle-Isle himself should be the first to do so. He was instructed to return to Versailles via the imperial court at Frankfurt. There he discharged his thankless and ironic mission. This was to urge Charles VII to 'abate the vast ideas'[27] which Belle-Isle had himself so stimulated, and to revert in some sort to the line of accommodation advanced by the Bishop of Würzburg and widely supported in Germany: namely, that the emperor should dispense with his French auxiliaries and should submit his dispute with Austria to the imperial diet or a European congress. This thinly veiled proposal for a French defection provoked an emotional scene between the marshal and the emperor, who, however, was pursuing his independent soundings in Vienna, Berlin and London, with a view to securing sufficient terms upon which to withdraw from the luckless conflict. The primary calculation for both France and Bavaria was how far each might advantageously be able to cut her own losses. Such was the wreck of Belle-Isle's grand design for Germany.

[26] Marquis de Stainville to Grand Duke Francis II, Paris, 5 Jan. 1743: Esteri del Granducato di Toscana, vol. 2295/1286, fos. 214–15 for the following.

[27] Instructions from Amelot de Chaillou to Marshal de Belle-Isle, Versailles, 12 Jan. 1743: Arch. Aff. Étr. C.P., Bavière: Broglie/Fréd-LXV, i. 390.

The strength of opinion against Belle-Isle at the French court corresponded to the extent of his previous ascendancy and of his present discomfiture. When, however, the marshal at last returned to Versailles on Sunday, 3 March 1743, the king received him graciously. Not formally in disgrace, Belle-Isle soon retired from court to nurse himself back to health, and was for a spell scarcely consulted. It was the end of his glory though not of his career, subsequently destined to overlap again with that of the future Duke de Choiseul.

CHAPTER V

ADVANCEMENT

I

THE Count de Stainville was now to rise as the Marshal de Belle-Isle was eclipsed from a court at Versailles very different from that at their outset for Bohemia.

On 5 January 1743 the French Minister of War, the Marquis de Breteuil, not yet sixty, died of an apopletic fit which came on while he was visiting Fleury at Issy. And at last the cardinal himself was marked down. A month earlier the Marquis de Stainville had described Fleury as 'continuing to waste away day by day, which causes an inexpressible ferment and stir at court'.[1] Losing his hearing and his eyesight, he had shrunk from five foot seven to under five foot three. On 30 January the marquis wrote of his old friend: 'After having fought long and after an agony of a fortnight the Cardinal de Fleury died yesterday half an hour after noon.'[2] It had taken death itself to terminate his tenacious rule of seventeen years, which had begun almost at the same time as the first mission to Paris of the marquis. The cardinal expired in his ninetieth year, one of the oldest chief ministers in history to die in office.

Fleury's death was among his most popular actions, except with the king himself. Never, one is assured, had there been 'an agony rendered so comic by all the songs, epigrams and demonstrations'.[3] Before very long, however, thoughtful opinion began to render greater justice to Fleury 'whose pacific and mild ministry', in the words of an eighteenth-century appreciation, 'constitutes an epoch in our annals less brilliant, but more fortunate than that of the celebrated Richelieu'.[4] The economic benefits which had accrued to France under Fleury's prudent administration have already appeared, as also the diplomatic successes, notably in his artful extraction of Lorraine from the War of the Polish Succession, and, upon these foundations, the superior position of France in Europe, in rapproche-

[1] Marquis de Stainville to Grand Duke Francis II, Paris, 8 Dec. 1742: Esteri del Granducato di Toscana, vol. 2295/1286, fo. 128.
[2] Marquis de Stainville to Baron de Richecourt, Paris, 30 Jan. 1743: Ö.S./H.H.S., Lothringisches Hausarchiv 189/III 126, fo. 221.
[3] D'Argenson, iv. 49.
[4] Abbé Millot, *Mémoires politiques et militaires* (Paris, 1777), v. 319.

ment with Austria before Frederick of Prussia took a hand. The
virtues of Fleury's statesmanship have since become fashionable –
this economic awareness coupled with unusual personal frugality, his
political pacifism, his good relations with England. It is high-handed,
though, just to dismiss contemporary criticism.

Another French cardinal who was also to conduct French foreign
policy once wrote of Fleury that 'he lived too long for his glory'.[5] If
Fleury in his closing years was indeed too old to be a wartime
minister, old gentlemen are to be censured, not excused, for
conceitedly clinging to power after they are past it.

Fleury's parsimony and slim finesse might redound to his success
in peacetime but not in war: his mind had not proved large or flexible
enough to adapt itself to radical change of circumstance. He had
grudged expensive cavalry for the French campaign in Bohemia and
compromised it still more gravely when, having failed to withstand
Belle-Isle's impulsion into war, he tried to hamper his activity and
support Broglie against him. The French failure in the Bohemian
campaign must largely be debited against Fleury for his fatal
duplication of the command. If his craven letter to Königsegg had
indicated duplicity towards Belle-Isle, duplicity had been a crooked
strand throughout Fleury's policy, whose Austrian inflection was yet
to be significantly evoked by Choiseul.

Fleury's hardly reconcilable engagements to Austria and to Bavaria
concerning the Pragmatic Sanction had afforded Belle-Isle his
opening. The latter's failure to combine Spain and Sardinia against
Austria largely reflected the resentment which Spain especially bore
against France as a slippery ally in the War of the Polish Succession,
notably in regard to French soundings with Austria during the siege
of Mantua in 1735. The French negotiations of 1739 over the Berg-
Jülich succession had further illustrated the comment of the Duke de
Luynes: 'This manner of acting by subtleties and underhand means,
and of wishing to satisfy both parties at the same time, was very
ordinary with the Cardinal [Fleury], as much in large matters as in
small.'[6] Duplicity might often enough be practised as a fine art in
eighteenth-century statescraft but even contemporaries considered
that Cardinal Fleury's, not controlled by a commanding intellect
such as Cardinal de Richelieu's, reflected the later cardinal's 'too little
elevation of mind'.[7] He had, as now apparent, recruited the future
Choiseul for France and in general he was undoubtedly a valuable

[5] Cardinal de Bernis, *Mémoires et lettres de François-Joachim de Pierre, Cardinal de Bernis
(1715–1758)*: ed. Frédéric Masson (Paris, 1878: henceforth cited as Bernis), i. 44.
[6] Luynes, v. 161.
[7] 'Portrait de M. le Cardinal de Fleury' in Luynes, v. 240.

minister to her: that he was a great minister does not appear either in the light of history or in the estimation of contemporaries. For the idealistic Marquis d'Argenson the Cardinal Fleury, 'as supple as a glove',[8] prompted the reflection that 'Punic bad faith must be left to little states like Savoy'.[9]

Now perhaps they might be. The emaciated cardinal had finally faded out like an obscuring film dispersed to reveal – the king. The cry went up: 'The cardinal is dead. Long live the king!'

II

King Louis XV of France is chiefly remembered for his licentious amours at the court of Versailles. So, naturally perhaps, he has tended to be assimilated to the popular tradition of a Merry Monarch: naturally, that is, for those who do not know what Louis was like.

Louis XV had been born on 15 February 1710, fourth in line of succession to his great-grandfather, Louis XIV. By the time that the puny infant became king on 1 September 1715 medical incompetence had ministered to the deaths of his grandfather, the Grand Dauphin, his father, the hopeful Duke of Burgundy, his mother, volatile Marie-Adelaide of Savoy, and his elder brother, the Duke of Brittany. In after years the Duke de Choiseul, a searching psychologist, wrote of the lonely little orphan that 'at the age of five he had been the object of the love and the wishes of the nation: the apparent weakness of his health, the precious preservation of his life in the position wherein France and Europe found themselves, the flattery and attentions of those charged with bringing him up were, I believe, the origins of the soft weakness of his spirit and of his body, as they were likewise of the vanity which made him believe that he was of a kind different from other men; sometimes he did not hide this conceited opinion.'[10]

Louis, cherished by his spoiling governess, the pious Duchess de Ventadour, had grown into a handsome boy with darkly vivid eyes, curling eyelashes, and long, thick hair. Already, though, the elderly duchess was writing presciently to Madame de Maintenon: 'He is a child who needs to be taken care of, for he is not naturally gay, and the big pleasures will be injurious to him because he will apply himself too much to them ... You will laugh at me if I tell you that he has the vapours; nothing, however, is more true, and he had them in the cradle. Hence these sad airs and this need to be aroused.'[11] Louis

[8] D'Argenson, ii. 255.
[9] Ibid., ii. 228.
[10] Choiseul, *Mémoires*, p. 374.
[11] Duchess de Ventadour to Marquise de Maintenon: cited, Casimir Stryienski, *Le dix-huitième siècle* (Paris, 9th ed., 1933), p. 13.

XV was a melancholic from the cradle to the grave. In this he resembled his Bavarian grandmother from the moody Wittelsbachs.

With Versailles abandoned under the regency of Orleans, the little king had been brought up in the Tuileries by his *chère maman* till, upon his seventh birthday, clinging sobbing to the skirts of the Duchess de Ventadour, he was ceremoniously transferred to a governor, the seventyfour-year-old Marshal de Villeroy. This courtier, nicknamed the Charmer, was credited with the maxim: 'One must hold the chamber-pot for ministers so long as they are in office, and pour it on their heads when they are so no longer.'[12] Villeroy did teach Louis regal deportment but at the cost of putting him through his paces, literally, making him strut around at different speeds before the Turkish ambassador, making him dance ballets in public. Louis XIV, the ultimate in all things for Villeroy, had as a child carried off such performances with that exhibitionist éclat wherewith he was later to dazzle Europe. Louis XV loathed it. A sensitive child, he became a shy one. The Regent did a good day's work when, on 12 August 1722, he had Villeroy bundled out of court and left the king primarily in charge, in practice, of his subordinate tutor, the Bishop of Fréjus who was thus to attain to the highest office as the Cardinal Fleury.

The maxims corrected by Fleury in his pupil's Latin exercises included: 'If kings knew all that God requires of them, they would tremble every day.'[13] Perhaps that timid king did partly know, did tremble. Fleury, indeed, was no Fénelon, whose *Télémaque* had taught the king's father that the monarchy was a contract to be fulfilled by the monarch on behalf of his subjects. Louis XV, however, was instructed by the best masters including noted teachers from Louis-le-Grand. The king retained a lifelong interest in geography, history, and botany. In after years Louis preferred scientific savants to freethinking literati, thus exposing himself to a bad press.

From the age of thirteen Louis XV received increasing tuition in all branches of state administration. A revisionist memorandum prepared for him on his revenues reminded that 'the King can only be as rich as his subjects are'.[14] Louis, however, had no head for figures or finance, an important factor in his reign.

If Fleury did not neglect the king's education as contemporaries alleged, with stories of card-games and even some horseplay during lessons, yet the cardinal was intent especially upon securing his own political supremacy in relation to a young king only too willing to

[12] Cited, Carré/Lavisse, p. 67.
[13] MSS. Bibliothèque Nationale: cited, Pierre Gaxotte, *Le siècle de Louis XV* (Paris, 1933), p. 84.
[14] Ibid., p. 87.

concede it. One political authority remarked that Fleury's 'policy consisted in inspiring in the King a sovereign dislike of business. He too is to be reproached for that general mistrust which became part of the character of this prince. Accustomed to think ill of all men, he believes that attachment is to be found only in the train of love.'[15]

The lifelong passion of the amatory Louis XV was, first almost, hunting and shooting. The Duke de Bourbon had confirmed his early devotion to the chase. One hears of the king, proficient in whatever he did, bagging 250 head of game in one day, on another, 100 in 153 shots in under two hours – good shooting with the guns of that day. Louis is reported to have killed 6,400 stags in thirty years. A weakling grown strong, he exhausted hounds and huntsmen. And in mid-December 1741 at Choisy, for instance, Louis regularly stayed out gardening the whole afternoon 'until nightfall, despite the winds and the rain'.[16] In those long hours in the open air he may have found relief from the stifling atmosphere at court.

'If I were king of France', Frederick the Great is reported to have said, 'my first edict would be to appoint another king, who should hold court in my place.'[17] French kingship was clogged with ceremonial, and since the return to Versailles in 1722 the costly etiquette of the Grand Monarque had been resumed. If less haughtily frigid than that of Vienna, less gloomily old-fashioned than that of Madrid, ceremonial at Versailles yet probably placed the greatest burden of all upon the sovereign, rendering his most private acts a public performance from morning till night. It has been suggested that no other person in the world was so unremittingly subject to the glare of publicity as was the King of France, exalted by hierarchy upon hierarchy of great officers of state, lesser officers, chamberlains, stewards, and flunkeys, usually buying their way in, standing upon their dignity and rank, jealous of each other, watching for any breach or neglect of that ritual which conditioned their existence.

When Louis XV had married Marie Leszczynska over four hundred new officers were promptly created, a queen's household beside the king's to multiply heart-burnings and disputes. Louis himself, for instance, had to adjudicate as to which household should supply the candles for a royal supper in the queen's antechamber one evening in 1743: the women of the queen's chamber made a tidy five thousand francs per annum from selling once-lit candles. The queen's first woman of the chamber enjoyed a two-thirds cut on the profits from the supply of playing-cards, 'which makes a very considerable

---

[15] Kaunitz/Mémoire, pp. 445–6.   [16] Luynes, iv. 55.
[17] Cited in the present translation by James Breck Perkins, *France under Louis XV* (Boston and New York, 1897), i. 11.

revenue'[18] over and above any nominal salary. The king's first groom of chamber did likewise over the supply of powder and pomatum. At almost every turn within the labyrinth of this spoils-system there was a rake-off for some hanger-on. The grand master of the household split with king himself the fat profits from the sale of household offices. At the French court, remarked a foreign observer, 'there is nobody who has not paid dear for his post, and who does not want to recoup himself as fast as possible.'[19] There was a multiple interest, financial no less than social, in conspicuous consumption and organized extravagance. Here again the court was but the concentration and epitome of defects which, in greater or lesser degree, permeated French society. The court crowned the fiscal inequality, venality of office, and financial inadequacy which flawed the prosperity of the old regime.

The economic dichotomy in France, flourishing commercially as never before while yet experiencing such distress that many starved and begged, was mirrored by the dichotomy at Versailles, never more splendid or sumptuous at that time when nearly everybody at court, from the highest to the lowest, was borrowing, scrounging, eking out his precarious personal economy. The Dauphin when already fourteen in 1743 received only 500 livres a month for petty expenditure including gambling, the great indoor recreation. He was consistently overdrawn, through his first valet. Some years later the Dauphin begged the king to rescue him from debt. 'I will deliver you from this embarrassment', said Louis, 'and you shall even have a tip as well (*vous aurez même encore quelque chose pour boire*).'[20] But then the king was 'the most tender father',[21] and he needed to be asked. He was reproached 'with not being generous, with letting himself from weakness be touched for what he would refuse by temperament. Madame de Mailly . . . [was] too proud to ask',[22] unlike her successors. So, noted another witness, 'Mme de Mailly is poorer than ever . . . Her shifts are worn out and in holes . . . The other day she did not have five crowns to pay at quadrille.'[23] At lansquenet she once lost heavily at a time when she was buying some diamond earrings by monthly instalments. Louis teased her: '"The girandoles will be ill paid for this month." He gave her nothing.'[24] One is scarcely surprised that the court musicians, unpaid, were 'dying of hunger'.[25]

Such were living conditions behind the brilliant façade of Versailles, notoriously badly built for comfort, very cold (whence Belle-Isle's concern for his wife), the courtiers mostly packed into

[18] Luynes, v. 215, n.   [19] Kaunitz/Mémoire, p. 840.   [20] Luynes, x. 171.
[21] Kaunitz/Mémoire, p. 443.   [22] Ibid., p. 445.   [23] D'Argenson, ii. 211.
[24] Kaunitz/Mémoire, p. 445.   [25] D'Argenson, v. 411.

cramped quarters. All this did the greatest nobility of France eagerly
covet. Because, while mostly possessing that mercenary grasp of the
French, they yet blended with it a concept of existence which France
was not destined to retain: the old ideal of the absolute and mighty
monarch, whose power was equalled only by his virtue, the Most
Christian King, God's temporal vicegerent holding sway by divine
right over that fairest portion of christendom, the father and possessor
of his people, the glory of his realm, whose habitation must match the
splendour of his heritage, whose existence must exhibit that living
grandeur which it is the delight and honour of courtiers to reflect, the
supreme sovereign to whom service is unconditional, from whom
favour is fulfilment.

That this august ideal had become tarnished and eroded is obvious:
less obvious, perhaps, that its inspiration still lingered on and needs
to be understood in order to make full sense of the way in which
leading men and women in France felt and behaved during the
eighteenth century. As one of them was to remark, 'In all courts one
meets base intriguers and abject flatterers... But in these same
palaces one finds men of elevation and dignity in feelings as in
manners, in short great lords noble in heart as in birth.'[26]

Versailles was not only the apotheosis of French monarchy but
also the centre of its government. From the shimmering Galerie des
Glaces on the first floor one could enter the sumptuous Cabinet du
Conseil, the focus for the king's personal participation in government
through the royal council. This amorphous council epitomized the
high and secretive complexity, overlapping and overbearing, of
central government in an autocracy not subject to a separation of
powers. All branches, executive, legislative, and judicial were
embraced by the royal council, constitutionally one but in practice
articulated in several component councils. At the head the Conseil
d'État, the old Conseil d'En Haut, dealt especially with foreign and
military affairs. The Conseil des Finances, tending to decline under
Louis XV, the Conseil des Dépêches, increasingly active in internal
matters, and the intermittent Conseil de Commerce completed the
main Conseils de Gouvernement, normally held by the king in
person. Below them came the more routine Conseil de la Grande
Direction des Finances, the Petite Direction, and in the judicial
sphere the Conseil Privé, otherwise Conseil des Parties, held at
Versailles in a larger Salle du Conseil, usually under the chancellor,
then the eminent d'Aguesseau. But the chancellor, the erstwhile
secretary-general of the monarchy and still its only irremovable
functionary, was no longer a member of the Conseil d'État, a

[26] Duc de Lévis, *Souvenirs et portraits, 1780–1789*, p. 45.

diminution promoted by Colbert in the administrative modernization of the conciliar structure after the death of Mazarin and fall of Fouquet in 1661.

Under Louis XV the Conseil d'État met twice a week, sometimes oftener. The meetings of the royal council formed part of that ritual of the court of France which persisted in stately prolongation, week after week, year after year, controlling brilliant galaxies of men and women with almost celestial regularity. On Sundays, more than merely devotional, there was a regular meeting of the council of state and in the evening gaming; every Monday there was a concert, on Tuesday reception of ambassadors, council of finances or of commerce if still scheduled, and French comedy, on Wednesday another council of state for a diplomatic roundup from the day before, also another concert, Thursday, tragedy, Friday, gaming, Saturday, Italian comedy preceded by a meeting of the Conseil des Dépêches unless it had been moved back to Friday to facilitate some weekend excursion or hunting fixture, especially hunting.

The appointed seasons brought the progresses to outlying palaces, Marly, delicious in spring, Choisy, Compiègne in summer (but not in wartime), in the autumn Fontainebleau where each visit cost at least a million livres. But, central everywhere, a royal boredom came to reign. Louis XIV had been the living inspiration of a court and ceremonial which were to Louis XV, more intelligent and more sensitive, a lasting imposition.

A vigorous reform of Versailles was not for Louis XV. His was another way. He retained almost the full façade of the French court while behind it, in accordance with his introverted nature, he operated a dual withdrawal, physical and psychological.

The ceremonial *lever* of the royal arising and the evening *coucher* continued to be enacted daily at Versailles in the first-floor apartment where the Grand Monarque had slept and died, centred behind the Galerie des Glaces and looking out over the main entrance in the Cour de Marbre. From 1738, however, Louis XV had begun a personal withdrawal up the northern wing along the marble-paved courtyard, so as to sleep in fact in a warmer bedroom and develop intimate living-rooms in exquisite taste, with woodwork mainly by Verberckt, in what became known as the king's cabinets. Above the cabinets Louis had fitted up a maze of truly private, almost secret, little rooms, the so-called little cabinets or little apartments. 'Delicious retreats'[27] for those few admitted, those excluded tended to call them 'rat-nests'.[28] Divergent also were opinions of the royal character. Even

[27] F.-V. Toussaint, *Anecdotes curieuses de la cour de France sous le règne de Louis XV*, p. 83.
[28] D'Argenson, v. 464. Cf. Pierre de Nolhac, *Versailles au XVIIIᵉ siècle* (Paris, 1926), p. 175.

as Louis XV devised his apartments in gradations of remoteness, so did he hold his spirit aloof, and in numerous compartments.

Those privileged to consort with their king in his interior privacy, as at his little suppers in his little cabinets, mostly succumbed to the attraction of this handsome and clever man, finding him 'gentle, polite, gay, amiable, talking much, very well, always justly, with wit and charm'.[29] The caustic Duke de Choiseul was to strike a characteristically different note in looking back on those suppers. He remarked that Louis 'had studied the culinary art much more than the art of governing. He amused himself by making up a large number of ragouts. Often half the dishes served in the evening, at his supper, had been seasoned and prepared by him; he took such a pride in the success of his buttery work that I have seen him jealous of the talent of his head cook.'[30]

Louis, however, was considerate of his servants, himself lighting the fire in his bedroom upon awakening and remarking of the valets: 'One must let these poor people sleep.'[31] A fond father to his eight surviving children, he bestowed upon them typically mocking nicknames; the ardent Adelaide (born 1732) was Torche, plump Victoire (born 1733) was Coche, sow, and lastborn Louise-Marie (1737), Madame Dernière was Chiffe, rag.

Retentive in memory, Louis XV possessed acumen and judgement verging upon sagacity. His intelligence led him, indeed, to enjoy the companionship of young intimates such as the wittily malicious Duke d'Ayen, eldest son of the Marshal de Noailles. But the aftermath of Belle-Isle underlined the king's habitual preference for industrious administrators rather than brilliant politicians. He himself preferred working alone on papers, as he regularly did without any secretary, to debates in council. He esteemed the blunt Controller-General Orry in accordance with his liking for 'frankness and honest people'.[32] 'His essential character', wrote the Duke de Luynes, 'is truth.'[33]

Small wonder that high hopes were entertained of such a sovereign. But there were other, less reassuring facets of his complex character. Fleury, as the Dauphin once observed to him, had 'kept a pretty good window into the heart of the King'.[34] Now few, few men certainly, were destined to find that window again. The king, almost always on view to courtiers almost always on the make, pulled down blinds of impassivity and secrecy. His personality was opaque. 'The foible of the king', commented d'Argenson, 'is *not to want to be fathomed*.'[35]

---

[29] Duc de Groÿ *Journal inédit du duc de Croÿ*, ed. V.te de Grouchy and Paul Cottin (Paris, 1906–7), i. 91.   [30] Choiseul, 'Mémoires inédits', 3/26/15/820/1.
[31] Luynes, i. 402.   [32] D'Argenson, ii. 322.   [33] Luynes, iv. 305.
[34] Ibid., iii. 209.   [35] D'Argenson, iv. 42.

The king hated new faces and needed to thaw out even with an old friend who had been absent. Once, while Belle-Isle was being besieged in Prague, Louis had been in the company of the marshal's wife and hurt her by addressing to her not a word; on being subsequently reproached by the Countess de Mailly, the king replied: 'You know my embarrassment and my timidity; I am in despair about it; ten times did I open my mouth to speak to her.'[36] Ten years later, even, an ambassador to the French court was reporting that at diplomatic audiences the king 'contents himself with moving his lips, to make a demonstration of having replied. It has needed twenty years at that to overcome his natural shyness, which went so far that it was the Cardinal or the Secretary of State who proceeded to speak when it came to replying. In private he expresses himself very well... He never does foreigners the honour of talking to them. When they are presented to him he hardly deigns to greet them.'[37]

A shy person, let alone a shy king, is not apt to find much sympathy among the apposite and pointed French. The respectful adulation which Louis XV received from his courtiers was not uniform. As one aristocrat was to observe of the court of Versailles, 'under an almost absolute monarchy, the tradition of chivalric equality ... was far from being lost.'[38] Distrustful of himself, unable to dominate his court through personality, Louis yet did, remarkably, secure his ascendancy by the inverse method of withdrawal and aloof impenetrability.

Impenetrability has its sinister aspect. There are stories from the king's childhood of his pleasure in slitting the throats of little birds, of his having stabbed a tame hind to death. In the last years of his reign the Duke de Choiseul wrote: 'After a sustained study, from which nothing has ever distracted me, I saw the king as a man without soul and without parts, fond of evil as children are fond of making animals suffer ... He talks continually of burials, illnesses, surgical operations. He evinces satisfaction at the death of all those whom he knew, and if a person does not die, he predicts that he will. I am persuaded that what makes him most attached to hunting is its destruction.'[39] Choiseul, not caring for hunting and loathing cruelty, writing later with a grievance against a deteriorated ruler, went too far in depicting Louis XV as a potentially vindictive despot restrained only by his pusillanimity. In that year of 1743 Louis certainly missed Fleury and, for instance, commuted to life imprisonment a sentence of torture and hanging passed upon a woman for forging the royal assent on a document. Yet there is evidence enough in general support of Choiseul's criticism, in confirmation that the afflictions of

[36] Luynes, iv. 245.
[37] Kaunitz/Mémoire, p. 446.
[38] Duc de Lévis, op. cit., p. 45.
[39] Choiseul, Mémoires, pp. 216–17.

others positively ministered to the king's disconcerting sense of humour.

One shrewd observer balanced up the complexities of Louis: 'One could not be more human, nor have greater gentleness in dealings ... He lets slip from time to time unkind shafts, which seem to clash with his natural kindness.'[40] Perhaps his petty cruelties, often psychological, imparted a cutting edge to that truth which he valued. Choiseul was not alone in finding that 'the king is very hard and insensible to humanity'.[41] Louis, almost the reverse of Choiseul, was a morbid man.

Kings are apt to have an invested interest in religion. Louis XV was considerably religious, again in contrast to Choiseul. The minister once observed that the king, 'in the midst of his greatest debauches, preserves a puerile respect for the most indifferent aspects of religion, while every moment violating its most sacred precepts. He imagines that he will secure his salvation by abstaining from laughing at the saints, and by allowing in his kingdom only the practice of the catholic religion. He believes that the exact observance of these two rules of conduct will get his turpitudes pardoned. I have never found anybody who had such a silly way of understanding and practising religion. The king thought himself quit towards God when he had heard a mass and a sermon according to court ceremonial.'[42]

Louis's censorious minister wrote upon another occasion: 'All his life, Louis XV had but one fear: that of the devil. It was his fixed idea, and, even in the midst of his orgies and debauches, he used always to see hell before him.'[43] There is concordant testimony that Louis 'is afraid of eternity and its horrors'[44] and, one gathers, did not respond readily to the Countess de Mailly's assurance that hell is 'an old wives' tale'.[45] One of his pastimes was reading aloud to his mistresses the searching moralities of that subtle Jesuit, Bourdaloue.

The disillusioned detachment which underlay the king's boredom embraced himself, his mistresses, and his government. This elevated defect did not escape contemporaries. The king, wrote one of them, 'accustomed himself too much to seeing through the eyes of others, or to allowing things to be done, although he saw that they could be done better'.[46] 'Unfortunately', wrote another, 'he relates too historically [current] events which, it would seem, should affect him.'[47] Such was the royal outlook, remote through 'large eyes, dark and naturally sad ... Some days he is alert and brisk, but usually one finds him dejected and languid. His health however is most robust.'[48]

[40] Kaunitz/Mémoire, p. 444.   [41] D'Argenson, iv. 60.
[42] Choiseul, 'Mémoires inédits, 2/6/3/179/3.   [43] Ibid., 3/26/15/820/3.
[44] D'Argenson, ii. 395.   [45] Ibid., p. 374.   [46] Abbé Millot, op cit., v. 318.
[47] Luynes, v. 96.   [48] Kaunitz/Mémoire, p. 443.

King Louis XV was not the man to appeal to the future Duke de
Choiseul, whose excoriation of him in his memoirs calls for some
subtraction, but only some. For the fundamentals of Choiseul's
gravamen against his king are to a striking extent borne out by
another eminent but more dispassionate observer, even in the sober
terms of a diplomatic report. The future Prince Kaunitz closed his
bleak analysis of Louis:

Equally insensible to the pleasure of commanding men and to that of rendering
them happy, hardly able to form a wish without finding it immediately accomplished,
meeting everywhere only slaves, a lover always adored, a master never contradicted,
it is impossible that he should not experience this condition of languor, this satiety
which follows passions satisfied, a situation which soon engenders boredom. That is
the cruellest enemy which this prince has ... He himself fears only solitude. Hence
this real need of continual dissipation, hence this immoderate passion for the chase,
hence finally this necessity to have a mistress.[49]

A monarch so accustomed to standing back was unlikely to have
missed the significance of the earlier course of his own reign. The
regency of the Duke of Orleans had betokened an aristocratic
revolution based upon the relegation of the testament of the Grand
Monarque, had in effect placed the crown of France in commission
in a series of interlocking councils inspired by Fénelon's Polysynodie.
The abandonment of Versailles for Paris had marked a loosening in
morals, in finance, not only by Law but also under the Duke de
Noailles's abortive initiative of 1717–18 towards reforming the
inequitable incidence of the *taille*: similarly, indeed, in politics what
with the revolutionary rapprochement towards England but also
with suggestions, as in the ridiculous Conspiracy of Cellamare, that
the factions of the high nobility might yet revive the civil discord of
the Fronde. The early Regency created a break in French history,
potentially of far-reaching significance. That it came to figure as
scarcely more than an episode was, for good or ill, due not only to the
political moderation and acumen of such statesmen as the Duke of
Orleans and the Cardinal Fleury but also probably, more than is
usually appreciated, to the traditionalism of King Louis XV.

After 1715 France lacked political stability almost as much as the
king lacked personal stability. But by ritual perseverance Louis XV
came to associate his name lastingly, and scarcely less than that of
Louis XIV himself, with the palatial pre-eminence of Versailles. This
has come to be so taken for granted that the magnitude of the
achievement may not always be fully apparent. It was a passive
achievement certainly, in keeping with the new king, but an

[49] Ibid., p. 447.

achievement none the less. This monarch, who 'was all habit',[50] consolidated his precarious succession to his great-grandfather at the price of prolonging his forbear's system of government: a clue to much throughout the artificially static reign of Louis XV. That, however, is to look ahead.

The opening of the year 1743 might seem to invite Louis, now mature, to take a new stand upon his kingship, now secure, and clinch his sovereignty. Ten days before Fleury died the Marquis de Stainville forecast: 'I am persuaded that after the death of the Cardinal the King will wish to take cognizance of his affairs himself and will work with his ministers, each in his own department. I do not say that this will last, but it will begin like that.'[51] The prediction proved precisely accurate. And the king was encouraged in personal rule by two dukes, very different but both figuring largely in the annals of their nation and in the life of the future Duke de Choiseul.

III

The Duke de Richelieu was the handsomest man at court. At forty-five he looked thirty. At sixteen, as the Duke de Fronsac, his ardour towards the Duchess of Burgundy, mother of Louis XV, had earned him a first spell in the Bastille, whereas his third had resulted from treacherous leanings in the Conspiracy of Cellamare. As brave as he was beautiful, Richelieu shone in battle and in duel, wherein he had killed that Prince de Lixin. Richelieu excelled, however, as 'the lady-killer of the century . . . He reduced the daughter of the regent to going to find a husband in Italy. Very often at a gathering he [Richelieu] has not been able to recall if such and such a woman had yielded to him.'[52] Another lady of the blood, lovely Mademoiselle de Charolais, sister of the Duke de Bourbon, was the mistress of Richelieu as he led the bloods of the regency into that licentious frolic from which the eighteenth-century aristocracy of France did not fully recover. Richelieu himself, a lifelong friend of Voltaire, grounded his excesses in a deliberate licence of thought said to have extended to black magic during a ceremonial embassy to Vienna which earned him his lasting nickname of Son Excellence. The erotic decorations in Richelieu's little house beyond the Vaugirard tollgate out of Paris proclaimed a system of libertinism in which this impertinent and impure courtier involved his king. Richelieu's

[50] *Journal inédit du duc de Croÿ*, iii. 110.

[51] Marquis de Stainville to Grand Duke Francis II, Paris, 19 Jan. 1743: Esteri del Granducato di Toscana, vol. 2295/1286, fo. 218.   [52] Hénault, p. 106.

carouses were upon occasion liable to involve the Count de Stainville, who was yet to observe in a later context: 'The unhappy character of the King ... had been sustained and manipulated by vice itself personified in M. de Richelieu.'[53]

Among those who promoted the power of the house of Bourbon in the seventeenth century there stood pre-eminent the Cardinal de Richelieu. Specially answerable among those who undermined the French aristocracy and monarchy in the eighteenth century was the cardinal's great-nephew, the Duke de Richelieu.

Louis XV had found early but not lasting happiness with his Polish wife, who was afraid of him. Six years older than her husband, kindly Queen Marie, plain and somewhat insipid, was piously given to good works and overeating, frightened of fresh air, reading big books she did not quite understand. Even her sleeping with her husband had been liable to the constraints of attendants and physicians till they advised her not to risk another pregnancy. Louis had been slow to imitate his loose-living courtiers but the Duke de Richelieu had not missed such an opportunity to promote his characteristic opinion: 'For the king to be his own master it is indispensable to make him have a mistress.'[54] If the initial sponsoring by Richelieu and Bachelier, the king's valet, of the Countess de Mailly had not been wholly unwelcome to Fleury, the ultimate danger was evident. But good-natured Madame de Mailly, who had had to compound with her short-lived younger sister, the Marquise de Vintimille, for the royal favour, had herself proved disappointing to Richelieu as a political instrument, failing to bring down Fleury by her advocacy of Belle-Isle.

Since Madame de Mailly had become 'bored and boring',[55] Richelieu, a classic cad, contrived, in keeping with the king's shy conservatism, to retain the royal amours within the family by promoting yet a third daughter of the impecunious Marquis de Nesle, who could do with the financial favours accruing from his daughters' physical ones. The youngest sister of the Countess de Mailly, the twentyfive-year-old Marquise de la Tournelle, was also the prettiest, besides being conveniently widowed. But, whereas Madame de Mailly loved Louis, the affections of Madame de la Tournelle were centred upon her acknowledged lover, the young Duke d'Agenais, then serving in Bavaria. And Agenais was nephew to Richelieu. In the words of Choiseul, 'neither honesty nor relationship are curbs upon the baseness and the contemptible ambition of M. de Richelieu. M. d'Aiguillon[56] was absent; his uncle facilitated the means of the

[53] Choiseul, *Mémoires*, p. 222.   [54] Broglie/Fréd-LXV, i. 199.
[55] D'Argenson, iii. 414.   [56] i.e. the Duke d'Agenais, subsequently Duke d'Aiguillon.

intrigue, persuaded Mme de la Tournelle, since Mme de Château-roux, that she should sacrifice to the King not only his nephew and the sentiments which she might have for him, but the whole universe.'[57] One of the reassuring qualities in Choiseul is his contemptuous disgust for Richelieu.

In the autumn of 1742 Richelieu concerted his intrigue with one of his former mistresses, literary Madame de Tencin, who had started life as a nun. She maintained a salon and wrote novels not nearly so spicy as her own existence as almost a feminine counterpart to Richelieu. Few women, probably, even in the eighteenth century, embraced so much history in the flesh. Leaving aside her alleged incest with her brother, the Cardinal de Tencin, a conservative tally of her lovers would include her nephew, the Count d'Argental, the Count d'Argenson, father of the marquis and himself chief of police (an ugly lover but useful for an unfrocked nun), Matthew Prior and Lord Bolingbroke, Law the financier, the Cardinal Dubois, the Regent Orleans himself, said to have come to reject her with the remark that 'he did not like whores who talked business between the sheets'.[58] Madame de Tencin once wrote to Richelieu: 'A clever woman knows how to mix pleasure with general interests',[59] not least financial ones. On her way up one minor lover, Cannon Destouches of the artillery, fathered upon her the philosoph, d'Alembert, whom Madame de Tencin promptly abandoned. This squalid woman so swindled another lover that his suicide cost her a spell in the Bastille to match up with her lasting friend, the Duke de Richelieu.

On 23 October 1742 Richelieu had to interrupt his intrigue to plant the Marquise de la Tournelle, and briefly left for the army which the Marshal de Noailles was concentrating in Flanders to replace that of the Marshal de Maillebois. On 5 November Madame de Tencin wrote a cryptic and sinister letter to inform Richelieu that she had 'talked myself hoarse this morning with the Slowcoach [*Guimbarde*, i.e. the king][60] to prove to him that the evil was much less than a double adultery'.[61] (Adultery with the Countess de Mailly, whose husband was living, was 'double'; with the widowed Marquise de la Tournelle it would be 'simple'.) 'I shall begin again tomorrow',

[57] Choiseul, *Mémoires*, p. 20.   [58] Duclos, op.cit., ii. 44.
[59] Madame de Tencin to Duke de Richelieu, 1 Aug. 1743: [L.-F. Faur,] *Vie privé du maréchal de Richelieu* (Paris, 1791), ii. 423, appendix: cited, Pierre-Maurice Masson, *Madame de Tencin 1682–1749* (Paris, 1909), p. 46. (For the grounds for Masson's acceptance of authenticity see ibid., pp. 261–2.)
[60] For Masson's acceptance here of the key furnished by Soulavie, see P.-M. Masson, op.cit., pp. 94–5.
[61] Madame de Tencin to Duke de Richelieu, 5 Nov. 1742: [Soulavie,] *Correspondance du Cardinal de Tencin, ministre d'état, et de Madame de Tencin sa soeur, avec le duc de Richelieu, sur les intrigues de la Cour de France depuis 1742 jusqu'en 1757* (Paris, 1790): cited, P.-M. Masson, op.cit., p. 95.

Madame de Tencin continued, 'to fill the head of this slowcoach with what I want him to say on Wednesday when he shall see the cardinal [Fleury]. He believes that the forsaken woman [de Mailly] loved him passionately . . . Would you have expected, when you gave yourself so much trouble to get them to see each other, that their liaison would become a snag?'[62]

The same day the Marquis d'Argenson entered in his diary: '5 November – Great news: the king has dismissed Mme de Mailly, to take her sister, Mme de la Tournelle . . . with a harshness which one cannot understand of a Most Christian King: it is the sister who is having the sister expelled; she exacts her exile'[63] from court. Soon the inevitable ditty was commenting:

> Si la canaille ose crier
> De voir trois soeurs se relayer,
> Au grand Tencin renvoyez–la,
> Alleluia.[64]

'Great Tencin', the cardinal, was indeed on the way up, partly under the propulsion of his sister. His appointment as a member of the council without departmental responsibility already dated from August 1742, as did that of the Count d'Argenson, the younger, suppler brother of the recording marquis. Tencin was regarded as the nominee of the failing Fleury anxious to retain control of affairs by means of such a pliant instrument: the younger cardinal had lately ingratiated himself despite the fact that the elder had once banished him, as Archbishop of Embrun, to his remote see on account of Tencin's 'bitter and imprudent zeal'[65] against the Jansenists at the ecclesiastical Council of Embrun in 1727. Tencin was also, characteristically, 'an intimate friend'[66] of Fleury's enemy, Richelieu, and was a leading figure now in the latter's creation of 'the new court of the cabinets'[67] to supersede the influence of Fleury. In the previous summer the Marquis de Stainville had reported that while it was believed that Tencin had been designated by Fleury 'to the King as his successor the Countess of Toulouse is working for her part for the Marshal de Noailles, her brother'.[68] Now Noailles, also helped on by a sister, was the other leading duke, besides Richelieu, who was

---

[62] Ibid.   [63] D'Argenson, iv. 36–7.
[64] 'Recueil de chansons, anecdotes satyriques et historiques depuis 1709 jusqu'en 1756', vol. xvi, fo. 132: Bibliothèque Mazarine, MSS. fr., no. 3988: cited, P.-M. Masson, op.cit., p. 97.
[65] Cardinal Fleury to Cardinal Corsini, 3 Sept. 1731: Arch. Aff. Étr., Mémoires et documents: Rome, vol. 73, fo. 240: cited, ibid., p. 83.
[66] Luynes, iv. 266.   [67] Ibid., iv. 469.
[68] Marquis de Stainville to Grand Duke Francis II, Paris, 2 June 1742: Esteri del Granducato di Toscana, vol. 2295/1286, fo. 113.

urging Louis XV to throw off the tutelage of Fleury and enter fully into his kingly heritage of governance.

The Duke de Noailles was dissimilar to the Duke de Richelieu. Belonging to an older generation, tall and pleasant-featured at sixty-four, the affinities of the martial Noailles matched the reign of Louis XIV, his friend, as much as those of Richelieu did the regency of Orleans. Under the regency Noailles's attempt at fiscal reform had earned his Council of Finance the nickname of the Bureau de Rêverie and himself the shrill invective of his fellow duke, Saint-Simon. The less excited and exciting Luynes, closer to that juncture of 1743, observed that Noailles 'knows a great deal ... but it is the practice at court that superficial knowledge is sufficient to give brilliancy; he is however capable of projects, one might even say of singular system. His natural character is ambition but a supple ambition capable of taking all kinds of forms.'[69]

For some twenty years the ambition of the Duke de Noailles had been more or less in eclipse, though he had conducted the Italian campaign of 1735. At the outbreak of the War of the Austrian Succession the duke, living in political retreat and religious piety, disapproved of Belle-Isle's aggression against Austria and the 'air of haughtiness and conquest with which they entered into Germany.'[70] After the military reemergence of Noailles in the autumn of 1742, to replace Maillebois in Flanders, the duke had done his best there with barely twenty thousand men to bolster the neglected defences at what he termed the 'critical point'.[71] His opponent, the Earl of Stair, commanding the Pragmatic Army, had certainly sought to make it so.

Stair, a not unworthy pupil of Marlborough, had projected a drive straight for the headwaters of the Oise, navigable for Stair's transport, and, bypassing the main French force up by Dunkirk, a swoop down the river directly upon Paris itself. Given the weakness of the French defence under Noailles, this hardy project was scarcely chimerical. Stair, however, was frustrated by 'the men of skill in England',[72] as he derisively described the council of war at Whitehall, and by his Austrian allies, with the Dutch not yet fully squared.

It had been a close shave for the Duke de Noailles, who represented to Louis XV: 'There is, Sire, not a moment to lose for putting this frontier in state of defence for the next campaign.'[73] This letter was

---

[69] Luynes, v. 92.
[70] Duke de Noailles, memorandum to the Marquis de Breteuil, 2 August 1742: cited, Camille Rousset, Correspondance de Louis XV et du maréchal de Noailles (Paris, 1865: henceforth cited as Rousset), i. xxiii.
[71] Duke de Noailles to Marquis de Bretreul, 21 Nov. 1742: cited, Abbé Millot, op.cit., v. 310.
[72] Cited by the Hon. J.W. Fortescue, A History of the British Army (London, 1899 f.), ii. 86.
[73] Duke de Noailles to King Louis XV, Saint Omer, 20 Nov. 1742: Rousset, i. 5.

one of the first in the intimate correspondence which Noailles now struck up with the king, here for once observable at work rather than at play.

Noailles, representing one of the very great families of France, was on close terms with Louis XV, as he had been with Louis XIV and also Philip V of Spain. The duke had married the favourite niece of Madame de Maintenon, while the latter's legitimized bastard by the king, the Count of Toulouse, had, by marrying Noailles's sister, made her a princess of the blood. By the unhappy marriage of the duke's eldest daughter to Prince Charles d'Armagnac the house of Noailles was further allied to that of Lorraine and, now, of Austria. Noailles's sons, the Duke d'Ayen and the Count de Noailles, had been largely brought up with the young King of France and were among his closest friends, while one of the queen's favourite ladies-in-waiting was the Duchess de Villars, Noailles's pious younger daughter, dubbed 'the good idiot'[74] by the king. Such was the royal intimacy of 'an old man who saw Your Majesty born.'[75] Now Louis replied to Noailles's quoted letter of 20 November 1742: 'The late King, my great-grandfather, whom I wish to imitate as much as shall be possible for me, enjoined me, on dying, to take counsel in everything and to seek to perceive the best in order to follow it always ... Thus I open your mouth, as the Pope to the Cardinals, and permit you to tell me what your zeal and your attachment for me and my kingdom shall inspire in you.'[76]

Upon Fleury's death Noailles communicated to the king a long memorandum, including significant allusions to two French kings famous for their sexual favourites, Henry III and especially Charles VII, with whom Louis XV had more than a little in common. To his memorandum Noailles appended the hoarded duplicate, confided to him by Louis XIV himself, of that monarch's private guidance in 1700 to the Duke of Anjou, setting out to found the Spanish Bourbons as Philip V. This political testament comprised thirty-three pregnant and lonely maxims of absolute monarchy – the fifth, for instance: 'Never have any attachment for anybody':[77] a lesson wherein Louis XV became a very perfect pupil. The last article, stressed by Noailles, sounded 'one of the most important warnings ... Do not let yourself be governed; be the master. Never have either favourite or prime minister. Listen, consult your council, but decide.'[78] The complete wisdom of this, notably as to no prime minister, came to be doubted

[74] King Louis XV to Duke de Noailles, Choisy, 1 Sept. 1743: ibid., ii. 9.
[75] Duke de Noailles to Louis XV, Spires, 8 Aug. 1743: ibid., i. 207.
[76] King Louis XV to Duke de Noailles, Versailles, 26 Nov. 1742: ibid., i. 10–11.
[77] King Louis XIV, 'Mémoire donné par Louis XIV à Philippe V, partant pour l'Espagne, le 3 décembre 1700': ibid., i. 27.   [78] King Louis XIV, ibid., i. 33.

even by French eighteenth-century opinion, but not by Noailles, who cited the personal rule of the Grand Monarque 'since the death of Cardinal Mazarin',[79] incidentally the exemplar for the now departed Cardinal Fleury.

At this juncture the receptive king is reported to have said to his courtiers: 'Gentlemen, so here I am prime minister!'[80] Indeed his active reign arguably began not upon his coming of age in 1723 but just twenty years later. The reign of Louis XV was retarded. Now, however, French ambassadors were instructed to report to the king personally, as they had to Louis XIV, and the ministers worked direct to their sovereign.

IV

Louis XV, with his qualities of good sense and goodwill, took the responsiblities of government seriously and may not have wearied of them so quickly as he seemed to do. He could work conscientiously for long hours at his desk, but a steadfast technique of ministerial co-ordination and collaboration was alien to his indirect temperament. If, as a contemporary then remarked, the king 'brings to his work and to his conduct with the ministers a distaste and unpleasantness which do not seem natural',[81] that largely reflected the fact that Louis, being personally timid, was politically weak. True, he was only following the Grand Monarque in council when, in case of difference, Louis habitually subordinated his own opinion to that of the majority: such was the moderate reality behind the grandiose facade of absolute monarchy in France. More than that, though, Louis XV tended to agree with a minister in council or consultation and later to act or decide contrariwise behind his back. The loyalty of the ministers was to a king who was disloyal, who was subsequently to evolve an entire personal policy in foreign affairs through organized duplicity.

Another procedural complication was that classic short-cut to the top whereby a French minister could to some extent bypass the royal council in a personal working-session or *travail* with the king. With no doctrine of collective ministerial responsibility, loyalty of ministers to one another was scarcely prescribed in theory and certainly did not prevail in practice. In the absence of a chief minister such as Fleury each was responsible to the king alone, who only could coordinate. Coordination was more than ever necessary in time of war when, as usual, foreign policy either determined or was

---

[79] Duke de Noailles, memorandum addressed to King Louis XV, Jan. 1743: ibid., i. 22.
[80] Cited, D'Argenson, iv. 49.   [81] D'Argenson, iv. 64.

determined by military strategy, and both in turn by financial policy. Without unified direction there could be no coherent determination. But with Louis XV it was defective. Of his secretaries of state Frederick the Great observed that 'France was governed by four subordinate kings independent of one another'.[82] Fleury, however, had bequeathed to Louis five chief ministers.

The 'plain and simple'[83] Controller-General Orry was described by the Marquis de Stainville as 'the only one in whom the King seems to have confidence'.[84] Orry was not so simple as to allow his burden of war-finance to inhibit money for the royal pastime, for instance, of palatial building. Orry, however, made a point of refusing to push his brother-in-law, La Galaisière, and could mainly be reproached, perhaps, for the fat profits on the Compagnie des Indes scooped by his grasping and managing brother, Fulvy, whose long-faced wife was also, compactly, Orry's mistress.

Less considerable than Orry, than most people, was the stuttering foreign secretary, Amelot de Chaillou, who knew 'a great deal of natural history'[85] but less of foreign policy. Under Fleury poor Amelot had 'performed but the function of a chief clerk, and trembled at every step'.[86] This dry little man, fiftyish, was matched, though not faithfully, by his bourgeois wife who was supposed to be rather a favourite with the king as the only person at court shyer than himself.

Amelot was an adherent of one of the cleverest and most ambitious members of the administration, the Count de Maurepas, Secretary of State for the Marine. Maurepas had inherited that office from his father twenty years before, at the age of twenty-two. His tenure appreciably vindicated in practice the dubious principle of hereditary office, which incidentally did not always turn out so badly in other spheres, notably the legal as attested by such outstanding dynasties as those of d'Aguesseau and Maupeou. In the naval compass 'one cannot have more intelligence than M. de Maurepas, nor a happier memory'[87] as to personnel. The Anglo-French alliance from the regency had primed cuts in the French navy and Fleury had displayed but slight understanding of naval affairs, which owed nearly everything to Maurepas.

The active young minister maintained pressure for funds from the parsimonious old cardinal, who normally kept the naval budget pegged to about nine millions. Maurepas, however, extracted

---

[82] Frederick, iii. 3.   [83] Luynes, v. 86.
[84] Marquis de Stainville to Grand Duke Francis II, Paris, 26 Jan. 1743: Esteri del Granducato di Toscana, vol. 2295/1286, fo. 222.
[85] D'Argenson, i. 272.   [86] Luynes, v. 89.   [87] Ibid., v. 88.

supplementary grants (to a total of 19,200,000 livres in 1739) so that by the time that hostilities with England loomed up again the French navy comprised something over sixty ships, two-thirds of them larger than frigates. Even that was barely more than half the British strength, [88] a long way from that naval parity with England enjoyed in the good old days when the nautical Count de Choiseul-Beaupré had been serving: whereas French land-forces were well over six times superior numerically to the British. Maurepas pled with reason: 'I have often heard foreign envoys say that our navy was too neglected, that it would be much better for the King to have 50,000 less troops and 50 more vessels.'[89] That logic had to await the Duke de Choiseul, soldier though he was.

The French commercial expansion promoted by Fleury's administration was imperilled by lack of adequate naval protection, as also by the embedded flaw that the French merchant marine lagged behind French foreign trade. Apart from the flourishing Levant trade and profitable runs to Africa and the Antilles, the traffic in the ports and along the coasts of France was largely directed by shippers from England, Holland and Hamburg. The expansion of France was navally handicapped from the start when it came to the commercial and colonial clash with England in the middle years of the eighteenth century.

If Maurepas could not supply enough ships he multiplied technical improvements, getting around to see and organize for himself at Cherbourg, at Brest where he had turned Choquet de Lindu on to engineering new magazines, at Bayonne with a view to deepening the draught of the Adour, and at Toulon. There new installations included a masting machine while improvement of sails and rigging was promoted by Maurepas's inspector-general of marine, the expert Duhamel du Monceau. Improved standards were pursued, for instance, in hydrography but although French naval officers might be better equipped theoretically than their English counterparts they tended, despite training cruises, to lack the islanders' traditional sea-going experience. This defect was deepened by internal hostility in the French fleet between the Navy of the Red, the aristocratic captains who commanded the precious ships of the line, and the despised Officers of the Blue, bourgeois injections from the merchant marine, as a rule only for the duration of hostilities. Nor did Maurepas in practice help by promoting a bureacratization of the navy in yet

---

[88] Cf. A. McC. Wilson, op. cit., p. 75.

[89] Count de Maurepas, cited, René Jouan, *Histoire de la marine française* (Paris, 1932), i. 223; cf. W. L. Dorn, op. cit., p. 117 passim. (This suggestive survey leans in favour of Cardinal Fleury on naval policy.)

another illustration of that administrative clamp which was being imposed as the pattern of French, of continental government in the eighteenth century.

If the Count de Maurepas, whose spry simplicity of manner yet imposed respect, was not a great or greatly successful minister, he 'really was a man of intelligence and sense; besides business ability, he had experience and discernment.'[90] To an appreciable extent the future Choiseul was to stand in line with Maurepas ministerially, perhaps also personally. Maurepas's important influence at court, however, was, typically in the France of that time, not derived merely or perhaps even mainly from his activity as Minister of Marine. Despite the fact that the ministry then controlled all colonial administration, the French navy remained a cinderella. At that period, however, the French administration resembled the British at least in the way in which, in the absence of a department of the interior, the functional attributions of the secretaries of state overlapped with territorial jurisdictions. A reversion here too from attempted reform under the regency meant that the Minister of Marine was, as noticed, departmentally responsible for the affairs of Paris at a time when 'Paris is all the kingdom'.[91] Maurepas was thus the superior of Marville, particularly important as lieutenant-general of police in Paris. The minister was also able to keep up with the stream of political ditties which were then the most spontaneous expression of public opinion in Paris. The ribaldries multiplied against Maurepas himself in allusion to his sexual impotence. Maurepas, however, piqued himself upon collecting and indeed composing such lewd lampoons. One observer of this minister's 'cold exterior' came to suspect 'that he affects to be so serious only in order to render his jests the keener'.[92] Maurepas was also, incidentally, a collector of antiquities, sometimes picked up on his naval tours which he would vary, for instance, by posting off to Fréjus to sketch the Roman ruins.

The marine, the colonies and the capital did not exhaust the sum of the power of the Count de Maurepas. It reached into the very penetralia of the realm. Maurepas was also the secretary of the households of both the king and the queen, offices which, as the Duke de Luynes observed with his habitual lack of exaggeration, 'much increase his credit and his consideration at court'.[93] Though that did not go for the Marquis d'Argenson, who qualified the Count de Maurepas as 'a dandy, a eunuch fertile in words and even in

90 Duc de Lévis, op. cit., pp. 3–4.   91 Hénault, p. 151.
92 Duc de Lévis, op. cit., p. 19.   93 Luynes, v. 89.

imagination and short of strength, enemy to all virtue which he turns to ridicule, friend of all vices, the plague of the ministry which he corrupts, as M. Orry ruins the poor people'.[94] If d'Argenson's abundant criticisms of the court and administration of Louis XV reflected an exceptionally independent and imaginative mind, they also characterized the disgruntled intellectual long disappointed of office.

The position of the suave and confident Count de Maurepas was now menaced by the very fact that he was a cousin of the sisters Nesle. His support of the Countess de Mailly during the crisis of her dismissal primed the accusation of her sisterly supplanter that he had previously neglected her and her other sisters in their straitened existence in Paris with their aunt, the Duchess de Mazarin. The promoter of the new mistress, Richelieu, could not abide Maurepas, threatened now by the reign of 'the three sisters', the close association of the Marquise de la Tournelle with her two immediate elders, the also pretty Marquise de Flavacourt, nicknamed The Hen, and the indolent but sprightly Duchess de Lauraguais, said to have made up an occasional fourth in the family team of royal mistresses.

The Minister of Marine was good at tacking. He managed to patch it up, more or less, with his cousin, and was heartened by the decline of his rival Belle-Isle, less so by the death of the amenable Marquis de Breteuil. He was succeeded as minister of war by the recently created minister without portfolio, the Count d'Argenson. The promotion of the Count d'Argenson was calculated to exasperate his elder brother, the marquis, still passed over himself in favour of his taller, suppler junior with an intelligence that was the more prompt and apposite but the less reflective and original of the two. The younger had been the favourite with his father as he now was with the court.

The Count d'Argenson's main support in the ministry was the fifth of the leading ministers bequeathed by Cardinal Fleury, the Cardinal de Tencin. He was the last of them left as a minister of state, as a member of the royal council of state but without the departmental responsibility of a secretary of state. What Tencin lacked in attribution he at first supplied in influence. Indeed he provided one of the earlier examples from that reign of the somewhat neglected importance of the potential influence of a French minister of state as a member of the council in the absence of strong government by a leading minister, as now. The pre-eminence of a cardinal was now Tencin's and, before sessions of the council, it was in his house that ministers tended to meet in an approximation to a committee, the

[94] D'Argenson, iv. 8.

designation then of a meeting of ministers without the king in a development of appreciable importance under Louis XV.

Tencin was adept at 'proportioning himself to the times and the circumstances'[95] and one of the more amiable traits in this shaded, shady character was a genuine diffidence. He had come far under the impulsion of his sister but even her latest protégée, the Marquise de la Tournelle newly created Duchess de Châteauroux, was soon to be writing of Madame de Tencin to the Duke of Richelieu himself: 'She intrigues and cabals everywhere. I have received several anonymous letters which without doubt come from her.'[96] Later, at least, the king 'nearly had gooseflesh when she was spoken of'.[97] Later again Louis XV was to confide that Fleury 'had had some desire to have as his successor the Cardinal de Tencin; but his sister was such an intriguer that Cardinal de Fleury advised me to do nothing about it, and I behaved in such a way as to deprive him [Tencin] of all hope, and disabuse the others. M. [the Count] d'Argenson fathomed me, and finally deprived him of all consideration.'[98]

For the present, however, the Cardinal de Tencin was a leading figure in that French government which, while it included no great ministers, was not wholly incompetent, drawn as it was from the *noblesse de robe*, professional men who had worked their way up. In that it was typical. If France was traditionally a home of aristocratic privilege, yet for a generation after the Regent Orleans and the Duke de Bourbon, as earlier under Louis XIV, it was exceptional for the great nobility, the old *noblesse d'épée* or nobility of chivalry, to assume the direct conduct of government, certainly to the extent that their counterparts did under the more liberal system in England. The equation of aristocracy with authoritarianism is, here as elsewhere, superficial. True, the assimilation of the nobility of the robe with that of the sword was by then largely and significantly under way.[99] This tendency can, however, be exaggerated. It was a notable event when a great nobleman was now included in the new French government.

Louis XV creditably selected not, after all, the fascinating Duke de Richelieu but the aged Duke de Noailles. On 10 March 1743 Noailles entered the royal council as a ministerial overlord without departmental attribution. This, commented the Marquis de'Argenson, 'makes life very hard for the ministers; they have been given not a

[95] Luynes, iv. 212.
[96] Duchess de Châteauroux to Duke de Richelieu, Versailles, 3 Nov. 1743: [L.-F. Faur,] *Vie privée du maréchal de Richelieu* (3rd ed., Paris, 1803), iii. 315.
[97] D'Argenson, vi. 142.
[98] Cited, Madame du Hausset, *Mémoires de Mme du Hausset*, ed. Hippolyte Fournier, (Paris, 1891), p. 67.
[99] This is the thesis of such modern authors as Franklin L. Ford, *Robe and Sword*, e.g. pp. 138 f., and François Bluche, *Les Magistrats du parlement de Paris au XVIIIe siècle*, e.g. pp. 303 f.

prime minister, but an importunate inspector, who interferes in everything, although he is master of nothing'.[1] The central problem for the government now was how to carry on the war, and the ducal marshal's political authority was matched by his military. Noailles was assigned the command of the French armies for that year 'from the Rhine to the sea.'[2]

V

Beyond the Rhine, back in Bavaria, the Marshal de Broglie meanwhile found himself in yet another fix. He was in command of what he described as 'enervated armies'[3] worn down by disease and, still more, discouragement. Since the Army of Bohemia had pulled back into France, the Army of Bavaria mainly hoped to follow suit. Broglie, by now notoriously inactive, responded little to rather timid stimulation from the new French minister of war, young d'Argenson, discounted co-operation with Marshal Seckendorff and went from bad to worse in his relations with the Bavarian emperor. In April 1743 Broglie did manage to run through to now isolated Eger a convoy of reinforcements and supplies under the command of du Chayla, one of the few of Belle-Isle's generals to be actively employed that year. But this success, isolated in every sense, was scarcely reassuring upon the wider horizons of the future.

The focus of forward activity was not Broglie's residual army, reinforced though it was, but that new army, to replace the one wasted by Belle-Isle, which was now assigned to Noailles, of better birth than Belle-Isle, of better brain than Broglie. In that time of stress the government launched a recruiting drive of exceptional vigour. Paris always needed to be treated gingerly, but early in 1743 recruiting-sergeants converged upon the busy bottleneck of the Pont-Neuf and set up their booths decorated with flags and patriotic slogans. There were also less elevated enticements: free food and wine, women and jingling bags of coin. Victims might be fuddled or abducted to isolated old houses or inns known as *fours*. One contemporary judged that for about twenty years after 1740 half the men enlisted were so by fraud.[4]

In that old pattern of the French army true volunteers were traditionally recruits of gentle birth for the self-supporting gendar-

[1] D'Argenson, iv. 61. [2] Luynes, iv. 425.
[3] Marshal de Broglie to Emperor Charles VII, 27 Dec. 1742: B. N. MSS.: Fonds de nouvelles acquisitions: cited, Broglie/Fréd-LXV, i. 303.
[4] Cf. André Corvisier, *L'Armé française de la fin du XVII siècle au ministère de Choiseul: le soldat*, i. 189.

mery, the residual men-at-arms (*gens d'armes*). Much more broadly, the more or less voluntary enlistment of mercenaries, in their cups or otherwise, for the regular regiments was supplemented by the conscription of militiamen drawn by lot between the ages of sixteen and forty. This French militia had been revived in 1726 at a strength of around a hundred battalions. Now included in this net was Paris, an innovation nervously introduced by the government. Sure enough February 1743 found the capital in a hubbub, not least over the complicated categories of exemption, often graded according to tax-assessment, for the employees of merchants, lawyers, printers, and so on. (It was plausibly supposed that the real object of the government in these upper categories was to augment revenue by inducing the rich to apply for increased assessment of polltax – *capitation* – in order to buy off their household.) Other exemptions, besides of course the nobility and the clergy, included the municipal officers, sanitary employees, cabmen and, to popular disapproval, 'those prodigal Puppies the Lacqueys'.[5] It was reckoned that there were that year in Paris some forty thousand liveried servants, who were 'for the most part ... the strongest and best built.[6] These hangers-on of the rich were, however, riding high: standing up behind their masters' carriages, they used to cock snooks at those militiamen who were coming to characterize the Parisian scene, often tight, not yet in uniform but sporting blue and white cockades in their hats.

Bourbon France, no omnipotent absolutism, was still a good long way from the new Prussian system with the triple obligation imposed by King Frederick-William I upon every citizen: *Steuerpflicht, Schulpflicht, Wehrpflicht,* levies upon the fortunes, minds and lives of the subjects of the jealous state. Whereas the recruitment now of Parisians, whose mood was followed by the government day by day in vivid police-reports, illustrated the way in which the French monarchy was in practice tempered not only, or perhaps mainly, by popular pressures but also by the vested interests of the estates of what was still largely a corporative realm. If in the basic countryside the peasant tended to huddle within the confines of his community, the custom of his lordship, so among his betters did the individual habitually find purpose and protection within the sphere of provincial estates and codes, of hierarchies legal, ecclesiastical or academic, or, by no means least, in guilds and commercial corporations. Those of Paris, especially the ancient *six corps des marchands,* now set up a privileged outcry against the call-up, wangled concessions and waved

---

[5] Baron von Pöllnitz, op. cit., ii. 285.
[6] Duke de Chaulnes, memorandum addressed to King Louis XV, 2 Oct. 1743: Luynes, v. 282.

medical certificates at the harassed chief of police. Numerous recruits, incidentally, had to be rejected for failing to measure up to the required minimum height of five foot.

Troops stood by as the twenty-one districts of Paris balloted in turn for the militia, in the courtyard of the Invalides, starting with the Faubourg Saint-Germain on 17 April 1743. Marville and the governor of the Bastille presided personally over the draw from a hat conducted in batches of thirty, twenty-five white tickets to five black, the future soldiers. In the event all passed off quietly: 'those who have white tickets go running off in good heart; those who have black tickets bear it patiently, and all of them . . . drink to the return'.[7] Paris still responded to the call of the country in danger. Once again, in the War of the Austrian Succession as in the War of the Spanish Succession, the reserved strength of France was brought to bear. In 1743, so soon after the wreck of the Army of Bohemia, the overall strength of the French army rose to 330,000 men.

Amid the national call to arms one young soldier who was active was the Count de Stainville, back at last. In February 1743 his reduced regiment, the Roi, had marched back from Amberg in a rear division of the retreating remnant of the Army of Bohemia, along that route which it had taken in full pride in the autumn of 1741: Fürth, Uffenheim, Wimpfen, Wiesloch, the names reeled off backwards now. Roi-Infanterie kept discipline to the last, duly securing from each neutral German township through which it passed that certificate of good conduct which was the requisite safeguard for a regiment against subsequent claims to damages. In the last days of February 1743 the royal regiment of infantry duly returned to its starting-point of Spires, whence on again into quarters at Nancy, the capital of Stainville's homeland.[8]

VI

Anyone who had come through the Bohemian campaign and the retreat from Prague had some claim to be considered quite a soldier, and Stainville had distinguished himself. But on that grim campaign his endeavours to match valour with gaiety among the adherents of the Marshal de Belle-Isle had prejudiced his prospects. The eclipse of Madame de Mailly had, as Stainville senior observed, made 'the stock of Monsieur de Belle-Isle fall prodigiously at court, for it was

[7] Barbier, iii. 440–1.
[8] Cf. 'État de la marche des Troupes de l'Armée de Bohème pour revenir en France': Arch. Guerre C., vol. 3006, no. 107; Count of Bavaria to Marshal de Belle-Isle, Spires, 26 Feb. 1743: ibid., vol. 3007, no. 117; 'État de la Distribution des Troupes de l'Armée de Bohème à leur rentrée en France et de celles revenant de l'Armée de Bavière': ibid., vol. 3007, no. 129.

the dominant party for him'.[9] The following spring found 'Monsieur de Belle-Isle and his adherents ... drowned (*noyés*)',[10] largely by those of Broglie. Back from Bavaria, they had got in first at court that winter, working upon the Marquise de la Tournelle and other new personalities, notably the incoming minister of war, the Count d'Argenson. So now:

The Count de Stainville learnt from the refusal of a regiment which he received from this minister, when a promotion rendered a large number vacant, that he was included in the list of the adherents of the disgraced marshal with whom he had had no connection, and in that of the enemies of the Marshal de Broglie whom he did not know; and that, on this double head, he was deprived of all hope of the most just advancement. It was no longer then, as [in the refusal] two years earlier, a mortification which he was experiencing; he was suffering a manifest injustice; he was twenty-three; thirty of his juniors, aged eighteen to twenty, were colonels; he beheld himself the object of the resentment – all the more to be feared, the less reasonable it was – of the mistress, the favourites and the minister. The uprightness of his character was revolted by it, and his pride refused to make or suffer any demarche to destroy the unjust and groundless prejudices whereof he was the victim.[11]

Another factor in the person of the Grand Duke of Tuscany now contributed to this hitherto unpublished crisis in the early career of the Duke de Choiseul. His father looked to Francis as a protector for all three of his sons. The second, Leopold Charles then aged eighteen, was destined for the church and almost a year earlier his father had been writing to Francis as a likely intermediary for a request to Maria Theresa 'to grant my son one of the abbeys vacant in the Duchy of Milan'.[12] In the event this ecclesiastical son was to find early preferment through the supplanter of Francis in Lorraine, King Stanislas. An Austrian niche was, however, found for the youngest brother, Jacques, then fifteen and destined like the eldest for a career of arms, but in the opposite camp. At the end of the same year of 1742 the marquis had written to his master: 'I know the favours wherewith Your Royal Highness is honouring the son which I have left with you as your page. I venture to beg you most humbly to be good enough to ... place him in the service of Our August Queen. War is a profession which one cannot begin too soon, so I hope that Your Royal Highness will be good enough to place this child in some regiment.'[13] Jacques de Stainville, handsomer and harder than Stephen, duly became an Austrian captain of dragoons, and thence upwards. Now, early in 1743, the career of Stephen

[9] Marquis de Stainville to Grand Duke Francis II, Paris, 10 Nov. 1742: Esteri del Granducato di Toscana, vol. 2295/1286, fo. 188.
[10] Ibid., 30 Mar. 1743: fo. 259.   [11] Essai/Arsenal 5808, fos. 23–5.
[12] Marquis de Stainville to Grand Duke Francis II, Paris, 27 Apr. 1742: *u.s.*, fo. 104.
[13] Ibid., 29 Dec. 1742: fo. 206.

became the focus of concern. The Marquis de Stainville wrote that March concerning his eldest to the grand duke:

The King [of France] has just made a promotion of new colonels, in which he has bestowed fifteen regiments, and my son is not included in it despite all the well founded hopes which I had been given. I know well that the honour which I have of being attached to Your Royal Highness is the cause of the bad treatment which he is receiving, but I would sacrifice the fortune of my whole family rather than fall short of what I must feel from honour, duty and gratitude. If I am obliged to take an extreme course, by making a total transplantation, I venture to flatter myself that Your Royal Highness will not abandon my children and that Her Majesty Our August Queen will honour them with her protection. I expect to take my decision on this shortly, and I am taking the liberty of warning Your Royal Highness of it while very humbly begging you to be good enough to honour me with your advice, which for me will be orders.[14]

For the Marquis de Stainville to adumbrate the threat of a 'total transplantation' in regard to his service of Francis was an exceptional step, taken on behalf of his eldest son. It looks as though Francis, not unmindful perhaps of young Stainville's military reputation, for once rose to the occasion. One is told that the grand duke 'wrote to the Marquis de Stainville and proposed to him, for his son, the post of adjutant-general to his own person, the rank of colonel, and assurances of everything which could thereafter most serve his fortune and flatter his ambition . . . In this painful position, in the cruel alternative of abandoning all hope of fortune, of dedicating himself to mortifications or of renouncing France which he would have chosen for his fatherland if the choice had been within his power, to which he was held by ties of duty and of honour, where he would be leaving friends behind, torn at the same time by the disheartening idea that a base intrigue by a corrupt minister was going to upset for ever the natural course of his life, tormented by the certain perspective of a failed career if he decided to remain, flattered by the fortune whereof he was given the assurance [by Francis], and which would not have escaped him, more flattered still by the very gracious manner in which it was offered to him, agitated by a thousand different impulses and more unhappy than one can conceive'[15] – he was perhaps overwhelmed as much as the reader of this nonstop catalogue of youthful perplexity and distress.

In this predicament the young Count de Stainville was not entirely without friends and relations at the French court. He had at one time attracted the favourable notice of Mademoiselle, as Mademoiselle de Charolais was habitually called – 'all the charms imaginable', wrote one, 'are united in her person: she has a noble aspect, a very lively sparkling wit.'[16] After giving herself to the Duke de Richelieu, Mademoiselle had passed on to become the mistress of the Bishop of Rennes and, he leaving upon embassy to Madrid, of the Abbé d'Aydie, the king's almoner: 'a time always comes', commented the unkinder Marquis d'Argenson, 'when whores give themselves to churchmen by a natural destiny.'[17] Mademoiselle had earlier promoted the Countess de Mailly rather as Madame de Tencin, that other former mistress of Richelieu, had promoted the supplanting sister. So Mademoiselle was rather in eclipse. 'This already super-annuated princess'[18] was liable to be a less influential patron for young Stainville than his older cousin, the Marquis de Meuse.

Henri-Louis de Choiseul, Marquis de Meuse, was the leading representative of the branch of Choiseul-Meuse and the owner of Sorcy, east of Stainville. 'Little Meuse'[19] was a member of the king's closest circle along with such other intimates as the Duke d'Ayen, the Count de Noailles and the Count de Coigny, son of the old marshal of that name. (Young Coigny was another of those who had consoled Mademoiselle for the absence of her bishop.) Meuse had been one of the youthful *arracheurs de palissades*, a nickname recalling an epicene scandal from back in July 1722, just after the court had returned to Versailles.

Meuse had gone on to become a soldier of merit, rising to lieutenant-general, and 'an assiduous and entertaining courtier':[20] such a keen one that in 1743 Louis XV was sensibly rejecting his suggestion for the institution of insignia of personal rank at court, approximating to the Russian model. The Marquis de Meuse had been closely associated with the favour of the Countess de Mailly and had made his nominal rooms at Versailles available for her private suppers with Louis in accordance with the king's orders to him: 'You will have a bed there, but you will not sleep there at all; you will have a closestool, but you will not use it ... You can bring M. de Luxembourg and M. de Coigny in there when they have returned from the army; but you will have to dine there. What do you want to have for your dinner?'[21] Asked by Louis to cost it, the embarrassed Meuse, with the assistance of Madame de Mailly herself, thought he might do them decently at supper for 1,200 to 1,500 francs (some £50–60) a month. Such were the practicalities of pleasure at Versailles.

The subsequent switch to the Marquise de la Tournelle had found Meuse equal to the situation. He had the unenviable assignment of tapering off Madame de Mailly's hopes of reinstatement; but on the morning after her sister's first night with the king at Choisy, in the

[16] Baron von Pöllnitz, op. cit., ii. 217.   [17] D'Argenson, ii. 231.   [18] Ibid., ii. 44.
[19] Ibid., iv. 81.   [20] Ibid., vii. 5.   [21] Cited, Luynes, iv. 6–7.

blue room still furnished with the silks worked by Madame de Mailly herself, it was to the Marquis de Meuse that the Marquise de la Tournelle exhibited the king's snuffbox left at the head of her bed. The exacting Marquise tended, however, to be jealous of Meuse's own little suppers, at that period, alone with Louis, who refused his repeated requests to proceed on active service. Meuse's young cousin in search of a regiment might well have reckoned that such a favourite would be well placed to advance his fortunes. Not for the last time in his career, however, was the Count de Stainville to avoid looking mainly to relations in pursuit of an advancement which he was to secure more cleverly, more certainly through others. His present course was manly and direct:

He attempted one more method in order to remain in the service of his prince; he went to find the Marshal de Noailles, nominated for the next campaign to the command of the army on the Rhine; [he] expounded to him, without being [previously] known to him, his cruel perplexity, acquainted him with his position, opened his heart to him; he received a consoling welcome full of kindness. The marshal begged him not to take any decision yet, went to find the king, attacked the minister [d'Argenson] in his prejudices, surmounted them, though with difficulty, brought back to the Count de Stainville the assurance of the first vacant regiment, and thereto joined the offer of a place in the general staff of his army, the only one which he was in a position to confer.[22]

In the words, largely, of one of Choiseul's best friends, this 'circumstance, which fixed the Count de Stainville for ever in France, is not unworthy of attention because it again proves that in an age which might have excused the levity wherewith he has since been so often and so unjustly reproached, on the contrary he shewed none: that he had remained firmly attached to what he believed to be his duty, and resisted upon the one hand mortifications and injustices, and upon the other the well-founded hope of a brilliant career'[23] in Austria.

In point of fact, even if the Marshal de Noailles had not hitherto been personally acquainted with the Count de Stainville, he had been with his father in his special position in the margin of the central issue of war or peace between France and Austria. In that context the marquis reported just about then of Noailles: 'This Marshal, whom I saw on Tuesday, said in my ear that he much wished that this business was finished. "You have long known", he said to me, "how I think in regard to Your August Master. My feelings are still the same, and I beg you to be good enough to assure

22 Essai/Arsenal 5808, fos. 26–7.
23 Ibid., fo. 27: passage amended by Duke de Nivernais.

him of it"':[24] which the elder Stainville thus did. Such were the accommodating sentiments of the French commander for the next campaign, and the confidential context of the appointment of his new staff-officer. Somehow politics never seemed very far away from young Stainville.

Explaining away high motives in terms of baser ones is a favourite pastime with clever and unkind historians. In no such spirit, while accepting for what it is worth the assurance of young Stainville's high sense of duty, one may yet admire the deftness with which that young hopeful exploited the Austrian offer in order to lever a regiment out of a hostile French government. But then the future Duke de Choiseul had a winning way with him in more senses than one. If on this occasion he had not needed Meuse's assistance, he had exemplified the motto borrowed from this cousin: *A force d'aller mal tout ira bien.*

The Count de Stainville declined with gratitude the flattering offer of the Grand Duke Francis. According to a moralist of the French eighteenth century, serenely disillusioned Chamfort, the only two ways for a man to preserve his liberty and character are to know how to say No, and how to live alone. As to saying No, young Stainville, precocious perhaps from family pressures, was graduating early. And in the later outlook of the Duke de Choiseul there are sudden glimpses of secret distances to suggest that perhaps he may also have learnt how to live alone, at least in spirit, at least occasionally, as in the present crisis. But a less lonely or more sociable person than the then Count de Stainville might be difficult to imagine. The personal pattern of his life largely derived from his exceptional success in preserving his liberty and character within the heart of a traditional and high society attaining to its aesthetic apogee in the ordered civilization of the French eighteenth century and the courtly conformism of Versailles. One secret of this success was Stainville's knack of directing his spontaneous emotions into politically profitable quarters. So now it only remained 'to add that gratitude for the Marshal de Noailles's welcome, full of kindness, and for the important service which he rendered the Count de Stainville was present to his memory all his life, that he did not cease to render to the marshal, so long as he lived, a continual tribute of respect and attachment, and that he lost no opportunity of testifying to his children how imbued he was with a sense of what he owed to their father.'[25]

Lasting gratitude is rather seldom prominent in politics, certainly

[24] Marquis de Stainville to Grand Duke Francis II, Paris, 13 Apr. 1743: Esteri del Granducato di Toscana, vol. 2295/1286, fo. 263.
[25] Essai/Arsenal, 5808, fo. 28.

in French politics then. But it was of a piece with the warm and generous nature of the later Duke de Choiseul. The French start in life which he largely owed to the Duke de Noailles, as now revealed, was a formative influence upon his career.

CHAPTER VI

DETTINGEN

I

'THE Marshal de Noailles left on Wednesday morning to proceed to Landau, which he has given as the rendezvous for all the general officers and his general staff on the 27th of this month.' Writing on 20 April 1743, the Marquis de Stainville continued to the Grand Duke Francis: 'The King [of France] having had me informed by M. d'Argenson that he wished my son to remain in his service, and that when he went so far as to retain in it a person of condition one could be sure that he would not be forgotten in the distribution of his favours, I took the course of sending him to serve on this campaign in the quality of Aide Major Général of the army of M. de Noailles, who seemed to me to take care of this with pleasure.'[1] That was one way of putting it.

This time the favours to come for the Count de Stainville did come quickly, on 21 May 1743. His father could further report to his master:

The King has just given my son an infantry regiment which will bear his name. Your Royal Highness has deigned to interest yourself in this with so much kindness that I feel that I should inform you of it while very humbly begging you to be good enough to continue the same favours to my family, for whose attachment to you I vouch, although I have been forcibly obliged to have my eldest son adopt another course.[2]

In such delicate fashion did the Count de Stainville come to command one of the French *régiments de gentilhomme* or 'grey regiments' usually uniformed in greyish white and bearing the names of their colonels in contrast to crack regiments of territorial designation. The retirement now of Colonel d'Auroy thus transformed the Régiment d'Auroy into the Régiment de Stainville, the latest designation of what had originally been the Régiment de Vendôme, raised in 1651 during the Fronde. Under d'Auroy it had served in the Corsican campaign of 1739 and most recently in Bohemia, at Sahay, the siege of Prague and the retreat. So Stainville

---

[1] Marquis de Stainville to Grand Duke Francis II, Paris, 20 Apr. 1743: Esteri del Granducato di Toscana, vol. 2295/1286, fo. 265.   [2] Ibid., 25 May 1743: fos. 291–2.

had very likely familiarized himself with the regiment, its greyish uniform set off by the usual tricorn trimmed with gold and by large collars and cuffs in scarlet. Also scarlet was the long waistcoat faced, in the case of the Régiment de Stainville, with a rather unusual amount of gold braid. The regimental colours carried the regular white cross quartering, in this case, plain fields of, respectively, blue, brown, mauve, and green.

It was a fine thing to be a colonel, which partly explains why little regiments like Stainville, comprising but one battalion, struggled to maintain their strength instead of being used to keep up the cadres of the main regiments, as would almost certainly have been more efficient and economical in time of war. It would of course have been less satisfactory for colonels and indeed, on the short view, for the government which got its regimental rake-off. The Count de Stainville had to pay 40,000 livres for the Régiment d'Auroy. It sounds as though it was a good one since the price seems to have been appreciably higher than was usual for a grey regiment at that period. In any case, well over £1,500 was probably quite enough for the family finances; although the income from the Stainville estate for 1743 was the highest for those war-years, at 25,719 livres, when balanced against expenditure and reprises it became a deficit of 1,845 livres.

A French colonel then paid dear for his rank of honour but relatively restricted authority. Since Louvois he was pretty strictly subordinate to his brigadier commanding four battalions irrespective of regimental attribution. And the newer rank of brigadier went by merit, as also did that of major, who largely replaced his colonel in the administration of the regiment. The intermediate lieutenant-colonel was appointed by seniority from the regimental captains, each commanding a company of forty men (thirty in peacetime) except for the colonel's own company directly under the lieutenant-colonel commanding the battalion. Each infantry battalion then normally comprised sixteen companies of fusiliers plus one of picked grenadiers. Each company was the purchased property of its captain who was directly responsible for the recruitment and maintenance, was thus the key-officer in the army. Governmental allowances in this respect were quite inadequate so that one retired captain had lamented a few years earlier: 'There is in the kingdom a nobility which is at the same time very old and very poor, which is born for the infantry and which, owing to the venality introduced in our time into this said infantry, is so to speak excluded from the service of the king.'[3] Many captains ruined themselves if their colonel did not fulfil

[3] Captain Cervin de la Rivière, 15 Feb. 1739: Arch. Guerre C. A1, vol. 3072, no. 51, cited, A. Corvisier, op. cit., i. 135, n. 14.

his moral obligation to subvent them. Thus the colonel was the regimental entrepreneur for whom the price of the regiment by no means necessarily ended the financial calls upon him. These obligations upon the nobility in the military service of their king could heavily counterbalance their tax-exemptions.

In the French army of old such was the inefficient system to which the Count de Stainville was then subject, and which he was within twenty years largely to sweep away. The logic of the later reforms of Choiseul stemmed not a little from just that year of 1743. For it was at that time of military stringency that the Count d'Argenson compounded the confusion by drafting conscripts into not only militia battalions but also the regular ranks of the mercenaries. Doubtless, though, recruiting-sergents and captains were glad enough at the time of any recruits whatever. Traditional French recruiting-grounds were the frontier-provinces, especially in the north-east. The new Régiment de Stainville, blooded in Bohemia, was not assigned to active duty that year but was garrisoned at Strasburg, the main French place of arms near Stainville's native Lorraine.

The new colonel, however, was not one, then or ever, to let the grass grow under his feet. He busied himself with his benefactor's handsome supplement at headquarters: staff appointments were then few and a considerable mark of recognition based, more than colonelcies, upon merit. Stainville had been gazetted an *aide-major-général* to Noailles's major-general, the Count de Chabannes. Major-general was at that time not a substantive rank in the French army, but a staff appointment. Besides the separate establishment, already explained, of the civil intendant of an army (Noailles's intendant was Chauvelin, an expert like Séchelles) the normal articulation of a French army-staff was then threefold. The quartermaster-general and chief of staff to the commander-in-chief was the *maréchal-général des logis de l'armée*. Subordinate to him were the quartermasters acting as chiefs of staff of the cavalry, the *maréchal des logis de la cavalerie*, and of the infantry, the *major-général*. Stainville thus became an infantry staff-officer for the campaign of 1743, the only staff-posting of the war held by that fighting officer.

II

By the end of April that year the Marshal de Noailles reached the advanced base of the French army at Spires. After the extravagant ventures of Belle-Isle, the traditional technique of Noailles promised a return to the good old days, the good old ways of soldiering along the Rhine and the eastern approaches to France. It was to man those approaches, as their fathers had before them, that the newly raised militia went marching out from Paris that May in their white uniforms 'with a yellow button and a hat trimmed with gold – imitation of course'.[4] The problems of equipment and supply, on top of that of manpower, as usual bore heavily upon the French government. In regard to the expensive cavalry Noailles reckoned that on average every troop back from the Army of Bohemia comprised, instead of the full complement of thirty-five horses, eight. The king wrote to his marshal at the front: 'As regards the repairs to the Army of Bohemia, we are making them so far as we can; but we are not God. As for provisions, they are very costly hydra'.[5]

On the other side costs were cushioned for Austria by British subsidies, now matched by Dutch ones in the ratio of two to three. Holland at last promised to contribute twenty thousand men to the Pragmatic Army, then building up on the northern bank of the Main atop the French angle of projection in Alsace. The British contingent had come marching through from Ghent, crossing the snow-swollen Rhine below Coblenz to find their Austrian allies, typically of warfare then, preoccupied not least with dominating the election occasioned by the recent death of the Archbishop of Mainz, the imperial arch-chancellor. This manoeuvre at least was successful. On 22 April 1743 the election of Count von Ostein, lately envoy in London, to be Elector meant that Mainz and its vote had passed from French into Austrian influence. In such an atmosphere the generalissimo of the Pragmatic Army, the mettlesome Earl of Stair eager to emulate Marlborough's campaign of 1704, failed to win approval for a bold drive from the Rhenish Palatinate across to the Upper Palatinate so as to link with Lobkowitz and Charles of Lorraine and all converge to smash Broglie's army in Bavaria.

Frustrated likewise was Noailles's counterplan for pre-empting Stair's strategy of junction with the Austrian army in the Bavarian theatre by himself advancing upon the lower Main and even occupying Frankfurt. Thus might Noailles have exploited his start over the Pragmatic Army in grouping his large force of seventy thousand men centrally along the Neckar eastward from Spires. Such a thrust seemed unduly bold to the French government, influenced as it was by the busy Pâris-Duverney who, as Noailles observed to Louis, was 'a very good munitioneer but whose weakness is wishing to make plans of war, and who . . . has begun by inflaming and seducing M. Orry'[6] to work upon the Minister of War. The

---

[4] Barbier, iii. 444.
[5] King Louis XV to Marshal de Noailles, Versailles, 8 May 1743: Rousset, i. 48.
[6] Marshal de Noailles to King Louis XV, Worms, 27 May 1743: Rousset, i. 85.

resultant directive of 20 May 1743 constrained Noailles not only to remain for the present upon the Neckar, which would keep him closer to Broglie in Bavaria, but also to detach thither a corps of twelve battalions of infantry and ten squadrons of cavalry. The forces in the Rhineland were the principal ones on either side but Broglie's battered army in Bavaria remained the strategic magnet of the whole campaign. And it was yet again in trouble.

Early in May 1743 Prince Charles of Lorraine, eagerly on the go again, crossed the river Inn at Schärding, defeated and captured the Bavarian General von Minutzi at Griesbach, and carried through to take Braunau and threaten Dingolfing upon the Isar. This aimed a wedge in more senses than one between Seckendorff's Bavarians and their allies under Broglie. The French commander stood out 'as firm as a rock'[7] against all adjurations to speed to succour Braunau and protect Munich on the Franco–Bavarian right flank. It was on his left flank that Broglie, understandably if unfortunately frightened of spreading his forces, was mesmerized by danger from Prince Lobkowitz ultimately backed by Stair and the ghost of 'Milord Marlborough in the campaign of Hochstedt'.[8]

Since Broglie would not go after the Austrians they came after him. In the ensuing clash the forward commands on both sides were held by up-and-coming young generals of whom more was to be heard. These were the Count von Daun and the Prince de Conti.

The Prince de Conti was the ablest and most mettlesome of the French royal princes. He had annoyed Louis XV the year before by disobeying his ban upon princes of the blood taking active service. Conti had slipped away from court and, implicitly shewing up the others, joined Maillebois's army of relief where he was placed under brief arrest before being assigned to duties in keeping with his keenness and the public consideration which it won him. The spirited Lieutenant-General the Prince de Conti now sympathized with Seckendorff against his own commander, Broglie, whose mainstay still was his principal lieutenant, Count Maurice de Saxe. Conti had just extruded Saxe from the critical command of the rearguard: the first but not the last military passage between that French royal prince and the Saxon royal bastard, the self-styled Duke-Elect of Courland and Semigallia whose own amours were earlier said to have embraced the wife of Conti. Now serving under Conti in command at Dingolfing was the Marquis du Châtelet, the neighbour of the Stainvilles and husband of Voltaire's bluestocking mistress.

[7] Marshal de Broglie to Count d'Argenson: Broglie/Fréd-LXV, i. 311.
[8] Marshal de Broglie to Count d'Argenson, Burglegenfeld, 12 Apr. 1743: Pajol, ii. 303.

Du Châtelet took the edge of Daun's attack against Dingolfing or 17 May 1743. Daun set Dingolfing alight and Châtelet on his way back to Landau, also to be burnt. It was the beginning of the long retreat of the Army of Bavaria, less inspiring than that of the Army of Bohemia.

On 27 May Daun and Prince Charles pushed Conti out of his headquarters at Deggendorf. Lobkowitz and Khevenhüller came closing in from north and south respectively. Broglie, abandoning his Bavarian allies to their fate, beat it back along the Danube, through Straubing, Ratisbon, Kelheim, Ingolstadt. The French garrisoned Ingolstadt but by 23 June 1743 the main army was back a Donauwörth leaving a trail of 'corpses scattered in every direction and deprived of burial'.[9] If Broglie had a positive plan it was to join Noailles and let the rest go hang. The reinforcement of Broglie'. army from that of Noailles was dimly viewed by both and secured the worst of both worlds, swelling Broglie's demoralized retreat while weakening Noailles over against the threatening Stair.

On 3–4 June 1743 as the 12,000 reinforcements were leaving Noailles's army for Broglie's, advanced elements of the Pragmatic Army under General Ligonier came probing south across the Main Stair was keen to give battle, not least with the solid object of securing sufficient freedom of movement to overcome the crippling dearth of fodder, also a cardinal consideration for Noailles. Once again did fodder-supply provide the rationale of much of the manoeuvring. As not infrequently in war, the opposing generals both made out how eager they were for a battle which somehow did not materialize Ligonier drew back his hazardous point and Noailles, reacting promptly northwards, reported that the enemy withdrawal 'resembles a flight. We have found in their camp trunks, some barrels of beer and bottles of brandy; ... there remained on this side [of the river] a number of women who were in tears; I have had them reassured, and have sent back the lot, not wishing to begin hostilities by so small a matter.'[10] Ligonier had reported that German women were a good deal less obliging than the English.

Forage remained the draw for 'these Anglo-Austrian gentlemen' as King Louis now called them, adding to Noailles, 'You see that I conform to new words, when they seem good to me.'[11] The Anglo Austrians scoured up the Main to strategic Aschaffenburg and were joined on 19 June by King George II, arrived from Hanover to

[9] Count de Saxe to King Augustus III, Ingolstadt, 13 June 1743: Comte C.F. Vitzthum d'Eckstaedt, *Maurice de Saxe et Marie-Josèphe de Saxe, Dauphine de France* (Leipzig, 1867 henceforth cited as Vitzthum/Saxe), p. 471.

[10] Marshal de Noailles to King Louis XV, Gross-Gerau, 12 June 1743: Rousset, i. 103.

[11] King Louis XV to Marshal de Noailles, Versailles, 22 June 1743: ibid., i. 109.

assume personal command. The same day brought a skirmish with the contact-keeping French, whose commander reported: 'They say that Lord Stair has had a bullet which pierced his hat, which I cannot approve; for I think that it is very indecent to fire upon a General.'[12]

If Noailles was a gentlemanly general he was also a methodical one. He bottled up the bridgehead at Aschaffenburg by a well-sited redoubt and encamped over against it, at Stockstatt. There the Count de Stainville's superior staff-officer, the Count de Chabannes reported: 'Our camp is very healthy; the soldiers lack nothing; they seem contented and very willing. Daily there reach us twelve or fifteen deserters from the enemy who bring us the very bad bread which they are eating and of which they are not even given a whole ration. The lack of provisions will oblige them to adopt a course within a few days.'[13]

The expectation of the Count de Chabannes was the intention of the Marshal de Noailles. In the accurate appraisal of his keen young staff-officer, Stainville:

In coming from Aschaffenburg, whither the army of the King of England had very indiscreetly advanced, to fall back upon Frankfurt, where the supply-depot of the English army was, one had either to pass [along the Main] by Dettingen, to traverse the village and the ravine [there] in order to enter upon the plain of Hanau, or else to take the mountain road [away from the Main] which was very difficult, for the King of England would have had to convey his whole army over into the mountain by a single road, which was a defile, which course was extremely dangerous and regarded as impracticable in the face of an enemy army. From the moment that the King of England had advanced to Aschaffenburg, the Marshal de Noailles arranged all his projects to render communications difficult from Frankfurt to Aschaffenburg, in order to oblige the King of England to retreat. Since the two camps had only the Main between them, movements were known in one camp as in the other. The Marshal de Noailles had two bridges established [at Seligenstadt] two leagues below his camp, fortified these bridgeheads, had posts occupied on the Main above and below, established on the bank of his side a hundred pieces of park-artillery which should sweep the plain which approached Dettingen and prevent the enemy from marching by this road. He sent a considerable corps to these bridges, not only to guard them, but to constitute the advance-guard of the army and to proceed to place it at Dettingen and the hollow road, if the enemy made a movement. I believe that there are few examples of a military position so advantageous and so well concerted. This position established, the Marshal de Noailles actively busied himself with harassing the resources of the English army which came from Frankfurt, in order to oblige the King of England to make a movement and to profit from it.[14]

Choiseul's admiration of these dispositions was shared by a more eminent and less implicated military critic. 'Noailles', wrote Frederick

[12] Marshal de Noailles to Count d'Argenson, Stockstatt, 20 June 1743: *Campagne de Monsieur le Maréchal Duc de Noailles en Allemagne l'an MDCCXLIII* [ed. P.F. Du Moulin] (Amsterdam, 1760–1; henceforth cited as *Campagne/43*), i. 218.

[13] Count de Chabannes to Count d'Argenson, Stockstatt, 24 June 1743: ibid., i. 228.

[14] Choiseul, *Mémoires*, pp. 7–8.

the Great, 'conceived a design worthy of the greatest captain.'[15] A little earlier Noailles had explained to Louis XV: 'I have as a maxim, Sire, that it is better to defer than to begin feebly.'[16] Now, after patient manoeuvring, he was ready to begin strongly.

III

At one o'clock in the morning of Thursday, 27 June 1743, the Marshal de Noailles received intelligence that the enemy was on the move. Alerting all troops under his command, Noailles swung into the saddle and rode off to the river-bank where he confirmed for himself that the Pragmatic Army was indeed 'in full march in two columns, and that they were taking the road to Hanau.'[17] As Choiseul commented: 'Everything succeeded for him according to wish.'[18]

Galloping down to Seligenstadt, Noailles ordered his nephew, the young Duke de Gramont, to cross the two bridges with twenty-eight thousand men, to occupy the village of Dettingen and to line out there against the enemy advance: a solid and menacing disposition since, in Choiseul's words, 'from this village up to the marshes which reach to the woods that bound the mountain, there is a hollow-way impracticable for the passage of an army in the face of another'.[19]

Gramont was across the river by dawn and took up his strong position covered by a brook in the nasty little dip. This was Noailles's northern, frontal block to the Pragmatic Army, constricted between the Spessart hills and the river Main. Splashing back across a ford to the west bank, Noailles attended to the remaining aspect, the enemy rear. The Pragmatic Army, as it marched north into the box, could observe French units on the opposite bank marching in the opposite direction, southwards, and officers in the two armies chatted as they passed each other. The French design was to cross the river at Aschaffenburg and hook round to take the allies in the rear, which was what they most feared. Noailles had sprung what he described as a mousetrap.

By seven o'clock the march of the Pragmatic Army, led by the British and Austrian cavalry, reached the village of Klein Ostheim, between Aschaffenburg and Dettingen. The route there was bottle-necked through the village street and the cavalry, once past it, were wheeled round facing the river and halted while the infantry marched

[15] Frederick, iii. 12.
[16] Marshal de Noailles to King Louis XV, Spires, 4 May 1743: Rousset, i. 47.
[17] Marshal de Noailles to King Louis XV, Seligenstadt, 28 June 1743: ibid., i. 109-10.
[18] Choiseul, *Mémoires*, p. 8.   [19] Ibid., p. 7.

up. Foreseeing such a situation, Noailles had sited his batteries on the opposite bank accordingly. These opened up across the river in a 'very well serviced'[20] cannonade. The confusion caused in the allied army was increased by its now observing, about eight o'clock, that Gramont was positioning his force at Dettingen across their route to Hanau. In order to confront this challenge the allied units facing to the river needed to deploy back on their right flank while the infantry passed up through the cavalry and the ill-ordered column of route was sorted out. All that morning the Pragmatic Army, still pounded by the French guns, was struggling into order of battle, with King George II excitedly prancing around on horseback.

The Duke de Gramont was content to observe the elaborate evolutions of the enemy till towards noon. Then 'despite the wise representations of M. de Cherizy, lieutenant-general and lieutenant of the bodyguard',[21] Gramont decided to depart from the defensive dispositions of Noailles, still away on the other bank, and to advance across the brook to the attack. This advance, while contrary to the intention of Noailles, was not, as the Count de Stainville emphasized soon afterwards, contrary to any express order of his. The marshal had given no explicit command either for or against an advance, had left too much to the discretion of his ardent nephew. To this extent did the ultimate responsibility rest with Noailles.

The critical initiative of the Duke de Gramont has been commonly ascribed to his impetuous urge towards glory, and recently[22] to a reasoned endeavour to take the enemy in the flank or in the act of redeploying. That may indeed have been a factor, though if it was the main one, as simply as that, it might seem a little surprising that he should have left it till so late, when the allied confusion was mainly mastered. Another explanation, which would seem to fit the timing rather better, was provided by the future Duke de Choiseul, who was on the spot; though his account has hitherto been used but little, if at all, by military historians.

'Those who commanded the [French] advance-guards,' wrote Choiseul, 'preoccupied with the idea that the enemy would not dare attempt the passage of the hollow-way and the village, but would on the contrary adopt the course of withdrawing by way of the mountain, feared that, if they awaited the rest of the army which the marshal [de Noailles] was fetching, the enemy would have time to clear off (*se*

[20] Marshal de Noailles to King Louis XV, Seligenstadt, 28 June 1743: Rousset, i. 113.

[21] Luynes, v. 66.

[22] Cf. Rex Whitworth, *Field Marshal Lord Ligonier* (Oxford, 1958), p. 76. General Whitworth's fresh interpretation of the battle of Dettingen lays emphasis, derived from Ligonier, upon the significance of the allied redeployment from the river. This tends to agree with the implications of Choiseul's account; at the same time Choiseul's explanation in some respects modifies such an interpretation of the battle and fills it out from the French side.

déblayer) by the mountain, that they would lose the whole advantage of the day and of the preceding dispositions if one did not press measures. They deceived themselves in taking one of the two suppositions for the other. In consequence, the Duke de Gramont had the two reserves cross the hollow-way and the village.'[23]

The Duke de Gramont, who was incidentally shortsighted, appears to have attributed to the allied wheel-round from the river, over towards the hills, a wider scope than it actually possessed. His advance was based upon the faulty supposition that he had to deal with English rearguards covering a turning movement into the hill-country: an error encouraged, possibly, by good use by the English of wooded cover.

The then Count de Stainville significantly recorded that 'the marshal [de Noailles] arrived at the moment when the troops were marching in the belief that they were going to attack a rearguard. He had not the conscience to make his advance-guards withdraw, to replace them in the position whence they had started and there to await his [main] army. It arrived, this army, at full speed; they pushed it successively into a terrain which could not contain it. It lacked order and fled; but it was only noon.'[24]

Both sides had piled rather breathlessly into the engagement. It opened to some ragged cheering and shooting, which startled King George's horse into bolting away to the rear till he was able to dismount and resume on foot his gesticulations of encouragement. And it was the steadfast British infantry who were especially to signalize themselves. Warming to their work in triple rolling fire, they staggered the French. The French weakness in drilled discipline was shewn up, especially in their infantry, the immediate concern of the Count de Stainville. The foot reflected all too clearly its hasty composition from batches of raw militia drafted in to replace the veterans destroyed in the Bohemian campaign. The French turned tail. Their cavalry indeed, especially the tough regiment of mounted gendarmery under the Duke de Picquigny, did conspicuously better in the savage melee which preceded the breakup of the battle. Choiseul's surviving account of Dettingen, owing to a lacuna in his memoirs, begins abruptly at this point in the middle of a sentence, literally in mid-flight, perhaps in reference to the fact that the close engagement 'of the cavalry rendered impossible all idea of restoring order, and consequently of preventing an almost general flight. In fleeing the troops passed the hollow-way and the village. They had without doubt lost some men in the three general discharges of the enemy army, but there were only some corps in particular which had

[23] Choiseul, *Mémoires*, pp. 8–9.   [24] Ibid., p. 9.

suffered. The head of the infantry was in condition and they recovered themselves, at noon, without being pressed by the enemy, who, as seems incredible, contented himself, without advancing, with watching the French army flee.'[25]

In describing the position at this turning-point, Choiseul characteristically probed the central riddle of the controversial combat of Dettingen: 'The troops which had not been able to enter upon the field of the battle were in the plain, on the other side of the village and the hollow road. The enemy was not following. The [French] artillery on the left of the Main had regained the advantage which it had lost when our troops had masked it and passed beyond the village of Dettingen. The whole army had subsequently reached the village on the other side of the hollow-way. Why did not they resume the position which was the object, the sole object of the operation?'[26]

That question has puzzled modern authority, which has suggested that Noailles merely lost his nerve and became paralysed with dismay.[27] His young staff-officer, however, provides an eye-witness, and a different, answer. 'The Marshal de Noailles', wrote Choiseul, 'wished it [i.e. to resume the original position]; I heard him give the order three times and himself make efforts to rally the troops and put them in battle-order. If they resumed this position, the enemy were lost, despite the skirmish of the morning wherein they had had some advantage. They did not resume this position because the troops would never obey the command. Ignorance, fright, noise, lack of silence rendered all pains useless, and a cannon-shot fired at random by the enemy scattered the army of the King and rendered impossible all means of restraining it.'[28] That would partly have been the job of the young staff-officer who was ruefully to record: 'The only thought was to make it [the French army] recross the Main and to put this barrier between it and the enemy.'[29] Some units needed little encouragement in this direction. The French footguards of the household troops made especially good time across the river so that for long afterwards this nominally elite regiment went by the nickname of Canards du Main.

[25] Choiseul, 'Mémoires de la main d'Étienne-François de Choiseul-Stainville, Duc de Choiseul': Bibliothèque de Versailles, MS. F850 (henceforth cited as Choiseul, 'Mémoires de la main'), fo. 5. The text of this passage as printed by F. Calmettes, op. cit., p. 7, does not include the first, incomplete, sentence. The second sentence, beginning in the original 'Les trouppes en s'enfuyant', there starts a new paragraph which would appear to have been subsequently and somewhat arbitrarily headed in Choiseul's hand as '3ᵉ' to designate a revised commencement of the third of the twenty letters comprising this text of his memoirs. Thus Calmettes's text might seem to follow Choiseul's intention as to the termination of a lacuna for which the author was himself responsible. It seems likely that this omission may have included the account of Choiseul's rejection of the offer of the Grand Duke Francis, and of his indebtedness to the Marshal de Noailles, as given above from Essai/Arsenal 5808: cf. p. 405.

[26] Choiseul, Mémoires, p. 9. [27] See Hon. J. W. Fortescue, op. cit., ii. 100.
[28] Choiseul, Mémoires, pp. 9–10. [29] Ibid., p. 10.

Choiseul's notably accurate account, so far as it goes, of the battle of Dettingen is primarily that of an infantryman. Yet it was after all the deadly shooting of the stolid English foot which had chiefly won the day. Such was the latest recurrence of that antique and expensive pattern, persisting through war after war, century upon century, wherein the two peoples pre-eminent in the west gave expression to their hereditary enmity. And the tradition came down even tactically. Those social divergencies exemplified in the tactics at Crecy were still appreciably relevant just on four hundred years later, upon the field of Dettingen.

This was the last battle wherein a King of England in person led his troops against the enemy. For England as for the continent of Europe the age of chivalry persisted but was passing: as was symbolized by the uncertainty attendant upon the initiative of the elated George II towards reviving the creation of knights banneret upon the field of battle, last performed by Charles I at Edgehill. Well might the king rejoice now at his lucky deliverance. 'The enemy, on their side,' wrote Choiseul, 'thought only of marching upon Frankfurt, even abandoning their wounded, and of profiting from the good fortune which had extracted them from so dangerous a situation, a good fortune which they owed only to the indiscipline and the ignorance of the French army; for, with a disciplined army acquainted with order, the tactical faults of the generals would have been repaired.'[30] Choiseul went on to explain that, exceptionally, he gave 'this lengthily detailed account'[31] of the battle of Dettingen because it had lastingly impressed him and led him to draw certain lessons therefrom when, twenty years later, his opportunity came for military reform.

IV

The day after Dettingen the Marshal de Noailles addressed to Louis XV a notably frank dispatch which fully bore out the then Count de Stainville's appraisal of the French indiscipline. Noailles warned 'that if one does not work, with the most serious and most sustained attention, to remedy it, the troops of Your Majesty will fall into the utmost decadence. I never could have believed, Sire, what I saw yesterday.'[32] The marshal had some grounds besides social partiality for further reporting to Louis on Dettingen in a private letter that

[30] Ibid.   [31] Ibid.
[32] Marshal de Noailles to King Louis XV, Seligenstadt, 28 June 1743: Rousset, i. 118.

'the princes and first lords of your realm have distinguished themselves all the more there in that they have been little supported by the troops'.[33]

The defeated chivalry of France had paid the price of valour. The already ailing Duke de Rochechouart, wounded but refusing to withdraw, had laid down his life: also the Marquis de Fleury, nephew of the cardinal. The Duke d'Harcourt, disdaining a cuirass, was gravely wounded. Seriously injured in the arm was the Marquis de Gontaut, brother of Stainville's old colonel, the Duke de Biron, who himself again reaped glory. And again had the Duke de Richelieu proved himself as valiant upon the battle-field as in the boudoir. Numbered likewise among the brave were the dukes de Luxembourg, Boufflers, and Chevreuse, the Prince de Soubise, the priestly Count de Clermont, great-grandson of the great Condé, the Duke de Picquigny at the head of his stout gendarmery, the Duke de Gramont himself, of whom Noailles indulgently reported that, 'a little too inconsiderate in his first dispositions, although he was not in command and had seniors, [he] has performed prodigies of valour, and this occurrence should correct him'.[34] To that Louis XV had something to say:

Since you speak to me of the Duke de Gramont, I will tell you that I have never doubted his valour, but that I much fear lest the precipitation with which he seems to me to have drawn you into this affair should do him great harm among the troops . . . I have always been fully persuaded also of the valour of our young nobles; but the thing which it is expedient that you should study in them is the talents which they develop, in order that you may cultivate them so that they can become good generals, whereof it is agreed by everybody that we are absolutely lacking, and yet it is that whereof this state will always have an extreme need.[35]

For an officer to be a valiant fighter in the ancient tradition of the *noblesse d'épée* was no longer in itself sufficient. The generalship of the future lay with those who, like the Count de Stainville, could learn to validate valour by staffwork. The Marshal de Noailles, rather exceptionally for those days, had singled out the work of his staff-officers at Dettingen for special commendation: 'I ought not to forget, Sire, to speak to you of the three general staffs of the army, with which I have every grounds for being very satisfied. The *maréchal général des logis de l'armée* has greatly distinguished himself, as well as the major-general [de Chabannes] and the *maréchal des logis de la cavalerie* and their aides; they betook themselves everywhere with

---

[33] Marshal de Noailles to King Louis XV, Seligenstadt, 29 June 1743: ibid., i. 120.
[34] Ibid., i. 121.
[35] King Louis XV to Marshal de Noailles, Choisy, 5 July 1743: ibid., i. 127.

activity and courage, and much contributed to the rallying of the troops and to the good order of the retreat.'[36]

It is reasonable to suppose that Stainville had made his contribution to the battle, more particularly since it was he whom Noailles designated to carry back to court the full account of it: a circumstance which lends additional weight to his evidence on the battle, or combat as it was termed. The heavy tidings of Dettingen had first reached Paris, fragmentarily, on 1 July 1743 in the person of one Charpentier, valet to the killed Duke de Rochechouart. He had posted off even before the battle was fully finished and his devotion enabled the duke's step-mother, the Duchess de Mortemart, to speed from her retirement to Versailles where, that same evening, she broke down before the king and got in first to secure for her grandson, aged four, the dead duke's valuable office of first groom of the royal chambers. Her news threw the court into agitation. Louis waited up that Monday night till four o'clock next morning for the official courier, who only arrived twelve hours later with Noailles's dispatches. The Marquis de Stainville reported a French clamp upon private correspondence from the front and 'general desolation'[37] amid a dearth of facts in Paris. In order to amplify and explain them his son arrived at Versailles towards the middle of July.

To return to the pleasures of Paris and Versailles once Dettingen was over, the climax evidently passed, was a common aspiration among the colonels serving under Noailles. 'I have learnt', wrote the king to his marshal, 'that several colonels wished to have leave, under pretext of the re-establishment of their regiments. I do not believe that you will give them any, and I warrant you that none will be issued from here. That has never been seen in full war.'[38] Young Stainville managed better than the rest by what looks like a combination of good luck and good positioning: a recurrent pattern in his career. He had sound reason for returning from the front, as a staff-officer absent from his regiment, which was now, however, on the move in the spreading scope of hostilities. So Stainville's place as aide-major-général on the staff was filled by a brother of Chauvelin, the intendant of the army of the Marshal de Noailles. It may well have suited that general to entrust the narrative of his defeat to an officer so beholden to him and, it seems likely, already judged proficient in accurate and plausible exposition. With Stainville riding back to Versailles with the tidings of Dettingen, one has a first sense,

---

[36] Marshal de Noailles to King Louis XV, Seligenstadt, 28 June 1743: op. cit., i. 117.
[37] Marquis de Stainville to Grand Duke Francis II, Paris 6 July 1743: Esteri del Granducato di Toscana, vol. 2295/1286, fo. 303.
[38] King Louis XV to Marshal de Noailles, Versailles, 25 Aug. 1743: Rousset, ii. 2.

as perhaps he had, that he might be going far. Only, prefiguratively for his career, they were tidings of defeat.

On reaching the court the Count de Stainville found, perhaps understandably, that his details of Dettingen 'were received coldly enough. Mme de Châteauroux[39] was mistress; court intrigue was more interesting than military deeds; the Minister of War was more skilled in the way of intrigue than he was instructed and interested in the details of the army.'[40] Not much love was lost, evidently, between the young colonel and the minister who had tried to thwart his colonelcy.

One person at least was interested in what the Count de Stainville had to tell the court. The Duke de Luynes, on to a first-hand source for his great diary, recorded on 16 July 1743 that young Stainville 'has told me that the disposition of our army [at Dettingen] was as it is indicated in the reports, and that it is not to be doubted that it is the vivacity of the Duke de Gramont which engaged the action; but that one cannot say that it had been against the precise orders of the marshal; that M. de Noailles had not forbidden him to pass the village, but that he had not ordered him to; that too much confidence in the Duke de Gramont on the part of this general is the cause of what happened; that M. de Noailles was well aware of it since, in returning after the affair: "too much complaisance," said he – they are pretty nearly his terms, "has spoilt everything which I have done up to the present." He [Stainville] added to me that the fright was so great among our troops that when the marshal wished to reform them in battle-order on the edge of the hollow-way, it had never been possible for him to stop them.'[41]

Stainville's contemporary description of Dettingen bears out the assurance that while putting up a good case for Noailles, he told his melancholy story 'without, however, listening to his feelings and his gratitude'[42] to him. It is indeed striking that Stainville's stiffer criticism of his commanding general should occur in his contemporary, rather than in his safely subsequent, narrative, incomplete though that be. That this young colonel should shrink so little from telling the truth, even when it rather told against his eminent benefactor, may perhaps have contributed towards the cool reception of his report at court.

In assessing his discussion of Dettingen with the Count de Stainville the Duke de Luynes commented, 'He has intelligence and talks very well.'[43] For the future Choiseul that would be valued

[39] i.e. the Marquise de la Tournelle, shortly to be created Duchess de Châteauroux.
[40] Choiseul, *Mémoires*, p. 11.
[41] Luynes, v. 74.   [42] Essai/Arsenal 5808, fo. 29.   [43] Luynes, loc. cit.

praise. That statesman, himself sparing of praise in writing of others, from experience suspicious of their motives, was upon a later occasion to support an assertion with the words: 'I have this fact from the Duke de Luynes . . . whom I have always regarded as a man incapable of giving credit to a lie.'[44] Such was the memorialist to whom we owe almost the earliest printed encomium of the future Duke de Choiseul.

[44] Choiseul, 'Mémoires inédits', 2/25/10/756/2.

CHAPTER VII

DIPLOMACY

I

THE details of defeat supplied by the Count de Stainville were not the only ones to reach Versailles about then. If things had gone ill with the Marshal de Noailles they had gone worse with the Marshal de Broglie.

Louis XV wrote to the former marshal in allusion to the latter: 'I am doing my best. Bavaria makes my head swim, if that is [still] possible.'[1] An eighteeenth-century historian judiciously observed that in this correspondence the king 'shewed an amiable modesty which one cannot praise too much when it does not degenerate into weakness'.[2] But it did. Louis did not impose himself. One hears of his ministers shouting at one another in the royal council, where Amelot supported Broglie's retreat, Tencin opposed it. The divided counsels of governmental indecision, compounding the obstinate incapacity of the old marshal, showed through the instructions sent him by the Count d'Argenson on 22 June 1743. They rejected a junction with Noailles and enjoined Broglie to keep the enemy in play in Bavaria so long as possible with 'the firmness with which you so long sustained your camp at Pisek'.[3] Whereas the lesson which he drew from the Bohemian campaign was 'what it is to lose communication with France'.[4] And he was now granted discretion 'in the case wherein every other course except that of retreat shall appear impracticable to you'.[5]

These instructions reached Broglie at Donauwörth at noon on 26 June. Disobeying their spirit, at least, Broglie that same day ordered that his selfish and inglorious retreat should recommence. There at Donauwörth the French in a scramble destroyed their magazines, dumping sacks of flour into the Danube or just anywhere.

The intendant of the Army of Bavaria, de Vanolles, echoed experience from Bohemia in later accusing Broglie of 'intolerable

---

[1] King Louis XV to Marshal de Noailles, Versailles, 4 June 1743: Rousset, i. 98.
[2] Abbé Millot, op. cit., v. 347.
[3] Count d'Argenson to Marshal de Broglie, 22 June 1743: Arch. Aff. Étr. C. P. Bavière: Broglie/Fréd-LXV, i. 409, appendix i.
[4] Marshal de Broglie to Count d'Argenson, 26 June 1743: Arch. Guerre C.: ibid., i. 330.
[5] Count d'Argenson to Marshal de Broglie, 22 June 1743: u.s., i. 410, appendix i.

temper' and of spreading 'general discouragement in the army' by his 'determined will'[6] to retreat. Back they went, all the way to Wimpfen where Broglie's army passed under the command of Noailles while Broglie himself passed on to his governorship of Strasburg, snugly back in France. And Broglie was more popular than Noailles. There are times when France is defeatist in defeat, turning to ancient and unworthy generals who, in the dark days, seek to withdraw within the internal solace of their beloved France and to ignore commitments of peril and of honour towards allies abroad, left to bear the brunt.

Frederick the Great, a few months later, wrote of France: 'This monarchy is a very strong body, without soul and without sinew.'[7] The French government and its king did not match the spirit of his eleven-year-old daughter Madame Adelaide, ardent Torche, nabbed one morning that summer as she was slipping out of Versailles, with fourteen golden *louis* in her pinafore, in order to join forces with a donkey-boy and 'place herself at the head of the army of Papa King and bring the King of England to the feet of Papa King'.[8] In reply to remonstrance the lively girl retorted that after all the Prince de Conti had won forgiveness for having run away to join the army, as she would do the more easily because she would win a battle, which Conti had not yet achieved. Another day Madame Adelaide, who cherished 'a sovereign aversion for the English', came up with a plan for inviting their leaders 'one after the other, to come and sleep with me; they will surely be very honoured by that, and I shall kill them all in succession'. The respectable Duke de Luynes hastened to add that 'since she did not understand what she was saying, they did not judge it opportune to make her understand further', only suggesting that to murder your enemies in your bed was not a very sporting form of warfare. Madame Adelaide – seemingly not an easy girl to put down – intimated that it was the best she could think of since her father had seen fit to prohibit duelling.

If the French court generally lacked Madame Adelaide's spunk, it was not so supine as to approve the Marshal de Broglie's miserable performance. It was estimated that all the campaigning of Belle-Isle and Broglie in Germany and Bohemia had cost France at least 80,000 men and 300 million livres. 'The pen falls from one's hand', wrote the Marquis d'Argenson, '... The Marshal de Broglie has just brought back our troops while abandoning the baggage and the sick, who have been killed in cold blood. It was all the same to him provided that he absolutely ruined the affairs of the emperor and put the rope round his neck.'[9]

[6] Luynes, v. 116.
[7] King Frederick II, marginalia upon a memorandum by Voltaire, Sept. 1743: Frederick, xxii. 144.   [8] Luynes, v. 99–100 for the following.   [9] D'Argenson, iv. 83.

The abandoned Emperor Charles VII wandered back from refuge to refuge, from Augsburg to Frankfurt. On the same day as the battle of Dettingen his Marshal Seckendorff concluded with the Austrians a separate suspension of hostilities. By an ingenious transformation, characteristic of German affairs at that time and in accordance with Charles' dual sovereignty, the Bavarian army technically became the imperial army, neutral, assimilated to protective detachments of the Swabian circle of the empire. For the German army of the eighteenth century was the confederate army of the Holy Roman Empire, an extraordinary conglomeration which was at once a direct survival of feudalism and an early essay in an integrated international force.

'My situation is the most terrible ever to be seen in history',[10] wrote Charles VII to Noailles, who, some days after Dettingen, visited him at Frankfurt. The emperor flourished Broglie's letters to himself at Noailles, who 'found the reading of them very embarrassing'.[11] Noailles personally lent the stricken sovereign forty thousand crowns so that he should not 'die of hunger'. Also, with a view to preserving the disgusted emperor's attachment to the French interest, Noailles represented privately to Louis that, although he himself had 'always had friendship and esteem' for Broglie, he considered it indispensable to make an example of him.

The Marshal de Broglie was banished to his estate at Chambray in Normandy, where he shortly afterwards had an apoplectic stroke. He died two years later, bequeathing to his eldest son his recent dukedom and his inveterate animosities.

Louis XV, explaining to Noailles why he had not punished Broglie more severely, observed that 'they are already saying that he has saved the army by this fine retreat; but I should say too much of that and should do too much about it, if I gave way to my ill temper; but you know that I do not like big punishments, and that often by punishing little and by rewarding little we do more than by the greatest rigours and the most lucrative rewards.'[12]

The King of France, who sardonically discounted what he termed 'the insipid adulation of the flattering courtier',[13] further informed Noailles with reference to Broglie's disgrace that 'the Abbé [de Broglie] is playing the hero over it, and the Belle-Islists are rejoicing at it, especially from my having said two words to d'Aubigny, which

[10] Emperor Charles VII to Marshal de Noailles, 24 July 1743: Arch. Aff. Étr. C.P., Allemagne: Broglie/Fréd-LXV, i. 354.
[11] Marshal de Noailles to King Louis XV, Steinheim, 8 July 1743: Rousset, i. 133–44 for the following.
[12] King Louis XV to Marshal de Noailles, Versailles, 13 July 1743: ibid., i. 163.
[13] King Louis XV to Count de Coigny, Saint-Léger, 22 Sept. 1741: Duc de Broglie, 'Lettres de Louis XV au comte de Coigny (1737–1745)' in Revue d'histoire diplomatique (1887 f.), 1ʳᵉ année, p. 514.

they had begged me to do, to prevent him from dying, and from La Fare's having supped with me. They will not rejoice so much when they see that he [Belle-Isle] is not going to Metz',[14] his old command: Belle-Isle had been proposing to edge back by 'setting out in the direction of Metz from the 20th to the 25th July in order to betake myself from there to Plombières'.[15] He was, however, left in continued retirement to digest the disgrace of his old rival as a sweetener to the asses' milk which was restoring him to health.

A more likely beneficiary from Broglie's disgrace than his old rival was his stoutest lieutenant, the Count de Saxe. Saxe, whose friendship with Noailles dated from the siege of Philippsburg back in thirty-four, was now addressing him as 'his master'[16] and securing his support for the succession to Broglie's command in Alsace. Louis, however, had something to say that:

I grant that the Count de Saxe may be the best officer to command whom we have, but shall we confide to him, alone, the guard of a province which they desire to take from us at any price, which was so short a time ago dismembered from the empire, to him who is a Huguenot, who wishes to be sovereign, who is always saying that if he is opposed he will pass into another country's service? Is that zeal for France? ... He has nothing at all to lose in this country except a mistress, and he will always find one again, being, as he is, of a changeable and little caring disposition; being, besides, brother of a king who is perhaps going to declare against us. That does not mean that he could not be excellent, especially so long as he shall remain under your orders, and perhaps, with time, we shall be more sure of him, and it is to that that I beg you principally to apply yourself, for I see scarcely any of our own people who think in large terms like him.[17]

Louis reflected a widespread feeling in his army against the Saxon soldier of fortune, but the young king's balanced judgement again commands respect: more than for his alternative choice of a commander in the seventythree-year-old and by now pacific Marshal de Coigny: typical of the king's wan adoption of a course recognized to be inferior. Louis admitted to the unenthusiastic Noailles that Coigny 'has little intellect' but he was the father of the king's intimate, 'little Coigny, who is said to be feeble and narrow',[18] in a jealous echo, perhaps, against one of the most successful and more creditable of the younger courtiers. The 'pretty count',[19] as the king called his polite

[14] King Louis XV to Marshal de Noailles, Versailles, 17 July 1743: u.s., i. 170-1.
[15] Marshal de Belle-Isle to Abbé de Ravannes, Bizy, 21 June 1743: Arch. Guerre C., vol. 3009, no. 125.
[16] Count de Saxe to Marshal de Noailles, summer 1743: cited, Abbé Millot, op. cit., v. 374.
[17] King Louis XV to Marshal de Noailles, Choisy, 1 Aug. 1743: Rousset, i. 178, and for the following.
[18] D'Argenson, ii. 43.
[19] King Louis XV to Count de Coigny, Fontainebleau, 20 Oct. 1743 (letter beginning: 'Eh bien! joly comte ...'): Duc de Broglie, 'Lettres de Louis XV au comte de Coigny (1737-1745)' in Revue d'histoire diplomatique, 1re année, p. 517.

friend, was Colonel-General of Dragoons and governor of the royal château of Choisy, yet held aloof from factional intrigue. On good enough terms with the king's successive mistresses, the Count de Coigny steered clear of any self-interested familiarity; during the Broglie–Belle-Isle conflict he had remained neutral and, fond son though he was, had not sought to push the fortunes of his father. That was a type Louis appreciated.

Thus did the peace-loving Marshal de Coigny assume the shield and buckler of France in Alsace, seemingly about to bear the brunt. For, except for two almost symbolic remnants of the Bohemian and Bavarian campaigns, the isolated French garrisons still bravely holding out at Eger and at Ingolstadt respectively, the armies of France were everywhere expelled from German soil and driven to defend their own – and against odds. Prince Charles of Lorraine was marching from Bavaria to swell the Pragmatic Army upon the Rhine. Noailles was reduced to manoeuvring through till winter should afford respite for recuperation and, chiming with his earlier confidence to the Marquis de Stainville, 'for seeking some means of managing to terminate a war in which there have been only misfortunes'.[20]

The King of England, confessed the Count de Saxe, had caused him 'some insomnia with his nasty great army',[21] standing in strength upon the confines of France. The frontier-provinces were in danger and alarm. Charles of Lorraine was thirsting to reconquer the patrimony of his forefathers. 'He has', wrote Louis XV to Noailles, 'got his Lorraine on the brain; you know what self-esteem and the desire to succeed are.'[22] Noailles did. He had already warned Louis that, if Prince Charles once penetrated into the duchy, 'Lorraine will be overthrown in a moment, and the inhabitants will receive him with open arms.'[23] Already there were rumours of secret intelligence between Prince Charles and the Beauvau-Craons. In the teutonic reaches of eastern Lorraine especially, in isolated mansions and farmsteads, in the little country-towns people still yearned for their affable dukes of old. At the approach of Prince Charles in person watchfires blazed out by night upon lonely crests of the Vosges, beckoning the invaders, threatening the new court of Stanislas at Lunéville. It dispersed in fear.

The local threat of military action was primed internationally by diplomatic calculation. Lorraine once conquered might prove more

[20] Marshal de Noailles to King Louis XV, Steinheim, 11 July 1743: Rousset, i. 160–1.
[21] Count de Saxe to King Augustus III, camp at Langen-Schleital, 10 Oct. 1743: Vitzthum/Saxe, p. 473.
[22] King Louis XV to Marshal de Noailles, Fontainebleau, 27 Sept. 1743: Rousset, ii. 32.
[23] Marshal de Noailles to King Louis XV, Spires, 27 July 1743: ibid., i. 175.

generally acceptable than Bavaria as the ever requisite equivalent for the Austrian loss of Silesia: not, of course, acceptable to France but then an Austrian liberation of Lorraine might well introduce the invasion and dismemberment of France herself by enemies who, thought Louis, might 'eat my country'[24] regardless of the technicality whereby France was still not at war with England or Austria. During a conversation on 30 July 1743 the French foreign minister exclaimed to the Marquis de Stainville: 'Well, Sir, so you are declaring war on us ... for Prince Charles is showing signs of wanting to cross the Rhine.'[25]

Prince Charles had sent on ahead to the Pragmatic Army 'John Daniel, Baron von Menzel, Colonel-in-Chief of the new Regiment of Hussar-Carabiniers ... and Commandant of a flying Camp of the Army of the High Allies',[26] now thrusting against France. Menzel so described himself in the proclamation which he now issued to 'the Provinces formerly of the Empire, which France has seized by her unmeasured intrigues and ambition ..., to inform the States of Alsace, Burgundy, Franche-Comté, Lorraine and Bar, the Bishoprics of Metz, Toul and Verdun, and also that which formerly belonged to the province of Luxemburg that the intention of H.M. the Queen of Hungary and Bohemia is to [regard] ... them as to her belonging, although France has for long years enjoyed them. We wish however to testify to all subjects with what grief we have seen them languishing beneath so unbearable a yoke ... In the said provinces nobody shall oppose our victorious armies and those of our High Allies ... And in case those whose employments are not military should have the audacity (which is however not to be presumed) to wish to interfere in the war, and to take arms directly or indirectly to the prejudice of these provinces, they will be punished by fire and sword, as well as corporally, by being hanged and mutilated, and being regarded as rebels, by setting fire to your provinces, as France has done in the Empire and in the hereditary provinces of my very gracious Sovereign.'

Menzel's sinister ranting may help to correct any assumption that eighteenth-century warfare, even in the western reaches of the Rhineland, was invariably a politely restricted exercise. In that century as in others Germanic and Central European armies deliberately employed the policy and propaganda of frightfulness. It was, though, still rather early days for its western application. The

---

[24] King Louis XV to Marshal de Noailles, Versailles, 9 Aug. 1743: ibid., i. 213.
[25] Amelot de Chaillou cited by Marquis de Stainville to Grand Duke Francis II, Paris, 3 Aug. 1743: Esteri del Granducato di Toscana, vol. 2295/1286, fo. 313.
[26] Proclamation by Baron von Menzel, Trarbach, 20 Aug. 1743: enclosed by Marquis de Brezé to Count d'Argenson, Saarlouis, 7 Sept. 1743: *Campagne/43*, ii. 121–5 for the following.

Marshal de Noailles drew the attention of Field-Marshal Kheven-hüller to 'the indecency of the writings which have been spread by Colonel Menzel and which were more in the style of an incendiary than in that of a man of war'.[27] Noailles himself had earned the thanks of the Earl of Stair 'for all your gracious and polite ways of acting',[28] more particularly in caring for the allied wounded left at Dettingen. And the newly arrived Marshal de Coigny civilly tried to restrain his men from circulating unflattering ditties about Prince Charles, who had got stuck literally half way across the Rhine, upon the island of Rheinau over from the sugarloaf hill of Altbreisach. Inaction was inspired by allied headquarters, which to Prince Charles 'seemed a republic, for everybody talks and seems to have a different opinion'.[29] He and mettlesome Stair came up against the cautious Hanoverian influence of George II, whose ear had been secured by Field-Marshal Neipperg, who seems to have had a way with princes. Allied headquarters stayed put at Worms, with a few of Menzel's raiding-parties probing up remote tracks in the Vosges as the closest that he came to fulfilling his sweeping manifesto.

The French meanwhile were toiling to strengthen their eastern outworks. Early in September 1743 they pushed Prince Charles out of his bridgehead at Rheinau and repulsed a second Austrian crossing at Rheinweiler. These symbolic little actions almost ended the hostilities then along the Rhine, though not the nervousness of Marshal de Coigny, suffering from an urinary disorder and begging support from Noailles up north at Landau. Their king, though, typically contrasted to Noailles that marshal's unpopularity in Paris as against its good opinion 'of Marshal de Coigny, but probably, that will not last long. No factions, I beg you . . . By our Lady, if everybody were as you and I, and the good God above all, it would go well.'[30]

If the factions subsided, so did the fighting on all fronts. That September brought the ultimate surrender at Eger and Ingolstadt of those isolated French garrisons whose protracted resistance had redeemed Linz. Upon the Rhine, all the armies went into winter quarters. France was relieved. Noailles wrote to Louis, 'It is very fortunate, Sire . . . that there are among your enemies no Eugenes, no Marlboroughs or no Starhembergs. We are heavily indebted to the irresolutions of George the Second.' [31] This verdict Louis the

---

[27] Marshal de Noailles to Field-Marshal Khevenhüller, 28 Oct. 1743: Arch. Aff. Étr. C. P., Allemagne. Lettres de divers généraux étrangers, cited, Broglie/Fréd-LXV, ii. 10–11. (The date of this letter is incorrectly cited by Broglie as 28 Oct. 1742.)
[28] Earl of Stair to Marshal de Noailles, Hanau, 30 June 1743: *Campagne/43*, i. 283.
[29] Prince Charles of Lorraine to Grand Duke Francis II, 27 July 1743: Arneth, ii. 518, n. 15.
[30] King Louis XV to Marshal de Noailles, Fontainebleau, 27 Sept. 1743: Rousset, ii. 31–3.
[31] Marshal de Noailles to King Louis XV, Hagenau, 16 Oct. 1743: ibid., ii. 39.

Fifteenth characteristically inverted. 'This century', he replied, 'is not prolific in great men, and it would be very unfortunate for me if this sterility existed only for France.'[32]

II

One man of that age who felt himself great was Lord Carteret, dominant at allied headquarters now that the frustrated Earl of Stair had withdrawn in dudgeon. The French prisoners whom he had captured at Dettingen were the occasion of a parley some days later between Lord Carteret and the Marquis de Silhouette, who, with his English connections, had been sent by Noailles as his emissary to the British camp. Silhouette cited Carteret: '"They accuse me," he said, "of despising France: but . . . my courage against her comes only from fear, and if I had feared her less, I should have been less bold in undertaking all that I have done against her; I shall deprive her of all her allies, and not a single one of them shall remain to her" . . . I[33] replied to him that he did me honour in esteeming me worthy of his wrath.'[34]

Carteret had indeed for months been bending his imperious energies to the accomplishment of his master-plan for isolating and reducing France. The two main fields of his diplomatic activity were the two disunited middle-lands, Germany and Italy, twin objects of the covetous combinations of the great and nearly great powers of Europe.

A prominent aspiration of Lord Carteret was to detach the Bavarian emperor from his French alliance. Charles VII was quite ready to parley behind the backs of his allies but he had taken the poorest view of the Anglo–Austrian project of 1742 for an exchange of his Bavarian patrimony for a Burgundian. His optimistic counter-proposals, renouncing all pretensions to the Habsburg inheritance in return for territorial pickings in Germany, had been angrily ruled out by Maria Theresa, intent upon any cessions being made the other way on, and were miserably disavowed by the emperor himself, in trouble over the liberties of the imperial constitution. The territorial aggrandizement of Bavaria was no longer seriously in question in the negotiations which Carteret resumed after Dettingen, at Hanau through the local Prince William of Hesse. These produced the much-disputed so-called Treaty of Hanau, which was in fact a document drafted by the evening of 14 July and headed 'Projet et

---

[32] King Louis XV to Marshal de Noailles, Fontainebleau, 21 Oct. 1743: ibid., ii. 49.
[33] i.e. Marquis de Silhouette.
[34] Marquis de Silhouette to Count d'Argenson, Steinheim, 8 July 1743: *Campagne/43*, i. 295–7.

Idées'. The project and ideas were, primarily, for Charles VII to change sides in return for the elevation of Bavaria to a kingdom and a British subsidy. But this scheme required the assent not only of the Austrian court but also, Carteret suddenly maintained, of the British ministers and parliament at home. There the distrustful Duke of Newcastle, the other foreign secretary of state, took a dim view of the production of 'my lively Brother abroad'.[35] So too did Frederick the Great and Charles VII himself. The Treaty of Hanau was stillborn.

Earlier that year a vain threat by Frederick to oppose the march of British troops onto German soil, if it had suggested that it was early days for patriotic Prussia to impose herself as the self-interested saviour of Germany, had yet cast shadows ahead. Frederick was also frustrated in his attempt to insert 'by hook or by crook'[36] into the negotiations at Hanau his envoy, Count von Finckenstein, described by Hyndford as a 'little spy ... he is the quintessence of Prussian *fourberie* ... extremely polite, insinuating, and affected.'[37] Frederick took it out of Hyndford in what that indignant minister termed the 'brutalities' of Glogau, demanding: 'Is it for the islanders to lay down the law to the Empire?'[38] As to that, Newcastle remarked: 'The scheme abroad is certainly to set ourselves at the head of the Empire.'[39] But all who ventured within the circles of the Holy Roman Empire seemed to fall under its paralysing spell.

Austria, as always unyielding about the Bavarian equivalent for Silesia, was hardly better pleased than Prussia by British policy in Germany. In a public protest launched on 16 August 1743 Maria Theresa replied in effect to Carteret's diplomacy at Hanau as well as to a communication of 26 July wherein Louis XV had pacifically assured the imperial diet that France had intended no invasion of German liberties but only support of its emperor, now intended anyway to withdraw her forces from German soil, and would welcome accommodation with Austria. Her ruler only heightened if anything the note of indignant injury and implacable retribution sounded the preceding summer in the reply conveyed by the Marquis de Stainville to Cardinal Fleury's overtures.

The long and angry reverberations of the Austrian declaration of August 1743 were fed by Austrian pressure to bring the protest to

---

[35] Duke of Newcastle to Earl of Orford, 22 July/2 Aug. 1743: British Library, Add. MSS. 32,700 (Newcastle Papers, vol. xv). fo. 314: cited by Sir Richard Lodge, *Studies in Eighteenth-Century Diplomacy 1740–1748* (London, 1930: henceforth cited as Lodge), p. 23.
[36] King Frederick II to Count Podewils, Breslau, 26 July 1743: *Politische Correspondenz*, ii. 390.
[37] Lord Hyndford to Lord Carteret, 20 July 1743: Hyndford Papers, vol. ix, fo. 164: cited, Lodge, p. 19, n. 1.
[38] Cited, ibid., p. 27.
[39] Duke of Newcastle to Earl of Orford, 22 July/2 Aug. 1743: *u.s.*

Dictatur, to have it dictated to the imperial chancery and officially laid before the diet: against this partisan initiative an outcry came to be led by Frederick, who rasped at Podiwils: 'You are the greatest milksop I know ... One must speak out loud of the liberties of Germany which the Queen of Hungary wishes to oppress ... The tocsin must be sounded against the Queen of Hungary.'[40] The tocsin traditionally rang in hostilities.

So much for Lord Carteret's high endeavour to weld a great germanic alliance against the archenemy of England, France. Even this, however, was but one part, and the lesser one, of Carteret's grand design. It has even been suggested that the Treaty of Hanau was for Carteret all along not so much an aim in itself as a power-political device for, in particular, exerting pressure upon Austria in furtherance of his other and more important combination. Though this is probably going too far,[41] too cleverly, certainly the chief concern for Carteret was that long negotiation which centred not upon Bavaria but upon Sardinia. This reopened the Italian perspective, which was to throw into relief the next stage of importance in the upward career of the Count de Stainville while rendering the diplomatic position of his withdrawn father more than ever central.

III

In the Italian theatre of events, more than any other, the War of the Austrian Succession came as a direct sequel to the wars of the Polish and of the Spanish Successions. The empire of Charles V, from being divided among Habsburgs had come to be divided between Habsburgs and Bourbons. That was the massive shift in the balance of power which had ushered in the eighteenth century. And after the peace settlement of Utrecht it was in disunited Italy, still, that the precise incidence of this shift was largely fought out in the wars of 1717-1720, 1735-1738 and 1740-1748, in this respect approximating to a war of Italian Succession. It has been suggested[42] that the equilibrium of Europe then came to hinge upon that of Italy. The ambitious policies of two Italians, first Cardinal Alberoni, then Queen Elizabeth Farnese had stirred up a limited but distinct revival of Spanish national energy under new Bourbon rule. Spain was out on the make in Italy, where the nice equilibrium, established by the War

---

[40] Minute by King Frederick II, Oct. 1743: *Politische Correspondenz*, ii. 438-9.
[41] Cf. Lodge, pp. 28-30, as corrected by Basil Williams, op. cit., p. 244, n. 1.
[42] Cf. Guido Quazza, 'La politica dell' equilibrio nel secolo XVIII' in *Nuove Questioni di storia moderna* (Milan, 1964), ii. 1194.

of the Polish Succession, between Bourbons and Habsburgs was too fine to secure prompt acceptance from either dynasty as a permanent solution. The dynasty which it did suit was that of Savoy, set upon maintaining the precarious balance to its own advantage and aggrandizement, throwing its weight now into one scale, now the other, seldom without profit. It struck contemporaries that 'the King of Sardinia is the King of Prussia in Italy'.[43] The parallelism between the two dynastic promoters of new nationalism was already striking, and in some degree overlapping in European impact. The Prussian grab of Silesia had begun to focus European concern upon Germany even more than upon Italy. This shift was to become pronounced after 1748 but as yet Italy remained immediately contentious.

In 1713 the Treaty of Utrecht had accorded international recognition of the new kingships erected in favour of the houses both of Hohenzollern and of Savoy. Thereafter, while King Frederick William I of Prussia was impressing the bureaucratic and military stamp upon his regimented dominions, King Victor Amadeus II of Sardinia was likewise welding into shape his new realm of some three million souls, notably through military and economic reforms. The Piedmontese nobility were deprived of fiscal immunities, as indeed of disputable landholdings, while the power of the catholic church was reduced. Thus did Victor Amadeus largely convert his realm from a feudal conglomeration of privilege to a benevolent despotism affording a good measure of equality before the law.

The parallel between King Frederick William I and King Victor Amadeus II extended from their political achievements to their personal relationships. Both were men of strong will and violent temper, not least towards their more sensitive heirs. Victor Amadeus, who had cherished and lost his elder son, vented his disappointment upon the younger, Charles Emmanuel, of unprepossessing appearance and a gentle and, it was expected, frivolous disposition. Victor Amadeus had determined to knock his seeming softy of a son into some shape as a ruler, thrust him into the whole machinery of government and in 1730 had abdicated in his favour, only to reclaim his throne next year. Perhaps the example of Philip V of Spain from 1724 proved contagious. But the anxious and amiable King Charles Emmanuel III, advised by the expert Ormea whom Victor Amadeus had raised from humble origins to be chief minister, now had his father arrested and confined till his death in 1732. This proceeding scandalized the still patriarchal society of Europe. Voltaire called it 'a terrible event which had no consequence';[44] though, long after

---

[43] Capello, 6 Jan. 1742: Arneth, ii. 496, n. 10.
[44] Voltaire, *Précis du siècle de Louis XV* (Garnier edition), p. 38.

Voltaire, it did inspire a play from one of England's celebrated poets.[45]

Such was the inheritance of King Charles Emmanuel III. His third queen was that Elisabeth-Thérèse of Lorraine whose matrimonial affairs had cost the Marquis de Stainville no little trouble. In the summer of 1741, however, she died of the miliary fever then prevalent in Piedmont. The Austrian affiliation by marriage of King Charles Emmanuel may well have exercised an additional influence upon the cool manner in which, as previously noticed, he toyed that year with the diplomatic approaches of Fleury. Sardinian conversations with France were, however, calculated to play up Maria Theresa who, in that summer of 1741, had proposed to Sardinia a treaty between the two of them and Tuscany also as underpinning to an Italian league for collective security against foreign invasion. This suggestion, containing no hint of territorial cessions to Sardinia, earned the contempt of the Marquis D'Ormea. Maria Theresa, however, retained a shrewd idea that in the last resort the King of Sardinia would reckon even as Solar, his envoy in Paris, once put it to the Marquis de Stainville, that 'the aggrandizement of the house of Bourbon in Italy . . . would put him squarely in the goffering-iron'.[46]

This consideration was sharply pointed by startling intelligence that on 20 November 1741 the first seaborne elements, 13,600 strong, of a Spanish expeditionary force had landed at Orbetello in the Presidii (Neapolitan coastal enclaves in Tuscany) despite the fact that a British squadron under Admiral Haddock was cruising in Spanish waters: so surprising as to arouse some ill-founded suspicion of Anglo–Spanish collusion. The Spanish command in Italy was assumed by the Duke of Montemar, who had conquered Naples in the preceding war and was now joined by a Neapolitan contingent under the Duke of Castropignano. In January 1742 another Spanish convoy came sailing through, partly under French escort. It daunted ailing Haddock. Once again, so soon after Carthegena, had Spain demonstrated to all Europe that English seapower was not invincible. It was a happy augury for the cause of Don Philip, recently created Grand Admiral of Spain.

Against this British background the Spanish landings disconcerted both Austria and Sardinia, now drawn together. The Marquis de Stainville had long represented to the Grand Duke of Tuscany, who indeed agreed, that 'the principal point for the Queen of Hungary

[45] Robert Browning, *King Victor and King Charles: a Tragedy* (1842).
[46] Marquis de Stainville to Grand Duke Francis II, Paris, 26 May 1742: Esteri del Granducato di Toscana, vol. 2295/1286, fo. 109.

was to make an indissoluble alliance with the King of Sardinia, whatever it may cost'.[47] An alliance now was achieved though hardly rendered indissoluble. By the remarkable Austro–Sardinian convention of Turin of 1 February 1742 Charles Emmanuel, while securing no definite pledge of territorial aggrandizement, yet undertook to support Austria with his forces in the defence of Lombardy and the occupation of Modena; at the same time he specifically reserved the claim upon Lombardy which he had cooked up genealogically through female inheritance from Philip II and had been pursuing diplomatically through recent soundings with Spain via Paris for a division of northern Italy at Austrian expense. It had been hoped in Madrid that the Spanish landings would clinch Charles Emmanuel. Instead he now contracted with Austria to abstain from pressing his claim during the period of the convention; but it was further stipulated that whenever he saw fit Charles Emmanuel might, upon one month's notice, denounce the convention and assert his territorial claims against Austria by any means, including alliance with other powers.

The Convention of Turin, almost stipulating disloyalty between allies, was something new even by eighteenth-century standards of slim diplomacy. The French foreign minister considered it 'the oddest treaty which has ever been concluded'.[48] The Marquis D'Ormea, classed by Frederick the Great as a very fair pupil of Machiavelli, was now created High Chancellor of the Kingdom of Sardinia by his grateful sovereign, who regarded the convention as their masterpiece. It was indeed rather more bizarre in form than in fact. The court of Vienna did not think it very likely that Sardinia would in fact invoke the escape-clause, while the latter court would not have gone so far had it not been fairly confident that in the long run Sardinian interest this time lay with Austria rather than with the French. Their unpopularity with the Piedmontese people was another factor, not negligible even in the eighteenth century.

Soundings to the potential detriment of allies was a game at which two could play. Towards the middle of February 1742 the Marquis de Stainville was dining in a large company with the Dutch envoy in Paris when, to the surprise of the marquis, the Spanish ambassador earnestly sought to engage him in discussion. Stainville subsequently called upon Campoflorido, who said: 'If we Spaniards reach agreement with the King of Sardinia we shall divide between us what the Queen of Hungary has in Italy, and nothing will remain to her; whereas by reaching agreement with us, not only will we leave

[47] Ibid., 27 Dec. 1741: fo. 79.
[48] Amelot de Chaillou to Cardinal de Tencin, 13 Feb. 1742: Hénault, p. 382.

her a large part of what she possesses there, but subsequently we will
even undertake to have restored to her what the King of Sardinia has
had from her by the last treaty.'[49] The Spaniard went on to suggest
that the Grand Duke of Tuscany 'could become the negotiator
between the Queen, France and Spain ... and that the negotiation
once broached, one could attain to a general accommodation'.
Stainville, this time handling this large overture with discreet skill,
received it with due reserve while artfully eliciting that it had been
made in concert with Fleury. Stainville relayed this overture to the
grand duke under pledge to Campoflorido of 'inviolable secrecy,
upon which he can count for my part': so much so, in this instance as
in others, that the father of the future Choiseul is one of the
subordinate figures who has hitherto concealed most lasting secrets
in the high diplomacy of Europe.

   Francis replied on 10 March 1742 in terms complimentary to
Campoflorido himself, with whom he had some acquaintance, and
responsive to the extent of intimating that Maria Theresa would
never reject proposals for accommodation that were just and
reasonable. On 23 March Stainville transmitted this to Campoflorido
'whom', he reported, 'I found in bed very troubled by a heavy cold'.[50]
The invalid undertook to try to secure definite Spanish proposals in
concert with Fleury, represented by Campoflorido as even keener
than himself upon such a negotiation. Stainville subsequently had
some talk on this with both Amelot and Fleury, who said to him: 'I
assure you that I desire nothing so much as peace.'[51] To which the
marquis in effect suggested that the sentiment might be a little
belated. In the event Campoflorido seems to have vouchsafed not so
much any Spanish offers to Austria as Sardinian ones previously
made to Spain, while commenting upon them that 'his master would
prefer that the Queen [of Hungary] kept the Milanese rather than see
it pass to the King of Sardinia'.[52]

   If the Spanish overture through Stainville was to peter out, that
diplomatist was already indignantly exercised by the march of the
second Spanish contingent through Tuscany, neutral but acquiescent
more or less under constraint. Stainville was protesting to the
converted in Fleury, himself concerned to maintain the guaranteed
neutrality of that territory in return for which Lorraine had been
lopped off in French favour. The cardinal had put pressure on the
Spanish government and, through it, upon the Duke of Montemar.
He, however, resented it, being keenly on the go in Italy with the
campaigning season now at hand.

---

[49] Marquis de Stainville to Grand Duke Francis II, Paris, 15 Feb. 1742: u.s., fos. 80-2 for the
following.
[50] Ibid., 23 Mar. 1742: fo. 93.   [51] Ibid., 6 Apr. 1742: fo. 99.   [52] Ibid., fo. 98.

After all the flimsy Convention of Turin was to usher in the period of solidest Austro–Sardinian collaboration in that war. King Charles Emmanuel, gratifyingly the commander-in-chief of the combined forces in Lombardy, got on well with the Austrian commander, Field-Marshal Count Traun. They bore down and ultimately captured the unenviably strategic duchy of Modena, whose Duke Francis III had on 30 April 1742 secretly allied himself with Spain by the Treaty of Aranjuez and had, after an ugly interview with the Marquis D'Ormea, fled to the Bourbon camp east of the Panaro river: for the Spaniards had marched slap across Italy to establish an advanced base at Rimini. By the beginning of August the Duke of Montemar was back across the Rubicon on to his base. At about the time that the retreating Spaniards were pulling in, three British men-of-war joined with an Austrian squadron ominously appeared off Rimini. The British warships had been sent into the Adriatic by Admiral Mathews, the tough old successor to Haddock, whose failure had further weakened the administration of Walpole. Whereas now Carteret, the patron of Mathews, was talking typically of bringing the Mediterranean to the boil; and that threatened to include the Adriatic. The Anglo–Austrian naval demonstration made Montemar fear an enemy landing in his rear in the classic manoeuvre for whoever has superiority at sea while fighting through the Italian peninsula, perennially subject to the technical considerations of mountain and amphibious warfare.

From Rimini the Duke of Montemar fell back south and south again to cover the kingdom of Naples. There, however, Admiral Mathews had just administered another nasty lesson in the application of seapower. On 19 August 1742 there appeared off Naples the sails of a British squadron under Captain Martin. He summoned King Charles of Naples to withdraw his contingent from the army of the Duke of Montemar and to undertake for the future to abstain from any support of Spain in Italy. The captain gave the king half an hour to acquiesce under threat of immediate bombardment of Naples by the British squadron, instructed in that case 'to lay the said city in ashes'.[53]

This robust threat did the trick. Naples was neutralized. The humiliation was not speedily forgotten by King Charles, destined one day to rule a greater kingdom.

This swift stroke of British seapower threw out Queen Maria Theresa scarcely less than King Charles. Naples neutral doomed her scheme of southern reconquest, as urged by the Austrian liaison-

---

[53] Admiral Mathews, instruction of 22 July (O.S.) 1742 to Captain Martin: H. W. Richmond, *The Navy in the War of 1739–48* (Cambridge, 1920), i. 212.

officer with Mathews, an adventurer styled Lieutenant-Fieldmarshal Ladislas Kökenyesdi von Vettes, a former adherent of the revolting Rakoczy. Maria Theresa had aspired to sweep the Bourbons clean out of southern Italy, restore the recent Austrian rule in Naples and, hopefully, buy off Charles Emmanuel from the sensitive north by according him Sicily, which still remembered the reforms introduced under the brief rule of King Victor Amadeus before he had swapped islands in 1720. In fact Victor's son, in the true tradition of the *condottieri* of the renaissance, now pointed out that he had only contracted to co-operate in the defence of Lombardy, certainly achieved. He had, moreover, set up a landmark in Italian history. Sardinian forces had for the first time stood upon the shores of the Adriatic.

The British government under pressure disavowed Martin's imposition of neutrality upon Naples, and rebuffed her king's deft attempt (the Fogliani mission to London) to get it underwritten by a British guarantee of her territorial integrity. It was a fine balance. If there was little British keenness to shelter the Bourbons at Naples, yet Osorio, the Sardinian minister in London, shrewdly suggested in the following year that prevention of an Austrian restoration there was 'the price wherewith the English will seek to buy their accommodation with Spain and some sort of freedom for their navigation in America',[54] the prime cause of the British opening of hostilities. The same idea was to strike Capello, the artful Venetian minister in Vienna.

For the present the Austro-Sardinian advance of 1742 against Naples stopped short of Pesaro. The King of Sardinia sped back from the Adriatic coast upon receipt of heavy intelligence that a new Spanish army, under the nominal command of the Infant Don Philip in person, had invaded his homeland in the rear, in ancestral Savoy. This large development was in origin yet another illustration of the compelling logic of strategic seapower. The comparatively few ships of Admiral Mathews, cruising centrally off Toulon, chiefly determined the march of armies for hundreds of miles all around the continental seaboard.

Since Mathews now stopped the seas against the third contingent of the Spanish Armada against Italy, Elizabeth Farnese had by April 1742 badgered Fleury into permitting the 17,500 troops to march round through Provence, a severe imposition upon that sparse region. The main towns, however, offered sumptuous entertainment to the

---

[54] Osorio to King Charles Emmanuel III, 29 Nov. 1743: Archivio Stato Torino, Lett. M.stri Ingh., docket 49: cited, Carlo Baudi di Vesme, *La Politica mediterranea inglese 1741–1748* (Turin, 1952), p. 53.

stylish Don Philip, said to have included 24 state coaches and 59 barouches in his personal train and to have 'charmed everybody in his passage ... He is French to the fingertips and has adopted corresponding manners, clothes, cooking, even down to the vivacity.'[55] Under this frenchified prince the operative Spanish command was exercised by General de Glimes. Very briefly, this general occupied southern Savoy and was then pushed out by Charles Emmanuel who, against the advice of the prudent Ormea, came marching over the Alpine passes. De Glimes was written off by the unquenchable Queen of Spain as 'the second volume of Montemar',[56] himself dismissed and succeeded by General de Gages, a Walloon, a reminder of how recently the Austrian Netherlands had been Spanish, and of how a ranker might occasionally become a general even in the eighteenth century. Though indeed the Spanish army was then, somewhat surprisingly, exceptional in that bourgeois officers were already becoming a majority: an object-lesson to those who argue that more middle-class officers should automatically have spelt increased efficiency.

General de Glimes was succeeded by the Marquis de Las Minas, recently Spanish ambassador to France where, haughtily imposing himself and failing to pay his bills, he had achieved a wide unpopularity. In December 1742 Las Minas in turn forced Charles Emmanuel into that retreat which Ormea had foreseen since the sundering snows of the Alps made it impossible in winter for Piedmont to maintain an army in outlying Savoy. On the Italian front, no less than the Bohemian, war that winter did not merely spell winter-quarters. By the end of the year not only had Las Minas come closing back against Savoy, but De Gages, from the south, against Lombardy.

De Gages, disliked by most of his noble Spanish officers, was an efficient disciplinarian who also had the sense to amnesty deserters. This apparently helped to build up his little army more effectively than had Montemar's earlier dispatch of disguised recruiting-officers through neutral Tuscany, much to the indignation of the Marquis de Stainville when he heard about it from the Count de Richecourt in Florence. Tuscan neutrality was more precious and more hostile to the Bourbons than that of the Papal States. As Pope Benedict XIV had lamented to Ormea: 'We are without a farthing and without soldiers, and are between the pincers.'[57] Such was the eighteenth-century reduction of the temporal power of the papacy, flouted now

[55] Cardinal Fleury to Cardinal de Tencin, 13 Apr. 1742: Hénault, p. 388.
[56] Cited, Spencer Wilkinson, *The Defence of Piedmont 1742–1748* (Oxford, 1927), p. 63.
[57] Pope Benedict XIV to Marquis D'Ormea, 4 Nov. 1741: Archivio Stato Torino, Lett. M.stri Roma 1741, cited, C. Baudi di Vesme, op. cit., p. 39, n. 48.

by the advance of the revived forces of De Gages, back through Rimini into winter-quarters at Bologna.

Snow or shine, Spanish generals then were constantly exposed in their rear to drumfire injunctions from the queen to attack, attack or be dismissed. Hence the battle of Camposanto upon the Panaro river, fought on 8 February 1743 by the Spaniards against the Sardinians and the Austrians, whose Field-Marshal Traun there anticipated Frederick the Great's oblique deployment at Kolin. Only towards dusk did this manoeuvre of daring deliberation lead into a battle of fearful in-fighting and bayoneting attack. Till nine o'clock that night the mêlée swayed back and forth beneath the pale light of the moon. Camposanto was one of those eighteenth-century engagements not widely remembered but terrible to be in.

Both sides claimed victory in the ding-dong carnage of Camposanto. De Gages sent captured standards back to Madrid and was promoted captain-general, the marshalcy of Spain, with rather better reason than Las Minas for his success in Savoy. But contrary rejoicings at Turin and Vienna came closer to strategic truth. De Gages and his army, struck by an epidemic, fell back from Bologna in the footsteps of Montemar, back to the Spanish base-area Cesena-Rimini. This static check endured throughout the summer of 1743. And as across the Lombard plains, so before the Alpine passes. The military intentions both of Captain-General de Las Minas and of King Charles Emmanuel were subject to diplomatic preoccupation.

IV

Sardinia, more even than Bavaria, was a key-piece in Carteret's commanding design for the reassertion of British initiative against the house of Bourbon in Europe, perhaps even in America. In the diplomatic underworld of covert double-crossing a leading Jacobite, Lord Sempill, was writing in May 1743 to De Bussy, an important clerk in the French Foreign Ministry and secretly in British pay, that British exertions 'in Germany are only designed to force us not to interfere in Italian affairs, which are closer to their hearts because they are the knot of American affairs'.[58] If Spanish aggrandizement in Italy could be prevented then England might hope to use Italian counters, such as Bourbon retention of Naples, in order to extract those economic advantages in South America which were her primary concern. And the most effective resistance to Franco–Spanish enterprises in Italy was to be expected from Sardinia rather

[58] Lord Sempill to De Bussy, 23 May 1743: Arch. Aff. Étr. C.P., Angleterre, vol. 417, cited, C. Baudi de Vesme, op. cit., p. 33, n. 15.

than from Austria, preoccupied in Germany. Economically, again, England wished to avoid any extension of Spanish protectionism in Italy and to counter the Hispano-Genoese commercial axis, typified by the Genoese Banco di San Giorgio, by promoting trade with Sardinia, also needed to protect Tuscany and in particular the important English trade through Leghorn. The canny Grand Duke Francis had eluded British attempts to recruit him as an allied belligerent: which allowed Sardinia a local preponderance unusual then in the balance of Italian affairs.

In Italy the main difference between the wars of the Polish and of the Austrian successions was that Sardinia had, temporarily at least, changed sides. Carteret needed to clinch the transitional convention of Turin between Sardinia and Austria, and he swiftly set about it.

From May 1742 the second main phase of the Austro-Sardinian negotiations had been conducted in London. This enabled Carteret to steer negotiations across the clumsy division whereby Austrian affairs fell to his northern department whereas Sardinia in the south appertained to the critical Newcastle. The venue also suited the Marquis D'Ormea, who liked to cushion his downy diplomacy, dealing whenever possible with Spain through France and with Austria through England in accordance with his nice sense of power-political realities. And now England actually increased a Sardinian demand upon Austria for either Finale or Piacenza into one for both. Carteret might characteristically disdain Charles Emmanuel as 'a shopkeeper king',[59] but the lordly baron did not fail to secure from Sardinia, in return for thrusting her pretensions down the throats of the Austrians, the promise of very favourable terms and improvements for British trade in the Mediterranean: where its concentration upon Tuscan Leghorn at the expense of Genoa was beginning to be matched by British commercial development of Austrian Trieste as against Venice. In the Mediterranean–Baltic trade Venice was an old partner of Holland, also disgruntled by the rise of Sardinia, now reaching for the sea at Genoese Finale. But it would suit England admirably if in the south a progressive and strategic Sardinia became to her rather what Holland, commercial and maritime, now was in the north, almost a client state or, as Frederick the Great put it in a famous simile, a skiff towed in the wake of the British man-of-war.

After months of stubborn negotiation Maria Theresa, by the beginning of August 1743, at last screwed herself up to authorize Wasner, now her negotiator in London, to agree to the cession of Piacenza in the last resort ('*nur in pessimum casum*').[60] As usual she

---

[59] Lord Carteret to Wasner, reported by Wasner, London, 29 Jan. 1743: Ö.S./H.H.S.: Arneth, ii. 507, n. 11.

[60] Queen Maria Theresa to Wasner, 4 Aug. 1743: ibid., ii. 524, n. 25.

made counter-stipulations. In particular Maria Theresa, intent as ever upon her Bavarian equivalent, now mooted a proposal that Charles VII be compelled to swap Bavaria for Naples. This bright idea may possibly have originated with the Austrian minister in Turin, young Count Kaunitz, then upon the threshold of his brilliant career. Whatever the paternity of the plan, Carteret rejected it out of hand. George II was set against it and Frederick II would never acquiesce in an Austrian absorption of Bavaria to tilt the scales against Prussia. For Carteret, if not the more cautious Newcastle, menaced Lorraine might well be preferable to Bavaria as the Austrian equivalent for the loss of Silesia and now, indeed, of Piacenza also. Carteret carpeted Wasner and told him that if Maria Theresa did not accede to the demands of the King of Sardinia the latter would be advised to go in with France and Spain, and would be asked to mediate for a British accommodation with those two powers. Nor was this rasping threat devoid of substance.

In May 1743 Ormea had renewed his gambit of negotiating with France and Spain in order to exert pressure upon England and Austria. In Paris the Commander de Solar resumed his conversations with the French government and threw his old colleague, the Marquis de Stainville, into considerable and doubtless intended anxiety. In fact, however, Charles Emmanuel and Ormea retained their basic preference for the other side and were attracted by comparatively modest cessions in Lombardy by agreement with Austria, having the prompt disposal, considerably more than by Bourbon lavishness with Habsburg domains yet to be conquered. It is related that King Victor Amadeus had used to say: 'My son, the Milanese is like an artichoke; it must be eaten leaf by leaf.'[61]

At this juncture, after Dettingen had reinforced the argument of Camposanto, an Austrian line of argument in Paris was illustrated in a conversation which the Marquis de Stainville had in the middle of July with the Marquis d'Argenson. The latter recorded that Stainville told him that 'if France were today willing to interfere no more in the affairs of Spain and of Italy, peace with us was certain, and that the high allies would not encroach at all upon our frontiers. He confessed that the design of the allies was to chase D. Carlos out of Naples and Sicily, that all the forces of Her Hungarian Majesty were going to pass into Italy, that the Count de Gages would be obliged to withdraw into the Kingdom of Naples where they would make short work of him; that we were espousing the follies of the Queen of Spain and that they were going to attack us in all parts upon the Rhine and in Flanders.' Whereat d'Argenson, never one for the Spanish connection,

[61] Frederick, ii. 31.

reflected, doubtless as intended: 'Would it not be better to lose our credit at Madrid for some time rather than to lose two or three provinces?'[62]

French fears for the eastern provinces at that critical period when the Austrian forces of Prince Charles of Lorraine were looming up against his homeland, the French announcement on 26 July of withdrawal from Germany and willingness to come to terms with Austria, French promotion of the Bourbon interest in Italy: such was the heavy setting of preoccupation for the French foreign minister at a dinner which he gave at Versailles on 6 August 1743 to foreign envoys, including the Marquis de Stainville. The marquis reported that as he was making to leave, Amelot 'pulled me by the sleeve into the embrasure of a window in the presence of the numerous company who were there, and said to me: "So you want, Sir, to institute a general conflagration in Europe. The Queen of Hungary wants to declare war on the King of France, whereas the king desires only tranquillity.... We have never acted except as allies and auxiliaries."'[63] Maria Theresa, though, had been '"made to believe that we are much lower than we are in fact".'

With this specious and plaintive prologue, Amelot proceeded to assure Stainville that France did not aim to detach Maria Theresa from her British allies, but that equally '"she must not think that we shall ever break the indissoluble ties which we have with Spain; but I warrant", continued the minister, "that [in return] for something very small which the queen would cede to the Spaniards in Italy, she could make her peace at the same time as bring about that between England and Spain. That is the only means of pacifying everything. I have not an order from the king to say it to you, but I say it to you, however, as a minister."'

The Marquis de Stainville told the French foreign minister that he would accordingly report the conversation word for word to the Grand Duke of Tuscany, but:

That for my part I knew only of a simple answer which contrasted totally with his proposition: ... by what right, in the victorious condition wherein the queen was, could they claim that she should make new sacrifices for the establishment of a new Spanish branch in Italy? – that I did not know how far her engagements with the King of Sardinia went but that I was sure, knowing her way of thinking, that, whatever it might cost her, she would never break her word; that it was not the moment to demand new cessions from her, who had suffered so and who was well qualified to demand indemnities for the infinite wrong which had been caused her by the unjust war which had been stirred up against her. At that M. Amelot replied

---

[62] D'Argenson, iv. 81–2.
[63] Marquis de Stainville to Grand Duke Francis II, Paris, 10 Aug. 1743: Esteri del Granducato di Toscana, vol. 2295/1286, fos. 315–18 for the following.

to me that we should see in course of time which power would be the first to succumb. And there ended our conversation, which was beginning to become lively as the spectators perceived.

If not an adept diplomatist, the Marquis de Stainville was a vivid reporter. He concluded:

Without wishing to make any reflection for my part, I simply take the liberty of saying to you that the power of France is very strong when she remains upon the defensive, and that the French example of sending troops [through Germany] far from home should naturally make one think before undertaking a ruinous war. I have the honour to speak to you as a true subject.

Stainville's personal predilection, thinly veiled, in favour of some accommodation with France was not then shared by the grand duke nor, effectively at least, by his queenly wife. And Stainville himself had stressed to Amelot the stumbling-block of Spanish claims in Italy. Italian affairs were assuming a central significance in the grand strategy of that war which, originated by Prussia against Austria, was merging with the prior conflict between England and Spain. To complete the secret crisscross in that wartime diplomacy of catch-as-catch-can, England was said to have been pursuing arcane soundings at the Hague with Spain, only to run up against that same stumbling-block in Italy.

The Sardinian court had been disconcerted to learn that France accepted all its deliberately augmented demands and undertook to compel Spain to do likewise. At the same time the Sardinian negotiations with Austria via England were at last upon the verge of completion, save only for final attempts by Maria Theresa to save Piacenza. The crux had come. At the beginning of September 1743 the two sharp lines of Sardinian diplomacy converged in an acute angle of decision.

The Marquis D'Ormea did not falter. This expert diplomatist concluded that it was time to supplement cunning with candour. Ormea told Villettes, who told Carteret, that he proposed to tell Senneterre the exact position of the Austro–Sardinian negotiation, in which he had now instructed Osorio to insist upon Piacenza. It would be explained to Senneterre that, if Austria gave in, 'the King of Sardinia must refuse the considerable advantages now offered him by France and Spain, as having been made too late. But, that if the Austrian minister persisted in his refusal to admit this controversial point, Monsr. Osorio was directed to disengage himself and break off all farther treaty or negotiation, and immediately to despatch a courier to Paris.'[64] There the Marquis de Stainville subsequently confirmed that in that case 'the commander de Solar had orders to sign the Treaty with Spain and France'.[65]

This ultimatum suited Carteret nicely since he had by now so offended Austria that it had seemed quite likely that her resistance would cap his failure at Hanau with another at Worms, whither the negotiations had migrated along with the headquarters. Carteret shewed Wasner the despatch from Villettes and instructions to Osorio. Ormea had calculated right. Wasner submitted. On 13 September 1743 the Treaty of Worms was signed by the plenipotentiaries of Great Britain, Austria and Sardinia. The Marquis de Stainville commented: 'Although the Queen is making a great sacrifice, I freely confess ... that it is one great anxiety the less to see this business completed.' Two days after the signature Solar in Paris gave a snug little dinner of celebration whereat, as he told Stainville in inviting him, 'We shall only be friends and allies.'[66] The other chief guests were Stainville's Austrian associate, Gundel, the inevitable Don Louis d'Acunha, and Anthony Thompson, the chargé d'affaires of Great Britain.

The provisions of the Treaty of Worms fell into three main groups, first, military and economic for the prosecution of hostilities. Large contingents for the allied army in Italy were promised by Sardinia and by Austria, whose reluctance to oblige incidentally illustrated how far reality differed from the picture painted for d'Argenson by Stainville. England subsidized as usual and for the first time also formally bound herself to maintain 'a strong squadron'[67] in the Mediterranean in return for a promise from Sardinia, and indeed Austria also, of increased economic privileges to British subjects (article XV).

On the second, political and territorial, plane the Treaty of Worms enshrined Sardinia's guarantee, for the first time, of the Pragmatic Sanction, and also the renunciation of her claim to the duchy of Milan (subject to a secret, contingent, in fact nonoperative reservation regarding a Habsburg–Bourbon marriage). Austria, under the heavy article nine, ceded to Sardinia the town and territory of Vigevano, all Austrian lands west of Lake Maggiore and the Ticino, the 'Pavese oltro Po', Bobbio included, finally long-contested Piacenza with its district stretching to the river Mura; Maria Theresa also (article X)

[64] Villettes to Lord Carteret, 2 Sept. 1743: P.R.O./S.P.F. Sardinia, vol. 47: cited, Lodge, p. 74.
[65] Marquis de Stainville to Grand Duke Francis II, Paris, 21 Sept. 1743: Ö.S./H.S.S., Lothringisches Hausarchiv 77/177B, third docket: and for the following.
[66] Marquis de Stainville to Grand Duke Francis II, Paris, 14 Sept. 1743: Esteri del Granducato di Toscana, vol. 2295/1286, fo. 328.
[67] Article VII of the Treaty of Worms, 13 Sept. 1743: A. F. Pribram, Österreichische ·Staatsverträge: England (Vienna, 1907f.), i. 615.

made over to Charles Emmanuel all her rights pertaining to the Genoese town and marquisate of Finale: all this rigorously subject to one stipulation, that the King of Sardinia should remain true to his alliance till the end not merely of the war in Italy but also of that in Germany and, significantly, even of Anglo–Spanish hostilities.

In the third group of secret and contingent provisions for future application a separate article looked hopefully towards the total expulsion of the Bourbons from Italy, and the treaty was accompanied by a separate Anglo–Austrian declaration wherein the King of England undertook to assist the Queen of Hungary 'to procure for her with divine aid all the compensation possible and surety for the future'.[68] This piece of pious nebulosity was all that Wasner in his final bargaining had been able to extract from Carteret in place of a promise of the long-sought Bavarian equivalent; as to which Carteret had characteristically advised Wasner verbally that 'since her Majesty the Queen was in possession of Bavaria, let her hold it without saying whether or no she means to keep it'.[69] Maria Theresa took more notice of the advice than of the declaration, which she scornfully refused to ratify. The British cabinet on its side refused to ratify another supplementary declaration guaranteeing that the subsidy to Austria should be upon terms of equal favour to those artfully extracted by Sardinia. These reciprocal refusals were foreboding for the future. Nevertheless the proud accomplishment of the central treaty stood, signed, ratified and pregnant for the future. Lord Carteret himself is said to have thought like Cardinal de Tencin, who remarked to the Marquis de Stainville in the aftermath of Worms that 'he foresaw that one day the King of Sardinia would be master of all Italy'.[70]

The terms of the Treaty of Worms were a triumph for Ormea. Its existence was a triumph for Carteret. It seemed as though his threat to Silhouette to strip France of her allies was no empty one. For Carteret the Treaty of Breslau was redoubled in success by the Treaty of Worms. Having broken Prussia off from France, he had now, beating France and Spain to it at the post, definitely engaged Sardinia against the house of Bourbon. At the same time this new arbiter of Europe, while concentrating his coalition against the Bourbons as the secular enemies of England, was yet skilfully checking Austrian might against Prussia in Germany and against Sardinia in Italy in a a brilliant balance of power. In this the Mediterranean assumed for England a central importance which it was not to regain for fifty

[68] Anglo–Austrian declaration of 13 Sept. 1743: ibid., i. 624.
[69] Dispatch from Wasner, Hanau, 27 July 1743: Ö.S./H.H.S.: ibid., i. 603.
[70] Marquis de Stainville to Grand Duke Francis II, Paris, 7 Dec. 1743: Esteri del Granducato di Toscana, vol. 2295/1286, fo. 344.

years and more. Not since Cardinal Wolsey had an English minister so dominated the diplomacy of Europe, where the sensation caused by the Treaty of Worms was prompt and profound. This was diplomacy in apogee.

One of the deepest dangers in diplomacy is not mere failure but excessive success. It is, after all, undiplomatic to be too conspicuously successful. The gods may or may not punish undue pride and prosperity in individuals, as was anciently supposed. Certain it is that those strictly diplomatic, as distinct from military, triumphs which do not contain the seed of their own dissolution are rare. The Treaty of Worms was not among the exceptions. Here again Lord Carteret diverged from English norms of conduct: for one of the secrets of the astonishingly consistent and solid success, upon the whole, of British diplomacy has lain precisely in its avoidance, perhaps partly instinctive, of selfish and spectacular triumphs. With Lord Carteret it was otherwise. He relished and he tasted triumph. But the price of it was to be exacted in heavy and in long instalments.

It has been justly observed that, in regard to the original disputes over the Pragmatic Sanction and Silesia, the year 1743 should have marked the end of the War of the Austrian Succession. Instead the Treaty of Worms ensured it a long continuation and tended to promote other consequences more far-reaching yet.

In the first instance the Treaty of Worms, with its disreputable intention of grabbing neutral Finale, verified the warning of the sagacious Ormea that it would promote local hostility between Genoa and Sardinia: a circumstance of import for the later campaigning in all Italy. On the wider horizon the treaty provoked not only active French participation against Sardinia but, quite quickly, that fully weighted and formidable Bourbon counterpoise which had hitherto been lacking. By the Treaty of Fontainebleau of 25 October 1743 France and Spain contracted a permanent alliance in what was known as the Second Family Compact, cementing the first made ten years earlier. France now fully underwrote the Spanish design on Italy. Louis XV would wage war in order to secure for Don Philip Lombardy, Parma, and Piacenza. The pronounced Austro–Sardinian military superiority in Italy was to become a thing of the past. And not only that. France further pledged herself to assist Spain to recover Gilbraltar and Minorca from England, also, and importantly, to be stripped of the commercial Asiento. So far from ending, the War of the Austrian Succession was evidently opening out into the full-scale sequel to the War of the Spanish Succession.

This was not the sum, however, of the adverse results for British interests of Lord Carteret's brilliant treaty-making at Worms. The

Franco–Spanish combination was, after all, an easily foreseeable and, it might be hoped, manageable counterstroke. Rather less so, perhaps, were the Prussian repercussions. Frederick the Great, already exasperated by Carteret's diplomacy at Hanau, was alarmed by that at Worms. He now felt not merely cold-shouldered but positively menaced. Among those treaties guaranteed by that of Worms were the settlements of 1731 and 1738, both incompatible with the Treaty of Breslau. The signatories of Worms had guaranteed the Pragmatic Sanction with no reference to the cession of Silesia. Frederick's thoughts began to turn in the direction least favourable to British designs, to turn against Austria again. And the preliminary to reentering the war against her was Prussian rapprochement with France.

Against this heavy background Voltaire in the autumn of 1743 undertook his would-be diplomatic mission to delicious Sans Souci. Frederick the Great, not to be lured by an amateur, mockingly annotated the memorandum presented to him by the French poet. 'To talk politics to you,' Frederick wrote, 'is precisely to offer one's mistress a dose of medicine.'[71] The most positive result of this serio-comic interlude was produced by the sentimental attachment which Voltaire conceived or feigned for the princess Ulrike, who was Frederick's prettiest sister, as Wilhelmina was the cleverest. Voltaire was inspired to one of the most exquisite of madrigals:

> Souvent un peu de vérité
> Se mêle au plus grossier mensonge:
> Cette nuit, dans l'erreur d'un songe,
> Au rang des rois j'étais monté.
> Je vous aimais, princesse, et j'osais vous le dire,
> Les dieux à mon reveil ne m'ont pas tout ôté;
> Je n'ai perdu que mon empire.[72]

Frederick, who like most enlightened despots of the day retained at bottom a sharp sense that mere authors should keep their place, composed private replies treating Voltaire as an impertinent rascal (*faquin*). The king was indeed proposing to bestow the hand of Princess Ulrike upon a person very different from Voltaire, in furtherance of the next stage of Prussian policy in Europe, now opening out through less poetic diplomacy.

In signing the Treaty of Worms Lord Carteret had, as it were,

[71] King Frederick II to Voltaire, Potsdam, 7 Sept. 1743: Frederick, xxii. 140. (For the dating of this letter cf. ibid., p. 139, n. *a*.)
[72] Voltaire, 'A Madame la Princesse Ulrique de Prusse' in *Œuvres complètes de Voltaire* [ed. L. Moland], (Paris, 1877–85), x. 528–9.

dropped a stone into a pool, starting ever-widening rings of repercussion across the surface of affairs. Fresh antagonism to British policy was aroused in Genoa, Spain, France, Prussia and, on the longest term, even in Austria. As it turned out, indeed, England, in her extraordinary maritime and commercial upswing of the eighteenth century, was not to suffer badly in the long run, rather, reaped rich profit by and large. But the analysis stands in terms of diplomatic technique and accomplishment. For the present proud Maria Theresa had to submit to the bullying policy of her English ally. But she did not forget, even if the famous reversal of alliances still lay far in the future. And the future Duke de Choiseul, the great patron of the Austro-French connection, was in some measure involved in those early stirrings back in 1743. So also was his father.

V

During the negotiation of the Treaty of Worms Robinson had urged upon Carteret from Vienna that if there was risk of an unsatisfied Sardinia siding with Spain there was also the countervailing danger of driving an aggrieved Austria into the arms of France. Feelers had already been put out in this sense, predictably in that diplomatic game of catch-as-catch-can with almost everybody negotiating behind everybody else's back. At that time as at others neutral Switzerland was a classic channel for secret soundings between enemies at war. Since the spring of 1743 the French Marquis de Coëtlogon had been in touch with the Marquis de Prié, Austrian envoy at Basel. The Austrian government seems to have shewn some interest but this sounding ran out, perhaps overlaid by another in a further instance of dual negotiation.

Dettingen had sharply increased in the disarrayed French government such inclinations towards accommodation as had been confided to the Marquis de Stainville, as we now know, by the Marshal de Noailles himself even before his campaign. Now Noailles appears to have taken a hand in soundings initiated by Hatsel, a subintendant in Alsace, with the new austrophil Elector of Mainz and prosecuted in correspondence with Bartenstein himself. The French proposal in this obscure episode was that Austria should make peace with France in return for French and Bavarian military co-operation with Austria with the object of reconquering Silesia from Prussia, and French support of Austrian candidature in the imperial succession. Carteret got wind of this underhand manoeuvre, as is fair to remember in estimating his treatment of Austria even though the initiative had been evidently French. Carteret further exasperated Maria Theresa by promptly denouncing the affair to Frederick, who called it 'an abyss of bad faith: it would have needed a new Oedipus to explain this mystery'.[73] Modern authorities have agreed that this mystery has persisted to an appreciable extent, more particularly as to the true designs of the amorphous French government.[74] Now, however, it is possible to provide some further elucidation.

Frederick the Great was particularly suspicious of the Austrian inclination of the other leading French minister besides the Marshal de Noailles, the Cardinal de Tencin. It was indeed the adherent of another French cardinal, Rohan's librarian, the Abbé Oliva, who had made an initial approach under Amelot's authority to an Austrian diplomat in Germany early in June 1743. Tencin himself, however, was said to have been mooting a separate Franco–Austrian accommodation hardly more than a month later;[75] and internal evidence leaves little doubt that he was the carefully unnamed French 'accredited minister, who is becoming more so every day'[76] and who was beginning about then to signal to the Marquis de Stainville. On Tuesday 23 July the Cardinal de Tencin opened up with him.

With the enemy standing before the eastern gates of France the cardinal now confided in secret to the marquis 'what he had imagined: that the King his master being at war with nobody, and free of his engagements with the Emperor owing to the neutrality which had just been concluded', could enter into a separate accommodation with Maria Theresa to the extent of a French guarantee of her 'peaceful possession of her hereditary lands'. Stainville reported: 'As I saw that this speech tended towards breaking the alliance' between Austria and England, he honourably scouted this, telling Tencin 'that he must allow something for gratitude' towards England. 'The Minister replied to me that, by France guaranteeing to the Queen her Italian lands, Spain would be obliged to try to make peace, since she would see no further way of being supported in that quarter; in short that he looked upon this first demarche as an approach towards a general peace ... He begged me to pass his ideas on to Vienna, while nevertheless asking for them an inviolable secrecy, without which all his projects would vanish.' If secret approaches through the Marquis de Stainville seldom produced

---

[73] Frederick, iii. 18.

[74] Cf. Braubach, p. 365; Dr. Fritz Wagner, *Kaiser Karl VII und die grossen Mächte 1740–1745* (Stuttgart, 1938), p. 448.

[75] Cf. F. Wagner, op. cit., p. 447.

[76] Enclosure in Marquis de Stainville to Grand Duke Francis II, Paris, 27 July 1743: Esteri del Granducato di Toscana, vol. 2295/1286, fos. 308–9 for the following.

positive reactions, they hardly ever produced damaging leaks, which may have been one reason why he was still selected.

Tencin put it to Stainville in conclusion that 'by the mediation of the Queen [of Hungary] the English would move towards rapprochement with Spain', and reciprocally through French mediation with Spain. One may mark the critical differences between these propositions put by Tencin to Stainville on 23 July 1743 and those already noticed as received by him a fortnight later from Amelot, who posited the maintenance of alliances, indissoluble French ties with Spain, and Austrian cessions to her in Italy, the point upon which Stainville rounded against Amelot. Another week later, on 13 August in Paris (the king being absent from Versailles), Stainville himself pointed out this discrepancy to 'the Cardinal Tencin'[77] – he named him this time. 'He was surprised', reported Stainville, 'and told me that he did not understand with what object I had been treated to this talk.' Tencin asked him not to report Amelot's abrasive approach (but Stainville already had) pending a 'reply to a little memorandum which I sent to M. Toussaint to inform your Royal Highness on the 27th of last month'. Thus did a French minister of state try to sidetrack his own foreign minister in that inchoate government under a nerveless king. Ten days earlier Stainville had observed: 'The ministry here is in great agitation. Disunion reigns in it. Cardinal Tencin is increasing in credit and it is absolutely necessary that there should be a prime minister, for it is impossible for things to remain in the state in which they are'.[78] But they did, for quite a while.

Tencin's sounding with Stainville was not only more amicable than Amelot's but, by the same token, deeper. The marquis related that the cardinal, in opening up on 23 July, 'expatiated much upon the bad system which had been followed in this country. He told me that if he had had the honour to be in the ministry at that time he would have opposed it with all his strength and would always have insisted upon keeping the engagements which had been contracted with the late Emperor [Charles VI], and that his own system was to profit from the present position in order to guarantee to the House of Austria all her possessions and to conclude with it an indissoluble alliance. According to him this was the only means of pacifying Europe.'[79]

[77] Marquis de Stainville to Grand Duke Francis II, Paris, 17 Aug. 1743: ibid., fo. 320, and for the following.
[78] Marquis de Stainville to Grand Duke Francis II, Paris, 3 Aug. 1743: ibid., fo. 314.
[79] Enclosure in Marquis de Stainville to Grand Duke Francis II, Paris, 27 July 1743: ibid., fo. 309.

Tencin's retrospective criticism was of course directed at the prussophile Belle-Isle rather than at Tencin's mentor, Fleury. He made this plain a fortnight later when Stainville, after his set-to with Amelot, went with Gundel just to pay their respects to Tencin. The cardinal treated them to his 'continual prayers for the pacification of christendom'[80] and his confession 'that he had never conceived anything so fine as the project of the late cardinal [Fleury], which was to make an immutable alliance between the House of France and that of Austria . . . [as] the only means of maintaining continual peace in Europe since these two powers united would infallibly be the arbiters of the others . . . It was his sole point of view.' A week later again Tencin reiterated his desire for 'a stable alliance with the Queen [Maria Theresa] . . . "So long as I have the honour of being in the ministry I shall not change my system."'[81]

These tentative approaches towards a Franco–Austrian accommodation, notably made in hitherto secret conversations between the Cardinal de Tencin and the Marquis de Stainville, formed the immediate setting of the first episode of diplomacy in the career of the latter's son, the Count de Stainville, back at court with the tidings of Dettingen.

Young Stainville was, as he explained, on his way 'to go to join my regiment, which was to march into Savoy'[82] in a contingent drawn from secondary regiments, largely salvaged from the Bohemian campaign. His father had reported at the end of June: 'All the battalions returned from Prague, which are still far from restored, have received orders to march into Languedoc. Some say that this is because there are some stirrings among the protestants of the Cevennes, others that it is in order to go into Provence and guard the coast there, and others again, who seem to me better informed, do not doubt that it is in order to join the army of Don Philip: which might make one think that the [French] negotiation with the King of Sardinia still subsists':[83] as indeed it did, with this French politico-military pressure vainly endeavouring to secure the Sardinian alliance.

Some twenty battalions were thus projected across France to converge towards Savoy from peripheral garrisons all round the north, from Belle-Isle in the west round to Strasburg, whence the Régiment de Stainville was detailed by the French ministry of war

---

[80] Marquis de Stainville to Grand Duke Francis II, Paris, 10 Aug. 1743: ibid., fo. 317, and for the following.

[81] Ibid., 17 Aug. 1743: fos. 320–1.

[82] Choiseul, *Mémoires*, p. 11.

[83] Marquis de Stainville to Grand Duke Francis II, Paris, 29 June 1743: *u.s.*, fos. 301–2.

to stage 'to Antibes, stopping at Lyons'.[84] Leaving Strasburg on 18 June 1743 Stainville's regiment was due beyond Lyons, at Pont-Saint-Esprit, by 17 July. In this march down the eastern side of France the young count did not lead his little regiment, still short of a number of officers held as prisoners of war from the Bohemian campaign. The count's capacity as colonel of the Régiment de Stainville yielded precedence for the present to that as a messenger from Dettingen and, perhaps now, to Vienna. He recalled:

I did not join my regiment, because it remained in Provence. Besides, the King's Council had thought of sending me to Vienna, under pretext of the exchange of prisoners and in order to be able, by my means, to have passed to this Court propositions of peace on behalf of the King. The Cardinal de Tencin spoke to me of this project and asked me what was my opinion on this mission. I asked him for some days to reflect upon it. I was not long in deciding not to accept this commission; I judged from the first moment that it was very subordinate, which was enough to make me feel that it did not suit me. Besides, without having reflected much upon politics, I easily perceived that the object of the commission which they wished to give me would have no success; that the court of Vienna was not the mistress of her resolutions, which were subordinated to her allies, so that what I should propose would be communicated to England, who would divulge the true motive of my journey to Vienna, and that after having been badly received in Austria I should be sent back to France rather in disgrace. Without my being a personage who could embarrass the King's ministers who would have sent me, if by an impossible chance my propositions were accepted at Vienna and in England, I reflected that they would not leave me the glory of making peace and that they would send personages other than me to reap the fruits of the first démarche.

In accordance with these reflections I resolved to refuse this commission; but, as I desired to remain at Paris and not to go to join my regiment in garrison in the provinces, I bethought myself not to say to the Cardinal de Tencin that I refused absolutely; I simply offered him some objections; I told him that I ought to confer about it with M. d'Argenson, Minister of War, and with M. Amelot, Minister of Policy; at each conversation I raised quite reasonable difficulties. Apparently events supervened which effaced this project from the heads of the ministers; I took good care not to question them; they spoke to me of it no more, any more than of going to join my regiment, so that I remained quietly delivered over to my pleasures alone and to the vexations of society during the year 1743.[85]

This first proposal that the Count de Stainville should enter upon the field of diplomacy wherein he was subsequently to shine was made at just about the time of Hatsel's approach to Bartenstein (letters of 22 and 24 July), of the French declaration to the imperial diet in favour of accommodation with Austria (26 July), and of Tencin's overture to the elder Stainville (23 July onwards) – a significant

---

[84] 'Estat des 20 Batt.ons a porter en avant, contenant les jours de marche pour arriver a leur Entrepost', June 1743: Arch. Guerre C., vol. 3009, no. 22. Cf. also the 'Estat des Reg.ts que sa Ma.té reserve pour servir au secours qu'Elle destine d'envoyer en Italie', ibid., no. 23.
[85] Choiseul, *Mémoires*, pp. 11–12.

conjunction. The future Choiseul in his memoirs no more mentioned his father in this connection than the marquis mentioned the approach to his son in his dispatches to the grand duke: though each probably had some idea of the other's business, with Tencin as the common term. The proposition to the Count de Stainville might also seem to relate to some extent to the other French ministerial overlord then in favour of accommodation with Austria, the Marshal of Noailles, the influence behind Hatsel. Noailles's keen young staff-officer would have been a plausible negotiator about prisoners. And one may agree with Choiseul's earliest biographer that he might have been expected to be dazzled by the exciting prospect 'of playing, at twenty-four, a role in politics, and in an occasion which was of interest to the whole of Europe'.[86] But young Stainville again said No.

The French government, according to the same source, wished to advance peace-propositions through young Stainville 'more in order to become acquainted with the disposition of the cabinet at Vienna, than in the true intention of [achieving a] pacification. But the Count de Stainville wanted to be able to carry to this court only positive utterances; those wherewith he was charged were not.'[87] His first introduction to diplomacy thus found him looking to French advances to Austria. Such advances across the divide of conflict are not, however, simple; and even if, as might appear, Tencin was sincere in making them, the countervailing intervention of Amelot suggests that the cardinal may not easily have had it his own way any more than Maria Theresa herself upon the other side. But then her true attitude towards France just then seems to have been one of some complexity if not ambivalence. She apparently evinced, not for the last time, a woman's capacity for regretting the course of action she felt compelled to take. Within ten days of the Austrian protest of 16 August 1743 in uncomprising terms which cut across Tencin's approach, one finds her privately assuring Count Ulfeld that she would 'always gladly have treated France with greater consideration and have left the door open after the example of the court of Turin. How often have I not desired a paper on this from Bartenstein. One time it is said that it is contrary to good faith (*Einmal heisst es, es ist contre la bonne foy*), at another that it would be abused; it was not the right time, circumstances had changed, it was no longer to the point (*nicht mehr der casus*). Now he himself comes back to it, but too late, for I positively believe that there is nothing more to be done and that we shall get the worst peace. Yet must we seek by all means to bring

[86] Essai/Arsenal 5808, fo. 33.
[87] Ibid., fo. 32.

it about, for otherwise it could turn out worse still.'[88] The Queen of
Hungary now appeared to regret her intransigence against Cardinal
Fleury the year before, and even in September 1743 she was still
exclaiming: 'Peace, peace with France, then all the others, who are
false friends, would come along too.'[89]

To the fading echo of Too Late a perverse fatality seemed to be
frustrating the inclinations towards peace in the highest quarters
both at Versailles and at Vienna, hence any opportunity for mediating
diplomacy by either Stainville. One may wonder whether a
contribution to this may have come from the hostility to France
which had possessed the Grand Duke Francis, more even than his
wife, within the very penetralia of Austrian policy. In this connection
some archival peculiarities may attract attention; but before supposing that Francis was withholding dispatches from his wife one needs
to take careful stock not only of their internal evidence[90] but also, for
instance, of the circumstance that later that autumn, even after the
Treaty of Worms, when the Austrian court was said to be wondering
whether Fleury's propositions of the preceding year were still open,
it was precisely Francis's confidant, Toussaint, who was reported as
indicating to Vincent, the French Chargé d'Affaires in Vienna, that
it only needed the offer to Austria of a possibility of her recovering
Silesia in order to bring hostilities in the west to a quick conclusion.[91]
But then Maria Theresa herself had said weeks earlier that it was
already too late, owing, especially, to the pressures of her English and
Sardinian allies, already approximating to her category of 'false
friends'. The secret history of her abortive Franco–Austrian soundings in the summer of 1743 suggests the extent of British responsibility
for the fact that the War of the Austrian Succession did not end then,
as might have been logical, but was prolonged for five more bitter
years, to a considerable extent as a war of the Italian succession, with
obdurate Spain linking back to that introductory War of Jenkins' Ear
which, in terms of British interests, came almost to encapsulate the
greater conflict upon the continent.

[88] Queen Maria Theresa to Count Ulfeld, 25 Aug. 1743: Alfred Ritter von Arneth, *Briefe
er Kaiserin Maria Theresia an ihre Kinder und Freunde*, iv. 185.
[89] Queen Maria Theresa, Sept. 1743: cited, Braubach, p. 371.
[90] A copy of the Marquis de Stainville's dispatch of 10 Aug. 1743, reporting his set-to over
he inapposite approach of Amelot, was, rather exceptionally, entered in the Austrian archives
reserved at Vienna: Ö.S./H.H.S., Lothringisches Hausarchiv 77/177A, fos. 32–3. (For the
riginal text preserved at Florence in Esteri del Granducato di Toscana, vol. 2295/1286, fos.
15–18, cf. p. 443 above.) Whereas copies of his dispatch of 27 July and related memorandum
o Toussaint, reporting the defter appeal of Tencin, were apprently not entered in the Austrian
rchives, any more than Stainville's follow-up of 17 August on the cardinal's overture: these are
nly to be found in the Tuscan archives. However, the Austrian copy of Stainville's dispatch
f 10 August included indications of his contacts with Tencin, though there unnamed.
[91] Vincent, dispatches of 23 Oct. and 2 Nov. 1743: Arch. Aff. Étr. C.P., Autriche, vol. 236:
Braubach, p. 371.

That the young Count de Stanville should then have reckoned so soon with the underlying factor of British preponderance over Austria is an index both to the early development of his political intelligence and to the later tendency of his foreign policy: especially impressive in a Lorrainer, whose horizon might well have been bounded by Austrian and continental considerations. Possibly, though, his father's English experiences and contacts, and indeed the maritime fate of his grandfather, may have suggested a corrective here. Even allowing for some claim by the later Choiseul to an anachronistic acumen, yet its superiority over that of his father is suggested here by the latter's frustrated eagerness, once again, to play a role in the kind of doubtful diplomacy which his son was careful to eschew, if at a lower and less accredited level.

Young Stainville had prudently calculated to avoid almost exactly what in fact befell Hatsel in his secret soundings with Austria. The latter's initiative was, as noticed, promptly relayed to British quarters, which promptly stymied it as damagingly as possible for purposes of political warfare, especially with the Prussian king and the Bavarian emperor. 'Really', wrote Louis XV to Noailles, 'M. Hatzel has got us into a pretty mess with the Emperor.'[92] By October the French line was to make out to the unhappy Charles VII that the whole Hatsel affair was a mare's nest, 'an invention of the court of London'.[93] The secret and informal diplomacy that year of Hatsel, as indeed of Voltaire, did its negotiator no good. One cannot but admire, as presumably intended, the precocious correctness of the Count de Stainville's equation, self-confessedly calculated entirely in terms of self-interest rather than of any urge to serve the two great nationalities to which he was affiliated but did not belong – as a Lorrainer, as a character, liberated from large and emotional loyalties.

While the future Choiseul artfully abstained from the Franco–Austrian stirrings towards rapprochment in 1743, yet they had prefiguratively brushed him, not to put it higher from our knowledge now of their hidden implication for his father. And one can see more broadly upon the French side how the long War of the Austrian Succession, wantonly fostered by Belle-Isle and now wantonly extended, has obscured the early and persistent inclination towards going in with Austria on the part of leading statesmen, Fleury himself and both of his most prominent successors, Tencin and Noailles, all of them in discreet touch with the Marquis de Stainville. On the

[92] King Louis XV to Marshal de Noailles, Versailles, 16 Aug. 1743: Rousset, i. 221.
[93] 'Mémoire pour servir d'instruction au sieur de Chavigny, allant de la part du Roi près l'Empéreur', Fontainebleau, 4 Oct. 1743: *Recueil des instructions données aux ambassadeurs et ministres de France depuis les traités de Westphalie jusqu'à la révolution française* (Paris, 1884 f. henceforth cited as *Recueil des instructions*), vii (Bavière, Palatinat, Deux-Ponts), 226.

Austrian side disillusion with the old connection with England was lastingly promoted by Carteret's triumphant Treaty of Worms, compounding that of Breslau. Maria Theresa was already beginning to look wistfully towards catholic France, in the direction of a reversal of alliances. This early evolution, even in wartime, nourished the inner logic of that Diplomatic Revolution which was to be largely achieved for Austria by her brilliant minister, Kaunitz, and largely cemented for France by hers, by Choiseul.

CHAPTER VIII

SOCIETY

I

NIMBLY evading the pitfalls of secret diplomacy, young Stainville plunged into the pleasures of Parisian existence. That existence was in his time upon the turn.

Paris, with a population around half a million and increasing, was largely the cultural and social focus not of France only, but of Europe. The capital of Bourbon France exemplified the continental transition, accented in the first half of the eighteenth century, from the lingering of the middle ages to the inception of modern times. The working-class quarter of the Faubourg Saint-Antoine was still symbolically dominated by the Bastille, and it was through the adjacent Porte Saint-Antoine that foreign ambassadors made their ceremonial entries into the Paris of old. There the forbidding donjon of the Temple was offset now by the magnificent residence of the French Grand Prior of the successors to the Templars, the Knights of Malta; and by the Hôtel de Soubise by Delamair, among the earliest and finest examples of French urban architecture in the eighteenth century, and among the last evidences of the willingness of so great a family as the Rohans to live at the east end of the market of the Halles, swarming around the elaborate pillory in an ancient setting of timbered houses. Hard by, the insalubrious charnel-house of the Innocents was the pitch of the public scriveners plying their quills for illiterate servant-girls and the like.

From the renaissance Hôtel de Ville on the Place de la Grève one could cross from the right bank to that island holding the ancient heart of the capital in Notre-Dame and the Palais of the Parliament of Paris with the Sainte-Chapelle. There the windows were already allowed by that age of classicism to be 'the most beautiful that can be seen' even though their radiant compositions were 'in truth very crudely delineated'.[1] To the west of the palace of the parliament the Place Dauphine led out on to the Pont Neuf, still edged with expensive houses and nearly always thronged with traffic. In the middle, out on the westward bastion looking down the Seine there triumphed the equestrian statue of King Henry IV. Thence the view

[1] Germain Brice, op.cit., iii. 267–8.

was accounted by one traveller of the time to be one of the three finest in the world, ranking along with the Golden Horn and the port of Goa:

This magnificent view extends to the right to the Louvre which presents a long succession of magnificent buildings on the bank of the river; to the left to the Hôtel de Conti, to the Collège des Quatre Nations, very remarkable by its dome and by its two large square pavilions, a little too far forward in truth . . . Mont Valérien . . . rises above . . . an excellent perspective in distance.[2]

In this new spread of Paris to the west, royal and aristocratic, it was still through the massive medievalism of the Petit-Châtelet, where debtors languished, that one passed from the Cité to the university quarter of Stainville's schooldays on the left bank. There the westward thrust of the select Faubourg Saint-Germain in the direction of the Invalides had lately produced fresh expressions of nobility. The Palais-Bourbon had been begun in 1722, after the duke had cashed in on Law. In 1739 Bouchardon had finished his fountain in the Rue de Grenelle. Those were the days when improvement in water-supply could still be effected through an outstanding work of art.

The opposite bank of the Seine, over by the Cours de la Reine, had been revetted with stone by that Marshal de Bassompierre who was the Count de Stainville's forbear on his mother's side: elsewhere in the city the river-banks still often sloped down, enabling the horses to drink. The Cours de la Reine, planted with elms by Marie de Medici, already formed a westward prospect for the gardens of the Louvre and the Tuileries while those of the Palais Royal, thrown open by the Duke of Orleans, were a favourite resort. Towards the Champs Élysées, lined for pleasure under Colbert, were new mansions like that built by the Count d'Evreux in 1718.[3] The Rue Royale on its present axis was barely ten years old in 1743 and as yet lacked both its terminal layouts. Already there, though, was the Place Vendôme, centred then upon the monumental bronze of an equestrian statue of Louis XIV. His most significant memorial, however, was to be found perhaps in the raised boulevards, often fringed with trees, which had been growing up along the levelled ramparts of the old city in a westward circuit from about the Bastille, round by the boulevards of the Temple, of Saint-Martin, and Saint-Denis. Warlike progress under Louis the Great had firmed the ramparts of the realm along the frontiers, in the masterpieces of

[2] Ibid., pp. 199–200.
[3] Now the Palais de l'Élysée.

Vauban, with the French boulevards of war projected out to Flanders and the Rhine so that those of Paris could make their civilized contribution to 'the most beautiful city in Europe':[4] that from a foreign visitor responsive to her special lift: 'This Country is my centre, and Paris is to me the Spring of Youth'[5] – in that, already, of the Count de Stainville.

A cultivated English visitor, even, found Paris then 'a most magnificent town, not near so big as London, but much finer',[6] largely paved and built of stone, less grimed by smoke if otherwise scarcely as salubrious: despite civic efforts, as in police-ordinances of 1726 and 1730, to mitigate the lasting simplicity of Parisian ideas as to the disposal of refuse. Twice a day in summer the bellman summoned householders to sluice down the streets, in winter those citizens designated to attend to street-lighting by hoisting candlelit lanterns on ropes slung across the streets. Feeble though the illumination might be, by about 1720 it had already been costing more than a hundred thousand écus a year. The bellman in his gaiters and three-cornered hat stands out in timeless precision from Bouchardon's drawings just about then of the Cries of Paris, the vociferous hucksters, the billposter – an important person in those days of limited news-media – and the inevitable crier of the 'list of winners in the lottery'.[7] This throng jostled in the narrow streets with sedan-chairs, fine coaches, and hackney-carriages for hire, already familiar as *fiacres*. Parking could even then be a problem and at the end of that year of 1743 the king himself had to sort out a nasty brawl involving the coachman of the Duchess of Modena, still hanging around Paris.

Behind the vivid concourse of the capital lay long hours of labour for the tradesfolk and their apprentices. But saints' days afforded frequent holidays when the humblest could enjoy themselves in an age which, looking to its aristocracy, believed in pleasure as an end in itself. The eighteenth century encouraged Parisian gaiety. It was already the inspiration of feminine fashion. Such a society throve upon the spicy scraps of gossip, the latest news-items, and the satiric ditties hummed in the pleasure-gardens and the hundreds of cafés which already characterized the Parisian scene. There, besides flirting with the *cafetière*, men could increasingly quicken their minds in assessing the newspapers and discussing ideas, even, now, those

---

[4] Baron von Pöllnitz, op. cit., ii. 191.

[5] Ibid., p. 197.

[6] Earl of Chesterfield to Philip Stanhope, Paris, Aug. 1741: *The Letters of Philip Dormer Stanhope, 4th Earl of Chesterfield*, ed. Bonamy Dobrée ([London,] 1932), ii. 471.

[7] Cited, with reproduction, by Marcel Poëte, *Une Vie de cité: Paris de sa naissance à nos jours*, Album (Paris, 1925), p. 296.

daring ideas beginning to be put about by the philosophs, whose rendezvous on the left bank was to be the Café Procope opposite the Comédie Française. Almost as much of an institution as the Comédie or the Opera was, at a more popular level, the Ramponneau tavern with dancing, smoking, and wine a sou cheaper than elsewhere. More dubious resorts were the numerous gaming establishments where young gentlemen could procure 'a bad supper'[8] and the pleasure of ruining themselves at biribi or faro. The Governor of Paris himself, the decadent Duke de Gesvres, had till recently made a nice thing out of running a gambling saloon. The police, in raiding such dens, usually confined themselves to making an 'example of some poor madam among the most unprotected'. In that summer of 1743 they raided Madame de Mazières, the keeper of one of these 'places of ruin and prostitution'.[9]

Sexual licence was a recurrent topic in the secret reports of the Paris police, notoriously omnipresent and driving pretty steadily against the lower class of prostitution, always liable to be rounded up and, like poor Manon Lescaut, packed off to populate the colonies. But it was uphill work against a hostile public opinion – and an unchanging human nature. 'There are many places of ill fame in the Rue Soli', ran a police report of 9 July 1743. '... At the Palais-Royal, from nine o'clock in the evening to ten, there occur things which are very little compatible with the piety of the Duke of Orleans.'[10]

Also attractive of a summer's evening was an outing to one of the little houses of refreshment which dotted the rural environs of Paris. These *guinguettes* led on topographically, perhaps also logically, to those outlying villas of delight which were becoming a feature of Paris, conveniently for young noblemen wishing to set up their actress or other mistress of the moment. According to the Marquis d'Argenson:

A perfect life with one's mistress would be this: to have a little house in a suburb or in the town itself ... several sessions a week, according to age, strength and health. Each session of six hours, from one o'clock to seven; the first three hours in bed, the second three hours at table, and with no third person. Dress oneself again, lay aside one's dressing-gown, and for the rest of the week let one appear unoccupied with love. That is how I lived in my youth.[11]

This was the kind of model before Stainville in his youth.

[8] D'Argenson, ii. 92–3 for the following.
[9] 'Journal de police sous Louis XV (1742–1743)': Barbier, viii. 341.
[10] Ibid., viii. 317.
[11] Marquis d'Argenson, MSS. no. 2338, in D'Argenson, i. 20.

II

The little Count de Stainville found himself with an increasing number of young French aristocrats in preferring the astringent gaiety of the capital to the ceremonious licence of the court. Zestful Paris, not constricting Versailles, was for him the formative atmosphere.

Stainville belonged to that not too congenial type of smart, witty, womanizing young man whom Paris particularly bred in the eighteenth century as in others. One foreigner had already observed that the French needed 'to get over the four or five Years of juvenile Fury, and to surmount the tumultuous Passions which their great Vivacity kindles in their Breasts, and prompts them to do things at twenty Years of Age, which at thirty they detest and abhor ... The Nobleman is infinitely more so ... He thinks that to be debauch'd gives him a fine Air; and many of 'em really boast of being greater Deboshees, than in Fact they are.'[12]

No type, though, could cover Stainville, who was nothing if not himself. A later description of him yet fits his youth, especially since he conspicuously retained his youthful disposition: 'Good, noble, frank, generous, gallant, magnificent, liberal, proud, audacious, fiery and even passionate, he recalled the idea of the French knights of old: but he also joined to these qualities several defects of his nation; he was light, indiscreet, presumptious, libertine, prodigal, petulant and conceited.'[13]

Recovering from this adjectival avalanche, one notices that the listed defects are mainly the extravagant faults of youth, not the mean deficiencies of middle age. As another observer put it, the then Count de Stainville possessed 'an impetuous character, which wanted to bend everything to his least wish; very great penetration, which depicted every possibility and indicated to him every means of realizing them, great prodigality, even when he was without fortune',[14] as now in 1743. This went with 'a generosity without equal, which was not formerly restrained by the mediocrity of his fortune'.[15] Always keen to help friends, as well as himself, young Stainville characteristically took less credit for his kind actions than for his sharp tongue. He was too clever and amusing not to be imprudently malicious in what he said, which gave enemies a handle. However, Stainville, said another acquaintance, 'possesses much

[12] Baron von Pöllnitz, op. cit., ii. 275–6.
[13] Gleichen, p. 61.
[14] Prince de Montbarey, *Mémoires autographes de M. le prince de Montbarey* (Paris, 1826–7), i. 201.
[15] Hénault, p. 278.

warmth and empressement, has no fatuity. More seductive than faithful, generous even to prodigality, but without ostentation; one sees that he combines just about what succeeds the most with the fair sex', who could thus overlook his 'not being the handsomest man of the century'.[16] It was generally agreed of this quick-tempered, snub-nosed little redhead that 'although he be ugly, his face has something agreeable in it; his mien is open. He has noble ways, full of grace.'[17] Another contemporary was struck by 'an inconceivable charm in his conversation'.[18] This was amplified by yet another (all these witnesses were men): 'Never have I known a man who has known how to spread around himself joy and contentment as much as he does; when he enters a room, he rummages in his pockets and seems to draw from them an inexhaustible abundance of pleasantries and gaiety.'[19] And gaiety breeds love.

Stainville was a fashionable charmer. A serious young English officer, who had just had his baptism of fire as an adjutant over against Stainville at Dettingen, was to remark a decade later: 'A Frenchman that makes his mistress laugh has no favour to ask of her; he is at the top of his ambition.'[20]

The Count de Stainville 'led a dissipated and libertine life in his earliest youth'.[21] By way of balance one may turn here to an authority who cherished no very warm regard for Stainville. Charles Pineau Duclos, fifteen years older than Stainville, was the son of a hatter at Dinant. This future Historiographer of France, noted for his frank acerbity, led a pretty fast life in youth and had at that time just published a couple of light novels (*Histoire de Madame de Luz*, 1741; *Confessions du comte de ***, 1742). He was then moving in that Parisian society of bright young men which was already being recruited from both the literary world of Duclos and the aristocratic one of Stainville: another instance, after that of Fréron, of Stainville's early acquaintance with young literati of humble origins. Duclos characteristically wrote of Stainville:

He is of distinguished birth, small and disagreeable in form, with worth, wit, and still more audacity. He chose, in entering into society, the role of a lady-killer, which proves that everybody can aspire to it. He was at the same time ambitious of a reputation for malice for which he had wonderful propensities, and of which he was

[16] Baron de Besenval, *Mémoires de M. le baron de Besenval* (Paris, 1805–6: henceforth cited as Besenval), i. 322.
[17] Ibid., i. 316.
[18] Prince de Montbarey, loc. cit.
[19] Gleichen, pp. 61–2.
[20] Lieut.-Colonel James Wolfe to Mrs. Henrietta Wolfe, Paris, 12 Dec. 1752: Beckles Willson, *The Life and Letters of James Wolfe* (London, 1909), p. 194.
[21] Gleichen, p. 65.

vain. With that one does not fail to impose upon fools, and to make oneself feared by them. His actions, however, served him better than his sallies. The former were complained of, the latter were not quoted; I have known him, and kept company enough with him since his youth, up to the time in which he entered the ministry. Before he played a role, I have seen him denied access to several houses; he was not far from being regarded as a scapegrace (*espèce*);[22] I have once heard him defend himself against this imputation which he has never deserved; but it was at least very humiliating for him that there should be a question of it.[23]

The testimony of Duclos is not lightly to be set aside, and one has the impression that with Stainville, as with so many Frenchmen, the sharper side of his character was pronounced in youth, when Duclos knew him. At the same time one suspects that Stainville and Duclos were both too confidently clever and independent to hit it off very easily, especially, perhaps, in view of the count's social superiority. And in reading an adverse assessment of a witty person one is always inclined to wonder which particular witticism it may be that is being avenged. After Duclos's careful denigration one rather prefers Choiseul's own description of how, in particular, he spent that autumn of 1743 in Paris: 'I thought only of my own pleasure and I delivered myself during this year to everything in the way of disorder which dissipation and inexperience occasion in a young head.'[24]

While Stainville enjoyed himself along with loose-living literati, and while he may well have been somewhat scouted by more sober circles, he was already beginning to make his way, in his fashion. In his youth, according to yet another witness, the 'Count de Stainville ... long had a kind of celebrity in society through his wit, his gaiety and a light and presumptuous air'.[25] Nor would it be correct to infer from Duclos that this celebrity was not already penetrating high society. The Prince de Montbarey testified:

From his first beginnings in society, the wit of M. de Choiseul [Stainville] secured him a real friend in Madame the Maréchale de Luxembourg, who, even before her second marriage, being Duchess de Boufflers, was at the head of the most striking women of the court and the town; who set the tone; at whose house there gathered the élite of good company; in whose salon the reputation of a man of wit, a jest even though offensive caused to be excused the impudence and perhaps even the depravity of the morals.[26]

---

[22] Duclos elsewhere (*Considérations sur les moeurs de ce siècle* in *Œuvres complètes de Duclos* – Paris, 1806 – i. 143) defined this word: '*L'espèce*, terme nouveau, mais qui a un sens juste, est l'opposé de l'homme de considération ... *L'espèce* est celui qui, n'ayant pas le mérite de son état, se prête encore de lui-même à son avilissement personnel ... Un homme d'un haut rang peut être une *espèce*.'

[23] Duclos, *Mémoires secrets sur les règnes de Louis XIV et de Louis XV*, ii. 498–9.

[24] Choiseul, *Mémoires*, p. 11.

[25] Sénac de Meilhan, *Portraits et caractères du XVIIIᵉ siècle* (Paris, 1945), p. 133.

[26] Prince de Montbarey, op. cit., i. 202–3.

The Duchess de Boufflers, as she then was, was the grand-daughter of The Charmer, of that Marshal de Villeroy who had made his questionable contribution towards the education of the king. Madeleine-Angélique de Neufville de Villeroy had been barely fourteen when, in 1721, she married the fifteen-year-old Duke de Boufflers, who within a year signalized himself as one of the *arracheurs de palissades.* The lively couple were, however, soon readmitted to court where the duchess was appointed a lady to the newly married Queen Marie Leszczynska, who developed a soft spot for the duke. Boufflers had, like Stainville, come through the Bohemian campaign, the siege of Prague, and that retreat. He had further, as noticed, distinguished himself at Dettingen along with the Duke de Luxembourg, the acknowledged lover of the Duchess of Boufflers. She, 'sensing all the advantages of having a stupid and opulent lover, sought to fix M. de Luxembourg, without making him any sacrifice [as regards fidelity]. She succeeded in this all the more easily in that, to the habit which women have of assuming sway, she joined her superiority over him. She formed a circle of Madame de L[uxembourg], wife of her lover, of the Duchess de la V[allière], and of all men of fashion of that time.'[27] Among them the Count de Stainville had, if he needed them, several lines of introduction, not only through his ducal comrades-in-arms but also perhaps through the affiliations of the Boufflers with Lorraine: a cousin had married one of the Beauvau-Craon girls who, as the Marquise de Boufflers de Remiencourt, revived with the new dynasty in Lorraine the tradition of the Craons, becoming the mistress of Stanislas and presiding over his delightful little court at Lunéville as the so-called Dame de la Volupté.

The dominating disposition of the tallish Duchess de Boufflers matched the imposing beauty of that great lady in the great tradition. Writing of her as she was at about that time, in her thirties, her friend the Marquise du Deffand described her as 'beautiful without having the air of suspecting it; her physiognomy is lively and piquant', her gestures gracefully winning. Thus:

She dominates everywhere she finds herself, and she always makes the sort of impression which she wishes to make; she uses these advantages almost in the manner of God ... She is so penetrating as to make one tremble; the smallest pretension, the slightest affectation, a tone, a gesture which are not exactly natural are sensed and judged by her with the utmost rigour ... Men do not love us for the merit which they find in us, but for that which we find in them. Madame de Boufflers, in general, is more feared than liked; she knows it, and she does not deign to disarm her enemies by regards which would be too contrary to the truth and the

[27] Besenval, i. 211.

impetuosity of her character. She consoles herself by the justice which is done her by those who know her more particularly, and by the feelings which she inspires in them. She has much wit and gaiety, she is constant in her engagements, faithful to her friends, true, discreet, obliging, generous. In short, if she were less discerning, or if men were less ridiculous, they would find her perfect.[28]

A masculine tribute nevertheless confirmed that the malice of the then Duchess de Boufflers 'was vented in sallies; her heart was no whit implicated. She was incapable of doing anything spiteful, or even of making mischief ... She was frank and natural ... She combined sound judgement with that prompt understanding which in men we call grasp, without which there would be neither great painters, nor clever doctors nor great generals: a happy quality granting dispensation from reflection, indicating the best of all courses, and ... inspiring the confidence given to authority. It is recognizable in replies that are simple, concise and admirably exact.' Asked once which of two favourite authors, Molière and La Fontaine, was the greater, this lady replied that La Fontaine was 'more perfect in a less perfect kind'.[29]

A marked affinity was liable to attract the Count de Stainville to the Duchess de Boufflers, to indebt the future Duke de Choiseul to the future Maréchale de Luxembourg, noted for her way with younger people. He had what it took to measure up to her formidable calibre. Someone, one suspects, who did not was that Swiss gentleman of fortune, the Baron de Besenval, whose memoirs – doubtful indeed – supply most of the nasty stories about her: the duchess's 'advantages were tarnished by a lack of equanimity, a temper which led her at every instant to make embarrassing scenes, ... most often for no reason'.[30] Even if one discounts something from this denunciation of 'her spitefulness and slander', it is less easy merely to dismiss[31] the circumstantial accounts of her 'excessive libertinage'.

If the more persuasive Duke de Lévis judged that Besenval's own widespread gallantry 'was in bad taste,'[32] the duke himself ascribed to Madame de Boufflers 'a conduct more than light.'[33] According to the Prince de Montbarey 'fidelity in love was, for her, a word devoid of meaning.'[34] The Count de Tressan, one of the literary young

---

[28] Marquise du Deffand, 'Portrait de Madame la Duchesse de Boufflers depuis Madame la Maréchale de Luxembourg' in *Correspondance complète de la Marquise du Deffand*, ed. de Lescure (Paris, 1865: henceforth cited as Du Deffand/Lescure), ii. 760-1.
[29] Duc de Lévis, *Souvenirs et Portraits, 1780-1789*, pp. 55-60.
[30] Besenval, i. 203-4 for the following.
[31] As is encouraged by Hippolyte Buffenoir, *La Maréchale de Luxembourg, 1707-1787* (Paris, 1924), p. 14.
[32] Duc de Lévis, op. cit., p. 136.
[33] Ibid., p. 54.
[34] Prince de Montbarey, op. cit., i. 203.

aristocrats of that circle (he translated Ariosto), circulated a ditty beginning:

> Quand Boufflers parut à la cour,
> On crut voir la mère d'amour:
> Chacun s'empressait à lui plaire,
> Et chacun l'avait à son tour.[35]

For that she slapped Tressan hard. This patroness of the Count de Stainville, if imperfectly likeable, yet embodied that truly aristocratic spirit which confidently takes for granted its pre-eminence in rank, in privilege, and in performance; which easily combines the correct conduct of noble living with the gay insouciance of frank indulgence by expressing both naturally in terms of high-spirited superiority, gallant in both senses.

'The thing in the world which Madame de L[uxembourg] likes best', wrote Besenval, 'is supping away from her home, especially with men.'[36] At about the time that Stainville figured in her set it was said to have 'supped five or six times a week in the Rue Cadet, at the little house of M. de Luxembourg, where everything of the most exquisite which good fare could provide was united with the most outrageous licence. When the wine heated heads, and especially that of Madame de B[oufflers], who, in whatever place she supped, rarely left the table with composure, they used to begin to talk what was called *English*.' That meant calling a spade a spade, a tool a tool, most often leading to demonstrations.

Besenval's spicy stories of the duchess may or may not be exactly accurate. Certainly accurate is another glimpse from a very different source, dating from the beginning of Stainville's season of 1743 in Paris. The secret police, who kept an eye on high and low alike in the capital, reported on 17 August 1743: 'Mesdames de Boufflers and de Luxembourg made themselves much remarked at the Opera yesterday, because of the bursts of laughter and badinage, which lasted a very long time, with the men who successively came to see them in their box.'[37] That was all. The police had just noticed, and noted.

It is not a long shot to suppose that one, at least, of the topics of merriment in the opera box that evening related to the immediately preceding item in that police report. This concerned a Mademoiselle Rotisset, sister of the private secretary to the Minister of War, who had set Paris humming the week before by making her début as a

[35] Cited, Besenval, i. 202.
[36] Ibid., i. 211–15 for the following.
[37] 'Journal de police sous Louis XV (1742–1743)': Barbier, viii 342.

singer at the Opera under the name of Romainville. The virtue of
actresses was, with goodish reason, automatically assessed as easy, so
that the Count d'Argenson had had to endure 'many mordant
shafts'.[38] Society was in commotion but the girl's parents, petitioning
everybody up to the king to have her restrained, could not prevail
against her support by Maurepas, the minister in charge of Paris. He
was relishing the discomfiture of his colleague d'Argenson. And now,
on that evening of 16 August when the Duchess de Boufflers and her
party were laughing away at the Opera, at the centre of it all, the latest
was that d'Argenson's secretary had come to Paris and had barely
been restrained from killing his sister. She survived, however, with
nothing worse than a recurrent stomach-trouble, and continued to
sing under the protection of Maurepas.[39]

Opera and the stage were to be lasting interests for the Count de
Stainville. A German in Paris had recently remarked: 'The Players
are much more respected here than they are elsewhere, which makes
them insolent to the last Degree. The Nobility are fond of their
Company, and admit them to their Parties of Pleasure.'[40] This kind
of social relaxation in France extended, for the same observer, to
valets, 'not to be confounded in the Lump with the European
Lacqueys ... Such, I say, as are in the Service of some young
Noblemen, are commonly Equals and Companions with their
Masters. There are others who are the Darlings of the Fair Sex.'[41] If
Stainville was a liberal yet sharp employer, he was indeed forming
theatrical and literary, as well as aristocratic, associations.

III

In tracing the career of the later Duke de Choiseul it happens time
and again that the conduct and policies of this self-advertised
lightweight reveal, upon closer and more patient inspection, an inner
reality that is more secret, more serious, often more creditable. What
is surprising is that this analysis would appear to apply appreciably
even to his giddy youth.

One of the Count de Stainville's contemporaries, a year younger
than himself, was the Duke d'Agenais, married to the only daughter
of the valiant Count de Plélo and, till recently at all events, the

---

[38] Ibid., viii. 338.
[39] Cf. Mademoiselle Rotisset de Romainville to Count de Maurepas, 29 Oct. 1745: *The
Maurepas Papers* (Parke-Bernet Galleries Inc., sale catalogue no. 2092: New York, 1962), p. 108.
[40] Baron von Pöllnitz, op. cit., ii. 266.
[41] Ibid., p. 274.

accepted lover of the Marquise de la Tournelle, now royally preempted with the complicity of Agenais's uncle, the Duke de Richelieu. Emmanuel-Armand de Vignerot du Plessis de Richelieu, Duke d'Agenais, had campaigned in Bavaria under Harcourt and Saxe, and in Bohemian operations. If now a less lucky colonel than Stainville – Agenais was serving that year in Alsace under Marshal de Coigny – he was soon to become a particular friend, soon an inveterate enemy. It appears, however, that it may even have been earlier, as well as more lastingly, that Stainville became friends with Agenais's mother, the Duchess d'Aiguillon, then in her early forties.

Anne-Charlotte de Crussol-Florensac was maintaining the century-old tradition of feminine distinction in the dukedom of Aiguillon, created in 1638 in favour of a niece of the Cardinal de Richelieu. In 1731 it had, by a judgement of the Parliament of Paris, been revived from a lapse through female issue in favour of Anne-Charlotte's husband, Armand-Louis. He was supposed to have owed his dukedom to his love for the Duke de Bourbon's unappealing sister, the Princess de Conti. 'Indeed', remarked Duclos, 'they lived together in such a way as to edify ... [the] public, if they had been husband and wife.'[42] The Duchess d'Aiguillon, only intermittently jealous, is said to have teamed up with them both in order to produce in 1735 the *Recueil de pièces choisies, rassemblées par les soins du cosmopolite*, regarded as a piece of impious licence. Her literary claims were, however, more considerable.

One of the stronger suggestions of the authenticity of the 'Mémoires inédits' of the Duke de Choiseul is to be found in the convincing detail with which they explain his otherwise unknown friendship with the Duchess d'Aiguillon in the earlier and less political part of his life:

It was impossible to enjoy her society without feeling for her a kind of admiration mingled with attachment. She knew four languages. The wits of the century consulted her taste, profited from her intelligence and regarded her as an infallible guide in the way of the sciences. Rich in learning, she dispensed it with particular grace without for a moment ceasing to be the first of the women whose erudition arouses astonishment and render her almost the equal of the superior men who sought her approval and support.

Although she only had twenty-five thousand livres a year as her whole income, she constantly refused offers which could have increased it without her self-esteem having to blush for it. She found the means to give every Saturday a supper to which there were invited celebrities, notable foreigners, former ministers and ministers in office, men of letters. There all ranks were mixed. The only nuances detected were in the complexion of the wit. Since the pedantry of knowledge was never granted a

<hr />

[42] C. P. Duclos, 'Morceaux historiques et matériaux pour l'histoire' in *Œuvres complètes de Duclos* (Paris, n.d.), x. 258.

place in this agreeable circle, it would have been difficult for malice to disturb its calm by acerbity of discussion or offensive satires. As the free flow of easy conversation gave everyone a chance of unfolding the real meaning of what he had in mind, people there thought out loud. But, it must be admitted, the Jesuits were not much spared there. One often saw there Montesquieu, Hénault, Duclos and many other writers.[43]

Such were the circumstances in which the Count de Stainville became familiar with leading French men of letters of his time and in particular with those who were to record impressions of him in youth, Duclos and President Hénault. The presidential title from the parliament of Paris had become something of a decoration for literary Hénault of the French Academy, the epicurean son of a rich farmer-general, the urbane versifier who had known Racine, the friend of the Duke and Duchess de Luynes, leading through to the queen, whose household he came to superintend. In 1743 Hénault at fifty-eight was steeped in history, perhaps in that intellectual intensifcation liable to quicken an author upon the threshold of publishing a major work. The following year was to produce his *Abrégé chronologique de l'histoire de France,* whose fashionable popularity fell short of lasting renown. For the future Choiseul the President Hénault figured among those 'writers known for their talents and their works', although the duke was in time to grumble good-naturedly about 'the mischief-making of the President'.[44]

Choiseul came to write that to a special friend of Hénault as also of the then Duchess de Boufflers and of the future Duchess de Choiseul. This central figure was Marie de Vichy-Chamrond, Marquise du Deffand, about forty-five in 1743. This clever lady was thus two or three years older than her friend, or acquaintance, the Duchess d'Aiguillon, whom she rivalled in the rather more modest salon of her little house in the Rue de Beaune. Madame du Deffand, separated from her husband and formerly the mistress of Hénault, was a remorseless and gifted egotist who specialized in generosity and in friendships preserved for posterity in her correspondence and character-sketches. Of this charming woman it has been said[45] that her soul wrinkled before her face. Such was the authoress of a portrait, divergent from Choiseul's, of his admired duchess:

The Duchess d'Aiguillon has a pursed mouth, a crooked nose, a bold, foolish look, and despite that she is beautiful. The brilliance of her complexion triumphs over the

---

[43] Choiseul, 'Mémoires inédits', 3/34/17/117/2, and for the following.
[44] Duke de Choiseul to Marquise du Deffand, 13 May 1761: *Lettres autographes et documents historiques* (catalogue of Maison Jacques, Étienne et Noël Charavay, Paris, for Jan. 1950) no. 680, p. 10.
[45] Cf. Du Deffand/Lescure, i. xxxv.

irregularity of her features. Her figure is coarse, her bosom and arms are enormous. Yet she does not appear heavy or thick. In her, force takes the place of lightness. Her mind much resembles her form. It is, so to say, as badly designed as her face, and as dazzling. Abundance, activity, impetuosity are her predominant qualities. Without taste, grace or proportion, she astonishes, she surprises, but she neither pleases nor interests ... One could compare the Duchess d'Aiguillon to those statues made to figure aloft, which would appear monstrous upon the pavement. Neither her face nor her mind are to be seen or examined from too close. A certain distance is necessary to her beauty.[46]

If distance lent enchantment, Madame du Deffand specialized in close-ups. However, another and more considerable friend of the Duchess d'Aiguillon was scarcely more enthusiastic about her. Charles de Secondat, Baron de Montesquieu, wrote: 'She has intellect, but it is of the poorest kind; she has the pride of a pedant and all the faults of a lackey';[47] 'the duchess was the woman in France who lied most in a given time;'[48] 'she is fonder of her enemies than of her friends.'[49] Since the President de Montesquieu was one of the Duchess d'Aiguillon's closest friends one may wonder which particular grievance he was here avenging. Despite his disparagement, he was one of those intellectuals noticed by the then Stainville as submitting points to her judgement. Although the president's relations with the duchess had their ups and downs, including a lawsuit, when he was in Paris her home was almost his, and she was to be faithful to him to the end, there when he died.[50]

In 1743 Montesquieu was a shy and shortsighted Gascon of fifty-four, member of the French Academy, Fellow of the British Royal Society, already known throughout Europe, chiefly as the author of the *Letters persanes*, frivolous distillations of penetrating thought, and of the *Considérations sur les causes de la grandeur des Romains et de leur décadence*. These considerations of ranging scope had in 1734 illuminated historical studies, not least in their methodological distinction between ultimate and proximate causes. Thence followed the preparation of the masterpiece upon which Montesquieu was at that time engaged, thrusting out far beyond Hénault. Other of Montesquieu's earlier writings were also contributing towards what was to emerge as *L'Esprit des lois*. To this end he was in 1743 completing the revision of one of them, the *Considérations sur les richesses d'Espagne*, originally titled *De la véritable cause de la décadence de l'Espagne*: in that variation lay the riddle.

[46] Marquise du Deffand, 'Portrait de Madame la Duchesse d'Aiguillon': ibid., ii. 741–2.
[47] President de Montesquieu, 'Pensées' no. 1370 in *Œuvres complètes de Montesquieu*, ed. André Masson (Paris, 1950 f.), ii. 407.
[48] Ibid., no. 1393, ii. 412.
[49] Ibid., no. 1394.
[50] Cf. Robert Shackleton, *Montesquieu* (Oxford, 1961), p. 184.

If the future Duke de Choiseul was in time to ruminate upon the *Esprit des lois* and its exaltation of the British constitution, the then Count de Stainville was soon to be particularly concerned with matters Spanish and also to develop an interest in that new field of political economy which Montesquieu broached in his Spanish considerations. In the salon, too, of the Duchess d'Aiguillon the young count may well have discussed contemporary politics with the author who regretted that he had not secured a position in the French foreign ministry since in that case 'I should have thwarted the projects of that fool of a Belle-Isle, and I should thereby have rendered the greatest service that a citizen could render his country'.[51]

Montesquieu and young Stainville were in the same circle not only in respect of the Duchess d'Aiguillon. The president had a link with court through Stainville's early patroness, Mademoiselle de Charolais, with whom Montesquieu had been staying in the previous year in the Palais de Madrid. Also, Montesquieu was by common repute the lover of that Marquise de Mirepoix whose marriage had intrigued the Count de Stainville when in Vienna: Montesquieu described her with poetic partiality as, '*Naïve, simple, naturelle, et timide sans embarras*';[52] in another's eyes she possessed 'warmth without enthusiasm, calm without insipidity'.[53] Montesquieu, too, was probably upon friendly terms already, as he certainly was a few years later, with the count's father, the Marquis de Stainville.

Two of Montesquieu's other friends were to figure as specially close ones of the Count de Stainville, namely the admired Prince de Beauvau and the captivating Duchess de Chaulnes. For Montesquieu, likely for Stainville also, the aristocratic salon of the literary Duchess d'Aiguillon led through to others, not only those of the Marquise du Deffand and the Duchess de Boufflers but, for instance, that of the clan of Brancas. Its elder branch was then represented by the worthy Marquis de Brancas, Marshal of France, and its youthful verve by the salon featuring his daughter of twenty-seven, the already widowed Countess de Rochefort, and her pretty sister-in-law, the Countess de Forcalquier. This rich relict of the Marquis d'Antin had been remarried for a year now to the Countess de Rochefort's elder brother, the delicate, caustically intelligent Count de Forcalquier. That shimmering salon specialized in performing his comedies, the 'charming trifles of M. de Forcalquier,'[54] as Montesquieu called them. They were scarcely tracts for marital fidelity even though

---

[51] President de Montesquieu, 'Pensées' no. 1466: *u.s.*, ii. 422.
[52] President de Montesquieu, *Œuvres complètes de Montesquieu* (ed. cit.), vol. i, 'Vers' p. 608 *bis*.
[53] Duc de Lévis, op. cit., pp. 62-3.
[54] President de Montesquieu to Duclos, Bordeaux, 15 Aug. 1748: op. cit., iii. 1125.

Forcalquier was reputedly religious. One of them was, already, a take-off of rosicrucians; another was significantly called *Les Blasés*, a word which Forcalquier helped to introduce in its modern meaning.

In addition to the Brancas team the casts featured the Marquise de Mirepoix in coquettish parts, the handsome young Duke de Nivernais who played the male lead of Lindor in *Les Blasés*, the Duke de Duras, the Marquis de Gontaut, and Duclos always as the valet. That abrasive character, who lived for a time in the Hôtel de Brancas, so condescended since he had fallen for the Countess de Forcalquier. But then nearly everybody seemed half in love with somebody else, which was half the fun of it. Every one of those actors was or was to be a particular friend or acquaintance of the Count de Stainville, though he himself is not mentioned among the casts any more than another stage-struck acquaintance of Montesquieu, the pleasure-loving, opera-going Abbé de Bernis. Bernis was to figure with Stainville not only politically but, for instance, in the latter's close friendship with the Duke de Nivernais, an aristocrat who was notably a gentleman, two years older than the future Choiseul with whom he has very likely overlapped at Louis le Grand. The name of Lindor, incidentally, was to echo in some association with Choiseul.

Nivernais was said to have a tenderness for one of the most beautiful of the spectators, the easy-virtued Duchess de la Vallière, who was also to belong to Stainville's set. Another of the audience at the Hôtel de Brancas was Nivernais's brother-in-law, Maurepas, himself the leader of a coterie known as the Académie de ces Messieurs. These gay dilettanti may well have included young Stainville who, in society a few years later, was to associate himself more particularly with the Count de Maurepas. To complete the circle, that alert minister was an especial friend of the Duchess d'Aiguillon, who in turn figured in another aspect of the Brancas set, provided by an elderly cousin from the junior and more distinguished branch in the person of Marie-Angélique Fremyn de Moras, Duchess de Brancas.

A sprightly sixty-seven in 1743, the Duchess de Brancas had just married off her son, the Duke de Lauraguais, to the interesting Mademoiselle de Montcarvel, Diane-Adélaïde de Mailly, sister to the royal stud. It is in the salon of the Duchess de Brancas that one glimpses Montesquieu and the Duchess d'Aiguillon concerting against Voltaire and the Marquise du Châtelet over the social differentiation between Paris and Versailles. This darting debate was surprisingly clinched by an elderly bore called the Marquis de Flamarens: noting the gradual assimilation between capital and court, he recalled that in his youth "'they were not inhabited by the same people ... [For courtiers] Versailles was their country: they really were foreigners in Paris." At this Madame d'Aiguillon could not restrain herself and started calling out at us: "He is right, he is right."[55] Such was the subtly shifting society which the Count de Stainville was entering through the salons of the aristocracy turning to literature at a high point of European civilization.

The Stainvilles have already figured as the neighbours of Madame du Châtelet back in the Barrois and were well enough known to Voltaire, as through Madame de Graffigny, though that lady was at a low level just then and had quarrelled with Madame du Châtelet. A closer link, perhaps, between Voltaire and the Count de Stainville lay through a Praslin cousin, César-Gabriel, Count de Choiseul-Chevigny, seven years older than Stainville, and richer, in the cavalry. The Count de Choiseul, a school-chum of Nivernais, had seen service in the War of the Polish Succession as also in the Austrian one in the army of Maillebois and on the staff of the French cavalry in Bohemia; promoted brigadier early in that year of 1743, he was campaigning in Alsace under Noailles, was to proceed next upon the same campaign as Stainville and, ultimately, to be closely associated with him politically as the Duke de Praslin. The then Count de Choiseul was a neighbour and intimate friend of the special friends of Voltaire, the theatrical Count d'Argental and his wife. Voltaire had written to them both that April from Passy that he was there 'taking the waters, which are not doing me much good, and from time to time working upon some canto of *Jeanne la pucelle* to amuse you and divert Mr. de Choiseul when he has indigestion'.[56]

Not in literature alone was the Count de Stainville liable to be honed in the salon of the Duchess d'Aiguillon. He particularly referred to her scientific attainments, which she worked up through her friendship with the celebrated Maupertuis, flattener of the earth. This early champion of Newton in France and instructor of Voltaire in this field was quite the scientist in vogue since his expedition of 1736–7 to the Arctic Circle under the ministerial impulsion of Maurepas. In the circle now of the Duchess d'Aiguillon, Maupertuis was in that year of 1743 assisted into the French Academy by Montesquieu, more successful than Richelieu and Madame du Châtelet had just been in similarly trying to promote Voltaire's perky

[55] Duchesse de Brancas, *Mémoires de la D.sse de Brancas*, ed. Eugene Asse (Paris, 1890), pp. 20–1.

[56] Voltaire to Count and Countess d'Argental, Passy, 16 Apr. 1743: *Voltaire's Correspondence*, ed. Theodore Besterman (Geneva, 1953 f.), xii. 227. (The ascription of this reference to the then Count de Stainville – cf. ibid., xxxix. 222 – would seem less plausible than one to the Count de Choiseul.)

pretension to succeed Fleury there. Madame du Châtelet was not the only aristocratic and scientific bluestocking in that remarkable society. The Duchess d'Aiguillon took to geometry and one need not be too surprised, perhaps, to find Stephen de Stainville some years later plunging into geometrical disputation.

The literary and, seemingly, mathematical interests of the Count de Stainville in youth were already set off by a love of pictures. He was to recall in a letter of 1749 to the Duke de Nivernais, with whom he corresponded particularly about art:

One does not always act from reason and I have perhaps departed from it as often as anybody. I admit for example that I scarcely followed it when I bought my Gerard Dous, but I had been tempted, and you would admit that one is more tempted by pictures that one sees than by those which one does not. I was [then] in better health, I was seven or eight years younger, my desires were more impetuous ... Do you know that I still owe a part of their price? ... It is not just presently that I know and admit that I did a silly thing in buying my Gerard Dous.[57]

Thus the Count de Stainville was already buying pictures in the early seventeen-forties,[58] long before he could really afford them, thanks to what he termed 'the unhappy facility of buying without paying'.[59] It was a facility of which he was to make full use in life.

It would also appear that Stainville was already pursuing his inclination towards Dutch and Flemish art, naturalistic, humanistic, then comparatively modern, and cheap. During the seventeenth century French collectors had concentrated upon Italian painting in the classic taste of Louis XIV himself. In this sphere as in others the Regent Orleans had heralded change. Parisian dealers drew increasingly upon those in Brussels and Amsterdam so that by about 1740 the italophile President de Brosses was already rather in the rearguard in disparaging as trivial the genre of the Dutch and Flemish schools. A few years later the dealer Gersaint wrote in the introduction to a Parisian sale-catalogue that 'the Flemish school ... is much in fashion here and is universally liked'.[60] While the enthusiasms of the Count

---

[57] Count de Stainville to Duke de Nivernais, 17 Nov. 1749: W. N. A., docket V/1, fo. 15.

[58] Such is the more certain answer which can now be given to the question posed by Émile Dacier in 'La Curiosité au XVIIIᵉ siècle: Choiseul collectionneur' in the *Gazette des beaux-arts*, 6th period, xxxvi (1949), 52: 'A quelle époque fit-il [Choiseul] ses premières armes de collectionneur?' Dacier proceeded to suggest that Choiseul's first purchases of pictures, or at least of old masters as opposed to works by living artists, were not earlier than 1758. F.J.B. Watson in *The Choiseul Box* (London, 1963) notices (p. 8) that 'between 1750 and 1770 he [Choiseul] was an important buyer at all the main Parisian art-sales' but refers (p. 16) to the seventeen-forties as a period 'before he began to collect'.

[59] Count de Stainville to Duke de Nivernais, 17 Nov. 1749: *u.s.*

[60] Gersaint, sale-catalogue of Quentin de l'Orangère collection, 1744: cited, F. J. B. Watson, op. cit., p. 7.

de Stainville were genuine enough they were also usually, as now already, modish.

If Stephen de Stainville's early keenness as a collector is now established, the particular grounds for his rueful assessment of his Gerard Dous remain unclear. While Stainville's taste was discriminating it hardly seems likely that he tired in general, certainly anything like so early as 1750, of the somewhat repetitive charms of Dou's genre of *nisstuk* or artistic snapshot of a domestic scene through an open window or door. Prize exhibits in Stainville's subsequent collection were to be two famous Dous, 'The Sick Woman' and 'The Poulterer's Shop',[61] the latter described by a subsequent owner, Beckford, as 'the famous, stupendous and purest Dou ... the first Flemish painting in the world.'[62] There is nothing to show that these were the Dous which Stainville bought so early. He came to own a number of works by this pupil of Rembrandt, including the 'Girl Cutting Onions'.[63] Stainville may have grown to regret his early purchase of Dous for having paid too much for them at a time when he could ill afford it; or, quite as likely since he was not much given to financial regrets, he may later have judged that those particular pictures did not measure up to the exacting standards which he developed. He was to write to Nivernais in the same letter: 'I would rather have fewer pictures and ones which are distinguished. You know my taste in this, and I know that I would rather buy a fine picture for a hundred louis than two mediocre ones.'[64]

The future Choiseul regularly rejected the subordinate, whether in art or in diplomacy as in the sounding proposed to him in that year of 1743.

The Count de Stainville developed a critical appreciation not only of painting but also, it now appears, of music. He was himself, like Frederick the Great, to be something of a flautist and his musical interests were stimulated by those in the theatre and the opera. Some years later at all events he was on terms of more than merely social acquaintance with leading French composers of his time such as Mondonville and, notably, Rameau. From that period dates a piece of Stainville's musical criticism which may already serve to illustrate the style that he developed. He wrote of the rehearsal, which he attended, of an opera by Rameau:

The fifth act is musically terrible and cannot pass as it is. Everybody thought too that the words of it were not good ... It has always seemed to me mediocre, but we had

---

[61] Now respectively in the Hermitage at Leningrad and the National Gallery in London.
[62] Cited, ibid., p. 10.
[63] Now in the collection of Queen Elizabeth II.
[64] Count de Stainville to Duke de Nivernais, 17 Nov. 1749: *u.s.*

imagined that it would lend itself to the music and would favour the musician. We have experienced just the contrary. This act is full of several successive noises without any intervals. The music cannot manage to distinguish these different noises in a sufficiently striking way. There is the noise of a fight, then a victory, and then a defeat and one finishes up with a tempest. It is a terrible and continual din. One is deafened without being moved, and you know that of all kinds of monotony that of noise is the most grievous.[65]

The keen involvement of the Count de Stainville in youth in the artistic and literary currents of his time balances the traditional picture of him as given over to womanizing. Though women of course are part of pleasure and that early friend of the sexual Duchess de Boufflers was not one to pretend otherwise. Stainville's known mistresses were almost all persons of notable intelligence, that quality which he and the society of his time particularly prized. A generation later he was to write to his sister: 'The fact is that when one is stupid one is neither a good soldier, nor a good politician, nor a good friend, nor a good lover – one cannot be anything at all.'[66] In his youth he exemplified the converse. One of those with whom his name was to be tenderly linked was the intellectual Duchess de Chaulnes, the captivating friend of Montesquieu, the friend of that Duchess d'Aiguillon from whom, stressed the then Stainville, young men had much to learn.

IV

The reservations which the older friends of the Duchess d'Aiguillon entered against her partly reflected, one feels, a personality which stood out oddly from the polished regularities of the age of reason. 'I said of Madame d'Aiguillon', recalled Montesquieu, 'that she was now a dream, now a delirium.'[67] Pronounced Madame du Deffand:

Everything that she says comes from a disordered imagination. She is sometimes a prophet who is moved by a demon, who neither foresees nor chooses what he will say: there are several noisy instruments from which no harmony results. It is a play loaded with machinery and decorations, in which there are some wonderful touches without sequence or order, admired in the pit but hissed by the boxes... Like the last trump she is made to waken the dead. It is the impotent who should love her, the deaf who should listen to her.[68]

[65] Count de Stainville to Duke de Nivernais, 17 May 1751: ibid., fo. 66: cf. p. 897 below.
[66] Duke de Choiseul to Duchess de Gramont, Chanteloup, 15 Mar. 1774: Gaston Maugras, *La disgrace du duc et de la duchesse de Choiseul* (Paris, 1903), p. 290.
[67] President de Montesquieu, 'Pensées' no. 1406 in *Œuvres complètes de Montesquieu* (ed. cit.), ii. 413.
[68] Marquise du Deffand, 'Portrait de Madame la Duchesse d'Aiguillon': Du Deffand/Lescure, ii. 742.

The Count de Stainville was neither impotent nor deaf. But he admired and listened to 'the old duchess',[69] of whom he wrote:

'One of the most laudable cares of the Duchess d'Aiguillon, when she wished well to a young man starting out in the world, was to forearm him against the false affectations (*simagrées*) and gossip at court; to warn him that, among certain people of high degree, modesty was taken there at its word and assimilated to inferiority, and a noble assurance to a consciousness of one's own intrinsic value.

... I have often heard her say: Youth must have amusement so that its features and manners contract the sunny expression of delicate pleasure. The face of happiness always carries influence. It imposes itself. There is no momentary action which does not lay a stone towards the edifice of our future. To frequent one's relations is good, one's friends, still better. The former have a merely inherited value, the latter that of distinction by merit. The protocol of ceremonial visits implies time to waste. It is the pastime of idle people. Not to be fond of the sterility of empty chatter, of prattle which ought to be called cackle, tacitly proclaims a mind capable of demonstration and penetration ... Those who possess the art of appositely striking the chords of another's fancy are the most adroit practitioners of the art of pleasing. To fall silent before people are tired of listening to us preserves our right to begin talking again with the same precaution. What is the enemy? Moral indigestion produced by monotony of situations.

In the 'sallies of this truly philosophic woman' long ago one comes closest, almost, to the core of Choiseul. Her maxims, which he so vividly recalled, of noble assurance, imposing happiness and the subtle art of pleasing were precisely the ingredients of his exceptional charm and success. Originally, at all events, his insouciant superiority may have been less effortless than appeared both then and since. Choiseul was a sensitive, emotional man with some of the characteristics, almost, of a shy one. Too clever to be self-important, he was considerate of the feelings of others, relating his own to theirs, while flattery of himself tended to render this flatterer ill at ease. One or two subtle critics have indeed wondered long since how far Choiseul's happy and open temper was natural or the acquired mask of a spirit of secretive depths, shadowed, presenting to history something closed and hitherto inaccessible.[70]

The spirit of each person is indeed manifold. Perhaps, though, there were inner distances which Stephen de Choiseul-Stainville needed to span in that French high society whereof a foreign contemporary was to observe: 'Perhaps there is no country where pride of birth is pushed so far as it is here. Since most of the great lords are of fairly recent date or are somehow connected with finance, those who are not in this case derive from it an astonishing vanity.'[71]

[69] Choiseul, 'Mémoires inédits', 3/34/17/117/1 f. for the following.
[70] Cf. Edmond and Jules de Goncourt, *Madame de Pompadour* (new ed., Paris, 1896), pp. 318-19.
[71] Kaunitz/Mémoire, p. 449.

The social span of the Duchess d'Aiguillon was to earn her the title, recalled by the then Count de Stainville, of 'the living journal of the court, the town, the Academy and the provinces. Like the Duchess of Burgundy, the mother of Louis XV, she was often heard to repeat that she never moved without being accompanied by all her friends, living and dead.'[72]

Such was the person who would warn a young man of the court of Louis XV in words recalled by Stainville:

This place, she would tell him, is the vain land of the wind (*le pays du vent*). There blow there waterspouts of ambition, jealousy and pride. Illusions abound there. By daylight everything takes on an air of harmony. People there know to a marvel how to hate politely and to mint in every mansion secret libels against the neighbouring one ... To hear us talk in private one would think us all to be of the race of Jupiter, so high do our pretensions reach. Chérin[73] never fails to prove their legitimacy, whatever one's origins. This mania for extolling our own birth is inspired in us by experience showing that the greater that one makes oneself the less risk one runs of being crushed. Illusions agreed upon in guise of realities are a kind of power with which sharper people may long secure superiority of consideration over the simple ones. Such is the irresistible influence of the reign of prejudices. They are criticized but they rule, and rule till what is too full finally spills over. Perhaps you will be present at the movement which sooner or later will change the face of things among us. If I am still alive at the time of this change, which will perhaps be a revolution, I shall rejoice at it. For frankly I care little for the baubles of the peerage, but much that objects should resume their true place. Reason does not cease to advise. If they would listen to it, everything would go better.

One begins to see why contemporaries found the Duchess d'Aiguillon an uncomfortable prophetess, if not crazy. But the future Duke de Choiseul did not. Under the name of this statesman of the old regime figured this accurate and revolutionary prediction of the shape of things to come. Here as elsewhere Choiseul supplied an interior critique, often neglected, of the old regime.

Such were the counsels to youth which the Duke de Choiseul was to recall, although one cannot ascribe them precisely to that year of 1743. There are suggestions of a rather later date for, for instance, so philosophic an estimate of the baubles of the peerage by a woman who, when her husband had been elevated to a dukedom, was unkindly said to have been so excited that she contracted smallpox. In any case, for the Count de Stainville then the future of immediate concern was not so much social revolution in a new age as military operations in a new theatre.

---

[72] Choiseul, 'Mémoires inédits', *u.s.*, and for the following.
[73] Bernard Chérin became the leading genealogist at the French court.

PART III

COMMANDING
1744-1748

CHAPTER I

ALPINE

I

WITH the approach of the new year of 1744 Italy became a fresh focus for French campaigning, for the Count de Stainville. On Don Philip's front in Savoy during the preceding summer Captain-General de Las Minas, building up his depleted army to 30,000, had evaded orders from the Queen of Spain to commence active operations, only to plunge into them in late September. The Spanish army marched out from Briançon for the Varaita valley upon an Alpine excursion into Piedmont. Also participating was a small French auxiliary corps under the Count de Marcieu, Governor of Dauphiny, and Chevert, who had advised against the offensive. Sure enough, after the Spanish capture of the half-ruined castle of Castello di Ponte in Don Philip's baptism of fire on 7 October 1743, King Charles in that late season of incipient snowfall lost no time in bundling the enemy back across the frontier with loss of baggage including Don Philip's plate, politely returned to him, and, non-returnable, of some two hundred French lives, five hundred Spanish, upon a 'terrible march'.[1]

This superficially stupid offensive could, once again in eighteenth-century warfare, have had a deeper point in diplomacy. The French came to consider that the Spaniards had launched out in order to activate Franco-Spanish co-operation in reply to the Treaty of Worms by committing France to intervention with larger forces for the Italian campaigning of the following year. Certainly that was what came to pass, though the headstrong offensive of Captain-General de Las Minas cost the Spaniards from the outset the confidence of their French comrades in arms.

Some ten days after the termination of this inglorious introduction to Franco-Spanish military co-operation in that war, France formally pledged herself to the Second Family Compact, to uphold the interests of ambitious Spain to such an extent as to support, here again, the future Choiseul's criticism of French foreign policy during the War of the Austrian Succession for its quixotic failure to look, above all, to its own national advantage in espousing the cause of

---

[1] Captain-General de Las Minas, 13 Oct. 1743: Correspondence of Las Minas, cited, *Erbfolge-Krieg*, viii. 406, n. 1.

others. But French feeling was running high in the aftermath of Worms and the influential Maurepas, in particular, was on intimate terms – rather too intimate – with the Prince of Campoflorido, Spanish ambassador to France. Nor was it, maybe, coincidental that four days before the signature on 25 October 1743 of the Treaty of Fontainebleau the Marquise de la Tournelle had been created Duchess de Châteauroux with more generous and distinguished provision than the famous mistresses of Henry IV or Louis XIV had enjoyed. It was said that she, like her crony Richelieu, came to touch large sums from Spanish sources. So nothing came of desultory peace-feelers put out that winter towards the Marquis de Stainville by specialists in that line, Don Louis d'Acunha and the Cardinal de Tencin. The French government had decided that in 1744 it would, for the first time in that war, intervene in substantial support of Spanish arms in the Italian theatre.

The Italian theatre of war was one of four in the massive master-plan for French campaigning evolved at Versailles in reply to Carteret's ambitious diplomacy upon the continent. The war was spreading with a vengeance into its second and more stubborn phase.

In the German theatre, with French forces of intervention thrown back upon the Alsatian borders of the Rhine, the Emperor Charles VII, abased, yet held the political key. Reciprocal need tied him to Louis XV, who was under no illusions, remarking that Charles was 'surrounded by people who ... would wish to see us a hundred feet below ground'.[2] The emperor was playing the current gambit of German princes, threatening ugly consequences unless France stepped up her subsidies: likewise Frederick the Great who wanted French 'corruptions' to German princelings channelled through himself, as he propounded to Valory almost in caricature of Prussian diplomacy in a 'Plan which the French should follow, if they are sensible'.

Distrusted Prussia, however, was in danger of being left out in the cold, especially since Austria concluded a defensive alliance with Saxony on 20 December 1743. This ominous pact was of prime importance in German affairs; in Italian ones it significantly embodied Austrian renunciation of Naples, now under a Saxon queen. Far from wholly congenial to Frederick the Great, moreover, was the design of Chavigny, back from Portugal, to win round Bavaria and others. His aim, more practical than the earlier ambitions of Belle-Isle, was a revival in some sort of the Rheinbund, the famous league whereby Mazarin had consecrated French ascendancy over

---

[2] King Louis XV to Marshal de Noailles, Versailles, 13 July 1743: Rousset, i. 166.

the Rhineland after the Peace of Westphalia. Prussia and France were henceforth jockeying for position.

By the beginning of 1744 the pace with Prussia was quickening. Frederick the Great sent to Versailles a special envoy, his dashing favourite, the gossiping Count de Rottembourg (Rothenburg). The frenchified Rottembourg, cynically coached by Frederick, began by excluding all the French ministers with departmental responsibilities, turning rather to another gay favourite, the Duke de Richelieu, who afforded him privileged access to the king via the Duchess de Châteauroux. Rottembourg went to work through them and through Noailles and Tencin. In this congenial atmosphere Rottembourg exceeded his instructions by presenting a memorandum of Prussian desiderata for a renewed alliance with France. 'My dear Rottembourg,' wrote Frederick, 'you have been dazzled by the Court of Versailles ... Take a white powder every morning and do not push anything. One does not make up alliances like parties of pleasure.'[3]

One of Frederick's main concerns, lest France might slip out of hostilities as convenient if not formally at war, was already being met. France at long last declared war on England on 15 March 1744, on Austria on 26 April. The French court was mainly accommodating, too, in other respects but Frederick maintained that he could not campaign before August; apart from military preparations he needed to complete precautions with Sweden and Russia. Throughout that winter the King of Prussia had been safeguarding his rear to north and east in preparation for his next stroke to the south.

The hand of the fair, and ambitious, Princess Ulrike of Prussia was pledged not to Voltaire but to Prince Adolphus Frederick of Holstein-Gottorp. This nephew of the Empress Elizabeth of Russia had become Crown Prince of Sweden in accordance with the Peace of Abo, imposed by Russia upon Sweden on 7 August 1743 in conclusion of the unlucky hostilities which the Swedish Hats had initiated under Belle-Isle's impulsion. Russia had now reinforced the heavy terms of the Peace of Nystädt, and also took a slice of Finland. The betrothal of Princess Ulrike was thus for Frederick a neat reinsurance and rapprochement with both sides in the recent war in the north.

At the time of the Peace of Abo, which might have furthered the Austro-British orientation favoured by the powerful brothers Bestuchev, the Franco-Prussian faction at St Petersburg struck against their opponents by unearthing an alleged conspiracy for the restoration of the little Ivan VI. There was staged one of those sensational but obscure political trials of alleged plotters which have

---

[3] King Frederick II to Count de Rottembourg, Berlin, 30 Mar. 1744: *Politische Correspondenz*, iii. 73.

been a recurrent feature of Russian politics. A wretched catspaw
called Lapuchin was tortured before Elizabeth herself, and efforts
were made to incriminate the Bestuchevs and the Marquis Botta, the
Austrian minister recently transferred from Saint Petersburg to
Berlin.

Frederick the Great commented in glee: 'One must take the ball
upon the bounce.'[4] The Empress Elizabeth was more or less bounced
into granting her accesssion and guarantee to the Treaty of Breslau,
her agreement to Frederick's promotion of another marriage,
personally as well as politically related to the Swedish one. A niece of
the new Crown Prince of Sweden, Princess Sophia of Anhalt–Zerbst,
was now betrothed to another nephew of Elizabeth, her heir, Peter of
Holstein–Gottorp. The princess was a timid little thing, not yet
fifteen and under the thumb of her mother. At her marriage this
princess took the echoing name of Catharine, one day to be great in
rivalry to Frederick himself. As yet she was but a pawn like Botta,
whom Frederick expelled from Berlin on the strength, or weakness,
of the Russian accusations of complicity in the alleged conspiracy of
Lapuchin. Diplomatically such an expulsion was then a most serious
step. Austro-Prussian relations were tensely strained against this
Russian background.

The continent of Europe watched and, largely, waited upon the
King of Prussia. The French Army of Alsace under Marshal de
Coigny became for the time being an army of observation. Although
the Marshal de Noailles favoured Rhineland campaigning, he was
designated to lead out against Flanders in 1744. The high days and
designs of the Roi Soleil were seemingly revived. This year, it was
decided, the King of France in person would ride forth to inspire his
greatest army in renewed attack upon those Austrian Netherlands
which were pre-eminently the British place of arms upon the
continent. Nor was this, even, the sum of French strategy in Europe
for that year. It designated yet a fourth theatre, most secret and most
daring. To Italy, Germany, and Flanders the government at
Versailles added nothing less than England.

II

To suppose that all great designs must emanate from great men is too
much like imagining that all such designs must succeed. It was
remarked by the Marquis de Stainville, doing his imperfect best to
probe French strategic aims:

[4] King Frederick II to Count Podewils, Potsdam, 21 Aug. 1743: ibid., ii. 408.

For the execution of these fine plans there would need to be greater concert in the French ministry. But the ministers of state are occupied only in destroying one another. The Minister of Finance would be very happy for the naval operations to fail, because he does not like the Minister of Marine. He is even more decidedly against the one for war, and they all come together again only in order to exclude from a premiership the Cardinal Tencin, the Marshal de Noailles and the Marshal de Belle-Isle. That is their main occupation.[5]

The ascendancy and acumen of the Count de Maurepas were reflected now in a boldly amphibious strategy. At either extremity of the continental battlefront of France there were to be naval extensions, southward from Toulon in relation to the Italian theatre and northward from Dunkirk in relation to that of Flanders. In the northern sphere the concentration against the Austrian Netherlands was to mask an invasion of the British Isles. This deep project was not imparted to all the royal council but in the summer of 1743 Louis XV had himself briefed a sporting James Butler to spy out in England in the Jacobite interest.

That autumn, with France not yet formally at war with England, Maurepas and his henchman Amelot had been secretly concerting with Jacobite agents, Lord Sempill and Macgregor of Balhaldy. Sempill promoted a bold project for a midwinter invasion of England in the worst and most unlikely season without giving her warning of a French declaration of war, without attracting attention by assembling a powerful fleet, without even running the gauntlet of the English Channel, but nipping in from behind, attacking from the east. A French expeditionary corps of ten thousand picked troops was to be concentrated in stealth around Dunkirk, under cover of winter-quarters upon the front in Flanders. In the port, which the French had been remilitarizing in contravention of the Treaty of Utrecht, miscellaneous transports, fishing smacks, and small craft were casually to converge. On the appointed day the troops would pile in with their gear and set sail if possible in the early darkness of the winter evening, under the escort of a mere couple of frigates or so. The invaders would necessarily be travelling light, planning to live off the country and round up horses in thinly garrisoned England. If all went well they should be able to slip across in a matter of twelve hours so that the following dawn should find them swooping upon the selected point of French attack. This was focused upon the inconspicuous coast of Essex, up the estuary of the Blackwater, against the sleepy little town of Maldon, singled out, not for the first or last time, in the invading plans of England's enemies.

[5] Marquis de Stainville to Grand Duke Francis II, Paris, 1 Feb. 1744: Esteri del Granducato di Toscana, vol. 2295/1286, fo. 360.

Essex supposedly nurtured Jacobites and three of her members of parliament were privy to the plan. The determinant, however, was strategic. By landing at Maldon the French would turn the Kentish bulge and the Thames, to stand at the start of march a bare forty miles from London, the capital objective of this sudden stroke of war. They would go straight for London, advancing from the least expected and most advantageous quarter, from the north. Ten thousand would be a sufficient strength, it was reckoned, to enable the invaders to interpose themselves against any English regiments which might be switched from the Midlands and the north to relieve the capital. Then, while the threat to London magnetized the English forces inwards, popular uprisings would, it was hopefully expected, be fomented in their rear in the outlying regions of Jacobite sympathy, in the west country, said to be disaffected by economic depression, in Wales and in the northern counties backing on to Scotland, where a further landing and rebellion were projected to swell the turmoil in the British Isles. At the centre the French swoop on London would, it was further anticipated, send the stock-exchange crashing so that a financial panic would stoke the military into chaos for the British government. And if once London fell the whole situation of Great Britain might open up towards 1688 in reverse.

The captain of war selected to command this venture of almost breathtaking possibilities was Lieutenant-General Count Maurice de Saxe. He was a protestant and proven at Prague in audacious unorthodoxy. Indeed he is said to have now slipped over to England on personal reconnaissance.

The French ministers appreciated the high risk. Saxe's instructions envisaged the possibility that, even if his expedition made England, he might have to capitulate there. It was coolly reckoned though at Versailles that the very attempt would so have shaken the British government that it would tend to bottle up in England troops which it would otherwise have sent to the Netherlands to oppose the main campaign by the Marshal de Noailles. The boldness of the fling against England was closely reasoned.

The plan ran into complication and delay. Unescorted invasion seemed after all too risky. On 15 November 1743 orders were issued for the concentration not only of transports and escort-vessels at Dunkirk but also of a covering squadron which was to come sailing round from Brest under the command of an ancient veteran, the Count de Roquefeuil, lieutenant-general of the naval armies in the significant French nomenclature of that date. It took precious time to make ready his twenty-two ships of the line. The delaying Jacobites imposed another important modification. Instead of making for

Maldon the French armada would, more boldly still, strike up the Thames itself, if possible right up to Blackwall by the East India Docks. Saxe, concentrating his expeditionary force around Dunkirk, studied the operations of de Ruyter in his famous sweep of the Thames. Then the Young Pretender surreptitiously left Rome and in the latter half of January 1744 landed at Antibes in defiance of the French treaty-obligation not to harbour Stuart princes. British agents were alerted but his destination and that of Roquefeuil remained obscure.

While uncertainty prevailed, the British Admiralty had indeed, already on 6 January 1744 (26 December 1743 in the old style of England), ordered a hot press in accordance with their rough and ready method of bringing crews up to complement. At one o'clock on the afternoon of 6 February 1744 Captain Brodrick, out scouting in little *Phoenix*, sighted the whole French fleet from Brest sailing out from Broad Sound. Storm-tossed for days in beating up the Channel, the Count de Roquefeuil on 28 February, at about the level of what he termed the Île de Huyt (Isle of Wight), detached four vessels under another senior sailor called de Barrailh to sail ahead to Dunkirk and provide the close support for Saxe's invading squadron. De Barrailh took a politely dim view of the 'many embarrassing cares'[6] of this hardy mission and caused Saxe to complain that the squadron 'is pitiably equipped. The sailors which constitute it are more fit to drive a cart than to navigate.'[7]

Nevertheless Saxe and his staff, which included the Count de Stainville's old commander from the Bohemian campaign, Lieutenant-General du Chayla, lost no time in embarking their expeditionary force. They were assisted on 4 March by a temporary clearing in the thick weather. The troops went ferrying out in fishing smacks and lighters to the transports fitted out by the commandant of the port, Bart, son of the celebrated Jean Bart. He had riding at anchor thirty-eight vessels ranging from 70 to 400 tons, such as Captain de la Vigne Buisson's *Comtesse-de-la-Rivière* from Saint-Malo, 250 tons all victualled up, or Captain Billeveld's local *Hareng-Couronné* of 110 tons, a blue flag at the stern. The Crowned Herring, the Goldfish, the Renown of Lorient, the Queen of the Angels – such were the ships of the troops against England.

---

[6] De Barrailh to Count de Maurepas, aboard *Dauphin-Royal*, six leagues south-west of the Lizard, 26 Feb. 1744: cited, J. Colin, *Louis XV et les Jacobites* (Paris, 1901), p. 93. (Colin's basic study has been updated and in some respects amended by Eveline Cruickshanks, *Political Untouchables*—London, 1979—to which the present account is also indebted.)

[7] Count de Saxe to Count d'Argenson, Dunkirk, 8 Mar. 1744: J. Colin, op. cit., p. 148. (H. W. Richmond, in *The Navy in the War of 1739–1748*, ii. 79, incorrectly cites this letter as addressed to the French Minister of Marine.)

Mounting a long-distance amphibious operation in midwinter is not an enviable operation. And the French embarkation was effected under louring portents of politics as well as weather. A French embargo on mail and shipping could hardly compete with the shrill squabbles of the Jacobites in the time-honoured tradition of political refugees. Their wildly optimistic expectations left the French authorities increasingly sceptical. By mid-February, furthermore, De Bussy, agent '101', had for £2000 betrayed to the British the whole French plan of invasion.

England was now in alarm. On 23 February 1744 the British government had ordered action-stations against invasion. Regiments were to concentrate on London, where Jacobite suspects were arrested. Reinforcements were drawn from the strategic reserve in Ireland, Scotland was seen to, marines drafted to garrison-duty, officers to command the forts of Tilbury and Sheerness. Trinity House was ordered to lift all buoys at the Nore and to blind the beacons at the North Foreland and elsewhere in case of enemy approach. The threatened island once again in her history kept watch and ward for her liberties.

The front line of the British defences was the home fleet based on Spithead under eightythree-year-old Admiral Sir John Norris in his hundred-gun flagship, the *Victory*. Norris recalled to the Duke of Newcastle his precautionary fears for the Channel in the preceding year, 'but I was treated then as an old man that dreamed dreams'.[8] Now, on 6 March 1744, he steered his superior fleet round the Downs to attack the Count de Roquefeuil's ships standing out from Dungeness.

But Norris was held off in a flat calm that night. The French men-of-war noiselessly cut or weighed anchor and, making no sail, drifted away upon the ebb-tide. At midnight a north-easter sprang up, soon blowing in an equinoctial gale. First light on 7 March found the British fleet scattered and scudding down the Channel under reefed canvas or bare poles. Not a French ship was in sight. The enemy vessels were blown right out of the Channel and day by day came dropping back to Brest,[9] where the Count de Roquefeuil died within a month.

The gale lashed Dunkirk, 'blowing horribly'[10] to wreck transports and wherries with loss of arms and stores. Saxe and his officers rode into the sea on horseback to further rescue operations. Barrailh reported dolefully that his own flagship was 'unstayed in her

---

[8] Admiral Sir John Norris to Duke of Newcastle, Feb. 1744: H. W. Richmond, op. cit., ii. 69.
[9] Cf. H. W. Richmond, op, cit., ii. 84.
[10] Bart to Count de Maurepas, Dunkirk, 2 p.m., 7 Mar. 1744: J. Colin, op. cit., p. 145.

toptimbers which play like a spinet'.[11] The invasion of England was cancelled.

The year 1744 was added to 1588 in the long tally of failed invasions of the British Isles. However, the threat against the English shores had at least the calculated effect of halting military drafts from England to Flanders, and even of reversing the flow by diverting some six thousand Dutch troops (regiments Eck de Pantaleon, Linsman, Bedarrides, Schaumburg–Lippe, Glinstra, Mulert) to stiffen the defence of those British Isles whose surest shield, however, was as always in her seamen and the sea.

'The Count de Saxe says that the wind is not Jacobite.'[12] Prince Charles Edward's premature arrival in France was, however, chiefly blamed by Louis XV in explaining to Philip V of Spain how the planned invasion had been frustrated by 'an infinity of contretemps'.[13] The court of Spain, which seemed to have a vested interest in invading England, was particularly exasperated by the failure. Still greater, though, was its concern with the other, southward extension in the ambitious strategy of Maurepas.

The year 1744 was to bring, for the first time in that war, a planned application of French military power to the affairs of the Italian peninsula. In November 1743 the French court had submitted to the Spanish a plan of campaign for a joint invasion of Italy in order 'to succour the army which the Duke of Modena is commanding in the Ecclesiastical States and to guarantee the Kingdom of Naples from the invasion of the English, the Austrians and the Piedmontese', hopefully by 'having transported thither a part of the Army of Don Philip'.[14] This Neapolitan perspective, diplomatically presented, lay behind the whole campaign from the south of France into the north of Italy. A glance at the map shews the importance here of the command of the sea, with its apex jutting up to Genoa.

The French expeditionary force against Italy was to muster thirty thousand men under the command of the dashing Prince de Conti, now designated at twenty-seven to serve as second-in-command of the combined Franco-Spanish army under the nominal orders of Don Philip in person. Conti's 'ambitious impatience',[15] as his aide-de-

---

[11] De Barrailh to Count de Maurepas, Dunkirk, 5 p.m., 11 Mar. 1744: ibid., p. 164.

[12] Dispatch of 8 Mar. 1744 from Dunkirk, enclosed in Marquis de Stainville to Grand Duke Francis II, Paris, 21 Mar. 1744: Esteri del Granducato di Toscana, vol. 2295/1286, fo. 381.

[13] King Louis XV to King Philip V, 15 Mar. 1744: Arch. Aff. Étr. C. P., Espagne, vol. 478, fo. 158: cited, Alfred Baudrillart, *Philippe V et la cour de France* (Paris, n.d.), v. 189.

[14] 'Mémoire envoyé en Espagne par la cour de France sur l'entrée des troupes françaises et espagnoles en Italie', 18 Nov. 1743: *Les Guerres des Alpes: Guerre de la succession d'Autriche (1742–1748): Mémoire extrait de la correspondance de la cour et des généraux, par F.-E. de Vault*, ed. P. Arvers (Paris and Nancy, 1892: henceforth cited as *Guerres des Alpes*), i. 93.

[15] Marquis de Saint-Simon, *Histoire de la guerre des Alpes* (Amsterdam, 1770), p. 17.

camp termed it, in playing truant from court to join the Army of Westphalia had already pointed towards what the later Choiseul was to describe as his 'large views of glory and command'.[16] Louis XV had written to Noailles of Conti's 'extreme desire to arrive'.[17] The ablest of the Bourbon princes, Conti had powerful promoters in the Châteauroux–Richelieu combination. Indeed it was said that this young prince had in his time been in love with the royal mistress. Now was his chance to embark upon what Choiseul called 'his romance of ambition'.[18]

Conti's command was announced on New Year's Day but, following usual practice, he did not at once leave court, where he had been engaged in marrying his young sister to the Duke de Chartres, intertwining the Bourbon branches of Condé and Orleans. The then Count de Stainville considered Conti lucky to land this marriage 'despite the bad state of his affairs' financially and the fact that 'the two families of Orleans and of Conti used not to see each other. It was the Duke of Orleans who took the first step ... by coming to ask point-blank for Mademoiselle de Conti for the Duke de Chartres.' In regard to the Duke of Orleans the writer assumed that 'everybody knows that he had withdrawn from the court in 1741 because the king had been unwilling to give his daughter, Madame Henriette, to the Duke de Chartres': the House of Orleans should not be dangerously elevated. So, continued Stainville:

The Duke of Orleans, cut to the quick and long tormented by ideas of devotion, went to figure as an anchorite in a cell at Saint-Geneviève, to follow processions on foot, argue over passages of the scriptures and get the little scamps of the parish to repeat the commandments of God ... The Duke de Chartres took good care to avoid these whims. He began by being much in love with his [Conti] wife, who fully returned it. It was said at Versailles that these young people at the beginning of their love could not resist the pleasure of demonstrating their feelings even when with strangers.[19]

For the present this mordant observer was prolonging the benefit of that wangle which had exempted him from joining his regiment and kicking his heels in distant Provence. There, however, the new year was already spelling activity for the Régiment de Stainville, more particularly in connection with mounting a naval introduction to the Franco-Spanish campaign in the Italian theatre.

It was with a slant upon the sea that the French and Spanish courts had agreed, at any rate, upon their opening strategy. A combined fleet was to put out from Toulon with the object of dealing at last with

[16] Choiseul, *Mémoires*, p. 22.
[17] King Louis XV to Marshal de Noailles, Versailles, 19 July 1743: Rousset, i. 172.
[18] Choiseul, *Mémoires*, loc. cit.   [19] Choiseul, 'Mémoires inédits', 2/16/8/497/3.

the truculent Admiral Mathews and so facilitating the conquest of
what was then cisalpine Piedmont, namely Nice and the naval base
at Villefranche. Maréchal-de-Camp the Marquis du Châtel, the
officer sent ahead by Conti for preliminary staff-work with the
Spaniards, wrote to the Minister of War: 'One must not have any
illusion; success on land depends upon that at sea.'[20] D'Argenson
largely agreed. France had decided to challenge British naval
supremacy in the Mediterranean no less than in the Channel. And
that while winter yet prevailed.

III

Toulon like Brest was all abustle. 'In the arsenal of Toulon', wrote a
local official, '... they have been working without respite for two
months, holidays and Sundays, on the armament of twenty-one
French vessels, and on that of the sixteen of the Spanish Squadron',[21]
also lying there under the command of Admiral Navarro. His French
colleague was de Court de la Bruyère, the senior lieutenant-general
of naval armies in the service. This eighty-year-old dugout was well
matched against Admiral Mathews, in command after eighteen years
ashore. Mathews had been holding council of war in Turin with
King Charles Emmanuel, the Marquis D'Ormea, Villettes, Count
Kaunitz, and Lieutenant-Fieldmarshal von Vettes. The Austrian
plea for all-out action against Naples was once again shelved in
favour of the more pressing preoccupation of Piedmont. Mathews,
with his forward base at Villefranche strengthened by British guns
and marines, sailed thence on 7 January 1744[22] to join his fleet, lying
in Hyères roads under Vice-Admiral Lestock.

On 25 January a French report glimpsed Lieutenant-General de
Court, who 'was yesterday incognito at Hyères with M. de la
Jonquière his flag captain and the major of marines; M. de Mauriac,
Lieut. Colonel of the Regt. de Stainville, and M. de Nollant, Captain
of the Grenadiers of the same regiment in quarters at Hyères,
accompanied him to the salt-marshes which are on the edge of the
roads of the Îles d'Hyères, whence, with spy-glasses, he discovered
and counted at his ease even down to the [number of] English on the
decks of each vessel. Admiral Mateus [sic], who is informed of

[20] Marquis du Châtel to Count d'Argenson, Grenoble, 13 Feb. 1744: Arch. Guerre C., vol.
3059, no. 95.
[21] De Portalis to Count d'Argenson, Hyères, 11 Jan. 1744: Arch. Guerre C., vol. 3127, no. 127.
[22] New style, as throughout unless specified to the contrary. The date of 27 Jan. 1744 given
for this sailing by Spenser Wilkinson, *The Defence of Piedmont 1742–48* (Oxford, 1927), p. 101,
is apparently due to a confusion.

everything which happens here, was so of the arrival of M. de Court at the salt-marshes. He saluted him with eleven salvoes of cannon. Vice-Admiral L'Estok, and the rear-admiral each did as much.'[23]

Mathews' mock salute of the ancient French admiral peering at him out of a salt-marsh was the kind of little incident which helps to explain why his name was a detested byword along the coasts of Provence.

The stationing at Hyères, over against the British fleet, of the Régiment de Stainville may have seemed appropriate in view of its recent Corsican experience. To swell the amphibious concentration on the Toulon area the regiments of La Reine, Lyonnais, Foix, Blaisois, and Tournaisis likewise came marching in. On Friday the 7th February 1744 the picked company of Stainville grenadiers under Captain de Nollant was one of those embarked on the French fleet in Toulon harbour to further de Court's plan to hit the depleted crews of the long-cruising British men-of-war by grappling and boarding them with reinforcements of French and Spanish troops. De Court 'had prepared cockades of white paper for the sailors and soldiers destined for the boarding; the sailors have represented that a cockade can come unfastened from a hat or cap, which they might even drop in the heat of battle, and that it is simpler that each mariner should pull his shirt outside his trousers for the reason that they are informed that the shirts of the English are blue or striped in several colours.'[24]

While contrary winds checked the sailing of the French squadron, Toulon was ringing with cheers and musketry as 'the grenadiers and soldiers were trained in shooting'.[25] At last, at one o'clock in the afternoon of Wednesday, 19 February 1744, the Franco-Spanish fleet began to weigh anchor. All that afternoon there unfolded the lovely spectacle of an eighteenth-century battlefleet sailing out to sea. Between three and four o'clock it was observed by a little British scout-vessel, the frigate *Winchelsea*. She sped back flying a red flag, the alarm-signal. The last seven or eight Bourbon vessels 'followed the others by moonlight'.[26] A collision earlier had reduced de Court's fleet to thirty-one, nineteen French and twelve Spanish, plus fire-ships. The reinforced British fleet was superior by some half a dozen warships but laboured under years of scornful antipathy between Lestock, in indifferent health, and Mathews, a peppery salt of the old

[23] De Portalis to Count d'Argenson, Toulon, 25 Jan. 1744: Arch. Guerre C., vol. 3064, no. 36.
[24] Memorandum of 8 Feb. 1744 enclosed in de Portalis to Count d'Argenson, Toulon, 8 Feb. 1744: Arch. Guerre C., vol. 3064, no. 75.
[25] De Portalis to Count d'Argenson, Toulon, 16 Feb. 1744: Arch. Guerre C., vol. 3127, no. 147.
[26] Geoffroy to Count d'Argenson, Toulon, 20 Feb. 1744: Arch. Guerre C., vol. 3127, no. 150.

breed of John Bull, described by Horace Walpole as 'a hot, brave, imperious, dull, confused fellow'.[27]

First light on 22 February 1744 found the Franco-Spanish fleet stretching away, ever south, from the roughly parallel British in line ahead some three miles westward. Mathews, refusing to be led away from the coastal waters critical for troop-transport, took a decision deemed to have anticipated Nelson's at Trafalgar and determined to cut in against the Spaniards, beginning to straggle back in the direction of sulky Lestock to the north. About noon the British flagship, ninety-gun *Namur*, and her second astern, H.M.S. *Marlborough*, came bearing down upon the Spanish flagship, Admiral Don Juan Navarro's *Real Felipe*, a magnificent vessel of 114 guns and a complement of 1,400.

The most formidable unit in that engagement, the Royal Philip, kept up a furious, hour-long cannonading, returning broadside for broadside at half pistol-shot against her two British assailants mounting 180 guns between them. Admiral Mathews and Captain Cornwall of the *Marlborough*, both his legs shot away, found little assistance astern where Lestock was sitting in an armchair on the quarterdeck of his ninety-gun *Neptune*, conning the end of the Spanish line. Only the little fireship *Ann*, about four o'clock, steered out against the *Real Felipe*, a grim hulk now, stripped of every mast, with twice-wounded Navarro knocked out of the command, his flag-captain shot down amid the carnage, 238 of the crew killed, 262 wounded. It was a French officer aboard, Captain de Lage, who, in the French version at least, commanded the Spanish guncrews to keep on pounding with the only three cannon that could still be brought to bear. This desperate discharge blew up the fireship in a cascade of 'an immense quantity of artifices, grenades, bomb-heads and firebrands, whereof a part fell upon the *Real*, without causing any damage'.[28] The indomitable *Real Felipe* had fought through to survival.

Forward of the British and Spanish flagships the brunt of battle had again been borne by the Spaniards, especially their smallest ship, the heavy frigate *Poder*. Her captain, Don Rodrigo de Urrutia, matched her fifty-four guns against not less than six British men-of-war, for the last two hours against the larger H.M.S. *Berwick* commanded by Captain Hawke, destined to be one of the celebrated admirals of his century. One understands why a Spanish or French

---

[27] Horace Walpole to Mann, London, 15 Apr. 1745 (O.S.): Walpole Correspondence, xix. 33.

[28] 'Relación de la batalla dada entre la Armada inglesa y la de las dos Coronas, delante de Marsella el dia 22 de Febrero de 1744': Archivo General Central; Estado; Legajo 4818: cited, D. Manuel Danvila y Collado, *Reinado de Carlos III* (Madrid, 1893), i. 237, n.

ship of some fifty guns was then reckoned a match for an English one of seventy, such was the superiority of continental construction and armament, validated now by valour. *Poder* was dismasted, had two fires blazing aboard and over two hundred killed or wounded of her crew of four hundred and fifty before she at last struck her colours about a quarter past four. Hawke sent a congratulatory capture-party aboard his reeking prize, only to be forced later to abandon it with its British prize-crew. *Poder* was recaptured by French grenadiers from the *Aquilon* in what was apparently the only exploit of those troops in the battle of Toulon.

The French intervention signified Lieutenant-General de Court's success at last in signalling a 'countermarch'[29] to what he called his 'little army'.[30] The whole French battlefleet had gone about – a moving sight – and stood to the northward on a starboard tack, compelling the British van under Rear-Admiral Rowley to follow suit. With but a short hour of daylight left, as the van and rear of each fleet now came converging, de Court interposed his ships to protect his mauled allies. But not before the stubborn Spaniards had exchanged last broadsides with the English ships as each passed into the shelter of the night.

Next morning, 23 February 1744, the Franco-Spanish fleet began to run westward across the Gulf of Lions before a chill north-easter and a British pursuit. Crippled *Poder* had to be abandoned and blown up. Next day Admiral Mathews called off the chase. It was one of his most debatable decisions in the much-debated battle of Toulon.

The strategic pull on both Mathews and de Court was back northeastward to the coasts of Provence and Piedmont where rival armies were assembling in anticipation of naval support. But the gathering gale was blowing contrariwise towards Spain, penning Mathews in Port Mahon while the Spaniards came limping into Carthagena, where they were joined by the French squadron on 10 March 1744. Thus came the Stainville grenadiers to be widely separated from their comrades in the outcome of the first battle wherein elements of that regiment were engaged.

The indecisive battle of Toulon ended in a welter of controversy. The Spaniards had shewn that their traditional prowess at sea was not yet extinguished, whereas the British navy, as Admiral Anson lamented that year, had struck a poorish patch. In its long annals few battles have been so injurious to the careers of so many officers.

[29] Journal de la Volage, M. de Beauffremont: Archives de la Marine: cited, H. W. Richmond, op. cit., ii. 41, n. 1.
[30] Lieutenant-General de Court to Bishop of Rennes, Feb. 1744: Luynes, vi. 222.

Admiral Mathews was ultimately cashiered, culpable Lestock, a good Whig, was acquitted; eleven of their captains were also courtmartialled. The battle of Toulon was, however, accurately appraised by the Marquis de Stainville: 'It is easy to see that all the advantage lay with the English, that the Spanish squadron was very roughly handled, and that the French one gave it little or no succour. So there is the plan for transporting troops into Italy by sea now stranded.'[31] Mathews, for the loss of one little fireship, had clinched his strategic menace and given the Bourbon fleet such a drubbing that it was to remain passive for the rest of that year.

Lieutenant-General de Court was rusticated while Navarro was created Marquis de la Victoria. In Cadiz posters appeared urging people to slit the throats of the treacherous French. The collaboration of the Bourbon monarchies was compromised almost from the outset. And their build-up on land now had to be pursued, as the Count d'Argenson observed to the Prince de Conti, 'in circumstances in which the sea could again be infected by the English'.[32]

The English infection spread to the waters of the Adriatic and influenced action along those coasts even as d'Argenson was writing. On the night of 6 March 1744 Captain-General de Gages had disengaged his Spaniards from their strong position at Pesaro over against the Austrian army of Lobkowitz. That dilatory prince followed down against the Spanish retreat, nominally under the supreme command of the Duke of Modena, just back from wintering in Venice. On 16 March his little army of 13,000 crossed the river Tronto, into Neapolitan territory. De Gages stood at Atri, Lobkowitz at Fermo, where he and the campaign halted. If Lobkowitz oversimplified in crediting the unexpected retreat of the enemy to the battle of Toulon, British seapower it was which had ultimately impelled de Gages, deprived of any Neapolitan expeditionary corps and fearful of landings in his rear. In fact the British squadron in the Adriatic had confined itself to inshore bombardment of the retreating Spaniards.

The Neapolitan objective which France had spelt out to Spain seemed receding in advance. The Bourbon fleet had been scattered away to Spain while the Spanish army in central Italy had been prized further apart from the Franco-Spanish one in southern France. It was now for the latter and larger, building up in Provence, to bear the brunt in that Italian theatre which was to be formative for

---

[31] Marquis de Stainville to Grand Duke Francis II, Paris, 14 Mar. 1744: Esteri del Granducato di Toscana, vol. 2295/1286, fo. 373.
[32] Count d'Argenson to Prince de Conti, Versailles, 10 Mar. 1744: Arch. Guerre C., vol. 3059, no. 157.

the Count de Stainville in 1744. On 22 February his father had written from Paris: 'All the officers are leaving for the army of Provence.'[33]

IV

The campaign against Italy remained secondary in the grand strategy of France for 1744. And in secondary theatres troops tend to go short. The Marquis du Châtel in his logistical preparations with the Spaniards in Provence was almost as tried as the Marquis de Beauvau some three years earlier by the Bavarians. Don Philip's army was, for instance, virtually innocent of mules for transport, and provisioning by different Spanish and French syndicates competed wastefully in those arid parts. It was partly in order to spare Provence an early imposition of a second staff and princely retinue that the Prince de Conti did not join Don Philip's headquarters at Aix-en-Provence till 14 March.

Colonel de Stainville was at last terminating his winter of pleasure in Paris, a winter which had brought to his second-in-command in Provence, Lieutenant-Colonel de Mauriac, promotion to the rank of brigadier as from 1 February, the date of the official appointment of Conti's staff. It comprised the dubious Count de Maillebois, son of the marshal, as quartermaster-general and chief of staff, Stainville's successor with Noailles, Chauvelin, as major-general of infantry, and the Jacobite Lord Tyrconnel as quartermaster of cavalry. Serving in the horse as a brigadier was Stainville's elder cousin César-Gabriel, Count de Choiseul-Chevigny, later Duke de Praslin.

The French forces concentrated on Grasse and Saint-Paul whence the Régiment de Stainville moved forward with the rest to Villeneuve where, in the last week of March, it was brigaded with Île de France, Blaisois, and Agenais, the young duke's regiment. The Spaniards advanced coastally, and allied headquarters to Antibes, whence Conti informed d'Argenson of the glum outset 'without meat and without money; the item of forage . . . is but very indifferently assured . . . in such sort that at the opening of the campaign I am already constrained to reduce the ration . . . We are as much destitute of resources as if we were in a foreign country two hundred leagues from our frontiers . . . I am much obliged to you for what you tell me about the pension which the King has granted to the woman for whom I have interested myself.'[34]

[33] Marquis de Stainville to Grand Duke Francis II, Paris, 22 Feb. 1744: *u.s.* fo. 368.
[34] Prince de Conti to Count d'Argenson, Antibes, 24 Mar. 1744: Arch. Guerre C., vol. 3059, no. 185.

Logistical adversity was sharpened by the strategic in the aftermath of the battle of Toulon. Villefranche was reinforced for the King of Sardinia by British marines and four ominous warships. Two British men-of-war put right in between Antibes and Cagnes to shoot up Bourbon mule-trains, while their intendant, Berthier de Sauvigny, commented that such ships 'absolutely prevent anything from entering Antibes by sea'.[35] Conti likewise had to drop plans for a leapfrogging landing in the rear of the enemy, at convenient Monaco: that nominally independent principality traditionally enjoyed, or suffered, a rather special form of neutrality under French protection and garrison. The Gallispan Army, as the Franco-Spanish forces were dubbed, in seeking to open its campaign with the capture of cisalpine Piedmont, notably Nice and Villefranche, was left with only a frontal attack across the frontier of the river Var.

The grand total of the army of the Infant Don Philip comprised 44 Spanish battalions of infantry and 36 French, 137 squadrons of Spanish cavalry and 134 French, some 46,000 troops in all. (The strength of a French battalion was up to about 550 men, of a Spanish to about 350.) But for the first phase of the campaign through the hills around Nice the heavy cavalry was left in Languedoc, and the troops lined up against the Var amounted to about half the total. French troops selected for the vanguard of attack camped at Cagnes, where French headquarters had also squashed in, as their quartermaster-general remarked, by 'a kind of miracle ... but ... not ... without altercation with the Spaniards'.[36]

The colonel commanding the French spearhead was the Count de Stainville. His vanguard was mainly to comprise picked companies of grenadiers. Only, his were among those stranded hundreds of miles away at Carthagena. Conti ordered that in regiments so affected fresh companies of grenadiers should be scraped up for service 'until the old ones shall have rejoined their formations'.[37] This not very startling intelligence was minuted in the French ministry of war, 'R[endre] C[ompte] au Roy',[38] inform the king. Louis XV might have been less bored by administration if his administration had had more sense of delegation.

The Count de Stainville was serving under the Marquis du Châtel, whose Spanish opposite was Maréchal-de-Camp de Corvalàn with the young Duke of Berwick as one of his brigadiers. From nine

[35] Berthier de Sauvigny to Count d'Argenson, Antibes, 24 Mar. 1744: Arch. Guerre C., vol. 3064, no. 183.
[36] Count de Maillebois to Count d'Argenson, Cagnes, 27 Mar. 1744: ibid. vol. 3059, no. 190.
[37] Major-General de Chauvelin to Count d'Argenson, Cagnes, 31 Mar. 1744: enclosing 'État des neuf bataillons dont les compagnies de grenadiers sont embarquées et qui ont formé de nouvelles': ibid., vol. 3064, nos. 217–18.   [38] Ibid.

o'clock on the night of 31 March 1744 vanguards went probing ahead of the march of the Gallispan Army against the Sardinian enemy across the river Var. At ten Stainville and Lieutenant-Colonel de Chauze led out from camp.

It was a filthy night of 'horrible rain, cold and darkness', reported Conti.[39] In the line-out along the hither bank of the Var, the place of honour on the right of the attack went to the Spaniards, due to cross from Saint-Laurent down towards the sea. Upstream the French under Stainville were to force the ford at Sainte-Marguerite. Each detachment of the vanguard comprised five companies of grenadiers and 250 mountain-fusiliers, light troops from the Pyrenean border-lands, called by the Spaniards the Mignones and by the French, to their annoyance, Miquelets. These nimble toughs wore rope-soled shoes, and their hair in nets topped by little bonnets in the style of Béarn. The Miquelets were expert with the carbines which they carried along with dirks, sometimes pistols, stuck into their belts: not the kind of troops one would relish coming up against on a dark night like that one.

At about first light on 1 April the advanced units of the Gallispan Army went splashing across the Var. The Count de Stainville, never one for leading from behind, was probably among the first to come over, attacking, on to enemy soil in the Italian campaign of 1744. It was to be the big campaign of his military career and was to promote influences, for good and ill, reaching out across the later statesmanship of Choiseul. For Stainville the crossing of the Var marked the beginning of a climb to peaks higher than the foothills of the Maritime Alps.

The Var was in itself reckoned to be 'not a very imposing barrier'.[40] Once across, Stainville's vanguard met virtually no resistance and the French forthwith carried the castle of Aspremont.

'The Var crossed,' ran a contemporary French appreciation, 'one enters into a plain of five miles in extent, adorned with fortified manors (*bastides*) and planted with vines, olives and all kinds of trees, which leads to Nice. The town is defenceless, and from the beginning of the last campaign the principal inhabitants had sheltered their effects in the principality of Monaco.' This gambit was now repeated and the open town of Nice duly surrendered its keys to the invaders. Conti admitted that 'as soon as we had crossed the Var there was terrible marauding; it is however true to say that it was pushed much

---

[39] Prince de Conti to Count d'Argenson, Saint-Laurent, 1 Apr. 1744: ibid., vol. 3060, no. 5.
[40] 'Mémoire envoyé en Espagne par la cour de France sur l'entrée des troupes françaises et espagnoles en Italie', 18 Nov. 1743: *Guerres des Alpes*, i. 94, and for the following.

further by the Spaniards than by the French. An example has been made [of delinquents] in both the nations.'[41]

Inland from Nice the strongpoint of Utelle also fell and the Marquis du Châtel drove through Castelnuovo to L'Escarène in a turning sweep on the left flank, carried forward by the Spanish Lieutenant-General the Marquis de Castelar. He took Peglia (Peille) and Castillon before swinging south to join hands with Colonel the Marquis de Montcalm: later to be immortalized in Canada, Montcalm now had led out the French garrison from Monaco to capture La Turbie. Despite the cancellation of a landing at Monaco the Gallispan army had by 12 April 1744 inversely closed its ring round the fortified base of Villefranche. The detailed accounts of these operations are particularly obscure but breasting through them came the vanguard of Colonel de Stainville, recorded as present in person 'at the capture of the castles of Aspremont and Utelle, Nice, Castelnuovo, L'Escarène, Peglia, Castillon and La Turbie'.[42]

Now battle loomed. Don Philip and his generals boldly decided that, although terrain and time did not allow them the usual artillery preparation, they would go slap for strongly held Villefranche in a storming assault, no later than the night of 13–14 April. For on the morning of 12 April the sails of the British fleet appeared off Villefranche. Mathews was back from Port Mahon to succour the Marquis of Susa, bastard brother of King Charles Emmanuel, in command of some seven thousand defenders in Villefranche. And inland Sardinian pressure from Sospel was already building up against the allied perimeter.

On the night of 13 April the Gallispan forces marshalled for attack in seven columns. The Régiment de Stainville was stationed in the second column, on the right flank down towards the sea. Stainville was brigaded with Agenais and two battalions of the Spanish Regiment of the Asturias under the command of his old acquaintance from Vienna and the Bohemian campaign, the Marquis de Mirepoix. As Maréchal-de-Camp, Mirepoix was himself subordinate to the Spanish Lieutenant-General Don Joseph d'Aremburu in a rather impressive integration of the French and Spanish commands. While d'Aremburu commanded the first three columns on the right, the fourth was under Lieutenant-General the Marquis de Senneterre. Having failed in his mission to the Sardinian court at Turin, Senneterre, in eighteenth-century style, now had the satisfaction of

[41] Prince de Conti to Count d'Argenson, Saint-Jean, 8 Apr. 1744: Arch. Guerre C., vol. 3060, no. 25.
[42] Pinard, *Chronologie historique-militaire*, v. 686.

launching the attack against the Sardinian base at Villefranche at ten o'clock that night.

Senneterre's column had effected a lodgement across the River Paillon when that black night was suddenly split open by a terrific thunderstorm, and the vanguard of attack found itself cut off by the Paillon swirling down in spate. Don Philip himself was said to be nearly drowned and 'a lieutenant, his sergeant and five men were reduced to ashes' by lightning while eighteen others were knocked 'silly and died a little while later without one of them having recovered his reason'.[43] Foul weather continued to delay resumption of the Franco-Spanish assault till the evening of 19 April, when forty-six battalions were concentrated much as before, this time in six columns of assault. The Régiment de Stainville was again brigaded under Mirepoix and d'Aremburu in what was now the first column, out in front of Nice on the extreme right of the line.

Around Villefranche the ridges and peaks of her natural ring of landward defence had been further fortified by the toiling garrison with the traditional skill of Italian engineering. To the west, confronting the first two Gallispan columns respectively under Lieutenant-Generals d'Aremburu and Campo Santo, the fortifications began on a headland with Fort Mathews, armed with the British naval guns supplied by that admiral, himself in Villefranche that night while his fleet stood offshore. From Fort Mathews an entrenchment, with batteries sited for cross-fire, ran inland to Fort Mont Alban, followed again by two more batteries, Lympia and Anima, on either side of the cartroad from Nice to Villefranche as it crossed the intervening Col de Villefranche. This was the objective of the first two columns of assault. In the wider plan of battle, however, their attack, which was to go in first, was designed as a diversion to draw Sardinian strength away from the key position of the Colimaçon, the Snail atop Mount Pacanaglia, marked down for assault by the sixth and strongest corps under Lieutenant-Generals de Castelar and du Châtel operating from Èze on the extreme left of the Gallispan front.

By eleven o'clock on the night of 19 April 1744 the Count de Stainville was leading his regiment into its first pitched battle on land. The initial objective of the advanced elements of d'Aremburu's column was what had become a blockhouse, known as the Cassine Thaon. It was held by fifty men under Colonel Keller who put up a spirited resistance in the darkness. Only after three hours, when the defenders had exhausted their ammunition, did they surrender. Even after the capture of the Cassine Thaon the attackers kept on firing. By

[43] Marquis de Saint-Simon, op. cit., p. 30.

this artifice they furthered their overall assignment of creating a din to attract enemy forces from elsewhere. The Sardinians supposed that the attack was still held up, while the noise of the further Gallispan advance through the olive trees was drowned.

Between three and four o'clock on the morning of 20 April a rocket went shining up on the left of the allied line. This was the signal from Castelar for the general assault. Part of d'Aremburu's column now worked too far to the right, but the main attack was duly delivered against the batteries Lympia and Anima. The Sardinians were chucked out, the Col de Villefranche captured, and a Sicilian battalion routed further inland by Mont Vinaigrier. The Gallispan capture here ultimately came to eleven Sardinian standards, over a thousand men and the commander-in-chief himself, the Marquis of Susa. It was a smashing start.

Out on the allied left troops stormed the Snail and were only checked at the valley of the Murta by the British marines. Between Castelar and du Châtel on the left and Campo Santo and d'Aremburu on the right, the columns of Senneterre and Danois were assaulting very tough objectives, Mont Vinaigrier and Mont Gros, which became the swaying battle-centre as the outnumbered Sardinians, now favoured by daylight, fought back inch by inch under Susa's Lieutenant-General Cinzano, veteran of the battle of Camposanto.

Meanwhile the attack of Lieutenant-General d'Aremburu, crisply assessed by Conti as 'an idiot',[44] had run into difficulty, into heavy artillery-fire 'from Fort Mont Alban, from the citadel of Villefranche, and even from the English fleet'[45] – a practical lesson for the Count de Stainville among others in the meaning of British seapower. Conti repeatedly ordered d'Aremburu to close up in support of Campo Santo. D'Aremburu did send a detachment, including part of the Régiment de Stainville, over that way, to his left. In the main, however, he veered off right against Fort Mont Alban and Fort Mathews. Fort Mont Alban comprised a donjon flanked by four towers with a terraced platform for artillery. It was against this fortification that the Régiment de Stainville was mainly employed, and there that the Count de Stainville signalized himself.

Under d'Aremburu's slack command a column, rather likely a Spanish one, had, in Conti's words, 'had the foolishness to ascend without orders'[46] the foot of the entrenchments of Fort Mont Alban,

[44] Prince de Conti to Count d'Argenson, camp before Villefranche, 4 May 1744: Arch. Guerre C., vol. 3060, no. 130: Guerres des Alpes, ii. 148.

[45] Major-General de Chauvelin to Count d'Argenson, camp before Villefranche, 22 Apr. 1744: Arch. Guerre C., vol. 3065, no. 79.

[46] Prince de Conti to Count d'Argenson, camp before Villefranche, 24 Apr. 1744: Arch. Guerre C., vol. 3060, no. 67.

where it evidently got into trouble. Stephen de Stainville went charging to the rescue, himself bearing one of his regimental standards up to the verge of the enemy entrenchments. Stainville was wounded and hit, though not seriously, in several places, in arm and foot. It was a high feat of personal gallantry and leadership.

The occasion of Stainville's valour might, however, seem to illustrate the way in which the troops under d'Aremburu were coming to operate in smallish packets unable to give each other effective support except, perhaps, through such a special effort as Stainville's. Whereas Cinzano was exploiting his advantage on Mont Gros in a turning movement against the whole western flank of the Gallispan army. The Piedmontese fusiliers standing before Fort Mathews came charging back to speed the good work while the artillery of Fort Mont Alban and the British fleet kept pounding at the ragged French and Spanish battle-groups. Those from over by Mont Gros were now in flight or something like it; they were joined, probably in somewhat less precipitate disorder, by d'Aremburu's main force, including Stainville's. They scrambled back and did not halt till they reached Nice itself.[47] The whole of the western perimeter of defence before Villefranche was recaptured by the Piedmontese and purged of the Gallispans, back on their starting-lines.

The Prince de Conti, at this discouraging juncture towards four o'clock in the afternoon, halted the whole attack upon Villefranche. According to the French returns that day-long combat had cost them just over a thousand casualties though total Gallispan casualties may well have been up to thrice as high.[48] But, as can well happen in war, the Gallispan Army had fought better than it knew. Despite Cinzano's counter-attack Castelar to the east remained master of the dominating Snail while Sardinian casualties including prisoners ran up to 2,500, leaving a bare five thousand to hold the breached positions. This was not enough.

Stout Cinzano and his men began to embark, covering their retreat only with small garrisons left in Fort Mont Alban and the citadel of Villefranche. Once again the British Royal Navy was affording succour to valiant troops pressed back to the limit of endurance and of the land. Escorted by British frigates, the Sardinian army sailed off east to Porto Maurizio and Oneglia in a coastal enclave of Sardinian territory within the republic of Genoa. (One notices again how

[47] This would appear to be the most coherent reading of the somewhat differing accounts of this incoherent retreat. French accounts, in particular, tend to play down or contradict the elements of rush and disorder. For instance, the Marquis de Saint-Simon stated, op. cit., p. 36, that the troops 'withdrew slowly and in good order'. But Conti himself, writing to Louis XV on the day of battle, admitted 'the precipitate retreat' of some units: *Guerres des Alpes*, i. 151.

[48] Cf. *Erbfolge-Krieg*, viii. 438, n. 4.

convenient, as well as tiresome, the territorial fragmentation of the eighteenth century could be.) The main British fleet sailed west, back to Mathews's old haunts off Hyères whence he could keep an eye on the French squadron, returned to Toulon. Bourbon activity, though, continued to be on land, where the British fleet now lost its main base.

Back at battered Villefranche the Fort Mont Alban easily surrendered. The citadel of Villefranche followed suit after the attackers had gingered up its eightyfive-year-old governor by lobbing a mortar-bomb into his room during the hour which the old gentleman reserved for his nap. By 25 April 1744 the reduction of Villefranche was complete. It was an auspicious opening to the Franco-Spanish campaign against Italy.

V

The conquest of Nice and Villefranche was celebrated in Paris with fireworks and a Te Deum at Notre-Dame. The churches on the spot were turned into hospitals for the numerous French and Spanish wounded. There the affable Prince de Conti endeared himself to his troops by doing the rounds and cheering the wounded. Among those in bed with wounds was the Count de Stainville, back in Nice. Numbers of the officers and men of his regiment were in like case, as may be gathered from the letter which, on 25 April, the day of the final fall of Villefranche, the Count de Stainville wrote on gilt-edged paper to the Minister of War, the Count d'Argenson:

Sir,
    The Regiment which I have the honour to command was in the attack on the entrenchment on the 20th of this month; it attacked opposite the castle of Mont Alban. One could not be more pleased than I was at the lively and bold way in which it addressed itself. The Prince de Conti has had me informed that he was pleased with it. In the affair I had one Captain killed, four wounded, of whom one seriously, four Lieutenants wounded, thirty-five soldiers killed and sixty-two wounded. As for me, my bruises are going wonderfully (*mes contusions vont à merveille*); it is only the one in my foot which makes me still keep my bed.
    I shall have the honour to address to you the ordinary evidence, the nomination of employments, and the favours whereof the regiment is susceptible.
    I have the honour to be with profound respect, Sir, your very humble and very obedient servant

Choiseul de Stainville.[49]

[49] Count de Stainville to Count d'Argenson, Nice, 25 Apr. 1744: Arch. Guerre C., vol. 3060, no. 71. (A contemporary or near-contemporary clerk indexed this letter incorrectly under date of 24 April: an early but far from isolated example of the difficulty which even Choiseul's contemporaries were apt to find in deciphering his handwriting. It was, however, appreciably more legible at that period than it later became.)

What Stainville characteristically called his bruises included a broken arm, as his parents in Paris were informed. Others were likewise apprised. The aristocratic compactness of European society then is incidentally suggested by the way in which the new Danish minister in Paris, just arrived, troubled to inform his sovereign, in a dispatch of 26 April,[50] of Stainville's wound at Villefranche. The young Baron von Bernstorff may hardly have guessed that he was soon to become one of the Count de Stainville's closest and most important friends.

Scarcely a friend of Stainville's was the Count d'Argenson. He minuted on the young colonel's letter to him: 'He should be complimented on his personal conduct but one must abstain from speaking of what concerns his Regiment.'[51] So the minister on 7 May 1744 replied to the count, hazily addressed as a marquis, that he had spoken from his letter to Louis XV: 'His Majesty has learnt with pleasure of the good state of your wounds; he is well informed of the distinguished manner in which you conducted yourself in the affair of the 20th and you will find him always very disposed to give you marks of his satisfaction'[52] – though not quite so disposed as Conti and, doubtless, Stainville had been hoping.

The Prince de Conti had drawn the minister's attention to Stainville's 'very fine action'[53] before Fort Mont Alban. Conti did this, however, not in his main dispatch after the battle but in another a few days later wherein he particularly marked his earlier omission of this exploit. One wonders whether he had been jogged; Stainville certainly had a sharp eye as to his mentions in dispatches. Conti made handsome amends for any tardiness by recommending Stainville, still only twenty-four, for the cross of the Order of Saint Louis, distinguished by that scarlet ribbon of military merit which was coveted only less than the Cordon Bleu of the Order of the Saint-Esprit.

Generals commanding in the field are apt to be disappointed by the unimaginatively rigid manner in which bureaucracies at home deal with their recommendations for decorations. The Count d'Argenson replied to the Prince de Conti on 24 May: 'I am vexed that M. de Stainville is not in a position to obtain the grace which Your Serene Highness would procure for him, but the actions are not

[50] Baron von Bernstorff to King Christian VI of Denmark, Paris, 26 Apr. 1744: Danish State Archives: Rigsarkiv, Tyske Kancelli: Udenrigsministeriet Arkiv (henceforth cited as Rigsarkiv/T.K.U.A.), Frankrig, C.253.
[51] u.s.
[52] Count d'Argenson to Count de Stainville, Valenciennes, 7 May 1744: Arch. Guerre C., vol. 3060, no. 146.
[53] Prince de Conti to Count d'Argenson, camp before Villefranche, 24 Apr. 1744: Arch. Guerre C., vol. 3060, no. 67.

sufficient; to have the cross of Saint Louis, one needs, under the terms of the institution of this order, a number of years of service which M. de Stainville has not yet got, and which can be made good only by wounds of a kind to which he is not subjected, fortunately for him.'[54] In after years the Duke de Choiseul himself was to call the Order of Saint Louis 'the reward of the blood of warriors'.[55]

Stainville had at all events ensured that, as he later wrote, 'the Prince de Conti, whom I had not known before this year [of 1744], treated me with kindness, and even with distinction'.[56] This favour was to promote Stainville's military career. Now, however, their friendship was speedily tested by an unhappy incident which marred the aftermath of Villefranche for Stainville.

The strained relations between the French and Spanish troops had been exacerbated by the disappointing day of 20 April. As, after the battle, Don Philip and Conti set up their headquarters at Nice, their respective officers spent their time wrangling and fighting duels. 'And the soldiers so well followed the example of their Officers that on a single day one saw a hundred sabres of the Allies crossed against each other.'[57] The harassed French major-general represented the difficulty of maintaining discipline in Nice, where the troops were 'finding an abundance of wine dirt cheap'.[58] Allied headquarters clamped down with stringent orders against brawling. Thereafter Conti insisted upon punishing some Spanish soldiers caught fighting, while assuring their protesting officers that he would deal faithfully with any French delinquents. Brawling between allies would now incur the death penalty.

'The occasion', one is told, 'was not slow in presenting itself.'[59] Two seasoned grenadiers, one from the Régiment de Stainville and the other from the Spanish Regiment of Galicia were 'surprised and arrested, both of them with sabre in hand and fighting each other with fury'.[60] However, 'their quarrel had not at all had for object the national discord, and was but a consequence of their mettle excited by a little wine: the Council of War could not fail to condemn them, but everything spoke in their favour. The officers of the two nations

[54] Count d'Argenson to Prince de Conti, camp before Menin, 24 May 1744: *Guerres des Alpes*, ii. 163–4. – The habitually accurate Ritter von Hoen states incorrectly, *Erbfolge-Krieg*, viii. 441, n. 5, that the Count de Stainville was promoted Maréchal-de-Camp after the capture of Villefranche. Ritter von Hoen was here confusing the Count de Stainville with his cousin, the Count de Choiseul, who was so promoted on 2 May 1744.
[55] Choiseul, 'Mémoires inédits', 3/30/16/949/3.
[56] Choiseul, *Mémoires*, p. 13.
[57] Marquis de Saint-Simon, *Histoire de la guerre des Alpes*, p. 40.
[58] Major-General de Chauvelin to Count d'Argenson, Nice, 9 May 1744: Arch. Guerre C., vol. 3060, no. 165.
[59] Marquis de Saint-Simon, loc. cit.
[60] Major-General de Chauvelin to Count d'Argenson, Villefranche, 2 May 1744: Arch. Guerre C., vol. 3060, no. 122.

desired with equal ardour that they should not be sentenced. One of them had been a grenadier for more than twenty years in one of the first regiments of Spain, and was considered to be the bravest and steadiest of his unit; the other had served nearly thirty years in the Regiment of the Count de Stainville with that honourable distinction which renders a soldier respectable and in some sort superior to his fellows; he had signalized himself on every occasion and displayed twenty-two scars on his body: he had given recent proof of his valour in the attack on the entrenchments of Mont Alban, where he had received two wounds which had detained him in the hospital, whence he had come at that very hour. He had not had time to be informed of the severe prohibitions which set limits upon his honour.'[61]

This was not the kind of situation which the warm-hearted Count de Stainville would take lying down. He threw himself into a passionate agitation to save the life of his stalwart grenadier. The latter's 'Colonel interested himself as keenly in his fate as if he had been his son or his relation; he [Stainville] solicited, pressed the Prince de Conti with all ardour of a heart as full of vivacity as of feelings; the Spaniards associated themselves with him; but the inflexible severity of his General ... yielded not at all to the circumstances.' Not that Conti was an unfeeling commander. The prince 'in private mingled his tears with his [Stainville's] own for the loss of so gallant a man'. For a general and a colonel to weep together over the fate of a simple grenadier may seem ridiculous to those who do not share their warm recognition of human valour within that eighteenth-century code which was not ashamed to unite sensibility with duty. Conti – the most attractive and promising of the Bourbon princes at that time – was, like Stainville, youthful, clever, ambitious and dashing, winning in manner, generous in disposition. Their respect for one another was perhaps liable to be more enhanced than impaired by the cruel divergence now between them.

On 2 May 1744 the two brave grenadiers were paraded before 'all the pickets of the two armies', French and Spanish, and were there 'executed ... to death'.[62] Such disciplinary severity was then rare, especially in the French army. The effect was corresponding. 'The death of the Grenadiers', one is told, 'became such a striking example, that no more talk of brawling was heard during all the rest of the campaign.'[63]

To those who take account of such things, the early sacrifice of Stainville's grenadier for the promotion of Franco-Spanish accord

[61] Marquis de Saint-Simon, op. cit., pp. 40–1 for the following.
[62] Major-General de Chauvelin to Count d'Argenson, Villefranche, 2 May 1744: Arch, Guerre C., vol. 3060, no. 122.
[63] Marquis de Saint-Simon, loc. cit.

present discern any more than the house.'[72] Such was the 'voluntary prison' wherein these alpine troglodytes spent more than half their lives, healthy and contented with their bare self-sufficiency. Their staple bread, keeping for a year and more, was eked out with cheese, fruit, and vegetables:

They are not eager to have either eggs, or salted meat, or a thousand resources which are regarded elsewhere as absolute necessities ... and very often dispense with having a fire; their houses not having any chimney-pots, the smoke evaporates as in the barns of Westphalia, without the least opening. If one of the family or of the cattle dies, he is carried to the loft, where he spreads no infection and is preserved without any precaution. These not very sociable beings ... are nowise impatient in the spring to go to seek their fellow-creatures.

Even so civilized a country as France retained pockets of such primitive existence though the omnipresent bureaucracy of the enlightenment was already reaching out to tax them and make 'them see that there is no place in nature, however wild, however hidden it be, where man does not owe a tribute to other men and where he may govern himself by laws which should certainly be those of pure nature, cultivating and reaping the fruits of the earth without hindrance and without charge'. One may recall the extent to which alpine Savoy formed the background for Jean-Jacques Rousseau and his doctrine of natural man, and notice, here again, that while despotism is so often a domination of the plains, it is mountains, as well as oceans, which tend to promote freedom and hardy independence.

The geography of immediate concern, however, was that not of politics but of strategy.

The wintry reconnaissance lay behind the Régiment de Stainville's march north from Nice at the beginning of June 1744 so that it stood at Levens at the start of the main march into Dauphiny on 24–25 June. The French march was divided into four divisions, with Stainville designated to head the second under the command of Maréchal-de-Camp de Courten while Stainville's cousin, the Count de Choiseul, led the first, both under the orders of Lieutenant-General de Lautrec. Theirs was a punishing march through the hot season and the Maritime Alps east of the Durance where troops had to scramble up mule-tracks, usually in single file so that orderly staging required that not more than three or four thousand men a day should traverse any given stretch. Nor was it easy to stock up supplies across that corrugated countryside, described by Conti as 'so

---

[72] Marquis de Saint-Simon, op. cit., p. 57, n. for the following. (The reproduction of this footnote in *Guerres des Alpes*, i. 175, n. 1, is not invariably verbally exact.)

odd that your most detailed maps could give you no notion of it'.[73] At last they hit the river Ubaye at Barcelonnette, whence upstream into camp at Tournoux.

Don Philip and Conti themselves skirted the foothills round by Draguignan, Sisteron, Embrun, Guillestre. This relatively easy route was calculated to impress those remote provinces with the rare spectacle of two princely progresses and correspondingly, perhaps, to lull the King of Sardinia. This design was favoured by the spontaneous exuberance of welcome in Provence and Dauphiny. The march of the conquering princes became almost one of those carnival processions so dear to Provence. From the wayside towns mummers and mimers issued in greeting with prancing hobby-horses, the so-called Chevaux-Flûtes, and, one is assured, even oldsters of fourscore years 'jumping and dancing like the youngest to the sound of their pipes and tabors'.[74] Also especially of Provence, in that age as in others, were the giant grotesques nodding to musical accompaniment in processional set-pieces, one, for instance, of the Queen of Sheba coming to visit King Solomon.

This joyride through the blaze of midsummer was tiring enough for the troops, especially the Spaniards, before their exertion ahead. By the beginning of July the Gallispan Army had taken up its new positions in a great arc along the Alps based upon six main camps running from Cervières, up by Briançon to the north, through Guillestre, Embrun, Tournoux, Barcelonnette, to Saint-Étienne. The Régiment de Stainville as part of Lautrec's corps occupied the advanced centre at Tournoux.

The Gallispan Army was poised for attack across the Alps in accordance with the strategic concept of an infantry captain in the Régiment Royal Vaisseau. Captain Pierre Bourcet from that alpine borderland was seconded to be assistant quartermaster-general (aide-maréchal-général des logis) upon the staff of the Prince de Conti, who acknowledged his debt more generously than had Belle-Isle in regard to Folard. Bourcet was another example to set beside Chevert of the fact that a humbly born officer of exceptional capacity was by no means wholly denied recognition in the French army of the eighteenth-century.

Conti and Bourcet were confronted by their problem rearing up in the shape of the Alps, their soaring summits 'still covered with a great quantity of snow', as Bourcet reported on 26 June, while adding: 'But, since we shall not be operating for a fortnight, all our openings will

---

[73] Prince de Conti to Count d'Argenson, Embrun, 7 July 1744: Arch. Guerre C., vol. 3061, no. 139.

[74] Marquis de Saint-Simon, op. cit., p. 60.

be free by then.'[75] The snowy peaks, observed a contemporary appreciation, were 'fortified to the clouds by nature and art'.[76] The Marquis de Stainville, following from Paris that Italian campaign wherein his eldest son was engaged, wrote of the Franco-Spanish switch from the Mediterranean to the Alps: 'This countermarch at least gives the King of Sardinia time to put himself in condition to defend these passages'[77] through the alpine passes. The most important of these six valleys were, from north to south, the Dora Riparia where Exilles and Susa guarded the exit to Turin itself, the Varaita with Casteldefino, already the objective of the preceding autumn, and the valleys of the Maira and the Stura, opening on to Coni.

The Stura was approached from France by the Col de l'Argentière, the most practicable even in winter, and this was the only valley equipped with a road that was something more than a mule-track. The defences here were corresponding, comprising not only the fortified township of Demont but, nearer the frontier, between Pietraporzio and Bersezio, a horrid gorge deserving its name now of the Barricades. The valley there scarcely afforded room for the river and the road which crossed it. The Piedmontese had broken the bridge and multiplied fortifications to seal this bottleneck against what must be almost suicidal attack. Nor were the other valleys neglected by King Charles Emmanuel and General Guibert, the chief organizer of the Piedmontese defence. Before Casteldelfino nasty surprises awaited upon Monte Cavallo in the shape of dismountable cannon invented by Engineer-General Count Bertola and transported by mules to otherwise inaccessible positions. From Monte Cavallo the new Strada dei Cannoni or Cannon Route, practicable even for artillery, ran down laterally to hit the valley of the Stura by the Col del Mulo. This strategic link did much to overcome the mountain handicap upon the usual advantage to the defence of interior lines. Flexibility was imparted to the Piedmontese forces whereof Charles Emmanuel had concentrated upon the Alpine frontier no less than forty-three of his fifty-four battalions, giving himself a probable strength of about 26,000 men against the Gallispan Army of perhaps rather over 33,000, a very fair ratio wherewith to hold such formidable defences.

[75] Captain Bourcet to Count d'Argenson, Mont Dauphin, 26 June 1744: *Guerres des Alpes*, ii. 218.

[76] 'Relation de ce qui s'est passé de plus intéressant à l'armée des deux P[rin] ces en Piedmont depuis le 1er Septembre jusqu'au 18 Octobre 1744', French memorandum of 18 Oct. 1744: Arch. Guerre C., vol. 3065, no. 177.

[77] Marquis de Stainville to Gundel, Chaillot, 26 June 1744: Ö.S./H.H.S., 23 Frankreich Varia 1736–1749, docket 'Choiseul de Stainville, Grossherz. toskanischer Gesandter in Paris an Gundel, 1744', fo. 15.

Captain Bourcet, as he was to explain in his classic *Principes de la guerre des montagnes*, also believed in flexibility. He intended to threaten not just one or two of the six valleys but every one of them, stretching the Sardinian defence to the uttermost, punching through at any weak spot which might develop and then packing the punch with the weight of the whole army, swiftly reunited.

VI

On 5 July 1744 the Gallispan Army opened up against the Alps with two divisions, one French, one Spanish, which marched out from the northernmost camp at Cervières, over the Col de Bousson to Cesana in the direction of Exilles and the Dora Riparia. Bourcet was seeking to exploit the fact that the Cannon Route did not run up beyond the valley of the Varaita. If Sardinian forces could be attacked to the less accessible north, that should help to uncover the way to strategic Coni, along the Stura from Barcelonnette. The Marquis de Stainville came close to the mark in writing to his friend Gundel, the Austrian chargé d'affaires who had had to leave Paris for Brussels after the French declaration of war: 'The Prince de Conti is going to attack the mountains of Piedmont again by the valley of Barcelonnette; my son informs me as of the 6th [July] that he does not yet know to which sugarloaf his division is destined':[78] an illustration both of the early factorization of warfare in terms of divisional formations and also of the typically jaunty approach of the Count de Stainville to the alpine barrier. But a week later his father, roughly relaying Conti's plan of multiple attack, added: 'The French officers who are in his army report that they will execute the orders of their general, but they seem very doubtful of the success of their sacrifice.'[79]

On 10 July the Prince de Conti inspected the troops at Bousson and Cesana as part of what he called his 'demi-demonstration'[80] against Exilles. The feint failed to draw enemy forces north, partly perhaps thanks to 'the ill will and little intelligence of M. de La Mina', as Conti put it. He lamented to d'Argenson on 12 July: 'Indiscretion unmasks all our movements; there is not one of the valets of the Infant who does not know, at the precise moment, not only the day of his departure, but the term of his arrival ... In the long run this situation is absolutely insupportable.' Next day the

---

[78] Marquis de Stainville to Gundel, 18 July 1744, ibid., fo. 23.
[79] Marquis de Stainville to Grand Duke Francis II, Paris, 25 July 1744: Esteri del Granducato di Toscana, vol. 2295/1286, fo. 442.
[80] Prince de Conti to Count d'Argenson, Guillestre, 12 July 1744: *Guerres des Alpes*, ii. 221-2 for the following.

whole Gallispan Army was upon the move. From the great arc of
menace sweeping round between the districts of Nice and of Briançon
the French and Spanish invaders were now advancing in nine main
divisions to launch their grand attack across the Alps.

At the southern extremity of the arc of attack the first column
comprised eight infantry battalions under Lieutenant-General de
Castelar. From the upper valley of the Var he advanced by way of
Saint Étienne into remote and forbidding mountains in the direction
of Les Planches, a village lying eastward of the Barricades. The
second column was a small one of five battalions plus oddments
scraped up from garrisons around Nice by their commander, the
Count de Mauriac, Stainville's erstwhile second-in-command. Mauriac led up the path over the gruelling Col de Fer in support of
Castelar against Les Planches on Mauriac's right. On his left
Maréchal-de-Camp de Villemur was heading in from the west with
the eight battalions of the third column against Ferrière to swell that
flank-attack. Frontally the Barricades were approached over the Col
de l'Argentière by the fourth and fifth columns respectively
commanded by Lieutenant-Generals Don Francisco Pignatelli and
Don Joseph d'Aremburu, covering the headquarters staffs of the
Infant Don Philip, the Prince de Conti, and Captain-General de Las
Minas.

The Count de Stainville's regiment was included in the fourteen
battalions from the camp at Tournoux which Lieutenant-General de
Lautrec led by Mont Maurin and the Col Marie in the direction of
Prazzo in the upper valley of the Maira, whence he might support
operations in either the valley of the Stura on his right or that of the
Varaita to his left. Co-operating with Lautrec was the smaller seventh
column of Lieutenant-General Don Luis de Gandija. The eighth,
under Lieutenant-General the Marquis de Campo Santo, came in in
five battalions farther to the north, over by the Col des Traverses,
while the ninth column of ten battalions under Lieutenant-General
the Bailli de Givri completed the threat to Casteldelfino itself.

Thus, that July, did the seventy battalions of the Gallispan Army
come weaving their several ways through the alpine peaks in a
complicated operation of military co-ordination. It stood the test of
performance in 'these frightful parts, where the least stumble can cost
one's life'.[81] Despite some disorder during a night of pelting rain on
16–17 July next day found every column advanced to its appointed
position, poised for attack.

If, on 16 July, the Piedmontese commander at the Barricades,
Lieutenant-General Pallavicini, had been able to watch with some

[81] Marquis de Saint-Simon, op. cit., p. 66.

equanimity the Franco-Spanish columns debouching on to the Col de l'Argentière opposite, less palatable were the reports coming in of the aggressively skirmishing advance of the Gallispan sixth column under Lautrec and his two lieutenants, Lieutenant-General Don Pedro Arteaga and Maréchal-de-Camp de Bissy. The Régiment de Stainville was one of those participating in their intricate marches[82] against Preit, the strategic Col del Mulo and indeed the whole northern flank of the Barricades. Meanwhile, still masked by the high ranges south of the Stura valley, the battalions of Castelar and Mauriac, brushing aside the few small enemy posts encountered in those desolate regions, had come toiling over and down to their appointed objectives. Castelar straddled the Stura at Les Planches and Mauriac at Pietraporzio, both directly behind the Barricades. This was the decisive clinch in Bourcet's complex strategy of mountain embrace. For Pallavicini the game was up. His eight battalions forthwith retreated from the Barricades by the only route still open, up by the Col del Mulo. On the morning of 18 July 1744 the confronting columns of the Spanish and French princes occupied the abandoned fastness of the Barricades without firing a shot. The Piedmontese defence had been pinched right out by the brilliant co-ordination of a great pincer-movement through the Alps.

The princes sent tidings of success to their courts, and two French aides-de-camp were despatched to inform Givri, out north on the tough flank against Casteldelfino, of the strategic stroke in the Stura valley, now the one upon which all should concentrate for the punch through. But one messenger fell and did not get through, the other only late. Meanwhile Givri's advance-guard was thrusting ahead under the expert guidance of a Piedmontese deserter – he had escaped from a disciplinary escort by pushing them over a precipice and he was subsequently adopted by Conti, at whose château of Isle-Adam this nimble peasant was to thrive as the Doux Berger. Givri's advance-guard was commanded by the ever-enterprising Chevert who, contrary to the spirit of Conti's original orders, won round Givri and his second-in-command, the tough Lieutenant-General Count de Danois, to an attack upon the redoubt of Monte Cavallo, the key position in the Piedmontese defence of the precipitous ridge of Pietralunga before Casteldelfino.

At three o'clock on the afternoon of 19 July the French surged in to assault the main palisade behind the entrenchments of Monte Cavallo, whose stubborn defence was commanded by King Charles Emmanuel in person. Chevert's men, lacking tools, tore at the

---

[82] For contemporary uncertainty concerning these operations, cf. *Erbfolge-Krieg*, viii, 466, n. 2 *et passim.*

stockade with their bare hands, were reduced to crouching for hours in the ditch right in front of it, crossing their guns with those of the Piedmontese upon the same parapets, shooting point-blank at one another's heads. After four hours of carnage a diversionary attack at last enabled men of the regiment of Poitou to scramble in over the corpses which cumbered a cannon-embrasure. Once through, the French fell to with cold steel. They gave no quarter. The Piedmontese officers, who had sustained a magnificent defence before their king, mainly preferred to perish rather than retreat. Retreat, indeed, offered no sure escape. French pursuit forced the fleeing Regiment of Saluzzo over the edge of a precipice, sent rolling and hurtling down into the valley far below.

The victory of Casteldelfino cost the French about eight hundred killed and as many wounded, over a third of their estimated strength of 4,500. Mortally wounded was the Bailli de Givri himself. His command passed to the lightly wounded Count de Danois who, on that evening of victory, 'was calmly whistling in the midst of the horrible carnage'.[83] His preoccupation was his supper. Danois was grumbling that wounded Givri 'will carry off the mule which was bringing the provisions for us both; and I, I shall have nothing to eat'. A Piedmontese senior officer, lying mortally wounded, took pity on the predicament of the Count de Danois and 'interrupted the cries which it [his wound] tore from him to instruct him [Danois] where his [own] canteens were: the Count de Danois had them fetched, and ate near the dying man; but as the latter did not cease to moan the Count de Danois said to him, "Sir, could you die in peace and let us eat in peace."' At which the Italian was struck dumb by 'astonishment or death'.

Not two hours after the last shot had been fired there Danois received the delayed tidings from Conti of success against the Barricades, with instructions not to attack the trenches before Casteldelfino. When, in return, news reached Conti of how his plan of campaign had been disregarded, and at what fearful cost, that feeling prince burst into tears and 'publicly gave himself over to the most immoderate grief.[84] This is said to have caused Don Philip to ask Conti, 'What then would you do if you were defeated?' Conti replied, 'I should be ashamed of my defeat; but I cannot be so for lamenting my friends and the loss of so many brave fellows.'[85] Perhaps the tears of the Prince de Conti counted against the munching of the Count de Danois.

[83] Marquis de Saint-Simon, op. cit., p. 85, n. 19 for the following.
[84] Ibid., p. 86.
[85] Cited, Luynes, vi. 38.

The grim tale of battle, magnified, reached the Marquis de Stainville 'just now', as he promptly wrote off to Gundel on 28 July, 'as I was celebrating Saint Anne's day at Chaillot.'[86] His exaggerated intelligence was that the Gallispan forces had captured not only Casteldelfino but also Demont at a cost of over 4,000 casualties, the dead including the Count de Danois and young d'Agenais (also in fact only injured there), the wounded the Count de Choiseul with 'all the general staff killed or wounded; judge in what anxiety I am for my son. Adieu my friend, I embrace you with all my heart. [P.S.] By the next post I will tell you more of it for today my head is in a whirl.'[87]

The concern of the Marquis de Stainville over the fate of his heir reflected some uncertainty, apparently persistent, as to his precise whereabouts in relation to the battle of Casteldelfino. One early authority describes the Count de Stainville as having been present at the attack on the entrenchments and the capture of Casteldelfino.[88] It is, however, certain that his regiment was operating farther south under Lautrec; and two days after his heavy letter of 28 July 1744 the Marquis de Stainville wrote further to his friend in Brussels: 'The other day I wrote you a little scrap, of which you will have understood nothing, for my head was muddled by anxiety. Yesterday I received the account whereof I attach a copy here.[89] You will easily guess from whom it comes; my son this time was not where the guns were firing; of those who were there is not a single officer who was not killed or wounded.'[90] The Marquis de Stainville appears to have been fonder of his eldest son than one might gather from the memoirs of the future Duke de Choiseul.

Next day another diplomatist was writing from Paris: 'For the last two days they have forgotten in this town that there are other countries in the world besides Piedmont. The only talk is of the brilliant success which the Prince de Conti has had there and which very far surpasses all hopes that had been formed for it.'[91] If the battle of Casteldelfino came to rank as one of the finest infantry engagements of that century, brilliant was the word for the Gallispan capture of the Barricades. Just fifty years later Napoleon, a disciple of Bourcet in mountain warfare, proposed to imitate the suggestive campaign of 1744 and with the same objective, to capture the

[86] Marquis de Stainville to Gundel, 28 July 1744: Ö.S./H.H.S., 23. Frankreich Varia 1736–1749, docket 'Choiseul de Stainville' etc., fo. 25.
[87] Ibid.
[88] Pinard, op. cit., v. 686.
[89] Now evidently missing.
[90] Marquis de Stainville to Gundel, 30 July 1744: u.s., fo. 24.
[91] Baron von Bernstorff to Count von Schulin, Paris, 31 July 1744: Rigsarkiv/T.K.U.A., Frankrig, C.253.

Barricades and carry through to besiege Coni. But for the present, for Conti, between the Barricades and the siege of Coni lay that of uncaptured Demont, described by the later Choiseul as 'a small fortress which closes an outlet onto the plain of Piedmont'.[92]

VII

The Barricades surmounted, the French and Spanish princes camped with their right wing at Sambuc on the Stura. Thence Brigadier de Mauriac was sent back to Provence with a small force 'upon advice of some movements by the English upon the coasts of Nice'.[93] Seapower was still exerting its long pull even upon that alpine campaign. Mauriac returned to command the southern shores under the Marquis de Mirepoix, who lamented that summer that the British fleet was bottling the French one up in Toulon and was 'doing us all the harm possible by sea. The town of Marseilles is suffering to the extent of more than twelve millions in loss from captures since the declaration of war. Money is becoming very scarce there and confidence is almost lost.'[94]

While the British navy was imposing this significant background of economic blockade upon the alpine campaign of the Gallispan Army, the Piedmontese peasantry were coming to the fore against it with their own brand of economic warfare. At first these hard-living mountaineers had mostly been ready enough, apparently, to draw profit from supplying the invaders; but the French, especially, so ground them down by severities and pillage that the peasants took to scattering their grain to destruction and staving in their casks. The land laid waste, its sturdy inhabitants, impoverished and aroused, took to their native mountains in order, as the French viewed it, 'to follow the trade of robbers and assassins under the name of militia'.[95] This ominous development for the Gallispan army was not slow to be felt.

The troops of the Prince de Conti received extra issues of mutton and brandy to reward their ardour and sustain it in their further advance, begun on 26 July, from Sambuco to Vinadio. The Gallispan columns, stiffened now by the cavalry come through from Dauphiny, went swirling down the valley of the Stura, round about the resistant

[92] Choiseul, *Mémoires*, p. 17.
[93] Major-General de Chauvelin to Count d'Argenson, Sambuc, 21 July 1744: Arch. Guerre C., vol. 3061, no. 177.
[94] Marquis de Mirepoix to Count d'Argenson, Marseilles, 10 Aug. 1744: Arch. Guerre C., vol. 3062, no. 31.
[95] Marquis de Saint-Simon, op. cit., p. 87.

fortress of Demont and probing out beyond, down to Mount Valoria by Gajola. There Franco-Spanish advance guards coatless in the heat, barefooted for surer foothold, had to clear a considerable body of Piedmontese peasantry off the heights. In the rear, meanwhile, the occupied village of Planches, incited by its priest, rose in arms against the invaders. They burnt the village and set the priest along with his flock to work in labour-gangs upon the precious roads through that rugged country, penetrated now to Demont. There the siege of the fortress was opened on the night of 9–10 August. Next night the partisans set ablaze the allied headquarters in the nearby village of Aisone. The two princes had narrow escapes, Bourcet's maps and papers were burnt, and among the officers who lost all their belongings and had to live hard for the rest of the campaign was the ancient Marquis de Maulévrier, the senior lieutenant-general in the French army. To him Conti now entrusted the completion of the siege of Demont while the bulk of the army pressed on towards the strategic prize of Coni.

While the militia of Piedmontese peasantry had been robustly harrying the invader around Demont, the army of the King of Sardinia had been concentrating for what Bourcet termed 'active defence' in the valley of the Varaita at Sampeyre, whence it might strike against the flank or rear of the advancing enemy, now confined to the valley of the Stura by the Sardinian dispositions. The forces of the Spanish generals on the northern sector and of Danois and Lautrec, including the Régiment de Stainville, bore south and consolidated on the main force around Demont. With Charles Emmanuel on the move from Sampeyre time pressed for the besiegers, consisting of seven Spanish battalions and as many French, including the Régiment de Stainville.

On 13 August two Gallispan batteries began the bombardment of Demont. Getting up ammunition for the siege-artillery was a grinding problem for an army short of precious mules, a favourite target of the partisans. On the morning of 17 August Maulévrier hotted up the siege and his shot, banging it red hot into the fortress. By five that afternoon Demont was ablaze, with some of the garrison throwing themselves out through embrasures. The governor, de Violet, said to have lost his wife from a bomb-splinter, ran up the white flag.

Through the night of 17 August Demont was left to blaze while the Spaniards looted it. Next evening the Prince de Beauvau, Stainville's friend serving in that campaign as Colonel of the Guards of Lorraine, visited the smoking ruins with de Violet and had an altercation with him as to responsibilities for so much damage. The same day Captain-

General de Las Minas brayed: 'We are going straight to Coni, which will naturally have the same fate as Demont.'[96]

They did not go quite straight through. If King Charles Emmanuel had failed to raise the siege of Demont, he had concentrated thirty battalions and thirty-two squadrons on Busca, whence he drew back to Saluzzo, seeking to lure the enemy on against him, away from strategic Coni. Conti prevented Don Philip and Las Minas from falling into the trap. Gallispan advance-guards went thrusting out to reconnoitre Coni. Once again, on 26 August 1744, they were set a fighting example by the eager Count de Stainville:

The Count de Maillebois, Maréchal-Général des Logis de l'Armée, upon whom devolved all the detail of the marches, and who everywhere made the most exact reconnaissances of the country, went ahead of the army with the Major-General of the Army of Spain and the chief engineers of both nations in order to reconnoitre an advantageous camp whence the army might at its ease conduct the siege of Coni, and receive the enemy if he presented himself. Some small Piedmontese detachments came to meet him, but the Count de Stainville with some companies of grenadiers and of the cavalry scattered them without losing many men, although he was attacked several times over; he even brought several prisoners into the French camp.[97]

At Conti's headquarters Stainville's running fight was evidently regarded as a creditable little engagement. Just as, at the opening of the campaign, Stainville had been one of the first to lead the French vanguards in attack across the river Var, so now at last did this keen campaigner lead them out from their toiling passage of the Alps, against the long-sought objective of Coni.

[96] Captain-General de Las Minas, camp at Gajola, 18 Aug. 1744: cited, C. Buffa di Perrero, *Carlo Emanuele III di Savoia a difesa delle Alpi nella campagna del 1744* (Turin, 1887), p. 164, n.
[97] Marquis de Saint-Simon, op. cit., p. 101.

CHAPTER II

CONI

I

CONI, Cuneo the wedge, occupies an extraordinary position. The fortified town had stood out steeply on a bluff, wedged into the confluence of the Stura and the Gesso, since about 1120 when, according to romantic report, it had been founded by rebels against a lord seeking to exercise the feudal right of first nuptials upon a local bride. Commanding the plain stretching flat away north-eastwards to Turin, Coni is cupped upon the other three sides by the mountains. So that, looking either way up many of the streets, one sees framed in the middle distance Alps at one end, Alps at the other, north-westward up by Busca and back towards Casteldelfino, then sweeping right round south in the direction Boves, Mondovi, Ormea.

Two and a half centuries after its fitting foundation of resistance Coni had acquired a shortlived English connection through the second son of Edward III, Lionel, first Duke of Clarence, to whom the town was made over by his father-in-law, Galeazzo Visconti. Subsequently Coni had become a standing bastion of Italy against France, and a stout one, enduring sieges in 1542, 1557, 1639, 1641, 1691. Only in 1641 had it fallen, to the renown of Caesar de Choiseul, that forbear and example for young Stainville. Coni remained 'the essential object ... at the outlet of the mountains ... whereof one could make a place of arms to sustain communications with Dauphiny or Provence'[1] and nourish an advance out on to those Lombard plains for which the Spanish court had been waiting, wrote its effective prime minister, the Marquis de la Ensenada, 'like the Jews for the Messiah'.[2]

If the Spaniards longed for Lombardy, they were slow in getting down to Coni. The French engineers, notably 'old Razeau ... grown grey in the business of sieges',[3] urged a quick crack at Coni while the season lasted but they could not prevail against the preference of the chief engineer of the Spaniards, an Italian called Amici, for a limited and carefully dug-in attack on the obvious southern front between the confluence. This was imposed by Las Minas whom Conti now

---

[1] Instructions to Prince de Conti, Feb. 1744: *Guerres des Alpes*, i. 130.
[2] Marquis de la Ensenada, San Ildefonso, 22 Aug. 1744: Correspondence of Captain-General de Las Minas: *Erbfolge-Krieg*, viii. 493.   [3] Marquis de Saint-Simon, op. cit., p. 102.

denounced in crescendo for 'impertinence upon impertinence ... M. de La Mina commands as a master, and refuses to obey even the Infant's orders; the Infant is as feeble towards me as towards him.'[4]

Two days before this outburst Conti had been writing to his Minister of War:

Three army corps are needed to succeed in making the investment, one to hold in check the army of the King of Sardinia, the second to sustain the trenches, the third beyond the Gesso to confront some battalions and 10,000 peasants who are assembling in the Mondovi district. The [present] army, weakened by the necessity of maintaining communications via the Stura, which become more troubled from day to day, is far from being able to suffice all these objects.[5]

As it was, the Piedmontese army up beyond Busca at Saluzzo had to be screened off by a Gallispan corps of observation based between Madonna dell'Olmo and Caraglio. The siege-corps itself, with headquarters between the Stura and the Gesso at Saint-Roch and Madonna delli Angeli, had to reckon with over three thousand defenders under Lieutenant-General Baron von Leutrum, of proven courage from Camposanto, of set intent that Coni should not falter in its proud tradition of resistance. Meanwhile beyond the Gesso, as Conti ominously noted, 'the environs of Mondovi are stuffed with peasants'[6] in arms thanks to the endeavours of the Marquis D'Ormea upon his home ground in the aristocratic tradition of supplementing diplomacy with war.

A force under the Marquis de Campo Santo struck out to quell these Piedmontese levies and get a grip on the area Boves–Peveragno–La Chiusa, whence the Gallispan army hoped to draw its main supplies. Soon, though, things reached such a pass that those three villages were burnt by order of Don Philip. It was a grim grip, and unproductive. More ominous still, three or four thousand partisans actually launched a full attack upon Borgo San Dalmazzo, a burg in the rear of the siege-lines, where the French and Spaniards had established their hospitals and depots. The attack was repulsed but not the attacking spirit of the countryside, notably against the long line of communication along the Stura back to France. The French were driven to make an example, executing thirty peasants captured in arms. The Spaniards followed suit. Thereafter the partisans mostly confined themselves to sniping from rocky fastnesses. But their hatred grew. Such was the baleful background to the opening of the siege-trenches against Coni on the night of 12–13 September 1744.

[4] Prince de Conti to Count d'Argenson, camp before Coni, 5 Sept. 1744: Arch. Guerre C., vol. 3062, no. 112.
[5] Prince de Conti to Count d'Argenson, Saint-Roch, 3 Sept. 1744: *Guerres des Alpes*, i. 216.
[6] Prince de Conti to his uncle, Count de Clermont, camp before Coni, 7 Sept. 1744: Arch. Guerre, Série Supplémentaire (Fonds de Suède), vol. 23, no. 33.

II

'I remember', wrote the later Choiseul, 'that in 1744, on arriving at Coni, M. d'Aiguillon, who had the regiment of Brie-Infanterie, was in my brigade with the Régiment de Conti. We were covering the headquarters and the rear of the trenches in the siege of Coni. We became fairly intimate, M. d'Aiguillon and I; we used to spend our days together. He confided in me his rage against the king, who had carried off his mistress, Mme de Châteauroux.'[7] The Duke d'Aiguillon, son of the Count de Stainville's philosophic duchess and nephew of The Duke de Richelieu, was then the young Duke d'Agenais, conveniently relegated to the remoteness of that secondary theatre of operations: a little before Agenais had left Versailles he had brought the royal displeasure down upon the Marquise de Flavacourt, sister to the Duchess de Châteauroux, for being so tactless as to accompany him to a masked fancy-dress ball given by the princesses. Louis had gone as a bat, Agenais and his partner as blind people, not daring to unmask. Some years later Agenais was still to be subjected to the cold treatment by his king, who 'does not forgive someone for having been fancied, even earlier than himself, by one of his mistresses'.[8]

Louis, however, had not blocked the promotion of Agenais to be a brigadier after the action before Casteldelfino, where he was wounded and held to have done well. When the new brigadier came to know Stainville before Coni there was special reason why Agenais should be full of his translated mistress. For while the Gallispan army had been crossing into Italy, back in France things had not stood still.

After the Prince de Conti and his officers had left court to campaign, King Louis XV had occasioned two important events. First, on the evening of Sunday, 26 April 1744, the Count de Maurepas, during a dinner which he was giving to Mademoiselle among others, was summoned forthwith to the king, who typically chose him to inform his own client, Amelot de Chaillou, still at table, that he was dismissed and banished from court. Like most of Louis's dismissals it was completely sudden. That very day the foreign minister had apprised Gundel of the French declaration of war, and Madame Amelot had been playing cards with the queen. Within forty-eight hours they were both gone, though Amelot kept his 20,000 livres a year while his wife was granted another 12,000 – not bad recognition of their inoffensive mediocrity. It had, however, not only

<hr/>

[7] Choiseul, *Mémoires*, p. 14.   [8] Kaunitz/Mémoire, p. 444.

bored King Louis but exasperated King Frederick, with his germanic hatred of weakness and his personal contempt for incompetence. He had seldom wearied of cruel jokes against Amelot, described by another clever German as 'this gentle man who only possesses the art of bending'.[9]

Within hours of the French renewal of war against Austria little Amelot was sacrificed to that Franco-Prussian rapprochement which Rottembourg was promoting. Amelot's dismissal was also a sharp warning to Maurepas, whose stock had fallen since the failure of the invasion of England; it had mainly succeeded in antagonizing in Germany the lesser protestant princes who, like the Dutch, viewed with alarm any attempt to overthrow the Hanoverian succession in England. Chavigny, trying to revive the Rheinbund under French aegis, had been urging upon Louis that the Jacobites 'are good for nothing ... Let us unite to save the empire with the protestants of Germany; it is by this way, sire, that your ancestors have marched and they have been fortunate therein.'[10]

In German affairs Louis was indeed trying to concert with the leading protestant power. He now assumed personal conduct of foreign affairs left without a minister, in an administrative concentration exceeding anything attempted by Louis XIV, and perhaps designed partly to overawe Maurepas and those others who had served under Fleury and retained a lively distrust of fresh negotiations with Frederick, especially since they had been initially excluded from them. Having given the old team a warning and Frederick a nod as to the determination of his foreign policy, Louis proceeded to do likewise in regard to his warlike intentions. A week before Amelot fell the Marquis de Stainville had observed: 'What they call the interior, which are the [royal] cabinets, wish the King to go [to the front]. But it is on the contrary to the interest of the ministers, except the one for war, to prevent it.'[11] Perhaps Amelot had here been pushed to push too hard. A week after his fall the king precipitated his second main event. At a quarter past three on the morning of Sunday the 3rd May 1744 Louis XV drove out from the Cour de Marbre at Versailles on his way to the main front in Flanders. He was entering upon his first campaign.

Louis left his ministers behind but was accompanied in his coach by two intimates of the interior, Ayen and Meuse. A week later the

[9] Baron von Bernstorff to Count von Schulin, Paris, 8 June 1744: Rigsarkiv/T.K.U.A., Frankrig, C.253.
[10] Chavigny to King Louis XV, Mar. 1744: Arch. Aff. Étr. C.P., Bavière: Broglie/Fréd–LXV, ii. 212.
[11] Marquis de Stainville to Grand Duke Francis II, Paris, 18 Apr. 1744: Esteri del Granducato di Toscana, vol. 2295/1286, fo. 391.

Marquis de Stainville, a significant source here, commented: 'It is the Marshal de Noailles who has contributed most to the king's journey. They claim that it is a courtier's sleight so as to be in a position, alone with M. de Richelieu, to render themselves so to say the masters of the kingdom by sequestrating the king from the counsel of his other ministers',[12] left behind. One of them, Maurepas, sneered of the royal advance: 'Is it sure that the King is so brave?'[13] Most Frenchmen liked to think so as he seemed to symbolize the renaissance of that French war-effort which, beaten down by the preceding autumn, was now expanding on all fronts, formalized by declarations of war, formidable in its total muster, militia included, of some three hundred thousand troops. This presented a heavy bill to the tax-shy but patriotic French.

The economic and sociological basis of the French war-effort was, at just that period, subjected to a striking analysis, broad yet acute. Baron von Bernstorff, outstandingly able, recently arrived as the Danish minister in Paris, was an early proponent of that new science of political economy in which he was subsequently to interest the future Duke de Choiseul. On 8 June 1744 Bernstorff sent the Danish foreign minister, Count von Schulin, by special bearer a survey after two months' residence in France:

She is supposed to be drained of men and money, her people discouraged, the court only wishing for peace ... Nothing of all that seems to me to be so ... It is true that France has provinces much less populated than those of some other countries and, in particular, of Germany. The long wars of Louis XIV, the Revocation of the Edict of Nantes, the colonies in America whither many people are going in order to establish themselves, the misery of the country caused by the harsh impositions beneath which it groans and still more by the hard way in which their payment is torn from it, finally the libertinage which has infected the generality of the nation in all classes, have diminished the number of inhabitants, which the two unfortunate campaigns of 1742 and 1743 have further lessened; but ... the loss of eighty or a hundred thousand men does not exhaust so large and extensive a kingdom as France.[14]

The shortage of manpower in France was, Bernstorff estimated, less severe than it had been back in 1709 and 'the drain of money is even less noticeable'. The heavy war-expenditure of the past three years had naturally 'diminished the amount of cash circulating in commerce' but, he explained:

This country, more favourably situated than any other in Europe, ... has infinite resources. At all events one does not see the least diminution of the luxury either of

---

[12] Ibid., 9 May 1744: fo. 401.　　[13] Cited, Broglie/Fréd–LXV, ii. 217.
[14] Baron von Bernstorff to Count von Schulin, Paris, 8 June 1744: Rigsarkiv/T.K.U.A., Frankrig, C.253 for the following.

the court or of individuals; shares keep on steadily; trade does not vary; they have not yet had recourse to those extraordinary remedies which Louis XIV so often employed even in the midst of his prosperity; and yet, as I know from certain knowledge, last March they had an assured fund of 298 million livres to meet expenses for the year to March 1745. This fund consists of the 204 million livres which form the ordinary revenue of the crown; of the Dixième (a hard tax but, even so, more tolerable than many others) which, from the 47 millions which it was worth, has been raised today to 54 millions; and of 40 millions which the edicts published this winter, for the increase of several dues, have yielded. It is true that all that makes the subject suffer, but his cries nowise reach the throne; the sovereign does not suspect this and it will take many years yet before he is aware of them and many more again before he listens to them.

This pregnant prophet continued:

I have as much to say of the discouragement of the people. It curses the war whereof it bears the weight, it sighs after peace, but it is its genius that it is not less prompt to sacrifice itself for the glory of the French name so soon as it is urged to or as the least success animates it. It is inconceivable how much irritation the ill-considered attempt of the Austrians to enter France last year has caused, and how much its ill success had raised the spirit of the nation.

Two days before Baron von Bernstorff tendered that analysis the Marquis de Stainville had bracketed him with Count John Loss, the Saxon minister in Paris, in observing that the Danish one 'also seems entirely devoted to the Court [of Charles VII] at Frankfurt, and to this one'.[15] And two months later, writing again of Loss, 'I should be sorry indeed to do him wrong but he is too abject a courtier to do his job well, as also M. Bernstorff, the new Danish envoy, an intimate friend of M. de Belle-Isle'[16], then eclipsed by fresh initiatives.

A French army over a hundred thousand strong in Flanders now came bearing down upon a conglomerate force of hardly half as many British, Hanoverian, Austrian, and Dutch troops. France was drawing her dividend from the attempted invasion of England, alarmed into suspending Habeas Corpus and reluctant to commit herself heavily upon the continent despite the renewed threat to Hanover. Frederick the Great was looking to France again while Maria Theresa rather relished the predicament of the British government, so prone to accompany its subsidies with lectures. Austrian assistance to the Anglo-Hanoverians under Field-Marshal Wade in Flanders was limited to a small contingent under the Duke von Arenberg. In vain had Prince Charles of Lorraine urged that the main Austrian armies be switched to Flanders in defence of his own holding. For that prince, splendidly married in January 1744 to

¹⁵ Marquis de Stainville to Grand Duke Francis II, Paris, 5 June 1744: *u.s.* fo. 414.
¹⁶ Ibid., 8 Aug. 1744, fo. 452.

Maria Theresa's sister, the Archduchess Maria Anna, had been appointed governor-general of the Austrian Netherlands, now with Count Kaunitz by his side: Kaunitz had latterly got across Ormea and was replaced in Turin by a suppler Lorrainer, Stainville's friend, Henry de Richecourt. In the military field, however, Prince Charles was ordered still to stand over against Alsace and his homeland of Lorraine.

With Austria and England preoccupied upon either hand the brunt of French attack in Flanders bore upon the Dutch garrisoning the frontier-fortresses under the Barrier Treaty. For Dutchmen the dark days of 1672 seemed to have returned. Only, now they tended to squeal, as in the intercepted dispatches of Van Hoey, still accredited to the French king. News of the capture of Villefranche had just reached him in camp at Cysoing beneath Lille when, advised by Noailles, he gave the brush-off to a Dutch emissary, the Count of Wassenaer-Twickel, bearing peace-propositions which in some respects adumbrated those to be adopted – ultimately. Next day Louis left to open the trenches against the Dutch in Menin. A siege suited a campaigning king nicely, as it had the Grand Monarque before Maestricht in 1673. Now they knocked down Menin in a week, on 4 June 1744. Louis triumphed back to Lille.

This military stroke for France coincided to within a day with a diplomatic one. When Louis, and Richelieu, had gone on campaign the negotiations at Versailles with Rottembourg had been entrusted to Tencin and Orry, encouraged by the example of Amelot to support rapprochement with Prussia. Tencin, unknown to his king, discussed the negotiation with Frederick's favourite, the Marshal de Belle-Isle, who was incidentally giving the cardinal tips on the stock-exchange. The pair were potential rivals to Noailles, and Rottembourg promoted a rapprochement between Belle-Isle and the Duchess de Châteauroux, withdrawn to Pâris-Duverney's house at Plaisance but kept in on the negotiations. Frederick had been writing to her that May: 'It is a pity that Prussia should be obliged to remain ignorant of her obligation to you.'[17]

The negotiations were indeed advancing. France and Prussia agreed to pickings in Flanders and Bohemia respectively. France undertook to carry the war into Germany once Prussian pressure in the rear had primed an Austro-British retreat from the Netherlands and the Rhine. Frederick stood pat upon the end of August as the term for a Prussian intervention and meanwhile insisted upon secrecy. The Cardinal de Tencin and the Count de Rottembourg

[17] King Frederick II to Duchess de Châteauroux, Potsdam, 12 May 1744: *Politische Correspondenz*, iii. 130.

signed the compact in Paris on 5 June 1744, the third anniversary of the ill-starred Franco-Prussian Treaty of Breslau. For the present, however, the new agreement with Prussia, like the earlier one, clinched French policy in Germany. Four days later Chavigny's union of German princes was achieved at Frankfurt am Main upon Frederick's reluctant consent to specific participation by France in this revival of the Rheinbund, though resort to a secret, separate article spared German sensibilities. The German lands were once again to be set against one another under French auspices as in the times of Cardinal Richelieu, of Marshal de Belle-Isle in his erstwhile glory.

Belle-Isle now advanced at least to Metz, where he was governor still. Richelieu meantime was concerting with the ladies, the Duchess de Châteauroux, Madame de Tencin, and, now, the dowager Princess de Conti, mother of the general. This ambitious lady, having 'all the intelligence possible',[18] decided that it would be good for morale to take her daughter, the newly married Duchess de Chartres, to join her enamoured husband in Flanders; and it so happened that among those accompanying the princess would be the Duchesses de Lauraguais and de Châteauroux. On 6 June 1744 they advanced on Lille.

The Marshal de Noailles, nicknamed her Godfather by the Duchess de Châteauroux, had not been keen to sponsor so close a repetition of the precedent from 1673, when Louis XIV had enjoyed having Madame de Montespan by the front. But then he, unlike Louis XV, had campaigned complete with queen and court. Now, too, the royal interior had failed to reckon with an increasingly lively public opinion, expressed as usual in low ditties, sung in Lille under the windows of the spirited mistress who was inciting her king to martial vigour. The then Count de Stainville explained that 'in order that there should be no mystery for the population as to the happiness of the King, they built an external gallery in the towns in which they slept, to communicate from the apartment of the King to that of Mme de Châteauroux.'[19]

After Menin, Ypres where Louis XV appeared on 17 June. Some ten days later Ypres capitulated and Knocke too submitted. The Barrier Fortresses were falling like a row of ninepins. The Duchess de Châteauroux exulted for Louis that 'his great-grandfather, great as he was, never did so much.'[20]

While the next siege, at Furnes, was preparing Louis toured the

[18] Barbier, iii. 517.
[19] Choiseul, *Mémoires*, p. 18.
[20] Duchess de Châteauroux to Duke de Richelieu, 27 June 1744: Broglie/Fréd–LXV, ii. 301.

Channel ports and made his acquaintance with the sea. 'It was very gentle', he wrote from Calais on 4 July, 'and the weather was so fine that I perfectly well saw the coasts of England and the tower of Dover',[21] so near and yet so far. His gaze, though, was swiftly turned in the opposite direction.

On 3 July Prince Charles of Lorraine had completed a crossing of the Rhine in force, foiling Marshal de Coigny and attacking into Alsace. Lauterbourg fell to the Austrians. They advanced by way of Wissembourg, the Pandours scouring ahead, though Menzel a few days earlier had paid with his life for a typical piece of drunken bravado against a French outpost. The court of Lunéville withdrew to Metz while Louis, his kingdom invaded, waited not upon his Flemish conquests – Furnes fell on 11 July. The king assured Noailles that he was 'very impatient to be at Metz and to confer with you and M. de Belle-Isle, who knows my way of thinking as well as you. I know how to do without my equipage, and, if need be, the shoulder of mutton of infantry lieutenants will nourish me perfectly.'[22] There was a good deal more than that at the feast given by Louis at Metz on 7 August, three days after his advent, in honour of Field-Marshal von Schmettau, arrived from King Frederick to concert Franco-Prussian strategy. The day after this copious repast Louis was indisposed and could not attend the Te Deum for the capture of Casteldelfino.

The later Choiseul wrote:

The King, while we were forcing the Alps to penetrate into Piedmont, fell ill at Metz, in passing from the Army of Flanders to the Army of Germany ... At first the illness was regarded as light. M. de Richelieu advised Mme de Châteauroux, and his opinion is always for doing something silly. They confined the King, without letting him see anybody except the intimate circle. He was like a kind of sultan in his seraglio; for Mme de Châteauroux had several women in her retinue, and M. de Richelieu and others, by their baseness and intrigues, were rather like eunuchs. The illness worsened and became serious enough to frighten the seraglio as to its consequences ... The doors opened; they gave the King to understand that he was in danger, which is not difficult ...

The effect of his pusillanimity was very extraordinary upon this occasion: Mme de Châteauroux, whom he loved as much as he can love, whom he had had come for this journey, upon whom he doubtless lavished proofs of the greatest weakness and the greatest submission, Mme de Châteauroux had just left him when they judged it opportune to have the doctors come into him. At this very moment he became frightened to the point not only of wishing to receive the Sacraments, of asking pardon of everybody for his past conduct, but of publicly ordering that they should expel this same Mme de Châteauroux from Metz, should inform her that he deprived her of her office with the future Dauphine ...

[21] King Louis XV to Duke de Charost, Calais, 4 July 1744: Luynes, vi. 6.
[22] King Louis XV to Marshal de Noailles, Rheims, 31 July 1744: Rousset, ii. 175.

He displayed eagerness to have his orders executed, and the ladies, whom he had brought with him with so much scandal, were obliged to return to Paris in a manner still more scandalous for the honour of the King. For the rest the King was not so ill as was thought and said. His absolute lack of courage was taken by the doctors for collapse. He was not even troubled in his head; he did not speak because fear had deprived him of all his faculties, even that of speaking. He recovered fairly promptly and was at the siege of Freiburg, to make himself despised in another kind of lack of spirit and of courage.[23]

Choiseul's rasping estimate of the court at Metz was written years afterwards in the bitterness of his own fall from favour. Yet his feeling censure of weakness and corruption carries conviction. His memoirs, from so high a personage of that court, stand apart even by comparison with those of the Marquis d'Argenson. The antipathy to the treacherous, lecherous Richelieu is one of the things which warms one towards Choiseul. As to fact, considering that he was not present then in Metz, his description is one of pregnant accuracy subject to one or two checks: the gallery across the street is otherwise heard of only at Metz, where it became a notorious scandal. Choiseul's agreement with Maurepas concerning the king's cowardice may have led him to underestimate the gravity of Louis's illness; but there was general agreement as to his fear of death and divine retribution, his undignified disloyalty in hastily dismissing his mistress at the behest of the young Bishop FitzJames of Soissons, who required this before affording the king the last sacrament.

With the king out of action, Belle-Isle mainly carried on the government, evoking for one admirer at Metz 'a shipwreck wherein the ablest and bravest person takes the helm and commands the ship without anybody wishing to dispute it him so long as the danger lasts'.[24] The danger caused the queen to travel forty-eight hours on end. She was accompanied by the Marquise de Flavacourt, and at Bar-le-Duc they passed her two sisters in their shrouded retreat from Metz. Upon arrival there at midnight on 18 August Marie Leszczynska learnt that Louis had turned the corner and was turning over a new leaf. He apologized for his previous conduct, and the queen is said to have tried to preen herself into renewed attractiveness. But her spirited rival was prophesying: 'So soon as he shall be a little restored, I wager that I shall trot furiously through his head, and that at last ... quite quietly he will ask Lebel or Bachelier what has become of me. Since they are for me, I shall do well.'[25] Looming was

[23] Choiseul, *Mémoires*, pp. 17–20.
[24] Baron von Bernstorff to King Christian VI, Metz, 16 Aug. 1744: Rigsarkiv/T.K.U.A., Frankrig, C.253, no 38.
[25] Duchess de Châteauroux to Duke de Richelieu, Aug. 1744: Broglie/Fréd.-LXV, ii. 348.

an interior battle not less real in its way than that impending in the camps of war.

III

In the trenches before Coni, with these events at Metz as hot news over the Alps, the jilted Duke d'Agenais impressed the Count de Stainville, in retrospect, as 'malignant and vain'. The then Stainville wrote of the then Agenais:

He was in despair and, in the bitterness of his heart, he did not know whom he should the most hate or despise, the lover, the mistress or his uncle. He was in this frame of mind when I made a fairly intimate acquaintance with him during the campaign of 1744. Although I could not have been less interested in the intrigues of the Court, in the amours of the King and even in his preservation, . . . M. d'Aiguillon explained his sentiments to me. He was very glad that the King should die, because the death of a rival can never cause pain; he overwhelmed the King with contempt for having treated Mme de Châteauroux so unworthily; for his vanity made him believe that a person whom he had loved should be treated with contempt by nobody but himself. It is not that this treatment did not transport him with joy; he often used to repeat to me: 'She has behaved like a whore; she has been treated as a whore should be'.[26]

Choiseul explained that at the time Agenais's 'confidences increased our intimacy and in good faith, without plumbing his character, I thought I was fond of him'.[27] Such was the beginning of that troubled friendship with the future Duke d'Aiguillon who was one day to supersede the resentful Duke de Choiseul. That, though, lay far ahead. For years yet d'Aiguillon was to experience the disfavour of the king in his resentment of the duke's priority with his mistress. Years later again, though, Louis had softened into some affection 'because', as he told Choiseul, 'of the trick which I played upon him a very long while ago.'[28] That was then, when the future Choiseul and d'Aiguillon were sharing the rigours of the siege at Coni, a different proposition from the so-called Barrier Fortresses.

The opening of the Gallispan siege-trenches against Coni had got off to a poor start, delayed till the night of 12–13 September. Leutrum set that night alight with red-hot shot and fascines blazing with pitch to illuminate the besiegers at work. Thus spotlit, he pounded them all night long with cannon and mortar fire. Dawn enabled the gunners

[26] Choiseul, *Mémoires*, p. 21.   [27] Ibid., p. 14.
[28] King Louis XV to Duke de Choiseul, 6 June 1770: Gabriel, duc de Choiseul, 'Lettre de M. le duc de Choiseul sur les Mémoires de Mme du Barry' in *Revue de Paris* (1829), iv. 57. For the dating of this letter cf. J. Levron, op. cit., p. 43.

of Coni to concentrate upon a redoubt newly constructed by Spanish troops. The cannonade kept up till two o'clock next afternoon when crack troops of the Piedmontese garrison came charging out. They swept the Spaniards back from their redoubt and inflicted a hundred casualties before French reserves helped to master the swaying combat and drive the assailants back. This virile sortie clogged Spanish siege-operations into caution.

Before opening the bombardment of Coni on 16 September 1744 the polite Prince de Conti sent an ensign under flag of truce to ask Baron von Leutrum to indicate his personal residence so that the French artillery might try to spare it. To which Leutrum 'graciously replied that his lodging was upon the ramparts'.[29] On 17 September the allied artillery, beginning to establish an ascendancy, set fire to a number of houses. Leutrum, on the scene, heard some citizens of Coni indulging in defeatist talk. He hanged five of them upon the spot. Coni held out.

Shingly soil, difficult to entrench, helped to settle the siege into the cumbersone routine of sieges, of saps, redoubts, battery and counter-battery, zigzags, gabions, and fascines, with regiments rotating in the trenches: on 23 September the Régiment de Stainville was one of the reliefs taking over the French front under the command of Chevert.[30] That night working-parties of Stainville and Gatinois were in the trenches when jumpy Spanish sentries mistook them for an enemy sortie and loosed off. This delayed the French diggers and cost them some twenty killed or wounded: the kind of little incident that does not improve relations between allies. And all this while September was slipping by. Autumn had arrived.

Conti at length gained his point. On 27–28 September siege-trenches were opened in a new attack against Coni by picked troops under the Marquises de Camposanto and du Châtel from the eastern front across the Gesso. This initiative of calculated risk, stressed by Las Minas, was critical. Leutrum sounded the alarm. But the alert Charles Emmanuel was already on the march from Saluzzo, bearing down in full force by way of Vottignasco, Murasso, Ronchi.

Charles Emmanuel had been 'awaiting some succour from Germany and the Milanese'[31] against the invaders, now debouched in superior force onto the spreading plain. His main army, however, received only some three thousand Austrian reinforcements under

---

[29] 'Journal du siège de Coni' in Henri Moris, *Opérations militaires dans les Alpes et les Apennins pendant la Guerre de la Succession d'Autriche* (Paris, 1886), p. 341.

[30] Cf. Major-General de Chauvelin to Count d'Argenson, camp before Coni, 24 Sept. 1744: Arch. Guerre C., vol. 3065, no. 156. Cf. also ibid., no. 183: 'Mémoire du siège de Cony'.

[31] Marquis de Saint-Simon, op. cit., p. 111.

Lieutenant-Fieldmarshal Pallavicini. They were mainly Warasdin Croats led by Colonel Maguire, another of those Irish expatriates who bob up in outlandish contexts throughout the eighteenth century. In the kingdom of Sardinia indeed, in what had become a patriotic war against the invader, conscription was now proclaimed for all fit males between sixteen and sixty: another corrective to too rigid an assumption that warfare then involved only small professional armies. Yet Charles Emmanuel's army remained small enough – something over 25,000 men advancing against a force about twice as strong, notably in that cavalry which a pitched battle would favour. That nevertheless was what the king intended in accordance with Ormea's advice 'that there is everything to gain thereby and little to lose'[32] even in case of defeat in that geographical layout and late season. Their march, merely, had already secured the initial advantage of compelling Conti to do as he had feared, promptly abandoning his flying camp and enterprise beyond the Gesso. The fortress of Coni was freed from immediate check.

The bulk of the Gallispan army was now concentrated north of Coni along the road to Caraglio running westward from the outlying church of Madonna dell'Olmo, Our Lady of the Elm, fortified into a strong-point with a redoubt to cover the extreme right of the allied line. In the rear a siege-corps was left under Counts de Lautrec and de Danois to contain Coni itself within the wedge of the confluence. The Régiment de Stainville had been out in the trenches again, along with Île de France and Vivarais, on the night of 28–29 September. The little Count de Stainville, however, was not one to be left, if he could help it, to kick his heels in the rear while other regiments distinguished themselves upon the field of battle. In his own words: 'We had a battle during the siege of Coni; I entreated vigorously to be relieved of the siege in order to go thither with my brigade. I obtained this.'[33] So on 29 September Conti, leaving his headquarters behind the siege-trenches, was 'betaking himself with the brigades of Lorraine and Stainville into the camp on the left bank of the Stura'.[34] Stainville's regiment was giving its name to the brigade which it had come to head up, with Stainville himself acting as second-in-command to the young brigadier, his friend Agenais. The two brigades joined the line of battle westward from Madonna dell'Olmo late that evening.

[32] Memorandum from Marquis D'Ormea to King Charles Emmanuel, Sept. 1744: 'Réponse du Marquis D'Ormea, et reflections sur les dispositions à donner et parti à prendre': C. Buffa di Perrero, *Carlo Emanuele III di Savoia a difesa delle Alpi nella campagna del 1744*, p. 211, n.
[33] Choiseul, *Mémoires*, p. 14.
[34] French memorandum, 'Bataille de Coni', 30 Sept. 1744: Arch. Guerre C., vol. 3065, no. 162.

IV

On the night of 29–30 September darkness spelt tension at Franco-Spanish field-headquarters. The thickly cultivated countryside made it difficult to reconnoitre the approaching enemy, especially by night when the local population was liable to pick off too venturesome patrols from the Gallispan army.

From the dawn of 30 September 1744 the French and Spanish army outside Coni could hear the bugles and drums of the advancing enemy, sounding into battle. Though this advance was to some extent masked by trees which the Gallispan forces had omitted to cut down, Charles Emmanuel attempted little stealth. It rather suited him that the attention of his antagonists should be concentrated upon his approach rather than elsewhere.

Drawn up to receive the army of the King of Sardinia was that of the Infant Don Philip and the Prince de Conti. This allied army to block the relief of Coni deployed twenty-three cannon, thirty-nine battalions of infantry and fifty-eight squadrons of cavalry. In the place of honour on the right of the line the redoubt of Madonna dell'Olmo was held by Spanish units including the Edinburgh Dragoons and dismounted hussars. Thence the front line was manned by Spanish infantry as far as a fortified farmstead, the Cassine Pasquale, held by the French infantry brigade of Lyonnais under command of stout old Count de Beaupréau. This line of battle was backed by a second, successively comprising more Spanish infantry, some Spanish and French dragoons and, somewhat west of the rear of Cassine Pasquale, the French units up from the siege-camp. That, therefore, was where Stainville stood, in the rearward line on the right of Don Philip's headquarters. These were shielded in front by some cavalry, including Conti's own regiment, holding the line on from Cassine Pasquale to the fortified redoubt of Picca-Rocca, occupied by more French infantry. Westward from Picca-Rocca again, over towards other farmsteads, the allied line ended with the bulk of its cavalry, massed thus at the extremity of the left wing with a view to exploiting its superiority in a broad turning movement against the whole of the Piedmontese right while the infantry fought a holding battle upon the hinge of Madonna dell'Olmo.

From about the middle of the morning the Austro-Sardinian army was taking up a broadly confronting position behind the road which led off from Madonna dell'Olmo to Tarantasca. 'The King of Sardinia,' observed a French tribute, 'having reconnoitred the position of his enemies, knew how to penetrate its intention, and to profit like a great general from the advantage of the terrain ... He made quite other dispositions from those which had been conjectured.'[35]

The Warasdin Croats and some Piedmontese grenadiers took stand on the Sardinian left over against the fortifications of Madonna dell'Olmo. Thence the main infantry, somewhat stronger than that of the Bourbons, extended westward in a single line, mainly, till, on the right wing, it was stepped back on to the Piedmontese cavalry, facing the allied, which was about twice as strong. To parry this enemy superiority, Charles Emmanuel sited his right and centre so far as possible behind the irrigation trenches which characterized that landscape, and further boxed them in with chevaux-de-frise garnished with artillery. Thus did the artful king swiftly fortify his whole line upon his exposed flank while canalizing the opening for attack in his chosen direction of Madonna dell'Olmo. If this choice could be criticized, notably by Bourcet, its implementation was indeed ingenious.

From the Franco-Spanish lines that morning King Charles Emmanuel could be discerned exhorting his troops. Don Philip for his part treated his Spanish regiments to a succinct allocation: 'Soldiers, remember that you are the vassals of my invincible father, and that I am your general.' This was apparently enough to touch off their enthusiasm in shouts of *Viva el Rey, y el real Infante*. Thereafter Don Philip withdrew to his command-post in the rear, where the captain of his bodyguard, Don Thomas Corvalán, was in Spanish fashion answerable with his head for the safety of his prince. The Prince de Conti led somewhat differently. Eschewing any harangue, Conti passed along the French lines, concerting last instructions with his commanders. He then took up position in the front line at the head of his own regiment of cavalry.

By about noon the Warasdins bearing down towards Madonna dell'Olmo were running into a protective screen of corresponding Gallispan troops, their sharp-shooting Miquelets. A scrap ensued. Some outlying houses before Madonna dell'Olmo went up in flames. The Croats secured the advantage and pressed it home till they found themselves coming up against the redoubt itself. A Piedmontese battery swelled the confused fighting, opening up against Madonna dell'Olmo with concentrated fire. This clinched the premature slide into battle contrary to the methodical intention of King Charles Emmanuel, himself at that time out on the other wing on his right,

---

[35] Marquis de Saint-Simon, op. cit., pp. 118 f. for the following.

where he had most to fear from the allied cavalry. The firing was extending all along the line so that it now appeared to the king more risky to try to break off the engagement than to continue it. The battle of Coni had begun.

The Warasdin Croats went storming in, right up to the entrench-ment of the redoubt. There the Spaniards held them, bent them back. Piedmontese grenadiers took up the attack upon Madonna dell'Olmo, both sides tending to reinforce in that direction. On the opposite flank meanwhile, the Gallispan cavalry was balked of its sweep forward by the cunning combination of spiky chevaux-de-frise with uninviting ditches. In this situation Conti refused the entreaty of the Count de Beaupréau, on his knees, 'his white hair dishevelled', to be allowed to lead out his infantry against the enemy batteries opposite. Conti was then intent upon himself leading a cavalry charge by his own regiment. This he did with conspicuous gallantry, and was slightly injured in the ankle when the heel of his boot was shot away. His troopers, though, could not dent the encrusted enemy position, spouting fire. His charge but served to confirm the general inability of the French and Spanish cavalry that day to exploit their superiority. But their artillery kept pounding away with such effect that 'it carried away whole ranks'[36] of Piedmontese. Meanwhile, in support of his own attack, Conti had been reinforcing the infantry to his right, pushing in regiments from the second line – Flanders, Foix, Brie, and Stainville. Thus Stephen de Stainville and his men advanced into the main line of battle at half past one that afternoon. The little count was going into action along with his friend, of whom he subsequently wrote: 'I was not too pleased with M. d'Aiguillon's style. At the beginning of the battle he remained on foot, although a brigadier, and, although on foot, he put on a cuirass. That did not look at all good.'[37]

At about that time[38] the blaze of the houses out in front of Madonna dell'Olmo had set alight a Piedmontese munition-wagon and blown up a forward battery of the Savoy brigade with ugly loss of life. This had been Beaupreau's chance to profit from the enemy

---

[36] 'Relation de la bataille gagnée par l'armée combinée de France et d'Espagne sur celle du Roy de Sardaigne le 30 7bre 1744', memorandum by Count de Maillebois to Count de Clermont: Arch. Guerre, Série Supplémentaire (Fonds de Suède), vol. 23, no. 47.

[37] Choiseul, *Mémoires*, p. 14.

[38] The detailed chronology of the battle of Coni, as of most battles, is appreciably confused. Thus the Marquis de Saint-Simon, op. cit., pp. 122–4, places Conti's charge earlier than the infantry reinforcement and Beaupreau's attack. This is not, however, easy to reconcile with other accounts, including Choiseul's, and is rejected by Ritter von Hoen, *Erbfolge-Krieg*, viii. 520. One is inclined to endorse the latter's verdict (loc. cit., n. 4) upon Saint-Simon's narrative of this engagement: 'Der Stil ... ist unklar und es drängt sich die Erkenntnis auf, dass seine Erzählung die Tatsachen richtig, die Zeitfolge aber falsch wiedergibt.' The present account represents a collation of French, Spanish, Italian, and Austrian sources.

confusion. The old warrior led Lyonnais charging out to assault the batteries of Savoy confronting them. They took the enemy guns. Savoy, though, was under the command of Lieutenant-General Cinzano, who had already given the enemy a taste of his mettle at Villefranche. Cinzano punched back at once and sent the French reeling into retreat.

The battle was getting going. Lyonnais were braced by the reinforcements from the second line under the overall command of Lieutenant-General the Marquis de Senneterre, once again in the thick of the fray against that monarch whom he had earlier failed to win by his diplomacy. At two o'clock Senneterre put in a fresh assault in two waves, himself heading the Lyonnais brigade in the first while in the second the Maréchal-de-Camp de Courten led the brigade of Stainville.

The later Choiseul wrote:

The battle had been begun about an hour when they came to order the brigade to march to attack a battery behind an irrigation trench in the enemy line. This attack was ordered in order to favour that which the Prince de Conti was making in person on our left. We marched, and scarcely had we done fifty paces when I saw that four men were bearing back M. d'Aiguillon upon halberds. I could not go to him because I had to march with my regiment to this battery, but I felt extreme grief at seeing him wounded. I sent an officer to ascertain what was the matter with him, and he reported to me that it was thought that he had a leg broken by a primed cannon-ball. I was truly in despair.[39]

For the moment, though, the battery of Savoy lay out there ahead, offering the Count de Stainville one of the great dangers and great opportunities of his career.

Lyonnais were finding it tough going again when Stainville and his soldiers came charging through to carry the brunt of the mortal combat swaying around the guns. Stainville captured the cannon, at once had them slewed around and set them pounding the broken enemy. This focus of conflict had by now attracted the King of Sardinia in person: throughout that day he displayed conspicuous personal courage and is said to have rejected attempts to restrain him with the words, 'Have I not, then, a son and successor?'[40] – just the kind of thing a king in battle ought to say, and *ben trovato* is an Italian expression. Charles Emmanuel now launched a savage counter-attack at close quarters against Stainville's left flank, threatening to roll it up. Stainville was prized out of the captured battery. But they budged him back only thirty yards. There, full within range of the enemy, the Count de Stainville reformed the brigade which he now

[39] Choiseul, *Mémoires*, pp. 14–15.   [40] Cited, *Erbfolge-Krieg*, viii. 523, n. 2.

commanded since Agenais was wounded. And Stainville had not yet finished. He led his brigade surging back in a second assault, and a second time did they wrest the cannon from the Piedmontese. By now it was a carnage of confusion, with fresh French infantry coming in under the Marquis du Châtel, some dragoon elements intervening on either side, and the Spanish infantry, which had charged alongside Senneterre, mixing it in their sector on the right of the French. In general, though, the lack of any sustained cavalry support was critical for Stainville out there in front. For the Piedmontese still refused to accept their repulse in that ding-dong set-to. On that day at any rate they shewed that Italians could know how to fight. Courten, seeing that the Stainville brigade was insufficiently matched by others in offensive prominence, pulled it out. By now the Count de Stainville's troops were terribly thinned away: not so, however, his own courage; and he was their leader. Yet a third time did the little colonel lead his men back to the attack.

As the Count de Stainville was marching his regiment for the third time along the way of duty and of death, a countermand reached him from the Prince de Conti. The troops were reformed on their starting-point, and for the rest of that afternoon the opposing lines on that part of the field stood in check. This was tensely exasperating for the French infantry who complained in particular that, in the words of the Marquis de Senneterre:

If M. de la Mina had been willing to comply with the reiterated entreaties of MM. d'Aremburu and Gandija, and with mine, that he should place behind the right 25 or 30 Squadrons, useless on the left which in any case was not their post, they would have entered sabre in hand ... so that the affair would have been determined very differently from how it was: but in vain were aides-de-camp after aides-de-camp sent to him [Las Minas] from the beginning of the action. He would only send M. d'Aremburu two squadrons of dragoons who were not sufficient to profit from the disorder into which our charge had thrown the enemy, besides which they [the dragoons] made no movement.[41]

The criticism of the dragoons may have been exaggerated: according to another account Conti himself, sabre in hand, had led them forward in support but had been unable to make headway against the sustained fire of the Sardinian infantry. One should also probably allow for the regular French tendency at that time to blame things off upon the Spaniards, and in particular upon Captain-General de Las Minas.

Obstinate Las Minas might be, but not afraid. He was constantly

---

[41] Marquis de Senneterre to Count d'Argenson, Embrun, 29 Oct. 1744: Arch. Guerre C., vol. 3065, no. 187.

in the thick of it and had several holes shot through his clothes and hat. The Spaniards not only supported the French charges but were locked in combat all the while with the Austro-Sardinian assailants of the redoubt of Madonna dell'Olmo. The Croats came charging back time and again but those ugly customers at close quarters met their match. The Spanish defences remained impervious. They were at one time bombarded also from behind by Leutrum's garrison in Coni, but it had to desist since its fire tended to harass the attackers even more than the Spanish defence, strengthened by fresh units under d'Aremburu. That officer, so criticized at Villefranche, now entered into his own in the battered redoubt at Madonna dell'Olmo. Even the French conceded this time that that general, 'as brave as he was experienced from long service, gave his orders with extreme sangfroid; he remained seated on a chair at the foot of the parapet in the midst of his soldiers, whose blows he directed, receiving without cease the enemy's fire, which lasted from noon till half past eight. The King of Sardinia having seen the uselessness of his efforts, and full of other objects, had for some hours been fighting only in order to gain nightfall, so as to cover his retreat.'[42] This was further covered, about seven o'clock that evening, by a last feinting attack put in by twelve companies of grenadiers, switched from the Sardinian right wing, under command of a Prince of Baden-Durlach. Cannonading continued more than an hour after darkness. The Austro-Sardinian rearguards of retreat were followed up towards Ronchi by Maréchal-de-Camp Don Thomas Corvalán, unleashed at last from his headquarters duty and subsequently supported by further cavalry operating under Lieutenant-Generals Pignatelli and du Chayla. There was, however, no general pursuit against an enemy who had imposed respect.

The Gallispan army had just won the battle of Coni, also called the battle of Madonna dell'Olmo. 'Your army, Sire,' wrote Conti to the king, 'has done prodigies of constancy and vigour.'[43] That constant vigour of the French and Spaniards had cost the Austro-Sardinian army the formidable total of nearly 4,400 dead and wounded. Franco-Spanish losses amounted to about 2,700,[44] which was tough

[42] Marquis de Saint-Simon, op. cit., p. 125.

[43] Prince de Conti to King Louis XV, camp before Coni, 1 Oct. 1744: Arch. Guerre C., vol. 3063, no. 1.

[44] The figure of 4,000 French losses given by Spenser Wilkinson, The Defence of Piedmont 1742–48, p. 171, for 'the battle of Madonna dell'Olmo' is misleading. French and Spanish losses taken together did not approach that figure. For French losses alone the official casualty return gave 351 killed and 800 wounded: 'État des officiers généraux et particuliers tués ou blessés à l'affaire du 30 7bre 1744': Arch. Guerre C., vol. 3065, no. 17: Guerres des Alpes, ii. 245. The total French and Spanish losses on 30 September, including the siegeworks, the Mondovi region, Borgo San Dalmazzo, and the Stura valley (see below) were, however, reported to be about 4,000.

considering that the bulk of the cavalry had scarcely been engaged. The little Régiment de Stainville lost eight captains wounded, two lieutenants killed among, it is said, the wounding of every officer but three; thirty-nine of their men were killed, seventy-nine wounded. Among the French senior officers wounded were Senneterre, du Chayla, Chauvelin, and Agenais. Later Choiseul was to recall:

The battle lasted till night. It was not possible for me to leave the field of battle; but the next day, when it was quite decided that the Prince de Conti had won it and that the enemy had withdrawn, nothing for me was so urgent as to fly to the quarters where I lodged with M. d'Aiguillon, which was two leagues from the battle-field. I arrived more dead than alive, in the fear that they might have cut off his leg. They were saying so in the army; the Prince de Conti had indicated to me his anxiety about it when I had gone to ask his permission to go to see M. d'Aiguillon. They were dressing his wound at the moment in which I entered his room. What was my surprise to see that they were putting water and salt upon a pretended scratch which he had on his leg, and which the most lively friendship could scarcely perceive! I spoke to him little of his wound and returned very easy as to the dangers which M. d'Aiguillon would henceforth run in war. I have extended myself a little upon this anecdote because I shall have occasion to speak of M. d'Aiguillon hereafter; but I shall speak no more of his courage; for, once said for all, he is absolutely lacking in it.[45]

The early intimacy of the future dukes of Aiguillon and of Choiseul was suddenly split across by that irrevocable cleavage which sunders brave men from cowards. Few circumstances could be better calculated to make the craven hate his detector with an abiding hatred. At the same time it is fair to recall that Agenais had been credited with courage in the grim work at Casteldelfino, which may conceivably have broken his nerve; though his superior officer in the battle of Coni itself, Maréchal-de-Camp de Courten, listed Agenais among the brave. 'I cannot render too much justice', wrote Courten, 'to the eight battalions which I had the honour to command. Messrs. de Beaupréau, d'Agenais, de Crussol, and de Stainville distinguished themselves extremely. In these eight battalions there were more than a hundred officers killed or wounded, which is much more than half those who were there.'[46] Courten himself was awarded the Cross of Saint Louis, a decoration which the generous Conti incidentally suggested for Agenais among others. There is confirmation that his leg-wound was a slight one. And another engagement in which he was to participate twelve years later was to confirm with the public Choiseul's poor opinion of his prowess.

[45] Choiseul, Mémoires, pp. 15–16.
[46] Maréchal-de-Camp de Courten to Count d'Argenson, camp before Coni, 2 Oct. 1744: Arch. Guerre C., vol. 3065, no. 167.

It was characteristic of Choiseul in later life that in his account of Coni he revealed the cowardice of Agenais but said not a word about his own exploits. This kind of omission increases the respect with which one is inclined to listen to anything that Choiseul did mention about himself in those memoirs in which he was, unlike many autobiographers, so ready to recall his own failings. It was, however, equally characteristic of Stainville at that time that, still with a career to carve out ahead of him, he swiftly sought to profit from his valour. Four days after the battle he addressed to the minister of war the following letter:

In Camp before Coni this 4th Oct. 1744.
Sir,
I have the honour to address to you the return of the officers, sergts. and soldiers of the regt. who have been killed or wounded in the affair of the 30th Sept. The regt. arrived upon the field of battle at half past one. It was formed up like the rest of the brigade, of which it was head, opposite the line of the enemy; it charged them half an hour afterwards under the orders of the Chevalier de Courten; we entered into the enemy battery of cannon, we took it, and even made it fire upon them; the brigade was obliged to fall back, being taken in the flank from very close by the second line of the enemy who were marching in column to outflank us upon our left. I was commanding the brigade at the moment, the Duke d'Agenais having been wounded. I reformed it at thirty paces from the battery. We attacked it again and took it again. The Chevalier de Courten, seeing that we were not being supported, made us reform on our first ground, where I remained till night to be relieved. I forgot to tell you, Sir, that we were on the march to attack a third time when the Prince de Conti sent us the order to remain. H[is] S[erene] H[ighness] and the Chevalier de Courten who commanded us seemed to me pleased with the way in which the regt. and in general the brigade conducted itself upon this occasion.
I have the honour to be with profound respect, Sir, your very humble and very obedient servant

Choiseul de Stainville.[47]

Courten's tribute to Stainville has been noticed. Conti wrote to d'Argenson: 'I could not tell you enough good of the way in which M. de Stainville comported himself, as well as of the ardour and the sangfroid which he displayed throughout all the action',[48] as also through later life in telling combination.

For the present the minister of war minuted upon Stainville's letter: 'Compliment him in the reply upon the distinguished manner in which he has conducted himself and of which the King is informed.'[49] So Stainville was assured from the camp before Freiburg in regard to his regiment's performance at Coni: 'The King is

[47] Count de Stainville to Count d'Argenson, camp before Coni, 4 Oct. 1744: Arch. Guerre C., vol. 3065, no. 168.
[48] Prince de Conti to Count d'Argenson, camp before Coni, 6 Oct. 1744: Arch. Guerre C., vol. 3063, no. 15.   [49] Loc. cit.

informed of the part which it had therein and of the distinguished manner in which you conducted yourself there personally. I gladly present you with my compliment upon it.'[50]

Two days after Stainville had reported to d'Argenson, the stout little thruster was addressing to a friend at court a missive which, as often then, bore no introductory address of greeting and no concluding signature. The name of the recipient is thus unknown, though it was certainly one of those influential Abbés who then characterized the French court: like the Abbé de Broglie or, to take the rival faction, Belle-Isle's correspondent, the Abbé de Ravannes, a counsellor of state with military interests; or, perhaps more likely were not the tone of the letter perhaps a little too assuming, it might have been one of Stainville's swarm of relations, Antoine-Cléradius, Abbé de Choiseul, the primate of Lorraine and royal almoner at Versailles. As to the sender, it was certainly Stainville.[51] Indeed the letter affords one of the rare glimpses at first-hand of his intimate outlook in youth:

In camp before Coni this 6th Oct.

We have fought, and we have beaten. (*Nous nous sommes battus, et nous avons battus.*) It is our custom. The affair was very lively. You will gather more circumstantial details of it from the reports which the Prince de Conti will be sending to the Court, and from Bissy whom he has charged to render account of it [at court] although this affair has been purely one of the infantry, and the cavalry could not even see the fight.

I come to the main point. My regiment was of the number of 7 French btns. which crossed twice against the enemy corps. I found myself commanding the brigade in the 2nd charge, from the wound of M. d'Agenais; we were on the march to attack again a 3rd time against a new column of the enemy, when the Prince de Conti sent order to the Chevalier de Courten, who was commanding us (very brilliantly in parenthesis), to stop and to stand his ground, which we did until night when I was relieved. I myself have returned as the seventh [surviving] officer of my regt. with twelve grenadiers and about a hundred and fifty soldiers; that is called being in a battle. Now they say that they wish to do something for me; see Bissy, I pray you, about it, and engage the cardinal [de Tencin] to interest himself in my being a brigadier; it is the essential point of my fortune. The Prince de Conti is very anxious to render me service. I beg you, my dear Abbé, to sound as to the disposition in which the King and M. d'Argenson are towards me; you will infallibly learn it through Bissy; for the rest, I shall never in my life have such a fine or such a brilliant opportunity of advancing myself; if that should fail after what my regiment has done, my word, one must no longer think of this trade; I was the only French colonel in the attack, M. de la Force having been wounded at the beginning of the affair; in all I beg you, my dear Abbé, to watch a little after my interests, to send me news about it. You know my inviolable attachment to you.

[50] Count d'Argenson to Count de Stainville, camp before Freiburg, 24 Oct. 1744: Arch. Guerre C., vol. 3063, no. 72.
[51] Both the handwriting and the internal evidence are conclusive, apart from the contemporary or near-contemporary indexing under his name.

I have written to Meuse for him to give the wheel a push. They have written to me that Mademoiselle is fairly well with the King. I have known a time in which she had some kindness for me, and I even believe that she would have still, if Meuse spoke to her to see if she were willing to intrigue for me; see if you think it necessary and in that case do me the kindness of telling him. I write to you but currently because we are in the air as we have never been. Our siege is going very badly. It is detestable weather, and I greatly fear that despite our victory we may be obliged to raise it.[52]

Vivid is what Choiseul was throughout his life. He possessed that quick flame of the spirit which, especially among Latin peoples, can inspire a magnetism more captivating to contemporaries than explicable to posterity. At the same time, whereas Choiseul in his memoirs stressed his lack of interest in intrigues at court or even in the survival of the king, he evidently did rather care about the latter's approval; and some intrigues, at all events, did not leave him quite cold, as his letter demonstrates with characteristic frankness and incision.

Stainville's spirited letter yet ended sombre. On the very night after the battle Conti had been receiving reports which 'delivered him over entirely to anxieties'.[53] This intelligence revealed that the King of Sardinia's challenge of battle had been but one main element in a masterplan embracing no less than four others. While the main Gallispan army had been disputing the field of Madonna dell'Olmo, Baron von Leutrum in Coni itself had not let slip his planned opportunity. His sortie against the enemy's principal siegeworks between the Stura and the Gesso was indeed so stiffly met by Lautrec that he had to employ it mainly as a covering operation behind which elements detached from Charles Emmanuel's army hooked round on Coni from the northeast and, profiting from the incompletion of the enemy circuit of investment, ran through convoys of supplies and munitions to the beleaguered garrison and relieved them, on the journey out, of the wounded and other useless mouths. This stroke was further covered by a second and more successful sortie from Coni against the abortive siege-camp beyond the Gesso, where the Piedmontese destroyed the works and captured abandoned ammunition. In this raid the garrison was supported by detachments of peasant militia closing in from Mondovi as part of Ormea's corps, stiffened by some Austrian infantry shipped across from Lobkowitz's army against Naples. The offensive sweep from the Mondovi country, the third element in the overall plan, further included successful attacks against the Gallispan outposts at Perveragno and

---

[52] Count de Stainville to Abbé . . ., camp before Coni, 6 Oct. 1744: Arch. Guerre C., vol. 3065, no. 169.   [53] Marquis de Saint-Simon, op. cit., p. 131.

Boves, where some hundred and fifty were taken prisoner. These operations were in turn co-ordinated with the fourth element, a more formidable assault against Borgo San Dalmazzo, the Gallispan supply and hospital depot in the rear of the main siegelines.

Looking out over the promised plains of Piedmont, backing on to the ending mountain to the west, battered Borgo crouched then in decay, shrunken and sinister. 'Its circuit had of yore been contracted by walls which seemed as old as the first ones and the space between was full of hovels and the ruins of houses. A large part of the walls had considerable breaches ... Castle ... ruins ... dominated the town; it is at present no more than a sorry burg.'[54] Closing all around that rotten borough, lightly held, there came that 30 September three Piedmontese battalions and picked grenadiers at the head of five thousand local levies from the mountaineering peasantry, creeping up under cover of 'the most tufty chestnuts, which however allowed freedom of movement underneath'.[55]

Borgo San Dalmazzo was attacked from every side. The French and Spanish garrison, heavily outnumbered, were joined on the broken walls by army bakers and sutlers, by virtually every man jack of them able to shoulder a musket. Even the wounded from the hospitals 'dragged themselves on to the breaches' and loosed off against the swarming assailants. Word of this desperate struggle got through to the Count de Lautrec at Coni, himself engaged against Leutrum's sortie but prompt to detach the cavalry regiment Dauphin against Borgo. Colonel the Marquis de Volvire led his men charging to the rescue. The French cavalry scattered the attack on Borgo and went fanning out against the fugitive levies, scouring up into the hills in grim pursuit. No quarter was given to those peasants armed outside the laws of war. There was an especial slaughter by the French of those seeking refuge in a chapel near Roccavione.

Borgo, even, did not complete the sum of the enterprises mounted by Charles Emmanuel against the invaders of his kingdom. Beyond Borgo again, over in the valley of the Stura, the peasant insurrection, again stiffened with regulars, was unleashed all along the vital line of allied communication back to France. The partisans 'had presented themselves against so many points and with so much confusion, that it would not have been possible to distinguish which post was most in danger, and to which aid should rather be sent; each individual [Gallispan] officer maintained himself as long as he could upon the ground which he was defending', till at last the enemy numbers and the need to concentrate in self-preservation compelled them to close

---

[54] Ibid., pp. 105–6.   [55] Ibid., pp. 126 f. for the following.

into one body. That gave the attackers their chance over the terrain abandoned. Accompanied by engineers, they swooped on the several bridges where the highroad crossed the Stura, and managed to blow up those at Rocca-Sparviera and at Oulme below Gajola. This successful coup was one of the most serious developments for the army of Don Philip and the Prince de Conti.

King Charles Emmanuel had framed the set-piece of battle by Madonna dell'Olmo against a wide and lurid background of partisan and patriotic warfare blazing up behind the besiegers of Coni. The issue of the battle itself assumed a more anxious perspective for Conti that night as there came in from all around first reports of the hostile turmoil throughout the countryside. And that same night there fell another heavy blow. It began to rain.

V

It kept on raining. The weather had broken with a vengeance. From the 1st to the 6th October it mostly came down in torrents and made torrents of the rivers. Not only was the bridge built by the besiegers across the Gesso swept away, but the Stura too, deeply channelled by Coni, came roaring down in spate, more than twelve feet above its former level, raging along with stones and rocks, smashing everything in its path. That included all the fourteen pontoon-bridges linking the siegecamp with the main Gallispan army on the left bank of the Stura. The two bodies of troops were for some days sundered. Stainville's regiment was, however, back in the trenches, under Lieutenant-General du Châtel, on the night of 4–5 October and again on that of 7–8. It was dismal work, with the soldiers splashing around and baling out, for the driving rain had 'brimmed the trenches, sapped the parapets' so that, wrote the harassed French chief of infantry staff, 'there is no sort of horror that we have not experienced'.[56] Such was the background to Stainville's sprightly epistle to his Abbé.

The state of the Stura hampered repair-work upon the strategic bridges at Oulme and Rocca-Sparviera. The supply-line was cut and the emboldened partisans, 'renewing their efforts, attacked, man to man and mule by mule, everything which did not pass with sufficient escorts; they had carried off a convoy near the [Col de] l'Argentière',[57] right back by the frontier. These extending operations were nourished

---

[56] Major-General de Chauvelin to Count d'Argenson, camp before Coni, 8 Oct. 1744: Arch. Guerre C., vol. 3063, no. 20.
[57] Marquis de Saint-Simon, op. cit., p. 132.

by Charles Emmanuel, who excellently grasped the potentialities of partisan warfare and now stiffened it with the Tarantasia regiment. From its headquarters at Dronero it co-ordinated all the alpine levies of the region.

The Piedmontese pressure told. Gallispan rations gave out. The soaked French or Spanish soldier was reduced to scrounging the local produce: 'excessive in his drink which he made himself by pressing grapes, eating with avidity chestnuts much heavier and more difficult of digestion than bread, this regime must necessarily cause illnesses in the train of which exhaustion always brings discouragement'.[58] It was nourished by fell reports from every quarter. Partisan hostilities were increasing in cruelty also. The peasant patriots of Piedmont were now torturing prisoners before killing them: which invited further reprisals. The grimly consequential cycle of partisan warfare, embracing the extremes of heroism and of horror, was already a familiar pattern. Now in Piedmont, as previously in Bohemia and Bavaria, the formal campaigning of armies was inset in the savage hostilities of populations, irregular and omnipresent. War, then as at other times, could be almost simultaneously atrocious and chivalrous. The Prince de Conti, that humane general, saw to the Piedmontese wounded left upon the field by Madonna dell'Olmo with such solicitude that he aroused discontent among his own sorely tried troops.

'You will grant me, Sir,' wrote Conti to d'Argenson on the same day that Stainville applied to his Abbé, 'that it is indeed terrible after so fortunate a campaign ... to be fought and perhaps beaten by the weather and the torrents.'[59] However, Conti in his 'indefatigable patience and work ... sustained the army by his example'.[60] He was credited with the idea of rigging up a makeshift suspension-bridge, sagging ominously in a span of over a hundred and fifty feet, in order to restore communication across the swirling Stura until pontoons could be re-erected. Supplies began to trickle through again but Conti had to announce that they still afforded only a two-day bread ration in three days to fighting men, excluding staff. His troops responded Vive le Roi! Vive le Prince de Conti, le père des soldats et de l'armée. Yet when French cavalry again began to patrol beyond the Gesso, in one day fifty-seven troopers, seventeen from the Dauphin regiment and forty from the Régiment du Commissaire-Général, deserted and just rode away.

[58] Ibid., p. 137.
[59] Prince de Conti to Count d'Argenson, camp before Coni, 6 Oct. 1744: Arch. Guerre C., vol. 3063, no. 14: Guerres des Alpes, ii. 244.
[60] Major-General de Chauvelin to Count d'Argenson, camp before Coni, 8 Oct. 1744: Arch. Guerre C., vol. 3063, no. 20.

The depleted Gallispan army had for the past fortnight been seeking to consolidate its position both tactically and also strategically from the rear. Two fresh initiatives were staged, one on either hand. From upper Dauphiny a Spanish thrust sought to attract the enemy northwards from the critical Stura, and at the other extremity French battalions from Provence aimed up the difficult valley of the Vésubie and across to menace the Mondovi district. The pouring rain, with torrents in spate and the mountain-tracks going to pieces, helped to wash out both initiatives. And the downpour was closely followed by reports, already, of upland snowfall. Out at Coni the night of 7–8 October brought the Piedmontese garrison some twelve hundred reinforcements run through from over by Fossano whither Charles Emmanuel was advancing. On 11 October 1744 Don Philip called council of war at his headquarters in camp before Coni.

Captain-General de Las Minas plumped for prompt withdrawal from Coni, where even Conti now envisaged 'this conquest as no longer aught but a chimera'.[61] The strategic focus was already shifting back from Coni to still smoking Demont. Aiming to gain time for defensive preparation there, Conti persuaded Don Philip to cling on a little at Coni. But the siege dwindled, with the heavy stuff beginning to move out and the Spaniards by now token besiegers. At a further council of war on 17 October they blandly proposed to ignore the tiresome fact that Coni was uncaptured, abandon alpine communications and march ahead to push Charles Emmanuel back and winter in Piedmont while stretching south towards Genoa and coastal communication with France – roughly the Spanish plan from the spring, only effected the other way on. Conti was having none of this and renewed the earlier dispute, remarking: 'The most vexatious misfortunes tickle M. de La Mina.'[62]

Conti's men at least had kept on at it against the now aggressive defenders of Coni. The morale of the French remained surprisingly high. On 18 October they managed to explode a mine which blew a breach in the walls with considerable loss of life to the defenders. French grenadiers swarmed to the attack. Leutrum, though, was on the spot, forced them back and closed the breach for a Piedmontese loss of some eighty-five men. Next day only eleven siege-guns were still in position against Coni, and the day after, five. On 20–21 October small combats were fought, mainly before the Gesso redoubt. That was how it petered out. Withdrawal was in the autumnal air. On 22 October 1744 it began.

[61] Prince de Conti to Count d'Argenson, camp before Coni, 6 Oct. 1744: *u.s.*
[62] Prince de Conti to Count d'Argenson, Demont, 24 Oct. 1744: Arch. Guerre C., vol. 3063, no. 66.

Conti had failed before Coni, once again standing inviolate against the invaders from France. It was reckoned that during each of the forty days of siege the assailants had on average hurled against the town and its defences one thousand cannonball, more than one every other minute, day and night. That was not counting mortar-bombs. But the stalwart defenders had kept on hitting back. The Prince de Conti, in a letter to the Marshal de Noailles, put the overall Franco-Spanish losses up to 12 October at 10,529; and it is estimated that over the whole period of the siege and battle in the Coni area the total Gallispan loss probably reached up to about 15,000 men. As a French appreciation put it, 'the army is weakened by its glory'.[63]

On 24 October 1744 King Charles Emmanuel III of Sardinia triumphed into Coni. If local lore rated men from Coni as notoriously none too bright, that was their day in their citadel of resistance, ringing now with cheers and joybells to welcome the monarch who had skilfully sustained those defenders whom he now delighted to reward.

The Count de Stainville's father, for whom Gallispan victory at Coni had represented 'really too many ills at once',[64] subsequently wrote to his friend, the Baron de Richecourt, of Conti's campaign: 'The victories, so vaunted, are turning to the profit of the King of Sardinia. It is long since, indeed, that I have learnt that battles are to be decided only by their sequel. They announce from the army of the Gallispans that it is reduced to 14 thousand men of both nations without what they will still be losing in the passage of the Alps, which I do not think will be made without difficulties.'[65] However fond of his son the marquis may have been, their relations were pulled asunder.

VI

The Gallispan army wound its way back to Demont on 23 October, and there halted for a spell. Piedmontese forces followed up but made no superfluous attack. So active on the other hand was the everlasting menace of the partisans against Franco-Spanish communications along the Stura that twenty-three battalions were required to guard them. Another headache for Conti at Demont was hospitalization, at

[63] Arch. Guerre C., vol. 3063: eighteenth-century 'Table des lettres et matières contenues dans ce volume': summary of no. 84, Major-General de Chauvelin to Count d'Argenson, Demont, 30 Oct. 1744.
[64] Marquis de Stainville to Grand Duke Francis II, Paris, 11 Oct. 1744: Esteri del Granducato di Toscana, vol. 2295/1286, fo. 482.
[65] Marquis de Stainville to Baron de Richecourt, Paris, 9 Nov. 1744: Ö.S./H.H.S., Lothringisches Hausarchiv 189/III 126, fo. 217.

that period habitually contracted out for the French army to private entrepreneurs in the same way as the provisioning. The Marquis de Saint-Simon wrote:

Illnesses continued to reign in the army; new abuses slipped into the hospitals and the troops suffered cruelly. The Prince de Conti redoubled his attentions ... By a misunderstanding which alone can excuse so barbarous an action, the employees of the hospital had [in retreating] carried off on their carts the sheets, bedclothes and utensils used for the sick, and had left the soldiers upon straw, doubtless being confident that other carts would come to take them away. The Prince de Conti, informed of this action within the very moment, granted but one hour wherein to retrieve it ... The gallows were actually erected, but they were not used ... Each sick soldier beheld himself placed upon a hastily made stretcher and carried on the shoulders of soldiers in full health, with whom there was no bargaining as to the price. The sick were transported to a new hospital where they received a quite different treatment. The Chevalier de Chauvelin, Major-General of the Infantry, went every day himself, as did several other officers, to visit the hospitals ... So many generals have been the victims of these millionaires of obscure and powerful protection that humanity groans at these abuses and is consoled when it sees a powerful man employ authority to repress them and merit to maintain himself thereafter.[66]

If the sidelights shed here upon military corruption are sufficiently clear, yet in the French army at least, medical services were evidently a matter, already, of appreciable organization and concern. The assumption, too, that the soldiers acting as stretcher-bearers would be specially paid reflected one aspect of a pretty widespread practice then in the French army, reinforcing the impression that all in all its troops were probably better paid in the eighteenth century than in later ones. Soldiers at that date tended to be treated still as strictly men of war, there to fight and march, so that even the manual labour of digging trenches was liable to be regarded as a remunerated extra: so much so that during the recent siege of Coni and dearth of provisions the French troops had for the moment been apt to do better than their officers, whom Conti had assisted, however, by keeping open table.

Conti found himself embroiled at Demont in further strategic conflicts that for once were more than merely interallied. The French command was divided as to whether to try to hold Demont through the coming winter, as Conti rather naturally hoped, or to abandon it, as Bourcet deemed necessary. The prince picked stout Chevert as the likely man to hold out at Demont, in echo of his last stand at Prague, after the main army had retreated to France, behind the sundering snows. Chevert argued strongly against Conti on military grounds,

---

[66] Marquis de Saint-Simon, op. cit., pp. 144 f. for the following.

observing incidentally of himself that he 'neither blushed nor was puffed up at having carved out for himself the path from one rank to another up to that of Maréchal-de-Camp, wherewith the King had honoured him in the course of this campaign'. Occasionally even then could two French officers argue as man to man across the gulf of class and caste. The argument now was bodied out in rival gangs of labourers set to work upon the castle of Demont, one to repair it for holding out, the other to mine it so as to demolish it if abandoned. So, simultaneously 'the repairers and the destroyers were working with equal ardour.'

The two French experts of humble birth came to be supported by the two courts at Versailles and at Madrid. On 14 November 1744 the Gallispan army set forth from Demont upon the last stage of its retreat across the Alps. Conti, 'in order to avenge himself like a prince upon Chevert', gave him the honour of commanding the advance-guard. Away to the rear the Count de Danois blew the bridge at Rocca-Sparviera before consolidating on the main rearguard under d'Aremburu, detailed to cover the demolition of Demont. He did not prevent Piedmontese partisans from swarming in even before the French engineers had pulled out. A squad of them was reduced to hurling stones to keep the peasants at bay till, struggling too long, the demolishers were demolished by their own explosion, whereas their assailants largely queered the destruction of Demont. And all along the line of retreat there raged the atrocious hostilities against the guerrillas, with the French by now tormenting their tormentors. 'In vain', confessed Conti, 'we practise the most horrible cruelties to intimidate the Piedmontese militia. They serve only to encourage the Piedmontese to avenge the blood of their compatriots and to double their efforts against us.'[67] Such, in that century as in others, was the imperfect logic of terror to quell terror.

The Sardinian regulars did not, however, press the pursuit. They scarcely needed to. It was bitterly cold now, as cold as was usual in January. On 15 November the Franco-Spanish army trudged on from Sambuco:

Towards the end of the day ... it passed the defile of the Barricades. There the coldest wind hurled fine dust mingled with hard and stinging sleet which clung to everything which it encountered, and in a moment was there converted into a thin coating of ice; the road became like glass, upon which neither the men nor the horses could support themselves; more than 100 soldiers perished ... All the column arrived but late and worn out with fatigue and cold. The camp occupied a small plain covered with snow, where there were neither trees, nor shelter nor resources. The

[67] Prince de Conti, 16 Nov. 1744: cited in the present translation by Spenser Wilkinson, op. cit., p. 167.

pegs of the tents could be driven into the ground only by great efforts. The soldiers
... finding absolutely nothing to cover the ice-coated ground whereon they were to
sleep, several removed the thatched roofs of the houses [at Brezés] to carry them
beneath the tents. The officers lodged in these houses had not the cruelty to set
themselves against so necessary an expedient ... After the thatch, the timbers were
knocked down to make fires with; then the soldiers added to them the doors and
mangers of the cattlesheds and stables. The whole night was spent in pitying them,
in letting them act and sometimes restraining them ... When daylight ended this
grievous night, the army resumed its march by the Col de l'Argentière.[68]

What with the retreat from Prague two winters before, and now
this other one from Demont, the Count de Stainville was becoming
a campaigner inured to one of the most exhausting forms of all
warlike enterprise. His father had been observing: 'One cannot depict
the state in which the Combined Army, which has raised the siege of
Coni, is returning.'[69]

The retreat continued. The day of 16 November was colder still.
The march back through those alpine crests became a series of scenes
from some white hell. Labourers toiled to clear the congealed road,
not least of the men, horses and mules frozen stiff upon it. At one
point three mules laden with silver coin of the military chest
stumbled, sank and could not rise. They were escorted by a sergeant
and twenty-two soldiers. Those following on from behind came upon
them all in one frozen tableau, mules and men posed lifeless and
rigid. (Passing troops pillaged some 50,000 francs, which were mostly
recovered.) That same day a French unit under Lieutenant-Colonel
de Kermelec was escorting a baggage-train over the Col de
l'Argentière when suddenly a terrific squall came whipping over the
crests to hit them at high velocity. An enemy ambush, one is assured,
could not have scattered Kermelec's men with greater loss, sending
them rolling down the mountains.

On 17 November it began to snow in earnest. The surviving horses
and mules could scarcely drag the cannon. At one point Conti,
coming upon a Swiss regiment toiling under this incubus, galvanized
it with an offer of twenty-five golden louis for every cannon lugged
to the top of the Col de l'Argentière. The mercenary and mountaineering Swiss produced ropes and, two hundred men to each gun,
hauled them up 'with singular ease'.[70] Humped back along with the
rest were trophies of captured Sardinian cannon, despite the
particular attentions of guerrillas. The partisans indeed combined
with six companies of Piedmontese grenadiers to take a last crack at
the French rearguard, now operating under Chevert, always, it

---

[68] Marquis de Saint-Simon, op. cit., pp. 155–6.
[69] Marquis de Stainville to Grand Duke Francis II, Paris, 8 Nov. 1744: *u.s.*, fo. 493.
[70] Marquis de Saint-Simon, op. cit., pp. 159 f. for the following.

seemed, at the point of prominent danger. Conti ordered the Count de Lautrec to reinforce Chevert but the latter proudly said that he could settle the enemy on his own, and did so. By 19 November the last allied troops were across the alpine divide. That night there fell four foot of snow. The retreat had ended none too soon.

Such was the severe conclusion of all the campaigning through the Alps in that year of 1744. It was a famous campaign, for so long so successful, capturing the county of Nice and driving right through the peaks, out on to the promised plains of Piedmont only to be frustrated and turned back not merely by the patriotic valour of the Piedmontese but almost as though by some implacable momentum of geography beyond the range of that human endeavour whereby the unsuccessful French and Spanish armies had yet afforded 'for all time models of prudence, of activity, and of courage'. And all this had they done not for any compelling national interest but in search of glory and a princely apanage for a younger son of the King of Spain. Such was the spirit of that age.

Choiseul, one feels, did not exaggerate in observing that 'the campaign was long and tiring'.[71] He himself had been present, in the words of that old citation, 'at the passage of the Var, at the capture of the castles of Aspremont and Utelle, Nice, Castelnuovo, L'Escarène, Peglia, Castillon and La Turbie; at the siege and capture of the fort of Montalban and of the citadel of Villefranche in the month of April,'[72] at the siege of Demont, of Coni, and at that battle there which witnessed the greatest feat of arms in his career.

One may, indeed, sense that the campaign of 1744 was formative for the Count de Stainville. It was on that first campaign in which he commanded a regiment that he formed a friendship and an enmity, with Conti and Agenais respectively, which were importantly to influence the course of his career. He had been campaigning, too, with his future ministerial associate, then Count de Choiseul, and with the Marquis du Châtel, the father of his future wife. More broadly, again, the young Count de Stainville had secured an intimate introduction to the valour, as well as the limitations, of Spaniards as working allies in that campaign which was further calculated to bring home the long realities of British seapower to one whose regiment saw its first service against it off Toulon and, frustrated there, had learnt the cost in charging through the fire of the British naval guns at Villefranche. It may or may not have been coincidence that a central theme of the policy of the later Duke de Choiseul was Spanish alliance against British domination across the waters of the world.

[71] Choiseul, *Mémoires*, p. 13.   [72] Pinard, *Chronologie historique-militaire*, v. 686.

CHAPTER III

REGROUPING

I

'I WAS no longer thinking of all that had happened at Metz', recalled the Count de Stainville, 'when I arrived at Grenoble, where M. d'Aiguillon was. The Prince de Conti, who was amusing himself at Grenoble, forced us to remain there.'[1] Yet, as Stainville implied, their party of pleasure in the capital of Dauphiny at the end of 1744 was set against a sweep of events at the French court and in the German theatre as well as the Italian.

From Italy 'little Bissy' had brought tidings of the battle of Coni to Louis XV at Strasburg on his way from Metz to rejoin his army now beleaguering the Austrian fortress at Freiburg im Breisgau once again, a generation after that siege wherein the Marquis de Stainville had served. He now wrote of Freiburg: 'Knowing its situation as I do, I doubt not that it will be defended long enough to bring destruction upon part of the army which is going to besiege it, and it will be glorious for the troops of the Queen to give the first example in this war of the way in which fortresses should be defended.'[2] If Coni was to do that more notably, yet despite the presence before Freiburg of Louis and a galaxy of competing marshals, Belle-Isle, Noailles, Coigny and Maillebois, it was not till 7 November that they took it and so mastered Anterior Austria. If that siege was less damaging than the then Count de Stainville made out to the reputation of King Louis, it was the count's protector, the Marshal de Noailles, whose credit suffered most.

The siege of Freiburg had only followed upon the enforced withdrawal across the Rhine of the army of Prince Charles of Lorraine that August when Frederick the Great had come bursting back into the war, sweeping through Saxony and on to Prague, swiftly taken once again. Noailles had just let Prince Charles march away apart from a tumbling skirmish on the so-called Journée des Culbutes. Frederick opened up once more to the liaison-officer sent by Noailles, the Marquis du Mesnil, against 'the follies' of French

---

[1] Choiseul, *Mémoires*, p. 21.
[2] Marquis de Stainville to Grand Duke Francis II, Paris, 13 Sept. 1744: Esteri del Granducato di Toscana, vol. 1286/2295, fo. 470.

generals, and also incidentally upon his own sex-life 'with a frankness,' wrote Mesnil, 'which I can scarcely get over'.[3]

To French displeasure Frederick's seizure of Prague incited Charles VII, in alternative to 'dying of chagrin in a hole like Frankfurt',[4] to sweep back with his Field-Marshal Seckendorf and liberate Munich, jubilant in what was about the emperor's last time of happiness. Maria Theresa for the present played down the advance of that 'lout Seckendorf (*du grobianus Seckendorffe*)', ripe for 'the gallows',[5] in concentration upon 'uniting in Bohemia to fall upon the King of Prussia ... to crush that devil at a blow'.[6] The incensed Grand Duke Francis wrote thus to Prince Charles of Lorraine whom he now longed to replace. Maria Theresa confessed that she had 'by my wickedness induced a fever in the old man (*aux vieux: sic*). Suddenly he got the idea of joining the army ... I had recourse to our usual instruments, caresses, tears, but what can they avail with a husband after nine years of marriage? So I obtained nothing, though he is the best husband in the world. I at length resumed my anger, which has served me so well that I and he have fallen ill'[7] while Prince Charles, with old Traun at his elbow, remained in command in Bohemia. For Frederick, standing out ahead of Prague in familiar parts, Pisek was now as pivotal as once for his old butt, Broglie. It was the Prussian turn to be pushed out and harried by the Pandours through a devastated countryside, right back into Silesia. Frederick too had to abandon an isolated garrison in Prague. His winter retreat, lacking any Chevert, was speeded from Prague by savage street-fighting and, despite a hardy initiative by the Count de Rottembourg, was much less successful than that of Belle-Isle. Frederick's gibes at French campaigning in Bohemia were repaid with interest.

So the pendulum of war had swung to rest that winter in a Central European equilibrium which demonstrated that if the Austrians could not evict Frederick from Silesia, neither could he dislodge them from Bohemia. In Bavaria a little Franco-Prussian auxiliary corps under the Marquis de Ségur supplied a tenuous link with the French army under Maillebois wintering along the lower Rhine. The stalemate there was more favourable, at least, to Bourbon arms than the dramatic retreat upon the Prussian front. This pattern in the German theatre had been appreciably matched in the Italian where,

[3] Marquis du Mesnil, 'Mémoire sur ce que j'ai fait auprès du roi de Prusse', 12–17 Sept. 1744: Arch. Aff. Étr. C.P., Prusse, cited, duc de Broglie, *Marie-Thérèse Impératrice* (Paris, 1888: henceforth cited as Broglie/Impératrice), i. 13–18.
[4] Emperor Charles VII: Arch. Aff. Étr. C.P., Bavière, Sept.–Oct. 1744; ibid., i. 22.
[5] Queen Maria Theresa to Archduchess Marianne, 3 Oct, 1744: Ö.S./H.H.S.: Arneth, ii. 563, n. 126.
[6] Grand Duke Francis II to Prince Charles of Lorraine, Schönbrunn, 22 Aug. 1744: ibid., ii. 557, nn. 69–70.   [7] Queen Maria Theresa to Archduchess Marianne, *u.s.*

largely thanks to Conti's siege of Coni, his subsequent retreat stood against a better Bourbon showing after all against Lobkowitz in Central Italy.

The standstill of Neapolitan and Spanish forces against those of Prince Lobkowitz up at Fermo had yielded to an indecisive action across the peninsula at Velletri on 17 June 1744, to an abortive insurrection in the Neapolitan Abruzzi stimulated by Austrian levies under a Catalan adventurer called Soro, to another Austrian enterprise mounted at dawn on 11 August by the Jacobite General Browne with the object, no less, of kidnapping in Velletri the whole Bourbon high command, Don Carlos, the Duke of Modena, and Captain-General des Gages. After the narrow failure of this lively initiative the strategic pull from Coni increasingly extended even to Velletri. On 1 November the Austrians began to pull back through papal territory to Perugia and Nocera, spared by Colonel Soro in surrendering it to des Gages, who made a fell example of the colonel's cut-throats. This dark chapter closed that campaigning with Lobkowitz going into quarters around Faenza while des Gages stood in the districts superbly overlooked by Orvieto.

Such success for Don Carlos may not have soothed the sulks of his younger brother. Don Philip had failed to put over a medical certificate against the likely effects of his residence at Nice, not yet appreciated as a winter resort. Las Minas was recalled in disgrace. If the earlier disgrace of the Duchess de Châteauroux at Metz was not worrying the Count de Stainville as he joined Conti at Grenoble, he found there the Duke d'Agenais 'flattering himself that the King would not take her back as Mistress and that he [Agenais] would regain his ascendancy over her, which he would employ not in order to forgive her, to love her and be loved by her, but to punish her, martyrize her and avenge himself'.[8]

'I tell you now that we shall return more brilliant than ever',[9] the Duchess de Châteauroux had written to the Duke de Richelieu even as the king turned the corner at Metz. And again: 'I am thinking of making myself as hale as a navvy so as to enrage our enemies as long as I can and to have the time to punish them, as they will be, you can rest assured.'[10]

This duchess whom adversity did not discourage proved correct in fathoming 'her very weak lover',[11] as the later Choiseul called the king. By the end of November 1744 the Marquis de Stainville was reporting: 'The whole court is in combustion. It is nothing but

[8] Choiseul, Mémoires, p. 22.
[9] Duchess de Châteauroux to Duke de Richelieu, correspondence of Aug.–Sept. 1744: Broglie/Impératrice, i. 38.
[10] Ibid, pp. 39–40.   [11] Choiseul, Mémoires, p. 23.

intrigues and cabals'[12] concerning the return of the royal mistress. As the son of the marquis was to explain, the Duchess de Châteauroux indicated to Louis 'the victims whom he should immolate to her vengeance'. Thus:

The Bishop of Soissons, the Duke de La Rochefoucauld, grand master of the wardrobe, the Duke de Châtillon,[13] governor of the Dauphin, were exiled. She ordered that the king should send to her the Count de Maurepas, for thirty years a minister and secretary of state, in order to tender to her at her home, in Paris, his excuses for what had happened at Metz, and to pray her to return to court. This minister had incurred the disfavour of the Mistress; she wished to humiliate him and was little concerned, or did not sense, that it was the King whom she was humiliating. This ridiculous embassy was made, and the minister, a few days afterwards, was to have been dismissed and sacrificed to the vengeance of Mme de Châteauroux. She fell ill [however] the day after she had publicly received the King's excuses. Her illness was a malignant fever, which ended her life in a few days. The courtiers, who very frequently have criminal thoughts in proportion to their base actions – notably M. de Richelieu, wished to have it believed that M. de Maurepas had poisoned Mme de Châteauroux. M. de Richelieu would indeed have had the black audacity to commit a crime for his lightest interest; but, besides the fact that the honesty of M. de Maurepas protects him from all suspicions, I verified the facts, and there were elements of impossibility and absurdity in this accusation, as there are in all those which come from M. de Richelieu. The King let the exile stand for those who had incurred it a few days before the death of Mme de Châteauroux, and there remained of this Mistress but the scandal of Metz and a part of the evil which she had ordered.[14]

It was on 25 November 1744 that the Count de Maurepas had tendered apologies to the Duchess de Châteauroux, whom he found in bed. It was in fact on 8 December that the duchess died. Meanwhile the good time at Grenoble had been going with such a swing that, as Choiseul wrote, 'in truth I believe that we should never have left it without the death of this same Mme de Châteauroux, which threw the Prince de Conti into despair. He lost a very effective protector. His absence had preserved him from all the vexations which had prevailed during the past eight months ... The Prince de Conti had large views of glory and command ... Not only did he lose much in losing the last Mistress, but he was uncertain of his credit as regards the next one. The Prince de Conti ... allowed us to leave.'[15] And he left himself.

On 19 December the Prince de Conti arrived at Trianon, whither the king had withdrawn in his grief, rendered still lonelier perhaps

---

[12] Marquis de Stainville to Grand Duke Francis II, Paris, 28 Nov. 1744: Esteri del Granducato di Toscana, vol. 2295/1286, fo. 504.
[13] The text printed in Choiseul, *Mémoires*, p. 23, here read 'Chaulnes' in a misreading for 'Chatillon', as Choiseul wrote it: Choiseul, 'Mémoires de la main', fo. 11.
[14] Choiseul, *Mémoires*, pp. 23-4.   [15] Ibid., pp. 21-2.

by the death four days earlier of another duchess, his 'dear Mama',[16] Madame de Ventadour. Madame de Châteauroux may not have exaggerated in claiming to know 'all the windings of his soul (*tous les replis de son âme*)'.[17] Choiseul, as noticed, described Louis as having loved her as much as he could love. Choiseul was never to say that of Madame de Pompadour, his own future friend. Years later, after the death of Madame de Pompadour, a true friend of Louis XV, the respectable Countess de Séran, once 'asked him if he had ever been really in love. He replied that he had been with Mme de Châteauroux.'[18]

The Duchess de Châteauroux had been loved by Conti too. On his return he was closeted alone with Louis. They supposedly wept together.

The king plunged into melancholy. The circle of his consolation included her sister, the Duchess de Lauraguais, perhaps inevitably said to have afforded him rather personal consolation, and the Duchess of Boufflers, another friend of the Count de Stainville. Also from his set was the fair Countess de Forcalquier, said to have been promoted now by that persistent pander, Richelieu: but in vain, as too with Madame Portail, supposed to have had too rough a way with her for the royal pleasure.

No special friend of Madame de Châteauroux had been Stainville's relation, the Marquis de Meuse. Yet he was on New Year's Day awarded the coveted Cordon Bleu of the Saint-Esprit. Stainville's own star was in the ascendant since his feats in Italy. His return to Paris was not prevented by the Minister of War's preoccupation with the fact that, as he had pointed out to Conti, 'the regiments of Anjou and Stainville have several officers who, having been taken prisoners of war in Bohemia, have not yet been exchanged and constitute a fairly considerable gap independently of a quantity of other officers who, against orders and the good of the service, under pretexts of illness or boredom with their sojourn, have absented themselves without passport or leave'.[19] The under-officered Régiment de Stainville was, however, no longer the limit of its colonel's ambition.

II

When the young colonel returned to Paris the Stainville residence was soon draped in mourning for the death of yet another duchess,

[16] King Louis XV to Duchess de Ventadour, Versailles, 2 May 1744: Luynes, vi. 235.
[17] Duchess de Châteauroux to Duke de Richelieu, correspondence of Aug.–Sept. 1744: Broglie/Impératrice, i. 39.
[18] Marmontel, *Mémoires d'un père pour servir à l'instruction de ses enfants* (Paris, 1804), iii. 74.
[19] Count d'Argenson to Prince de Conti, 6 Dec. 1744: Arch. Guerre C., vol. 3069, no. 231.

the Dowager Duchess of Lorraine, released from her sad retreat at Commercy, from recent fits of apoplexy and dementia. At Versailles, however, the court in February 1745 went gayer than for years in celebration of the marriage of the Dauphin.

The Dauphin Louis of France was at that time a heavy youth of fifteen. This, it now appears, was the then Count de Stainville's recollection of him from early days:

The Dauphin was born with the same inclinations towards libertinage as the king his father. At the age of ten he used to like to sit himself upon women's knees, to tease them over their bosoms and rumple them, which Louis XV found charming. His son gave promise of great impetuosity of character. He gave orders haughtily, and went quite red with anger at however little hesitation in obeying him. But all that changed thanks to the education which was given him. M. de Châtillon, his governor, was given over to jesuitical and intolerant ideas. The Bishop of Mirepoix, the Dauphin's tutor, and his assistant, the Abbé de Saint-Cyr, were two Jesuits. The exile of the Duke de Châtillon, after the illness from which the king expected to die at Metz, changed nothing in the monastic plan of education which had been adopted for the young prince. They kept him posted on all the king's conjugal infidelities: which is, in my view, a disgrace. The duty of his tutors was to leave him in ignorance of them, because the natural effect of these confidences was altogether to ruin the feelings of respect which the Dauphin should have had for his father.[20]

This disgrace was now to be compounded by the very occasion of the Dauphin's marriage. He who was to become the temperamental opposite and enemy of the Duke de Choiseul, was then betrothed to Maria Theresa Raphaele, Infanta of Spain, four years older than the Dauphin and the younger sister of the Infanta Maria Anna Victoria, rudely rejected long ago as a bride for Louis XV himself. Now this Spanish marriage completing the French one of Don Philip, was calculated to heal old injuries and embody the Second Family Compact of the house of Bourbon. Towards this the large-nosed Infanta Maria Theresa, serious and well educated, contributed 'a pretty plumpness well distributed'[21] with accentuated hips. She was very fair of skin and hair as she shimmered forth in silver brocade and pearls for a solemnization of the marriage at Versailles on 23 February 1745. The celebration that evening included a topical ballet and recitative, *La Princesse de Navarre*, in which the music of Rameau was judged superior to the libretto by Voltaire. Though one line at least may be preserved:

Et toujours les héros ne sont pas sérieux.[22]

[20] Choiseul, 'Mémoires inédits', 2/16/8/498/1.
[21] D'Argenson, iv. 174.
[22] Voltaire, *La Princesse de Navarre*: cited, Broglie/Impératrice, i. 371.

It was the authentic echo, perhaps epitaph, of the French nobility in a century bent on frivolity and torn by war. The ensuing week of classic celebration at Versailles was to usher in what has been termed the last year of glory for the old regime of the French monarchy. The patron of its decadence, the Duke de Richelieu, organized one of the most sumptuous balls ever held at Versailles, on the evening of 25 February.

This masked ball in fancy dress was a public festivity proclaiming the popular aspect of absolute monarchy in France. 'The bourgeois of Paris of every quality'[23] thronged out in coaches, in hackneys, in anything going. In they squashed in a solid jam so that in the gallery, according to the dismayed Luynes, 'one was carried almost from one end to the other without setting foot to the ground . . . The indiscretion of those masked was extreme.'[24] They fell upon the buffets stacked with salmon, fillets of sole, trout pâté 'and everything which one could wish upon a Friday night',[25] including oranges which the thriftier revellers were said to have pouched and resold. Into this turmoil of enjoyment emerged eight grotesques got up as yewtrees. They were the king and his intimates.

The royal yew made the acquaintance that night of a fair Diana of twenty-four, questing, her bow and quiver upon her shoulder. Diana, christened Antoinette, was one of the Parisian bourgeoises, Madame Le Normant d'Étioles. She coincided again with Louis at another crush three nights later at the town hall in Paris. This future Marquise de Pompadour, so important for the career of the future Duke de Choiseul, did not as yet specially signify for the Count de Stainville who, one gathers, participated in those 'fêtes for the marriage of the Dauphin'[26] as one of that warrior people then celebrated by Voltaire as

Enchanté d'un loisir, hélas! trop peu durable.[27]

The war continued. The common people of France longed to read peace into a New Year which in fact opened with a heavy reminder to the bourgeoisie also of the economic incidence of war. The Marquis de Stainville provided advance intelligence: 'They are turning here to the last resort in order to find money. They have taken the funds of the Compagnie des Indes which were used to pay the dividends on the shares; so that, this interest being no longer paid, how many families, who have but that upon which to live, are going to be reduced to beggary?'[28] Suspension of payment was announced on 2

---

[23] Barbier, iv. 20.   [24] Luynes, vi. 324.   [25] Barbier, loc. cit.
[26] Choiseul, *Mémoires*, p. 25.   [27] Voltaire, *La Princesse de Navarre, u.s.*
[28] Marquis de Stainville to Grand Duke Francis II, Paris, 29 Dec. 1744; *u.s.*, fo. 536.

January 1745. The shares, normally standing at about 2,000 livres and paying 7½ per cent, had by 4 January slumped to 950. This crisis produced a rather rare measure of public accountability. Controller-General Orry had to face a special meeting of shareholders, which he was said to have done with ability. The company, directed by his brother, Fulvy, was pushed into publishing its accounts, or as much as seemed opportune. On these figures it had, from its trading in the Indies and China from 1724 to 1743 inclusive, increased its capital from 39,385,940 to 61,148,817 livres: over and above which, the company was in reality the creditor, to the tune of 100,000,000 livres, of the king who figured as holding 11,600 shares out of a total of 51,500. Countervailingly, the government was making substantial annual payments to the company, which, grumbled Orry, never had enough floating capital of its own to finance its voyages. In his eyes at least, the Compagnie des Indes had been paying dividends on an artificial basis and tiding over on governmental advances, which he had now decided to stop. In the event the company pulled through with shares standing at around 1,200 till a settlement, involving further subvention at interest by shareholders, was subsequently effected.

Orry's financial programme also included increases in capitation, on the *gabelle*, in dues upon a spread from playing-cards to copper. These yields were for the future since the prudent controller-general, at least, was planning for the campaign after next. For 1745 he is reported to have budgeted for an expenditure of 353 million livres. It was the price of glory.

In this time of financial stress the Marquis de Stainville, while not one of those depending only upon unpaid dividends, was yet suffering another kind of financial loss. Back in the Barrois the iron-foundry of Châtelet had again run into trouble amid the hazards of industrial enterprise in that early phase. Nicolas Cochois the younger had fallen down on his previously noticed contract of 1738 for the exploitation of the Châtelet–Fruze–Attignéville complex at an annual rent of 3,600 livres to the Marquis de Stainville. By the beginning of 1743 the arrears due to the marquis had amounted to 'a sum of nine thousand and some hundred livres',[29] while Cochois also owed back-wages to the workers. Stainville had secured an order of distraint upon Cochois but subsequently, making the best of a bad job, had tried to salvage him by a new lease of 19 March 1743 granted to

---

[29] Plea entered on behalf of the Marquis de Stainville by Maître de Braux to the lieutenant-general of the bailiwick (*bailliage*) of Neufchâteau, 7 Oct. 1744 *in re* 'François J^h. de Choiseul, Marquis de Stainville contre N^ic. Cochois, amodiateur des forges et fourneaux du Châtelet et de Fruze, Virla et autres' etc.; Arch. Vosges, Série E, no. 116, and for the following.

Cochois and his wife Margaret by a local agent acting for the Marquise de Stainville under the full powers of 1738 from her husband.

The new lease, which now included the château of Châtelet and its seigneurial revenues as well as the foundry, was to run from 1 October 1743 at an increased rental of 4,600 livres per annum. Shaky Cochois was obliged to set aside as security for his rent a weekly production of iron at the rate of 72,000 pounds a year for sale each December and March. This incidental index to the price of iron was adjustable to it. The contractor further undertook 'to keep the factories working without discontinuation, to pay the workers and smiths' – eight or nine master-smiths were the key men needed to keep the factory of Châtelet working to about capacity in this small instance of the tentative emergence of an industrial economy within a feudal one.

The recent expiry on 1 October 1744 of the first year of the new lease had revealed 'the abuse committed by Nicolas Cochois of the goodness'[30] of the Marquis de Stainville in giving him another chance. Not only was the annual rental not forthcoming but something over 6,000 livres from the earlier arrears were still owing to the marquis, and substantial back-wages to the workers. Cochois had been up to his old game of selling for ready cash the iron which he should have stocked as surety; 'he had only given something at a low rate to the workers to appease them'[31] and had let the factories run right down to no more than one master-smith. The defrauded workers were threatening to seize the stocks of iron in their own interests and also to sue Stainville himself for their unpaid wages. Industrial unrest could already spell ugly possibilities even for an aristocrat like the unlucky marquis, now faced with the prospect 'of seeing the factories unemployed ... and of suffering an enormous loss'. To cap all, the price of iron had recently 'fallen extremely'.

The Stainville estate through its lawyer, de Braux, now moved quickly to distrain and on 13 October 1744 Cochois came to terms for a 'friendly liquidation' in acknowledgement of a total debt to the estate of 14,312 livres, 9 sous, 8 deniers exclusive of the arrears of wages and an item of 371 livres in compensation for injury to adjacent meadowlands caused by the industrial workings. This was but the beginning, though, of further troubles. Bankruptcy brought the usual crush of creditors, notably Laurent Virla, merchant of Toul, and Georges Pierson, merchant of Nancy, both of whom had been lessors

---

[30] 'Requette contenant causes et moyens de préférence et servant de contredit pour M. le Marquis de Stainville, saisissant et deffendeur, contre Nicolas Cochois fils, partie saisie et deff^e., Laurent Virla, Georges Pierson et autres', plea entered on behalf of the Marquis de Stainville before the Chambre des Comptes of Lorraine, 7 May 1745: ibid.

[31] Plea of 7 October 1744: u.s., and for the following.

to Cochois in another example from those parts of bourgeois
entrepreneurship in landed property. Another action concerned
unpaid dues for hallmarking iron from the factory. It became a
question of 'the decision of the preferences'[32] with the Marquis de
Stainville struggling to salvage what he could for himself from among
the acrimonious creditors.

The 14,300 livres or so owing to the Marquis de Stainville from his
iron-foundry was a relatively small sum but then he was a relatively
small man, certainly by comparison, for instance, with his son's
patron, the Prince de Conti, considerably interested in coal.[33]

Conti in his big way and Stainville in his small illustrate how
industrial enterprises, like those of finance, were already being
exploited to flush the fortunes of the aristocracy in France in the
eighteenth century. At the same time the risk and litigation accruing
from Stainville's industrial venture suggest the kind of factors
restricting such exploitation. Such was the depressing background to
an observation at the celebrations for the Dauphin's marriage that
the Marquis de Stainville, 'whose son is a colonel in our troops, has a
suit of silver cloth embroidered with gold, lined with sable. The
lining alone costs, they say, twenty-five thousand livres.'[34] Not
everybody could make such a splash as the Marquis de Stainville.
Dress-hire was already operating, at a price. The Marquis de
Mirepoix, last noticed guarding the coasts of Provence behind the
Gallispan army, hired three suits to be worn once each for six
thousand livres, some £250. The Marquis de Stainville relayed a
comment upon the court celebrations that February, that 'on this
occasion the King's subjects are doing what they owe to him but they
owe for what they are doing, and indeed everybody is ruining
himself'.[35] If that did not quite apply to the Stainvilles, they had to
reckon in addition with military expenses.

The Count de Stainville's ambition after Coni to be promoted a
brigadier had been characteristic of his cheeky optimism. At that
time he was a colonel of less than two years' seniority whereas even
one of three was then normally reckoned in the French army to be
unripe for such advancement. Stainville's valour in the Alpine
campaign did, however, earn him reward, and one almost more signal
than the coveted promotion. On his return to Paris he received a
letter for the Minister of War proposing that he should change his
regiment and giving him the pick of the regiment of Champagne or

[32] Plea of 7 May 1745: *u.s.*
[33] Cf. Marcel Rouff, *Les Mines de charbon en France au XVIIIᵉ siècle* (Paris, 1922), *passim.*
[34] Barbier, iv. 13.
[35] Marquis de Stainville to Grand Duke Francis II, Paris, 20 Feb. 1745: Esteri del
Granducato di Toscana, vol. 2295/1286, fo. 568.

of Navarre. It was a flattering choice for the young colonel of a little *régiment de gentilhomme*. For Champagne and Navarre, each of four battalions, were two of the oldest and finest regiments in the French army, in all Europe.

Both regiments stood out in the army-lists among the first six of the Vieux Corps. Champagne and Navarre rotated annually along with Piedmont in seniority since all three looked back in pride to their traditional incorporation as regular regiments in 1569, after Jarnac, Champagne in the catholic camp of the future King Henry III, Navarre in the protestant camp of the future King Henry IV.

Subsequently Choiseul affected a typical nonchalance: 'I had a regiment of my name, with which I had just completed the Italian campaign: I was pleased enough with it and I did not care about changing. However the change which occurred in the command of the armies, the Prince de Conti being due to command that of Germany, where were the two regiments which they proposed to me, decided me to choose Navarre.'[36]

In Conti the Count de Stainville was looking to 'the general in fashion'[37] at court that winter despite the disparagement of the rival Saxe: 'The feats of the Prince de Conti in Italy have not gone down very well here. Since his return the officers of his army have arrived and the public is informed that he has fruitlessly lost two-thirds of it. So he is no longer called the invincible Conti.'[38]

Recent associations may have contributed to Stainville's preference for Navarre. After the War of the Polish Succession the Regiment of Navarre had been stationed at Metz and Toul and had detached its second battalion as guard of honour for Stanislas Leszczynski upon his arrival at Lunéville. And Navarre, unlike Champagne, had been all through the Bohemian campaign, largely bearing the brunt at Sahay. Stainville could thus have got to know this regiment resplendent in its white uniform with gilt buttons, formidable beneath those dun-coloured standards of Navarre which it had borne in the Wars of Religion, the Thirty Years War, the Fronde, the Dutch War, the War of the League of Augsburg, the War of the Spanish Succession, and of the Polish and now this Austrian one, most lately at the siege of Freiburg.

By rotation, furthermore, the Regiment of Navarre was to be the senior of the competing trio for the coming year. The regiment was then available for Stainville because its former colonel, the Count de

---

[36] Choiseul, *Mémoires*, p. 25.

[37] Baron von Bernstorff to King Christian VI, Paris, 12 Feb. 1745: Rigsarkiv/T.K.U.A. Frankrig, C. 254.

[38] Marshal de Saxe to Princess of Holstein, Versailles, 1 Feb. 1745: *Lettres du maréchal de Saxe à la princesse de Holstein, sa soeur*, ed. H. de Chateaugiron (Paris, 1831), p. 8.

Mortemart, one of the Rochechouarts, has just thrown up his commission in disgust at not being included in the New Year's promotions for 1745. This resignation of aggrieved officers was an accepted gambit even in time of war and was constantly being threatened in order to prise promotion out of the harassed Minister of War.

Louis XV, in a working session with the Count d'Argenson on 15 January 1745, had granted the Regiment of Navarre to the Count de Stainville. It cost the formidable sum of 75,000 livres, nearly twice the 40,000 to be raised on the little Régiment de Stainville, now to become de La Roche-Aymon.

The industrial restriction just then of the Marquis de Stainville's budget may have contributed to his son's heavy borrowing in order to buy his new regiment. However, when a colonel invested in a regiment more expensive than the one he already owned it was normal then to borrow the balance at five per cent, the capital repayable when the borrower attained the rank of *maréchal-de-camp*, that is, of a general officer, who would then sell out his regimental holding to his successor in the colonelcy. It was for such a transaction that young Stainville now turned to an old comrade-in-arms from the Régiment du Roi, Captain de Tondeboeuf,[39] with funds to spare although he was himself just acquiring the Régiment de la Sarre.

Stainville, while still a colonel, assimilated himself with Conti's 'general officers of whom several are particularly attached to him',[40] getting themselves transferred along with their commander. The author of this observation, Baron von Bernstorff, was, as a good diplomat, clearly paying attention to such up-and-coming officers. It is probably from about this period that one should date the long and pregnant friendship between the future Duke de Choiseul and the future Count von Bernstorff, one day to be foreign ministers of France and of Denmark respectively, to be acclaimed, the one as the Coachman of Europe, the other as the Oracle of the North.

III

Baron Johann Hartwig Ernst von Bernstorff, born in Hanover in 1712, was the grandson of the main founder of the family fortunes. Andreas Gottlieb Bernstorff had been the trusted counsellor of the

---

[39] R. H. Soltau, *The Duke de Choiseul* (Oxford, 1909), p. 7, states, in a confusion of ranks, that the Count de Stainville contracted to repay his debt 'when he got his marshal's baton'. He never got it.

[40] Baron von Bernstorff to King Christian VI, Paris, 15 Mar. 1745: Rigsarkiv/T.K.U.A. Frankrig, C. 254.

elector who became King George I of England, whence the Hanoverian minister had acquired Irish citizenship and a pension of £2,500 per annum on the Irish revenues. His grandson, who revered him, had been admirably educated at Tübingen and, especially, through the tutoring of an outstanding polymath, Johann Georg Keyssler, author of one of the best guides to the Europe of his day, as noticed in connection with Duke Leopold's academy at Lunéville.[41] Young Johann von Bernstorff had spent some time at that little court where he had dined with the then Duke Francis back in 1731 during a grand tour with Keyssler. Bernstorff may well have become acquainted with the Stainvilles either there or just afterwards in Paris. The winning youth, very handsome, made friends wherever he went, all over Italy and in England where he took in Windsor and Oxford and was rather taken up by Queen Caroline. Lord Chesterfield was a family friend, though the increasingly English orientation of the Hanoverian dynasty is said to have alienated the elder Bernstorff. So it was in Danish service that Johann von Bernstorff at twenty had, as one of his friends remarked, 'stepped, still as a youth, into the office of a man'[42] as envoy to the court of Saxony.

Baron von Bernstorff had been brought up a pious Lutheran, versed in theology by Keyssler, steeped in religious emotion by his pietistic sister-in-law Dorothea, reading his bible daily and earnest in prayer even upon the crest of his diplomatic career. This serious and conscientious young bachelor had in 1737 graduated from Dresden and Warsaw, where he had deplored the expense of having to harness six horses to drag a coach through the appalling streets after rain, to the imperial diet at Ratisbon. He profited from a post that was 'but a school of German public law'[43] before becoming Danish minister to the Emperor Charles VII at Frankfurt where the glittering ascendancy of Belle-Isle had reminded him of the Russian ambassador in Poland. Belle-Isle and, later, Choiseul were the only French statesmen whom Bernstorff truly admired, and he became the closest friend of the Duchess de Belle-Isle. She described their platonic relationship as 'eternal and unalterable'.[44] This tenderness is said to have earned him the jealous enmity of the Cardinal de Tencin when Bernstorff achieved his heart's desire and arrived in Paris to represent King Christian VI early in 1744.

[41] Cf. p. 57 above.
[42] H. P. Sturz, *Erinnerungen aus dem Leben des Graften Johann Hartwig Ernst von Bernstorf* (Leipzig, 1777), p. 11.
[43] Bünau to Baron von Bernstorff, 6 June 1737: cited, Aage Friis, *Bernstorfferne og Danmark: Bidrag til den Danske Stats Politiske og Kulturelle Udviklingshistorie, 1750–1835* (Copenhagen, 1903–19), i. 76.
[44] Duchess de Belle-Isle to Baron von Bernstorff: Wotersen archives, cited, ibid., i. 123.

In Paris the reverse side of Bernstorff's complex character blossomed. He was a young man of fine and expensive taste, dressing elegantly and, though eating little from a weak digestion, a considerable gourmet. At Versailles it was allowed that 'he has wit, finesse and taste; he knows the French language much better than many Frenchmen ... He is a kind of philosopher, who however readily lends himself to society; he has made friends in this part of the world [at court] and is capable of great attachments. He is extremely measured in his proceedings, listens much, speaks little, and always cogently and to the point.'[45]

Bernstorff was soon frequenting the best salons including that of the Duchess d'Aiguillon. Thus he met Montesquieu, also Maupertuis, Bernis, Voltaire, Fontenelle. Bernstorff moreover used to visit the Château d'Étioles near Versailles. He got to know the beautiful Madame Le Normant d'Étioles so early as the spring of 1744, before her royal ascent to be Madame de Pompadour. He came to be reckoned one of her closest friends. And she was not one to forget. The Danish minister took part in the glittering ball of the yewtrees at Versailles on the evening of 25 February 1745. After it he noted in his diary: 'Beginning of the adventure of Madame d'Étioles (*Anfang der Avanture von Madame d'Étiolles*).'[46] It sounds like a prepared adventure.

If the Count de Stainville was in youth notoriously no friend of the Marquise de Pompadour he became one of the closest ones of one of her closest. Bernstorff had the knack, so valuable to diplomatists, of choosing young friends destined for fame and fortune. His shrewd attention is said[47] to have been drawn from the first to the vivid figure of young Stainville because he always attracted a circle around himself without possessing any special influence, or luck. Certainly, Stainville was no rich or regular courtier.

Bernstorff was seven years older than Stainville and, one might have thought, basically dissimilar from the dashing colonel. Yet they had much in common, intelligence, taste, fondness for the theatre, means that by no means matched their extravagant standards of superior living – Bernstorff had run into heavy debt to a Jewish banker of Hamburg called Michael David. Bernstorff's neglect of his own affairs was offset by his growing recognition of the importance of economics in international relations, till one finds him writing to his foreign minister: 'Of all the means of increasing the consequence,

---

[45] Luynes, vi. 452.
[46] Baron von Bernstorff, diary, cited, A. Friis, op. cit., i. 184. This entry provides evidence that the affair began at this ball at Versailles rather than at the Hôtel de Ville in Paris three nights later, as had earlier been supposed: cf. ibid., p. 438, n.
[47] Ibid., i. 193.

riches and power of the kingdom, the development of trade is the least dangerous, the smoothest and surest.'[48] This was a lesson particularly learnt by the future Choiseul from one whom he was to acknowledge as 'his master'.[49] For the present they further shared an easy confidence in their nobility, special kindness towards servants and, more broadly, dislike of Prussia, affection for France. These two young men from small states were both seeking their fortunes with larger ones since, as Bernstorff had bitterly put it at his outset, 'my fatherland is reduced to a province'.[50] That was even truer of the Count de Stainville.

One is tempted to suggest that the two friends further shared the quality of integrity. While Stainville was the brighter spark, sexually relaxed, yet his friendship with Bernstorff already illustrated his capacity, noticeable throughout life, for winning the respect and confidence of good people outwardly more solid than himself. Bernstorff's religious feeling may even have deepened rather than restricted their friendship. It was not every French aristocrat who was then close friends with a keen protestant; though doubtless one should not overstress the coincidence whereby Stephen de Stainville acquired a regiment with earlier protestant associations at about the time that he was getting to know the man who resisted the attempts of the Duchess de Belle-Isle to convert him to the Romish church and what Bernstorff termed 'its spiritual tyranny'.[51] He was, however, anything but a protestant sectary in his perception of one church-general in Christ behind its several organizations. He observed of the catholic church that 'the councils were never assembled in order to decide how far one should worship God, fear and obey him, or whether ... one should be humble, chaste and compassionate. The elucidation of speculative dogmas and difficult texts can make a man cleverer but never better.'[52] Bernstorff was confident that God would not hold against poor, weak men and women any errors of understanding but only sins of the heart against a religion of the heart. That matched the elevated and warmhearted inclination of the Count de Stainville, whose contempt – perhaps excessive – for the prudential conformism of Louis XV in religion has been noticed.

Baron von Bernstorff held that the politicking and obscurantism of the Vatican had reduced the contemporary Italian to a state, essentially, of atheism or paganism 'because they teach him only fables and tell him nothing of the miracles and commandments of

---

[48] Baron von Bernstorff to Count von Schulin, 14 Apr. 1748: ibid., i. 156.
[49] Cited, ibid., p. 195.
[50] Baron von Bernstorff to Billerbeck, Jan. 1732: ibid., p. 46.
[51] Baron von Bernstorff, cited, op. cit., i. 224. [52] Baron von Bernstorff, ibid., pp. 222–3.

the Almighty, so as to inspire in him veneration only for the daydreams and puerilities of men.'[53] The Count de Stainville was to use the same expression in remarking to a French friend in Rome that in society 'they laugh at the puerilities with which our poor religion is tricked out'.[54]

During the ministry of Choiseul there was to be a notable increase in French toleration of Huguenots, not Jesuits. Before Choiseul attained power Bernstorff, some years on, described him as 'a man lively, satirical and agitating, but full of sense and wit, and made to play a large part in the world, or to perish in the effort'.[55]

IV

The world now stretching ahead of the Count de Stainville, while still torn by war and riddled with diplomacy, was by the spring of 1745 substantially altered. In its regrouping two figures had disappeared and a new one arrived.

The newcomer was fiftyone-year-old Louis René de Voyer d'Argenson. The Marquis d'Argenson had become French foreign minister because by November 1744 Louis XV had wearied of that immediate burden and it had, exceptionally for then, been declined by the Marquis de Villeneuve, the veteran diplomatist from Constantinople, because of 'the bad choice of our ministers in the foreign courts, and of the chief clerks of the [foreign] office'.[56] Whereas d'Argenson was said to have been pushed by the chief clerk, Du Theil, as well as by the royal valet, Bachelier. D'Argenson's younger brother was of course already in the ascendant as Minister of War even though characterized by his jealous elder as jesuitically hostile, 'l'inimicus homo'.[57]

The Marquis d'Argenson was a prototype of the progressive intellectual. He had introduced the Abbé de Saint-Pierre to the Club de l'Entresol in the Place Vendôme, an early forum of the intellectual enlightenment in discussing current affairs in the Abbé Alary's agreeable apartment, where one could find 'even the English papers'.[58] D'Argenson's other, suggestively different mentor, Chau-

---

[53] Baron von Bernstorff to his nephew, Baron A. P. von Bernstorff, Sept. 1755: Aage Friis, *Bernstorffske Papirer* (Copenhagen, 1904–13: henceforth cited as *Bernstorffske Papirer*), i. 136.
[54] Count de Stainville to Duke de Nivernais, 17 May 1751: W.N.A., docket V/1, fo. 69.
[55] Baron von Bernstorff to Baron A. P. von Bernstorff, *u.s.*, p. 141.
[56] D'Argenson, iv. 148.
[57] Cited, Edgar Zévort, *Le Marquis d'Argenson et le Ministère des Affaires Étrangères du 18 novembre 1744 au 10 janvier 1747* (Paris, 1880: henceforth cited as Zévort), p. 10.
[58] [Marquis d'Argenson,] *Essais dans le goût de ceux de Montaigne* (Amsterdam, 1785. Reprinted as *Les Loisirs d'un Ministre*, Liége, 1797), ii. 181.

velin, had been disgraced in the year in which the marquis produced a work originally entitled *Traité de politique dans lequel on examine à quel point la démocratie peut être admise sous le gouvernement monarchique en France*: in a measure of local self-government and tax-assessment was roughly his answer. The appointment of such a thinker to high office was striking in a society wherein, as he himself remarked, 'the foundation of the character of the ministers is that of being the first courtiers'.[59] That internal tension was largely to condition the ministries both of the Marquis d'Argenson and, very differently, of the Duke de Choiseul.

One of the Marquis d'Argenson's few supporters at Versailles was the Marshal de Belle-Isle. Both looked to Frederick the Great as the pivot, still, of French foreign policy. December 1744 had found Belle-Isle, faithfully accompanied by his brother, once more heading into Germany to confer with his client, the emperor, before concerting with his patron, the King of Prussia, whose retreat from Prague had helped to reduce Charles VII almost to collapse before an Austrian comeback.

Upon his snowbound journey to Berlin across the German principalities Belle-Isle on the morning of 20 December 1744 drove into the courtyard of the posting-house, displaying the Prussian escutcheon, in the little village of Elbingerode north of Nordhausen. The gates slammed to behind. The Marshal of France was the prisoner of the bailiff of Elbingerode. Because under a traffic convention this one Prussian posting-station was sited in a little Hanoverian enclave. The territorial entanglement of Germany could catch out even contemporaries.

Triumphant Hanoverian guards made the two Belle-Isles in their coaches lie up in woodland till after dark when they smuggled them across an outlying strip of the duchy of Brunswick to the Hanoverian heartland at Osterode. The startling intelligence was sent to England, and Belle-Isle, his sciatica intensified, had to endure a horrid crossing of thirteen days before landing at Harwich in February 1745. Thence he was conveyed to Windsor Castle under a cavalry escort to head off the robust English populace who turned out along the way to hoot the French marshal and chuck stones and filth at his coach.

At Windsor the prisoner was confined in the main tower in order to scotch unfounded suspicions of collusion with the Broadbottom Administration of the Pelhams who were moderating the haughty pretensions of Earl Granville, as Carteret had become upon losing office just when the Marquis d'Argenson assumed it. Belle-Isle was solaced by an English allowance of fifty pounds a day, by the

[59] D'Argenson, iv. 160.

politenesses of the Duke of Newcastle and the Duke of Grafton, the
Great Chamberlain, and by the fact that, as he wrote, 'at Windsor
... the air is extremely pure, and proper to my health'.[60]
  From Paris the Marquis de Stainville reported to Vienna: 'At the
present juncture the French regard ... as a great good fortune the
detention of Messrs. de Belle-Isle, who by their intrigues would
surely not have failed to get approved, perhaps, projects as
extraordinary as the first ones'[61] culminating in the election of the
Emperor Charles VII. The juncture now was his death on the night
of 20–21 January 1745.
  Autopsy upon this emperor broken after three years, dead after
forty-seven, revealed, in the words of Voltaire, 'his lungs, his liver and
his stomach gangrened, stones in his kidneys, a polyp in his heart; it
was judged that for a long time he could not have been a moment
without suffering ... He was buried with the ceremonies of the
empire; and ... they bore the globe of the world before him who,
during the short duration of his empire, had not possessed even a
small and unhappy province.'[62]
  The most important act of the Emperor Charles VII was his death.
Puppet though he had been, the strings were the convergent threads
of European policy and war, all suddenly fallen slack in a tangle.
Distracted Germany was, as Frederick the Great wrote to Louis XV,
plunged into a 'terrible crisis'.[63] Watchers looked back fearfully to the
baleful times of imperial interregnum just on five hundred years
before. A more frivolous but pertinent French comment ran:

> La nuit du vingt au vingt et un
> Monsieur l'Empereur est defunt ...
> S'il donne la paix à la France,
> Il ne peut qu'en être approuvé.[64]

Here was a chance for France to drop that imperial commitment
which had been the stickiest, still, of the terms for an 'ultimatum for
peace'[65] extracted from Louis XV before Christmas 1744 by the
foreign minister whom he nicknamed 'Monsieur d'Argenson de la
Paix' in distinction from 'Monsieur d'Argenson de la Guerre'. That

---

[60] Marshal de Belle-Isle to Count d'Argenson, Windsor, 18 Mar. 1745: Arch. Guerre C., vol.
3096, no. 224.
[61] Marquis de Stainville to Grand Duke Francis II, Paris, 27 Jan. 1745: Esteri del Granducato
di Toscana, vol. 2295/1286, fo. 555 (copy in Ö.S./H.H.S., Lothringisches Hausarchiv 77/177A,
fo. 34).
[62] Voltaire, Précis du siècle de Louis XV, pp. 93–4.
[63] King Frederick II to King Louis XV, Berlin, 26 Jan. 1745; Politische Correspondenz, iv. 24.
[64] Broglie/Impératrice, i. 140.
[65] King Louis XV to Marquis d'Argenson, 23 Dec. 1744: D'Argenson, iv. 254.

same December a French envoy had significantly arrived in Warsaw for the first time since Augustus III had ousted Stanislas Leszczynski. This special ambassador was the subtle Count Louis de Saint-Séverin d'Aragon, who had switched from the service of Parma when she passed to Austria in 1736. Saint-Séverin was an old friend of the Marquis de Stainville, both friendly with the Duke de Noailles who now stood behind the despatch of Saint-Séverin, after his success in Sweden,[66] to try his hand at building up relations in the other constitutional monarchy of Poland. Even before the death of the emperor the Saxons had been alerting the French that faithless Frederick had been up to his old tricks though with little response, indeed, from either George II or Maria Theresa. Those two sovereigns had on 8 January 1745 gone in with Holland and Saxony to sign the Quadruple Alliance of Warsaw, not immediately ratified, however. This secret treaty of mutual defence meant that in the Saxon court, its lesson learnt and now subsidized by Britain, an alarmed animosity against Prussia had taken precedence over that against Austria. Whereas the Marquis d'Argenson would not after all follow up the let-out from Prussia towards peace, refusing to entertain denunciations of Frederick, making every kind of foolish excuse for the faithless ally whom he admired. This contrasted with his attitude towards the Spanish ally. Elizabeth Farnese is said to have complained subsequently of this true disciple of Chauvelin that she knew he 'only spoke of her as a f... and a b...'.[67] D'Argenson's crudity of language was notorious. He had been assured by Louis that he had only unwillingly concluded the Second Family Compact. This was almost certainly a lie, typical of that monarch's timid and often insincere acquiescence in the views of his ministers. It was enough, however, to allow d'Argenson to push, as he did in the first half of 1745, the curious policy of encouraging Spain to make a separate peace with England: only it might not have stopped at England, as was shortly to be suggested to the Marquis de Stainville.

V

The European crisis of 1745 was to afford the Marquis de Stainville his most significant, most secret role in history. At Versailles on 19 January, just before the imperial demise, the Marquis d'Argenson

---

[66] Cf. p. 229.

[67] Note of 29 June 1763 to Duke de Choiseul by Count de Noailles on his mission with his father, Marshal de Noailles, to Madrid in 1746: Arch. Aff. Étr. C.P., Espagne, vol. 461: Zévort, p. 42.

asked the Marquis de Stainville to take a seat and addressed him thus: 'So there is no means of reaching an accommodation. I assure you that I am so anxious for it that I would give two fingers from my hand for it to be made, and it would not be so difficult as is thought if . . .'[68] Maria Theresa would make the first overture. Stainville did not see why the injured queen should do so, remarking that 'the greatest princes do not cease to be human. Upon this we separated, very little in agreement upon our principles':[69] a new sidelight upon d'Argenson's later contention that but for the death of Charles VII 'peace would have been signed before the opening of the campaign of 1745'.[70] D'Argenson disliked diplomatic friends of Noailles like Stainville and Saint-Séverin, whom he described as 'an old friend of the bottle of the Marquis de Stainville, a Lorrainer as false as the Italian'.[71]

The next conversation between the French foreign minister and the Tuscan envoy was on 26 January 1745. D'Argenson, reported Stainville, 'said to me on my entering his room that he foresaw that the unexpected event of the death of the emperor was going to plunge the whole of Europe back into greater chaos than she had been in previously. I replied to him quite simply that sometimes such events produced good effects, and that on the contrary I envisaged that perhaps this one might provide means of procuring repose for Europe, that it broke many engagements which were troubling it, if it were only the Union of Frankfurt which naturally dropped by the death of its head. On that the minister replied to me that the engagements of the king [of France] with the house of Bavaria subsisted none the less'[72] and that any Austrian attempt against it would compel Louis to make every effort in its favour. The temper of the conversation rose. D'Argenson, said Stainville, proceeded: 'I am greatly the servant of your master, but it is not in the interest of the king or of the kingdom to let him reach the imperial throne, and to that there will always be opposition on the part of France. At this remark I broke off short with the minister, saying to him that the arguments which we might advance would only be based upon our own ideas since in order to establish a solid system one had to know the intentions of the interested courts. And upon that we finished.'[73]

It was only months later that the Marquis de Stainville further reported in this connection that the Marquis d'Argenson had said

[68] Marquis de Stainville to Grand Duke Francis II, Paris, 23 Jan. 1745: Esteri del Granducato di Toscana, vol. 2295/1286, fo. 549.
[69] Ibid., fo. 550.   [70] D'Argenson, iv. 260.   [71] Ibid., v. 158.
[72] Marquis de Stainville to Grand Duke Francis II, Paris, 27 Jan. 1745: Esteri del Granducato di Toscana, vol. 2295/1286, fo. 553 (copy in Ö.S./H.H.S., Lothringisches Hausarchiv 77/177A, fo. 34).   [73] Ibid., fo. 554.

that, rather than consent to the imperial election of the Grand Duke Francis, Louis XV would 'make war for forty years, a declaration which he made to me personally, and to all the foreign envoys'.[74]

Such advance animosity perhaps suggested the natural strength of the imperial candidacy of the husband of Maria Theresa. The King of France was indeed unenthusiastic about such an elevation for his former vassal, the erstwhile Duke of Lorraine. But the Marquis d'Argenson's stiff interchange with the Marquis de Stainville on 26 January 1745 was not matched in a conversation which the latter had that same day with another French minister, the Cardinal de Tencin.

The cardinal offered Stainville a glimpse of the prospect of 'a general conciliation'[75] of Europe if only Maria Theresa would recognize the rule of Maximilian Joseph in his ancestral lands as the new Elector of Bavaria, instead of stoking up war against him. Tencin hinted that the elector might prove a useful ally for Maria Theresa against Frederick and that in such circumstances France would not oppose the imperial election of her husband. Stainville refused to be drawn as to the latter's prospects. And in reporting his dissimilar conversations that day with the two French ministers he displayed greater interest in another German ally for the Queen of Hungary when venturing one of his rather rare expressions of personal opinion upon high policy: 'I think that the principal object for the Queen is to be indissolubly connected with the King of Poland, to do nothing except in concert with him and if possible with the Empress of Russia, and the old allies.[76] In that case, the King of Prussia will find himself isolated, and abandoned for sure by France.'[77]

Such indeed was the pivotal position of Augustus III of Saxony and Poland, the importance of Russia and England, the anxiety of Frederick. As he quickly perceived, the balance of forces was inclining towards the imperial election of the Grand Duke Francis, so that one French minister wondered 'if one should not even concur in what one could not prevent ... so as to extract thereby a peace suitable to the king and his allies'.[78]

This writer was the Marshal de Noailles. The Cardinal de Tencin had been too modest in making out to the Marquis de Stainville on 26 January that he was the only French minister inclined to look towards Maria Theresa. About a fortnight later the Princess

---

[74] Marquis de Stainville to Emperor Francis I, Paris, 14 Nov. 1745: Ö.S./H.H.S., Lothringisches Hausarchiv 77/177B.
[75] Marquis de Stainville to Grand Duke Francis II, Paris, 27 Jan. 1745: Esteri del Granducato di Toscana, vol. 2295/1286, fo. 554.
[76] Notably England and Holland.
[77] u.s., fo. 555.
[78] Marshal de Noailles to Count de Chavigny, 6 Feb. 1745: Abbé Millot, *Mémoires politiques et militaires* (Paris, 1777), vi. 101–2.

d'Armagnac, the estranged wife of Prince Charles of the house of Lorraine and the daughter of the Marshal de Noailles, told the Marquis de Stainville that her father would like to see him on the following Tuesday at Versailles. So on 16 February Noailles quietly asked Stainville what the foreign minister had been saying to him. Stainville related in confidence d'Argenson's broadcast threat of the hostility of Louis to the candidature of Francis, adding that the diplomatic corps in Paris had been 'extremely surprised by it. "I am very much so myself," replied the minister [Noailles], "and all that I can say to you is that the King thinks very differently." At this moment the Dutch ambassador was announced. This seemed to cause annoyance since it was desired that our interview should be secret.'[79] Noailles asked Stainville to keep in touch and said that he would give him an appointment in Paris, away from court observation.

Between six and seven o'clock on the evening of 5 March 1745 the Marquis de Stainville called by arrangement at the town-house of the Princess d'Armagnac. There he had a very long conversation with her father.

The Marshal de Noailles began by declaring that he was not speaking on any instructions. He told Stainville 'that, so far as it lay with him, he was fighting the fear which they had here of the might of the house of Austria; that they would not get it into their heads that she was no longer the same power as when she possessed all Italy and the Spanish monarchy'.[80] Noailles believed that if Maria Theresa, with the participation of Britain but not of the too public Dutch, were to advance 'some reasonable propositions' and accept 'very slight sacrifices', France would support the imperial election of her husband. A free election could be ensured by the withdrawal from Germany of all foreign troops, and a general armistice would favour negotiations for that peace which France was represented as desiring. 'Provided', said Noailles, 'that the King [Louis] could emerge from this business honore salvo, he would be content, not wishing to aggrandize himself in any way.' To all of which the Marquis de Stainville 'only listened, as is my wont'. The listener recorded: '"In God's name" he [Noailles] continued, "urge His Royal Highness [Francis] to send you a prompt reply".'

One may understand why the Marquis d'Argenson denounced as 'a great Austrian at heart'[81] that French marshal whom Stainville now described to the Grand Duke Francis as 'the man at the court

---

[79] Marquis de Stainville to Grand Duke Francis II, Paris, 20 Feb. 1745: Esteri del Granducato di Toscana, vol. 2295/1286, fo. 567.
[80] Ibid., 6 Mar. 1745: fo. 574–5 for the following (copy in Ö.S./H.H.S., Lothringsches Hausarchiv 77/177A, fo. 35).
[81] D'Argenson, vii. 66.

who makes the most profession of being attached to Your Royal Highness'.[82] Francis was in fact writing that same day to give his minister in Paris a rather rare assurance of satisfaction with his recent services. A prompt reply to the overture from Noailles was another matter. Ten days later Tencin took up the running, expressing surprise that Stainville had not been authorized to make any opening towards peace. The marquis, evidently rating the cardinal's advances lower than the marshal's, contrasted Tencin's language with that of d'Argenson and rather unkindly intimated 'that it was not possible to address oneself to a divided ministry'.[83]

Four days earlier, on 12 March 1745, the Tuscan minister had complied with a request that he should call upon the Spanish ambassador in Paris. Campoflorido told Stainville 'that he had proposed that they turn totally to the side of the Queen of Hungary, while supporting the views which she might have upon the imperial throne, on condition that she cede some little thing to the Infant Don Philip; that that had not been totally rejected; that he had written of it to his court, and that although he had said to me at first that he regarded it as an extravagant project, he thought that it was the only means of making a solid arrangement. I replied to him that according to the language which M. d'Argenson had held to me, he would not be of this opinion; upon that the ambassador replied to me "that that talk was extraordinary, and that he had himself said so to M. d'Argenson".'[84] This was as much as Stainville had been able to make of the conversation since 'the ambassador does not explain himself very clearly'.

Since the Marquis d'Argenson had treated the Marquis de Stainville to what the latter termed 'his fine declaration at the death of the Elector of Bavaria'[85] a constrained silence had supervened between them. Contemporary canons of diplomatic courtesy had been outraged by the blunt hostility of d'Argenson, an early advocate of open diplomacy, characteristically maintaining that he had nothing to hide since he had nothing but good intentions. D'Argenson did share Stainville's appreciation of the central importance of Saxony, and now put forward Augustus to rival Francis as a candidate for imperial election in preference to the new Elector of Bavaria, described by Noailles as 'without troops, without money, without consideration and perhaps without counsel'.[86]

[82] Marquis de Stainville to Grand Duke Francis II, Paris, 6 Mar. 1745: *u.s.*, fo. 573.
[83] Ibid., 20 Mar. 1745: fo. 586.
[84] Ibid., 13 Mar. 1745: fo. 580 (copy in Ö.S./H.H.S., Lothringisches Hausarchiv 77/177A, fo. 37), and for the following.
[85] Marquis de Stainville to Grand Duke Francis II, Paris, 1 May 1745: Ö.S./H.H.S., Lothringisches Hausarchiv 77/177B.
[86] Marshal de Noailles to Count de Chavigny, 6 Feb. 1745: Abbé Millot, op. cit., vi. 101.

Augustus III was flattered but already going over to the other side. Frederick the Great, in refusing to underwrite his promotion by the French government, adduced Russian opposition to the elevation of the King of Poland and went on to ask the awkward questions which Saint-Séverin had already answered for d'Argenson: 'Saxony is incapable of shaking off the yoke of England and Vienna; there is nothing to be expected from Dresden.'[87] Yet d'Argenson persisted in his silly policy of trying to prod the Roi de Porcelaine, as Frederick christened Augustus, into competing for a second elective throne. Meantime the Bavarian elector, still France's ally, received a jog from Maria Theresa.

VI

On 21 March 1745 Count Batthyany burst across the lower reaches of the Inn in command of a small army braced by two of Austria's most forward generals, Bernklau and Browne, switched up from Italy. It was almost a repeat from two years before. The Austrian advance reeled off the same names westwards, only quicker now: Passau, Schärding, Braunau, Landau, Straubing, Dingolfing, Landshut. Once again was Bavaria cruelly bent beneath the marauding Pandours. Browne was wounded by his own troops in trying to restrain them at the capture of Vilshofen, where the Bavarians had actually resisted for five days. On 15 April at Pfaffenhofen, nearly midway between Munich and Ingolstadt, Austrian advance-guards had the better of the little French force of the Count de Ségur, always the unlucky general in those parts. The French beat it back to Donauwörth, twice so humiliated within two years. Only this time the Bavarian ruler did not come along.

Earlier representations of the Bavarian plight by Chavigny had caused the Marquis d'Argenson to discount him as 'a darling who was spoiling her child'.[88] On 17 April d'Argenson informed Chavigny that he had felt justified in telling Louis that he would answer for the Bavarian elector's 'fidelity in any event'.[89] Five days later the Elector Maximilian Joseph contracted out to Austria by the Treaty of Füssen.

By secret articles of the treaty the Bavarian elector undertook to furnish a corps of troops to his erstwhile enemies provided they replaced his subsidies from France; and he would vote Austrian in the imperial election, would work in that sense upon his relatives, the

---

[87] Count de Saint-Séverin to Marquis d'Argenson, 13 Mar. 1745: Zévort, p. 101.
[88] Cited, Zévort, p. 116, n. 2.
[89] Marquis d'Argenson to Count de Chavigny, 17 April 1745: ibid., p. 120.

electors Palatine and of Cologne. A Hessian contingent had just marched away from the engagement at Pfaffenhofen in ominous defection from the French connection, left derelict in Germany by the Bavarian collapse. Frederick would have to fend for himself against an exultant Austria with whom Augustus of Saxony now ratified the Treaty of Warsaw in furtherance of a juicy negotiation for the dismemberment of Prussia, seemingly a more hopeful prospect for him than the always implausible one of imperial election.

Now more than ever was the time for France to drop the Saxon candidature and cut her losses in Germany. But such clear decision in adversity was not for the Marquis d'Argenson. In the melancholy words of Voltaire: 'This general war continued because it had begun ... The king, abandoned by those for whom he had begun the war, was obliged to continue it without having other object than to make it cease: a sad situation which exposes the peoples, and which promises them no indemnity.'[90]

Within the French government political differences tended to become strategic. The Marquis d'Argenson advised his king: 'Your Majesty should conduct only a defensive in Flanders ... In Italy another defensive ... but in Germany we should make our greatest efforts.'[91] This would suit the book of d'Argenson's favourite ally, who subsequently represented to Louis XV: 'If the Spaniards make a descent in the Canary Islands, or if the King of France takes Tournai, or if Thamas-Couli-Kan [sic] besieges Babylon, these events are entirely one ... in the war of Bohemia and Moravia.'[92] But a French hit-tune that season ran:

'Je n'irons [sic] *plus, je n'irons plus à Prague.'*[93]

Louis XV held that his foreign minister, as he told him, did not understand war: 'which was very true'[94] admitted d'Argenson. It was against fair-lying Flanders, the traditional field of military renown, that the main French army was ranged that spring in over a hundred battalions and 160 squadrons under the Marshal de Saxe,

[90] Voltaire, *Précis du siècle de Louis XV*, pp. 94–5.
[91] Marquis d'Argenson, memorandum to King Louis XV, Feb. 1745: de Flassan, *Histoire générale et raisonnée de la diplomatie française* (2nd ed., Paris, 1811), v. 243–4. The authenticity of this so-called Flassan Memoir has been questioned but it was probably printed by him from the bulk of the d'Argenson manuscripts which perished in the burning of the Library of the Louvre in 1871. The memorandum was subsequently ignored by Zévort, written down by the duc de Broglie (Broglie/Impératrice, i. 209, n. 1), written up, convincingly, by Arthur Ogle, *The Marquis d'Argenson: a study in criticism* (London, 1893), appendix A (cf. also, in particular, D'Argenson, iv. 261 with Flassan, v. 245), and apparently accepted by Lodge, p. 92.
[92] Memorandum enclosed in letter of King Frederick II to King Louis XV, Camenz, 16 May 1745: *Politische Correspondenz*, iv. 166–7.
[93] Broglie/Impératrice, i. 374.   [94] D'Argenson, iv. 261.

dropsically reduced to 'a pitiable state',[95] said the Marquis de Stainville, by the rigours of campaigning and debauch. Nevertheless Saxe set forth that April, with a wagonload of whores among his impedimenta. The subsidiary French army was to be that upon the Rhine under the command now of the Prince de Conti, who had swopped the Italian theatre with the Marshal de Maillebois.

A week after the Bavarian defection the Marshal de Noailles was urging Louis that, since the decision was for an offensive in Flanders, Conti's army should be defensively pulled back behind the Rhine as 'nothing would be more useless'[96] than to keep it in Germany. Such withdrawal would accord well enough with the policy which Noailles had adumbrated to the elder Stainville, and the advice might have been good but for d'Argenson's policy of contesting the imperial election at Frankfurt. The tug between d'Argenson and Noailles had promoted muddle. In place of a possible policy of profitable peace Monsieur d'Argenson de la Paix had, perhaps more than has always been appreciated, assimilated himself to his brother in an ill-adjusted bellicosity. The concentration upon Flanders represented the implementation of a poor policy by a worse strategy.

The Prince de Conti himself had not hurried from Isle-Adam to activate the German theatre. His delay hung over his subordinate officers whose arrival at the front was postponed to 15 April. On the third the Marquis de Stainville reported that for the past week he had discontinued his probing contacts with French ministers, 'not having anything to say to them, and having been indispensably occupied for the departure of my son'[97] for the Rhine. Another boulevard of war was opening ahead for the Count de Stainville.

---

[95] Marquis de Stainville to Grand Duke Francis II, Paris, 10 Apr. 1745: Ö.S./H.H.S., Lothringisches Hausarchiv 77/177B.
[96] Memorandum by Marshal de Noailles to King Louis XV, 29 Apr. 1745: Rousset, ii. 192.
[97] Marquis de Stainville to Grand Duke Francis II, Paris, 3 Apr. 1745: Ö.S./H.H.S., Lothringisches Hausarchiv 77/177B.

CHAPTER IV

RHINELAND

I

AT THE outset of the Prince de Conti's campaign of 1745 he was described by Bernstorff as 'passionately fond of everything which relates to falconry'.[1] But Conti's assumption of his command had been liable to delay by bigger game than falcons could provide, by the beginning of a long secret which was to be constantly active against the foreign policy of the Duke of Choiseul.

Conti's ranging ambitions in Eastern Europe, as in an earlier project for his marrying the Empress Elizabeth of Russia, were now revived in a new form which seemed almost to personalize the perennial issue for French eastern policy: whether to look primarily to Russia or to Poland. At the austrophil court of Augustus III the Count de Saint-Séverin had 'been reduced to living everywhere like an outcast, at Grodno, at Warsaw, at Dresden'[2] but had nevertheless established important connections in Polish society, notably through a literary Frenchman called Duperron de Castéra who was tutoring young Prince Adam Czartoryski. In March 1745 Castéra was back in France conferring not only with Marquis d'Argenson but also, secretly, with the Prince de Conti to whom he remitted a letter from Count Francis Bielinski, Grand Marshal of Poland. Bielinski and other Polish magnates wished, through the secret agency of Castéra, to run Conti for the Polish throne if it should fall vacant, as was considered not unlikely since Augustus was in bad health, with ulcerated legs. For Bielinski and the powerful clan of Czartoryski, aspiring to lead a patriotic faction, the dashing young Prince de Conti stood out as a grandson of that Conti elected King of Poland in 1697 but forcibly frustrated by his successful rival, the Elector of Saxony.

A Polish fear was that the Saxon dynasty would, with Russian support, seek to render the Polish crown hereditary: which Saint-Séverin had thought might profit France. Conti properly informed his king of the Polish proposal. Louis XV approved it but reasonably required particular secrecy and no personal involvement at that stage

[1] Baron von Bernstorff to Count von Schulin, Paris, 4 June 1745: Rigsarkiv/T.K.U.A. Frankrig, C. 254.
[2] Count de Saint-Séverin to Marquis d'Argenson, Frankfurt am Main, 15 Oct. 1745: Arch. Aff. Étr. C.P., Allemagne, vol. 543, fo. 105.

in view of his commitment to the Marquis d'Argenson's policy in favour of Augustus III for the imperial succession. So Conti pretended that he had not consulted his sovereign and confined himself to sending Castéra back to Poland with a memorandum of pertinent questions for elucidation before proceeding further.[3] Such was the operative beginning of that Secret du Roi of King Louis XV and the Prince de Conti which was to become one of the classic paradiplomacies in its strange complexity and concealed persistence for just on a generation, outlasting the ministry of him who was now serving under the prince as the Count de Stainville.

Conti was to collaborate closely with Saint-Séverin both in his Polish designs and also, now, in his campaigning upon the Rhine in support of the imperial candidacy of the sovereign whose interests in Poland he might be setting out to rival. One might not be surprised if his military keenness were now somewhat moderated.

News of the Bavarian defection, which earlier action by Conti might at least have delayed, reached that prince at Strasburg on his way to headquarters at Spires. From the outset he had to master this earliest of the external pulls upon his campaign that year. Conti's first concern was to succour Ségur and effect a junction with him, achieved at Zuffenhausen just north of Stuttgart on 25 April 1745. Only then could Conti join his main army which Maillebois, in the last weeks of his command, had been artfully manoeuvring north of Frankfurt am Main so as to bend the Austro-Hanoverian army of the Duke von Arenberg back from the line of the Lahn. The Regiment of Navarre had advanced to capture Weilburg on the Lahn on 7 April from the retreating Hanoverians.[4] Three weeks later French headquarters had been established at Langenschwalbach by Conti and his faithful band of officers, du Châtel, du Chayla, Villemur, and Stainville's 'little Bissy'. Only, the impetus ran down under perennial difficulties of supply and communications.

Conti's marching orders from the king, dated on April Fools Day, had been at least as much political as military: to hold the Austrians off from the circles of the Rhine, Swabia and Franconia while imposing upon local princes in French interests for the imperial election at Frankfurt. Conti corresponded with the Marquis d'Argenson as well as the count, and direct with French diplomatic missions in Germany, holding as he did plenipotentiary powers

[3] The foregoing account of the origin of the Secret du Roi is indebted to the analysis by Didier Ozanam and Michel Antoine, *Correspondance secrète du comte de Broglie avec Louis XV* Paris, 1956), i. xvi–xxi.

[4] Cf. Count de Berchiny to Count d'Argenson, Hofheim, 19 Mar. 1745, and de Cornillon to the same, Usingen, 7 Apr. 1745: Arch. Guerre C., vol. 3096, no. 265 and vol. 3097, no. 60 respectively.

provisionally to conclude treaties in case of urgency with 'Princes and States of the Empire who shall wish to unite themselves with His Majesty'.[5] But they did not so wish. Conti's position contrasted sadly with that of Belle-Isle four years earlier. Even in regard to Chavigny's diplomatic achievement of the previous year the Marquis d'Argenson now minuted on a French memorandum assessing the Bavarian defection: 'The confederal union [of Frankfurt] was a great enterprise ... but inordinate in expense with regard to the circumstances and above all to the directorial strength of the French government; it would have needed the strength of the Cardinal de Richelieu and the riches of the ministry of Colbert.'[6] Their successors, d'Argenson and Orry, were confessed unequal.

The French policy of subsidizing German princelings had become muddled and weak. The French government was reduced to haggling even with the beholden Elector Palatine, inclining towards neutrality. The electors of Mainz and Cologne had been bought by Carteret the year before. It was a shaky basis for Conti's campaign wherein strategy must ever look to diplomacy.

II

After the Count de Stainville had left Paris to serve under Conti, the Marquis de Stainville had continued to attend the prolonged festivities for the marriage of the Dauphin, notably at the Bourbon embassies of Spain and Naples. At the latter the marquis one Sunday, 25 April 1745, murmured to Tencin that he had heard that the cardinal had written that strictly according to the laws of the Holy Roman Empire the Grand Duke of Tuscany was ineligible for the imperial throne. Tencin exclaimed that it was untrue, asked Stainville to dinner two days later, when he told him that he had now recalled something written to Rome which might have been misinterpreted. The cardinal proffered specious explanations. The marquis 'made pretence of believing him'.[7]

'Upon that,' Stainville continued, 'the Cardinal de Tencin proceeded to business, and said to me that this was indeed the moment to make some overture for peace.' Stainville agreed and suggested that it was now for France to withdraw her forces from Germany

[5] 'Pleinpouvoir pour Mgr. le Pce. de Conti', Versailles, 3 Apr. 1745: Arch. Aff. Étr. C.P., Allemagne, Diète de Francfort 1745, vol. 538, fo. 12.
[6] Minute by Marquis d'Argenson on memorandum 'Sur l'accomodement que l'Elr. de Bavière vient de conclure avec la Reine de Hongrie', Versailles, 25 Apr. 1745: ibid., vol. 538, fo. 92.
[7] Marquis de Stainville to Grand Duke Francis II, Paris, 1 May 1745: Ö.S./H.H.S., Lothringisches Hausarchiv 77/177B, and for the following.

where they no longer had the pretext of supporting Bavaria: which was just about what Noailles was advising Louis in his memorandum two days later. Tencin, however, told Stainville 'that he did not think that anybody would dare make this proposal to the king ... "You yourself, Monsieur de Stainville, laying aside your prepossessions – if you were in the King's Council, would you give him this advice?" "Yes, without doubt," I replied affirmatively to him, "because ... it is more glorious for a great prince to acknowledge his faults than to wish to sustain them."' Tencin, still demurring, changed tack to ask why '"is not the Queen of Hungary, who formerly made such advantageous propositions to France, willing to make any at present?" Upon which I replied to him, "I ask you, Monseigneur, laying aside all partiality, if you were in a position to give advice to the queen, would you advise her to be the first to make démarches with regard to a power which had been the first in declaring war on her contrary to the most sacred previous undertakings, and without any just motive? It is for the aggressor to make the first démarches and never the opposite."' Stainville termed the conversation 'very lively'.

The trenchant marquis proceeded to emphasize to the supple cardinal that 'the whole French nation ... looks upon this war with nothing but horror. "Well then", said the cardinal, "so we have to see this war perpetuated for a little point of honour as to who shall make the first démarche."' To which Stainville retorted as before, adding that negotiation needed confidence, whereas:

'In truth the queen had not been rewarded for displaying it; and without wishing to hark back', I continued, 'to the engagements undertaken with the late emperor [Charles VI], reiterated at his death, from the very mouth of the king [Louis XV] to the Prince of Liechtenstein, it was enough to see what had happened through me myself, what the late cardinal [Fleury] and Monsieur Amelot had said to me at the time of the march of Monsieur de Maillebois into Bohemia, the word which they had given me to bring back all the French troops behind the Rhine, if the garrison of Prague was allowed to leave freely; and then after breaking their word as they had done when it was a question of the performance, giving me in writing quite the contrary of what they had said to me verbally, and thereby making me risk destroying myself in the estimation of my master, who, if I had not been known by him, could have suspected me of having imposed upon him over it. And after such proceedings you wish', I continued, 'that the queen should make proposals. In truth that is not natural.' This conversation, which was to have been for a moment, lasted five quarters of an hour.

That altercation of 27 April 1745 provided one of the most vivid records, hitherto unpublished, from that century of a debate on the heavy issue of peace or war between two great enemy powers. And it is rather refreshing to find an eighteenth-century diplomatist denouncing the regular trickeries of his calling. Though one notices that Stainville did not let on – indeed he was bound not to – to Tencin that he had in fact already received suggestions for peace, if only personal ones, from Noailles. As to that, Stainville had something to say in another dispatch of even date.

Stainville wrote to Molitoris, who from Vienna had relayed to him Tencin's remark about the imperial election, that the Spanish ambassador had lately spoken much to the marquis of the election, observing:

Tencin, Noailles and Maurepas were all of opinion to seize the moment to give consent to the views of Her Majesty the Queen [Maria Theresa] since it was the only opportunity to extract therefrom some advantage for Don Philip; that for the rest the other ministers did not know what they were doing in their arrogance and that he, the Spanish ambassador, was awaiting the latest orders from his court to say so clearly to the king in an audience which he would request to that end. You will judge well that I answered nothing because they do not put me in a position so to do; but you will also judge well that they are very wrong not to reply to me.[8]

Maria Theresa may well have been exalted by the recent successes of Austrian arms against Prussia and against Bavaria. Still Stainville received no word for Noailles in reply to his overture of 5 March. The marquis had to tell the marshal as much at their further rendezvous at five o'clock on the afternoon of Friday, 7 May, the eve of Noailles's departure for the front in Flanders. Noailles replied to Stainville: '"Never mind; one must not be disheartened" . . . He again assured me anew that the declaration of [French] exclusion [of Francis as emperor] which they [d'Argenson] had made to me, had been against the intention of the king.'[9] Noailles thought it would be much better for Francis to be elected emperor unanimously, and begged that he be written to again. Stainville reported Noailles as saying:

He repeated to me anew that the reign of madness [by d'Argenson] would have but a term and that he hoped that soon it would yield place to that of wisdom and prudence. After this discourse he fell again upon the ministers in favour, saying to me that since they had been in office he had not yet been one single time of their opinion in the council, and that he had said there out loud that it was more glorious for a king to avow his faults than to sustain them, which is in conformity with what I replied to another minister.

On the reverse side of the medal stands d'Argenson's denunciation of Noailles for 'showing himself in the council to be a great Austrian, and all the appearances are that he betrayed the state. He is continually in conference with the Marquis de Stainville.'[10] The

---

[8] Marquis de Stainville to Molitoris, Paris, 1 May 1745: ibid.
[9] Marquis de Stainville to Grand Duke Francis II, Paris, 8 May 1745: ibid., and for the following.   [10] D'Argenson, iv. 184.

purport of those secret conversations, now revealed, entail some revision of previous estimates of the European balance for peace or war that spring.[11]

III

The Marshal de Noailles, after his significant conversation with the Marquis de Stainville on 7 May 1745, had to make speed to join the king and the Dauphin who had preceded him to the French camp before Tournai, and to impending battle. If Noailles was not exactly loyal to the d'Argensons, he was to Saxe. The senior French marshal with exceptional disinterestedness now acted as assistant to his former protégé against a somewhat motley force of English, Hanoverians, Dutch under the conceited Prince of Waldeck, and an Austrian remnant led by old Königsegg, all under the overall command of the twentyfour-year-old Duke of Cumberland. This second son of George II came bearing down from Brussels to relieve Tournai and, on 11 May 1745, to engage the battle of Fontenoy.

Noailles's impetuous nephew, the Duke de Gramont, now redeemed Dettingen with his life. His command was promptly assumed by the Duke de Biron, whose quenchless valour cost three or four horses killed beneath him. And this time the French infantry was a different proposition, battering back at an intrepidly advanced British column which came to stand at bay, shooting and killing and being killed. The French hacked into the enemy with everything they had till at last, after nearly four hours, the British remnants slowly went back fighting, back on their starting-lines. King Louis XV, who had borne himself imperturbably under fire at his observation-post in the hamlet of Chapelle-de-Notre-Dame-aux-Bois, had outrivalled generations of his ancestors in imposing defeat upon an English army in pitched battle. The weak king, his ailing marshal, and their gallant troops had won the battle of Fontenoy.

The Cardinal de Tencin, talking over Fontenoy with the Marquis de Stainville, observed that it had been a costly and a narrow victory 'and that he was very glad that the King should have seen for himself how much princes risked in making war'.[12] It is said, indeed, that

---

[11] Cf. the argument that since by the Treaty of Füssen 'ein wichtiges Hindernis für den österreichisch-französischen Frieden aus dem Wege geräumt wurde, möchte doch auch Maria Theresia wieder optimistischer stimmen. Aber war man in Frankreich nun wirklich bereit, dem alten Gegner die Hand zu reichen? Es hat doch bis zum Sommer 1745 gedauert, ehe ernsthafte Versuche unternommen wurden, miteinander ins Gespräch zu kommen': Braubach, p. 372.

[12] Marquis de Stainville to Grand Duke Francis II, Paris, 22 May 1745: Esteri del Granducato di Toscana, vol. 2295/1286, fo. 591.

Louis commented upon the field of slaughter: 'Learn, my son, how dear and painful is victory';[13] and that the Dauphin, silent, wept. By the same account, Louis, asked how the wounded British prisoners should be treated, replied: 'Like our own men. They are no longer our enemies.' This philosophic sensibility, suggesting a growing refinement in the western outlook, found practical expression in the new standard of efficiency set by French hospitalization after Fontenoy.

'Admit with me, my dear Valory, that it is of no use to me':[14] thus Frederick on Fontenoy. Though to Podewils he privately admitted benefit. Four days after Frederick had lectured Valory ('You are afraid of embroiling yourselves in Germany, my dear friends') he lured the luckless Prince Charles of Lorraine and his Austrian army into a pretty trap. The battle of Hohenfriedberg was one of Frederick's finest victories.

Fontenoy and Hohenfriedberg illuminated the Franco-Prussian alliance with a new and sudden brilliance. But its effective focus upon the discomfited Austrians called for a central consolidation. Frederick wrote from the battlefield to Louis: 'You will have seen that I have not delayed in following your example; it is now the turn of the Prince de Conti.'[15]

Conti was well aware. A week after Fontenoy, however, renewed instructions were sent to him to detach twenty battalions of infantry and forty squadrons of cavalry, some twenty thousand men, to reinforce the already stronger army in Flanders. 'I cannot get over this detachment for Flanders', exclaimed Frederick when he heard of it. 'In the name of God what good is it? ... You should on the contrary have detached from Flanders for Germany.'[16] And Voltaire, so often the mouthpiece of his Prussian patron, now admonished the Marquis d'Argenson: 'You have abandoned the solid for the brilliant ... But that is not my business; and I have only to sing to you.'[17] His *Poème de Fontenoy* advanced the claims of his friend Richelieu in a long controversy with Saxe for chief credit for the most brilliant of the last victories of the French monarchy. This triumph was as though symbolically embedded in the vicious and superficial strategy

---

[13] Mouffle d'Angerville, *Vie privée de Louis XV*, ii. 222, and for the following.
[14] Report by Marquis de Valory of a conversation with King Frederick II in camp at Faulbruck, 31 May 1745: Zevort, p. 159, and for the following.
[15] King Frederick II to King Louis XV, Hohenfriedberg, 4 June 1745: *Politische Correspondenz*, iv. 182.
[16] Report by Marquis de Valory of a conversation with King Frederick II in camp at Krolowatotta, 21 June 1745: Zévort, p. 161.
[17] Voltaire to Marquis d'Argenson, Champs, 4 July 1745: *Voltaire's Correspondence*, Ed. T. Besterman, xiv. 189.

of what the Prince de Conti, on the very day, rather tactlessly termed 'a diversion in Flanders'.[18]

Sulky Conti, reduced in strength and seemingly in spirit, fell back from the Lahn to concentrate with Ségur's corps. Their manoeuvring did not prevent Field-Marshal Traun, Count Batthyany's successor up from Bavaria, from swerving round to effect his junction with Arenberg's army which in turn came under Batthyany, a little east of Frankfurt am Main on 27 June 1745. The Austrian joint command was now assumed by the Grand Duke of Tuscany, a fair indication that by then not much trouble was expected from Conti on the other bank of the Main where he established his headquarters at Steinheim, with a detachment under the Marquis du Châtel close in to Frankfurt at Offenbach. Conti had written waspishly to the Marquis d'Argenson: 'The King judges that the army of which he has given me command is still stronger than those of the Duke von Arenberg and of Count Traun united. I am very much obliged to learn that the King is of this opinion and it is a real service which you render me, although doubtless innocently, being yourself probably in error.'[19] D'Argenson subsequently admitted the mistake of weakening Conti's army but observed with some reason that that prince in that campaign 'did nothing which counts, and . . . shewed but an extreme prudence where temerity was needed'.[20]

It was all very well, though, for d'Argenson to urge Conti, as he had done, to engage the enemy 'even to beneath the walls of Frankfurt'[21] when less than a fortnight earlier the foreign minister had sent the prince a manifesto for publication, announcing among other things that Louis XV 'wishes to do nothing to cramp the liberty of the Imperial Election . . . whereof he has already just given an example in having the army of the Prince de Conti move away from Frankfurt'.[22] This vapid effusion, typical of d'Argenson's predilection for open diplomacy and propaganda, horrified Chavigny who sent Conti from Munich a passionate denunciation of the utter muddle of French policy under d'Argenson. His manifesto was related to his reply to the Saxon King Augustus III who, as Vicar-General of the Empire, had now formally requested the withdrawal of French troops from German soil in the interests of a free election: this from

---

[18] Prince de Conti to Marquis d'Argenson, Langenschwalbach, 11 May 1745: Arch. Aff. Étr. C.P., Allemagne, Diète de Francfort 1745, vol. 538, fo. 165.
[19] Prince de Conti to Marquis d'Argenson, Dieburg, 16 June 1745: Arch. Aff. Étr. C.P., Allemagne, vol. 539, fo. 179.
[20] D'Argenson, iv. 260.
[21] Marquis d'Argenson to Prince de Conti, camp before Tournai, 12 June 1745: Arch. Aff. Étr. C.P., Allemagne, vol. 539, fo. 139.
[22] Manifesto enclosed by Marquis d'Argenson to Prince de Conti, camp before Tournai, 1 June 1745: ibid., fo. 24.

the very prince whom d'Argenson persisted in supporting as the French candidate.

Even the French foreign minister came to wonder, 'if the King of Poland continues to conduct himself so badly, why should not one think of the Elector Palatine?'[23] (Because scarcely anybody in Germany would do so.) Two days later d'Argenson was suggesting to Chavigny that imperial prospects be dangled before the Elector of Bavaria in order to lure him 'from the Austrian paws';[24] he should seek refuge with Conti's army and have Seckendorff arrested. It was all utterly chimerical. Yet the philosophic marquis, who resented Conti as an aristocratic intruder, 'a libertine pedant, an ambitious misanthrope',[25] could sneer at him for acquiring 'a smattering of a quantity of germanic pedantries wherein memory could scarcely follow him'.[26] The trouble was that German politics were largely conditioned by germanic pedantries, by them and by power-relationships. Conti represented that under Austrian preponderance there was virtually 'no scission in the Electoral College'[27] so that, as another wrote from his camp: 'If the Prince de Conti were in condition to attack the Austrians and he were to beat them ten times, we should not prevent the election, which will be made in one place or another.'[28] This cogent if somewhat unenterprising argument came from the ailing Count de Saint-Séverin, back from Poland and designated to be the special envoy of France to the Electoral Diet at Frankfurt.

Another less conspicuous arrival from Poland at Conti's head-quarters that summer was a Frenchman called Guintard, surgeon to Count Bielinski. Guintard brought more or less hopeful replies to Conti's questions as to his royal candidature, plus requests from the Polish magnates for money and protection, for the communication of their proposal to Louis without the intermediary of any French minister and, once again, for de Castéra to be appointed French resident at Warsaw. Conti may well have been inclined for the present to wait upon events closer to hand, and at his headquarters meanwhile Saint-Séverin, if not formally initiated into the secret, was certainly close to it. The Marquis d'Argenson subsequently claimed proof that 'the Count de Saint-Séverin, since his return, was working with the Prince de Conti to prepare everything for the future election

---

[23] Marquis d'Argenson to Prince de Conti, camp before Tournai, 28 June 1745: Arch. Aff. Étr. C.P., Allemagne, vol. 539, fo. 236.
[24] Marquis d'Argenson to Chavigny, 30 June 1745: Zévort, p. 122.
[25] D'Argenson, iv. 176.
[26] Ibid., iv. 408.
[27] Prince de Conti to Marquis d'Argenson, Dieburg, 10 June 1745: u.s., vol. 539, fo. 91.
[28] Count de Saint-Séverin to Marquis d'Argenson, Steinheim, 29 June 1745: ibid., fol. 251.

of [himself as] the King of Poland'[29] in opposition to the interests of that Saxon monarch whom Saint-Séverin was now due to support as the unlikely French candidate at Frankfurt. Saint-Séverin, perhaps understandably, struck Conti as being 'frightened of the new burden with which he finds himself charged'.[30]

IV

The Count de Saint-Séverin's old friend, the Marquis de Stainville, was also entering upon a phase of activity more important than anything to which a minor diplomatist might ordinarily aspire. A month earlier, on 28 May 1745, Stainville had had another of his talks with Tencin wherein the latter had assured him, so soon after Fontenoy, that Louis was most anxious for peace; and, again, that the French king and government did not in fact wish to prevent the imperial election of the Grand Duke Francis. Tencin, however, rather pathetically added 'that having for five years waged a war, costly in money and in men, to prevent the imperial crown from being perpetuated in the house of Austria, they [at Vienna] must at least save the king from self-contradiction by displaying some desire to have his consent, which he certainly would not refuse'.[31]

Stainville reported in the same dispatch: 'Everybody is eager to pay me compliments upon the forthcoming greatness to which Your Royal Highness is to be raised. I accept them from my particular friends.' Whereas others, fishing for reactions, 'should not be pleased with my replies which are assuredly very laconic. Whatever happens I shall remain in my usual condition, which neither prosperity nor misfortune shall ever be capable of making me change',[32] of devotion to the grand duke.

A fortnight later, on 12 June 1745, Stainville at last received a reply from his master to his dispatches reporting Noailles's overture of 5 March. Francis had in fact made this answer so long ago as 4 April. Stainville did not know why it had been delayed and 'retained at Brussels; these are secrets which I ought to respect',[33] and which history probably must.

The Grand Duke of Tuscany expressed full confidence in the Marshal de Noailles – still not by name, 'but his language seems to

---

[29] D'Argenson, v. 49.
[30] Prince de Conti to Marquis d'Argenson, Steinheim, 29 June 1745 :u.s., vol. 539, fo. 247.
[31] Marquis de Stainville to Grand Duke Francis II, Paris, 29 May 1745: O.S./H.H.S., Lothringisches Hausarchiv 77/177B.
[32] Ibid.
[33] Marquis de Stainville to Grand Duke Francis II, Paris, 15 June 1745: Esteri del Granducato di Toscana, vol. 2295/1286, fo. 597 (copy in Ö.S./H.H.S., Lothringisches Hausarchiv 77/177A, fo. 41.)

me too vague for it to be possible to draw therefrom any conclusion as to what his court wishes to do; so it is not possible to open up on that basis'.[34] As to Noailles's assurances of the sincerity of the French for peace, 'I shall still be doubtful of them,' wrote Francis, 'so long as I see them animated and so closely connected with the enemy of public tranquillity and the true torch of war in the whole of Europe.' That was the kind of feeling which Frederick the Great aroused.

The grand duke would, however, listen in due secrecy to anything further that Noailles might have to say, if it was clearer and more official. All this Stainville was authorized to tell and indeed, as though on his own initiative, without instructions, to read to Noailles, but without giving him a copy. This authorization was conveyed in a covering note wherein Francis added that the suggested armistice 'is impossible and seems rather to render a solid peace more distant'. The marquis was further instructed to try to get the French ministers 'to open up more with you upon their ideas for peace. Write to me henceforth upon this matter in cypher.'

At last Stainville had received instructions from Vienna to do something, however tentatively, in the sphere of high policy. That critical hold-up at Brussels may have been due to chance, to policy in relation to military developments or even in part to jealousy. Stainville's correspondence via Brussels passed there through the hands of Count Kaunitz.

This time, however, the Marquis de Stainville did not trip even if he may have somewhat exceeded his instructions when writing on 14 June to Noailles at the front to tell him that he had now received replies to his overture, and that he, Stainville, would be very happy 'to be able to shew them to you, as I am ordered to do'.[35] The marquis considered, however, that it would create undesirable publicity if he left Paris to find the marshal, and intimated that it was for him to contrive a secret meeting. In enclosing to the grand duke a copy of this letter, Stainville explained that he 'simply wrote to the friend in question in order to preserve and nourish his confidence'.[36] For the rest, 'I am remaining totally inactive ... I dare flatter myself that you will never have grounds to reproach me for imprudence. The news of a victory gained by the King of Prussia in Silesia swells the natural pride of the nation. This is why I believe that it would be misplaced

---

[34] Grand Duke Francis II to Marquis de Stainville, 4 Apr. 1745: Ö.S./H.H.S., Lothringisches Hausarchiv 77/177A, fo. 39–40 for the following.

[35] Marquis de Stainville to Marshal de Noailles, 14 June 1745: Esteri del Granducato di Toscana, vol. 2295/1286, fo. 600 (another copy in Ö.s./H.H.S., Lothringisches Hausarchiv 77/177A, fo. 42).

[36] Marquis de Stainville to Grand Duke Francis II, Paris, 15 June 1745: Esteri del Granducato di Toscana, vol. 2295/1286, fos. 597–8 for the following.

to make demarches in such case. So I repeat again, Monseigneur, Your Royal Highness can be easy. I am not using cypher in this dispatch which is going to Brussels by the express which they have sent me, and as a traveller by the stage-coach. I am moreover having request made to Monsieur the Count de Kaunitz to transmit this packet by a sure route.'

On the same day that he wrote to Noailles, Stainville in fact contrived to see Tencin on the pretext of confirming news of Hohenfriedberg. On the real point, the possibility of peace, the cardinal maintained his earlier line, though with significant respect for the Prussian victor. Reviving his previous fiction with Stainville of swapping places in the counsels of the nations, Tencin depicted himself as advising Maria Theresa to make every sacrifice in order to '"make the grand duke emperor. The King [of France] will consent to it. Let the Treaty of Breslau be executed." At that', reported Stainville, 'I stopped him. "What, Monseigneur?" I said, "You require the execution of a treaty to which the King of Prussia has been so expressly unfaithful?" "Well then" he replied, "to punish him for having broken the peace, let something be subtracted from what he was at first ceded."' Tencin went on to suggest Savoy for Don Philip, Austro-Sardinian accommodation in Italy, no trouble about French conquests in Flanders, and commercial concessions to England.[37] In his earlier conversation of 28 May the cardinal had worked himself up against the British, assuring Stainville that 'the English nation will soon get tired of the war. She has no other object but her trade, and nobody can dispute it her, since she has and will always have the superiority at sea.'[38]

The rich reach of seapower in the British ascendancy was very present then even to continental calculations of international affairs. Certainly, it was the allies on either side, England and Spain and Prussia, who now mainly clogged Austro-French rapprochement. The Marquis de Stainville commented that it was evident 'that so far France will make peace only in conjunction with the King of Prussia ... that before all they [the French] have the intention of satisfying their allies.'[39]

With the news bad from Silesia, Stainville had adoped an attitude

---

[37] Ibid., fo. 598. The latter part of this report is printed in extract by Arneth, iii. 437, n. 28. This would appear to be the only part of all the conversations that year between the Marquis de Stainville and French ministers and intermediaries which has hitherto been published and extensively noticed.

[38] Marquis de Stainville to Grand Duke Francis ii, Paris, 29 May 1745: Ö.S./H.H.S., Lothringisches Hausarchiv 77/177B.

[39] Marquis de Stainville to Grand Duke Francis II, Paris, 23 June 1745: Esteri del Granducato di Toscana, vol. 2295/1286, fos. 605–8 (copy in Ö.S./H.H.S., Lothringisches Hausarchiv 77/177A, fo. 44).

of some reserve with Tencin; though when the cardinal urged secrecy for his proposals, the marquis had replied 'that the Queen had given unequivocal proof of her discretion, not having made any use of the letter of Hazel [Hatzel] in 1743'.[40] Now other letters, from more important personalities, were being directed in more successful secrecy towards the same goal of Franco-Austrian accommodation. On 18 June 1745 Noailles wrote in reply to Stainville that he could not get away from the front, must know what was the grand duke's answer, was therefore sending Stainville by safe hand a cypher for correspondence between them. But the marquis, prohibited from giving anything in writing, assured Francis on 23 June that he did not propose to conduct such a correspondence with Noailles. At about that time, however, Stainville received a new and more significant approach for peace.

On 30 June 1745 the Tuscan minister in Paris sent word to Vienna:

One who is an intimate friend of Monsieur d'Argenson, and who has been mine for thirty years, came to see me some time ago and said to me that he asked me as a favour to tell him if Her Majesty the Queen [Maria Theresa] would be inclined to listen favourably to proposals for peace. I answered him that from everything which I had seen till now I could render assurance that she would never refuse to listen to proposals based upon justice and equity, in concert, always, with her allies.[41]

This approach came from the French foreign minister then absent at the front, from the prussophil Marquis d'Argenson himself, who had begun that year so roughly with the Marquis de Stainville. It was only considerably later that the latter revealed that the old mutual friend who had acted as intermediary was the learned Abbé Alary, once a tutor to Louis XV, a friend of Bolingbroke and president of the erstwhile Club de l'Entresol. If Alary's personal relations rendered him a suitable choice, so too, perhaps, did his interest in German affairs – in his snug priory at Gournay-sur-Marne he was always writing a great history of Germany which never saw the full light of day. If his literary output did not match that of his fellow academician, Voltaire, his diplomatic activity may for a period have been not less important: certainly it was more professionally shrouded in a secrecy unbroken until now.

Alary relayed Stainville's prudent reply and on 29 June, reported the latter, returned to assure him:

One could count upon his word, even as the King [Louis] also counted upon the good faith of Her Majesty the Queen, and upon his discretion: if they wish to listen

---

[40] Marquis de Stainville to Grand Duke Francis II, Paris, 15 June 1745: Esteri del Granducato di Toscana, vol. 2295/1286, fo. 599.

[41] Marquis de Stainville to Grand Duke Francis II, Paris, 30 June 1745: ibid., fos. 609–10 for the following (copy in Ö.S./H.H.S., Lothringisches Hausarchiv 77/177A, fo. 47).

to talk of peace, they have but to say. France is ready to enter into negotiation. The surest means which they conceive for attaining it [peace] is to leave things in the state in which they are, to propose the *uti possidetis*, and France on her side will leave the [imperial] election entirely free, and will keep her word exactly on this head, as upon all the others which shall be agreed. Inviolable secrecy and a positive reply are requested.

The secrecy was forthcoming but not the reply. From Vienna there ensued one of those prolonged and pregnant silences to which the Marquis de Stainville and his French contacts were becoming gloomily accustomed. This heavy pause in secrecy may well explain the hitherto somewhat inexplicable failure of the Marquis d'Argenson for so long to provide the aggrieved Count de Saint-Séverin with 'either orders, or instructions, or credentials'.[42] Saint-Séverin was left kicking his heels at the headquarters of Conti, subsequently indeed recommended to the count by d'Argenson as 'the depository of the secret intentions of His Majesty upon the affairs of Germany'.[43]

V

At the headquarters of the Prince de Conti during the Rhineland campaign the Count de Stainville, from being a familiar, had been becoming something of a figure. By a coincidence, if that was the word, his emergence almost matched in time both the increasing importance of his father in high diplomacy and the beginning of Conti's secret connexion with Polish affairs: too secret doubtless for the then Count de Stainville, though straws in the wind might not escape him, and he was more than likely already acquainted with his father's old friend Saint-Séverin. He was subsequently described by Choiseul as having first made his way by appealing 'to the Cardinal de Fleury by his appearance and a sort of rather naughty gaiety'.[44] The then Count de Stainville was not alone in his low opinion of the capacity of the admittedly honest Italian, to whom was applied Voltaire's oxymoron of self-satisfied inadequacy, *le plus insuffisant suffisant.*

Conti's headquarters were then liable to afford young Stainville another early insight into the diplomatic incidence of war, if a less exhilarating one than Villeneuve's encampment before Belgrade. And through his father he was already apt to be involved in the chores of international relations in time of war. On 11 July 1745 the

[42] Count de Saint-Séverin to Marquis d'Argenson, Frankfurt am Main, 15 July 1745: Arch. Aff. Étr. C.P., Allemagne, vol. 540. fo. 116.
[43] Marquis d'Argenson to Count de Saint-Séverin, Liplo, 20 Aug. 1745: ibid., vol. 541, fo. 258.
[44] Choiseul, *Mémoires*, p. 45.

Marquis de Stainville informed the grand duke that 'Mr Ogara writes to me from Spa'[45] that he wished to pay his respects to Francis in Vienna and asked Stainville 'to get him a passport from the Prince de Conti. I have consequently written to my son, who is in his army, and I doubt not that in passing that way he [Ogara] will find there all the facilities which he desires.' A Charles Ogara or O'Hara was a chamberlain to Charlotte of Lorraine. There is no evidence that the Count de Stainville was involved in the secret underside of international affairs then any more than in 1743, any more than in Conti's schemes. Such, however, was the setting of that campaign for the colonel of Navarre even while his main preoccupation was doubtless military.

Conti's staff came to be criticized for comprising 'only mediocre lieutenant-generals'. ('Is this policy or negligence?' asked Barbier.)[46] Another, possibly connected, criticism was that 'the Prince de Conti consults little the general officers who are under his orders, and they complain that in everything he is not communicative enough'.[47] This background throws into relief an anecdote from that campaign related by Choiseul:

I recall that a certain Brother Latour, a Jesuit and newsmonger of the Prince de Conti, informed him, each post, that the talk of Paris was that I had all the influence on his mind and that I was directing the operations of his army. The self-esteem of the Prince de Conti was doubtless wounded by such a rumour; he spoke to me of it at supper, not entirely in a tone of jest, but with an irony which indicated to me that he was offended by this rumour. I at first replied jestingly; but, upon its repetition, I said to him that he should be easy on the score of the rumours devoid of foundation which seemed to offend him, and that it was not possible that people should imagine that a head as mad as mine should be conducting a campaign as prudent as that which we were executing.[48]

Those who employed irony against the Count de Stainville were apt to get as good as they gave. And he was not much afraid of superiors, of anybody.

Here is an early example of Choiseul's habit of gaily depreciating himself as a lightweight, a fashionable role in that age and society. Such self-depreciation can denote an inwardly conscious superiority, but a man who employs it should perhaps not be too aggrieved if his contemporaries assess him at his own ostensible valuation. To accept it is, however, not necessarily the function of history.

Here too is a further suggestion that even in youth Choiseul was not on specially cordial terms with Jesuits, not even with the

[45] Marquis de Stainville to Grand Duke Francis II, Paris, 11 July 1745: Esteri del Granducato di Toscana, vol. 2295/1286, fo. 613 for the following.
[46] Barbier, iv. 66.
[47] Luynes, vii. 125.
[48] Choiseul, *Mémoires*, pp. 25–6.

headmaster of his old school. Father Simon de Latour was then principal of Louis-le-Grand and the literary friend of another old boy, the gossiping Voltaire. For the present, however, it was probably the military point of the then Count de Stainville's anecdote which most closely concerned him.

On 10 July 1745 the Count de Saint-Séverin, significantly revising his earlier military assessment after a two-day visit to Frankfurt, wrote to the Marquis d'Argenson: 'It scarcely appears that they will proceed to the election so long as the King's army commanded by the Prince de Conti shall remain in this countryside. The question is whether it can maintain itself there.'[49] This was soon answered.

On 14 July Saint-Séverin left Conti at Steinheim to assume his mission to Frankfurt. Three days later the prince was in full retreat from the Main. He was reacting as intended to pressure from Austrian advance-guards under the enterprising Bernklau, who had threatened Conti's rear by crossing the Rhine before Mainz and hooking round to capture two French detachments at Oppenheim. As the then Count de Stainville drily observed in his memoirs, it was for the French army 'not a very brilliant campaign ... We retreated successively as far as the Rhine.'[50] What he did not record in his memoirs was the distinction of his own part in that retreat.

On 17 July 1745 Stainville's regiment of Navarre was one of the French units which camped and entrenched at Nordheim covering Rheindürkheim where two pontoons were thrown across the river. Next day detachments under the Count de Ségur passed over to the west bank of the Rhine. At about dawn on 19 July Conti's main force moved out to make the crossing. Staunch Navarre formed part of the rearguard under command of the Count de Berchiny. His troops had to resist repeated skirmishing attacks from a follow-up of Austrian light forces, the ubiquitous Croats and Pandours.

In this minor fighting the Regiment of Navarre suffered the heaviest infantry casualties in officers, with a captain mortally wounded and three brother officers less severely; the other ranks lost two killed and eleven wounded.[51] Their new colonel was not behindhand in valour. According to the official record of the personal dossier of the Count de Stainville's military service, this crossing of the Rhine was one of the actions wherein 'he very much distinguished himself'[52] – even upon that flat campaign.

[49] Count de Saint-Séverin to Marquis d'Argenson, Steinheim. 10 July 1745: Arch. Aff. Étr. C.P., Allemagne, vol. 540, fo. 105.
[50] Choiseul, Mémoires, p. 25.
[51] 'État des officiers d'infanterie, sergents et soldats tués ou blessés ou pris prisonniers à l'arrière garde du 19ᵉ. juillet 1745': Arch. Guerre C., vol. 3097, no. 272.
[52] Arch. Guerre: Archives Administratives 967: Duc de Choiseul.

Conti put his total casualties in this engagement at around 250 as against about 800 of the enemy. Such French prisoners as were taken by the Austrians were led off to a captivity wherein they were to be subjected to horrible cruelties. The French army, however, had by the early afternoon of 19 July beaten off the enemy and had effected its crossing in good order. Austrian activity was reduced to sporadic sniping against the methodical retraction of the French pontoons when, 'the anchors having been raised, the lashings, although double, broke all at once; the pontoons were carried away by the rapid current'.[53] Only a few could be retrieved. The rest had to be burnt. Conti attributed the simultaneous snapping of the hawsers to dirty work by two boatmen, said to have been seen hacking at them. Conti was uncomfortably aware that, in the words of his intendant, 'this event is all the sadder since it gives a fine retreat an air of precipitation which it did not have at all'.[54]

A fine retreat can create a lamentable impression. Conti back across the Rhine meant that French arms had virtually abandoned Germany. One would like to think that the Marquis d'Argenson did not believe his own argument that this would now dispose Augustus of Saxony to declare his imperial candidacy. Such rubbish might have been a fill-in pending, still, an Austrian answer to d'Argenson's overture through Alary to the elder Stainville. More crisply Frederick the Great wrote to Louis XV of Conti's retreat: 'It is he who is crowning the grand duke.'[55] Louis himself was said to be so angered that he thought of transferring Conti's command to that prince's uncle, the royal-blooded Count de Clermont, grandson of the line of the great Condé and held to have done well the year before in Anterior Austria. Conti, however, scraped through. For one thing, other fronts soon presented for French headquarters in Flanders 'such great projects and such brilliant successes [which] occupy all minds so agreeably that they trouble themselves but very moderately about what had just occurred on the Rhine'.[56]

On 23 July 1745, four days after the Prince de Conti had recrossed the river Rhine, Prince Charles Edward landed upon the island of Eriskay, in his own words, 'without men, without money, but with seven friends of my own'.[57] The high adventure of the Fortyfive had

[53] Prince de Conti to De La Noue the younger (French envoy at Stuttgart), Horchheim, 24 July 1745: Arch. Aff. Étr. C.P., Allemagne, vol. 535, fos. 360–1. (Cf. the corresponding account sent by the Prince de Conti to King Louis XV on 21 July: Arch. Guerre C., vol. 3097, no. 265.)

[54] De Vanolles to Count d'Argenson, Leiselheim, 20 July 1745: Arch. Guerre C., vol. 3097, no. 264.

[55] King Frederick II to King Louis XV, Chlum, 23 Aug. 1745: *Politische Correspondenz*, iv. 265.

[56] Baron von Bernstorff to King Christian VI, Ghent, 31 July 1745: Rigsarkiv/T.K.U.A., Frankrig, C.254.

[57] Cited, Basil Williams, *The Whig Supremacy 1714–1760*, p. 252.

begun. Away up in Scotland yet another front had opened in that vast war.

The Young Pretender had been conveyed in a French privateer but, in contrast to the preparations of the preceding year, with no French military support. This reflected fairly accurately the usual divisions in the French council, where the Cardinal de Tencin, that persistent Jacobite, had been arguing in this also against the Marquis d'Argenson, justifiably sceptical and apprehensive of the reactions of Frederick the Great. D'Argenson, too, was already involved in desultory peace-feelers towards England which, though offering even less hope than those aimed at Austria, were maintained by a variety of agents including the Marquis de Silhouette, busy as usual with English affairs. This activity was now swept away, most opportunely for French arms. The new peril to England from Scotland sucked back from the Netherlands all available British units together with their commander, the Duke of Cumberland. The Marshal de Saxe's promenade became almost a walkover.

Once Tournai had fallen, on 20 June 1745, the French invaders swept ahead. On 10 July Saxe's Danish protégé, the venal Count de Lowendahl, together with du Chayla burst into Ghent. Oudenarde, Bruges, Dendermonde followed and, on 23 August, Ostend. The hook round to the coast was completed on 5 September by the capture of Nieuport. The French had burst clean through the Barrier Fortresses and, knocking back citadels like ninepins, had overrun all the coastal reaches of the Austrian Netherlands. There was nowhere left there for British forces to land, or embark. British entrance into the continent was restricted now to menaced Holland. Just then, however, came a reminder of the scope of British seapower across the world.

News reached Europe that June that a British amphibious assault had captured Louisbourg and Cape Breton Island, the key to the French expanse of Canada. This heavy blow, striking the Marquis d'Argenson as the revenge of Neptune against Jupiter, ushered in that mid-century contest between England and France for the domination of the New World which was to test and temper the statesmanship of the future Duke de Choiseul. For the present his father promptly observed that 'the capture of Cape Breton by the English causes much more harm to France and the nation than the conquests [in the Netherlands] of the Most Christian King procure him advantage'.[58]

---

[58] Marquis de Stainville to Grand Duke Francis II, Paris, 15 Aug. 1745: Esteri del Granducato di Toscana, vol. 2295/1286, fo. 630 (copy in Ö.S./H.H.S., 23 Frankreich: Varia 1736–1749: docket, 'Frankreich Varia 1745–1748', fo. 4).

VI

The Marquis de Stainville's long-range assessment was made in a dispatch of 15 August 1745 wherein he also reported that he had received another visit from the Abbé Alary, who expressed surprise that no reply had come from Vienna to his overture to Stainville on 29 June. 'I replied to him', wrote the latter, 'that that did not astonish me at all because he had spoken to me in one way while they were acting in another which was diametrically opposite.'[59] Whereas Stainville had reported Alary's proposal that Louis XV should consent to the imperial election of Francis, the French sovereign 'had had all his ministers at the courts of Germany declare that he would never consent to the said election'.[60] Alary conceded that Stainville was right but argued:

So long as they did not have an answer, it was natural to act along the old lines, especially as the King had reason to believe that his proposals were despised. 'In order to show you, however,' he continued, 'that despite the advantages which the king is gaining, he is still disposed to contribute towards a general pacification, I come once more charged with proposals, and here they are: The King will consent, and even contribute, to the election in favour of Your Royal Highness provided that suitable proposals are laid down, and the king will make no demand for anyone at all (*pour qui que ce soit*) save for Don Philip.[61]

The Marquis de Stainville continued that 'the same person' – he still did not name the Abbé Alary – asked him if he could write him a letter, 'which he could shew', in which Stainville should give a positive assurance on behalf of Maria Theresa that, if the French contributed towards the election of Francis, 'they could count upon a general pacification, and that the Queen would forget all the past ... I replied that I was not empowered to write such a letter, that I would report on it, but that I warned him in advance that if I were to have permission to write it, it would never be except in reply to a letter which he himself should have written me, wherein the proposals which he was making me would be indicated.'[62] In conclusion Alary urged Stainville to write at once for a prompt reply in complete secrecy since 'the more things go ahead [in the war], the more difficult they will become'.[63]

Stainville's warning to Alary, during their diplomatic fencing about committal in writing, apparently produced swift results. Three days later, on 18 August 1745, the Tuscan minister informed the grand duke most secretly in cypher that the still mysteriously

[59] Ibid., fo. 627.   [60] Ibid.   [61] Ibid., fo. 628.   [62] Ibid., fo. 629   [63] Ibid.

anonymous Abbé Alary had 'come to see me once more with a very lengthy letter from the minister[64] which was read to me from one end to the other'. Stainville recapitulated:

Here is the précis of what it contains: [of the] three allied powers, equally independent, the principal one[65] wants nothing or little for herself, to which indeed she will find it difficult to hold the two others, not to be taken on trust owing to the madness of a woman[66] and the small [?][67] confidence that one can have[67] in the fidelity of a man.[68] It is a question of getting them to agree to what the principal and most disinterested [ally] shall wish.[69]

In this secret missive the Marquis d'Argenson proceeded to rehearse the reasons which should incline Maria Theresa towards peace and make her see that 'it is prudent to offer some little sacrifice in order to ensure the principal.' Stainville's summary continued:

The following articles were contained in the same letter and the commissary [Alary] had orders to dictate them to me. Here they are word for word:
1. That the grand duke and Her Majesty the Queen [of Hungary] should, verbally if they wish, make some offer, for nothing in the world would make us be the first to speak, for one must get Prussia and Spain to decide and we for our part must decide to clinch them, so an offer must be made to us.
2. We will allow the grand duke to be elected emperor and we will recognize him.
3. The treaty of Breslau confirmed on behalf of the King of Prussia.
4. We will keep Furnes and Ypres and we will return the rest.
5. For Don Philip, Savoy. For the Queen of Spain the duchy of Parma and Piacenza for the lifetime of this queen in the way that the Duchess of Lorraine had had Commercy. They would indemnify the King of Sardinia as they wished. Finale would remain to the Genoese.
6. English trade and navigation regulated by the treaties of the Pardo and of Utrecht. The *assiento* and the permitted vessel to be renewed.

Such were the six articles of August 1745 in this early French peace-proposal to Austria, hitherto suppressed from history. The suggestion is that the terms were communicated to the Marquis de Stainville in the seclusion of a rural retreat since, as he explained shortly afterwards, he was 'spending my summer in a little country house near Paris'.[70] Alary subsequently confirmed to Stainville that on the French side the proposals were known only to himself, the Marquis d'Argenson, and the King.

The Six Articles, dubbed by Stainville Alary's 'second proposals',[71] were significantly stiffer than the first which a few days earlier he had

---

[64] Marquis d'Argenson.   [65] France.
[66] Queen Elizabeth Farnese.   [67] The decypher is here defective.
[68] King Frederick the Great.
[69] Marquis de Stainville to Grand Duke Francis II, Paris, 18 Aug. 1745: ibid., fo. 632–4 for the following.
[70] Marquis de Stainville to Grand Duke Francis II, Paris, 29 Aug. 1745: ibid., fo. 644.
[71] Ibid., 5 Sept. 1745: fo. 648.

outlined verbally: as Stainville complained when he met Alary at dinner with Don Louis d'Acunha on 4 September. The revised proposals also exceeded those advanced on 14 June by Tencin, though following them in the main, as also the reported terms of a supposed French 'plan of pacification'[72] of which Stainville had got wind towards the end of July from Acunha and Mendez. Stainville transmitted the Six Articles initially without comment though, as he later recalled, he accurately predicted to Alary that they would evoke no reply from Vienna 'since the first of them all was the execution in entirety of the Treaty of Breslau'.[73]

For the present Stainville added that at the conclusion of their conversation that August 'the commissary seemed to me in a great hurry to have these articles passed to your Royal Highness',[74] suggesting that the marquis should send a special courier. Stainville pointed out that it would be quicker to use the ordinary route since it would take time to procure the French passport which a special courier would need: otherwise, 'falling into the hands of the Prince de Conti, he would infallibly seize my dispatches'.[75] The marquis scouted the French headquarters where his son was, and perhaps reckoned that in this instance at least the French foreign minister would also wish to do so.

The Marquis de Stainville, as the Abbé Alary had partially allowed, had good grounds for complaint over the Marquis d'Argenson's ambivalence towards the imperial election. At the beginning of August d'Argenson had already been admitting to Saint-Séverin that they could 'only hope for a very short delay before the fatal election of the Grand Duke of Tuscany; but this election will do even more hurt to the Empire than to us'.[76] From this the wishful theorist went on to wonder whether the Germans might not draw back after all: he dreamed up a typically advanced solution whereby the states of Germany, abjuring an emperor altogether, should form a free association on the model of the Swiss Cantons or the United Provinces of the Netherlands. It was to Conti that Saint-Séverin, at grips with realities in Frankfurt, lamented that 'the Elector of Bavaria as well as those of Trier, Cologne and Saxony are laughing at us'.[77]

[72] Ibid., 25 July 1745: fo. 619 (copy in Ö.S./H.H.S., Lothringisches Hausarchiv 77/177A, fo. 48).
[73] Marquis de Stainville to Emperor Francis I, Paris, 31 Oct. 1745: Ö.S./H.H.S., Lothringisches Hausarchiv 77/177B.
[74] Marquis de Stainville to Grand Duke Francis II, Paris 18 Aug. 1745: Esteri del Granducato di Toscana, vol. 2295/1286, fo. 634.
[75] Ibid.
[76] Marquis d'Argenson to Count de Saint-Séverin, Ghent, 2 Aug. 1745: Arch. Aff. Étr. C.P., Allemagne, vol. 541, fo. 22.
[77] Count de Saint-Séverin to Prince de Conti, Frankfurt am Main, 12 Aug. 1745: ibid., fo. 183.

The mission of the Count de Saint-Séverin to that election contrasted miserably with its dazzling predecessor under the Marshal de Belle-Isle. The count was now moving into the Junghof, an old house of lath and plaster converted from flats although 'one could descend the principal staircase only, so to speak, by going backward as on a ladder and by holding on to a rope so as not to break one's neck'.[78] Owing to fire-risk cooking had to be done out in the courtyard, whereas it was essential to entertain, 'for with the Germans one can only do business *inter pocula*',[79] amid the winecups. Not only did the necessary alterations find the French government reluctant to foot the bill, but its envoy in Frankfurt had to cope without his wife. She was in Paris badgering her old friend, the Marquis de Stainville, for passports to bring her through the Austrian lines to join her husband. Stainville did his best for her, writing to Toussaint, to the grand duke himself. Saint-Séverin reported, however, that the Austrians were violating even their own safe-conducts besides maltreating French prisoners against all the laws of war and of humanity so that he actually recommended that his friend, Stainville, be held personally answerable even though 'one cannot strictly lay the blame on him'.[80]

The Austrian army camped around Frankfurt did not follow Conti's sporting precedent of allowing free access. Saint-Séverin was separated from Conti's headquarters and his own diplomatic staff there, notably Dufour, designated to be Saint-Séverin's secretary and to bring him his long-delayed letters of credence to rescue him from 'the pitiless formalists'[81] of a hostile German bureaucracy. Dufour was moreover involved in an intrigue by Ledran, chief clerk of the foreign ministry, at the expense of Saint-Séverin, himself bitter against the Marquis d'Argenson and liable, indeed, to be relegated by the secret approach to Stainville. Louis XV himself finally lost patience with Dufour. ('All this falls like lead',[82] confided Ledran.) But Saint-Séverin ultimately thought it too late anyway to present his credentials, and folded up under 'a very violent curvature'[83] with the shivers, with pains all over. Incipient consumption was diagnosed, milk and mineral water prescribed, though the Marquis d'Argenson thought that Saint-Séverin had made himself ill by excessive drinking of stiffer stuff. The invalid could not face the exodus from Frankfurt

---

[78] Count de Saint-Séverin to Marquis d'Argenson, Frankfurt am Main, 12 Aug. 1745: ibid., fo. 161.
[79] Count de Saint-Séverin to Marquis d'Argenson, Frankfurt am Main, 3 Sep. 1745: ibid., vol. 542, fo. 33.
[80] Ibid., 4 Sept. 1745: fo. 44.   [81] Ibid., 17 Aug. 1745: vol. 541, fo. 198.
[82] Ledran to Dufour, Ghent, 22 Aug. 1745: ibid., fo. 280.
[83] Count de Saint-Séverin to Marquis d'Argenson, Frankfurt am Main, 21 Aug. 1745: ibid., vol. 541, fo. 267.

traditionally required on the eve of the election as a symbol of its freedom from foreign pressure. (The Austrian army camped all around was presumably another matter.) But the German authorities would not accept a medical certificate from Saint-Séverin's doctor because he was a Jew. A racially acceptable practitioner was found to enable the sufferer to remain in Frankfurt. 'He did not go out of his room',[84] scornfully recalled the later Duke de Choiseul.

At a quarter to two on the afternoon of 13 September 1745 the Count de Saint-Séverin was subjected to the boom of a triple discharge of artillery from the ramparts of Frankfurt, announcing to the world that an election had been made. 'I thought', he wrote, 'that I could dispense myself from making enquiry as to who had been elected King of the Romans.'[85] The gunfire set off all the bells in the city and 'the acclamations of a very numerous, frenzied populace, which diminished nothing of its clamour till far into the night. The [Austrian] ambassadors of Bohemia threw money to the people.'[86]

VII

In the week preceding the triumphant election of the Grand Duke of Tuscany to be King of the Romans, Louis XV had returned in glory to Paris from his campaign in the Netherlands, which 'everybody agrees . . . is the finest that has ever been conducted by any king of France'.[87] The credit, though, mainly went to Saxe, still at the front. This time the enthusiasm with which Parisians greeted this rare visit from their king, gay and thinner, did not match the streets decked for the Te Deum at Notre Dame on 8 September 1745 and royal junketing at the Hôtel de Ville. There waiting in an upper room was the recently created Marquise de Pompadour, still incognito but already liable to impair the popularity of Louis. Public opinion sided politically also with the injured queen. At Versailles on 24 August Marie Leszczynska had called the Marquis de Stainville to her and confided her longing for 'a progression to peace. Conquests hardly move me unless they serve towards reaching this goal desirable for all Europe.'[88] This rare expression of her personal viewpoint in politics did not carry the poor woman far. In reply Stainville 'made a deep bow so as not to start in upon such matters.'

[84] Choiseul, *Mémoires*, p. 45.
[85] Count de Saint-Séverin to Marquis d'Argenson, Frankfurt am Main, 13 Sept. 1745: Arch. Aff. Étr. C.P., Allemagne, vol. 542, fo. 146
[86] De La Noue the elder to Marquis d'Argenson, Frankfurt am Main, 14 Sept. 1745: ibid., fo. 189.
[87] Barbier, iv. 83.
[88] Cited, Marquis de Stainville to Grand Duke Francis II, Paris, 29 Aug. 1745: Esteri del Granducato di Toscana, vol. 2295/1286, fo. 643, and for the following.

The withdrawn diplomatist now at the hub of so much wheeling and dealing for European peace was able to use his rural residence as a pretext for not illuminating his house in Paris in celebration of the king's return. Stainville was, however, among the foreign envoys who, headed by the nuncio, participated in the Parisian celebrations of 8 September by proceeding in a body to the Louvre in order to congratulate Louis, after his toilet, upon his happy homecoming. He had returned with his foreign minister, and it was in the king's apartments at the Louvre that the Marquis d'Argenson promptly told the Marquis de Stainville that he had a lot to talk to him about. The latter agreed to call upon d'Argenson at five o'clock the following afternoon, Thursday, the 9th September.

Stainville reported that at this interview d'Argenson began with 'a great preamble about everything which he had transmitted to me by our common friend',[89] Alary. This approach, said d'Argenson, had resulted from Louis's keen desire for peace, which had made the minister 'think that he ought to advise him, in order to attain it, to address himself to his enemies rather than to his allies'. The French foreign minister maintained that it was not a question of either party letting down their respective allies, but that once France and Austria had agreed upon 'some proposal for the basis of the peace', the other powers could be brought along. He emphasized 'that the principal matter was to negotiate in impenetrable secrecy, that it was the only means of succeeding in this great work, that he alone was charged with it on the part of the king'. The secrecy of these soundings has been preserved till now.

'"But it must not be thought", this minister [d'Argenson] continued, "that the [French] king will recognize the grand duke as emperor except that agreement be previously reached upon some principal points such as the articles which I had remitted to you"' by Alary. D'Argenson pointed out that Louis 'was master of the whole of Flanders or nearly so, that he was making a pretty large sacrifice in restoring it all with the exception of Ypres and Furnes, that the capture of Ostend was easily worth that of Cape Breton by the English', whose king 'would perhaps have enough to do at home' now that the Young Pretender was raising Scotland against him.

The Marquis de Stainville said that it seemed to him extraordinary that the French government should stipulate the maintenance of the Treaty of Breslau in favour of Frederick the Great, who had negotiated it without the participation of France 'and even to her prejudice. He [d'Argenson] told me that that did not matter, that the

[89] Marquis de Stainville to Grand Duke Francis II, Paris, 12 Sept. 1745: Ö.S./H.H.S., Lothringisches Hausarchiv 77/177B, and for the following.

King of Prussia had returned [to his French connection] in good
faith and that the Most Christian King would not fail in the
engagement which he had contracted with him, come what might.
They had tempted him in every way on this subject, wishing to make
him suspicious that the King of Prussia might fail him.' Louis,
however, remained constant in 'preferring to run the risk of his
infidelity rather than give him an example of it. Our conversation
lasted a good three hours, the [French] minister having talked the
whole time.'

In conclusion d'Argenson told Stainville 'that in order the better to
hide the little negotiation which he had broached with me he was
affecting to publish it everywhere that the [French] king would never
consent to the election of Your Royal Highness but that I could give
assurance that that was not true since, upon their giving the mere
word that they would concur in the peace, the king would make no
difficulty about recognizing Your Royal Highness as emperor.'

It was only ten days after this important conversation that the
Marquis de Stainville received from Vienna a reply, not indeed to the
French Six Articles but to 'his accounts of the 15th, 23rd and 30th of
the month of June last',[90] reporting his caution in executing his
delayed instructions with regard to the Marshal de Noailles, his
conversation in mid-June with the Cardinal de Tencin, and the first
approach of the Abbé Alary. The undated Austrian memorandum of
reply to Stainville was enclosed in a despatch of 28 July 1745 which,
like the earlier one of 4 April to him, had been somewhat mysteriously
delayed.

Stainville was at last informed that the contents of his three
despatches under reply had been communicated to Maria Theresa,
who highly approved his prudent interpretation of his earlier
instructions and regretted their delay at Brussels 'by mistake'.[91] The
Queen of Hungary confined herself to generalized and high-flown
reiteration of her loyalty to 'her good and faithful allies', her 'just and
natural resentment' against France, and her sincere desire for 'the
succour of the poor populations, crushed by the calamities of war',
by ending them 'the sooner the better in a manner which could
promise a long and happy tranquillity, that is to say, upon the
footing of the engagements which subsisted at the time of the death
of her late August Father'. In other words, in particular, Silesia
should not remain to Frederick. It always came back to that, and

[90] 'Mémoire pour servir de reponse à Mr. le Comte [sic] de Stainville à ses relations du 15, 23
et 30 du mois de Juin passé:' Ö.S./H.H.S., Lothringisches Hausarchiv 77/177A, fo. 52. Cf.
Arneth, iii. 437, n. 29. Arneth (ibid., p. 129) briefly summarized but did not quote this
memorandum.
[91] Ibid., and for the following.

him. As he himself put it, Maria Theresa would rather lose her shift than Silesia.

The loyalty of the French king to the Prussian was already one-way again by the time that d'Argenson defended it to Stainville on 9 September 1745. A fortnight earlier, on 26 August, Frederick II, victorious at Hohenfriedberg, and George II, harried at home, had concluded the Anglo-Prussian convention of Hanover. England thereby undertook to exert pressure upon Austria to renew the terms of the Treaty of Breslau, that is, to allow Frederick, regretful at having rejoined the war, to quit it again and still get away with Silesia. The Convention of Hanover was the next step ahead from the Treaty of Worms towards a new political configuration of Europe. For England had acted now without her Austrian ally, and Prussia still more blatantly in disregard of France.

Already at the beginning of July the Prince de Conti had sniffed possible danger from diplomatic activity in Hanover. A month later he was writing to the heedlessly honest Marquis d'Argenson: 'But if one could discover if the King of Prussia is trying to be unfaithful to us, would it be to deceive him to try to injure his negotiation, or if it could not be upset, to begin one [of our own with Austria] whereby he should be the dupe?'[92] The French foreign minister was in fact going further than was known then or subsequently in approaching Austria through Stainville, but was frustrating all these soundings by stubbornly clinging to Silesia for Frederick. Louis XV himself had been 'unshakable on the subject of the King of Prussia'[93] when sounded that August about an accommodation by the Marshal de Saxe, primed by the Saxon Counts Brühl and Loss. Now, however, Brühl communicated to the French minister in Dresden, Count Vaulgrenant, proof of Frederick's perfidy, a copy of the Convention of Hanover obtained through Count Saul, Saxon minister in Vienna. Brühl said 'we told you so', said he had reason to believe that if Louis XV now desired to repay Frederick in kind, he would find Maria Theresa receptive. Concordant intelligence came from Chavigny at Munich where the Bavarian government was only too eager to cover its recent switch by reconciling France with Austria. Here was that opportunity for peace which France had earlier neglected, after the death of Charles VII, now renewed in more concrete form.

In favour of seeking to exploit this opportunity were Tencin and Noailles of course, Orry, always out to cut the cost of war, and

[92] Prince de Conti to Marquis d'Argenson, camp at Oggersheim, 1 Aug. 1745: Arch. Aff. Étr. C.P., Allemagne, vol. 541, fo. 3. (Cf. the somewhat incomplete version cited in Broglie/Impératrice, ii. 159–60.)

[93] Count J. Loss to Count Brühl, General Headquarters at Opdorp, 22 Aug. 1745: Vitzthum/Saxe, p. 493.

Maurepas, that subtle minister never under the Prussian spell. It continued, however, to fascinate the Marquis d'Argenson even in the face of the latest evidence. One probably needs to reckon also, as a new factor, that disappointment with his unanswered soundings through Stainville disinclined him to count much on any at second-hand through Brühl. Such disappointment may further, perhaps, have helped to incline d'Argenson in another direction.

The Marquis de Stainville had not omitted to report that on the same day as he had had his conversation with the French foreign minister, 9 September, the Dutch envoy Van Hoey, though recently reprimanded by his government for his French proclivities, had had a private audience of Louis: 'which has astonished the French as much as the foreigners'.[94] Among the foreign envoys at Versailles the worthy but silly Van Hoey was the special crony of d'Argenson and encouraged his earlier-expressed belief that 'peace can come through Holland'.[95] Now, that September, the able and sceptical Abbé de la Ville at the Hague was, under typical instructions from d'Argenson, proposing a general congress for the pacification of Europe upon the liberal soil of the expiring Dutch republic. This flimsy proposal was premature and was to peter out amid what the Marquis de Stainville had termed 'the almost always certain indiscretion of the Dutch'.[96]

Such was the inwardness of the international windings towards peace at that time of European expectancy of change from the new elevation of the sovereign of the Marquis de Stainville. Yet, the day after the Grand Duke Francis II was elected King of the Romans, there was inaugurated another new ascendancy of greater renown in history, of closer concern for the future Duke de Choiseul.

The Marquise de Pompadour, nervously resplendent in her youthful beauty and panniered court-dress, was presented at Versailles at six o'clock on the evening of Tuesday, 14 September 1745. Her socially somewhat superior cousin and confidant, the Countess d'Estrades, herself presented two days earlier, attended the marquise in this formal round of introduction to the embarrassed king, the injured queen, who carried it off with gracious dignity, and the disapproving Dauphin. This presentation at court of the king's mistress was made by his cousin, the raffish old Dowager Princess de Conti, always keen for her gambling debts to be paid and for the advancement of her son in his military career in competition with the

[94] Marquis de Stainville to Grand Duke Francis II, Paris, 12 Sept. 1745: u.s.
[95] Minute by Marquis d'Argenson on memorandum 'Sur l'accommodement que l'Elr. de Bavière vient de conclure avec la Reine de Hongrie', Versailles, 25 Apr. 1745: Arch. Aff. Étr. C.P., Allemagne, vol. 538, fo. 93.
[96] Marquis de Stainville to Grand Duke Francis II, Paris, 25 July 1745: Esteri del Granducato di Toscana, vol. 2295/1286, fo. 620.

Marshal de Saxe: he had recently confided to his half-sister, a Princess of Holstein, that he supposed Conti to be 'a little jealous'.[97] The Prince de Conti, lamenting the local dearth of supplies, was unlikely anyhow to be ordered into a vigorous offensive while France was still feeling for a peaceful opening with Austria in relation to the imperial elevation of Francis at Frankfurt. That left Conti and his troops, as one of them remarked, encamped for two months at Mutterstadt 'a short league from Mannheim, the residence of the Elector Palatine . . . The palace and the gardens . . . are charming and there is a very pretty theatre there . . . One was occupied only in gaming and in pleasures':[98] apart from occasional skirmishing between outposts wherein some credit accrued to the young Duke de Broglie, setting out upon what was to prove rather a repetition of his father's inglorious military career. The second Duke de Broglie was later to run foul of the Duke de Choiseul, who was then a participant in Conti's enclave of pleasure around Mannheim, as at Grenoble the year before.

The future Choiseul wrote of the inauguration of the royal mistress who was to be his friend and protector:

At that time such a presentation appeared monstrous, for it seemed that all the rules of police, of justice and of etiquette were being violated by carrying off the wife of a farmer-general in the middle of Paris and, after having had her change her name, making her a woman of rank fit to be presented. The spectacle of this indecency made it difficult to find a woman who was willing to present her. The Princess de Conti offered herself and had this honour. In this connection I cannot refrain from writing a reflection which I have very often made since: it is that in general all the princes of sovereign houses are naturally baser than other men, and that, among all the princes of Europe, it is the princes of the house of Bourbon who have as their share the most contemptible baseness. I should say, however, that I then saw the Prince de Conti very affected by that of his mother, and that this prince always appeared to me very far removed from basenesses which have for motive money or favour.[99]

One understands why the memoirs of the Duke of Choiseul have not been popular with French monarchists, who have done their imperfect best to discredit them. One also gathers that the installation of Madame de Pompadour at court shocked people, if largely for snobbish reasons, more genuinely than is often supposed. The Marquis d'Argenson considered that the Princess de Conti had accomplished an act of 'baseness without shame'.[1] It would appear

[97] Marshal de Saxe to Princess of Holstein, camp at Hortegems, 29 July 1745: *Lettres du Maréchal de Saxe à la Princesse de Holstein, sa soeur*, ed. H. de Chateaugiron, p. 15.
[98] Arch. Guerre. Mémoires Historiques, vol. 199: 'Journal de la guerre présente', vol. ii, fo. 402.
[99] Choiseul, *Mémoires*, pp. 27–8.   [1] D'Argenson, iv. 175.

that her son never wholly forgave the marquise for this humiliation of his house. They were to form opposite factions at court and, significantly, in foreign affairs.

Choiseul's memoirs illustrate the extent to which the politics of love at Versailles then preoccupied French officers on active service, at Metz, Coni, Grenable, and Mannheim now. And for the present the Count de Stainville was following the Prince de Conti.

CHAPTER V

SECRETS

I

THE Marquis de Stainville wrote to the new King of the Romans on 26 September 1745 that the Cardinal de Tencin, 'whom I saw some days ago at his house, complimented me upon Your Majesty's election, saying to me that he was very sorry not to be able to signify his joy to me publicly, that he still wished that this event could lead to peace.[1]

Francis was shortly to be crowned emperor, alone. All his persuasions had failed to move Maria Theresa to share in his coronation: it would be too expensive, she was as usual pregnant – as if that would deter so stout a maternalist. One of her courtiers had written more frankly to Francis: 'Your Royal Highness well knows how it is when Her Majesty has once formed an opinion ... Perhaps she rates this coronation lower than the two masculine crowns which she wears, for she once said that in the matter of crowning she did not wish to change sex again, and she repeated to me today that this coronation [as empress] was but a comedy, and that she did not want to play it.'[2] So it was incognito that she made her last journey outside her hereditary dominions to the imperial rendezvous. She was to be a spectator together with Francis's sister, Princess Charlotte of Lorraine. The day after Maria Theresa's entry into Frankfurt, however, 'only she is talked about, and one does not even hear the name of the Grand Duke advanced in his own apartments.'[3]

At eleven o'clock on the morning of the feast of Saint Francis, 4 October 1745, the disconsidered Grand Duke of Tuscany rode forth from a mansion in Frankfurt, once occupied by Belle-Isle, in order to seal the defeat of that marshal's policy and to be crowned the first Holy Roman Emperor not of germanic origin since that disputed election, close on five hundred years before, of Richard, Earl of Cornwall, and King Alfonso of Castile. A yellow canopy blazoned with the imperial eagle was borne above Francis, mounted upon a

[1] Marquis de Stainville to King Francis of the Romans, Paris, 26 Sept. 1745: Esteri del Granducato di Toscana, vol. 2295/1286, fo. 651.
[2] Count Ulfeld to Grand Duke Francis II, Vienna, 22 Aug. 1745: Ö.S./H.H.S.: Arneth, iii. 429, n. 13.
[3] De La Noue the elder to Marquis d'Argenson, Frankfurt am Main, 26 Sept. 1745: Arch. Aff. Étr. C.P., Allemagne, vol. 542, fo. 358.

black charger and wearing as yet the jewelled crown of Jerusalem as Duke of Lorraine in a challenging resumption of that title. By three o'clock that afternoon his crown had become the imperial diadem. The new reign had begun in completion of the sovereign's triple elevation and numerical reduction from Duke Francis III of Lorraine to the Grand Duke Francis II of Tuscany to the Emperor Francis I of the Holy Roman Empire.

Almost at the time that Francis was crowned Maria Theresa received word that his brother, Prince Charles, had yet again been heavily defeated by King Frederick in the battle of Soor upon the borders of Silesia and Bohemia. A skilful plan by the Prince of Lorraine for enveloping the Prussian army had been more skilfully destroyed. While Frederick's forces, however, were pursuing the beaten enemy, some Hungarian light cavalry overran and pillaged his camp. Their captures included two of his secretaries and part of his confidential correspondence. The tattered fragments ('the hussars care very little about papers'[4] explained Prince Charles) vividly confirmed Frederick's latest diplomatic trickery and caused Maria Theresa tears of mortification. When the unhappy Robinson duly urged her to fall in with the Convention of Hanover he only incurred another dose of what he ruefully termed her imperial vivacity. The convention secured the looked-for adhesion of neither Austria nor Saxony.

Meantime, on 22 September 1745, the Marquis d'Argenson had sent Count Vaulgrenant instructions and full powers to treat with Austria through the Saxon intermediary in the light of Frederick's defection, at last recognized reluctantly and conditionally upon confirmation. The French price for peace remained substantially as stipulated a month earlier to Stainville though with some variation in the Italian terms and with the mooted addition of recently captured Nieuport plus Tournai to desiderated Furnes and Ypres. And again, Vaulgrenant was to entertain no proposals tending to deprive Frederick of Silesia 'or, moreover, to cause him any prejudice'.[5] These soundings through Vaulgrenant were thus stillborn even if the fault was still to some extent Austrian. Those dilatory procedures so dear to the Austrian chancellery and so familiar to Stainville were again deployed by Bartenstein. He shrewdly suspected that France might not have spoken her last word and he found it difficult, besides, to lay aside the animosity against her which he shared with Francis.

The obverse drag could be expected in some French quarters at

⁴ Prince Charles of Lorraine to Emperor Francis I, 4 Oct. 1745: Arneth, iii. 434, n. 15.
⁵ Marquis d'Argenson to Count Vaulgrenant, 22 Sept. 1745: Arch. Aff. Étr. C.P., Saxe: Broglie/Impératrice, ii. 229.

least. That August the Marquis de Stainville had reported French dismay at the return from captivity in England of the bellicose Marshal de Belle-Isle who had ended up there as the lion of the season, feted at a water-party on the Thames, at Richmond, and at Blenheim. Stainville himself had described Belle-Isle to Alary as 'an insurmountable obstacle to every kind of accommodation'[6] and on 4 September the Abbé had assured Stainville from d'Argenson that the marshal would have no knowledge of their sounding. In fact Belle-Isle composed a memorandum, dated 25 September 1745, wherein he described himself as 'the man in the kingdom, perhaps, to whom the King of Prussia has shewn most kindness and confidence', yet now joined with Conti in urging that France should seek to equip herself against 'the reiterated bad faith of this prince'.[7] Belle-Isle contended that if Frederick were left to make his peace separately with Austria the new emperor would become so strong against France that 'the balance of power *(équilibre du pouvoir)* which is so talked about would no longer subsist'. Whereas, the marshal maintained, Maria Theresa would prefer to conclude a separate peace with Louis if he once dropped Frederick: as she did apparently convey to Count Saul, hopefully active as a go-between at the time of the imperial coronation.

The Marquis d'Argenson read Belle-Isle's memorandum to King Louis on 27 September. But the foreign minister scarcely abated his policy, persuading himself that Frederick's fault at Hanover lay only in his not having informed his ally beforehand of his useful initiative towards a general pacification. When d'Argenson assured Conti that October that 'the King of Prussia declares at present that he wishes to remain inseparably united to the French alliance'[8] the answer was that Conti was not surprised that Frederick 'is increasing his treachery by his false protestations'.[9] Conti was well aware that his military inaction despite Frederick's angry prodding was likely to be adduced by the king as a let-out. As October ended Conti, apprised that the Austrians against him were withdrawing into winter quarters, marched his army away to Spires and soon stood it down. He does not appear, however, to have been in much hurry to reach Versailles, which he did on 9 December. Young Stainville was kept away still longer. 'At the end of this campaign', he wrote, 'I had a leg broken from a kick from a horse. I had myself transported to Strasburg, where I remained till the end of the year.'[10]

[6] Marquis de Stainvillle to Grand Duke Francis II, Paris, 5 Sept. 1745: *u.s.,* fo. 647.
[7] Memorandum by Marshal de Belle-Isle, 25 Sept. 1745: Arch. Aff. Étr. C.P., Allemagne, vol. 542, fos. 363–5 for the following.
[8] Marquis d'Argenson to Prince de Conti, Fontainebleau, 17 Oct. 1746: Arch. Aff. Étr. C.P., Allemagne, vol. 543, fos. 154–5.
[9] Prince de Conti to Marquis d'Argenson, camp at Mutterstadt, 23 Oct. 1745: Ibid., vol. 543, fo. 224. [10] Choiseul, *Mémoires,* p. 26.

That autumn fell gloomily also for the elder Stainville, fearful for his job at each translation of his chilly master to a higher sovereignty. The Marquis de Stainville resumed his nervous pleas, familar from the time when Lorraine was abandoned: 'The public informs me of bad news as regards myself . . . After thirty years of laborious service I ought not to fear when I see my august master at the summit of greatness.'[11] In the event the marquis was kept on at Paris, but in a diplomatic twilight which contrasted sadly with the hope expressed to him by the Queen of France, in her yearning towards peace, that she would 'see me this winter having a very brilliant public audience'[12] as imperial envoy. Instead Stainville was now forbidden to frequent Versailles since the French government refused to recognize Francis as emperor. The marquis told him that he had been 'morally certain' that d'Argenson would not accept the formal notification, in Latin under date of 5 October 1745, of the imperial dignity pending 'some sort of reply to the six articles'[13] transmitted on 18 August. In his secret soundings with Austria d'Argenson sought to use French recognition as a bargaining counter.

When the Abbé Alary about 20 October relayed surprise at the silence from Vienna his interlocutor replied, he reported, 'merely that for my part I was not surprised since the declarations of the Abbé de la Ville at the Hague seemed to me to be diametrically opposite to what had been said to me'.[14] Alary, returning to the charge a week later when notifying Stainville of the French refusal to recognize Francis, was reminded this time of French insistence upon the Treaty of Breslau. Stainville shrewdly added that 'it was not natural that the Queen Empress should do for France what she was not doing for her closest allies; that without doubt he knew of the convention signed at Hanover on 26 August and ratified at London on 22 September; that if the Queen Empress had been willing to make the sacrifice of Silesia, she would have made it upon the request of England, her ally, rather than upon that of the Most Christian King who was indissolubly attached to the King of Prussia only in order to injure her.'[15]

Nearly a month later, on 23 November 1745, d'Argenson himself resumed the debate with Stainville, sitting in the foreign minister's study. He accused Maria Theresa of holding back in constant hope

[11] Marquis de Stainville to Emperor Francis I, Paris, 31 Oct. 1745: Ö.S./H.H.S., Lothringisches Hausarchiv 77/177B.
[12] Marquis de Stainville to Grand Duke Francis II, Paris, 29 Aug. 1745: Esteri del Granducato di Toscana, vol. 2295/1286, fo. 643.
[13] Marquis de Stainville to Emperor Francis I, Paris, 31 Oct. 1745: Ö.S./H.H.S., Lothringisches Hausarchiv 77/177B.
[14] Marquis de Stainville to Emperor Francis I, Paris, 24 Oct. 1745: ibid.
[15] u.s., 31 Oct. 1745.

of improved terms from the march of events, latterly the imperial election, now a 'demarche by the Empress of Russia'. But Stainville's remarks to Alary may have sunk home. D'Argenson went so far as to say 'that if the proposal for the maintenance of the Treaty of Breslau had shocked them, they should have said so, and in that case some expedient would have been found; that one did not always get everything that one asked, and that first proposals put forward were only to broach the negotiation, but that to answer nothing at all was a total refusal of willingness for a rapprochement'.[16]

The Marquis d'Argenson had a point there, as the Marquis de Stainville very likely felt. But then he was used to the cold treatment from Vienna. It remained doubtful, too, how far d'Argenson's verbal advances really abated his settled predilection for Prussia. A week after his conversation with Stainville, on 1 December 1745, d'Argenson was instructing Vaulgrenant in Dresden that the keener Maria Theresa shewed herself about recovering Silesia, 'the more we should set our hearts upon the King of Prussia being able to keep it'.[17] During the intervening week, however, the French foreign minister may have been swayed back by news of violent new developments which had burst upon the European scene on the very day of his conversation with Stainville.

II

King Frederick the Great had a flair for potential manoeuvres, both military and diplomatic, directed against himself. A fortnight before the d'Argenson–Stainville conversation of 23 November he had written to his confidant in French affairs, Count de Rottembourg: 'Cardinal Tencin is negotiating, from what they tell me, with the Marquis de Stainville. The system of Europe is becoming daily more confused. God knows what will become of us.'[18] D'Argenson concealed his own soundings with Stainville beneath assurances to the Prussians that he was Prussian from head to foot but even his relations with the Prussian king had been reduced to angry bickering. In reply to a French invitation to protest against the imperial election Frederick had suggested French concentration upon the Rhine and declaration of war against Saxony. France risked getting the worst of both worlds, lacking the resolution either to drop Frederick adroitly or to support him vigorously.

[16] Marquis de Stainville to Emperor Francis I, Paris, 28 Nov. 1745: ibid.
[17] Marquis d'Argenson to Count de Vaulgrenant, 1 Dec. 1745: Arneth, iii. 443, n. 51.
[18] King Frederick II to Lieutenant-General Count de Rottembourg, Potsdam, 8 Nov. 1745: *Politische Correspondenz*, iv. 334.

Saxony yet again was pivotal, the ally both of Austria and of Russia, the latter aloof yet still preponderant in European calculations, as indicated by d'Argenson's remark to Stainville. Frederick had also urged France to try to counter the evident Russian swing in favour of Austria and Saxony. Those two powers, undeterred by the convention of Hanover and the battle of Soor, were secretly concerting to implement their Treaty of Warsaw by a hardy plan. Leaving contested Silesia aside this time, Austria was covertly to insinuate troops through Saxony who, in that unlikely season of winter, would join in a surprise smash against Brandenburg, the heartland of Prussian power which Saxons would dearly like to see dismembered.

When the Austrian army confronting Conti on the Rhine had withdrawn, as was supposed, into winter-quarters, part of it marched slap through Bohemia to swell the concentration in Saxony where a secret council of war was held in Dresden on the evening of 14 November 1745. Frederick got wind of it, sprang into action and, risking Russian intervention against himself, struck first into Saxony. On 23 November he swooped upon Saxon elements of the army of Prince Charles of Lorraine at Gross-Hennersdorf, routed them and threw the enemy dispositions off balance, drove ahead in a lightning campaign clinched for him by the Old Dessauer on 15 December at Kesselsdorf. There Prince Leopold of Anhalt-Dessau inflicted a resounding defeat upon an Austro-Saxon army under Saxe's half-brother, that Count Rutowski who had figured earlier at Prague. (Marshal de Saxe sent Frederick adulatory congratulations upon his victory over the writer's own family and homeland.) Kesselsdorf was added to Hohenfriedberg and Soor as a third brilliant in the Prussian diadem of victory that year, which won for Frederick the designation of Great. Three days later he was to triumph into Dresden, which he set out to charm.

Dresden had been in a turmoil of alarm on the night after Kesselsdorf. That very night Vaulgrenant had a critical conversation with Count Frederick Harrach, the Austrian envoy just arrived in order to pick up urgently those threads of negotiation for peace via Saxony which had for so long hung slack. Harrach was anxious to pull it off with Vaulgrenant but made it clear to him that failure to do so would compel unwilling Austria to come to terms with Prussia. Yet Vaulgrenant, a nervous and reluctant negotiator, adhered rigidly, even upon minor points, to the tenor of his instructions from the prussophil Marquis d'Argenson, such as those of 1 December for denying Silesia to Austria. That stubborn purpose most likely nourished the ostensible break between Vaulgrenant and Harrach upon the lesser point of the precise extent of Don Philip's apanage in Italy. When the morrow of Kesselsdorf dawned over Dresden the French and Austrian negotiators separated with nothing achieved.

An Italian establishment for Don Philip was something of a luxury for France if not Spain. Otherwise France had nothing really left to fight for, except faithless Prussia. If the Marquis d'Argenson's policy of using Frederick against Maria Theresa was comprehensible enough, his preferring Prussia to peace was becoming costly. In the critical year of 1745 French foreign policy had been fumbled by an unimpressive and disunited government. The meteoric rise of Prussia within the last four years had confronted France with problems of European policy which were to exercise her in one form or another for decades, for centuries to come. In this climacteric some, like the Marshal de Noailles, already sensed that France's future lay if anything with her hereditary enemies, the Habsburgs, rather than against them. If, as he had confessed to the Marquis de Stainville, he rather naturally still needed to educate others in the council, that was less so as regards the king and, now, his closest circle.

Vaulgrenant's clumsy failure with Harrach, complacently related in his dispatch of 16 December 1745, was liable to reach Versailles as a heavy blow to the protagonists of peace with Austria.

III

After dark, at about six o'clock, on the evening of Tuesday the 28th December 1745 the Marquis de Stainville betook himself to the residence in Paris of his old and influential acquaintance, Pâris-Duverney. He had asked Stainville to call for a talk. The latter reported at that time that 'M. Pâris Duvernet [*sic*] and M. Pâris Monmartel, his brother, are all powerful at court; they do not wish to be ministers but they make them and unmake them.'[19] Just recently, at the beginning of that December, the brothers had engineered the dismissal, after so long, of Controller-General Orry who had censured some of their dealings in military supply. Now Monmartel joined Duverney in his conversation with Stainville.[20]

[19] Marquis de Stainville to Emperor Francis I, Paris, 29 Dec. 1745: Ö.S./H.H.S., Lothringisches Hausarchiv 77/177B. Cf. Rohan Butler, 'Paradiplomacy' in *Studies in Diplomatic History and Historiography in honour of G.P. Gooch, C.H.*, ed. A.O. Sarkissian (London, 1961), p. 21.
[20] The Marquis de Stainville reported on his conversation of 28 December 1745 in his dispatch of the following day: cf. preceding note. He related further particulars of this conversation in his succeeding dispatch of 3 January 1746: cf. below. In the former dispatch the marquis recounted only his exchange of remarks with Pâris-Duverney, and in the latter only that with Pâris-Monmartel. The second dispatch, however, specifically referred to the same conversation as the first; and the Marquis de Stainville clearly did not confuse the brothers, both old acquaintances: cf. the quotation at preceding footnote. The inference therefore is that both brothers were present at the conversation, in part at least.

Pâris-Duverney opened with a long disquisition upon d'Argenson's Six Articles of 18 August which had remained unanswered, Duverney now conceded, because of their insistence upon the full execution of the Treaty of Breslau. He represented that 'the moment was favourable for renewing the said proposals'[21] upon a more likely footing. Now was the time for a mutual dropping of allies. England, in the high alarm of the Fortyfive with the Young Pretender so lately thrusting down to Derby, now had no troops or – alleged Duverney – money to spare for Austria; while 'from another side, the Most Christian King could withdraw with honour from intrigue with the King of Prussia in representing to him that the first demands which he had made upon Her Majesty the Empress, before the war, extended only to four estates, lordships or duchies in Silesia, ... that he should content himself with being given what he asked for then, the rest being but a usurpation which France was not willing to support. He was persuaded that the King [Louis] would be disposed to make this démarche provided that Her Majesty the Empress was willing to reply a little handsomely upon what concerned Don Philip.' Duverney did not enter into detail here, nor specifically mention subordinate issues in the six proposals of August, such as French pickings in the Netherlands: Harrach had been prepared to offer Ypres, Furnes, and Beaumont. The central issue remained Silesia. Here Duverney went far beyond anything that d'Argenson or Vaulgrenant had offered when he now envisaged the return to Austria of all Silesia except the four districts, recalling prewar Prussian pretensions to Jägerndorf, Liegnitz, Brieg, and Wohlau.

Pâris-Monmartel urged upon Stainville the need for speed in clinching the proposals with regard to Silesia and Italy, adding that France could, without resort to fresh financial expedients, wage war for another three years – an interesting if coincidental approximation to the actual term of the continuation of hostilities. Monmartel made out that he was not saying this merely in order to drive home the French proposals, and he confessed 'that at the end of these three years they would be obliged to have recourse to violent means, that that was what they wished to avoid by making peace no later than now'.[22] In the eighteenth century as in others economic considerations could weigh heavily in issues in war and peace.

Paradiplomacy, that is, personal diplomacy at the highest level, outside the foreign ministry, may require special protection against disclosure, even to the practitioners of the regular diplomacy of the

---

[21] Marquis de Stainville to Emperor Francis I, Paris, 29 Dec. 1745: *u.s.*, and for the following.
[22] Marquis de Stainville to Emperor Francis I, Paris, 3 Jan. 1746: loc. cit., and for the following. Cf. Rohan Butler, op. cit., p. 22.

governments concerned. Pâris-Monmartel insistently begged the Marquis de Stainville 'not to compromise him'. The envoy promised 'an inviolable secrecy', most truly preserved for over two hundred years. The Pâris brothers emphasized that if the Austrian reply were favourable, they would answer for the success of the negotiation. It would seem that they cautiously omitted to specify in so many words on whose authority they were initiating it with such new and critical proposals. There was quite likely no need for them to do so, and it appears to have been sufficiently understood between them and Stainville. The authority scarcely came from the French foreign minister. Stainville reported that Duverney 'told me in the course of the conversation that the ministry of France was not agreed *(n'était point d'accord)*, but that he could assure me that the King ardently desired peace and that I could report it as something certain.'[23] King Louis XV, unlike the Marquis d'Argenson, probably preferred peace to Prussia. Already on 6 December 1745 he had addressed a pretty chilly communication to King Frederick II.

Throughout their conversation of 28 December Pâris-Duverney made it appear to Stainville, an experienced if not a brilliant diplomat, 'that he was not holding it of his own accord, but that he was authorized to do so by the king himself, to whom he was in a position to report personally'. In this secret initiative from Louis XV the choice of the brothers Pâris as diplomatic intermediaries was suggestive. Those who are responsible for financing great wars are apt to be particularly keen to end them. Through the two brothers French financial pressure for peace found an expresssion which was both influential and intimate. For it is a fair guess that in describing them as all-powerful at court the Marquis de Stainville may very well have had in mind their influence upon the king not only through his ministers whom they made and unmade but also through his mistress, then in the first flush of royal love.

The Marquise de Pompadour was notoriously in very close relations with the brothers Pâris, who were old family friends. Her father, François Poisson, in his chequered financial career, had been their agent, and her mother more or less intimate with Pâris-Duverney. Pâris-Monmartel was the godfather of Madame de Pompadour. The earliest aspect of her political influence was her connection with this financial power-centre. The first, premonitory indication of it had been the recent dismissal of Orry, ascribed to her intervention.

The brothers Pâris and the Marquise de Pompadour were at that

[23] Marquis de Stainville to Emperor Francis I, Paris, 29 Dec. 1745: *u.s.*, and for the following.

time, each of their own reasons, anxious that France should find peace. Madame de Pompadour sought to influence Louis in the opposite sense from that favoured by her predecessor, the dominating Duchess de Châteauroux with her patronage of the Franco-Prussian alliance and incitement of the passive monarch to emulate the military glory of the Roi Soleil. The eclipse of the duchess while on campaign at Metz was scarcely an encouraging precedent for her successor, liable to be resentful too at not herself being allowed to the front. The object of the Marquise de Pompadour was to be constantly on the spot with delicious distractions for the king in his overhanging boredom. His absence on campaign, as when he had left her for Fontenoy, was something to be prevented so far as might be for the future. And the ultimate preventive would be peace.

It may or may not have been coincidence that the Pâris brothers put out feelers from the king for peace with Austria at the expense of Prussia three months after the formal inauguration at Versailles of the long ascendancy of the Marquise de Pompadour. There is no conclusive evidence to connect her with their intervention. But it is not always tactful for the records of secret paradiplomacy, or the influence of royal mistresses, to be too specific. The fall of Orry had just suggested how closely Madame de Pompadour was collaborating with her financial backers in working upon the king for political objects. Nor was she any friend of the Marquis d'Argenson, who described her as 'the graceful instrument of sorry designs'.[24] To suppose that it was without any participation of Madame de Pompadour that the Pâris brothers were then in secret and intimate concert with their king behind the backs of his ministers, and promoting for him a policy which would among other things precisely suit his mistress, might perhaps strain credulity almost more than to suppose her already actively concerned to some extent, even if only as intermediary, with the foreign policy of France: as had been the Duchess de Châteauroux the year before in an opposite, Prussian orientation. And subsequent developments were to tend, if anything, to strengthen such a supposition.

Hence the possibility that the Marquise de Pompadour may have been attempting in some degree to participate in French foreign policy almost from the beginning of her ascendancy, earlier than has hitherto been demonstrated. And one would rather expect that initially any such activity on her part would be more discreetly veiled than subsequently, in the established fullness of her favour. It may be that it was during the unfortunate ministry of the Marquis d'Argenson in that critical year of 1745 that there originated not only

24 D'Argenson, iv. 179.

the Secret du Roi, directed by the Prince de Conti and withheld from Madame de Pompadour, but also her occasional intervention in other, sometimes opposite, secret phases of French foreign policy. If so, there was to be a suggestive thread of continuity, personal as well as political, between the secret Franco-Austrian soundings at about the time of the Anglo-Prussian Convention of Hanover and those a decade later at that of the Anglo-Prussian Treaty of Westminster and the celebrated Diplomatic Revolution, lastingly associated with the light influence of the Marquise de Pompadour. One of the chief executants for France of this revolution was to be the Count de Stainville, the more brilliant son of the marquis to whom the proposals for rapprochement between the two great antagonists of the continent had now been secretly transmitted.

In relaying to the emperor at Vienna the proposals advanced by the Pâris brothers, the Marquis de Stainville wrote: 'I submit all this to the enlightened judgement of Your Imperial Majesty but at the same time I have the honour to observe to you that this proposal appears too advantageous in itself not to merit a reply; provided that it be handsome it could be put to good use. France was not attached to the affair in England, and if the Queen of Spain wishes to make peace with this power, the means thereto will not be difficult so soon as she shall be given something for Don Philip, for the establishment of whom she will willingly concede to England advantages in trade.'[25] It was a deft analysis of allied angles around the still central, but opposite, Convention of Hanover.

Only it was all just too late. In fact three days before the Marquis de Stainville's conversation with the brothers Pâris, at noon on Christmas Day in Dresden in the presence of a British mediator, Count Harrach in heaviness of heart had signed a treaty of peace between Austria and Prussia. The Treaty of Dresden confirmed the Convention of Hanover and the Treaty of Breslau. Frederick kept Silesia. Also included in the settlement were Saxony, Hanover, Hesse-Cassel, and the Palatinate. Peace was imposed upon distracted Germany, and France was diddled again. Thus was the Second Silesian War extracted from the War of the Austrian Succession, which had originated from the struggle for the province in question. Frederick the Great was already the winner. Austria with England and France with Spain were left to finish the fighting. The treaty of Dresden stipulated that hostilities in Germany should cease on 28 December 1745, the very day upon which the French approach was made to the Marquis de Stainville. As now appears, it was a fine-run thing.

[25] Marquis de Stainville to Emperor Francis I, Paris, 3 Jan. 1746: u.s.

From the beginning of the year, since the death of the Emperor Charles VII, France, committed to the inexpert policies of the Marquis d'Argenson, had bungled opportunities for attaining that peace which was the logical and keen desire of the nation and, ultimately, of the king with his elevated aversion from war. Now, at the end of that crowded and critical year, the paradiplomatic attempt of Louis XV to pursue peace beyond the limitations of his foreign minister had itself also come too late when only a few months, a few weeks earlier it might have changed the course of European history.

IV

The Marquis d'Argenson himself noted, as a prompt consequence of the Treaty of Dresden, that Maria Theresa switched large Austrian forces from Germany to Italy, the other fragmented and disputed middle-land: and not before they were needed there.

In the spring of 1745 the Marshal de Maillebois had arrived at Antibes to find Italian prospects much brighter than those which had confronted the Prince de Conti. The Bourbon powers, with Spain here in the lead, swung over to them the republic of Genoa by the Treaty of Aranjuez of 30 April 1745, and a week later Captain-General des Gages pushed into Genoese territory. This put a new complexion upon the coastal advance from France earlier resisted by Conti. Maillebois, now in operative command under Don Philip, successfully accomplished the dangerous passage of the Riviera di Ponente and on 23 July linked with des Gages south of Alessandria. Together, on 27 September, they defeated Charles Emmanuel at Bassignano in a victory rather forgotten but not unworthy of Fontenoy and Hohenfriedberg in that year of victories against Austria and her allies.

Two days before Bassignano the legitimized half-sister of Charles Emmanuel, the lately widowed Princess de Carignan living in Paris, had asked the Marquis de Stainville to ask the Grand Duke of Tuscany to come to the aid of Charles Emmanuel, who 'was in great straits'.[26] Bassignano indeed led through to the Gallispan capture of the town, but not citadel, of Alessandria and on 17 November the ever thrusting General Chevert took Asti less than thirty miles from Turin. Casale on the Po followed and as winter came the district of Montferrat was under Bourbon occupation.

The Franco-Spanish tug of strategic opinion from the previous

---

[26] Marquis de Stainville to King Francis of the Romans, Paris, 26 Sept. 1745: Esteri del Granducato di Toscana, vol. 2295/1286, fo. 652.

year was repeated further east. While Maillebois concentrated in the Montferrat to keep Piedmont menaced, des Gages and Don Philip, as ever impelled by their queen, marched away to winter over towards the promised lands, Piacenza, Parma, and the Milanese. On 16 December 1745 the Spanish Infant occupied the city of Milan and prepared to besiege the citadel of the capital of Austrian Lombardy. Whereas in the Austrian Netherlands nobody seriously imagined that in the classic reckoning of bargaining-counters France would ultimately claim more than a border-town or two, contemporaries felt, and rightly, that in more keenly contested Italy the destinies of principalities for decades to come hung hovering in the balance of war.

King Charles Emmanuel, hemmed in ever more closely by his Bourbon enemies, returned from the front to Turin on 20 December 1745. That same evening a French negotiator secretly entered his capital. Three months earlier, on 17 September, eight days after Stainville had received d'Argenson's personal overture, the foreign minister had taken what can now be discerned as a significantly comparable sounding with the Count of Mongardino, intendant of the household of the Princess de Carignan. This time the French intermediary was Levesque de Champeaux, French Resident at Geneva then resident in Paris, a crony of d'Argenson from the Entresol Club in the same way as Alary, whose soundings with Stainville were so much longer concealed than those of Champeaux. The influence of the Entresol Club upon d'Argenson's foreign policy makes a nice little subject for research. Its thrust had come through when Champeaux met Mongardino on 27 October 1745 in the autumnal garden of the Capuchins in the Faubourg Saint-Jacques.

If Champeaux, a diffuse and rather clumsy enthusiast, was not perfect for a secret negotiator he was just the man to expound, as he now did, his patron's largely prophetic but immediately impractical projects for a national reordering of the Italian peninsula. D'Argenson, inheriting Chauvelin's penchant for Italian affairs, was keen that 'the Germans be expelled from Italy for ever',[27] together with the theoretical suzerainty there of the Holy Roman Empire. Champeaux now proposed that the Emperor Francis be required to make Tuscany over to his brother Charles; the King of Sardinia was to become King of Lombardy and patriotic leader of an Italian federation of some half-dozen rounded-out principalities. When Villettes subsequently heard of the scheme he promptly suggested in accordance with Sardinian suspicions that thereby the French king

[27] Memorandum by Marquis d'Argenson, 'Ligue pour rétablir et maintenir la paix en Italie', Jan. 1745: Arch. Aff. Étr. C.P., Sardaigne, vol. 214: Zévort, appendix xiv, 388.

would become emperor in Italy in rivalry to the Austrian emperor in Germany.[28] Indeed, if the Marquis d'Argenson's revolutionary aspiration 'to form a republic or eternal association of the Italic powers, in the way that there is a Germanic one, a Batavic and a Helvetic'[29] looked back via the Abbé de Saint-Pierre to Sully's Grand Design, it also reached forward towards that Napoleonic radical-imperialism in Italy which was to come to full fruition more than a century later.

D'Argenson's idealistic scaffolding was promptly knocked down by the cautiously scheming court of Turin after Champeaux, disguised as the Abbé Rousset, had slipped in on 20 December 1745. More interesting to Charles Emmanuel and the Marquis of Gorzegno, who had succeeded Ormea upon his death in June, was that part of the French proposal which Louis XV himself, with his favourite maps, had largely sketched out for the carve-up of Austrian Lombardy. Such was the military predicament of Piedmont that Gorzegno on 26 December signed his agreement to the territorial provisions as terms upon which a treaty might be based.

The details of the Franco-Sardinian preliminaries, and of the complicated negotiations which they initiated, have, unlike those with Austria through the Marquis de Stainville, often been analysed.[30] Suffice it here that these preliminaries produced a multiple muddle whereas the sudden Austro-Prussian peace of Dresden, signed the very day before, rendered an armistice in Italy at least as urgent as a treaty: only, the preliminaries were at first unknown to Maillebois, des Gages, and even the Count d'Argenson. Bringing in the Minister of War led to the initiation of Spain and a comprehensible outburst of indignation. Not only had the Treaty of Fontainebleau prohibited separate negotiations with the enemy but it ran counter to the proposed assignment, now, of Milan to Charles Emmanuel. The Marquis d'Argenson's slim secret exploded into uproar.

The hubbub rendered the Sardinian court further suspicious, particularly of a design to get it in wrong with the Austrians. An armistice was nevertheless signed in Paris by Mongardino on 17 February 1746; only, Charles Emmanuel, true to form, stipulated that it must be proclaimed and operative by 1 March, or else he was free to renew hostilities; only, this crucial proviso was not commu-

---

[28] Villettes to Duke of Newcastle, 31 Dec. 1745: P.R.O./S.P.F., Sardinia, 50: Lodge, p. 102.
[29] D'Argenson, iv. 267.
[30] Cf. d'Argenson, iv. 266 f.; Duc de Broglie, *Maurice de Saxe et le Marquis d'Argenson* (Paris, 1891: henceforth cited as Broglie/Saxe), i. 114f.; Zévort, pp. 286f.; Lodge, pp. 100f.; Spenser Wilkinson, *The Defence of Piedmont 1742–48*, pp. 226f.; Arthur Ogle, *The Marquis d'Argenson: a study in criticism*, pp. 138f.

nicated to the Marshal de Maillebois whose son the count, son-in-law
to the Marquis d'Argenson, arrived at Rivoli only on 4 March in
order to haggle with the Sardinians over the previously agreed terms
of armistice, notably the critical point, still, of the beleaguered citadel
of Alessandria.

By ten o'clock on the morning of 5 March 1746 Sardinian units
under tough Leutrum had surrounded the surprised French garrison
in Asti. The secret preparations of the artful Sardinians went
punching home against an enemy caught off balance and divided,
with the Spaniards cursing the French betrayers. Alessandria was
relieved, Casale recaptured. And an Austrian relief-force under
General von Browne was bearing down. On the night of 18–19 March
Milan was evacuated by the Infant Don Philip. The whole Gallispan
position in Piedmont was folding up. From Turin the British
minister was already exulting at the swift triumph achieved 'with the
loss of about thirty men and a subaltern officer of artillery' by the
King of Sardinia's sudden switch from negotiation to 'this other
string to his bow'.[31]

The Marquis d'Argenson's pet negotiation with Sardinia had been
conducted in a number of respects with ineptitude, disloyalty, and
disastrous result. On the broad view this failure resulted not a little
from his earlier failure, owing to his Prussian predilection, in his
potentially more important but actually less productive soundings
with Austria through the Marquis de Stainville. As it was, the
military coup in Piedmont encouraged Austria and her allies to
persevere in the war despite the recent shock of an equally dramatic
stroke delivered against them that winter in the northern theatre of
war.

The New Year of 1746 found two pleasure-loving French generals,
Saxe and Richelieu, absent in the field from the distractions of
Versailles. Richelieu was now to command an adventure wherein
Saxe had earlier failed, an invasion of the British Isles in support, this
time, of the hardy enterprise of the Young Pretender, now penned
back, though, in Scotland after his swoop to Derby – the initial
setback. British troops in French service had, however, been allowed
to volunteer and the Régiment Royal-Écossais under Lord John
Drummond and elements of the Regiment of Fitzjames, some three
thousand men in all, had already slipped across in merchantmen to
Scotland. A further eleven or twelve thousand were now affected to
Richelieu at Boulogne from Saxe's army in Flanders. Protestant Saxe,
glad enough to be out of it this time, commented to his old friend

---

Noailles: 'The protestant party will always exist in England because of the church property which is owned by the nobles of the nation, and this fear will never leave them.'[32]

The ostentatious Richelieu, aiming at Folkestone, had his bluff at Dunkirk called. Yet again did winter weather support cruising squadrons from the British Isles. Richelieu's flimsy projects against their Jacobite and Celtic fringes – if not in Scotland, then Ireland, Wales, or Cornwall – became increasingly implausible. By February 1746 he was ostensibly ill. Another invasion was off. The irrepressible Parisians greeted the returning Richelieu:

> *Ce pilote ignore les vents*
> *De l'Angleterre:*
> *Il ne sait qu'embarquer les gens*
> *Pour l'île de Cythère.*[33]

It may well have suited deeper calculations that the trumpeted preparations of Richelieu had overlaid silent ones by Saxe, dawdling in Ghent with his sister, the Princess of Holstein, and ostentatiously given over to cockfighting with English birds. At the end of January Saxe suddenly struck. In the heart of winter French forces went lunging out from the line Ghent–Oudenarde–Ath, slap against the capital of Brussels, all unprepared under its governor, Count Kaunitz, more skilled in politics than war. Whereas Saxe backed a swift siege by an artful correspondence with Kaunitz, of whom he was yet to form a high opinion, presciently suggesting that he would make a good envoy to France. On 20 February 1746 Brussels fell. French booty included fifty-two standards including that captured with King Francis I upon the field of Pavia.

Saxe triumphed back through traditionally French attentions, from little girls in white frocks pushing bouquets at him all along the road and from implacable customs-officers who tried to search his coach. 'What are you doing, scoundrels?' cried the marshal. 'Are laurels contraband?'[34] Saxe was indeed crowned by Mademoiselle de Maix representing Glory when, back in Paris on 18 March, he went with the Duke de Biron to Quinault's opera, *Armide,* and to a rapturous ovation. The Marquis de Stainville noted of this classic scene that the victor accepted his crown 'with modesty'.[35]

---

[32] Marshal de Saxe to Marshal de Noailles, Ghent, 25 Dec. 1745: Archives de Mouchy, cited, Broglie/Saxe, i. 17.
[33] Ibid., i. 24, n. 1.   [34] Ibid., i. 50.
[35] Marquis de Stainville to Emperor Francis I, Paris, 20 Mar. 1746: Ö.S./H.H.S., Lothringisches Hausarchiv 77/177B.

V

Against that wintry background of action in Italy, Scotland, and the Low Countries the Count de Stainville with his broken leg was this time confined to the more traditional winter-quarters for young officers amid the gaieties of court. From his hospital in Strasburg the road for Stainville back to Paris lay directly through Lunéville. The miniature court of King Stanislas was a regular halt for French officers travelling to and from the German front. Conti and Maillebois both called there, and there was a special welcome for Lorrainers like the Count de Stainville, who was a visitor, perhaps about then since his ties with Lorraine had recently been strengthened.

In April 1745 Stephen de Stainville's seventysix-year-old cousin and godfather, Count Jean-François de Stainville, had bequeathed to his godson his estates of Beurey and Mussey, down the river from the patronymic château. Under the long legalism of the old regime, however, the requisite letters-patent were not to be given at the court of Lunéville till 16 July 1746. For young Stainville to have been keeping things warm there meanwhile would have accorded with his talent for combining business with pleasure, both concentrated in that little enclave of delight amid a world at war.

One tribute to the uniform sway exercised from the prototype of Versailles was the fact that Lunéville was the only French specimen of those miniature courts which decorated Germany and Italy like embossed jewels in the advancing age of the rococo. The delicious court of Stanislas Leszczynski combined the best of both worlds, with gallic elegance and wit unlaced from the strictness of Versailles, as befitted a bonhomous sovereign who usually drove himself around in a one-horse gig, smoked a six-foot hookah, did charity by stealth, and had his personal accounts totted up every Friday. His treasurer, like his doctor, was a protestant. Not strictly French, either, was Stanislas's predilection for sauerkraut and meat cooked with fruit. By the enjoyment, and employment, provided by his court the benign Stanislas went a good way towards reconciling his subjects to the stern rule of his chancellor, the usual exactions which war had again brought upon Lorraine, and the break with the old dynasty.

Duke Leopold's architectural activity at Lunéville was carried forward by Stanislas's director-general of buildings, Héré. This local architect was soon to give Europe one of its great squares in the Place Stanislas at Nancy, leading into that Place de La Carrière where the Count de Stainville had been born. Just about then, though, there was plenty to do at Lunéville where a fire in 1744 had destroyed one wing of the palace. There the reigning lady was not the disapproving and asthmatic Queen Opalinska but, true to the model of Versailles, the king's mistress, the Marquise de Boufflers, lately bereaved of her twenty-year-old brother, Alexandre de Beauvau, killed at Fontenoy as a brother-in-law had been at Dettingen – another family instalment of the grim price of aristocratic enjoyment. The Marquise de Boufflers was devoted to her other brother, that fit friend of the Count de Stainville, the Prince de Beauvau, finely described by Belle-Isle as 'the aide-de-camp of all who march against the enemy'.[36] She was also close to her sister, the Marquise de Mirepoix.

Less faithful than her sister, wittier than she was beautiful, disinterested in money, the Marquise de Boufflers was prodigal of her favours. The accommodating Stanislas had to share his self-styled Dame de La Volupté with his chancellor, La Galaizière, with the frigid poet Saint-Lambert, and, so far as physically might be, with the duke's more amiable reader, young Devaux, Madame de Graffigny's Panpan. Unlike him the superior Marquise de Boufflers was an enemy to gossip. She once sent the Prince of Beauvau a little poem with the refrain:

> *Il faut dire en deux mots*
> *Ce qu'on veut dire;*
> *Les longs propos*
> *Sont sots.*[37]

The society of the Marquise de Boufflers and King Stanislas, who loved a good discussion, attracted intellectuals from the circles in Paris frequented by the Count de Stainville. The visitors to Lunéville included Montesquieu, Maupertuis, Moncrif, Hénault with messages from Stanislas's royal daughter, also Helvétius, the farmer-general of extreme philosophy who actually married a Ligniville, and the Abbé Morellet who was educating the son of La Galaizière. It was the court theatre of Lunéville which launched Mademoiselle Clairon towards stardom at the Comédie Française and Mademoiselle Chantilly towards the embrace of the Marshal de Saxe.

Thus, almost as a lasting houseparty for friends, flourished the miniature court of the last Duke of Lorraine. Now, though, the Count de Stainville was to receive a small but typical reminder of the less congenial temper of the French court, whither he returned from Strasburg in order to pay his respects.

From the middle of January 1746 King Louis XV with his family and more favoured courtiers was in residence at Marly. Perhaps the

---

[36] Cited, Gaston Maugras, *La Cour de Lunéville au XVIIIᵉ siècle*, p. 184.
[37] Ibid., p. 180.

most lastingly evocative of the elegant satellites setting off the palace of Versailles, Marly that month remains focused in a transient brilliance. The weather was consistently bright, and cold. Frost reduced the king from hunting to promenades, especially to admire Coustou's splendid Chevaux de Marly, just erected at the end of the gardens in fitting apogee of the last brilliant year of the old regime.

Indoors Madame de Pompadour was just then finding fault with the main salon at Marly; whereas the Dauphine enjoyed the glitter of the gambling there after the dreary card-games in the queen's apartments at Versailles, and teased her unamused husband for being 'like an owl'.[38] The men's clothes that season were held to be at least as magnificent as those of the women. Many were *salonistes,* the term at Marly for those who, without being resident in the crowded palace, enjoyed permission to attend the salon, where the four mirrored doors often confused them on leaving. The *salonistes* most probably included the Count de Stainville, who now visited that court forbidden to his father and had a brief but publicized encounter with the Dauphine.

One day at Marly at the end of January 1746 the Count de Stainville, doubtless because of his broken leg, was being carried in a sedan-chair appertaining to the palace, by porters in royal livery. They met the Dauphine with her lady, the Duchess de Brancas. Stainville called to his bearers to halt in token of respect but, unheeding, they plodded on to the indignation of the duchess who thought not only that they ought to have stopped but that the count should have alighted. The incident provided professional courtiers with a fascinating debate over multiple considerations: whether the correct etiquette was the same for the Dauphine as for the king, at Marly as elsewhere, on a highroad as on a path, for a sedan-chair as for a coach, for a male occupant as for a female, with royal porters as with ones in private liveries – a splendid variety of precedents and possible permutations. After a fortnight the king gave his ruling that Stainville's porters, being royal, had done right in conforming to a regulation of Louis XIV that those at Marly should not halt even on meeting his own person. 'If', commented the disappointed Luynes, 'it is indeed the will of the king, there is nothing for it but to obey; but it is difficult not to imagine that it would be more respectful, especially for men, to get out of the sedan-chair.'[39]

The Count de Stainville himself recalled another kind of formalism during that visit to Marly: 'I found Mme de Pompadour the appointed mistress of the king and of the kingdom'[40] – a significant

---

[38] Luynes, vii. 212.   [39] Ibid., pp. 218–19.
[40] Choiseul, *Mémoires*, pp. 27–8 for the following.

tribute to the reality, already, of her political influence. The later Choiseul added: 'I was at Mme de Pompadour's at Marly. One was presented to her as to the queen. I found her etiquette much more exalted than had been that of Mme de Châteauroux, who had preserved social politeness and equality. Since the king has no head for proportion, because he has no measure of co-ordination *(aucun degré de combinaison)* and since Mme de Pompadour, having no knowledge of the court or its customs, only took her ideas from the king, it is not extraordinary that she should have thought that it was for her idol, who was the king, that people paid her the basest respects and homage.'

Another future statesman, Kaunitz, was to confirm precisely Choiseul's account of Madame de Pompadour at that period: the early inception of her political influence, obeisance to her that 'surpasses anything one can imagine'[41] although initially, 'full of false airs, she had an insufferable manner from bad company'. One of her early affectations was not to be able to stand the smell of truffles. The king ordered truffles to be set before her at table. And somewhere about then 'she was complaining bitterly one day at not having been born a boy, for, said she, "I should travel, I should go to the war, I should make women mad about me." – "You would have done nothing of the kind", replied the King drily, "for you would have remained a little Fish *(un petit Poisson)*."'

Louis XV would hardly have made that kind of joke to the less agreeable Duchess de Châteauroux, and that, one suspects, for more reasons than one.

The then Count de Stainville, however, explained: 'I was not, at that time, at all concerned with making reflections upon the situation at court and I viewed everything with gaiety and from the aspect which most affected me. My profession, some literary occupations and my pleasure wholly absorbed me. I did not see Mme de Pompadour again that winter.[42] He did not stay at court.

War, literature, and love were the ideal combination in the life of the Count de Stainville at twenty-six. His glancing reference to his literary occupations remains characteristically unelaborated. While he was familiar with intellectual and literary circles of an aristocratic stamp such as the salon of the Duchess d'Aiguillon, his contacts from Louis-le-Grand may already have included not only Fréron but also Jean-Baptiste Gresset, the poet who was in the following year to produce a comedy somewhat associated with Stainville. Gresset had founded his reputation ten years earlier upon his charming evocation

---

[41] Kaunitz/Mémoire, pp. 449–51 for the following.
[42] Choiseul, *Mémoires*, p. 28.

of Ver-Vert, the pious but peccant parrot. For the known literary works of Choiseul himself one has to wait long years till his retirement. Then, among other things, he tossed off in a day a theatrical divertissement, *Le Royaume d'Arlequinerie*. This 'comedy in the heroic manner', described by its author as 'neither interesting nor amusing',[43] does include a splendid take-off of a meeting of that French royal council which he had by then come to know so well. Now, however, it appears possible that there may survive one, at least, much earlier composition of the then Stainville. The manuscript copy stands under date of 1747 but it seems quite likely that it could have originated in the previous year both from internal indications in the source and from the shape which his life now was to assume.

For the present it may be enough to notice, for instance, the possibility that Stainville was already familiar, as he certainly was a few years later, with such a liberal litterateur as the Abbé Chauvelin, brother of the marquis who had served with Stainville under Noailles and Conti. Some years later at least, Stainville was also to be theatrically involved with the Abbé de Bernis; and Stainville's previously remarked assimilation to the Count de Maurepas and his Académie de Ces Messieurs might quite easily have been involving him in the production of light pieces like those just presented in 1745 in the *Recueil de ces Messieurs*. Formerly attributed to the cultivated Count de Caylus, this miscellany was probably a joint production, with which the names of Maurepas and Duclos have also been associated. It evoked the *Lettres Persanes* of Montesquieu in such morsels as a Turkish commentary upon the christian idea of love and marriage 'to one woman alone, and for ever . . . Your senses [are] more enlightened.'[44]

While any connection in literature just then between Maurepas and Stainville remains uncertain, this is a little less so in regard to Stainville's 'pleasure'. It would appear that about then the Count de Stainville's mistress, or one of them, was the Duchess de Chaulnes. The evidence is a story in doubtful taste from a source of dubious reliability, the memoirs of the Count de Maurepas, clever and salacious though not depraved in the manner of the Duke de Richelieu. Staunch Choiseulists can thus reject the story but on balance it seems rather more likely than not that there may be some truth in it.

The Duchess de Chaulnes, a year older than the Count de Stainville, was the type which, one gathers, appealed to him. She was a woman of high birth, intelligence, and idiosyncrasy, striking

[43] Duke de Choiseul, *Mémoires de M. le Duc de Choiseul* (Chanteloup, 1790), ii. 167.
[44] *Recueil de ces Messieurs* (Amsterdam, 1745), pp. 121–4.

contemporaries as a whit fantastical, like her friend, and his, the Duchess d'Aiguillon. The Marquise du Deffand wrote:

The intellect of the Duchess de Chaulnes is so singular that it is impossible to define. It can only be compared to space. It has so to say all its dimensions, depth, extent and nothingness. It assumes all kinds of shapes and preserves none ... She lacks no attribute of intellect and yet one cannot say that she possesses one – reason, judgement, ability, etcetera. All these qualities are perceptible in her but in the manner of a magic lantern. They disappear even as they materialize. All the gold of Peru passes through her hands without her being any the richer. Devoid of feeling and passion, her spirit is but a flame without fire and without heat but never ceasing to spread a great light.[45]

The light shone high. The dissecting critic conceded: 'She will never be concerned or interested except by things which call for a kind of effort. The most abstract sciences are the only ones to which she is attracted ... The Duchess de Ch[aulnes] is a being who has nothing in common with other beings except external form. She has the practice and appearance of everything, and she has the property and reality of nothing.'

This elusive creature was further described by Madame du Deffand, with present relevance: 'The extreme activity of her imagination makes her abandon herself without examination and without recourse to all her initial impulses. She will engage in a gallantry and disengage from it with such precipitation that she could well forget even the name, the face even, of her lover.' While this may hardly have applied to the Count de Stainville, such was the mistress of whom the Count de Maurepas seemingly told a story that looked towards what was probably the end of their association.

The Duchess de Chaulnes, according to the Maurepas memoirs, 'having at the fêtes at Versailles in March 1746 seen an officer, a handsome and well-made man, who pleased her and whom, from her temperament, inconstancy or curiosity, she wished to get to know, she made all the advances and the adventure was pushed further than she would have wished.'[46] Her lover gave her gonorrhoea, which she passed on to her husband and to the Count de Stainville, 'her ordinary lover, and to some others; and all that before she was aware of her condition. Having been the first to perceive it, she sent for Morand', a surgical doctor of leading reputation.

The Duchess de Chaulnes warned Morand that her husband might be consulting him on the same account. The doctor, 'sharp and adroit', in due course fobbed off the innocent duke on account of his

[45] Marquise de Deffand, 'Portrait de Madame la duchesse de Chaulnes' in Du Deffand/Lescure, ii. 745–6 for the following.
[46] Comte de Maurepas, *Mémoires du comte de Maurepas* (3rd ed., Paris, 1792), iv. 154.

having slept with his wife during menstruation. The story went sniggering around court and King Louis characteristically teased cuckolded Chaulnes. 'But Stainville', according to Maurepas, 'raised an outcry. He related the adventure, it is said, to whomsoever was willing to listen.'

Supposing the Count de Maurepas to be approximately accurate, the Count de Stainville's misadventure with the transitional Duchess de Chaulnes may have inclined him the more towards a very different and more significant mistress, whose association with him embraced one of his best friends. This was Charles-Antoine-Armand, Marquis de Gontaut, the congenial younger brother of Stainville's old colonel, the Duke de Biron. After his wound at Dettingen, Gontaut, a brigadier of thirty-five, had quit campaigning for the court. There, very much a well-bred man of the world, he became a favourite of the king and of his favourites, the Marquis de Choiseul-Meuse, the Duchess de Châteauroux, and, especially, the Marquise de Pompadour. The latter's personal maid, the shrewd and honest Madame du Hausset, wrote of the Marquis de Gontaut: 'He was very gay, and had the reputation of *creating* gaiety; he was, somebody said, an excellent piece of furniture for a favourite: he makes her [Madame de Pompadour] laugh, he asks nothing, either for himself or for others; he cannot excite jealousy, and interferes in nothing. He used to be called the White Eunuch.'[47]

This significantly nicknamed banterer had at the beginning of 1744 married sixteen-year-old Antionette-Eustachie, elder daughter to the Marquis du Châtel. Still more to the point, she was the paternal grand-daughter of the millionaire Antoine Crozat, distinguished as Crozat the Rich from his younger brother, the lesser millionaire Pierre, Crozat the Poor. This valuable family of Crozat was to be lastingly and intimately associated with the Count de Stainville, whose friendship for the Marquis de Gontaut embraced his wife.

The brothers Crozat had come of banking stock at Toulouse. Antoine was already reputed to be worth twenty million livres in 1707, the year in which he bought the marquisate of Moy in Picardy from the indebted Prince de Ligne and also supplied a dowry of two million for his clever and only daughter, Marie-Anne, in marrying her into the princely house of Bouillon, to the nasty Count d'Évreux. His mother, the Duchess de Bouillon, said to have been tipped 50,000 livres, referred to her daughter-in-law as 'her little gold ingot'.[48] Such was the backing to the building in the Rue Saint-Honoré of the

[47] Madame du Hausset, *Mémoires de Mme du Hausset*, ed. Hippolyte Fournier (Paris, 1891), p. 169.
[48] Cited, Baron Desazars, 'La Famille Crozat' in *Revue des Pyrénées*, xix. (1907), 160.

sumptuous Hôtel d'Évreux, later acquired by Madame de Pompadour, later the presidential Élysée.

The French aristocracy of the eighteenth century was less exclusive than sometimes supposed, in relation to finance at all events. In France then, as usual, money talked. And Crozat the Rich kept on making it. He promoted the Picardy Canal, also known as the Crozat Canal, and if in 1717 he prudently relinquished his monopoly in Louisiana in favour of Law's Mississippi Company, he had made huge profits from other commerce overseas. In 1716 a special levy on profiteering during the War of the Spanish Succession cost him 6,600,000 livres compared with four million from his competitor, Samuel Bernard. In the previous year a loan of three million to the French government had procured for Antoine Crozat the office of grand treasurer of the order of the Saint-Esprit, entitling him to wear the Cordon Bleu without being a full member. And the purchase of another marquisate in Brittany made him the first Marquis du Châtel of his line.

On the death of Antoine Crozat in 1738 his title had passed to his eldest son, Louis-François, who had married a Gouffier girl from a very old family rich in court favourites back to the time of Charles VII. This daughter of the Marquis d'Heilly, also a Luynes on her mother's side, was a match for the vivid intelligence of the Crozats. The second Marquis and Marquise du Châtel, parents of the young Marquise de Gontaut, were a clever and charming couple. The younger marquis had chosen the correctly aristocratic profession of arms and had figured in the same campaigns as had the Count de Stainville, through the long severities in Bohemia and then into Italy in 1744, commanding Stainville's crossing of the Var which du Châtel's preliminary staff-work had prepared. That May he was promoted lieutenant-general. Here again it would seem that shared campaigning cemented another valuable connection for the winning Count de Stainville, who described the Marquis du Châtel as 'very much one of my friends'.[49]

The Count de Stainville's happy touch in allying material benefit with disinterested worth was nowhere more evident than in his friendships. The Marquis du Châtel furnished this wry self-portrait:

M du Châtel is ugly and small; without having an ignoble air, his physiognomy is sombre; his extreme shyness is hidden beneath harsh and immobile features ... It would be tempting to believe that M. du Châtel is but a draft of a nature; it appears that he owes to it neither his tastes, nor his ideas, nor his feelings, and that he has acquired them all by dint of cultivation and labour; his heart and his intellect seem to be foreign guests domiciled with him, and he seems to have withdrawn them in order to complete and perfect his being ... He is properly a man of art ... Since M.

[49] Choiseul, *Mémoires*, p. 61.

du Châtel has moulded himself upon excellent models, all his feelings are honest and most of his ideas are sound and fairly just . . . If he could have bestowed upon himself vanity and ambition, he would perhaps have made himself a great man.[50]

The wealthy Marquis du Châtel was a man of art in more senses than one. For France the eighteenth century, distinguished by the spreading power of her great financiers, had opened under the auspices of the three great financial empires of Samuel Bernard, the brothers Crozat, and the brothers Pâris. How the latter projected finance into politics has recently appeared. Whereas the more amiable Crozats had reversed the progression of Bernard, sprung from a protestant family of artists, and had deployed finance into the realm of art. The uncle of Stainville's friend, Pierre Crozat, had been one of the first among modern millionaires to devote his wealth to art. Crozat the Poor or Crozat le Curieux, as he was also called, scorned to follow his elder brother, Crozat le Traitant, in buying feudal lands and titles. Of pictures Pierre Crozat, a bachelor, formed one of the great collections of all time.

Together with his partners in art, the elegantly classicist Count de Caylus, and Mariette, the slim scholar, Pierre Crozat was indeed a prototype of the eighteenth-century *curieux* or connoisseur. Art had become this Crozat's real profession after visiting Italy where he bought everything worthwhile which he could lay hands on, the whole Boschi collection at Bologna, splendid pastels in Venice, above all perhaps a magnificent lot of Raphael's first drawings from Urbino. Raphael's pellucid painting of Saint George and the Dragon from the collection of Charles I of England figured among the four hundred and more first-rate canvases displayed in Pierre Crozat's magnificent mansion, one day to be Choiseul's, in the Rue de Richelieu. As Mariette said of Crozat the Poor, 'everything went to him and he let nothing escape',[51] though in fact much put out when the Duke of Devonshire got in first on the famous Flinck collection in Rotterdam. The Crozat collection further included sculpture and carved gems but its chief glory lay in 19,000 drawings by old masters. Modern opinion has supported Mariette in supposing this to be probably the greatest collection of drawings ever assembled. After Pierre Crozat's death in 1740 the gems and drawings had, by his characteristic direction, been sold for the profit of the poor, and the enrichment of French national collections.

Pierre Crozat left his mansion to his eldest nephew and, it was

[50] Marquis du Châtel, 'Portrait de M. du Châtel fait par lui-même' in Du Deffand/Lescure, ii. 748–9.
[51] Pierre-Jean Mariette, foreword to *Description sommaire des desseins des grands maistres d'Italie, des Pays-Bas et de France du cabinet de feu M. Crozat* (1741), cited, Baron Desazars, op. cit., xix. 342.

reported at the time, the bulk of his property including paintings also passed 'into the hands of the Marquis du Châtel, who recognises their value and takes pleasure in showing them to connoisseurs',[52] almost certainly including his young friend, the Count de Stainville. Also beneficiaries were the two younger brothers of the marquis, the Baron de Tugny (another estate bought by his father from the Prince de Ligne) and the Baron de Thiers, both notable collectors, especially the latter. Thiers was, like du Châtel, a lieutenant-general and had, like Stainville, fought at Coni. The baron was for ever deploring that France had gone to the dogs since the high days of Louis XIV and now possessed no generals or statesmen except his friend, Belle-Isle. Thiers shared this admiration, and a keenness for the theatre, with his particular friend, the Baron von Bernstorff. Through his friendships with Bernstorff, the du Châtels, and the Gontauts the Count de Stainville was edging further into a world not only of taste and high art but also of high finance, and love, and grief.

Military connections and friendships with both the father and the husband helped to steer the Count de Stainville towards the young Marquise de Gontaut. Antoinette-Eustachie was tall, with a good figure and agreeable features, though, it was judged, lacking in grace. She inherited, however, a lively intellect. Certainly, if she was anything like her younger sister, Louise-Honorine, who lived much longer and left more mark, she must have been an enchanting creature. Likely enough the Marquise de Gontaut was then that anyway, being eighteen in the winter of 1746. She and the Count de Stainville formed a deep attachment. She adored him and became his mistress. For him, as noticed, the point of having a mistress was to love her and be loved. He did not dilate upon her for the benefit of posterity. But from rare hints, and the circumstances, one is inclined to suspect that this may have been the true love in the life of the future Duke of Choiseul.

From about this time comes the literary composition which may possibly originate from the Count de Stainville. It is one of the little literary pieces in a manuscript compilation of a kind common enough in those days.

The miscellany is entitled 'Mélanges en Vers et en Prose par Madame de Graffigny et ses Amis', one of several volumes. This one includes a number of poems dated 1746 and quite a few featuring aristocratic rather than purely literary figures. As one would expect, contributions fairly often suggest connections with Lorraine. There is a 'Chanson pour Madame de Meuse'[53] and a monorhymed

---

[52] *Mémoires de Trévoux*, Apr. 1741, pp. 761f., cited, ibid., p. 357.
[53] B. N.: Cabinet des Manuscrits, former collection of Sir Thomas Phillipps/Graffigny 23900, vol. lxxxvii (Poésies), fo. 35.

epigram on the Marshal de Belle-Isle with a Beauvau ascription[54], as well as poems by the Duke de Richelieu. Pieces by friends and acquaintances of the Count de Stainville also include an 'Impromptu' on love by the Abbé de Bernis[55] under date of January 1746 and a 'Portrait de Madame de Rochefort par M. le Duc de Nivernais'.[56] Both the dating and the personalities thus assembled bring one close to young Stainville about then, himself known to Madame de Graffigny, still the friend of his parents. And one item in her collection, under date of 1747, is entitled 'Madrigal de Mr. de St.'[57]

It would seem possible that in some cases at least the dating of poems in Madame de Graffigny's 'Mélanges' may relate more to their incorporation than to their composition. Nor is their order of inclusion strictly chronological. The 'Madrigal de Mr. de St.' is followed by a 'Madrigal de Monsieur De St. Lambert'[58] of December 1746 and another[59] by that poet, here copied in inverse order and dated June 1746. The heading of these two madrigals under St. Lambert's full name would suggest that it was hardly he who figured a few pages earlier under what would be partial abbreviation to Mr. de St. Mr. de St. Aulaire was another name so written out in the succeeding volume.[60] Hardly, either, would King Stanislas Leszczynski be thus abbreviated even if he could have composed the poem. At the same time there is no proof that St. stands for Stainville. Yet in Madame de Graffigny's circle the person whom it might appear to fit most closely was the Count de Stainville: not only from his circumstances around 1746–7 but even, may be, from the style, so different from the reflective correctness of Saint Lambert in its throb and uninhibited urgency of love and truth. Not best suited, perhaps, by contemporary canons to overt attribution or publication, here is the poem:

Madrigal de Mr. de St.

> *Sur tes beautés au gré de mes désirs*
> *Laisse égarer, et ma bouche et mon âme.*
> *Ah, dans les transports de ma flamme*
> *Est-il des riens, qui ne soyent des plaisirs?*
> *Livre à l'ardeur qui me dévore*
> *Tous tes charmes les plus secrets;*
> *Laisse-moy les baiser, et les baiser encore.*
> *Philis, chacun de tes attraits*
> *Est une part de ce tout que j'adore.*[61]

---

[54] Ibid., fo. 127. [55] Ibid., fo. 182. [56] Ibid., fo. 228.
[57] Ibid., fo. 239. [58] Ibid., fo. 245. [59] Ibid., fo. 247.
[60] *u.s.*: Phillipps/Graffigny 23900, vol. lxxxviii (Miscellanies in Verse and Prose), fo. 260.
[61] *u.s.*, vol. lxxxvii, fo. 239.

I

THE restless scurry of secret diplomacy characterized the War of the Austrian Succession more persistently even than the clash of arms. Both carried suggestions towards the future career of the Duke de Choiseul.

In March 1746 the French government decided to send the Count de Stainville's old patron, the Marshal de Noailles, on special mission to Madrid to try to retrieve the Sardinian fiasco. And indeed separate negotiation with the enemy was a game which two could play. Yet another Abbé on secret assignment, the Abbé Armani from the entourage of Don Philip, was sounding an Austrian representative in Padua for nothing less than an Austro-Spanish alliance against France; similar but more substantial, most secret soundings were conducted some months later at Wiener-Neustadt with the Genoese patrician Girolamo Grimaldi speaking for Spain. The Marshal de Noailles, however, could look to his special connections in both Austria and Spain – he was an old friend and protagonist of King Philip V from the War of the Spanish Succession. If the Marquis d'Argenson confessed to 'a great moment of delight in causing to be absent from the council, for several months, so importunate and mischief-making a minister',[1] in fact the mission of the Marshal de Noailles accompanied by his younger son, the pious and homosexual Count de Noailles, marked the ascendancy at Versailles of the Spanish faction against the largely discredited d'Argenson, let down by Sardinia, let down by Prussia.

While Noailles now stood over against the French foreign minister on the Spanish side, on the German stood Conti, the other patron of the Count de Stainville and critic of the Marquis d'Argenson.

The foreign minister who had refused to recognize the Emperor Francis I sneered that Conti 'was cited in the council as a doctor in the affairs of Germany',[2] where the princes were now liable to swing behind their new emperor in the Austrian war against France. On 13 December 1745 Conti produced a 'Mémoire concernat la neutralité

---

[1] D'Argenson, iv. 308.　　　　[2] Ibid., iv. 408.

des cercles'[3] and on New Year's Day 1746 the French royal council resolved that for the coming year it would renounce grand gestures in Germany in favour of separate negotiations with German states for their neutrality. This tedious and unspectacular policy, lubricated with palm-oil, produced what was probably the solidest achievement in the foreign policy of the Marquis d'Argenson. For handsome considerations France more or less lined up Bavaria and critical Saxony. In dealing with the King of Poland, however, d'Argenson was once again running into the special sphere of Conti. In March 1746 Louis XV insisted upon the appointment of Conti's agent, Duperron de Castéra, to be French chargé d'affaires to Saxony as earlier proposed by Saint-Séverin and requested by Bielinski's Poles, now also subsidized. To follow was an ambassador to Dresden in the person of Charles-Hyacinthe de Galéans de Castellane, Marquis des Issarts, warmly recommended by Conti. The Secret du Roi was getting under way.

Prefigurative for Conti was his immersion in German complexities and Polish chimeras while the effective sphere of action, diplomatic as well as military, was increasingly the Low Countries. The lead towards pacification through Holland, never technically at war with France in that conflict, had been tenuously following through from Count de Wassenaer-Twickel's abortive mission to the French court on campaign at Lille and Arras in the summer of 1744. Saxe's swoop on Brussels gave the frightened Dutch another push towards peace. On 20 February 1746, driving with his son into Paris, the longfaced Count de Wassenaer-Twickel reappeared upon the scene, this time openly and feted at Versailles to the mortification of the discredited Van Hoey. Twickle, as he was to his British colleagues, held his most specific conversations with his old friend from the Hague, the able Abbé de la Ville, lately returned in order to succeed Du Theil as the chief clerk in the French foreign ministry. But their soundings bristled with difficulties, starting with Cape Breton whose recent capture by the British was positively regretted by Henry Pelham as 'a stumbling-block to all negotiation'.[4] As often happens at the initiation of heavy negotiations, the two parties were still too widely separated for any rapid realization of the generalized inclination towards agreement expressed in social courtesies. These included the performance of music by the Dutch diplomat, who was quite a composer though slightly deaf.

D'Argenson grumbled that Wassenaer-Twickel, who talked too

---

[3] Arch. Aff. Étr. C.P., Allemagne, vol. 544, fos. 259–60.
[4] Pelham to Trevor, 11 December 1745 O.S.: William Coxe, *Memoirs of the administration of the Right Honourable Henry Pelham* (London, 1829), i. 284.

much, had been 'told at the Hague that our government was such that the court and the town [of Paris] influenced affairs, that the ministry had little credit permitting it to adopt resolutions; and he thought he ought to treat us as a republic wherein one has to capture the votes of the multitude':[5] another suggestion to modify a picture of eighteenth-century France as a monolithic autocracy. In fact she had to endure considerable periods of ephemeral ministries under weak kings and insignificant ministers in conditions which approximated more than always allowed to those which later undermined republican regimes in France. Besides the everlasting scrape of trying to govern the tax-shy French, they paid for their social brilliance by allowing it to outshine their government so that ministers and policies were too often subordinate to coteries, mistresses, financiers, and interested factions with influence in the right quarters.

In seeking to probe what, besides Dutch alarm, lay behind Wassenaer-Twickel's mission d'Argenson correctly deduced that he was to some extent able to speak with the consent of the British government, but not of the Austrian. The court of Vienna in fact viewed the separate and unconcealed peace-feeler of the Dutch count with great suspicion. So did the Tuscan minister in Paris.

II

A week after Wassenaer-Twickel arrived in Paris the Marquis de Stainville gave the emperor his own opinion: while Maria Theresa's loyalty to her allies was admirable, 'it is much to be desired that these same allies should have the same delicacy, but ... '[6] he doubted it. Anglo-Dutch feelers were now to be reckoned with and he had long suspected, he wrote, the secret Franco-Sardinian negotiation: 'It is some months ago now that I warned the Count de Richecourt at Turin of my fears; I have even taken the liberty of writing of them to Your Imperial Majesty ... I am still keeping myself in retreat which has been prescribed to me, but ...' he advised the counterploy of an Austro-French negotiation. And 'when it shall be a question of negotiating here, I dare to say that nobody is better placed than I to do so advantageously'.

Maria Theresa, however, was sore at having just signed away Silesia and embittered against the prussophil Marquis d'Argenson. Nor does this resentment appear to have been much moderated by the secret and belated approach of the brothers Pâris to the Marquis

---

[5] D'Argenson, iv. 338.
[6] Marquis de Stainville to Emperor Francis I, Paris, 27 Feb. 1746: Ö.S./H.H.S., Lothringisches Hausarchiv 77/177B for the following.

de Stainville, himself perhaps scarcely more trusted by the Austrian government that Van Hoey now was by the Dutch – a significant relegation of two obvious middlemen in the slow swing towards peace.

At Versailles, however, there lingered a not unnatural inclination to turn to the Marquis de Stainville as a secret intermediary. He was now approached for peace by no other than the military idol of the hour in Paris. The connection of the Marshal de Saxe with the house of Holstein included a nephew. Saxe, on his triumphal return from Brussels to Paris, had the Prince of Holstein's governor, a Florentine called Count Philippi, pass word to the Tuscan minister that the marshal would like to see him. Just a week after Saxe's coronation at the opera, on Friday the 25th March 1746, the Marquis de Stainville went to keep an appointment at the marshal's residence.

Stainville recorded of his most secret conversation with Saxe: 'He spoke to me very frankly of the extreme wish he had to see peace re-established in Europe, and he said to me openly that, raised as he was to the highest point of glory, he had nothing to wish for but the complete restoration of his health. He feared those reverses which are so common in the profession of war and, knowing the French nation as he did, he was sure that if he suffered the least little check they would forget everything good that he had been able to accomplish till now. Thus he could only lose from the continuation of the war, without hope of gaining anything.'

'After having spoken to me of his personal interest,' Saxe, reported Stainville to the Emperor Francis, 'assured me that the [French] king also greatly desired to see tranquillity re-established; and in the rest of the conversation he made me feel that he believed that that depended only upon Your Imperial Majesty and upon the Queen Empress.'[7] Stainville replied as usual that he was sure 'that they themselves desired nothing so much as a general and stable peace, that in accordance with these views they did not ask better than to enter in and listen to all the just and reasonable proposals which might be made to them.'

'"What," the marshal answered me, "you are sure of that? . . . Then why do they not make peace, for the king wants nothing for himself? He is very glad, by returning his conquests, to finish a war which is not only useless, but very burdensome, to him. Have you told our ministers what you have just told me?"' Yes, replied Stainville, but 'they had not believed me. The marshal said to me on that that he was leaving that day for Versailles, that he begged me to call again at his

---

[7] Marquis de Stainville to Emperor Francis I, Paris, 27 Mar. 1746: Ö.S./H.H.S., Lothringisches Hausarchiv 77/177B for the following.

house next day, that he would make use of what I had told him with the king personally.'

On 3 April the next instalment opened: 'Sire, The Marshal Count de Saxe having asked for an appointment at my house upon his return from Versailles, he kept it, and . . .' told Stainville 'almost word for word' (cypher begins):

I can and I must tell you that the king very sincerely desires peace. If démarches have not been made to the court of Vienna it is that the Dutch have seized the negotiation for themselves, and that they seem very glad on either side that it should pass through them. That is why I see them as the mediator of this whole affair, and for them it is in truth a fine position for getting out of the embarrassment in which they are; for if the war were to continue they would be ruined from top to bottom. They put their hope in vain in the King of Prussia. This prince will not allow them to be invaded or destroyed, but he will not be sorry that their power should be diminished. For he will always draw his strength from the enfeeblement of others.

Saxe continued to the reporting Stainville:

I think then that I can tell you that the negotiation with Monsieur Wassenaer is far advanced, but in rendering the Dutch mediators it is desired that they should remain absolutely neutral, and that they should no longer afford any passage to the allies upon their soil. In that case there will be established a congress whereat each shall have his interests discussed. The Queen of Spain will be obliged to content herself with something very small for Don Philip, still leaving the Queen Empress the strongest in Italy. The [French] king will not abandon little Prince Edward *(le petit Prince Edouard)*, who has shown too much courage and resolve, but he [Louis] is great lord enough to create a state for him himself; so he will be brought back from Scotland and the tranquillity of the House of Hanover in its kingdoms will be disturbed no more. In addition the English nation will be given a permitted vessel.[8] The Marshal de Noailles has left to go to persuade the Queen of Spain to accept this plan as a whole; and if he cannot make her consent to it, he has orders to declare to her that France does not intend to make war for her eternally, and that she will not give her any more help for the pursuit of her too ambitious views.

I do not doubt that the Dutch are negotiating in concert with your court. So it is informed of everything that I am telling you. But you can however report it as something which I have told you on good authority. And once again give good assurance that the king sincerely wants peace, and that all his ministers think the same despite the great efforts which we have made, being all ready to enter upon campaign in Flanders with one hundred and fifty battalions of regular troops and fifty battalions of militia for guarding fortresses. With such forces the king can lay siege of Antwerp, and he will have another army between the Sambre and the Meuse, which can at the same time lay siege to Mons or Namur, without the allies being able to raise any obstacle to it. But for my part I am of opinion that one must not make sieges when one does not reckon to keep the fortresses which are attacked. That always means losing men uselessly. As for the siege of Luxemburg, since happily the fine projects of the Marshal de Belle-Isle are no longer listened to, I do believe that they are not thinking of this enterprise.[9]

[8] i.e. *navio permiso* for trade to South America.
[9] Marquis de Stainville to Emperor Francis I, Paris, 3 Apr. 1746: ibid. for the following.

Perhaps it was not very often even in the eighteenth century that a general gave the enemy so obliging and accurate a preview of his forthcoming campaign. The Marshal de Saxe concluded his striking exposition to the Marquis de Stainville on a personal note, duly reported: "'I can tell you further that, knowing your uprightness as they do, it is greatly desired that you should be employed in this great matter, and I for my own part assure you that I much wish it.'"

The second conversation, at least, of the Marshal de Saxe with the Marquis de Stainville suggests a carefully concerted communication. The question is with whom, if anyone, besides the king himself, Saxe had concerted. For his peace-feeler to Stainville differed in notable respects from that put out three months earlier by the brothers Pâris. Now England and Holland were to be included in the reckoning, and the French ministers, instead of being depicted as divided in their views, were represented as unanimous in their desire for peace, if not, perhaps, as to the best means of attaining it. It is even possible that the Marshal de Saxe may have consulted the Marquis d'Argenson, whom he was supporting in his negotiation for Saxon neutrality. On the whole, however, it seems more likely as well as more creditable for d'Argenson's good faith that he was not in on Saxe's démarche to Stainville.

Some weeks earlier, towards the middle of March 1746, the Marquis d'Argenson had drafted some 'Idées sur la Paix entre Messieurs le Marquis d'Argenson et le Comte de Wassenaer'. This important French memorandum, remitted to the British government by the Dutch, had proposed among other things that Maria Theresa should cede Limburg and Austrian Gelderland to the francophil Elector Palatine, should cede to France herself the enclaves of Hainault – Chimay, Beaumont, and Saint-Hubert – and should dismantle the fortress of Luxemburg. Though conceivably these French terms may have been written off as trifles scarcely worth a mention, Saxe had not breathed a word of them to Stainville in representing Louis as quite ready to restore his conquests. It may be that Saxe's indications reflected, rather, views which his confidant and mentor, Noailles, would now have liked to inject into d'Argenson's negotiations. Saxe may well have shared Noailles's preference for seeking peace through Austria rather than through Holland, which Saxe had militarily overawed. The Marshal de Noailles had in fact not yet left, but was just leaving, for Madrid. He and Saxe had certainly been in touch the month before, while Saxe was yet beseiging Brussels, concerning the mission of the Count de Wassenaer-Twickel.

Wassenaer-Twickel had reported home that even the Marshal de Saxe desired peace, contrary to the more obvious view of the hero, to which he may himself, outwardly at least, have lent some colour.[10] In seeking peace Saxe was at one with both the king and the king's mistress. And in seeking peace with Austria through Stainville Saxe was following the line recently traced by the Marquise de Pompadour's financial backers, the brothers Pâris: with whom, in turn, any general commanding a French army needed to be on close terms. Saxe established cordial relations with Madame de Pompadour and later that year was to earn her gratitude by discouraging Louis XV from proceeding to the front. That would be more radically achieved by promoting peace. There is no direct evidence to associate Madame de Pompadour with Saxe's secret approach to Stainville, any more than with that of the brothers Pâris. But all the intermediaries for France were her particular friends, all spoke to Stainville of peace, which suited her, as though direct from her royal lover; and in looking towards Austria they were taking a direction which the Marquise de Pompadour herself was to follow pretty steadily till it led, just ten years later, to the Diplomatic Revolution of the Franco-Austrian alliance, as subsequently clinched by her then protégé, the younger Stainville.

The very fact that the Marshal de Saxe sought peace with Austria in the spring of 1746 has hitherto remained an unopened chapter of his life thanks to the secret loyalty and inconspicuous positioning of the Marquis de Stainville. About a week after their second conversation Stainville for the first time in three months appeared at the French court, where the ministers had been grumbling that they never saw him. He reported on 10 April 1746: 'I paid them a visit of decorum, giving them as an excuse for my long absence my incapacity for walking owing to the erysipelas which I have had in my legs for three months and which still subsists.'[11] So both the Marquis and the Count de Stainville had had gammy legs that winter. The Marquise with her passion for cleanliness had been unable to protect her husband against the then common affliction of erysipelas, the malignant rose of fiery anguish promoted by dirt.

When the halt Marquis de Stainville re-emerged at court the Marquis d'Argenson typically pitched into him about a seemingly unfriendly communication by the emperor to the imperial diet. D'Argenson threw in a pointed allusion to French respect hitherto for Tuscan neutrality. 'This minister', reported Stainville, 'then spoke to me again of his previous proposals, and finished by saying to me that the Court of Vienna should treat secretly with Spain; that would certainly shorten the negotiation, and once Spain was content peace

---

[10] Cf. Broglie/Saxe, i. 69–70.
[11] Marquis de Stainville to Emperor Francis I, Paris, 10 Apr. 1746: *u.s.* for the following.

would no longer be difficult to conclude. He talked to me all the while without giving me time to reply.' If Spain scarcely needed such encouragement, d'Argenson's rather naive suggestion chimed with his previous suggestion to Wassenaer that for the present Italian questions should be excluded from the Dutch negotiation. This did not prevent d'Argenson later from upbraiding Noailles for favouring just then, as between Spain and Austria, direct negotiations which were liable to be conducted, at the expense of Sardinia, 'rather for Spain alone than for France and Spain'.[12]

A slightly different tack was pursued with the Marquis de Stainville by his old acquaintance, the Cardinal de Tencin, who still presided over a ministerial committee every Monday. Tencin asked why the emperor did not instruct Stainville to put forward, noncommittally as from himself, 'some proposal as to what the Queen Empress would be willing to give to Don Philip'. The French government would assuredly prove receptive and such an imperial overture, insinuated the cardinal, might shew the way 'to abridge all other negotiation'[13] – a little twist, perhaps, to d'Argenson's Dutch proclivities. Though it would indeed seem as if the French government as a whole was, in its pacific inclination, anxious to complement the feelers extended towards England through Holland by bringing Austria, by one means or another, into an Italian negotiation in order to assuage Elizabeth Farnese's territorial ambition for Don Philip, the main stumbling-block to peace in Europe now that the only other ruler who matched her remorseless appetite had just been appeased with Silesia.

The exhortation of the Cardinal de Tencin in favour of an Austrian proposal regarding Don Philip was repeated and significantly reinforced to the Marquis de Stainville in the most interesting of his conversations with leading Frenchmen upon that crowded day. 'I found myself', he explained, 'in a position to see the man who has formed the subject of one of my previous dispatches written in cypher. I gave him my word of honour not to name him.' From internal evidence this shy personage was certainly not Tencin, Noailles, or Saxe. And it could scarcely have been the Abbé Alary, who was little more than a subordinate go-between with d'Argenson, whom Stainvillle saw in person that day. That chiefly left the brothers Pâris and perhaps most probably Pâris-Duverney, always influentially in the background.

'He said to me first of all,' wrote Stainville, 'that if my master would have me propose something at the present moment it would be a fine

[12] D'Argenson, iv. 315.
[13] Marquis de Stainville to Emperor Francis I, Paris, 10 Apr. 1746: *u.s.* for the following.

opportunity to supersede *(faire tomber)* all the other negotiations and to finish the great work of peace ... The proposals for the treaty with the King of Sardinia are not discontinued, and if the Marshal de Noailles can get them accepted by the Court of Spain, the business would soon be done, and thereby the empress would infallibly lose all Italy.' Because, made out Stainville's interlocutor with appreciable exaggeration, the empire would remain quiescent, the Dutch wanted to be neutral, and the English would not be sending any men to the Netherlands so that Louis XV could, if he wished, dispatch a hundred thousand troops into Italy. If, on the other hand, Elizabeth Farnese were to refuse to come to terms with Sardinia she would turn to the English, granting them many commercial concessions as the price of their putting pressure upon Maria Theresa to yield more, perhaps, to Don Philip than France would have required.

This ingenious argument was driven home to the Marquis de Stainville with the words: '"I assure you that the [French] king would rather treat with the Court of Vienna than with that of Turin, that he is not anxious to despoil the empress of her states in Italy, and that on the contrary he would prefer that she should be more powerful there than the King of Sardinia. In the name of God put yourself in position to say something. Time presses. Your master risks nothing since you would only speak as from yourself." '

Stainville concluded his vivid report: 'I have been struck by the resemblances which I found between these latest remarks and those which were made to me by the Marshal de Saxe ... and those of the Cardinal Tencin ... I should say further – and I am sure of it – that the Marshal de Noailles ardently desires that the negotiation should be conducted rather with Your Imperial Majesty than with the King of Sardinia ... If ... you are good enough to honour me with your orders, time presses. I have not dared to send a [special] courier for fear of making a news-item, but for the reply it would be good to send one at least as far as Basel so that I receive it sooner.'

In this latest conversation, as in Stainville's earlier one with the brothers Pâris, one suddenly glimpses the most secret springs of French foreign policy. More than anything else of the kind in that phase of high policy they probably bring one close to Louis XV himself, that secretive monarch, and also, maybe, to his mistress. The allusion to superseding the other negotiations, the intimated preference for an Austrian preponderance in Italy, though perhaps deliberately deceptive in part, were probably not wholly so. They conveyed, rather, a slightly sinister suggestion of the inimical forces with which the Marquis d'Argenson had to contend within those penetralia of Versailles known to contemporaries as 'the interior'.

The persistent, almost beseeching, French approaches for peace to the Marquis de Stainville do suggest, however, that the French court, whatever its failures and shortcomings, in 1745–6 may have been keener and more sincere in its desire for peace with the stiff-necked and suspicious Austrians than has hitherto appeared. Though one person, at least, suspected as much at the time, and the hidden channel.

Frederick the Great was maintaining his astute interest in the inconspicuous Marquis de Stainville. Barely more than a week after the latter had reported his critical conversations it so happened that Frederick's secretary of cabinet, Eichel, was writing to his minister of state, Count Podewils, that the king desired his minister in Paris, Baron Le Chambrier, 'to observe that Stainville well and not let him out of his sight, but he should pay attention whether he is secretly negotiating something *(ob derselbe secrètement etwas negociirte)* or is keeping quiet'.[14] Only two days earlier Frederick himself, in instructing Le Chambrier to deny indignantly a suggestion by the French that he was trying to queer their negotiations with the Dutch, wrote: 'I have my suspicion whence the thrust comes. It is too like the usual contrivances of the court of Dresden, or perhaps of the Marquis de Stainville, to seek another origin for it.'[15]

True enough the Saxons, middlemen politically as well as geographically, were, like Stainville, still active in the direction of Franco-Austrian rapprochement. But both alike were rebuffed from Vienna. The Saxon envoy there reported to Brühl about ten days later that Ulfeld had orders to reply to any French peace-feeler with the mocking question: 'Is France ready this time to fall upon Prussia with us? So long as we do not have this guarantee, there will be nothing doing with her. We cannot treat with people who want to make the King of Prussia the dictator of the empire.'[16] Somewhat more diplomatic was the phraseology, as least, in which the Emperor Francis I a week later, on 4 May 1746, did reply at last to the Marquis de Stainville in a dispatch which the French government intercepted. The emperor wrote from Vienna to his envoy in Paris:

I have received yours consecutively till that of the 17th April and I have seen from that of the 10th that you have visited the ministers. Yet I had ordered you to the contrary and I wish that you shall henceforth abstain therefrom, it not being suitable that my minister should go to see those of a power which does not recognize me in the dignity which is due to me, being recognized unanimously by all the Empire. Concerning all that all the ministry, and another, said to you, you answered well that

---

[14] Eichel to Count Podewils, Potsdam, 18 Apr. 1746: *Politische Correspondenz*, v. 59.
[15] King Frederick II to Baron Le Chambrier, Berlin, 16 Apr. 1746: ibid., v. 58.
[16] Count C. Loss to Count Brühl, Vienna, 27 Apr. 1746: Arch. Aff. Étr., C.P., Vienne, cited, Broglie/Saxe, i. 259.

I as much as the Empress still held the same pacific sentiments, but I should warn you that all the Court of France is not acting in good faith with you; what I know for certain renders me, moreover, much more circumspect and should also render you so, besides my not finding it seemly that you should frequent either the court or the ministers till further order.[17]

The Emperor Francis continued:

If France was so anxious to make peace as she would have it believed, she would have gone, and would go, about it differently, for everything that is said to you is talk in order to see what is thought, without their putting forward from their side anything as to what they are willing to do; so from that you can rightly judge of the little sincerity of their words, and that is not the way to further a negotiation or to propose one and does not draw us out any further from our general terms for peace, which are however very really sincere.

Thus was the Marquis de Stainville rebuffed into seclusion for the rest of the war. If the court of Versailles was now closed to him that of Vienna remained open to his wife, who was actually to be found there a year later, in May 1747, attending a gala performance of a French comedy got up by Prince Charles and Princess Charlotte of Lorraine. Also in the select audience was Baron von Pfütschner. It was not only Madame de Pompadour who could stage court theatricals, and the Marquise de Stainville may have been reconciled to these in Vienna by the fact that every actor was titled. One was Count Kaunitz,[18] soon to figure upon a wider stage of European diplomacy.

For the present the Marquis d'Argenson was left to make the diplomatic running with the Dutch in soundings still withheld from Austria. If, however, the Emperor Francis had already got wind of the latest development in that quarter, his discount of French sincerity was indeed explicable.

Wassenaer had been reinforced by yet another Dutch negotiator, Jacob Gilles, closest confidant of the Grand Pensionary Van der Heim. Their task was facilitated by the Jacobite collapse at Culloden on 16 April 1746. Soon afterwards Wassenaer and Gilles had given their discussions with d'Argenson an important push by suggesting that Don Philip should for the present be suited by the cession of Tuscany. This approach towards the main Bourbon desideratum was welcomed by d'Argenson even though he had recently, typically, been toying with a more radical destiny for the grand duchy, asking

---

[17] Emperor Francis I to Marquis de Stainville, Vienna, 4 May 1746: Arch. Aff. Étr. C.P., Autriche (intercepted dispatch), cited, Zévort, pp. 239–40 for the following.

[18] Cf. Prince J. J. Khevenhüller-Metsch, *Aus der Zeit Maria Theresias: Tagebuch des Fürsten Johann Josef Khevenhüller-Metsch,* ed. Rudolf Graf Khevenhüller-Metsch and Dr. Hanns Schlitter (Vienna and Leipzig, 1907f.), ii, 160.

Count Lorenzi in Florence whether he did not see 'in the State of Tuscany any disposition to re-establish there a republican government such as existed previously?... Certainly the opportunity today is a fine one.'[19] Now, however, a Tuscan apanage for Don Philip, however delicate in relation to Lorraine, was incorporated in d'Argenson's counter-projects of terms of peace, remitted to Wassenaer and Gilles on 9 May 1746. Though the French foreign minister, who has been aptly termed a clumsy humanitarian, largely spoilt the chances of his proposals by associating them with insistence upon British clemency towards the Jacobites.

The Tuscan proposal for Don Philip was withheld by the Marquis d'Argenson from the Marshal de Noailles, now in Madrid enduring the robust sarcasms the Queen of Spain regarding the separate negotiation with the Dutch by d'Argenson, who was deceiving her with what he himself termed 'false confidences'.[20] And he as good as admitted, without regret, that this stultified from the start Noailles's task of restoring Spanish confidence. The Spanish queen could expect a measure of sympathy from Noailles, whom she wooed with favours, an extraordinary bestowal of the Golden Fleece upon his son while the marshal himself netted the back-pay of a Spanish captain-general since 1711, variously estimated at over half a million livres or, by the Marquis de Stainville, at a million.

The Emperor Francis I, in suppressing Stainville, had added insult to injury by instructing him to continue to report all news 'even of trifles which may be droll or curious, songs, verses and all kinds of diverting novelties'.[21] The marquis complied stiffly, observing that such ephemera turned 'but upon the bickerings or love-affairs of society, wherewith one must be familar in order to be amused by them'.[22] Stainville reported rather, in the same dispatch, his attentions, including an unaccepted offer to lend his house, to the Vice-Chancellor of Russia, the Count Voronzov, just arrived in Paris upon a grand tour of Europe with his young wife and little girl of three. Stainville's concern reflected his concert with the Russian minister in Paris, Gross, especially disliked by d'Argenson for his Austrian proclivities. Count Voronzov was in fact received almost regally by the French, constantly afraid that Russia, leaning towards England, might bear down upon the continent with critical effect on

---

[19] Marquis d'Argenson to Count Lorenzi, 11 Jan. 1746: Arch. Aff. Étr. C.P., Toscane, vol. 103; cited, Zévort, pp. 244–5.

[20] D'Argenson, iv. 342.

[21] Emperor Francis I to Marquis de Stainville, Vienna, 4 May 1746: Arch. Aff. Étr. C.P., Autriche (intercepted dispatch), cited, Zévort, p. 240.

[22] Marquis de Stainville to Emperor Francis I, Paris, 22 May 1746: Ö.S./H.H.S., Lothringisches Hausarchiv 77/177B.

the fortunes of that war which was then opening out into yet another year's campaigning.

III

If the extensive hostilities in the spring of 1746 swung against France and her allies upon the Scottish moorlands and through the Italian tilth, in the focal area of the Low Countries the Marshal de Saxe exploited his grab of Brussels along almost exactly the lines which he had obligingly prefigured to the Marquis de Stainville.

After some criticized dawdling the main army of the Marshal de Saxe, honoured by the presence of Louis XV, arrived before Antwerp. The siege was entrusted to a prince of the blood, the Count de Clermont, one of the last ecclesiastical generals in European history, drawing 180,000 livres a year from his abbey of Saint-Germain des Prés and further gratification from Mademoiselle Camargo and other facile beauties. Meanwhile the Count de Clermont's more ambitious nephew, the Prince de Conti, had assumed command of a second and smaller army concentrating to the south at Maubeuge. For the third year running the prince was to command the Count de Stainvillle, required to join his Regiment of Navarre by 20 April, after he had briefly returned to court, for the first time since his appearance at Marly, in order to take ceremonial leave.

Conti, headed off from Germany to central Hainault, retained an independent command owing, it was said, to Madame de Pompadour's obligation to his mother; though that complaisant princess seems to have embarrassed her protégé nearly as much as her son. Conti and his adherent generals could march from Maubeuge either to cover eastern France if necessary or to co-operate with Saxe in the Netherlands, in the first place by besieging Mons. On 9 June 1746 the princely army, including Navarre, came up, passing near Malplaquet, to beleaguer Mons while the surrender of Antwerp at the beginning of that month had enabled King Louis to return to Versailles for the confinement of the Dauphine. According to the then Count de Stainville since the king 'had experience, from the episode at Metz, that to have his mistress come to the army could bring misfortune, he took the course of going to rejoin her at Versailles'.[23]

The besiegers of Mons were entertained by court gossip of a rival to Madame de Pompadour, a young lady-in-waiting to the princesses. This Madame d'Andlau, continued the writer, 'was the mistress of Monsieur de Soubise and of his brother, the cardinal – so far as one

---

[23] Choiseul, *Mémoires*, pp. 28–9 for the following.

could be ... the silliest counsellors that one could have had at that time. She took it into her head one day to lend to Madame Adelaide *Le Portier des Chartreux*, a notorious piece of pornography 'full of abominable prints.'[24] Upon discovery 'the king on the spot, without considering that for the reputation of his daughter this anecdote should be hushed up, had Madame d'Andlau publicly expelled from court'.[25] Stainville's criticism was to be borne out by Kaunitz, who observed that 'Madame Adelaide became the laughing-stock of all Europe'.[26] Her relationship with her father suffered for years. Meantime the eclipse of Madame d'Andlau left the court clear to Madame de Pompadour and their mutual friend Charles de Rohan, Prince de Soubise, a leading courtier recently married to a swarthy Hessian princess.

The Prince of Hesse-Philippsthal was commanding the garrison of Mons and lost little time in surrendering it on 10 July 1746. Stainville's regiment, which had been nourishing the siege from the north, was detailed to secure the gates. He politely called upon the Prince of Hesse, whose third surrender it was, and culled a specimen of his fatuous delivery to provide subsequent entertainment. 'After the capture of Mons', continued Stainville, 'the army of the Prince de Conti proceeded towards Charleroi and undertook its investment. The Prince de Conti had some anxieties during this siege.'[27] For the allied army of Prince Charles of Lorraine was bearing down from the Dutch frontier and threatening to separate Conti from Saxe. That marshal was criticized by Stainville for dawdling at Louvain before at last reacting by forced marches to cover Charleroi at the end of July from Walheim at little behind Ramillies in that countryside of classic campaigning. There Saxe met up with a force thrown out ahead by Conti under the command of the Count d'Estrées, the erstwhile admirer of Stainville's mother. Now d'Estrées's limiting orders vexed Saxe, who had been vainly urging Conti to effect their junction the other way on, by abandoning the siege of Charleroi. The tug between the two formed a dreary sequel to the French campaigns in Bohemia and Germany.

Before Saxe had got going, on the night of 28–29 July 1746, Conti had anxiously opened the siege of Charleroi, a strong fortress extensively mined. The French besiegers were suffering even more than Saxe's men from such sicknesses as purples and, especially, smallpox. All the villages around Charleroi were reeking of it so that the French generals and even their batmen were afraid to venture into their billets. It had turned terribly hot.

---

[24] Luynes, vii. 332, n. 1.   [25] Choiseul, *Mémoires*, p. 30.
[26] Kaunitz/Mémoire, p. 836.   [27] Choiseul, *Mémoires*, pp. 31–2 for the following.

The French attempted to abridge the siege by working upon the Austrian governor of Charleroi, described by Stainville as 'an old man of more than eighty years, who was called Monsieur de Beaufort. He was run by an old valet, whom we seduced by means of a spy, promising him a very large sum of money for himself and his master'. This episode supplied Stainville with another of the comic little stories with which he enlivened that flattish campaign.

Before the ancient governor could be seduced, however, Conti's men had gone punching into the siege of Charleroi in a triple attack on the night of 28–29 July. In this two battalions of Navarre were deployed from the direction of Montigny on the lower Sambre under Lieutenant-General the Marquis de La Fare, just up from capturing Saint-Ghislain. The pressure on Charleroi was maintained 'with much intelligence and vivacity',[28] and on 1 August it was subjected to a general bombardment. The defence, mostly Dutch, began to crumble. At four o'clock in the dawn of 2 August a French working-party of a score of pioneers leapt into an enemy outwork and, related the Count de Stainville, 'pursued the soldiers who were defending this work right into the body of the fortress, having no other arms but their tools. They[29] were supported in a moment by the troops in the trenches.'[30] Others from the captured lower town promptly boated around the moats, shouting *Vive le Roi!* The alarmed inhabitants made old Beaufort hoist the white flag. So, said Stainville, 'the town was taken by chance in the moment at which it was least expected'. An 'incredible event'[31] exulted another of the French besiegers. 'Anger and disappointment'[32] tersely commented the nearby General Ligonier commanding the few British troops in the Netherlands that year. The French conquest of Austrian Hainault was complete.

The helter-skelter storm of Charleroi after only four days of trench-warfare was a brilliant feat in that age of dragging sieges like the one which young Stainville and Conti had had to endure at Coni.

On the afternoon of 3 August 1746 Conti, who had been suffering from a 'very uncomfortable bile',[33] took the initiative in going to meet Saxe and concert at a lively conference in the château of Conroy near Saxe's headquarters. The successful Conti urged upon the more cautious Saxe a joint attack against Prince Charles of Lorraine. The Count de Stainville, who is a prime authority for this phase of the

---

[28] Major-General de Chauvelin to Count d'Argenson, camp before Charleroi, 31 July 1746: Arch. Guerre C., vol. 3139, no. 240.
[29] The French party.   [30] Choiseul, *Mémoires*, p. 32 for the following.
[31] Major-General de Chauvelin to Count d'Argenson, camp before Charleroi, 2 Aug. 1746: Arch. Guerre C., vol. 3148, no. 15.
[32] Lieutenant-General Ligonier: cited, R. Whitworth, *Field Marshal Lord Ligonier*, p. 129.
[33] Prince de Conti to Marshal de Saxe, Charleroi, 7 a.m., 2 Aug. 1746: Arch. Guerre C., vol. 3148, no. 19.

campaign, explained the strategic necessity of the French junction, but the question was which of the two 'should command the two armies reunited. It was scarcely possible to propose to the Prince de Conti that he should serve under the Marshal de Saxe. Besides his quality as a prince of the blood, he had been a lieutenant-general before the Count de Saxe; he had commanded an army at the same time as him; he thus had the infinite superiority of rank, of length of service, of equal army-command, and had just captured two important fortresses. On the other hand, how could they dare to remove the command from the Marshal de Saxe, who was regarded as the hero of France . . .?'[34]

'The Marshal de Saxe', continued the Count de Stainville, 'recognized all his advantages, maintained them with the German and indeed ridiculous haughtiness of a royal bastard, and all the more strongly and haughtily in that he had for antagonist a prince of the blood . . . Yet it was necessary either that one of them should serve under the other, or that one of them should quit the army.'

IV

In this dilemma the Prince de Conti chose the young Count de Stainville to carry to Versailles the astonishingly good news of the capture of Charleroi. Not only had the intrepid colonel evidently distinguished himself once again at Charleroi, but once more when his general was likely to be in a fix, as Noailles had been after Dettingen, was Stainville selected as spokesman to a court where his influence, perhaps, was already not negligible.

The Count de Stainville was, he explained, entrusted with letters from Conti to the king and the Minister of War as to the necessity of joining forces 'as well as his rights to the command of the whole.' Stainville added:

He explained himself very clearly . . . admitting no middle term and saying that, if the king did not entrust to him his Army of Flanders, he would return to court at once. The more the commission wherewith I was charged was agreeable for my promotion, which was not in doubt since I carried such interesting news as the capture of Charleroi, the more I felt the delicacy and the little success of my negotiation. I was not unaware, moreover, that Madame de Pompadour favoured infinitely the Marshal de Saxe and that, despite her presentation by the Princess de Conti, she neither esteemed nor liked her who had committed a base action for her.

Stephen de Stainville, riding some hundred and fifty miles, reached Paris at three o'clock on the morning of Thursday, 4 August 1746, and pressed on to Versailles. His tidings came to gladden a

---

[34] Choiseul, *Mémoires*, p. 33-4 for the following.

court plunged into mourning for the Dauphine, who had died a fortnight earlier after giving birth to a daughter and receiving news of the death of her father, King Philip V, on 9 July.

'On arriving at Versailles,' wrote the later Choiseul, 'I informed Monsieur d'Argenson, Minister of War, of the object of my commission. He did not disguise from me from the first moment that he would be very happy to assist the Prince de Conti in preference to Marshal de Saxe, but that he had not the strength. I handed to the King the letter from the Prince de Conti; I handed to Madame de Pompadour that which was addressed to her. I was very coldly received by this last.'

On that same day of 4 August 1746, however, the Count de Stainville duly received the promotion which had eluded him after Coni. His brevet as brigadier now recognized his 'good and faithful service ... wherein he has given proofs of his valour, courage, experience in war, activity and sound conduct'.[35] Next day he was accorded a gratuity of six thousand livres, though it looks as if it may have taken a little while for the money to materialize. The same treatment was given to the Chevalier de Maupeou, bearer of the standards captured at Charleroi; his military advancement was to run curiously parallel with that of Stainville, one day to fall foul of the elder brother, the Chancellor Maupeou. For the present Stainville's promotion in particular injured such as Colonel de Bonnac, in Saxe's army at Conroy, pained 'to see my junior pass in front of me.'[36] The career of successful men is strewn with jealous second-raters.

The Count de Stainville stayed two days at court. From the subsequent event it seems rather likely that he yet found time to celebrate by making love to his cherished mistress, the Marquise de Gontaut. Meanwhile everyone was buzzing with his news, just suited to its bearer, of the comical knock-down of old Beaufort. 'The more one learns', wrote Stainville's friend, Bernstorff, 'of the circumstances of the capture of Charleroi, the more this event seems singular and incredible.'[37] But the Marquis de Stainville hastened to assure the emperor that 'although my son, who has brought this news, has thereby found his promotion, I am none the less indignant at the poor defence which all the fortresses of the Low Countries have made, and this is most shameful.'[38]

[35] 'Brevet de Brigadier d'Infanterie pour M. le Mis. de Stainville du 4 Aoust 1746': Arch. Guerre: Archives Administratives 967: dossier of Duke de Choiseul.

[36] Colonel de Bonnac to Count d'Argenson, Conroy, 8 Aug. 1746: Arch. Guerre C., vol. 3140, no. 48.

[37] Baron von Bernstorff to King Christian VI, Paris, 8 Aug. 1746: Rigsarkiv/T.K.U.A. Frankrig, C. 255.

[38] Marquis de Stainville to Emperor Francis I, Paris, 7 Aug. 1746: Ö.S./H.H.S., Lothringisches Hausarchiv 77/177B for the following.

In the same dispatch the Marquis de Stainville reported: 'The public is praising highly the action of the Prince de Conti in having been to join Marshal de Saxe without knowing to which of them the general command will belong ... The largest party is for the prince, but the confidence of the king is in the marshal. I believe that when they shall be sure of not having any battle they will separate the two armies again in order to avoid this conflict.' The marquis could have had a tip here from his son.

On 6 August 1746 the Count de Stainville, reappointed that day in his new rank to Conti's army, set off for it from Versailles. He bore:

A reply from the King, who proposed to the Prince de Conti that he should command an army-corps on the Meuse, which army should be employed upon the siege of Namur when Marshal de Saxe should have thrown the enemy off the track. This middle term was not what was best for the King's service, but it showed the Prince de Conti the desire which the court had to satisfy him as much as was possible. The Prince de Conti, whatever the entreaties which I made to him, as did all those who were in his confidence, absolutely would not accept the course which the King proposed to him.[39]

Conti's military assessment was correct, his personal resolve fixed. From camp at Conroy at noon on 12 August 1746 he wrote tersely to Saxe: 'I am leaving, Monsieur the Marshal. You should have received orders to issue them to the armies. All is arranged in conformity with what we had agreed. You know, Monsieur the Marshal, the sincerity of my sentiments for you.'[40] Saxe disingenuously asked him that same day: 'Could I have had the misfortune to displease you, Monseigneur?'[41]

In both French armies mettlesome officers like the Chevalier de Belle-Isle had supported Conti's offensive inclinations. If Parisian opinion swung against the young prince for quitting, at court his reception was unexpectedly gracious. Madame de Pompadour was well suited by Conti's withdrawal, and the unification of command under her protégé removed the most pressing reason for the king's return to an infected front. Conti resumed the intimate round at court, to Choisy, to Crécy where he joined the king, the Marquis de Gontaut and the Marquise de Pompadour, who was to remain excluded from Conti's chief employment for the next decade at the head of the King's Secret. Now, indeed, he was granted the patent of a generalissimo, precluding subordination of his command in any

---

[39] Choiseul, *Mémoires*, pp. 34–5.
[40] Prince de Conti to Marshal de Saxe, camp at Conroy, noon, 12 Aug. 1746: Arch. Guerre C., vol. 3139, no. 263.
[41] Marshal de Saxe to Prince de Conti, 12 Aug. 1746: Arch. Guerre: Broglie/Saxe, i. 351.

future campaign. Only, there was none. The 'interval',[42] as Conti's absence was described to his own army, ended the military career of that hopeful prince of twenty-nine.

The then Count de Stainville wrote with understandable feeling that Conti 'left the army the next day but one[43] after my return, greatly to my regret, and this army, the very day of his departure, began to march to join that of Marshal de Saxe, who a little while later threw the enemy off from beneath Namur.'[44] It was besieged by the Count de Clermont while Saxe's main army, including Stainville's Regiment of Navarre, held off the enemy under Charles of Lorraine and Ligonier by skilful manoeuvring out ahead by Tongres. Saxe, still disinclined to punch the siege home, was incited by Noailles, back from Madrid. The citadel of Namur capitulated on 1 October. Virtually complete was the French conquest of the Austrian Netherlands.

V

With the Barrier Fortresses going down like ninepins the main soundings for peace that summer had swung over to Holland, following upon the Franco-Dutch conversations in Paris. It had been on campaign at Antwerp that the Marquis d'Argenson thought he detected in the king, mindful perhaps of other soundings, a measure of doubt and disparagement when his foreign minister proposed to him to send to the Hague as unofficial harbinger the Marquis de Stainville's old schoolfellow, Louis-Philogène Brulart, Marquis de Puysieulx, lately French ambassador at Naples. Puysieulx went, nominally for his health ('a finesse much out of season',[45] thought the Marquis de Stainville), only to be described by d'Argenson himself as a mediocrity of 'commonplace ideas which he made use of beneath an exterior of wisdom and reserve; nourished in the seraglio, he knew its folds and windings perfectly. Thus he is a nice courtier; he possesses all the wheedling ways of the Jesuits and the Italians and all the profundity of trifles.'[46] Puysieulx was subsequently to replace d'Argenson.

The Franco-Dutch soundings were at the beginning of July 1746 at last communicated by the British government to the Sardinian

[42] Count d'Argenson to Marquis de La Fare, 10 Aug. 1746: Arch. Guerre C., vol. 3139, no. 262.
[43] This would date the Count de Stainville's return to the Prince de Conti's headquarters as 10 August 1746, whereas he indicates that his departure from Versailles was on 6 August.
[44] Choiseul, *Mémoires*, p. 35.
[45] Marquis de Stainville to Emperor Francis I, Paris, 19 June 1746: Ö.S./H.H.S., Lothringisches Hausarchiv 77/177B.   [46] D'Argenson, iv. 346.

and Austrian allies. Maria Theresa was just then even less pacifically inclined than hitherto, hoping to recoup the loss of the Austrian Netherlands in Italy. There, since the Gallispans lost Milan, their fortunes had been going from bad to worse till on 16 June Don Philip and Maillebois were defeated by the Austrians and Sardinians at the battle of Piacenza. The first Austrian victory in pitched battle against the French in all that war was largely attributed to the skill of General von Browne, the unskill of General d'Aremburu who got himself and many others captured by involving troops in another fumbling attack like that at Villefranche wherein the Count de Stainville had participated two years earlier. A month after Piacenza Louis XV was writing of the Italian apanage proposed for Don Philip: 'I think that Tuscany would today occasion great difficulties.'[47] Parma, that prince's ultimate billet, was now proposed instead.

The fortunes of Don Philip were further depressed by the death, four days before Louis wrote, of King Philip V and the accession of Ferdinand VI, Don Philip's half-brother by the sister of Charles Emmanuel of Sardinia. Ferdinand was a well-intentioned but debile melancholic under the influence of his Portuguese wife, the graciously ugly Queen Maria Barbara, no friend of France. Her patronage of Farinelli, an Italian singer soothing to her moody husband, had the sprightly Bishop of Rennes reporting that only Portuguese and musicians could look for favour at the new court of Spain, where it was mainly Maria who succeeded to Elizabeth Farnese, to the gratification of d'Argenson. But the British government employed an Iberian expert, Benjamin Keene, and a certain Marquis of Tabernuiga, who had found refuge in England from the hostility of Elizabeth Farnese, to mount a diplomatic offensive through the Portuguese ally towards a separate peace with Spain.

The English offensive was said to be specially feared by Puysieulx. On return from the Hague 'he had confided everything to the brothers Pâris, who had constituted him the adviser and friend of Madame de Pompadour; he soon passed himself off as a great man',[48] significant confirmation of the direction of Madame de Pompadour in foreign affairs by the brothers Pâris. Puysieulx was now to be her confidant in foreign policy, and to return to Holland that September to represent France at the conference that was to meet at Breda to discuss terms of peace and, in the English intention, spin things out pending any results via Portugal. On 2 September 1746 the Marquis de Stainville was visiting an acquaintance in Paris when in walked the Marquis d'Argenson. He drew Stainville aside and expressed the

---

[47] King Louis XV to Marquis d'Argenson, 13 July 1746: ibid., p. 348, n. 1.
[48] Ibid., p. 350.

comprehensible fear that the Pragmatic Powers would spoil things at Breda by seeking to transform a snug Franco-Anglo-Dutch colloquy for peace into a general congress.

When, reported Stainville, he attributed his own diplomatic withdrawal to his 'indispositions' the French foreign minister 'received my excuses with a laughing and ironic air'.[49] The embarrassed envoy left and reluctantly reverted to his round of chores, dealing with the usual French complaints of infringements of Tuscan neutrality, securing passports, taking a creditable initiative, despite his awkward position, to protect the interests of Austrian prisoners of war who were being hauled into France from Mons and elsewhere. The disconsidered Marquis de Stainville was apparently instrumental in preventing 'these poor troops'[50] from being packed off to remote Roussillon in reprisal for the Austrian dispatch to Hungary of French prisoners taken in Italy; he also saw to the financial support of Austrian captives, raising funds for them privately with the help of friends in Paris, notably an English banker called Lambert who was already subventing Dutch prisoners.

The overture made to the Marquis de Stainville by the Marquis d'Argenson at the beginning of September 1746 suggests a certain disingenuousness in the indignant surprise evinced by the Marquis de Puysieulx a month later, at the opening of the Conference of Breda, when the introduction of the absent allies was proposed by the new Grand Pensionary, Gilles, and the British representative in the person of the fourth Earl of Sandwich, the ambitious protégé of the Duke of Bedford at the Admiralty. In disputing the composition of the conference for the rest of that year Puysieulx played considerably rough with d'Argenson's favourite Dutch, agreeably to others at Versailles, while rating young Sandwich 'a greenhorn (*blanc-bec*)'.[51] To him the French diplomatist one day explained: 'So long as your master shall have a hope of concluding something at Lisbon, he will make you here play the part of a chump (*soliveau*).'[52].

Keene was finding it heavy going at the remote court of Portugal where the palsied old King John V, father of the new Queen of Spain, was given over to religious mania and inaccessible even, it was said, to his prime minister, Cardinal da Mota. The Marquis d'Argenson sensed an opportunity to mount in concert with Don Louis d'Acunha another ultrasecret negotiation: only to come to grief once more, with Motta suggesting the dismissal of the tricky d'Argenson: a suggestion

---

[49] Marquis de Stainville to Emperor Francis I, Paris, 4 Sept. 1746: Ö.S./H.H.S., Lothringisches Hausarchiv 77/177B.

[50] Ibid., 9 Oct. 1746.

[51] Marquis de Puysieulx to Marquis d'Argenson, 7 Oct. 1746: Arch. Aff. Étr. C.P., Hollande; Broglie/Saxe, ii. 33.   [52] Ibid., 9 Oct. 1746.

which the excluded Chavigny, back in Lisbon, did not minute in a
dispatch reaching Versailles on 9 or 10 January 1747. At Lisbon,
meanwhile, Keene's hand had been weakened rather than strengthened by the arrival of Count Rosenberg to represent Austria at a
court which was for practical purposes headed by an Austrian queen,
the stupid sister of the late Emperor Charles VI. Now his daughter
in Vienna was again insisting that under the Treaty of Worms the
equivalent for her cessions to Sardinia should be allied assistance for
the Austrian reconquest of Naples. The poison injected by Carteret
into Anglo-Austrian relations was working through to kill any
English idea of detaching Spain from France.

Franco-Spanish relations in the Italian theatre had not, however,
been improved, after the defeat at Piacenza, by King Ferdinand's
replacement of des Gages by Conti's old antagonist, Las Minas. He
helped to fold up a campaign starved of reinforcements till the
Gallispans, abandoning their Genoese ally to enemy retribution,
found themselves by 18 October 1746 right back on the west bank of
the Var, back out of Italy. The invasion across the Var, in which the
Count de Stainville had led out in 1744, was rebounding against
France.

Count Rosenberg in Lisbon might urge the reconquest of Naples
but the Duke of Newcastle was particularly keen for the allies to take
a smack at Provence as a powerful diversion from Flanders, directly
against France. And the British government which paid the piper
mainly called the tune. The invasion of Provence was made ready by
one of Austria's most aggressive commanders, General Maximilian
von Browne. This new menace looming up against the French
homeland was part of the price of the victorious campaigning of the
Marshal de Saxe in the Netherlands.

VI

The Low Countries rather than the Latin south were to remain the
principal theatre for military, as for diplomatic, operations. The then
Count de Stainville wrote:

After the capture of Namur, the Marshal de Saxe, who had a mind to go into winter
quarters, waited with impatience for the enemy to recross the Meuse. They had
abandoned the headwaters of the Demer and had encamped with their left at Liége
and their right at the entrenched camp at Maestricht, the Meuse behind them. This
camp certainly had the air of a camp of separation. Yet they did not quit. The Court
pressed the marshal to attack them and proclaimed that he was going to march
against them in order to settle them. They remained. He marched slowly to give

them time to withdraw. A Prince of Waldeck, who was commanding the Dutch, induced the enemy army to receive battle. The Marshal de Saxe had advanced so far that it was no longer possible for him not to attack.[53]

The Count de Stainville clearly did not take kindly to Saxe after Conti. The emphasis upon Saxe's initial reluctance to attack was, however, accurate. Saxe told Frederick the Great that after taking Namur 'there was nothing left for us to do',[54] and had earlier indicated his desire to avoid taking on Charles of Lorraine with French troops, upon whose steadiness Saxe did not rely – not the general to endear himself to French infantry-officers such as Stainville. So late as 9 October 1746 the Chevalier de Belle-Isle, for instance, was reproaching Saxe for not exploiting the mistake of Charles of Lorraine in stringing out his allied forces along too broad and broken a front in a 'nursery-garden of ravines'[55] between the Meuse and its tributary Jaar. But the Saxon too had an eye to an opportunity, as well as pleasure.

Saxe and his dissipated generals, the Counts de Clermont and de Lowendahl, had been indulging themselves in camps of unprecedented luxury nourished by the rich and populous countryside. As one participant explained, 'the considerable expenditures which all these amenities involved were drawn from the immense contributions which could be exacted thanks to the rapid conquest of the Netherlands. It was through these channels of dissipation, and the costs which they necessitated on the spot, that the Belgian dominions of the house of Austria could provide the sums which were demanded of them.' [56] Amongst other things Saxe had been entertaining himself and his officers with a troupe of comic opera led by the poet Favart and his pretty little bride from Lunéville, La Chantilly, said to be fancied by the marshal. At the close of her performance on the evening of 10 October 1746, under secret orders through Favart, La Chantilly sang

Demain nous donnerons relâche . . .
Demain bataille, jour de gloire.[57]

Such was the announcement to the French army of the battle of Rocoux. La Chantilly was followed on the stage by the duty-officer:

---

[53] Choiseul, *Mémoires*, p. 35.
[54] Marshal de Saxe to King Frederick II, Tongres, 14 Oct. 1746: Arch. Guerre C., vol. 3143, no. 82.
[55] Lieutenant-General de Belle-Isle to Marshal de Belle-Isle, 9 Oct. 1746: Broglie/Saxe, i. 421, n. 1.
[56] Prince de Montbarey, *Mémoires autographes de M. le prince de Montbarey*, i. 30.
[57] C.S. Favart, *Mémoires et correspondance littéraires, dramatiques et anecdotiques de C.S. Favart*, ed. H. F. Dumolard (Paris, 1808), i. xxv. n.

post that night would call to action-stations: units would draw powder and ball at ten: 'each went to his duty with the same gaiety which had sped him to the play.'[58]

It rained that night. At dawn heavy mists of autumn shrouded the deployment of the armies, enormous for those times, possibly some 120,000 French troops elaborately ranged against an estimated 80,000 of the allies upon a frontage of about ten thousand yards: 'never was there a sight to compare with that presented by this immense plain to the first shafts of the sun on 11 October 1746.' The forces at Rocoux were indeed larger than in any previous battle of the eighteenth century. They loomed forward towards mass-warfare between hosts of national conscripts in crueller generations to come. The War of the Austrian Succession was enlarging the scale of continental warfare.

Immediately, however, there was a lull of two hours while the mists lifted and Saxe reconnoitred. His front-line troops meanwhile played leap-frog and danced with the *botteresses*, delivery-women out from Liége as usual, carrying upon their heads the daily milk, butter, and other provisions 'for the breakfast of these happy-go-lucky fellows ... until the moment when a drumbeat, repeated along the whole front of the army, recalled each to his post.'

From about noon the two armies were in confrontation, the enemy line based upon Ans, Rocoux, and Voroux. To the French 'the three entrenched villages seemed three citadels. In Flanders the villages are all entrenched naturally since, in almost all, each property is surrounded by an orchard enclosed by defensive hedges', with ditches.

It was afternoon before the French right under the Count de Clermont really got going in their successful drive against the Prince of Waldeck's Dutchmen in the village of Ans and in Sainte-Walburge, a suburb of Liége, itself yielded to the French the previous night. The Count de Clermont was known in the army as Clermont-Prince to distinguish him from the Marquis de Clermont-Gallerande who was commanding over towards the opposite, left flank. There in front of a Roman camp the Austrians under Prince Charles were cut off by broken terrain and held away from the critical centre where the Marshal de Saxe confronted the elite of the enemy, General Ligonier with twelve battalions of English, Hanoverian, and Hessian infantry strongly entrenched in the villages of Voroux and Rocoux. The two places were separated only by a little clearing planted with barley but cut into strips by hedges, preventing the French cavalry from intervening, as throughout the day in that broken terrain. Rocoux was a battle of infantry.

[58] Prince de Montbarey, *u.s.*, pp. 31f. for the following.

Looking from the French lines, Rocoux was covered on the right by 'a virtually impenetrable hedge'[59] bordering a sunken road. The main French attack on the village was therefore weighted on the left, over by Voroux. There, confronting the two villages centrally with Voroux to its left and Rocoux on the right, stood the pick of the French infantry, massed in four brigades. The first brigade consisted of the four battalions of the Count de Stainville's Regiment of Navarre.[60] It was about half past three that October afternoon, a little after Clermont's attack on Ans away to the right, that Stainville led his spearhead into the thick of the battle, this time against British, not Italian, infantry. But, as at Coni, Stainville's intrepid dash once again drove his men ahead of effective support from other units, some of which wilted at first under the remorseless fire of the Anglo-Hanoverians. A bit of confusion over precise objectives contributed to the French hold-up. In the words of an old narration: 'The Marquis [sic] de Stainville led on the brigade of Navarre; at half musket-shot from the villages of Rocoux and Voroux he received the order to halt until the columns which were marching on his left were come up equally to his own. Here he was very exposed to the enemy cannon and musket-fire, and lost very many men. The gallant Marquis de Stainville scaled the hedges of the village of Voroux and chased the enemy from one orchard after the other.'[61]

At about four o'clock Navarre stormed into Voroux at the bayonet-point, took it and thrust on to dent into Rocoux. Only at this critical juncture did the general directing this French attack, the Marquis d'Hérouville, unleash the brigades on Stainville's right, slap against Rocoux. Here the regiments of Orleans and Beauvoisis suffered comparably to Navarre. In all, it is said, fifty-two battalions of French infantry went surging into that milling conflict in less than one hour, wave upon wave of them rolling forward, breaking against the villages, swirling round about them. One French cavalry-general, the Duke de Boufflers, went in as an infantry volunteer in support of his son of fourteen, serving as a colonel and thrown over the entrench-ments by his father as they battled together. It took another half hour of 'frightful carnage'[62] before the outnumbered and resistant British with their German auxiliaries were prised out of Rocoux also. Many Hessian prisoners including their general, Prince von Issemburg, were stripped naked by the rapacious French soldiery.

[59] Lieutenant-General de Belle-Isle to Marshal de Belle-Isle, Saint-Siméon, 15 Oct. 1746: Arch. Guerre C., vol. 3149, no. 84.

[60] French order of battle at Rocoux, 11 Oct. 1746: ibid., no. 45.

[61] Baron O'Cahill, Geschichte der grössten Heerführer neuerer Zeiten (Rastadt, Karlsruhe, and Frankenthal, 1785–90), v. 242–3. Cf. Baron d'Espagnac, Histoire de Maurice, Comte de Saxe (Paris, 1775), ii. 256–7.   [62] Prince de Montbarey, u.s. p. 34.

The Marshal de Saxe set about rolling up the enemy from his right with his superior forces. British, Hanoverians, and Dutch beat it back across the Meuse in a hazardous but skilfully protected retreat. The broken terrain hampered exploitation by the French horse, and the early nightfall of autumn clamped down upon it. Saxe said that with two more hours of daylight the enemy would have been utterly destroyed. As it was, Rocoux, purchased with some 1,250 French lives and twice as many wounded,[63] remained a victory with no immediate morrow. The Chevalier de Belle-Isle, who had again distinguished himself, was to be disappointed in his hope that the political fruits of Rocoux would be richer than the military.

Brigadier de Stainville had come through unscathed but the price paid by his regiment was, in significant modification of overall proportions, 140 men killed and 128 wounded, plus 26 officers – some quarter of their total – with 'terrible wounds':[64] Captain Malpoix shot through the lower abdomen and with a broken arm, another captain with a large part of one thigh shot away by a cannon-ball, and so on and so forth: the grim reckoning of their response to the commands of Saxe and the singing of La Chantilly. As had been announced on the eve of battle, the night of its morrow was duly graced by a performance of *Les Amours grivois*, to which Favart contributed a magnanimous verse in praise of English valour also.

Never a flowery chronicler, Stainville later recorded simply that his regiment 'had carried Rocoux and had done very well':[65] once again no description of his own valour in battle. He had, however, played a leading part in what was, in that century, the largest battle to date and one of the few infantry engagements wherein the French defeated the British. One may feel that the personal valour of the future Duke de Choiseul against the English redcoats at Rocoux in some sense blooded him as the great antagonist of Great Britain in the world-wide conflict of after years.

Typical, again, of Choiseul was that in his memoirs, instead of playing up a victory to which he had signally contributed, he played it down in criticism of his commander:

We won a battle which we could not lose,[66] but we nowise profited from it to destroy the enemy, because the Marshal de Saxe was very careful to preserve the enemy so as to have an army to fight the following year. The Marshal de Saxe has been much

---

[63] Following 'État des Officiers et Soldats tués ou blessés à la Bataille de Raucoux le 11 8ᵇʳᵉ 1746': Arch. Guerre C., vol. 3149, no. 58. Somewhat lower figures are, however, given without source in Pajol, iii. 490, no. 1.

[64] De Séchelles to Count d'Argenson, Tongres, 12 Oct. 1746: Arch. Guerre C., vol. 3143, no. 55.

[65] Choiseul, *Mémoires*, pp. 35–6 for the following.

[66] Cf. the similar if more generous judgement of Pajol, iii. 489.

praised because he has been fortunate and because good luck always has the advantage of being exalted. Yet one must admit that the good fortune of Monsieur de Saxe was sustained by an army at least twice as strong as that of the enemy, and that this army was operating in Flanders where he had every means of subsistence and commodities in profusion. I noticed, besides, that the Marshal de Saxe in no way had at heart either the interest or the glory of the king's arms; he thought only of perpetuating his command at the head of the army and in Flanders in order to extract for his profit as much money as he could from his conquests. So he left the enemy every facility for conducting their retreat quietly to beneath Maestricht. He so to speak suspended victory, and no profit was derived from the battle of Rocoux.

The future Duke de Choiseul's criticism of the Marshal de Saxe may have tended towards excess, for instance by reference to the latter's approach earlier that year to the critic's own father on behalf of peace – assuming, as one is inclined to, that it was sincere. But independent evidence in relation to Saxe's next victory at Lawfeldt[67] lends rather sinister point to Choiseul's critique of Rocoux.

The geographical context of Choiseul's military criticism is in any case suggestive. Despite such unpleasantness as the smallpox around Charleroi, one can appreciate that the gradual French advance in strength across the familiar fields of fertile Flanders may have seemed almost cushy campaigning to one who had seen distant service in Bohemia and in the terrible retreat from Prague, and to and fro across the very Alps, both campaigns infected by the cruel warfare of total enmity with partisans. Saxe too had briefly shone at Prague and again shewn his sudden daring, if not against London itself, then in seizing Brussels. Yet it remains true that his famous victories – Fontenoy, Rocoux, Lawfeldt – stand rather as the final term in that classic tradition of limited warfare unfolded in the Low Countries by the great captains of the Roi Soleil. Whereas the later Duke de Choiseul, man of his time though he was, in military as in other spheres, went reaching out ahead of it. More modern and more ruthless were the ideas of one who was later to project, as a pioneer, the mechanical propulsion of artillery and, in the midst of peace, no declaration of war to lame sudden invasion of the inviolable fastness of the British Isles.

All that, though, lay in the mists of the future. The immediate concern of the youthful Brigadier de Stainville was the ever interesting one of leave now that the battle was won and the army about to disperse into winter-quarters in the good old tradition. When, two days after Rocoux, Stainville applied to his commander, 'the Marshal de Saxe, to whom I had never spoken in my life, paid me a compliment upon the conduct of my regiment and upon my own'.

[67] Cf. p. 694.

On the evening after Rocoux the hitherto critical Saxe had said over supper, 'Now I have made it up with the infantry.'[68] The marshal reported to the Minister of War: 'I have never seen such valour.'[69]

VII

At Rocoux the Count de Stainville had earned his permission from the Marshal de Saxe 'to go to Lorraine to receive an inheritance which was inconsiderable but which gave me all the more pleasure in that the lands which I was inheriting were the first real property which I had possessed'.[70] This inheritance was the barony of Beurey and Mussey from his godfather, Count Jean-François de Stainville, who had died there at the age of seventy-eight the day before Rocoux, on 10 October 1746. From Rocoux to Beurey is less than a hundred and fifty miles, and Stephen de Stainville was never one for dawdling with opportunity. No later than 18 October did he assume legal possession of his inheritance by the intermediary of Sieur Jussy in a deed drawn by Jussy's partner, Armand, notary of Bar-le-Duc.[71]

The death of the Count Jean-François extinguished the old line of Stainville. Its merger into that of Choiseul was now completed. For Beurey it was an extreme change of fortune. Its late lord, the crusty old bachelor, had been born, had lived and died at Beurey. Now the little village underpinned the resounding career of the future Duke de Choiseul. And there is evidence,[72] apart from the suggestion of his memoirs, that he did visit and remain at Beurey at least till the end of October 1746.

Beside the river Saulx that autumn, briefly at all events, the young Count de Stainville was to be found in his first enjoyment of 'the goods, rights and revenues depending upon the lands and barony of Beurey and Mussey, having domainal jurisdiction and woodmote (*prévôte et grurie*) ... the seigneurial house with its gardens appurtaining and its dependencies, a dovecote, a house for the farmer near the château, another for the vinedresser'.[73] The banal winepress

[68] Marquis de Valfons, *Souvenirs du Marquis de Valfons*, ed. Georges Maurin (Paris, 1906), p. 175.
[69] Marshal de Saxe to Count d'Argenson, Château de Bettot, 13 Oct. 1746: Arch. Guerre C., vol. 3143, no. 65.   [70] Choiseul, *Mémoires*, p. 36.
[71] Arch. Meuse, C. 596, fo. 7: cited, H. de La Perrière, *Beurey: ses seigneurs et leurs demeures*, p. 35.
[72] Arch. Meuse, J 18[19]: 'Comptes de la baronie [*sic*] de Stainville, 1741–1785': account for 1747, 'chapitre de dépence', item 1 for a payment of 521 livres 'suivant l'arreté de Compte de mon dit seigneur [Choiseul] à Beuré le 30ᵉ 8ᵇʳᵉ 1746 cy': cf. also p. 772. Thus Henri de La Perrière, op. cit., p. 39, was too unassuming in describing Beurey, in relation to Choiseul, as 'la modeste baronnie qu'il ne visita sans doute jamais'.
[73] Arch. Meuse, J 18[27]: 'Baronnie de Beurey-sur-Saulx. Titres généraux. Biens et droits à Beurey-sur-Saulx, 1315-1786', docket III, 'Beurey. Bail de la Baronnie'.

was just beside the Jardin de l'Isle, a large property acquired back in 1713 by Count Jean-François so that his new house, facing south, should look out on something better than a huddle of hovels and plots – they gave way to an outlying orchard for their lord, down by the river with the warren of Robert-Espagne out beyond. That way lay the lands of the superior Count de Couvonges.

When the lordship of Couvonges had been held by that widowed countess, Catherine Diane de Beauvau, who became Countess de Rouerke and the young Count de Stainville's godmother, she had given his godfather quite a bit of trouble. She had originally enjoyed the high justice of Beurey while he held the low and middle justice. This involvement had been sorted out in favour of the elder Count de Stainville but dependent Mussey had apparently remained different again. And when young Stainville now took over at Beurey he found, for instance, that in the ownership there of the mills, banal in origin, he was still going halves with the Count de Couvonges, who had leased his share to the under-farmer of his revenues, one Nicholas Seroux. Such was the gradual though incomplete shift of emphasis from feudal jurisdiction to leased utilities, such the muffled advance in social and economic relationships under the old regime.

That there was some real advance is suggested by the evidence of several mills at little Beurey, some at least, apparently, of fairly recent construction and for processing not only grain but also hemp. Hemp-growing was one strand in that mixed economy in miniature; another was sheep-farming, with a sizeable seigneurial flock. Young Stainville moved into Beurey in good time to cash in on the half-yearly rent due on 25 October under the nine-year lease of 1740 for the mills of Beurey. Their total annual rental was five hundred French livres plus a depreciation-allowance of six livres 'for the diminution of the millstones of the said mills', plus 'twelve pounds of processed hemp in kind, six fat capons alive and in feather, and six oranges, half to the said lord Count de Stainville, the other half to the said Seroux'.[74] Unless the latter had exercised their option of a six-year break, all this was still due from 'Jean Maybel, wheelwright, and Françoise Eloy his wife residing at Vassincourt': another instance, after those from Stainville itself, of the leased delegation of a feudal squeeze to little rural entrepreneurs, and of the legal association of husband and wife in such undertakings.

The lease of the mills at Beurey contrasted with the commutation back in 1710 of the rights of the banal oven, presumably more onerous and less useful to the villagers than the milling. They accordingly

[74] 'Bail des moulin[s] de Beurey ... le 25 avril 1740': ibid. docket VII, 'Beurey: Moulin', and for the following.

now owed the Count de Stainville an annual 'due of twenty sols per each full household, and of ten sols per half household [i.e. single persons], to take the place of the banal right of the oven'.[75] But, as is apt to be the way with commutations of unpopular rights, by 1746 the villagers of Beurey were refusing to pay up. If this was in the nature of a try-out against a new lord, they had picked the wrong man, as was to appear next year.

Almost inevitably, things were rather different in the rest of the little barony, at the hamlet of Beurey-la-Petite and at Mussey. There, for instance, the banal oven had been commuted some fourteen years later than at Beurey and upon a tariff more complicated and more than twice as stiff: fifty sols per full 'husbandman's household'[76] and forty for a labourer's, with bachelors and spinsters also differentiated as between those at work (twenty-five sols) and the aged who paid twenty. These higher rates apparently included an allowance for the making over to the villagers of the oven-house itself – a suggestion, perhaps, that at Mussey at least its communal function was not exhausted. The Count de Stainville, however, drew only marginally more in proportion from the oven of Mussey than from that of Beurey because he had to halve the proceeds from the former with the chapter of Saint-Pierre at Bar-le-Duc. Feudal prolongation rendered a clear separation of domains as rare locally as one between nations was upon the international level. Hence, partly, the close-knit society of that age and the difficulty of any partial reform of vested interests endlessly overlapping.

There was plenty for Count Stephen de Stainville to learn that October when he came to settle up accounts at Beurey. His agent there was François Carré, who became a favourite and faithful retainer of the future Choiseul and was in a few years to replace Nicholas Mathieu, not without grievous heartburning, as procurator-fiscal and receiver of the whole marquisate of Stainville. There too a new regime under the new master was already getting under way. The marquisate significantly headed the other estates in the following item of account: 'Paid to the Chancellery of Lunéville for the letters of faith and homage of Stainville, Beurey and Mussey of this 10th April 1747, 177 livres, 12 sous, 6 deniers'[77] – it cost a further 90 livres, 18 sous a fortnight later to have these letters registered by the Chambre des Comptes at Bar-le-Duc. On 3 June 1747 another 9 sous,

[75] Plea of the Count de Stainville against the inhabitants of Beurey, 26 June 1747: ibid., docket VIII, 'Beurey: Four banal'.
[76] 'Acte par lequel M. le Comte de Stainville et M. M. de St. Pierre de Bar ont abandonné aux habitants de Mussey l'emplacement du four banal et la bannalité d'iceluy', 1 Apr. 1724: Arch. Meuse, J 18²⁸, docket II.
[77] Stainville accounts for 1747: ibid., J 18¹⁹.

6 deniers procured for the Count de Stainville a legal power of attorney to authorize the provost of Stainville, Jacques de Lescaille, to act for his master in 'taking possession of the estate and marquisate of Stainville by, for and in the name of the said Lord of Stainville'.[78] Such was the legal registration of that act, executed before a solicitor at Bar-le-Duc on 21 June 1747 at a cost of 3 livres, 6 deniers and as much again for a separate transaction in respect of Ménil-sur-Saulx as a distinct dependency of the marquisate now passing into fresh hands.

It is not entirely clear what legal and financial arrangement the Marquis de Stainville may have made with his son and heir for his taking over the marquisate. It was nine years since the marquis had granted administrative power of attorney to his wife; now he may have taken the opportunity of his son's enthusiasm for his inheritance at Beurey to combine generosity with a further devolution upon him of the cares and chores of the management of the main family property already entailed on him. It may indeed have been then, in 1746 or 1747 rather than three years later, that the Marquis de Stainville gave his son further cause for gratitude by taking the very handsome initiative, in legal phraseology from 1750, 'of the abandonment which the said lord has made and approved to the profit of the said lord . . . his son of the usufruct and enjoyment of the said estate'[79] of Stainville. Certain it is that, after a suggestive gap for 1746 in the series of Stainville estate-accounts, those for 1747 onwards were rendered by Mathieu no longer to the Marquis de Stainville but 'to the very high and mighty lord, Monseigneur the Count de Stainville, brigadier of the armies of the King, colonel of the Regiment of Navarre, lord (*seigneur*) of Stainville, Lavincourt, Montplonne and Ménil-sur-Saulx, dependent upon the marquisate of Stainville':[80] but not of separate Bazincourt.

Immediately, however, the chief pride and interest of the Count de Stainville in that autumn of 1746 lay in that little barony of Beurey which had been created five days before he was born thanks to his godfather's patient policy of territorial expansion by purchase. Four years after the erection of 1719 Count Jean-François had further rounded out his estates by buying from a widow Poupart houses and lands, with fields of corn and hemp. Despite such expenditure the thrifty old bachelor had left his godson with something better in

---

[78] 'Registre des acts des Nottaires et sous seign privé', 16 April–4 July 1747: ibid., C. 599, fo. 43.
[79] Marriage contract, 'Mariage, 6 & 12 X^bre 1750: Mr. le Comte de Stainville avec Mlle Du Châtel': Arch. Nat., Minutier Central des Notaires, dossier XXX/319.
[80] Stainville accounts for 1747: *u.s.*

hand than that tribute of capons and oranges. The young count recalled: 'I found in the estate twenty thousand écus in ready cash, which the Marquis [sic] de Stainville, from whom I was inheriting, had been sixty years in amassing and which I consumed in the course of the winter.'[81] Years later the Duke de Choiseul was to write to Voltaire: 'One must never be afraid of things done.'[82]

A spending spree in Paris was indicated for the lucky young blade in that winter of 1746–7. And one does catch or nearly catch one glimpse of him at about that time, spanking by in his equipage with a running footman in splendid livery out in front, to echoed comment from bystanders that 'Monsieur de Stainville is a good economist. He has a year's revenue ahead of him.'[83]

The later Choiseul was notoriously extravagant. That was precisely the impression which he wished to create. Conspicuous consumption and extravagance, like frailty in a woman, were among the fashionable failings, than which there is no truer mirror of an age. For the then Count de Stainville, however, the underlying reality comprised all those petty dues and tangled revenues back in the Barrois, the care with which he was to see to his estate accounts, as later to the budgets of his government departments.

Youth, though, is for pleasure, and so is a mistress. The Count de Stainville's Marquise de Gontaut was pregnant that winter. The Marquis de Gontaut as usual spent much of his time at court dancing, or acting, attendance upon the Marquise de Pompadour. Her celebrated theatre rigged up by the Escalier des Ambassadeurs at Versailles was in full swing that season. In the New Year of 1747 one hears of Gontaut acting 'mediocrely'[84] – not up to Stainville's other friend, the Duke de Nivernais – in La Chaussée's Le Préjugé à la mode and Dufrény's L'Esprit de contradiction. Half the fun of it of course lay in excluding from the little auditorium all but the chosen few. A week earlier, for a performance of Tartuffe featuring Nivernais, d'Ayen, and Meuse, admittance had been refused to the Prince de Conti, the Marshal de Noailles and his younger son, the count, d'Ayen's brother. A fairly frequent spectator, however, was Madame de Pompadour's old friend, Bernstorff. Whereas his friend Stainville probably focused his immediate interest more upon the Gontaut–Biron residence in the Rue de Richelieu than upon the Pompadour's theatre in exalted circles which were as yet hardly for him.

[81] Choiseul, Mémoires, p. 36.
[82] Duke de Choiseul to Voltaire, Versailles, 28 May 1759: P. Calmettes, Choiseul et Voltaire, p. 22.
[83] Cited, K. von Schlözer, Choiseul und seine Zeit, p. 29.
[84] Luynes, viii. 91.

VIII

In Paris that was the winter of dancing jacks (*pantins*) 'so that one could not go into any house without finding some hung upon every chimneypiece'.[85] This Parisian craze for cardboard cutouts, with limbs worked from behind by strings, employed even such artists as Boucher. Often manipulated by hidden threads of policy were those dancing jacks who postured for a spell upon the crowded stage of European diplomacy towards the close of the long complication of the War of the Austrian Succession.

More active than the desultory soundings for peace at Breda and at Lisbon was the partly related scheming at this crux of affairs for an advantageous bride to fill the 'furious void'[86] left for the Dauphin by the death of his Spanish wife. The later Duke de Choiseul recalled:

This prince wished to marry the second Infanta, sister of the late Dauphine. Spain passionately desired this marriage. The court of Rome would have made no difficulty as to the dispensation[87] ... The king objected to the very ardent wishes of his son, to the soundest policy, which was beyond question to unite himself to Spain by all possible ties. The same man who very illicitly had had all the sisters of one family was not willing to allow his son to have in marriage two Infantas of Spain.

In accordance with this ridiculous scruple a daughter of the King of Sardinia, cousin-german of the king [Louis], was assuredly what best suited the Dauphin. The King of Sardinia was at war against France. I do not think that the marriage of his daughter would have made him change his system; but it would have been possible, in the negotiation of the marriage, to induce him to be a mediator. The English were tired; the house of Austria had lost Flanders and the Breisgau; I think that, by means of the King of Sardinia who must have desired the end of the war, one could have made at Turin a more honourable and more advantageous peace than that which was made the following year at Aix-la-Chapelle. This peace deserved all the more attention in the Italian part in that King Philip V had died at the same time as the late Dauphine and that, by his death, the Spanish army had lost all zeal for conquests in Italy for the Infant Don Philip.[88]

Choiseul added:

The King, by nature without any sense of political combination, would have been disposed to marry his son to a princess of Savoy. He even had it spoken of to the King of Sardinia, and a negotiation regarding this alliance was broached and some promises given; but all of a sudden Marshal de Saxe persuaded Madame de Pompadour that it would be infinitely more suitable that the Dauphin should marry a Saxon princess ... It happened that the Marquis de Paulmy, son of the Marquis

[85] Barbier, iv. 212.

[86] King Louis XV to Bishop of Rennes, Choisy, 26 July 1746: Arch. Aff. Étr. C.P., Espagne, vol. 461: Zévort, p. 51.

[87] To marry a deceased wife's sister.   [88] Choiseul, *Mémoires*, pp. 37–9 for the following.

d'Argenson, was travelling in Germany and had not been so badly received at
Dresden as his demeanour and his face might make one fear; this induced his father
... to applaud the will of Madame de Pompadour; so that, without considering that
Saxony, after having been France's ally at the beginning of this war, had abandoned
us in our distress in Bohemia and had connected herself with the house of Austria,
without examining the fact that this [Saxon] alliance could be of no use to the
kingdom [of France] either for the present or for the future, after having rejected the
Spanish alliance and been wanting in good faith and honesty regarding that with
Turin, they decided in favour of a Saxon one.

The Marquis d'Argenson himself confirmed that the Saxon bride's
'personal qualities were of more interest than the political conditions
of her alliance ... after having averted the Spanish one'.[89] Whereas
Choiseul's scathing retrospect was in keeping with the Spanish
sympathies of his two early protectors, Noailles and also Conti,
scarcely likely to welcome an alliance with his Saxon competitors for
Poland. Choiseul's analysis was, as often, broadly accurate even if he
neglected, for instance, the eviction from Italy of the Gallispan armies
and corresponding elevation of the terms of the King of Sardinia (at
least Savona, now, in addition to Finale). Louis XV had in fact
mentioned the possibility of a Saxon princess, as well as a Sardinian
one, in his letter of 31 August 1746 to King Ferdinand VI, turning
down the Infanta Antonia under stimulus from d'Argenson. Two
months later the Marshal de Saxe, mobilized by the artful Saxon
minister in Paris, was reporting to his half-brother, Augustus III:
'Madame de Pompadour has been very useful to us, for she is on the
best terms with the queen, who still has a little corner of
Stanislasism'[90] against the Saxon supplanters of her father in Poland.
Choiseul was well informed here since Saxe's part remained secret, as
had his soundings that spring with the Marquis de Stainville.

The Marshal de Saxe swung over his old patron, Noailles, and
Maurepas, another leading hispanophil and lever on the queen. Saxe
also acknowledged great help from 'the Pâris ... They have ever been
my intimate friends and they are the most honest people and the best
citizens: which few Frenchmen are.' On 26 November 1746, two days
after the memorial service in Notre Dame for the late Spanish
Dauphine, it was announced that the Dauphin would marry the
fifteen-year-old Saxon Princess Maria Josepha. Saxe had given his
word that she would 'have a Duke of Burgundy before the end of
next year'.[91]

---

[89] D'Argenson, v. 63.
[90] Marshal de Saxe to King Augustus III, Brussels, 27 Oct. 1746: Saxon archives, cited
Vitzthum/Saxe, pp. 63–6 for the following.
[91] Marshal de Saxe to Queen of Poland, Brussels, 26 Oct. 1746: ibid., pp. 68–9 for the
following.

The marshal entered into the trousseau of the princess, who preferred dark colours. Silk dresses of Indian or Persian design would, suggested Saxe, score off the ladies at Versailles ('all as witty as devils, and equally spiteful') since such imports into France were normally prohibited. Nor, in that feminine century, did he overlook her underclothes. Nowhere, pronounced Saxe, did they make 'whalebone corsets so well as at Dresden'; only, one should watch 'that the tailor does not make the waist too long. It is a fault into which our tailors fall, and it gives an awkward appearance and renders the skirts too short, which is not to the taste of the master of this court'.[92]

One point which Saxe could not encompass was Count Brühl's plea to be spared 'the embarrassment of the visit of the Duke de Richelieu with his train'[93] of eighty, including young Paulmy, on special embassy to Dresden to conclude the marriage-contract. For the Marquis d'Argenson this would further the Franco-Saxon rapprochement inaugurated by a treaty of the preceding April[94] and, in general, that appeasement and neutralization of the Holy Roman Empire which was one of the most successful aspects of his policy. Here nothing was more important for the prussophil d'Argenson than the promotion of detente and concert between Frederick and Augustus 'even if it should only be in appearance',[95] as Louis, in his wan realism, intimated to Saxe.

Count Brühl, much more of a diplomatist that the Marquis d'Argenson in the best and worst senses, was set on giving the Franco-Saxon rapprochement an opposite, Austrian orientation against Prussia, as might have happened the year before, and was to a decade later. And Saxon ties with Austria tended towards Russia, especially since the conclusion on 26 July 1746 of an Austro-Russian defensive alliance, terminating the estrangement over the luckless Botta, now busy on behalf of Austria in mulcting his compatriots, the overrun Genoese. This Saxon set hardly flattered d'Argenson's other aim, against the interests of the Prince de Conti, of bolstering Saxon authority and even hereditary succession in Poland as a neutralizing buffer against Russia. The policy of Saxony and her Polish apanage was conditioned by the circumjacent power-factors, Prussia, Austria, and Russia. As Choiseul indicated, France could no more draw solid support from that policy than when Saxony had let her down over the Bohemian debacle: even less so, indeed, since no French troops

---

[92] Marshal de Saxe to Queen of Poland, Versailles, 1 Dec. 1746: ibid. p. 100.
[93] Count Brühl to Marshal de Saxe, Warsaw, 26 Nov. 1746: ibid., p. 105.
[94] Cf. p. 637.
[95] Marshal de Saxe to King Augustus III, Brussels, 27 Oct. 1746: Vitzthum/Saxe, p. 64.

now stood on German soil. A good deal of the Duke de Choiseul's later statecraft in regard to the Russian and Spanish extremities of Europe was implicit in his critique of the affiance of the Dauphin to the Princess Maria Josepha.

If the marriage did little immediately for France, it did less for her foreign minister for all his boasting that his part in it was 'rather that of a prime minister than of a simple secretary of state'.[96] Whereas the title of prime minister was now to be conferred upon Count Brühl, whose fall the Marquis d'Argenson had in his time clumsily sought to stimulate. This was reciprocated by the 'dearest little rascal (*allerliebst Schelmchen*)',[97] as Saxe called Brühl, assuring him by 10 December 1746: 'The d'Argensons are tottering ... The one for foreign affairs is so stupid that the king is ashamed of it ... Here they are beginning to suspect Messieurs d'Argenson of not sincerely wanting peace. It is a petard. If it is lit, they will be blown up ... All are persuaded that I desire it [peace]; and that is true ... The marquis [d'Argenson] is not disposed to listen to anything which comes in the name of the court of Vienna, and says very strange things on that head.'[98] Choiseul's doubts as to Saxe's loyalty to the French government were explicable.

Five days later Saxe's mentor and confidant, the Marshal de Noailles, addressed to the king a long memorandum attacking the whole policy of his old enemy, the Marquis d'Argenson, and calling for his dismissal. Now was the time, wrote Noailles, 'to turn towards the court of Vienna and to renounce the idea of annihilating the house of Austria, a project equally unjust and chimerical'.[99] Noailles particularly recalled d'Argenson's statement 'to M. de Stainville and to M. Gross that Your Majesty would oppose the [imperial] election of the grand duke, and that you would use your last soldier against it. Those are the terms which were used, and which have never left my memory ... A false system has been the cause of all these mistakes.'

The alternative, Austrian system was that of the French powers behind the scenes, Noailles and Saxe, the brothers Pâris, the Pompadour. For her, opposition to d'Argenson was a perfect lay, enabling her for once to gratify both the rival heroes, Conti as well as Saxe. D'Argenson was also coming under fire from Lisbon. And now in Dresden the Duke de Richelieu, as the luckless minister came to realize, was working behind his back. Richelieu revealed to Brühl on the Boxing Day of 1746 that his secret mission was to encourage

[96] D'Argenson, v. 69.
[97] Marshal de Saxe to Count Brühl, Brussels, 27 Oct. 1746: Vitzthum/Saxe, p. 72.
[98] Marshal de Saxe to Count Brühl, Paris, 10 Dec. 1746: ibid., pp. 109–10.
[99] Memorandum from Marshal de Noailles to King Louis XV, 15 Dec. 1746: Rousset, ii. 255–7 for the following.

Saxon good offices in promoting a direct arrangement between France and Austria. From Dresden a courier was dispatched next day to Count Christian Loss, who represented Saxony at the Austrian court as his brother, Count John Adolf Loss, did at the French.

Count John Adolf had already been trying to edge the Marquis d'Argenson in the same direction. But he seemed wedded to the terms mooted with the Dutch the previous spring, including the cession of Tuscany to Don Philip, and to the treaties of Worms and of Dresden, consecrating Austrian losses to Sardinia and Prussia. After Loss had heard of Richelieu's overture, he reported on 6 January 1747 that d'Argenson still 'did not relish the idea of making Dresden the centre of the negotiation'.[1] Rather more lay behind that than has hitherto appeared. For d'Argenson was already seeking, if only in despair, to give renewed effect to his preference of the preceding year for seeking accommodation with Austria most secretly in Paris.

[1] Count J. Loss to Count Brühl, Paris, 6 Jan. 1747: Vitzthum/Saxe, p. 146.

CHAPTER VII

LAWFELDT

I

Sire,
The Abbé Alary, an intimate friend of Monsieur d'Argenson, Secretary of State for Foreign Affairs, who eighteen months ago had put some proposals to me on behalf of this minister, and whom I had not seen since, has come to see me and has told me that there had come into his head an idea with which he wished to acquaint me, but that it was only as from himself that he was speaking to me.[1]

Thus began the Marquis de Stainville to the Holy Roman Emperor on New Year's Day of 1747. Stainville reported 'word for word' on Alary:

He thought that at present it would be a favourable time for broaching a negotiation between the Queen Empress and France, that he saw that the conferences at Breda would produce nothing, and that even if they turned into a congress at the Hague, as appeared likely, it would be subject to protractions very prejudicial to the two parties; that it would be thus more to the purpose, under an inviolable secrecy, to establish a negotiation here, into which there would enter only the Minister of Foreign Affairs, the Duke of Huescar, the [special] Spanish ambassador, and myself; that everything was divided into parties in England, where the government was composed but of three sorts of person, frantic and furious people, pacific people, and flabby people (*gens mous*) who were neither for nor against. That as for the king [George II], everybody knew what that was – those were his [Alary's] own terms; that it would thus be much more to the purpose to treat directly with France. One must get out of the hands of these Dutch, who were the cause of all the mischiefs which had happened, not having known how to make either war or peace. He thereafter tried to flatter my self-esteem by presenting me with the fine picture of contributing in some sort to the general pacification of Europe.

'After all this rigmarole of useless words', continued the marquis, I replied to him that he apparently did not remember what I had said to him at the time of his first proposals ... that the Queen Empress would never listen to any proposition except in concert with her allies ... It would be simply useless for me to report what he said to me, because I should not receive any answer, or else it would be the same as I had already received.'

[1] Marquis de Stainville to Emperor Francis I, Paris, 1 Jan. 1747: Ö.S./H.H.S., Lothringisches Hausarchiv 77/177A for the following.

Alary drew right back and begged Stainville 'not to make any use of what had been said to me'. Two days later, however, the Abbé returned to say that upon reflection 'he thought he had found a means of contenting everybody; that a negotiation had been secretly broached at Lisbon in order to make peace between Spain and England, that France was not entering into it but that she wished that this negotiation should succeed since it would be one difficulty less in arriving at a general peace; it was natural that France' should broach a parallel negotiation with Austria to complement that at Lisbon towards procuring a general pacification. Stainville agreed to report this while reiterating its uselessness. For Alary, he observed, 'was proposing an injustice to me, in wishing to have the Spanish ambassador as an associate in the proposed negotiations, and not wishing to admit into it the allies of the Empress'. Stainville concluded:

The proposal seemed to me revolting ... I judge that two motives have occasioned it: the first the [Austrian] irruption into Provence; the second and the more urgent for the minister is that he sees himself as so to speak overthrown and soon out of office unless he finds means to render himself necessary in some respect. I believe this second motive to be the stronger, for unhappily one only too often sees ministers in office thinking more of maintaining themselves there than of the true good of the state.

The Marquis d'Argenson might not, perhaps, have attempted his last fling towards Austria had he not previously failed to bolster his position through his favourite foreigner, the King of Prussia, reluctant just then to let France in on his pursuit of a defensive alliance with Sweden against Russia, already impending over the political combinations of Europe. Frederick was well enough aware that d'Argenson's stock was sinking and on 10 January 1747 the king authorized Le Chambrier to tell him 'that it nowise suits me to play Don Quixote for France'.[2]

That same evening of 10 January 1747, the Marquis d'Argenson had just finished a dinner given by his brother to celebrate the marriage of the latter's son to little Mademoiselle de Mailly-d'Hautcourt when a letter from the king was handed to the foreign minister to inform him that he was dismissed. At the same time a letter to his brother confirmed him as Minister of War and further granted him the privileged access of the grandes entrées at court. The price of his escape was said to have been a little arrangement concerning the Marshal de Saxe, who informed Count Brühl: 'Well,

---

[2] King Frederick II to Baron Le Chambrier, Berlin, 10 Jan. 1747: Politische Correspondenz, v. 288–9.

my dear count, the petard has blown up!... They have made me a
marshal-general of camps and armies ... On the military score I
cannot climb higher, or it will become a breakneck business (*je ne puis
monter plus haut, oder es wird halsbrechende Arbeit daraus*).'[3] Since
Louis XIV had suppressed the rank of Constable of France, the
highest was that of marshal-general, conferred only exceptionally,
upon such captains as Villars and Turenne. Saxe was now the richer
by 30,000 francs a year, the first of all the marshals of France and, not
least, entitled to command even princes of the blood. Conti's patent
of generalissimo was swiftly overtrumped.

II

Saxe had reported that Versailles was so absorbed by the remarriage
of the Dauphin that 'they are not thinking more of Provence than if
it was in China,'[4] even if the Marquis de Stainville had not overlooked
its possible bearing upon events. They now primed the comeback of
one of the Marquis d'Argenson's few remaining friends, the Marshal
de Belle-Isle, despite his vain attempt, reminiscent of the Bohemian
compaign, to evade an unhopeful command. On 3 December 1746 he
had arrived at headquarters in Provence to take over from Maillebois
the French element of the Gallispan Army three days after General
von Browne had crossed the Var to invade France under British
naval cover. England had primed this hardy attempt to repay the
threatened French invasion of 1744 and the Fortyfive, to carry
Toulon where Prince Eugene himself had failed just on forty years
before, to offset Marshal de Saxe's victories in the Low Countries by
counterattacking right into France so as to render her more
accommodating in the desultory pourparlers at Breda.

England had already delivered a preliminary instalment out west
at Lorient in the first of a long series of combined operations against
the coasts of France. More successful initially was the allied thrust
against the soft underbelly of the enemy, with the Marseillais fearful
for their trade and Count de Marcieu at Grenoble only able, as he
wrote, to sleep with one eye open, to spy out subversive protestants,
still a local element allegedly incited now by flitting agents, the
Chapeaux Noirs; whereas catholic Jacobites were appropriately
prominent under General Browne, whose invasion was spearheaded
by the Slavonian levies of General Count Maguire of Inniskillin,

---

[3] Marshal-General de Saxe to Count Brühl, Versailles, 24 Jan. 1747: Vitzthum/Saxe,
pp. 154-5.
[4] Marshal de Saxe to King Augustus III, Versailles, 6 Jan. 1747: ibid., p. 139.

noticed at Coni. Now Maguire occupied Draguignan and Austrian patrols went probing forward to within thirty miles of Toulon.

Midwinter subsistence, though, was grim in that deliberately denuded countryside where Austrian outposts were grubbing for edible roots. Then on 21 January 1747 the Gallispan forces punched out all along the line to execute Belle-Isle's plan for expelling the invaders by multiple outflanking movements down through the mountains on the Gallispan left, already projected by Chevert nearly to Castellane and now stiffened from the fresh direction of Savoy by a corps of mountaineering Swiss in the Spanish service. Pivotal Castellane and Draguignan were retaken. Mirepoix relieved the unsubdued garrison of Antibes. By 3 February all Austrian and Sardinian troops were back across the river Var. Gallispan losses were minimal. The Marshal de Belle-Isle had not lost his touch.

If Browne's eviction had been speeded by lack of sustenance, that in turn had been aggravated by events at his base, which became for him 'cursed Genua'.[5] Her oppression by Botta d'Adorno savoured of personal revenge. Hatred had risen against the Austrians as the ramparts had been stripped of their artillery for use by Browne against Antibes. On the evening of 5 December 1746 an Austrian working-party had been lugging towards the harbour a heavy mortar when it toppled and stuck in a ditch. The Austrian non-commissioned officer in charge called upon Genoese bystanders to lend a hand and sought to thrash them into looking lively. They did. They became a swarming mob, snatching up cobblestones and pelting the Austrians back into quarters. Next morning the popular insurrection spread with barricades and sniping against the Austrian garrison, depleted on behalf of Browne and slackly organized by Botta. Parleys and a local truce only afforded time for further Genoese mobilization, for swinging over the cautious Doge and Senate and for echoing the tocsin through the surrounding countryside. Breasting their way through bands of armed peasants, the discomfited Austrians had reached safety at Gavi by 13 December. Nor did the wretched Botta contrive a prompt comeback, whereas his Sardinian allies five days later captured coveted Savona further down the coast.

Once again had the pattern of eighteenth-century warfare proved anything but formal as the republican virtues of a moribund regime at Genoa flamed up to overthrow the troops of alien oppression and to change the ways of war along the Ligurian seaboard. Botta had been booted out of Genoa even more ignominiously than out of Berlin, to a chorus of exasperation: 'It seemed as if destiny was saving

[5] General von Browne to Cobenzl, Milan, 25 Apr. 1747: Ö.S./H.H.S., Grosse Correspondenz 301 of 1747, cited, Christopher Duffy, The Wild Goose and the Eagle (London, 1964), p. 161.

up a blow like this just for Marquis Botta';[6] 'I wish Botta had been hanged when the Czarina would have had him hanged.'[7]

III

At the beginning of the seventh year of hostilities in 1747 the affairs of the Italian peninsula, with their bearing upon those of the Iberian, importantly affected the Austrian reaction to the French peace-feeler put out by the Duke de Richelieu through Saxony and pushed through to Vienna despite an ultimate proposal from the Marquis d'Argenson that the negotiation be switched to Paris by the despatch thither of an Austrian envoy to treat with him and Huescar: in effect, Alary's proposal of a few days earlier to the Marquis de Stainville, now minus that diplomatist. This was actually taken up in a letter which King Augustus III now addressed to the Empress Maria Theresa while Brühl sent to Vienna his factotum, Saul, instructed on 23 January 1747 to drive in a hackney-coach to the Hofburg where he would 'find a man in a green suit. He will lead you in the courtyard and up a mean spiral staircase into the room of Princess Trautson'[8] and the presence of the empress, Count Ulfeld, and rasping Baron Bartenstein.

Saul presented a seven-point programme devised by Richelieu and Brühl but the seven points received from the Austrians a scarcely more favourable reception than had the Marquis d'Argenson's six articles transmitted to Vienna eighteen months earlier by the Marquis de Stainville. An Italian establishment for Don Philip caused trouble yet again, even as it stymied Austro-Spanish rapprochement via Lisbon. Furthermore the English veto upon an Austrian conquest of Naples still stood. Naples in the south and Prussia in the north, both lately wrested or aggrandized from Austria but now with British approval excluded from hostilities, formed two heavy drags upon pacification with the injured Empress Maria Theresa.

Frederick the Great, sitting pretty, was as conscious as Maria Theresa that his Silesian grab remained the real stumbling-block for her rapprochement with France. The more ostensible obstacle of Don Philip now recalled the abortive Harrach-Vaulgrenant negotiation at the end of 1745, as also did the Saxon setting and some relationship once again to more direct and still more secret French

---

[6] General von Browne to Cobenzl, 17 Feb. 1747: ibid, p. 146.
[7] Lord Hardwicke to Duke of Newcastle, 26 Dec. 1746 (O.S.): British Library, Add. MSS. 32,709, fo. 383: cited, Lodge, p. 203.
[8] Count C. Loss to Saul, Vienna, 23 Jan. 1747: [Count C.-F. Vitzthum d'Eckstaedt,] *Die Geheimnisse des sächsischen Cabinets. Ende 1745 bis Ende 1756* (Stuttgart, 1866), i. 142.

approaches to Austria through the Marquis de Stainville, most notably by the brothers Pâris.

Frederick expected that after the fall of the Marquis d'Argenson the greatest influence in French foreign policy would lie with the brothers, the inspirers of Saxe and of Madame de Pompadour who, wrote the Saxon minister in Paris, 'blindly follows their advice'.[9] Their favoured Marquis de Puysieulx was now recalled from Breda and appointed foreign minister.

'The Pâris only want lackeys in office'[10] remarked the displaced Marquis d'Argenson. He described his successor as 'a man as vain as he is limited . . . He believes himself to be a very honest man with the frankness of the old school, without [in fact] being anything of the kind; he holds in adoration his fathers, who began to make a mark under Henry IV and who are said by the memoirs of the time to have been little men like himself and great knaves, especially the Chancellor de Sillery.'[11] This acid etching depicted Puysieulx as 'singularly ignorant, never having read anything . . . He smacks of education by the Jesuits, and on top of that the lackey's lacquer (vernis de valet) which one takes on at court has rendered his character fit for any deceit . . . He is peevish, morose, sly, dreary; he has always taken particular care of his health; he has not been very fond of women, fairly so of wine, some riotousness in youth, clothes and equipages in good taste, exacting as a householder, meddlesome, cruel with his servants, pettily vindictive, adroit, his small stature well set up. That is the way in which our state is going and will go to ruin.' More balanced was a later foreign minister: 'Puysieulx has a judicious and sure intelligence; he speaks with nobility and dignity; his principles and his proceedings are honest . . . but one senses the difference which there is between a skilful and virtuous courtier and an able minister, between a judicious intelligence and a broad intelligence.'[12]

'Monsieur de Puysieulx', wrote the Marquis de Stainville from Paris on 15 January 1747, 'should arrive here today or tomorrow, and upon his arrival it will be announced that the Count de Saint Séverin is to go to replace him at Breda. For nearly thirty years I have been living on most intimate terms with Monsieur de Puysieulx and Monsieur de Saint Séverin.'[13] So Stainville could be useful in Paris if only he were trusted in Vienna.

Upon his return Puysieulx succumbed seriously to smallpox. His duties were temporarily discharged by the Count de Maurepas.

---

[9] Count J. Loss, 12 Jan. 1747: Vitzthum/Saxe, p. 148.   [10] D'Argenson, v. 85.
[11] Ibid, pp. 143–5. for the following.   [12] Bernis, i. 138.
[13] Marquis de Stainville to Emperor Francis I, Paris, 15 Jan. 1747: Ö.S./H.H.S., Lothringisches Hausarchiv 77/177A.

Towards the end of January the Marquis de Stainville visited Saint-Séverin and expressed his concern over Puysieulx and the hold-up. Saint-Séverin, reported Stainville, 'answered me coldly . . . that, as for the present . . . he firmly believed that only military operations would enable them to arrive at proposals for peace, and that if he had the honour of being Minister of Foreign Affairs at this moment, he would say to the Count d'Argenson, the Marshal de Saxe and Monsieur Duverney: "Gentlemen, it is your business to put me in condition to act usefully in my office."'[14] When Stainville took him up on this, Saint-Séverin 'unbuttoned himself entirely', reasoning thus:

The lynchpin for the continuation of the war is England. She is at a much higher degree of power than when the war began, since she is absolute mistress of the sea, and she has acquired settlements which she had not possessed. Mistress of commerce as she is, she will not lack resources for . . . subsidies which she will always be in a position to furnish to . . . her allies. The Queen Empress has everything that she can wish, no more enemies against her either in Germany or in Italy, and her husband emperor. It matters little to her that we be masters of the Netherlands, for which she is only moderately concerned since it is the business of her allies rather then hers, and they will always have to be returned. 'I regard Flanders', he continued, 'as a table upon which one is gambling. Flanders still belongs to her old master, and that does not prevent the obstinate gamblers from winning or losing a lot.'

Saint-Séverin told his friend that he had accordingly eluded the thankless mission to Breda, which was entrusted to Du Theil, restored to favour after the fall of d'Argenson. Also restored, after long exile, was seventyseven-year-old Don Melchior Macanaz, granted a passport by Stainville as Spanish envoy to Breda and accurately described by him as being 'of a singular petulance and vivacity'.[15] As for Saint-Séverin, the marquis suggested that he might have been less reluctant to appear at Breda if adorned with the blue riband of the Saint-Esprit. Also, the Marshal de Saxe had been intriguing against the mission of Saint-Séverin, judged inimical to the interests of King Augustus. In any case, before the desultory conversations at Breda resumed, the Marquis de Stainville received yet another secret approach from the hidden inspirer of French policy.

'Ministers in France . . . will never speak to you so intelligibly as Sieur Duverney has done',[16] wrote Frederick of Prussia to Le Chambrier on 10 February 1747. Two days later the Marquis de

---

[14] Marquis de Stainville to Emperor Francis I, Paris, 29 Jan. 1747: ibid. for the following.
[15] Ibid., 26 Feb. 1747.
[16] King Frederick II to Baron Le Chambrier, Potsdam, 10 Feb. 1747: *Politische Correspondenz*, v. 317.

Stainville reported: 'Monsieur Pâris Duverney having informed me through my son that he much wished to see me, I have been to his house and I am going to render to Your Imperial Majesty an exact account of a conversation lasting three hours.'[17] The high probability is that the intermediary was Count Stephen de Stainville, already known at both the French and Austrian courts, rather than a younger brother: Leopold–Charles, the Abbé de Choiseul, was probably steeped in examinations just then; within a fortnight he was to sustain a thesis, dedicated to the Dauphin, for a degree of Bachelor of Theology at the Sorbonne in the presence of the influential Bishop of Mirepoix.[18]

It would thus appear that the future Duke de Choiseul was already on terms with his father's powerful friend, Pâris-Duverney. And while the young man may well have remained ignorant of their political intercourse, yet in view of his father's habitual withdrawal, of his own earlier reckoning with secret soundings towards Austria, of his facility for putting two and two together, it seems likely that the general drift, at all events, of what was in the wind did not altogether escape him. His early appearance in the setting of secret moves towards accommodation with Austria is suggestive for his later policy.

Pâris-Duverney now renewed to the Marquis de Stainville his assurance of the previous year that Louis XV greatly desired peace. So, thought the financier, should everybody, 'even the English'. He therefore did not regard peacemaking as impossible or even very difficult. Duverney, subtler than the Marquis d'Argenson and his Abbé Alary, held that one should not seek peace 'by detaching any ally upon either side, that it must be made in concert, and that for that there was but one means which was to have the plan made by the Dutch in concert with the Queen Empress'.[19] It would then be up to the English to fall in or out. Otherwise, continued Duverney, 'the English will make peace all alone and will lay down the law to all Europe, for they will find a way of making a good accommodation with Spain . . . One fine morning they will say to you, "Peace is made upon such and such conditions; if it does not suit you, Empress, and you, King of Sardinia, and you Dutch, make the best of it you can; as for us, we are outside." Then no more subsidies, and perhaps in order to make a better bargain with Spain they will further impose some sacrifice upon the Empress.'

---

[17] Marquis de Stainville to Emperor Francis I, Paris, 12 Feb. 1747: Ö.S./.H.H.S., Lothringisches Hausarchiv 77/177A.
[18] Cf. *Lettres de M. de Marville, Lieutenant Général de Police, au Ministre Maurepas*, (*1742–1747*), ed. A. de Boislisle (Paris, 1896–1905), iii. 165.
[19] Marquis de Stainville to Emperor Francis I, Paris, 12 Feb. 1747: *u.s.* for the following.

Thus did Duverney skilfully deflect against Austria the English thrust against France in treating separately with Spain. He drove his sharp point home: 'As for us, we shall not oppose the peace which they [the English] may make with Spain, not demanding anything for ourselves.' When Stainville asked what made Duverney suppose the English set upon an early peace, he said because with them 'it was already a question ... of the demolition of Cape Breton, that it had been said in their government that it would cost a lot to put it in good condition, that the troops which they were sending there were all dying, and that it would be more useful to the state to demolish it altogether'.

Duverney's analysis cut deep. Within a fortnight the Earl of Sandwich was writing from Holland to the Duke of Newcastle of 'the danger we are in hourly of being abandoned by our treacherous ally the Republick.'[20] And Newcastle was soon to tell Sandwich: 'Many of your best friends, and formerly the most zealous advocates for Cape Breton, begin to think that Cape Breton alone without Quebeck and Canada will be such an immense expense and of so little use that the best we could do with it would be to purchase better conditions of peace.'[21]

The Marquis de Stainville rightly regarded the approach from Pâris-Duverney as being of a different order of importance from that lately made to him by the sinking Marquis d'Argenson. The financier's shrewd factorization around England contrasted with the sterile colloquies pursued by the Duke de Richelieu via continental Saxony and with a flimsy suggestion of 15 February from Saxe to Brühl that Don Philip might be fitted up in the Austrian Netherlands, as though England would allow that – pretty much Saint-Séverin's point to Stainville.

Saint-Séverin was also correct in his conviction that the Conference of Breda would achieve nothing. It remained technically, under d'Argenson's arrangement, an Anglo-Franco-Dutch affair with the envoys of Spain (Macanaz), Austria (Count Harrach), and Sardinia (Chavanne) as consultants in the wings. The resumption of conversations was further complicated by the doubts of the Earl of Sandwich as to whether Du Theil was gentleman enough to deal with, of others as to whether Don Melchior de Macanaz was rational enough. That terrible old man, said by Sandwich to have only one tooth left, was described by Harrach as 'a real Spanish fantast, who

[20] Earl of Sandwich to Duke of Newcastle, 24 Feb. 1747: British Library, Add. MSS. 32,807, fo. 99: Lodge, p. 231.
[21] Duke of Newcastle to Earl of Sandwich, 6 Mar. 1747 (O.S.): *u.s.*, fo. 176: Lodge, p. 239.

has a great facility for building Spanish castles in the air'.[22] For the ancient Don the chief rival of Spain remained France, causing Du Theil to ask his furious ally: 'But whom, then, do you want to kill here, Monsieur Macanaz?'[23] Their altercation turned upon the composition of the conference, still unresolved at its last formal meeting on 16 March 1747. Even by eighteenth-century standards this was a poor performance.

While the Conference of Breda was in its death-throes the new French foreign minister, pustular, had been convalescing from his smallpox at Plaisance, the sumptuous country-house of his patron, Pâris-Duverney. A week after the last meeting of the conference the Marquis de Stainville reported that the Marquis de Puysieulx, back at his residence in Paris, had proposed a meeting through Duverney, 'our common friend'. Stainville found Puysieulx 'confined to bed by an accidental fever caused by ... rheumatism on the chest'.[24] The invalid spoke to his old friend of 'the pear being not yet ripe. "We solicit peace", continued this minister, "and we do not make it ... Only events ... can procure it."' But, he added, the war 'must be finished'. Further:

The court of Vienna is on its guard against us, as we are against it; and I will freely confess to you that its mistrust is better founded than ours. You see that I am not speaking to you as a minister, but you can do me the justice of saying that I am not a rascal, that I do not want to deceive anybody, and your masters much less than anybody at all ... I have even long thought that one will never be able to make a durable peace except by reuniting your court intimately to ours.

In conclusion Puysieulx took up Duverney's suggestion of the danger to Maria Theresa from a separate English peace. Within a month indeed the Earl of Sandwich, who got so far as to draft a treaty with Macanaz in Holland, was writing to Newcastle anent Austria that 'nothing is to be done in any pacifick negotiation if we determine to act in everything fairly in concert with that court'.[25] But soon the Sandwich–Macanaz negotiation too dribbled away. England would not yield Gibraltar and there was the usual trouble over Don Philip. In the last resort France, with her marriage-tie to him, was likely to prove more forthcoming than England. That was a decisive

[22] Count Harrach to Empress Maria Theresa, Breda, 9 Mar. 1747: Ö.S./H.H.S: Arneth, iii. 469, n. 32.
[23] Du Theil to Count de Maurepas, 1 Mar. 1747: Arch. Aff. Étr. C.P., Hollande, Conférence de Breda: Broglie/Saxe, ii. 160.
[24] Marquis de Stainville to Emperor Francis I, Paris. 23 Mar. 1747: Ö.S./H.H.S., Lothringisches Hausarchiv 77/177A for the following.
[25] Earl of Sandwich to Duke of Newcastle, 17 Apr. 1747: British Library, Add. MSS. 32,808, fo. 15: Lodge, p. 245.

consideration for the Spanish government, whose policy changed less than might have been expected under the new foreign minister, the Count de Carvajal.

Criticism[26] of the Marquis de Puysieulx for neglecting the opportunity of the elder d'Argenson's fall for a cast towards Austria must now reckon with fuller knowledge. Only Puysieulx was not for peace at any price, at that of Prussia and her Silesian nub. He instructed the Marquis des Issarts to assure his Prussian colleague in Dresden that Richelieu's mission represented 'nothing serious ... It suits us no less than the King of Prussia himself that this prince, at the general peace, should be able to remain the peaceful possessor of the acquisition which his victories have procured for him.'[27] Richelieu had to lament to Brühl the failure 'of our great peace plan'.[28]

Not now to recur was that critical French offer, to abandon to Austria nearly all Silesia, which Pâris-Duverney had made to the Marquis de Stainville at the end of 1745. Yet Puysieulx's latest profession to him of special inclination towards Austria was to prove something more than a tactical assurance. Puysieulx's significant reference to the need for an intimate Franco-Austrian reconciliation was even to be echoed back to Richelieu in an Austrian communication remitted from Vienna by Count Christian Loss on 21 April 1747. The Austrian message, however, insisted that any negotiations should be conducted not in Paris, as proposed by the French, but in Vienna. This difference regarding venue, with its Austrian implication against Stainville, was important and remained unresolved.

So all the intricate soundings and negotiations, secret and more secret, towards peace that winter at Breda, Lisbon, Dresden and the controlling capitals of Europe came to nearly nothing, certainly nothing immediate. The Marquis de Puysieulx's pear was not yet ripe. Apropos of the soundings with Austria the Marshal de Saxe had written grimly that in the Austrian Netherlands 'I have actually under my command 250 thousand men'.[29] With this huge host he was now to seek once more to compel such success in war as might match his success in love in promoting the marriage of the Saxon Princess to the Dauphin of France. Only, love was not at first the mainspring of that marriage.

---

[26] Cf. Broglie/Saxe, ii. 139.

[27] Marquis de Puysieulx to Marquis des Issarts, 11 Apr. 1747: Arch. Aff. Étr. C.P., Saxe: ibid., ii. 146. (The date is there misquoted as 1745.)

[28] Duke de Richelieu to Count Brühl, 30 Mar. 1747: Arch. Aff. Étr. C.P. Autriche, vol. 240: Braubach, p. 383.

[29] Marshal-General de Saxe to Count Brühl, Versailles, 15 Feb. 1747: Vitzthum/Saxe, p. 170.

IV

Maria Josepha, proceeding to Versailles for the final instalment of her marriage, had been met by Maurice de Saxe at Nangis. There by a mischance she received cutting confirmation of the fact that, as she later confessed to her mother, the Dauphin 'was very cross to see me filling the place of a wife whom he had loved tenderly; he regarded me but as a child; all this repelled him from me and caused me mortal grief.'[30] The poor girl was married with all pomp at Versailles on Thursday, 9 February 1747, in a skirt which Saxe, who had earlier held it, estimated to have 'weighed a good sixty pounds. There are none of our cuirasses which weigh so much. I do not know how she could have kept on her feet for eight or nine hours with this enormous weight.'[31] When she finally got out of her clothes it was to join her bridegroom in being ceremonially put to bed, 'which is terrible, for the whole court is in the room . . . It had the air of a sacrifice.' As with the homage of Duke Francis of Lorraine some fifteen years earlier, one notices that antique ceremonies, religiously perpetuated, were beginning to jar upon a more sensitive generation.

The Dauphin pulled the coverlet over his head. He and his bride only wept together that night. Such were the nuptials of the future mother of three kings of France.

A bad foot was given out as the reason for the Dauphine's not dancing at the ball at Versailles on the evening of her marriage. But plenty of others did, likely including the young Count de Stainville. 'I was', he later recalled, 'little occupied then with political affairs; but I, like all those who thought, was sensible of the absurdity of this marriage, which did not prevent me from diverting myself greatly at it. But the pleasures of this winter were for me followed by a very lively unhappiness.'[32] It was rare that Choiseul, even thus briefly, recalled grief in his life. This grief emerged from joy.

On Thursday, 13 April 1747, the Gontaut-Biron residence in the Rue de Richelieu was eagerly astir. The young Marquise de Gontaut that morning gave birth to a son. 'It is', commented the Duke de Luynes, 'considerable news for this family, Monsieur [the Duke] de Biron, who is the elder, not having any boy till now.'[33] The duke, the Count de Stainville's former colonel, was to remain childless so that it fell to his younger brother, the White Eunuch, to perpetuate the proud line of Biron. But now, thanks most probably to the vigorous Count de Stainville, this had been achieved.

[30] Dauphine to Queen of Poland, 19 Feb. 1752: ibid., p. 212.
[31] Marshal-General de Saxe to King Augustus III, Versailles, 12 Feb. 1747: ibid., pp. 161–4 for the following.
[32] Choiseul, *Mémoires*, pp. 39–40.   [33] Luynes, viii. 182.

The Birons lost no time in registering the happy succession. On that same day of 13 April the infant was christened in the parish church of Saint-Eustache, a name-saint of his mother. He became Armand-Louis, Count de Gontaut, later to revive the amorous renown of the title of that Duke de Lauzun who had been the lover of Mademoiselle de Montpensier and a favourite Knight of the Garter at the exiled court of King James II of England. The baby, however, derived his first name from his grandfather, who stood as his godfather that day. This was Charles-Armand, Duke de Gontaut, premier Marshal of France, the military restorer of the renaissance lustre of the house of Biron. The godmother was the infant's maternal grandmother, 'Marie-Thérèse-Catherine Gouffier, spouse of the very high and very mighty lord My Lord Crozat, Marquis du Châtel, lieutenant-general of the armies of the King'[34] upon those campaigns which evidently cemented his friendship with the Count de Stainville.

The mother of the little Count de Gontaut was swiftly seized of a violent fever, presumably puerperal. At first there was hope of taming it. But upon the third day she died. Antoinette-Eustachie, Marquise de Gontaut, had lived nineteen years. They buried her five days after the birth and baptism of her son, in the same church of Saint-Eustache. The Lord giveth and the Lord taketh away.

For the family of Gontaut-Biron the death, one supposes, was sad, the birth gladder. But for the young Count de Stainville that thirteenth of April had indeed proved a day of misfortune, as his memoirs suggested years later with pregnant brevity and reticence. Whether or no it was to this loss, as has been suggested, that Voltaire referred in a little-known allusion to his respect 'for the grief of M. de Choiseul',[35] the count's bereavement had almost certainly, by contemporary consent, gained him a son he could not call his own. It was to be his only known child. Five years later when he was expecting another by his wife he confided to one of his closest friends that his proud hope of her pregnancy 'is however often mingled with fear from the remembrance of the misfortune which I have experienced'.[36] The future Duke de Choiseul did not often confess to fear or reveal the shadowed underside of his resolutely sunny

[34] Baptismal register of the church of Saint-Eustache, Paris, 13 Apr. 1747: cited, Gaston Maugras, *Le duc de Lauzun et la cour intime de Louis XV* (Paris, 1893), p. 24, n. 1.
[35] Voltaire to Countess d'Argental, ? Apr. 1747: V. S. Lublinsky, *Pis'ma Vol'tera* (Moscow & Leningrad, 1956), p. 111. In suggesting this date for the undated letter Lublinsky noticed, ibid. n. 6, that the future Choiseul was then called Stainville. Voltaire's reference could have been to Stainville's cousin, the Count de Choiseul (future Duke de Praslin), a particular friend of the d'Argentals. In that case the cause of the Count de Choiseul's grief is uncertain though it might, for instance, have related to the death of his sister-in-law, Anne-Catherine, Countess d'Estrées. She had died childless at the age of twenty-eight on 19 July 1743. This would date the letter to that year, for which Lublinsky prints five others from Voltaire to the d'Argentals.
[36] Count de Stainville to Baron von Bernstorff, 30 Jan. 1752: *Bernstorffske Papirer*, ii. 639–40.

existence. And behind those few words to Baron von Bernstorff there could have lain a still closer relevance.

As she lay dying that April, about to leave her lover so soon and for ever, the Marquise de Gontaut is supposed to have spoken with her little sister, Louise-Honorine Crozat du Châtel than aged about ten, and to have made Louise-Honorine promise that she would marry the Count de Stainville, perhaps also induced to promise. The Marquise was said to have done this in order to assure the material fortune of the man she loved by introducing him to the riches of the Crozats through that closest and legal tie which she herself could not provide. If such was indeed the parting gift to Stephen de Stainville from Antoinette-Eustachie, it was to provide a rich foundation for the whole of his subsequent career. It is, however, at least possible, at least additionally, that young Stainville's mistress also loved and sensed the quality of her little sister and made her over as a still greater bequest to him so that Antoinette-Eustachie's association with her lover might, so far as humanly possible, outlast death itself.

In terms of the above, Louise-Honorine was to remain faithful to her word. According to a more prosaic story[37] her union with the Count de Stainville was to be promoted by a preceding marriage between her lady's maid and his valet. The two accounts are not incompatible. The immediate certainy was that for the Count de Stainville the death of the Marquise de Gontaut was 'a very painful misfortune which caused me to leave very early for the army'[38] in the contested Netherlands. For Stainville there could have been a double relevance in the imposition by Louis XV upon his army of mourning for his mother-in-law, Queen Catherine Opalinska, deceased dropsically swollen at Lunéville a month before the Marquise de Gontaut. It was a black spring.

V

The campaign to which the Count de Stainville returned was assuming a new, Dutch dimension.

'We will do a good job, if it pleases Gott, that god of the Germans ... The Dutch will cry Ow! Ow! but whether they cry or not scarcely matters': Marshal-General de Saxe to the Count de Clermont, 10 April 1747.[39] Whereas Saxe's mentor wrote to him next day: 'In attacking the Dutch the resolve here is yet to treat the country and

[37] Cf. J. N. Dufort, comte de Cheverny, *Mémoires sur les règnes de Louis XV et Louis XVI et sur la révolution*, i. 138.
[38] Choiseul, *Mémoires*, p. 40.
[39] Arch. Guerre, Papiers de Condé: Broglie/Saxe, ii. 181.

people with many regards' so as to constrain them 'to enter sincerely
into views of peace to ensure the very preservation of the republic. It
is an extreme remedy which they want to administer gently, without
however prejudicing the firmness and vigour of the execution . . .
You should be informed of the true dispositions of the king's council
upon this subject.'[40]

Noailles's tone was hardly that of his old master, Louis XIV, in
regard to the decision taken at last, almost anxiously, by the French
government to attack the generally respected and useful Dutch, till
now protected combatants. Topical, however, was the allusion to the
preservation of the Dutch republic, unready and rattled by the
French notification of attack addressed to the Estates-General on 17
April. Grand Pensionary Gilles was haunted by the mob-murder of
his great predecessor John de Witt after the French had come bearing
down in 1672 and provoked the elevation of William III of Orange in
a national resurgence. That precedent prevailed remarkably and the
Dutch in their new extremity veered back towards princely
government in the crook-backed person of Prince William IV of
Orange, the thirtyfive-year-old son-in-law of King George II of
England. The Earl of Sandwich had been encouraging the Orange
faction under William Bentinck, another evocative name, and a
British squadron in the Scheldt stimulated the province of Zeeland
to rise up and appoint Prince William IV its Stadholder. This was a
provincial, not federal, office in the monarcho-republican mishmash
which then made the Dutch constitution almost comparable to the
Polish. On 3 May 1747, after rioting at the Hague, William was
further proclaimed Stadholder of the critical province of Holland,
and he became the first of his line to hold that office in all seven of the
United Provinces. Some months later it was made hereditary in male
and female descent. Thus began in the Netherlands that hereditary
rule of the house of Orange which has since endured.

On 4 May Prince William assumed the federal offices of Captain-
General and Admiral of the Union. They were not sinecures just
then. Lowendahl got going in Dutch Flanders and skittled down
every strongpoint masking the strategic estuary of the Scheldt.
Between 1 and 17 May he took Sluys, Sas de Gand, Hulst, and finally
Axel, perhaps the most striking example of 'a Dutch defence' in
Fielding's phrase from *Tom Jones*, written in the following year. The
island fastness of Axel was broached by a young French officer under
flag of truce, the Count de Broglie, second son of the late marshal and
exact contemporary of the Count de Stainville. Young Broglie's

[40] Marshal de Noailles to Marshal-General de Saxe, 11 Apr. 1747: Archives de Mouchy:
ibid., p. 178.

application of diplomacy to warfare, securing the surrender of Axel without a shot fired, helped to single him out as a competitor against Choiseul in long years to come.

The Marshal de Saxe brayed from Brussels, 'Here I have once again got the wolf by the ears.'[41] He was dissuaded by gentlemanly Noailles from his project of setting privateers to prey upon Dutch shipping to his personal profit. Saxe was in any case in funds as marshal-general commanding in conquered territory. This satisfactory location procured Saxe's whole army a special bounty on a scale prescribed by ordinance of 15 June 1747. The Count de Stainville, as a brigadier now, stood to have his pay augmented by no less than 2,500 livres a month. Something of the value of his recent promotion to general rank may be inferred from the corresponding increase for a colonel: 120 livres a month. Inequality of reward according to rank was dear to the old regime.

After Dutch Flanders had been mopped up there ensued a lull. The Duke of Cumberland, once more in aggressive command of the allies, failed to draw out Saxe, sitting pretty in the area Mechlin-Louvain, able to lunge at choice against either of the main Dutch prizes, Bergen-op-Zoom upon his left flank by the coast or, inland upon his right, Maestricht. Saxe, once more a good deal preoccupied with La Chantilly, may have rather rationalized his inaction in subsequently explaining to Frederick the Great that he had sought to test the enemy supply-position while giving 'the crops time to ripen in order to keep my cavalry in good condition for the rest of the campaign.'[42] Frederick had recently been assured by his own envoy, chiming with the opinion of the Count de Stainville, that Saxe 'will always consult his personal interest'.[43] That largely turned upon Louis XV who had recently left Madame de Pompadour again in advancing on campaign to Brussels. There, as often, he became bored. Towards the middle of June 1747 the Marshal de Saxe reluctantly consented to do something.

The then Count de Stainville crisply described the opening of the main campaign:

The army of Flanders ... assembled beneath Louvain. The Marshal de Saxe let himself be pinched upon the headwaters of the Demer by that enemy army which he had not been willing to destroy the year before at Rocoux. He put in danger the corps of his advance-guard commanded by the Count de Clermont and the Count d'Estrées, which he had pushed forward to beneath Tongres. He was obliged to

---

[41] Marshal-General de Saxe to King Augustus III, Brussels, 4 May. 1747: Vitzthum/Saxe, p. 499.
[42] Marshal-General de Saxe to King Frederick II, July 1747: Arch. Guerre C., vol. 3210, no. 3.
[43] Baron Le Chambrier to King Frederick II, 16 June 1747: Broglie/Saxe, ii. 231.

impose upon his army three forced marches so as to arrive before Tongres upon the heights of Elderen [Heerderen]. The enemy, as is inconceivable, gave him all the time necessary to reassemble his troops.[44]

This critique largely reflected contemporary opinion as instanced by the writer's father. The Marquis de Stainville was reporting from Paris on 2 July 1747: 'Upon the movement which the allies have made to cover Maestricht, they have for several days been very anxious here for the detached corps of the Count de Clermont, the prince, and the Count d'Estrées, which they feared might be cut off; it seems however that they have been able to withdraw in time.'[45]

Saxe, all activity now, had pressed ahead of his main army, ordered to march out eastward from its camp at Louis' headquarters at the Abbey du Parck outside Louvain, starting at half past eleven on the morning of 29 June 1747. Stainville's Regiment of Navarre set forth in honourable distinction in 'the first column on the right'[46] at the beginning of those forced marches for forty miles in midsummer on the road to Tongres and beyond – long remembered by such an infantry officer as the Count de Stainville.

King Louis XV, that tireless huntsman, set an example to his troops in haste – 'not relaxing',[47] as he characteristically put it to the absent Dauphin. After midday on Saturday the 1st July the king, now driving in his coach with a small escort, was pressing on from Tongres when he was met by one of Saxe's favourite young colonels, the Chevalier de Valfons, galloping up from the front. About halfway between Tongres and Maestricht, in the area Bilsen–Lawfeldt–Heerderen, the opposing armies were running up against one another in heavy rain and mutual surprise at the weight of enemy deployment. From about noon the main columns of the Duke of Cumberland were winding into view. At Heerderen the unenthusiastic Saxe is said to have represented to Louis that there was still time to avoid a battle. But the king held firm for attack.

So it was to be battle once again in that long and sanguinary war. All through the night and the rain French infantry came squelching and straggling into battle-stations. A little to the rear, in a wretched billet at Old Elderen or Heerderen, the King of France slept in the keeping of his weary and devoted troops.

The dawn of the battle of Lawfeldt on Sunday the 2nd July 1747

[44] Choiseul, *Mémoires*, p. 40.
[45] Marquis de Stainville to Emperor Francis I, Paris, 2 July 1747: Ö.S./H.H.S., Lothringisches Hausarchiv 77/177A.
[46] 'Ordre du 29ᵉ juin au Camp du Parck 1747': Arch. Guerre C., vol. 3209, no. 208.
[47] King Louis XV to Dauphin, Commanderie des Vieux Joncs, 2 July 1747: Vitzthum/Saxe, p. 196.

was balefully illuminated. In the early hours the hamlet of Vlytingen, just west of Lawfeldt over towards Bilsen, was going up in flames. British Guards were deliberately burning it. Lawfeldt followed. The inhabitants were driven out. Somewhat surprisingly the British reoccupied positions in among the smoking ruins: the British second-in-command, Sir John Ligonier, General of Horse, had insisted upon the value of defended villages in breaking an attack. In this as in other respects Lawfeldt was to form a sequel to Rocoux.

Looking from the French lines over against Lawfeldt, away to the left in front of Bilsen on the allied right, across a little valley, the Austrian whitecoats were holding the villages of Grosse Spauwe and Kleine Spauwe, with Field-Marshal Batthyany's headquarters at the Commanderie des Vieux Joncs. Some Dutch units, again under the Prince of Waldeck, were sandwiched between the Austrians and the British holding Vlytingen and, with Hanoverian and Hessian support, Lawfeldt in difficult surrounds as at Rocoux. Eastward again of Lawfeldt, in the direction of strategic Maestricht, the four-mile line ended at about the villages of Kisselt and Wilre with the toughest regiments, the allied cavalry under Ligonier being massed against the superior French horse standing to the east of Remst.

The brunt of the French attack fell to the vanguards of the Count d'Estrées and the Count de Clermont opposite Lawfeldt. Their troops had been spared those forced marches whereas the regiments which had endured them, such as Stainville's Navarre, were mostly stationed rearwards in support. A little after ten o'clock that morning Clermont launched the infantry attack against Lawfeldt itself. There ensued four desperate hours of killing.

The fire of the British infantry sliced its habitual swathes through the attacking French. Cumberland had enfilading cannon join the mowing with mutilating caseshot. The French, too, were advancing against driving rain, pitilessly persistent, the ditches running with water, the banks slippery and sliding away underfoot. The attackers suffered terrible casualties in thrice capturing the burnt buildings of sinister Lawfeldt, only to be thrice thrown out by ever-reinforcing units from Cumberland's reserve, plenished by some Austrian detachments. Yet a fourth time was the French attack resumed, primed now by Irish regiments which fought the English with habitual fervour. Even when they too were bent back, they partially clung on. Meantime a local charge by French cavalry westward of Lawfeldt toppled a Dutch regiment of horse and sent it careering back through the allied lines, breaking the infantry wide open. Marshal de Saxe skilfully switched the weight of his attack, catching the enemy off balance from an unexpected quarter. At this crux Saxe, sword in hand, himself led the fifth and final surge which broke into Lawfeldt and, this time, went swirling through it 'with frightful cries and shooting',[48] sweeping the British and German troops back into a milling retreat pounded by French artillery.

It was two o'clock and the allied line was broken through the centre. Out on the allied right the main Austrian strength had all the while stood virtually immobile, till Batthyany prudently concluded that it was time to retreat. For Saxe now was the time to unleash the cavalry of Count d'Estrées, who had already carried Wilre on the allied left. But Ligonier, unaware of how ill things were shaping over by Lawfeldt, could no longer resist the opportunity for a mighty slap against the French cavalry. On his own initiative he sent his horse charging into one of the greatest cavalry combats of that century, of all time. Sixty allied squadrons threw more than twice as many French into disarray and recaptured Wilre. Only, with Lawfeldt lost clumsy Cumberland countermanded the cavalry attack, then, upon Ligonier's protest, reordered it. But, in battle certainly, resumption is not equivalent to continuation. A second attack must now be a forlorn hope to cover the allied withdrawal.

Ligonier gathered up his staunchest horse, the Greys, the Inniskillings and the Duke of Cumberland's, and led them headlong back into the massed enemy. Once again the British burst clean through. But they ran onto enemy infantry freshly posted to play upon them while French reserves of cavalry dashed in against their flanks and Saxe threw in the carabineers to complete a knockout. The British attack was suppressed in a furious mêlée. In the midst two French troopers of the carabineers, a certain Haude and Guillaume Ibère, recognized the star of the Order of the Bath upon the uniform of a mounted general. They captured General Sir John Ligonier. He had no loaded pistol left. Refusing his purse and jewelled watch as the price of freedom, they led him through the ugly press towards King Louis who, at any rate according to Ligonier, was hard by, 'having been in the thick of the fight'. [49] It is said that Saxe introduced Ligonier to Louis with the words: 'Sire, I here present to your Majesty a man who has defeated all my plans by a single glorious action.'[50]

Now, however, Ligonier was much afraid. For he was by birth a Frenchman, a protestant southerner from Castres in Languedoc,

---

[48] Marshal-General de Saxe to King Frederick II, Camp de la Commanderie, 20 July 1747: Baron d'Espagnac, *Histoire de Maurice, Comte de Saxe*, ii. 358.

[49] General Sir John Ligonier to Prince William of Hesse: Camile Rabaud, *Jean-Louis de Ligonier* (Dôle, 1893), pp. 21–2.

[50] Translation as in R. Whitworth, *Field Marshal Lord Ligonier*, p. 158. The present account is indebted to this work.

arguably a renegade in arms against his rightful king, hardly entitled to treatment better than that of the wretched Scottish rebels in the Fortyfive. Ligonier's talents were among those whereof France had stripped herself in the revocation of the Edict of Nantes. But King Louis, related Ligonier, 'greatly reassured me with a gracious smile: "Well, General, so we shall be having the pleasure of supping with you this evening"... I thought I was dreaming... The king was very gracious to me that evening ... which set an example to the others. Finally, when I was taking leave of His Majesty and mustering all the remaining French in my vocabulary, the King said to me: "Monsieur de Ligonier, your captivity will not be hard; for you know that I am not very spiteful (*méchant*)." At that my heart swelled and I could answer only by putting a knee to the ground, and then the king stretched out to me his beautiful gloveless hand, on which I planted, I swear you, a very warm kiss seasoned with some tears. The King of France is a great and good king believe me.'[51]

Louis XV, often subjected to denigration, was kingly in the hour of victory and, as he recked, of carnage. Now after Lawfeldt 'never was anything so frightful seen.The surrounding plains and villages were strewn with dead and wounded.'[52] Such was the backcloth to Louis's hospitality, more appreciated by Sir John Ligonier than by the Count de Stainville.

Lawfeldt was the last pitched battle whereat the Count de Stainville was present. For him it was also, one may imagine, one of the least satisfactory. Instead of leading the charge as at Rocoux, he had to kick his heels in the rear, standing over towards the right of the central reserve under Lieutenant-General the Marquis de Brézé and Maréchal-de-Camp the Count de Saulx; while old comrades in arms were gloriously active out in front. There went Lieutenant-General de Lautrec heading the first attack against Lawfeldt through terrific enfilading fire which broke his hand. Among the next to plunge in was valiant old Beaupréau, contriving to be in the thick of it no less than at Coni. A veteran from the Bohemian campaign, the Count of Bavaria, laid down his life for France at Lawfeldt. Stainville's erstwhile colonel, the Duke de Biron, had yet another horse shot under him. Their old Régiment du Roi was thrown in by Saxe in his last desperate assault to overcome the magnificent stand of the British infantry. Navarre had indeed been one of four brigades next ordered against Lawfeldt but it fell even as they were advancing into action. Saxe pulled them back to the heights of Heerderen to overawe Batthyany. So vanished Stainville's only hope of action that day, in

[51] General Sir John Ligonier to Prince William of Hesse: *u.s.*
[52] [L. B. Néel,] *Histoire de Maurice, Comte de Saxe* (Dresden, 1770), ii. 227.

exploitation of the capture of Lawfeldt. This aspect was the only one treated by him in his recollections of the battle.

At the end of the battle of Lawfeldt, observed the future Choiseul, the same thing happened for Saxe as had occurred at Rocoux:

The left of the Duke of Cumberland had folded and was withdrawing by the left on Maestricht. All the enemy right, composed of Austrians and other German troops, ... had no other way to rejoin Monsieur de Cumberland except by traversing a very narrow defile, which was situated behind what was roughly the centre of the enemy army when it was in line of battle. If Marshal de Saxe, after having carried Lawfeldt and divided the two parts of the enemy army, had extended the right of his victorious army on to this defile, it is evident that Marshal Batthyany and all the Austrians would have laid down their arms.

Instead of this manoeuvre, which was very simple, ... the Marshal de Saxe ... suspended all movement among his troops and conducted the prisoners to the king, who had remained the whole day like an image upon the heights of Elderen. The king's speech upon the arrival of the marshal was not more military than his actions had been. The king proposed luncheon to Monsieur de Saxe, Monsieur de Ligonier and other prisoners. Monsieur de Ligonier did not refuse this little revel, which saved the army in which he was one of the principal generals.[53]

The critique continued, 'After the luncheon, which was long, they minded that there were armies in the plain. The Marshal de Saxe gave orders for the movement of that which he commanded; but, ...' too late:

The next day and even during the night the Marshal de Saxe made pretence of wishing to draw advantages from the battle ... and to undertake the siege of Maestricht. The impossibility of the siege was easily proved when day broke. So no advantage resulted from this victory, wherein the losses in men had been equal on each side. This battle confirmed my opinion of the Marshal de Saxe and presuaded me that he was either a very mediocre general, despite his successes, or a general perfidious to the power whose armies he was commanding.

The then Count de Stainville's judgement of the battle of Lawfeldt most likely reflected his frustration at not being unleashed for action, his regular animus against Louis XV, probably some exaggeration regarding the dinner which he calls a lunch, possibly some inaccuracy regarding losses.[54] But his searching analysis is independently confirmed on salient points regarding military dispositions and Saxe's responsibility, which incurred strong criticism at the time. If the future Choiseul, with his modern outlook and grim concentration upon destroying the enemy, was inclined to rate Saxe a mediocre

[53] Choiseul, *Mémoires*, pp. 40–2 for the following.

[54] Choiseul's account of equal losses at Lawfeldt may be compared with figures given by Pajol, iii. 542: over 8,700 French casualties as against at least 10,000 allied. But R. Whitworth, op. cit., p. 155, gives, without source, about 5,000 allied casualties and twice as many French.

general despite his victories, the Emperor Napoleon was to do likewise. Even Choiseul's imputation of possible perfidy may not seem entirely far-fetched. The adventurous marshal has already appeared in a not wholly reassuring light, perhaps, in his secret contacts with the Marquis de Stainville and with Count Brühl. Now from Lawfeldt rather ugly evidence against Saxe was supplied precisely by one of his chief protégés and admirers, the Chevalier de Valfons, gallantly active there upon his staff in that capacity of *aide-major-général* which the Count de Stainville had exercised at Dettingen. Valfons related that after the French capture of Lawfeldt:

There were still in line of battle nine Dutch squadrons, behind which a part of the beaten infantry was filing back in great disorder. I proposed to the marshal, with whom I was alone at this instant, to have them charged by our squadrons from the right, which would have captured them all; he could not prevent himself from saying to me: 'Yes, here is a good moment.' But, making a gesture with his arm and raising his hand, he proved to me that, not wishing to finish the war, he was only to win battles by halves; and, telling the Marquis de Clermont-Tonnere not to make any attack, he went galloping off to the heights of Heerderen.
    ... The king gave a very gracious reception to the marshal, who said to him: 'Sire, we must win two battles in one day and march against the Austrians who are upon that plateau.' But our dawdling facilitated the retreat of Marshal de Batthyany, who would have been irretrievably lost if the marshal [de Saxe], instead of coming to Heerderen to seek compliments of the king, had had His Majesty advance at the head of his household troops and with all the cavalry ... From then onwards we should have invested Meastricht ... but, I repeat, the marshal was like all generals, too great in time of war to desire peace and get it for sure by too marked successes. ... That evening, all the French military came to congratulate the marshal, who was being served at supper; he forced me alone to sit down at his table ... Imbued with his marks of favour, I did not let myself be intoxicated and, still preoccupied with his not having wanted to win the battle completely and crush the enemy, ... I could not prevent myself from saying to Monsieur de Soubise: 'Sir, advise the king to make peace; I cannot tell you the clue to the riddle, but advise peace.'[55]

The Count de Stainville's accusation after Rocoux, that Saxe deliberately spared the enemy to fight another day, was precisely repeated by Valfons after Lawfeldt. Saxe confessed to Frederick the Great his surprise on the morrow of Lawfeldt to learn that the enemy had all crossed the Meuse to Maestricht; and to Noailles the victor admitted that 'the combat of Lahweld [*sic*] was delivered in the intention of being able to undertake the siege of Maestricht. The mistakes which we committed that day have deprived us of the advantages which we should have drawn from it.'[56] Lawfeldt was injurious to the reputations of both commanders-in-chief, to Saxe

[55] Marquis de Valfons, *Souvenirs du Marquis de Valfons*, pp. 213–18.
[56] Marshal-General de Saxe, memorandum of 17 Aug. 1747: Arch. Guerre C., vol. 3203, no. 240.

scarcely less than to Cumberland, who for his part described the battle as a 'brisk but not very successful affair between our left wing and almost the whole of the enemy's army'.[57]

French criticism of Saxe's generalship at Lawfeldt was primed by his sharpening feud against the Minister of War, as usual involving rival factions at court. The Marquis de Stainville was reporting from Paris later that July: 'All the French nation, and even the army, is declaiming greatly against the affair of the second of this month, because of the considerable losses ... They claim that this affair was fought against the advice of the Marshal de Saxe who, from what they say, has used this opportunity to destroy Monsieur d'Argenson ... They were even saying yesterday in Paris that he was recalled.'[58]

Saxe did not in fact topple the Count d'Argenson, who incidentally managed to block the marshal's special request that gallant Valfons be promoted brigadier. Two days after the battle[59] Valfons was detailed to escort Ligonier at a victory-parade of the French army. Valfons related that an 'imprudent' young French officer pointed out to Ligonier the Count de Stainville's Regiment of Navarre, spared for once at Lawfeldt, and said to the British general: 'Sir, there is the finest regiment in Europe.' 'Yes, Sir', replied Ligonier. 'I know it. I saw it taken prisoner at Hochstadt',[60] back at Blenheim more than a generation ago.

The imprudent French officer may or may not have been Brigadier de Stainville, just turned twenty-eight. Navarre that day probably paraded something less than three thousand whitecoats[61] under about a hundred and ninety officers, massed in five battalions beneath their dun-coloured battle-standards of renown.

The future Duke de Choiseul had in youth scaled a pinnacle of military perfection not always fully appreciated but not irrelevant to his subsequent career. Though his later policies arguably bore still greater relation to the broader setting of all those battles and campaigns across the classic reaches of the Low Countries. For it was not tactically alone, but in the grand strategy of that War of the

[57] Duke of Cumberland to Duke of Newcastle, 3 July 1747: British Library, Add. MSS. 32,711, fo. 473: Lodge, p. 260, n. 1.
[58] Marquis de Stainville to Emperor Francis I, Paris, 23 July 1747: Ö.S./H.H.S., Lothringisches Hausarchiv 77/177A.
[59] R. Whitworth, op. cit., p. 159, seems to place the following incident on the very afternoon of the battle. This dating would scarcely seem the most probable or in accordance with the narrative of Valfons, who related the story only after specifying, op. cit., p. 221; 'Deux jours après, l'armée prit les armes pour faire la réjouissance de nos succès.'
[60] Marquis de Valfons, op. cit., p. 222.
[61] According to an official return of a week later, 'État des Regimens d'Infanterie de l'Armée du Roy au Flandre commandés par M. le Maréchal de Saxe, au camp de la Commanderie le 10 Juillet 1747' (Arch. Guerre C., vol. 3202, no. 195), the Regiment of Navarre mustered under arms the impressive strength of 2,929 men out of a total nominal strength of 3,140. The difference comprised 207 soldiers absent sick and four officers on leave.

Austrian Succession which was so much more besides, that the costly victory of Lawfeldt shone out for France with spoilt effect, like a precious gem set in base metal. Despite her military prowess, so much advanced since the beginning of the war and thrice proven now even against the English redcoats, France was being clamped around as in a ring owing to English command of the sea and of enterprise, both military and commercial, across the wide waters.

VI

The predicament was already evident to thoughtful Frenchmen. In describing French disillusion over Lawfeldt the Marquis de Stainville, setting it against the successful string of French sieges in the Low Countries, reported: 'In talking some days ago to a very sensible man, he said to me that while the king [Louis] was capturing towns, the English were besieging the kingdom of France, which they were sapping at its foundations by totally destroying its trade. Though this remark be repeated from King William [III of England] during the war of 1700, it is not the less exact at the present moment.'[62] On the large view this was but another phase of that great Anglo-French contest for hegemony, military, commercial and colonial, which in the main lasted a century and a quarter, from 1689 to 1815. The colonial expansion of this struggle to worldwide proportions was one of the two main developments in international politics during the eighteenth century, and the one which was chiefly to stamp the statesmanship of the future Duke of Choiseul. For the present the War of the Austrian Succession, in this respect the direct precursor of the Seven Years War, promoted the expansion overseas of that conflict which, already during the War of the Spanish Succession, had incidentally cost the life of Choiseul's grandfather in the succulent West Indies.

The riches of the East Indies also were increasingly coming into dispute between the commercial harbingers of the British and French empires during the disintegration of the Mogul empire in the decades after the death in 1707 of the exacting Emperor Aurangzeb. At present the tide was flowing in favour of France, first in the field of planned expansion in India as in North America. After Anglo-French hostilities had been formally inaugurated in Europe in 1744, the British East India Company had rejected a proposal for local neutrality from Dupleix, Commandant-General of the establishments of the Compagnie des Indes centred upon Pondicherry. In the light

---

[62] Marquis de Stainville to Emperor Francis I, Paris, 23 July 1747: Ö.S./H.H.S., Lothringisches Hausarchiv 77/177A.

of this significant failure of one of the last proposals for insulating territories overseas from European conflict, the French in India had got cracking. Vaulting Dupleix called up the ships of the enterprising La Bourdonnais, governor of the French islands of the Indian Ocean, the Seychelles and Île de France, otherwise Mauritius. La Bourdonnais temporarily seized local command of the sea, swooped upon the British in Madras and captured it in September 1746. The disposal of so rich a prize provoked ugly contention, yet again in that war, between two French leaders; and a cyclone speeded La Bourdonnais back to his islands while Dupleix stripped down Madras. Later, an English riposte against Pondicherry was to prove abortive.

Madras was to be a prime pawn for France in that peace-bargaining with England which also largely related to America. Yet those initial French successes in India helped to promote European intervention in local politics, leading towards British empire in that sub-continent. Soon, too, the French attempt to encompass the English hold upon the Carnatic and the Coast of Coromandel by hooking round to mobilize the barren reaches of Mahratta power in the Deccan, with the questing Marquis de Bussy thrusting through Hyderabad even to Aurangabad, was to instil an empire-building lesson at French expense: that wide sweeps of imaginative enterprise with tenuous grounding are no match in the long run for what may be less calculated expansion spilling outwards, as under its own momentum, from more consolidated areas of productive settlement. This lesson for the French was to be strikingly paralleled upon the American continent.

In New England the old British colonies and their affiliates, still looking mainly to the Atlantic seaboard, were already in rapid expansion during the first half of the eighteenth century. New crops, like rice and indigo in South Carolina, were being exploited, commerce was on the up, with new ports such as Baltimore opening out, while the total population roughly trebled from some 400,000 to a million and a quarter. This rise was already primed by foreign immigrants, notably the Pennsylvania Dutch, largely Germans fleeing the devastation of the Palatinate by the War of the Spanish Succession, mostly Lutherans but also including Moravians, Dunkards, Swenkfelders, and other religious weirdies in the pietist footsteps of Penn and his Holy Experiment, on towards such as Jonathan Edwards and missionary Whitefield.

The newcomers and bolder spirits in that nascent America were already tending to thrust inland towards virgin freeholds. Thus began a century and more of westward enterprise and transcontinental exploration across thousands of miles to the shores, at last, of that farther ocean. For the present the migration was still towards the Blue Ridge and, out beyond again, the Great Smoky Mountains, the Iron Mountains, and the Shenandoah, on through the back-country of Virginia and Maryland, spilling across the barrier of the Appalachians and, quite soon now, over into the lands lying between the Monongahela and Great Kanawha rivers, looking across to the Red Indian territories upon the Ohio. But already the Indians there were not quite alone.

Pioneering Frenchmen were probing towards the Ohio from the opposite direction, from right back in the Illinois country, establishing little fortified posts and calling in support from the Shawnees, the Miamis and, if might be, the balancing Iroquois with their Confederation of the Six Nations centred upon Onondaga. Though there was already some tendency for the Indians to favour overtures from the commercial British, as with the Creeks and Chickasaws down by the Mississippi, where the French could usually rely upon the Choctaws. For backwoodsmen from the Carolinas, out after deerskins, were also running up against the French in those southern parts. Already in 1721 the British government had built a fort upon the Altamaha River in what was soon to become the colony of Georgia, founded by the philanthropic General Oglethorpe as a dual-purpose refuge and buffer against the Spaniards in Florida and, west of them, the French.

France had set about ordering her American dominions after the Treaty of Utrecht had diminished them to British benefit in Newfoundland and Acadia, soon to become Nova Scotia. But between those two, at the gateway to all French Canada, France yet retained Cape Breton Island where, in 1720, she had begun to build at Louisbourg the strongest fortress in North America. Two years earlier and two thousand miles to the south New Orleans had been founded to head the province of Louisiana, only just separated administratively from French Canada. The French ambition, though, was to link the two geographically from either end, pushing up the mighty valleys of the Mississippi and the Ohio and down the spacious navigation of the Saint Lawrence to draw a grand cordon of containment round behind the English colonies. Loose control by France of vast and largely empty stretches of the wilderness was picked out by her few and far-ranging fur-traders, the hardy *voyageurs*, one index to French failure to consolidate her North American economy and populate its settlements in sufficient density. The advent of war in 1744 had found French Canada with a diminutive population of some fifty thousand *habitants* reproducing the agricultural inadequacies of France and her administrative clamp through intendants and the governor-general up aloft at Quebec, himself directly subordinated to the Minister of Marine.

The seemingly unlikely combination of rigid bureaucracy and military adventure is a recurrent feature of autocratic government. It then afforded the French colonists initial advantages against their opposites in New England, loosely and more popularly organized, often parochial in the relations of one colony with another and not invariably of the strictest loyalty towards their mother country. Shippers in New England brazenly, and profitably, continued to supply timber, grain and Irish beef to French islands in preference to British in the West Indies, where renewed hostilities brought inconclusive results. But William Shirley, vigorous governor of the colony of Massachusetts, had promoted that colonial capture from the surprised French in 1745 of Louisbourg, a precious pawn to play off against French captures in the Netherlands and in India.

A year after the British reduction of Louisbourg its recapture was planned by the active Count de Maurepas and entrusted to a relation, one of the La Rochefoucaulds styled the Duke d'Enville, lieutenant-general of galleys and Vice-Admiral of the Levant. This noble favourite was short of experience of the rougher waters of the Atlantic. His squadron was wrecked, his own life lost upon the rugged coasts of Nova Scotia. French failure at sea was repeated in the following May of 1747 off Cape Finistère. Seventeen men-of-war under Admiral Anson overcame the gallant resistance of the Marquis de La Jonquière in command of an inferior French fleet escorting a valuable convoy outward-bound for the Compagnie des Indes. Magnificent prizes of bullion and booty were triumphantly paraded on wagons through London: a crude but telling illustration of how England, so long worsted upon the continent, could yet make war pay. In France one of the charges brought by the Marshal de Noailles against the Marquis d'Argenson had been 'his antipathy and prejudice against commerce and the colonies. He has no hesitation in saying that nothing is more useless. In vain does one represent to him that they are what constitute the strength, greatness and power of the English':[63] a strikingly colonial emphasis from the patron of the Count de Stainville. The Marquis d'Argenson was soon sneering that it was difficult to know which had been worse managed by Maurepas, the navy or, in his Parisian capacity, the opera, faced with bankruptcy.

Bankruptcies and soaring prices were by 1747 being brought home to Frenchmen and their wives under the British clamp. 'Nothing',

[63] Marshal de Noailles, memorandum of 15 Dec. 1746 to King Louis XV: Rousset, ii. 271.

wrote Barbier, 'is arriving here from the islands of Martinique; sugar, which was fourteen sous a pound, costs twenty-seven sous; coffee has gone up by half as much again; no cod for lent except by way of the Dutch. Money is scarce so that all is at a stop.'[64] By the end of the year the Marquis de Stainville was reporting from Paris: 'In discoursing the other day with a big merchant of this country he told me that it was proven that French commerce for the ports situated upon the ocean had diminished by fifty millions a year, that of Marseilles by more than twenty, and that all the manufactures of the kingdom were falling off. And he calculated that [French] trade in general had diminished by one hundred millions, which constitutes a considerable article for the kingdom and the total ruin of many individuals. Another considerable article, which greatly worries the ministry, is the dearth which is already making itself felt in many provinces; and it is very difficult to remedy it, the harvest having generally nearly failed and it being impossible to draw cereals from abroad, the sea not being free.'[65] That same day the emotional Marquis d'Argenson was proclaiming 'famine this year in half France'.[66]

Of course England too had her troubles. There champagne was by now in very short supply – a French officer captured at Cape Finistère accordingly sent Admiral Anson a consignment of the best champagne he could find in Calais upon his repatriation that same year. (This was to offset a gold watch which the Frenchman had won from Anson in a bet upon the outcome at Lawfeldt, 'not wishing to be behindhand in generosity with an English lord, however rich he may be'.)[67] If England's subsidies to her allies were to reach the alarming level of £1,750,000 in 1748, a longer significance attached to the extent to which London was by then becoming an international centre for marine insurance. On the French side, necessity being the mother of invention, the Compagnie des Indes in 1747 brought out a diving-bell to help fish up ships and their cargoes which had gone to the bottom.

If France fared badly in her commercial and colonial struggle in what were then known as the *pays éloignés*, the far countries, not even in the European sphere was her showing uniformly good. In Italy, in some ways the most interesting European theatre of that war, fortune turned against France some months after the brilliant opening of

[64] Barbier, iv. 215.
[65] Marquis de Stainville to Emperor Francis I, Paris, 17 Dec. 1747: Ö.S./H.H,S., Lothringisches Hausarchiv 77/177A.
[63] D'Argenson, v. 124.
[67] De Saint Georges to Count d'Argenson, Paris, 6 Sept. 1747: Arch. Guerre C., vol. 3204, no. 114.

1747 with the eviction of the Austrians from both Genoa and Provence.

Marshal de Belle-Isle followed through with transports to sustain beleaguered Genoa despite British sea-power. The first convoy mostly slipped through under the Count de Stainville's former second-in-command, now something of an old hand at amphibious operations, so that Maréchal-de-Camp de Mauriac with some three battalions, about two thousand men, came marching into Genoa in triumph.

The French gripped the mountainous perimeter held in bitter partisan-warfare by local peasants, notably under a certain Barbarossa, against the vengeful Austrians under General von Schulenburg in succession to Botta. In Genoa itself the partiotic uprising had an egalitarian edge with workers' brigades like the Arts Battalion of artisans keeping a lookout for any backsliding by patricians. Hundreds of priests, too, shouldered muskets, and women and girls were to toil at constructing defences. The whole republic of Genoa stood at bay. Another knock to conventional warfare then was given by the arrival of the French Colonel de Roquépine specializing in atrocity-propaganda – the Pandours eating babies and so forth. Indeed the conduct of the teutonic enemy and his slavonic auxiliaries was grisly enough.

On 15 May 1747 the Austrians took Barbarossa's stronghold at Voltri, ravaged it atrociously and drove ahead to Masone and Rivarolo. The French under Chauvelin, young Stainville's successor of the staff after Dettingen, punched back. At the beginning of that month the Genoese had been reassured as to French support by the arrival from Antibes of Lieutenant-General the Duke de Boufflers, husband of the Count de Stainville's friend and patroness. Boufflers took over from Mauriac, galvanized the defence, wore himself out in the blazing sun, expired at the age of forty-five on the morning of 2 July, just before the dawn of deliverance. Within a few days the enemy were falling back from their close investment of Genoa and the environs. King Charles-Emmanuel had once again given precedence to a threat to his Alpine rear in the broader strategy and dominant geography of the Italian theatre.

After the Austrians had recrossed the Var the only scrap of French soil still held by them was the Îles de Lérins off Cannes, important in that phrase of coastal convoy towards Genoa. On 25 May 1747 Chevert, ever on the go, nipped over and captured the Île Sainte-Marguérite from the Austrians. British naval protection had been entrusted to Rear-Admiral John Byng, who had glumly forecast the coup by the French 'without having it in my power to prevent them'.[68] The Austrians blamed Byng for lack of support in ominous prefiguration of his greater failure nine years later to succour a greater island in Mediterranean waters. The Îles de Lérins once mopped up, the Marshal de Belle-Isle struck out again to recross the Var and recapture the objectives familiar to the Count de Stainville from three years earlier, Nice, Villefranche, Ventimiglia on 1 July.

The parallel with Conti's compaign of 1744 was ominously close. The Spanish commander still was Captain-General de Las Minas, as intent as ever upon plunging along the coast 'to land us', complained Belle-Isle to Noailles 'in this Genoese vice through a defile of fifty or sixty leagues'.[69] Belle-Isle, echoing Conti, held out for another attack across the Alps from Dauphiny, only to receive instructions to conform to a coastal strategy, recognized though it was by the French Minister of War as 'nonsense, an infatuation'.[70] Noailles explained that this unpromising decision, taken in a Franco-Spanish council of war at Tongres as Louis XV was passing through to Lawfeldt, was inspired by French fear that Spain, from her soundings with Austria at Lisbon, might enter into 'a separate settlement ... if she were provided with a plausible pretext'.[71]

The coastal command reached the Marshal de Belle-Isle too late to pull back his brother, the chevalier, from thrusting out from Guillestre down the Dora Riparia against Exilles. On 19 July 1747 he led into an uphill, desperate battle against Austro-Sardinian forces artfully entrenched upon the Col de l'Assiette, the key to Exilles. The Chevalier de Belle-Isle, fighting furiously, laid down his life upon that alpine battlefield where the finally retreating French left nearly six thousand men, mostly corpses. The Chevalier, once reputed so cold and wise, was denounced for his temerity by the bereaved nobility of France. Saxe smugly deplored the overweening ambition of his old enemies, the Belle-Isles.

VII

If the Marshal de Saxe himself was scarcely scatheless after Lawfeldt, the then Count de Stainville was to comment further:

Not being able to undertake the siege of Maestricht, they decided upon an enterprise

---

[68] Rear-Admiral Byng to Vice-Admiral Medley, H.M.S. *Superbe* off Île Sainte-Marguérite, 27 Apr. 1747 (O.S.): *Report on the manuscripts of Lady Du Cane*, Historical Manuscripts Commission, Cd. 2367 (London, 1905), p. 175.

[69] Marshal de Belle-Isle to Marshal de Noailles, 7 June 1747; Archives de Mouchy: Broglie/Saxe, ii. 258.

[70] Count d'Argenson to Marshal de Belle-Isle, 26 July 1747; ibid., p. 267.

[71] Marshal de Noailles to Marshal de Belle-Isle, July 1747: ibid., p. 263.

equally dangerous, much more costly and perfectly useless, for indeed they had to do something. So they conceived the idea of undertaking the siege of Bergen-op-Zoom. Marshal de Saxe himself undertook the containment of Monsieur de Cumberland [before Maestricht], and he sent Monsieur de Lowendahl to Bergen-op-Zoom. This Monsieur de Lowendahl had pretty nearly all the vices that one can have; but he was distinguished on account of his fawning upon everybody in general, but especially upon the Marshal de Saxe, whose courtier, and even humblest slave, he was. The marshal charged him with the siege of Bergen-op-Zoom, saying to him: 'If you do not succeed, all the blame for the small success of the campaign will fall upon you; but, if you succeed, I will have you made a Marshal of France.' Monsieur de Lowendahl very humbly thanked the marshal and went to Bergen-op-Zoom. The King, who had not so much at heart the appearance of having fought a fine campaign, awaited, with impatience mingled with the greatest boredom, the issue of Bergen-op-Zoom, which they had made him believe to be very significant, for fear lest he should too abruptly leave the army.[72]

The multiple malice of this ironical analysis largely matched the truth. The reputation of the adventuring Lowendahl, the Danish royal bastard now adhering to the Saxon one, was no better than might be expected of one who had figured in Russia as a protégé of the sinister Empress Anne and had, to contemporary scandal, been twice divorced. As to strategy Saxe himself confessed to Noailles that after his failure to exploit Lawfeldt, 'nothing presented itself to be done to justify the result of this combat except the siege of Bergen-op-Zoom, which was regarded as a poor fortress',[73] perhaps on the strength of the previous string of Dutch capitulations. For Bergen-op-Zoom was a military fastness unsubdued by the fierce skill of Parma in 1588, of Spinola in 1622, and now, artfully enlaced with waterworks, was the masterpiece of Baron Cohorn, the Dutch Vauban. For weeks Lowendahl, who had arrived there on 12 July 1747, was unable to make any significant dent. If King Louis, still in the field before Maestricht, was bored, the combination of activity and boredom was shared by his mistress, left behind to recover from 'a terrible bile'[74] due to his departure. From around then comes a rare glimpse of Madame de Pompadour at war. Probably in touch with Pâris Duverney:

She received her courier from the army every day during the last campaigns in Flanders, when she lived at Choisy in the absence of the king. Nothing was concluded without her. Her decision upon everything was awaited. She spent whole nights in replying. Her conduct was in charge of the Marquis de Gontaut, who was derisively called her chief eunuch. She saw hardly anyone. The princesses of the blood used to come to supper there and returned home to sleep. This life very

[72] Choiseul, *Mémoires*, pp. 43–4.
[73] Marshal-General de Saxe, memorandum of 17 Aug. 1747: Arch. Guerre C., vol. 3203, no. 240.
[74] Marquise de Pompadour to Count de Clermont, 19 May 1747: Broglie/Saxe, ii. 232.

quickly bored her. A crowned lover causes double anxiety; another could steal his heart. These considerations contributed not a little to the promotion of peace. Besides, she was piqued at not having followed the King to the war whereas Madame de Châteauroux had gone to it.[75]

The embrace of boredom may well have included the Count de Stainville, also stuck before Maestricht in inaction – and expense. Stainville was still at Saxe's headquarters at the Camp de la Commanderie when he received from Mathieu, the receiver of the patrimonial marquisate, an advance of 1,500 livres representing the payment for the July quarter of Brigeat's general lease at 6,000 livres a year; and Stainville drew a further thousand livres from his personal inheritance at Beurey. By the middle of August his Regiment of Navarre was standing just south of Tongres, 'its right at the large hollow-road of Glaen, its left on the Joar, near the gate of Troyes called that of Liége'.[76]

Stalemate in the camps of war was, however, offset by their diplomatic involvement. On 8 July 1747, within a week of the battle of Lawfeldt, General Ligonier had returned to the headquarters of the Duke of Cumberland on parole as the bearer from Saxe, with whom he shared scientific and womanizing interests, of the first French pursuit of peace in a directly English quarter in that war. Cumberland relayed Ligonier's report that 'the Marshal de Saxe owned to him that the battle was not worth winning ... that the King of France disliked war, and that he [the Marshal] was sensible of the slippery path he trod, as he knew they would never forgive him being a German.'[77] The ensuing Saxe–Ligonier interlude in diplomacy is well known but now appears less as a colourfully isolated episode than as the latest term in Louis's secret soundings for peace through Saxe and others, hitherto aimed towards Austria as in the marshal's overture to the Marquis de Stainville in the spring of 1746 and in the following winter through the court of Saxony. The continuity was to be underlined by Saxe's comment to Brühl on his dealings with Ligonier: 'If I had been the master to direct this negotiation according to my lights, or rather according to my inclination, I should have preferred to treat with His Excellency the Count Batthyany.'[78]

As it was, the Saxon marshal in the French army encouraged the French general in the British one to treat behind the backs of the

[75] Kaunitz/Mémoire, p. 448.
[76] 'État général de la position actuelle des troupes qui composent l'armée du Roy', French memorandum of 16 Aug. 1747: Arch. Guerre C., vol. 3210, no. 175.
[77] Duke of Cumberland to Earl of Chesterfield, 10 July 1747: British Library, Add. MSS. 32,711, fo. 587; Lodge, p. 268.
[78] Marshal-General de Saxe to Count Brühl, camp at Tongres, 14 Aug. 1747: Vitzthum/Saxe, p. 507.

French 'King and politicians. I must deceive them in order to serve them. Courtiers and ministers are like women; you have to guess their desires and it is easier to make them do things than to make them say things.'[79] Saxe's letter was next day described by the Duke of Cumberland to the Duke of Newcastle as 'either the frankest or falsest I ever met with'.[80] Perhaps, as could happen with Saxe, it was a bit of both. Here at all events is a further pointer to the kind of distrust which he inspired in such as the future Duke de Choiseul.

Saxe's approach to Ligonier rather than Batthyany turned upon the nub now of British rendition of Cape Breton, substantially in return for the Netherlands, whereas Saxe subsequently attributed to Ligonier a lapse over Spain, while he himself had forgotten to include the necessary restoration of Genoa and Modena: suggestive not only of military amateurishness in negotiation but also of military subsidence in Italy after the bloody day upon the Col de l'Assiette. In that theatre allies upon both sides were at odds. The Spaniards, fed up with the discomfited French, took separate soundings with the Austrians which chiefly served to embroil the latter further with the Piedmontese. That autumn a small Austro-Sardinian reversal of Conti's march of 1744 up the Stura, now just into France by the Col d'Argentière, achieved no greater effect than Belle-Isle's little comeback coastwise to succour the citadel of Ventimiglia at the western tip of Genoese territory. Genoa herself remained ringed around but she had been braced by the landing of a successor to the Duke de Boufflers in the person of the Duke de Richelieu, accompanied by his nephew the Duke d'Agenais, written off by the Count de Stainville after Coni. Genoa held out and in Turin General Wentworth renewed the British veto to the south. In the British book, which was largely the allied account-book, Austria was no more to regain Naples than she was to lose her Netherlands.

The Marshal de Saxe's overture to the Duke of Cumberland evoked a ready response from him and from the pacific element in the British cabinet headed by the prime minister, Henry Pelham, and the Earl of Chesterfield. Less keen were others like the Earl of Sandwich and the Duke of Newcastle, who scotched the French design for a separate negotiation by insisting upon full communication to allies. This may have critically postponed peace-preliminaries and provoked a cry against them from the formerly pacific, newly royalist Dutch, who offered to go halves with England in hiring

[79] Marshal-General de Saxe to General Ligonier, 30 July 1747: translation as in R. Whitworth, op. cit., pp. 161–2.
[80] Duke of Cumberland to Duke of Newcastle, 31 July 1747: British Library, Add. MSS. 32,712, fo. 163: Lodge, p. 276.

thirty thousand Russian troops to swing the next campaign. Bentinck described Ligonier's behaviour as 'scurrilously ridiculous'[81] and valuably secured an English undertaking to consult the Dutch in future peace-negotiations in advance of the other allies. When Maria Theresa was apprised of the Saxe–Ligonier sounding she quickly authorized Field-Marshal Batthyany to treat and even to 'sign the peace with the Most Christian King and his allies ... , being very glad that matters are being handled by the Count de Saxe whom I greatly esteem'.[82]

Batthyany was at present to act without Cumberland in putting to Saxe direct Austrian proposals, at last, for peace with France, so long sought in secret through the Marquis de Stainville. Austria would now concede the French demands for the cession of Furnes and the restoration of Modena and Genoa in Italy, significantly prominent in the Austrian scheme; Maria Theresa at last contemplated an Italian apanage for Don Philip but only by an ingenious shunt to Corsica, in perennial revolt against Genoa; and mere renunciation by Austria of designs on Naples would hopefully recover her Lombard cessions to Charles Emmanuel by the bitter treaty of Worms. It was the French turn now to play the allied gambit in consideration of Spain though Saxe favoured dragging along the Spaniards who, he assured Ligonier, were 'a *canaille* and more obstinate to deal with than their own mules'.[83] But Ligonier had to inform Saxe that Cumberland himself, unlike Batthyany, had no power to conclude peace. The heady prospect of a quick peace between soldiers had been destroyed. The role of Saxe and Ligonier was reduced to arranging, despite Austrian protest, the meeting which took place between the Earl of Sandwich and the Marquis de Puysieulx in a convent at Liége on 11 September 1747.

Puysieulx and Sandwich spent hours going over, once again, the well-worn issues leading towards, or away from, long-elusive peace. English insistence upon French dismantling of Dunkirk and repudiation of the Stuarts was especially wounding. The negotiators were reduced to an echo of Puysieulx earlier to Stainville: 'the fruit was not yet ripe'[84] – but ripening. France really did want peace, while Puysieulx twigged that Sandwich was perfunctory in his defence of Austrian, as distinct from Sardinian and Dutch, interests. The two agreed that a peace-congress to include allies might usefully

---

[81] Bentinck to Earl of Sandwich, 12 July 1747: Sandwich Papers: Lodge, p. 270, n. 1.

[82] Empress Maria Theresa to Field-Marshal Batthyany, 17 July 1747: O.S./H.H.S: Arneth, iii. 478, n. 14.

[83] Cited in the present translation by R. Whitworth, op. cit., p. 162.

[84] Earl of Sandwich to Earl of Chesterfield, 11 Sept. 1747: P.R.O./S.P.F., Holland 426, fo. 135: Lodge, p. 288.

be held on neutral soil at Aix-la-Chapelle. Sandwich artfully encouraged Puysieulx with the prospect, still, of an Anglo-French dialogue at the centre of a general congress. This improved its chances because it corresponded to reality. As yet, though, room for rapprochement between the prime antagonists remained limited. A campaign for 1748 was preparing even as that of 1747 flared into final activity.

Four days after the Sandwich-Puysieulx conversation at Liége, on the night of 15–16 September, the Count de Lowendahl, ever before Bergen-op-Zoom, launched a sudden attack by storm into and over its battered defences. In an instant, it seemed, the ramparts sprouted French standards. The sleepy Dutch defenders resorted to street-fighting and sniping. They were punished. Amid a spreading conflagration the victorious assailants, in a French narration, came bursting in 'like lions in fury ... They massacred, raped and pillaged the town ... Our officers generally agree that our troops are crueller and harsher in pillaging than any others.'[85] Bergen-op-Zoom became a mercenary charnelhouse that grim Saturday. In the wake of the drunken despoilers came Jews and other squalid campfollowers, buying up and reselling loot although the French 'officers are not sufficiently in funds to buy from the soldiers'. Young Stainville, pulling in his rents while on campaign, was not the only one to feel the pinch. Bergen afforded another illustration after Coni of the economic inversion between officers and other ranks which could arise in the supposedly rigid armies of the Ancien Régime.

This further instance, too, of cruel warfare, even in western Europe, shocked contemporaries. A French officer present at that shambles was to write: 'Far from depicting it, I want to forget it for ever'.[86] Nasty Lowendahl, however, expressed offhand regret at having been unable 'to guarantee this wretched town from pillage ... It has enriched the army prodigiously, and I hope that it will render it as audacious as it will humiliate that of the enemy.'[87] The Marshal de Saxe, who had six years earlier conspicuously spared Prague such a fate, is alleged to have advised Louis XV that the only thing to do with Lowendahl was either to hang him or to make him a marshal. Saxe extracted the baton from the reluctant king.

Louis returned to Compiègne and Versailles in the company of his intimates including the Marquis de Gontaut. Units began to pull back for the winter and the long confrontation of unreduced

---

[85] Barbier, iv. 259–60 for the following.

[86] Chevalier de Ray, *Réflections et souvenirs du Chevalier de Ray*, ed. L. Mouillard, p. 39.

[87] Lieutenant-General de Lowendahl to Count d'Argenson, Bergen-op-Zoom, 17 Sept. 1747: Arch. Guerre C., vol. 3204, no. 217. (Broglie/Saxe, ii. 365–6, prints these extracts in a slightly variant context and gives the addressee as Saxe.)

Maestricht was stood down. By 9 October 1747 the Count de Stainville's Regiment of Navarre was due into camp at Wavre[88] before passing on to snug down in his native Lorraine. Also returning were the foreign envoys who had followed the king to the front that summer, leaving behind the Marquis de Stainville, isolated and reduced to consular concerns. Out of allied loyalty Stainville made it his own rule not to grant a passport to a British traveller unless he could produce a British one 'because there are many people attached to the house of Stuart on whom I should not wish passports of mine to be found; I hope that your Imperial Majesty will approve my delicacy.'[89]

Most of the returning diplomatists took up again with the Marquis de Stainville and his good dinners. Such was the occasion at the end of that September for the Swedish Minister to France, Baron de Scheffer, to urge upon the Marquis de Stainville that the allied powers should clinch with the pacific inclination of France. 'He spoke to me', reported Stainville, 'as Monsieur de Puysieulx might have done.' But Stainville's other crony, Saint-Séverin, dining with him a fortnight later, was less sanguine about peacemaking, saying that he would not be representing France at Aix-la-Chapelle any more than at Breda, and proceeding to give an analysis which generally corresponded to that of Stainville's interlocutor in a still more interesting conversation which he had had the previous day, 12 October 1747.

'Last Thursday', reported the Marquis de Stainville, 'there came to see me a man who has exacted my word of honour that I should not name him. He had arrived the day before from the army. Your Imperial Majesty will easily recognize him from his remarks, if you will recall a conversation which I had last winter with the same man.'[90] That cut out the Marshal de Saxe, who was in any case to remain in Brussels for another couple of months yet. Nor could the nameless visitor have been Alary, Saint-Séverin, or Puysieulx, who had returned earlier from the Netherlands. It is as certain as anything now can be that it was Pâris-Duverney, further indicated by Stainville's assurance that 'the man who talked to me is better informed than anybody of the most secret intentions'.

The Marquis de Stainville opened their conversation with the latest campaign and reported that Pâris-Duverney 'frankly confessed to me that it would have been a very wretched one without the

[88] 'État des troupes qui seront demain 9 aux camps de Wavre et de Florival aux ordres de M. le Comte d'Estrées', 8 Oct. 1747: Arch. Guerre C., vol. 3206, no. 65.
[89] Marquis de Stainville to Emperor Francis I, Paris, 1 Oct. 1747: Ö.S./H.H.S., Lothringisches Hausarchiv 77/177A for the following.
[90] Ibid., 15 Oct. 1747 for the following.

miracle of Bergobzoom [*sic*]. He called it a miracle, saying that the enterprise had been extravagant and that it should never have been expected to succeed, but it had succeeded.' Nevertheless Louis XV still sought peace and had himself formulated 'the sincere observations which he had made on this subject to Monsieur Ligonier'. The Marquis de Stainville had in his time had complementary indications of the personal diplomacy of the King of France, who 'ardently desired peace'; though Pâris-Duverney now seems not to have mentioned the French evasion of the overture through Batthyany. That evasion might even have reflected, in part, the French predilection, matching the Austrian distaste, for dealing through Stainville. Though now – another factor – Duverney's line with him was significantly varied from that of earlier occasions.

Stainville related that he proceeded to question Duverney:

What, then, was responsible for this peace, so desired, not being made; because I was sure on my side that my masters asked nothing better than to contribute to it. 'I am willing to believe it', he replied to me, but in a tone which made me judge that he was not persuaded of it. 'But', he continued, 'England does not want it. She is mistress of the sea, and thinks to exhaust France by destroying her commerce. However, let her not deceive herself in that. Let her remember that the late King Louis XIV made war for fourteen years without having a vessel at sea, always unfortunate, losing a battle and several fortresses per campaign, having consumed his revenues for four years in advance; yet he finished in 1714 by making an honourable peace. We are not in the same case. We are winning as much per campaign as the other lost. The king has not drawn for one quarter upon his revenues of next year, the kingdom is inexhaustible in resources. The conquered territories are actually bringing the king in thirty-five millions, which help greatly to meet the expenses of the campaign, and if it is still necessary to wage war for thirty years, the king will be in condition to sustain it for thirty years.

The great French financier could usually be relied on to cut through to essentials, beneath all the trappings of that age, and to instruct with economic data even when it was politically angled in optimistic support of his challenge for war or peace. Pâris-Duverney, in Stainville's vivid record, knew of only one means of making that peace, so desirable and dependent upon Maria Theresa:

Let her insinuate to the King of England her desire for peace; and here is the way to do it: let her say that, whatever wish and whatever need she may have for peace, she will never make it except in concert with him, but that she asks that he should examine with care, and without flattering himself, the state wherein the allies find themselves; that if, in undertaking one more campaign, there is hope of rendering their situation better than it is, one must unquestionably make every effort to prosecute this campaign with vigour, that if on the contrary the [allied] situation can only become worse, it is necessary sooner rather than later to finish a war which is becoming more onerous every day without hope of changing the general situation.

The latter alternative, argued Duverney, represented the true position in view of French strength in the Netherlands. In the next campaign there, explained the military financier:

There are three principal objects which we should have and for which the allies should be upon their guard, Zealand, Bois-le-Duc and Willemstadt, and Maestricht. It is certain that the allies cannot be in force everywhere. If they thin out one side we shall perceive it – we cannot fail to aggrandize our conquests further. In consequence the conditions of peace will become more onerous for the allies, and if the King of England manages to extend his commerce in the New World as the [French] king extends his conquests in Flanders, he [George II] will soon say to his allies that he wishes to make peace and enjoy the wellbeing which he has procured for his subjects, and will further make them [his allies] make sacrifices to attain to this peace; whereas, his object not being fulfilled, he is unwilling that these same allies should re-enter into their possessions through a reasonable peace, and moreover he is even making them risk losing much more still. That is what I should vigorously represent to the King of England if I had the honour to be in the council of the emperor and the empress.

All this the Marquis de Stainville reported 'word for word ... without ... even the reflections which my attachment suggests to me.' The confidant of the innermost counsellors of the French king was a broken diplomat.

As for Pâris-Duverney, one can well appreciate his secret sway over the government of France. His essay in diplomatic persuasion must rank as brilliant, frank yet acute, elaborated with gallic logic and precision upon the highest plane of policy, taking into realistic account both the economic conditionals and the primacy of England now for attempts at peace, modifying the role of Austria accordingly in recognizing her dependence upon her British ally while yet sowing distrust between them, artfully seeking, in effect, to pass on to Vienna the political pinch of British economic warfare against France. And King Louis XV was reaching out from victory to peace. But authoritative governments which employ their best men in deep secret, as France was now doing, need to reckon, perhaps, that in the long count of history – if not the very longest since truth will out – they stand to see their case go rather by default in comparison with more open dealers who, as already then in England to a considerable extent, do not shrink from tempering their policies in the forum of public opinion, through press and parliament.

Any idea, however, that the French government in the middle of the eighteenth century merely ignored public opinion is a misconception now again confirmed. Pâris-Duverney might put a bold face upon economic stringencies in France for the benefit of Stainville, who had recently (6 August 1747) reported sombrely upon her financial pinch. Its incidence upon the population, and pressure towards peace, did not escape the French government. Pâris-Monmartel's forecast to Stainville, at the end of 1745, of a three-year economic term for the French war-effort without extreme measures may not have been so far out. In that October of 1747, indeed, Monmartel was strikingly successful in raising funds through a public lottery on ingeniously attractive terms, and a surcharge of four sous per livre had just been slapped on all the dues previously imposed by edicts of 1730 and 1743. Barbier commented that this 'will send up all provisions, which are already very dear ... It is solely to subvent the expenses of the present war, which imposition [however] is for nine years ... The edict is not too clear, but its levy will be real.'[91]

It was all very well for Frederick the Great, snugly neutral still, to lecture the French government as he now did for its flabbiness in going along unduly with the pacificism of 'the people and the public of an inferior order'[92] in the time of French triumph in the Netherlands. If Puysieulx like Duverney was conscious enough of the countervailing maritime and economic factors, his reply to the King of Prussia stressed the psychological one:

We are governing a nation ... [of] vivacity and levity ... which, having seemed to desire war, today sighs only after peace. The king's administration should not subject itself blindly to this inconstancy: but it must also know how to subscribe to it in favour of the great qualities which this nation moreover possesses, above all at a time when she is lavishing her blood and her goods for her king with a generosity and a disinterestedness whereof only she is capable.[93]

In this elevated spirit was the Marquis de Puysieulx to direct for France that long-sought peacemaking from which his old friend, the Marquis de Stainville, was to remain excluded. The latter, furthermore, was now stricken by one of his recurrent bouts of illness, with a fever lasting several weeks. Whereas his son and heir was heading back into the swim.

[91] Barbier, iv. 261.
[92] King Frederick II to Baron Le Chambrier, 10 Oct. 1747: Arch. Aff. Étr.: Broglie/Saxe, ii. 388.
[93] Marquis de Puysieulx to Marquis de Valory, 25 Nov. 1747: ibid., pp. 390-1.

CHAPTER VIII

PEACEMAKING

I

'THE army of the Marshal de Saxe has separated', reported the
Marquis de Stainville on 22 October 1747. 'The regiments are
marching to the winter-quarters ... and all the general officers and
colonels are successively arriving here',[1] among them the Count de
Stainville. He may have returned to Paris via Lorraine and was
certainly there a month later, at the seat of the marquisate at
Demange-aux-Eaux. There on 22 November 1747 he had a stiffish
and premonitory accounting for the year with Nicholas Mathieu.
The accounts then presented to young Stainville were necessarily in
interim for that whole year; and since those for the earlier war-years
were only to be checked off by the elder Stainville in the following
summer, that may have been the point of impact by his son upon the
estate-management. On the following day of 23 November he gave
orders for repairs to the château de Stainville, which may have fallen
into wartime neglect. For the present, however, the main concern for
the Count de Stainville was probably that he got Mathieu to pay over
to him a thousand livres in cash. Following upon the advances to
Stainville at the Camp de la Commanderie, he seems to have lost
little time in cashing in on the estate.

The Count de Stainville was set for a jolly season after his black
spring. Life beckons to swift youth. And, after breath itself, the
certificates of life are love and laughter.

'I passed the winter of 1747 to 1748 at Paris, solely occupied by my
pleasures', he was to recall. 'I often heard talk of the intrigues at court,
or rather of the activities to which the courtiers devoted themselves
in the suite of Madame de Pompadour and even of a Madame
d'Estrades, whom Madame de Pompadour had placed at court as her
follower; but I took so little interest in the court intrigues and
ambitions that I have forgotten what I may have known of that
time.'[2] At the time, though, the ambitions at court of one friend, at
least, did not leave him indifferent.

---

[1] Marquis de Stainville to Emperor Francis I, Paris, 22 Oct. 1747: Ö.S./H.H.S., Lothringisches
Hausarchiv 77/177A.
[2] Choiseul, *Mémoires*, p. 44.

If the count was kept posted on the favourite and her circle by mutual friends such as Bernstorff and Gontaut, Stainville's preference was still for the pleasures of Paris, perhaps also the circle of her enemy, the Count de Maurepas. According to a later friend of Stainville, 'some thoughtless remarks had earned him the hatred of Madame de Pompadour, and he used to boast of it. He called himself, though in jest, the Chevalier de Maurepas to show that he was second in the mistress's scale of resentment.'[3] Nor perhaps was it only in mordant wit that Stainville learnt from Maurepas. He was one of the few ministers of that period of whom the later Duke de Choiseul spoke with some respect. Choiseul was to be the great developer of just those themes of policy which the alert Maurepas had been largely unsuccessful in seeking to promote: French commercial activity abroad, naval expansion against England and furtherance of empire overseas.

The Count de Stainville was not one to neglect the ministerial status of an acquaintance. And despite the self-depreciation in his memoirs of his early years, he was already commanding consideration with such influentials as Bernstorff, Noailles, Conti. This chimed with an allusion by Stainville himself to a development now concerning his friend who was Maurepas's brother-in-law, the charming Duke de Nivernais.

Nivernais, proud of his membership of the French Academy, was something of a poet, to be rated by Horace Walpole as 'at the top of the mediocre'.[4] This duke, who shared Stainville's taste for music and the theatre, had graduated from the Hôtel de Brancas to become one of the best actors in the famous Théâtre des Petits Cabinets recently instituted at Versailles by Madame de Pompadour for the royal distraction. In her sphere, certainly, one thing was apt to lead to another. Towards the close of 1747 there was question of an embassy for Nivernais. It is said that Maurepas wanted him to secure Rome, especially appropriate in view of Nivernais's Roman origins and his relationship by marriage with the then French ambassador there, the Cardinal de La Rochefoucauld. Whereas Stainville subsequently made the rather unexpected admission to Nivernais that 'before your destination to the embassy was entirely fixed, I fought against it. I did not lack means then, and I knew all the value and extent of philosophic arguments. I believe that one can attain to public esteem ... by different ways. I believe also that whatever path you had taken you would have arrived and that you could never miss your goal.'[5]

---

[3] Sénac de Meilhan, *Portraits et caractères du XVIIIe siècle* (Paris, 1945 ed.), p. 134.
[4] Horace Walpole to Gray, Paris, 25 Jan. 1766: Walpole Correspondence, xiv. 184. ·
[5] Count de Stainville to Duke de Nivernais, 24 May 1751: W.N.A., docket V/1, fo. 71.

Perhaps the relative backwater of Rome seemed inadequate, though it rather sounds as though Stainville scouted a diplomatic career for the delicate friend whom he was to assure some years later: 'I have long known of what you are capable, of everything which is good, honest and decent.'[6] As a careerist Stainville was no common one. It would appear that deeper values and farther horizons already informed his thinking and made his directness difficult to gauge. His acute angles raised problems of scale, as in his strategic critique of Saxe. Stainville's claim to influence so early as 1747 is noticeable, noticeable also the announcement on 29 December 1747 that the Duke de Nivernais was appointed ambassador to Rome. French ambassadors then did not usually proceed to their posts for some while and Nivernais's departure was delayed by a difficult pregnancy for his wife, set upon accompanying him. This delay may have helped to underline some association then of Nivernais with Stainville in another respect, through their shared involvement in the theatre.

A comedy call Le Méchant, first performed on 15 April 1747, became the hit of that war-winter in Paris. The author was Jean-Baptiste-Louis Gresset, the former pupil at Louis-le-Grand who had already made his name with his pious parrot, Ver-Vert. If Madame de Pompadour was unenthusiastic about supporting Gresset for the French Academy, to which he was shortly to be elected, she gave his new play a puff by putting it into study by her troupe, featuring Nivernais, at just about the time that he received his embassy.

For a second-rate play Le Méchant abounded in first-rate lines. One especially, slightly improved, echoed on among contemporaries: Les absents ont toujours tort. This poignant generalization was never more so than in its original setting under a king from whom absence spelt displeasure, under a court which was to its initiates 'this country' of enchantment against outsiders, in a capital which notoriously monopolized the best (the original ran: Mais Paris guérit tout, et les absents ont tort),[7] in a society which decreed that far the greater number of its men and women should pay the penalty of issue from humble wombs and should live out their lives, contentedly or not, as absentees from world-history, from those opportunities, delights, dangers and high responsibilities reserved for the noble few, for such as the youthful Count de Stainville. The Méchant's valet, Frontin, was already coming to reflect:

On est bien malheureux d'être né pour servir:
Travailler, ce n'est rien: mais toujours obéir![8]

[6] Ibid., 14 Feb. 1751, fo. 46.
[7] Gresset, Le Méchant in Œuvres de M. Gresset (revised ed., London, 1765), ii. 271.
[8] Ibid., p. 280.

For the quality the immediate fun, as in any close society, was spotting the allusions and characterizations. By December 1747 the Marquis d'Argenson was writing: 'The more times that I see this piece at our theatre, the more I find in it studies drawn from life.'[9] When a creative writer is really successful nothing is more agreeable to his public than to crib his originality by proving it derivative. According to the marquis, Cléon, the principal character who was the Méchant, was compounded of the Count de Maurepas, the Duke d'Ayen, and the Count d'Argenson. Another contemporary, however, testified that Count Stephen de Stainville's 'talent for persiflage and the vexations which he had stirred up in several circles had caused it to be believed that Gresset had had him in mind in tracing the character of the Méchant'.[10]

While Gresset may indeed have compounded his titular character from several, he was perhaps less likely to have looked to ministers and exalted courtiers at Versailles than to such as the young blade from his old school who was roystering in Paris upon the fringes of literary and fast society. Gresset was almost certainly already, as later, acquainted with the stagestruck Stainville, whose 'seductive voice'[11] he was to celebrate. Gresset was an intimate of the salon of the Duchess de Chaulnes, lately linked with the Count de Stainville, and of the so-called Cabinet Vert of the Countess de Forcalquier, another member of his circle. In the Chaulnes salon Gresset encountered not only figures from Louis-le-Grand like Father Bougeant but also, for instance, such a friend of Stainville as the anti-Jesuit Abbé de Chauvelin, the brother of his fellow-officer. This salon was noted for its barbed persiflage (*méchanceté*) in the tradition of the *Médisant* by Destouches. And the germination, now, of Gresset's *Méchant* has been particularly associated with the brilliant circle Chaulnes–Forcalquier–Stainville:[12] and that at just about the time that Stainville was allegedly making himself the talk of Paris by his unedifying complaints against the sexual contretemps of the Duchess de Chaulnes.[13] Such an adherent of hers as Gresset might well have conceived it an apt little revenge to cast him as the unattractively broiling Méchant.

Aside from the question just how far young Stainville may have supplied the model for the Méchant, the fact was that a good many people thought he had. Stainville indeed could not just be written off

[9] D'Argenson, v. 132.   [10] Sénac de Meilhan, op. cit., p. 133.
[11] Gresset, *Epître à M. le Duc de Choiseul*, 20 Jan. 1762, in G. L. van Roosbroeck, *Unpublished Poems by Voltaire, Rousseau, Beaumarchais, Anne d'Urfé, Helvétius, Gresset, etc.* (New York, 1933), p. 44.
[12] Cf. Feuillet de Conches, *Les Salons de conversation au dix-huitième siècle* (Paris, 1891), p. 106.   [13] Cf. p. 631.

in terms of squalid malice. Yet a comparison of his character with that of the Méchant is instructive.

As a play Le Méchant was in many ways typical enough, a brittle comedy intertwining stratagems around love for Chloé, the nominal heroine. But the true one, by a rather bold device, is her waiting-woman, Lisette. She has the last word in the first act wherein the traditional introduction by seconds is an effective and rather unusually psychological debate and build-up upon the character of Cléon, already dominant off stage. For Lisette the Méchant is:

> Un fourbe, un homme faux, déshonoré, perdu
> Qui nuit à tout le monde, et croit tout légitime. [14]

In reply Frontin defends his master, liberal as the future Choiseul often was to his devoted servants. And Chloé's old uncle, Géronte, counters in defence of Cléon:

> Toujours la calomnie en veut aux gens d'esprit,
> Quoi donc! parce qu'il sçait saisir le ridicule,
> Et qu'il dit tout le mal qu'un flatteur dissimule,
> On le prétend méchant! C'est qu'il est naturel:
> Au fond, c'est un bon coeur, un homme essentiel. [15]

The Count de Stainville too was adept at winning the good graces of older people, and 'natural' was very much how he struck contemporaries in that formal age.

The development of the plot was the vindication of the analysis of Lisette. She mainly unmasked the falsity of Cléon in contriving endless mischief for the sheer fun of it beneath the guise of generous affection. Lisette gave this incidental glimpse of the Méchant:

> A son air, où l'on voit dans un rire ironique
> L'estime de lui-même et le mépris d'autrui,
> Comment peut-on sçavoir ce qu'on tient avec lui?
> Jamais ce qu'il vous dit n'est ce qu'il veut vous dire. [16]

This enigmatic touch of superiority was precisely present in the Count de Stainville. In the words of Cléon himself:

> Les sots sont ici-bas pour nos menus plaisirs. [17]

Not far from fools came clogging relatives – in his view fit only for the lower orders: a revolutionary tilt against the supremacy of the

---

[14] Gresset, Œuvres de M. Gresset, ii. 219.   [15] Ibid., ii. 226.   [16] Ibid., ii. 238.
[17] Ibid., ii. 246.

family. But Cléon's philosophy had a sunny side closely matching Stainville's:

> Tout ce qui vit n'est fait que pour nous réjouir,
> Et se moquer du monde est tout l'art d'en jouir.[18]

The Méchant was socially mobile in his emancipated independence. In the words of his duped friend Valère, Chloé's lover:

> Il passe, il se promène
> Dans les cercles divers, sans gêne, sans lien,
> Il a la fleur de tout, n'est esclave de rien.[19]

Cléon himself explained that he had no intention of burying himself in any coterie. On the contrary, wherever he went, society was created. When bored, he moved on, preferring amusing people he did not like to dull friends. Often, indeed, this might be rather making a virtue of necessity, after having been virtually shewn the door. (Compare the testimony of Duclos regarding young Stainville.)[20] But when people shewed they hated him, Cléon merely laughed at them – a trait which was in later life to cost Choiseul dear. For the present, Cléon could afford it, rejoicing in being both feared and sought, an ornament of Parisian society. Valère speaks again:

> Je l'ai vu quelquefois
> A des soupers divins retenu pour un mois ;
> Quand il est à Paris, il ne peut y suffire ;
> Me direz-vous qu'on hait un homme qu'on désire?[21]

Cléon is the many-sided tone-setter, vividly on to the latest thing, this time according to Chloé's competitively courted mother, Florise:

> Cléon a tous les tons, tous les esprits ensemble ;
> Il est toujours nouveau.[22]

The Méchant, like Stainville, liked method. He docketed letters from his mistress and toyed with the idea of publishing an edition of them, or perhaps of writing some wonderfully revealing memoirs. His intellectual interests, again like the later Choiseul's, particularly ran to dramatic criticism. Says Valère:

> Il faut l'entendre après une pièce nouvelle :
> Il règne, on l'environne, il prononce sur elle,
> Et son autorité, malgré les protecteurs,

---

[18] Ibid., ii. 262.   [19] Ibid., ii. 326.   [20] See p. 464.   [21] Ibid., ii. 324.   [22] Ibid., ii. 317.

Pulvérise l'ouvrage et les admirateurs.
. . . Enfin Cléon est respecté
Et je vois les rieurs toujours de son côté. [23]

In keeping with his age, one of the secrets of Choiseul's power was to have on his side, if not always the laugh, then the laughter.

The courageous ambition of the then Count de Stainville likewise inspired the Méchant, who closed the second act with the curtain-line:

On ne va point au grand, si l'on n'est intrépide. [24]

Later, too, Cléon went deeper in epitomizing his philosophy:

Tout le monde est méchant, et personne ne l'est. [25]

That pellucid line echoed on with philosophic implications. It could arch lightly across, an elegant bridge, from the religious doctrine of original sin to that rationalistic yet in isolation mistaken concept of the perfectibility of man wherewith Voltaire and the Philosophes were conspicuously to emancipate French thought in the following decades of that century. As it was, that line from Gresset might almost seem to echo and complement another from a more famous play by Marivaux some two decades earlier. In *Le Jeu de l'amour et du hasard* Monsieur Orgon says: '*Dans ce monde, il faut être un peu trop bon pour l'être assez.*' [26]

Those voices in their disillusioned benevolence carry much of what was best in the old regime towards its close. If the serene disillusion was to decline, so, perhaps, was the assured benevolence, till the logical terminus became that Terror which Choiseul just did not live to see.

In *Le Méchant* it is rather difficult not to take Cléon, for all his base and unsuccessful stratagems, less as a villain than as an early if involuntary type of the antihero. His mischief is limited, largely to verbal shafts. But when finally his wiles are all exposed, the Méchant is no whit cast down but utters, as his last word, 'revenge', leaving the others to huddle together in a final scene that is essentially his aftermath. If the Méchant, one of the most striking characters of French drama in that century, indeed nodded acquaintance with the Count de Stainville, many traits naturally indicated dramatic licence and exaggeration. Perhaps it was fair enought to satirize the satirist.

---

[23] Ibid., ii. 322–3.   [24] Ibid., ii. 276.   [25] Ibid., ii. 334.
[26] Marivaux, *Le Jeu de l'amour et du hasard* in *Théâtre de Marivaux* (ed. Garnier; Paris, 1947), i. 232.

Though it was an unkind coincidence to have Cléon recall of a mistress:

> *Elle mourut, je fus enchanté de sa mort.* [27]

That was first declaimed upon the evening before the death of the Marquise de Gontaut. All in all, however, the vivid indirection of *Le Méchant* may seem to bring one close to the young Stainville in Parisian society. Cléon indeed affected boredom with it but Valère described it thus:

> *Tout est colifichet, pompon et parodie,*
> *Le monde, comme il est, me plaît à la folie.*
> *Les Belles tous les jours vous trompent, on leur rend:*
> *On se prend, on se quitte assez publiquement;*
> *Les maris savent vivre, et sur rien ne contestent:*
> *Les hommes s'aiment tous: les femmes se détestent*
> *Mieux que jamais: enfin c'est un monde charmant,*
> *Et Paris s'embellit delicieusement.*
> Cléon. *Et Cidalise?* ... Valère. *Mais* ... [28]

After Paris came Versailles. On Monday, 5 February 1748, the Marquise de Pompadour staged *Le Méchant* in her little theatre. Besides the fun of private theatricals, a spice of naughtiness was imparted by contemporary estimation of the theatrical profession. Madame de Pompadour now played Lisette to the Cléon of the Duke de Duras. Another of her best actors, the Duke de Nivernais, was well cast as Valère. Nivernais triumphed in his tender rendering of the part, and the actor Roselli, who had been playing it less happily at the Théâtre-Français, was allowed to attend and learn. Géronte was taken by the Duke de Chartres and Florise by the Dowager Duchess de Brancas, another regular in that select company.

This highly ducal performance of *Le Méchant* was a great hit. The Duke de Luynes blandly recorded that at Versailles the play was 'very highly esteemed for the benevolence of the moral and the beauty of the verses'. [29] There are morals and morals, and such fun exacted its price at court, as the Duchess de Luynes had been reminded in the preceding autumn, in a rather rare glimpse of the suppressed element there. Queen Marie had written to her dear friend of 'the rocks of Fontainebleau. I shall tell them my grief but they are so deaf, and I am rather fond of people who listen and understand me (*gens qui m'entendent*); besides, they are so hard ... so one must arm oneself; but not with patience, that sad remedy, especially against rocks. The

---

[27] Gresset, op. cit., ii. 339.   [28] Ibid., p. 267.   [29] Luynes, viii. 442.

fight would not be equal ... So it will be by trying to make myself inaccessible like them. There is a fine fruit to pluck from a journey. Do not show this letter to anybody, for it is without common sense. It is a result of the absence of my vapours.'[30] A week later she wrote of 'the true me, which is not my body'.[31]

The body is frail. A month later the Marquis de Stainville was reporting that at Choisy 'the day before yesterday Madame the Marquise de Pompadour was attacked by a fairly violent fever with a pain in the side which obliged them to bleed her from the arm and from the foot on the same day'.[32] Another fortnight later, in December 1747, she was described as growing thin, with a weak chest. Within a year she was said to be coughing blood. But she was 'a well trained odalisque'.[33] The king must be amused. In Madame de Pompadour's production of Le Méchant it fell to the Marquis de Gontaut as Frontin to address to her the opening line of the play:

Te voila de bonne heure, et toujours plus jolie.[34]

Thus Cléon's valet was the husband of the late mistress of the Count de Stainville, and was his special friend – 'les hommes s'aiment tous'. As for the Méchant himself, Stainville subsequently indicated to Nivernais that he did not care for the Duke de Duras. Nor did others. The Count de Stainville was not then in, but pretty closely on the edge of, the highest theatrical society in the circle of Madame de Pompadour. Whereas he himself, as noticed, held off from court at that period, adding: 'I was only interested in the news of the assembly of a congress at Aix-la-Chapelle, because I feared peace. The war was agreeable and interesting to me in Flanders; I much enjoyed spending seven months on campaign and five months at Paris, and I was infinitely afraid of the success of the congress. I was a little reassured by the plenipotentiary whom they sent to it on behalf of the king.'[35]

The shaft was worthy of the Méchant. The later Duke de Choiseul can scarcely be accused of attributing an anachronistic gravity and elevation to his spanking youth. He was 'natural'.

II

The diplomatic butt of the then Count de Stainville was his old acquaintance from Conti's campaign before Frankfurt, the Count de

[30] Queen Marie to Duchess de Luynes, 13 Oct. 1747: ibid., p. 416.   [31] Ibid., 21 Oct. 1747.
[32] Marquis de Stainville to Emperor Francis I, Paris, 26 Nov. 1747: Ö.S./.H.H.S., Lothringisches Hausarchiv 77/177A.
[33] D'Argenson, v. 242.   [34] Gresset, op. cit., ii. 217.   [35] Choiseul, Mémoires, p. 44.

Saint-Séverin, conscripted after all to represent France at Aix-la-Chapelle, allegedly to the disappointment of Belle-Isle, sick of war since the Alpine debacle and the death of his brother but still too compromised as the promoter of hostilities to make him a popular choice for their termination. Nor was it popular, however, that now an Italian would be leading France into peace while a German still led her in war. The later Choiseul described Saint-Séverin as 'born hard, brutal, without wit, without even knowing the value of words. By his imperious and decisive manner he had subjugated the poor feeble Marquis de Puysieulx, who, in choosing him, made the worst choice that one could make.'[36] Back in 1745 young Stainville may conceivably have got wind of Saint-Séverin's ruthless proposal against his own friend, the Marquis de Stainville, or of some similarly cold-hearted craft. The Marquis d'Argenson accused the 'Italian traitor'[37] of every kind of crime from seducing his bride to having failed to die under 'a horrible operation on the liver' occasioned by his excessive drinking; but 'the emissaries of his protectors, the Marquise de Pompadour, the Pâris, M. de Puysieulx, the Prince de Conti, the Marshal de Noailles, have always cried out that he is the only one to be the ambassador for making peace'. And in fact his capacities were far from nil.

In the New Year Honours of 1748 Saint-Séverin, always a hard bargainer for his services, achieved the order of the Saint-Esprit at the same time as Puysieulx himself and also that Duke de Luynes to whom history is so indebted. The decoration and liberal remuneration of the French envoy to Aix-la-Chapelle matched the local brilliance of the French position. Thanks to the resounding victories and captures of Marshal-General de Saxe, the king of France now lorded it over the Netherlands more absolutely than in the great days of the Roi Soleil. At the opening of 1748 the plight of the United Provinces was yet grimmer than in 1672, the Dutch themselves less sturdy and their Stadholder not William III but only William IV. French hegemony upon the continent was unmatched, perhaps, since the turning-point just one hundred years earlier when the Peace of Westphalia had begun the history of modern Europe under, so largely, the auspices of France.

This French command upon the continent to some extent masked an inward hollowness to match the hollow men at court. Yet their military advantages were primed by others diplomatic. France's great antagonists, England and Austria, were already pulling apart and exposed to play-off by Saint-Séverin. Immediately, for concluding

---

[36] Ibid., pp. 45–6   [37] D'Argenson, v. 176 for the following.

peace, England was the more difficult and important, alone capable of restoring Cape Breton, raising her blockade and relaxing the economic pressures against France. But in the longer run, for winning the peace, Austria was a cardinal factor. Both George II and Newcastle, who in February 1748 switched from south to north to replace disconsidered Chesterfield, were set against an alliance with Prussia but the poison injected into Anglo-Austrian relations by Carteret's treaties of Breslau and of Worms, to the advantage of Prussia and of Sardinia, was beginning to work through. This gave lasting importance to those now more fully uncovered Franco-Austrian soundings without immediate effect, through the Marquis de Stainville and, becoming topical again, through the Saxon court.

The court of Vienna was at last beginning to take account of that desirability of peace and distrust of England which Pâris-Duverney had artfully preached through the Marquis de Stainville in October 1747. Shortly after the receipt of his despatch Maria Theresa, on 15 November, addressed to Wasner in London a suspicious denunciation of British policy which, as in the War of the Polish Succession, seemed to her liable to leave Austria in the lurch and sacrifice her to her enemies and, still bitterer, to her 'false friends'.[38] By 20 December Count Kaunitz, designated for Aix-la-Chapelle, was attending a discussion in the Austrian council of 'the secret negotiation with France through the channel of the Saxon court',[39] again preferred to that of the Marquis de Stainville. Vienna now looked to some renewal of Count Brühl's grand design for containing Prussia. When in January 1748 Count John Loss broached this to Puysieulx the latter exclaimed: 'But what will Prussia say? And if the accommodation which we might negotiate is not to the taste of England, do you not think that the king of Prussia would be capable of letting himself be carried away by her and of replacing the empress against us?'[40] That was the nub for the peacemaking and thereafter. Loss went so far as to suggest to Puysieulx, more afraid than fond of Prussia, that, even after the war, a catholic alliance between Austria, France, and Spain might confront the protestant courts of London and Berlin.

On 16 February 1748 Maria Theresa addressed to Count John Loss full powers to sign on her behalf fifteen articles and two separate secret articles now proposed for preliminary peace with Austria. They went beyond the Batthyany proposals in that Don Philip was

---

[38] Empress Maria Theresa to Wasner, 15 Nov. 1747: Ö.S./H.H.S., cited, A. F. Pribram, *Österreichische Staatsvesträge: England*, i. 772.

[39] *Aus der Zeit Maria Theresias: Tagebuch des Fürsten Johann Joseph Khevenhüller-Metsch*, ed. Rudolf Graf Khevenhüller-Metsch and Dr. Hanns Schlitter, ii. 195.

[40] Count John Loss to Count Brühl, 27 Jan. 1748: Saxon archives: Duc de Broglie, *La Paix d'Aix-la-Chapelle* (Paris, 1892: henceforth cited as Broglie/Paix), p. 56.

at last allowed an apanage upon the Italian mainland. Maria Theresa would concede him Parma and Piacenza, the latter, however, being already ceded by her to Sardinia under the Treaty of Worms. She disinterested herself in Franco-British issues except that, if England reimposed dismantlement upon Dunkirk, she would throw in Furnes for France. The three counterparts stipulated for Austria were: the return, still, to Austria of her cessions (except now Piacenza) to Charles Emmanuel at Worms; Tuscany to acquire the coastal enclaves, the Stati dei Presidii, from Naples; a secret stipulation that, while Maria Theresa had no intention of infringing the Treaty of Dresden so long as Frederick exactly observed it, his title to Silesia should not be newly guaranteed.

The French reply to these terms strung Austria along. Her two large desiderata in maintaining an edge against the greedy upstarts, Sardinia and Prussia, were accepted in principle though Puysieulx thought it superfluously offensive to Frederick to spell things out. Furnes should be no problem but there was some dickering about other pickings, for the loyal Elector Palatine, against the Emperor Francis scooping the Stati dei Presidii, for a Savoyard satisfaction for Don Philip. A hint, however, that this might not be pressed was conveyed about the beginning of March 1748 to the Marquis de Stainville, who may have known more than he let on to Vienna of the Franco-Austrian soundings from which he was now excluded. Stainville's anonymous informant, by now easily guessable as Pâris-Duverney, postulated the restoration of Modena and Genoa but intimated that France, apart from advocating moderation, would leave Spain to negotiate her own terms.

The same French informant told Stainville, probably with Furnes in mind, of a draft stipulation in the French 'plan of proposals for peace, that the [French] king would retain some little thing from his conquests . . . but that he [Duverney] had represented that since the king had always openly declared that he wanted nothing, that he was making war only in order to have justice done to his allies, one must keep to this and not change one's language if one wanted to establish that confidence so necessary for the re-establishment of public tranquillity; and this had been granted him.'[41] It would appear that Pâris-Duverney, again a prime mover, was considerably responsible for good or ill for that early endeavour by France to attain to a peace without victory, peace without annexations.

A month earlier, as Puysieulx was getting down to it with Loss, Saint-Séverin had secretly confided to Stainville that Louis XV

[41] Enclosure in Marquis de Stainville to Emperor Francis I, Paris, 3 Mar. 1748: Ö.S./H.H.S., Lothringisches Hausarchiv 77/177A.

himself 'really desired peace, but that the different opinions of those who compose his council embarrassed him as to the choice of means; that for himself he had made up his mind to talk to the Count de Kaunitz with an open heart.'[42] Kaunitz in Aix-la-Chapelle rather than Loss in Paris was to make the further running with France. 'But', remarked the presumed Pâris-Duverney to Stainville, 'be sure that your court will again be sacrificed to England. It is very unfortunate although I am quite aware that she [Austria] cannot do otherwise.'[43]

The English squeeze on France was telling. In Paris austerity was increasingly dictating simplified models in coaches, clothes and trinkets – cardboard snuffboxes and the like. Coin was disappearing beneath a flood of bills and even solicitors were doing badly, a sure sign in that litigious age. By the end of February 1748 the Marquis d'Argenson was exclaiming: 'Here, within a fortnight, are eight large bankruptcies at Bordeaux ... Lyons is still going, but Marseilles has stopped her trade to the Levant.'[44] March brought a swingeing new range of war-taxes to make 'everything which is necessary to life, food, wood, candles ... beyond price'.[45] Even the Marquis de Stainville found 'living so dear in Paris that it is almost impossible to manage to subsist there'.[46]

Such was the price paid by the people of France for her military glory reaped by the Marshal-General de Saxe, now additionally dignified as Commandant-General of the Low Countries where he provoked comparisons with the extortionate Verres. The fighting, though, was not yet over in the Low Countries and beyond. The Duke of Newcastle was exulting to the future British plenipotentiary for peace: 'Two hundred thousand in Flanders, ninety thousand in Italy, and a fleet to sweep all before it! I begin now to talk a little big.'[47] And there was another factor looming daily larger.

Already by the end of 1747 the forthcoming peace-congress was being overshadowed, for French opinion at least, by the westward march of an expeditionary force from Russia. At long last the Russians were really coming – 'the best troops in Europe'[48] exulted Sandwich – upwards of thirty-six thousand of them, lured by the two Maritime Powers by a convention of 30 November 1747 following on

[42] Marquis de Stainville to Emperor Francis I, Paris, 28 Jan. 1748: ibid.
[43] Enclosure in Marquis de Stainville to Emperor Francis I, Paris, 3 Mar. 1748: ibid.
[44] D'Argenson, v. 202.   [45] Barbier, iv. 289.
[46] Marquis de Stainville to Emperor Francis I, Paris, 31 Mar. 1748: u.s.
[47] Duke of Newcastle to Earl of Sandwich, 22 Jan. (O.S.) 1748: British Library, Add. MSS. 32,811, fo. 102: Lodge, pp. 302–3.
[48] Earl of Sandwich to Duke of Newcastle, 26 Jan. 1748: British Library, Add MSS. 32,811, fo. 53: Lodge, p. 301.

from the Austro-Russian defensive alliance of 2 June 1746. France might lord it over the Low Countries but the net around her whole position upon the continent now looked like being roped in. Not so far from being reversed was the sweeping strategy wherewith the Marshal de Belle-Isle had launched France into the long expansion of the War of the Austrian Succession. It was all very well for him now to concoct a characteristic 'project for toppling the whole power of Russia into the sea'.[49] When the French minister in Saint Petersburg requested an explanation of the Russian march, Count Bestuchev reminded d'Alion that the Empress Elizabeth had asked for none when King Louis had seen fit to march auxiliary contingents through Germany against her allies.

The auxiliary status of the Russians in their advance through Poland and Germany in theory permitted the attachment of a French observer with Russian experience in the person of Colonel de La Salle. He was promptly clapped into gaol at Danzig on a Russian charge of earlier desertion. Always adept at perverse legalism, Russian authorities are apt to give short shrift to unwelcome liaison-officers. The French government had rather greater success in planting less official observers and it sought to slow the Russian advance by stimulating Polish contacts into 'increasing the difficulty of provisioning along their route',[50] already sufficiently great for the rudimentary Russian commissariat.

This long-range attempt in contemporary terms at economic warfare overland was largely directed by Marshal de Lowendahl. While in the service of the Empress Anne he had commanded the Russian generals now leading the thrust across Europe. Lowendahl had supplied an appreciation of them, beginning with Prince Repnin, 'aged about fifty, consumed by gout, scurvy and the stone ... He is extremely gentle and lazy beyond imagination.'[51] Lowendahl surmised that this somewhat reassuring commander of the dreaded Russians was under orders to concert with the fiftytwo-year-old Lieutenant-General Prince Lieven of the distinguished Baltic family which was already to the fore in Russia. Prince Lieven was described as 'extremely thin and delicate ... an upright man, intelligent and brave'.[52] In general, however, Voltaire commented that 'the Russian soldiers, become so good ... no longer had at their head a Münnich, a Lascy, a Keith or a Lowendahl'.[53] But on they came despite wishful

[49] D'Argenson, v. 104.
[50] Count d'Argenson to Marshal de Lowendahl, Versailles, 21 Apr. 1748: Arch. Guerre C., vol. 3276, no. 231.
[51] 'Les Généraux Russes qui commandent le Corps qui passe au service des Puissances Maritimes', memorandum by Marshal de Lowendahl enclosed in Marshal de Lowendahl to Count d'Argenson, Namur, 19 Jan. 1748: ibid., vol. 3280, no. 40.
[52] Ibid.   [53] Voltaire, *Précis du siècle de Louis XV*, i. 177.

rumours to the contrary in Paris. This subjected the Russian minister, Gross, and his close colleague the Marquis de Stainville to 'unendurable questioning at every instant'.[54]

The Prince de Conti, whose agents remained active in Poland, might elaborate a classic combination of Poland, Turkey, Sweden and Prussia in order to break Russia off from Austria and force her back into her wastes, out of the European orbit. Only, Russia was in fact heading into it to the discomfort of Augustus III and Frederick the Great, angrily aware that Silesia came after Poland in this advance by Russia, who was paid by England to keep a further contingent handy upon the Livonian confines of East Prussia and upon the Baltic seaboard where 30,000 Russians were supposed, even, to be awaiting British shipping to ferry them round to measure up against the French in the Low Countries in a second thrust. Such was the eastward escalation of fear across the northern continent from Hanover, herself menacingly overlooked by Prussia. If George II could not compass his wish that his cousin of Prussia were, as he put it, the Khan of Tartary, yet England was already calling in from the Slavonic east, emergent and gigantic, a new world to redress the balance of the old. Prussia was indeed to remain the catalyst, with her retention of Silesia now virtually agreed between England and France, though Saint-Séverin successfully resisted British attempts to secure the representation at the peace congress not only of King Frederick but, even more, of the assertive Empress Elizabeth. It may have been more evident to contemporaries than to some historians that the wars of the Polish and of the Austrian successions both terminated in conditions which included a Russian advance into Germany: and the next war was to present that same pattern in striking emphasis and variation.

Long afterwards the Duke de Choiseul in a characteristic conspectus recalled that at that juncture Great Britain, besides having captured Cape Breton, 'had had great advantages at sea against our trade, but she had been obliged, in India, to raise the siege of Pondicherry'.[55] He held that for Britain:

The expenses of this war far surpassed her strength; the interruption of her trade with Spain and France prevented her from making good the efforts she had been obliged to make. Although the enterprises in Scotland and in England of the son of the Chevalier de Saint-George had not succeeded, they had caused perturbation within the English administration and in the credit of this nation, so that in 1748 England was at the point of going bankrupt, which is certainly the most humiliating defeat that a great power can experience.

[54] Marquis de Stainville to Emperor Francis I, Paris, 3 Mar. 1748: Ö.S./H.H.S., Lothringisches Hausarchiv 77/177A.   [55] Choiseul, *Mémoires*, p. 55 for the following.

This analysis, if it reflected the later Choiseul's standing preoccupation with the economic foundations of policy, also betrayed considerable exaggeration of England's plight, partly derived, as likely as not, from the pacific Duke of Bedford, who was to negotiate with Choiseul to end the Seven Years War and who, at the end of the present one, had just acquired the southern department when Newcastle succeeded Chesterfield in the northern.

England had in fact come nearer, at least, than the other belligerents to making war pay. Now, however, she took a financial knock when the Dutch fell down on their quota of the subsidy to Russia and suddenly seemed to be at the end of their resources, financial and military. 'And yet', lamented Newcastle to Sandwich, 'it was the Stadholder and Holland that caused us to reject Marshal Saxe's proposals, and to engage in the immense expense of this year. You must forgive me, my Lord, if I am a little warm.'[56] The British cabinet inclined towards peace and in particular towards countenancing some Italian provision for Don Philip, prominent in those French counter-proposals through Loss upon which Saint-Séverin opened his sparring with Kaunitz at Aix-la-Chapelle. Saint-Séverin had hoped to see the elder Stainville there but the marquis was not to cap his appearance twenty years earlier at the Congress of Soissons. It was with Kaunitz that Saint-Séverin now became almost cordially confidential in their joint pursuit of peace, privily from England or Spain, and in contemplation, even, of a catholic league just a century after that peace of Westphalia which had terminated the last of the great conflicts of religion.

For the present the very aspect of the city of Aix-la-Chapelle and its environs reminded the plenipotentiaries for peace that war was still lapping through those fringes of distracted Germany. Following a useful precedent from the Congress of Nimwegen in 1678, every road leading into Aix, at a distance of three-quarters of a league all around, was studded with mobile barriers and signboards inscribed in French and German with the word 'Neutrality'. These fragile barriers excluded all troops from the little zone of neutrality and, be it hoped, eventual peace. As yet the negotiators at imperial Aachen could listen to the booming of the cannon twenty miles to the west, around the latest focus of those long years of conflict.

III

In order to give peace a warlike nudge the Marshal de Saxe in concert with the best French brains, Belle-Isle, Noailles, and the

---

[56] Duke of Newcastle to Earl of Sandwich, Mar. 1748: Lodge, p. 316.

ever-present Duverney, had been secretly laying urgent plans. Already in March 1748 French units including the Regiment of Navarre from Lorraine were marching out through landscapes still icy after the heavy snowfall which had ushered in that month of biting cold and frost. Several weeks earlier than usual French officers were under orders to rejoin their regiments. By the beginning of April the invaders in Flanders were massing against the next prize after Bergen-op-Zoom, that of Breda, against which forces went probing forward under Lieutenant-General d'Estrées.

So early as 31 March 1748, however, the Marquis de Stainville had dispatched hot intelligence from Paris regarding seventy-two French battalions from winter-quarters:

Instead of proceeding to Flanders as was their first destination, are actually in full march to proceed towards the Luxemburg country without its being known till now what is the project which has been formed in that direction, all the senior officers who have gone to join this corps being due to receive their orders only when it shall be assembled beneath Montmédy. It is easy to conjecture that it is not against Luxemburg that they have designs but that it is hoped, by following the right bank of the Meuse and crossing the province of Limburg, to invest Maestricht from that side, while the Marshal de Saxe marches against this fortress from his side ... It seems likely that they will lose many troops in executing this, for it is terribly cold.[57]

The strategic prediction of the Marquis de Stainville proved exact. As Saxe doubled back up the familiar road from Tirlemont through Tongres past Lawfeldt to before Maestricht, Lowendahl struck out with a corps in six divisions from the arc Namur-Longwy, bunching up from the Meuse through the windy Ardennes to converge on Verviers and hook up to spring a surprise against Maestricht from the east. In this nimble operation the Regiment of Navarre marched in the sixth division on the eastern flank.

Saxe's swift stratagem and stringent clamps of secrecy caught out not only the enemy but some of his own officers, including the Marquis de Valfons, who had difficulty in gaining the front in time: and not only he. The then Count de Stainville in later years recalled that at this juncture:

I guessed by pure chance that it would be the siege of Maestricht. As my regiment was coming from Lorraine and was to cross the Meuse at Longwy, I thought that I could stay in Paris longer than those whose regiments were in Flanders ... I was in the country and left a fortnight after everybody. That fortnight of pleasure was fatal for me; for Marshal de Saxe had prohibited no matter whom from crossing the Meuse after the troops destined for the siege had crossed it; this obliged me to skirt

[57] Marquis de Stainville to Emperor Francis I, Paris, 31 Mar. 1748: Ö.S./H.H.S., Lothringisches Hausarchiv 77/177A.

along this river from Longwy to Namur and in this last town to bribe the garrison-commander into letting me through. I made Louvain whence, at the risk of being captured by the enemy hussars, I marched day and night and arrived at Liége, where I found the Regiment of Navarre. I had been excessively anxious from the moment that I felt that my regiment might be at the siege without me and that this dereliction, which was a question of honour, was assuredly my fault without by being able to exculpate myself to myself; this anxiety, which causes great unhappiness if one has any sense of honour at all, should teach young people how dangerous it is to forget the exactitude required by the profession of arms.[58]

When the future Choiseul waxed serious, it could be at his own expense.

Saxe's artful swoop on Maestricht aroused general admiration. Even the then Count de Stainville conceded:

The enterprise of the siege of Maestricht was, I think, the finest which was executed in this war. The marches of the troops and the arrangements of supply were a masterpiece of co-ordination and precision; and, after the manoeuvres which made the enemy anxious upon our left at Bois-le-Duc and upon our right in Luxemburg, Maestricht found itself invested upon both banks of the Meuse. Many people were keen to claim the credit for the plan. I have since been concerned to fathom from whom it proceeded. I have verified that it was a certain . . . [sic], a captain of the guides, who formed it. He came to Paris to impart it to Monsieur de Crémilles, chief of staff (maréchal des logis) of the army of Flanders . . . I know from the Chevalier de Bauteville, who was with Crémilles, that they could not get the plan accepted by the Marshal de Saxe. Then recourse was had to Duverney in order to persuade the marshal. This last succeeded. It must be granted that, once the marshal had adopted the plan, he executed it with much ability.

The then Count de Stainville was apparently not the only adherent of Conti to seek to deprive Saxe of credit for the plan against Maestricht, whose strategic importance was fully evident to the marshal. However, it rather looks as if the later Choiseul may have been drawing in part upon researches stimulated by him when Minister of War. He was to take a lively interest in archival matters generally: another seeming paradox in his complex and dégagé character, on a par with the way in which that spender scrutinized accounts.

The siege of Maestricht was begun in earnest by Marshal de Lowendahl just after Easter, on the night of 15–16 April 1748. The start was slow, with rain clogging the trenches into mud. The Regiment of Navarre was operating on the east bank of the Meuse, closing in against Maestricht from around Wyck. The night of the 16–17th found the five battalions of Navarre in the trenches under the superior command of the duty-generals for the day, Lieutenant-

<hr />

[58] Choiseul, *Mémoires*, pp. 46–8 for the following.

General de Lautrec who was to run into jealous trouble with Lowendahl, and, as Maréchal-de-Camp, the Jacobite Lord Tyrconnell. Two nights later grenadiers from Navarre were once more active and the Count de Stainville was the orderly brigadier commanding siege-works on the right bank.[59]

On 22 April the defenders of Maestricht under the Dutch command of stout Baron d'Aylva smashed pontoon-bridges linking the siege-camps upon either bank of the Meuse, swollen by foul weather worsening once more into snow. And the Austrian garrison followed through with offensive sorties. All this and something more besides lay behind the then Brigadier de Stainville's terse account: 'The siege followed the usual course of sieges. The besieged defended themselves better than the enemy had defended the fortresses which had been captured from them during this war.'[60] Stainville had personal proof of this on the night of 27–28 April 1748.

Around Maestricht the early hours of 28 April were very dark, with driving rain. In the siege-trenches over by Wyck squelched two battalions of the Regiment of Navarre, commanded by the Count de Stainville and, as orderly officer that night, Maréchal-de-Camp the Count de Saulx. At three o'clock that morning the Austrians with some thousand picked infantry and two hundred cavalry sortied against rather rashly advanced French batteries. While the Austrian horse stood in battle-order by the grim landmark of some gallows, and troops of their hussars scoured around, the infantry achieved initial surprise against the French trenches, sprang through the embrasures and spiked most of the cannon, if ineffectively in the scramble, before the picquets of Navarre reacted on either side of the battery and the Count de Stainville brought his two battalions to bear, more particularly against three bodies, each of some two hundred Austrian infantry, who were in close support of the first wave of attack. Navarre's shooting, reported de Saulx, 'was so much to the purpose, so lively and so sustained that these three troops, although very close to the parapet, did not dare to advance upon us and on the contrary withdrew much in disorder, leaving some thirty dead or wounded upon the field of battle'.[61]

So ran a supplementary report of the action sent by Stainville's superior in order to correct 'the ill-founded rumours which have spread in the army, and of which I only learned yesterday, concerning the manoeuvre of two battalions of the Regiment of Navarre on the

[59] 'Ordre du 16 au 17 Avril 1748 au camp devant Mastrick'; ditto for 18–19 Apr.: Arch. Guerre C., vol. 3276, nos. 189 and 204.
[60] Choiseul, *Mémoires*, p. 48.
[61] Count de Saulx to Count d'Argenson, camp before Maestricht, 30 Apr. 1748: Arch Guerre C., vol. 3277, no. 70 for the following.

night of the 27th to the 28th . . . The two battalions . . . had only two men wounded and the smallness of this loss caused the falsest allegations in the world that they gave way and that the whole trench was overthrown. . . . These two battalions manoeuvred most firmly and most worthily for the reputation of their regiment . . . I have rendered the same account to the Marshal de Saxe.'

There has already been some suggestion from the Alpine campaign of 1744 that the Count de Stainville had a keen eye for mentions in dispatches. It was a pity that he had been forced on to the defensive by that little action out by Wyck, the last one in all that war for the count and his seasoned troops.

Concentric were the military pressures towards peace at Aix-la-Chapelle. The Russians still were squeezing in but, having crossed the Polish frontiers at the beginning of February, very slowly, still remote. Saxe assured Saint-Séverin on the way to Aix that he would easily beat the Russians to it at Maestricht, and on opening the siege he wrote to the adjacent diplomat: 'You are going to hear the cannon rumble. I do not know if the sound of this agreeable music will incline spirits to thought of peace or to martial ardour.'[62] Newcastle thought that French capture of Maestricht might shake the British government.

Winning the Austrian government for peace remained the apparently sincere preference of the astute Count de Saint-Séverin as he also negotiated with the Earl of Sandwich, a clumsier performer. Saint-Séverin loyally resisted pressure for Genoese cession of Finale to Charles Emmanuel and, loyally too, apparently did not reveal that the British plenipotentiary had even mooted British acquisition of Austrian Ostend, which would fairly have set the cat among the eagles and also have ruffled Dutch memories of the Ostend Company. Considerable progress had nevertheless been made when on 24 April 1748 Sandwich received instructions empowering him, in the case of need, to sign preliminaries of peace without the consent of Britain's allies. Maestricht now was closely threatened. Saint-Séverin suddenly found Sandwich markedly more co-operative. The Italian, who enjoyed negotiating latitude, judged that at last the diplomatic iron was hot. He pressed.

IV

On 27 April 1748 Saint-Séverin elicited from Kaunitz that he expected it would be about a week before he received the Austrian

---

[62] Marshal-General de Saxe to Count de Saint-Séverin, 12 Apr. 1748: Arch. Aff. Étr. C.P., Bréda et Aix-la-Chapelle: Broglie/Paix, pp. 107–8.

reply regarding the latest and now hopeful phase of their separate
negotiation. On 28 April Saint-Séverin followed up a previous
warning to Sandwich with hot news that Austria and Spain had
practically concluded a separate treaty whereby Maria Theresa
would recoup cessions to Don Philip by revoking those made to
Charles Emmanuel at Worms. The only way to prevent this
European upset was, Saint-Séverin urged upon Sandwich, for them
both to sign at once a preliminary treaty of their own upon terms for
peace by now virtually agreed. A request by Sandwich for production
of the compromising Austro-Spanish documents was eluded by
Saint-Séverin, since they did not exist. His whole story of the Austro-
Spanish compact was a mendacious invention, while the previous
secret soundings between those two powers rendered it, even without
proof, sufficiently plausible to such an austrophobe as Sandwich. So
much for Saint-Séverin's assurance just three months earlier to the
elder Stainville that in treating with Kaunitz, to whom he was willing
to swear faith on the gospel, Saint-Séverin would 'rather fall into
indiscretion than into dissimulation or falsehood'.[63]

Sandwich, after insisting upon informing the Dutch and, ultimately, the Austrians, got down to drafting preliminaries of peace
with Saint-Séverin. That unscrupulous diplomatist had given a
masterly push towards peace. His sudden turn of speed may have
been winged by fears of renewed military success entertained by
French partisans of peace even including Saxe's friends at court,
ranged behind Saint-Séverin in ascendant order, Puysieulx, Pâris-
Duverney, Madame de Pompadour, the king himself.

Saint-Séverin and Sandwich drafted the preliminaries, roughly
enough, in twenty-four articles plus one secret article. They reposed
upon the reciprocal restoration by signatories of all conquests made
'in Europe equally as in the East and West Indies'[64] (India and
America). This settlement, to be effected when all interested powers
had adhered to the preliminaries, would embrace the full restoration
of Genoa and Modena, general recognition of Francis I as Holy
Roman Emperor, renewal of the Pragmatic Sanction for the residual
Habsburg territories including the Austrian Netherlands, after
subtraction of Silesia, guaranteed to Frederick, and the cessions to
Sardinia under the Treaty of Worms. Don Philip was at last to get
the duchies of Parma, Piacenza, and – hotly disputed – Guastalla,
with reversion to present holders if he should succeed his elder

---

[63] Marquis de Stainville to Emperor Francis I, Paris, 28 Jan. 1748: Ö.S./H.H.S.,
Lothringisches Hausarchiv 77/177A.
[64] Article 2 of the Peace Preliminaries of Aix-la-Chapelle, 30 Apr. 1748: Broglie/Paix,
appendix B, p. 308.

brother in Naples or die without issue. Britain should regain the Asiento and Navio Permiso. Saint-Séverin neatly wrapped up in allusions to previous treaties the wounding British conditions for French abandonment of the Young Pretender and destruction of the seaward (but not now the landward) fortifications of Dunkirk. Signature was to spell cessation of hostilities between all belligerents, not only signatories, within six weeks on land and twice that term at sea. This pointed towards the separate and secret article wherein the contracting parties undertook to concert coercive measures against any other belligerent if it did not submit to the preliminaries.

On 30 April Saint-Séverin and Sandwich appeared together at a dinner given by Kaunitz, due to be apprised of the agreed preliminaries and of the bitter fact that he had once again been imposed upon by the British ally and, now too, fooled by the negotiator for France. Saint-Séverin blandly explained to Kaunitz that he had really had to hurry into the preliminaries with Sandwich because Spain was alarmingly advanced in separate negotiations with – this time – England: another plausible lie to round off a dual exercise in machiavellian diplomacy worthy of the Marquis D'Ormea. On the same evening of 30 April 1748 the Count de Saint-Séverin signed the Peace Preliminaries of Aix-la-Chapelle together with the Earl of Sandwich and also William Bentinck, jollied along by insinuations from Saint-Séverin that failure to follow England now would be liable to cost Holland commercial favours from France and also her great fortifications at Bergen-op-Zoom, mined by the French and all ready to be touched off.

An advance indication, even, of the preliminaries had been enough for the Empress Maria Theresa. On the evening of 26 April, pregnant again, she had let fly at Sir Thomas Robinson: 'I am neither a child nor a fool ... And why am I always to be excluded from transacting my own business? My enemies will give me better conditions than my friends ... *Your King of Sardinia* must have all, without one thought or care for me! Good God! how I have been used by that Court! *There is your King of Prussia!*[65] The Marquis de Stainville had the slim consolation of pointing to his verified warnings against England; and if France was not yet as forthcoming as Maria Theresa had significantly indicated, it was Saint-Séverin, already tacking back, who persuaded Kaunitz to adhere to the preliminaries two days after the three original signatories had, on 21 May 1748, exchanged ratifications. Sardinia too came into line and Genoa joined Spain, ever the slowcoach, in signing on 28 June. Though she had been

[65] Sir Thomas Robinson to Duke of Newcastle, 1 May 1748: Willaim Coxe, *History of The House of Austria*, ii. 353.

rudely excluded from Saint-Séverin's negotiations, he had not done so badly for Don Philip. Thus Spain could fairly be ranked with Sardinia and Prussia as the powers which had actually extracted territorial advantage from the war. They were all lesser or marginally great powers. Of the truly great, Austria was the loser, especially to the most striking winner, now neutral Prussia. England and France for the present held the balance of the ocean and the continent level against one another in reciprocal restitution of conquests.

The future tilt of the Anglo-French balance of world-power was perhaps already suggested by the way in which remote British successes by small forces across and upon the high seas now counterbalanced sweeping victories by great French armies in classic campaigns that subjugated the whole of the Austrian Netherlands and overawed the Dutch. At the end of it all France in her altruistic resignation was to acquire nothing. While Saint-Séverin was held to this by such as Pâris-Duverney, at Aix the plenipotentiary, looking beyond the peacemaking to the peace, pursued and prepared arcane advantages: such as would cut across the design of the Duke of Newcastle that Prussia 'should be gained by way of additional strength (if possible) to the old alliance, but not be substituted in the place of the House of Austria to form a new chimerical system'.[66] Saint-Séverin was already at work to shift the odium of the brusque preliminaries. Two days after their conclusion he was writing to Puysieulx: 'The best that I see in this business is that for long hence the courts of Vienna and of Sardinia will not forget the trick which the Maritime Powers have just played on them, and I am completing the beginnings of distrust and bitterness which are established among our enemies.'[67]

Both Saint-Séverin and Sandwich were soon reassured as to the reactions of their governments to the peace into which their enterprising plenipotentiaries had dared to plunge them. True, French public opinion was not slow to deduce an almost nil return from a 'war which has cost us immense sums and the loss of three to four hundred thousand men'.[68] The Marquis de Stainville, though, reported from Paris: 'It is not possible to depict the joy which the news of the peace has spread through the public.'[69] Details, however, were scarce so that 'everybody has been drawing up preliminary articles in his own way'. In the depressed French provinces the

[66] Duke of Newcastle to Duke of Cumberland, 7 June 1748 (O.S.): British Library, Add. MSS. 32,715, fo. 166: Lodge, p. 360, n. 1.
[67] Count de Saint-Séverin to Marquis de Puysieulx, 2 May 1748: Arch. Aff. Étr. C.P., Bréda et Aix-la-Chapelle: Broglie/Paix, pp. 173-4.
[68] Barbier, iv. 309.
[69] Marquis de Stainville to Emperor Francis I, Paris, 12 May 1748: Ö.S./H.H.S., Lothringisches Hausarchiv 77/177A for the following.

reaction was less sophisticated. Into Bordeaux, bottled up by the implacable British, there came galloping a courier, shouting out the famous news of peace to a hungry crowd milling around for bread. Nine-tenths of them, one is told, started running around like madmen, dancing, singing, embracing one another. Their joyous cries of 'Peace is made!' are also relevant to the slim diplomacy at Aix-la-Chapelle of the Count de Saint-Séverin d'Aragon.

Less enthusiastic was the reception of the news from Aix by the nearby French before Maestricht, still under siege. Three nights after the Count de Stainville's scrape out by Wyck, on 30 April – 1 May, he was again the brigadier superintending the extension of the right-hand siege-trenches.[70] By May 2 1748 all was ready for assault, to be led that night by the French guards till the Marshal de Lowendahl represented that their terminal casualties would shake Paris whereas '"tomorrow", said he, "it will be the turn of the Swiss; their deaths will pass unnoticed, for the cries from their mountains will not be heard." "You think of everything", Maurice had said, laughing. "Till tomorrow then!"'[71] Fate, though, was kinder than they.

Next day, Friday, 3 May 1748, one Saxe's officers wrote to the French Minister of War: 'I hope, Sir, that here is the last list of killed or wounded that I shall be sending you on this campaign.'[72] Reports were spreading that day in the French camp before Maestricht as, in the words of the then Count de Stainville, 'there arrived an English officer from Aix-la-Chapelle with the news of the signature of the preliminaries of peace and an order from the enemy courts to the commander of the fortress to surrender it to the Marshal de Saxe'.[73] Cumberland's staff-officer was Lord George Sackville with proposals for the arrangement of an armistice.

The armistice would be in execution of a supplementary protocol concluded by the signatories of the preliminary articles at Aix on the same day, 30 April. In this protocol the French, British, and Dutch plenipotentiaries provided an important gloss to article 16 stipulating cessation of hostilities on land within six weeks: 'Wishing to prevent ... the continuation of the shedding of Christian blood, we have agreed that all ulterior hostilities, except the siege of Maestricht, already begun, shall cease in all the Netherlands'[74] on a day to be agreed between commanders. The six-week term was thus anticipated

[70] 'Ordre du 30 avril au 1er. May 1748 au camp devant Mastrick': Arch. Guerre C., vol. 3277, no. 68.
[71] Marquis de Valfons, *Souvenirs du Marquis de Valfons*, p. 246.
[72] Chevalier de Vaudreuil to Count d'Argenson, Maestricht, 3 May. 1748: Arch. Guerre C., vol. 3277, no. 121.
[73] Choiseul, *Mémoires*, p. 48.
[74] Anglo-Franco-Dutch protocol of Aix-la-Chapelle, 30 Apr. 1748: Pajol, iii. 594.

in the Netherland theatre to the specific if probably formal exclusion of Maestricht, artfully stipulated by Saint-Séverin in order not to cheat the disgruntled Saxe of his prey and also, it may well be, to maintain French pressure for peace. Now Baron d'Aylva insisted upon specific orders from the Dutch States-General before running up the white flag over Maestricht on 6 May 1748.

On the morning of 10 May the French army was lined along the exit from Maestricht to salute the gallant garrison as it came marching out with honours of war. D'Aylva's Dutch troops, though, made sorry showing compared with the Austrian auxiliaries under Baron Marschall, included in the capitulation even though their government had not yet signed the preliminaries. The Marshal de Saxe meanwhile had a collection of recaptured French deserters decimated, in grim accompaniment to the Te Deum upon his entry into Maestricht through 'the dungheaps and filth which were in the streets and which had not been cleaned for three years'.[75] That stinking conquest, even in the absence of a major assault, had cost the French army just on two thousand wounded and seven hundred killed. The Regiment of Navarre had come off lightly with three dead and two dozen wounded.[76] Stainville's 'little Bissy', the erstwhile messenger of victory from Coni, now minus a leg from a mortar-bomb, died at the age of thirty-two, just at the arrival of news of peace.

On the morning of Saturday, 11 May 1748, trumpeters at the head of all French detachments and garrisons throughout the conquered Low Countries sounded the cessation of hostilities. Those long years of war were at last now over. However, wrote the then Count de Stainville, even without the armistice 'Maestricht would have been taken in a few days ... The Marshal de Saxe was in despair and could not hide his mortification over the end of the war. His whole army shared his feelings in this respect.'[77] Saxe himself, the royal bastard always aspiring to be something better territorially than a titular Duke-Elect of Courland and Semigallia, would have been nicely suited by a captured 'titbit' in the retroceded Netherlands. He grumbled to the Count de Maurepas: 'I know nothing of your devil of politics. I see, I know that the King of Prussia has taken Silesia and that he has kept it, and I would that we could do the same ... If the faldals of the negotiations once begin to get mixed up in it, we are in for ten years without firing a shot. That is your business ... I promise

[75] Chevalier d'Hallot to Count d'Argenson, Maestricht, 9 June 1748: Arch. Guerre C., vol. 3278, no. 18.
[76] État des officiers et soldats tués ou blessés devant Mastrick pendant le courant du siège': Arch. Guerre C., vol. 3277, no. 157.
[77] Choiseul, *Mémoires*, p. 48.

you, too, to fight until death for truths which I do not understand.'[78]
One resource for generals is to play the bluff old soldier.

For many of Saxe's officers peace brought a sizeable sweetener. On
10 May 1748, the day that Saxe entered Maestricht, Louis XV
promulgated a valedictory promotion of no fewer than ninety-three
new lieutenant-generals, eighty-five Maréchaux-de-Camp, and one
hundred and twenty-six brigadiers. Brigadier Stephen de Stainville
was promoted Maréchal-de-Camp. Though not rich and the son of
the representative of the inimical emperor, young Stainville,
displaying a courage to match his intelligence, had in rather under
seven years risen in the French army from subaltern to the equivalent
of major-general, at the age of twenty-eight.

The war was petering out. The armistice in the Low Countries
evidently extended along the French shores of the English Channel,
still subject to the unremitting pressure of British seapower. Less
than a month before the signature of the peace preliminaries all the
northern coasts of France had been alerted in what the Minister of
War drily termed 'an interesting moment'.[79] This reflected sufficient
confirmation by the Minister of Marine of intelligence received by
the French chief of staff at Antwerp on 31 March 1748 from a young
English girl arrived from England. She was apparently the daughter
of an officer in French service in the Jacobite regiment of Ogilvy, one
Thomas Taylor, then spying in London. Miss Taylor, who spoke
French 'very badly',[80] had under interrogation produced, in her
clear, sloping handwriting, two documents in English, 'An Exact
Account of a Secret Expedition to be directly Executed' and 'An
Exact Account, out of the War Office Books, of all the Forces in
England, and their destination for the next Campaign',[81] not in the
Netherlands only but throughout the world.

The most urgent intelligence was of British plans for a combined
operation to land troops 'at Saint Vallery near Dieppe, where they
expect to be joined by the Hugoneaus [sic] of the Country'.[82] If the
reported co-ordination of this descent with another against Brest,
indeed the whole story, remained dubious, and if in the event a
British landing in force at Saint-Valéry was to wait for long years,
minor incursions against the French coastline continued even a day

---

[78] Marshal-General de Saxe to Count de Maurepas, camp before Maestricht, 15 May 1748:
[Count de Grimoard,] Lettres et mémoires choisis parmi les papiers originaux du maréchal de Saxe
(Paris, 1794), v. 270–1

[79] Count d'Argenson to Lieutenant-General de Crémilles, Versailles, 7 Apr. 1748; Arch.
Guerre C., vol. 3276, no. 81.

[80] Lieutenant-General de Crémilles to Count d'Argenson, Antwerp, 1 Apr. 1748: ibid., no.
26.

[81] Ibid., nos. 27–8, enclosures in no. 26.

[82] Ibid., no. 27.

or so after the signature of the preliminaries. May Day of 1748 was signalled at the village of Sangatte, some miles west of Calais, by ultimate hostilities for four hours between coastguards and a small English landing-party.

More persistent and important were operations upon the Mediterrean seaboard. Sizeable reinforcements had reached Richelieu in Genoa, though the Duke d'Agenais in March 1748 muffed a surprise landing against Savona, destined to be not his last coastal failure. A main objective there had been enemy dumps to nourish another insurrection in Corsica against its hard-pressed Genoese masters. Both sides landed troops to hold the balance of international intervention in Corsica and contain for Genoa, for a while yet, that troublous island one day to loom large for the Duke de Choiseul.

France and England had by then signed the preliminaries of Aix-la-Chapelle. So soon as the news reached Marshal de Belle-Isle, commanding the main French army on the Italian front, he notified Admiral Byng, commander of the British fleet in the Mediterranean in succession to Admiral Medley who had died of fever and been pickled in five gallons of rum in a naval hospital at Savona. But angry Richelieu was still starved of full relief by sea. In the additional protocol of 30 April 1748 a prompt armistice had been envisaged only for the Netherlands while article 16 of the preliminaries muffled the cessation of hostilities at sea, to English advantage. To the landward of Genoa meanwhile Austria and Sardinia had not even nominally ceased hostilities.

That spring General von Browne was massing an army at Parma for a big push against Genoa from this new direction, through the Apennines while from the opposite flank General Nadasty came closing in against La Bocchetta. At the end of May Teutonic and Slavonic warfare bore down upon the valley of the Vara in a grim finale, less meaningful in the history-books than, say, to the stout peasants of Zembrano, reduced to ashes by Browne to punish patriotic resistance. Local cessation of hostilities was at last fixed for 15 June, the six-week term of the peace-preliminaries. Till then there was little let-up. One Austrian commander, Clerici, seized the Strada Romana between Brugnato and Matterano in a near breakthrough to the coast. On the day that the Franco-Austrian armistice finally entered into force Genoese peasantry wildly assaulted Clerici's position at Brugnato. In the age of supposedly conventional warfare the last European hostilities in all that war had been mounted by infuriated irregulars.

V

The awkward failure of the Italian Count de Saint-Séverin to include the Italian theatre in the supplementary protocol was perhaps understandable since the governing peace-preliminaries were not signed till weeks later by four of the six main belligerents in the Italian peninsula, Austria, Sardinia, Genoa and Spain. Spanish ire against distrusted France flared up against Richelieu at Genoa, at Versailles where the Duke of Huescar created scenes that made the mild Marquis de Puysieulx nearly ill, while at Aix-la-Chapelle the Marquis de Masones silently turned his back on the Count de Saint-Séverin to join Count Kaunitz in musical accompaniments and mutual complaints against allies. This renewal of Austro-Spanish rapprochement was nourished by shared antipathy to Charles-Emmanuel who, grumbled Kaunitz, had become 'England's fad'.[83]

Staggered armistices mean military muddle and diplomatic dickering, especially then in the erratic conglomeration of hostilities which had swelled the war, and in the diplomatic flux that was sapping old alignments even before the attainment of peace. Another aspect, looming up behind, was that the new warriors 'from so far were at last arriving. The Russians were already in Franconia. They were indefatigable men trained with the strictest discipline.'[84] And, characteristically, the less the 'Russian devils' (Marquis de Puysieulx) were now wanted, the quicker they came on in order to stake out political influence for the Empress Elizabeth who, along with her Grand Chancellor Bestuchev, had been much put out by the swift signature of peace-preliminaries. If Russia is traditionally good at getting in on an international kill, England after a war quickly succumbs to what the Duke of Cumberland then termed 'the improper spirit of economy',[85] as over subsidies. With no word once again to Count Kaunitz, the Earl of Sandwich and the Count de Saint-Séverin on 2 August 1748 concluded a separate convention whereby the Russians were to turn back in their tracks while the French correspondingly withdrew and stood down thirty-seven thousand men from the Low Countries. Maria Theresa, who especially prized the Russian lever, plausibly regarded this as a delusive bargain since the Russians unlike the French would be withdrawn for good. Kaunitz was to pay Sandwich out in kind on 25

---

[83] Tercier to Marquis de Puysieulx, 15 June 1748: Arch. Aff. Étr. C.P., Conférences de Bréda et d'Aix-la-Chapelle: Broglie/Paix, p. 204
[84] Voltaire, *Précis du siècle de Louis XV*, i. 176
[85] Duke of Cumberland to Duke of Newcastle, 20 May 1748: British Library, Add. MSS. 32,715, fo. 40, cited, Lodge, p. 369, n. 1.

September by concluding a separate Franco-Austrian convention for the withdrawal of thirty thousand men from each of their respective forces in the Netherlands. Thus did the allied powers, even reluctant Austria, move towards peace by angry jerks while that smooth operator, the Count de Saint-Séverin, sitting pretty between them, exerted a controlling influence.

Reduction of French forces in the Netherlands swelled the dregs from that long war which were being sucked back to Paris in dangerous eddies, as was already represented to the Minister of War on 19 June 1748 by Berryer: this protégé of Madame de Pompadour had succeeded Marville as lieutenant-general of police. He faced an influx of soldiers and batmen who, presumably to save their officers' pockets, were said to have been summarily discharged with nothing more than three livres, mostly without even coats. Several, famished, went begging in vain and resorted to the argument 'that since they were given nothing, they had to take what they might find'.[86] Such, for them, were the fruits of that victory which brought to the generals and nobles of France fame, riches, and advancement. The Count d'Argenson, politely pressed by Berryer to do something about it, proposed to make an example of 'officers capable of such a manoeuvre', while pointing out that in the postwar scrimmage many troops had taken french leave and were drifting back illegally. According to the Marquis de Stainville it was the dismissal of irregular levies 'which, it is claimed, renders the highroads unsafe'.[87]

French deserters were roaming the Austrian Netherlands in gangs. One of their leaders, when caught, was broken on the wheel in Brussels. At a higher level the rapacious soldiers of fortune, Saxe and Lowendahl, were said to be leading the horrid plunder. Early in July the Marquis de Stainville was writing to Vienna: 'If the evacuations are delayed some time longer, the districts which the French troops are occupying will be totally devastated. The [French] nation itself is indignant at the excesses which are being committed there; and they are very surprised here that I have not been charged to make complaint of it.' If he were given such orders, 'I would execute them with zeal and perhaps with success'.[88]

A fortnight earlier the marquis had reported that French colonels were being strictly held to their regiments, apparently to supervise the stand-down. Even a leave-pass from Saxe did not always save a colonel in Paris from being clapped into gaol by the Minister of War

---

[86] Berryer to Count d'Argenson, Paris, 19 June 1748: Arch. Guerre C., vol. 3278, no. 40.
[87] Marquis de Stainville to Emperor Francis I, Paris, 23 June 1748: Ö.S./H.H.S., Lothringisches Hausarchiv 77/177A.
[88] Ibid., 7 July 1748.

in his feud with the marshal, 'and the poor officers are the victims of it'.[89] Those of general rank, however, were already pouring back with impunity, apart from a few retained by Saxe for duty in the Netherlands behind the cordons of disengagement. Among those few marked with a cross for retention on the return was the Count de Stainville, incidentally still listed as a brigadier.[90] By the end of August 1748 his regiment of Navarre along with that of Ogilvy was standing at Mechlin[91] in the regrouping of the forces of occupation in connection with the reduction covenanted between Saint-Séverin and Sandwich.

All was astir as the clamps of war at last came off. A month earlier Paris had already been subjected to a daily influx of 'foreigners and above all English people,'[92] as usual set on crossing to the continent so soon as hostilities ceased. Meanwhile a belated tack back by the Duke of Newcastle towards conciliating Austria in accordance with the Hanoverian interest only succeeded in antagonizing Frederick at Berlin and shaking Sardinia and Holland while strengthening the position of Saint-Séverin. The latter's aim of rapprochement now with Austria was assisted by Saxony, always on that tack, through her observer at Aix-la-Chapelle, Baron von Kauderbach. He renewed to Saint-Séverin the grandiose theme of a catholic alliance, supported by Kaunitz himself and, as the Marquis de Stainville had been apprised, not by him alone.

In the middle of June 1748 Saint-Séverin had returned briefly to Versailles to report, and on his way through Paris he had a three-hour conversation with his old friend. The plenipotentiary for France told the Marquis de Stainville that he was consoled over the ignorant criticism of his peace-preliminaries by his having been received by Louis 'with the last degree of perfection'.[93] After eulogizing the conduct of Kaunitz at the peace-congress, Saint-Séverin told Stainville 'that all that had pained him had been the fact of having left intact all that had been ceded to the King of Prussia, but that England had absolutely insisted upon it. As for the French system, it had totally changed. The old one had been to diminish the power of the house of Austria, but at present it was on the contrary to maintain her in the state wherein she is, without allowing any diminution ever to be made therein. He judged that the large contacts which there

[89] Ibid., 21 July 1748.
[90] 'Estat des Officiers Généraux, Brigadiers et de l'Estat Major de l'armée des Pays Bas', June 1748: Arch. Guerre C., vol. 3278, no. 1.
[91] 'Tableau général de la position des troupes de Campagne et des milices dans la Flandres et dans le pays conquis', 30 Aug. 1748: ibid., no. 171.
[92] Marquis de Stainville to Emperor Francis I, Paris, 21 July 1748: u.s.
[93] Ibid., 16 June 1748 for the following.

were between the King of England and the King of Prussia were for
the establishment of a protestant league in Germany' which they
would try to enlarge by demanding 'the creation of a tenth electorate
in favour of the House of Hesse . . . In order to thwart this alleged
Protestant League and maintain the Catholic Religion, Their
Imperial Majesties must be very careful to have on their side all the
other Electors' and mutually reconcile them 'in concert with France
. . . He repeated that to me several times, saying always that there
must be a true union between Your Imperial Majesty and the King,
his master . . . and that what he was saying to me could be relied upon
because, once again, the system of today was diametrically opposite
to that of yore.'

This intimation by the Count de Saint-Séverin to the Marquis de
Stainville in June 1748 of a fundamental alteration in the French
system of foreign relations, from alliance with Prussia to support of
Austria, is one of the earliest and clearest pointers towards the shape
of things to come. Saint-Séverin doubtless spoke so for immediately
tactical reasons. But this time his palaver clothed an inward and
strategic truth. In the sphere of Franco-Austrian relations as in others
those uncertain months of 1748, suspended between war and peace,
already signalled not only the end of one conflict but, hardly less, the
origins of another with reversed alliances, as was indeed to occur
after an interval of armed truce for regrouping in the middle of that
contentious century.

Close to the secret hub of this forewheel of change there stood, with
little doubt, the scintillating figure of the Marquis de Pompadour on
one side, and upon the other, with none, the inconspicuous figure of
the Marquis de Stainville. Held away from Aix-la-Chapelle and the
preceding Franco-Austrian soundings through Saxony, Stainville in
his diplomatic backwater had yet first received the secret offer from
Pâris-Duverney to rat on Frederick over Silesia at the end of 1745,
the subsequent approach from Saxe himself and now Saint-Séverin's
spelling out of the French reversal. Formalized in 1756 under the
patronage of Madame de Pompadour after the embassy to Paris of
Kaunitz, this reversal now stands revealed in its longer and more
secret antecedents through the virtual predecessor of Kaunitz in
Paris, the father of the future Duke de Choiseul. The political
background to Choiseul's policy of Franco-Austrian alliance was for
him a personal one.

For the present, for the generally francophil Marquis de Stainville,
it was bad luck that his master the emperor remained appreciably
more anglophil than his wife, as often stressed from Vienna. The
slant towards the emperor was evident in Saint-Séverin's religious

picture of his empire. Though that diplomatist, upon return from Paris to Aix, largely retraced it for Kaunitz too, this time with the variant embellishment that Frederick the Great was thinking of turning catholic with the object, opposed by France, of ousting Austria from the imperial succession: a tale which apparently also reached English ears. Almost equally chimerical, from the opposite quarter, was a Dutch suggestion that the peace treaty should stipulate better treatment for protestants in both France and Hungary. It was, however, rather more than a formality that, after a lapse of exactly a century, the treaties of Westphalia were to be the first of those specifically renewed and confirmed by article III of the treaty of Aix-la Chapelle.

The tale of the catholic conversion of Frederick was but one of the iridescent bubbles which the Count de Saint-Séverin, always good with the soft soap, was then blowing towards Austria. He had earlier described the preliminaries to Kaunitz as soft wax for remodelling while dropping reminders that France had participated in none of the treaties that Maria Theresa specially resented, Breslau, Worms, Dresden. Now Saint-Séverin returned loaded with warm messages for the Austrians from the whole French court including Madame de Pompadour. Upon this tide of hot air the nimble Italian launched another trial-balloon.

The Saxon Secret was reactivated. Saint-Séverin complained to Kauderbach, 'a good and clever lad',[94] of the trouble he was having with Sandwich over the execution of the preliminaries in regard to timetables for the evacuation of conquests: if – a critical conditional – England reneged the preliminaries that might open up a whole new landscape wherein Austria could reclaim her entire irrendenta in Lombardy while France, then, made substantial acquisitions in the Netherlands. And there were other attractive features in Saint-Séverin's imaginative prospect. Apprised of it, Maria Theresa perceived that the French price for supporting her ambitions in Lombardy would be tolerably high. It would really suit her better if France, more moderately, merely agreed to disinterest herself in any subsequent reckoning with Prussia or Sardinia. This was in effect proposed in ponderous Latin in connection with Austrian counter-proposals which, unlike Saint-Séverin's bright suggestions, in the main followed the peace-preliminaries.

Saint-Séverin was not biting on this, and Kaunitz may scarcely have expected him to do so. The Italian had previously reassured Puysieulx 'about what I have said through Kauderbach; we are

<hr/>

[94] Count de Saint-Séverin to Marquis de Puysieulx, 26 June 1748: Arch. Aff. Étr. C.P., Conférence de Bréda et d'Aix-la-Chapelle: Broglie/Paix, p. 218.

compromised and committed to nothing. I am of your opinion that one must in preference to everything follow the plan [of the preliminaries] which we have formed, but I do not think there to be any harm in throwing out remarks which one can follow up or abandon as the case may demand.'[95] For Saint-Séverin treaties were serious, for clinching peace, essentially with England; whereas words were cheap, for sketching the future, essentially with Austria.

Perceptible now is the extent to which oversimplification and faulty focus distorted the truth latent in the Duke de Choiseul's retrospect: 'During the negotiations of Aix-la-Chapelle, Monsieur de Kaunitz made overtures to Monsieur de Saint-Séverin regarding an alliance between France and Austria. Monsieur de Saint-Séverin imagined that Monsieur de Kaunitz was making fun of him and informed Monsieur de Puysieulx, who found the idea of an alliance with Austria most extraordinary. So it was Monsieur de Kaunitz who was first of all made fun of for his advances and vexation at having failed in his design.'[96]

Puysieulx in Paris on 20 August 1748 received Choiseul's father 'with demonstrations of the most tender friendship'[97] while indicating that that between France and Austria was not yet far advanced. Puysieulx would, however, work for it, instancing 'his hereditary attachment' to the house of Lorraine. The occasion of their meeting was in fact some personal business which Stainville was negotiating for Princess Charlotte of Lorraine, and Puysieulx expressed his astonishment at the delay by her brother in sending Stainville new letters of credence which would give formal notification of the imperial election of Francis, now recognizable by the French government. Stainville had not failed to urge this, with incidental reinstatement as a full minister plenipotentiary but, with both sides intent upon fishing in the troubled waters of the slowly subsiding tide of war, he had been informed 'that it was not the time to send him letters of credence'.[98] The interests of Francis were receiving scant recognition and Stainville had especially resented the assignment by the preliminaries to Don Philip of Guastalla since 'I have always thought that this fief belonged by right to Your Imperial Majesty'.[99] Stainville's idea of exchanging it for the Stati dei Presidii got nowhere. Nor was the final Treaty of Aix-la Chapelle to include any specific

[95] Count de Saint-Séverin to Marquis de Puysieulx, 9 July 1748: ibid.
[96] Choiseul, 'Mémoires inédits', 2/16/8/498/2.
[97] Marquis de Stainville to Emperor Francis I, Paris, 25 Aug. 1748: Ö.S./H.H.S., Lothringisches Hausarchiv 77/177A for the following.
[98] Endorsement on dispatch of Marquis de Stainville to Emperor Francis I, Paris, 16 June 1748: ibid.
[99] Marquis de Stainville to Emperor Francis I, Paris, 12 May 1748: ibid.

recognition of Francis as emperor: so slack had the original threads of the Austrian succession fallen in that straggling patchwork of a war.

For the present Puysieulx made out to the discountenanced Stainville that 'if the preliminary articles had displeased my court, it was not his fault if these articles had not been drawn up with it rather than with England. He would indeed have wished that, and our common friend, M. de Saint-Séverin, could tell me one day'[1] that Austrian unforthcomingness had driven him into the arms of England. Such, now, was the deceptive French gloss. One wonders, too, what the Marquis de Stainville as a Lorrainer would have made of the striking twist to the tangled threads with Austria which Puysieulx himself gave ten days later in passing to Saint-Séverin proposals which included a temporary niche for Don Philip in Luxemburg or Hainault till he could succeed Stanislas in Lorraine. Saint-Séverin led Puysieulx's proposals to Kaunitz rather as an accompaniment to the Franco-Austrian military convention of 25 September 1748. Maria Theresa had lately been encouraging Kaunitz to follow up the French ideas advanced earlier through Kauderbach who, however, now seems to have overreached himself in imaginative implausibility. Kaunitz came to write later of 'the nasty intriguing (*vilain tripotage*) of Sieur Kauderbach'.[2]

In that diplomatic game of catch-as-catch-can there were almost as many try-ons to be resisted as loose ends to be caught up or tucked away, as with the Hanoverian desiderata of George II, notably for imperial investiture for Bremen and Verden. In order to guarantee that the French withdrawal at earliest from the Low Countries would be matched in good faith by the remoter British withdrawal from Cape Breton the Earl of Sandwich ingeniously rigged up, for one of the last times in European diplomacy, the ancient expedient of hostages. The young Earl of Sussex, who needed to improve his French, and the handsomer Lord Cathcart, already a veteran from Dettingen, Fontenoy and Lawfeldt, appear to have had a splendid time at the court of the gracious Louis XV. Less agreeable all round was to be the subsequent execution of the stipulated withdrawal of all French support from the Jacobite cause and in particular from the romantic Young Pretender, the determined darling of the Parisian public.

Austria for her part secured some advantage over renewal of Dutch

---

[1] Ibid., 25 Aug. 1748.
[2] Count Kaunitz to Baron von Koch, Paris, 18 Dec. 1750: Hanns Schlitter, *Correspondance secrète entre le comte A. W. Kaunitz-Rietberg, ambassadeur impérial à Paris, et le baron Ignaz de Koch, secrétaire de l'impératrice Marie-Thérèse, 1750–1752* (Paris, 1899: henceforth cited as Kaunitz/Koch), p. 51.

garrisoning of the Barrier Fortresses, Spain over renewal of the Asiento. Now that Don Philip was pretty well fixed up with Parma and Piacenza, and the Italian settlement firmly outlined, the influence of Charles Emmanuel was diminishing. For once he could not secure the support of Newcastle for his further introduction of 'absurd Sardinian demands'.[3] A Piedmontese corridor to the sea through Genoese territory came to seem hardly less chimerical than the flimsy realms which the Marshal de Saxe, territorially baulked in the Netherlands, was to project for himself in Madagascar, Tobago, Corsica or even at the head of a Jewish colony in the New World. Saint-Séverin described greedy Saxe and Lowendahl as Sarmatian Devils. Puysieulx, quietly sensible, holding that the peace-preliminaries had been in turn excessively praised and criticized, had written that June to Belle-Isle: 'I think I have seen things as they are ... It would seem that the allies would like to give forced interpretations to the preliminaries; if that happens, we shall soon have taken up arms again ... The peoples, who should be counted for something, would be grieved to see the hopes which they have formed, vanish.'[4] Aix-la Chapelle, however, showed once again that resentment has an isolating quality. The disgruntled were too disunited to make much impression upon the common purpose for peace of the two prime antagonists. Madame de Pompadour was said to have told Saint-Séverin not to come back without peace. The later Choiseul analysed:

King Louis XV wanted peace by reason that he did not want to leave for the army, where indeed his deportment was more indecent than heroic. Madame de Pompadour for her part desired peace, so as to be no more separated for so long from the King. Monsieur de Puysieulx wanted everything that Madame de Pompadour wanted, and did not bethink him that, without making the King leave Versailles, he might have been able to derive the greatest advantages from the conquests of Marshal de Saxe, and above all to avoid discontenting Spain and her allies even to despair by signing the preliminaries of peace with England without informing them.[5]

Choiseul added:

Monsieur de Saint-Séverin and Monsieur de Puysieulx were without doubt honest people, but very limited and above all very ignorant. They did what they could. They even thought they were doing well since they were acquiescing in the wishes of the King, of his mistress and of the ministers of the council. They were mistaken only in the manner of making it [peace]. Talent is needed. The council can have a general will (une volonté générale) without embarrassing itself with political formulations. Then, for example, Monsieur [the Count] d'Argenson wanted peace

---

[3] Duke of Newcastle to Sir Thomas Robinson, 21 Sept. 1748: Lodge, p. 402, n. 2.
[4] Marquis de Puysieulx to Marshal de Belle-Isle, 17 June 1748; Arch. Guerre C., Série Supplémentaire: Broglie/Paix, pp. 260-1.
[5] Choiseul, Mémoires, pp. 369-71 for the following.

because he wanted to get rid of the Marshal de Saxe, his enemy; Monsieur de Machault because he was controller-general and in time of war a controller-general is haughty in vain; events command him; he must obey the [political] departments and especially the Department of War: it so happened that Monsieur de Machault was the friend of Madame de Pompadour and the particular enemy of Monsieur d'Argenson.

Choiseul piercingly dissected the personal rivalries which weakly united the French government in favour of peace. Choiseul's father had been told by Saint-Séverin in the middle of June 1748 that if the congress were prolonged it would move to Mechlin, which Louis had offered to evacuate, since Aix was 'not habitable, above all during winter'. However, the French plenipotentiary hoped 'to be able to finish the job completely in the space of three or four months':[6] a strikingly accurate estimate. In this cause Du Theil, a dab at drafting, was in August appointed the second French plenipotentiary to match Sir Thomas Robinson. The French bureaucrat outflanked Kaunitz's traditional preference for multiple treaties by blandly proposing that they should all be identical, and then kept everyone on tenterhooks as he slowly redrafted the preliminaries. The draft of the final peace was unveiled at Aix on 23 September, in the main to a chorus of English satisfaction. For, after so much haggling and dispute, the proposed treaty in essentials closely followed the preliminaries.[7] Both documents comprised twenty-four main articles.

VI

The peace treaty of Aix-la-Chapelle was signed by the French, British, and Dutch plenipotaries, and still by them alone, on 18 October 1748, one hundred years, to within ten days, after the signature of the peace of Westphalia. Spain, for once the first of the sulky laggards, signed two days later, Austria on 23 October, peeved Sardinia not till 20 November 1748. That really was the end of that great war which had arisen, in its introductory phase, just nine years earlier as a conflict over Spanish riches in the New World and the severance of a seaman's ear, a conflict later encapsulated in that yet fiercer one originating in the Central European grab of Silesia by the then untried, now neutral, Prussian king of twenty-eight, and extended especially, by the vaulting French ambitions of the Marshal

[6] Marquis de Stainville to Emperor Francis I, Paris, 16 June 1748: Ö.S./H.H.S., Lothringisches Hausarchiv 77/177A.
[7] Cf. p. 732, above. The text of the Treaty of Aix-la-Chapelle is conveniently printed in A. F. Pribram, Österreichische Staatsverträge: England, i. 791–808.

de Belle-Isle and his like to rob still further the eighteen-year-old Austrian queen, to lay low the empire of the Habsburgs and recast the Holy Roman one, which ambitions, going all awry, had yet given the hostilities a mighty spread to the battlements of Prague, the confines of Naples and the crests of the Alps, the Low Countries and the Scottish highlands and out across the oceans to European annexes in Canada and in India also.

Rather seldom do the issues at the end of a great war closely match those at the beginning. The momentum of war itself crushes some and pushes others open. The War of the Austrian Succession, even more than most, had gone lopsided in a new slant upon the future, at the cost of many thousand European lives.

Hostilities had dragged on longest in the Italian theatre after the signature of the preliminaries of peace, and now that the peace-treaty itself was signed, its application still lagged in that peninsula. While history-books are apt to skip the practical tidying-up at the end of any great conflict, article VIII of the Treaty of Aix-la-Chapelle had prescribed that this should be done by commissions sitting at Brussels and at Nice. Not till 26 February 1749 did the last French troops recross the Var and leave Italy to the Italians, Austrians and Spaniards. Saint-Séverin's failure first to stipulate a prompt armistice in Italy, and then to carry with him any other power with an army there when signing peace with England, lay behind the later Choiseul's exaggerated accusation that the Italian representative of France 'totally forgot that France and Spain had an army, an Infant... and interests in Italy. This forgetfulness is perhaps the most extraordinary political fact which has ever occurred. They had to have a recourse to establishing conferences at Nice for this part of it.'[8]

Pace the Duke de Choiseul, the future of Italy now owed not a little to the Count de Saint-Séverin d'Aragon, who is reported to have transmitted to Maria Theresa a heeded warning against attempting simultaneous comebacks against her two subtractors, the Kings of Prussia and of Sardinia. Apart from Don Philip's acquisition of Piacenza along with Parma, Charles-Emmanuel was left in enjoyment of all his gains from Austria at Worms and, not less important, relieved of his bugbear of an exclusive hegemony of either the Habsburgs or the Bourbons in the peninsula. The nice balance now achieved there might seem particularly delicate. In fact it proved the solidest part of the whole settlement, largely outlasting the Napoleonic interlude and even, for a spell, that national-liberal awakening just

---

[8] Choiseul, *Mémoires*, pp. 56–7 for the following.

one hundred years after the Treaty of Aix-la-Chapelle in the false dawn before the real one for the unification of Italy upon the ruins of the old regime.

Choiseul's more substantial criticism of the southern aspect of the peace of Aix-la-Chapelle was of Saint-Séverin's push towards it 'without the knowledge of Spain, our sole ally'. Choiseul learnt this lesson and was signally to reverse such French neglect of Spanish susceptibilities while reinforcing the new French set towards Austria, critical though he was of the immediate French failure even to 'recall the sacrifices which the Empress had offered before the war . . ., without even thinking to arrange those boundaries which, since the treaty of Utrecht, had provided daily discussion between the court of Versailles and that of Vienna . . . They praised the King to the skies for his moderation, whereas they should have criticized his imbecility and that of his ministers.' Frederick the Great did so, as the neutral nonparticipant in the Treaty of Aix-la-Chapelle who came through, even more than Charles Emmanuel, as the real winner from it. The judgement of Frederick and of Choiseul chimed with the French catch-phrase now, bête comme la paix. Though Voltaire defended French abstention from the acquisition of two or three towns in Flanders, which would have been an 'eternal object of jealousy',[9] liable to prejudice rapprochement with Austria.

Saint-Séverin himself was reported to have said 'that he did not build his reputation on the making of the Peace', which might even be called 'infamous; but he founded his glory . . . on having sowed the seeds of dissension between the Courts of London and Vienna, and having made an irreparable breach between them'.[10] That was in itself largely true. Austria was, ominously for Prussia, swinging from one of the great outliers of Europe, England, towards the other, Russia, already almost the rival of Prussia as the dominant neutral in the peace-settlement. If Saint-Séverin had already sown some seeds for a more spectacular Franco-Austrian rapprochement, that would not suffice to win the peace as he aspired, to win more than a truce and breathing-space, as Frederick was to describe it. That was the inward flaw of the peace for France. Eschewing conquest, she had not achieved tranquillity, and so stood to get the worst of both worlds. Her elevated attempt at peace without victory, based upon the status quo with only local exceptions, proved highly insecure, leaving the broader issues unsettled. This was the underlying justification of Choiseul's critique of the diplomacy of Saint-Séverin. It was the deep

---

[9] Voltaire, Précis du siècle de Louis XV, p. 199.
[10] Colonel the Hon. Joseph Yorke to Lord Hardwicke, Paris, 8 Mar. 1749: Philip C. Yorke, The Life and Correspondence of Philip Yorke Earl of Hardwicke (Cambridge, 1913), ii. 15.

diplomacy of a shallow man, largely tactical even in its strategic slant towards Austria, lacking, as Choiseul put it, 'even foresight for the preservation of this same peace. That did not prevent the King, Madame de Pompadour and Monsieur de Puysieulx from being enchanted with this fine piece of work.'[11]

A less exalted Frenchman considered that the outcome of that war 'will teach the ministers to come that it is not enough that we should be almost sure of conquering on land so long as we have not got a navy which can face at sea the maritime powers who, by reason of trade, will always be allied against us'.[12] One future minister who was conspicuously to grasp that lesson was the Duke de Choiseul, the soldier from inland Lorraine with a sweep of vision to embrace the continents beyond the Continent. In them lurked England's proudest destiny. In them, especially, was France to learn the cost of Saint-Séverin's business unfinished. The later Choiseul, left with so much there to try to redeem, succinctly recorded of the peace of Aix-la-Chapelle: 'England returned Louisburg, but nothing was stipulated for the Asiatic boundaries. The Canadian boundaries were referred to commissioners. This article was the ground of the war of 1755.'[13]

Choiseul reverted more than once to this leading theme: 'It is surprising that France, who could and should have laid down the law at Aix-la-Chapelle, did not think of deciding [in Acadia] the question of boundaries, which will always be a sharp point in discussion, but chiefly when these boundaries are situated in America where there are no titles to support one's right other than that of force and usurpation'[14] – and, as he stressed elsewhere, ambiguous treaties: 'Monsieur de Saint-Séverin, who was a man of profound nullity, had been so silly as to allow the insertion in the Treaty of Aix-la-Chapelle, after the clause for the reciprocal restitution of conquests, of a provision that all things should be put back upon the footing on which they were or ought to have been (ou devaient être) before the war.'[15] This was an accurate citation from the second paragraph of article IX of the treaty. 'The boundaries of Acadia and Canada', continued Choiseul, 'not being fixed by the Treaty of Aix-la-Chapelle, and being so by that of Utrecht in a manner which lent itself to every imaginable supposition, the English, armed with these unfortunate words devaient être' – could lay about them almost at will in North America.

The Duke de Choiseul was remorseless in his elegant criticism of the imperfect treaty which was to loom so large for his later policy:

[11] Choiseul, Mémoires, p. 57.   [12] Barbier, iv. 309–10.   [13] Choiseul, Mémoires, p. 57.
[14] Ibid., p. 147.   [15] Choiseul, 'Mémoires inédits', 2/16/8/498/1 for the following.

If Monsieur de Saint-Séverin had had the slightest knowledge of the situation in Acadia and of the subject of its boundaries, he would have foreseen that by referring this matter to commissioners there would sooner or later result either war between France and England or the cession of French pretensions and even possession of a part of Acadia. For the English, not being constrained by a treaty of peace to a repartition of these boundaries, could not agree in a negotiation between commissioners that we should remain in possession of lands which were behind their most essential colonies and which took them in the rear. Thus politically it would have been better to compromise on the boundaries at Aix-la-Chapelle, as the English would have liked, rather than to have referred the decision to a negotiation between commissioners, under reserve of having such complaisance rewarded in the treaty upon other matters. Monsieur de Saint-Séverin and those who were directing him had not applied themselves to a policy of foresight. They were acting for the moment, which is perhaps one of the greatest faults in politics. It was not the only one which they committed in this line; but the mistake which they made at Aix-la-Chapelle was only ... the pretext for the proceedings of England against France.[16]

Such was the verdict of the greatest antagonist of the British Empire in the middle of the eighteenth century. Yet this imperial inheritance for the policy of the Duke de Choiseul was largely conditioned, politically as well as personally, by that continental diplomacy wherein his father, as now appears, had been a secret link, and by that continental warfare in which he himself had shone.

Choiseul's acid appraisal of the peace of Aix-la-Chapelle may well have included, even in retrospect, something of the disgruntlement of the fighting soldier who, after helping to pull his country through the long haul of war, believes that his efforts were sold short by diplomatic incompetents in the peacemaking. And it had been a long war for a young man, a long decade since his smallpox in Vienna and preliminary baptism of fire at distant Groczka against the Turkish infidel: then the big war itself, marching out as subaltern to Bohemia, beleaguered in Prague before the Marshal de Belle-Isle's terrible retreat in midwinter; the critical choice for young Stainville between the service of Austria and of France, and that heavy day at Dettingen upon the staff of his benefactor, the Marshal de Noailles; the Duchess d'Aiguillon, too, and his social initiation in artful preference to a premature one in that secret diplomacy between the two antagonists, already familiar to his father; his first little regiment wrung from a hostile Minister of War, the wound at Villefranche, the scaling of the Alps, heroism upon the field of Coni and squelching duties in the trenches, friendship with the young Duke d'Agenais turned to contempt of cowardice, but friendship with the dashing Prince de Conti cemented to survive even the flat campaign next year in the Rhineland before the delights of Marly in the days of his youth, grim

16 Choiseul, *Mémoires*, pp. 147–8.

and gay, extravagantly spanking around Paris, successful with women as with war, grieving indeed for young Antoinette-Eustachie but making a fashionable hit, like the Méchant, as a mordant man about town; and in the field ever leading his famous Regiment of Navarre in Saxe's classic victories over the English at Rocoux and at Lawfeldt, present again at the ultimate capitulation of Maestricht, rising to the equivalence of a major-general at the age of twenty-eight.

Soon this military apprenticeship for France was to be rounded out by a diplomatic one. That called for some consolidation in society and at court of a free-living youth. The Count de Stainville, after looking around a little, set about securing three powerful resources for a young man, however able, in any drive to the top. These were a loving wife, great wealth, and high opportunity.

PART IV

CLIMBING
1748-1754

CHAPTER I

SEIGNEURIAL

I

THE years between the close of the Count de Stainville's active military career in 1748 and the opening of his diplomatic one in 1754 might seem the emptiest of his mature life, given over to personal concerns and social pleasure. Those six years were in fact formative for his future.

Not only was Stainville now to acquire a wife and a fortune but he went thrusting ahead in business administration, in social consideration and, at the questionable crux of his career, in political influence. And all this, significantly, just at the hinge of the French eighteenth century, turning now towards a new dispensation economically, with the immediate distress in postwar France yielding place at last to sunnier revival from long depressions of seventeenth-century type, politically, with the personal decline of the king coinciding with the advancing initiative of the parliaments, and intellectually in the next great reawakening after the renaissance, this time with France in the lead in encyclopedic enthusiasm for the new-found perfectibility of man. It was precisely from 1750 onwards that the philosophs came to form an ideological movement.[1] Such was the mid-century turning-point for France emergent from a seigneurial society under authoritative monarchy towards a renovation so revolutionary as to cast into the shade even the landmarks from its inception.

If the peace of Aix-la-Chapelle further opened out fresh perspectives overseas for the policy of the future Duke de Choiseul, yet the termination of the War of the Austrian Succession, confirming that of the house of Habsburg-Lorraine, strengthened the ties of the then Count de Stainville to the inland duchy of his birth.

The accommodating Leszczynski Duke of Lorraine provided Stephen de Stainville with his share in a regular reward for general officers. At Lunéville on 14 March 1748 'Stanislas by the grace of God King of Poland, Grand Duke of Lithuania, Russia, Prussia, Mazovia, Samogitia, Kiovia, Volhynia, Podolia, Podlachia, Livonia, Smolensk', and so on down to humdrum Lorraine, proclaimed that 'Messire Stephen, Count de Choiseul, Marquis [sic] de Stainville' had

---

[1] Cf. Robert Shackleton, 'When did the French "philosophes" become a party?' in *Bulletin of the John Rylands University Library of Manchester*, vol. lx, no. 1 (1977), p. 197.

given King Stanislas such proof 'of his valour, zeal, fidelity and affection for our service'[2] that he was the man to fill the newly created office of governor of the town and castle of Mirecourt.

Stainville was nicely suited, one might think, by the little country-town of Mirecourt less than thirty miles south of Nancy and about the same to the west from the ducal court at Lunéville and from the Count de Stainville's sisters snugly ensconced at Remiremont. Mirecourt, manufactory of musical instruments, is tucked down in the tufted country of the northern foothills of the Faucilles as they hook out westward from the Vosges. The town lies a little upstream from Haroué on one of the earliest tributaries of the Moselle, the little river Madon, crossed at Mirecourt by the bridge of Saint Vincent. The aspect of the place, as of so many others in the eighteenth century, was still largely gothic with its narrowly irregular main-street, twin-turreted marketplace, and houses jostling beneath the hexagonal church-spire.

Before the Count de Stainville could assume authority over even such a little place, Louis XV had to consent, as he formally did five days later, to this attachment to a nominally foreign sovereign. Then it was the turn of Counsellor Gallois as a commissioner appointed to attest to the governor-designate's zeal, 'life, morals, catholic, apostolic and Roman religion'.[3] This regular procedure for appointments and honours must have caused referees in that century to turn a remarkable number of blind eyes. Upon satisfactory certification Stainville at last repaired to Nancy and there, on 18 July 1748, took the oath to Chancellor de La Galaizière 'faithfully to serve the King and the public', actually mentioned.

The new governor of Mirecourt was to see to 'the safety and preservation of the said town and castle, to maintain the inhabitants in good union and intelligence with one another, and the said soldiers [local militia] in good discipline and police'.[4] In 1744 Mirecourt had sent to the war, to guard the eastern frontiers, a respectable little battalion of 710 militia though with only 500 guns and bayonets between them. Their return, plus the transit no doubt of other units, was a major preoccupation of the townsfolk, not least of Anne-Catherine Fromantau, a 'young widow . . . afraid of having a military man staying in her domicile. Her situation is most unhappy.'[5] It became the concern not, indeed, of the Count de Stainville but of

---

[2] 'Provision de M^r· de Choiseul Gouverneur des Ville et Château de Mirecourt,' 14 Mar. 1748: Arch. Vosges, Série E, BB.25 ('Canton de Mirecourt: Enregistrement des resolutions, remontrances et sentences de l'Hôtel de Ville 1748–1772'), fo. 1.

[3] Ibid., fo. 5–7 ('Extrait des Liasses du Greffe du Conseil d'Etat') for the following.

[4] Ibid., fo. 2.

[5] Ibid., fo. 16–18 ('Placet et décret pour la D^lle. Fromantau pour l'exemption de logement de Gens de Guerre') for the following.

officials at the townhall and La Galaizière himself, who granted her 'appropriate consideration', not legal exemption from billeting. And it was the indefatigable Chancellor of Lorraine who, that September, sent detailed instructions to the Subdélégué and chief of police at Mirecourt, one Louis Alba, for the preparation of a magazine for the storage of the militia's arms and equipment in 'ten racks of two or three rows each'.[6] They were to be in charge of a resident caretaker instructed 'to beat out the clothes, or have them beaten out, every month, to rub the arms with pieces of rag soaked in oil, and to see that dust does not settle on the equipment'.

La Galaizière was a stout fighter in the everlasting battle against dust, rust and moth. For France the eighteenth century, so far from being one slow decline, has been assessed as a golden age of her bureaucracy. The municipality of Mirecourt duly built for its returning militia 'an arsenal in the old town hall',[7] for which the local carpenter, François Bailly, charged 114 livres. Another extraordinary item of municipal expenditure that year, a new pulpit for the parish church, netted Bailly over 700 livres in all. Still, looking at the pulpit, one feels that he earned his money. It compared with a little over forty-five livres that year for keeping the town clock in running order and no less than 1,140 paid to a contractor as 'the price of the lighting of the parish'[8] in the enlightenment of Lorraine. These items and many others, including 500 livres for Alba's salary as chief of police, brought the municipal expenditure of Mirecourt for 1748 to 18,281 livres, 7 sous, 10 deniers. This represented a deficit on the municipal budget of something more than 2,000 livres: total receipts for that year were rather over 16,000 livres, mostly from the local tax of the subvention, netting 9,614 livres, plus just over 6,000 livres received on account of the Ponts et Chaussées. For those interested in long trends on a small scale, the graph of the municipal receipts of Mirecourt rose from 12,152 livres in 1725 to 14,711 in 1740, 17,864 in 1750, 19,560 in 1760, 21,574 in 1770, then dipping rather ominously to 18,874 in 1780, 17,455 in 1789.[9]

In this little community then steadily on the up the representative of the absent governor was to be a lawyer called Godefroy, who was a demesne lieutenant (*lieutenant à la gruerie*) at Mirecourt. After, in

---

[6] 'Mémoire sur ce qui doit être observé à l'égard des magasins qu'il s'agit d'établir dans les quartiers d'assemblée des bataillons de milice pour y garder en réserve les effets d'habillement, d'équipement et d'armement qu'ils y déposiront à leur retour des provinces frontières', enclosure in La Galaizière to Alba, Lunéville, 14 Sept. 1748: ibid., fo. 13 for the following.

[7] 'Compte de Sieur François Maréchal, marchand bourgeois de Mirecourt, en qualité de receveur des deniers patrimoniaux et d'octroys de la ditte ville de Mirecourt: pour l'hôtel de ville pour l'année 1748': Arch. Vosges, Série E, CC.56[2], fo. 27.

[8] Ibid., fo. 19.

[9] Arch. Vosges, Série E, CC.4 ('Livre de comptes des collecteurs, 1725 à 1790'), *passim*.

turn, verifying the morals and capacity of Godefroy, the Count de Stainville appointed him to be 'secretary to our government at Mirecourt'[10] on 1 August 1748. This brevet of appointment was signed and sealed that day by Stainville and countersigned by 'our ordinary secretary', Carré, as being 'done in our château of Demange-aux-Eaux'.

II

The Count de Stainville, on his way back from taking oath of office at Nancy, had evidently looked in at Demange, agreeable amid its waters in high summer. Once again, though, it provided a rural setting for financial preoccupation. It looks as if, with hostilities at last ended, young Stainville took this opportunity to have a grand accounting with his father and the agents. At Demange-aux-Eaux next Saturday, 3 August 1748, the Marquis de Stainville took up the backlog of war and checked through the estate-accounts for the years from 1740 to 1746.

The bare entries in the accounts, as rendered by Nicolas Mathieu, procurator-general and receiver of the marquisate of Stainville, indicate how little, even during the war-years, the slow tenor of life there had changed, outwardly at least, from the earlier picture for the seventeen-twenties. Prickly du Tertre was still being bought out of Bazincourt in quite a big way and was drawing five per cent interest on the twenty thousand livres owing to him till it had at last been paid off in February 1741. Jacques Colin, chief forester at Stainville for thirty years, continued to draw his annual hundred francs in the old currency of Bar, making the tiresomely odd figure of forty-two livres, seventeen sous. Morel remained the gardener though of course there were new faces too, like Vadet, that 'young servant'[11] of the Marquise de Stainville. Local deals in timber remained constant, as also derelictions. In April 1740 an oak illegally cut in the Bois du Petit Val had been sold off to Jean Pitois for twenty livres plus two livres, ten sous in respect of the suggestively entitled levy of *franc vin*. The ancient due of formarriage still caught up with two or three girls marrying outside the marquisate each year and brought in an annual revenue of six or seven livres.

More interesting probably to the Marquis and Count de Stainville was the broad balance, or rather imbalance, of Mathieu's accounts.

---

[10] 'Brevet du Sr. Godefroy, Secretaire du Mr. le Gouverneur', Demange-aux-Eaux, 1 Aug. 1748: Arch. Vosges, Série E, BB.25, fo. 7 for the following.

[11] Arch. Meuse, J 18[19] ('Comptes de la baronie [*sic*] de Stainville, 1741 [*sic*]-1785'), account for 1740 (wrongly endorsed on original as for 1748) for the following.

That for 1740 totalled the receipts of the marquisate at 18,170 livres, 3 sous, 8 deniers, wherein much the largest single item was the 6,000 livres paid by Brigeat as his rent for the general lease of the farmlands; it nearly equalled all income from sale of timber, standing at just over 6,200 livres that year. Brigeat's six thousand were, however, paid over in full to the Marquis de Stainville, as were other sizeable sums, such as a thousand that year from timber; and these payments were entered as expenditure. As against the total receipts, the expenditure and the accounts outstanding as offsets or reprises taken together came to 18,569 livres, 2 sous, 5 deniers. Hence, following Mathieu's form of accounting, the expenditure plus rebates slightly exceeded receipts to give a deficit of 406 livres, 8 sous, 11 deniers. This might not seem so bad till one appreciated the fact that the incoming reprises, amounting to over five thousand livres, were included in the total of the receipts, and only thereafter separately re-entered as rebates in a somewhat confusing form of double entry. Such was the inwardness of the Marquis de Stainville's endorsement of the account for 1740: 'Which account is allowed at this figure on condition of carrying over as reprise the five thousand three hundred and sixty-one livres, three sous, five deniers of rebate. Choiseul de Stainville': certified as 'done at Demange the 3rd August 1748'.

One begins to see why the young Count de Stainville looked upon such offsets in the estate-accounts with a sharp and unfriendly eye. It may have been he who stiffened his father to make that endorsement. The inclusion of reprises in the receipts largely represented an artificial reckoning of bad debts, often carried over from year to year: twelve listed for 1740, nineteen in 1741, twenty-one in 1742 and in 1743, thirty in 1744, twenty-five in 1745. In the accounts for 1742 onwards this was indeed balanced, if rather less clarified, by the inclusion, as the first item of expenditure for the current year, of the true deficit from the preceding year, found by extracting receipts from the total of expenditure plus reprises. Disregarding sous and deniers, Mathieu's round figures in livres for these years from 1741 in the marquisate were as follows:

Year	Receipts	Reprises	Expenditure	Deficit
1741	23,948	10,544	16,593	3,189
1742	24,157	13,294	15,785	4,922
1743	25,719	10,194	17,370	1,845
1744	22,553	11,080	17,100	5,627
1745	25,153	8,355	17,211	412

The high tally of reprises may have approximated to a local index to the pinch of war. Though doubtless there were also elements of dishonesty, bad luck or, as with one of the largest debts, illness. That of a third party called de Brau was held responsible for the nonpayment to the marquisate by a former ironmaster, Bonnau or Bonneau, of 1,138 livres, 4 sous, 5 deniers on account of wood supplied to him so long ago as 1734. Ten years later legal proceedings over this were dragging on in the courts of Ancerville. But of course litigation cost more money and even that might not be the end of it. The accounts for 1742 itemized not only 63 livres, 12 sous, 11 deniers for legal proceedings against another defaulter called Thumelin, but a further outgoing of 330 livres, 6 sous 'according to the receipts of the gaoler for the food for three years of Claude Thumelin, a prisoner for timber debts . . . at six sous per day'.[12] If the lot of Thumelin and his like was not a happy one, nor, one feels, was that of the receiver of the marquisate of Stainville. And now, under Count Stephen, it was to become still less so.

In the postwar reckoning at Demange in that summer of 1748 the Marquis de Stainville was not concerned, formally at all events, with the most recent account which his son had gone through when there the previous November, and which afforded something of a contrast to its predecessors. Mathieu's interim account, to November, for the marquisate in the year 1747 was rendered to the young count in accordance with his previously noticed act of possession that June.

In this 'first account' for 1747 the largest single receipt remained Brigeat's rental of 6,045 livres. And it maintained almost the same balance as in 1740 against sales of timber, which in 1747 totalled 6,367 livres. These sales ranged much as usual, from the biggest adjudication of 348 oaklings for 2,228 livres plus 278 livres *franc vin* to a combine formed by Nicolas Varin, François Rotou, and Jean Labreche, down to half an acre (*arpent*) of the Putiot woodland to Jean Pilerel the locksmith for thirty-five livres and, for fifteen, a quarter of an acre of copsewood to half-hogshead René – René Demymuid. The lease, too, of the tile-kiln at Montplonne was once more bringing in four hundred livres.

There was, however, one sizeable new item of receipt: one thousand livres 'which the accountant has received from Beurey at the hands of Messire Carré from the proceeds from the corn and forage'.[13] This was the thousand from young Stainville's own inheritance which, as noticed earlier, was sent to him that year at Saxe's Camp de la Commanderie. The other 1,500 livres, from Brigeat's rent of 6,000, which Stainville received there, slotted in suggestively with a new item in the outgoings, for 'the sum of 4,500 livres which Messire

[12] Ibid., account for 1742.
[13] Ibid., 'Compte premier de 1747', and for the following.

Brigeat has paid to Madame the Marquise from the rental of this property'. If its running had, in effect, passed from the Marquise de Stainville to her son, not all the profits had, not yet at all events.

The most striking innovations in the account for 1747 were two omissions: first, of the traditional first item under expenditure, namely the deficit from the previous year; secondly, of the whole 'chapter of reprises'. Mathieu might perhaps reassure himself that this one was only a 'first account'. But the outlook here was not encouraging, more particularly in view of the fact that the telling omissions were evidently convenient to the Count de Stainville, permitting him to endorse the account in his own tight handwriting: 'The receipts of this account amount to thirteen thousand eight hundred and thirty-one livres, twelve sous, seven deniers; the expenditure to 9,217 livres. Mathieu owes me 4,614 12s. 7d. I have passed this account thus. The 22nd Nov. 1747.' This was followed by a further endorsement: 'I have received from Mathieu, on account of the 4,614 l., 1,000 l.' Countervailingly, Mathieu specified that he rendered the account 'under protestation of carrying over in reprise the sums which remain due and whereof he has not been able to secure payment'. The Count de Stainville would see about that, in the absence of any subsequent account for 1747, when the time came at the end of that year of 1748.

If the Marquis de Stainville, in the accounting at Demange that summer, kept clear of this financial tussle deriving from his son's take-over in 1746–7, yet the father at that period remained fully implicated in other aspects of his heritage in Lorraine, notably in his half-share, through his wife, of the marquisate of Removille. This was providing a little case to suggest how the dusty litigation of feudalism could largely supply the terms wherein conflicts of class were fought out in that century.

In 1746 the Marquis de Stainville in his capacity of half a marquis of Removille had got together with his lesser partners for the other half, the Bassompierre Marquis de Baudricourt and the Choiseul Count de Savigny, to go to court at Bourmont in the bailiwick of Bassigny in order to secure payment every Martinmas by each inhabitant of Jainvillotte to the plaintiffs, as territorial lords (*seigneurs fonciers*) thereof, of 'an annual quitrent of one bushel of oats, one pullet and one denier of Toul'[14] in respect of the communal woods of that locality. In the face of this demand the inhabitants of Jainvillotte 'thought that it would be to their interest to call to their help the venerable Benedictines of Saint-Mihiel in the hope that they would

---

[14] Ibid., 4 H 51, 'Bénédictins de l'abbaye de St. Mihiel', no. 47, record of deliberations of the monks of Saint-Mihiel, 20 Dec. 1746.

afford them the means to ward off the judgement which was threatened against them'.[15] The townsfolk argued that if they had to pay up to the Marquis de Stainville and his consorts then the monks in their capacity of lords enjoying high justice (*seigneurs hauts justiciers*) over Jainvillotte could no longer claim their due of the third penny on sales of timber from the communal woods. One sees how this triangle of forces, involving the three estates of the realm in miniature, was building up at Jainvillotte.

On 20 December 1746 Prior Toussaint of Saint-Mihiel together with the sub-prior and seventeen monks assembled 'as a chapter to the sound of the bell'.[16] They shrewdly decided that the inhabitants of Jainvillotte did owe the marquises of Removille their due, but in respect not of quitrent for the communal woods but of legal dues (*droit d'avouerie*) and therefore without prejudice to the monkish third penny. Though it was for arrears of quitrent that the men of Jainvillotte were on 24 January 1747 condemned to pay up to the Marquis de Stainville and the others. Behind the legal formulae of the serried documents it rather looks as though the monks may have been inclined to gang up with the marquises against the local representatives of the third estate in a microcosm of much of the old regime. Though the worsting of the third estate was by no means invariable in those parts, as was being strikingly confirmed at Stainville itself in a more important case then grinding towards its ultimate settlement by the young Count de Stainville in person.

For the Marquis de Stainville the grand accounting of 3 August 1748 at Demange-aux-Eaux represented something of a signing off from his active concern with the Stainville estate, apart from separated Bazincourt. The very next day he was trying, unsuccessfully, to promote his diplomatic comeback by a 'very respectful remonstrance'[17] to the Emperor Francis for neglecting to send the French court formal notification of his imperial election. While Stainville's despatch of 4 August was dated as from Paris, it was rather unusually in his own hand, suggesting that he was in fact away from his secretary of legation. One may notice incidentally that if diplomatic existence then was often an agreeable one, like that of courtiers, like them ambassadors and envoys were expected to be pretty constantly on duty, sometimes for years on end at a foreign court, apparently with few holidays or even journeys home for consultation. Only, the Marquis de Stainville still could not even appear at the court to which he was accredited. And if, even upon his

---

[15] Ibid., no. 48.   [16] Ibid., no. 47.
[17] Marquis de Stainville to Emperor Francis I, Paris, 4 Aug. 1748: Ö.S./H.H.S., Lothringisches Hausarchiv 77/177A.

inherited estates, he was now heading into limbo, so was the procurator-fiscal of his marquisate.

III

Nicolas Mathieu, busy with the accounts of Stainville for over twenty years, had evidently been running into trouble over them with his new master. The next account, for the year 1748, even suggested some reversion to old ways. A rubric of 'extraordinary receipts' included a small intake of 16 livres, 13 sous 'for the price of thirty-seven pieces of sawn timber coming from the demolition of the partitions between the rooms in the new building, sold to M. Brigeat'.[18] On this the Count de Stainville wrote in the margin: 'Pray inform me why thirty-seven pieces of timber were sold for 16 *ll.* and by what order.' Mathieu subsequently explained that they were joists 'which had been valued at this price by two experts'.[19] But there was worse to come.

The same rubric in Mathieu's account for 1748 concluded: 'The accountant observes that in his account he does not render the dues of receipt (*droit de recette*), seeing that they have been ceded and surrendered to him to indemnify him for the costs and expenditure which he is obliged to incur during the year both for the meals which he gives to the officers of the forestry on the days when the timber is sold, and to the merchants who come to buy it, as also for other expenses.'[20] The count countered: 'As I give wages to my receiver I do not wish that he should levy these dues and I wish him to inform me of what he has drawn.' The answer was 387 livres on auctions of timber in the two years of 1747–8, as Mathieu's rake-off in dues of receipt at the rate of one sol in the livre or five per cent of the purchase-price. This was a tidy sum by comparison with his regular wages of 300 livres per annum. Mathieu was to be constrained to agree to refund the 387 livres to the Stainville estate.

At Stainville the easygoing days of old, with their woodland jollifications, were being sharply revised in the takeover of the young count and, perhaps, through accompanying intrigues in the estate-agency. Mathieu subsequently lamented, evidently to his successor as receiver: 'You can also recall that you wrote to me from Paris that I had enemies who had done me much harm, beginning with Monsieur Cazin who had spoken at Demange to Madame and

---

[18] Mathieu, 'Compte de l'année 1748': Arch. Meuse, J 18[19] ('Comptes de la baronie de Stainville, 1741–1785') for the following.
[19] Mathieu's account for 22 Nov. 1747–1 May 1749: ibid.
[20] Mathieu, 'Compte de l'année 1748': ibid. for the following.

Monsieur about the dues of receipt.'[21] Madame and Monsieur in that order suggest, as one would rather expect, the Marquise de Stainville and her incoming son. Monsieur Cazin may well have been Claude Cazin, who had rendered the accounts of the marquisate for, apparently, a suggestively short period back in the early seventeen-twenties (Cazin's account for 1724 had been succeeded in the following year by a considerably fuller and more satisfactory one rendered by a certain Jean Colin and countersigned, already, by Mathieu).

If the receipts, and non-receipts, of the estate in Mathieu's account for 1748 provoked trouble, the items of expenditure spelt more: especially with regard to that order which the Count de Stainville had given him on 23 November 1747 for repairs and additions to the château de Stainville. These had involved the 'purchase of materials in stone, wood and windows to shut, the workmanship and daily labour employed on the construction of the planks, doors, lintels, shutters, ceilings, walls, window-glazing and staircase of the prisons'[22] to a total of 1,203 livres, 8 sous.

Here is proof that just about the middle of the eighteenth century a feudal landowner in Lorraine was still actively concerned with maintaining his château as, in part, a gaol to back his seigneurial justice. Such was the grimmer background to young Stainville's pleasures in Paris. At the same time it looks as though he may already have been preparing the pattern which he was to trace in larger affairs: that of working within the old-established order while trying to modernize and humanize it. There is later evidence of the Count de Stainville's concern for the conditions of neglected prisoners, and he may well have been setting an example at home (the emphasis now on windows might even suggest previously unglazed apertures). There should, however, be a limit to improvements. The count annotated the account: 'I did not give such an extensive order as is supposed and this item must be modified by at least half.'

The immediately following item was 'for the repairs made to the [banal] presses of Stainville and Lavincourt and to houses at Montplonne in accordance with and execution of the judgement of the provostship of Stainville of the month of August 1747', seven hundred livres. This incurred the countly comment: 'When the provostship of Stainville had the impertinence to give judgement against me, I wrote about it to mark my astonishment and I was informed that it was but an advance which I would be making and that the money would return to me. That was nearly two years ago

---

[21] Mathieu to (?) Carré, Blainville, 30 Sept. 1752: ibid.
[22] Mathieu's account for 22 Nov. 1747–1749: ibid. for the following.

and I have been told no more of this matter. So I do not allow it.' So much for local action then against a lordly landowner. Though, be it noted, the required repairs had been effected.

Unpleasantness over the receipts and expenditure of the Stainville estate for 1748 was compounded by the fact that Mathieu's account for that year, unlike his interim one for 1747, once more concluded with a rubric for nagging reprises. The first item here went back to that sharp calculation wherewith the count had clinched the reckoning for 1747, namely that Mathieu owed him 4,614 livres, 12 sous, 7 deniers. Of that amount Mathieu had been able to recover from the actual debtors to the estate less than half, leaving outstanding as a reprise the sum of 2,657 livres, 12 sous, 2 deniers. Roughly corresponding, the account for 1748 closed with an exceptional section headed: 'Account of the old debts carried over as reprises in the account for 1746.'[23] These debts due from a dozen individuals had amounted to 6,679 livres, 12 sous, 4 deniers, subsequently reduced by recoveries to 4,891 livres, 8 sous, 5 deniers. Of this last the unhappy agent now asked to be discharged of responsibility for 2,067 livres, 7 sous, 11 deniers, the total of four bad debts owing from Sieur Bonneau, formerly an inspector in the tobacco farm in Hainault ('has gone bankrupt'), Sebastian Bidaut ('is ruined'), Sieur Molet, the lawyer ('there are proceedings'), and agricultural Claude Lamy ('he is ruined'): a bleak glimpse into rural insolvency and failure in the everlasting struggle to make a living.

Such was the hard core of debts outstanding which had confronted the Count de Stainville ever since he took over the management of the marquisate. So displeasing, evidently, was Mathieu's reckoning of them now, that his account for 1748 was not agreed or signed off in the usual way. Its main items were recapitulated and often elaborated in the fresh account which he had to render for the fuller period from 22 November 1747 to 1 May 1749. This new account, exceptionally all in Mathieu's own hand and presented by him on 7 May 1749, again included a rubric of reprises, rounded up to 2,657 livres. Stainville countered: 'I want no reprises in my accounts and I have declared that they are a charge upon my receiver.'[24] This annotation is one of many in the hand of Stainville's secretary, François Carré. Some months later one finds Stainville dictating when ill, or he may here have been anticipating his ministerial practice.

The showdown had come. The period covered by Mathieu's latest account ran from his accounting with the count at Demange back in the autumn of 1747 to the time, nearly, in the summer of 1749

---

[23] Mathieu, 'Compte de l'année 1748': ibid. for the following.
[24] Annotation on Mathieu's account for 22 Nov. 1747–1 May 1749: ibid. for the following.

when he was replaced as receiver of Stainville by the count's man, Carré.

Stephen de Stainville dictated to Carré the following endorsement on Mathieu's last account: 'I have allowed all the items of this account except those to which I have made apostils in my hand, which I declare to be of no value and which I forbid Sieur Carré to charge to the account. At Paris this 14th May 1749. Signed Choiseul de Stainville.'

For Nicolas Mathieu, so long the servant of the marquisate, that summer was a melancholy season of winding up and handing over, with numbers of embittered tangles to sort out. At last, there at Stainville on 8 July 1749, Mathieu reached a conditional settlement with 'François Carré, present receiver of the marquisate of Stainville in consequence of the power of attorney which has been given to me in writing by my said lord'.[25] This settlement was, by whatever device, endorsed on the back in the Count de Stainville's hand as having been approved by him in Paris on the very next day of 9 July.

Such crisp action might not suggest that in fact the younger Stainville was himself under the weather just then. On the previous day he had begun a course of the waters, sipping those of Passy 'in small quantities. At present it is so terribly hot that one does not know what to do with oneself. This circumstance, together with the travail of the waters, depresses and prostrates me. Still, it is a good thing that I am equally afraid of the heat and the cold. I find cold more disagreeable and heat more unhealthy. It is exhausting me and draining me of the little strength I have left.'[26]

In those years, which one might take to be mainly halcyon days of enjoyment for the Count de Stainville, he is strikingly often to be found indisposed and sorry for himself in the French tradition of physical concern verging upon hypochondria. Though he may indeed have been suffering in reaction to years of arduous campaigning, already perhaps from the onset of his later bouts of acute nephralgia or gravel of the kidneys.

For the present Stainville persevered with his cure of the waters for twenty-two days, at the end of which, he further explained to the Duke de Nivernais, 'I was doing very badly... I am at present resting and doing nothing. My stomach is working very badly, and in consequence I am much subject to the vapours.'[27] Nearly three weeks later again, that troubled summer, the terms of Carré's settlement

---

[25] Carré, 'Récapitulation et formule de l'arrêté du compte de M. Mathieu pour l'année 1748', Stainville, 8 July 1749: ibid.
[26] Count de Stainville to Duke de Nivernais, 13 July 1749: W. N. A., docket V/1, fo. 3.
[27] Ibid., 4 Aug. 1749, fo. 5.

were engrossed at the end of Mathieu's last account: 'Today the twenty-third of August one thousand seven hundred and forty-nine I the undersigned François Carré, present receiver of the marquisate of Stainville, testify that in consequence of the orders in writing which my Lord the Count de Stainville gave me under date of ninth July last, I have settled the present account as follows: by removing from the present account the reprises, which shall belong to Sieur Mathieu, the accountant, by means of the cession and transfer thereof which is made to him by my said lord the Count de Stainville.'[28] Instead of Mathieu having to make up the bad debts, he was made a present of them. But he had to refund 387 livres for the dues of receipts and presumably carry the can for the excision from the account of the 700 livres for repairs for the provostship and of 601 livres, 14 sous, being half the cost of the repairs to the prison.

All this meant that in the account Mathieu's total figures of 24,291 livres expenditure, 3,406 in reprises and 23,051 in receipts, producing a deficit of 4,646 livres, were altered to a total 'expenditure of 22,989 livres against 23,438 in receipts, yielding a profit for once of 448 livres, further payable by the luckless Mathieu to the estate. That sum was, however, deducted from the 1,863 livres which was agreed to be owing to him from the account for 1746. For the balance Mathieu had to be content, or discontent, with the assignment of local debts still outstanding from that year.

IV

The settlement between the old and new receivers of Stainville proved anything but conclusive. Mathieu clearly had the losing end of it. His worries persisted and also, one gathers, unfriendly treatment of him. So late as the end of September 1752 he was unburdening himself, evidently to Carré, in an enormous epistle from Blainville whither he had withdrawn eastwards from Stainville, over by Nancy. It began by acknowledging Carré's letter of the fifteenth instant 'by which you inform me that the count has sent you back my letter and that he charges you to finish with me concerning my demands. I am charmed that he should have had this kindness. It is long enough that I have been making the advances. It is true that I have or should receive from Sieur Jullien and Gaillet one hundred and ninety-seven livres.'[29] Mathieu plunged off into his petty concerns of debts, worries and grievances. They were probing right back to his part in

[28] Carré, endorsement of 23 Aug. 1749 on Mathieu's account for 22 Nov. 1747–1 May 1749: Arch. Meuse, J 18[19].
[29] Mathieu to (?) Carré, Blainville, 30 Sept. 1752: ibid. for the following.

that slim little business of omitting from the accounts for 1741 the supply of oaks to Pitois for repairing the mill at Ménil.[30] Mathieu now pointed out that the Count de Stainville himself had been in on that short cut past official bumbledom on an urgent job:

Besides, we accounted and consequently receipted this business together. I do not doubt that my conduct in everything is suspected since everything is being investigated, and that does not worry me because I shall justify myself when I have to, and with regard to the 1,070 livres I shall, then, address myself again to His Excellency [the Marquis de Stainville]. It is not just that I should lose such a sum, having given it from my money and you can ascertain that Charlier has still been persecuting me since I have been here. You can see it too from my accounts since you have been leafing through them again.

The emotion beneath the dreary figures came welling up. Mathieu proceeded:

It seems that you are very angry from the expressions of your letter against me. Tell me, I beg you, what wrong I have done you. Am I not allowed, then, to complain of the bad treatment which I have received? Do you find that in the letter which I wrote to the count I was speaking of you? In no wise. If I speak of people of bad character who have done me harm, have I not cause? And you know that I have always sought opportunities of pleasing you. Who was it who introduced you to the count? Remember that my wife fell out with the Marquise at Beurey because of you, and I too.

Then as to Cazin's doing the writer down at Demange over those dues of receipt, Carré himself had written of it to Mathieu from Paris, as also that:

Monsieur de Lescaffort had said to you coming out of Madame's room at Paris that I had been made out to be as black as ink in their minds, that it was Monsieur Robert who was to replace me, that he had been soliciting for that for a long while, that in consequence you advised me to ask for my retirement for fear that [otherwise] it might be dishonourable for me, that Monsieur de Lescaille was also suspected of conniving with me to deceive them and that he would share in it and that he would be ignominiously dismissed if he did not make his decision, and never had I said a word to him nor to Monsieur Cazin because I do not like bickering and nobody can say that I have said anything to him against you.

Mathieu's breathless indignation went surging on:

It is true that on your return from Paris you tried to despise us and to make us despised and much vexed when we had only rendered you politeness and offers of service. But you followed another feeling. If we were strangers perhaps you and your bad behaviour could be excused. You should at least spare a relation, who has only sought to please you on every occasion, without getting into a temper. You are right

[30] Cf. p. 282.

to serve well a master who likes you and gives you your bread. I praise you for upholding his interests against everybody, but you should at least have told me what you thought before advising the count about the business of Pitois, and you would have learnt the truth, but at present there is no more charity in this world. I am only thinking of finishing off the little business that I have if I can before dying and with all my heart I forgive the men and women who have slandered me and the wrong and injury which I have suffered from it. I know that people were trying to injure me long before you were in the household, so you are wrong to take to yourself complaints which I am making to the master, who knows the truth. I think that you would not be very pleased if they gave you similar treatment. God preserve you therefrom ... I ask of the Lord only peace and good concord and after this life paradise for us all, and do not think that I wish you any ill, but on the contrary all kinds of happiness and contentment. I am very perfectly, Sir, your very humble servant N. Mathieu.

Elevated sentiments have never been the monopoly of elevated rank. Conversely, intrigue in old France was anything but confined to her courtiers, merely most prominent, hence almost excessively censured in relation to what others were at, then as always, valets as well as masters, commoners along with nobles. From court Madame de Pompadour had written to her brother with cool clarity in a letter two years earlier than Mathieu's: 'I have seen a lot and reflected a lot since I have been here. From it I have at least gained a knowledge of human beings, and I assure you that they are the same at Paris, in a provincial town, as they are at court. Difference in subjects renders things more or less interesting, and displays vices in a clearer light.'[31] It may just be that, compared with the plethora of court memoirs, the thousands of diplomatic dispatches, letters like that of Nicolas Mathieu were rare and long neglected.

Those with first-hand experience of trying to disentangle the sly reservations and labyrinthine ramifications of rural grievances and disputes will know better than to attempt any ultimate judgement at this time of day upon the issues that sundered those two relations, Mathieu and Carré. The latter's side of it, prevailing at the time, is by chance less present to posterity. Perhaps the farthest one can go is to say that Mathieu does not read like a rogue, more like a decent agent who had got himself snugly built in over the years, not above the usual little wangles and rake-offs, making allowances for himself as well as others, contriving to get by more or less and used to managing things his way, the old one. This was not a person to hit it off with such a new broom as the Count de Stainville. The young master, for all his insouciant charm, had a touch of that ruthless decision which is apt to drive people, not least a soldier such as he, to the top. The

---

[31] Marquise de Pompadour to de Vandières, Mar. 1750: M. A. P. Malassis, *Correspondance de Mme de Pompadour avec son père, M. Poisson, et son frère, M. de Vandières* (Paris, 1878), p. 41.

impetuous Stainville was always impatient of muddle, seeking short cuts to efficiency, authoritatively working within the context of tradition while irreverently testing it by the logic of results. In this instance the youthful incomer to the sleepy tangle of the marquisate had swiftly got an impressive grip on it, put in his own man and gingered it into running his way towards the result he wanted. This takeover at Stainville already demonstrated, even more fully than later and larger fields of ministerial activity, that the future Duke de Choiseul possessed the qualities of a considerable administrator.

The result which the Count de Stainville mainly wanted from the estate was cash, the index of efficiency, the purveyor of pleasure. A harassed note had latterly crept into Mathieu's accounts: 'I will at least do all I can to have a hundred louis from the timber and a hundred louis from Monsieur Brigeat for the 15th April next.'[32] Mathieu vainly suggested shifting on to Brigeat the thankless corollary of chasing up persistent defaulters like Bonneau and Lamy. The squeeze from the top upon insolvents down below was reflected in a new rubric of estate expenditure 'concerning the sums paid to Monsieur the Count',[33] including the 3,056 livres, 11 sous, 8 deniers 'paid into the hands of Monsieur Cornu to take them to my said lord at the army'[34] in accordance with the count's order of 30 March 1748 and receipts of 3 and 8 May following – a little something with which to round off the long campaigning. The following October, after the Michaelmas intake, Cornu brought 3,100 livres to the count in Paris. There followed a further 1,705 livres in that currency of Lorraine, representing another fifty-five louis which he had received in Paris, this time via Carré. Another 1,545 livres was provided by a quarterly payment of Brigeat's general lease, while the latter further paid to the Count de Stainville 6,200 livres as the price of 104 acres of copsewood sold to Brigeat for annual exploitation by a contract of 'November 1747 for the remainder of his lease' which was running from 1 January 1746 for nine years with an optional break after six.

The large sale to Brigeat looks like an exceptional extra, contrasting with a windfall of 14 livres, 12 sous, 6 deniers 'for the price of a beech forming the boundary between the [lands of the] inhabitants and the lord in the Bois du Tiers, adjudged to Nicolas Braye the younger on the fifteenth of January last, fallen in the gale, everything included'.[35] The same purchaser paid another 27 livres for two smashed oaklings plus six cherry and other trees 'broken by the wind on the first of

[32] Mathieu, 'Estat de ce qui est deub a la Recepte de Stainville pour l'année 1748 tant bois taillis que chesne adjugé': Arch. Meuse, J 18[19].
[33] Mathieu's account for 22 Nov. 1747–1 May 1749: ibid.
[34] Mathieu, 'Compte de l'année 1748', ibid. for the following.
[35] Mathieu's account for 22 Nov. 1747–1 May 1749: ibid. for the following.

March last'. That winter in the early year of 1749, as in most, the winds and the gales were blowing through the forgotten landscapes of history.

If timber was the traditional source of ready cash for landlords, it was not the only one now in the keen reckoning of the Count de Stainville. The same account included a further payment by Braye of one hundred francs Barrois, making 42 livres, 17 sous in respect of the capital sum of 2,000 francs for which he had bought the sheepfold of Stainville on 14 March 1748 'in accordance with the orders of my said lord dated at Paris on the 1st February 1748'. On the day before that purchase Father Petitpain, chaplain of the chapel of Saint Nicholas in the church at Stainville, had bought his house for 600 livres, also in pursuance of an order of 1 February from the young master. The same two dates determined the transaction which had produced at Easter a revenue of 170 francs Barrois, another five per cent, on a principal of 3,400 francs for the sale 'of the house of the Gros Gaignage, that of the gardener and dependencies adjudged to Jean Leclerc, labourer, and his wife'. Although not paid on the nail, so substantial a buy by a labourer and his wife balances against the ruin of such as Claude Lamy and the fiscal fear of conspicuous prosperity among the canny peasantry. By such little transactions, alienating parts of his patrimony, did the young Count de Stainville scrape up enough or nearly enough to cut a figure in society. In the static one of Stainville the very buildings were beginning to hint at some progress or at least change, the poorer acquiring property from the richer, the prison in the château under renovation.

One of the carriers of the proceeds to the count, both at the army and in Paris, has been noticed as a Monsieur Cornu. This was Michel Cornu, conveniently placed in both spheres since he was a military contractor who lived hard by the Count de Stainville in Paris, in the Rue du Cherchemidi near Saint-Sulpice. Cornu was agriculturally active in Stainville's subsidiary properties of Beurey and Mussey. It was, partly at least, in succession to an earlier arrangement that the count, in his then residence in the Rue de Grenelle on the morning of 24 April 1750 in the presence of lawyers, granted Cornu a general lease of the barony of Beurey and Mussey for nine years to run from a year thence, Saint George's Day 1751. By payment of two thousand livres a year Cornu would be to Beurey what Brigeat was to Stainville, both estates now being run under the same convenient arrangement of general leases. That for Beurey comprised feudal dues and fines, tilth and pasture including the stead 'coming from the Pouparts',[36]

---

[36] 'Bail pour 9 ans des D[o] m[ain] es de Beurey et Mussey', Paris, 24 Apr. 1750: Arch. Meuse, J 18[27] for the following.

the fields of hemp and the vineyards, shooting and fishing 'from the bridge to the mill'. The only exception was the timber, reserved to the count. He was also still to have 'the enjoyment of his château of Beurey for occupation when shall seem good to him, as of the garden which is in front of the said château'. Cornu was to keep it up and could live in the château in Stainville's absence; upon his advent, Cornu 'shall occupy only the room which is above the kitchen'. If Stainville was an absentee landlord, yet he was no stranger to his little residence at Beurey.

It was provided in conclusion that Cornu could sublet in whole or in part without further reference to the owner. It may or may not have been some complication arising from this slightly surprising provision which caused the Count de Stainville some six months later, on 6 October 1750 in Paris, to cancel the lease before it had come into operation. All was arranged in consequence, Cornu undertaking tenant's repairs (*réparations locatives*) 'with the exception nevertheless of the windows, whereof the said Lord Marquis [*sic*] de Choiseul de Stainville discharges him as of this present'. One wonders why those windows were out.

V

Such was the background in the Barrois to the Parisian existence of the Count de Stainville. The little concerns of the marquisate of Stainville and the barony of Beurey lay close to him in terms of sentiment, of money and of administration. The displacement of Mathieu by Carré was not the only innovation introduced by the young count, nor the most significant in historical perspective. A longer shadow was cast ahead by a dispute at the lowest level which had been grinding on at Stainville for the last five years, from 1745 to 1750.

The lax and absentee landlordism of the Marquis de Stainville may, partly at least, have encouraged the labourers of Stainville back in the summer of 1745 to refuse to perform their feudal service of *corvée de bras*. At Stainville, it may be recalled, all labouring men or households which did not qualify to commute the *corvée de charrue* of the ploughing were required instead to contribute to their lord a *corvée de bras* of two days' work in the year, one at haymaking and the other at harvest-tide. This might seem a scarcely excessive stint, and each day entitled a worker to an allowance of bread to the value of four deniers of Bar. But the refusal to work had confronted Brigeat when his new lease began at the start of 1746, and there was nothing doing again when haymaking came round that year. It was not the family of Choiseul-Stainville but the farmer-general of their estates, Jean Brigeat, who directly bore this loss of labour.

Brigeat began to take legal action in July 1746 and on 6 August formally summoned those liable in Stainville to turn out in due course for the corvée of the harvest. On 14 September Jean-François Gillet, syndic of Stainville and spokesman of its inhabitants, was required to make a declaration before the registrar there that he had, as demanded by Brigeat, called upon the community to provide twenty-five harvesters; but not one had appeared. Each thereby incurred a statutory fine of up to three livres. This testimony formed part of what were now legal proceedings in the provostship of Stainville between Brigeat and Gillet, respectively represented by Antoine Molet, the former procurator-fiscal now active as a lawyer, and by Maître Champion. One notices incidentally that at Stainville at least the crude notion of a nobleman and his peasantry scowling across at one another under the old regime is much oversimplified. The principals were respectively represented by the farmer-general and the syndic, and they in turn by lawyers. The whole dispute was given a legal form twice removed from an extreme confrontation of class, however relevant.

A fortnight after Gillet's declaration, on 28 September 1746, he was again ordered by the provotal court of Stainville, on pain of personal responsibility, to get on with rounding up the recalcitrant harvesters. Again he failed. On 12 October judgement was given for Brigeat, who five days later appealed to the lieutenant-general of the bailiwick of Bar for enforcement. By now it was a question of fines. One gathers, though, that they were more easily imposed than collected. Winter came.

July 1747 found the dispute still straggling, haggling, on. Mathieu wrote from Stainville on the seventh to tell Brigeat at Ligny that he and Sebastian Lecoy, a legal officer of the marquisate described as lieutenant-assessor and controller of the provostship and woodmote, had done what they could at a general meeting of the villagers held to discuss the disputed corvée. Lecoy, reported Mathieu, told them 'that he would arrange that you should give them quittance for one franc [Barrois] each for the two days. In the end they maintained that they do not owe any [corvée] either at haymaking or at harvest-tide. They must be constrained thereto in good time and we shall see what they will do. I have informed the count that Madame de Choiseul has been persecuting you in order to get six hundred livres and that you gave them to her on the quarterday. My wife, family and lady cousin present a thousand very humble compliments to you and Madame

Brigeat.'[37] The middleman was being squeezed from both ends. If the Choiseul lady was expensive, with the haymakers and harvesters the sums were small, the issue large.

A month later, on 11 August 1747, Brigeat once more referred his case against the inhabitants of Stainville to the bailiwick of Bar-le-Duc. By then he was resorting to another lawyer, Gerard of Bar, probably of higher calibre than Molet at Stainville; though there may have been more to it than that since Molet was subsequently briefed by the other party. On the same day of 11 August Brigeat sent Gerard the papers of the case, requesting him to shew them to the Count de Stainville's own lawyer, Aubry, and ask him 'if it is by way of appeal that I should sue or else by a new action'.[38]

This reversion by Brigeat to the higher instance stirred the recalcitrants of Stainville into calling another meeting of their community. It instructed the syndic that it was now prepared, more or less, to accept Lecoy's possibly unauthorized offer of commutation at one franc per annum, though only as from 1 January 1748, leaving the interim somewhat unclear; it further looks as though the canny peasants pared down the franc of Bar, worth a little over two-fifths of a livre, to a traditional five sous or a quarter-livre: an example, perhaps, of the convenience of a dual currency for fine gradations and manipulation.

On 15 August Brigeat wrote again to his lawyer:

Sir, I return to you enclosed the application[39] with the assignment given to the syndic of Stainville, upon which I have put three livres instead of five sous as a fine, which I have thought just since the rolls, which are very numerous, all say a fine of five sous which can rise in case of refusal [of the corvée] to three livres, [whereas] they are diminishing rather than increasing it, and I think that, besides the fine, I ought to have damages and interest, for if the inhabitants could only [? be held to][40] five sous they would never go to the corvée and the payment for having this fine imposed would cost more in expenses than its proceeds would be worth.[41]

One notices that the farmer-general was apparently thinking in terms of a fine (*amende*) rather than commutation, and still hoped to secure the labour. That was what he really wanted and what the peasants did not. This unresolved conflict swiftly came to a head over the other contentious point: what was to happen about the corvée in the interval till the New Year of 1748.

[37] Mathieu to Brigeat, Stainville, 7 July 1747: Arch. Meuse, J 18²¹ ('Stainville: droits seigneuriaux, banalités, logement des gens de guerre 1405-1807'), docket I ('Stainville: Corvées et droits. 1652-1758').
[38] Brigeat to Gerard, 11 Aug. 1747: ibid.
[39] Probably to the bailiwick of Bar-le-Duc.
[40] The text here is torn.
[41] Brigeat to Gerard, Ligny, 15 Aug. 1747: ibid. for the following.

Brigeat continued to Gerard: 'Yesterday I had the inhabitants subject to this corvée notified that they were to be present tomorrow at five o'clock in the morning at the fields which I have indicated to them, in order to fulfil the corvée. I strongly believe that they will do nothing of the kind. I shall be there, however. I will acquaint you with what shall come of it.' Next day he did so. He had been right. Once again, not a soul turned up. So Gerard was to 'do what is needed, and always in consultation with Monsieur Aubry'.[42]

Gerard promptly went into action against the inhabitants of Stainville who, apparently not to be done down, had also briefed a new and presumably superior lawyer, a certain Maître Husson. On 19 August the bailiwick of Bar-le-Duc instantly ordered the villagers to assemble, deliberate the issue and submit their deliberations for official sanction. The inhabitants of Stainville ignored this order. On 16 September the order was repeated, this time with provision for the village meeting to be held in the presence of a counsellor to the bailiwick, Sieur de Vassimont. Nothing happened. The insubordinate labourers of Stainville were getting away with it all along the line.

On 13 November 1747 Brigeat was still prodding Vassimont to hold the meeting at Stainville. Six days later the village did at last meet in the presence of that official. The assembled inhabitants of Stainville maintained that they were not liable for the corvée. They authorized their syndic to press on in their legal defence. It looked as if things were if anything moving backwards from the financial haggling of the summer. Possibly this was a tactical mistake by the peasants. On 23 December 1747 the bailiwick of Bar-le-Duc sentenced them to pay Brigeat seventy-nine livres, five sous in costs. Things were getting serious. Five days later Brigeat put in a plea to the lieutenant-general of the bailiwick for permission 'to have subpoenaed before you the Count de Stainville, lord of the said place, in order to cause to cease'[43] – the maddening behaviour of his peasantry.

After three years of dispute both the farmer-general and his adversaries were beginning to be pressed. As happens in diplomatic disputes, so in this agricultural one, the time had evidently come at last for informal parleys and compromise towards a settlement. Brigeat several times got together with the labourers in the auditory or seigneurial courthouse at Stainville and apparently came to agree to drop the costs which he had mobilized against them and even arrears, provided that the issue of principle was settled tolerably. Then on 17 February 1748 'a larger number of the said inhabitants'[44]

---

[42] Brigeat to Gerard, Stainville, 16 Aug. 1747: ibid.
[43] Plea by Brigeat to lieutenant-general of the bailiwick of Bar-le-Duc, 28 Dec. 1747: ibid.
[44] 'Extrait des registres du greffe de la prévôté de Stainville', 21 Apr. 1748: ibid. for the following.

of Stainville – a restricted formulation probably excluding the rustic extremists – privately subscribed to a declaration that in lieu of the corvée they were each willing to pay one franc (a retreat from five sous) a year to the Marquis de Stainville. As one might expect, Brigeat had cited the young count but now his milder father made a reappearance, perhaps in some mediatory capacity. It was still necessary to validate the declaration of 17 February 'and render it more solemn and authentic' by having it ratified by a general meeting of the whole community of Stainville.

And so one evening in that spring of 1748 Nicolas Rostaine, successor to Gillet as syndic of Stainville, had 'the said inhabitants summoned to the sound and ringing of the bell in the usual way on coming out from vespers said and sung in the church of the said Stainville'. The peasants came crowding in 'and having all halted in front of the banal bakehouse in the public square, on the advice of the said Sieur Husson to them communicated, they all with one voice unanimously determined among themselves that they would charge and empower their said syndic and the said Sieur Husson', their lawyer, at long last to conclude a legal agreement in commutation of the *corvée de bras* at Stainville. The assembled peasants stipulated that the terms should be as now agreed: each to pay one franc a year, only as from 1 January 1748: Brigeat to get no arrears, nor any costs. All this was duly recorded and legally validated in the registers of the provostship of Stainville by the lieutenant-assessor, Sebastian Lecoy, on 21 April 1748.

So far so good. There was local agreement. But the case had been referred to the higher instance of the bailiwick of Bar-le-Duc, which had to sign it off and ratify the terms of agreement. This took just over two more years. The provisions engrossed at Stainville on 21 April 1748 were registered at Bar-le-Duc on 2 May 1750. The cause of the delay is not clear. But it looks as though it may have been relevant that the young Count de Stainville was never a person whom it was easy to bypass, or to constrain. The cited extract from the register of the provostship of Stainville for 21 April 1748 is endorsed as follows at the foot, in the tight handwriting of the count: 'We approve these presents, on condition that the inhabitants discharge them. At Paris, the 1st March 1750. Choiseul de Stainville.' It was signed with a flourish and sealed with his arms.

The future Duke de Choiseul was to sign many more important documents than that, was to be concerned with the abrogation of larger rights and possessions, such as French sovereignty over Canada. Yet he was to conclude few agreements of more immediate significance in human terms of the social order of the eighteenth

century. What had happened at Stainville between the years 1745
and 1750 was a revolt by the poorest peasants against established
authority. And in essentials that revolt had succeeded. In 1750 the
rebellious peasantry had, in return for an annual and nearly nominal
payment, finally thrown off that obligation of labour for their lord in
the *corvée des bras* which had lain, heavy or light, upon their fathers
and upon their fathers' fathers before them for generations, for
centuries immemorial.

As the discomfited Brigeat had said, there were quantities of rolls
and deeds, plenty of precedents to prove the long legality of the
corvée. They had counted for little in the face of the stubborn resolve
of the labourers of Stainville that enough was enough. Nor is it easy
to suppose that they were quite isolated from surrounding districts in
that resolve and in the climate of opinion which nourished it. News
of local doings and defiances such as those at Stainville was of the
kind that spreads like wildfire through a countryside even in that age
of limited communications, perhaps especially then. If public opinion
in the Barrois in the later seventeen-forties had not had some
appreciation that the peasants had something to argue about, it is
difficult to imagine, even allowing for such wartime callup of militia
as was noticed at Mirecourt, that the revolt at Stainville could not
have been severely punished by either the seigneurial or the regional
administration. Whereas the prudence, not to say forbearance,
wherewith the humble recalcitrants were treated by authority at all
levels remains most striking.

Already obtruding is the fact that for something like the last half
century, gradual commutation by the peasantry of old feudal
obligations for small cash payments had been a feature of local
development upon the estates of Stainville as also at Beurey and,
most likely, across the lands lying between. An early disappearance
had been the corvée of ploughing at Stainville itself and at Ménil,
while at Beurey the banal oven had undergone commutation forty
years before the latest liberation at Stainville.

Another likely factor here was the seigneurial policy of leasing,
first of feudal utilities or dues to various locals, then of a whole estate
to one general lessee or farmer. One could not have it both ways. The
convenience to the lord of securing a fixed and regular income from
the lessee-general was bought by a weakening of the feudal tie with
the peasants: at Stainville they apparently yet displayed some
preference for settling with the marquis rather than with Brigeat.

Even under the caretaker administration of Stanislas Leszczynski
and La Galaisière, Lorraine was not quite France, not quite yet. By
an apparent paradox the Count de Stainville could keep his

seigneurial prison in repair and, one gathers, use it to punish accepted torts; but a social revolt, broadly based, against his – and in the last resort it was his – feudal imposition of the corvée was apparently beyond the scope of such sanctions. One is reminded, rather, of the noble grumbles from so early as the reign of Duke Leopold that the peasants were for ever going to law against their lords. The labourers of Stainville had fought and mainly won their bad case in law with an astonishingly assured legalism, instructing Maître Husson in popular assembly on that spring evening in front of the bakehouse on the public square at Stainville. It might be difficult to know how democratic initiative and control could be carried further down.

The upshot for Stainville back in the Barrois, suddenly illuminating the slow underflow of social change, brooks comparison with a vignette of another rural community in that same month of March 1750 in a different part, outside the French capital. The Marquis d'Argenson was spending that spring in a house which he had taken at Segrez. There he wrote:

The inhabitants of this countryside are not badly off. It is only ten leagues from Paris. The owners of the estates or country houses of the district are rich people from Paris ... The complaint here is of a great scourge. The game, rabbits especially, eat the vines, corn and all the fruits which would be gathered by individuals. Suzerainty is a great evil, especially when it is connected with some authority deriving from the court. The poor peasant is afraid of everything and dare not complain. His complaints would draw down upon him new vexations. These are the remains of tyranny and barbarism which we still have in France. Diminish the power of the nobility as that of the clergy in France has already been suppressed, but do not substitute for it that of the extortioner, as is happening to-day. Substitute for it that of the commune, of democracy conceded with equanimity, and you will have a good government.[45]

The atmosphere at Segrez evidently differed from the robust temper of Stainville, already almost exemplifying the kind of democracy based upon the rural commune which d'Argenson could have had in mind. And precisely because the peasants of Segrez, as of Stainville, were on the whole not so badly off, feudal remnants were apt to irk the more. Whereas even in liberal England the game-laws then were of notorious severity. In French lands the peasantry were indeed partially oppressed, and regional variation forbids confident generalization. Yet from developments like that sanctioned by the Count de Stainville in 1750 one would infer that sometimes at least, scarcely less than in England, aristocratic domination by the few was apt to be tempered by a healthy respect for the crude reality of the masses and their ready passions. In this rather imprecise but

---

[45] D'Argenson, vi. 181.

important respect, underlying and modifying the institutional crust, the leading nations of western Europe were already diverging from Teutonic and Slav dominations to the east: a divergence which was to develop in after centuries with increasing impact.

CHAPTER II

ARTISTIC

I

In the same month that the Peace of Aix-la-Chapelle was signed there was also published *L'Esprit des Lois* by the Baron de Montesquieu, already known to the Count de Stainville. Which of these events was in the long run the more important for the world, America as well as Europe, remains uncertain.

If *L'Esprit des Lois* in appreciable degree drew upon flimsy sources derided by Gibbon, if it was precisely its legal grounding which was disappointing from one legally trained (*'de l'esprit sur les lois'*, said the wits), if its vast canvas was in places inadequate and quirky, yet was it one of the seminal works of all time, largely introducing the modern study of comparative politics, sociology, and the philosophy of history, leading through, not least by its novel stress upon climatic conditioning, to the deeper and more disturbing reaches of a comparative morality. An eminent biologist observed to Montesquieu: 'Newton has discovered the laws of the material world: you, Sir, have discovered the laws of the intellectual world.'[1] In the later perspective of centuries this exciting distillation of witty wisdom could be ranked as almost certainly the greatest book of the French eighteenth century. At the time it was for Horace Walpole simply 'the best book that ever was written'.[2]

L'Esprit des Lois went into twenty-two editions in something like fifteen months. It was devoured in the intellectual circle of the Count de Stainville. He was lastingly interested and, it may be thought, influenced by it. Thirty years later the then Duke de Choiseul was to reflect in retirement:

President de Montesquieu, in the book *L'Esprit des Lois*, seems to give preference to the government of England over all the other governments which he examines; it is natural that a book which deals with the spirit of laws, when it talks of monarchy, should prefer that wherein the laws and not arbitrary will are the immutable principle and force of the government. True it is that English government fulfils absolutely the idea which should be conceived of a monarchical government, which,

[1] Charles Bonnet to Baron de Montesquieu, Geneva, 14 Nov. 1753: *Œuvres complètes de Montesquieu*, ed. A. Masson, iii. 1478. Cf. R. Shackleton, *Montesquieu*, p. 252.
[2] Horace Walpole to Horace Mann, London, 10 Jan. 1750 (O.S): Walpole Correspondence, xx. 107.

in my view, consists in the absolute power of laws made by the people conjointly with the magistrate called king, set up (*préposé*) by the nation in order to have them carried out. In England it is law which governs; the king himself is subject to it . . . The king without parliament would be without effect . . . These two authorities can do nothing without one another; together they make law and law rules all parts of the English administration. The king by his prerogative is the dispenser of favours; he can do good: the law alone does justice and punishes crime. There is no need to go into more detail upon English government in order to sense that this monarchical administration is the happiest known in the world, for each individual in the English nation and even for the king; I say for the king, for the prince upon the throne of Great Britain can do all kinds of good to his people and can never reproach himself with an injustice as to ownership of property, personal liberty and the honour of his subjects. I do not believe that there is another monarch who enjoys a similar satisfaction.[3]

Choiseul, in his enthusiasm for British constitutional monarchy, was as usual not wholly uncritical:

One cannot conceal from oneself that the form of the English constitution, as it is at present, has defects; and the defect which incontestably entails most drawbacks is that of corruption. The members of the House of Commons are in effect nearly always elected by bribes or from motives foreign to the good of the districts which elect them; people intrigue to be elected by the counties in order to go to the court; for even when a person sits in the opposition it is only with a view to being bought by the court and getting places; so that there is corruption in order to be elected a member of parliament, and corruption either in fact or in expectation when one is sitting in the House . . . Although the king has at his disposal a superior number of votes in parliament, the opposition, which is the opposition only because it desires places and especially those of the ministers, is an active supervisor of the administration, which restrains the king and his ministry in operations which could injure the state so that, despite the corruption, the state and the individuals in the state are safeguarded.

If Choiseul somewhat overdid the corruption of even the unreformed House of Commons, was silent on the House of Lords, he went as usual for essentials, and proceeded:

However, one must admit that everything that is corrupt is vicious, that moreover the precautions against despotism taken in England would be impossible in France; one could even add that French minds, accustomed to the yoke, would be more difficult to contain if they were freed from it all of a sudden, and that the impetuosity, warmth and levity of the French would produce trouble if they followed exactly the same laws as are followed in England. I have become worked up in comparing the governments of the two nations which one could call preponderant in Europe, and like the Abbé de Saint-Pierre I have composed a political romance upon the administration of France.

---

[3] Duke de Choiseul, 'Projet d'États provinciaux' in Choiseul, *Mémoires*, pp. 436–8 for the following.

With that characteristic flick at the good Abbé, and himself, Choiseul moved into his romance for the reform of the administration of France before the revolution which he adumbrated. That, though, belongs to a later period.

It is striking to find the prime antagonist for France against England so enthusiastic for the British constitution in an elevated impartiality avowedly indebted to Montesquieu, to find the chief minister of the latter years of King Louis XV a monarchist of such radical liberalism and, not least, to find the Duke de Choiseul so stressing the satisfaction of truly benevolent rule, of benevolent constitutionalism as against the benevolent despotism of his own government. Choiseul's English enthusiasm echoed Voltaire. It has been fairly suggested, though, that, compared with the more scintillating and superficial Voltaire, Montesquieu has never quite been taken by Frenchmen to their hearts. Much the same is true of Choiseul and for similar reasons. If Voltaire largely promoted the French fashion then for admiring England, yet Montesquieu like Choiseul evinced a dispassionate and pragmatic liberalism that might seem almost English in its cast of mind. Rather few of that stamp have been lasting heroes to Frenchmen.

The future Choiseul's discerning wife, for whom Voltaire came to seem superficial beside Montesquieu, was to observe that it was from England, 'a generous rival', that her husband 'has always received the most flattering praise'.[4]

It is possible that a further association with some British bearing between Choiseul and Montesquieu may have been freemasonry. Montesqieu was a mason; it is said or implied that Choiseul was one, apparently without clinching evidence.[5] The then Count de Stainville may, however, have followed the fashion in that as in other respects. During the second quarter of the eighteenth century freemasonry had spread in France under initial influences both Jacobite, with the Scottish lodges, and also more Hanoverian and English: in 1735 Montesquieu was reported to have participated in a lodge in Paris along with the Count de Saint-Florentin and several English including the Earl Waldegrave. It has been suggested[6] that an even

---

[4] Duchess de Choiseul to Lady ? Cholmondeley, Chanteloup, 6 Feb. 1771: *Correspondance complète de Mme du Deffand avec la duchesse de Choiseul, l'abbé Barthélemy et M. Craufurt,* ed. Marquis de Sainte-Aulaire (3rd ed., Paris, 1877: henceforth cited as Du Deffand/Ste-Aulaire), i. 336-7.

[5] Cf. recently Renée Lelièvre, 'Un trio de francs-maçons ignorés' in *Dix-huitième Siècle* (Société française d'Étude du XVIIIᵉ siècle, Paris, 1969f.), viii. 372. Some confusion has arisen from the masonic involvement of other Choiseuls, notably the duke's heir, Claude-Antoine-Gabriel, Duke de Choiseul. Such confusion is evident, for instance, in the indexing of Albert Lantoine, *Histoire de la franc-maçonnerie française* (2nd ed., Paris, 1927 f.), and Paul Filleul, *Le Duc de Montmorency Luxembourg* (Paris, 1939).

[6] Cf. Gustave Bord, *La franc-maçonnerie en France* (Paris, 1908), i. 120.

earlier reference to a masonic Choiseul may have been to the Marquis de Meuse. In 1738 Pope Clement XII had proscribed freemasonry under pain of excommunication in the bull *In eminenti apostolatus specula*. That suited Fleury: freemasonry, like a good deal else then in France, was officially, tolerantly, disapproved of. Sporadic French moves against it were petering out by the middle of the century when the grand master of the significantly styled English Grand Lodge of France was the militant Count de Clermont. He had been elected in 1743 against Conti and Saxe. And, later at least, two eminent clans associated with the Count de Stainville, the Luxembourgs and the Noailles, were to figure in French freemasonry. The future Choiseul was to be in correspondence with the Duke de Bouillon,[7] who was a leading freemason. But then, besides the Bouillon associations both with Lorraine and with Navarre, that duke was, most interestingly, perhaps, an intimate of the Young Pretender.

The liberal spirit of freemasonry, in superimposing upon aristocratic rank elaborate hierarchies of proclaimed merit, upon religious creeds a tolerant outlook of international beneficence was quite likely to appeal to the Count de Stainville. On the other hand he was never much of one for mumbojumbo. If he was indeed a freemason then for him, as for Montesquieu, it was probably not of special importance. Whereas his interest in the president's political analysis was enduring.

Montesquieu's immediate renown leapt across Europe. The King of Sardinia had his son read *L'Esprit des Lois* and take notes. In Vienna the imperial librarian – no other than Duval from Lorraine – encouraged its dissemination in opposition to clerical hostility. It was in this context that Montesquieu began a letter to the Marquis de Stainville on 27 May 1750:

The kindness wherewith Your Excellency has always honoured me causes me to take the liberty of unburdening myself to you about something which concerns me greatly. I have just learnt that the Jesuits have succeeded in having the sale of the book *L'Esprit des Lois* forbidden in Vienna. Your Excellency is aware that here I already have to endure quarrels, as much against the Jansenists as the Jesuits ... Your Excellency is apprised of the success which my *Défense* [*de l'Esprit des Lois*] has had, and that there has been a general outcry here against my adversaries. I thought that I was going to be at peace when I learnt that the Jesuits have been and carried to Vienna the quarrels which they excited in Paris.[8]

In applying to the Marquis de Stainville for assistance Montesquieu had unwittingly exaggerated the need since clerical pressure had not

[7] Cf. Bibliothèque Nationale, Fichier Charavay 44, p. 127, no. 2368, also no. 2486.
[8] President Montesquieu to Marquis de Stainville, Paris, 27 May 1750: *Œuvres complètes de Montesquieu*, ed. cit., iii. 1308–9.

in fact managed to suppress his book in Vienna, where it was widely read. Such pressure was stronger at Rome. There Montesquieu had mobilized the Duke de Nivernais, who on 1 February 1750 remitted an emollient memorandum to the scholarly Cardinal Passionei. Pope Benedict XIV himself was also sympathetic to Montesquieu. But liberal popes have to reckon with Roman reaction. On 29 November 1751 *L'Esprit des Lois* was enrolled upon the Index of Prohibited Books, at the same time as a publication by another friend of the Count de Stainville. This was the more closely topical *Examen impartial des immunités ecclésiastiques* by the Abbé Chauvelin. Such was the latest recruitment, also including Pufendorf, to the noble company of the papally proscribed, Montaigne, Descartes, Montesquieu.

II

The departure of the Duke and Duchess de Nivernais upon embassy to Rome in December 1748 had been a heavy loss to the Count de Stainville. Not only was Nivernais a special friend but Stainville was close to nearly all the family: the charming duchess, her mother, the Countess de Pontchartrain, and the duchess's two daughters, of whom the younger, six-year-old Diane-Délie-Adélaïde, Mademoiselle Mancini, was reluctantly left behind, to console her maternal grandmother and doting paternal grandfather, the Duke de Nevers. The elder sister by two years, Hélène-Julie-Rosalie, Mademoiselle de Nevers, accompanied her parents. So did Nivernais's devoted secretary, Charles-Antoine Le Clerc de La Bruère, inclined, however, to skimp his duties in favour of the theatrical interests which he shared with the Count de Stainville, five years the younger of the two.

La Bruère, to be described by Luynes as 'a lad of wit and merit',[9] was yet not an entirely amiable character. The Duke de Nevers called him Malagrazia. The Count de Stainville regularly called him The Little Man. He probably owed it to the Duchess de Nivernais's half-brother, the Count de Maurepas, that, together with another dramatic author, Fuzelier, he held the profitable printers' licence for the *Mercure*, actually edited then by a journalist called Rémond de Saint-Albine, who scored with a critique of *Le Méchant*. So early as 1734 La Bruère had put on his *Les Mécontents* at the Comédie Française, where after a fortnight it had been cut from three acts to one. Five years later, however, he had contributed the libretto of *Dardanus*, perhaps the most successful of all Rameau's operas. Now,

[9] Luynes, xiii. 366.

a month before La Bruère left for Rome, he had one evening been reading to some friends including Charles Collé, the literary gossip, a rather risky little comedy called *Les Congés* and also *Le Prince de Noisy*, a three-act opera apparently based upon a druidical tale by William Hamilton, the bard who had followed the Young Pretender into French exile after the Fortyfive. La Bruère's script seemed to Collé in that October of 1748 to be 'divine ... There is nothing better written in the lyric style.'[10] On 13 March 1749 *Le Prince de Noisy* was performed as a 'heroic ballet',[11] set by Rebel and Francoeur, at Versailles in the private theatre of Madame de Pompadour. She played the title-role of the prince, alias little Poinson. Four days later Stainville began a letter to Nivernais in Rome: 'They acted Poinson at court last week, and it succeeded very well. I congratulate the little man, and you, my dear friend.'[12]

Stainville, more at home then in the Parisian theatre, carried on to Nivernais: 'We are at present showing *Sémiramis* again, revised and corrected. It is being a great success. The large number of changes which he has made to it, and especially to the fifth act which is unrecognizable, has been very well received, and it seems to me that besides the applause, the crowd and the receipts, which prove the success, it has greatly gained in what is said of it and that its reputation is [now] quite different.' If Stainville was not alone in his opinion, Collé this time was less enthusiastic: 'On the 10th [March 1749] M. de Voltaire put on his *Sémiramis*, with corrections and additions. The fifth act is much less bad than it was, but it is still worthless ... Twenty verses, at the end of the fourth, would finish the play ... Sémiramis is still the same as he had painted him: that is to say, it is not Sémiramis at all.'[13]

The background had been Voltaire's personal supervision of the first night of *Sémiramis* on 29 August 1748. Despite his precaution of issuing all the tickets himself, two or three young people in the stalls, according to Duclos, 'had clapped *while yawning out loud*, which caused much amusement to everyone, except Voltaire'.[14] That had set the tone of the reception of his unworthy challenge to a play on the same theme by Crébillon the elder, now old and moving into a revival against Voltaire under the patronage of Madame de Pompadour. If *Sémiramis* was the darkest of Voltaire's tragedies, it could not rival the tragic intensity which Crébillon had long since

[10] Charles Collé, *Journal et mémoires de Charles Collé*, ed. Honoré Bonhomme (Paris, 1868), i. 14.
[11] Luynes, ix. 354.
[12] Count de Stainville to Duke de Nivernais, 17 Mar. 1749: W. N. A., docket V/1, fo. 1 for the following.
[13] C. Collé, op. cit., i. 60.   [14] Ibid., p. 2.

achieved, in part at least, in his *Rhadamiste et Zénobie*. Now, with the revised *Sémiramis* of 1749, Stainville was strikingly concerned with Voltaire as a playwright, in a faction distanced from that of the royal mistress.

Stainville's use of the first person plural in writing of the revival of *Sémiramis* does not prove that he was himself actively involved in it. But it might suggest that he was, especially since he was not usually one to imply a personal connection where none existed. Slightly disconcerting, once again, is the extent to which one so gregarious in inclination, so open in manner was deeply secretive about his more important concerns, at that time literary and dramatic, later political and diplomatic. In this at least he may have owed something to his father. Small wonder that full appraisal of the future Choiseul has been slow. He was writing to Nivernais later that year about another theatrical project: 'It is in the last degree essential to keep it in profound obscurity, come what may.'[15] The Count de Stainville has hardly figured hitherto in the theatrical chronicles of that time.

Sémiramis had been revived two nights after the withdrawal of *L'École de la Jeunesse* by the 'very illustrious and very mediocre La Chaussée',[16] leader of the new fashion in *comédie larmoyante*, tearfully blurring the separation of comedy from tragedy to produce what Voltaire described as bourgeois tragedy and the beginning of decadence. In his own life the moralistic playwright, nicknamed Le Révérend Père Chaussée, was a member of the gay set and contributor to the *Recueil de ces Messieurs*. A precursor of sentimental comedy had been Marivaux and it was at supper with him and Helvétius that La Chaussée now ascribed his failure to a cabal inspired by Voltaire, who in fact described him as one of the first authors after those who have genius. Stainville continued his letter of 17 March 1749 to Nivernais:

La Chaussée, stubborn and vain as you know him to be, would not admit the failure of his play by taking it off. He defied the murmurs of the public and its indignation, the despair of the poor players who thought themselves ruined, the wise advice of his friends and the contempt to which he exposes his work. By the rules it failed twice in seven performances. It was scoffed at by everybody, and will be the cause of a new regulation for the rules of the theatre in order to protect the public and players from the obstinacy and bad temper of unfair and boring authors. I own that I am overjoyed that this example is being made and is falling upon this haughty personage. You really should get the little man to work for you in leisure moments. If you do not shake up his laziness he will do nothing. But that is enough talk of the theatre.[17]

[15] Count de Stainville to Duke de Nivernais, 17 Nov. 1749: *u. s.*, fo. 17.
[16] C. Collé, op. cit., i. 197.
[17] Count de Stainville to Duke de Nivernais, 17 Mar. 1749: ibid., fo. 1.

III

Stainville's letter was answered by La Bruère himself, who was getting to work on the libretto of an opera called *Linus*, the mythological son of Apollo in the elegiac class of Adonis, Hyacinth, Narcissus: in a Theban version musical Linus, the inventor of threnody, was the teacher of apt Orpheus and inept Hercules, who killed his master with a blow from a lyre. The stock of mythological and classic themes for eighteenth-century drama was limited and it is not always simple to disentangle one minor version from another. If the overlap in the case of *Sémiramis* was deliberate enough, La Bruère's recent *Prince de Noisy* may or may not have looked back to a comedy of that title by a certain Dumas d'Aigueberre, produced in 1730. Similarly obscure is the relation if any of La Bruère's *Linus* to an act under that name apparently extracted from *L'Empire de l'Amour* by Moncrif, another member of those literary circles.

In the summer of 1749 the Count de Stainville wrote in connection with *Linus*:

I have received from La Bruère a letter thanking me I know not why nor wherefore. I am not answering him for I have nothing to tell him yet. The Abbé de Bernis, newly Count de Lion [*sic*], is in charge of the negotiation to get the work taken by Rameau. It seemed to me the last time I saw him [Bernis] that he augured ill of it. I did not find in him that air of confidence which gives hope of success. If we do not succeed with Rameau we must certainly have recourse to Mondonville. He is the only one with some genius. All the others are wretched scribblers from whom one can hope for nothing.[18]

So much for French music in the middle of that century. Cassanéas de Mondonville was musical superintendent of the chapel at Versailles, echoing to his motets.

Two months later Stainville was 'replying to La Bruère' who had sent him a draft for *Linus*:

It seems a little odd at first look, however I am not averse from lending a hand. We are in such a horrible dearth of musicians that, God forgive me, I would rather send my script to Quito than give it to Bury, Royer etc. But we should like the same musician to do the whole work, and we are frightened of the patchwork (*bigarrure*) of having the recitative done here with the music done in Rome ... But what you must, please, prevent is that La Bruère, who prides himself upon composing, should want to do the recitative ... It is a mistake to think that one need not be a musician in order to do recitative. Perhaps one does not need such great depth but one must possess perfect modulation.[19]

[18] Ibid., 4 Aug. 1749, fos. 5–6.   [19] Ibid., 6 Oct. 1749, fos. 13–14 for the following.

Stainville may have learnt from Rameau whose recitatives, more musical than Lully's, maintained the continuity of his operas, not yet fully symphonic. Stainville, here again, proceeded to recommend strict secrecy in any Italian venture: 'It could very well miscarry and in that case, if nothing had been said about it, no [? great][20] harm would be done. We could always find a Bury; and perhaps we should no longer find a musician willing to take it on if it were known that it had been done and spoilt by an Italian.'

Stainville's impartiality, in the interest of securing the best result, in the reviving controversy as between French and Italian music may be prefigurative of his attitude in more important disputes. Remarkable also is his association already, through the theatre, with the Abbé de Bernis, like himself a benevolent enthusiast with slender resources, unlike himself a particular friend of Madame de Pompadour: yet another of Stainville's circle to be standing close to her. The allusion to Bernis's new nobility was to his recent election to an exclusive canonry at Lyons: it required proof of sixteen quarterings and conferred the privilege of wearing an enamelled cross on a ribbon of crimson and blue.

Stainville was soon at it again:

The essential point is to know if the Roman musician really has genius. He could have done beautiful motets and beautiful church music without having a great stock of genius. This what we meet with in Mondonville. He only had a glimmer of genius sufficient for motets; ... for opera, his was not fruitful enough, varied enough, extensive enough, and he has composed bad operas. The last is less bad, but it has no greater genius ... M. de Duras, the commonplace protector of bad works and proclaimed defender of the detestable opera which Mondonville has most recently given us, is declaring publicly and boasting to everybody of having persuaded you in favour of Mondonville. He is making out that he has had a letter from you telling him that your view is for giving him [Mondonville] *Linus* and that La Bruère seems to be resolved on it provided that the Abbé de Bernis and I have not disposed of it otherwise.[21]

Stainville had heard nothing of this from Nivernais himself, as he coldly explained when 'M. de Duras came to see me two days ago all gushing as you know that he is, all triumphant and quite full of this business ... He pressed me with his usual delicacy to know what I thought of it. I told him that I thought that La Bruère would do very badly [to turn to Mondonville] ... but that he was the master of his work.'

Finally the Duke de Duras, from a rival coterie to that of the Duchess de Boufflers, asked the recording Count de Stainville:

[20] The text here is torn.   [21] Ibid., 17 Nov. 1749, fos. 16–17 for the following.

'What do you want me to say to M. de Nivernais, for I really must reply?' 'Nothing', I said to him. 'I write by every post to M. de N. I am big enough to express my thoughts myself, and I am not in the habit of using secretaries of such good family.' He said to me, 'You are getting angry.' 'Not at all. I do not know how to get angry, but I do know how to write.'

This passage between the supposed Méchant and the interpreter of the role in Madame de Pompadour's theatre may seem worthy of the play itself.

'Finally', proceeded Stainville, 'he let go, but I am afraid that he may make a quackquack [sic] of this, telling everybody that La Bruère is determined to give it to Mondonville, that he may tell him himself, that he may tell it to Mme de Pompadour, and that all this may cause me vexation.' As yet Stainville was scarcely in her circle but their common friends and interest in the theatre, if not also other things, meant that his set already overlapped with hers.

'As for me', continued the count of the Duke de Duras, 'when I see him [again] I am quite determined to tell him that I have received a letter from La Bruère in which he seems to me anything but decided. Perhaps that will restrain him a little if there is indeed any brake upon him, for he is a horse that obeys neither bridle nor spur. I do not know what you were thinking of in introducing him into all this, unless it be a refinement of Roman policy the better to hide our project' – particularly, it would seem, the possibility of an Italian orchestration. Stainville urged such secrecy in the setting of *Linus* 'whether it succeeds or not. If it is good, it will be the more striking. If it is worthless', one could still mobilize some French hack like Royer or Mondonville, 'seeing that it would not be known that it had already been set to music . . . Goodbye, my dear friend. I am exhausted by such a long dispatch. For some days I have been as sick as a dog. I have had a very lively bout. It is lessening but it is not over.'

The Duke de Duras appears to have given a somewhat inexact account of his letter from the Duke de Nivernais, who subsequently offered to send the Count de Stainville a copy of it. The count refused this as unnecessary:

I quite believe your word and, even were I not so familiar with your veracity, I would in any case trust you rather than the man in question. He has not spoken to me of it again, nor I to him, but I still have a little negotiation for Rameau. It has not yet either failed or succeeded. I confess that I should much like him to take our script . . . It could well be that his genius is wearing itself out and ageing, but it does not seem so in this latest opera, whatever they may have told you of it, and believe me I am telling you the truth; but I thought I did notice this [decline] in *Zaïs*, and *Naïs*. Perhaps too he did them too quickly. However that may be, in such a matter one can never be sure of success in advance. All one can do is to give one's work to the best musician and commit one's soul to God. Now Rameau is certainly not only the best, but the only one, and I am so much of that opinion that I am very much in favour of having it set to music in Rome if Rameau does not undertake it. This project could be a chimera, but I do not regard it as madness.[22]

Balanced boldness and secret originality were the stamp of the policy of the future Duke de Choiseul. Hitherto unknown has been his early application of these qualities in the musical sphere. Stainville continued to his friend in Rome:

If you have a man of genuis who does good music, I am persuaded that it would score a great success [here], greater than if it were done by a Frenchman. You know the taste of this nation for novelty. Italian music is gaining ground every day. Rameau is already the mean term. We should have a very large party for us, and we should only have to defend ourselves against the sect of the old Lullists. I am only afraid that they might poison us, but above all mum's the word (*motus*), for they would laugh at us if our plan got out.

An Italian setting, Stainville appreciated, could yet produce complications:

What worries me most is the airs for violins. I do not know if in their operas they do them in our style, or at least in a style which might please us. For the rest have no anxiety for the execution. I am sure that our orchestra would manage it well, and perhaps better than Lully's operas for which people are daily losing the taste, while Italian is encroaching.

Stainville was one of the Ramoneurs or Chimneysweeps as the supporters of fertile Rameau were called, supposedly in play upon his relatively complex scores, so sprinkled with semiquavers that they looked as though splotched with soot to the supporters, still, of the dry simplicities of classic Lully. If that Florentine, then dead sixty years and more, had largely founded French opera, indeed French music by breaking it off from Italian, it was Rameau, more inventive again within a terminating tradition, who opened out opera towards its true self through his new music with its expansion of pizzicato playing, of bassoons and clarinets in progression from the strung-along melody of Lully to a textured harmony. Rameau has been saluted as the prime grammarian of the musical language employed by the west for three centuries.[23] Radiantly French, Rameau enriched the tradition of Lully in not being afraid to learn from the Italians. Such was the perceptiveness of Stainville's description, already, of

---

[22] Ibid., 29 Dec. 1749, fos. 20–1 for the following.
[23] Cf. Samuel Baud-Bovy, 'Rousseau as a musician' in *The Times Literary Supplement* no. 3724, p. 830, of 20 July 1973; also, *passim*, Cuthbert Girdlestone, *Jean-Philippe Rameau* (London, 1957) and Norman Demuth, *French Opera* (Sussex, 1963).

Rameau as the mean term in relation to the gathering Italian comeback.

The Count de Stainville was regularly on to the latest thing. His, now, is the suggestion of the strength in Paris of musical influences from the school of Pergolesi so early as 1749, two years and more before the celebrated Guerre des Buffons between the French and Italian persuasions was to enable Jean-Jacques Rousseau, the amateur of insight, to drive home his personal vendetta already being pursued against Rameau. For the present, however, it proved unnecessary to pursue Stainville's willingness to have unorthodox recourse to Italian composition for *Linus*.

By 6 April 1750 Stainville was writing the Nivernais: 'The Abbé de Bernis, whom I met this week, promised me to write to La Bruère. I do not know whether he has done so despite the positive promise which he gave me. Rameau has decided to do *Linus* but he does not want to work on it till La Bruère has made the necessary changes and connections and has got it quite in shape. So get the little man to work on it as soon as possible. The Abbé de Bernis should be telling La Bruère of the changes which he thinks necessary',[24] especially in the fifth act. Six weeks later 'Rameau is becoming impatient'[25] and, feared Stainville, liable to turn back to a composition earlier put in hand in case of a firstborn son for the Dauphin. The great composer, however, did get ahead with *Linus* even though Stainville in the following November was still receiving revised verses for it from the Little Man.

Stainville explained to Nivernais that he had not given these verses to Rameau from a scruple that they should be remitted by Bernis, the Pompadour's friend, to whom Stainville was then deferential: 'We have need of him during the whole of this business, so he must be treated tactfully. I told you that I saw Rameau. He seemed to me very pleased with what he has done [on *Linus*]. He seemed to me to have worked on it with relish, and to be taken by it. The haste with which he did it gave me misgivings, and I was afraid that he had hurried to get rid of it, as of something which one takes on to oblige, but the way in which he spoke to me of it has reassured me. Indeed he told me that he had shewn it to Mlle Lemmery [?Lemierre], who had been pleased with it.'[26] The interest of this conversation is that, while the manuscript of La Bruère's libretto survives, what mattered was the music, and *Linus* is the only one of Rameau's operas that is lost, except for a part for the first violin.[27]

[24] Count de Stainville to Duke de Nivernais, 6 Apr. 1750: *u. s.*, fo. 22.
[25] Ibid., 18 May 1750, fo. 26.   [26] Ibid., 16 Nov. 1750, fo. 31.
[27] Cf. C. Girdlestone, op. cit., pp. 307–8.

While Stainville tactfully forbore on this occasion from himself communicating La Bruère's revised verses, he did shew them to a literary friend, Voltaire's best one:

M. d'Argental . . . is as interested as we are in *Linus*. In general we were content with them, but we both think that the fête in the 5th act leaves something to be desired. The words are pretty enough, but there is nothing to distinguish it from all the fêtes of nereids and Tritons which are to be found everywhere. They [the words] could indeed do for every kind of fête. We should like him [La Bruère] to find a way of giving his divertissement a particular character, to provide the musician with a subject to depict, so that by offering a less vast and less ordinary scope he affords matter for music that is distinguished and characterized. What we are asking is easier to imagine than to execute, I know, and perhaps indeed the way in which I express myself might seem to anybody but you as vague as the fête that I am complaining about.[28]

Stainville, however, was sure that Nivernais would 'perceive how important this fête is for the success of the work . . . and that it should offer scenes which have not yet been presented'. The writer left it entirely to the ambassador whether or not to pass on the joint criticism of the two counts to touchy La Bruère:

We certainly do not want to vex him. We are inspired only by the interests of the author and the work, and we should not be looking at it so closely if we were less interested in it. It is for you to see if what we are asking is possible, . . . if sunset, the freshness of a summer's night, the soft voluptuousness which should reign in the palace of Thetis upon the return of the sun are sufficiently marked subjects to give him ideas for characterizing the fête, or if it would be better (without departing too much from the subject), by means of some new supposition or invention, to introduce into this fête another divertissement susceptible of tableaux and of some novelty. I was told yesterday that the Abbé de Bernis was back. I will try to see him this week . . . I forgot to tell you that Rameau has finished [*Linus*]. He is letting the work rest a while so as to take a fresh look at it later. He has promised me to let me hear it one day on the harpsichord with the Abbé de Bernis. I am very curious to hear it.

IV

If *Linus* was the main theatrical preoccupation of the Count de Stainville in those years, he kept up as usual with the new productions. The 24 July 1749 had seen the first night in Paris of a play by the wife of a tax-collector from Dieppe. Ten days later Stainville was writing:

We have just had a tragedy by Mme Dubocage, called The Amazons. It has been received with all the indulgence that one can expect from French gallantry. They let it finish and replay. There is even a scene in the fourth act which Mlle du Mesnil

---

[28] Count de Stainville to Duke de Nivernais, 16 Nov. 1750: loc. cit. for the following.

acted in such an admirable manner that she forced applause ... For the rest it seemed to me about as badly done as a play can be, and the style inferior to that of her poem. There are, however, here and there some verses fairly turned and some others that are dazzling.[29]

Stainville's balance was kinder than Collé's conviction that 'nothing has ever been seen that is feebler, more ordinary, more like everything, worse botched together than this tragedy. The first four acts are pillaged, taken, basically copied from *Le Comte d'Essex, Bajazet, Ariane* and Crébillon's *Sémiramis*.'[30] Collé further recorded early that September: 'In an assembly, where the Maréchale de Boufflers was, they were exaggerating the ridiculousness of Madame du Châtelet's producing a child at her age; upon which the good Maréchale maintained that it was not so great as that of Mme Dubocage producing a tragedy.'[31] The tragedian at least was to live into her ninety-second year in 1802. Voltaire's mistress with whom he had fallen out of love died on 10 September 1749 at the age of forty-two after giving birth to a girl by Saint-Lambert.

Another literary lady connected with Lorraine received some attention about that time from the theatregoing Count de Stainville. Madame de Graffigny and her young companion Minette, the Ligniville girl, were invited to a popular performance by the pupils of Louis-le-Grand of the *Mort imaginaire* in the elegant new theatre which had been fitted up there in 1748. The authoress's Jesuit familiar, the Canadian Father Martel, wrote that he had heard 'that M. de Stainville would be coming: he is your friend. So tell him to pick you up on the way'[32] or else to send his coach back for her.

The Count de Stainville participated in a theatrical occasion of closer interest to Madame de Graffigny, whose salon he sometimes visited. She was also keeping up, more or less, her wry relations with his mother as also her distinguished ones with Prince Charles of Lorraine in Brussels and the theatrical Princess Charlotte in Vienna. At the end of 1748 the princess had graciously received from her 'dear Grosse' a little fairy-tale called *Phaza* for acting, so she hoped, by the little archduchesses. Thence Madame de Graffigny was now approaching her dramatic zenith, casting and rehearsing her major play, *Cénie*.

For the lady playwright, as she confided to her ever devoted Panpan, the 1st June 1750 proved a proper Monday morning. She had slept rottenly, her pet Acajou had disappeared, and she had been

---

[29] Ibid, 4 Aug. 1749, fo. 6.   [30] C. Collé, op. cit. i. 86.   [31] Ibid., p. 96.
[32] Father Martel to Madame de Graffigny, *c.* 1750: cited, G. Noël, *Madame de Graffigny*, p. 266. (Father Martel's reference would seem less likely to be to the marquis than to the count, the youngish former pupil of Louis-le-Grand and devotee of the stage.)

unable to get out of going to luncheon with the Marquise de
Stainville. Meanwhile she had to cope, as French authors then largely
did, with casting her play and histrionic quarrels over parts. This
'deathly morning'[33] lasted till after one o'clock, while Madame de
Graffigny kept 'the cursed coach' sent by the Marquise de Stainville
waiting. 'I had one of those moments in which one does not know
which way to turn' – no time to do her hair or even to dress properly,
only it would not matter since the Marquise 'spends her whole life
alone'. Only of course she did have guests after all, a Choiseul-Beaupré
relation from the branch of Daillecourt, Claude-Antoine, Bishop of
Châlons-sur-Marne, plus a rather dim Chevalier and a lady featured
as the Little Bitch: a ghastly meal for Madame de Graffigny looking
such a sight and hardly able to utter, feeling 'as ashamed as a sick
wolf'.

Very different, after another nearly sleepless night, was Madame
de Graffigny's great day, Thursday, 25 June 1750, date of the first
performance of *Cénie*. She awoke feeling fine, in a singing mood and
actually did a little dance of excitement and relief that at last the
waiting was all but over. After sending off complimentary tickets for
the stalls that day – 'they have cost me a fine louis'[34] – and reciting
Cénie over to herself, Madame de Graffigny had that morning driven
out in a borrowed coach to the Cours. It was a lovely day, all green
and windy, blowing away even her heady awareness of being 'the
woman of the day' till on her way home about one o'clock she passed
the theatre which in a few hours now was to be 'my tribunal. The wall
was already lined with valets there to get seats' for their masters and
mistresses. She herself could not face the first performance but after
luncheon she sent her own valet dressed up as a gentleman with a
sword, under orders to hurry back in the interval to tell her how it
had gone with the first two acts, the ones that were worrying her
most.

So Madame de Graffigny sat writing all this to Panpan as she
waited, with 'Minette at the window to see my lackey arrive'. It was
rather after half past five. Suddenly there he was:

He says that the applause hardly left time for the acting, that it happened at every
word, every minute, that in the pit they were saying 'Oh, how beautiful that is. Who
is it by?' 'It is by Mme de G.' 'Ah, I am not surprised' was the reply ... Minette is
bursting. She is beside herself and, as for me, I am quietly going on writing to you.
It still does not seem true to me. I am stupefied for my satellites are making a horrible
racket over my being so cold ... I must stop.

[33] Madame de Graffigny to François Devaux, Paris, 1 June 1750: Yale/Beinecke:
Phillipps/Graffigny 23900, vol. l, fo. 247 for the following.
[34] Ibid., 25–6 June 1750, fos. 289–93 for the following.

News of victory floods into spate. Between the fourth and fifth acts the clapping was nonstop, they assured her, for a quarter of an hour with people drumming applause with their feet till asked to stop 'because of the dust'. All her friends came pouring in to congratulate her. 'They were mad. There was nowhere to sit. They were jostling ...shrieking. Oh what chaos.' Madame de Graffigny had attained her literary apogee. A day or two later she attended a performance of *Cénie*, holding court in her box for admirers. 'And who? The Duke de Duras, the Duke de Lauraguais and the Duke de Biron. They showed me their eyes, red and swollen'[35] just as they should be with a sensitive duke in the new fashion of *comédie larmoyante*. *Cénie* came to be classed with *Le Méchant* as the best plays of that flattish period.

Madame de Graffigny did not escape the usual suspicions of cribbing, centring this time upon *La Gouvernante*, one of La Chaussée's 'rhapsodies'. Analysis and development of character within the classic unities yielded to a scenario of lachrymose romance articulated in telling episodes, in this case around the heroine, Cénie, of interestingly dubious parentage known only to her scheming suitor, Méricourt – and so on. For many contemporaries this stuff was charged with novel delight deriving, perhaps, from a compassionate sensibility less developed before the age, now already dawning, of Rousseau's rediscovery of nature, of naturalness, as a pointer to the romantic movement.

La Chaussée's prototype was, thought Collé, surpassed by *Cénie*, which 'extracted from me some semi-tears... You begin to be moved, and you are left in mid-air.'[36] Some spectators were moved still less upon that first night of 25 June 1750. It is easy to make fun of emotion. If insipid, it asks for it. Even the triumphant reports to Madame de Graffigny allowed that a hostile 'cabal in the pit' had had to be suppressed, with one gallant champion of the lady playwright calling out 'Are there women here dressed as men?'[37] There was one formidable woman dressed as a woman. 'All through the play Madame de Boufflers made fun of it, and so abused it that the next box, where Madame de Rochefort and company were, were scandalized by it.' The Countess de Rochefort championed the play afterwards at supper at the Brancas mansion. At Madame de Graffigny's that evening a friend 'finished a tirade' against the Duchess de Boufflers, in three days to become the Duchess de Luxembourg, by exclaiming, 'Nobody, by God, has ever carried hatred of virtue so far as she.'

If the Count de Stainville was not in the Duchess de Boufflers's

[35] Ibid., 27 June 1750, fo. 295.   [36] C. Collé, op. cit., i. 189.
[37] Madame de Graffigny to Devaux, Paris, 25–6 June 1750: *u.s.*, fos. 291–2 for the following.

box that evening, he was almost certainly treated to her caustic estimate of *Cénie*. For his own part he reported: 'Cénie, a comedy in five acts by Mme. de Graffigny, has had a fair success. The controller gen. has as yet said nothing positive to the clergy.'[38]

This terse intelligence was conveyed in another of Stainville's chief correspondences just then, with his old friend Bernstorff. Some weeks later Stainville was informing him: 'Voltaire has sent in his resignation from his office of historiographer and his pensions.'[39] The death of the Marquise du Châtelet had unsettled Voltaire, clinging now to his niece and newer mistress, Madame Denis. He had become more susceptible to renewed blandishments from Frederick the Great. Stainville continued on 22 August 1750 that Voltaire was going to settle 'in Prussia; he is having Madame Denis go there, and the King of Prussia is giving them, for them both, a pension of 20 thousand francs. D'Argental and the Abbé Chauvelin are desolated, but I console myself because perhaps we shall have a good edition of his works in which the poem of the Pucelle will figure; moreover I think that Voltaire, Mde. Denis and the king of Prussia are committing a great folly.'

Voltaire, who had in fact left Paris for Berlin just on two months earlier, had scarcely arrived at the Prussian court before he began to share Stainville's view and to regret a move which marked the beginning of an absence of twenty-eight years from his beloved Paris, till the last months of his life. The brittle philosopher had set out from the old ordering of France upon his long pilgrimage, often squalid in its squabbles and intrigues while bravely aspiring towards something finer in an age which he largely kindled to enlightenment.

By October 1750 Stainville was already writing that 'Voltaire is coming to us at the end of this month, decked out with a chamberlain's key and the Order of Merit. They say that he will only be here long enough for us to admire the new decoration. I hope, however, that he will spare a moment to give us a tragedy and let us see a Prussian chamberlain in dispute with the actors.'[40] A month later the sharp correspondent corrected: 'Voltaire is no longer coming so soon to this part of the world, for Voltaire is also making news. His friends, and apparently he more than they, seem amazed that his post of historiographer has been given to Duclos. He wanted to give up and to retain, which is sometimes difficult.'[41]

The wit of the later Choiseul approached that of the literary lion with whom he was to have considerable dealings, more particularly

---

[38] Count de Stainville to Baron von Bernstorff, Paris, 1 July 1750: *Bernstorffske Papirer*, ii. 635 (there misdated 1751).
[39] Ibid., 22 Aug. 1750, p. 623 for the following.   [40] Ibid., 8 Oct. 1750, p. 626.
[41] Count de Stainville to Baron von Bernstorff, Paris, 8 Nov. 1750: ibid., p. 627.

in relation to Frederick the Great. Already the Count de Stainville was striking his usual note with Voltaire, one of amused amity overlaying a reserve of high admiration tinged with scorn: which one may think a just enough estimation of that flawed genius.

V

Literary and theatrical interests were not the sum of young Stainville's artistic involvement. He was too keen a collector not to respond to advice from Nivernais that there were bargains in pictures to be had in Rome, possibly from two cardinals. Stainville was writing to him in September 1749:

I in no way refuse the proposal that you make about pictures and I have full confidence in your taste so far as serious subjects are concerned, but here is what could make me uneasy:

1. I have always heard it said that there is much deceit in Italy and that the ablest people have been caught there. They make out that in Italy there are few pure pictures entirely from the hands of the great masters. They used to touch up the works of their pupils, and they are sold today as being by them. They [also] had excellent copyists whose pictures are sold today as originals, and it is very difficult to distinguish them.

2. You are French and an ambassador. If they do not deceive you, at least they will overcharge you. These two heads seem to me really to rule out bargains.

3. You say that pictures are very common and at a very reasonable price. I am afraid that they may be mediocre pictures by second-rate masters, ... that fine pictures by the great masters with famous names are rare and dear, as excellent things are everywhere. Now you know that my taste is not for the mediocre, and that I should prefer one beautiful picture to ten ordinary ones.

4. You also know how averse I am from holy subjects. Sometimes there are agreeable ones which might find favour with me, but they are rare.[42]

This was the kind of crisp and searching analysis which Choiseul was to bring to bear upon politics, and with much the same object: to secure the best most economically. While Nivernais had apparently suggested ten or twelve paintings for as many thousand francs, his exacting correspondent argued:

With four pictures for the upper walls I should have enough to furnish my study ... I could lay out a thousand Ecus this year, if you could get me for that or thereabouts two beautiful pictures, agreeable above all, really pure, really original and by a fine name, for names count a lot in these parts ... I could perhaps devote a similar sum to it again next year, and gradually build up an Italian collection, that is

[42] Count de Stainville to Duke de Nivernais, 21–2 Sept. 1749: W. N. A., docket V/1, fo. 12 for the following.

to say of Italian pictures for the upper walls, for I believe that this is what we must
go for. However, if you should find some pretty little picture, as charming as those of
which we have some in France, I would not exclude them, but I know that they are
very rare, and I need pictures for the upper levels.

So much for any assumption that Stainville's concentration upon
the Flemish and Dutch schools implied a rigid exclusion of Italian
interest. But it was liable to be costly. He still had not paid off those
Gerard Dous bought years earlier nor 'the fittings of my house and
the ground at the end of my garden. Now in sound morality
necessities take precedence over superfluities. The superfluities are
the pictures; the necessity is to pay the debts ... It is in general true
that I have very little money to spend on this, and it is cheapness that
tempts me. That is so much so that I have not bought 50 livres worth
of pictures since you left.' If Choiseul was to be extravagant, and he
was, he was not a spendthrift. 'But', he added, 'I should prefer to
spend rather more to have something beautiful rather than to fall into
mediocrity.'[43]

In terms of artists this meant, explained the count to the duke, that
'I should much like you to be able to unhook me some beautiful
Guido, Titian, Albani, Forti, Barocci, Caracci, even Correggio or
Raphael if necessary. I should agree very well with your two
cardinals. Their conscience is perhaps at bottom not more timid than
mine, but my exterior is less reserved, and I should take with pleasure
these subjects which they dare not allow themselves. It is one which
I like best, as you know, and I ask of you above all bright pictures and
agreeable subjects.'[44] It may well have been a question of nudes.
Stainville was later to enjoin the respectable Nivernais not to worry
about nakedness in a Titian. The future Choiseul did not include
himself among what he termed 'timid consciences'.[45]

For the present Stainville added: 'I know that there are no Raphaels
and that Correggios are infinitely rare, so I do not count on them and
I should make do very well with the folk you mention to me,
especially Titians, Guidos and Albanis. However, I exclude neither
Caraccis nor Pietro da Cortonas, nor Baroccis, of which I am also
very fond.'[46] If Stainville's taste in Italian art for the sweet tradition
of Raphael and the eclectic school of Bologna was then conventional
enough, his emphasis upon Titian stands out.

Stainville continued directly to Nivernais: 'The Ste Palayes's
pictures have not yet arrived. I am very curious to see them.' The

[43] Ibid., 17 Nov. 1749, fo. 15.   [44] Ibid., 6 Oct. 1749, fo. 14.
[45] Duke de Choiseul to Voltaire, 21 Mar. 1768: P. Calmettes, op. cit., p. 224.
[46] Count de Stainville to Duke de Nivernais, 17 Nov. 1749: W. N. A., docket V/1, fos. 15–16,
and for the following.

Sainte-Palayes were devoted twin brothers, bachelors. Jean-Baptiste, then rather over fifty and the one usually called Sainte-Palaye, was a delicate and dedicated scholar, spared mundane cares by his brother, La Curne. In that age of reason Sainte-Palaye was a medievalist steeped in the age of chivalry and its troubadours. He had just been to Rome to add to his great collection of manuscripts and also, apparently, of pictures. The Count de Stainville with his background in Lorraine was friendly with this protégé of Stanislas Leszczynski, with whom Sainte-Palaye had earlier had diplomatic dealings and under whom he graced that Academy of Nancy which he had helped to found. Stainville had recently been telling Nivernais how sorry he was 'for you about the departure of the Sainte Palayes. They are good company everywhere, but they are still more precious at Rome.'[47]

Now the brothers' pictures were ages in following them on from Rome. As for any acquisitions of his own, however, Stainville assured the ambassador that 'there is no hurry. One must await a favourable opportunity.' This was to mean waiting a year and more. Meanwhile developments in Stainville's social life were to change his circumstances and promote a signal expansion of his collection of paintings.

The future Choiseul collection was to reflect its owner's insistence from the beginning upon quality over quantity: not specially large, it was to abound in masterpieces, those 'pure pictures' demanded by this connoisseur who was to be seldom taken in by that subordinate work of the schools against which he was early upon his guard. (One exception, probably, was to be a landscape by Rubens not now generally accepted as such.) It has been suggested[48] that no picture-collection formed and dispersed in the eighteenth century has made a richer contribution than Choiseul's to today's national collections in Paris, London, Berlin, and Amsterdam, in America and in Russia. If this should prompt some caveat in respect of the Crozat collection, precisely a Crozat connection was to lead, soon now, through to Choiseul.

A keen concern and knowledge, already, in painting, music, literature and drama stamp the future Choiseul as something more than a rich dabbler in good taste. He was one of the most artistically implicated men to hold high political office in any age.

[47] Count de Stainville to Duke de Nivernais, 6 Oct. 1749: ibid., fo. 14 for the following.
[48] Cf. Emile Dacier, 'La Curiosité au XVIIIᵉ siècle: Choiseul collectionneur' in *Gazette des beaux-arts*, 6th period, xxxvi (1949), 74.

CHAPTER III

FOREIGN

I

EXACTLY one month after the main signature of the Treaty of Aix-la-Chapelle the father of the Count de Stainville was at last sent instructions, historic in relation to the War of the Austrian Succession, from Count Colloredo, imperial vice-chancellor, to remit to King Louis XV 'in an audience in accordance with the usual practice'[1] the letter of notification of the imperial election of Francis I, still under the original date of 5 October 1745.

This was the Marquis de Stainville's chance: no royal audience for him without new letters of credence as his friend, Puysieulx, obligingly insisted. Stainville represented to the emperor that in granting him such letters 'it would cost you nothing to honour me with the quality of your ambassador',[2] even if only temporarily. Yet again there was nothing doing for the marquis. He was never to be an ambassador, however briefly, nor, even, were any new letters forthcoming. At the close of the year of 1748 Stainville executed instructions to give to Puysieulx for remission to his king, over three years late, the notification from Francis I that he was 'crowned yesterday amid agreeable applause (*hesterna die festivos inter applausus*)'.[3]

If Francis for once was 'very satisfied'[4] with the discharge by his minister in Paris of his disappointing commission, Stainville himself was less so, pleading: 'My fate must of necessity be decided.'[5] His fate still was limbo, enlivened by such occasions as a smart wedding or, on 16 December 1748, a day spent with the Count de Saint-Séverin, dining in the family circle at the home of his father-in-law. Saint-

---

[1] Count Colloredo to Marquis de Stainville, Vienna, 18 Nov. 1748: Ö.S./H.H.S., Hofkanzlei: Frankreich/Varia (1736–49), Varia 1745–8, fo. 57.
[2] Marquis de Stainville to Emperor Francis I, Paris, 4 Dec. 1748: Esteri del Granducato di Toscana, vol. 2295/1286, fo. 672.
[3] Emperor Francis I to King Louis XV, Frankfurt am Main, 5 Oct. 1745: Arch. Aff. Étr. C.P., Autriche, vol. 239, fo. 100. (The filed original carries the following French annotations: 'Nᵃ. Cette lettre n'a été présenté au Roi que vers la fin de 1748 ... Nᵃ. Cette lettre n'est point contresigné du Vice Chancelier de l'Empire.')
[4] Count Colloredo to Marquis de Stainville, Vienna, 25 Jan. 1749: Ö.S./H.H.S., Hofkanzlei: Frankreich/Weisungen (1749) 117, fo. 77.
[5] Marquis de Stainville to Count Colloredo, Paris, 5 Jan. 1749: Ö.S./H.H.S., Hofkanzlei: Frankreich/Berichte (1749–50) 119.

Séverin, back from Aix, had been appointed a Minister of State and had on the previous day attended his first meeting of the royal council of state, already comprising Tencin, Noailles, the younger d'Argenson, Maurepas, and Puysieulx.

Saint-Séverin recalled to Stainville his important communication to him in the previous June of the French desire to follow a new system of rapprochement with Austria.[6] And now, a fortnight earlier, Puysieulx in the course of a two-hour conversation about those letters of credence had assured Stainville that Louis XV wished 'to cement an immutable union with the august house of Austria ... The King had totally changed system.'[7] For the present Saint-Séverin added that 'he had long been shocked'[8] at the way in which foreign envoys dealt direct with ministers of state, such as he now was, instead of channelling their approaches properly through the foreign minister. In order to avoid 'disunion' in the council Saint-Séverin proposed to hold aloof. '"Of course", he continued, "there is no general rule without an exception and I shall always have great pleasure in seeing Monsieur de Stainville, my special friend, and there is nothing that I would not do ... to support the negotiations wherewith he shall be charged by his master."' In point of fact Stainville was not even warned of the arrival in Paris towards the end of January 1749 of a preliminary emissary from the Austrian government in the person of a secretary of embassy called de Launay. Two days later he died there of an apoplectic fit. Stainville had to cope, sealing up Launay's official papers after seeking out 'the furnished apartment where he had lodged in a very remote quarter of the town. There I found his wife and family in a state of desolation.'[9]

Austria was thus still without a direct representative at the French court when the Marquis de Stainville at last made his reappearance at Versailles on 11 March 1749. It was one of the Tuesdays for the diplomatic corps. Stainville, still denied new letters of credence, explained that he had agreed with Puysieulx that he should return to the royal apartments 'as though I had never discontinued going there, in order to avoid all ceremony of presentation'.[10] Thus did Stainville slip back into circulation, to report that by the royal family he was 'received with distinction, and the Dauphin, who is little talkative, came up to me and said to me in a kindly manner that he was very glad to see me again for all sorts of reasons, and that those

---

[6] Cf. p. 742 above.
[7] Marquis de Stainville to Emperor Francis I, Paris, 4 Dec. 1748: Esteri del Granducato di Toscana, vol. 2295/1286, fo. 673.
[8] Marquis de Stainville to Emperor Francis I, Paris, 22 Dec. 1748: Ö.S./H.H.S., Lothringisches Hausarchiv 77/177A for the following.
[9] Ibid., 2 Feb. 1749.   [10] Ibid., 16 Mar. 1749 for the following.

which were personal to myself played a large part therein'. The Dauphin was destined to see more and approve less of the eldest son of the Marquis de Stainville.

On the same day that the Tuscan minister was reinstated at Versailles he was negotiating with the French foreign minister on the usual run of everyday business: leftovers, still from Lorraine, with Stainville trying to realize the best price for the emperor on some inherited French bonds, now depreciated by sixty or eighty per cent; also the perennial question of the financial liquidation of French obligations towards the former government of Lorraine, notably in respect of the fodder extracted during the War of the Polish Succession. Here, after more than ten years, Stainville, supported by the emperor's agent, Molitoris, was still arguing the issue with the French controller-general and La Galaizière. Tuscan issues included the subjection of French couriers to new measures against smuggling and the straightening out of a quarrel between the Count de Richecourt and Count Lorenzi, whose family, as Puysieulx explained, 'from father to son, had been the king's chargé d'affaires at Florence for more than sixty years', so that the present one was in no hurry to accord the grand duke imperial recognition.

Tuscany had a closer interest just then for the Marquis de Stainville. A fortnight later, he reported, he 'gave M. de Puysieulx a little memorandum to procure a passport for the effects which the Prince de Craon was having brought back [from Tuscany] to Lorraine. After having ... promised me the requested passport, he [Puysieulx] said to me with heartfelt emotion, "So that informs me of the moment of our separation. I assure you without flattery that it really touches me. The friendship which there has been between us since our childhood"' had led him to expect Stainville to remain with the prospect, continued Puysieulx, of their doing '"good work together with regard to the respective interests of our masters. But I quite see that you are going to leave us and that the rumours which are circulating, that you are going to replace M. de Craon in Tuscany, are only too true." Upon that I assured the minister that I knew nothing of it'[11] – as usual.

The Prince de Craon was retiring that spring to Lorraine from his Tuscan regency, needled by 'that man (*cet homme-là*)', as Richecourt was called by the princess. Mann suggested that her daughter, the Marquise de Boufflers, might now have to look to her laurels at Lunéville, and further commented that in Florence:

The Earl [Richecourt] hopes to succeed, though some people talk of Monsieur de Stainville who is at Paris, where they are obliged to keep him, as he has no place at

[11] Ibid., 30 Mar. 1749.

Vienna. He is *grand maître* to the Great Duke, but not as Emperor, and then he can't remain at Paris as *envoyé* of the Great Duke when the Empress sends a minister with a superior character, so that I always thought the *mezzo termine* would be Tuscany.[12]

As Mann's colleague in Turin, however, remarked of Richecourt: 'It would be a cursed bite upon this last, after all the trouble he has had in undermining and working Prince Craon out of the way, to have Count [*sic*] Stainville step in between him and supreme power.'[13] Three days earlier Stainville himself had reported that Queen Marie Leszczynska had asked him about the Tuscan report, remarking that 'if it was for my good, she would be very glad of it despite her sadness at seeing me leave this part of the world. On this subject everybody is offering me congratulations, which I do not accept, and I am replying to everybody alike that I am still in uncertainty as to my fate.'[14] Stainville was to be kept dangling in that Tuscan uncertainty for a year and more.

Meanwhile specks of high diplomacy yet brushed off upon the Marquis de Stainville, the first envoy in Paris after the Peace of Aix-la-Chapelle to receive French overtures to Austria in a further stage towards their momentous rapprochement and reversal of alliances. Puysieulx's comment upon the Prince de Craon's passport had been preceded by an assurance to Stainville that 'it had lain only with the Queen Empress to treat directly with the King [of France], and that since four years, and in the last instance at Aix-la-Chapelle'.[15] The Frenchman knew that the Lorrainer knew, as did few others, the inwardness of that assertion. Stainville replied along regular lines as to her 'very rare' scrupulousness in fidelity to allies.

'Upon this', related Stainville, 'the minister answered me that he too did not blame her but on the contrary, all the more, continued Monsieur de Puysieulx, "since it was quite simple to understand that she should not have great confidence in us, for we scarcely deserve it; and besides, the little stability of the French ministry, my arrival in this same ministry – I who had not the honour to be known by this august princess – all that did not contribute towards giving her confidence. But I hope to deserve it eventually, and a time will come when we shall perhaps contribute towards restoring the house of Austria in its old brilliance; but once again one must not be precipitate. One must let time do its work, and profit from events."'

[12] Mann to Horace Walpole, Florence, 8 Mar. 1749: Walpole Correspondence, xx. 29.
[13] Villettes to Mann, 30 Apr. 1749: P.R.O./S.P.F. 105/309, fos. 107–8, cited, ibid., xx. 45, n. 27.
[14] Marquis de Stainville to Emperor Francis I, Paris, 27 Apr. 1749: Ö.S./H.H.S., Lothringisches Hausarchiv 77/177A.
[15] Ibid., 30 Mar. 1749, for the following. Cf. Alfred Ritter von Arneth, 'Biographie des Fürsten Kaunitz: ein Fragment' in *Archiv für österreichische Geschichte*, lxxxviii (Vienna, 1899), 185.

The French foreign minister concluded this suggestive effusion by looking towards the restoration of confidence between Louis XV and Francis I, swearing to Stainville 'that the king desires it ardently and that there remains in his heart no shadow of pique or animosity': once again an assurance of the personal predilection of King Louis for appeasement with Austria.

At inferior level a memorandum prepared in the French foreign ministry at the end of January 1749 was still arguing conventionally from a basic opposition of French and Austrian interests. Their appeasement, however, inspired the instructions of 25 March to Blondel for his mission to Vienna as French chargé d'affaires and harbinger to match the ill-fated de Launay. Before leaving, Blondel did not fail to call upon the Marquis de Stainville to assure him, truthfully enough, of his austrophil conversion.

II

The return to Versailles of the Marquis de Stainville in March 1749 coincided with a crux in an international crisis, now mainly forgotten, which threatened to plunge Europe back into war. Storm-signals were out in the north. Prussia and Russia, neither blooded most recently by war, were the two fierce powers in the aftermath of Aix-la-Chapelle. And peace renders the warlike ill at ease. Four days after Austria, the critical power-factor between Prussia and Russia, had adhered to the peace-treaty, the Marquis de Stainville had been reporting to Vienna: 'They seem very anxious at Fontainebleau about the great preparations which the Empress of Russia is making in Finland. That together with the Russian troops in Bohemia and Moravia, and the state wherein the King of Sweden finds himself, causes much argument among the politicians.'[16]

The frivolous old King Frederick I of Sweden was as usual unenviably placed. When Sweden had been kicked out of the war by Russia in the humiliating Peace of Abo of 1743, the powerful peacemaking of the Empress Elizabeth had imposed as the Swedish heir Prince Adolphus Frederick of Holstein-Gottorp, cousin and heir-presumptive as yet of that young Duke of Holstein-Gottorp, Charles Peter Ulrik, whom the Czarina had lately proclaimed her own heir, the future Czar Peter III. This had threatened a Holstein-Gottorp clamp from Schleswig-Holstein and, now, Sweden also against Denmark. She was overawed by Russia and a conciliatory

[16] u.s., 27 Oct. 1748.

Swedish move towards marrying Adolphus Frederick to a Danish princess was frustrated, not least because England no less than Russia, the other great outlier, was opposed to any suggestion of a Scandinavian union controlling access to the Baltic. Instead Adolphus Frederick had been married to the attractive sister of Frederick the Great, Voltaire's Princess Ulrike, fond of the arts and politically ambitious, going in with Count Charles Tessin and his francophil party of the Hats. She swayed her weakly stupid husband accordingly, away from the tutelage of the Empress Elizabeth, who thereupon reverted to an older pattern of relationships by inducing Denmark, still lured by Schleswig-Holstein, to join Russia and England in fomenting factional strife on behalf of the Caps. Under the Hats the Swedish government, defensively allied with Prussia in 1747, by 1748 found itself holding out against the formidable diplomacy of the Russian Grand Chancellor Bestuchev.

Those who, like Montesquieu looking to the richly protected British Isles, extolled the excellence of parliamentary government, needed to reckon that the two large countries of the continent wherein parliamentary institutions really counted for something in that age of enlightened despotism were Sweden, in such precarious enjoyment of her Frihetstiden or age of freedom, and Poland, already heading towards foreign subjection. (Little Holland had just had her revolution towards authority.) Both the Swedish and Polish governments, between the pulls of France and Russia, were so weak, venal and menaced as to constitute danger-spots for Europe. For both regimes the support of distant France was a precarious stay against neighbouring and ascendant Russia, too strong now for either to take on. That was the grim reality just a century after the Peace of Westphalia which had left expanding Brandenburg still gripped in Swedish pincers. Since then not only had Charles XII lost out to Peter the Great but Sweden had been overhauled by Prussia, significantly standing behind her in the northern crisis of 1748–9 and the multiple threat from Russia.

Bestuchev had survived the dark days of the conspiracy of Lapuchin and had been in English pay since 1746. Next year he married his son to the daughter of his empress by her splendid Cossack, Count Alexis Rasumovsky, the so-called Night Czar endowed with everything 'needful to a Hercules upon Cythera, [but] denied ... the gift of intelligence'[17] according to Mardefeld. This Prussian minister to the Russian court had omitted to win over the

---

[17] Baron von Mardefeld, cited, Reinhold Koser, *König Friedrich der Grosse* (3rd ed., Stuttgart and Berlin, 1904), i. 467.

grand chancellor, and the prussophil vice-chancellor, Count Voront-sov, was cowed. Frederick confessed the failure of his diplomatic wooing of the empress. Now, at the end of 1748, Bestuchev used Rasumovsky to complete the elimination of the Franco–Prussian faction in the person of the favourite's former confederate in the interest of Elizabeth's accession, Count Lestocq. The empress now consigned him to the grim routine of political change in Russia: imprisonment, torture, Siberia. While these dark designs were working out, the Russian expeditionary corps to the west was ominously wintering in Bohemia. Bestuchev was still scowling in the direction of Sweden, and of Prussia.

During that summer of 1748 Bestuchev had already propounded to Austria, England, and Denmark his plan for falling upon Sweden and, with Saxony and Hesse-Cassel joining in, replacing the ungrateful crown prince by Prince Frederick of Hesse, son-in-law to George II of England, or perhaps by the Duke of Cumberland. The inwardness and danger here was that Frederick the Great would be likely in his own interests to honour his defensive alliance with Sweden against Russian attack or, if necessary, could perhaps be provoked into doing so. Once Frederick resorted to war again he would trigger the secret provision of the Austro–Russian treaty of 1746 whereby, in that eventuality, he was to be stripped of Silesia: Austria in fact would have another go at him. If for the present the Austrian government, like the British, was preoccupied with the peacemaking of Aix-la-Chapelle, not so the Russian, aggrieved, not for the last time in history, at being excluded from the European settlement, and alarmed by the rise of Prussia.

From February 1749 onwards the French government for its part was letting it be known that it could not view with indifference any attack upon Sweden. There was much talk in France, war-weary as she was, of sending an expeditionary corps to Sweden. By the beginning of March intelligence of ominous troop-movements was filtering through from both Finland and Bohemia. The spring had brought the crisis darkly intended by Grand Chancellor Bestuchev in the exhausted aftermath of war.

So Frederick the Great took a hand. In Prussia all military leave was cancelled. At Potsdam he held council of war. Supplies were to be stocked up in Silesia where the spring manoeuvres would, it was explained, be upon an increased scale that year. In fact the plan against attack was for Frederick himself to attack into Bohemia. East Prussia was coolly written off. General Lehwaldt in Königsberg was to make ready to pull out in good time all troops, men of military age, horses and bullion, back across the Vistula to Pomeranian shelter.

That Teutonic retreat before the overwhelming Slavs was, however, yet to come.

On 15 March 1749 the Berlin press carried articles explaining that the measures of military alert were strictly defensive; but, in good German style, the assurances were so grimly worded as to increase European consternation. A German war of nerves was operating by means of what Frederick described to his sister in Sweden as his 'little ostentations'.[18] He sent to Versailles a special envoy, Count Finkenstein fresh from Saint Petersburg where he had succeeded Mardefeld, to reinforce Le Chambrier in bracing the Franco–Prussian alliance in that hour of need. On 18 March an open communication from the Prussian government blandly asked the British one, regarded as a promoter of Russian designs in the north, whether it would join in Frederick's endeavour to save the peace. A week later a Russian note formally enquired of England, Austria and Saxony whether, in the event of war with Sweden, Russia could count upon the assistance of her allies. The crisis was at crux.

It was on the same day of 25 March 1749 that the Marquis de Puysieulx had extended his feeler towards Austria to the Marquis de Stainville. That diplomatist related that when he next visited Versailles on the following Tuesday, the 1st April, he was told by Le Chambrier, in the queen's apartments, that Puysieulx was asking for him. The French foreign minister began by telling Stainville that Louis XV, having 'sacrificed everything to re-establish tranquillity in Europe', was sad to see that:

My court, by being too precipitate, wanted to reintroduce disturbance there; that under pretext of the treaty of 1746 which it had made with Russia, it was giving her thirty thousand men; that Russia was making the greatest preparations for war while still declaring that she did not want to attack anyone, but that this finesse was covered by too fine a veil of gauze for one not to see through it; that it was easy to see that by setting fire to one corner of Europe the conflagration would soon become general. 'And all', continued the minister, 'because the queen empress [Maria Theresa] has not been satisfied over one article [regarding Silesia] in the Treaty of Aix-la-Chapelle. It is not our fault if we did not contract directly with her. She did not want it. But on our part there is no means of breaking a treaty whose signatures are not yet dry . . . England, as much as ourselves, ought to uphold the engagements which we have undertaken together, and above all the guarantee of Silesia.'[19]

This was a direct French warning to Austria of the tougher reverse of Puysieulx's policy for understanding with Austria within the context of upholding the hard won and already threatened peace.

[18] King Frederick II to Princess Ulrike of Sweden, 4 Apr. 1749: ibid., i. 475.
[19] Marquis de Stainville to Emperor Francis I, Paris, 6 Apr. 1749: Esteri del Granducato di Toscana, vol. 2295/1286, fos. 675–7 for the following (copy in Ö.S./H.H.S., Hofkanzlei: Frankreich/Berichte 1749–50, 119).

Blondel was instructed accordingly. The Marquis de Stainville commented wryly: 'It is easy to see that the ... Prussian minister ... had also procured for me this long harangue to which I replied but with a word': he would report but 'did not believe that my court was desirous of disturbing the tranquillity of Europe'.

Stainville was right. The Russian summons of 25 March 1749 drew the Austrian and British governments closer once more in a joint endeavour to restrain Bestuchev. Maria Theresa gave reassurance of her moderation. Puysieulx, in his next conversation with Stainville on 8 April 1749, redressed the balance of his policy with the assurance that 'if any of the [French] king's allies should give occasion for some rupture, either directly or indirectly, the king would make common cause with my court',[20] the Austrian one. Puysieulx had said the same to Colonel Yorke, British envoy in Paris, and, significantly added the foreign minister, 'I have declared it without evasion to the Prussian minister. As for Sweden, I answer for her. She asks only peace and repose.' She received notes of loud menace from Bestuchev but they covered a Russian retreat. The wars of the Spanish, Polish, and Austrian successions were not after all to be rounded off by a war of the Swedish succession. The northern crisis in its acutest phase was over. Yet that nearly forgotten crisis of March 1749, when war-weary Europe shrank back from yet another conflict, had stimulated an Austrian set towards France, restrained though it was to be by cross-currents.

III

On 7 March 1749 Maria Theresa had asked the members of her council, the secret conference, for their written views as to the desirable course for future Austrian foreign policy, to be rendered within a fortnight: almost indecent haste by Austrian canons of grave deliberation. The Emperor Francis, the traditional anglophil, led the argument in favour of maintaining the old alliance with the maritime powers against the hereditary enemy, his erstwhile French overlord. The Emperor's strongest supporter was his vice-chancellor, Count Colloredo: such were the two chief correspondents with whom the francophil Marquis de Stainville had to contend. They had the agreement, too, of the other members of the conference, Field-Marshal Königsegg, Khevenhüller, Harrach and Ulfeld, all except one, the youngest member. The celebrated memorandum put in by

[20] *u.s.,* 13 Apr. 1749, fos. 682–3 for the following (copy *u.s.* Cf. Dr. J. Strieder, *Kritische Forschungen zur österreichischen Politik vom Aachener Frieden bis zum Beginne des Siebenjährigen Krieges*, p. 34).

Count Kaunitz was nearly twice as long as all the others put together, and was opposite. Prussia, argued Kaunitz with coldly compelling logic, was now Austria's real enemy marked down for revenge. Russian support against Prussia was most necessary but England, looking overseas, was no longer to be counted on, not after Maria Theresa's bitter experiences over the treaties of Breslau and of Worms, the convention of Hanover and the peace of Aix-la-Chapelle. So Austria now might need to win over France for an alliance against Prussia. Maria Theresa was convinced by Kaunitz's argument, if indeed she still needed convincing. The others soon fell in. A remarkably warm welcome awaited Blondel at Vienna. Such, in the middle year of the eighteenth century, was the effective beginning of its diplomatic revolution by reversal of alliances.

The leading inspiration of this revolution towards Franco–Austrian alliance has traditionally been ascribed to the successful Kaunitz, largely rightly but not wholly so. The later Choiseul was to wonder whether Kaunitz had derived from Bartenstein, still state-secretary, 'notions of the projects of the Emperor Charles VI'[21] with Fleury in the direction of Kaunitz's own project, judged by Choiseul to be 'really fine and really useful for the house of Austria'. The suspected influence here of Bartenstein was real enough,[22] but Choiseul ignored the effaced role of his father. Thanks, especially, to the circumstantial reports of the unsuccessful Marquis de Stainville the Austrian government, Kaunitz not least, stood to appreciate Puysieulx's point well enough: that for nearly four years, on and off, roughly coincident with the sway of the Marquise de Pompadour, the French government had been secretly probing towards that understanding with Austria already cultivated by Fleury and his confidant, the father of the future Choiseul.

Now corroboration of this secret continuity was for once provided from Vienna in a memorandum of instruction to the Marquis de Stainville conveying the gratification of Maria Theresa at the assurance from Puysieulx which he had reported on 13 April, and giving Stainville discretion to allude now to that heartcry from Fleury, incriminating Frederick and envisaging Austrian compensation, which the marquis had reported on 28 July 1742.[23] Now too, on 20 April 1749, the Emperor Francis I at last sent Stainville an agreeable communication, friendly to France and favourable to peace, with instructions that he should, as by his own initiative and in confidence, read it over to Puysieulx.

Stainville executed the emperor's instruction at Versailles on 10

[21] Choiseul, *Mémoires*, p. 152 for the following.   [22] Cf. Braubach, p. 406.
[23] Cf. p. 331; also J. Strieder, op. cit., p. 35.

May and reported that the French foreign minister 'was enchanted'.[24]
In return Puysieulx underlined his important assurance that he had
warned the allies of France that if they directly or indirectly 'should
cause disturbances, not only shall we not support them, but that we
should take sides against them with the powers whose tranquillity
they wished to disturb. I swear and vow to you that those are our true
intentions.' Puysieulx continued this striking avowal: even if he
himself should quit office, the policy would still be that of Louis XV;
as for Frederick the Great, he was 'too shrewd to dare to attempt
anything on his own account, and it would be so much the better for
your court if he did'. Frederick would then be faced with the
encircling coalition which Russia had just tried to mobilize. 'As for
us', the French foreign minister added in regard to the Prussian
monarch, 'not only will he secure no support but, as I repeat to you
again, we will make common cause with you. The Emperor and the
Queen Empress can count upon this, and I beg you to assure them of
it affirmatively.' The contingent undertaking offered by the French
government to the Austrian could scarcely have been plainer.
Puysieulx said that he was going at once to communicate the
emperor's letter to Louis XV, who read it with 'the greatest
satisfaction'.[25]

Thus did the effaced Marquis de Stainville receive French
assurances that went further than anything that Blondel had been
authorized to convey. But the marquis was not to harvest what he
had tried to help to sow. He was still no ambassador, and the time was
coming for those who were. Back in March Stainville and Puysieulx
had already been going over ambassadorial possibilities for both
capitals. Stainville had heard Puysieulx's son-in-law, the Count
d'Estrées, canvassed for Vienna. The French foreign minister
negatived the chances of this ertswhile admirer of the Marquise de
Stainville, as also those of the Duke de Chevreuse, the Duke de
Chaulnes, once cuckolded by Stainville's son, and of the little count's
unfavourite Duke de Duras, described by Puysieulx as 'too young
... and, while possessing much intelligence, he has rather too light a
head for your court'.[26] Two months later the foreign minister
confided to the elder Stainville that he was thinking of the rich
Marquis de Hautefort, a mutual friend for thirty years, and was
confident that his appearance would be redeemed by his character.
Upon being asked, Stainville testified to Puysieulx as to Hautefort's
'extreme gentleness in society, no temper at all, a fund of probity

[24] Marquis de Stainville to Emperor Francis I, Paris, 11 May 1749: Ö.S./H.H.S.,
Lothringisches Hausarchiv 77/177A, and for the following.
[25] Marquis de Puysieulx to Marquis de Stainville, Versailles, 28 May 1749: ibid.
[26] Marquis de Stainville to Emperor Francis I, Paris, 23 Mar. 1749: ibid.

proof against anything, sufficient application'.[27] The writer, however, added to the emperor that Hautefort, tallish, not yet fifty, had 'rather an ugly face, holding himself badly and with an awkward air, a little shortsighted, absent-minded by nature but when it is a question of something said to him he replies better than another'. Stainville's son, as will be seen, was to sum up Hautefort more succinctly.

The Marquis de Stainville helped the Marquis de Puysieulx to recruit the Marquis de Hautefort for Vienna, no arduous task. The two cronies were soon mooting Hautefort's counterpart as Austrian ambassador to France in the person of Kaunitz himself, indicative of Austrian desire for rapprochement. Pending his advent Stainville as usual 'was not even warned'[28] of the arrival in Paris on 17 August 1749 of the successor to the ill-fated de Launay, secretary of embassy Mareschal. Two days later the aggrieved but obliging Stainville presented him to Puysieulx. Austria was at last directly represented again at the court of France. The diminished Marquis de Stainville stayed on through the summer exodus, already fashionable, for the country so that, as he wrote: 'Paris is at present peopled only by foreigners, above all by English, who swarm there.'[29] And a curious episode of English significance had recently refocused international speculation upon this withdrawn diplomatist.

The future Duke de Choiseul reflected French opinion of the period in judging that at Aix-la-Chapelle the French government 'conceded the most humiliating conditions regarding both Dunkirk and the Pretender'.[30] Louis XV abandoned the forlorn cause of Bonnie Prince Charlie, the darling of the Parisian populace, arrested outside the opera on 10 December 1748 in a swoop mounted by Choiseul's old commanding officer, the Duke de Biron. The Young Pretender, who had earlier rejected French entreaties that he should quietly leave the country, thereafter repaired to the papal enclave at Avignon where his angry thoughts apparently turned towards the recent enemy of France.

On 13 July 1749 there was left at the door of the Marquis de Stainville's residence in Paris a double envelope incorrectly addressed to the Count de Stainville. Inside was an anonymous letter to the marquis dated 26 May that year. It purported:

To express the sentiments of a prince in exile so unworthily abandoned by his allies. The zeal which you have shewn to his adherents makes him have this confidence in

---

[27] Marquis de Stainville to Emperor Francis I, Paris, 25 May 1749: Esteri del Granducato di Toscana, vol. 2295/1286, fo. 693 for the following.
[28] Marquis de Stainville to Emperor Francis I, Paris, 21 Aug. 1749: Ö.S./H.H.S., Lothringisches Hausarchiv 77/177A.
[29] Ibid., 28 Sept. 1749.   [30] Choiseul, *Mémoires*, p. 57.

you, Sir. It is a question of knowing if the Emperor or the Queen of Hungary would receive in their states such a prince . . . He is ready to carry a musket for the prince who would be willing to protect a soldier and an honest man. P.S. The reply will reach me at the following address, to Mr. John Douglas – for the attention of M. Waters the elder, Rue de l'Université at Paris.[31]

The downy Marquis de Stainville, whatever he may have guessed, did not answer this letter but copied it to the emperor 'since people who write such letters are capable of inventing replies to them'.[32] It rather looks, though, as if something did lie behind this one. The pope, with a Stuart pretender in each of his territories, was well up in their doings. On 24 September 1749 Benedict XIV was writing to his old crony, the Jacobite Cardinal de Tencin:

Prince Edward . . . has had recourse by letter to the Marquis de Stainville, envoy of the Emperor as Grand Duke of Tuscany, . . . for a refuge for himself in his dominions, at the same time proclaiming his ardent desire to devote himself for ever to his service. We are afraid that the imagination of the prince may be a little heated, and we are much pained by the displeasure which it will awaken in the King his father . . . The King knows how much he owes to France, is hoping to obtain from France the subsistence for his worthy son the cardinal [York].[33]

Benedict concluded that Francis was in no condition to receive his princely applicant. The pope in negotiation with whom the Duke de Choiseul was to win his diplomatic spurs was a shrewd as well as a good man.

If Choiseul's father, as a seasoned diplomat, had friendly enough contacts with the Jacobites, he remained correctly loyal to the British ally and now reestablished relations with one of the chief suppressors of the Jacobite cause. The Marquis de Stainville reported that on 30 July 1749 'Lord Albemarle had his first audiences . . . at Compiègne. I have renewed with him an acquaintanceship of 32 years'[34] dating from the Englishman's education at Duke Leopold's academy at Lunéville. The Earl of Albemarle now recalled the good duke's kindness to him. Since he and Stainville first met back in 1717 Albemarle, of medium build and looks, had been Governor of Virginia, a lucrative sinecure, had been ranged against Stainville's

---

[31] Enclosure in Marquis de Stainville to Emperor Francis I, Paris, 13 July 1749: *u.s.*

[32] Marquis de Stainville to Emperor Francis I, Paris, 13 July 1749: ibid.

[33] Pope Benedict XIV to Cardinal de Tencin, Rome, 24 Sept. 1749: *Le lettere di Benedetto XIV al Card. de Tencin*, ed. Emilia Morelli (Rome, 1955 f.: henceforth cited as Benedetto-Tencin), ii. 200–1. (Since publication of this modern edition of this correspondence has not been completed, I reluctantly resort, by advice of its editress, where necessary to the earlier and less satisfactory edition: Émile de Heeckeren, *Correspondance de Benoît XIV* – Paris, 1912: henceforth cited as Benoît-Tencin.)

[34] Marquis de Stainville to Emperor Francis I, Paris, 3 Aug. 1749: Esteri del Granducato di Toscana, vol. 2295/1286, fo. 717.

son upon the days of Dettingen and Lawfeldt, between which he had also figured gallantly at Fontenoy and at Culloden, carrying on from the Duke of Cumberland's subsequent butchery as British Commander-in-Chief in Scotland, in the Low Countries in the last phase of 1748 as a lieutenant-general, colonel of the Coldstreams, Knight of the Garter and, now, postwar British ambassador to Paris. This earl of Dutch extraction had done better than the marquis from Lorraine.

If the Marquis de Stainville regained a friend through British diplomacy, the Count de Stainville was now to lose one through circumstances with another British bearing.

IV

The close friendship of the Count de Stainville contributed towards the Baron von Bernstorff's delightful incorporation in French society. Still more important were his tender ties with the Duchess de Belle-Isle and his long friendship with Madame de Pompadour. So Bernstorff was trying to avert the looming prospect of his succeeding Schulin as foreign minister in hyperborean Copenhagen. By March 1750 Count Schulin, in writing to him, was resigning himself to losing the successor he desired. But King Frederick V insisted upon a visit at least from Bernstorff, whom he had not seen since his accession. Bernstorff was packing for this temporary departure from Paris when he heard that Schulin, still in his fifties, had suddenly died on 13 April.

Bernstorff's future came closing in. The call of Danish duty would now be much harder to resist, at all events without divulging the concealed reason against it. During the preceding winter Bernstorff had received a message by a very secret channel from Frederick, Prince of Wales, who had been keeping an eye on him from afar. He was now reminded that his patrimonial estate at Wotersen was a fief of Lauenburg and himself a vassal of Hanover. The baron was not asked to relinquish his Danish legation but only to forgo the more binding commitment by contemporary canons of assuming office in Copenhagen. Because, intimated the Prince of Wales, in the quite likely event of his soon succeeding his hated father he proposed to make Bernstorff his chief minister in Hanover in an about-turn from the Münchhausen regime to match a new ministry in England. Such was the Hanoverian design of the Prince of Wales whose contradiction of George II, however, began that English orientation which was to be projected by George III.

Bernstorff little wished to be plunged into the dynastic broils of England. The Hanoverian offer was more flattering than attractive. He had concluded years ago that his ambitions called for wider scope now that his homeland had been reduced to an English province. His fatherland it yet remained, and now his German fidelity, his personal honour, had brooked no doubt. Baron von Bernstorff had secretly promised the Prince of Wales that he would be his man. That was what would now need a little explaining to King Frederick V of Denmark. On 28 April 1750 Bernstorff took leave of King Louis XV and his queen, who once said that she had never met a more lovable person than 'the little baron'.

Such was the international straddle of the eighteenth century then exercising Bernstorff, rather as his friend Stainville had earlier been torn at a lower level between larger countries, Austria and France. Back in Denmark, Bernstorff, reported the French minister there, soon became 'the oracle of the king and the spoilt child of the crowd'.[35] No later than 1 July the Count de Stainville was assuring his friend 'that we are all plunged into grief by your letter of the 13th June'[36] indicating that he would not be returning after all. So now Stephen de Stainville, already writing weekly to Nivernais and his wife, was embarking upon another of the most intimate correspondences of his life. The best correspondents are often produced by the loneliness of being single, or left.

For Stainville now there was nothing comparable to the glittering competition for Bernstorff's services in the highest offices at the age of thirty-seven. Stainville's other friends and acquaintances were moving up in what were still for him unpenetrated fields of politics and diplomacy. With Nivernais already in Rome, Stainville was writing in his next letter of 9 July 1750 to Bernstorff of the forthcoming departure for Vienna of the selfconsciously noble Marquis de Hautefort, delayed by the invariable difficulties of protocol, not least with the house of Lorraine. 'The French ambassador will go to the apartments of the archdukes and archduchesses, and will not see Prince Charles [of Lorraine] nor the princess [Charlotte], consequently no Royal Highness.'[37] And Stainville, who wrote more of politics to Bernstorff than to his still closer friend Nivernais, had closed his preceding letter of 1 July: 'Madame de Mirepoix left on Saturday for Lorraine, where she

[35] Abbé Lemaire to Marquis de Puysieulx, Copenhagen, 22 Sept. 1750: Comte Edouard de Barthélemy, *Histoire des relations de la France et du Danemarck sous le ministère du comte de Bernstorff, 1751–70* (Copenhagen, 1887), p. 25.
[36] Count de Stainville to Baron von Bernstorff, Paris, 1 July 1750: *Bernstorffske Papirer*, ii. 634 (there misdated 1751).
[37] Ibid., 9 July 1750, p. 618.

expects to stay only two months. M. de Mirepoix is established at Vaugirard where, I think, he is a little lonely',[38] but not for long. Stainville's old acquaintance as French ambassador at Vienna before the War of the Austrian Succession was, now that it was over, packing up to leave as ambassador to London in counterpart to the Earl of Albemarle.

In the same letter of 1 July 1750 the Count de Stainville wrote to his Danish confidant:

I am no further on in what I told you of; I have not been to Compiègne since I wrote to you, and shall only go in eight or ten days; what I do know is that Madame de Pompadour has spoken of it very favourably to my father; in decency I am not shewing too much eagerness. I am astonished by what you tell me upon this head, which makes you incline to Naples. I have dreamt of it, and I do not understand it; if I get this commission, there I shall be further away from you than ever.

By the end of the month Stainville was adding:

I believe that the business which I told you of is for Naples; I even believe it to be fairly advanced. However it is not concluded, and indeed there is nothing absolutely decided. Thus I do not regard it as certain but as the more agreeable, indeed, if it succeeds since you are interesting yourself in it. I am so much afraid of [interception in] the post that, although there is no harm in all this, I do not dare to explain to you all that was said and done on this head, but what I can assure you is that so soon as I am certain of something, you will be the first to be informed of it. In this part of the world[39] I am with the greatest care hiding everything that can relate to this mission, and up till now nobody suspects it. I would wish, if it takes place, that that holds till the departure.[40]

In this he was to be doubly disappointed. Once again, though, Stainville was insistent upon secrecy. Aristocratic existence at court was a natural school for diplomatists. And diplomacy in peacetime matched leadership in war for the pick of the nobility.

So the Count de Stainville was already preparing in stealth for the next step in his career, up to the rank of ambassador. And it now appears that at least as early as June 1750 the interest of Madame de Pompadour in his career was being mobilized in concert with her friend, Baron von Bernstorff, and with the Marquis de Stainville, in diplomacy as in war more concerned with promoting his son's advancement than one would infer from the latter's write-off of his father. The Count de Stainville, never one to neglect the distaff side, was also keeping well in just then with the foreign minister's wife. He had talked a lot with the Marquise de Puysieulx that July about the next stage in the career of Bernstorff. On this the baron was assured by his friend: 'You have many more friends and admirers here than

[38] Ibid., 1 July 1750, p. 635 for the following.   [39] i.e. at court (dans ce pays-cy).
[40] Ibid., 27 July 1750, pp. 618–19 for the following.

you could have imagined ... There is nothing so agreeable [as] to hear those of whom one is fond being praised, and there is nothing so uncommon in this part of the world.'

V

Chance or not, the future Choiseul's earliest aspiration in diplomacy can now be seen already directed towards the Latin south, to a Bourbon embassy within that family compact which was later to supply a mainstay of his foreign policy. Italy was already engaging his attention, not Naples alone but also those papal relations which may have figured particularly owing to his friendship with Nivernais, and which were in fact to provide his diplomatic debut. A few days after his preceding letter the Count de Stainville, never much of a huntsman, was reporting northwards: 'The only talk at present is of hunting in the various captaincies of the chase. The king is going there next week to hunt and sup with the captains. Otherwise there is not the slightest news, for there is no talk, as you can well imagine, of the disputes between the republic of Venice and the pope.'[41]

Papal relations with the Venetian republic had for centuries produced the habitual rubs between competing, still more, adjacent Italian states. In 1749 papal accommodation with Venice had just about assuaged some fifteen years of border-dispute in the rich reaches of Ferrara, only to yield place to that more complex contention over the patriarchate of Aquileia which apparently interested the Count de Stainville more than other Frenchmen.

The ancient seat of Aquileia by the northern shores of the Adriatic lay in Austrian territory but its ecclesiastical jurisdiction straddled into Venetian Friuli where the patriarch, regularly Venetian, had long resided at Udine. So centuries of Austro–Venetian strife had signalled yet another international dispute engendered by the emergence of nation-states to cut across the ancient intricacies of feudal and ecclesiastical jurisdictions. The spiritual needs of the imperial population were left to an archdeacon while episcopal functions were nominally performed by the nuncio in Vienna, in useful collusion with the patriarch. This had lately broken down and the Venetians had encouraged papal intervention, 'flattering them-selves', remarked Benedict XIV, 'that we should follow the example of some of our Predecessors, who did not think it opportune to displease the Venetians.'[42] They had misjudged a rare pontiff who

---

[41] Count de Stainville to Baron von Bernstorff, Paris, 1 Aug. 1750: ibid., p. 620.
[42] Pope Benedict XIV to Cardinal de Tencin, Rome, 29 Apr. 1750: Benedetto-Tencin, ii. 268.

put pastoral before political considerations. With no animus against either party to the dispute, Benedict had reiterated that 'we have no other aim but that of not leaving these souls [in Austrian Aquileia] without spiritual government'.[43]

Benedict XIV had accordingly revived a project of Urban VIII and on 29 November 1749 issued a brief authorizing in principle, as a temporary solution, the appointment of a vicar apostolic with the character of a bishop *in partibus* to reside in Gorizia. If the nerveless Patriarch Delphini of Aquileia merely meekly protested, not so the dominant faction at Venice, spearheaded at Rome by Cardinal Quirini. Setting his fellow cardinals by the ears, he created such a hullabaloo that Benedict was writing to Tencin on 24 June 1750: 'If we eat, we are eating Aquileia, if we are asleep we are dreaming Aquileia, if we want to read anything, here comes a note about Aquileia.'[44]

Three days later the pope, having secured imperial assent to his earlier brief, issued a brief of establishment whereby a canon of Basel, Karl von Attems, was appointed vicar apostolic of Gorizia. Benedict had quietly gone ahead in the face of persuasions and threats to which, as he explained, 'we have always replied that we had nothing to fear either in life or after death; we did not ascend to the Supreme Pontificate by the devious road of flattery and intrigues, and not wishing that our own family, after our death, should be anything more than it was when we left Bologna to come to the conclave':[45] that classic conclave of 1740 which had lasted for more than six months, longer than any since the Great Schism, and had, in the two hundred and fifty-fifth scrutiny, elected as successor to Clement XII one who in the two hundred and fifty-fourth had not received a single vote, the learned but humble Cardinal Prospero Lambertini, Archbishop of Bologna, Pope Benedict XIV.

The Venetian authorities protested vehemently against the papal brief of 27 June 1750. Benedict commented that his vicar apostolic would be proceeding to Gorizia 'despite all the contrary cackling: only what displeases us is that if the [Venetian] protest falls into the hands of the Germans, who are offensively treated in it, they will not fail to reply ferociously in wretched Latin, which nevertheless will not fail to be understood'.[46] The Venetian republic withdrew its ambassador from Rome and was shortly to expel the nuncio. Such was the tense position when the Count de Stainville wrote of it at the

[43] Pope Benedict XIV to Cardinal de Tencin, Castel Gandolfo, 11 June 1749: ibid., ii. 166.
[44] Ibid., 24 June 1750, ii. 285.
[45] Pope Benedict XIV to Cardinal de Tencin, Rome, 1 July 1750: ibid., ii 289.
[46] Ibid., 15 July 1750, ii. 294.

beginning of August in that Holy Year of 1750. Subsequently French mediation was to assist the substantial solution of the inveterate dispute within a couple of years though Venetian spite envenomed its aftermath right through the pontificate of Benedict XIV and the embassy to Rome of the Count de Stainville.

If the just are rewarded, so, often, are the artful. The pope's stand over Aquileia likely contributed to his eventual success in another border-dispute, this time with the Emperor Francis I arising from the recent death without heir of the Count of Carpegna, a papal district backing on to Tuscany and occupied now by Tuscan troops in fulfilment, maintained Francis, of his coronation-oath to the German princes 'to claim the imperial fiefs which exist in Italy'.[47] Thus did the medieval contest in Italy between the two great dominations of the christian world linger on into the height of the eighteenth century. And a larger international question just then was the election of a King of the Romans.

In April 1750 the Marquis de Stainville's old friend, Count Henry de Richecourt, for some months now the imperial minister in London, received an overture from the austrophil Duke of Newcastle towards promoting the election of the little Archduke Joseph to be King of the Romans. Richecourt that summer accompanied George II to Hanover where Münchhausen pursued the imperial project more keenly than the Austrians themselves. The Emperor Francis was not thrilled by the prospect of his more German son coming up on him, while the Empress Maria Theresa scouted those further concessions which, as she shrewdly anticipated, would be the price of electoral suffrages for Joseph. She was understandably suspicious of British tactics after the treaties of Breslau, Worms, and Aix-la-Chapelle. Sure enough the British government, which had merely wished to ingratiate itself with Maria Theresa, was soon irritating her by actually arguing on behalf of France's client, the Elector Palatine, over his claims which had got elbowed out at Aix. And there was other sterile haggling. Such was the diplomatic ineptitude of the Duke of Newcastle within the labyrinths of the Holy Roman Empire. The future Emperor Joseph II was to wait another fourteen years for that Roman title of kingship which he then held for not much more than one.

By October 1750 young Stainville was writing to Bernstorff: 'The politicians are discussing three subjects: the election of a King of the Romans, the pretensions in America of the English, who, from what is said, are sustaining them with stubbornness and injustice; and the eternal business of the north. I believe that on all these heads it would

[47] Ibid., 20 Aug. 1749, ii. 191.

ill become me to reason with my master.'[48] Stainville did not call a man his master for nothing – he never did so to Nivernais. In politics the future foreign minister of France began as a pupil of the future foreign minister of Denmark.

The eternal business of the north was to be that of the Baron von Bernstorff for the next twenty years. Indeed developments after the northern crisis of March 1749 had largely centred upon Denmark. On 14 August following she had, to the consternation of the Anglo–Russian camp, concluded a subsidy-agreement with France. Denmark also entered into a treaty of friendship with Sweden whose governing Hats, agreed the Crown Prince Adolphus Frederick, persuaded by his wife, should renounce his possible claims in Schleswig-Holstein in exchange for the outlying Danish principalities of Oldenburg and Delmenhorst plus a financial sweetener. This *mageskifte* dear to Danish policy had led through towards an initiative in 1750 by Tessin for Sweden and Bernstorff for Denmark to do better than their predecessors in allying the royal families. This was warmly welcomed by the King of Denmark. The Swedish royal couple were indeed less enthusiastic about the imposed betrothal of their four-year-old son Gustavus to the Danish Princess Royal.

By 1750 British and Russian policy had lost out not only in Sweden but in Denmark too. This largely reflected, yet again in European politics, the ascendancy of France. Her Swedish client of tradition was now doubled up with Denmark. The Marquis de Puysieulx was justly confident that 'the system of the late M. de Schulin'[49] would now be followed by Bernstorff for whom the French hegemony from the high days of Louis XIV seemed anything but over. The northern crisis of the preceding year had thrown Frederick the Great himself back upon France, still preponderant in such lesser German courts as that of the Elector Palatine. All this added up to a large bloc interested in maintaining peace in Europe under a French aegis embracing the Three Fredericks of the north, King Frederick I of Sweden, Frederick II of Prussia and Frederick V of Denmark. Because the Marquis de Puysieulx and the Count de Saint-Séverin were not brilliant figures it is too often forgotten that, after the War of the Austrian Succession as before it, France stood impressively predominant in Europe. That did not apply overseas, a heavy drag on France's future, as Choiseul was to emphasize in his castigation, already noticed, of the two earlier statesmen for their failure at Aix-la-

---

[48] Count de Stainville to Baron von Bernstorff, Paris, 8 Oct. 1750: *Bernstorffske Papirer*, ii. 627.

[49] Marquis de Puysieulx to Abbé Lemaire, 2 July 1750: Count Edouard de Barthélemy, op. cit., p. 22.

Chapelle to define the frontiers of Canada. And so early as 1750 the future Choiseul was observing developments in America.

If the Count de Stainville now modestly forbore from treating Bernstorff to an American commentary, in after years he furnished an authoritative sketch of what resulted from the failure at Aix-la-Chapelle to clarify and clinch that American settlement of Utrecht which had notably subjected to British rule the French inhabitants of Acadia, sundering them from their compatriots to the west in Quebec and to the north in contested Louisbourg, now just restored to France and being fortified more strongly than ever as her strategic hold over the misty waters of the North Atlantic.

Choiseul explained that, armed with the ambiguities of Aix, the English 'invaded the borders of Canada and the territories occupied by our establishments along the banks of the Ohio'. For the English he allowed:

Their colonies in America were much threatened by ours, because they [the French] were busy at that time with the execution of a plan which was already an old one; it consisted in establishing, first by way of the lakes and then by a chain of forts and settlements, a communication between Canada and Louisiana. I do not know how the knowledge of this project reached the English ministry. It was pained to see that the French settlements were disposed in such a way that the English colonists could no longer cross the Appalachian Mountains, and that all the western part of America, occupied by savage tribes, would in the long run be subject to our domination. So the English ministry began encroaching upon Canada directly after the peace in order not to allow us time to collect ourselves.[50]

It would be difficult to find a statement of the mid-eighteenth-century strategy of France in North America that was clearer, more concise, more authoritative, coming as it did from the very captain of French opposition to English expansion overseas. Choiseul's analysis was also characteristically fair. He in no way disguised the provocation of France's grand design even if, in the Canadian section, he emphasized the forward policy of Britain rather than of France. The two were already on collision-course.

From Cape Breton the French sought to protect their communications overland to Quebec by planting Fort Beauséjour on the very neck of Acadia, where the British government for its part in 1749 founded the port of Halifax in what became the new colony of Nova Scotia under Governor Cornwallis. The British administration had for a generation applied politic leniency to the *habitants* of Acadia. Their dominance threatened now by the thud of British axes chopping inland, the French settlers were especially incited, or cowed, by the militant Abbé Le Loutre and his pack of nominally

[50] Choiseul, 'Mémoires inédits', 2/16/8/498/1.

catholicized Indians like the Mic-Macs. If the Acadians responded insufficiently to the fear of hellfire for acquiescing in the heretic rule of the British, the Mic-Macs still enjoyed a bit of scalping on the side. The Governor-General of Canada, doughty La Galissonnière in Quebec, had primed a comeback against the British not only in the maritime east but continentally, way down south.

The end of the War of the Austrian Succession, King George's War in America, had found the English probing out from the Appalachians, their fur-traders penetrating French preserves from such posts as Pickawillany upon the Miami river, over beyond the Ohio. So in 1749 La Galissonnière sent a notable little expedition under Céloron de Blainville, formerly commanding at Detroit, to toil right through the wilderness to the forks of the Ohio, clamping down leaden plates of sovereignty, nailing shields to trees so that remote forests glinted with the lilies of France. Already, though, it was beginning to be more than just a question of sending some English traders packing. By 1750 English settlements were in places spilling over the western slopes of the Appalachian Mountains. Out ahead now lay a fertile emptiness, those stretching lands of the Ohio that invited land-investment by colonial magnates and purposeful surveying by the commercial English.[51]

Such were the conflicting pressures to give definition to the great criss-cross of vague claims and aspirations athwart North America: a horizontal claim by the English to whatever lay westward within the parallels of their seaboard colonies, and a vertical claim by the French, heirs to La Salle's early explorations, to all the basin of the Mississippi with headwaters up to Lake Erie. Already the sharpening pattern was beginning to look like the crossed swords of conflict renewed, conflict of heavy destiny for the policy of the Duke de Choiseul.

[51] Cf. especially Frank Thistlethwaite, 'Rivalries in America' in *The New Cambridge Modern History* (Cambridge, 1957), vii. 528 f.

CHAPTER IV

DOMESTIC

I

CHOISEUL recalled:

After the peace the only concern in France was with court intrigues. That is natural enough in every court wherein a weak king has a mistress and ambitious ministers. Madame de Pompadour had more confidence now in one minister, now in another, which produced jealousy between them. The entourage of the mistress sought to form her impressions in accordance with their passions. Among the ministers there was one, Monsieur de Maurepas, who in the mind of Madame de Pompadour was excelled by Monsieur d'Argenson, his rival. They put it into the head of the mistress that this minister wounded her vanity at every word. Monsieur de Maurepas rather assisted the intrigue of his enemies by helping with the composition of songs which were written against Madame de Pompadour; and in these songs the King was featured with the ridiculousness which was his. A Madame d'Estrades, who had come to court in the train of Madame de Pompadour by title of relationship, had had a discussion with Monsieur de Maurepas for a position with the princesses. She had not been at all pleased with the minister's replies. She was given over to Monsieur d'Argenson and became the mainspring of the intrigue to undo Monsieur de Maurepas. It was not very difficult, after the business of the songs, to injure him and to give Madame de Pompadour the courage to turn the King effectively against this minister.[1]

The bleak analysis continued:

Since Monsieur de Richelieu must needs try to enter into all the nasty intrigues of the court, he repeated the ugly language which he had held some years previously, namely that Monsieur de Maurepas had poisoned Madame de Châteauroux, thus giving it to be understood that Madame de Pompadour should fear the same fate. They caused to arrive a box full of contrivances and acid, which was brought to Madame de Pompadour as though this box contained jewels. Somebody primed put to Madame de Pompadour the atrocious reflection that it was not prudent to open this box without precautions ... They masked a valet, who with infinite precautions opened this dangerous casket, and they found there what those [conspirators] ... all knew well, namely powder and glass phials which, in breaking, caused an explosion. Then poor Madame de Pompadour did not doubt that they had wanted to assassinate her, and, amid her fear and her prepossessions, it was very easy to persuade her that Monsieur de Maurepas was the author of this infernal project. I believe for sure that the idea of the intrigue of the casket came from [the younger] Monsieur de Maillebois, so well known since for his dark and dishonest intrigues, for in this sort he is still deeper than Monsieur de Richelieu.

[1] Choiseul, *Mémoires*, pp. 58–60 for the following.

When the Count de Maillebois, son of the marshal and son-in-law of the Marquis d'Argenson, was subsequently chief of staff to the Marshal d'Estrées, he was accused of disloyal manoeuvring in action from perfidious ambition, was disgraced, and confined in the citadel of Doullens.

Choiseul continued his indictment: 'The King could not bear up against the fright of his mistress, supported by such likely facts. Monsieur de Maurepas, who had intelligence, probity, an infinity of useful knowledge as to the court and the administration of Paris – Monsieur de Maurepas, who was agreeable to the King, who had been his minister for thirty years, was dismissed and exiled.' All unsuspecting, he was so notified by the Count d'Argenson about eight o'clock on the morning of Thursday, 24 April 1749. At that hour the Duke de Richelieu was at the Parliament of Paris for a formal reception of the Marshal de Belle-Isle as a peer of the realm. Richelieu, who had further fallen foul of Maurepas over his abortive expedition to Britain, looked beside himself with glee.

Choiseul added:

Some months[2] previously Monsieur de Maurepas, foreseeing that he would succumb, tired of a ministerial office subject to intrigue, depicted to the King, during a working session, his disgust and the event which he foresaw. In consequence he asked the King for permission to quit his ministry and represented to him that it seemed to him impossible that the King should uphold him; that when he should abandon him, he [Louis] would believe, so as to justify it, that he [Maurepas] had displeased him; that it would grieve him [Maurepas] that he [Louis] should think this .... This language and this resolve of Monsieur de Maurepas were those of a wise man. The King praised him much for his services, insisted upon his remaining, assured him that if subsequently there were something in his conduct which displeased him, then he promised to let him know of it ... Some weeks later, at the moment when he least expected it, he received the King's letter which exiled him. It began with these words: Monsieur de Maurepas, I have promised you to let you know when your services should no longer please me. I order you to give your resignation, etcetera, to the Count d'Argenson, and you will proceed to Bourges, where you will remain until further orders on my part.[3]

Choiseul, whose own ministerial experience of Louis XV was to be not wholly dissimilar, explained that this episode 'has singularly struck me and it depicts not only the weakness of the King, but his falsity and malignity when he has the pleasure of having the courage to hurt'.

Choiseul, later the great friend of Madame de Pompadour, was to

---

[2] 'Quelques ans', ibid, is a misreading of 'quelques mois' in Choiseul, 'Mémoires de la main' fo. 28 (cf. 'quelques semaines' below, p. 61 and fo. 28 v.). Nor are the inverted commas printed ibid p. 60 present in the original on fo. 28.

[3] Choiseul, *Mémoires*, pp. 60–1 for the following.

be exceptionally placed for verifying this story, which is substantially borne out. The sober Luynes, for instance, adds that the unpleasantness between Maurepas and Madame d'Estrades led to a scene wherein Madame de Pompadour called him 'a liar and a rogue'.[4] From that proceeded an enmity so great that she was saying almost openly that he wanted to poison her. Choiseul, writing in another context of this murky affair, did moderate his encomium upon Maurepas down to his having been 'a bad and even a very bad Minister of State and of the Marine, but a fairly good minister for Paris and the royal household'.[5] As to his alleged designs against the favourite, however, Choiseul added:

It is astonishing that a gentle and good person like Madame de Pompadour should have had the pusillanimity to believe it, and that the king should have had the weakness not to dissuade her and to yield to the wickedness as though he believed it. Doubtless it is vexatious for a state that its sovereign should be born with a weak character; but the weakness which merits the most contempt and which removes all idea of a sentiment of honour in a prince is when, against his personal conviction, he submits to the weaknesses of those who surround him, and lends his authority to the most odious and most punishable calumny ... From the acquaintance that I have had with Louis XV, the wish of Madame de Pompadour, the weakness of the king and the calumny of the poison would have sufficed to have the whole council exiled. Thus, if Monsieur de Maurepas diverted himself, as I do not doubt that he did, at the supper at which those songs were made up, he has nothing to reproach himself with; for he did not advance his disgrace by this giddiness, even though one could say that it was of a major kind.

It was by a heartless combination that the intriguers had triumphed. Neither the Duke de Richelieu nor the subtler Count d'Argenson, nor indeed the treacherous Countess d'Estrades, was truly the friend of the exploited Madame de Pompadour.

A true friend to the queen, who was undergoing a change of life about then, had been the Count de Maurepas. Now she disobliged the king by crying for two days on end; and little Amelot de Chaillou, who had been killing himself in retirement by overeating, died of grief as well a fortnight after the exile of his protector. Honest Puysieulx, still foreign minister, earned disfavour by reacting adversely. The Count d'Argenson, still minister of war, picked up perhaps the most influential part of Maurepas's multiple portfolio, the superintendence of Paris. There he curried favour with the lieutenant-general of police, Berryer, a protégé of Madame de Pompadour. Another was Rouillé, who succeeded Maurepas as Minister of Marine, allegedly in accordance with a long design of Pâris-Monmartel, still a power behind the royal mistress. Rouillé,

---

[4] Luynes, x, 117, n. 1.   [5] Choiseul, *Mémoires*, pp. 371–2 for the following.

whose path was to cross that of the Count de Stainville, was an honest little man, rich, elderly, delicate. In that ministerial carve-up of Maurepas's estate the third main slice went to diminutive Saint-Florentin, who was to exercise long sway over the royal household. He, Rouillé, and Puysieulx were christened by the embittered Marquis d'Argenson the 'three dwarfs, and very ugly'.[6] In the French government it was still mainly the season of little men. The wife of Saint-Florentin was to figure as the mistress of the biggest man among them, Machault d'Arnouville, still controller-general.

II

Machault, no unworthy successor to Orry, sought to overhaul the postwar financing of French government, to bring to book the peculation of such farmers-general as Lallemant de Betz. Their general farm of taxes now provided just over 100 million livres out of the total French revenue of 230 million, compared with the 200 million of a decade earlier. If wartime levies on wax, tallow, copper, paper, hair-powder were suppressed early in February 1749, those which hurt most, as on butter, eggs, and wood, were retained. This, together with abominable weather, helped to dampen rejoicing on the twelfth of that month when the end of seven years of war for France was formally proclaimed with pomp in Paris under the auspices of Berryer and Bernage, as Prévôt des Marchands the chief magistrate of the municipality. At the close of the proclamations the popular response to *Vive le Roi* was thin, the king next day was unexpectedly absent from the Te Deum at Notre-Dame, and in the ensuing celebrations, remarked the Marquis de Stainville, 'everything went off in the most gloomy silence'.[7]

As with indirect taxation so, rather, with direct under Machault. He was now bound by a royal promise to end the wartime Dixième but, by the decrees of Marly of May 1749, he slapped on the Vingtième, a new tax of five per cent designed to cover a simultaneously announced loan at that rate to meet war debts and also to service a sinking-fund. This innovation in time of peace opened up an endless vista of direct taxation; the Vingtième was moreover a comprehensive levy whereby Machault sought to correct the inequitable incidence of such other imposts as the *taille* upon the little man rather than the big, Pays d'Élections rather than Pays d'États. The Vingtième was designed to levy five per cent upon the

---

[6] D'Argenson, v. 475.
[7] Marquis de Stainville to Emperor Francis I, Paris, 16 Feb. 1749: Ö.S./H.H.S., Lothringisches Hausarchiv 77/177A.

incomes of all alike, regardless of birth or condition, upon income
from real and personal property, sale of offices, commerce and
industry. To attempt such a bold sweep under the old regime was to
court resistance and evasion at every turn. The Parliament of Paris
finally registered the decree of the Vingtième only under constraint
by royal injunction, and that was far from the end of it, as was soon
to appear in the Pays d'États of Languedoc and Brittany.

Public resentment of sharper taxation was quickened by increasingly critical appraisal of royal expenditure. At Versailles the
department of the petty pleasures, the Menus Plaisirs, was said to be
costing an annual 2,700,000 livres as against 400,000 under the Roi
Soleil. It was said that the King's fondness for building cost him as
much per foot of masonry as six foot would cost a private person. The
royal household, excluding its ceremonial military, absorbed some
twenty-five millions a year, nearly a tenth of the total revenue and
more than the whole French navy even with its increased estimates
for 1749 of twenty million, rather less than half the peacetime cost of
the army. Poor Rouillé, the new Minister of Marine, lamented to
Luynes 'that he had found debts for 21 to 22 millions outstanding
upon the funds of the marine, of which about 12 millions were to
various contractors, and 8 or 9 millions due since four or five years
back to unhappy sailors, who were dying of hunger ... M. Rouillé
gave me all these particulars with tears in his eyes.'[8]

There was some attempt, indeed, to popularize the neglected navy
and Louis XV was actually persuaded to forsake his palatial round
for a few days in September 1749 in order to visit Le Havre, then
with a population of around 24,000. On the return he stopped off to
see Belle-Isle's residence at Bizy. The royal party included the royal
mistress. Her nautical initiative subsided into an unpopularity that
was acquiring new intensity. Everything, economic or political,
tended to be blamed upon the woman who monopolized the king,
who had acted Europa for him in an operatic piece at Versailles on
the evening that he had cut the Te Deum for victory in Paris. Next
month the Marquise de Pompadour was reported to be 'continually
in tears',[9] a month later again, in April 1749, to have had a
miscarriage – at least her third since her favour, it was said. The lewd
lampoons against her ominously began to embrace him whom she
had rendered no longer Bien-Aimé:

Lache dissipateur des biens de tes sujets,
Toi qui compte les jours par les maux que tu fais,

---

[8] Luynes, x. 141.   [9] D'Argenson, v. 425.

Esclave d'un ministre et d'une femme avare . . .
Tu verras chaque instant ralentir notre zèle,
Et souffler dans nos coeurs une flamme rebelle.
De guerres sans succès fatiguant les États,
Tu fus sans généraux, tu seras sans soldats . . .
Crains de voir bientôt sur toi fondre l'orage:
Des maux contagieux empoisonnent les airs.[10]

The reign of Louis XV was already turning sour in a hangover from wartime distress. Great wars are great looseners, of politics as of economics, and morals. Parisian increase in cost of living nourished popular criticism, a new self-awareness. By May 1750 the Marquis d'Argenson was writing: 'When the people fears nothing, it is everything.'[11] This pregnant reflection was prompted by an extraordinary outbreak in Paris of mob-violence against the arrest of stray children, common enough with mangy ragamuffins, apt to be abandoned if their parents could not feed them, but a very different matter in regard to respectable 'artisans' children whom they returned to their parents for twenty livres'.[12] That, now, was one story among many, that it was wished to populate the Mississippi, that the new minister for Paris, the Count d'Argenson, was seeking to stamp out vagrancy by abductions which, remarked Barbier in his detailed account, 'offend nature and the law of nations'.[13] If Barbier, unlike the Marquis d'Argenson, was in Paris during the disorders, so was the Count de Stainville, hitherto an unheard witness.

On 25 May 1750 Stainville wrote to Nivernais:

In the last few days we have had kinds of barricades in Paris. M. Berryer, in accordance with old and reasonable custom, has had the police constables pick up vagrant children and little scamps who were playing in the streets. In doing so he was only following a police-regulation which has been in force for more than thirty years and which seems very sensible, for these little libertines can only become good-for-nothings and it is the seed-ground for thieves. It may well be that in executing this these constables, who are vulgarly called bum-pushers (*pousse cul*) and who have not the best reputation in the world, may have abused their orders a little and that the bait of six francs per capture, which they gave them, may have made them extend their functions too far . . . What is sure, however, is that they have returned them so soon as they have been claimed, and since the first riot . . . about ten days ago it is further certain that they have not taken one.[14]

Nevertheless, continued Stainville:

There has spread among the populace an infinity of fables of every kind, as for instance that they were taking the children so as to cut their throats and provide a

[10] Ibid., p. 402, n. 1.   [11] Ibid., vi. 205.
[12] Luynes, x. 266.   [13] Barbier, iv. 422
[14] Count de Stainville to Duke de Nivernais, 25 May 1750: W.N.A., docket V/1, fos. 28–9 for the following.

bath of blood for a leprous prince. You know how things that are likely and rational promptly spread among the common people. That moved their tempers to ferment and a spirit of sedition which produced effect. On Friday there were four riots in various districts, several men killed, houses pillaged. The watch and the police no longer dared shew themselves . . . A man dressed in grey was passing by. Someone took it into his head to say 'There is a police officer in disguise or a spy, there is one of those child-snatchers.' On the spot the populace set upon him and felled him or else if he escaped into a house the luckless fellow had to be rescued, or the house was sacked. Five or six houses of superintendants have been pillaged. Last Saturday M. Berryer was besieged in his house and had his windows broken.

The Count de Stainville added to his vivid and generally accurate account that baseless reports of further child-arrests had continued:

Which would make one think that those rumours were inspired by ill-intentioned people . . . It is even claimed that in some parishes catechisms have been interrupted and that there are priests who have told their parishioners not to let their children go out. However that may be, since I began taking things in I have never seen such a universal spirit of revolt. It has even reached the environs of Paris, where they certainly have not been arresting children. The day before yesterday the Regt. of guards was ordered in and distributed at various street-corners, and since yesterday all is quiet.

An emollient proclamation by the Parliament of Paris helped assuage this obscure upsurge of collective hatred. It was said to have cost at least twelve or fifteen dead or injured, enough to make the Marquis d'Argenson write: 'Here we have the people of Paris become extremely cruel, tearing men like savages.'[15] The full effect of such cruelty was not to be experienced for some decades yet. So sudden and transient was the warning that perhaps only those who had observed it personally, like the Count de Stainville, were likely to recall it. For the present one notices that, humanitarian as he was in general, he was no sentimental rebel against the established order, more of an independent conformist.

III

Stainville's independence of judgement came out in the next paragraph of his letter of 25 May 1750 to Nivernais, concerning another development in the internal politics of France, and one of more immediate consequence. 'Today', wrote Stainville, 'the assembly of the clergy is beginning. It is not yet known how it will go. A week or ten days ago there appeared a book which pulverizes the alleged privileges of the ecclesiastics in the strongest and most solid way. They do not say who the author is. Several people are named but

[15] D'Argenson, vi. 204.

Battle of Lawfeldt.   2 July 1747.

View from the French camp. Maestricht is in the distance at right. At left is the
French command-post upon the heights of Heerderen. King Louis XV, with arm
outstretched, is riding a white horse. At extreme left are French regiments standing
in reserve.

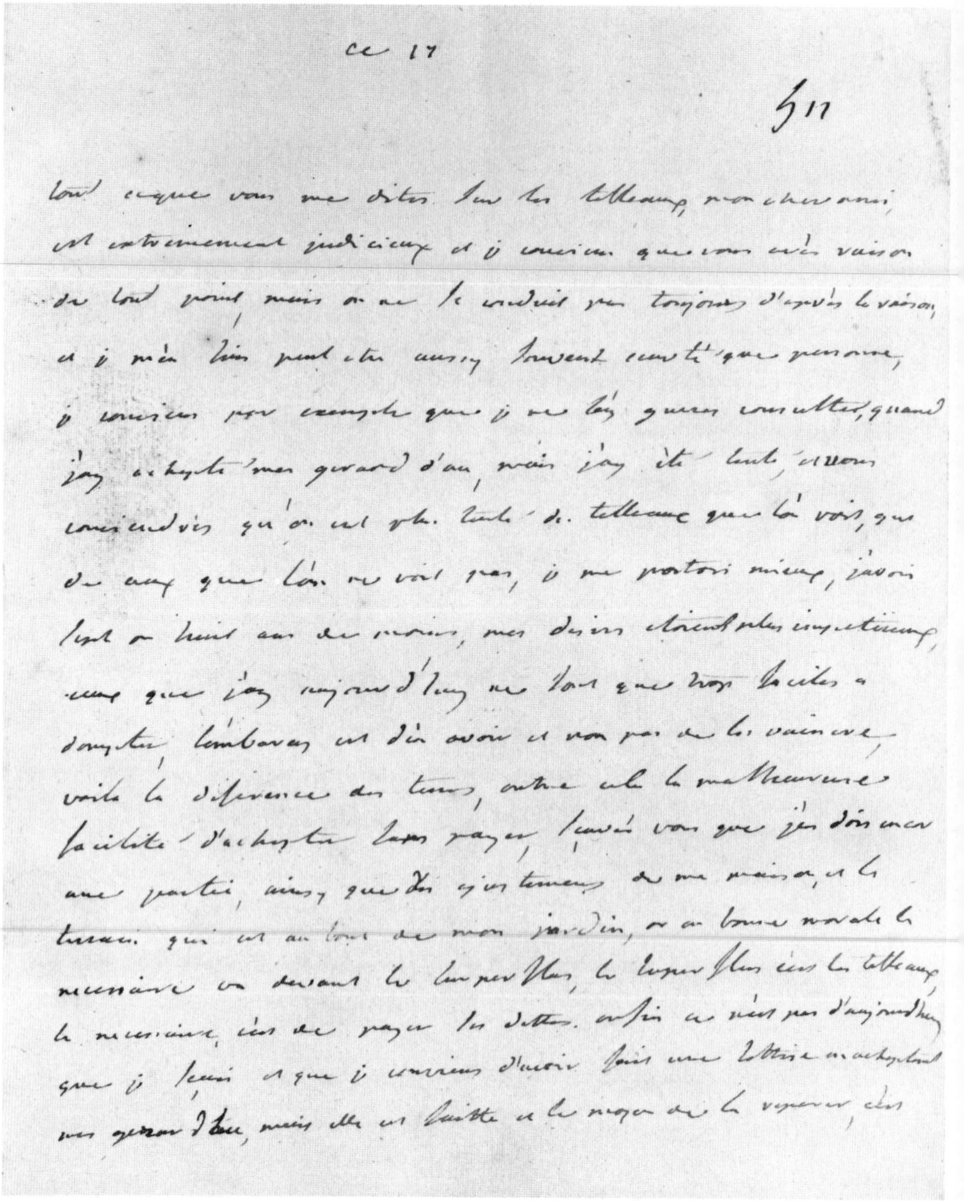

ce 17

511

[handwritten letter text]

Beginning of letter from Count de Stainville to Duke de Nivernais. 17 November 1749.

Begins: 'ce 17   Tout ce que vous me dites sur les tableaux, mon cher ami, est extremement judicieux et je conviens que vous avès raison de tout point, mais on ne se conduit pas toujours d'après la raison, et je m'en suis peut etre aussy souvent ecarté que personne, je conviens par exemple que je ne l'ay gueres consultée, quand j'ay achepté mes gerard d'ou, mais j'ay été tenté . . .' etc.

nobody confesses to it. What is certain is that it is very well done and puts them out of conceit.'[16] This passage is one of the earliest and most illuminating for Stainville's true attitude towards matters ecclesiastical, already within his keen focus.

The background here was the quinquennial assembly of the Gallican Church, if anything a more lively force in the eighteenth century than the Church of England. And the background to that assembly in the Grands-Augustins in Paris was the ecclesiastical aspect of Machault's comprehensive attempt to tune up the decrepit taxation of French resources. He reckoned the annual income of the French clergy at about 250 million livres, more than the budget of the state itself; of this 250 some 114 millions might be accounted properly taxable: so that the church's contribution to public funds, by her traditionally voluntary grants (*dons gratuits*), of about 182 millions since the beginning of the century worked out at less than a thirtieth or three and one third per cent of her taxable revenue. In August 1749 Machault had renewed earlier attempts to limit the sterilization of property by ecclesiastical mortmain and there was already talk of extending his new Vingtième as a flat-rate levy of five per cent on all ecclesiastical income.

In a characteristic complication the assembly of the Gallican Church did not include representation of the so called Foreign Clergy of peripheral and latterday provinces, notably the eastern Three Bishoprics along with Alsace, Hainault, Franche-Comté, Roussillon. Their subventions were, needless to say, organized somewhat differently and it was here that Machault had artfully sought to insert the thin end of his twentieth. The excited Bishop of Verdun invoked the example of Thomas à Becket as the more central clergy urged their outlying brethren not to create a precedent. For an ecclesiastical Vingtième was neatly calculated to increase yield while yet lightening the burden upon parish priests by pegging it at a twentieth of their true income in place of the swingeing tithes liable to be imposed by diocesan assessments – wealth once again silting up at the top end of the old regime.

As usual, again, there were multiple gradations wherein a beneficed Curé retaining his own tithe might do pretty nicely compared with a whole class of vicarial Curés scraping along upon slender stipends, designated with some irony as congruous portions (*portions congrues*), doled out by their rectorial Curé Primitif, often a rich abbey or chapter.[17] Such were the social tensions behind that dim controversy

[16] *u.s.*, fo. 29.
[17] Cf. John McManners, *French Ecclesiastical Society under the Ancien Régime* (Manchester, 1960), *passim*.

over clerical finance and behind one of the few truly popular movements towards reform in eighteenth-century France, the socalled cult of Richerism.

Edmond Richer (1560–1631) had been a turbulent theologian of the catholic faith in the time of the French Wars of Religion, a doctrinal leader of the Sorbonne and the Parliament of Paris, twin champions of gallicanism then as later. This editor of Gerson and author of the tellingly critical *De ecclesiastica et politica postestate* (1611) had evinced affinities that were republican, synodal, against prelatical pre-eminence in favour of a governance of the catholic church by the whole company of its pastors. This gallican version of ecclesiastical democracy significantly persisted, deriving as it did from a source that was rather older, more indigenous than that of popularly styled Jansenism. In eighteenth-century France the inclination of the lower clergy towards Richerism primed the political influence of Jansenism.

In 1727 a practical beginning of Richerist agitation among the parochial clergy had produced an appeal to the king, and now in the swelling controversy of 1750 the Duke de Luynes, brother of the Bishop of Bayeux, denounced radical pamphlets like the Abbé Constantin's *La Voix du prêtre* for their 'destestable maxims of irreligion, of fanaticism, of Richerism'.[18] Another advanced Abbé, the Count de Stainville's friend, the Abbé Chauvelin, was significantly one of those credited with the authorship of the anonymous work which Stainville described to Nivernais that May as pulverizing ecclesiastical privileges. This publication of *Lettres* with the epigraph *Ne repugnate vestro bono* was in fact written by Daniel Bargeton, a leading lawyer of Calvinist stock.

After an early spell in the Bastille for alleged complicity in the Conspiracy of Cellamare, which enabled him to figure as a victim of despotism, Bargeton had latterly been assisting Chancellor d'Aguesseau in his great work of legal reform and was now coming to the aid of Machault. The controller-general had consulted Bargeton about his plans for ecclesiastical taxation. The sympathetic Bargeton is said to have shrewdly advised Machault not to take on the clergy since he estimated, correctly, that in the long run the weak king would let his minister down. But Machault pressed for Bargeton's support so that he was now qualifying priests as the least useful part of the nation, promoting its depopulation. This was no longer ecclesiastical Richerism but legal anticlericalism. The government of eighteenth-century France was already finding anticlerical allies, even before that set against the Jesuits in which, Bargeton

18 Luynes, x. 426.

having meanwhile died, leading parts were to be played by the Abbé
Chauvelin and his early friend, the future Duke de Choiseul. Such is
the interest of the then Count de Stainville's admiration, already, for
Bargeton's anticlericalism.

The Abbé Henri-Philippe Chauvelin, a counsellor in the Parliament of Paris and spokesman there for the Jansenist interest, was a
cousin of another leading parliamentarian, the President Louis
Chauvelin. The Abbé was liable to work in with the President,
himself a nephew of the ever-exiled Germain-Louis Chauvelin, the
former foreign minister. President Chauvelin was a friend of
Machault and it was now said[19] that the president, perhaps his uncle
also, had been in on the controller-general's draft for the royal
declaration of 17 August 1750 to the ecclesiastical assembly. Three
days later the Count de Stainville began a letter to the Baron von
Bernstorff:

At last the king's commissioners have made their proposal to the clergy. Their
address was extremely wise. There was no question either of a 20th or of declarations
[to the Treasury of ecclesiastical revenue] ... His Majesty asks of his clergy an
annual fifteen hundred thousand francs which will be deposited in a sinking fund,
for the discharge of the debts due to the clergy; and as the king owes justice to all the
members of his state, and since he has learnt that the old register which the clergy
were using for its taxes was not just, he desires that the clergy should construct
another more just upon the basis of the declarations which it, the clergy, shall render
to its own representatives; and the king will confer upon this operation his authority,
as has been asked of him by the clergy upon divers occasions. Moreover His Majesty,
asking nothing for himself, wishes that the fifteen hundred thousand francs of the
sinking fund should be levied upon each individual possessing ecclesiastical property
and not in the form of a loan. – There in substance is the memorandum of the
demand, which is very judicious and to which there is very little to reply.[20]

As a minister the later Duke de Choiseul was to make much use of
précis-writers to expedite business. He evidently had himself some
early acquaintance with the art. His chief omission in the present
case was to explain that the royal demand for an annual million and
a half livres was, for the present at least, for five years only, making
seven and a half millions in all. The Count de Stainville continued:

The clergy ... has asked for time ... That is how the matter stands. I forgot to tell
you that in the harangue of the commissioners it is stated that the king, in order to
confer his authority upon the operation of the new register which he wants the clergy

---

[19] By Omer Joly de Fleury of the Parliament of Paris to the Count d'Argenson: cf. J.M.J.
Rogister, 'Conflict and Harmony in Eighteenth-Century France: reappraisal of the nature of
relations between the Crown and the Parliaments under Louis XV (1730–1771)' (Oxford thesis,
1971), p. 36, n. 60.
[20] Count de Stainville to Baron von Bernstorff, Paris, 20 Aug. 1750: *Bernstorffske Papirer*, ii.
621–2 for the following.

to compile, the commissioners have said [*sic*] that H.M. was going to issue a declaration [of intention] which he would have registered by his parliament, and it is this declaration of which the clergy is afraid.

Such was stubborn Machault's plausible alternative to the twentieth in reaching towards his main object. This was not even so much the immediate revenue from the clergy, over and above their *don gratuit*, as the new register of ecclesiastical income (there was a precedent from 1726) with its ominous implications for the future and heavy principle of royal supervision of clerical taxation.

Two days later Stainville added:

There has since appeared a declaration registered by the parliament [of Paris], which enjoins each benefice-holder to render to his bishop the declaration [of his revenue] so that, according to the revenue of each, the register should be revised and set at its true value. There are penalties for those who shall not conform . . . and although it be the clergy which is rendering the declaration to the clergy itself, the king reserves to himself the right to have it presented to him . . . I expect that the Danish secretary [of legation] will have sent you the address and the declaration, which are printed. Otherwise I would have directed them to you, for they are rather singular pieces.[21]

On 10 September 1750 the assembly of the French clergy presented long remonstrances to King Louis XV. They protested against initiative towards an ecclesiastical twentieth taken by the intendants of Metz and Perpignan, requested the withdrawal of the royal declaration of 17 August, observed that 'a terrible spirit of philosophy has spread like a deadly venom and has withered the root of faith in nearly all hearts',[22] and countered in the next paragraph with an edifying citation from Charles the Bald's council of Thionville in the year 845. Three days after their presentation, the Count de Stainville was writing that the remonstrances had been badly received and that the ecclesiastical assembly would be dissolved: 'but I do not know whether, afterwards, they [the government] will not be embarrassed. The matter is very delicate, and this affair is far from being finished'.[23]

On 16 September Louis XV sent the Count de Saint-Florentin to the assembly with a gently phrased missive assuring the clergy of 'his care for privileges',[24] disclaiming an ecclesiastical Vingtième but requesting obedience to the declaration. Saint-Florentin waited several hours for the answer which, related Stainville, represented the clergy as 'in despair at being able to respond to the intentions of H.M. only by tears. M. de Florentin, seeing this reply, gave them from the king a *lettre de cachet* which breaks up the assembly, orders

---

[21] Ibid., 22 Aug. 1750, pp. 622–3.   [22] Luynes, x. 537.
[23] Count de Stainville to Baron von Bernstorff, Paris, 13 Sept. 1750: *u. s.*, p. 624.
[24] Ibid., 27 Sept. 1750: p. 625 for the following.

each bishop to go to his diocese and there to see to the raising of the fifteen hundred thousand francs. They have obeyed the first order and have protested against the latter. That is how it stands. Nobody can foresee the sequel to this business, unless it is the controller-general. This business has absorbed all the other small news.'

The eighteenth century in France as elsewhere demonstrated that the close of the middle ages had no more completely terminated those national issues between church and state than it had international ones between papacy and empire. And now, as with most issues foreign or internal, that of ecclesiastical taxation produced rival factions at the court of Versailles.

The Count de Stainville's approval of Machault's hardy attempt to rope the clergy into his fiscal rationalization was, perhaps with some meaning for the future, more importantly matched by that of Madame de Pompadour. With her she had nearly all the government and even such as the Duke de Richelieu, her enemy, together with religious sympathizers like the Abbé de Broglie and the Duke de Noailles, who had unsuccessfully tried his own hand at fiscal reform back in the regency. Embattled against them on behalf of the church stood the Count d'Argenson and all the royal family. And behind the factions were ranged the two most powerful pressure-groups in France, on the side of the royal mistress the financiers, the brothers Pâris, on that of the queen the prelates led by the Archbishop of Paris, the virtuously honest, stubbornly unintelligent Christophe de Beaumont, by the Cardinal de Tencin and by Boyer, former Bishop of Mirepoix, the powerful adviser on preferment. Balancing the two parties was the inconstant king, at first swayed by his controller-general, perhaps as much by his mistress, but cherishing genuine religious scruples liable to be worked on when the going became rough.

The Count de Stainville was correct in sensing that the scattering of the bishops might not mark the end of the government's difficulties. Earlyish in October 1750 he informed Bernstorff that after their dispersal 'there appeared a *procès-verbal* of the assembly printed by their order, whereto there was appended the *procès-verbaux* of the assemblies since 1561. These two pieces are very singular. I dare not send them you because they have been suppressed by order of the court, but the Danish secretary ought not to be so scrupulous as I, and you would do very well to ask him for them.'[25]

These clerical *procès-verbaux*, designed to shew French clerical taxation to have been always voluntary by *dons gratuits*, were countered by Stainville's friend, the Abbé Chauvelin, in critical

[25] Ibid., 8 Oct. 1750, p. 626.

Observations upon them. And it was most probably he who followed these up with a more broadly entitled *Examen impartial des immunités ecclésiastiques.* If the *procès-verbaux* were hardly to the liking of the government, it contrived by royal decree of 21 May 1751 to suppress the most objectionable of them at the same time as the opposed publications of Chauvelin and others, notably Voltaire. That prime philosoph imagined a splendid decree of the Inquisition against the apologists of governmental taxation of the clergy: 'Antichrist is come already ... Satan has ... retailed a book worthy of him ... to prove that ecclesiastics form part of the body of the state, instead of admitting that they are essentially the masters of it ... He urges that those who have a third of the state's revenue owe at least a third in contributions, not recalling that our brothers are there to have everything and to give nothing. The said book furthermore is notoriously full of impious maxims ... wickedly tending to ... relieve the poor clerics hitherto righteously oppressed by the rich ones.'[26]

To an extent difficult to recall, that kind of persiflage, however exaggerated, sliced through the stuffy climate of right-thinking conformism, whether sincere, hypocritical or lazily muddled. Louis XV, standing for what he did, was right never to trust Voltaire, now relegated to protestant Prussia despite the sympathy of Madame de Pompadour, still scintillating in her ascendancy.

IV

'She was at her toilette, and the handsomest creature I think I ever saw, and looked like a rock of diamonds.'[27] Such was the impression of the Marquise de Pompadour upon a young British naval officer visiting Versailles in June 1749. Rather later another foreigner, but a critical one who knew her well, specified:

Her eyes are blue, set well apart, quite large, her look charming. The contour of her face is oval with a small mouth, pretty forehead, an especially nice nose. She has a good complexion and it would be much more so without the quantity of rouge that she puts on. Her ash-blonde hair falls in profusion to her waist. The care that she takes to hide her hands and bosom prove that they are not up to the rest. Her favourite attire is a kind of Greek dress which buttons up to the neck, with sleeves to the wrists. For the rest she is large rather than small, rather thin than fat; her carriage is noble, her graces touching ... Her form has something distinguished about it, so uncommon that even women find in her what they call the air of a nymph.[28]

[26] Voltaire, *Extrait du décret de la Sacrée Congrégation de l'Inquisition de Rome* in *Œuvres complètes de Voltaire,* ed. L. Moland, xxiii. 463.
[27] *Augustus Hervey's Journal,* ed. David Erskine (London, 1953), p. 87.
[28] Kaunitz/Mémoire, p. 447.

No friend of Madame de Pompadour was the Frenchman who wrote of her sway in 1749: 'For this winter they are preparing fine ballets and operas in the private apartments (*cabinets*), and she will sing in them. In this beauty there must be unknown forces which maintain her fresh and beautiful amid so much fatigue, and with a ruined chest. In former times one would have said that it was thanks to a spell, a talisman, a magic ring.'[29] If her recent miscarriage was overlaid by her magnetic brilliance, its setting also was imperfect.

Next year the favourite's uncle Le Normant de Tournehem in his sphere, as director-general of the royal buildings, was warning Louis XV of the 'general decay'[30] of the gardens at Versailles, described by a visitor a little later as soon inspiring 'melancholy and ennui . . . The verdure there lacks liveliness and freshness, and everything is extremely arid . . . The beds sanded in different colours bear rather mediocre flowers.' Even the proud waterworks only produced a full flow of 'dirty water' for some minutes 'twice or three times a year . . . The rest of the time one does not see a drop of water flowing, . . . only fountains run dry and basins half full of stagnant and stinking water.'[31] If Father Laugier was predisposed towards the greater rusticity of Lunéville, he yet supplies a convincing background to the court of Louis XV at its most brilliant, as conventionally focused in the bloom of the Pompadour in her twenty-eighth year and in the afterglow of the victories of the Marshal de Saxe.

The military framework, even, of the court was less than perfect in its household troops: 'The Maison du Roi, composed of about nine thousand men, is beyond contradiction the most magnificently dressed body of men in Europe. The French compare them to Darius's ten thousand who were covered with gold and silver . . . It is a pity that it does not give the appearance of being better maintained . . . The infantry is not gaitered. Their discipline moreover answers no better. The infantry is not drilled, and the cavalry marches even worse.'[32] Their commanders were largely ducal grandees but, again according to unkind Kaunitz: 'They say that the modern [French] dukes are a race of pygmies. It is the exact truth. One would be tempted to believe that the species has degenerated (*que l'espèce est dégradée*) . . . As for the ladies of the court, one would think that the Queen has been careful to collect all the ugliest in France. Of the fifty-two women who perform the duties, there are not three passable ones.

[29] D'Argenson, vi. 77.
[30] Cited, Pierre de Nolhac, *Versailles au XVIIIe siècle* (Paris, 1926), p. 325.
[31] Père Laugier, *Essai sur l'architecture* (revised ed., Paris, 1755), pp. 236 f.: cited, P. de Nolhac, op. cit., pp. 331–5.
[32] Kaunitz/Mémoire, pp. 839–42 for the following.

Above all, they have been careful to give monsters to Mesdames the princesses.' So the Pompadour shone.

Already, though, the beginning of the end of the sweetest time was at hand. At half past nine on Saturday evening, 18 April 1750, the curtain of the favourite's little theatre at Versailles went up for a repeat-performance of *Le Méchant*. Now, as two years previously, Madame de Pompadour starred as Lisette, Duras as Cléon; but Frontin, formerly Gontaut, was played by shady Maillebois the younger while Valère fell to the Prince de Monaco in place of the Count de Stainville's other friend, the absent Nivernais. The play was followed by a little ballet for six. At half past eleven the performance ended, and the theatre. That was the finish of the celebrated Théâtre des Cabinets. Next month workmen at Versailles began fitting up new apartments for Madame de Pompadour in the respectable region inhabited by the princesses below the state apartments. Their Mummy Whore was moving down from her little rooms of delight, not down, though, from her pre-eminence as the king's friend. Still, it was a change.

If the Count de Stainville was indirectly associated, through the Méchant, with the theatrical retreat of Madame de Pompadour, so was he also, through the Princess de Robecq, with the favourite's wider achievement in holding her own in a malevolent world, among mean-minded men and able-bodied women.

Tales of the extravagance of the Marquise de Pompadour were rivalled by ever-recurrent rumours, ever to be disappointed, that she was being superseded by some other beauty. In the summer before peace was signed at Aix-la-Chapelle the favoured rival had been the Princess de Robecq, the young daughter of the king's long-standing intimate from the noble house of Montmorency, the Duke de Luxembourg, also the long-standing lover of the Count de Stainville's patroness, the Duchess de Boufflers. There were stories that season that Luxembourg was seeking to promote his daughter as the king's mistress, that Louis was smitten and that, meeting the princess out walking one day at Bagatelle, he had disappeared with her for a quarter of an hour. However that may have been, Bagatelle itself was to become the domain of the politically, if not physically, invincible Marquise de Pompadour. The Princess de Robecq was substantially left for the enjoyment of other men, in particular of the young Count de Stainville.

It is uncertain just when the Princess de Robecq became the mistress of the Count de Stainville. It may not have been quite yet, though she was certainly an early intimate of his circle.

Anne-Marie de Montmorency had married the twenty-year-old

Count d'Estaires at the beginning of 1745; later that year the death of his father made her the Princess de Robecq. It had been a gratifying marriage since the Robecqs represented another branch of the house of Montmorency, separated seven or eight generations back from the Luxembourg line, once again convergent in her person. Tallish, with a good figure, the Princess de Robecq 'has a pleasing face and is very like her mother',[33] the first Duchess de Luxembourg, born Marie-Sophie-Emilie-Honorate Colbert de Seignelay of the stock of the great minister. This lady was a bibliophile and her daughter inherited the Colbert intelligence. The Princess de Robecq had a clever, oval face with large, dark eyes, very French, a contrast to the chubby countenance of the Count de Stainville. A possible bond between them may have been not only wit but also bereavement. He was still in the aftermath of the death of his loved Marquise de Gontaut when, in that year of 1749, his later mistress of longer accomplishment, the Princess de Robecq, lost her only son.

The Princess de Robecq was a fitting addition to the Count de Stainville's select collection of clever mistresses of high rank. His engrossment of her was liable to reassure the Marquise de Pompadour, described in July 1750 as now 'flying upon her own wings and no longer has known advisers; the offices are no longer listened to in affairs.'[34] The billowing out of petticoat government reduced the function of its financial stays. Three days earlier Stainville had closed a letter to economically interested Bernstorff: 'I was told yesterday that M. de Monmartel was voluntarily quitting all his employments in order to place in safety the income of two millions which remains to him for his pains. They add that it is M. Bouret, farmer gen., who will replace him. It is the same M. Bouret who gave the controller gen. the true return of the product of the [tax] farms and who by this infidelity caused the disgrace of M. de Betz. Adieu, Sir. Love still the most devoted servant that you have in the world.'[35] The Marquis d'Argenson carried the same gossip, characterizing Great Bouret as 'a very superficial and very incapable man',[36] and extending the retirement to both the brothers Pâris. Stainville's next to Bernstorff carried more gossip about the appointment of new counsellors of state and about Monmartel, concluding: 'What seems to me certain is that he has the intention of leaving the bank and the royal treasury; that makes me easy as to their sound future.'[37]

Earlier that month Bernstorff had been treated to another specimen of Stainville's deadpan reporting: 'The husband of Mme du Deffand

[33] Luynes, vii. 293.   [34] D'Argenson, vi. 226.

[35] Count de Stainville to Baron von Bernstorff, Paris, 9 July 1750: *Bernstorffske Papirer*, ii. 618.

[36] D'Argenson, vi. 225.   [37] Ibid., 27 July 1750, ii. 618.

is dead, which rejoices her.'[38] Such was Stainville's earliest recorded mention of his future wife's great friend in her happy release on 24 June 1750 from her worthy, injured husband. Some weeks later, reporting appointments to the household of the youngest French princesses, Mesdames Sophie and Louise, Stainville referred to the introduction of a Mademoiselle de Welderen, 'a Dutchwoman who has left her country for the catholic faith; apparently they want to give Mesdames a decided taste for transubstantiation'.[39] And of a change in their mother's ladies-in-waiting Stainville had written a year earlier, on 4 August 1749, to his other absent friend, Nivernais: 'Mme. de Boufflers has just handed over her position to her daughter-in-law. There is a furious recruit for the queen's palace.'[40]

It sounds as though Marie-Anne-Philippine-Thérèse, daughter of the late Prince de Montmorency, had inherited the spunk of her house. This product of yet another branch of it and of a Belgian baroness from Ghent had in 1747 married Charles Joseph de Boufflers, the twentyfive-year-old son of Stainville's formidable duchess. Young Boufflers succeeded to the dukedom after his father's death at Genoa, and to Stainville's colonelcy of the Regiment of Navarre in 1749 when the new duchess was also being set up in position. She, like Stainville, was an easterner in France, with a brother in the Austrian army. Another close but later link with the future Choiseul was to be the marriage of the only surviving daughter of the young duke and duchess to the Duke de Lauzun, Choiseul's putative son by the Marquise de Gontaut.

For the present the handover by the dowager Duchess de Boufflers to her daughter-in-law as lady-in-waiting represented a strategic retreat in discreet self-effacement for a time from court pending the dowager's expected marriage to her longstanding admirer, the Duke de Luxembourg, widowed father of Stainville's mistress, the Princess de Robecq.

The Boufflers dowager, widowed on a tidy income of 80,000 livres, joined forces with her Luxembourg lover on 6 May 1750 to purchase for sixty thousand the château of Montmorency near Paris. There an artistic arcady of sumptuous elegance had been contrived by Pierre Crozat the Poor of that family wherein the Count de Stainville was already implicated.

The Crozats had bought Montmorency in 1702 from the heirs of the painter to the Sun King, Charles Lebrun. His porticoed residence had become the Little Château by comparison with the new magnificence of the classic mansion built by Cartaud to command

[38] Ibid., 1 July 1750, p. 635.   [39] Ibid., 13 Sept. 1750, p. 624.
[40] Count de Stainville to Duke de Nivernais, 4 Aug. 1749; W.N.A., docket V/1, fo. 6.

lovely views. Within, corinthian pilasters in the central saloon rose through two storeys to support the heavens characterized, by Charles de la Fosse, with the impetuosity of Phaeton.

The gardens, though, at Montmorency with their terraces and fountains of delight struck a contemporary as still owing to Lebrun 'their chief beauty ... It seems as if the shade of this great painter still takes its pleasure in these same spots.'[41] They were commemorated too by a greater painter, in Watteau's little landscape entitled The Perspective. Enclosed, however, was a separate plot to set off a circular orangery by Oppenord. Other pleasures included a grotto, waterfall, and La Laitière as they called an octagonal lake surrounded by trees in quincunx. If it be heresy that art can improve upon nature, then the gardens of the high baroque and the rococo affirmed serene and unrepentant heresies. Those at Montmorency were to help seduce the very prophet of return to natural simplicity, the soon familiar Jean-Jacques Rousseau.

Now this splendid property was reverting from high finance to the high nobility in the person of a Montmorency himself, rather as Stainville had earlier been repurchased by the family in another inversion of the stereotype of social development. Even before the repurchase of the Château de Montmorency, however, it had figured under the Crozat aegis in the circle of the Count de Stainville. At the close of the preceding year he had been writing to the Duke de Nivernais about another member of it from the Brancas salon, the delicately literary Count de Forcalquier, to be unkindly described by Stainville's other mentor, the Duchess d'Aiguillon, as an eternal moribund (*éternel mourant*). According to Stainville in December 1749 'the condition of Forcaltier [*sic*] ... seems to me less worrying for his friends and more disagreeable for him. The choking fits have increased. He is suffering more, but for a long while he has had none of those mishaps on the chest to which he was so subject ... It seems to me that the illness has declined as to consumption and gained as to asthma. I saw nothing of him the whole summer for he was always at Montmorency, but since his return that is how I have judged it.'[42]

In addition to Montmorency the town house of the Duke de Luxembourg in the Rue Saint-Marc was giving him and the elder Duchess de Boufflers a lot to do, was indeed held responsible for delaying their marriage. At last they were united in her Parisian parish of the Madeleine on the night of Sunday to Monday, 28–29 June 1750. 'The marriage', wrote the attendant Stainville to Bernstorff,

[41] Dezallier d'Argenville, *Voyage pittoresque des environs de Paris*, cited, H. Buffenoir, *La Maréchale de Luxembourg*, p. 80.
[42] Count de Stainville to Duke de Nivernais, 1 Dec. 1749: W.N.A., docket V/1, fo. 18.

'went off very well. Amid it all my heart finds plenty of time to speak of you'[43] in sadness now that he would not be returning. Meanwhile the consecration in a second union of the true love of the conveniently widowed duke and duchess may remind those shocked by the immorality of the court of Louis XV that divorce and remarriage there were habitually forbidden by its catholic faith.

Stainville began his next to Bernstorff: 'There is nothing new to tell you today, Sir, and I am simply writing to remind you of me. I am going to Compiègne in two days to see the regt. of the Grenadiers of France which is arriving there tomorrow. It will make up the camp all by itself,'[44] being over two thousand strong. Such training-camps provided regular distraction in time of peace.

With drum and fife the grenadiers in eighteen companies came marching in from Arras. The royal review was held at five o'clock on the afternoon of 12 July. The troops engaged in mock combat, manoeuvred, and executed a new drill, according to the Duke de Luynes, 'singularly well for the little time that they have had to learn it'.[45] Whereas to the Marquis d'Argenson they 'seemed a piece of clockwork and virtually good for nothing – a strange garb of deep blue cloth with bonnets which hid their faces, a company of pioneers dressed as Roman Lictors, their drill strange and ridiculous, sulkily copying the Prussian drill'[46] then being promoted by the Marshal de Saxe. He and Lowendahl attended the exercise 'and gave it affected praise which turned this spectacle to ridicule. These two generals are badly received at court since there is no longer need of them,' whereas the inimical Count d'Argenson figured then 'very brilliant, very cherished by the King'.

Saxe was on his way out in more senses than one. His last visit to Versailles in the following month was for what Stainville then described to Bernstorff, a little prematurely, as 'the childbed at any moment of the Dauphine. There are great preparations for festivities which will not take place if, unhappily, she gives birth to a princess, as all Paris has decided that she will."[47] Paris was proved right by her shortlived firstborn, Marie-Zéphirine, painfully produced in sweltering heat under Saxe's sensible protection against the complimentary crush of sweating courtiers whose stench, he feared, might infect her.

Three months later, at the end of November 1750, the Marshal de Saxe himself died at Chambord. Despite long rumours of a fatal

[43] Count de Stainville to Baron von Bernstorff, Paris, 1 July 1750: *Bernstorffske Papirer*, ii. 634.
[44] Ibid., 9 July 1750, p. 617.   [45] Luynes, x. 295.
[46] D'Argenson, vi. 229–30 for the following.
[47] Count de Stainville to Baron von Bernstorff, Paris, 7 Aug. 1750: *Bernstorffske Papirer*, ii. 621.

encounter in the forest with his old rival, Conti, the marshal-general in fact succumbed to an orgiastic houseparty with a team of ladies from court. Madame de Pompadour is said to have commented, 'Poor Saxe has died in his bed like any old woman, believing nothing and hoping for nothing.'[48] At Chambord, vacant now, six cannon boomed in final salute every quarter of an hour, day and night for thirty days.

More interesting to the Count de Stainville was Versailles where, as he had told Bernstorff towards the end of that July, 'I have spent some days. Mme de Luxembourg has done her presentation [in her new quality], that is to say she has avoided all the ceremonial and has only made curtsies. On the same day her husband took the oath, and has entered upon the exercise of his commission [as a captain of the guards]. So there they are established as if all that had happened twenty years ago. They will only lodge in the same house upon the return from Fontainebleau, because the apartment in the Luxembourg mansion will only be ready then.'[49] Louis had appointed the Duke de Luxembourg to succeed the defunct Duke d'Harcourt and had characteristically explained to another ducal captain, Villeroy: 'It was your company that was destined for Monsieur de Luxembourg because I expected that you would die first.'[50] As it was, the Duke de Luxembourg on 23 July had placed his hands in homage between those of his king, and the queen had welcomed back the duchess, who was accompanied by the Duchess d'Antin and the Princess de Robecq. Another preoccupation for young Stainville at court just then was his previously noticed, carefully concealed aspiration towards an embassy.

Meanwhile Stainville gossiped on in his next to Bernstorff: 'I went to sup yesterday at St. Ouen. M. de Soubise gave a fête there to Mme de Luxembourg. Everybody that you know was there. He had had the various salons fitted up with fair taste and much magnificence. This fête is a rehearsal for a supper which he is to give for the king on the 11th of this month.'[51] The participation of the Count de Stainville in rehearsal for royalty may suggest how far he had, and had not, climbed as yet. In due course Louis XV was feasted by the Prince de Soubise with 'fireworks, ... illuminations and a great supper. The weather was not favourable, which greatly spoilt the illumination of the boats on the river.'[52]

Subsequent news from Stainville brought the sudden death of the

[48] Cited in the present translation by Jon Manchip White, *Marshal of France* (London, 1962), p. 255.
[49] Count de Stainville to Baron von Bernstorff, Paris, 27 July 1750: *u. s.*, ii. 618.
[50] Cited, Kaunitz/Mémoire, p. 444.
[51] Count de Stainville to Baron von Bernstorff, Paris, 1 Aug. 1750: *u.s.* p. 620.
[52] Luynes, x. 307–8.

archbishop of Tours and more about the ladies, not least the Duchess de Luxembourg, who had let her own house to her sister-in-law, 'Mme d'Antin and is going next week to establish herself in the Luxembourg mansion'.[53] It was a busy time for the new Duchess de Luxembourg, keen on furnishings and a great one for poking around the shops in her district of the Rue Saint-Honoré. Prominent there was Lazare Duvaux, the court jeweller dealing in objects of art and antiques, a prime supplier to Madame de Pompadour. Later that August, according to his accounts, he sold the duchess 'two large coffers of Dresden china, square, 120 livres'.[54] A month later again it was 'a cast eight-branch candelabrum and consols, very massive silver gilt, and to making the candelabrum, 350 livres', along with 'silken cord in three colours with two tassels, two ells long, 50 livres'.

On 13 September 1750 Stainville resumed to Bernstorff:

We are back from Liladam [l'Isle-Adam], Mde. de Luxembourg, Mde. de Robecq and I. The Prince de Conti has come out of his lair to gather together at his place a very brilliant company which he received with much grace and splendour. We were very pleased with our journey. We are going to make another to Villers Cotterets during the king's journey to Crécy, and then Mde. de Luxembourg will go to install herself at Fontainbleau, where she will maintain a house during M. de Luxembourg's quarter [of duty at court]. She is living at the moment in the Rue St. Marc and is keeping very great state there. It sets a very good tone, and no fakes [jetons] or suchlike company.[55]

Stainville added of this high living in the Rue Saint-Marc: 'I could indeed wish that it would put the lady who is our friend out of conceit, and that it should open her eyes, for this fault is the only one that I recognize in her. I love her with all my heart and this intrigue makes me suffer more than I can tell you. I hope that Mme. de Luxembourg, who has undertaken to break it and who is fortunate, will succeed in doing so.' Stainville's cryptic allusion was evidently to the passion entertained just then by his other leading duchess, Madame de La Vallière, for Jélyotte, the unhandsome, sunny-natured idol of the Opera.

The Duchess de La Vallière was to be described by Bernstorff as being, compared with the Duchess de Luxembourg, 'gentler, possessing much good sense and reason of a happy kind if she did not often let herself be carried away by other people's taste rather than her own'.[56] Both duchesses, wrote Bernstorff, had been 'amongst the

[53] Count de Stainville to Baron von Bernstorff, Paris, 7 Aug. 1750: *Bernstorffske Papirer*, ii. 621.
[54] Cited, H. Buffenoir, *La Maréchale de Luxembourg*, pp. 45–6 for the following.
[55] Count de Stainville to Baron von Bernstorff, Paris, 13 Sept. 1750: *Bernstorffske Papirer*, ii. 624, and for the following.
[56] Baron von Bernstorff to Baron A. P. von Bernstorff, Copenhagen, 17–25 Jan. 1757: *Bernstorffske Papirer*, i. 172–3 for the following.

most beautiful women in the kingdom' but it was not for their morals 'that I praise and like them'.

Such were these intimates of the Count de Stainville, who began a letter of 8 October 1750 to his graver friend to the north:

You have never seen anything so deserted as Paris, Sir. It seems to me that this year is even worse than the others. Everybody has taken their cue to go into the country. Mme de Luxembourg is at Fontainbleau, Mme de La Vallière at Champs; even Mme du Châtel has gone to stay for a fortnight with M. de Cambade . . . I am going to journey like everybody. I shall go to Champs this week and in a week's time to establish myself at Fontainbleau till the end of the month.[57]

The lovesick duchess, though, apparently induced the Count de Stainville to linger at the Château de Champs, one of the most beautiful in the Ile-de-France. Chamblain's masterpiece, finished about 1707 some dozen miles to the east of Paris, had been inherited by the Duke de La Vallière, a keen bibliophile and collector of pictures. He had lately been superintending the finishing touches to that interior glimpsed through the eleven bays of the facade in creamy stone.

The restrained elegance of this classic mansion led right through the mirrored doors of the great salon out on to the terrace with sphinxes flanking the slope of the garden between flowerbeds twisted into French embroidery and pleached avenues with fountains and statuary out across farther lawns and expanses of delight.

Internally the pleasure of the salon was being rather superseded by the grand cabinet recently redecorated by Christophe Huet so that the straight lines of the original woodwork were if anything enhanced by the rococo delicacy of his painting upon each panel of Chinese scenes and arabesques. On the other side, facing the forecourt, he also decorated the more intimate Chinese Room. Here the pinks and greens of the grand cabinet gave way to a smoky blue lending distance to suave visions of Cathay. Within a few years the decorative gem of Champs was to be let by the Duke de La Vallière to Madame de Pompadour herself.[58]

Such was the delicious milieu already frequented by the Count de Stainville in his fret over the passionate involvement of the duchess of the house, where he was prolonging his autumn. It was only on 17 November 1750 that his letter to Bernstorff opened: 'I have just arrived from Champs, alas! It was as usual. We had flattered ourselves, Mme de Luxembourg and company, that there would be

[57] Count de Stainville to Baron von Bernstorff, Paris, 8 Oct. 1750: op. cit., ii. 626.
[58] This account is indebted to John Cornforth, 'The Château de Champs, Seine-et-Marne' in Country Life of 21 Jan. 1965, vol. cxxxvii, no. 3542, p. 116.

a lessening, but it seemed to me stronger than ever, driving one further to despair, for I love her enough to be as angry about it as a lover or husband would be.'[59] In fact the Count de Stainville seems to have been more concerned than the Duke de La Vallière about that duchess's persistent passion for Jélyotte. The gallant duke had his own operatic preoccupation in pert Mademoiselle Lacour who made her 'old dukey (*vieille ducaille*)' kneel to her upon his ribbon of the Saint-Esprit. Stainville proceeded to Bernstorff: 'I will tell you anon how it all comes out. Mme de Luxembourg seems to me determined not to receive the histrionic fellow at her house. It is a great affair for our set, as you can well judge.'

Three days later the less involved Marquis d'Argenson was striking a rather different note:

The new Duchess de Luxembourg has resolved to assemble good company at her house in Paris this winter and for that men of wit are needed. She has obliged Mme de La Vallière to dismiss Jélyotte, the singer at the opera. The Duke de La Vallière has said to Jélyotte: 'Although henceforth you will no longer be my wife's friend, I want you none the less to be one of mine. We will have you to supper sometimes. Another lover has been chosen for this duchess. He is the Count de Bissy and, to ornament the set, it was decided to get him into the French Academy. They based his claims to it on a translation from the English of Bolingbroke's *Patriot King* and required Mme de Pompadour to remit the nomination of Piron to another time. The Marquise conducted this with much finesse, keeping behind the scenes, and it fully succeeded yesterday, Thursday, M. de Bissy being elected unanimously... Thereby they seek to set up the Luxembourg mansion against the Duras one, and Bissy against Pont-de-Veyle. Our French ways are becoming charming.[60]

The Marquis d'Argenson never made the French Academy. And if Bissy, cousin of the one killed at Maestricht, was outshone by Belle-Isle in speeches upon installation as academicians, in such a case as Bissy's it is more important to obtain than to merit the distinction. Different, though, were the values of an old friend of both duchesses and of the Count de Stainville, namely the Prince de Beauvau, brother of the less reliable Marquise de Mirepoix. Beauvau's disinterested charm was grounded in good judgment and good taste laced with wit, of which Stainville now rescued a specimen in sending Bernstorff a news-item about the Palatine minister in Paris: 'Grevenbrock has married a Mlle. Deschamps of the queen's music ... Odd that Grevenbrock should do anything so silly for love ... But if all must be said, apart from the Palatine quality there is no inequality between the couple.'[61] To which Stainville added a

---

[59] Count de Stainville to Baron von Bernstorff, Paris, 17 Nov. 1750: *Bernstorffske Papirer*, ii. 628 for the following.   [60] D'Argenson, vi. 292.

[61] Count de Stainville to Baron von Bernstorff, Paris, 17 Nov. 1750: *u. s.*, p. 628 for the following.

separate throw-away line: 'Somebody like M. de Beauvau has said that Mlle. Deschamps has been done in long enough to be a Palatine.' The memory of the vigorous mother of the Regent Orleans was still green.

Stainville began his next to Bernstorff at the end of November 1750:

I am back, Sir, from Fontainebleau where I have been for nearly a fortnight on end. I am little accustomed to pay such long visits to court, but Mde de Luxembourg and her family would make me do much more than that. She maintains a most considerable state there; the officers of the bodyguard furnish the substance and the honours of the establishment, and after them there is not a woman whoever she is nor a courtier who does not desire to be asked to sup with her. Her house does not empty from one o'clock after noon till four in the morning. Only very good company enters there. She is at her ease, extremely polite and paying singular attention to everybody. The master of the house also adopts that tone, and I assure you that she is acquiring the consideration of which we have so often talked.[62]

Stainville and Bernstorff had evidently been putting their judicious young heads together with a view to settling their fast friend into that sort of social intercourse of easy grandeur which was to distinguish the later Duke de Choiseul. If he then, rather in the taste of his father, preferred a private round of semirural visiting to the court, yet he was already, as noticed, interested enough in Madame de Pompadour, busy then with her new house at Bellevue, built upon sandy soil out by Meudon. 'On the 22nd', wrote Stainville of the court that November, 'there will be the first journey to Bellevue, which will only be for ten days, but there will be frequent ones this winter since the little shows of Versailles are to be played there.'[63] Such was the – relatively – economical migration of the theatre of the little cabinets, after that last performance of Le Méchant, to the new theatre at Bellevue in delicious chinoiserie by Boucher, Oudry, Verberckt, Caffieri. Bellevue itself, while usually viewed in relation to Versailles, contributes to the suggestion that, more than may sometimes be supposed, the French aristocracy then enjoyed country-house life, of a mondain kind, in such exquisite retreats as Stainville frequented at Isle-Adam, Montmorency, Champs.

V

To view the Count de Stainville's idyllic round of pleasure as the sum of that existence would be to romanticize a past free from those little

[62] Count de Stainville to Baron von Bernstorff, Paris, ?30 Nov. 1750: ibid., pp. 628–9, where dated 31 [sic] Nov. 1750.
[63] Ibid., 8 Nov. 1750: p. 627.

ills and worries which habitually clog the human condition even in
sunny times. The anxious underside largely related to diplomatic
evolution and its consequences for his father. Stainville had told
Bernstorff in July 1750: 'M. d'Authefort [sic] takes leave on 20th of
August and will depart [for Vienna] in Sept. I expect that my father
will also leave about that time. I shall remain an orphan piously put
out in the street, but I am trusting in Providence.'[64] He habitually
did.

The delivery of the Dauphine delayed d'Hautefort's departure,
while Kaunitz's dallying in Vienna deferred the elder Stainville's
journey thither 'to arrange the destination',[65] the long-mooted fresh
destination for that effectively superseded diplomatist.

'The affairs of my father, who assures you of his respect, are still at
the same point', wrote Stainville the younger to Bernstorff later that
August. 'The embarrassment of M. Richecourt is more considerable
than we could have imagined, even [knowing him] from our
childhood; however, it really must have an end, and a month from
now I expect that my father will be leaving for Vienna.'[66] A month
earlier the embarrassment of the Count de Richecourt had been
described from the Tuscan end:

He has been absent from Florence some time, and, to justify his long stay at the baths
[at Pisa], made the poor physician there make a certificate which was sent to Vienna
that they were necessary for his health. Does it not sound odd that an hitherto
despotic, favourite, first minister should think it necessary to have recourse to such
means to make the Emperor believe him? This, and many other circumstances,
persuade people that he is disgusted, and that he knows for certain what they believe,
that Marquis Steinville is to come here, they say in quality of regent, which must put
an end to his reign. The Florentines will be glad of any change, though they are not
sure of being bettered by it.[67]

During the previous winter Richecourt's patron, 'Baron Toussaint,
the great favourite of the Emperor'[68] had suddenly visited Florence
but at the same time it had been said that Richecourt was losing
favour. Now a false press-report spread across Europe to the effect
that 'on 11 Sept. this year [1750] the Marquis de Stainville departed
from Paris for Florence in order to take the place there of the Count
de Richecourt in the government of Tuscany'.[69] Two days after this
alleged departure the Count de Stainville was in fact writing from
Paris: 'My father cannot leave here for three months. He is leaving

---

[64] Count de Stainville to Baron von Bernstorff, Paris, 9 July 1750: ibid., p. 618.
[65] Ibid., 7 Aug. 1750: p. 621.
[66] Ibid., 22 Aug. 1750: p. 623.
[67] Mann to Horace Walpole, Florence, 18 July 1750: Walpole Correspondence, xx. 162
[68] Ibid., 28 Nov. 1749, xx. 97.
[69] Neue genealogisch-historische Nachrichten [1750] (Leipzig, 1750), p. 671: cf. also p. 1013.

his house and is being lent one for this time. As for me, I shall lodge at my house, but I hope that in one way or another I shall not stay out in the street.'[70] The count subsequently implied that he would have preferred to follow his parents.

By the New Year in Florence 'nobody even thinks of Monsieur Stainville. The Count [Richecourt] seems to have taken a resolution not to yield to anyone, and exercises his supreme authority with a high hand'.[71] Back in Paris Stainville was reduced to one or two chores such as the endless liquidation of French war debts to Lorraine and the introduction to court at Fontainebleau that October of a Count Paar, cousin and, evidently, harbinger of Kaunitz. Paar tactfully assured the queen that Maria Theresa 'takes no care of herself and drinks coffee with milk five or six times a day, which has much fattened her'.[72] At last, on 8 November 1750, the Count de Stainville wrote to Denmark: 'M. de Kaunitz reached Fontainebleau a week ago. The king has treated him wonderfully ... and I am told that he could not be more feted. He is held to be polite and witty. There are those who say that he has a German air, which is a very extraordinary thing. It is true that they could not say at Vienna that M. d'Hautefort has a French air.'[73] The sharp-shooter added: 'I have not yet seen M. de Kaunitz. I thought that of our family it was quite enough for my father to be in his train.'

Not much love was to be lost between the Count de Stainville and Count Kaunitz, however their policies might approximate. Rather more than a year later Kaunitz was to provide a glimpse of Stainville and his friend Beauvau in sharp contradiction of the later Choiseul's parade of early indifference to the court. In noting the etiquette for invitation to the intimate suppers of Louis XV, Count Kaunitz explained that after hunting the companions of the chase assembled while the king himself wrote out a list of those invited:

He pays much attention to this list; sometimes he does it twice over so as to see that there is nothing to add to it. Those who are in the antechamber and do not find themselves upon it are sure that it is not from forgetfulness. There are people who have presented themselves twenty times without having been able to procure it: the Prince de Beauvau, for instance, and the Count de Stainville, the eldest son of the Marquis. It is thought that it is their reputation for spitefulness (méchanceté) which has brought upon them this kind of disgrace.[74]

---

[70] Count de Stainville to Baron von Bernstorff, Paris, 13 Sept. 1750; Bernstorffske Papirer, ii. 624.
[71] Mann to Horace Walpole, Florence, 1 Jan. 1751: u.s., xx. 210.
[72] Duchess de Luynes to Duke de Luynes, Fontainbleau, 17 Oct. 1750: Luynes, vol. x, p. 357.
[73] Count de Stainville to Baron von Bernstorff, Paris, 8 Nov. 1750: Bernstorffske Papirer, ii. 627, and for the following.
[74] Kaunitz/Mémoire, p. 846.

Kaunitz observed also that those not bidden to sup 'return to Paris as fast as possible so as to hide their shame and despair'[75] – an angle, perhaps, on Stainville's preference for Paris. Even there uncertainty as to his father's destination now spelt uncertainty for his own lodging. Earlier that year the Count de Stainville had been 'residing in Paris at his town-house in the Rue de Grenelle in the district of Saint-Germain-des-Prés near Saint Sulpice.'[76] This was in fact his parents' residence, also described as 'near the fountain'[77] wherewith Bouchardon had graced their street, round the corner from their old house in the Rue du Bac. By 1 August 1750 young Stainville was thanking Bernstorff for wishing 'to get me a house. I have a little one at the end of the Rue de Sève which I shall occupy upon the departure of my father.'[78] Meanwhile, as he had written a few days earlier: 'It has been unbearably hot for the last eight or ten days; I am in a little room on the south where I am dying.'[79]

That summer of 1750 was a classic scorcher in France. At Versailles the reservoirs ran dry, with fountains silent, gardens parched, courtyards like ovens. One is told, if one can believe, that one day there during that heatwave at the end of July fifteen soldiers dropped dead during the ceremonial relief of the midday guard. Mowers were mown down lifeless in the fields. Though the country was preferable in that terrific heat punctuated by thunderstorms. The day before the Count de Stainville had reported it to cooler Denmark, the Marquis d'Argenson noted that the temperature 'is obliging quantities of people to abandon Paris'.[80] Young Stainville, though, was sweltering there in his little room confronting the pitiless sun. Few settings are more depressing than a city deserted in great heat, and it is in summer sometimes that life can seem almost like a death begun. The loneliness was compounded for him, far separated from such friends as Bernstorff and Nivernais, with his father leaving him, as he jested, like an orphan. And the previous year had already shown how the heat was liable to affect the Count de Stainville's health, already delicate.

VI

During his cure in the summer of 1749 Stainville had explained to Nivernais that the waters of Passy 'are affecting my head a little, but

[75] Ibid., p. 842.
[76] 'Bail pour 9 ans des D[o]m[ain]es de Beurey et Mussey', Paris, 24 Apr. 1750: Arch. Meuse, J 18[27] (Baronie de Beurey-sur-Saulx. 1315–1786), docket III.
[77] *Almanach Royal, année MDCCL* (Paris, 1750), p. 116.
[78] Count de Stainville to Baron von Bernstorff, Paris, 1 Aug. 1750: *u. s.*, ii. 620.
[79] Ibid., 27 July 1750, p. 619.   [80] D'Argenson, vi. 234.

I am not surprised at it. It is such a weak part that the least thing affects it.'[81] Despite this failure his doctor, Fournier, thought that Stainville would yet feel the benefit. But in another month his secretary had to take up the pen to tell Nivernais under dictation; 'Last Tuesday I had an attack of nerves which has so far given me no respite, for it is one of the most violent that I have had. I am in a state of extreme weakness and total incapacity.'[82] Nivernais, however, was not to worry for 'it is an habitual ailment which is not at all dangerous, but is more disagreeable than a real illness'.

The ailment lingered on into the autumn. On 19 September 1749 the Count de Stainville submitted to 'having leeches applied to the piles'.[83] They extracted from him 'two and a half pipkins of blood'. This was part of the treatment prescribed by a new German doctor, a specialist in chronic conditions, who concerted with Fournier and thought 'like all the other doctors' that Stainville's affliction was not dangerous, but slow to cure. The German switched him from Eaux de Passy to Eaux de La Motte, only to repeat the cycle from alleviation to relapse. 'It is the fate of nearly all the waters', reflected Stainville a fortnight later. 'Their weight and volume tire and upset my stomach so I have been forced to leave off. At present they are making me take a powder which I began the day before yesterday ... I doubt, however, whether it will succeed with me, for there is a lot of iron in it, and my nerves are already beginning to feel it.'[84]

Next month Stainville was laid low by another of his 'habitual ailments, a fairly heavy cold',[85] going on to his chest. He was spitting phlegm 'but the washing to which I have been forced to resort has ruined my stomach. I am no longer digesting anything and I am experiencing first-class vapours and great weakness. At this moment I am quite done for (*tout déconfit*).' However, he was patiently trusting to time and dieting, in which he was a firm believer. Yet the following spring found him suffering once more from his 'nasty ailment'[86] of the vapours and taking a course of baths. In the sweltering July of 1750 he was 'indisposed,'[87] as he more tersely informed his rather less intimate friend, Bernstorff; and by that November he was back again to leeches, a regular remedy which 'usually relieves me for some days, but it does not cure me'.[88]

---

[81] Count de Stainville to Duke de Nivernais, 13 July 1749: W.N.A., docket V/1, fo. 3.

[82] Count de Stainville to Duke de Nivernais, Paris, 1 Sept. 1749: ibid., fo. 9 for the following.

[83] Count de Stainville to Duke de Nivernais, 21–2 Sept. 1749: ibid., fo. 11 for the following.

[84] Ibid., 6 Oct. 1749, fo. 13.   [85] Ibid., 1 Dec. 1749, fo. 18 for the following.

[86] Ibid., 3 May 1750, fo. 24.

[87] Count de Stainville to Baron von Bernstorff, Paris, 27 July 1750: *Bernstorffske Papirer*, ii. 618.

[88] Count de Stainville to Duke de Nivernais, 22 Nov. 1750: W.N.A., docket V/1, fo. 32.

For the Count de Stainville it was only the lively concern for his health of his specially close friend, Nivernais, which 'authorizes me to be prolix upon this head, and the fonder one is of people the more inclined one is to talk to them about oneself".[89] It is indeed only from the intimacy of these unpublished letters that one now gathers the extent to which Stainville's outward ebullience was, in his own view certainly, precariously based even in earlier years: another secret and somewhat surprising truth about him.

Medically, as in other respects, Stainville spread his concern to include his friends, such as Forcalquier and Nivernais himself, who was incidentally a considerable gourmet. From Rome the duke wrote pages to assure his father that it was 'a country of very good fare. The beef here is delicious, that is to say at least as good as in Paris; veal is better. Mutton from the Roman *campagna* is mediocre, but that which is brought from the mountains is excellent ... All the greenstuff is delicious, especially the celery, broccoli, and lettuces of every kind. Here they have the roots of white chicory cooked and they eat it in the evening as a salad in the guise of supper ... Root-vegetables are not so good as in France, except the salsifies which are better.'[90] August 1749, however, had found Stainville writing to his friend in Rome that he had heard from the Duchess de Nivernais there 'that the heat is extreme and is impairing your digestions. I am not surprised for it is the usual effect I have always felt it, but I am sorry for it. There is however a sure and necessary remedy which is to eat hardly anything. You have given proof that you are capable of dieting, so I hope that by sobriety you will prevent the accidents which a succession of indigestions could cause. We have been very anxious about Mme Guerchy. They thought she was going to have smallpox, but it is only measles.'[91] (The Count de Guerchy was, like Duras indeed, another regular correspondent of Nivernais.) Medical particulars followed and led back to Stainville's own health. Also noticeable is the somewhat didactic note which Stainville was already apt to strike with the less sharp Nivernais in contrast to Bernstorff, with whom the roles were rather reversed.

Medical concern was to persist for the future Choiseul. Years later he was writing to another friend who had apparently sent him some ginseng, that fabulous medicament, only to be reminded: 'But I also need to be told how it is used, if as tea or else by eating the root and in what quantity and if, after resting, it might not do harm; in sum,

[89] Ibid., 21–2 Sept. 1749, fo. 11.
[90] Duke de Nivernais to Duke de Nevers, Rome, 12 Mar. 1749: Lucien Perey, *Un Petit-Neveu de Mazarin*, pp. 96–9.
[91] Count de Stainville to Duke de Nivernais, 4 August 1749: W.N.A., docket V/1, fo. 5.

how and at what time it is best for the digestion'.[92] Choiseul liked precision.

For the present, around 1750, while some hypochondria might enter in, there was certainly a suggestion that the Count de Stainville was highly strung and suffering from some chronic condition, possibly related to kidney-trouble if not to the rigours of his long campaigning on top of that fever from Belgrade. He himself also supplied a psychological clue to his ailment: 'despair and discouragement are mingled in it.'[93] This depression evidently related to the enigmatic persistence of his disorder, perhaps more broadly also to the unresolved interim in his fortunes in that aftermath of war with no assured occupation, no embassy to match the Roman assignment of his absent friend, with that other one soon off to Copenhagen, leaving Stainville, least lonely of men, a little lonelier. Such were the realities underlying what might seem a halcyon existence of enjoyment with fast friends in a round of country houses. Stainville, never one to brood, was tersely to write off that year of 1749 and its successor: 'I recall no event which interested me in the whole course of the year and of the following one'[94] – till its very end.

Meanwhile the Count de Stainville's parents had been packing up to leave and relegate him to his little house in the Rue de Sève. He indicated to Bernstorff that it 'will suffice until I get married or go journeying [as an ambassador]. In either case I trust that Mme du Châtel will conclude my business because, if I stay, it would be uncomfortable for me to lose the amenities which the residence of my father procured me and which I can only recover by a marriage; if I go, I shall be very glad for it to be concluded before my departure so as not to have to think of it any more. However I do not expect the decision on my journey till during the Fontainebleau [residence of the court], but according to appearances I do not think it at all in doubt, unless I myself should be in the position of making difficulties. You will be told everything, Sir, although I am much afraid of the post and still more afraid of wearying your friendship with my own affairs.'[95]

Three weeks later Stainville added to Bernstorff concerning the coveted embassy to Naples: 'I confess to you that I fear it at least as much as I desire it. We are beings composed of contraries which counterbalance our wishes tremendously. It is grievous at my age to

---

[92] Duke de Choiseul to Marquis   ?   , Versailles,   25   ?: Arch. Nat., M 825, dossier XXI bis, no. 46.

[93] Count de Stainville to Duke de Nivernais, 21–2 Sept. 1749: W.N.A., docket V/1, fo. 11.

[94] Choiseul, Mémoires, p. 61.

[95] Count de Stainville to Baron von Bernstorff, Paris, 1 Aug. 1750: Bernstorffske Papirer, ii. 620.

exile oneself and to leave real pleasures in the hope of things that are often very ideal. What is not so – and it sustains me – is the wish, which I have, to do something and to indicate my willingness.'[96] In Stephen de Stainville the springs of action were often more complex, more modest than might superficially appear in his gay confidence and clever success. Which was one reason, perhaps, why he was so attractive, not least to women.

That autumn of 1750 found both brilliant friends, Stainville and Bernstorff, similarly placed, still casting around in suspended animation, personal as well as professional. Bernstorff too had coolly begun to think of settling down with a rich bride even though his future was still floating: the Prince of Wales refused to release him from his word at the solicitation of the prince's sister, the English queen of King Frederick V. He, however, charmed Bernstorff into remaining in Denmark and cut his retreat to Paris by appointing a diplomatic successor there, a Reventlow: which, exclaimed Stainville, 'hurts me horribly. I am quite sure that I shall not get to know him. It would make me ill.'[97]

In the same letter of 27 September of 1750 Stainville wrote: 'The business of Naples will not be coming off. I do not know, but it seems to me that they are thinking of something else for the man in whom you are interesting yourself. He does not guess what it can be.' By the middle of November it was: 'I am off to Fontainebleau presently and I think that I shall stay there till the end of the month; they will have plenty of time to see me there. On my return I shall think seriously of my marriage so that it shall take place in the course of the winter.'[98]

Early that year the Count de Stainville's old comrade-in-arms and prospective father-in-law, the Marquis du Châtel, still not sixty, had died. It was a personal loss even if Stainville stood to gain financially from having been, as he said, 'long since attached to Mme du Châtel and it was long since too that my marriage with her daughter had been arranged. This marriage was on my part and on that of Mlle du Châtel more a marriage of sentiment than a marriage of interest.'[99] If that, on Stainville's contemporary showing, calls for a pinch of salt, the evident convenience of the marriage was not only financial but also domestic. Sexual satisfaction with a girl of thirteen would then be scarcely the main incentive for Stephen de Stainville, a youth no longer, turned thirty and entering a phase of change in his advance into matrimony, and wealth.

[96] Ibid., 22 Aug. 1750, p. 623.
[97] Ibid., 27 Sept. 1750, pp. 625–6 for the following.
[98] Ibid., 17 Nov. 1750, p. 628.
[99] Choiseul, *Mémoires*, p. 62.

CHAPTER V

MARRIAGE

I

'IN THE country where I am I hear it said that marriage and the population are dying out ... In my parish ... there are more than thirty lads or girls who have more than reached nubile age; no marriages are being made ... On being urged to it, they all answer the same thing, *that it is not worth while to breed wretches like them.*'[1]

If this was the voice of the people, swelling ominously, neither they nor the Marquis d'Argenson in making this last entry in his diary for the year 1750 could know that in that postwar depression they were yet standing nearly at the beginning of a demographic upswing in France. Earlier that December the diarist had noted even of the capital: 'Hardly any marriages are being made this winter in Paris. The penury is becoming great, even among the financiers.'[2] Among financial families, however, there were exceptions.

A few days earlier, on 4 December 1750, the Marquise du Deffand, special friend of the Marquise du Châtel, had written to Baron von Bernstorff: 'I have got back this moment from Sceaux'[3], the château where the Duchess de Maine, then ill, held literary court, not least for her old friend, who continued in her letter: 'Upon arrival I found a note from Madame du Châtel informing me of the marriage of Mademoiselle, her daughter, with M. de Stainville. It will take place a week tomorrow; you are sure to be very pleased about it.' Bernstorff was not the only one to be gratified.

Some days previously, on 29 November, the Marquis de Stainville had taken the opportunity to remind the Emperor Francis I 'of the former kindness wherewith you were good enough to honour my eldest son. It was only by your orders and with your consent that I attached him to the service of France, Your Imperial Majesty having deigned at that time to uphold the reasons which made me take this course. I am finding a very advantageous marriage for him. It is to Mlle. du Châtel, daughter of the lieutenant-general of this name, who died last year [*sic*], and who has left to this daughter a pretty

[1] D'Argenson, vi. 322–3.   [2] Ibid., p. 306.
[3] Marquise du Deffand to Baron von Bernstorff, 4 Dec. 1750: *Bernstorffske Papirer*, ii. 668–9 for the following.

considerable vested estate; she also has one assured; and in the state in which my affairs are, I am overjoyed to find such a good match for my son. So I venture to take the liberty to beg Your Imperial Majesty very humbly to be good enough to grant me your consent to this marriage, since I never wish to dispose of my family save with your permission.'[4]

That the future Duke de Choiseul had entered the service of France, nominally at least, rather upon the nod of the dynasty of Habsburg-Lorraine is a fact formerly absent from history. Perhaps, though, it was more form than fact: in the present instance one notices that the request for imperial consent was sent too late for a reply to have any effect upon arrangements for the wedding.

The Marquis de Stainville was, exceptionally, about to spend three days on end at Versailles. Part of his business there was still in interminable pursuit of a settlement of French indebtedness to the former government of Lorraine. Stainville lamented that he had been unable to see Controller-General Machault 'although I presented myself at his door more than fifteen times. This minister is too busy with his own affairs,'[5] having just assumed the additional office of Keeper of the Seals upon its being separated from that of Chancellor at the retirement of old d'Aguesseau in favour, now, of the lesser Lamoignon de Blancmesnil. However, the Marquis de Stainville also had his own, more satisfactory business at court.

Around midday on Sunday the 6th December 1750 the marriage contract between Stephen Francis Choiseul de Stainville and Louise-Honorine Crozat du Châtel was signed and witnessed in the palace of Versailles in the royal presence. By such means did the king hold patriarchal sway over the blueblooded kith among his subjects. There were that day three contracts to be signed, one of them on behalf of the only daughter of the Marquis de Stainville's old friend, the Marquis de Saint-Séverin, in an italianate match with a Marquis de Pignatelli. But the most considerable union, evidently, was that of the Count de Stainville with his heiress by a contract concluded, in its own wording, 'with the consent and permission of their majesties the King and Queen of France'[6] and their children: that was the royal consent which mattered. So this document, elegantly bound top and bottom with sky-blue ribbon, began its copious conclusion of signatures with Louis, Marie, Louis – a nasty scrawl from the Dauphin, Marie Josèphe, Henriette Anne, Marie Adélaïde, Victoire

---

[4] Marquis de Stainville to Emperor Francis I, Paris, 29 Nov. 1750: Esteri del Granducato di Toscana, vol. 2296/1287, no. 43.

[5] Ibid., 13 Dec. 1750, no. 45.

[6] Marriage-contract, 'Mariage, 6 & 12 Xbre 1750; M. le Comte de Stainville avec Mlle Du Châtel': Arch. Nat., Minutier Central des Notaires, dossier XXX/319 for the following.

Louise Marie Thérèse, Sophie Philippine Elisabeth Justine, Louise Marie – perhaps as good a collection of French royal signatures from the middle of the eighteenth century as one is likely to find. There followed those of the parents on both sides, then the bridegroom – 'Choiseul de Stainville' with a befitting flourish – the bride and other witnesses including her uncle, the Baron de Tugny, her brother-in-law, the Marquis de Gontaut, and the Count de Stainville's clerical brother Leopold-Charles, the Abbé de Choiseul.

This impressively subscribed contract listed the property of the Count de Stainville as comprising, beside the barony of Beurey and Mussey, the estate and marquisate of Stainville 'which belong to him in full ownership' by virtue of the entail and 'of the abandonment' of it to him previously by his father, who now added the cession of the adjoining property of Bazincourt as from 1 January 1751. In return, however, the younger Stainville contracted to pay off his father's longstanding debt to Pâris-Monmartel, now running at 48,000 livres. The Marquise de Stainville threw in her ironworking properties of Châtelet and Removille but only as from her own death and subject to the payment by her son of legacies amounting to 72,000 livres of Lorraine.

The bride's property was more briefly described as comprising, first, a fortune 'of three hundred thousand livres whereof gift was made to her by Master René-Joseph de Gouffier, Canon of the Church of Paris,' but under stipulation of 9 February 1747 that the income therefrom should belong to her mother during the lifetime of the Marquise du Châtel. The rest of the property resided 'in the rights of inheritance, real and personal, of the said young lady the future spouse in the inheritance of the said Lord the Marquis du Châtel her father'. That was the juicy marrow, potentially.

The terms of contract, while boldly declaring that the young couple 'will hold all property in common . . . in accordance with the custom of Paris', subsequently spelt out that each of them would pay 'into the said Community [of property] the sum of eighty thousand livres, to be taken respectively' from the property of each, 'and the surplus of property belonging to each . . . , real and personal, shall be and remain peculiar to them and theirs on each side and line of descent': except that the Count de Stainville's property must further provide his wife with a jointure of six, contingently eight, thousand livres. Her diamonds were subject to particular safeguards, as were future acquisitions or alienations, with the Marquise du Châtel designated to supervise her daughter's interests during her minority. As to the past, specifically excluded from the community of property, and assigned to individual responsibility, were 'the debts and mortgages of one and the other done and created before the celebration of their marriage'.

Such was the legal reality of the marriage commonly supposed, and indeed with reason, to have made the fortune of the future Choiseul. But if marriage is apt to be a rather distasteful blend of love and legalism, love, even then, could prove the determinant. Whereas, on the strictly legal side, it might appear that the bride's lawyers had done a good job in protecting her from being a little heiress handed over for the plucking. While the Count de Stainville's brilliant future remained as yet unknown, not so his conspicious extravagance.

Immediately, too, Louise-Honorine du Châtel's only large fortune in cash, that 300,000, yielded nothing either to her or her bridegroom – and it came, rather strikingly, not from the fabulous Crozats but from her maternal Gouffiers. True, the unspecified but crucial inheritance from her father did pretty promptly provide 40,000 livres. Of this the first 24,000 was delivered to the Count de Stainville by Sieur Petit, the Marquis du Châtel's executor and 'guardian in charge (*tuteur onéraire*)'[7] of his daughter, no later than 10 December 1750, two days before the marriage. The sum was just half of what he had to pay off for his father to Pâris-Monmartel. The count duly gave a receipt and the amount was accounted to Sieur Petit, together with two subsequent payments to Stainville on 3 and 30 March 1751 of three and thirteen thousand respectively, making up the 40,000 as registered in a codicil of the latter date to the marriage contract.

If the Count de Stainville characteristically lost little time in cashing in, up to a point, it would appear that the marriage did not immediately make him an outstandingly rich man: even were it the case that his bride would be worth 70,000 livres a year 'even in the event of the loss of several cases which Madame du Châtel has against her brothers-in-law,'[8] the President de Tugny and the Baron de Thiers, over her husband's estate. Choiseul was to recall succinctly that at the time of his engagement 'Mlle du Châtel then had a lawsuit upon which depended a large part of her fortune'.[9] Even if that were somewhat overstating it, the issue was a substantial one.

The Marquis du Châtel had inherited that Breton marquisate along with the lordship of Kérouarle under the will of his father, Crozat the Rich, as executed some years later in a family deed of 3 March 1742. The second of the three sons, Joseph-Antoine, the President de Tugny, a legal graduate from the Parliament of

[7] Receipt from Count de Stainville to Sieur Petit, Paris, 10 Dec. 1750: Archives de la Ville de Reims.

[8] Luynes, x. 389: the most favourable assumption is that a slightly unclear reference here to an income of 70,000 livres related to Mademoiselle du Châtel rather than to her mother.

[9] Choiseul, *Mémoires*, p. 62.

Toulouse to that of Paris, had inherited the barony of Tugny and other property in the Rethel district of the Ardennes. The lot of the youngest brother, Bernstorff's friend and Stainville's old fellow-campaigner, Louis-Antoine, Baron de Thiers had been that barony in the Auvergne, his father's mansion in the Place Vendôme and, apparently, the marquisate of Moy in Picardy. Theirs, however, never called himself better than a baron and from the litigation now arising it rather looks as if in some subsequent family transaction Thiers may have alienated Moy to the Marquis du Châtel, conceivably in the light of the death of the latter's only son in 1743 and of that further provision in the will of Crozat the Rich which was the nub of the main lawsuit now lumbering into action.

Not only had Louise-Honorine's father left no male heir, but her grandfather, Crozat the Rich, apparently wishing to be certain of keeping his main property in Brittany in the family, had bequeathed the estate of du Châtel to his eldest son under entail to his second son, the childless President de Tugny. This entail, confirmed in the marriage-contract of the Marquis du Châtel and in other family documents, had never been challenged by that amiable soldier. Upon his death Tugny had naturally claimed the property legally set aside for him, being already egged on, it would seem, by his younger brother, the Baron de Thiers. The Tugny–Thiers claim meant disinheritment of the estate for the Marquis du Châtel's only surviving child, Louise-Honorine, and for the future Duke de Lauzun, the three-year-old son of her deceased elder sister, the Marquise de Gontaut: too bad for the interests of the sisters: except that entail out of the direct line of succession was forbidden by the customary law of Brittany as spelt out in chapter 118 of the customary 'drawn up about the 14th century,'[10] as reinforced in a new customary by article 199 against gifts to heirs presumptive, as secured by decrees of 1682 and, especially, of so recently as 1746 regarding the jurisdiction of the Parliament of Brittany over its province, including the marquisate of du Châtel.

In all this the Count de Stainville could hardly have been more intimately involved, on behalf of his future wife, of his dead mistress and of his putative son. He and the friend he had cuckolded, the Marquis de Gontaut, weighed in for the Marquise du Châtel in the interests of her daughters, and their marriages. If Stainville was of a sanguine temperament his future mother-in-law was rather the reverse. A friend of the Marquise du Châtel, as of her brothers-in-law, the sympathetic Genevese patrician, Jean-Louis Saladin, was to

---

[10] Mémoire sommaire de la cause entre le Comte de Gontault et le Comte de Stainville et le Bn. de Thiers concernant la substitution de la terre du Châtel située en Bretagne', after mid-June 1751: Bibliothèque du Sénat, MS. no. 1103 (9455): 'Mélanges: XVIIᵉ–XVIIIᵉ', fo. 780.

write later of this case to another mutual friend, Madame du Deffand:
'It is a pity that the minority of the parties should not have allowed an
accommodation: it was a case if ever there was one for ending all the
claims by a compromise.'[11] Such a juicy case, though, just suited that
litigious age and it was beginning to grind into action shortly before
Stainville's marriage.

In August 1750 Stainville was telling Bernstorff: 'Our suit against
the President de Tugny will only begin at Martinmas. There have
been delays on both sides.'[12] There were to be more. At least the
family litigation was apparently at that stage as amicable as possible
in the circumstances in regard to the cultivated Tugny, described by
Stainville as 'amiable and charming company'.[13]

If people were surprised that the Count de Stainville with his
moderate means had hooked so rich a catch as the Crozat heiress,
they were also struck by his not waiting to land it by winning the
lawsuit before entering into marriage. The fondly worried Marquise
du Châtel would quite have understood a prudent delay. But
Stainville liked doing the big thing; and he liked getting things done.
So that, as a later friend remarked, if with some slight exaggeration,
'when he sought [the future] Madame de Choiseul in marriage, she
had hardly anything but hopes'.[14]

II

Financial legalities, happily, are not the sum of marriage. If dowries
were then important, so were trousseaux, not least perhaps for a girl
later distinguished for her fastidious taste in fashionable clothes
despite the solitary piece of advice allegedly given to Louise-Honorine
du Châtel by her mother – not to have any tastes. It was around the
time of her marriage or soon after that Louise-Honorine was
portrayed in a pastel, ascribed to Jean-Baptiste Deshays, as a vestal,
a fashionable one with silken topknot upon the neat coiffure of her
auburn hair. Bows graced her throat and breast. In this enchanting
portrait, though, fashion yields to her face, also very French, if not
exactly beautiful then fetchingly distinctive. The efficient elegance,
not least of her mouth, is set off by her large eyes gazing dark and
deep in a limpid candour already, maybe, serenely tinged with
disillusion. Grief, certainly, was for her no stranger. She, so young,

[11] Saladin to Marquise du Deffand, Geneva, 15 Aug. 1751: Du Deffand/Lescure, i. 141.
[12] Count de Stainville to Baron von Bernstorff, Paris, 7 Aug. 1750: *Bernstorffske Papirer*, ii. 621.
[13] Ibid., 10 Jan. 1751, p. 629.
[14] Dutens, *Mémoires d'un voyageur qui se repose*, ii. 83.

had but recently lost her father and before that the sister who had passed on to her the man now to become her husband.

The future Duchess de Choiseul is said to have remarked: 'I never had any youth except that happy deception which they so soon and so inhumanly took from me.'[15] She was to take issue with her confidante, Madame du Deffand, for supposing 'that I am without passions because I am reasonable, ... without reproach because I am without passions! ... Well, learn then that my character is, on the contrary, one of the most violent and passionate that has ever existed, and that if I have some merit, it is from having triumphed over it a little ... You believe, again, that my education was excellent, because my mother was a clever woman; but this education was the most null of all, and perhaps indeed that it is what was best about it; for at least they did not bestow upon me the errors of others. If I have learnt something, I owe it neither to precepts nor to books, but to some afflictions. Perhaps the school of misfortune is the best of all, when these misfortunes are not of a sort to debase the soul, or the soul is not of a cast to let itself be debased. Passions are perhaps the greatest masters as also the greatest obstacles; it is force proportioned to resistance. But that is enough and much too much said of myself. The exposures which I am making cannot be agreeable to you, and these confessions are but humiliating for me.'[16]

The Count de Stainville's little bride had the makings of a considerable woman, if one taking after her father, described by President Hénault as having 'infinite intelligence. He was a little too fond of dissecting his ideas ... He was a little too much the metaphysician, and had communicated this taste to Madame du Châtel', his wife, 'who was as intelligent as he, and who was charming company and with a character as solid as it was agreeable':[17] another of young Stainville's special friends of sterling quality.

The Marquise du Deffand, later blind and recalling the youthful Countess de Stainville, was to describe her to Voltaire: 'Picture to yourself a nymph, made like a model, as pretty as the day.'[18] This chimed with local tradition whereby Louise-Honorine was featured as the shepherdess Issa from Lesbos in Boucher's allegorical painting, in the year of her marriage, of Apollo revealing his divinity to Issa, wrongly identified of old as Latona. By the same tradition the figure of Apollo, advancing radiant upon his classic shepherdess in elegant disarray, represented an idealized Count de Stainville. This Apollo

[15] Duchess de Choiseul to Marquise du Deffand, cited, Du Deffand/Ste-Aulaire, i. cxxiii.
[16] Duchess de Choiseul to Marquise du Deffand, Chanteloup, 25 July 1766: ibid., i. 60–1.
[17] Hénault, p. 237.
[18] Marquise du Deffand to Voltaire, 21 Mar. 1769: Du Deffand/Lescure, i. 554.

and Issa, if not among Boucher's great compositions yet one of his more satisfying in its delicate interlacing of thrust and plane, had been commissioned by Madame de Pompadour's benefactor, Le Normant de Tournehem, as director of the Bâtiments du Roi for 2,400 livres in 1749. That was the year in which the court theatre at Versailles had put on the opera by Destouches which for the past fifty years had familiarized France with Apollo's passage with Issa from Ovid's *Metamorphoses*. For some reason, however, the painting was left on the artist's hands and was bought by Stainville, it is said[19] as a wedding-present for his wife.

Issa's expression of almost timid trust, sweetly grave, in straining towards Apollo might indeed suggest Louise-Honorine du Châtel but on other grounds there is much to be said for an alternative identification of Boucher's Issa and Apollo as disguises for Madame de Pompadour and the king. It is in any case supposed[20] that another woman who was to be enjoyed by Louis, a callipygian Irish miss, Louise or Louison O'Murphy, modelled for the naiad reclining among the reeds in a parallel to the bride, but naked, straining away from her own swain to cast a backward glance of tenderness, she too, at dazzling Apollo. This naiad is set against a dark background of woodland in contrast to the central effulgence, nearly heart-shaped, of frolicking cupids, of whom one aloft, up by the horses of the sun, brandishes the torches of love and marriage.

The contract of marriage between the future Duke de Choiseul and his potential heiress was additionally signed on the morning of Saturday the 12th December 1750 by such witnesses as were not 'lords of the court (*seigneurs de la Cour*).'[21] This signature took place in the du Châtel mansion 'in the street and by the gate de Richelieu,' smartly up the road from the massive building of the Royal Library. That same morning, 12 December, the marriage was celebrated in the chapel of the Marquise du Châtel in the parish church of Saint-Eustache. After the service it was back to the bride's home in the Rue de Richelieu for a grand reception for friends and relatives, foremost among them the witnesses to the contract.

Noticed among the witnesses was the bride's brother-in-law, the Marquis de Gontaut, and the Count de Stainville's youngest brother, the rather handsomer Leopold-Charles, Abbé de Choiseul, abbot still

[19] Cf. Barbara Scott, 'The Duc de Choiseul, a Minister in the Grand Manner' in *Apollo* (January 1973), xcvii, no. 131, p. 46. This version appears rather more plausible than the older one whereby the picture was a wedding-present from Louis XV to the Stainvilles.

[20] Cf, Boris Lossky, *Tours: Musée des Beaux-Arts: Peintures du XVIIIᵉ siècle* (Paris, 1962: vol. vii in *Inventaire des collections publiques françaises*), no. 5 *et passim* for discussion of this picture, with iconography.

[21] Marriage-contract between the Count de Stainville and Mademoiselle du Châtel, 6 and 12 Dec. 1750: *u.s.* for the following.

Louise-Honorine, Countess de Stainville,
later Duchess de Choiseul.

Apollo revealing his divinity to Issa.   François Boucher, 1750.

of local Jovilliers, now also vicar-general to their handy relation, the
Bishop of Châlons. The ascent of the Abbé de Choiseul was unlikely
to stop there if it could be helped by his eldest brother, already keen
upon assisting friends and, not least, close relations. In the previous
year the Count de Stainville had been prodding the Duke de
Nivernais in Rome to see to some unspecified 'business of the Abbé
de Choiseul,'[22] apparently also featured as the Abbé de Stainville.

One absentee from the wedding-reception of those who had
attended the signature of the contract at Versailles was the Duchess
de Luynes, friend and also relation since the Marquise du Châtel was
a Luynes on her mother's side: a significant connection for the future
Choiseul. At the court ceremony the duchess, in attendance upon the
queen, had been feeling hot and heavy. On the night of the following
day she came out with smallpox. Back at her house in Paris the
Duchess de Luynes was joined by another of the queen's ladies, the
Marquise de Flavacourt, who went down with the same disease of
mortal danger. Marie Leszczynska required seven or eight letters a
day about their condition.

Those who did attend the wedding-reception in what had been the
Hotel Crôzat, built in 1704 for Pierre Crozat the Poor, would drive in
from the Rue de Richelieu and up the stem of a T, past stables and
offices, into the main courtyard fronting the house, not all that large,
elegantly simple in its two main stories with ionic pilasters rising to
corinthian beneath a high-pitched roof. Deeper than it was wide, this
mansion by Cartaud, the architect who had done Montmorency for
Crozat the Rich, had received additions, not universally regarded as
happy, by the fashionable Le Carpentier to the order of the Marquis
du Châtel after he had inherited it in 1740 from his uncle together
with part of his magnificent collections. This was the home where the
Count and Countess de Stainville were to begin their married life.

For a wedding-reception there was the great gallery, right through
the house and running the whole width of the ground floor on the
inner frontage. Sixty foot by twenty-two, this gallery gave upon three
sides, through nine french windows, on to the garden which formed
the crossbar of the T. Some eight acres of garden constituted, even in
contemporary estimation, 'fairly considerable grounds for a private
house, above all in such an inhabited district'.[23] The central view was
of an onion-shaped lawn sloping away to an ornamental facade
'which seems to proclaim the entrance to a saloon but which is only
backed on to the wall which separates this garden from that of the
Hôtel de Gramont'. This dummy facade faced straight across to the

[22] Count de Stainville to Duke de Nivernais, Paris. 1 Sept. 1749: W.N.A., docket V/1, fo. 9.
[23] Jacques-François Blondel, *Architecture françoise* (Paris, 1752–6), iii. 90 for the following.

du Châtel mansion where the December afternoon was reflected in the back wall of the great gallery by large mirrors corresponding to the arrangement of the Galerie des Glaces at Versailles.

Reflected also was the interior surround of rich decoration 'in virile taste and without the affectation of any superfluous ornament'.[24] Gilt cherubs held girandoles above the focal fireplace in the mirrored wall. This delicately exuberant carry-through from high baroque had been crowned in 1707 by the chief glory of the gallery, its vaulted ceiling painted by Charles de la Fosse to set off Cartaud's architectural celebration in the same combination of artists as at Montmorency. This time La Fosse's renowned composition depicted the birth of Minerva, issuing from the brows of Jove against such a sky 'that the ceiling-vault appears actually to be pierced'.

The aged La Fosse had lodged in the mansion which he had embellished till his death in 1716 and his widow had been allowed to stay on. Since then others had moved or were moving in on the kindly hospitality of the Crozats and du Châtels in the Rue de Richelieu. The Marquis de Gontaut was now to be joined there by the other son-in-law. There is some suggestion, though, that the Count de Stainville did not move into this snug billet on the very night of his marriage in order to consummate it with his teenage bride.

That the bridegroom's concern on the day of his marriage was not with it exclusively is suggested by the opening of the letter which he wrote to Nivernais next day, the Sunday, to catch the weekly post on Monday for Rome:

The postal courier from Rome has been delayed this week, my dear friend, and arrived only yesterday. I was at first anxious at having no news from you, but ... when I got in again (*en rentrant*) yesterday evening I found your letter of the 25th [November 1750] ... I am very glad that the smallpox is lessening. That will set your mind at rest. I think just like you that it would be a good thing that your children should have it in such a favourable climate, but for all that I am wonderfully aware that one can wish it only in the past and never in the present. There is a prodigious amount of it in these parts. Mmes de Luynes and de Flavacourt have got it at Versailles. So far they are standing it well, and there is every ground for thinking that they will pull through successfully.[25]

It was only in the second paragraph that the happy man began: 'I am up to my neck in wedding (*Je suis en noce jusqu'au col*). Stainville got married on Saturday to Mlle du Châtel. I think I have already told you. I hope that when today is over there will be no more talk of

[24] Germain Brice, *Description de la ville de Paris* (Paris, ed. of 1752 f.), i. 380 for the following.
[25] Count de Stainville to Duke de Nivernais, 13 Dec. 1750: W.N.A., docket V/1, fo. 36 for the following.

it. It bores me to distraction (*Cela m'excède d'ennuy*), and we have not got much compensation (*grand dédommagement*).'

So much for marriage making the Count de Stainville promptly rich, or romantic. In his throwaway description of it, worthy of the Méchant, he was as in most things quite in fashion. Two months later his friend Bernstorff was to confess: 'One of the grounds which moves me to marry is the wish to satisfy my creditors without diminishing the fortune which I have inherited from my fathers ... Did I not have this aim ... then I should not think of uniting myself with a person who does not know my heart.'[26] For this young statesman 'the role of one betrothed is such an embarrassing part'.[27] Less coldblooded if anything was the Count de Stainville. His marriage may after all have been for him a bittersweet occasion, celebrated at Saint-Eustache where they had buried his loved mistress and, now, posthumous sister-in-law, where they had christened her son, never to be recognized as his.

III

To suppose that the Count de Stainville took it out on his little bride would be to slander his sunny nature. His kind consideration for her became recognized. A month after their marriage he gave an intimate glimpse of it in beginning a letter to Bernstorff: 'Mme du Châtel charges me, Sir, to remember her to you and to thank you for your kind concern with my marriage. I congratulate Mme de Stainville every day upon only having entered society after your departure. She has no regrets but she pretends that between the two of us, Mme du Châtel [and I], if we continue to talk about you in front of her, we shall cause her some, and that without her knowing you, which is more unhappy when one has no hope.'[28] The flirtatious teasing of newly-weds is of every age.

The same letter added: 'Mme. de Luxembourg is back from Versailles and settled for good in Paris where she maintains a large and fine house. Everything here in the way of good society comes and wants to come there. One no longer even sees there any doubtful characters.'[29] The Duchess de Luxembourg was turning over a new leaf in this inauguration of the most elevated and socially influential

---

[26] Baron von Bernstorff to Count H. W. von Schmettau, 6 Feb. 1751: cited, A. Friis, *Bernstorfferne og Danmark*, i. 261–2.
[27] Ibid., p. 266.
[28] Count de Stainville to Baron von Bernstorff, Paris, 16 Jan. 1751: *Bernstorffske Papirer*, ii. 630–1 for the following.
[29] Ibid., p. 631.

of all the salons of the French eighteenth century. It was also to be
almost the longest-lived, into the close of the Ancien Régime, and
lastingly intimidating to such as the new Countess de Stainville.
Twenty years later she could still write of the Duchess de
Luxembourg: 'Despite the velvet paw which she has always shewn
me, I cannot prevent my fear of the scratch of which I have heard so
much, and this fear inspires in me an insurmountable and probably
intolerable constraint, which must add further to my natural
sullenness; so that she has every reason to find me not nearly so
agreeable as I find her.'[30]

The future Duchess de Choiseul was to be described by Horace
Walpole, writing to the poet Gray, as 'not very pretty, but has fine
eyes, and is a little model in wax-work, which not being allowed to
speak for some time as incapable, has a hesitation and modesty, the
latter of which the Court has not cured, and the former of which is
atoned for by the most interesting sound of voice, and forgotten in the
most elegant turn and propriety of expression. Oh! it is the gentlest,
amiable [sic], civil, little creature that ever came out of a fairy egg! so
just in its phrases and thoughts, so attentive and good-natured!
Everybody loves it.'[31]

Yet Louise-Honorine was a spirited woman matched to her
husband. In the year of Walpole's description she was herself to
write:

Life is through fire, youth burns for pleasure, lively hearts for love, the ambitious for
glory, virtuous people for honour, for the good, that good whereby one creates
enjoyment and enjoys oneself. Those who have acquired some celebrity of whatever
kind it be, those who have handed down their names to us from the remotest
centuries were all alight with this fire divine; it extends its existence over the present,
it perpetuates it in future centuries. Those whose names are dead to posterity were
so already to their contemporaries. I know that one can acquire this celebrity by
criminal means, but it is not the crime which has become celebrated, it is this ardent
element which has produced the great efforts which have astonished the universe or
have changed its face.[32]

That ardent element was Choiseul's, and it was exacting. At first
repressed, his wife was still to write of him after nearly twenty years
of marriage: 'It seems to me that he is beginning to be no longer
ashamed of me, and it is a great point, already, no longer to wound the
self-esteem of people by whom one wants to be loved!'[33]

Even a happy relationship can conceal distances only to be bridged

[30] Duchess de Choiseul to Marquise du Deffand, Chanteloup, 4 Nov. 1771: Du Deffand/Ste-
Aulaire, ii. 82–3.
[31] Horace Walpole to Thomas Gray, Paris, 25 Jan. 1766: Walpole Correspondence, xiv. 154–
5.
[32] Duchess de Choiseul to Marquise du Deffand, 1766; u.s., i. 19.
[33] Duchess de Choiseul to Marquise du Deffand, Chanteloup, 13 May 1770: u.s., i. 265.

by love entire. In the present case one may suspect that distance was widened by discrepancy of age hardly less than by Choiseul's unfaithfulness. Yet, years hence, he was to write to a friend concerning a marriage projected between a young girl and a Marquis de Boufflers in a later generation: 'You will be sensible that a girl of fourteen is easier to mould than one of twenty. Besides, I do not doubt that M. de Boufflers will take all the precautions useful for the health of his wife. As for the disproportion [of ages], I do not understand why it should cause alarm. I think that one is still young at thirty-five, and that it is much happer for a woman to marry a man of that age than to marry one of twenty. I am an example under this head. I got married at thirty-three, my wife was not thirteen and I flatter myself that from the time of the marriage she has been pleased to have married me.'[34]

Stephen de Stainville, in fact thirty-one, began to mould his bride of thirteen and lead her into their union of happiness and of sadness there in the mansion du Châtel with its sheltering acres. Even in winter one could stroll in the stone-built orangery to the right of the central lawn, looking from the back of the house, and slantwise to it since this ornamental greenhouse, topped by a terrace, backed on to the old rampart of the capital, now planted out as a raised boulevard. This Cours flanked by four rows of trees sliced across the du Châtel garden and, by the orangery, steps led down to 'a subterranean passage pierced at much expense through the earthwork of the rampart'[35] to connect on the far side with a well-planned kitchen-garden running over to the gardener's house and backyards on the cul-de-sac of the Grange-Batelière.

The offices of the mansion itself were likewise commodious. They included water-closets supplied from a pump and cistern fitted in beneath a staircase. Nor was the great gallery the only sumptuous apartment calculated to foster in the young couple what may have been already a shared enthusiasm in keeping with the wedding-present which Stainville is said to have given his bride. He was later to recall that 'Mme de Choiseul liked painting and good pictures. How could it have been otherwise? For M. Crozat du Châtel, her father, was a great connoisseur and possessed one of the richest collections that there was in France.'[36]

IV

Beauties from the original collection of Crozat the Poor still graced the Hôtel du Châtel at the time of the wedding. Only the Marquis du

---

[34] Duke de Choiseul to Gabriel Sénac de Meilhan, Chanteloup, 20 Aug. 1772: *Mélanges de littérature et d'histoire* (Société des Bibliophiles Français), part I (Paris, 1856), pp. 303-4.
[35] Germain Brice, *Description de la ville de Paris*, i. 378.
[36] Choiseul, 'Mémoires inédits', 3/31/16/21/2.

Châtel's collection of sculpture, less attractive to the Count de Stainville, had as yet been sold. Pictures were massed in two symmetrical rooms upon either hand on traversing the house from the courtyard to the gallery. And jutting out along the eastern flank of the court was the dining-room featuring oval allegories of the four seasons painted for that room in 1712 by Watteau, another familiar of the Crozat household. Summer, celebrating corn-crowned Ceres with her sickle, and old Winter huddling away from the winds and the frosts towards a kindling fire were among the few paintings which the future Choiseul was to keep all his life. He is said to have acquired subsequently four other ovals of the seasons by Pater as well as a couple of his *fêtes champêtres*, notably the delicious *La Balançoire*.[37] The then Count de Stainville retained a taste for the fadingly fashionable, lastingly enchanted ambiance of *fêtes galantes*.

Another lifelong inheritance from the Crozats was a little portrait of a nun by Rubens (possibly one of his studies of a saint such as Theresa), also perhaps two large paintings 'of subjects from fables'[38] by La Fosse who had done the ceiling of the great gallery. The Countess de Stainville's relatively modest inheritance from the Crozat collection included a few Spanish paintings and, as one might expect, some Italian including three Guido Renis, as many Guercinos, and Tintoretto's Judith and Holofernes.[39]

The Count de Stainville, however, was not waiting upon a Crozat inheritance of pictures, any more than of money, in order to enrich his collection. His correspondence about the time of his marriage confirms that it was not to make him a promptly rich man. Less than a month before the event he began a letter to Nivernais:

You tempt me much, my dear friend, by the description which you give of the picture ... I think as you, five thousand francs would be too much money. My finances would not allow me to go to that if it were worth ten. I should even be accomplishing a great effort and an indifferently reasonable (*médiocrement raisonnable*) action in laying out a thousand Ecus of our currency on it, but I could lay this folly to the account of my illness. The whim of a man with the vapours is quite as good as that of a pregnant woman, so I could well go up to that.[40]

Stainville was apparently reckoning a thousand *écus* as being then worth about three thousand francs or livres. For the picture itself:

[37] Now in the Louvre.

[38] Paillet, sale-catalogue for 18 Dec. 1786, cited, Émile Dacier, 'La Curiosité au XVIIIe siècle: Choiseul collectioneur' in *Gazette des beaux-arts*, 6th period, xxxvi. 72.

[39] Now in the Prado.

[40] Count de Stainville to Duke de Nivernais, 16 Nov. 1750: W.N.A., docket V/1, fo. 30 for the following.

I am well aware that as to colouring there is a great difference between that of Poussin and of Rubens, and it is indeed the former's weak side, so I have hardly thought of having anything by him for this reason. I am by nature fond of colour, and you need it in Flemish collections and the pictures lacking it do not hold up in them. However, I know that Poussin did some that are beautiful enough in colouring. They are rare but there are some. I confess to you moreover that it is extraordinary to find a French painting in Rome, though it has happened several times, but places and names are nothing provided that the things are beautiful and, all that said, if the picture is as I imagine it from your report and your knowledge I shall be very glad to have it.

The Count de Stainville was almost literally a vivid person, and exacting. He subsequently dismissed an offer from the nervous Nivernais, to keep the Poussin for himself if his artistic mentor was not delighted with it, as being 'too noble and generous to be accepted'.[41] And again:

I see that you speak to me modestly of it ... but through this circumspection I perceive very well that you think a lot of it ... I am however a little sorry that the background be blackened, for in Flemish collections black pictures are even less successful than elsewhere, and in short I do not like them black, but I suspect you of making the harm out to be greater than it is, and I confess that I am very greatly impatient to have it in my home ... I only beg you to have it carefully rolled up and packed by somebody used to sending pictures.[42]

Poussin it was to be, perhaps not only he. Already by the end of 1750 Stainville had been writing to Nivernais: 'You tell me further of two other sales which are to take place and you ask me for letters of credit. You well know that I have not the courage to refuse you anything, and that I am very susceptible to the temptation of pictures. So do everything you wish, provided that our common mentor is in favour.'[43] The Duchess de Nivernais was a moderating influence upon this keen collector, who kept to his limit of a thousand *écus* per picture. So that were Nivernais to buy him another two at that price in addition to 'the one by Poussin, that would make 9,000 livres, which is a very large sum, and above my present capacity ... It is all that I could do and even more. I have got such a wretched head today that perhaps I explain myself rather badly, for I am sensible that I am not very much myself, so do not keep literally to what I am telling you, but rest assured that I shall always approve what you do for me.'

A month later: 'As for the Titian whereof you tell me, it is very difficult to defend myself against the temptation. Have no scruple about the nudity. The affliction of my nervous gender (*genre nerveux*)

41 Ibid., 28 Dec. 1750, fo. 38.
42 Ibid., 17 Jan. 1751, fo. 42.
43 Ibid., 28 Dec. 1750, fo. 38 for the following.

has changed nothing in me in this respect, unless it be to remove the danger while leaving me the taste for it.'[44] Thus intimate was this correspondence of the Count de Stainville, incidentally suggesting a venereal clue to his chronic indisposition at that period.

Some months later Stainville was to confirm his enjoyment of the nude in art by buying at auction for a modest 560 livres a delight from the Crozat collections, Rembrandt's Finding of Moses[45] by aquatic handmaidens in undress.

For the present the Count de Stainville treated the Duke de Nivernais to what he termed 'my little observations'. First, the Titian's price was a bit stiff, 'all the more since three and two make five, and I have heard that your wife has said that it was madness to spend so much on pictures. You know how afraid I am that she should disapprove of me, and incidentally she should be very pleased with me, for since your departure I have not bought one.' He continued:

Besides that you know that Titians are very suspect. They have nearly all been copied and that always casts doubt as to originality. At the very least it lessens their merit. I even believe that there is a sleeping Venus by him in this country, without my being able to recall where. Finally I have seen much by this artist in which the colour is worn, among others the fine Du Châtel Danäe which you know, and Mr. de Boexière has bought one which cost him very dear, of which the copy is in the Palais Royal, and which creates no effect in his house ... It is true that those which are well preserved and of his good period are most agreeable, and he is an artist of whom I am very fond.

One may now dismiss a further doubt previously entertained[46] about the future Choiseul as a collector: whether he was not just a rich fancier buying decoration through the taste of others rather than a connoisseur who really cared about pictures. Stainville's informed response to that tempting Titian speaks for itself. It sounds as though it may have been one version of several treatments by Titian of the theme of a sleeping Venus or sleeping nymph.

Stainville's mention to Nivernais of Boexière referred to a rich farmer-general whose taste for art assorted him with the count. There was some question of facilitating the transport of Stainville's Poussin from Rome through the good offices of Boexière rather than the official ones of Puysieulx which the impatient purchaser scouted. Couriers were expensive whereas Stainville was depressed to hear from Sainte-Palaye, back from Rome, 'that the route by sea was often very slow'.[47] More than a month later Stainville was telling Nivernais:

[44] Ibid., Paris, 1 Feb. 1751, fo. 45 for the following.
[45] Now at Philadelphia.   [46] By Émile Dacier, op. cit., xxxvi. 72.
[47] Count de Stainville to Duke de Nivernais, Paris, 1 Feb. 1751: u.s., fo. 44.

'I am awaiting my Poussin with great impatience, and I confess that it would be very well received if you would kindly pack yourself up in the same case.'[48] Another fortnight and the writer at last had word that his picture had reached Marseilles, though he was not to receive it in Paris till the latter part of May 1751.

V

Paintings were not the only preoccupation of the Count de Stainville about the time of his marriage. If he now had a real home to embellish and a legal need to secure its financing, he also, soon now, would have a new career to make. He was already comparting his concerns even in writing to his closest friends. While he hardly mentioned art in his letters to Bernstorff, those to Nivernais were almost innocent of Stainville's diplomatic aspirations. Whereas, back from Fontaine-bleau a fortnight before his marriage, he had confided to Bernstorff: 'They are talking again of the first journey which you approve without telling me why ... Your friend will lend himself to it if the proposals are decent. M. des Issarts, who is the ambassador to Poland, is dying and returning. I would not want to replace him for anything in the world, and I hope that you will approve.'[49]

If Bernstorff had not specially enjoyed his own posting to Poland some fifteen years earlier, he had, as a good diplomat, remained the abiding friend of 'the families', the proudly brief designation of the two great Polish ones of Czartoryski and Poniatowski. And Stainville was familar not only with Bernstorff but also with Conti, so one may not be surprised that evidence from a little later suggests that if the future Choiseul did not already know of or surmise the personal diplomacy of Louis XV in Poland, he was at all events on to Conti's covert intrigue for the Polish crown, and anxious to steer clear of it.

Stainville's set resolve, already, against service in Poland is as suggestive as his early inclination towards the Bourbon south, notably Naples. That, though, now seemed receding. Early in 1751 he informed Bernstorff: 'The rumour has circulated in Paris that I have been nominated to the embassy at Naples. That has amazed me because it is certain that M. de Puysieulx has not spoken to me about it, that probably he is not thinking of me, and besides that I still need to be in Paris for a fairly considerable time to look after my private affairs. So soon as they are finished, I should have great pleasure in

[48] Ibid., 7 Mar. 1751, fo. 50.
[49] Count de Stainville to Baron von Bernstorff, Paris, 31 Nov. 1750: *Bernstorffske Papirer*, ii. 629.

shewing my zeal for the king's service, but from now till then it is not possible.'[50]

Private affairs meant legal proceedings. Whether in law or love, war or politics, the future Duke de Choiseul seldom did things by halves. He was to recall: 'I was occupied, the year after my marriage, with Mme de Choiseul's case. With great application I followed through with this matter, which I had in common with the Duke de Gontaut, father of the Duke de Lauzun, who was then five [*sic*] years old.'[51] One notices the sidelong but specific attribution of paternity. The putative father continued: 'I was lodged in Mme du Châtel's house with the Duke de Gontaut. We lived together in intimacy and I should say that this intimacy has not slackened for a moment for twenty-three years.' At that time, incidentally, the widowed Gontaut was in love with a Madame Rossignol, wife of the intendant of Lyons. Gontaut was constantly on about her to Stainville, asking him over and over again, 'Brother, do you think Madame Rossignol loves me?'[52]

The answer, as Stainville conceived, might partly depend upon the outcome of the litigation shared with Gontaut. Here the year of 1751 had opened somewhat inauspiciously, precisely because their opponent at law, the amiable magistrate Joseph-Antoine Crozat, President de Tugny fell ill and died within a week. Stainville diagnosed correctly to Bernstorff: 'I believe that this event, in the circumstances of the lawsuit, is unfortunate for me.'[53]

Stainville went on to explain that immediately, as regards Tugny's undisputed slice of the Crozat fortune, 'he constitutes M. de Thiers, his brother, as his residuary legatee. Moreover he only makes bequests to some friends and servants, by virtue of which, the residuary legacy once satisfied, the rest of the real property belongs to Mme de Stainville; but since it appears that M. de Thiers will quit his capacity of residuary legatee, the inheritance will be divided in half between us. I do not know what we shall get out of it; I am afraid that it will be nothing much; it will depend upon the number of debts,' as legacies so often do. Still, nothing much by Stainville's standards might not be too bad after all.

The real property left by Tugny in Paris alone was worth three hundred thousand livres. On a smaller scale, it is uncertain whether the Countess de Stainville recovered her grandmother's gold cabinet which Tugny had inherited from the countess's father less than a

[50] Ibid., 16 Jan. 1751, ii. 630–1.
[51] Choiseul, *Mémoires*, p. 63 for the following.
[52] Louis Dutens, *Mémoires d'un voyageur qui se repose*, ii. 101.
[53] Count de Stainville to Baron von Bernstorff, Paris, 10 Jan. 1751: op cit., ii. 629 for the following.

year before. Put up for sale that summer was the bulk of Tugny's collection of paintings and sculpture, together with part of the late Marquis du Châtel's holding of pictures and prints as well as a residual 244 pictures from the founding collection of Pierre Crozat the Poor. The auction included his favourite Raphael as well as paintings by Titian, Tintoretto, Veronese, also Rubens, Rembrandt, Lebrun, a *Danäe* by Poussin which made 1,890 livres, a seaport by Claude Lorrain, and a Watteau study of a bodyguard. The sale made 31,000 livres that year. Such was the dispersal of probably the greatest art collection of all time, tantalizing to such a keen and relatively straitened collector as the Count de Stainville. His wife's modest inheritance of paintings and such small acquisitions as Rembrandt's Finding of Moses scarcely compared with the wealth of the Baron de Thiers, who was 'extremely rich in pictures by old masters which come for the most part from the cabinet of the late M. Crozat'.[54]

All this, though, was comparatively small stuff by the lush standards of the Crozats. The big prize remained the disputed entail of the estate of du Châtel. As Stainville proceeded to explain to Bernstorff, Tugny's death 'changes nothing in the first lawsuit. M. de Thiers will take the place of his brother. At the same time I have every ground to be pleased with a conversation which I had yesterday with M. de Thiers. He made me feel that in this pass he regretted your absence, and that touched me. His capacity as your friend will be a very powerful reason for me to redouble my attentions to him.'[55]

Thiers wrote Bernstorff letters giving him the other side of the lawsuit. Thiers, not a uniformly attractive character, apparently found it more difficult than Tugny to maintain amicable relations with his legal adversaries, although he was subsequently, at all events, to be friendly enough with his niece. Conceivably the many campaigns which Thiers had shared with young Stainville may have made them rather too well acquainted. Stainville confided to the pacificatory Bernstorff three weeks later.

The desire which you entertain, Sir, and which no doubt can only be advantageous to me, is becoming very difficult to fulfil with regard to M. de Thiers in view of the terms that he is on with my mother-in-law, and the considerable suits which we have got to have judged. But if it is impossible that we should live cordially together, it is at least very sure that I on my side shall pay all proper attention so that nothing happens which could shock him either in my behaviour or in my conversation. I wish that on this last head he had the same consideration as I, but when he may fail in what he owes to me, I am too vain to resort to recriminations.[56]

[54] Dézallier d'Argenville, *Voyage pittoresque de Paris* (2nd ed., Paris, 1752), p. 113.
[55] Count de Stainville to Baron von Bernstorff, Paris, 10 Jan. 1751: *Bernstorffske Papirer*, ii. 630.
[56] Ibid., 31 Jan. 1751, pp. 631–2.

A proud disdain of rivals and enemies was characteristic, for good and ill, of Choiseul's career from beginning to end. Thiers for his part was a formidable opponent and could indeed be an awkward customer. With his additional inheritance from Tugny he was in any case exceedingly rich. At the Château de Tugny the Baron de Thiers was to live in state, maintaining a private troop of sixty horsemen and pursuing a policy of territorial annexation. When, five years later, he expensively prised out from neighbouring Arson the maddening Madame de Fuschenberg, a sporting lady who had queered his own hunting, Thiers dismantled her château, toppled the towers of Arson, chopped down the surround of fine trees.

Such was Stainville's opponent in the engrossing lawsuit. It called for the best briefing and incidentally sorted out for the future statesman legal friends and opponents. Their subsequent fortunes are instructive. For the opposition the Baron de Thiers enlisted the support of his cousin and friend, the President de Meinières, learned compiler of a celebrated collection of legal texts. Twenty years earlier Jean-Baptiste-François Durey de Meinières had, like Hénault, become a Président des Enquêtes at the tender age of twenty-five, and he had since been brought into the literary fringe by his blue-stocking wife Octavie, known as Madame Belot. Now his legal intervention was to mark him down, so he subsequently pled to Madame de Pompadour, as 'the victim of the persecutions and calumnies wherewith the Marquis [sic] de Stainville and the Marquis de Gontaut have overwhelmed me.'[57] On the other hand Stainville was greatly assisted in his suit by a very swagger and adroit lawyer, President Ogier, like President de Meinières a keen Jansenist despite his schooling at Louis-le-Grand. Jean-François Ogier d'Enouville had a clever and amusing wife also known to Stainville, owned the splendid Hôtel Lauzun on the Île Saint-Louis, was a keen collector of china and a keen shot: in that year of 1751 he organized a shoot at Orly for friends like the Duke de Croÿ. It has been justly suggested,[58] as typical of that age, that the duke's sumptuous style of living did not differ much from that of the lawyer, also a friend of Gontaut as well as Stainville and himself a future ambassador. It was significantly Ogier who was to interpret the policy of the future Choiseul at Copenhagen and act as go-between with his particular friend and counterpart, Bernstorff.

For the present Stainville was writing to Bernstorff on 6 February

---

[57] President de Meinières, 'Conversations de la Marquise de Pompadour et du Président de Meinières', Première Conversation, 31 Jan. 1757: M. A. P. Malassis, *Correspondance de Mme de Pompadour avec son père, M. Poisson, et son frère, M. de Vandières*, p. 177.
[58] Cf. François Bluche, *Les Magistrats du parlement de Paris au XVIIIe siècle*, p. 372.

1751 that 'our case is at last going to begin in a fortnight'.[59] The rights and wrongs of the customary law of Brittany versus the Crozat entail were at last thrashed out that spring on behalf of the Marquis de Gontaut and the Count de Stainville versus the Baron de Thiers and his son-in-law, the Count de Béthune, an adherent of Stanislas Leszczynski. Towards the end of May judgment was due for delivery by the Chambre des Requêtes of the Parliament of Paris.

In its medieval origin the Parliament of Paris been an assembly of the king's lay vassals and prelates as still reflected in the eighteenth century in the legal personnel of counsellors both lay (*conseillers lais*) and ecclesiastical (*conseillers clercs*). Only lay counsellors served by rotation in the parliament's criminal jurisdiction of its grim Chambre de la Tournelle; whereas the counsellors generally were attributed to one or other of the main instances for civil suits, the Chambre des Enquêtes and the Chambre des Requêtes, both subdivided into several courts. While the Chambre des Enquêtes served as a court of appeal acting upon the briefs and documentary inquests (*enquêtes*) from courts of first instance such as those of the bailiwicks back in the Barrois, the Chambre des Requêtes, originally pronouncing upon petitions (*requêtes*) direct to the king, had become a jurisdiction for the civil suits of privileged persons, those enjoying the right of evocation or Committimus. Such were Stainville and the other noble litigants in the du Châtel case. A circumstance which was to prove of critical importance for them all was that the Chambre des Requêtes was not a court of final instance since appeal lay from it to the supreme organ, the primitive survival of the Parliament of Paris in its dignified Grand' Chambre with its special procedure and jurisdiction under seasoned judges.

On the morning of Thursday, 27 May 1751, the news sped out to Versailles: the Requêtes had given judgement 'in favour of M. de Thiers and M. de Béthune. The entail has been declared good and valid. M. de Gontaut has been sentenced not only to clear out of the properties of du Châtel and Moy, but even to the restitution of the [interim] proceeds from them, and with costs.'[60] That went, of course, for Stainville too. They had been sitting together in court, listening to the delivery of the heavy verdict calculated to deprive them both of a fortune. At one point during the reading Stainville said to Gontaut under his breath, 'My brother, do you think that Madame Rossignol loves you?'[61] The two discomfited young aristocrats burst out laughing to the astonishment of the court.

[59] Count de Stainville to Baron von Bernstorff, Paris, 6 Feb. 1751: *Bernstorffske Papirer*, ii. 633.
[60] Luynes, xi. 148.   [61] Dutens, op. cit., ii. 100–1 for the following.

The future Choiseul was evolving, in matters civil as well as military, a gay courage of which he was to have full need in years to come. It was now, one hears, that 'he told his mother-in-law, who was grieving, not to worry, that he would not give the game up till he had an embassy and had acquired a property yielding two hundred thousand livres a year'.

Three days after the verdict the Count de Stainville was writing to his Danish confidant;

On Thursday, Sir, I lost my case, not indeed unanimously, but very materially. We have appealed against it to the Grande Chambre, and although I believe that the business could not be in better shape, yet this verdict of the Requêtes is a disadvantageous detriment, more disadvantageous and more stinging with regard to the public than it will be with regard to our new judges. If M. de Thiers wins his case, it will throw me into a multitude of affairs that we do not see the end of, and the disunion that has come between us deprives us of hope of any accommodation. We are beginning to plead again on the first of July, and judgement will be given at the end of August.[62]

Meanwhile the friends of Madame du Châtel were expressing their concern through the intermediary of Madame du Deffand. In the middle of June Montesquieu wrote from Holland: 'I beg you to speak of me to Madame du Châtel. I learn that the Requêtes of the Palace [of Justice] have not been favourable to Madame de Stainville; tell her [Madame du Châtel] how much I feel everything that concerns her and this charming person who will never have a rival in anybody's eyes except for her mother.'[63] The little Countess de Stainville was already earning high praise from the high-minded. Three days later Saladin was chiming in from Switzerland:

I am very sorry that Madame du Châtel still has to spend several weeks between fear and hope. My friendship for M. de Tugny[64] had perhaps made me view the question in a prejudiced sense which I ought not to maintain. The battle before the judges of first instance is already good proof that in the point of law there are more problems than I had thought; and if in case of doubt one may have regard to the considerations, they come down with much more assurance for the daughters of the elder son than for those of the younger.'[65]

Saladin continued: 'This business has pained me extremely from its beginning, and I have looked on it as a relief that I shall be out of

[62] Count de Stainville to Baron von Bernstorff, Paris, 30 May 1751: *Bernstorffske Papirer*, ii. 634.
[63] Baron de Montesquieu to Marquise du Deffand, Breda, 15 June 1751: Du Deffand/Lescure, i. 130.
[64] Following the original edition of 1809 (*Correspondance inédite de Mme du Deffand*, i. 35) in preference to de Lescure's emendation to 'Thiers' in Du Deffand/Lescure, i. 131.
[65] Saladin to Marquise du Deffand, Geneva, 18 June 1751: *Correspondance inédite de Mme du Deffand* (Paris, 1809), i. 35 for the following.

Paris when it comes to be judged in the final instance. When heart
and mind are not in agreement, one is ill at ease.' He subsequently
explained: 'I wish and fear to learn the result of the case; I believe that
Thiers is right, and I am very fond of Madame du Châtel. I do not
think, like you, that women are eternal children; first, they cease to be
such before we do, and besides they withdraw much sooner than we
from a certain dissipation. It is as common for men to have the
vapours as it is for women. Those of Paris have always seemed to me
less frivolous than the men who could be their parallel.'[66] The
reflective Genevese concluded as to the fair sex in the current case:
'What I find consoling in it is that there is enough stuff for all these
ladies, married or to be married, to have been the best matches in
Paris.'[67]

Stainville had greater confidence in the merits of his case than did
Saladin, or some more malicious gossips. It may well have been, in
that society, that in the last resort the friendship of the Marquis de
Gontaut with the Marquise de Pompadour may not have done his
case, and Stainville's, any harm, to put it mildly. But the latter's
accounts to Bernstorff suggest that Stainville at all events was relying
primarily upon his brief. It was still a strong one, and being
strengthened.

The case still turned upon the du Châtel–Gontaut–Stainville
argument that the customary law of Brittany specifically forbade
entail, such as the Baron de Thiers now claimed. Stainville's side
mobilized an important precedent from 1708 when royal letters-
patent had been granted to the house of Rohan, outstanding in
Brittany, precisely in order to exempt it from the provisions of the
customary law against entail and deeds of gift: 'formal recognition by
the king', claimed Stainville and his colitigants, 'of the existence of
the law, and that it should be observed in all cases where letters-
patent do not derogate from it'.[68] Nor was that all.

As a prelude to the resumption of the case at the beginning of July
1751 the side for which Stainville was going all out procured the issue
of 19 June of an affidavit (acte de notoriété) as to the validity of the
Breton prohibition of entail.

It looks from the legal arguments as though Stainville's assessment
to Bernstorff was correct. It would appear that Thiers, despite his win
in the Chambre des Requêtes in respect of the evident intention of

---

[66] Ibid., 24 July 1750, i. 43.
[67] Ibid., 15 Aug. 1750, i. 47.
[68] Mémoire sommaire de la cause entre le Comte de Gontaut et le Comte de Stainville et le
Bn. de Thiers concernant la substitution de la terre du Châtel située en Bretagne', after mid-
June 1751; Bibliothèque du Sénat, MS. no. 1103 (9455): 'Mélanges: XVIIe–XVIIIe', fos. 783–6
for the following.

Crozat the Rich, was being bent back by massive legalism. For now came counter-argument from Thiers that even if the customary law of Brittany were valid against entails, in order to satisfy the terms of the Crozat bequest as closely as possible, the Crozat inheritance should be treated as solidary: that is, the inability to execute the entail in respect of the property of du Châtel in Brittany should be offset and compensated by transferring the entail to other family property outside Brittany, such as that of Moy in Picardy, which could have been legally entailed – if only Crozat had in fact done so.

That argument in turn was beaten down on behalf of Stainville and his partners in law. Their pleading against it unkindly concluded:

This is what causes it to be said with good reason that Sieur Crozat the Father did what he could not do, and did not do what he could. He did what he could not do in entailing the property of du Châtel situate in Brittany; he did not do what he could since he could have entailed his properties situate beneath other customary laws ... So one can confidently affirm that no regard can be had in this case to the method of compensation employed by the Baron de Thiers.

Approaching the crux, on 1 August 1751, Stainville closed a letter to Nivernais: 'I have a lawsuit which torments me and tires me greatly. That is no good for the vapours ... Goodbye, my dear friend. My head is in a miserable state.'[69] In his next, of 9 August, Stainville wrote; 'I am still taken up with my case. Judgement should have [been][70] given last week but there is a matter between the archbishop [of Paris] and the Parliament which has occasioned several meetings of the chamber at the expense of my hearings.'[71]

This delay was due to a classic pother over the administration of the General Hospital of Paris, which grouped ten institutions caring for the sick and destitute, feeding over twelve thousand of them.[72] As usual then, religion bulked large in the hospital, which had become a hotbed of Jansenism. Against this the archbishop had weighed in and had had his authority over the hospital reinforced by a royal declaration of 24 March 1751. Now the Parliament of Paris, the champion of the Jansenists, was refusing to register it as it stood. The governors of the hospital were divided while widow Moisau, put in by the archbishop to run it, managed to put everybody's back up. The unpleasantness dragged on till, as Stainville was to remark to Bernstorff by the end of November, 'the affair of the hospital which seemed in principle, Sir, to be a wretched wrangle, has become a very important and very singular affair'.[73]

[69] Count de Stainville to Duke de Nivernais, 1 Aug. 1751: W.N.A., docket V/1, fo. 91.
[70] Text torn.   [71] Ibid., 9 Aug. 1751, fo. 93.
[72] Cf. J. M. J. Rogister, 'Conflict and Harmony in Eighteenth-Century France', p. 39.
[73] Count de Stainville to Baron von Bernstorff, Paris, 27 Nov. 1751: Bernstoffske Papirer, ii. 636.

It had in fact become the first serious crisis between the parliament and the government since 1732. Some days after Stainville wrote parliament did grudgingly give in over the General Hospital but the broader context remained ominous. In its factious handling of that affair the Parliament of Paris had been venting its displeasure against the government for having constrained it that May to register an edict for a royal loan of fifty million livres on top of fifty million already borrowed plus thirty million raised since 1749 by Machault's Vingtième.[74] His attempt to impose it as a uniform levy was sparking the resentment not only of the Parliament of Paris but of the provincial estates of the outlying Pays d'Etat which had retained the right to levy their own taxation for the crown, notably in the form of so-called *dons gratuits* comparable to those voted by the clergy. On clerical taxation a royal retreat was indeed operated under the lee of the row over the hospital, which enabled the Count d'Argenson, in charge of Paris, to encourage the king against the parliament, in the direction once more of the church to the discomfiture of his ministerial rival, Machault. On 23 December 1751 a royal decree was to suspend the collection of the contentious clerical contribution of 1,500,000 livres. Machault's reform had failed against the vested interests of the church. Once again under the old regime it was the old order which prevailed.

The earlier opinion of the Count de Stainville, that people tended to underestimate the clerical comeback, was already being borne out. It was a dingdong struggle, though. If the clergy now won the battle of their taxation the parliament was to vex them yet more sorely in the looming conflict of faith and principle, already embedded in the affair of the General Hospital, in regard to Jansenism.

These stormclouds were pregnant for the future of the Count de Stainville. For the present, however, they imposed upon his lawsuit only temporary delay. In telling Nivernais of it on 9 August 1751 Stainville had yet added: 'I hope that I can secure judgement tomorrow. If so I will add a word to my letter.'[75] And indeed it ends: 'P.S. My case has been decided and I have won it.'

The news spread: the Grand' Chambre had subtantially reversed the verdict of the Chambre des Requêtes, 'at least as regards the property of du Châtel, which makes a difference of 60,000 livres in income... The judgement is without [further] appeal. They maintain that, according to the customary law of Brittany, Messrs. de Gontaut and de Stainville could not lose the property of du Châtel.'[76] But

---

[74] Cf. J. M. J. Rogister, 'Conflict and Harmony in Eighteenth-Century France', pp. 41 f.
[75] Count de Stainville to Duke de Nivernais, 9 Aug. 1751: W.N.A., docket V/1, fo. 93 for the following.
[76] Luynes, xi. 206.

their plea against compensation for Thiers in the property of Moy
was not upheld. Du Châtel, though, was the main inheritance.
Despite typical allegations of court influence in the courts, the verdict
on the du Châtel inheritance would appear to have been legally
correct.

The Count de Stainville and his brother-in-law had overcome
quite an adversary. Stainville was now, like Thiers, to be a really rich
man. The count's keen work on the case had paid off handsomely.
The regional incidence of customary law under the old regime had
largely set up the forward-looking Duke de Choiseul of the future.
Once again, not for the last time, his fortunes exemplified that motto
which he had taken over from Sorcy back in Lorraine, *A force d'aller
mal tout ira bien.*

CHAPTER VI

RELATIONS

I

THE marriage of the Count de Stainville was not the only one arranged in the clan of Choiseul in that winter of 1750 to 1751 with important effect for his future. And, more than with his own marriage, this effect was to turn upon the Marquise de Pompadour, then putting on weight and 'becoming more beautiful than ever'.[1] It was in that snowy February that she went sledging, the enchanting emblem for all time of Boucher's Winter. Coincident, indeed, were jeering suggestions that she was suffering from 'jubilee fever' in that religious jubilee of 1751 pressed home upon the king by the lenten sermons of Father Griffet with reference to the woman taken in adultery. Madame de Pompadour's friends countered that she had never been on better terms with Louis. At the same time she could claim that her role as royal mistress was, strictly, now completed. It was then that she had had made for Bellevue a statue of herself as the goddess of friendship.

That January, too, an edict had brought to fruition one of Madame de Pompadour's most beneficent enterprises. She had put her head together with the Pâris brothers to carry through their longstanding project of creating a royal military academy to provide free education, including languages, for five hundred future officers from the age of eight. For the Marquis de Stainville, kept posted by 'my friend' Pâris-Duverney, the École Militaire 'will be the finest monument which could be erected'[2] to the reign of Louis XV, through the intermediary of his zealous mistress. Rather different was the concern with her then of the Count de Stainville.

In his memoirs for this period the later Duke de Choiseul, embarking upon his most elaborate piece of personal explanation, laid the scene in his intimacy in the Rue de Richelieu with his brother-in-law and special friend: 'M. de Gontaut was a courtier by taste and habit. He was the friend of the king's mistresses, and as for me, in the time of Mme de Pompadour who was the reigning one, I

---

[1] D'Argenson, vi. 370.
[2] Marquis de Stainville to Emperor Francis I, Paris, 20 Dec. 1750: Esteri del Granducato di Toscana, vol. 2296/1287, no. 46.

went to court only when my pleasures induced me to. Since I had become a Maréchal-de-Camp I had no business to do with the ministers. Mme de Pompadour thought that she hated me and said so fairly openly.'[3]

This, it is clear by now, was a rather careful picture of careless pleasure, let alone his diplomatic aspirations. Yet there was probably some significant truth in the filling out of this picture by Choiseul's earliest biographer. This eulogist related that the then Count de Stainville found the brilliant court around the Marquise de Pompadour 'cramping and dull'. Thus:

He was bored there and he was, besides, little loved there. The sagacity and precision of his mind gave him an acute and prompt perception of the faults in the operations of the cabinet. The oddities which he came across in society, the frankness and freedom of his character did not allow him to keep silent on the judgments which he passed; and the gaiety, the charm, the thrust, which went with everything he said, rendered all the more stinging the censure and ridicule which he bestowed upon everything that shocked or amused him. He had spread himself upon crazy and immoderate sarcasms and jokes about Madame de Pompadour.[4]

The contrast between the originally bourgeois manners and increasingly regal state of the royal mistress 'had provided the gaiety of the Count de Stainville with a thousand shafts full of sallies which had all been repeated. His jokes were even mingled with more serious censure.' For:

Light as he seemed, gay as he was, the Count de Stainville from then onwards showed that respect for public opinion, for keeping the decencies which never deserted him in any of the positions wherein he has found himself. It seemed to him that this existence of Madame de Pompadour, whom the king had carried off from her husband, whose name he had changed, whom he had installed in the queen's household, was a monstrous existence: that it violated all the rules of society, of justice and of propriety. He explained his view of it with more gaiety than bitterness, but with a pungency and freedom which were restrained by no consideration. So Madame de Pompadour proclaimed that she hated him: for which one could not blame her.

Even if this is taken with a pinch of salt, Stainville's letters about then to his close friends do reveal in him a serious underside with moral implications, as in his almost paternal concern for settling down his flightier lady-friends such as the duchesses de La Vallière and de Luxembourg. What is now known, however, of his rebuffed endeavours and diplomatic feelers at court, to be extended to Madame de Pompadour herself, suggests a sharp corrective to his later story

[3] Choiseul, *Mémoires*, p. 63.
[4] Essai/Arsenal, fos. 36–9 for the following.

that 'I worried infinitely little about what she thought and said [about me] and I never talked about the court either to M. de Gontaut, or to all the courtiers with whom I used to live, except when there were some jokes to be made about it.'[5] According to one who knew Stainville well, 'M. de Gontaut did all he could to have him taken into the intimacy of the king and of the Marquise; but since M. de Stainville had the reputation of being a malicious man (*homme méchant*), his brother-in-law met with resistance.'[6] The poor standing of the supposed Méchant with Madame de Pompadour was liable to be lowered further by what now occurred.

The then Stainville began his story:

M. de Gontaut lived on intimate terms at Versailles with the Marquis de Meuse who, like him, had no other employment but that of a courtier. At M. de Meuse's he saw a M. de Choiseul, a stupid, brutal, coarse starveling, who had been all his life in an infantry regiment and who had managed to get [command of] a regiment by I know not what chance. This M. de Choiseul was poor and a gambler. He was my cousin german. He had spent his life in garrisons. Most recently he had just been serving at Genoa or in Corsica. I had never seen him.[7]

Such was the later Duke de Choiseul's rendering of François-Martial, Count de Choiseul-Beaupré, two years older than himself but actually of an earlier generation so that the careful Duke de Luynes was more accurate in describing the Count de Choiseul-Beaupré as a 'cousin german of M. de Stainville, the father',[8] the marquis. This lopsided cousinship derived from the thirty-three years which had separated the first and second marriages of the Marquis de Stainville's grandfather, Louis de Choiseul, Baron de Beaupré. Whereas the father of the marquis, the naval captain who married Nicole de Stainville, had been the eldest son of the first marriage, the eldest of the second had been Antoine, Marquis de Choiseul-Beaupré and head of the branch of Choiseul-Sommeville. Antoine's second son was François-Martial, born on 8 October 1717. He had indeed become colonel of the Regiment of Flanders even though Luynes confirmed that he had 'not one sou of property.'

Now, in the aftermath of the War of the Austrian Succession, the Count de Choiseul-Beaupré had at last quit his garrisons for Paris, where he went to see his younger and brighter cousin, the Count de Stainville. Looking back, the latter wrote that Choiseul-Beaupré

[5] Choiseul, *Mémoires*, p. 63.
[6] J. N. Dufort, comte de Cheverny, *Mémoires sur les règnes de Louis XV et Louis XVI et sur la révolution*, i. 138.
[7] Choiseul, *Mémoires*, pp. 63-4.
[8] Luynes, xi. 106 for the following.

'spoke to me of his mediocre fortune and the difficulty he had in maintaining himself at the head of a regiment.' In reply:

I advised him to acquire a reputation through love of his profession and willingness to volunteer for all the most distant and dangerous assignments, and even to go to America if that was necessary. I represented to him that with his name and with attachment to his profession, living with his regiment rather than being a gambler at Versailles, he would acquire respect; and that this respect would in the long run procure for him, with the support of his relations, the ease which he wished to obtain. M. de Choiseul did not seem to me to relish my advice. He was right, for the friendship of M. de Meuse, and of M. de Gontaut above all, was to lead him much more quickly to fortune. M. de Gontaut used to talk to Mme de Pompadour continually about M. de Choiseul, who had become his dominant passion and in consequence the perpetual subject of his conversation. Mme de Pompadour had in a very dark corner a relation of her husband who had a daughter. She conceived the idea of marrying this girl to M. de Choiseul. M. de Gontaut became very excited about this marriage. M. de Meuse joined him.[9]

The girl was Charlotte-Rosalie de Romanet whose father, a counsellor in the Parliament of Paris, had conveniently just died. Her mother had been born Marie-Charlotte d'Estrades, ultimately descended from the Marshal d'Estrades of the Roi Soleil and, more immediately to the point, the sister-in-law of the also widowed young Countess d'Estrades, the intriguing adherent of the Marquise de Pompadour and her cousin by marriage of the latter's husband's aunt. The obvious picture has been of the Countess d'Estrades putting her head together with Madame de Romanet to push Charlotte-Rosalie into the marriage; though by one account it was against the mother's wish that Madame de Pompadour arranged for the girl of sweet seventeen to marry the impecunious Count de Choiseul-Beaupré.

The then Count de Stainville continued:

One day M. de Gontaut came to Paris to tell me that he thought I would approve of what he had done for the fortunes of my cousin, and that he had got Mme de Pompadour to give him Mlle de Romanet, her relation. In thanking M. de Gontaut for his goodwill and his kindness I could not conceal from him that I disapproved infinitely of this marriage. I recall that I gave him two reasons for this: first, that I preferred that M. de Choiseul should remain in his military condition with a mediocre fortune rather than contract an alliance which seemed to me dishonourable; secondly, that I thought it was very imprudent to place at court, inside the king's circle, a man who seemed to me in the first place very little made for that part of the world, whose coarse style presaged nothing but vexations.

Young Stainville's pride in the clan of Choiseul was genuine enough. Conceivably more substantial, though, than the reasons

[9] Choiseul, *Mémoires*, p. 64–6 for the following.

which he advanced against the marriage was the underlying circumstance that it might by no means suit the ambitious Count de Stainville if another and so clearly inferior Choiseul count, whom he had not exactly encouraged, should leapfrog him into favour. If that is a little hard on Stainville, yet Gontaut maybe suspected something of the kind. According to the former:

M. de Gontaut seemed to me to be shocked by my observations. He shewed me honestly but sharply that my repugnance displeased him and he ended by saying to me that he looked on M. de Choiseul as his son and that, if I agreed, he would not miss an opportunity to make the fortune of a man of that birth, who had no other resources from his own family but the advice to go to America, which was about the same as advising him to throw himself out of the window. In vain did I represent to him [Gontaut] that this advice should not have seemed so extraordinary to M. de Choiseul since he already had two brothers established in Saint Domingo.

The Choiseul connection with Haiti or French Saint Domingo, harking back to the Count de Stainville's grandfather, was being maintained by the offspring of the latter's half-brother in the Sommeville branch of Choiseul-Beaupré. (The elder brother of François-Martial, Antoine-Nicolas, was another naval captain.) And it was the more natural for Stainville to suggest a West Indian destination to his soldier-cousin since the Minister of Marine was at that time actively recruiting forces to defend the French colonies as a counterpart to the postwar drive to reconstitute the navy. Saint Domingo, moreover, was then an active front in its small way owing to a boundary dispute over the division of the island between the two Bourbon powers of France and Spain.

But as young Stainville, in his vividly recalled altercation with Gontaut, defended his cousinly suggestion of Saint Domingo:

M. de Gontaut listened to me with impatience, and as for me, who did not want to quarrel with my brother-in-law over a matter which after all could not have interested me less, I ended the conversation with a joke and left the field clear for the little-enlightened enthusiasm which he entertained for M. de Choiseul. M. de Gontaut thought, however, that he ought to go and speak of this project to M. de Praslin who, without our having consulted one another, put to him the same reflections on this marriage which I had made to him. This did not produce anything except that M. de Praslin incurred his displeasure. The marriage of M. de Choiseul with Mlle de Romanet was concluded without their speaking to me any further about it.

So, that spring, 'everybody who bore the name of the bridegroom was invited to the wedding-feast at Bellevue, at Mme de Pompadour's'.

II

It was on a Sunday, 25 April 1751, that Madame de Pompadour's new residence provided a splendid setting for the uneasy celebration of this union of the proud house of Choiseul with the monied interest of the sexually compromised Le Normants. Writing of it next day to her brother, the Marquise de Pompadour noted of her fond sponsor: 'M. de T[ournehem] was very pleased and with good reason.'[10] Others saw less reason. The Count de Stainville was an ironic participant in that festivity at Bellvue, of which he recalled:

I perceived that M. de Gontaut had said something about the dissatisfaction which I had expressed over this marriage, for Mme de Pompadour, and above all Mme d'Estrades, the aunt of Mlle de Romanet, did not look upon me too kindly. This did not prevent me from diverting myself infinitely over the new relationship which I had acquired. Mlle de Romanet, who was getting married, was fairly well made with a common face and the air of a kept woman who has plenty of experience of the world. I have never seen such bold, one might even say loose manners. She had a mother, Mme de Romanet, who bore a perfect resemblance to the borrowed aunt of a woman of the town. I saw from the first moment that the new bride would get herself talked about, and I was certain of it when I perceived, at the end of the dinner, the marked flirting which she allowed herself with M. de Beauvau who, as a relative, had been invited to the wedding-feast.[11]

There is a story that Beauvau, then thirty-one, was to respond to the allurements of the new Countess de Choiseul-Beaupré. Someone more exalted certainly did.

For the present Madame de Pompadour lent Bellevue to the bridal couple for their wedding-night and 'procured for M. and Mme de Choiseul favours without number'. The king had endowed the bride and created two supernumerary appointments, of Choiseul-Beaupré as a gentleman to the Dauphin, and of the countess to be a lady-in-waiting to the princesses: lush enough even if people exaggerated in reckoning 'that this marriage is costing the king two hundred thousand livres a year, without any need or reason'.[12] But then to Dufort de Cheverny, more gallant than Stainville, the Countess de Choiseul-Beaupré, 'beautiful as an angel, tender, discreet, faithful, was a dish fit for a king. One could compare her to Mademoiselle de Fontanges under Louis XIV.'[13]

[10] Marquise de Pompadour to de Vandières, 26 Apr. 1751: M. A. P. Malassis, *Correspondance de Mme de Pompadour avec son père, M. Poisson, et son frère, M. de Vandières*, p. 83.
[11] Choiseul, *Mémoires*, pp. 66–7 for the following.
[12] D'Argenson, vi. 395.
[13] J. N. Dufort, comte de Cheverny, op. cit., i. 138.

Women tended to be angels in the generous enthusiasm of the Count de Cheverny. Whereas the Duke de Croÿ, an occasional intimate at court, rather went along with Stainville in describing the bride as a lively and personable young thing, 'fairly pretty'[14] with 'a giddy air'.[15] After the marriage of the Choiseul-Beauprés, explained Stainville, 'Mme d'Estrades undertook to keep them with her at Versailles and they were invited, as I had foreseen, into the intimate company of the king',[16] not behindhand in granting the new Countess de Choiseul 'marks of distinction'.[17] Within weeks she was one of only five ladies, including Mesdames de Pompadour and d'Estrades, chosen to accompany the king to Crécy. Besides the usual staghunting and gambling there, 'since there are many young people on this voyage, there have been games of prisoners' base on the terrace'[18] in which even elderly courtiers played.

The party at Crécy that June included the Marquis de Gontaut, like the Dukes of Luxembourg and Ayen. 'Without being in this intimacy', recalled the uninvited Stainville, 'and despite the repugnance and contempt which I had for the blunders and pretentious airs of M. de Choiseul, since his protection did not extend to me, I was careful not to give him advice'[19] – it seems that in some reversal of roles it was already a question of the blunderer protecting his nimble cousin. The latter continued: 'But, persecuted as I was by his solicitations that I should see his wife, and in order to destroy the view held by Mme d'Estrades and Mme de Pompadour that this marriage – which meant nothing to me – was casting me into despair, I went rarely, but from time to time, to see Mme de Choiseul. She shewed me a kind of familiarity and confidence which amused me.' With such a lady-killer as Stainville that would suggest something of a flirtatious friendship. He concluded: 'I have spread myself upon this marriage, very immaterial in itself, because this marriage was the first circumstance which partly determined the conduct which I pursued thereafter and the various events which have followed from it.'

At the end of July 1751 the Duke de Croÿ found the Countess de Choiseul-Beaupré, along with such as the Countess d'Estrades and the Marquis de Gontaut, gracing the king's intimate suppers at Compiègne. The Count de Stainville may indeed have had other preoccupations about then, as the Duke de Nivernais in Rome may

[14] Duc de Croÿ, *Journal inédit du duc de Croÿ: 1718–1784*, ed. Vicomte de Grouchy and Paul Cottin (Paris, 1906–7), i. 167.
[15] Ibid., p. 189.
[16] Choiseul, *Mémoires*, pp. 67–8.
[17] J. N. Dufort, comte de Cheverny, loc. cit.
[18] Luynes, xi. 159.
[19] Choiseul, *Mémoires*, p. 68 for the following.

have gathered from a somewhat cryptic letter, dated 7 August, from
the Marquise de Pompadour:

Since my first letter went Stainville has sent me one for you which you will find
enclosed. He begs me to commend to you the business about which he is writing to
you. I do not know what it is, but no matter. I commend it to you anyway on account,
and I beg you to do it, doable or not. I embrace Your Excellency very tenderly and
wish you better pens than the one that I am using.[20]

This is the earliest trace from Madame de Pompadour herself of
any connection with the Count de Stainville. Just how early is not
quite certain since her dating by month alone could relate to 1749,
1750, or 1751. Either of the earlier years, however, might render that
obliging letter still more surprising than it would be in 1751, after her
patronage of the Choiseul-Beaupré marriage and her entertainment
of Stainville at its celebration at Bellevue. A week earlier than that
dating of the favourite's letter Stainville in his regular concern for
helping others had significantly sent to Nivernais direct 'a little
memorandum which the Abbé Chauvelin has begged me to
commend to you. If you can get him what he asks I should be very
obliged to you.'[21] This controversial Abbé was more warmly
supported by Stainville than the Abbé de Saint-Sauveur whom he
had guardedly recommended some weeks earlier since 'I know his
brothers who are in the interest of the P[rince] de Conti'.[22] A week
later again to Nivernais it was the turn of Stainville's own family:

The Abbé de Stainville is still thinking of going to Rome if the news of the
archbishopric of Narbonne is true. I beg you to interest yourself for him so far as
your credit may be able to influence it. He believes that the Pope would like him
better than another, because he was at the same college . . . If they consult you about
this, you could turn to account here this disposition of the pope, apart from the other
good things which there are to be said about him, and I answer for it that you
yourself would be pleased with him.[23]

The Count de Stainville about then was already helping quite a
few people to keep irons in the fire at Rome. Whichever the one for
which he enlisted Madame de Pompadour, it is striking that he was
thus able to mobilize her, to the extent of prompting her to write
specially to Nivernais just after she had closed a letter to him. This
needs to be set against the future Choiseul's careful disparagement in
retrospect of his early relations with Madame de Pompadour. At the
same time each may judge for himself from her delicate brevity of

[20] Marquise de Pompadour to Duke de Nivernais, 7 Aug. ?1751: Maison Charavay, *Lettres
autographes et documents historiques,* no. 747 (Paris, Dec. 1972), p. 48.
[21] Count de Stainville to Duke de Nivernais, 1 Aug. 1751: W. N. A., docket V/1, fo. 91.
[22] Ibid., 21 June 1751, fo. 78.
[23] Ibid., 28 June 1751, fo. 80.

expression how far she was as yet enthusiastic, or otherwise, in discharging a commission for the young man who was shortly to consult her about his diplomatic aspirations, whose high destiny, soon now, was to begin to intertwine with hers.

III

With his inheritance by marriage tied up at last, Stephen de Stainville could revert to his ambition for advancement through diplomacy, hitherto limited as he had indicated to Bernstorff at the beginning of that year of 1751: 'I could much wish that the quarrels of the north should give birth to the idea of a temporary commission: I should strive for this course, which would bring me close to you for some moments. If you see any daylight in this idea, let me know what you think, because a journey of three months would not at all disturb my affairs.'[24]

Stainville's hopeful wheeze did not come off. He was never destined to visit those northern reaches which were still preoccupying keen observers of international affairs, such as he already was, and still in terms of lively danger. Three weeks earlier he had written from Paris: 'They are murmuring of war here, but I think that this rumour has no foundation other than the desire which some individuals have to see it happen. However I see from the gazette that the King of Prussia finds himself a little embarrassed, and that this accession of England to the treaty of Petersburg could have an effect in the north. It is certain that if ever they fire the guns it can only be by way of your districts that the fire will reach us.'[25]

George II had recently acceded formally to the alliance between the Russian and Austrian empresses, though not in respect of its fourth, secret, separate article stripping Frederick of Silesia if he again resorted to war. This was liable to be a heavy blow to France, to the prospects of Franco-Austrian accommodation, as Frederick did his best to ensure. At the same time, as the Duke of Newcastle put it some months later, Frederick could only be kept 'in awe ... by Russia':[26] again the eastward escalation of fear from Hanover through Prussia to Russia. Anglo-Prussian relations had deteriorated and there were personal aggravations. Frederick the Great demanded the recall of the new British minister, Sir Charles Hanbury Williams, credited with the reflection that 'it was better to be a monkey in the

---

[24] Count de Stainville to Baron von Bernstorff, Paris, 31 Jan. 1751: *Bernstorffske Papirer*, ii. 633.

[25] Ibid., 10 Jan. 1751, p. 630.

[26] Duke of Newcastle to Lord Hardwicke, Newcastle House, 6 Sept. 1751: William Coxe, *Memoirs of the administration of the Right Honourable Henry Pelham* (London, 1829), ii. 406.

island of Borneo than to be a minister at Berlin'.[27] The Marquis de Valory's successor there for France, the Count de Stainville's comrade-in-arms from his Alpine campaign, the Irish Jacobite Lord Tyrconnel, complained of Frederick that 'conversations with this prince are a continual storm'.[28] Perhaps as some counterpart to this French appointment, when trusty Le Chambrier died in harness in that summer of 1751 Frederick provocatively replaced him in Paris with the Scotch Jacobite Keith, the proscribed Earl Mareschal. Well might Podewils exclaim on hearing of it, 'What will Uncle say?'[29] Uncle George of England said quite a lot, if not so emphatically as the Empress Elizabeth over another upset among the envoys accredited to the formidable King of Prussia.

Frederick the Great, who really seemed to enjoy annoying people, had entirely succeeded with Elizabeth and Bestuchev in the preceding summer of 1750 by making much of an envoy from the Khan of Tartary. The prussophil Russian minister in Berlin, Count Keyserling, was replaced by Gross, the old friend of the Marquis de Stainville from Paris. When Frederick meted out his familiar rudeness to Gross, he had been instructed at the end of November 1750 to quit Berlin forthwith, without taking leave. Two months later the Count de Stainville was writing to his Danish friend:

I am certainly wrong, for I am not of your opinion as to the new quarrel between the King of Prussia and Russia. Squire Gross is surely but a pretext for the animosity of M. de Bestuchev against the court of Berlin. I do not think, however, that anything interesting can blow up (*éclater*) before the Swedish Diet; but everything is so much in preparation for that moment that it would seem to me very difficult for the ill temper which dominates all this not to produce some sanguinary effects besides the discussion. If M. de Bestuchev were a great man, I doubt not that, with his ill temper, he would make war; but I have been told that he is such a poor individual that he will perhaps be afraid of such a weighty burden.[30]

In assessing the critical conjuncture of the north young Stainville was already evincing his capacity for sifting the superficial from essentials. Looking ahead to the Swedish Diet, he could not know that within two months, in March 1751, that meeting would be overshadowed by the death of King Frederick I of Sweden, the accession of King Adolphus Frederick and his ambitious consort,

[27] Sir Charles Hanbury Williams to Duke of Newcastle, 27 Feb. 1751: P.R.O./S.P.F. Poland 71, cited, Sir Richard Lodge, *Great Britain and Prussia in the Eighteenth Century* (Oxford, 1923), p. 78, n. 2.
[28] Lord Tyrconnel, cited: duc de Broglie, *L'Alliance Autrichienne* (Paris, 1895: henceforth cited as Broglie/Alliance), pp. 42–3.
[29] Count Podewils, cited, R. Koser, *König Friedrich der Grosse*, i. 561.
[30] Count de Stainville to Baron von Bernstorff, Paris, 31 Jan. 1751: *Bernstorffske Papirer*, ii. 632–3 for the following.

sister to the greater Frederick. However, the expectation that
Bestuchev would pull back from the arbitrament of war proved
correct. Stephen de Stainville's sharp writing down of the Russian
Grand Chancellor, if it reflected the forceful judgement of a young
officer, already suggested why Europe would need to look lively
when the Duke de Choiseul, no respecter of persons, should assume
conduct of policy.

For the present Stainville the younger continued to Bernstorff:

There has appeared a reply from the King of Prussia to the Russian declaration: I
have been told that it was very civil to the empress and very insolent to M. de
Bestuchev, which has served to increase ill temper. There has also appeared a
circular letter from the court of Vienna to the ministers of the Electors except those
of Prussia and the Palatine. It is the dullest production that ever I read, in accordance
with the usual style of that court.

If Stainville here again evinced scornful dislike of the tone of
Austrian affairs, he was personally interested in their conduct in
relation to his father. Three weeks earlier he had told Bernstorff: 'M.
de Kaunitz has a kind of malignant fever; he is still fairly seriously ill;
my father is ever here without knowing when he will be leaving'[31] to
settle his future in Vienna.

At the opening of 1751 the Marquis de Stainville had been
deploring Count Kaunitz's 'extreme weakness ... I only leave him as
little as possible ... The delicacy of his constitution makes me
tremble.'[32] A fortnight later he was ungratefully better. The elder
Stainville related that he had presented himself at the door of
Kaunitz's room 'several times without avail, but for some days I
myself have been attacked by such a violent bout of gout that it is
absolutely impossible for me to support myself. I shall, however, do
what I can to drag myself to Versailles next Tuesday'[33] in order to try
to push ahead what he described to the evasive Machault as 'this
wretched business'[34] of the fourteen-year-old liquidation of French
indebtedness to Lorraine from the War of the Polish Succession and
the ensuing settlement.

Sure enough on 19 January 1751 the Marquis de Stainville, as he
explained, found 'M. de Machault at the Marquise de Pompadour's.'
There:

As I had much difficulty in supporting myself, he asked me why I was exposing
myself to coming to Versailles in this state. I answered him that I was astonished by

---

[31] Count de Stainville to Baron von Bernstorff, Paris, 10 Jan. 1751: ibid., ii. 630.
[32] Marquis de Stainville to Emperor Francis I, Paris, 3 Jan. 1751: Esteri del Granducato di
Toscana, vol. 2296/1287, no. 48.   [33] Ibid., 17 Jan. 1751, no. 50.
[34] Marquis de Stainville to Machault d'Arnouville, Paris, 16 Jan. 1751: ibid., enclosure in no.
51.

his question, since it was he who obliged me to come there in order to complain of the slowness which he was bringing to the dispatch of the business which concerned Your Imperial Majesty. To which he replied that he only asked me for a few days more to finish his work on it, which was well ahead. Madame de Pompadour, who witnessed our conversation, said to me, 'I have asked the Keeper of the Seals to clear you promptly, and he knows how much I interest myself in what concerns you.'[35]

The royal mistress herself was another friend at court for the Marquis de Stainville, the friend of her old protectors, the brothers Pâris: another suggestion that the marquis was a more useful father than his eldest son subsequently made out.

Even favourites can find the going difficult when it comes to finance. By March the French foreign minister, Puysieulx, was assuring his old friend Stainville in regard to Machault that he 'was not ceasing to persecute him'[36] for a reply. As usual one excuse succeeded another so that there was still nothing to hand by 21 May 1751 when the Emperor Francis at last granted Stainville 'the permission so much desired'[37] to depart. Some days later his son was describing him as 'leaving for Vienna at the end of next month. I hope that it will be the last journey there that he will be making.'[38] The marquis explained to the emperor that on his way through Lorraine he proposed 'to stop some days at my place, where I have not been for thirty years':[39] which might seem a slight exaggeration. There was also some question of redeeming a previous promise to the Duke of Würtemberg to visit Stuttgart. The French reply, though, remained outstanding.

Stingy French obstinacy was an unresolved irritation not only for Stainville and his master but also for numbers of his former subjects in Lorraine, still denied French payment for their supplies. It would appear that in representing their interests the Marquis de Stainville perpetrated a document wherein the emperor was described as willing that his claim to compensation should be adjudged by Louis XV: yet another suggestion of easygoing precipitancy by Stainville in negotiation with the congenial French. The opening did not escape them in the person of Trudaine, the administrative dynast who had geared the Ponts et Chaussées to notable success and himself become intendant-general of finances, working to Machault.

[35] Marquis de Stainville to Emperor Francis I, Paris, 24 Jan. 1751: ibid., no. 51.

[36] Ibid., 7 Mar. 1751, no. 57.

[37] Ibid., 6 June 1751, no. 71.

[38] Count de Stainville to Baron von Bernstorff, Paris, 30 May 1751: *Bernstorffske Papirer*, ii. 634.

[39] Marquis de Stainville to Emperor Francis I, Paris, 6 June 1751: Esteri del Granducato di Toscana, vol. 2296/1287, no. 71.

The French court was in residence at Compiègne throughout July 1751. There on the 26th the Marquis de Stainville was at last handed the French reply on the Lorraine liquidation. The document was entitled Draft Decision, Projet de Décision. The decision proposed in the name of Louis XV was to be regarded by Francis I as derisory in relation to the magnitude of his claim, by then evaluated at nearly ten million livres. It was not the happiest augury for the aspirations of the Marquis de Stainville who, upon receipt of the French reply, left forthwith for Vienna 'where', noted the Duke de Luynes, 'he expects to remain till October. It is believed that he much wishes to succeed M. de Kaunitz as ambassador to France. He prefers it to the regency of Florence, of which there was a question for him. The Emperor has a minister there who leaves the regent no authority.'[40] Whether Stainville indeed preferred not to cross Richecourt, or was putting a good face upon disappointment, either way one may surmise that Stainville's old opponent, Toussaint, was not quite without influence in holding him off from the regency of Tuscany.

A fortnight after the Marquis de Stainville left the French court his son won his lawsuit and could resume his own, ultimately more successful, quest for diplomatic appointment. For the present the Count de Stainville's legal success was complemented on 26 August when King Stanislas bestowed upon him the honorific office of Grand Balli d'Epée du Pays des Vosges, involving ceremonial duties in Lorraine. If this distinction emphasized, as it were, the dynastic divergence of father and son, it was an appropriate one for the governor of Mirecourt, historically the focus for the bailiwick of the Vosges as one of the chief territorial components of Lorraine. It was a pleasing office, too, for the great-nephew of the valiant Fieldmarshal de Stainville, who had himself figured with honour in that direction of the Vosges.

More prosaically, by September 1751 young Stainville had to reckon with the resignation from the French foreign ministry of his father's friend, the Marquis de Puysieulx, described some months earlier as 'absolutely snuffing out . . . He can hardly string two words together.'[41]

Looking back, the later Duke de Choiseul commented: 'With the peace [of Aix-la-Chapelle] there supervened what one sees almost everywhere, and principally in France: the only concern was with intrigue. Poor M. de Puysieulx felt that he was not up to his job; M. de Machault, the controller-general, who had the preponderant credit, had the post given to an imbecile, M. de Saint-Contest, a

---

[40] Luynes, xi. 195.
[41] D'Argenson, vi. 376.

relation of M. de Courteilles, a friend of M. de Machault ... After the
departure from the council of M. de Puysieulx and the exile of M. de
Maurepas, there remained the preponderant ministers, Messrs.
d'Argenson [the younger] and Machault',[42] respectively the enemy
and the friend of the Marquise de Pompadour. Within a month the
elder d'Argenson too was observing that 'it is M. Machault who is
directing M. de Saint-Contest totally, as M. de Maurepas used to
direct the late M. Amelot ... I have discussed political matters with
M. de Saint-Contest; I thought him more petty-minded than any
minister I have ever seen.'[43]

On the same day that that was set down, 10 October 1751, the
Count de Stainville was writing to Baron von Bernstorff in a vein to
be compared with his subsequent account:

M. de Puysieulx enjoys, Sir, the greatest esteem, and is at present enjoying it without
disturbance and without anxiety for the future. I think that his near relations and
special friends are as sorry as the foreign envoys about the course which he has taken,
but they are hoping that he will retain great influence without fear of the
mortifications, that his health will be restored; besides which he enjoys a very
considerable income and will not leave court. So it is only his friends who are really
sorry. His relatives seem to me very content.[44]

Stainville here was accurate all round. Puysieulx was moving into
the apartments at Versailles recently vacated by Tencin. The
cardinal, now a rheumatic seventy-two, grieved by Machault's drive
against the clergy, had gracefully retired to his archdiocese of Lyons.
Louis XV had politely intimated to Tencin that he would still be
'charmed to receive news from you often';[45] and for years yet he was
in fact to receive regularly from the cardinal important intelligence
of his old friend, Pope Benedict XIV, with a future bearing upon the
career of the Count de Stainville. For the present, back at Versailles,
Puysieulx was indeed nicely off from the fruits of office and of favour;
and from Paris the most eminent member of the diplomatic corps,
Kaunitz, had reported: 'I am really sorry about the resignation of M.
de Puysieulx. He did business like a man of quality and was a
thorough friend of peace and an entirely honest man'[46], worthy of his
friend, the elder Stainville. The foreign policy of the Marquis de
Puysieulx was more successful than has usually been allowed. And

[42] Choiseul, *Mémoires*, pp. 371-2.
[43] D'Argenson, vii. 8.
[44] Count de Stainville to Baron von Bernstorff, Paris, 10 Oct. 1751: *Bernstorffske Papirer*, ii.
636.
[45] King Louis XV to Cardinal de Tencin, La Meutte, 3 May 1751: Luynes, xi. 126.
[46] Count Kaunitz to Emperor Francis I, Paris, 11 Sept. 1751: Ö.S./H.H.S.,
Frankreich/Berichte (1751), 126.

it importantly paved the way towards Franco-Austrian rapprochement in the diplomatic revolution.

Whereas Puysieulx's successor was further described by the Marquis d'Argenson as a poor clerk 'who hardly sees Mme de Pompadour. He is without industry and without address ... M. de Puysieulx detests M. de Saint-Contest and loses no opportunity to vex and bring him into ridicule. Mme de Pompadour's party is thus splitting and supporting her badly. It is thus that these court factions, ... battening on the weakness of the sovereign and upon injury to France, fight and destroy themselves by God's command, by atrocious ingratitude.'[47] With the Count de Stainville one deduction may have been that for a young man on the make a weak minister increased the importance of the royal mistress. He was writing to Bernstorff that October: 'I expect to go to Fontainebleau on the 19th of this month until the beginning of next. Madame de Luxembourg will be going at that time, and I shall be very glad to be there with her.'[48] Hers, however, was not to be the only feminine company that he kept there at court. In the following spring Stainville recalled to the same friend:

Last year, at Fontainebleau, Md. de Pomp [sic] spoke to me of this embassy [to Poland] in connection with that to Spain of which I was speaking to her. I felt before the conversation that the Polish commission would not suit me at all; what she said to me justified my refusal still further. I thanked her for her good will, as also the ministers. I believe that you will approve my conduct on this head; it seems to me that it would have been imprudent to risk my fortune at that game.[49]

Already a year before that interesting conversation in the autumn of 1751 Stainville, as noticed, had been set against succeeding Des Issarts as ambassador in Poland. Yet the military patronage which Stainville had enjoyed from Conti might well have suggested him as a promoter of that prince's 'game' in seeking election to the Polish crown. There were liable, however, to be undercurrents, crosscurrents. Conti's confidant and Stainville's detractor from the abortive Rhineland campaign, the Jesuit father Latour, had been described at the beginning of 1751 as 'the soul'[50] of the prince's Polish aspirations. The Marquis d'Argenson proceeded:

The Prince de Conti, indeed, does not seek support in this election from the Muscovites but there is Don Quixotry in this. He claims to be strong enough with

[47] D'Argenson, vii. 45.
[48] Count de Stainville to Baron von Bernstorff, Paris, 10 Oct. 1751: *Bernstorffske Papirer*, ii. 636.
[49] Ibid., 20 Mar. 1752, p. 641.
[50] D'Argenson, vi. 339–41 for the following.

the forces of Prussia, Sweden and the Poles to maintain himself as the elected king of Poland against the Russians, Austria and England ... My son seems to me to be in this cabal through Father de Latour, and they are flattering him that thereby they will enable him to attain the position of minister for foreign affairs ... The Marquise de Pompadour wants to rid herself of the Prince de Conti and thinks it would redound to the glory of the king, but the injury to France touches her little.

The slur upon Madame de Pompadour's patriotism is unsubstantiated. The suggestion that she might be playing along with Conti's Polish project for her own ends is interesting but uncertain. The certainty was that Conti hit it off with her no better than with her ministerial supporter, Machault: Conti was said that year to be vainly seeking admittance to the royal council. Less certain, again, is just how much she may have known of Conti's game. She was a clever woman, though, and now she evidently added to what the clever Count de Stainville already knew of it. It becomes almost more than a suspicion that the shrouded paradiplomacy of the Secret du Roi was, in part at least, known to both of them that early. One might infer, too, that another person to some extent in on it was their mutual friend in Copenhagen.

Back in 1751, then, the Count de Stainville and the Marquise de Pompadour were already on fairly amicable terms of some confidence, warmer, at all events, than they had been five years earlier when she had received him frigidly as Conti's spokesman after the capture of Charleroi, just at the inception of that prince's military eclipse. Now the confidential conversation at Fontainebleau that autumn may have marked a stage in Stainville's smart switch from the faction of Conti, his former patron, to that of Pompadour, his future one.

Three weeks before that conversation the Marquis d'Argenson had already been writing: 'The mistress is prime minister and is becoming more and more despotic, such as no favourite has ever been in France.'[51] As for the would-be ambassador, even then it was not every nobleman of thirty-two who felt able to turn down the suggestion of an embassy and angle for one of the very greatest, that at Madrid – again the southern, Spanish orientation of Stainville's interests. For the present, however, at the end of that year, he tersely reported to Bernstorff: 'M. de Duras is still going to Spain; Dresden has not been nominated.'[52]

Subsequently the Spanish ambassador at Paris, Don Jaime Masones de Lima, confided to the Earl of Albemarle that after Duras's appointment to Madrid he, Massones, had told him in reply to a question that 'upon the Spanish Ministers enquiring whether he

[51] Ibid., pp. 472–3.
[52] Count de Stainville to Baron von Bernstorff, Paris, 26 Dec. 1751: *Bernstorffske Papirer*, ii. 638.

knew anything of him [Duras] he had said, that in his younger days he was famous for cutting capers better than any man in France – and what else, interrupted Mr. Duras? Why, replied he, I added that as, between that time and your being appointed ambassador, you had been in the army and had seen the world, you might possibly have acquired other talents, but which are as yet unknown to me'[53] – as they still were to the Spanish government according to Don Jaime. The Count de Stainville was not alone in his moderate opinion of the Duke de Duras or, as now appeared, in his high one of the Baron von Bernstorff.

In March 1751 the sudden death of the Prince of Wales, hit by a ball, had brought Bernstorff a Hanoverian release or, in counterpart, Danish constraint. By 11 May he was writing to Madame du Deffand from delicious Fredensborg, a country palace of the Danish king: 'My fate is decided. I am staying here. I have just been nominated Minister of State, and I am to take my seat in the council the day after tomorrow'[54] as a lead-in to the foreign ministry. Ten days later he was steering the Danish royal council through Swedish and Russian complications of the Schleswig-Holstein question, cardinal for his term of office. It was a question of clinching a recent renunciation by Adolphus Frederick, now moving up from Holstein-Gottorp to the Swedish throne, of his claim to Schleswig, and of ensuring the same of the Duke of Holstein-Gottorp, the Russian grand duke and heir to the Empress Elizabeth, while getting him to agree to yield Holstein itself to Denmark. Count Bestuchev insidiously suggested that Danish forces should walk in. Bernstorff, no admirer of Frederick the Great or his example, argued (in German) that 'this occupation, so easy to effect, would, however, not be at present legal',[55] would send repercussions rippling across Europe. Not for nothing had Stainville apprehended to Bernstorff that a northern conflagration could spread from Danish districts. Bernstorff's coolly calculated rectitude carried the day and validated his appointment as foreign minister on 1 October 1751.

Next day the French minister in Copenhagen observed of this erstwhile favourite in France: 'If I judge aright, this minister will wish to fly very high. He talks only of dignity and glory.'[56] The Abbé

[53] Earl of Albemarle to Earl of Holdernesse, Fontainebleau, 13 Nov. 1753: P.R.O./S.P.F., France, vol. 248, part ii.

[54] Baron von Bernstorff to Marquise du Deffand, Fredensborg, 11 May 1751: Du Deffand/Lescure, i. 128.

[55] Baron von Bernstorff, memorandum to the Danish royal council, Fredensborg, 21 May 1751: P. Vedel, Correspondance ministérielle du comte J.H.E. Bernstorff, 1751–1770 (Copenhagen, 1882), i. 3.

[56] Abbé Lemaire to Count de Saint-Contest, 2 Oct. 1751: cited, Count E. de Barthélemy, Histoire des relations de la France et du Danemarck sous le ministère du comte de Bernstorff, 1751–1770, p. 32.

Lemaire distrusted Bernstorff's distrust of France's ally Frederick, and would not have been reassured by a dispatch which Bernstorff addressed a week later to his successor in Paris on the vexed subject of Sweden, where Denmark naturally sympathized with the Russian and British preference for weakening Sweden by encouraging the factionalism of her parliamentary government as against the French inclination towards a more authoritative strengthening of her northern client. 'If France', wrote Bernstorff, 'continues in the system of Swedish liberty, which certainly best assures the stability of her credit in that nation, and whereof Monsieur de Puysieulx has so often and so well recognized the advantages, then she will find us upon the same road as herself.'[57] If not, not — the somewhat offhand attitude matched the fact that France, while richly subsidizing the Danish government, yet in the last resort could not provide support enough to guarantee Scandinavia against danger, especially, already, from Russia. That was the heavy handicap for France in pursuing her Scandinavian policy of trying to harness against Russia the northern rivals, Denmark and Sweden. Such, largely, was to be the future pull of policy between those two friends, Bernstorff and the future Choiseul.

IV

If one is struck by the extent to which the Count de Stainville's letters to his friend in Denmark were already concerned with foreign affairs, so is one also by their virtual exclusion from his letters to his friend in Rome with their keen concentration upon the arts. Early in 1751 the Duke de Nivernais's secretary, La Bruère, was back in Paris contending with delay in the setting of his opera, *Linus,* owing to the illness of Rameau. By 10 May, however, Stainville, still involved, was writing: 'Today they are doing a rehearsal of *Linus* at Mme de Villeroy's.'[58]

This was probably the 'full rehearsal (*répétition solemnel*)'[59] noticed by the Abbé de La Porte and described by the Count de Stainville in his next: 'The first four acts were pretty successful in general although they are by no means ready, and there are many things to recast in the music; but there are some fine and even distinguished ones, above all in the entertainments, the airs for violins and certain pieces of music. The vocal treatment is much weaker and needs to be

[57] Baron von Bernstorff to Count Reventlow, Fredensborg, 9 Oct. 1751: P. Vedel, op. cit., i. 24.
[58] Count de Stainville to Duke de Nivernais, 10 May 1751: W.N.A., docket V/1, fo. 65.
[59] [Abbé de La Porte,] *Voyage au séjour des ombres* [Paris, 1752], part ii, p. 161.

greatly touched up.'[60] Rameau himself had written shortly before: 'Harmonic proportion gives the finest harmony to be heard ... but the difficulty in it is to know how to proportion the voices and the instruments, and of this the composer is not always the master, so soon as he has not the choice of the subjects which he needs.'[61]

If Rameau excelled especially in instrumental passages, he was notoriously ill served by his librettists. Stainville now moved into his criticism, already noticed, [62] of the fifth act of *Linus*, musically unsatisfying, the words generally condemned, 'although we found it a little better than it had been formerly'.[63]

Stainville was a crisp if fairly conventional critic, in this instance of Rameau's inclination to project his mastery of the delicate register of the late baroque out into the violence of the tempest, of earthquake even, as already in the 'craggy and scabrous'[64] *Indes Galantes*. If Rameau came to exceed the range of contemporaries, he was himself now dissatisfied with *Linus*, as Stainville explained:

Besides, the setting which is not bad in itself is not lively enough for the setting of a fifth act. It is a little languorous, and that is not what is wanted at the end of a tragedy ... This is the opinion of all those who were there, and everybody thinks that by resuscitating Lully and Campra they cannot make a good musical act out of this fifth; but there has been a revolution in characters which much surprised all those who are up in it. Rameau is [now] the gentlest and most docile person in the world. He said ... after the rehearsal that there were many things in the music with which he was not happy, and that he even felt that he had not conveyed the words and situations ... He ... confessed that he had done this work very quickly, without eagerness and even with a little aversion, and that he felt that there was a lot to change ... All the same he thought that in it there were pieces good enough not to be abandoned, but he asked that the poet for his part should lend himself to making the changes judged necessary.'[65]

There came the unexpected rub. Stainville confessed:

Without being taken in by La Bruère's gentle air, and well knowing that he was an author as others are, very fond of what he has done, prejudiced enough in favour of his children and in addition very lazy, I did not believe that he was so intractable and so temperamental. For even before the rehearsal he had taken against the opera ... I have had two conversations with him since the rehearsal and assuredly they are quite the two last. The first was fairly gentle, because despite his stubbornness, his temper and his unreasonableness I had armed myself with gentleness and a patience

[60] Count de Stainville to Duke de Nivernais, 17 May 1751: *u.s.*, fo. 66.
[61] J.-P. Rameau, *Démonstration du principe de l'harmonie, servant de base à tout l'art musical* (Paris, 1750), p. 28, cited, Louis Laloy, *Rameau* (Paris, 1908), p. 209.
[62] Cf. p. 476 above.
[63] Count de Stainville to Duke de Nivernais, 17 May 1751: loc. cit., and for the following.
[64] Abbé Desfontaines, cited in this translation by C. Girdlestone, *Jean-Philippe Rameau*, p. 348.
[65] Count de Stainville to Duke de Nivernais, 17 May 1751: *u.s.*, fos. 66–8 for the following.

which did not desert me. In the second I again made use of all my reasoning, but finally he made me so impatient that I left him a little angrily and firmly resolved not to hear it mentioned again.

Stainville reflected wryly:

He who puts himself between two madmen is madder than they. I have done enough, too much even. The interest of La Bruère, that of our pleasure and the success of the matter have led and directed my actions. I much regret them now, not for myself but for the harm which it does the two authors. I had foreseen in advance the disadvantages of Rameau and I did not disguise them. You are witness to it . . . the difficulty of guiding him, the influence of his friends, and the defect of his talent, which is great in certain things but not universal. In short I hid nothing of what I thought for good and ill. It is true that despite all that I said I thought him the best. I think so still or rather I think him the only one.

As for the inferior La Bruère, it would have been all right if he had spoken up six months earlier. As it was, it was too late 'and now that I know with whom I am dealing, I shall not be had again. I have spread myself greatly on this because I am full of it and have been talking about it a lot these last days, but that is done now. I have let fly, and flung restraint to the winds (*J'ay jetté mon suc, et mon bonnet par dessus les moulins*). I shall speak of it no more nor hear it spoken of.'

The future Choiseul, liable to flare up, was bad at grudges. A weakness, or strength, with him was the difficulty he often found in cutting people off. Nivernais too was persuasive in kindness.

Three weeks later the Count de Stainville was telling his well-matched friend that La Bruère 'has put a little water in his wine. Since I wrote to you about it I have not spoken to him of anything, and I was quite resolved never to say anything to him, but on the eve of his departure [to rejoin Nivernais in Rome] he told me that he was determined to redo the fifth act. He said so too to the Abbé de Bernis and to d'Argental. I do not know if he will keep his word. What is certain is that everybody thinks that . . . it would be a great pity to lose such a work. As to the first four'[66] acts, if Rameau asked for minor alterations La Bruère should accede since 'authors who are working together owe one another some consideration, but I have advised him to make the Abbé de Bernis his proxy for that, because those things need to be done in concert, and it is not possible for him to do them himself 300 leagues away . . . The Abbé de Bernis is very capable of that, as also [of][67] setting words, and I assume that he has

[66] Ibid., 7 June 1751: fos. 74–5 for the following.
[67] The text here is torn.

not [such][67] bad taste or weakness as to spoil the work in deference to Rameau.'

'There are', concluded this even-handed critic, 'many good and beautiful things in it and I believe that it could make a very fine opera. You would do well to exhort La Bruère to rework the fifth immediately.' As Stainville further explained a month later: 'One must make the most of the time remaining to Rameau. He is old. He is becoming a little infirm and has been rather ill since La Bruère left, and he has not long left for working. He is better at present, and I should like him to make the most of the rest of this summer in order to put the last touches to the work. La Bruère will tell you that he would be very happy that it should not be finished, and that even the first four acts are worth nothing. Do not believe him.'[68] Purposeful prodding primed the thrust of the Count de Stainville. It now carried the day.

Another month and Stainville was congratulating the Little Man and assuring him that he would be very glad to see the revision of 'the 5th act of *Linus* but I think he would do well to send it to the Abbé de Bernis, for we have need of him. He must be treated with consideration.'[69] Inferiors who had dealings with Stainville were, however, often reluctant to relinquish them. On 16 August 1751 he scribbled briefly to Nivernais: 'By this post I have received a letter from La Bruère. I thank him for writing to me and you for not writing. I am sorry that he is sending *Linus* to me. He would have done better to send it to the Abbé de Bernis ... I will give it to M. d'Argental who will give it to the Abbé de Bernis.'[70]

So ends this contribution by the future Choiseul to an extended knowledge of the circumstances of the composition of one of the least-known works of Rameau, who in the event outlived La Bruère by ten years. Questions, however, remain: whether that summer's uneasy collaboration in revision did produce a later version; or whether the traditional location at the Villeroy mansion of the only performance of *Linus* was indeed restricted to that fraught rehearsal owing, apparently, to a supervening illness of Madame de Villeroy and dislocation of her household.[71] What is certain is the keen involvement of the future Choiseul in Rameau's *Linus*, in the musical world of his time. Less remarkable now may seem the attribution, at least, to Choiseul years later, in the plenitude of power, of the authorship of the libretto of an opera.

[67] The text here is torn.   [68] Ibid., 11 July 1751, fos. 84–5.
[69] Ibid., 9 Aug. 1751, fo. 93.   [70] Ibid., 16 Aug. 1751, fo. 94.
[71] Cf. L. Laloy, op. cit., pp. 245–6; C. Girdlestone, op. cit., pp. 307–8.

V

Better documented hitherto than Choiseul's feeling for music has been his fondness for pictures. Here too, however, his early letters to Nivernais cast new light, as upon that Poussin. On this the Count de Stainville began his letter on 22 May 1751:

At last our picture has arrived, my dear friend, and I am extremely pleased with it . . . It smacks of its great master, and I am not surprised that it is highly thought of at Rome . . . It is true that the background has come up a little, but it is horribly dirty, and I believe that it will lighten up. I do not know why you were afraid that I should think the man looks like somebody drowned. It would be very unfair . . . The children are charming, and the composition seems to me very true in nobility and grace. In short I like it very much, and in respect of the colouring, which is the weak side of our artist, it is one of the best that I have seen by him.[72]

The appreciation leaves it unclear which picture by Poussin was acquired by Stainville. For an identification the relevant considerations of subject, size and provenance are complex but of the known works one of the more plausible possibilities might be a version of Rinaldo and Armida or else of Cephalus and Aurora.[73]

Whichever the picture, its new owner had promptly brought in his expert: 'Colins has just left and has taken it to clean. He viewed it with admiration and appreciation and quite requested me to tell you from him that he thought it a perfectly beautiful picture . . . Colins valued it at two thousand Ecus. I told him that I did not know yet what it had cost, and that you had not wanted me to know before having had it but I knew, generally speaking, that it was dear and I quite expected it to come to that much at least. Repaying generous delicacy in kind, Stainville thus gave Nivernais an expert valuation as a hedge against undue reduction.

Stainville was soon impatient for his Poussin, but art is slow. By 14 June he was reporting:

The day before yesterday I saw our picture at Colins's. It is beginning to clean up. I found it much brighter and this suits it wonderfully. It badly needed this restoration. It is one of the most beautiful Poussins I have seen and one of the best coloured. Colins thinks the same and is very pleased with it. Since it has been cleaned they have discovered some places which have been repainted. It appears to have suffered previously, and they have had to repair it, but it does not hurt it, and I do not believe that one will be able to observe it when it is varnished and hung. I am very impatient to have it at home . . . I have ordered a beautiful frame.[74]

[72] Count de Stainville to Duke de Nivernais, 22–4 May 1751: W.N.A., docket V/1, fo. 70 for the following.
[73] Perhaps a version of the debated Armida carrying off Rinaldo in the Staatliche Museen in East Berlin: cf. in particular Anthony Blunt, *The Paintings of Nicolas Poussin* (London, 1966), no. 204; ibid., no. 145 for the Cephalus and Aurora at Hovingham Hall, Yorkshire.
[74] *u.s.*, 14 June 1751, fos. 76–7.

At last a letter could begin on 3 July 1751:

Your picture was hung in place this morning, my dear friend. It creates an admirable effect and I am enchanted with it. If only I could see you with it in my study, that would be a truly delicious moment ... Your picture ... ravishes and satisfies my eye, but my heart is sad [from absence] and I feel that I lack a benefit more precious than all the pleasures of the senses. I cannot prevent myself from touching this chord and I am aware that that is ill done both for you and for me. I reject this idea, but it assails me.[75]

The age of sensibility was in the offing. Stainville wrote a week later:

I am still revelling in your picture. I am growing more and more fond of it every day, and besides its intrinsic beauty the form and fashion of it go wonderfully in my study. It seems to have been made specially for the position ... I have put it in the largest place in my study, and it fills it completely. Only four inches are left clear between the frame and the beading [of the panel]. I still have one similar place and that is all. The other parts of my study are much smaller. So I warn you so that you should pay attention to it if you should subsequently find something which might suit me, and so that you should not get anything wider, that is to say about six foot. Six foot and a half would not do. Goodbye my dear friend. You know how tenderly I love you. I return to the places in my study. I have two (those beside my chimneypiece) which are not large and for which I am having much trouble in finding pictures. So far there are two portraits which go detestably there and dishonour my room ... So if you find any, my dear friend, by great masters, real originals and really beautiful, I beg you to think of me. I do not care about having full-length figures. I should like half-lengths or two thirds at most, but it must be fine for in this line the mediocre is dreary and flat. My places are about five foot wide, from which one must subtract the thickness of the frame and a distance of about three or four inches on each side between the frame and the beading, for so it needs to be. The pictures must not be more than three foot and a half, but it could be less provided they are very striking.[76]

So ended this exacting epistle, characteristic in its blend of warmth and precision. The exceptional quality of the future Choiseul collection was, it now appears, indebted to the detailed care and informed enthusiasm of its owner, worried now by some questioning, apparently, from Nivernais as to the Poussin having been varnished contrary to the custom then in Italy. Whereas in France it was considered advantageous at any rate for the finest pictures 'and above all the Flemish and Dutch which are the most sensitive and delicate. The authority of the Italians carries great weight in pictures, but they are not exempt from prejudices, and this could well be one. I am very far from being able to decide this question, but in my uncertainty I conform to [local] custom. Besides, an unvarnished picture beside one that is appears dull and is diminished. Well, your Poussin is not

[75] Ibid., 3 July 1751, fo. 82.
[76] Ibid., 11 July 1751, fo. 85.

so in my study ... In truth it increases the deformity of the other walls which are not so well stocked ... That is why I have asked you'[77] – to start again. Such is the way with keen collectors, and Stainville must always be on to the next thing.

While the daring Titian seems to have receded, there was some question of a second Poussin. Stainville, though, was not too keen from the sound of it:

Besides, I am happy with mine. I do not want to like another more and if it was inferior, it would not give me pleasure ... but you have talked of two pictures by Albano. If they were truly originals, really pure, well preserved, as agreeable as those that I know, they would suit me wonderfully although they are of medium [size][78] and could not hang high; and I am not so set upon large pictures ... Well, this Albano is one of the painters whom I like best. There is at present one for sale in the estate of M. de Tunis which is very beautiful, but it will sell very dear, for there are many enamoured of it. They think it will reach five or six thousand francs. It is, however, only two foot eight inches high by three foot two inches wide. But it is ... as fresh and brilliant as if it had just been painted.[79]

Such were the true restrictions upon Italian representation in the Choiseul collection, such the preoccupations of collecting and of sales which were to entertain Choiseul for most of his life.

VI

If the Count de Stainville's artistic enthusiasm had earlier been under check from the Duchess de Nivernais, that influence had been brought home thanks to the fragile health of her mother, the old Countess de Pontchartrain, pining for her absent daughter. By the new year of 1751 the Nivernais had decided that the duchess should return alone to France. On 7 January Stainville began a letter to the duke: 'I do not know if I am glad or sorry about what I learn from your wife's letter, my dear friend. In reading it I was in the highest degree surprised. Nobody here expected her to take this course. You cannot doubt the pleasure that it will be to me to see her again. It is assuredly the tenderest and purest that I could ever have, but'[80] – such a journey in winter, so cruel a separation for Nivernais. 'Mme. de Pontchartrain', added Stainville, 'was very surprised by the resolve you have taken, and she wanted to send you a courier to prevent Mme de Nivernais from leaving, but she reckoned that he would

---

[77] Ibid., 19 July 1751, fo. 87.
[78] The text here is torn.
[79] Ibid., 3 July 1751, fos. 82–3.
[80] Ibid., 7 Jan. 1751, fo. 40 for the following.

arrive too late.' She was still expecting them both back together after Nivernais had made his ceremonial entry as ambassador but 'since she has had grounds for hope of seeing her daughter again, distant though they be, the change that has come over her is unbelievable. She is no longer the same person.' Three days earlier the old lady had in fact begun a letter to her son-in-law: 'Dear Black Sheep, Since it is entirely to your affection that I owe my return to life and even the wish to preserve it . . .'[81]

The duchess did come without her husband, with her elder daughter, Mademoiselle de Nevers, and La Bruère. But by the end of February 1751 Stainville was still writing to the duchess at Turin, 'for it seems . . . that the flooding of the rivers has entirely upset her journey'.[82] Another month and he had 'news of her arrival at Bourges'[83] where she broke her journey to Paris in order to visit the family of her half-brother in his exile from court and, as the Count de Maurepas put it, give them 'a great pleasure, and the only one which we have tasted for a very long time'.[84] His wife broke down upon receiving the Duchess de Nivernais into their loneliness while Maurepas himself did his sprightly best to make things cheerful and amuse the little girl.

'She arrived at last on Tuesday', wrote Stainville of the duchess to the duke on 4 April 1751. 'I saw her only at Villejuif because I had not wanted to hamper her progress by taking post-horses. I found her very thin, but in good health . . . I hope that we shall fatten her up again, but . . . she needs to be quiet for that, and she has not yet had a moment . . . We were unable to talk of you without being moved and emotional.'[85] But it was much too brief and, he continued, 'I am experiencing what usually happens in such cases, which is that I have more questions to ask her now than I had before seeing her. However, I shall not be seeing her again for some days, for she went yesterday to Versailles.'

In his next the Count de Stainville reported of the Duchess de Nivernais:

She was unwilling to take again to rouge, which was very necessary for her. I confess to you that that pained us all extremely and that we were hoping that after having left it off in order to conform to the customs of the country where she was, she would resume it here for the same reason. If I had been born three hundred years ago I

---

[81] Countess de Pontchartrain to Duke de Nivernais, 4 Jan. 1751: Lucien Perey, *Un Petit-Neveu de Mazarin*, p. 219.
[82] Count de Stainville to Duke de Nivernais, 1 Mar. 1751: W. N. A., docket V/1, fo. 48.
[83] Ibid., 29 Mar. 1751, fo. 56.
[84] Count de Maurepas to Duke de Nivernais, spring 1751: L. Perey, op. cit., p. 228.
[85] Count de Stainville to Duke de Nivernais, 4 Apr. 1751: W.N.A., docket V/1, fo. 58 for the following.

should have let my beard grow, and I should not have put any powder on. Now I have myself shaved every day, and I cannot persuade myself that there is any good reason for making oneself look odd (*pour se singulariser*) and exempting oneself from common custom.[86]

No rouge for women at the Vatican contradicted the convention at Versailles. Its absence there was held to denote a disapproving Dévote. Pious the Duchess de Nivernais was – Stainville mentioned in the same letter that on Easter Day 'she spent the greater part of it, as you can imagine, at church'.[87] But the queen herself conformed to rouge. The Countess de Pontchartrain, however, had failed to persuade her daughter by producing a pot. Stainville's dismay was echoed to Nivernais by other friends such as Guerchy, Forcalquier, and Duras. The ambassador, whose ambassadress was busy on his behalf at court, took alarm and wrote to urge her into reverse. If this trivial pother seems excessive, so did it to Stainville.

'I believe I am partly responsible for it', he wrote a month later, 'and I am sorry, for I am in my week of repentance'[88] – in the previous paragraph he had abjured further involvement in contentious *Linus*. He continued:

Not that I have basically changed my opinion... If it had happened yesterday, one would have no hesitation, but she has been seen without rouge since she has been here. The news is made and past, as everything passes, especially in this country... They are no longer talking of it. To resume it would be another piece of news, another opportunity to get her talked about, explanations and manifestoes to be made, a kind of inconsequentiality in her conduct if you mix yourself in it to this end... They think you are busy with more serious things. So despite all my taste and fondness for rouge, Guerchy and I think it would be better to stay as one is.

The Count de Stainville's cool calculation of fine angles at the frivolous court of Louis XV was to carry him far in matters more important. For the present, summed up the count to the duke:

The Dévotes have triumphed over it. Good, let us leave them this little satisfaction. Men of the world have said, 'Why has she left it off?' 'It is that she is pious', they said, and upon that they go for the supporters. They laugh at the puerilities with which they deck out our poor religion (*des puerilités dont on affuble notre pauvre religion*).

Appropriately, perhaps, it is from a lady's toilet that one derives a clue to the personal approach of the future Duke de Choiseul to those

[86] Ibid., 12 Apr. 1751, fo. 61. Cf. L. Perey, op. cit., p. 232, where this passage appears to be wrongly ascribed to the Count de Guerchy.

[87] *u.s.*, 12 Apr. 1751, fo. 60: cited, M. Blampignon, *Le Duc de Nivernais* (Paris, n.d. [?1888]), p. 79.

[88] Count de Stainville to Duke de Nivernais, 17 May 1751: W.N.A., docket V/1, fo. 68–9 for the following.

religious issues wherein he was to play so large and contentious a part. The serene disillusion, the wry pity for the catholic overlay of christianity was the authentic note of that superior and benevolent man. He continued his analysis of the spirit of his age: 'Bigotry and superstition are turned to ridicule, but at bottom believers in good faith are spared, and they do not cease to do justice to true merit whatever may be the colour upon her cheeks.'

It was not only in regard to rouge that the Count de Stainville watched over the Duchess de Nivernais and, maybe, found his views disregarded. A fortnight later he wrote: 'She went yesterday to Versailles. I hope that she will be satisfied with her journey, but I do not expect so, and I believe that all the démarches which they are making her make are very badly calculated. I think very differently in every respect ... But she does well to do badly, since the people in whom she is interesting herself wish it so.'[89] Only a week earlier the duchess had shewn Stainville part of a letter from her husband about him: so that the count acknowledged his friend's high regard for 'my judgement and approval' while gracefully discounting them in comparison with the depth of 'my unalterable and tender friendship'.[90]

It might be simplistic to suppose that the early return of the Duchess de Nivernais related only to her mother's health. Rouged or not, the duchess proved no bad emissary on behalf of her husband at court, where she had promptly gone to work, especially with the queen and the Marquis de Puysieulx, especially over the ruinous expense of the ambassador's ceremonial entry into Rome, still to be performed. The Duchess de Nivernais secured for her 'dear little dearest (*cher petit chéri*)'[91] an assurance of a hundred thousand livres and, to go with it, the longed-for Order of the Saint-Esprit. Almost more difficult was the other question of his early return to join her thereafter. Meanwhile the Count de Stainville was deploring their separation with what, in one less emotional, might seem almost exaggerated feeling.

'The sacrifices which one makes for people of whom one is fond carry their recompense with them. I am well aware', continued Stainville to Nivernais, 'that the compensation is not equivalent. It is the stoppage of five per cent (*du vingtième*) which one makes on debts. Never mind, it is a compensation and I am sure that it takes effect upon you ... I judge your heart by mine, and I do not think that I do either an injustice.'[92]

[89] Ibid., 31 May 1751, fo. 72.   [90] Ibid., 22–4 May 1751, fo. 71.
[91] Duchess to Duke de Nivernais, Apr. 1751: L. Perey, op. cit., p. 235.
[92] Count de Stainville to Duke de Nivernais, 21 Mar. 1751: W.N.A., docket V/1, fo. 54.

The same letter ran in conclusion:

As for me, my dear friend, I am too fond of you both for my personal interest ever to be able to blind me. One can desire one's own good, but one should never achieve it at the expense of people of whom one is fond; since one shares their sorrows and griefs one causes them to oneself when one occasions theirs. By that I am not claiming that one should reckon oneself as nothing. That is an effort beyond humanity. I am very far from it for on the contrary I confess that I count myself for much. It seems to me that if I did not love myself, I should love nothing, and it is precisely for this reason that I desire the happiness of the people I love. I could not be happy if they were not. Such is my way [of] feeling. This is what inspires in me this appearance of personal disinterestedness, for which I do not want to do myself more honour than it deserves.[93]

Superficial the future Choiseul was not. A true but balanced benevolence was central in this man of good self-conceit and formidable penetration. His intimate analysis of the heart explains much of his attraction for women, his affinity with his wife, his charm in society. Two months later he was writing:

Ah my dear friend, if I were a little bird or an elf (*lutin*) you would see me often. I should go to share your afflictions and labours. I should relieve you in many little ways. The wretched state of my head would not allow me to take a larger department. Never mind, zeal opens intelligence. It gives strength and energy ... I should talk to you of what you love ... I should in some sort bring you closer to her. Then I should come back to tell her your news ... She would promptly send me back. I should leave each of you without regret, and you would see me go in the same way. How sweet it would be for me to divide myself thus between the two people in the world who are dearest to me, and to be so to say the point of reunion of two hearts so well made for one another.[94]

Such was the aerial shuttle of marital love in the imagination of one renowned for fast living. He proceeded:

But I am dwelling upon chimeras. Such is the lot of man. His happiness is hardly ever more than an idea and unhappiness is very real. You are 300 leagues away from us, and I am very far from being a bird. I have never been so heavy, so material, so terrestrial. For several days I have had symptoms of inflammation spread everywhere, external symptoms, a stiffness which exhausts and lays me out in the last degree. I even have a bit of a sore throat. However, since it is fine and even hot, I am hoping that it will disperse more quickly than it did this winter, and that there will not be any after-effects, but meanwhile it puts me in very sorry condition.

Perhaps it was a touch of influenza. The Count de Stainville's health had not been promptly improved by his marriage. And after his wry allusion to his wedding to the Duke de Nivernais there was

[93] Ibid., fo. 55.
[94] Ibid., 10 May 1751, fos. 64–5 for the following.

barely a mention of the little countess in her husband's letters that were so full of the duchess and her separation from her husband. In this context Stainville was writing to him by July 1751: 'I am delighted that La Bruère has rejoined you ... When totally abandoned as you were, the smallest resource becomes considerable. It is like a man who has lost all his money gambling, and who finds a louis in his pocket.'[95]

The victim of this swift wit had returned to Rome with not only his battered libretto of *Linus* but also the Count de Maurepas's diamond cross of the Saint-Esprit which he was giving his brother-in-law to decorate his ceremonial entry into Rome. Louis XV himself contributed three magnificent coaches, all gilt and velvet-finished, which were put on public show opposite the Louvre before being shipped to Rome. Over a hundred carriages in all drove in procession at the entry of the Duke de Nivernais on Sunday, 5 July 1751. Two days earlier Stainville had been commiserating with him for being 'crushed by the weight of representation'.[96] The writer was to make at least as great a splash at the next ambassadorial entry into Rome for France. But the future Choiseul was a more private and attractive person than might be inferred from the calculated éclat of his public performance, less effortless for him than he chose to suggest.

Nivernais performed his local apothesis to the plaudits of the eternal city. He decided, though, not to hurry home even now to his wife and eager friends: his little son out there with him was cutting his last teeth, he should stay to celebrate the childbearing of the Dauphine and, not least, as he explained to Puysieulx, in the first aftermath of his ruinously expensive triumph in Rome 'they would infallibly attribute my departure to sordid avarice'.[97] That was not at all Nivernais's style, as Stainville implied in a letter of 1 August 1751.

'Although men are very corrupt', the letter ran, 'they cannot prevent themselves from honouring and respecting true merit and virtue. Whatever bitterness our separation causes me, I confess that I take some consolation and pleasure in thinking that they are fond of you and do you justice 300 leagues away. It seems as if it justifies my taste and feeling, and that part of your success reflects upon me. Perhaps it is a result of amour-propre, for it pokes itself in everywhere. Perhaps it is oneself that one loves in one's friends. Happily I am not entering into this metaphysic of the heart ... What is moreover very sure is that I should like you still better here just as a private individual, even an obscure one, supping and talking together like

[95] Count de Stainville to Duke de Nivernais, 11 July 1751: ibid., fo. 84.
[96] Ibid., 3 July 1751, fo. 82.
[97] Duke de Nivernais to Marquis de Puysieulx, Rome, Aug. 1751: L. Perey, op. cit., p. 261.

good bourgeois with our feet in the embers, rather than as ambassador at Rome, representing the most powerful king in the world and glittering with glory and honours. But since you are, to our misfortune, it is at least a little compensation to know that it is with the approbation and consideration which you enjoy there.'[98]

This revealing missive wound down:

There you are quit of your labours and the fuss of your entry. Now at least rest, take great care of yourself, and think of your health. I do not like this tetter having returned. It is bad company. I expect you are at present at Frascati, and I prefer you there than at Rome, for I imagine that you have more leisure there.

In his next Stainville was worrying that Nivernais's labours in the heat were scarcely calculated to cure his nasty eruption of the skin:

But in God's name, my dear friend, use only internal remedies, and do not let yourself go in for putting on blisters. Nothing in the world is so dangerous. We have seen so many fatal examples of it that I regard use of them as a real poison. You are perhaps going to think that your wife has got me to speak to you of it. Not at all. It is true that she told me that a doctor at Rome had proposed it to you and that very becomingly you had not wanted to use it without her being brought in. Upon that I broke out and I told her that she should never agree to it, that for my part I should oppose it with all my strength, and that I would write to you about it. I have seen so many ill effects of blisters in such cases that I have become their sworn enemy.[99]

The Count de Stainville's keen concern for health still embraced his own. His next letter, of 16 August 1751, his last in this intimate series to Nivernais, was a scribbled note beginning: 'I am as sick as a dog, my dear friend, and I have business which wearies my head. When one is upon the point of departure, there is always an infinity of odds and ends (*chiffonage*). I am leaving on Thursday' for what he called 'my visit to La Flèche'.[1]

The little town of La Flèche lies westerly upon the Loir south of Le Mans. At La Flèche King Henry IV had founded for the Jesuits a college which became the celebrated Prytanée for the instruction of the sons of officers. So this pleasant spot had in the previous century acquired large college-buildings with a fine chapel. Links with La Flèche might have been expected of such as the Count de Stainville, a former pupil of Louis-le-Grand who had taken military service. This is not the first, nor the last, indication that in that interval of peace Stainville, despite indifferent health, maintained an active interest in matters military, beyond the routine inspections to be

[98] Count de Stainville to Duke de Nivernais, 1 Aug. 1751: W.N.A., docket V/1, fos. 90–1 for the following.
[99] Ibid., 9 Aug. 1751, fos. 92–3.
[1] Count de Stainville to Duke de Nivernais, 16 Aug. 1751: ibid., fo. 94.

expected of a Maréchal de Camp. Military education was in vogue at that time of its expansion through the École Militaire at Paris under the aegis of the Marquise de Pompadour.

VII

If the Duke and Duchess de Nivernais were the close intimates in the Count de Stainville's ducal circle, it still included his old benefactor, the Duke de Noailles, now withdrawn to Saint-Germain with a cancer of the jaw masked by a silver chinpiece. His sons were friendly with Stainville at court, where the count was, however, apt to avoid the wife of a new ducal recruit, the Marquis de Mirepoix now created, not indeed a titular peer of the realm (*duc et pair*) but a lesser duke by patent (*duc à brevet*). Stainville wrote drily to Bernstorff on 10 October 1751: 'The Duchess de Mirepoix, duchess by patent, arrived some days ago . . . I have not seen anything of her.'[2]

Another such letter at the beginning of that year had explained:

I have remained with Mme de Mirepoix at the point at which you left me. I have even added some slightly colder inflexions; for instance I have only been to her house once during all the time that she has been here . . . Everybody knows the attachment which I have vowed to you, but it has reached me that she is not fond of you, and I could fairly easily believe that the compliments are the outcome of her falsity and of that fickleness which we know to be hers. I think that every sensible man should beware of the heart and mind of this woman, these two parts of her being are spoilt by the most fearful defects. Be it said between us alone, because I have imposed a rule on myself never to talk about her either favourably or unfavourably.[3]

The ducal balance was held in France on 13 September 1751, which produced a royal grandson in the longed-for Duke of Burgundy and extinguished by smallpox the young Duke de Boufflers, only son of the first marriage of the Duchess de Luxembourg. Thus was the Count de Stainville's old regiment of Navarre to pass to another who particularly interested him, if in a different way. Next month he wrote of the bereaved duchess: 'Her grief is not abating yet; I hope that the stir of Fontainebleau will deaden it.'[4]

The stir of the incipient salon of the Duchess de Luxembourg was to enliven French society. Madame du Deffand's earlier appreciation of the duchess's delicate rigour was to be matched by Madame de Genlis's description of her as 'the governess of all the youth at court'[5]

---

[2] Count de Stainville to Baron von Bernstorff, Paris, 10 Oct. 1751: *Bernstorffske Papirer*, ii. 636.
[3] Ibid., 31 Jan. 1751, p. 632.   [4] Ibid., 10 Oct. 1751, p. 636.
[5] Comtesse de Genlis, *Mémoires inédits de Madame la Comtesse de Genlis* (Paris, 1825), i. 297.

including two of France's greatest foreign ministers, the future Duke de Choiseul and, later, that Prince de Talleyrand who was to look back from across the gulf to the incomparable sweetness of French society in the old regime.

This duchess leavened fashion with letters so that, as the Abbé de Voisenon was to put it, 'the courtiers learnt to argue, the men of letters learnt to converse: the former ceased to be bored and the latter from being boring.'[6] The reign of pedants and preachers was yielding to an intellectual emancipation that was also one between both classes and sexes. The novelty of lay conversation upon serious topics, just suited to the nimble clarity of the French intelligence, was especially important for enlightenment in an age when newspapers were for the most part still sparse and, with books and pamphlets, subject in France to censorship, indulgently erratic though it could be. And if the Parisian growth of salons was already familiar enough to such a frequenter as the Count de Stainville, by the middle of the century this social phenomenon was just beginning to become sociological, ideological, dangerously for the future of the old regime.

Small though the scale might be as yet, more people than ever before were seriously beginning to think for themselves, and to enjoy it. During the first half of the century salons were predominantly literary. That led on to the morality of censorship and, under the impetus of a Voltaire or a Montesquieu, to the basic morality of much else besides, both political and religious. What Voltaire had described in 1732 as the 'little kingdoms' of the salons were by about 1750 beginning to open out into a republic of letters. This coincided with an almost dynastic change in the ladies ruling two of the older and outstanding salons.

With the death of Madame de Tencin in 1749 her torch had been taken up by the ambitious Madame Geoffrin, relieved that year of her rich, peevish, nondescript husband. Her salon extended beyond literature to embrace artists, politicians and, in the Tencin tradition, distinguished foreigners from all over Europe. Lord Albemarle adorned Madame Geoffrin's assemblies, as had Baron von Bernstorff. Her cooking and cellar surpassed those of the Marquise du Deffand who in the later forties had rather hived off from the rural salon of the Duchess de Maine at Sceaux. Its devotees took to the celebrated salon of the maliciously bored, feelingly sceptical Madame du Deffand, the close friend of the Duchess de Luxembourg and of the young Stainvilles. Other drawing-rooms in that circle were kept by the worrying Duchess de La Vallière and by the Countess de Clermont, ducally born a Rohan-Chabot, the inamorata and future wife of Stainville's old friend, the Prince de Beauvau.

From Saint-Lambert, Beauvau's literary crony from Lorraine, one catches a rather rare glimpse at just about that time into those really smart salons where the Count de Stainville was most at home in an atmosphere significantly moderated from that of more radically intellectual and widely publicized assemblies. The Duchess de Luxembourg, however, might not have agreed with the loyal Saint-Lambert that:

Madame de Clermont was then incontestably the woman in Paris at whose house the most excellent company gathered ... In this so agreeable house and in the others of the same kind people were but little concerned with the quarrels of Jansenism and Molinism which were agitating Paris ... Since the printing of the *Esprit des Lois*, of the book called *L'Esprit*, of some works by the Abbé de Condillac and of the first volumes of the Encyclopedia, the philosophic spirit had found its way into every conversation. It was not yet a fashion, but a taste begun. Prudence, which is commoner among the first order of citizens, had not yet been banished from talk; but it was set a little further aside day by day ... Moderation in opinions was established in the house of Madame de Clermont. People there were hostile, not to every innovation, but to all sudden change which had not been prepared by a succession of intellectual advances (*des lumières successives*).[7]

Such was the outlook of the Count de Stainville. It was the future Princess de Beauvau who was to recall that the title of a musical hit was applied to the Duke de Choiseul as 'a philosoph without knowing it'.[8]

VIII

'I am not telling you other news; it cannot be told.'[9] The Count de Stainville's withholding from Baron von Bernstorff on 10 October 1751 remains cryptic but suggestive of the development which was now to prove critical for the writer.

While the initiation of the career of the Count de Stainville at the court of Versailles was entering a chequered and formative phase, the Marquis de Stainville had been trying that summer to crown his career at the court of Vienna. The elder Stainville, in the hope of supplementing if not succeeding Kaunitz in his high diplomacy, had evidently made the most of French friendliness and feelers to himself,

[7] Saint-Lambert, notice of Prince de Beauvau: Madame Standish, *Mémoires du maréchal prince de Beauvau* (Paris, 1872), pp. 49–50.
[8] Princess de Beauvau, memoir of 1 June 1793: Madame Standish, *Souvenirs de la maréchale princesse de Beauvau* (Paris, 1872), p. 19.
[9] Count de Stainville to Baron von Bernstorff, Paris, 10 Oct. 1751: *Bernstorffske Papirer*, ii. 636.

also, perhaps, of Kaunitz's notable lack of success after all with his own friend, Puysieulx. The Austrian ambition was to break France off from Prussia. But if Puysieulx seemed to the Austrian court 'to think less ill than other French ministers, especially Argenson',[10] recent developments had not encouraged Puysieulx to cut loose from Prussia in response to insinuations from Kaunitz, 'at first slight and then more positive as to an alliance between his court and France'. That came from the future Duke de Choiseul, who characteristically commented:

To present such a project to M. de Puysieulx was to try to get a canary to swallow an ox. So the proposal, honourably received and rejected in the most obliging terms, achieved no success. M. de Kaunitz was not disheartened. He knew M. de Puysieulx; he knew that, because he was fond of English horses and was selling his wine from Sillery to the English, his passion was to make an alliance with England; but he knew at the same time that M. de Puysieulx was a perfectly honest man, who would not succeed in his project regarding England, if he dared to attempt it: but that he was in any case incapable of compromising the proposals which he had insinuated to him. M. de Kaunitz had talked to M. de Puysieulx only so that he should not have grounds for complaint if he learnt that he [Kaunitz] had had conversations with the same object with Mme de Pompadour.[11]

Whatever Puysieulx's own predelictions for the English (his initial instructions to Mirepoix had been sceptically amicable), he could not really believe that Austria would break with England but did believe, wrongly, that Austrian overtures to France were concerted with London. Nor had Kaunitz's recourse to the Pompadour in fact prevented him from becoming considerably more disheartened than Choiseul was to allow: so much so that already by June 1751 Kaunitz had addressed to Maria Theresa a critical analysis substantially reversing his lead of 1749 towards France, in favour now of the old alliance with England and, so she deduced, of accommodation with Prussia.

That might seem the chance with the empress for such a steady francophile and quiet operator as the Marquis de Stainville. But it was to Kaunitz that her secretary, Koch, wrote on 1 October, enclosing in strict secrecy a somewhat earlier memorandum remitted by Stainville and known only to the emperor and empress:

M. de Steinville [sic] makes out that he stands very well with the [French] King and is above all in close relations with M. de St. Séverin. He insists upon knowing what he should say upon his return [to Paris] as to all the statements which are supposed to have been made to him. The Empress, who wants to do nothing without Your Excellency's approbation, wishes to know at earliest what you think of the whole

[10] Instructions to Mareschall, 11 July 1749: J. Strieder, op. cit., p. 44.
[11] Choiseul, *Mémoires*, pp. 152-3.

contents of the memorandum, whether M. de Steinville does indeed stand so well at court . . . if [he should] make some reply on his return to the observations or advances which he says have been made to him.[12]

Imperial disconsideration of the hapless Marquis de Stainville was unlikely to be alleviated by his contemptuous competitor, Count Kaunitz. Thanks to his reply Koch expected Maria Theresa to have Stainville told that 'she could not entrust him with any commission, already having her ambassador at Paris and being unable to use two ministers at once. The memorandum has incidentally passed into the hands of H.E. the Count d'Ulfeld',[13] the declining chancellor who was not initiated into the imperial paradiplomacy of the secret Koch-Kaunitz correspondence. Thence it transpired a week later:

Nothing has been decided yet in regard to M. de Steinville. The Count d'Ulfeld and M. de Bartenstein would like to give him a reply or instruction in writing, expressed, however, in such a way that apart from fair words it says nothing and could be seen by the whole universe; but Her Majesty is inclined not to give him any at all.[14]

The ministers of the unimpressed empress may have been trying to do something for Stainville, soon to return from Vienna via Lunéville. There he at least discussed European affairs with Stanislas Leszczynski, assuring him of the pacific disposition of Austria, whose rapprochement with France they both now had at heart. If effectively, however, it was to be curtains for the Marquis de Stainville, they were to be sumptuous, as he explained to his son upon his return to Paris about the middle of December 1751. On Boxing Day the Count de Stainville wrote of his father to Bernstorff:

He has a pension of fifty thousand francs, whereof ten are upon the head of my mother, with two hundred thousand francs [made over] on the liquidation of Lorraine to pay his debts, and the promise of the first [Golden] Fleece that is given. He is charged with no business; however, he is authorized to write to the emperor on behalf of the king [of France], and equally to render account here of particular matters which the emperor may wish to transmit, but without assuming any official capacity. That is his position, sir. It seems to me a very fine retirement, and we are all very pleased with it. He has charged me with his very humble compliments to you.[15]

The Marquis de Stainville was yet making the most of his diplomatic residuum. On the same day he wrote doggedly to the emperor:

My two friends, M. de Pusieulx and M. de Saint-Séverin . . . have advised me, both of them, not to assume any official quality so as not to be confused with all the little

---

[12] Baron von Koch to Count Kaunitz, Vienna, 1 Oct. 1751: Kaunitz/Koch, p. 131.
[13] Ibid., 30 Oct. 1751, p. 141.   [14] Ibid., 6 Nov. 1751, p. 145.
[15] Count de Stainville to Baron von Bernstorff, Paris, 26 Dec. 1751: *Bernstorffske Papirer* ii. 637–8.

Ministers of the second and third rank. They told me that my old letters of credence would suffice me . . . and that by not assuming any quality I could go whenever I wished to court, where I would always be looked on with the consideration due to my birth, merit and as a man honoured with the confidence of Your Imperial Majesty. That would put the King at his ease in regard to me, and he was fond of me.[16]

Nor was Louis XV alone in this. 'I know', added the Marquis de Stainville, 'that the Marquise de Pompadour also wishes me to be upon this footing, for she has had it reach me through my son.' Here was the young count, in his hidden contacts of some amicability with the royal mistress, conveying a friendly message from her to his father, and at a particularly interesting juncture.

In his Boxing Day dispatch the Marquis de Stainville had mentioned that he had still been too tired from his journey to attend a special festivity at Versailles on 19 December 1751. Not so the Count de Stainville who recorded that it 'did not come off as it should. Its principal merit should have been the sight of an [outdoor] illumination and the spectacle of the [royal] drawing-room held in the gallery. Bad weather made the illumination a partial failure, and the crush which got into the gallery made it very disagreeable to remain there. Thursday is to be the second day of the fête. It is to be hoped that it will be a greater success.'[17]

The fête of 19 December 1751 had begun soon after six that Sunday evening (young Stainville jumbled the day to Bernstorff) when Louis XV entered the Galérie des Glaces, specially decorated and lit by nearly three thousand candles doubled in the mirrors facing the curtained windows. In the middle of the gallery the Duke de Luxembourg, captain of the bodyguard that quarter, stood behind the king's armchair at lansquenet. The sixteen other players at the table included the royal children, the dukes of Chartres and of La Vallière, the Marquise de Pompadour. The British ambassador headed an English party.

Some time after seven the curtains were drawn back to reveal a further dimension of fairyland with lamps and lanterns twinkling against the classic façades and away through the gardens. It was just on eight when the queen rose from her cavagnole at the end of the gallery adjoining the Salon de la Paix and walked up for a central view of the outdoor illumination. But, as though in some sad symbolism across those contrived delights, a rising north-wind was already extinguishing a proportion of the guttering lamps – a partial failure, as the Count de Stainville crisply noted. Unfulfilled, too, was

---

[16] Marquis de Stainville to Emperor Francis I, Paris, 26 Dec. 1751: Esteri del Granducato di Toscana, vol. 2296/1287, no. 74 for the following.
[17] Count de Stainville to Baron von Bernstorff, Paris, 26 Dec. 1751: *u.s.*, p. 637.

to be his hope of improvement in the second instalment of the gala on 30 December when the fireworks were largely to fail and land two or three pyrotechnic experts in gaol in fitting sacrifice to the demanding pleasures of the old regime.

On the other main complaint of the Count de Stainville about the first evening, the horrid crush was swelled by intruders and pickpockets. Though the crowd around the king's table did protect the gamblers from the howling draughts through the windows in the rising wind. Yet the Marquis d'Argenson grumbled that there were 'not enough women'[18] there and that those who did attend hardly looked their best. Too many old costumes 'provoked comment on the lack of cash among the courtiers' while 'the women seemed aged, for the chandeliers, too strung up, made their eyes go dead.'

That flawed festivity stood out for d'Argenson as 'beautiful and gloomy'. Such could be the melancholy inflections of pleasure in the heyday of Madame de Pompadour – if her heyday it still was. 'What was principally remarked', wrote the same critic, 'was the gloomy sadness of the favourite, the Marquise de Pompadour. People saw, they say, something fatal in it. It was observed that it cost the king to look at her, and he brusquely turned his back on her as soon as he caught sight of her. The great finery in which she was decked increased these semblances of change and disgrace whereof the cause is unknown.'

Of course, though, there were whispers, and they touched more than one of those in the Galérie des Glaces that evening. Less than a week earlier d'Argenson himself had written: 'Mme de Pompadour is more beautiful than ever and looks content; however, people are still asserting the triumph of her young rival, Mme de Choiseul.'[19] This rivalry from the cousin of Count de Stainville was now to be formative for his future.

---

[18] D'Argenson, vii. 53 for the following.
[19] Ibid., p. 48.

CHAPTER VII

INTRIGUE

I

'IT IS the Marquise who got her married, and there she is now, able forthwith to play her the same trick as the sisters of Mme de Mailly played on her.'[1] Such had been the Marquis d'Argenson's gloss, already in November 1751, upon reports that Louis XV 'covets the young Mme de Choiseul, cousin of Mme de Pompadour'.

Wishful rumour had the king groping his unfamiliar way back from the Countess de Choiseul's room, had Madame de Pompadour fibbing so as to exclude her from his little suppers. Such tales may well have been untrue. True it was that the Count de Stainville's old regiment of Navarre, without a colonel since the death of the young Duke de Boufflers, was now given to the Count de Choiseul. This may not have wholly pleased Stainville, for whom the Beaupré branch of the clan was in some danger of becoming rather overshadowing, as also for Madame de Pompadour in her sphere. However, she was to carry it off so adroitly that in the new year following that wintry fete at Versailles the Duke de Croÿ detected no sign of her being put out by her young rival.

As for the Count de Stainville, he was more immediately concerned just then with another woman closer to himself. 'Mme de Stainville is three months pregnant although she is only fifteen years old', her husband was writing to Bernstorff at the end of January 1752. 'I hope that she will come through well because she is pretty strong, and the capital interest for me in having children makes me regard this event a fortunate one, though it is often mingled with fear from recollection of the misfortunes which I have experienced.'[2] Such was the terse restraint with which he recalled the death after childbirth of the Marquise de Gontaut. On 20 March Stainville began his letter to his northern confidant:

A misfortune has happened to me, Sir. Mme de Stainville has had a miscarriage at four months. I was anxious for some days but she has come through it wonderfully,

[1] D'Argenson, vii. 20 for the following.
[2] Count de Stainville to Baron von Bernstorff, Paris, 30 Jan. 1752: *Bernstorffske Papirer*, ii. 639–40.

and at present she is feeling better than ever. This accident has left me with but the loss of a boy, which is a real one for me but which, in view of both our ages, can be repaired in a little while.[3]

The Count de Stainville was ever an optimist, in matters personal as well as political. That dead son was to be his only one in wedlock. He was now never to have the child he longed for, a central lack in his life, still more in that of his adoring wife. She failed to hold his love to herself alone. She failed to give him an heir. The health of this brave and beautiful little creature was in fact lastingly injured. Recalling Stainville's childlessness and his marital relations, the unkind Talleyrand wrote some sixty years later: 'He had himself impaired her constitution by an enjoyment which had much preceded the period at which she had become a woman, and from this imprudence there had resulted for her incommodities which often obliged her to remain upon a chaise-longue.'[4] Talleyrand was here retailing later gossip which, almost inevitably perhaps, improved Stainville's premature enjoyment into premarital intercourse. This unlikely and malicious insinuation has not found modern acceptance.[5]

II

Young Stainville had meanwhile been keeping up as usual. 'I am going to spend my week at weddings', he wrote to Bernstorff on 5 February 1752. 'President Regnault thought himself obliged to give a wedding supper to the Viscount de Rohan; Monday is the marriage of M. de Montmorency and Mlle de Tingry; the next day it will be at Mme de Luxembourg's, and Wednesday is the marriage of Mlle de Choiseul, the daughter of the Blackbird (Merle), with M. de Montrevel.'[6]

Blackbird Choiseul was the Count de Stainville's older and richer cousin, César-Gabriel, his erstwhile comrade-in-arms upon the Alpine campaign and future political associate as the Duke de Praslin. Blackbird he may have been from Merle as slang for a fellow, and perhaps from a family holding whence the daughter in question was titled Dame de Chant-d'Oiseau. This girl of fifteen, Elisabeth-Céleste-Adélaïde, was marrying the fifteen-year old Count de Montrevel, one of the La Baumes. The bride was said to be,

---

[3] Count de Stainville to Baron von Bernstorff, Paris, 20 Mar. 1752: ibid., p. 641.
[4] Prince de Talleyrand, Mémoires du prince de Talleyrand, ed. duc de Broglie, v. 531.
[5] Cf. J. Levron, Choiseul: un sceptique au pouvoir, p. 59.
[6] Count de Stainville to Baron von Bernstorff, Paris, 5 Feb. 1752: u.s., ii. 640.

prospectively at least, about half as rich as her husband who enjoyed an income of around 80,000 livres.

The bride's age and the bridegroom's income would fit a cryptic allusion by Stainville to Nivernais in the preceding summer to 'a very important and very importunate affair'[7] anent match-making. The prospective bride had then been 'only fourteen and a half. That is early, but good matches are rare, and I am afraid of regretting subsequently what I would have refused at present. There are pros and cons in everything in life.' If this indeed concerned the Blackbird's daughter, it demonstrated the extent to which the forceful Stainville was already directing his cousin's affairs, as later politically, so now concerning the marriage which was to produce the adoptive heir of the childless Duke de Choiseul, and later holder of that title. Stainville was also closely involved in the second wedding in his round. The Duke de Montmorency was the only son of the Duke de Luxembourg by his first marriage and was brother to Stainville's mistress, the Princess de Robecq. The bride was the only daughter of the Prince de Tingry, himself a Montmorency-Luxembourg and the executor, incidentally, of the poor Countess de Mailly who had died a year earlier at forty-one in high piety and penitence.

By the end of January 1752 the Duchess de Luxembourg, reported the Count de Stainville, 'is in the throes of the wedding, which they want to be brilliant'.[8] It was solemnized on 7 February at the church of Saint-Roch 'and the wedding-feast in the house of Mme de Senozan in the Rue de Richelieu. Although no cousins, not even cousins-german, were admitted, there were more than fifty people including some special friends',[9] such as Stainville. On 20 February the Duchess de Luxembourg presented the little Duchess de Montmorency at court, where she was judged 'not at all pretty; however her face is not displeasing'. Compare Stainville a month later: 'Mme de Montmorency is sullen and badly brought up; it is making Mme de Luxembourg embarrassed and impatient, but she is restraining herself because she is held in by M. de Luxem. and M. de Tingry, who is madly fond of his daughter, although she is very like him for ugliness.'[10]

Stainville explained the third marriage in his crowded week: 'The Viscount de Rohan is marrying Mlle de Vervins, the grand-daughter of President de Massigny ...; she has an income of 70 thousand

[7] Count de Stainville to Duke de Nivernais, 21 June 1751: W.N.A., docket V/1, fo. 78 for the following.
[8] Count de Stainville to Baron von Bernstorff, 30 Jan. 1752: *Bernstorffske Papirer*, ii. 639.
[9] Luynes, xi. 437 for the following.
[10] Count de Stainville to Baron von Bernstorff, Paris, 20 Mar. 1752: *u.s.*, ii. 643.

livres. The Chabots have taken the marriage amiss'.[11] Stainville added that this catch had put out his uncle by marriage, the Baron de Thiers. Within two months 'all Paris has it that M. de Thiers is marrying his daughter to the Duke de Broglio [Broglie]; . . . that piqued by the marriage of the Viscount de Rohan to Mlle de Vervins, he [Thiers] arranged that with the Duke de Broglio straight away, and that what has delayed the publication is the embarrassment that he is in about announcing it to the Marshal and Maréchale de Belle-Isle. It is true that it will be odd that the brother-in-law of the brother-in-law of the Marshal de Belle-Isle should be the son of Marshal de Broglio, and the nephew of the present Abbé de Broglio.'[12] Thus had the enmity between the two marshals upon the Bohemian campaign ripened into a family feud.

The second bride now of the second Duke de Broglie was eighteen-year-old Louise-Augustine-Salbigothon Crozat, second of the three daughters (no sons) of the Baron de Thiers, and a sister-in-law at a remove of the Duchess de Belle-Isle. Thus did the future Duke de Choiseul, at least by the canons of that time, become related to his unfavourite Broglies.

If marriage were of clinching interest in that close society, love could be still more so, especially for such as the giddy Duchess de La Vallière. Her Jélyotte may have been discarded, but there was always a successor. 'Mme de La Vallière is absorbed in her Billy [?Bissy]', reported the Count de Stainville in March 1752. 'Her door is nearly always shut; I only see her still at supper; I believe that she is caught up in the mania for wit, which distracts her from the feelings which come from her heart . . . I much disapprove of her conduct.'

Love can drain, even through idyllic summers of long ago. 'We have been paying a visit to Montmorency, Sir, in the most beautiful weather in the world', wrote off Stainville to Bernstorff on 2 July 1752. ' . . . The illness of Mme de La Vallière, who has been in the greatest danger, has been the cause of our return. She has had a putrid fever with a kind of false pleurisy. She was very ill for several days. Happily she is out of danger.'[13] But convalescence was to be long and uneven.

By the beginning of October the Count de Stainville was 'back from Champs where Mme de Vallière is recovering a little slowly as it appears to me. Mme de Mirepoix has gone to Meudon; her condition is still the same. I doubt if it will ever change. I have seen little of her, and although my feelings for her have long been

[11] Count de Stainville to Baron von Bernstorff, 30 Jan. 1752: ibid., p. 639.
[12] Ibid., Paris, 20 Mar. 1752, pp. 641–3 for the following.
[13] Ibid., 2 July 1752, p. 643.

mediocre, her condition arouses my pity. M. de Mirepoix does not seem at all touched by his wife's condition; on the contrary; he came to spend four days at Champs – has hardly seen her for two months – is off to Fontainebleau to return to England at the end of the month. I believe that their reciprocal sentiments are at present very cold.'[14]

The Mirepoix were in fact to remain more constant than most in that high society. Maybe the duchess was already a martyr to those horrible headaches and migraines ascribed by her French friends to the bad habit that she picked up in London of drinking quantities of tea.

Other invalids that summer included the old patron of the Count de Stainville, who wrote: 'The Marshal de Noailles is still ill at St. Germain and will not be going to Compiègne any more than M. de St. Séverin, who is staying at Isly for his aunt's sake!'[15] And a greater illness now alarmed the court of France.

On Saturday, 29 July 1752, the Dauphin took a smart turn at Versailles round the Pièce des Suisses, circled that ornamental lake in twenty-five minutes, got hot, felt cold, was sick, feverish, down with smallpox under the best doctors, Senac de Meilhan – just become first doctor to the king – Ponce and Vernage, the two leading specialists in the disease.

The delirious Dauphin sang at times. When clear-headed, he was fobbed off with his having a touch of erysipelas, with the king not visiting him because of a bad knee. Mirrors were withheld from him and, when he asked to see the *Gazette de France,* they ran off a dummy copy to support their solicitous fibs. Whereas bulletins were issuing from the Hotel de Ville, special prayers from Notre Dame. The devoted Dauphine scarcely left the bedside of danger. Then on 7 August there came a turn. Ten days later Stainville began a letter:

The illness of the Dauphin, Sir, has produced the effect here which the dangerous state of a health so precious should produce. He is happily out of danger, has no more fever, and they told him yesterday that he had had smallpox, which he was much afraid of and had not suspected. Thus he has the pleasure of having passed through a great danger without knowing it, and the kingdom the advantage of seeing that he has had smallpox severely enough for there to be no fear of this illness on his account.[16]

Thus did the future Choiseul hail the survival of the prince who was to rank among his chief antagonists. By the end of August the Count de Stainville's bulletin ran: 'The Dauphin, who is at Meudon, is entirely recovered. The fêtes for his convalescence are multiplying, and never have fêtes had a more interesting motive. The poor

[14] Ibid., 1 Oct. 1752, p. 648.   [15] Ibid., 2 July 1752, p. 645.
[16] Ibid., 17 Aug. 1752, p. 646.

Marshal de La Fèvre [Fare] is very ill of the smallpox which he has caught from this prince. I should be very sorry for his death. He is a good man who has many friends and who deserves to have them.'[17] Stainville had campaigned with La Fare, described, however, in his obituary next month by the carping Marquis d'Argenson as 'a real marshal of the court . . . a friend of vice, gay and jovial, everybody's friend in appearance and fond of nobody.'[18] Yet La Fare, the chief adviser of the Dauphine, had shared her unafraid devotion to the Dauphin despite a premonition that were he to contract the smallpox it would do for him as it had for his father and grandfather before him.

At such forgotten cost did the Dauphin survive, unlike that other prince, the pious son of the Regent Orleans. Earlier that year the charitable Duke of Orleans, of a judgement less good than his intentions, a prey to whimsies of premature deaths, had himself been carried off at forty-eight from his austerities at the abbey of Sainte-Geneviève. He left his corpse to further anatomical studies. In it they found desiccated organs, a withered heart. The Count de Stainville had written on 5 February:

The Duke of Orleans died yesterday to the great regret of a very considerable number of people whom his death reduces to beggary. I do not yet know very positively about his dispositions . . . In his will he calculates the fortune which he had at the death of the Regent, together with the debts which amounted to nine millions. Thereafter he reckons the increase in fortune which he is leaving and, after all debts are paid, he is leaving [the amount of] this increase, which is said to be considerable, as a life-annuity for those poor whom he names in his will, with the capital reverting to the Duke de Chartres. This provision seems to me the wisest possible. It is not yet known if the Duke de Chartres will have his father's household; the princes are doing what they can to prevent the king from granting it to him.[19]

They did not succeed despite encouragement, it was said, from the new Duchess of Orleans, at daggers drawn with her frivolous husband. So the young duke could set up in his palatial residence at Saint-Cloud. By 1 October 1752 Stainville was writing to Bernstorff:

The Duke of Orleans has given, Sir, a fête at St. Cloud for the convalescence of the Dauphin which was the most beautiful thing that I have ever seen. One could not describe the pitch of perfection to which the attentions for each individual were carried without forgetting the populace in the tumult of a fête made brilliant by the abundance of different kinds of displays. I assure you that I do not think that there has ever been anything of this kind that was so fine, so elegant and so successful. The

[17] Ibid., 29 Aug. 1752, pp. 647–8.
[18] D'Argenson, vii. 296.
[19] Count de Stainville to Baron von Bernstorff, Paris, 5 Feb. 1752: *Bernstorffske Papirer*, ii. 640.

prince, indeed, has since the death of his father been doing everything needful to make himself adored, and it seems to me that he is succeeding in it.[20]

The exceptional enthusiasm inspired in Stainville by this classic festivity of Sunday, 24 September 1752, had been earned by toil for three weeks by two hundred workmen 'at prodigious expense',[21] noted the careful young Colonel James Wolfe, then improving his French in Paris. At Saint-Cloud on the evening 'there were more than two thousand chairs which the prince had placed upon the terrace and which were free for the bourgeois and respectable folk,'[22] wrote one of them in that blend, noted by Stainville, of popular entertainment with sumptuous enjoyment for the elect. The spectators that afternoon could enjoy shooting contests and jousts to fanfares upon the river while acrobats tumbled in a little theatre run up in one part of the park. Music lilted out from other groves.

As evening fell 'the Duchess of Orleans and the lords and ladies of the court, magnificent in their stuffs and diamonds, promenaded in the park for an hour in ten or twelve barouches in a row, all in the livery of Orleans: which made a beautiful sight'.[23] The fountains were playing and from half past eight fireworks across the river kept cascading into the night, putting into the shade that show at Versailles the preceding winter. Seaserpents blazed across the waters and fiery dolphins gambolled in compliment to the Dauphin. Dear to that age were fireworks, frivolously artificial, providing sheer pleasure in fragile defiance of the expectant darkness.

Pedestals supporting urns and flambeaux decked the river banks while the great château itself, illuminated from outside, blazed afar its princely message of meant magnificence. Within the cavagnole was presided over by the Duchess of Modena, by now a lasting expatriate in favour of this sparkling connection of the Orleans. Supper for over two hundred in the orangery was so well served that it 'only lasted about two hours'. Around midnight they cleared away the huge table so as to admit additional celebrants to the masked ball for which four thousand tickets were said to have gone out. Strongboxes were thoughtfully provided for the diamonds of the select ladies about to plunge into the masked revelry of anonymous hazard, and opportunity. Thus dawned the morning of 25 September 1752 for the Count de Stainville and the other chosen at the Château de Saint-Cloud at the summit of French civilization, then the highest in the world.

[20] Ibid., 1 Oct. 1752, p. 648.
[21] Lieut.-Colonel James Wolfe to Lieut.-General Edward Wolfe, Paris, 9 Oct. 1752: Beckles Willson, *The Life and Letters of James Wolfe*, p. 187.
[22] Barbier, v. 291.
[23] Luynes, xii. 157–8 for the following.

Beautiful as a picture, it was a picture to be actively created and lived as pleasure in the enlightenment, almost, of a religion of happiness.

It had not escaped Stainville that the pleasure had a purpose. Not wholly without reason did other princes of the blood suspect the house of Orleans. The Regent and his son had, in very different ways, both diverged from Bourbon orthodoxy. Now the new duke was already launching that policy of courting a wider popularity which was to be notably extended by his son, Philippe-Egalité, then five, and his grandson, Louis-Philippe, the future King of the French. If, in the inscrutable dictates of time, Philippe-Egalité was to vote for the execution of Louis XVI, the son of him whose recovery was celebrated at Saint-Cloud, Louis XV, as though prefiguratively, stood afar off from the fête of the father of the regicide. That was one celebration in the age of Madame de Pompadour which she did not grace: 'the king saw the fireworks from the terrace of Bellevue, but he could only see them sideways, even a little from behind. The Queen, the Dauphin, the Dauphine and the princesses did not go to Saint-Cloud.' But the future Duke de Choiseul had gone.

III

For the future Choiseul those early fifties might seem an idyllic time of affluence in early marriage and enjoyment of his beautiful mistress, the Princess de Robecq, and all the intimates of his high circle. During that sunny stretch, according to the earliest biography of the then Stainville, by 'distributing his days between pleasures, jokes and some occupations which he continued to make for himself, he led the most agreeable and happiest existence. Everybody who lived with him rejoiced in his good fortune and shared it.'[24] In accordance with 'his lively, gay character and his curiosity he divided his time between the pleasures to which he addressed himself with intoxication, whereof he was the life and soul, and that reading which he had made himself undertake from the earliest age in order to make good what had been neglected in his initial education'.[25]

Even then Stainville had a serious side, sometimes distressed, already disabused. If his precarious health was better about then, there was the anxiety of his wife's miscarriage, not to mention the fever that touched Bernstorff that summer.

Stainville wrote to him:

Your remoteness is a much greater void for me than it can seem to you, and that is very just. Dissipation replaces neither friendship nor trust and still less the charm

[24] Essai/Arsenal 5808, fo. 41.   [25] Ibid., fo. 36.

and profit which flow from the advantage of living with you. I see nothing here but dissipation. I confess to you that I am disgusted by it and that I feel that for me it is cloying everything that is called pleasure (*que j'en suis dégoûté et que je sense qu'elle me blase sur tout ce qui s'appelle plaisir*). It seems to me that after thirty a man of a certain condition must fill his life with great concerns, or else school himself definitely to adopt the course of moderation and philosophy. The latter is much the happier and by that very fact perhaps the more difficult to attain. I am giving myself daily lessons in philosophy, which so far have not had great effect.[26]

Such was the future Choiseul's own revision of his accepted image, promoted by himself, as an insouciant sensualist. The moral tone of his later memoirs may seem less hypocritical than some have previously suggested. His expression of disgust was made less than a month before his savouring of the sweet life at Saint-Cloud. Nor were the two just contradictory. The pursuit of happiness easily degenerates into one of enjoyment, sexual enjoyment not least. And for France the regency of Orleans, though it had failed politically, had largely set the moral tone. Stainville wrote of the surfeit of dissipation at a time when Casanova was in Paris and had been receiving 'certain privileges'[27] from the Duchess of Chartres, now of Orleans (he prescribed for her pimples). And Casanova, even, had found himself laughed at by teenage girls from the Opera, and their mothers too, for failing to measure up to their cynical parade of immorality.

Within a few months a different visitor was appraising the Parisian scene. Colonel Wolfe thought that the thoughts 'of the younger people of Paris ... are entirely employed upon the figure they are to make in public, their equipages and dress; and their entertainments within consists [*sic*] of luxurious suppers and deep play. Some of them are elegant enough to be pleased with music, and they all sing well. A few there are – a very small number – that read and think. I begin to be tired of Paris. The English are not favourites here; they can't help looking upon us as enemies, and I believe they are right.'[28]

Such was the ominous conclusion of the twentysix-year-old who, by his defeat six years later of Stainville's fellow-campaigner from fourty-four, the Marquis de Montcalm, was to open the way from Quebec to the signing away of Canada by the Duke de Choiseul. For the present Wolfe was presented to the silent Louis XV and to Madame de Pompadour, whom he found 'a very agreeable woman'[29] possessed, as he judged, of 'a great deal of wit and understanding'.[30] If she was now to be instrumental in the Count de Stainville's ascent

[26] Count de Stainville to Baron von Bernstorff, Paris, 29 Aug. 1752: op. cit., ii. 647.

[27] Casanova, cited in this translation by J. Rives Childs, *Casanova* (London, 1961), p. 73.

[28] Lieut.-Colonel James Wolfe to Mrs. Henrietta Wolfe, Paris, 1 Mar. 1753: Beckles Willson, op. cit., p. 306.

[29] Ibid., 26 Oct. 1752, p. 188.

[30] Lieut.-Colonel Wolfe to Lieut.-General Edward Wolfe, Paris, 10 Jan. 1753: ibid., p. 199.

towards his 'great concerns', it may or may not be coincidence that it was during the ascendancy of the Countess de Choiseul-Beaupré that Stainville, still excluded from the king's suppers, had yet begun to figure rather more noticeably at court. He is first recorded as performing a ceremonial office on 24 March 1752, as a pallbearer at the funeral of beloved Madame, scrofulous Madame Henriette, younger twin of Madame Infante, confidante of the Dauphin.

IV

Madame Henriette's 'gentle character, without temper and even without will',[31] had run like her mother's towards charity and mild overeating. After developing the regular symptoms of the grim casehistories of that time, putrid fever, convulsions, gangrene of the entrails, extreme unction, she had died aged twenty-four at about noon on 10 February. She had 'really loved the king; the king knew it.' Lonelier now, he left for Trianon.

Ladies in the circle of the Count de Stainville figured prominently in the obsequies with the white trappings of a virgin princess. After two days of Chapelle Ardente at the Tuileries the severed heart of Madame Henriette was conveyed to Val-de-Grâce on the evening of 17 February. It was carried in a coach by the Bishop of Meaux accompanied by the new Duchess of Orleans and, sitting opposite, the Duchess de Luxembourg with the Duchess de Beauvilliers, who had to receive and verify the heart fresh-cut from the corpse – 'a terrible spectacle'.[32]

Two evenings later at just on seven o'clock the body began its last journey from the Tuileries to the abbey of Saint Denis. Sixty poor, two by two, marched ahead with torches. Torchbearers also were the ensuing cavalry, Black Musketeers, Grey Musketeers, light horse, household troops. Behind came the court mourners in royal coaches, each drawn by eight horses caparisoned in silver silk bound with black velvet. Among those riding in the first coach was the Countess de Choiseul-Beaupré. Pages and trumpeters stretched back to the hearse itself, all white and silver and ermine. The procession, judged magnificent, took half an hour to wind past any part of the watching throng, up the Rue Saint-Honoré, out by the Rue de la Ferronnerie. Some of the mounted musketeers livened up the route by swishing their flambeaux to set alight the wigs of spectators, or throwing their brands into the crowd to watch it singe and scatter. Such was the compound of the old regime.

[31] Luynes, xi. 403, and for the following.
[32] Barbier, v. 163.

Madame Henriette had been viewed as a possible supplanter of Madame de Pompadour herself with a king who 'seeks pleasures less than friendship'.[33] He had not now arranged for the Marquise to accompany him to Trianon. 'But', wrote d'Argenson, 'since she shews great courage in the office which she fills for the monarch, she suddenly took her decision like a great captain: she left [for Trianon]; she had the king informed that she was there; she was shewn in; she took possession of the principal apartment even though the queen was at Trianon; the latter lodged where she could.'[34] By 20 March the Count de Stainville was writing: 'The court, which has been much afflicted, and the mistress very anxious, has resumed its ordinary course. Her credit remains as strong as it has ever been. The king, who hardly used to make any journeys in lent, has made many this year. He is going tomorrow to Bellevue'.[35] Stainville did not bother to tell Bernstorff that some days earlier he had been designated one of the four pallbearers at the funeral-service of Madame Henriette.

From about nine o'clock on the morning of Friday the 24th March dignitaries of city, church and court came filing in through the white-draped portals of Saint-Denis. Some two hours later drove up the cortege of the Dauphin, whose second coach bore the Count de Choiseul-Beaupré among others. In another carriage came the royal sisters, Mesdames Victoire, Sophie, Louise, not Adelaide, too moved, like the absent king. Detachments of the French and Swiss Guards presented arms as the royal children entered the abbey to don their regalia of grief and, if wanted, snatch a bite of lenten fare.

Absence of recent precedents for the ceremonial burial of a virgin princess had made it hard going for the Marquis de Brézé, Grand Master of Ceremonies. Now it was noon and after ere he led into church the procession of heralds in their tabards, walking ahead of the Dauphin with Madame Victoire on his arm, then Madame Sophie on that of the Duke of Orleans and so on back. Stainville's cousin, Meuse, was one of those carrying the train of Madame Victoire while Gontaut did likewise for Madame Sophie. The Count de Stainville himself was in attendance as pallbearer up by the coffin at the end of the long, narrow nave. Draped all in white, armorially embroidered, it contrasted with the black clothes and led the eye up to the columned catafalque, sprightly in white satin picked out with rose-pink and willow-green.

[33] Kaunitz/Mémoire, p. 833.
[34] D'Argenson, vii. 117.
[35] Count de Stainville to Baron von Bernstorff, Paris, 20 Mar. 1752: *Bernstorffske Papirer*, ii. 642.

The service was conducted by the Bishop of Meaux. There had been a wild hope that it might be curtailed by an illness preventing the Bishop of Troyes from delivering the funeral oration; but sure enough he waded in for some three-quarters of an hour upon the text *Dies mei sicut umbra declinaverunt, et ego sicut foenum arui; tu autem, Domine, in aeternum permanes.*

Then, at the elevation of the host, eight royal pages flourished torches. Mass over, four junior bishops censed the corpse to the chant of *Libera me Domine* and other prayers for the dead. Upholsterers with ladders undid the pall, canopied across the catafalque, and spread it out upon the ground. That was the moment when there stepped forward to take up the four corners the Count de Stainville and his fellow pallbearers from the youthful nobility, the Counts de Gramont, Rochechouart, and Lislebonne, eldest son of the Duke d'Harcourt – all three, indeed, from ducal families so that Stainville, listed ahead of them, was stepping high.

At the same time eight guardsmen, their bandoliers covered by scarves of white taffeta, shouldered the coffin and bore it to the vaults below. The service had lasted four hours. It was just on five when the Dauphin and his sisters left for Versailles.

It only remained to dismantle the trappings and distribute the pickings of death to its vulturine acolytes from the French court: 'the [mourning] mantles of the princesses belong to the heralds at arms. All the candle wax is in sequestration until there has been a decision about its division.'[36] The Swiss Guards claimed all candles from the nave. Also attributed by tradition to the mercenary Swiss and commuted for cash were the external hangings over the doorways. Whereas the pall which Stainville had helped to carry went to the royal valets. This time they were hoping it would net them thirty louis; the wartime one of mere plush used for the Spanish Dauphine had only fetched about 400 livres, a wretched return compared with the 1,800 said to have been paid them for the velvet model which had embellished the burial of the Italian one back in 1712.

Death is permanent only for the dead. For the living pleasure should prevail. Four days before he officiated at that funeral Stainville had been writing to Bernstorff of the operas to be performed after Easter at Bellevue even though Louis was still plucked by grief:

It was a great business getting the king to sanction the operas. The Duke of Zweibrücken, an intimate friend of the Marquise, has arrived and served as a pretext for the proposal. They say that he is going to change his religion. It would not

---

[36] 'Relation de ce qui s'est passé à l'enterrement de Madame Henriette à Saint-Denis, au mois de mars 1752': Luynes, xii. 255.

surprise me. It is certain that Mme de Pomp. has aims for him. The difficulty will be to carry them to success. I should have thought that it would have been more advantageous for him to agree to marry a daughter of the Prince of Wales, which I know has been proposed to him. For I regard the Polish crown and one of Mesdames as a chimera impossible to achieve, however much talent the Count de Broglie may have.[37]

The suggestion that Madame de Pompadour was trying, if in vain, to counter the Conti designs on Poland and exploit the embassy of the Count de Broglie in the interest of her own protégé came significantly from one who had himself discussed such an embassy with her, who was the intimate of her intimate, the Marquis de Gontaut.

At thirty the protestant Duke Christian IV of Pfalz-Birkenfeld-Zweibrücken, related to the francophil Elector Palatine, was a veteran French officer from that Bohemian campaign wherein Stainville had likewise served. The duke had developed the habit of dropping in incognito as the Count of Sponheim upon the French court where he was cherished by Louis XV. The Polish crown, however, was not for the Duke of Zweibrücken, nor a French princess. He was to contract a morganatic marriage, was to be dead three years later. If present pleasure looked to him at Bellevue yet a heavy cold contracted by Madame de Pompadour threw out the opera there towards the end of April 1752.

The first half of May found the king at delicious Marly with the gayer element of his court and such bright occasionals as the Count de Stainville. The later Choiseul was to recall of that period that 'since I never went to court except for pleasure, I saw those who lived there continually only at Fontainebleau and at Marly. Mme de Pompadour prided herself upon hating me and I prided myself upon making fun of her.'[38]

It was that May at Marly that the mordant Count de Stainville went into partnership with the Marquis de Castries, commissioner-general of the French cavalry, in gambling at cards. They were among the outstanding winners in specially high play even if they did not quite come up to the Marquis de Livry, first master of the king's household. According to the reliable Luynes 13 March 1752 proved Livry's lucky evening at Marly to the record amount of 3,000 louis. Play might last all night, till eight or nine in the morning.

It looks as though it was this classic coup by Livry, blurred in certain particulars, which later came to Choiseul's mind, unlike his

[37] Count de Stainville to Baron von Bernstorff, Paris, 20 Mar. 1752: *Bernstorffske Papirer*, ii. 642.

[38] Choiseul, *Mémoires*, p. 69.

own profitable performance, when he recalled more than twenty
years later:

Louis XV had begun to degrade himself from the middle of the war of 1741; after the
peace he proceeded to lose all noble feeling. He was taken with a furious passion for
faro. He played so high that in a single evening at Choisy [sic] Monsieur de Livry
won three thousand louis from him. The king played very badly because he was
preoccupied with the idea of raking in the gold that there was upon the table. When
he won he put his gains aside; when he lost he gave his adversary a chit upon the
treasury so that one would have thought him a man who lived by his work and was
afraid of want. When it was seen that he was venturing a lot of money, all the
courtiers did as he did, according to custom.[39]

A humble spectator of the play at Marly, where Stainville made his
killing with Castries, has preserved the fleeting emotions of 'the
curious spectacle of the royal gaming in the salon. There I used to go
to watch, around a table of lansquenet, the torment of passions
condensed by respect, the greedy thirst for gold, hope, fear, the grief
of losing, the ardour of winning, joy after a good hand, despair after
a dud, all quickly succeeding each other in the hearts of the gamblers
beneath the motionless mask of cool calm.'[40]
The then Stainville added to his own recollections:

Madame de Pompadour, who was the king's sincere friend, did everything she could
to divert him from his passion for gambling but could not manage to. It was the same
as regards champagne, which Louis XV drank beyond measure so that his royal
majesty was sometimes compromised upon leaving table. It followed that the king,
who was still used to listening to what was said in the council and sometimes joining
in the discussion, lost all concern for the affairs of the kingdom.[41]

Thus, according to the later Duke de Choiseul, it was not only
sexual indulgence which lowered Louis XV. Though that too was a
renewed preoccupation at court just then, if under camouflage as
regards the admiration inspired by the young Countess de Choiseul-
Beaupré, who came to be known as the Countess de Choiseul-
Romanet. The then Count de Stainville recalled of that same time:

On a visit to Marly, in 1752, I thought while gambling that I perceived that the
Dauphin was having a flirtation with Mme de Choiseul. I spoke to her about it; she
did not deny it. As she was interested in my gambling she was beside me at Trente
et Quarante and, all that visit, the Dauphin went to bed later [than usual] and did not

[39] Choiseul, 'Mémoires inédits', 2/16/8/497/2.
[40] Marmontel, *Mémoires d'un père pour servir à l'instruction de ses enfants*, ed. Maurice
Tourneux (Paris, 1891), ii. 8–9.
[41] Choiseul, 'Mémoires inédits,' 2/16/8/497/2f.

leave us. On the last day I said to Mme de Choiseul that I was afraid that this flirtation might not be free from trouble. She joked with me about it. I returned to Paris and thought no more either of Mme de Choiseul or of her flirtation.[42]

V

The Dauphin, a pious prince under Jesuit influence, was not above trying his luck with a pretty woman; only, he was apt to be promptly headed off by the Dauphine, 'the most jealous wife in the kingdom'.[43] Whatever her role in relation to the Countess de Choiseul-Romanet, the latter's charms were to take effect upon a level higher, even, than the Dauphin's and one more alarming to Madame de Pompadour. Some such preoccupation may have underlain a glancing reference in a letter which she wrote on 23 June 1752 to her brother about her pet project of the École Militaire: it looks as though the Count de Choiseul-Beaupré was involved in some typical trouble which the planners had run into over rehousing an institution for convalescent children on the Plaine de la Grenelle (the Marquis de Stainville's old house near The Convalescents may conceivably have pointed to some Choiseul property-holding). 'I have', wrote Madame de Pompadour, 'told M. de Choiseul to let me handle this dreary affair with you; he himself has one of a very different order of importance, and it does not allow him time to breathe.'[44]

The development of relations between the Marquise de Pompadour and the Count de Choiseul is a somewhat neglected aspect of the scandal of his wife's set at the king. The general report was that the giddy Countess de Choiseul-Romanet had lacked the skill to play a sufficiently waiting hand, had yielded too soon to the king's desire. An account of the crux comes from Dubois, first clerk in the Ministry of War and confidant of the Count d'Argenson, the lover of the Countess d'Estrades. At the critical juncture those three were in the minister's study together, it so happened, with Quesnay, the physiocratic doctor to Madame de Pompadour. They were anxiously waiting.

The Countess de Choiseul-Romanet entered in dishevelled triumph. The Countess d'Estrades ran to embrace her in eager

---

[42] Choiseul, *Mémoires*, p. 69.

[43] J. N. Dufort, comte de Cheverny, *Mémoires sur les regnes de Louis XV et Louis XVI et sur la révolution*, i. 101.

[44] Marquise de Pompadour to de Vandières, 23 June 1752: M. A. P. Mallasis, *Correspondance de Mme de Pompadour avec son père, M. Poisson, et son frère, M. de Vandières*, p. 95. (There the identification in the index of 'M. de Choiseul' with 'le duc de Choiseul' is evidently incorrect. It seems probable that this identification should be with the 'comte de Choiseul', that is Choiseul-Beaupré, specifically mentioned by Madame de Pompadour in her letter of 26 Apr. 1751 to her brother: cf. p. 884, n. 10 above.)

enquiry. 'Yes', replied the latest adultress, 'it is done. I am loved. He is happy. She will be dismissed. He has given me his word.'[45] There was general jubilation, except for Quesnay. The Count d'Argenson assured him that he would be all right. Quesnay, rising, replied: 'I, count! I was attached to Madame de Pompadour in her prosperity, and I shall be in her disgrace.' The doctor stalked out to their consternation. Madame d'Estrades reassured the others that Quesnay was not the man to give them away. She was right. Dubois, the silent observer of all this, closed his account: 'And indeed it was not through him that the secret was revealed and the Marquise de Pompadour delivered from her rival.' It was through the Count de Stainville.

Stainville now became enmeshed in an enterprise of chance for higher stakes than those upon the red and black of the gaming-table at Marly. His young cousin's light affair was to prove a turning-point in his career, and one that many of his contemporaries were to judge severely.

First, then, the case brought by the enemies of the future Duke de Choiseul, as set out by one who claimed to be a friend. The Count de Cheverny recalled of the Choiseul-Romanet affair:

At length the Marquise became highly anxious ... The Marshal de Richelieu, on the lookout for his master's pleasures, delighted to play a part for which he could not hope with the Marquise, as wittily officious as a courtier can be, set his emissaries to work. In short a correspondence was established between the king and the Countess de Choiseul-Romanet; but it could not be kept so secret that Madame de Pompadour was not informed of it.

All heads were put together. This nascent passion had to be foiled. They cast eyes upon M. de Stainville; Madame de Pompadour told him that the king would never confess his unfaithfulness, that she looked to him [Stainville] to secure proof. Nothing more was necessary. M. de Stainville deployed all his methods of seduction, for, although very ugly, his wit made one forget his face. Madame de Choiseul-Romanet succumbed. He played the jealous lover, made himself desired and by the subtlest device obtained the king's letters. As soon as he had them he took them to the Marquise, who used them so victoriously that the convicted king was obliged to give up this new attachment.[46]

The accusation proceeded:

M. de Stainville kept his word and lived with his new mistress without causing jealousy to the king, who, shocked by her preference, wished to think of her no more. But by the greatest fatality this affair had not been arranged three months before Madame de Choiseul-Romanet was carried off in a fortnight by a malignant fever. Malicious gossip made out that she had been poisoned. The king, foiled in his amours, could not have instigated this crime. The Count de Stainville, who had seen

[45] Dubois, cited, Marmontel, op. cit., ii. 26–7 for the following.
[46] Comte de Cheverny, op. cit., i. 138–9 for the following.

in the delivery of the letters but a means of assuring himself a woman whom he really loved, could not be suspected. However the jealousy which was inspired by the part that he was beginning to play was responsible for vile gossip. I was in a position to judge its value and upon my soul and conscience I have always believed him incapable of such a crime . . . He was above suspicion on that score.

While the emotional Count Dufort de Cheverny generously acquitted the Count de Stainville of being a poisoner, he otherwise lent support to a story calculated to delight Stainville's enemies. Though Cheverny himself admitted their jealous animus against the future Choiseul. There was indeed a substratum of truth in Cheverny's version; but in a number of respects it was, at least, an ignorant rendering. One may turn now to Stainville's own account of the part he played in October 1752 and in the months succeeding.

VI

The future Choiseul recalled:

When the court was at Fontainebleau the rumours about Mme de Choiseul increased. Some people thought that it was the Dauphin who was in love with her; others assured one that the king was in love with her and that she was in a position to replace Mme de Pompadour. I did not pay much attention to these rumours. I had, some months previously, remained persuaded of the flirtation by the Dauphin: I thought that it had continued and was the cause of the rumours that were circulating.[47]

Looking back to the time of his intimacy, in particular, with the Luxembourgs and the Princess de Robecq, the then Count de Stainville continued:

As a consequence of my social connections I was at Fontainebleau a fortnight after the court had been established there [on 26 September 1752]. On the very day that I arrived there I met M. de Choiseul [Beaupré] by chance in the king's apartment. He drew me aside, saying that he was looking for me, and asked me if I had heard tell of the things that they were saying about his wife. I told him that I had just arrived and that I had not heard tell of anything. Then he informed me, with exclamations and ridiculous displays of fury, that Mme de Pompadour was putting it about in society and was having it put about by her friends that the king was in love with Mme de Choiseul; nothing, he said, was so base and unforgivable as this behaviour of Mme de Pompadour, who saw fit to decry the wife of a man like him, and such a virtuous woman, doubtless in order to take revenge upon Mme d'Estrades.

So recently as 20 September the Marquis d'Argenson, the elder brother of her lover, had noted: 'The Countess d'Estrades has more

[47] Choiseul, *Mémoires*, pp. 69–70 for the following.

influence than ever: Mme de Pompadour believes that she will be ruined by her.'[48]

Choiseul-Beaupré, wrote Stainville, added:

He was capable of going to all sorts of extremities to avenge the mere suspicion of injury to his honour, and he told me without more ado that if he thought his wife capable of listening to the king, he would treat her as she deserved. The end of this tirade was that he would be capable of burning down the château of Fontainebleau. M. de Choiseul spoke to me with such especial vehemence and absurdity that, besides my not having time to stop him, I had to make a great effort to contain myself and not burst out laughing in his face. When he had finished, I observed to him that we were not in a fit place for such a conversation and I suggested to him that we should choose a secluded one if he wanted to continue it.

We went out. He wanted to repeat to me all that he had said. I begged him to listen to me. I represented to him first of all how ridiculous it was to make such an exhibition of himself for such a cause: how wise and noble it was to seem to ignore public gossip upon this subject. I said that I was pleased to see that he was as satisfied as he was certain of the good behaviour of his wife. As to blaming Mme de Pompadour for the public gossip, I observed to him that I was not fond of Mme de Pompadour so that naturally I was not disposed to soften imputations against her; however, I thought I ought to make him aware that it seemed to me that there was little plausibility in imagining that the king's mistress would wish to make public the king's love for somebody other than herself. So I did not think that Mme de Pompadour was guilty of what he accused her of. He ought to reflect, too, that even if she had made some indiscreet remarks out of jealousy or stupidity, he was under such a great obligation to Mme de Pompadour that I did not think that in decency it was right for him to let fly at her. Finally, the wisest advice that I could give him was not to upset himself over monsters which probably did not exist and to which, for sure, his person, his fortune and his honour would fall victim. I added that if he perceived that there was any reality in all that was disturbing him, that I should be the first to advise him to adopt the most decisive courses on behalf of his honour, but that I saw nothing in all that he had told me which merited what I had seen of his perplexity and rage.[49]

It would appear, incidentally, that Stainville was probably not the only recipient of his cousin's ill-considered outbursts against Madame de Pompadour. Stainville commented:

The sagacity of my arguments did not greatly persuade M. de Choiseul. It was time to go to supper, and I said to him that we should be seeing each other again. He begged me to see to this and above all to go to see his wife, to console and advise her.

From the moment that I had arrived at Fontainebleau I had seen nobody but M. de Choiseul. That evening I learnt from everybody that his jealous suspicions were well founded. People knew and related to me details of the king's intrigue with his wife, and this intrigue had infinite subdivisions within Mme de Pompadour's circle and at court. Next day I reflected that it would not suit me to play a part in all these

[48] D'Argenson, vii. 302–3.
[49] Choiseul, *Mémoires*, pp. 70–6 for the following.

intrigues. I took the course of not going to call upon Mme de Choiseul and of avoiding her husband. I had things to do at Fontainebleau other than taking care of the king's mistresses.

Events, though, were carrying the Count de Stainville in their direction:

Some days later I did not succeed in avoiding M. de Choiseul. He had been looking for me and at last he encountered me. He seemed to me that day more inclined than before towards jealousy and thinking ill of his wife. I reassured him as best I could. At the same time I repeated to him what I had given him to understand the first time, namely that nothing should make an honest man agree to being the husband of the mistress of the king but that, in order to avoid suspicion of such a misfortune, there was a very simple means; this was to remove his wife to Paris upon pretext of her pregnancy and to keep her away from court till her child-bed – she was only four or five months pregnant. In six months' time the rumours would have stopped and everything would resume its usual course. I thought I perceived from the way in which M. de Choiseul received my advice that Mme d'Estrades and M. d'Argenson were not giving him the same kind and that, whether from stupidity or from infamy, he did not have a taste for absenting himself but, it seemed to me, did have one for being the king's favourite.

That brought one to the inward labyrinths. They presented themselves to Stainville thus: 'M. d'Argenson stood badly with M. de Machault, controller-general of finances and favourite of Mme de Pompadour; in consequence he stood badly with Mme de Pompadour. Mme d'Estrades was also on very cool terms with Mme de Pompadour because she was passionately in love with M. d'Argenson and shared in his interests and intrigues. Both of them very easily controlled the mind of M. de Choiseul and keenly desired that Mme de Choiseul should get Mme de Pompadour dismissed from court and should replace her. Then probably M. d'Argenson would undertake to appease the husband', as a Minister of War might well do for a serving officer by promotion, perhaps conveniently combined with a distant posting. The then Stainville proceeded:

I sensed the whole extent of this intrigue from the reply which M. de Choiseul made to me when I proposed to him that he should take his wife away to Paris. He stammered. He told me that that would be throwing in his hand while he was being attacked by Mme de Pompadour. He added that he was under many obligations to the king, that his wife, besides, was more dependent upon Mme d'Estrades than upon him, and that Mme d'Estrades did not wish it. Upon this I could not prevent myself from posing him with this dilemma: either he believed that his wife was incapable of loving the king, which I believed like him, in which case he should not be affected nor even talk of this whole business; or he did believe her capable of it and did not want to adopt the means of preventing it. In the latter case, since he had informed me of the rumours which he supposed were circulating on this subject, I ought also to warn him that as Mme de Choiseul bore my name, I thought I owed it to myself to inform the public of the conversation which I had had with him, of the advice which I had given him, of the absolute aversion which I should maintain all my life from a woman of my name being regarded as the king's mistress, and of how he had refused me over taking his wife to Paris in order to cut short all suspicion of this shameful intrigue.

The Count de Stainville was formidably sharp. And though he himself enjoyed his own mistresses and was to profit especially from the king's, that is not to say that he was necessarily insincere in being violently opposed to one of his own kin acquiring influence by being publicly branded as the loose woman of a loose king. The dual morality of that age deeply underlay its careful code of misconduct.

At the same time Stainville's menacing intervention in his cousin's affairs was of course drawing him into them:

M. de Choiseul was rather struck by the vivacity with which I expressed myself. He told me that he thought as I did. He reproached me for not having been to see his wife for some days as I had promised him that I would. He added that she was sad not to see me, that she was expecting me, that I would be well pleased with her docility and touched by the mortification which the common talk was causing her. He made me promise to go to see her after dinner on the morrow. I promised him all the more willingly in that I was curious to penetrate the mystery of this intrigue and, if it were possible, to spare my name the opprobrium wherewith it was threatened.

The Count de Stainville continued his account of this crux at Fontainebleau in the latter part of October 1752:

I went next day after dinner to see Mme de Choiseul. She seemed to me to be delighted to see me. She told me that she had been impatiently awaiting me and, without other preamble, she confided to me the king's love for her and her inclination to respond to it; but she attached a condition to it, namely the dismissal of Mme de Pompadour so that she should occupy her place with the same influence. I listened to her without answering anything, for I was careful not to interrupt her. Mme de Choiseul went on, with inconceivable volubility and heedlessness, to tell me that she had announced this condition to the king. I would doubtless approve of it all the more readily in that I was the only person of the name which she bore to be in a position to profit from all the advantages of her favour. She would use her influence first of all to have me made a duke and to procure for me the favours which I might desire. At the same time she hoped that I would attach myself to her by the most intimate friendship and that I would find the means in concert with M. d'Argenson to get rid of her husband for her.'

It was an ugly if superficially seductive proposition, if solidly grounded. That was the first question for the Count de Stainville:

I had no difficulty in perceiving that Mme de Choiseul had a conspiratorial little head which regarded what she desired as being something certain; but I wanted to know if she would give me proof of what she was asserting to me. I made it appear to her that I doubted everything she was telling me. I observed to her that in such matters it was easy to be led astray by appearances. She bridled up at the word *appearance* and I explained to her that I regarded as such the mere desire of the king to sleep with her, and that even if this desire were satisfied it was a long way from there to all the ideas which she had conceived of her favour and the dismissal of Mme de Pompadour. She heatedly assured me that she would not lend herself to anything without this dismissal, that she had declared as much to the king. 'And how', I said to her, 'have you been able to declare it to him? Are you seeing him?'

This was the moment of truth. Her interlocutor continued:

She hesitated and then told me that she had spoken to him only in passing, in the Garden of Diana, but that she used to write to him. I asked her if she received any answers. 'Of course,' she said to me, 'for it is he who wrote to me first and who is pressing me infinitely.' I repeated that he was doubtless pressing her to consent to what he desired, but that it was necessary to weigh the words in the king's letters carefully in order to know whether his proposal was a serious engagement or a mere diversion, what was called in society a passing fancy. I doubted whether the king, who had just made Mme de Pompadour a duchess, who wanted her to be regarded as his prime minister, would at the same time be negotiating in order to dismiss her and to put in her place a woman whose marriage Mme de Pompadour had arranged, whom she had taken into her confidence and who existed at court only thanks to her.

These remarks incidentally confirm Stainville's chronology of the affair since it was on 17 October 1752 that Louis XV had bestowed upon his devoted mistress the rank and patents of a duchess, a title which she yet had the creditable tact to eschew. Stainville added:

I added that I could not believe the king to be thus false. Mme de Choiseul, impatient at my incredulity, went to fetch a casket in which I saw a number of letters from the king. She took the last one and gave it to me to read. It was very long. I do not exactly remember the words which were badly arranged in this letter as in all those that he wrote, but it seemed to me to be pressing. It compounded for the dismissal of Mme de Pompadour. I saw that Mme de Choiseul, as I had suspected, had not granted everything in the Garden of Diana and from this letter I feared that, if she continued to hold out and to be well advised, she might attain to everything that she sought and might, during that very sojourn at Fontainebleau, be declared titular mistress. I pictured to myself with dread the horror of having a woman of my name in this position.

Stainville here contradicted the general report, the circumstantial evidence of Dubois, perhaps even the inherent probability with so flighty a creature, that Madame de Choiseul had in fact yielded herself to Louis. Possibly she lied about it successfully to her cousin, perhaps even had the adroitness to show him one of the less compromising letters; perhaps for once he just misunderstood its application – conceivably to a permanent arrangement over and above any initial sampling; perhaps Stainville just preferred to misunderstand, not to acknowledge such a lapse in the proud house of Choiseul:

I did not hesitate to say to Mme de Choiseul that in the circumstances in which she found herself she could not have chosen a confidant more fitted than I was to give her good advice, especially as she would see that the advice which I was going to give her would be highly disinterested. I declined with thanks her goodwill on behalf of my fortunes. It would be shameful to wish to further them in any way by sacrificing the honour of my name; and since she had confided her secrets to me, I was obliged to inform her that she must get her husband to take her to Paris within four days from the moment at which I was speaking to her; otherwise I should tell this same husband of hers everything that she had told me and everything that I had read.

If she persisted, it would be war between the cousins. The anonymous author of the 'Essay sur la vie de M. le duc de Choiseul' wrote: 'I have sought with avidity, but with scrupulous care, to enlighten myself from him [Choiseul], from his friends, as regards all the events in his life to which I had heard culpable intentions attributed.'[50] Certainly Choiseul looked back in his memoirs at unusual length upon this cardinal and much criticized phase of his life. The possibility that his earliest biographer may have been the addressee of the autobiographical letters which form the core of the published memoirs is somewhat strengthened by the fidelity with which he follows them throughout, and notably in this account of how the Count de Stainville countered the intrigue of the Countess de Choiseul-Romanet. The biographer, however, adds certain particulars which might well have been supplied to him orally, more especially, in the present connection, as to those moods and passions which the later Choiseul may have evened out in writing. According to the Essay 'the horror of what the Count de Stainville gathered [from the Countess de Choiseul-Romanet] threw him into violent anger. He treated this woman with a harshness derived from contempt and indignation'[51] in presenting her with his four-day ultimatum. To return to his own account:

At these words Mme de Choiseul flew into a rage with me, insulted me upon how I was abusing her confidence and threatened me with the king's indignation. I assured her that I was well aware of the risks which I was running. If I had stayed at Paris I would probably not then have come to Fontainebleau in order to get myself mixed up in this business; but since chance had initiated me into her secrets it would be contrary to my honour and contrary to my conscience not to do everything that was within my power to put an end to rumours and intrigue which were dishonourable to our family. 'It is not', I said to her, 'that I am very scrupulously pedantic about love. I should, moreover, consent to all the tastes, whatever they were, which you might

50 Essai/Arsenal 5808, fo. 42.
51 Ibid., fos. 47–8.

have, and even to your satisfying those of the king provided that so far as the king is concerned it were in secret and with no appearance of your having influence. In a word the position of Mme de Pompadour would seem to me unendurable.'[52]

'The Count de Stainville', according to his biographer, also 'flattered her, consoled her, employed the seduction of his graces and his gallantry.'[53] As he himself put it, 'I joined to this firmness all the gentleness of which I was capable. I greatly praised Mme de Choiseul for her good nature, her taste for honesty, how susceptible she was to noble feelings. Finally I do not know how it happened but I moved her to such a point that she promised me to leave Fontainebleau on the following Sunday.'[54] He recalled:

It was on the Wednesday that she made me this promise. I repeated my praises with increased energy. She was crying as she looked at that casket where the king's letters were. Her husband came in. She promptly shut the casket. Her husband asked why she was crying. I told him that she was infinitely affected by the talk that was being put around in public and that she, like me, thought that the best way to stop it was to depart immediately from Fontainebleau and to remain in Paris till after her confinement. At once Mme de Choiseul said to her husband that she begged him to approve this plan. Her husband shewed some opposition to quitting and ceaselessly repeated that his wife's aunt, Mme d'Estrades, would not consent to this departure and that he did not want to decide anything about Mme de Choiseul without the consent of her aunt. As there could not be any other objection to their leaving, I proposed that I should go at once to Mme d'Estrades to explain to her my opinion upon this departure. M. and Mme de Choiseul agreed that I should go to her and, after having made them both promise, I was determined that, if Mme d'Estrades consented to their going to Paris, they should go for certain on the following Sunday.

The Count de Stainville was now plunging into the thick of it:

So I went to see Mme d'Estrades, whom I knew very little and who appealed to me even less. Happily I found her alone. I related to her quite simply that all that M. de Choiseul had told me on the day of my arrival and what I had replied to him. She was interrupting me every minute to tell me that she did not know what was meant by these follies that M. de Choiseul was retailing. I observed to her that these follies originated from the public rumours, that besides that there was mischief afoot in Mme de Pompadour's close entourage, and that it did not seem to me proper that she [his cousin] should be the object of Mme de Pompadour's jealousy, or of the public talk. I warned her that I had just advised the husband and wife to leave Fontainebleau at the first opportunity and that Mme de Choiseul should leave court till after her confinement in order to put a stop both to the mischief-making against Mme de Pompadour and to the public rumours. I added that I begged her to believe that I would not have got myself mixed up in this business if M. and Mme de Choiseul had not spoken to me of it but that, since they had asked my advice, I thought that I could

[52] Choiseul, *Mémoires*, pp. 76–7.
[53] Essai/Arsenal 5808, fo. 46.
[54] Choiseul, *Mémoires*, pp. 77–9 for the following.

not give them any that was wiser and, since I happened to be the closest relation of M. de Choiseul, I begged her not to oppose the advice which he would ask of me as to his conduct.

Mme d'Estrades was trying to make me understand that what I was saying to her was devoid of common sense when M. d'Argenson, who had just been working with the king came in. As soon as he appeared I called out to him that he was not intruding upon our conversation; I repeated to him everything that I had just said to Mme d'Estrades. After a discussion between the three of us, which, however, was not very long and seemed to me to embarrass Mme d'Estrades and M. d'Argenson, I repeated to them that I could not suffer that Mme de Choiseul should play the part that she was playing. I begged them to believe that I was well enough informed of what was going on to be in a position to declare to them that if she did not leave Fontainebleau on Sunday I should employ all means that might seem best to me to make her leave on Monday.

The subtle yet open boldness wherewith Stainville daunted the two schemers was prefigurative of his diplomatic technique:

Then M. d'Argenson agreed that I was right and it was decided that Mme de Choiseul should leave not on the Sunday but on the Tuesday. For this delay Mme d'Estrades gave a reason which I no longer recall but which seemed to me fairly plausible. I returned to Mme de Choiseul's where I found her husband still with her. I told her her aunt's decision and the view of M. d'Argenson. I noticed Mme de Choiseul's regret. However she renewed her promises and, upon leaving them, I said to them that I relied upon their word and that I hoped that we should have nothing further to say upon this subject.

Two days later I met M. de Choiseul, who told me that he was definitely leaving on the Tuesday. M. d'Argenson sought to see me and confirmed this departure to me. I was all the more pleased with my negotiation in that I congratulated myself upon having done what was a good deed in itself and without my being able to see that it would produce any disadvantage for myself. For the secret was perfectly kept and I was pleasurably enjoying the anxieties which Mme de Choiseul's intrigue was causing among Mme de Pompadour's courtiers, knowing as I did that in a few days this whole to-do would lose its substance.

The Méchant was by his own confession hugging himself in malicious glee and, in the words of his apologist, thanking 'his lucky star'.[55]

VII

On the morning of that Sunday which had been the original term of Stainville's ultimatum to his cousin to quit he went 'by chance to the apartment of my brother-in-law, the Duke de Gontaut, to talk to him about something which concerned me personally. I found him with

[55] Essai/Arsenal 5808, fo. 50.

President Ogier',[56] their legal friend. Ogier figured advantageously not only in the Grand' Chambre of the Parliament of Paris but also at Versailles, where he was superintendant of the finances of the Dauphine's household, perhaps in preference to taking up his nomination to Ratisbon as French envoy to the Imperial Diet. When Stainville entered the room Gontaut was discussing with Ogier 'the rumours which were circulating about Mme de Choiseul, reproaching himself for having helped to make a marriage which was mortally grieving Mme de Pompadour.' Stainville could not resist:

I reminded him of what I had told him at the time of M. de Choiseul's marriage and of the gibes which my repugnance towards it had then incurred. He admitted that I had been right and he continued, along with President Ogier, to deplore Mme de Pompadour's situation. I had seated myself by the fire while he walked up and down making all those exclamations of his which made me laugh. He reproached me for amusing myself with somebody else's unhappiness. I put it to him that since Mme de Pompadour made a point of not liking me it was natural enough that I should not like her and could not care less about her situation.

Choiseul's earliest biographer, in his corresponding account of this lively conversation, presented it with a somewhat critical implication against Stainville's crowing, possibly derived from personal evidence from Gontaut,[57] the obvious friend to ask about this episode. By this account Stainville, commenting on the Beaupré marriage to the other two, 'chaffed them with having, by this fine piece of work, effected the misfortune and ruin of their friend [Madame de Pompadour]; and by his sarcasms and his ironical remarks he had reduced his two unfortunate friends to deeper despair'.[58]

The account of the then Count de Stainville himself was naturally enough rather more restrained. It proceeded:

M. de Gontaut began again on all the matters of complaint which he personally had against Mme de Choiseul, on the justified anxieties of Mme de Pompadour, the embarrassment in which she found herself and his mortification at seeing her in this situation. I did not join in the conversation at all and as it was time to go to dinner I got up, saying that I could not help laughing at being conscious of the fact that, in an intrigue which concerned me so little, if I were to say a word I could set everybody's minds at rest.

[56] Choiseul, *Mémoires*, pp. 79-80 for the following.
[57] This might also explain why the author of the Essai made the third participant in the conversation not President Ogier but the Marquis de Meuse, a more memorable name for feeding up in a possibly blurred recollection years later. While it is possible that Meuse was a deliberate correction of Choiseul's version, it would seem that his mention twice over (cf. above) of the less conspicuous Ogier is to be preferred, more particularly since the Marquis d'Argenson had noted only the month before (23 Sept. 1752): '*M. de Meuse s'est retiré pour toujours dans ses terres de Lorraine; c'est un ennemi de moins pour la marquise de Pompadour et pour le duc d'Ayen*': D'Argenson, vii. 308.
[58] Essai/Arsenal 5808, fo. 50. (In the manuscript the last clause is struck through, evidently as reflecting unduly upon Choiseul.)

'And why not say it, this word?' exclaimed M. de Gontaut.

'My dear brother', I replied to him, 'because I have no desire to set Mme de Pompadour's mind at rest'.

With that I went out to dine where I was expected[59].

His biographer adds that Stainville went out singing to himself. No play could contrive a more effective exit for the Méchant.

By the same account Stainville had fired his parting shot at the other two 'as a consequence of the gaiety induced in him by the ridiculous aspect of their affliction',[60] and his remark was made 'without other object than to torment these gentlemen further'.

Back to Stainville on that eventful Sunday: 'Hardly had I left the dinner-table than they came to the place where I was dining to beg me on behalf of M. de Gontaut to go to find him in the quarterly apartment, at the Maréchale de Luxembourg's',[61] installed there since her husband was on duty that quarter as captain of the royal bodyguard: hence, too, his wife's employment of them as messengers to Stainville who, he was to recall, was 'far removed from thinking that this message had any connection with the business about Mme de Choiseul. I imagined that as we were used to exchanging pleasantries, Mme de Luxembourg, M. de Gontaut and I, they were summoning me to play some tricks on me. I did not at the moment want to leave the place where I was' – one wonders a little how carefully anonymous it may have been left in so circumstantial a story. It proceeded:

I said to the bodyguard whom Mme de Luxembourg had sent to fetch me that I would go to her as soon as I could. This bodyguard had hardly left before another arrived with fresh solicitations. Finally the major of the bodyguard came to urge me to go to Mme de Luxembourg. I went there. I found there M. de Gontaut who said to me: – My dear brother, you may perhaps take it unkindly against me that I could not help passing on to Mme de Pompadour what you told me this morning in my apartment as you were leaving. She charged me to look for you wherever you might be so as to take you to her in order that you should speak to her the word which can set her mind at rest.

Stainville's malicious laughter had shattered the thin ice over which he had been skimming:

'I shall do nothing of the sort', I retorted hotly. 'Beside the fact that what I said was not serious and was only a joke which I wanted to play on you, even if there were really something in it nothing could induce me to go to Mme de Pompadour's. Since I should not be going there from sympathy, I should have the air of playing a part of

[59] Choiseul, *Mémoires*, pp. 80–1.
[60] Essai/Arsenal 5808, fo. 50–1 for the following.
[61] Choiseul, *Mémoires*, pp. 81–2 for the following.

an intriguer, and this air does not suit me in the very least.' I reproached M. de Gontaut for having so heedlessly taken my name in vain. He said to me, as did Mme de Luxembourg, everything that could be said to persuade me to follow him. I replied to him everything that could be replied in order to resist it. This dispute, which was very lively, lasted a long time.

The Duchess de Luxembourg as usual played a leading hand. She drew the attention of the Count de Stainville to the delicacy of his position, saying:

'M. de Gontaut has indiscreetly told Mme de Pompadour that you knew a secret which could set her mind at rest. She has suggested that you should go to see her. You refuse to do so. She would inevitably think that, apart from your refusal being rude towards her, you are particularly her enemy and perhaps in the intrigue to get her dismissed. – You say', she added, 'that you will not hear any intrigue nor be suspected of it. You will be, however, by Mme de Pompadour, who will always believe that you support this intrigue since you are not willing to set her mind at rest.' To all these entreaties I replied that what I had said signified nothing, was devoid of any sense and that it would be ridiculous for me to go to Mme de Pompadour to tell her that I had nothing to tell her.

But he did have something to tell her: 'M. de Gontaut resumed: "I do not ask you to tell her anything other than that. But come to see her to make good the blunder that I have committed and prevent it from recoiling upon yourself."' According to the complementary account of Choiseul's biographer, while he was engaged in this anxious altercation with his friends he received and disregarded an urgent summons from Madame de Pompadour. But when it was repeated he gave in. 'I allowed myself', he wrote, 'to be carried off to Mme de Pompadour's apartment. M. de Soubise was there.' This was Charles de Rohan, Lieutenant-General the Prince de Soubise, Governor of Flanders for a year now, an upright man liked by the king and also one of the most assiduous friends of the Marquise de Pompadour. Soubise and Gontaut now left her alone with the Count de Stainville.

For Stainville it was to be one of the most important interviews of his life. According to his biographer, 'the conversation which he began with the gaiety which was habitual to him could not long be sustained upon this note. Madame de Pompadour was in tears and replied only with sobs to the assurance which M. de Stainville gave her as to the nullity of what he had said to M. de Gontaut.'[62] Stainville's own account ran:

She asked me what the remark which I had made at M. de Gontaut's signified. I told her that, being accustomed to joke with M. de Gontaut, I had made this remark to

[62] Essai/Arsenal 5808, fo. 52.

him and that it meant nothing, but that I had been punished for it since he had repeated it to her. Mme de Pompadour's crying redoubled. She became so emotional as to beseech me in the most touching manner to relieve her of her anxiety. I refused to do so for quite a time, still upon the pretext that I had nothing to say.[63]

It was as likely as not from Stainville himself that his collating biographer secured these particulars of the scene with Madame de Pompadour: 'After long and useless entreaties, the Count de Stainville saw her fall upon her knees, bathed in tears, imploring him with hands joined to deliver her from her cruel position, not to encourage the pretensions of Madame de Choiseul and declare himself her enemy to such an extent. The Count de Stainville [was] revolted by the suspicion that he could be dabbling in an intrigue which he detested.'[64]

'At last', recalled the later Choiseul, 'touched by her tears, I could resist no longer and I confided to her that I knew that Mme de Choiseul was to leave Fontainebleau in two days' time and would not be returning to court till after her confinement, in six months. I ought to have confined myself to this confidence, sufficient to set Mme de Pompadour's mind at rest, but the conversation between us became more confiding and I had the imprudence to confess to her how I knew of the departure of Mme de Choiseul. I confided to her in turn the various circumstances with which I was acquainted. In doing so I was committing a great fault, with which I have since reproached myself; but, when one is moved beyond a certain point, considered reserve is very difficult. So I told Mme de Pompadour that I had seen a letter from the king to Mme de Choiseul which proved a flirtation on both sides but which did not seem to me one that should cause her anxiety, above all since Mme de Choiseul was taking the course of withdrawing.'[65]

This reassurance, according to Choiseul's biographer, was prompted by Madame de Pompadour's notion that her loved Louis was then 'in the moment of passion bestowed by the first instants of happiness',[66] which she feared that he had just consummated with the Countess de Choiseul-Beaupré. As for Madame de Pompadour herself, one scarcely needs to be assured that she subjected the susceptible Count de Stainville to 'all the seduction of her sex and age'.[67] The same source adds that he explained his concern to prevent his cousin from smirching the family honour and that Madame de Pompadour was 'less humiliated by what was offensive to her in M. de Ch[oiseul-Stainville]'s motive than satisfied by the result that he

[63] Choiseul, *Mémoires*, pp. 82–3.   [64] Essai/Arsenal 5808, fos. 52–3.
[65] Choiseul, *Mémoires*, p. 83.   [66] Essai/Arsenal 5808, fo. 54.   [67] Ibid.

announced to her . . . Madame de Pompadour served his ends for the execution of this honourable project.'[68] The narrator went on to explain that his source for this whole episode was 'the Duke de Choiseul himself, by whose hand I have seen this story set down as I am writing it,[69] and who has several times talked to me about it'. The account from Choiseul's own hand continued:

Before deciding to give myself, or rather before letting myself be drawn into the satisfaction of setting Mme de Pompadour's mind at rest, I declared to her that what I was willing to do for her, by acquainting her with the removal of Mme de Choiseul from court, had no other end nor any other interest on my part except the pleasure of relieving her of a situation which grieved me. In this connection I even paid her compliments; but at the same time I assured her that I should regard it as dishonourable to myself to turn this event to account in order to profit from her influence; and I added that, although it might be dangerous for her if she informed the king of what I had just told her, I nevertheless left her free to do so if she should find it useful. Mme de Pompadour promised me the greatest secrecy. She did not keep her word to me, but she did then want to do so. We heard the king returning from evensong. I left her and cut short the thanks which she was rendering me with much feeling, as also her very lively entreaties to me to see to it that Mme de Choiseul did leave as I had assured her that she would.

When I had got outside Mme de Pompadour's apartment, on the way back to Mme de Luxembourg's, I confess that I felt uneasy about what I had just done. The sight of Mme de Pompadour in tears had excited my head a little. Upon reflection I felt remorse for a conversation which had the air of an intrigue and which consequently offended my natural delicacy. At Mme de Luxembourg's I reproached M. de Gontaut for his indiscretion. I told them what had happened, asking them to keep it the deepest secret.[70]

VIII

Choiseul's biographer says, however accurately, that he was now so worried that he left Fontainebleau next day and did not reappear there during that sojourn of the court. He himself merely wrote: 'I did not inform myself of the use with the king which Mme de Pompadour had made of my confidence. Mme de Choiseul left Fontainebleau on the day that she had promised me', the Tuesday. But in her last two days at court – the extension secured by the Countess d'Estrades – she had done one thing heavy with future import, which remained long unknown both to Stainville and to Madame de Pompadour. Because the king was better than either of them at keeping a secret.

[68] Ibid., fos. 53–5.
[69] This passage confirms the strong supposition from other internal evidence that Choiseul's earliest biographer saw the original manuscript of the memoirs of Choiseul which were subsequently published by Fernard Calmettes.
[70] Choiseul, *Mémoires*, pp. 83–5 for the following.

For the present Stainville, in perhaps merciful ignorance, went to see his cousin at Paris some days after her arrival. 'I perceived', he wrote, 'that she was extremely cold to me, as also her husband whom I found with her. I imagined that Mme d'Estrades, enraged by the departure of her niece, had made some trouble for me': in fact his cousin had made some for him on her own account. Still, he could reflect with satisfaction:

My object of preventing an affair dishonourable to my family was fulfilled. M. de Gontaut assured me that Mme de Pompadour was better in than ever with the king. I forgot and neglected the court and Mme de Choiseul, whom I only saw again some months later, at the moment of her confinement. I saw Mme de Pompadour twice by chance during the course of the winter. She told me nothing of what she had said to the king in the course of her explanations with him; she assured me that I had not been compromised; I thanked her for this not so much from fear of displeasing the king, whom I used not to see twice a year and who had always treated me with much indifference, but from fear of being suspected of having made a delation from interested motives.

The Count de Stainville was, as noticed, to be suspected of worse than that with regard to that cousin whom gossip turned into his mistress, an insinuation which his biographer, one would now think with reason, scornfully brushed aside.

Thus was the young Countess de Choiseul-Romanet evicted from court 'like a little whore, who was ogling the king and who had other lovers'[71] – according to the not wholly reliable Marquis d'Argenson. By his account Madame de Pompadour made out that her rival 'had had the Chevalier de Bissy', and now forbade the Countess d'Estrades to entertain her when she came out from Paris, as she still did when her week of duty as lady-in-waiting to the princesses came round. For the Countess de Choiseul-Romanet was not exiled, just relegated. And if the inner court of Louis and Madame de Pompadour was now closed to her that only earned her and her husband a warmer welcome from the Dauphin and his sisters. Paris, though, remained the base for the discomfited pair, who were shadowed.

The story which made the relegated countess the mistress of Stainville may seem particularly implausible in the light not of his memoirs merely but of his actual preoccupation in the first half of 1753. The Countess de Stainville was so ill as to render her husband so. She was apparently afflicted by some unspecified aftermath from her miscarriage the year before.

'Madame de Stainville', wrote her husband to Bernstorff that May, 'has relapsed, Sir, into a condition which disturbs me as much as the

---

[71] D'Argenson, vii. 382 for the following.

illness. I confess to you that she moves me piteously and that I greatly fear that she cannot gain the upper hand. I have been through three cruel months. Her condition and mine will serve as my excuse for having gone so long without telling you of my affection.'[72] This excuse for a gap since 1 October 1752 in the preserved correspondence apparently stretched back to the period of intrigue over the Countess de Choiseul-Romanet.

Stainville now added: 'I am going to Marly this evening, on business' seemingly related, still, to his diplomatic aspirations: further disproof of his later assertion that he only went to court on pleasure. Nor perhaps was he in the mood to try to repeat his gaming success of the preceding year at Marly. There, in a reversal of his fortunes, the king was now winning a lot; whereas 'Monsieur de Livry is ruined by gambling, and his estate of Livry is going to be sold'.[73]

Meantime it could have been more than coincidence at court that it was just after the disgrace of the Countess de Choiseul-Romanet that even the relatively uninformed Barbier had written in March 1753: 'They are telling stories in Paris. It is said that the king found in his path in the gardens of Choisy a young girl of fifteen to sixteen, extremely pretty, with whom he has been amusing himself, and that she is lodged in the Parc-aux-Cerfs',[74] the district of Versailles where Madame de Pompadour now made over to the king her retreat of the Ermitage. This is one of the earliest mentions of the famous little institution of the Parc-aux-Cerfs to which a succession of young girls were brought for the satisfaction of the 'virile pleasures'[75] of their king. One wonders whether it was about now that he may have reached some understanding, tacit or explicit, with Madame de Pompadour for his licensed indulgence with pretty little chits in consideration of his forgoing the Countess de Choiseul-Romanet and her politically dangerous sort.

It was not long before the French court was buzzing with gossip about the inmates of the Parc-aux-Cerfs, especially witty little Louise O'Murphy, Morfi to most, Helen to Casanova, 'the Irish Lady'[76] to the chaplain of the British embassy. She was succulently portrayed by Boucher. 'The court', observed the Marquis d'Argenson, 'is no longer anything but a seraglio of women and eunuchs, who govern everything by cursed Italian intrigues.'[77] But the sway of Madame de

---

[72] Count de Stainville to Baron von Bernstorff, Paris, 17 May 1753: *Bernstorffske Papirer*, ii. 649 for the following.
[73] D'Argenson, vii. 411.
[74] Barbier, v. 360.
[75] D'Argenson, viii. 29.
[76] Dr. John Jeffreys to the Hon. Philip Yorke, Paris, 14 Nov. 1753: Hardwicke Papers, vol. cclxxxii: British Library, Add. MSS. 35,630, fo. 109.
[77] D'Argenson, vii. 401.

Pompadour was now to endure. Such was the court at which the Count de Stainville had to make his way.

On 3 June 1753 Stainville wrote to Bernstorff from Paris: 'I will not talk to you of news; you used not to know a Madame de Choiseul, Mademoiselle Romanet, a niece of M. d'Estrades; she died yesterday as a result of childbirth. If you write sometimes to the Baron de Scheffer, I beg you to give him my compliments.'[78]

This was the only reference to his fateful cousin made by Stainville in his extant correspondence to Bernstorff. And that letter significantly set the context, beginning: 'Mme de Stainville still has a little fever. This illness seems very long to me, Sir. It has lasted for more than five days, and I do not yet know when it will end. Imagine my anxiety. However, I think that for two days now she has been better, and I am seizing this moment to give myself over to a hope which would console me for all my sorrows.' If he meant hope of still having a child by her, that consolation was to be withheld from him, for ever. He added in the same letter that 'for three months I have been thinking of nothing but my patient and how to capture my doctors'. They may well have included the most celebrated, Senac de Meilhan, the protégé of the Marshal de Saxe who had lately been appointed first doctor to the king, and superintendent of the mineral waters of the realm. Senac's literary-administrative son was to become an adherent of the future Choiseul.

Such was the Count de Stainville's medical preoccupation with his wife while Charlotte-Rosalie de Choiseul-Romanet was giving birth to her daughter, delivered on Monday, 28 May 1753. The mother died on the following Saturday.

It looks as though the Duke de Choiseul had somewhat advanced her pregnancy in the recollection of his memoirs, where he further recorded: 'Mme de Choiseul was brought to bed in the spring and died in childbirth so that I thought that with her this whole story would be buried in the deepest oblivion.'[79] And so indeed it seemed to be for a while, but for a while only. In the words of his earliest biographer: 'Calumny, which was silent for two years while he continued his youthful way of life, soon made itself heard from the time that he was picked out from the common run; and it spread further still in accordance as his fortunes increased; the most criminal intentions and actions were attributed to him.'[80] Two generations later, even, the Prince de Talleyrand was careful to revive the slander

---

[78] Count de Stainville to Baron von Bernstorff, Paris, 3 June 1753: *u.s.*, ii. 649–50 for the following. (This letter is there dated, evidently in error, 8 June.)
[79] Choiseul, *Mémoires*, p. 85.
[80] Essai/Arsenal 5808, fo. 59.

that Stainville had poisoned his young cousin; though one might perhaps think that the venom was Talleyrand's in his comment; 'It is not the only suspicion of this kind which they dared to form against M. de Stainville. However persuaded I may be that none of them was well founded, I feel a kind of embarrassment in not being able to derive my grounds for this conviction from the morality of his life and to be obliged to go to seek them in the levity of his character.'[81] At the time another person falsely accused of poisoning the Countess de Choiseul-Romanet was the Marquise de Pompadour.

Those who are conspicuously successful in life may be pretty confident that if they offer a handle to gossip it will be given an ugly twist against them. Because human malice is kept evergreen with envy.

Each may now judge for himself as between the then Count de Stainville and the many detractors of his conduct in regard to the Countess de Choiseul-Romanet in the years 1752 and 1753.

While one may take Stainville's assurance as to his 'natural delicacy' with a pinch of salt, yet honour was certainly more than just a word to him. The previously unused correspondence for this period modifies accepted assumptions by revealing now that the future Choiseul, even in youth, was at once quite something of a moralist yet also a good deal more concerned with the influence of the Marquise de Pompadour, and better known to her, than one would suppose from his memoirs. Still, his circumstantial story of intrigue does carry considerable conviction, if largely because it is so far from wholly creditable to himself.

The later Choiseul had the honesty to admit that he had betrayed his cousin's confidence to her rival and promptly regretted having done so. As to his explanation of motives, even clever men do make mistakes, do go too far under stress of emotion. As Choiseul explained of his critical conversation with Madame de Pompadour, a warm-hearted young man may indeed find it difficult to resist a beautiful young woman in tears. One little gloss perhaps suggests itself: it may be specially difficult if the young man is ambitious and the young woman wields power in the land.

That suggestion was specifically rejected in after years by the Duke de Choiseul, in moving terms.[82] It is natural to suppose that one understands oneself. And time softens perspectives.

---

[81] Prince de Talleyrand, 'De M. le duc de Choiseul' in *Mémoires du prince de Talleyrand* (ed. cit.), v. 518.
[82] Cf. p. 1000.

CHAPTER VIII

ESTATES

I

'I am still very anxious about the health of Madam the Countess. I beg of you to let me have news of it',[1] wrote the procurator-fiscal of Stainville to the count early in July 1753.

A fortnight previously the Count de Stainville had begun a letter to Baron von Bernstorff: 'At last I believe, Sir, that Mme de Stainville is quite over it . . . She has been so well for some days that the doctors no longer fear a relapse. It was time that the anxieties ceased.'[2] The flat reflection suggests long strain. Now Carré, also reassured, was soon writing: 'I am charmed that Madam the Countess is better. I have remitted to the Curé of Stainville the letter which you addressed to me for him. The prayers for her are being continued.'[3] Such was the intercession in the family church for the wasted girl who was to achieve spiritual self-reliance.

The Countess de Stainville, the count was now writing off to Denmark, was so recovered that:

It only remains for her to regain strength and put on weight, and I am hoping that the fine weather and her youth will promptly provide them. Her illness had worked me up so prodigiously that a fortnight ago they put me on to remedies, which has prevented me till now from going to Compiègne, whither I shall be going only the day after tomorrow. The camp of the Regt. du Roi is assembling there from the 20th to the 30th. This camp will be rather an expensive occasion for M. de Guerchy but, apart from the expense, it is an agreeable enough moment for him.[4]

Guerchy, successor to Biron in command of the Régiment du Roi, was expected to dispense refreshments as well as serving sit-down repasts in five marquees. The king lent three and Conti a beauty all hung inside with crimson damask with gold galloons, given him by Don Philip upon their Alpine campaign. One participant wrote from brilliant Compiègne on 20 July 1753: 'You must reckon that this part

---

[1] Carré to Count de Stainville, Stainville, 5 July 1753: Arch. Meuse, J 18[11], docket II ('Stainville. Bail seigneurial. 1660–an VII').

[2] Count de Stainville to Baron von Bernstorff, Paris, 22 June 1753: *Bernstorffske Papirer*, ii. 650.

[3] Carré to Count de Stainville, Stainville, 20 July 1753, *u.s.*

[4] Count de Stainville to Baron von Bernstorff, Paris, 16 July 1753: op. cit., p. 651. (Guerchy is there wrongly transcribed as Querchy.)

of the world is the golden age,'[5] bathed in the sunshine of grilling
heat. The Count de Stainville, however, was there not just for the
junketing of his old regiment but in pursuit of his interest then in a
camp more severely functional than that of the king's own regiment.

The court at Compiègne sparkled against the threat of war-clouds
banking up across the world. If the Peace of Aix-la-Chapelle was
widely considered but a truce in a conflict unassuaged, it was hardly
so much in India. After French rendition of Madras the masterful
Dupleix, playing off native rulers like Chanda Sahib against the
British, had conjured up an empire almost in a twinkling so that by
1751 he was hailed as the effective ruler of southern India from the
Kistna down to Cape Comorin. A former clerk of the British East
India Company, Robert Clive, proceeded indeed to hold captured
Arcot against Chanda, and next year saw the capitulation of French
troops under Jacques-François Law, nephew of the financier, before
resistant Trichinopoly. But if Dupleix's position in the Carnatic was
thus compromised, westwards in the Deccan his other lieutenant, the
brilliant Marquis de Bussy-Castelnau, was still thrusting ahead. A
swaying struggle for mastery in India was under way, already,
however, with some inclination against the French, in danger of
outrunning their resources, military and financial. If Dupleix and his
wife, the commanding 'Begum Joanna', were accused of rapaciousness,
he did likewise by Bussy and other officers; while back in Paris the
Marquis de Silhouette, now royal commissioner attached to the
Compagnie des Indes, argued against an expensive quest for empire,
in favour of peaceful profits from modest establishments. In that
month of July 1753 he was representing to the controller-general:
'The idea of laying down the law to the whole of the Deccan with a
handful of Frenchmen is madness.'[6]

Anglo-French rivalry in Southern India was conveniently if thinly
cloaked behind commercial companies whereas in North America,
where trade was also to the fore, the clash was more directly colonial,
graver. While Acadia continued distracted, the main struggle bore
down upon the Ohio. By 1753 Duquesne, worthy successor to
Governor-General La Galissonnière, was clamping new forts southward from Lake Erie down towards Fort Venengo and, soon now,
Fort Duquesne itself at the contested forks of the Ohio. Such was the
French thrust from Canada to link down to Louisiana in a specious
strategy to produce the clash with the English sketched by the future
Duke de Choiseul.[7]

[5] Letter to Duke de Luynes, Compiègne, 20 July 1753: Luynes, xiii. 19.
[6] Marquis de Silhouette, memorandum to Machault d'Arnouville, July 1753: cited,
Carré/Lavisse, p. 280.   [7] Cf. p. 820.

If French opinion remained apprehensive of the avid British navy, so did it also of the great Austrian army. British adhesion reinforced the Austro-Russian treaty of 1746. Austria and Prussia, France's ally, remained scowling at one another across Silesia while Kaunitz had not after all managed anything substantial in the way of Austro-French rapprochement. If the continent was not quite an armed camp, in France certainly camps were springing up and armaments being furbished. That July the Count d'Argenson was attending a successful demonstration of improved siege-mines by the celebrated engineer Bélidor in a hill which the Marshal de Belle-Isle had allowed him to tunnel at Bizy. Three months later the Régiment Royale Artillerie, encamped at Versailles, was to test lighter types of cannon. The culmination of French military endeavour that summer was to be in a series of camps interesting to the Count de Stainville.

A financial tussle between the Minister of War and the controller-general, who charged d'Argenson with having deliberately 'ruined the kingdom',[8] had squeezed out funds for some half a dozen training-camps around the confines of France. Down south Saxe's former chief of staff, de Crémilles, was to command a camp with characteristic precision near Beaucaire. Up by Alsace stout Chevert was forming the camp of the Saar where dragoon-training reached a new pitch with whole troops of horse jumping hedges and ditches in battle-order. The smartest camp probably was that of Flanders to be held at Aimeries in the classic campaigning-country of the Sambre under the princely command of Lieutenant-General de Soubise, friend of the Marquise de Pompadour. This was the one to which the Count de Stainville, whom she invited to supper at Compiègne, secured a nomination in his rank of Maréchal-de-Camp. As he had explained to Bernstorff in June 1753: 'I thought that one might as well occupy oneself with manoeuvring troops as stay doing nothing in Paris, all the more so as I am very pleased to be with M. de Soubise and M. de Séchelles',[9] Stainville's old fellow-campaigner from back in Bohemia.

Soubise should have left already for Flanders but, explained Stainville, was 'awaiting the judgement of a case which he has against the princes of the blood because of the titles which he assumed in the marriage-contract of his daughter', Charlotte-Godefride-Elisabeth de Rohan, in the previous month to the current Prince de Condé of the blood royal. The Rohan style of High and Mighty Prince de Soubise was contested by the princes of the blood championed by Conti pushed by Orleans who could in any case sign as Very High and

---

[8] D'Argenson, vii. 444.
[9] Count de Stainville to Baron von Bernstorff, Paris, 22 June 1753: *Bernstorffske Papirer*, ii. 650 for the following.

Mighty Princes. Soubise prevailed and left for Flanders where, explained Stainville, 'his camp will only assemble on the 1st Sept.'[10] By 19 August 1753 he was writing from Paris: 'I am leaving today, Sir, to take Mme de Stainville to my mother's in Lorraine and from there to rejoin M. de Soubise in Flanders, where we shall be encamped till the 1st Oct.'[11]

II

The Countess de Stainville should benefit from country convalescence at smiling Demange where her mother-in-law could at least be relied upon to feed up and fuss over the invalid. The Count de Stainville, however, had received warning that at Demange he would find one or two little matters to sort out with his managing mother in regard to those Stainville estates which he had been keenly supervising amid all his preoccupations in the capital and court.

In contrast to easygoing ways under the marquis, it had been no later than New Year's Day of 1752 that the count went through Carré's estate-accounting for the year 1751. This account was rendered in a new form sharply diminished from that of the forties. The main slice of income from Brigeat as the general lessee of the marquisate was now wholly absent. Only left to Carré as its receiver and procurator-fiscal were residual receipts from much reduced timber-sales, a few small rents and dues, plus fines from woodland contraventions to make a total of a mere 3836 livres, and that still in the currency of Lorraine.

This betokened no diminution in the total yield of the marquisate, rather the contrary. There is evidence that, as one would expect, Brigeat was rendering to the Count de Stainville separate accounts, more important but untraced. Never much of one for the slack of middlemen, the young count may well have preferred to deal with Brigeat direct and collect from him before the payments got tied up in the estate-account. Broadly viewed, the new arrangement seems to mark a third stage in the progression in the accounting of the Stainville estate through the eighteenth century. In its early years under the old line of the Stainvilles they and their procurator-fiscal had been scrabbling in annually a tangled mass of petty dues and payments, as their feudal forbears had been doing for generations past. Then around 1720 the advent of the Choiseuls in the person of the new Marquis de Stainville had roughly coincided with the grand simplification of offloading the main collection on to a general lessee.

---

[10] Ibid., 16 July 1753, p. 651.   [11] Ibid., 19 Aug. 1753, p. 652.

Now, a generation later, the take-over of the Count de Stainville was bringing a further reduction in the direct accounting of such a feudal officer as the procurator-fiscal whose functions as receiver were becoming residual after the separate accounting of the general lessee by financial contract.

If this gradual but suggestive evolution in finance might be taken to reflect some loosening of the feudal ties between the lord and his peasantry, yet the new rigour with which the Count de Stainville proceeded to control his estate-accounts promptly supplies some corrective, in a modernized form, to such generalisation. Also, there may be some suspicion that a separating off of Brigeat's rent could have brought tax-advantage to the Count de Stainville in minimizing the booked yield from his estate, perhaps even in unloading some taxation on to Brigeat. For, in distinction from the good old days of the forties, there now figured prominently under the heading of expenditure a series of nasty little items relating to 'twentieths', implying that the broad incidence of Machault's new impost had been duly matched in the co-ordinated administration of Lorraine: 'for the twentieth of the estate of Stainville to the charge of Monsieur the Count',[12] 150 livres. (Which might suggest others involved.) Another 75 livres were similarly charged against semi-detached Bazincourt, while the Beurey estate came in at 120. Next year Stainville figured again at 150, plus, however, an additional 112 livres, 10 sous 'for a supplement of three years of the twentieth of the said estate'.[13] The Count de Stainville endorsed the surcharge as 'allowed'.

Brigeat figured in a note at the end of Carré's account for 1751: 'The accountant does not enter as a receipt the yield of the farm of Bazincourt seeing that he is to remit it to M. Brigeat to be used to pay the instalment due to M. de Monmartel.'[14] Thus were the terms of the Count de Stainville's marriage-contract being fulfilled, with Bazincourt, which it had added to his estate as from 1 January 1751, providing an income tied to redeeming the counterpart, namely the count's assumption of his father's debt to the financier. The new acquisition was responsible now for an outgoing of forty livres 'for the expenses of taking possession of the estate of Bazincourt and of registering the deed at the bailiwick of Bar'. Whereas the enrolment there that same year of the marriage-contract itself cost just over 100 livres.

The other subsidiary estate of Beurey also figured only partially in the Stainville account, notably for an expenditure of 'thirty-six

---

[12] Carré's account for the Stainville estate for the year 1751: Arch. Meuse, J 18[19].
[13] Carré's account for 1752: ibid.
[14] Carré's account for 1751: ibid. for the following.

French livres, making forty-six livres, ten sous in money of Lorraine, paid to Madame Morinval for what she had advanced for repairs done at Beurey', possibly including those windows which Cornu had been let off when his lease was cancelled, and which Madame de Morinval would doubtless have wanted quickly shipshape when her husband had moved into Beurey in place of Cornu on Saint George's Day 1751, taking over the flock of sheep, the fields already sown with corn and oats, and a stock of 'vine-props to fit up the vines again'.[15] It was in that same year apparently that the Count de Stainville had been rounding out his holding at Beurey and subsidiary Mussey by making a sizeable purchase in the latter village of property, complete with title-deeds back to 1616, from another local lady.

While Stephen de Stainville could now well afford to extend his acres a little, he continued to keep a tight hand on outgoings. The largest of them in the Stainville account for 1751 was to the tune of 1,022 livres, 'to which amount the charges on the marquisate according to the return determined by Monsieur the Count, the whole having fallen due on the first of January 1751 for 1750'.[16] Once again, the Count de Stainville's personal intervention was towards streamlining the accounts, by cutting out tedious enumeration of small expenditures, mostly on wages, now relegated to a separate return and, for purposes of the main accounting, consolidated into a global figure: the 1,022 livres compared with 996 for 1748. The figure for 1751 was repeated in 1752 'according to the return signed by Monsieur the Count at Paris in the month of March'[17] 1752. This item in Carré's account for that year was annotated in Stainville's hand: 'Allowed. I must be sent a new return for the year 1750 which I will sign.'[18] So late as 1752 he was still sorting out the backlog of accountancy: it may be more than coincidence that the account for 1750 is missing.

After the consolidated charges on the marquisate the largest single outgoing in the account for 1751 was 775 livres, representing 600 French livres, 'paid to the Countess de Stainville according to the order of Monsieur the Count of 25 April 1751'.[19] Just which countess is not very clear. She may or may not have been that Madame de Choiseul who had been persecuting Brigeat for a like sum back in 1747,[20] or, most obviously, the count's wife, perhaps in payment of interest upon borrowings from her. Other countesses were Stainville's sisters at lush Remiremont, either the subsequently prominent

---

[15] 'Reçu de Monsieur de Morinval pour M. le Comte de Stainville à son arrivée au Château de Beurey, 24 avril 1751': Arch. Meuse, J 18[19].
[16] Carré's account for 1751: ibid.
[17] Carré's account for 1752: ibid.
[18] Annotation by Count de Stainville on Carré's account for 1752: ibid.
[19] Carré's account for 1751: ibid.   [20] Cf. p. 773.

Beatrix or, at least as likely just then, Charlotte-Eugénie. She, like her brother, was administratively busy with local affairs as working deputy to the abbess, the Princess of Salm, in the absence of that great lady. The year 1753, for instance, found 'Charlotte-Eugénie, Countess de Stainville, lieutenant of the abbess' appointing a clerk 'to the abbatial court of the town'[21] and dealing with an obstreperous juror who claimed to have been 'unjustly deprived of the said office by our act of revocation.'[22]

If Count Stephen de Stainville was to be the great one of the family, he did not monopolize its administrative ability. His payment to the countess in 1751 was repeated next year, unlike a smaller matter of 150 livres 'paid for the instalment due to the Countess de Rouerke by order of Monsieur the Count'.[23] This payment thereafter ceased upon the death of his godmother but was to provide one of the points at issue with his mother.

The Count de Stainville, like his father before him, was also indebted to his home reaches for direct nourishment in delicacies: twenty-four livres 'for the cost of fishing for three pots of trout sent to Monsieur the Count at Paris'[24] in 1752 and, the year before, 'ten livres for a roebuck sent to Paris',[25] eleven livres, twelve sous, six deniers (nine livres French) for a dozen pots of jam – the last item in an expenditure for 1751 totalling 2,986 livres of Lorraine. The addition of reprises, still unavoidable but reduced now to just on 825 livres, produced a figure of 3,811 livres to set off against the income of 3,836, giving the slim surplus for that year of 25 livres, 11 sous, 1 denier. For 1752 the corresponding figures were: receipts, 4,669 livres, 2 sous, 1 denier; expenditure, 4,456 livres, 15 sous, 2 deniers plus a reprise of 212 livres, 6 sous, 11 deniers to make a total offset of 4,669 livres, 2 sous, 1 denier in a neat balance.

Nearly three quarters of all the booked receipts came from sale of timber, just on 3,400 livres in 1752 as against a little over 3,000 the year before. The account for 1752 still included a few small sales of the traditional kind: 26 livres for 'an oak sold to the procurator of Jovilliers by order of Monsieur the Count',[26] 124 livres for '21 oaktrees and oaklings delivered to Charles Braye, miller of Stainville, for the restoration of his mill on 15 January 1752', 95 livres for a similar sale in May of fourteen oaks to that Jean Pitois whose slim purchase of an earlier lot of oaks to repair his mill at Ménil back in 1741 had spelt

[21] *Inventaire sommaire des Archives départementales antérieures à 1790: Vosges*, Série G (Épinal, 1887 f.), ii. 70.
[22] Arch. Vosges, G.996, dossier XVI D, no. 20.
[23] Carré's account for 1751: Arch. Meuse, J 18[19].
[24] Carré's account for 1752: ibid.
[25] Carré's account for 1751: ibid.
[26] Carré's account for 1752: ibid. for the following.

such trouble for Mathieu. Apart, however, from such incidental sales
to meet local repairs, the streamlining policy now in the marquisate
seems to have been to concentrate sales into one or two large
transactions a year. That in the account for 1752 was for 2,674 livres
as the price of 466 oaks and other trees adjudged to one, Jacques
Guinard de Bouchon. This seems to have been an improvement on
the previous year's sale to yield a significantly similar total in two lots,
1,818 livres for 295 trees sold to François Roton or Rotou, plus 800
livres for 64 sold to François Legros. Both purchasers had fallen short
when it came to paying, Rotou by 355 livres and Legros by 175.
These two debts together made up well over half that nasty figure of
824 livres for the rebates of 1751. Both defaulters were distrained on.
Such was the harsh reality behind the satisfactory entry of the total
rebate of 1751 as a receipt in 1752.

The balance of receipts in those years was partly made up by small
payments, still, from those who had bought property on the
instalment-system in the seigneurial sale of 1748 at Stainville.
Nicholas Braye continued to pay an annual 42 livres, 17 sous for his
sheepfold. Then the fishing at Montplonne was rented to Pierre
Herbillon for 12 livres a year. Finally there were the fines imposed by
the woodmote, still in the old currency of Bar, in 1752 to a total of 476
francs, 3 gros, making just over 204 livres of Lorraine. That figure,
though, possessed a notional quality since the reprise of 212 livres for
that year was described as the sum which Carré 'has not been able to
recover since he has been at Stainville': though it may be noted – the
Count de Stainville apparently did so – that the whole of the
preceding reprise of 294 livres for the woodland fines of 1751 had
been included in that write-off of 824 livres as a receipt in the account
for 1752.

Now Carré, in his turn after Mathieu, defensively pled that his
master should sanction the rebate of 212 livres, 'it not being just that
he [Carré] should pay from his own money fines which he has not
been able to extract from the individuals who have been condemned
and who are not in a position to pay'. Woodland pilferers
approximated to the really poor. The Count de Stainville, by now
really rich, noted against this item: 'I am willing to allow the article
of the reprises for this year only while observing that it seems to me
extraordinary that [? upon the article][27] of the fines there is due to me
for the year 1752 204 livres in fines and that I am charged 212 livres
in reprises, whence it ensues, first that there is entered as reprises
more than is due to me and secondly that not one sou has been
extracted from all the fines for the year. Carré will give me an

[27] The text is here torn and uncertain.

explanation of the debts and will in everything be warned to be more exact about the fines and more circumspect on the score of reprises, which he well knows that I do not like.'[28]

Thus did Stainville continue his struggle against those nasty reprises that were creeping back even under the new regime of Carré. Because rebates for future recovery are the standing drawback of rustic adversity, and cunning.

Stephen de Stainville seems to have been in particularly brisk form at his annual accounting on 30 December 1752 (Carré, knowing his master, had got in ahead with the account that month). The count's pithy annotations besprinkled even those new items of expenditure which testified that he was not just a grinder of the poor, as for instance the 150 livres 'for the pension of Madame Flouart'.[29] The count noted here: 'Allowed. Carré will evidently have rendered to himself each year a certificate straight from the said Flouart if he does not see her herself.'[30] Twice the amount of Madame Flouart's pension was now accounted as 'paid to the Curés of Stainville, Bazincourt, Ménil and Lavincourt for the charities ordered by Monsieur the Count in these parishes'.[31] On this he commented: 'Allowed. In the statement of annual expenditure the alms will be accounted to me and in the alms something for Montplonne. In sending me the account every year the statement of charges must be returned to me.'[32] He wanted to know just who benefited and how much. The poor of the neglected little village of Montplonne, at all events, would have reason to be grateful to the sharpness with which the Count de Stainville scanned even minor items in dull documents. He had already acquired this facility of importance for a man of business, a diplomatist, a statesman.

Another beneficent expenditure for 1752 was the sum of 27 livres, 13 sous, 2 deniers paid to Petitpain, the priest at Stainville, for a new missal for the chapel of Saint-Nicholas there. The count, the admirer of *La Pucelle,* allowed this item as also another for a like sum of just on twenty-eight livres, this time 'for the payment and carriage of the outfit of Maiziert, the mounted keeper, sent from Paris',[33] in likely stiffening against poachers. A further item of 40 livres, 2 sous, 6 deniers was booked 'for the remainder of the wages of Jacques Maltry, the superintendant (*surveillant*) until the day of the reception of Maiziert'. This incurred a comment from the count: 'Allowed while

[28] Annotation by Count de Stainville on Carré's account for 1752: ibid.
[29] Carré's account for 1752: ibid.
[30] Annotation by Count de Stainville on Carré's account for 1752: ibid.
[31] Carré's account for 1752: ibid.
[32] Annotation by Count de Stainville on Carré's account for 1752: ibid.
[33] Carré's account for 1752: ibid. for the following.

observing, however, that Jean Maiziert was included in the big statement[34] and that he should not be so separately seeing that this item has the air of being a duplicate entry whereof Carré will give me an explanation.'[35]

If young Stainville's keenness to get things straight made him a strict master, down on slackers, he could certainly be considerate. A further item relating to the incoming Maiziert was for twenty livres 'for the repairs done to the lodging of the mounted keeper according to the orders of Monsieur the Count'.[36] He endorsed this: 'Allowed; a copy of my orders, and still better the original, must be sent to me. In other years Carré sent me back my orders as proof.'[37] The count was good at noticing omissions, and if his quick perception sometimes led him to jump to the wrong conclusion in estate-accounting as later in foreign affairs, even where his questioning was misapplied it was often of that fruitful kind which clarifies by testing and keeping subordinates alert.

Carré's mauled account for 1752 was rounded off in Stainville's hand:

Carré will send me back a duplicate of this account with a copy of my observations, as well as an explanation about the pannage, which is yielding nothing since he has been at Stainville and which has always yielded for 30 years previously. I also bid him to put into yield for next year the tile-kiln of Monplonne.

Maximization of yield to match strict control of outgoings was the principle of this aristocrat who yet acquired – how deliberately is now suggested – a reputation for the fashionable failing of insouciant extravagance. Against such extravagance, which the future Choiseul certainly did practise, one may set one little entry in Carré's account for 1752: 'Fifteen livres for nails provided since I have been at Stainville for the maintenance of the roofs, without which the roofers could not have worked.'[38] To which the Count de Stainville had this to say: 'Allowed. Another year I do not want one nail driven in without my particular order.'[39]

Carré, with due deference in form, did stand up to Stainville in a manner creditable to both. There was an explanation of Maltry's wages; as to the house-repairs for his successor, the absence of the count's authorization was because 'it is contained in a letter which you did me the honour of writing to me, which contains several other

---

[34] i.e. under the preceding general heading of 1,022 livres for charges on the marquisate.
[35] Annotation by Count de Stainville on Carré's account for 1752: ibid.
[36] Carré's account for 1752: ibid.
[37] Annotation by Count de Stainville on Carré's account for 1752: ibid. for the following.
[38] Carré's account for 1752: ibid.
[39] Annotation by Count de Stainville on Carré's account for 1752: ibid.

things; another time I beg you to separate your orders when they are for some expenditure or repairs.'[40] As for those nails, the roofers of Vaucouleurs employed 'for the upkeep of the roofs of the château' were only under contract to supply the labour; the estate had to provide slates and nails; when Carré had taken it on 'there was still some slate, but not a single nail' in stock. Next summer it would be a question of buying not just nails but slates as well.

Pannage provoked another comeback from Carré:

I am not to blame, Sir, if the oaks produce no acorns, or rather, if the frosts and the rains destroy them. Since I have been at Stainville there has been no pannage except in 1749 ... I wish with all my heart that there was a good pannage every year; I should profit by it, because as procurator-fiscal I have the right according to the ordinance to put four pigs on it, and the other officers in proportion.

If at Versailles the spoils-system then of rake-offs for functionaries was open to just criticism, yet as so often it only reflected, as in a polished magnifying-glass, conditions and conventions which permeated the old regime at almost every level. Most built-in societies build in perquisites for the establishment. As to those acorns, the Count de Stainville may after all have been on to some little fiddle. Or perhaps it was just a happy coincidence that, after quite so many bad seasons, the pannage for the following year of 1753 should suddenly show a tidy little profit of 310 livres.

As for the rebarbative reprises, Carré made the perhaps expected point that those 212 livres were not in respect of fines for the current year. He would do all he could to eliminate the reprises and collect the debts, but the succinct realities were: 'those who are condemned [to fines] will pay, or you will let them off, or they will be in prison'. In any event not only should the bad debts not be charged against him but he should be reimbursed his costs of attempted collection: 'it is the rule and the purest justice.' However that might be, there were to be no reprises in Carré's account for 1753.

Carré was pretty clearly of lower financial calibre than Brigeat. (The procurator-fiscal's clerkly copperplate contrasted with the lively flow of the general lessee's handwriting, though both impress by their education.) While the Count de Stainville retained Carré to watch his personal interests on the spot, he evidently made Brigeat directly responsible for the main yield of the marquisate. By such a shrewd dichotomy the count may further have been seeking, largely at any rate, to cover his own overheads on the estate from the residual yield still accounted by Carré, releasing the main lumps from Brigeat to his

[40] Carré, memorandum of 1753 to Count de Stainville, undated and incomplete: ibid. for the following.

personal use. In any case the count's accounting was only the cutting edge of his close involvement in his estate, evident in the flow of letters which he received from both Carré and Brigeat.

III

On 1 August 1753, shortly before the Count de Stainville set out from Paris to take his wife to his mother's at Demange, Carré had warned him:

Madame the Marquise is claiming back the annual payment of 150 livres which you had to make to Mme de Rouerke till her death. I did not make any payment of it last year because it was not requested; she is also making out that you are saddled with paying the twentieth for Bazincourt, which, however, would not be just since, in making the annual payment to M. de Monmartel, the twentieth is withheld. It is for you, Sir, to make arrangements about this with Madame the Marquise.[41]

If the Count de Stainville was financially involved over his godmother, he had recently, it appears, been somewhat unattractively resolved that no such involvement should accrue from such a relationship contracted locally by his wife and himself. Carré had informed Stainville that February that Madame Carré had produced a lusty daughter:

She has been baptized and is called Louise Honorine. I had you and Madame the Countess represented by M. and Mme Lecoy; as regards the expenses of the ceremony, there will be no question of them in my accounts. I should be very sorry if there were; when I took the liberty of praying you to be the godfather and Madame the Countess the godmother of this child, I had no eye to my [financial] interest but to the honour of your protection for myself and my family, which I very humbly beg you to grant me. I should be much happier if it were a boy, so that presently he could be attached to you in some way, but it is a girl.[42]

One senses that beneath the formulae of proper submission Carré was capable of standing up to his formidable master whom he showered with letters crammed with local news and problems: 'I beg your pardon, Sir, if I bore you in this way; you want me to inform you of everything that happens on your estate',[43] whence the Count de Stainville continued to nourish his mondaine existence in the capital and court with local rents, dues, pots of trout, and other dainties. In the letter about the birth of his daughter Carré had also reported that in the name of his master he had faithfully presented to the lieutenant-

---

[41] Carré to Count de Stainville, Stainville, 1 Aug. 1753: Arch. Meuse, J 18[11], docket II ('Stainville. Bail Seigneurial. 1660–an VII').
[42] Ibid., 6 Feb. 1753.   [43] Ibid., 5 July 1753.

general of the bailiwick of Bar the head of 'a medium boar'[44] killed by the rangers of Stainville. Hunks of the meat had gone to leading locals like Aubry and Brigeat with one for Carré himself, who wondered whether the count would like some another time, allowing that 'one can only send this game by coach; it is slow and the carriage costs a lot. There are too many of these animals who do nothing but damage to the countryside. I do not know if you were pleased with the venison which I sent you, nor even if you received it, any more than the jam, the snails and the mustard.'

One Sunday later in that month of February 1753 a man had been found drowned 'near the Cense de Nantel, a dependency of the Abbey of Jovilliers'.[45] Carré, alerted, had led out Lieutenant Lecoy and his rangers together with the clerk of the manorial court. They carried the corpse back to Stainville where, as that of a stranger, it was for twenty-four hours exhibited for recognition in the square by the auditory. Then the body, unclaimed in that close community, was given religious burial in the parish cemetery on the hillside. The costs, the procurator-fiscal warned the count, were his but small, barring complications if 'this man was killed and thrown into the water, and his murderers are known, which I do not think to be the case'. If this might suggest the facility then of rural crime there were other legal angles. Carré continued:

I am sorry for the death of this poor man but I am not at all sorry that he should have been found on the territory of the Abbey; the raising of this corpse is an act of jurisdiction which affirms that which you have over the farm of Nantel, which the monks wanted to contest with you two years ago.

Such was the legalized bickering, decade after decade, between the marquisate of Stainville and the abbey of Jovilliers, even under the family tie of the count's younger brother, the pious Leopold-Charles, who had held those neighbouring acres for something like ten years now. A memorandum of about that time found Carré pleading: 'It is not my fault if the survey of the forest encroachments (acrües) of Jovilliers has not been done. I have pressed the provost to work on it; we went there last summer; we did nothing: the weather at present does not allow one to work on this operation. M. de Lescaille has gout.':[46] so many good reasons from the clutter of everyday for not getting on with the job.

In the eighteenth century boundary disputes were one indication that a marquis or count was still apt to be a little ruler. The same

---

[44] Ibid., 6 Feb. 1753 for the following.   .   [45] Ibid., 27 Feb. 1753 for the following.
[46] Carré to Count de Stainville, undated fragment of memorandum, probably early 1753: ibid. for the following.

memorandum included a heading 'Commissioners of Police', with reference to 'the disorders which are committed in the parishes of your estates with reference to the taverns, which are always full of people on holidays and Sundays'. The locals of Stainville could evidently afford their drink, and their pleasure needed policing.

In the same survey Carré urged that he should chase up the feudal quitrents, many of which had fallen into abeyance for lack of certain knowledge of who was still liable: 'it is an operation which will cost, but it [is] in the interests of a lord not to let the least right of his estate be lost.' Once again one notices how a middle-class professional, even in the feudal context, could sharpen the often oversimplified issue between peasant and noble.

The little matter of the quitrents may have been one of those outstanding for the attention of the Count de Stainville when he revisited his patrimony towards the end of August 1753. And it looks as though he may, in part at least, have transferred it from his procurator-fiscal to his higher-powered lessee-general. On 19 October Sieur Brigeat was promising the count that 'directly I am a little quit of my vintaging'[47] he would send him 'a fully detailed return of the domains of this county.' He proceeded to discuss the possibility of an apparently advantageous commutation of quitrents due from the villagers of Lavincourt for their woodland; it was, a little grimly, a good opportunity to persuade them 'since grain is very dear this year'.

IV

The background here was an involved row, one of many, between Brigeat and Carré, rivals on the estate for the favour of their count. Carré had expostulated to Stainville that July: 'You have reproached me too bitterly on the subject of the underlessees of Sieur Brigeat for me not to explain myself in this business.'[48] Off he went, back to December when one of them, Nicolas Chevalier, had been elected syndic of Lavincourt by the villagers. This significant dualism in a petty functionary soon produced tension. Chevalier, keener on his popular role of syndic than on that of under-farmer of the seigneurial revenues, had on the Easter Day of 1753 apparently gone ahead with a distribution by lot to the villagers of entitlements to cut firewood to the detriment of seigneurial interests. The Curé of Lavincourt complained, Carré told off Chevalier and took the opportunity to dun

[47] Brigeat to Count de Stainville, Ligny, 19 Oct. 1753: ibid. for the following.
[48] Carré to Count de Stainville, Stainville, 5 July 1753: ibid. for the following.

him for an unpaid fine. Whereupon, reported Carré to his master, 'this brutal fellow uttered a thousand insults at me ..., insults which reflected upon yourself. Next day I sent three tipstaffs to constrain this man' who promptly complained to Brigeat, 'who had the kindness to write me the most impertinent letter in the world'. Carré had sent a hot reply:

I sometimes catch fire when I see somebody who is going against your interests; it is not with regard to myself. According to Sieur Brigeat, then, one must let his underlessees cut your woods, damage your estates, and furthermore tell them that they are doing right. No, I will not endure it.

The Count de Stainville was significantly inclining towards the more modern operator and renewed Brigeat's lease for the general farm of his estates. This prompted Carré to ask the count whether, in doing so:

You have had the kindness to think of me over the gardens which he enjoys, and which you promised me in my commission. It is a small matter for you and big for me, for since these gardens consist of ploughland I should sow them with corn and barley, even with hemp to help me to live. Sieur Brigeat gave ... 45 livres a year for them. I should even prefer to give this sum for them rather than be pinched as I am. In everything you are the master ... Sieur Brigeat has already deprived me of a little vineyard which you had given me. So as not to importune you, I consented to it. It would not be a bad thing for there to be a copy of this new lease here so as to know to what M. Brigeat can be held.[49]

The Count de Stainville may sometimes have wondered wearily whether it was worth trying to run his estates in double harness. But it would tend to keep both agents keen.

'Here is a new matter to cause Sieur Brigeat to exercise his pen against me', wrote Carré to his master on 5 July 1753. 'The inhabitants of Stainville have long been complaining about the miller ... and are saying that the miller is a rascal and a thief; they reiterated their complaints at the [village] assembly on last Saint John the Baptist's day.'[50] Carré, having failed to appease the issue, had then advised the villagers to petition direct to the Count de Stainville with their complaints, which he considered just, as did Curé Petitpain. Carré preferred to forgo his perquisite of having his corn ground free at the banal mill of Stainville since the miller 'had it ground so badly that one could hardly eat the bread, it was so full of stones. Sieur Brigeat has eaten it several times' but, made out Carré, still wanted to keep his man, the miller, rumoured to be paying Brigeat an annual rake-off

---

[49] Carré to Count de Stainville, undated fragment of memorandum, probably early 1753: ibid.
[50] Carré to Count de Stainville, Stainville, 5 July 1753: ibid. for the following.

beside his rent of some 550 livres. It just happened, too, that Carré knew the very man to take over the lease of the mills at the present rate. He would further pay the Count de Stainville a lump sum of a hundred *louis* for it, in effect switching any surplus profit on the side from the lessee-general to the landlord.

This concise illustration of the practical working of the lease of a banal utility demonstrated that once again, as over the commutation of the corvée, public indignation found an effective outlet in the local assembly, while the manorial officer felt a dual loyalty, downwards as well as up. A fortnight later Carré was depicting Brigeat to the Count de Stainville as threatening those who addressed remonstrances to the count, and frightening others into signing up to support the miller: 'which only tends to make your subjects revolt. Sieur Brigeat is not here to see what is going on. It is misery to hear the inhabitants. I cannot go out of the château without being overwhelmed with complaints on all sides.'[51]

Carré sent his master copies of the legal charges now being preferred against the delinquent, and begged for secrecy since 'a denunciation is a secret document, and the ordinance forbids me to show it to anybody, till after the decision of the case'. Indignant villagers were clamouring not just for sacking the wretched miller but for damages. Initially inclined to get out, he waxed 'proud and arrogant'[52] under the wing of Brigeat, and himself began to cite, presumably for defamation, signatories of the petition against him. The litigious tendency of those sturdy peasants was, once again, to stand up for their own interests almost as much as did their noble masters. One can pretty much imagine the heated discussions of a Sunday in those crowded taverns at Stainville in the summer of 1753.

At a higher level the procurator-fiscal was giving the count an exposition from the feudal viewpoint of seigneurial relationships under a general lease of estates:

It is not for Sieur Brigeat to expel the miller or put in another. That is your concern, or mine under your authority. It is an emphyteutic lease which can be broken only with your consent, and providing that the lessee-general gets the rent for which the mill was farmed at the time of his lease, he has no say in the matter. So it is you, Sir who should render justice to your inhabitants and not Sieur Brigeat. It is indeed in your interest that it be done thus.[53]

Such was the dispute which very likely awaited the Count de Stainville on his return to Lorraine that August. He may have followed Carré's advice and settled the matter himself, on the spot:

[51] Ibid., 20 July 1753, for the following.   [52] Ibid., 1 Aug. 1753.
[53] Ibid., 20 July 1753.

whence our ignorance of how it went at the last with the miller of Stainville.

Yet another duel between Carré and Brigeat, and one which appears to have dragged on after their master's visitation, concerned an appointment to the little chaplaincy of Saint Nicholas in the parish church at Stainville. Carré pled for a resident chaplain since 'the parish is too large only to have one priest. M. Petitpain has been sick unto extremity'[54] and was convalescing at Ligny. Once again the procurator-fiscal had just the man for the job, 'Abbé Lamy, priest, a nephew of Morel, the gardener of Madame the Marquise de Stainville at Demange, and a relation of mine'. But Brigeat, too, had a likely relative, and appears here also to have carried the day with the Count de Stainville, who undertook to see personally to the 'negotiation' of the chaplaincy. This, Brigeat was to write to him in the following October, made his favourite 'so sure of success that I have the honour to send you my thanks in advance. My nephew, the Abbé to whom I have begged you to give it, left yesterday for Paris'[55] to form up to the count. Here again the contemporary way of doing things locally did not differ so much from that at Versailles. Both featured retinues and patronage, both liable to be honeycombed with nepotism.

When the Count de Stainville brought his wife to Demange that August he consulted both his rival agents about the main piece of rural negotiation which he and they then had on hand. This was an attempt to buy a sizeable property, adjoining the marquisate at Montplonne, from a certain Madame de Boncourt. She had begun by asking 45 thousand livres of Lorraine, then 40, 36, 30 thousand as they beat her down towards the 25,000 that the count was willing to pay. His figure represented some twenty-seven and a half years' purchase. For those interested, as Stephen de Stainville was, in local property-values at that time the Boncourt estate comprised plough-land, meadows, and hempfields lumped together by Carré as being worth 12,000 livres, forty-four acres of woodland put at 8,000, plus 4,000 for her large house with gardens and paddock, 1,500 for vineyards, and 500 for some waste land, in all 26,000 livres of Lorraine, less than 20,000 French. The total yield per annum on this property was put at 900 livres, 500 of it from the cultivable fields. The woodland was reckoned to produce 150 a year on the basis of cutting a yearly average of two acres plus some oaks so that the whole would be felled by rotation in roughly twenty years. The remaining 250 livres would come from the house and that vineyard which, explained

---

[54] Ibid., 5 July 1753, for the following.
[55] Brigeat to Count de Stainville, Ligny, 19 Oct. 1753: ibid.

Carré, often produced only enough to cover the cost of labour on it; but since it was the only vineyard in Montplonne it had scarcity value and could be sold off to advantage. He recommended the same for the outlying houses on the estate, which were in very bad repair. Whereas two good farming families could be doubled up in Madame de Boncourt's own dwelling.

The lady contended that the Count de Stainville's offer of 25 thousand had surely been in French currency – another instance of local play with the exchanges. Carré had to disabuse her and, not letting her suppose that his master was particularly keen on buying, had by the beginning of August got her down to 28 thousand livres of Lorraine, with a hope that she would take twenty-six. But Brigeat, who would quite have liked the property himself, also took a hand. He told the Count de Stainville, when the latter looked in on Demange and Ligny at the end of that month, that he had got Madame de Boncourt to accept the offer of twenty-five. Stainville said he would not go higher and stipulated conditions favourable to himself regarding arrangements for payment. The lady thereafter reneged in favour of twenty-six, making out that a merchant from Vitry was keenly interested. It was not till the end of October that Brigeat tied her down to twenty-five, though with somewhat improved modalities. Evidently the Count de Stainville's partici-pation in the Crozat fortune had not rendered him any less keen when it came to rounding out his own little estate.

Evidently, too, relations between the rival agents were kept up civilly enough. Earlier that year Carré had been writing to his master on behalf of another nephew of Brigeat. This trooper then on leave from the cavalry regiment of Penthièvre wanted an extension, did not dare broach it to his uncle but understood that the Count de Stainville, as a general officer of the rank of Maréchal de Camp, had the power to prolong his leave. More considerable military concerns, however, now awaited the count as he journeyed on northwestwards from Demange-aux-Eaux to join his training-camp at Aimeries near Maubeuge on the Sambre upon the confines of Hainault and the Austrian Netherlands. It began under the Prince de Soubise on 1 September 1753.

V

If the Stainville estates represented something less than a rural idyll even for their aristocratic master, the camp at Aimeries was not just a free-and-easy outing. The grudging French treasury was at least going to get its money's worth. Soubise was to see 'that the officers do not go hunting for the whole duration of the camp'.[56] Gambling there was also prohibited. With Stainville's friend, Séchelles, as the intendant, administrative precision prescribed in advance water-transport for any sick to hospitalisation at Maubeuge, tobacco-rations to troops as per the ordinance of 1 October 1743, and so on and so forth.

The troops in camp at Aimeries comprised thirteen squadrons of cavalry and as many battalions of infantry, the latter from the regiments of Auvergne, Poitou, Provence, Royal Écossais, Ogilvy, suggesting a significantly Jacobite proportion. In this command the Prince de Soubise was supported by two other lieutenant-generals, the Marquis du Mesnil and the Duke de Broglie, son and heir to the late marshal and elder brother of the diplomatic count. Under them served only one officer of the rank of Maréchal de Camp, the vigorous Count de Stainville. This might suggest that he was in for a busy time. He wrote from camp that September: 'Since we have been here, we have been spending our days on horseback and in exercising our troops. A camp in peacetime is more tiring by far than a camp in war, indeed I do not believe that we should be equal to it if it were to last longer'[57] than the prescribed month.

The coda of Aimeries to the active military career of the Count de Stainville stood out as an occasion when he, much less of a horseman than his father, was to be found regularly in the saddle and, as a general officer, in command of cavalry as well as infantry: as in an exercise there wherein Stainville directed an attack, with infantry in the centre and cavalry on either flank, against a village called Laval. The attack was down to begin along the outlying hedges when a defensive fusillade would compel Stainville to group his units in battle-order under fire: 'As soon as the corps has been formed, M. de Stainville will reinforce the attack on the hedges of Laval whence at a shot from a cannon, the Duke de Broglie will send out, through the main street of the village, some pickets which will take in the flank those attacking the hedges, will throw them into disorder and will push them back to the sunken road.'[58] That, in turn, should suck in the attacking horse and 'when the cavalry of M. de Stainville shall be but thirty paces from the others it will make a half-turn to right by half-troops.'

The Count de Stainville as a veteran, in particular, from that attack

[56] Instructions of 6 Aug. 1753 to Prince de Soubise: Arch. Guerre, Mémoires historiques No. 1815 (carton no.2/8): Camp d'Aymeries sur la Sambre, 1753. Mr. Le. Pr. de Soubise.
[57] Count de Stainville to Baron von Bernstorff, camp at Aimeries, 17 Sept. 1753: *Bernstorffske Papirer*, ii. 653.
[58] Order of September 1753, camp at Aimeries: Arch. Guerre, Mémoires historiques No. 1815, *u.s.* for the following.

on the village of Rocoux back in forty-six could presumably be relied on to handle that kind of exercise. In it he found himself pitted against the head of his unfavourite family in the person of the second Duke de Broglie. Their opposition in the field appears to have escaped previous attention. One wonders how far, in those exercises at Aimeries, Stainville may have got the military measure of the future Marshal de Broglie the younger, whether it was at all to inform Choiseul's opposition to him after his luckless day at Vellinghausen eight years hence.

Stainville for his part appears as usual to have earned the approbation of his general, of whom he wrote to Bernstorff: 'M. de Soubise is very popular with his army; he is behaving marvellously in it; as for me, I have every grounds for being well pleased with the attentions which he shows me. We have just been celebrating the birth of the Duke of Aquitaine; our general has given a magnificent fête to his whole army.'[59] They did have some fun in camp.

On 8 September 1753 the second Dauphine had produced her second son, Xavier-Marie-Joseph, short-lived Duke of Aquitaine. That month court gossip had it, truly or not, that his father, in the convenient absence of strait-laced Vauguyon and in the aftermath of the Countess de Choiseul-Romanet, was turning for a mistress to the young wife of one of his gentlemen, du Châtelet. It was almost as though from precedent in the Dauphin's suite that the Count de Stainville's old Regiment of Navarre now changed hands for the third time since his colonelcy. Du Châtelet ousted Choiseul-Beaupré, who received nothing in consolation. It was noted, though, that the Choiseul family was hoping 'to receive some favour from the king'.[60]

The greatest favour was soon to accrue to the rival branch of Stainville. The little count, whose fine old regiment had become the shuttlecock of courtiers, was of his own choice sweating it out in military application. If connection with Soubise might suggest higher things in store, yet that gruelling camp, while setting a seal upon Stainville as a soldier, scarcely did much to command attention. Stainville summed it up in his letter to Bernstorff from Aimeries: 'I am not telling you any news. An army without enemies has nothing of interest to report.'[61]

VI

Back from camp, Stainville picked up his wife at Demange on their way to Paris, their destination for the early October of 1753. Briefly

---

[59] Count de Stainville to Baron von Bernstorff, camp at Aimeries, 17 Sept. 1753: *u.s.*
[60] Luynes, xiii. 67.
[61] Count de Stainville to Baron von Bernstorff, camp at Aimeries, 17 Sept. 1753: *u.s.*

on his estates again, the local issues came crowding in. That negotiation with Madame de Boncourt at Montplonne was still hanging fire. Then there was a little matter of a couple of petitions from locals asking to be let off fines or debts. At Demange, probably under the influence of Carré, the count had rejected the petitions, only to grant them after all while passing through Ligny, probably under the countervailing influence of Brigeat. Carré of course could not approve 'but', he wrote to the count, 'you are the judge, and the master able to do what you want. Do it. I am happy about it. It will be one trouble the less for me, not to have to extract payment':[62] especially at the onset of a winter of stringency and dearth.

Brigeat's observation as to the price of corn had national application. By the close of the year the Marquis d'Argenson was noting: 'Nobody is having new clothes made this winter; nobody is leaving the countryside to come to Paris... The distress is terrific. One sees nothing but beggars. Provisions have doubled in price, especially vegetables.'[63] One person, however, who did come up from the country that winter was the procurator-fiscal of the summoning Count de Stainville. Carré arranged to travel to Paris 'by the Joinville coach'[64] early in the new year of 1754.

On 26 January Carré rendered to his master his estate-account for the preceding year. These accounts, in the slimmed, modernized form, underlined the count's personal concern for his dependent poor in those hard times. Following through from his eleemosynary annotation of the preceding account, the wages and other standing charges of the estate were this time lumped in with 'the alms according to the lists drawn up by His Excellency on the third and fifth of February 1753'.[65] The whole item was now up to 1,522 livres of Lorraine exclusive of the 150 livres still for Madame Flouart's pension.

A less agreeable outgoing had been 187 livres, 10 sous, this time, for the Vingtième 'according to the receipt of the collectors of Stainville'. These items of expenditure together with Carré's own wages, were the main ones for 1753, apart from the heavy debit of 3,217 livres, 16 sous, in respect of the sum of 2,491 livres, 4 sous in the currency of France sent to the Count de Stainville 'in two letters of change drawn on Sieur Mathieu, merchant, and at need on Sieur Ramé, banker at Paris'.

[62] Carré to Count de Stainville, Stainville, 9 Oct. 1753: Arch. Meuse, J 18[11], docket II ('Stainville. Bail seigneurial. 1660–an VII').
[63] D'Argenson, viii. 169.
[64] Carré to Count de Stainville, Stainville, 18 Dec. 1753: u.s.
[65] Carré's account for the Stainville estate for the year 1753: Arch. Meuse, J 18[19] for the following.

The estate might perhaps feel that it could stand such sizeable remittances since the main sale of timber in the account, to Jean Labreche in partnership with François Legros, had jumped up to 4,597 livres plus 574 in *franc-vins,* no longer the perquisite of Carré. At over 5,000 livres of Lorraine in all this was getting on for double the corresponding yield of 1752. Though as usual there were snags. Brigeat had written to the Count de Stainville on 26 November 1753: 'I am just back from Stainville where I learnt that the assignee of your timber last year is still indebted to you. Since he is solvent and has made a lot from this sale I advise you to make him pay up without paying any attention to the respites which Sieur Carré may have granted him.'[66] The two agents rarely seemed to agree about methods. Carré just then was having a brush about brushwood with one of Brigeat's subcontractors who wanted to slice into new forest instead of cleaning up an exploited one, less immediately attractive, in accordance with Carré's plan for methodical cutting 'so as not to sink all of a sudden from something down to nothing'.[67]

Behindhand with payments though the concessionaries of the Stainville timber might be, Carré at last eliminated from his accounts for 1753 those reprises which so displeased his master. The rasping annotations with which the count had peppered the reckoning for 1752 were now happily absent. This time his repeated marginalia of *'Alloué'* gave Carré a clear run in just about balancing the account for 1753 at some thousand livres more than last year, with a total expenditure of 5,764 livres as against receipts of 5,753 livres, 19 sous, 4 deniers so that ten livres odd were owing to Carré. The Count de Stainville subscribed to this in Paris on 8 February 1754.

The count, however, had been having his usual stint of worry about Bazincourt, the regular troublespot of the estate. This time it was an administrative difference with the local officials of the bailiwick of Bar. 'It is odd how there are all these vexations' commented Carré in suggesting that Stainville might like to write to La Galaizière about them. Carré, though, was kept busy with questions not only of local administration but also of popular representation. 'For a week', he wrote a month later, 'we have been working on the general assemblies of the communities of your estate, for the election of the syndics, assayers, keepers and others.'[68] Evidently, as one would expect, the seigneurial administration took a considerable hand in all this. Yet at the local level there were assemblies, there were elections, there was, in however rudimentary

[66] Brigeat to Count de Stainville, Ligny, 26 Nov. 1753: Arch. Meuse, J 18¹¹, docket II.
[67] Carré to Count de Stainville, Stainville, 19 Nov. 1753: ibid for the following.
[68] Ibid., 18 Dec. 1753, for the following.

a form, a kind of popular democracy at the base of the autocratic government of the old regime.

The same letter from Carré yet reminded the Count de Stainville that by no means all local appointments were elective. The multifarious procurator-fiscal was writing on 18 December 1753:

It is some days since the girls' school at Stainville fell vacant. The sister from Demange had been proposed to the Curé to fill this post. He wants none of this because he regards her as a spy of the bishop; but if he does his duty, as I expect him to, he has nothing to fear. This girl, who is in the favour of Madame the Marquise de Stainville, is well deserving of this position. She comes from Stainville. It is only obstinacy on the part of the Curé. You would do great good in the parish if you were willing to exercise your authority in this matter.

Such was the interpenetration of ecclesiastical and lay authority in local education, for girls by nuns of course. Another item of hot news in the same epistle to the Count de Stainville rated two marginal crosses for special attention:

On the night of the 11th to the 12th of this month the wind and the rain cast down a large part of one of the houses of the farmers of Monplonne. The poor wretch who occupied this part was nearly crushed together with his family and cattle. His grain was covered with stones, earth and tiles, and completely wetted. He was forced to transport it to another house in the village. This man is complaining greatly and not without reason since he is reduced to a pitiable condition. You will find enclosed an estimate of what is needed to repair this building. There is virtually not a year in which repairs are not done in these houses, but it does not make them more solid. Their situation has much to do with it, because, being at the foot of a hill, the water which runs off it rots the foundations of the walls, which are gradually sinking. You will have the goodness to give your orders to Sieur Brigeat to do what is necessary in this respect.

It seems to have been uphill work keeping things up at Montplonne, whether it was that tile-kiln or the property just bought from Madame de Boncourt. Brigeat complained that her 'house and garden-walls are in pretty poor condition and are threatening to crumble'.[69] So he could not get more than 500 livres a year when on 22 April 1754 he let the dilapidated dwelling with the main parcel of its land, but not the woods or the vines, for a term of three years.

Brigeat was careful to be prompt with his own payments to the Count de Stainville. By comparison with the 2,491 livres French remitted by Carré towards the end of 1753, Brigeat had on 19 October already sent the count a bill of exchange drawn on a banker in the Rue Truanderie at Paris in the sum of 3,200.

Brigeat's nephew had meanwhile been making himself useful, if

[69] Brigeat to Count de Stainville, Stainville, 23 Jan. 1754: ibid.

not popular with Carré, by inventorying the archives of the Count de Stainville, who liked papers properly kept. (Gresset's Méchant had docketed his love-letters.) One wonders whether this was the same nephew who had been after that chaplaincy at Stainville, whether in that case he may not have got it after all, whether his precipitate advance on Paris to further his cause might have contributed to his having somehow incurred the count's displeasure despite Brigeat's vehement assurances that the youth's conduct had been 'entirely innocent (*toutes affait inosente*)'.[70] This upset may have coincided with some swing in the count's favour towards Carré.

In his accounts for 1753 Carré had not failed to settle up his own emoluments as procurator-fiscal and receiver to the end of that year, at a figure of 295 livres: 225 for the last three quarters since 1 April of his salary of 300 livres per annum, plus 70 livres as a modest indemnity for those *francs-vins* which the Count de Stainville had disallowed him. Now, however, there was to be a step up in Carré's fortunes, calling for a new procurator-fiscal. Carré wrote to the count that he was 'very puzzled to find you a procurator-fiscal here'[71] at Stainville where there seemed to be nobody suitable. 'When I am at Paris', he continued, 'we will see what can be done in this matter.' Doubtless they did put their heads together and if it is not clear that they found anybody that may possibly chime with their apparent search at the same time for a new demesne provost for Stainville: and that perhaps not only from the recent death of the previous one, Lescaille, but as part of the reorganization of the estate necessitated by the higher calls now being made upon it and upon its master.

By the beginning of 1754 Carré's arrival in Paris on the way to higher things was related to recent advancement in the fortunes of the Count de Stainville. Those as sensitive to forms as were the men of the old regime will already have noticed that he now figured in Carré's accounts as His Excellency.

[70] Brigeat to Count de Stainville, Ligny, 17 Feb. 1754: ibid.
[71] Carré to Count de Stainville, Stainville, 18 Dec. 1753: ibid. for the following.

CHAPTER IX

EMBASSIES

I

THE career of the Count de Stainville could profit if anything from the fact that his father, as agreed upon his return from Vienna, had been presented anew at Versailles, in the political polymorphism of that age, in his private capacity 'as a Frenchman, and was very well received'[1] by Louis XV and the royal family. That had been on 30 December 1751, when the Marquis de Stainville had stayed on for the second instalment of the festival of fireworks there that month. For him at least 'this spectacle was magnificent'.[2]

The career, even, of the marquis himself was liable to benefit from the new arrangement. If he lost the privilege of diplomatic status, he was exempted from its restrictions, notably as to access to court. This was, he told the Emperor Francis I, underlined to him that day by the Marquise de Pompadour 'who strongly approved of my being here upon the footing that I have adopted. She promised me to arrange for me to have conversations with the king when that should be necessary for the interests of Your Imperial Majesty.'

Holding in reserve this talisman of direct access, the Marquis de Stainville wrote direct to Maria Theresa, as she had graciously ordered him after all, that he had first 'wanted to see for myself if the change in the ministry during my absence had affected the system which the court had been proposing to follow before my departure. To that end I wanted to have a private and confidential conversation with the Marquis de Puysieulx, whose probity has long been known to me.'[3] Stainville assured him how much the empress regretted his recent retirement. Stainville's friends were indeed fading into retirement, or death. Prince Charles d'Armagnac had died just recently at sixty-seven, maintaining his sporting interests nearly to the end, though unable to walk.

Influential people out of office can, however, provide good channels.

[1] Count de Stainville to Baron von Bernstorff, Paris, 6 Jan. 1752: *Bernstorffske Papirer*, ii. 638.
[2] Marquis de Stainville to Emperor Francis I, Paris, 2 Jan. 1752: Esteri del Granducato di Toscana, vol. 2296/1287, no. 75 for the following.
[3] Marquis de Stainville to Empress Maria Theresa, Paris, 16 Jan. 1752: Ö.S./H.H.S., Frankreich/Berichte (1752), 134 for the following.

The Marquis de Stainville told the Marquis de Puysieulx that January that it would not be difficult to convince Maria Theresa of the good intentions of Louis XV 'provided that facts corresponded to words'. This had not hitherto been so since France had always 'shewn suspicion; in the Russian disputes with Sweden they had at first thought that my court was fomenting them, whereas they subsequently perceived the contrary; as to the election of the King of the Romans, they had not been willing to believe Your Imperial Majesty when you said that you had no part therein nor even knowledge of the first démarches which had been made in this respect, and that you had informed the [French] king of it the moment that word of it had reached you; at present they saw clearly that you had spoken nothing but the truth, and that alone should suffice to establish this [Franco-Austrian] confidence, so desired and so desirable.'

Such was Stainville's criticism of Puysieulx to his face for having failed to respond to the overtures of Kaunitz. And Puysieulx, according to Stainville, actually agreed with all this and advised him to repeat it to Saint-Contest. When Stainville doubted whether he could be equally frank with a stranger, Puysieulx 'also advised me to see the Marshal de Noailles who has much influence in foreign affairs and who entirely directs M. de St. Contest. I have done so.'

Stainville continued on Noailles:

This marshal has long professed an inviolable attachment for the person of His Majesty the Emperor ... He was first in talking to me about the desire which the king had to see established between the two courts a confidence which constitutes the security and the happiness of Europe. I informed him of the disposition of Your Imperial Majesty. He appeared extremely pleased and told me that in the greatest secrecy he would find means for me to speak with the king upon this matter, and that he knew the pleasure which that would give him [Louis]. That is how I stand. I shall not hurry the conversation with the king, for I should be very glad to receive beforehand the orders of Your Imperial Majesty.

It would appear that the Marquis de Stainville was once again to be left standing. It now appears, however, that in the difficult field of Franco-Austrian reconciliation Count Kaunitz had too close a harbinger in the Marquis de Stainville, for ever probing in high places in characteristic secrecy, for the famous statesman to have much friendly feeling for the suppressed diplomatist or, perhaps, for his son.

Also remarkable is the disclosure of the secret influence on high, still, of Noailles. The convolutions and shifts, both in tactics and in personnel, in French foreign policy towards the middle of the eighteenth century may hitherto have obscured the broad circumstance that in the decade after the death of Cardinal Fleury, who had presided over foreign affairs from an elevation greater than that of foreign minister, he was to some extent succeeded in that capacity by the Marshal de Noailles. Louis XV had almost summoned him to that high sphere in their intimate correspondence in the first aftermath of Fleury. And the marshal's influence, sometimes outwardly overlaid precisely because of that intimacy, appears, in part at least, to have lasted on longer than has always been brought out.

True, there were quite a few others who manipulated or competed with foreign ministers, personalities such as the Count de Maurepas, the fading Cardinal de Tencin, the Prince de Conti, the brothers Pâris, and even Madame de Pompadour. It seems likely, though, that none of these, not even the last, stood politically so close to the king as the Marshal de Noailles, the great aristocrat from the great reign of yore, the king's mentor and old friend, father of the king's playfellow and intimate, the Duke d'Ayen. By March 1752 a hostile witness was writing: 'They say that the credit of the Noailles is increasing every day; added to that is the old friendship of the king for the Countess de Toulouse ... sister of the marshal.'[4]

Noailles and other high-level manipulators at court enjoyed elbowroom because none of the French foreign ministers in the aftermath of Fleury was politically outstanding. The most considerable though not the most successful of them, the Marquis d'Argenson, had found himself in some opposition to the Marshal de Noailles and, significantly, soon relegated. If Puysieulx had been rather more successful, more than generally allowed, the other foreign ministers before the later Choiseul were timid little men, Amelot, Saint-Contest, soon now Rouillé, dim even to their contemporaries. A broader perspective for French foreign policy during the reign of Louis XV after the regency might proportion Choiseul's policy rather as the third term in a progression: Fleury, Noailles, Choiseul.

Qualifications promptly suggest themselves. Noailles was not so prominent in power or preponderant in policy as the other two. There were, however, special reasons for that, both personal – in France the greatest nobility like Noailles did not usually stoop to governmental chores – and also political. The middle period of Noailles's ascendancy was one of uneasy transition and experiment. Earlier under the Regent and Fleury traditional hostility against England had been temporarily mitigated. That, though, had proved a false start into the age of imperial rivalry; so too, largely, had the new swing to Prussia begun under Fleury by Belle-Isle, who backed

⁴ D'Argenson, vii. 131–2.

d'Argenson against France's other hereditary enemy, Austria. D'Argenson, too, had clashed with Noailles most conspicuously over the latter's support of the Bourbon family compact of France and Spain against England. Not England but Austria was the hereditary foe to whom France would soon be turning in accordance with the steady inclination of the Marshal de Noailles, as indeed of the Marquise de Pompadour. In perspective the forthcoming diplomatic revolution in this reversal of alliances might, from the French side certainly, seem close to an evolution from the submerged inclination of Noailles towards the notorious policy of Choiseul, his protégé and the Pompadour's, in appeasement of relations with the great catholic powers of Spain and Austria.

The rather neglected links between Noailles and Choiseul were personal as well as political. Back in 1743 the marshal had clinched the then Count de Stainville for the French, instead of Austrian, military service. Ten years later, quite soon now, Noailles was once more to play a critical part in promoting the fortunes of the future Duke de Choiseul, this time in diplomacy.

II

While the Marquis de Stainville was active yet again upon the fringe of the high diplomacy of Europe, his thankless chore of that Lorraine liquidation had been transferred to Count Kaunitz. He was writing wryly to Francis I at the beginning of 1752: 'Your Majesty having the goodness to charge me henceforth with this affair, it would be fortunate and very agreeable for me that it were in a less grievous position.'[5] Three days later Stainville was assuring the emperor that 'after the pains that I have taken to extract this business from the chaos that it was in, I am nowise jealous that another should have the honour of finishing it'.[6] Whereas Kaunitz later sourly reminded the influential Koch that when he took over the dreary business 'it was at that moment nearly fifteen years old, consequently of an age that does not improve an affair and for that matter it had been very badly conducted since the peace, as, I think, neither H.M. the Emperor nor his ministers are unaware'.[7]

Kaunitz grumbled that he had to try to retrieve the tactical

[5] Count Kaunitz to Emperor Francis I, Paris, 20 Jan. 1752: Ö.S./H.H.S., Frankreich/Berichte (1752), 134.
[6] Marquis de Stainville to Emperor Francis I, Paris, 23 Jan. 1752: Esteri del Granducato di Toscana, vol. 2296/1287, no. 78.
[7] Count Kaunitz to Baron von Koch, Paris, 11 Nov. 1752: Kaunitz/Koch, p. 305.

disadvantage due to Stainville's having confided to the French government that decision in the matter so unsatisfactorily presented to him in the draft of the previous July. By February 1752 Kaunitz was conferring about this 'ulcerated' business with Stainville and Sieur Richard, an expert in the affairs of Lorraine, but derived 'little enlightenment'.[8] The Austrian disagreed with Stainville about the method of liquidating the French national debt to Lorraine, and ingratiatingly suggested to Francis that it was in his interest 'that the operation to be executed on your personal debts should precede that in relation to national debts'.[9] Kaunitz, however, did subsequently forward to the emperor a pathetic petition from an impoverished 'widow de Feuquières',[10] the kind of person who really suffered from French reluctance to repay.

On 30 April 1752 Kaunitz remitted to Saint-Contest a new memorandum tracing the business right through from 1733 and invoking the authority of the Declaration of 1736. By June the ambassador was writing to the emperor of the Lorraine liquidation:

I am in despair at the slowness with which business, and above all business of substance, is conducted in this part of the world ... The king's continual journeys are the reason why all the ministers are dispersed, making journeys of their own to different estates and so becoming unfindable. The most vexatious absence of all is that of the Marshal de Noailles who is fundamentally the only person at present to have some influence, together with the Keeper of the Seals and Controller-General [Machault], who is of all men the hardest when it is a question of giving away money. I am basing all my hopes upon the residence [of the court] at Compiègne, where the greater part of the ministers are collected and where they will not be able to escape me ... I am sensible that Your Majesty must be impatient ... and that you might even think that it was partly my fault.'[11]

It might almost have been the Marquis de Stainville writing.

Kaunitz did get going at Compiègne with 'Saint Contest, but he is a man with whom everything languishes and nothing happens. I, like all the other ambassadors and foreign envoys, have grounds for complaint over his slowness and irresolution. Matters which are a little complicated frighten him, and his small influence does not allow him to take the least risk. All the other ministers, from the example of the monarch, are always betwixt and between, hardly ever in Paris and very rarely to be found even at Versailles on Tuesdays',[12] even for the favoured Kaunitz. When he did manage to nobble Machault he found that he had only a superficial acquaintance

[8] Count Kaunitz to Emperor Francis I, Paris, 28 Feb. 1752: Ö.S./H.H.S., Frankreich/Berichte (1752), 134.
[9] Ibid., 13 Apr. 1752.   [10] Ibid., 23 Nov. 1752.   [11] Ibid., 5 June 1752.
[12] Ibid., 26 June 1752.

with the dreary business. 'For one thing the multiplicity of affairs', sighed Kaunitz, 'does not allow the [French] ministers, what with the time that they need for acting as courtiers, to have enough to inform themselves of their business.'[13]

Not that Machault was at all frivolous when it came to cash, as Kaunitz recognized. He warned the emperor that he could not hope 'to obtain anything like the sum of four and a half millions, or even that of four million'.[14] The French, he came to complain, 'are employing against us a thousand wretched chicaneries'.[15] It was just six months after he had presented his memorandum on the Lorraine liquidation that, on 30 and 31 October 1752, Kaunitz and Richard had two working sessions with Trudaine, 'unquestionably one of the ablest people in this country',[16] and a French expert called Courchetet. 'These two meetings', commented Kaunitz, 'had the usual fate of this way of working in business. Both sides pled their case very well, and on parting each remained of his own opinion.'[17] Kaunitz was by now moving towards higher things than 'this odious affair'. But if it remained unsettled when he left Paris to take office at Vienna, 'I should be afraid', he wrote, 'even for the little which was granted by the [French] memorandum handed to M. de Stainville last year.' Perhaps Stainville had not done quite so badly after all.

Kaunitz now lost little time in lifting the whole business on to a higher and less formal plane with Noailles, then enjoying 'one cannot say a decided credit but at least more credit than anyone else. I found means', continued Kaunitz, 'of interesting him and, in concert with him, Messrs. de Puysieulx and St. Séverin. In a word, I created for myself a party in the [royal] council',[18] precisely as Stainville had done long since. His successor proceeded:

I know that the marshal busied himself warmly with the Keeper of the Seals and M. de Trudaine...But unhappily he [Noailles] cannot by a long stretch achieve everything that he would wish, above all when it is a question of money, the disorder in the finances being at present at such a pitch that I know beyond doubt that the Keeper of the Seals does not know where to turn, so to speak, from one day to the next.

Noailles thus secured acceleration rather than accommodation. On 7 November 1752 he remitted to Kaunitz a reply to his memorandum.

[13] Ibid., 19 July 1752.   [14] Ibid., 8 Aug. 1752.
[15] Count Kaunitz to Emperor Francis I, Fontainebleau, 20 Oct. 1752: ibid.
[16] Count Kaunitz to Baron von Koch, Paris, 11 Nov. 1752: Kaunitz/Koch, p. 305.
[17] Count Kaunitz to Emperor Francis I, Paris, 11 Nov. 1752: Ö.S./H.H.S., Frankreich/Berichte (1752), 134 for the following.
[18] Count Kaunitz to Baron von Koch, Paris, 11 Nov. 1752: Kaunitz/Koch, p. 306 for the following.

The French resorted to the usual kind of let-outs, lack of adequate receipts and disputed priorities of reimbursement against an ominous background wherein the French government had in general settled its debts to German princes for military supplies at a level of roughly an eighth of what it owed: so might the costs of war be shuffled off on to disunited Germany.

Kaunitz lamented that this negotiation, the most tiresome that he had ever been saddled with, should be coming to the crunch 'exactly, so to speak, at the moment of my departure'.[19] Maria Theresa wanted him back to replace Ulfeld as chancellor. One gathers that she was not overmuch interested in the haggling of her husband, who indeed kept the particulars from her. Cutting out stubborn Machault, Kaunitz at last agreed with Saint-Contest that King Louis XV should pay the Emperor Francis 2,800,000 livres in full liquidation and upon terms largely agreed and embodied in a draft settlement communicated by Kaunitz shortly before he left for Vienna on the New Year's Day of 1753.

The inevitable French counterdraft, however, caught up with Kaunitz at Brussels. His shrewd successor as ambassador, Count George Starhemberg, brought to Paris the emperor's further redraft; but in September 1754 young Starhemburg was still complaining to the French government that he received 'only dilatory replies'.[20] The interminable dickering of Kaunitz and Starhemberg with the French over the Lorraine liquidation provides, negatively, appreciable vindication of the persistent diplomacy of the Marquis de Stainville. So too in a wider field did the failure of Kaunitz to make significant headway towards rapprochement with France.

III

While Count Kaunitz was drudging at the Marquis de Stainville's diplomatic leftover from Lorraine the latter in his semiretirement was, wrote his son at the beginning of July 1752, 'going to make a pleasure-trip to Brussels – I could well wish that the Fleece would arrive for him during his stay with Prince Charles [of Lorraine]. If the Queen of Hungary is brought to bed that might well be; at all events he has been promised that he shall have it at the first promotion. You know that the [French] king and queen are going to be the godparents of this child of the Queen of Hungary.'[21]

---

[19] Ibid., 17 Dec. 1752, p. 313.
[20] Count Starhemberg, memorandum to the French government, 3 Sept. 1754: Ö.S./H.H.S., Frankreich/Berichte (1754), 145, docket 4, fo. 8.
[21] Count de Stainville to Baron von Bernstorff, Paris, 2 July 1752: *Bernstorffske Papirer*, ii. 645.

The child was yet unborn a month later when Count Kaunitz put a somewhat different interpretation upon that jaunt of the Marquis de Stainville, 'from what he says, in order to pay his court to H.R.H. [Prince Charles], but I am tempted to think that he would like to succeed the Marquis Botta and that that is the object of his journey'.[22] If hunting with Prince Charles upon the Prince de Ligne's estates at Baudour was not the only objective, the elder Stainville was once again to be disappointed. He was no more to achieve proconsular office in succession to Botta in the Netherlands than he was in succession to Craon in Tuscany. Nor was Stainville to receive the Golden Fleece when Maria Theresa did on the thirteenth of August 1752 produce her thirteenth child and, third time lucky, an Archduchess Caroline who was actually to survive (two elder sisters of that name had died) to become queen of Bourbon Naples.

At the christening Louis XV was represented by his ambassador, Hautefort, and Marie Leszczynska by the Princess Charlotte of Lorraine, now a long-faced old maid of nearly forty, feeling increasingly out of things at the Austrian court where her precedence was diminished with depressing regularity by the ever-growing swarm of Maria Theresa's children, by this latest one in her arms. The ceremony symbolized Franco-Austrian rapprochement through both the old and the new dynasties of Lorraine.

That September, Stanislas Leszczynski on one of his regular visits to Versailles recalled to the Marquis de Stainville their conversation of the previous autumn at Lunéville: since when, Stanislas told the reporting diplomatist, 'he had not ceased to think about what could most effectively contribute to the views, full of equity, of Their Imperial Majesties and to the intention, which he knew to be that of his son-in-law, of maintaining the tranquillity of Europe. The surest means according to him was to establish perfect confidence between the two courts, and upon this he had composed a little pamphlet entitled *Lettre d'un Suisse à son ami* which he would send me so soon as he got back.'[23] It reached the Marquis de Stainville at Brussels.

King Stanislas I had grounds enough for resentment against the Austrian court, which had successfully opposed his restoration in Poland and unsuccessfully threatened his refuge in Lorraine. This self-styled Philosophe Bienfaisant, impressionable and eudemonic, had however been won round by the likes of the Marquis de Stainville in Lorraine, the one gallic territory where rapprochement

[22] Count Kaunitz to Baron von Koch, Paris, 7 Aug. 1752: Kaunitz/Koch, p. 250.

[23] Marquis de Stainville to Emperor Francis I, Paris, 26 Nov. 1752: Esteri del Granducato di Toscana, vol. 2296/1287, no. 103. This dating affords a corrective to that of 1743 given for this work by Louis Lacroix, *Les Opuscules inédits de Stanislas* (Nancy, 1866), p. 25.

with Austria was traditionally popular. In his *Lettre d'un Suisse à son ami* this inveterate pamphleteer now observed that for three centuries 'the fount which has flooded Europe with a torrent of almost continual wars . . . is the rivalry of the two predominant houses of Bourbon and of Austria.'[24] This torrent should be stanched by an alliance leading through, in the wishful thinking of the philosopher-king, to a system of perpetual peace: the steady policy of Lorraine, already pursued by Duke Leopold in connection with the Quadruple Alliance.

Stanislas gave this foreign policy a distinctive inflection in arguing that the two great antagonists, forming rival coalitions and weakening themselves in conflict, were running the risks of Athens and Sparta in the Peloponnesian War before their subjection by the common enemy from the Macedonian north. Now, he indicated, the common enemy of Europe was Russia. Stanislas was the only sovereign in Western Europe with close, only too close, experience of what he termed 'the imperious yoke of Muscovy'.[25] He seemingly came to look, more even than to the traditional cordon of eastern adherents of his French patron, to a Franco-Austrian reconciliation in the interest of uniting Europe so that 'Muscovy be reduced to her original obscurity (*son premier néant*)'. If it was to be only after two centuries more and four partitions of his Polish homeland that Western Europe was at last to ally herself effectively, against a broader background of nations uniting for peace, yet Russian intervention had significantly influenced the recent conclusion of the War of the Austrian Succession and was to influence yet more dramatically the conclusion of the Seven Years War, to the detriment of the Franco-Austrian alliance. And the first of those four partitions lay but twenty years ahead of Stanislas's warning.

The Switzer's letter to his friend exemplified the secular aspiration towards peace in such middle-lands as Switzerland and Lorraine deriving from the ancient kingdom of Lothair. If the letter was almost too interesting to be published, the Marquis de Stainville in Brussels now showed it to Prince Charles of Lorraine and forwarded it to the emperor, explaining that Stanislas had written to him 'that he had had it communicated to the king, his son-in-law, and that he implored me to seek every means of working for such a salutary end'.[26] So, already, sovereigns upon either hand were authoritatively apprised of this programmatic production featuring an overlaid Russian factor, unlikely to be acceptable in Vienna, in the approach to a diplomatic revolution in Europe.

[24] King Stanislas I, 'Lettre d'un Suysse à son ami', cited, L. Lacroix, loc. cit.
[25] King Stanislas I, cited, ibid., p. 22, and for the following.
[26] Marquis de Stainville to Emperor Francis I, Paris, 26 Nov. 1752: *u.s.*

IV

The diplomatic interests of the Count de Stainville that year had opened with the marriage of the Baron von Bernstorff. Just after Christmas 1751 Bernstorff had contracted his chilly union of convenience with eighteen-year-old Charitas Emilie von Buchwald from rich gentry in Schleswig-Holstein. He described her as not very pretty but not unpleasant. They were married very quietly at Fiurendal in Seeland. Congratulations poured in from all over Europe. The Count de Stainville avoided false sentiment:

So your marriage is done. I renew my compliments to you. I was afraid that the death of the queen [of Denmark on 19 December] might delay this matter, and I know how disagreeable it is when a marriage which has been arranged drags on. You will be busy marrying your master [again]. I would very much wish that for this ceremony religion may not be an insurmountable obstacle. You would have some good choices to make among our princesses, but the only thing that I fear for you is lest you choose a sister of the King of Prussia. When I say that I fear it, you well know that I believe that you will act for the best, but the Queen of Sweden and her example seem to me to be matters of fear for ministers, especially those for foreign affairs. I am very bold to acquaint you with my visions; you will forgive them, knowing that the motive is in my heart; you and your glory, that is the principle of my northern policy.[27]

Time would rather alter that principle. Such, though, is the earliest index to that antipathy to Prussia which Stainville already shared with Bernstorff. Stainville's pretty steady concern with the south lay behind his gossip to his friend two months later that 'Mme de Luxembourg is going to Montmorency this week till after Easter. She is put out by the departure of M. de St. Germain who often used to come to see her and with whom she had reason to be pleased. She was saying to me yesterday that this departure was reviving in her a much greater affliction.'[28]

The trigger of regret for the former Danish envoy in Paris was the forthcoming departure of the Sardinian one, the Marquis of San Germano. His wife was the mistress of his master, Charles Emmanuel, and San Germano was said to be going back to something good, perhaps even to succeed Osorio. Stainville, who shared the regret at San Germano's departure, further wrote: 'The Ambassador of Sardinia is just leaving, content enough to see his master alternating in signing a treaty with the King of Spain and the Queen Empress.'[29]

---

[27] Count de Stainville to Baron von Bernstorff, Paris, 6 Jan. 1752: *Bernstorffske Papirer*, ii. 638.
[28] Ibid., 20 Mar. 1752, p. 642.   [29] Ibid., 27 July 1752, p. 646.

Stainville was referring to the conclusion between the three powers of a new Treaty of Aranjuez of 14 June 1752, different from that of 1745. Sardinian adhesion this time to what was basically an Austro-Spanish compact had been delayed, not least, by a technicality of the protocol dear to old diplomacy, the so-called *alternat* or alternate. The often disputed precedence of contracting powers in signing copies of treaties could be resolved by the polite procedure of the alternate – the copy of a treaty which was to be preserved by a particular power was signed first by its plenipotentiaries so that each contractant enjoyed the honour of signing one copy first. That was what the jumped-up King of Sardinia, a kingdom for barely thirty years, had just imposed upon the Spanish monarch and even the Habsburg empress. The procedural issue, like many in that century, carried greater significance than might now appear. So did the Treaty of Aranjuez itself.

It is not a bad plan to keep an eye out for the lesser treaties which are apt to succeed great settlements of peace. Such settlements necessarily derive from the past whereas succeeding agreements can be tipped towards the future. Austria and Spain had been the main malcontents in the settlements both of Utrecht and of Aix-la-Chapelle but the aftermaths in Italy of the two treaties were in striking contrast. The peace of Utrecht had not embraced that Austro-Spanish conflict wherein Spanish forces seized Sardinia in 1717, Sicily in 1718. Subsequently the Quintuple Alliance and Ripperda's treaties of Vienna had provided only intermissions in that half-century of contest for Italy wherein Naples was batted back and forth between Spain and Austria, and the interests, largely, of Elizabeth Farnese's precious sons ensured that Spanish troops were still fighting the Austrians up and down the distracted peninsula in the wars of both the Polish and the Austrian successions. Aix-la-Chapelle left both antagonists, once again, ominously discontent. Only at last there had been a real shift in terms of personalities and power.

With Don Carlos now confirmed in Naples, Don Philip in Parma, their formidable mother was at last suppressed in the solitude of San Ildefonso, though still corresponding with the faithful Marshal de Noailles. The opposite, Anglo-Austrian, orientation represented by her successor, the also influential Portuguese Queen Barbara of Spain, was reinforced by an approach in favour of accommodation from her maternal relative, the Habsburg empress. Not only towards France but towards the Bourbon courts generally was the attitude of Maria Theresa evolving under pressure of the new power-factors embodied in the kings of Prussia and of Sardinia. The ambitions of the Emperor Charles VI – more grandiose than is always remembered, not least in Italy – had now contracted to the yearning of the

Empress Maria Theresa to recover Silesia. For that a prime desideratum, as the last war had cruelly underlined, was to secure the Austrian rear in Italy. And there the ascent of Piedmont-Sardinia was tending to bring Austria and Spain closer, if not in common interests then in related fears.

Back in 1750 muffled soundings in Rome had introduced an Austro-Spanish rapprochement. Maria Theresa hoped it might prosper her overtures to the neighbouring Bourbons in France. In this significant prodrome sublime Farinelli, the favourite singer at the Spanish court, supported an Austrian inclination in something of the way that Madame de Pompadour was to do at the French one in an age when it was diplomatic to bow to beauty. That had not of course ruled out the usual haggling, with Maria Theresa vainly seeking to exclude the island of Sardinia from her guarantee of the *status quo* on the plausible ground that she could deploy no fleet, while the Spaniards had resisted practical obligations in respect of Habsburg possessions outside Italy. King Ferdinand VI was prudently inclined to keep his war-worn half-brothers snugged down in Italy and his own war-worn country out of further trouble. He wanted no part in any war over Silesia. The high days of Spanish intervention in Germany during the Thirty Years War were already a century ago. And now, fifty years after the outbreak in Italy of the War of the Spanish Succession, it was over that peninsula that a seal was set at last upon the Spanish conflict of the dynasties of Bourbon and of Habsburg.

The Treaty of Aranjuez further carried a British impress. The Duke of Newcastle, through the adept Benjamin Keene at Madrid, aimed at distancing Spain from France in retaliation against Saint-Séverin's critical success at Aix in estranging England from Austria. For the present, though, British pressure once again brought Maria Theresa to put up with Sardinia, whose adhesion was critical for giving real effect to the treaty-provisions. Austria and Spain guaranteed one another's possessions in Europe; only in case of enemy attack against those in Italy, however, did their defensive alliance stipulate mutual assistance in troops or cash. The guarantee of the *status quo* in Italy further embraced Parma, Sardinia and Naples, grumblingly acquiescent. Almost the most important clauses in the short run were those to promote reciprocal commercial advantages, notably to the benefit of Austrian trade through Trieste and Ostend. This came too close to the Ostend East India Company of the Emperor Charles VI just a generation earlier for the outcome at Aranjuez to be wholly welcome after all to the British Government, which had for its part recently agreed with Spain to renounce at last the residual Asiento, against restoration of other British commercial privileges in Spanish reaches.

Great Britain, furthermore, had suffered the rejection of her striking offer of a naval squadron in the Mediterranean to support the guarantee of the Italian settlement. British inclusion in the treaty itself had also been refused on the plausible grounds that she held no Italian possessions and that her admission would involve that of France. As it was, the Treaty of Aranjuez seemed to contemporaries to prise Spain away from France. That was to prove no lasting set, yet in Italian terms it was the absence of further Gallispan combination against Austrian power that was largely to single out Italy as an exemplar of a successful balance of power, almost neutralizing her.

The aftermath of so much French diplomacy on behalf of an Italian apange for Don Philip now registered the elimination of any large French influence in that peninsula where Vendôme had been thrusting out just fifty years before. Henceforth the Marquis d'Argenson's dreams of French hegemony in Italy were destined for only transient realization through Napoleonic adventures. Whereas the Italian settlement sealed at Aranjuez under Austro-Spanish aegis was to persist, more or less, for a century to come. The treaty deserved its appellation of *Il Patto d'Italia*.

The Pact of Italy has, in the Anglo-French focus upon European history, naturally tended to be overshadowed by the larger settlement at Aix-la-Chapelle, which had indeed laid down the guidelines for Italy. But that was in essence an Anglo-Franco-Dutch arrangement. The voluntary coming together now of the opposite overlords in Italy together with her emergent leader gave the whole settlement of the peninsula a new solidity and (despite the Second Treaty of Versailles) an enduring quality which, precisely because it obviated any sensational sequel, could too easily be taken for granted. Yet it was to be a striking difference that, next time, the Seven Years War unlike that of the Austrian Succession saw no Italian campaigning. The Austrian rear had been secured; and if the Austrian alliance with France was severely disappointing to the British sponsors of 'the tranquility of Italy'[30] via Aranjuez, yet in the longer perspective British influence in introducing Piedmont-Sardinia, and even the British offer of naval support in the Mediterranean might seem distantly prefigurative of British championship of Italian aspirations in the Risorgimento. In closer perspective the Franco-Austrian alliance of 1756 was to suggest the extent to which, both then and since, the significance of the initial Austrian concert with the

[30] Sir Benjamin Keene to Castres, Madrid, 7 July 1755: *The Private Correspondence of Sir Benjamin Keene, K.B.*, ed. Sir Richard Lodge (Cambridge, 1933), p. 415.

Bourbons at Aranjuez was underestimated in relation to that which was to ensue at Versailles.

In years to come the Italian accommodation between Austria and Spain was to possess major importance for a French foreign policy which, under the Duke de Choiseul, largely rested upon alliance with both powers. His criticism, even to excess, of the neglect of Italy at Aix-la-Chapelle throws into relief his contemporary notice of the Treaty of Aranjuez. And if its full import was unrevealed to the then Count de Stainville as to others, yet it already stimulated him to a spacious evaluation of European statecraft significantly drawn from just the technicality of that alternate signature which King Charles Emmanuel, the needed party, imposed upon the Pact of Italy:

A hundred years ago the house of Austria could not have conceived that such a pretension could [even] be made. That is a good indication of the insufficiency of a policy which, however good it may be, does not prevent the revolutions which time produces. That would make me fancy that the ministers who only work from day to day are quite as good as the others in terms of the future. It is true that at the present moment they have some drawbacks.[31]

Ranging beyond the inadequate Saint-Contest and his little friends in office, the future Choiseul's philosophic estimate of the puny efforts of ministers against the long revolutions of time was to find poignant application in his own endeavour under Louis XV to turn back the decline of old France in the world. For the present, however, what mattered was to make a start by securing an appropriate embassy.

V

In March 1752 Stainville informed Bernstorff that the Count de Broglie, younger son of the old marshal, was getting Poland, and recalled his own refusal of it when Madame de Pompadour had broached it to him the preceding autumn. The Marquis d'Argenson commented on the Polish assignment of this 'very small man with a head as straight as a little cock ... The great question is to know if he enters into the interests favoured by the Prince de Conti.'[32] As Stainville put it:

The Count de Broglie does not know the extent of the commission which he is undertaking. He has no real property. He wants to do something. Perhaps he is right to risk this embassy. I am not in the same position. I would say the same to you about

[31] Count de Stainville to Baron von Bernstorff, Paris, 27 July 1752: *Bernstorffske Papirer*, ii. 646.
[32] D'Argenson, vii. 144.

the Berlin one, which is going vacant after the death of poor Tyrconnel and which I should also refuse if it were proposed to me. Duras is sure to have the Spanish one. So there are my political aims now become very remote.[33]

Paris had just heard of the incipient death in Berlin of Stainville's Jacobite comrade-in-arms, coughing blood for months while 'quantities of applicants',[34] unlike Stainville, sought to succeed him. It appears already that Stainville was as strikingly reluctant to get involved with Frederick the Great as with the paradiplomacy of the King's Secret on behalf of the Prince de Conti. Madrid was significantly different. But the Duke de Duras was a particular friend of Machault, so Duras was the one to grapple, unsuccessfully, with Keene for influence in the peninsula. Diplomatically disappointed, Stainville now confided to Bernstorff: 'I am thirty-two years old. I have still got some years in which to canvas for what would suit me, during which time I shall attempt a new tack towards buying some office of lieutenant-general of a province, which would bring me to command that province, which, for the ribbon [of the Saint-Esprit], would produce the same result as an embassy. I am boring you, Sir, with the details of my affairs.'[35] But he asked Bernstorff's advice in that phase of indecision for his career and of superficial enjoyment in society. That was to be the summer of his disgust with its dissipation.

It was all very well for the Count de Stainville to make out that the real lure was that blue ribbon, as it certainly was in part but in part only. He was soon back on the diplomatic tack: 'I am following up the idea of Sweden, and I hope that it may succeed if M. d'Havrincourt returns'[36] from the French embassy at Stockholm. On this Stainville had mobilized the Swedish ambassador in Paris, Baron Carl Frederick Scheffer. He was about to return to be a Swedish senator after nine years in Paris during which 'his gentleness, his politeness, the agreeable range of his mind . . . have gained him a large number of friends'[37] including Stainville, Madame du Deffand, Voltaire. By the end of August 1752 the diplomatic aspirant was writing to the foreign minister in Copenhagen:

You are going to see a man who has by his talk upset the plan for an idle life which I had proposed to follow. Baron de Scheffer had excited my interest in the embassy to Sweden; before leaving he was going to talk to the ministry and sound it out as regards myself. He told me that after the conversations which he was going to have, he would let me know how things lay. He has left without my having seen him and

[33] Count de Stainville to Baron von Bernstorff, Paris, 20 Mar. 1752: u.s., ii. 641–2.
[34] D'Argenson, vii. 161.
[35] Count de Stainville to Baron von Bernstorff, Paris, 20 Mar. 1752: u.s., ii. 642.
[36] Count de Stainville to Baron von Bernstorff, Paris, 27 July 1752: ibid., p. 646.
[37] Luynes, xii. 113.

without my having heard tell of him. Such behaviour proves that he did not find people as favourably disposed as he had wished. Perhaps he will talk to you about me. I beg you to throw light upon this enigma and to be sure that you will be the sole cause of the regrets that I shall have at not being able to be employed in the north.[38]

To the east there was speculation in Vienna that summer whether they might be receiving the Count de Stainville in the intermediate capacity of a minister or chargé d'affaires in the envisaged aftermath of the Marquis de Hautefort. Kaunitz wrote to Maria Theresa's secretary: 'I do not think that they have ever thought here of sending the Stainville son (*M*r *de Stainville le fils*) to Vienna; however, I will keep an eye on it'[39] – not a specially friendly eye, perhaps. But before so many years were out Kaunitz would have to deal with the Stainville son as French ambassador in Vienna to cement that diplomatic revolution lastingly associated with Madame de Pompadour.

Kaunitz's own embassy then in Paris, unproductive with Puysieulx and such a cypher as Saint-Contest, was looking especially to Madame de Pompadour. Kaunitz, explained the future Choiseul, established with her 'a particular relationship of friendship and confidence',[40] persuading her of Maria Theresa's regard for Louis XV and for herself, as expressed in letters in her own hand which the ingratiating ambassador shewed the favourite: 'these letters flattered the self-esteem of Mme de Pompadour, very easy to flatter' – a significant point from Choiseul. Kaunitz represented the logic of rapprochement for such friendly rulers while prudently adding that for the present all that Maria Theresa wished 'was that the King should be fully persuaded of her sentiments. Mme de Pompadour gave assurance that she was not leaving him in ignorance of them, which was true.' Before returning to succeed Ulfeld as chancellor, the ambassador secured permission to write to her and for his successor to see her. And Kaunitz, according to Choiseul at least, 'took away with him the certainty that he had laid toothing upon foundations good enough for the success of his project, when favourable opportunity should arise'.

Kaunitz in fact communicated no such certainty upon return to Vienna and an English orientation, though he may after all have had some measure of secret reliance upon Madame de Pompadour, and in the event the tendency stressed by the then Count de Stainville did prevail.

For the present Stainville himself was still looking north. By the

[38] Count de Stainville to Baron von Bernstorff, Paris, 29 Aug. 1752: op. cit., ii. 647.
[39] Count Kaunitz to Baron von Koch, Paris, 7 Aug. 1752: Kaunitz/Koch, pp. 249–50.
[40] Choiseul, *Mémoires*, pp. 153–4 for the following.

autumn he was writing to his friend there: 'You will have seen Baron de Scheffer. President Hénault is working very keenly to get M. d'Obterre [Aubeterre] nominated to the embassy to Sweden, and I am not sure that he will not succeed.'[41] Only, the Marquis d'Havrincourt was after all to remain in Stockholm for another ten years and was there to serve the future Choiseul. Now he wrote in the same letter; 'M. de Duras has left for his embassy to Spain and the Abbé de Bernis for that of Venice, so there are our women and our wits much forsaken. I do not know what will become of us during this absence.' If the Count de Stainville had shewn some deference towards the Abbé de Bernis in their artistic association over Rameau's *Linus,* their social acquaintance had already bred a bantering regard in the count who was before very long to overhaul the Abbé with the Marquise de Pompadour.

While Duras too was off to Madrid, the other Bourbon embassy to which Stainville had aspired, at Naples, was being filled by one who was to be a leading executant of the future Choiseul's foreign policy. This was Peter Paul, Marquis d'Ossun, seven years older than Stainville and, significantly like him, an officer beholden to the Marshal de Noailles, who particularly presided over French policy in the Bourbon south. D'Ossun had assured Noailles that it was on his advice that he had accepted Naples, and that Puysieulx had explained to Louis XV and his queen 'that I had the honour to belong to you'.[42] Another embassy of potential interest in Italy was Turin where the new French envoy, the ambitious Marquis des Issarts, had not arrived when Bernis passed through that October on his way to Venice. So it fell to him, a diplomatic beginner, to sound out Osorio as to the precise scope of the Treaty of Aranjuez, not less interesting to the French government than to the Count de Stainville. By artful ingratiation the Abbé succeeded so well in this that when, some months later, des Issarts fell mortally ill, the Sardinian government asked that he be replaced by Bernis, according to Bernis. Meantime, however, Stainville had been in the thick of his passage with the Countess de Choiseul–Romanet to the profit of the Marquise de Pompadour.

Coincident with the Choiseul–Romanet affair, the gap of over six months in Stainville's letters to Bernstorff cut out the writer's regular bulletins on his diplomatic ambitions. It is by the Abbé de Bernis, to whom Madame de Pompadour was 'to open her heart'[43] over that

[41] Count de Stainville to Baron von Bernstorff, Paris, 1 Oct. 1752: *u.s.,* ii. 648, and for the following.
[42] Marquis d'Ossun to Marshal de Noailles, 18 Apr. 1751: Arch. Aff. Étr., Mémoires et Documents: France, vol. 534, fo. 175.
[43] Bernis, i. 206–7 for the following.

affair, that one is told that the Count de Stainville, losing little time in seeking a reward, asked for Turin. Even the rescued favourite could not get it for him and 'M. de Saint-Contest hastened to have it given to M. de Chauvelin', Stainville's old comrade from the Régiment du Roi. He had done well as minister at Genoa and commander in Corsica, collecting that red ribbon of Saint Louis which Stainville had missed. The count's contemporaries seemed to be forging ahead of him.

Madrid, Naples, Turin, not to mention Stockholm, had all eluded Stainville. He seemed to be finding it almost as difficult to get an embassy as once a regiment. Success for him, as for most, was not automatic.

When Stainville resumed to Bernstorff in May 1753 there was no mention of Turin, assigned two months earlier. By now Stainville was explaining of his visit to Marly 'on business; I know nothing except what you have long known. They have offered Poland to him for whom you would wish Sweden. He will refuse it, and I believe that you will approve this.'[44] He confirmed in his next: 'I have refused what I told you of, and the man who is there will not remain very long in view of the dissatisfaction that there is with him. But I prefer that somebody else should go to cause dissatisfaction so far away. Besides'[45] – there was his prime preoccupation with his wife's health.

VI

If the illness of the Countess de Stainville had coincided with her husband's lesser preoccupation with the forthcoming camp at Aimeries, his visit in this connection to Compiègne that July also had a diplomatic background and coincided with the close of a ten-day visit there by his father. It was apparently just after the Count de Stainville's arrival at court, about 19 July, that the father was summoned by the Marquise de Pompadour who, he informed Francis I, 'begged me with the liveliest entreaty to write to Your Imperial Majesty in favour of the Countess de Marsan',[46] a lady-in-waiting then in the ascendant. Born a Rohan-Soubise, Madame de Marsan was descended through her mother from the ducal house of Lorraine though how legitimately was a point at issue in her recent

[44] Count de Stainville to Baron von Bernstorff, Paris, 17 May 1753: *Bernstorffske Papirer*, ii. 649.

[45] Ibid., 8 June 1753.

[46] Marquis de Stainville to Emperor Francis I, Paris, 22 July 1753: Esteri del Granducato di Toscana, vol. 2296/1287, no. 126 for the following.

litigation over a Guise inheritance, involving lands in Lorraine, with the Duke de Richelieu, the enemy of Madame de Pompadour. She now begged that the emperor should have justice done to the Countess de Marsan, 'vexed in her possession of estates which legitimately belonged to her ... by virtue of a treaty made with the late Duke Leopold and confirmed by the late Emperor Charles VI of glorious memory'. The Marquis de Stainville added that Francis 'will easily sense that I could not avoid promising that I would write': all the more, perhaps, since Madame de Marsan was the sister of the Prince de Soubise, the friend of Madame de Pompadour designated to command the camp which the Count de Stainville was about to join.

This despatch from the Marquis de Stainville was received in Vienna on 8 August 1753. The very next day the Emperor Francis, habitually so slow to answer him, sent a reply favourable to the Countess de Marsan, obliging to the Marquise de Pompadour. Being unable to see her, Stainville wrote the good news. Madame de Pompadour replied:

You surprise me agreeably, Sir, in informing me that you have acquainted the Emperor with the tender interest which I take in the Countess de Marsan. Would you kindly lay at the feet of His Imperial Majesty my very respectful gratitude for what he has deigned to have conveyed to me by you upon this subject; and would it be too daring to ask him to continue his protection of the Countess de Marsan? Be, I beg you, Sir, my guarantor to His Imperial Majesty of my zeal for everything which could please him.[47]

In such elegant fashion was the French favourite already cultivating relations with the court of Maria Theresa and in particular with the Holy Roman Emperor. More intimately informal by now were the relations of the Marquise de Pompadour with the Marquis de Stainville's son. The later Choiseul recalled of his keenness for camp that July:

This little commission obliged me to go to Compiègne both to see the Minister of War before going to Flanders and to take leave of the king. I went and in the crowd I perceived I know not how that the king viewed me with displeasure. Next day I saw Mme de Pompadour, who invited me to come to supper with her. I refused and told her of my suspicion of the king's ill-feeling towards me. She protested to me that he suspected nothing and she made fun of my lively imagination. It was in vain that I told her that, although the king's feelings could not interest me less, nevertheless I did not want to feel his aversion in public activity. She pressed me so much to come that I supped with her.[48]

---

[47] Marquise de Pompadour to Marquis de Stainville, probably late August 1753, as cited textually in Marquis de Stainville to Emperor Francis I, Paris, 2 Sept. 1753: *u.s.*, no. 130.
[48] Choiseul, *Mémoires*, pp. 86–7 for the following.

This account of that evening long ago at Compiègne continued:

After supper I was talking to her near a table which was turned towards a door through which the king came in. As soon as he perceived me I saw his face change to such an extent that it was thought in the room that he felt ill. Mme de Pompadour hurried over to him; she asked him what was the matter; he said that his stomach was not working well, and sat down to gamble. I played with him; chance would have it that I made impossible wins from him, which did not produce a more favourable expression towards me, but which consoled me infinitely for his sour look. He went to bed after the game. I took [formal] leave of him at his couchée. He did not say a word to me and I went upstairs again to Mme de Pompadour to ask her if she still had any doubts about the king's knowledge of my conversation with her at Fontainebleau. She told me that she did not understand what had happened, swearing to me at the same time that the king had never said anything to her which could have made her suspect that he was enlightened about it. I begged her to ascertain the facts during my absence, more so as to satisfy my curiosity and render myself free to see her without embarrassment than in order to efface the king's impressions, to which I was indifferent.

Yet it was the king who appointed to embassies, to which the Count de Stainville was then anything but indifferent. When setting out for Compiègne the count had written to Bernstorff: 'Your friend has to await patiently the events which could bring him closer to you; if lively desires brought the time closer he would soon join you.'[49] It looks as though there was still hope of a French vacancy at Stockholm, rather than at Copenhagen itself where one had recently been filled – but then it was only a legation. There the Abbé Lemaire was said to have intrigued with the Prussian minister for Bernstorff's overthrow, and had tried to retard the payment of French subsidies to Denmark. Finally the Danish government had suggested a more congenial envoy than the Abbé since, as Bernstorff had put it to Reventlow in Paris, 'in him we have but a sombre and prejudiced censor'.[50] The French government had obliged by altering from Ratisbon to Copenhagen the destination of the Count de Stainville's friend, Ogier, described even by Count Kaunitz as 'really a man of merit'.[51] That was echoed by Stainville to Bernstorff that August as Ogier was setting out with his wife, 'a clever woman who is a little bit of a hothead and who will amuse you'.[52]

If Ogier was long to interpret to the Danish court the policies of the future Choiseul, the latter was for the present still to pursue his

[49] Count de Stainville to Baron von Bernstorff, Paris, 16 July 1753: *Bernstorffske Papirer*, ii. 652.
[50] Baron von Bernstorff to Count Reventlow, Copenhagen, 25 July 1752: P. Vedel, *Correspondance ministérielle du comte J.H.E. Bernstorff, 1751–1770*, i. 62.
[51] Count Kaunitz to Emperor Francis I, Paris, 1 May 1752: Ö.S./H.H.S., Frankreich/Berichte (1752), 134.
[52] Count de Stainville to Baron von Bernstorff, Paris, 19 Aug. 1753: *u.s.*, p. 652.

inclination southward, through the instrumentality of a more distinguished friend from that quarter.

VII

In Rome the Duke de Nivernais had hit it off well with the benevolently liberal Pope Benedict XIV, less well with his Secretary of State, Cardinal Valenti, who had been intriguing with the nuncio in Paris, Durini, to have Nivernais replaced by someone hotter against Jansenism. It had been on leave, however, that he had eventually returned early in 1752 to Paris, and Versailles where he resumed his high favour with Madame de Pompadour: no bad development for the Count de Stainville, whose own career was to take a suggestively Roman turn.

A main reason for Nivernais's return had been concern for his delicate heir, affected by the Roman climate. The little Count de Nevers had improved and had recently made his first public appearance at the wedding on 23 May 1753 of his eldest sister to the Count de Gisors, only son of the Marshal de Belle-Isle, once befriended in time of need by Nivernais's father. It was no fault of the marshal if, for his son, his marriage to Mademoiselle de Nevers was clouded by his reciprocated love for Sophie-Septimanie, the alluring daughter of the Duke de Richelieu. Nasty as usual, Richelieu, hating Belle-Isle, had snobbishly refused to hear of her marrying a Fouquet, too comparable to his own moderate ancestry. So the great-grandson of the great Fouquet, instead of marrying a Richelieu, made do with the great-niece of that other cardinal who had relegated the lad's ancestor to perpetual imprisonment. If such families were relatively new, small wonder that they held themselves high. They were history personified.

Four months after his marriage the Count de Gisors wrote to the Marshal de Belle-Isle of his new in-laws: 'My dear father, I cannot depict the desolation which reigns here at the moment at which I am writing to you. Madame de Nivernais, on her knees in the chimney-corner is bursting into tears as she says her prayers; M. de Nivernais in the other corner is terribly prostrated, his head sunk forward. The little patient, who is in the next room, never stops complaining; everything sickens him.'[53] That was the Count de Nevers. He had gone to school at Louis-le-Grand as a part-boarder but this concession to his health had not saved him from an epidemic there of what was described as a gangrenous throat-infection, sounding like diphtheria.

---

[53] Count de Gisors to Marshal de Belle-Isle, Paris, 18 Sept. 1753: cited, L. Perey, *Un Petit-Neveu de Mazarin*, pp. 300–1.

He died the night after that letter was written. The Duke de Nivernais cried from half-past five the following morning till ten o'clock that night, 19 September 1753. With the death of his heir, commented the Marquis d'Argenson, 'there happily perishes the wretched name of Mazarin which has caused France such horrors. Perish thus, say Frenchmen, all these hateful names of ministers who have despoiled and tyrannized over the kingdom!'[54] Bloodthirsty rhetoric is the nourishment of revolution.

Some weeks after the boy's death the Count de Stainville was back in Paris from his summer in camp in Flanders and on his estates in Lorraine. Upon his return he received a letter from his old friend and protector, the Marshal de Noailles. As the recipient later recalled, it informed him 'that M. de Nivernais, who was in Paris, was resigning the embassy in Rome; that he [Noailles] had spoken to M. de Saint-Contest, the Minister of Foreign Affairs, to dispose him towards making me replace M. de Nivernais; that the dispositions of M. de Saint-Contest were very favourable and that he advised me, if I designed to be an ambassador, to come to Fontainebleau to follow up this matter'[55] – at last an opening that beckoned.

Nivernais, already reluctant to return to Rome, could not now face a place full of recent reminders of his extinguished son and hopes. That death, wrote the Count de Stainville, had caused his stricken friend 'to renounce all employment'.[56] Nivernais was a good friend to have, while 'the friendship of the Marshal de Noailles was kept active on behalf of the Count de Stainville, by the latter's feeling gratitude'.[57]

Besides cultivating his old benefactor, the younger Stainville seems to have been particularly friendly with the marshal's younger son, the Count de Noailles, some three years his senior. Comrades-in-arms at Dettingen, Rocoux, Lawfeldt, they now shared interludes of the sweet life at court, where the Count de Noailles figured prominently as governor of Versailles with sway too over delicious Trianon and Marly. Before so very long now Stainville was to be writing to him nostalgically: 'I send you a thousand thanks, Monsieur the Count, for the list of [those bidden to] Marly . . . This list has made me envious, and I have been recalling the times that I have spent in that spot.'[58] For the present the call was to Fontainebleau, from the elder Noailles.

[54] D'Argenson, viii. 126.
[55] Choiseul, *Mémoires*, pp. 87–8.
[56] Count de Stainville to Baron von Bernstorff, Fontainebleau, 18 Nov. 1753: *Bernstorffske Papirer*, ii. 654.
[57] Essai/Arsenal 5808, fo. 62.
[58] Count de Stainville to Count de Noailles, Rome, 1755: Archives de Mouchy, 2830, no. 9.

If the then Count de Stainville in his memoirs was to ascribe the Roman initiative to the ministerial level of Noailles and Saint-Contest, that may have been formally correct. Far from wholly implausible, however, is the contention of Bernis that when the Sardinian wish to have him as ambassador at Turin had been shelved, Madame de Pompadour had sought to console him by asking, already, that he should succeed Nivernais at Rome, as might seem fairly appropriate for an Abbé fresh from diplomacy in Venice. But when Stainville, her recent benefactor, was likewise disappointed of Turin then, according to Bernis, he 'was preferred to me for filling the embassy at Rome'.[59] It might even, of course, have been, partly at least, that at that critical juncture in France of the parliamentary struggle over the religious issue of Billets de Confession, it was judged that Stainville would make a more effective ambassador at Rome than Bernis.

'Till then', Stainville was to maintain, 'I had been fairly diligent in instructing myself and working on all sorts of matters, but I had not thought particularly of politics.'[60] Since politics here embraced diplomacy, that statement was a lie. His long search for an embassy ran right through his contemporary correspondence with Bernstorff; though that with Nivernais himself testified that Stainville, conscious that man is a creature of contraries, was genuinely fond of informal living so that it might well be with truth enough that he proceeded to recall his reluctance to give up his agreeable routine of morning study and afternoons of pleasure:

Besides I had married a child whom I loved tenderly; who, during the three years that I had been married, had had a miscarriage, had caught a horrible malignant fever from which she had not recovered; it had left her in a very worrying condition of weakness and exhaustion. I could not and would not leave her and I was sensible of the difficulty of having her make a journey like that to Rome at her age, and in such a delicate state of health.

All this was explained to the Marshal de Noailles in that October of 1753 when his protégé duly arrived at Fontainebleau, where the court was waxing 'resplendent and beautiful'.[61] Stephen de Stainville added 'how uneasy I should be, if war came, not to be serving in the army. The Marshal de Noailles reassured me as to war and told me that in time of peace there was no nobler occupation than that of politics, that, finally, I was of an age to settle down (*pendre de la consistance*) and win some public consideration, which would never happen if I remained idle.'[62] Even a French aristocrat of the

[59] Bernis, op. cit., i. 207.
[61] D'Argenson, viii. 147.
[60] Choiseul, *Mémoires*, p. 88 for the following.
[62] Choiseul, *Mémoires*, pp. 88–9.

eighteenth century, if he was to count for much, was expected to do something more than manage his estates and dance at court.

VIII

On the advice of Noailles young Stainville went forthwith to see the marshal's creature, the inadequate foreign minister. ('The clerks in his office laugh at him.')[63] Stainville found Saint-Contest 'warned of my visit and ... [he] received me as somebody whom he greatly wished to oblige. Next day I told Madame de Pompadour what I had done on the preceding one; she emphasized the reasons which the Marshal de Noailles had given so as to clinch my decision, and told me that she would speak to M. de Saint-Contest, to get him to finish this business at once. I took no further pains in this matter.'[64] The weak minister was not being allowed to repeat his gambit over Turin.

Thus the later Choiseul's account had him speaking to Madame de Pompadour only after matters were officially in train. His eulogist explained, if a shade too emphatically, that he 'had not wished, in all the embarrassment of this business, to address himself to Madame de Pompadour. His reasons are sufficiently apparent. She was sensible both of the delicacy of the Duke de Choiseul and of what it behoved her to do.'[65] Choiseul was, not least, a diplomatist of the emotions. In that realm a claim can at times be strengthened by not asserting it. It was now that the royal mistress and the future minister really began to draw together.

Choiseul, regularly relegating his father, explained that after these conversations at court:

I returned to Paris to inform my family and dispose them in favour of my nomination to this embassy, of which I had not yet told them; and I came back to Fontainebleau at the time when I thought that M. de Saint-Contest would be conferring with the king in order to obtain a decision. I saw him upon my arrival. I found him a little embarrassed with me. He told me that he had conferred with the king, but that the nomination to the embassy at Rome had been deferred to another session; he would have something to mention to the king in a few days' time and he would then put the [nomination] paper before him again. He advised me to wait. I did not imagine that this delay was on my personal account. The king's expression still showed strong disfavour towards me when he met me, but I was not unaware that his aversions or affections did not influence the proposals of his ministers. Madame de Pompadour thought no differently than I. So I very patiently awaited the new working-session [with Louis]. It came. I asked M. de Saint-Contest, as he was coming out of the king's apartment, if he had concluded my business; he told me that it was again deferred and that he was going to give an account of it to Madame de Pompadour. Then did this delay, and the way in which M. de Saint-Contest told me of it, strike me as

[63] D'Argenson, viii. 142.   [64] Choiseul, *Mémoires*, p. 89.   [65] Essai/Arsenal 5808, fo. 65.

extraordinary. Before the demarches which they had got me to make, which my family and friends knew about, I had felt repugnance, rather than desire for the embassy to Rome; but I felt injured by this refusal. I spoke in this sense to M. de Saint-Contest, who was as astonished as myself at the king's repugnance and did not know the grounds for it.[66]

Choiseul's apologist added that Louis XV appointed no day for further consideration of the matter and that 'the king had perhaps never, since he had been upon the throne, stood out twice over against a proposal by one of his ministers; and the Duke de Choiseul was grieved by it as it seemed to him cruel that he should have wrought such a baneful miracle in the king's character'.[67]

The same account supplemented that of Choiseul to the effect that 'being determined to see to what point the king's resolution against himself might extend, he begged M. de Saint-Contest to place his request before the king's eyes again, till he should have positively refused it. He [Stainville] was preparing himself for this decisive refusal.' The postulant himself merely wrote of the foreign minister:

He conferred yet again with the king and could not bring him to give a decision. I believe that I am the sole example of somebody who had the advantage of giving the king the strength to refuse for three weeks to grant his minister what he himself did not wish. Madame de Pompadour became much more heated than I over the king's resistance. I was beginning to accustom myself to the idea of being the object of the king's aversion. This condition suited me well enough. I had warned my friends and family that my hopes of success in this request had vanished, and I begged Madame de Pompadour to give up the idea, which could only bring unpleasantness upon herself. I had taken my decision over this disagreeable little event, all the more so since I had very seductive compensations of all kinds.[68]

The king's mistress, however, was made of stouter stuff than the king. Her new protégé was to recall that 'one morning I received from Madame de Pompadour a note proposing that I should go to her room. There I found M. de Saint-Contest who informed me that the king had sent for him before going hunting to tell him that he was nominating me to the embassy at Rome. I thanked him, saying in reply that I had not expected it. I remained with Madame de Pompadour', after the foreign minister had withdrawn that Friday, 16 November 1753. Then at last it came, a revelation of mysteries on high by the favourite:

She told me that that very morning she had had an explanation with the king. She had asked him the grounds for his resistance to my nomination, and after many meaningless subterfuges he confessed to her that he had a personal hatred of me

---

[66] Choiseul, *Mémoires*, pp. 89–90.   [67] Essai/Arsenal 5808, fos. 64–5 for the following.
[68] Choiseul, *Mémoires*, pp. 90–1 for the following.

because I had told her of the letters which he had written to Madame de Choiseul. Madame de Pompadour asked him how he could have known it. He told her that in the explanation which he had had with Madame de Pompadour about Madame de Choiseul one day at Fontainebleau, upon his denying to her that he had the least tenderness for Madame de Choiseul she had lost her temper and had reproached him with not being truthful; for it could not be said that one had no gallant feelings for a woman when one was writing her love-letters, and at that she repeated to him word for word a passage from one of his letters. He had been astonished that she had knowledge of it. He had continued to deny everything and to employ every means to quiet her down and end the explanation. But that evening he had, as was his custom, seen Madame de Choiseul and had reproached her with her indiscretion. She had confessed to him that she had indeed shown his letters to M. de Stainville but that she had shown them only to him and that he alone could have reported them or had them reported to Madame de Pompadour. Upon this indication he had made some researches to find out if I had seen Madame de Pompadour, or if I had got my brother-in-law to speak to her, and he had been informed that I had been to her room while he was at evensong the previous Sunday. With all the circumstances matching thus, he had taken an aversion to me. If I had lived in his intimate circle, he would have punished me for playing him such a perfidious trick, but since he did not consort with me, he had confined himself to not liking me and refusing me everything which might show some preference.[69]

This painful confession by Louis to his mistress for once exposed his withdrawn self, his stealthy procedure, patient checking, his elevated moderation in resentment. The earliest biography of Choiseul, however, here carries the deletion of a just acknowledgment that Louis XV 'often evinced good nature and sometimes ideas of justice'.[70] Though that was naturally not quite how it then struck Madame de Pompadour. She was later to remark to Stainville: 'I have been paid out for taking care of your cousins.'[71]

The then Count de Stainville remarked of that set-to with the king:

Mme de Pompadour, according to what she told me, made him sensible that it was against herself rather than against me that his anger and aversion were directed; and that she could not endure that I should be the victim of an indiscretion which she had committed, and that if he did not nominate me that very morning she would, she declared, take his refusal as her own dismissal, and she would go to Paris, not to return to court. She reminded him that previous explanations had put an end to the discussions between themselves relative to Madame de Choiseul, and how unworthy of him it was, after having made her agree that everything to do with this quarrel should be forgotten, to preserve in his heart a venom which would grieve her so. Since she spoke with a good deal of vehemence she intimidated the king, which is the surest way of persuading him.[72]

[69] Ibid., pp. 91–2.   [70] Essai/Arsenal 5808, fo. 67.
[71] Marquise de Pompadour to Count de Stainville, 1755: Général de Piépape, 'Lettres de Mme de Pompadour au comte de Stainville (Choiseul)' in *Revue de l'histoire de Versailles et de Seine-et-Oise*, 1917 (Versailles, 1917), p. 12.
[72] Choiseul, *Mémoires*, p. 92 for the following.

The king, related Stainville, forthwith 'sent for M. de Saint-
Contest, nominated me and went downstairs again to Madame de
Pompadour to tell her; but at the same time he added the condition
that he should not be pressed to make me a knight of the order' of the
Saint-Esprit, as was often done in connection with ambassadorial
appointments. Madame de Pompadour, thinking only of the victory
which she had won, raised no objection to this restriction; but I for
my part, feeling the restriction with more haughtiness than
gratification at being ambassador to Rome, protested strongly against
this condition; and I wanted it to be annulled or else I would resign
the embassy. Madame de Pompadour with extreme gentleness asked
me to make this sacrifice of my vanity, with all the more reason, she
said, because the restriction imposed by the king was a residue of its
humour which would have no lasting effect.' So Stainville swallowed
his pride along with his embassy. As she was to put it to him wryly in
another context: 'One has to be of service to one's friends in spite of
themselves.'[73]

On both fronts the spirited initiative of Madame de Pompadour
had brilliantly retrieved her earlier error in unintentionally putting
Louis on to Stainville's part in thwarting him. The count had long
suspected that she had done so but now all that was easily enough
obliterated by gratitude. As his biographer explained, it was only
now that Stainville had thus learnt 'that Madame de Pompadour had
courageously surmounted all these obstacles. He was grateful to her
for having acquainted him with them only after having triumphed
over them, and for having shown him her desire to be of service to
him only after having served him.'[74]

They had treated one another with that best of good faith which is
expressed both in courage and in delicate feeling. It had taken a year
for their association, curiously evolved from their preceding coolness,
to ripen into what has been termed a defensive and offensive alliance,
potentially of great strength. In the words of Choiseul's biographer,
he was 'from this moment bound to her by gratitude, by true
friendship which grew stronger every day, which she nourished by
the most regular attentions, by the most wholehearted preoccupation
with the interests of the Duke de Choiseul and of his family'. As she
was to assure him two years later: 'I shall never forget the intention
which you had of rendering me service.'[75] She, as it were, slipped her
hand confidingly into what she described as 'Your Excellency's pretty
little hand'.[76]

[73] Marquise de Pompadour to Count de Stainville, 23 Oct. 1756: Général de Piépape, u.s.,
p. 176.   [74] Essai/Arsenal 5808, fos. 67–8 for the following.
[75] Marquise de Pompadour to Count de Stainville, 21 Apr. 1755: Général de Piépape, u.s.,
p. 18.   [76] Ibid., 1755, p. 14.

The future Choiseul, looking back over the emotional origins of his political career, his cousin's royal liaison, his chance of an embassy at last, his critical friendship with the royal favourite, summed up thus:

There is the exact and detailed recital of the event which was the origin of everything which has happened to me since with the king. I have not been unaware, and it has hurt me, that it has been thought in society that I employed base means to satisfy my ambition. I did not have, and never have had, any ambition other than that of being esteemed by those with whom I had friendly or business relations. I believe that to deserve esteem is the first of all ambitions. It is so far above desires for fortune that the employments and dignities which one acquires seem but the means of cultivating the true and only estimable ambition.[77]

He proceeded: 'I felt a kind of inner uneasiness at not being able to confess the motives which induced Madame de Pompadour to show interest in me, but I thought that the embassy to Rome was a post which was not above what I could very reasonably aspire to, and consequently that I owed people no explanation of an event which seemed to me very simple.' But about twenty years later he did explain:

Now that I no longer am, and never shall be, anything in the administration of the state so long as King Louis XV shall live, I have been very happy to write down in the most detailed fashion an anecdote personal to myself so that those who shall read it may judge the purity and honesty of my conduct. God forbid that I should deny that this circumstance in my life was the occasion which made me acquainted with Madame de Pompadour, which associated me with her in the tenderest friendship and interested her in everything that happened to me. All my life I shall recall my attachment for her and the gratitude which I owe her for myself, my friends and my family.

The favourite had found a true friend. 'But', he continued, 'I should repeat, for it is the very truth, that my connection with Madame de Pompadour, at first the product of chance as has been seen, did not contain, either in origin or even in what followed, any ambitious design for my fortune.'

Such is Choiseul's own story of his climb to favour and preferment. His story is involved, as motives are, as truth often is. His evidence is revealing, inevitably partial, considerably convincing, sometimes not, in a balance which each may hold for himself.

IX

However chequered the grounds for advancement, an official appointment is a specific event. The Count de Stainville's nomination

[77] Choiseul, *Mémoires*, pp. 92–3 for the following.

as ambassador to Rome was a remarkable achievement. If Rome was by no means the most important post politically, it was probably more evident to contemporaries than it has since been to others that by the international protocol of that hierarchic age Stainville's first step in diplomacy set him above all other French ambassadors. Thanks to papal primacy he was to be proudly listed first in the *Almanach Royal*,[78] ahead of the envoy to the Porte, significantly second. Since Vienna, third, was to be vacant that put up the Duke de Duras at Madrid; the Duke de Mirepoix in London came fourth, Ossun fifth at Naples and so on down to the Count de Broglie eighth at Dresden, next Chauvelin at Turin, Ogier in Copenhagen, and at Venice, eleventh, poor Bernis, the more obviously appropriate choice for Rome. For him that ambition was now to be pushed back fifteen years and that by one whose appointment, when first rumoured, caused a friend of Montesquieu to write of 'the amiable Mr. de Stainville... That would not surprise me, for one must not be surprised by anything.'[79]

Such was the intimation to Baron Scheffer of the likelihood of Rome for the young man whom he had thought of for Stockholm. Whereas his correspondent, the Count de Bulkeley, a retired general related to the Duke of Berwick, confirmed the Count de Stainville's appointment by asking: 'What do you say, Sir, to our Roman ambassador?... Of all the choices that one seems to me the most absurd, for, apart from his capacity which I think mediocre everywhere except around beds, he can scarcely be regarded as a Frenchman, being one only from eight or ten years back, having been brought up in Vienna, and at the court of Lorraine; it seems besides that he will ill replace the Chaulnes, Créquis, Lavardins, Tessés and even Mr. de Nivernais. Although there be no difficulty about a birth fit for anything, I know of no goods that he has delivered.'[80]

Contemporaries were mostly more conscious than their successors of the external origin of the Count de Stainville. Criticism of him on that score was a good piece of Irish logic. Bulkeley was born in Britain. And as to extraction, one little noticed circumstance may well have meant something in those times of regional awareness. If, as reputed, Madame de Pompadour was the granddaughter of a peasant from La Ferté-sous-Jouarre, yet her stock may well have

[78] Cf. *Almanach Royal* for 1755 (Paris, 1755), p. 114.
[79] Count de Bulkeley to Baron C.F. Scheffer, Paris, 19 Oct. 1753: Gunnar von Proschwitz, 'Lettres inédites de madame du Deffand, du président Hénault et du comte de Bulkeley au baron Carl Fredrik Scheffer, 1751–1756' in *Studies on Voltaire and the Eighteenth Century*, ed. Theodore Besterman (Geneva, 1955 f.), x. 347.
[80] Ibid., 6 Dec. 1753, p. 356.

looked back to the village of Poissons, less than twenty miles from the village of Stainville. In any case those two clever easterners were liable to figure at the French court as outsiders, he by nationality, she by birth. And outsiders tend to draw together.

The Marquise de Pompadour, while wangling the appointment of the dissipated, diplomatically untried Count de Stainville, had been made disagreeably aware that he was not exactly an obvious choice for the Holy See. After his arrival there she was characteristically to urge him to incessant work: 'Give me the ammunition in order to make me forget what they said to me when you were nominated ambassador.'[81]

The future Choiseul did not let her down. Nor had the royal mistress been alone in her initial faith in him. The wittily superior Marquis Caraccioli, then in charge of the Neapolitan embassy in Paris, was to recall that once in company when, like Bulkeley, 'people were surprised that M. de Choiseul, then not far on at court, should have been nominated ambassador to Rome, a man of parts said: Gentlemen, you are astonished to see M. de Stainville (that was then his name) going as ambassador to Rome; whereas I should not be at all astonished to see him one day prime minister.'[82] If Choiseul was indeed to ride high, one notices the stealthy withholding from most contemporaries of his early favour with Madame de Pompadour.

On 18 November 1753 the Count de Stainville excused delay in writing to Baron von Bernstorff:

I have been at Fontainebleau for a month, expecting to return thence from one day to the next. A matter which should have been finished at the beginning of my visit has kept me here till it was decided the day before yesterday. The king has nominated me his ambassador to Rome ... Although I have not yet thanked the king, and consequently the grace which he has granted me has not been announced, I did not want to miss a post in letting you know of the destination of one of your servants. However brilliant it may be, it would have gladdened my heart much more if it had brought me closer to you either in place or in business ... We shall be two exiles from Paris who will have great pleasure in writing to one another.[83]

The day after that was written the recording Duke de Luynes heard of the Roman appointment for 'the son of the one who has for long been the minister here of the Duke of Lorraine, since grand duke, today Emperor'.[84] Luynes, proceeding to explain the pay-off of the Marquis de Stainville, was for once apparently confused in

---

[81] Marquise de Pompadour to Count de Stainville, 1 Feb. 1755: Général de Piépape, u.s., p. 14.
[82] L. Dutens, *Mémoires d'un voyageur qui se repose*, ii. 83–4.
[83] Count de Stainville to Baron von Bernstorff, Fontainebleau, 18 Nov. 1753: *Bernstorffske Papirer*, ii. 653–4.
[84] Luynes, xiii. 112 for the following.

including in it 'the expectation of the Golden Fleece for his son', then a quite unlikely beneficiary as compared with his father, denounced now by the Marquis d'Argenson as 'the greatest Austrian and the greatest enemy of France that we have had in Paris for a long time'.[85] In announcing to Bernstorff the appointment to Rome, young Stainville added: 'A little piece of good fortune has also come to my father. The Emperor has nominated him Kt. of the Fleece; it is in consequence of his retirement.'[86] A generation of inconspicuous service to the house of Lorraine had at last earned conspicuous recognition.

Father and son could rejoice together upon their almost simultaneous distinctions from opposite governments. The Austrian chargé d'affaires in Paris put an edge on this to Kaunitz:

Several people are doubtful whether the designation of the Count de Stainville for the Embassy at Rome, whereof I had the honour to tell Your Excellency in my last letter of the 19th, be certain as yet; but nobody doubts that his father will be included in the next promotion to the Golden Fleece since he himself is saying so with circumstantial particulars which display the generosity of His Imperial Majesty.[87]

Three days later, on 29 November 1753, the Marquis de Stainville was one of eight new knights nominated in a chapter of the Order of the Golden Fleece held in Vienna. This list seems to have been largely personal to Francis I from his earlier days. Stainville kept company with the emperor's old mentor, Field-Marshal Neipperg, a less felicitous general than Count Daun, also knighted that day. The only other creation of Germanic stock was Count von Salburg of no brilliant birth. Otherwise there was the Duke de Croÿ and a pack of Italians, the Marquis Doria and Counts Pallavicini and Montecucoli Caprara. The Fleece was still the order of honorific chivalry with the widest spread in christendom.

'This promotion', observed an Austrian courtier, 'has not won so much approval as the two previous ones.'[88] If the Marquis de Stainville was not one of those chiefly disapproved for the Fleece, it was upon that occasion that 'it was only to be deplored that H.M. the Emperor keeps himself so shut off concerning both the intended promotion in general and in particular the choice of candidates, and will not draw in to advise anybody discreet and experienced'.

Maybe the Marquis de Stainville was well absent from the

---

[85] D'Argenson, viii. 164.

[86] Count de Stainville to Baron von Bernstorff, Fontainebleau, 18 Nov. 1753: *u.s.*, p. 654.

[87] Mareschal to Count Kaunitz, Paris, 26 Nov. 1753: Ö.S./H.H.S., Frankreich/Berichte (1753), 141.

[88] Prince J.J. Khevenhüller-Metsch, *Aus der Zeit Maria Theresias 1752–1755*, ed. Rudolf Graf Khevenhüller-Metsch and Dr. Hanns Schlitter (Vienna and Leipzig, 1910), pp. 150–1 for the following.

traditional festivity for the new knights of the Fleece held in Vienna on 30 November 1753. Instead he was about to return to Brussels where the prince most nearly identified with his little homeland of old, Prince Charles of Lorraine, was to invest him with that high dignity of local creation more than three centuries earlier by Duke Philip the Good of Burgundy. The treasury and treasurer of the order of the Golden Fleece still remained in Brussels. Stainville's agreeable journey thither was now used by the Austrian representative in Paris, Mareschal, for the conveyance to Vienna of despatches and of recent pamphlets from the ebullient capital of taste. Thus did the Marquis de Stainville become the unlikely transmitter of the latest polemic from Jean-Jacques Rousseau, the *Lettre sur la musique française*. 'A number of people', explained Mareschal to Kaunitz, 'are taking this business tragically and are saying that Rousseau is a ... disturber of the public peace who must be punished or shut up for the rest of his days.'[89] Rousseau was indeed to prove himself in more serious respects a disturber of the public peace of the old regime. 'Since I am on the subject of music', concluded Mareschal, 'I would add further that the new ballet by M. Rameau, performed at Fontainebleau, fell quite flat at the first performance ... For the rest the cabals, enmities and loves continue upon the old footing at court.'[90]

Such were the tidings brought by the Marquis de Stainville to Brussels where the beneficent rule of Prince Charles of Lorraine, primed first by the Marquis Botta D'Adorno, burying his military bungle at Genoa, now by the popularly extravagant Count Charles Philip von Cobenzl, was retrieving the recent French invasion and stripping down by Séchelles. The Austrian Netherlands were reviving towards prosperity in furtherance of the constructive designs across Europe of the multinational Habsburg empire.

It was on the Boxing Day of 1753, the feast of Saint Stephen, that Prince Charles decorated the Marquis de Stainville with the gorgeous collar of the Golden Fleece in an investiture held in the Church of Saint-Jacques-sur-Coudenberg in the upper town of Brussels, the old citadel of the Dukes of Brabant and of Burgundy, of the Emperor Charles V. With Brussels rising anew after the great conflagration of 1731, Prince Charles planned a capital on the model of Vienna. However, Saint James, the church of the proconsular court, was so far, still, the old one of an Augustinian abbey atop cold mountain Coudenberg. This was one of the shrines of christendom in Northern

---

[89] Mareschal to Count Kaunitz, Paris, 2 Dec. 1753: Ö.S./H.H.S., Frankreich/Berichte (1753), 141.
[90] Ibid.

Europe, the spot where, more than six centuries before, Godfrey de
Bouillon had inspired the Flemings to follow that first crusade which
had stamped the chivalry of Lorraine.

If Francis Joseph de Choiseul must rank as one of the less
outstanding members of the order of the Golden Fleece, yet the
Austrian accolade was a long stretch from the impecunious orphan
with his little inheritance of pots and pans at Beaupré to back his
youthful enlistment in the musketeers of France. Now, upon return
from Brussels, came his brilliant moment at the French court. On 15
January 1754 the Marquis de Stainville, resplendent in his new
dignity, appeared at Versailles 'where', he told the emperor, 'I was
overwhelmed by the kindness which the king shewed me in
congratulating me upon the decoration wherewith it has pleased
Your Imperial Majesty to honour me. He said to me jestingly that I
should have a Fleece in diamonds: to which I replied that I had not
yet had time to have one made. But I managed to say nothing of the
real reason which is preventing me.'[91] Stainville was not one of the
great nobility and his golden handshake did not run to diamonds.

Characteristic of King Louis XV was both his kindness to a worthy
second-rater and the cutting edge to his joke. His graciousness to the
father over the Golden Fleece contrasted with his sulky refusal of the
Saint-Esprit to the son. Nor was it only with Louis that the Count de
Stainville had a past to live down in his elevation to be ambassador
to Rome. Some days earlier Baron Scheffer had been writing of it
from Stockholm to Madame du Deffand: 'How will Madame du
Châtel console herself for the absence of her daughter, who is
doubtless going to follow her husband to Rome, and how will other
fair ladies in Paris, to whom he cannot be indifferent, console
themselves for this journey? I expect that you will reply that they will
not be at all inconsolable, and in truth I should have supposed so for
the very reason that the journey is taking place. People who are very
fond of each other do not look for opportunities of leaving one
another.'[92]

The author of this rather weak equation of true love had in fact
been assured by Bulkeley that the Princess de Robecq was said to be
'already consoling herself for it. It is the attribute of princesses to
make such sacrifices'[93] – and the duty of ambitious ambassadors.
Stainville was now ostentatiously turning over a new leaf in keeping
with his entry into the strange field, for him, of ecclesiastical affairs.

[91] Marquis de Stainville to Emperor Francis I, Paris, 20 Jan. 1754: Esteri del Granducato di
Toscana, vol. 2296/1287, no. 143.
[92] Baron Scheffer to Marquise du Deffand, Stockholm, 4 Jan. 1754: Du Deffand/Lescure, i.
192.
[93] Count de Bulkeley to Baron Scheffer, Paris, 6 Dec. 1753: u.s., x. 356.

Here the Cardinal de Tencin, the old friend of the elder Stainville, was to lend a useful hand. But on 12 December 1753 Pope Benedict XIV had written to the cardinal:

The letters from France inform me that the Marquis de Choiseul [sic] has been nominated to succeed here to the Duke de Nivernais, whom we are very sorry to lose. The rumours which are current about the marquis are not to his advantage and, in confidence, it stabs us to the heart with grief because Rome in its present state has no need of a larger number of libertines. However, for fear of worse we shall not say a word. If we opposed his coming without success we should only have soured him and disposed him to be still worse.[94]

It was not the warmest of welcomes from the head of a state to an ambassador to be accredited to him. Stephen de Stainville's first diplomatic mission to Rome might seem to be opening hardly more auspiciously than his father's first one to London a generation earlier.

[94] Pope Benedict XIV to Cardinal de Tencin, Rome, 12 Dec. 1753: Benoît-Tencin, ii. 309.

CHAPTER X

IDEAS

I

THE Count de Stainville's diplomatic début was compromised in Rome not only morally, by the patronage of Madame de Pompadour, but also doctrinally by that of the Marshal de Noailles, suspect, like his uncle the cardinal, of Jansenist sympathies.

The marshal had become acquainted with the then Archbishop Lambertini during the Italian campaigning of the War of the Polish Succession. Pope Benedict was now to observe to Cardinal de Tencin: 'In matters of religion this marshal goes beyond bounds in what is superfluous and stops short of them in essentials. We used to know him well at Bologna, where he came with a submissive air to ask our permission to communicate at midnight mass on Christmas day, because he knew that that is forbidden in Italy; but as regards the decretals of the Holy See and the decisions of the church upon the constitution Unigenitus, he forgot all his submission.'[1]

Young Stainville was from way back in his military career significantly affiliated to the two exalted overlords then presiding over important phases of French politics, the Marshal de Noailles and the Prince de Conti. If Noailles had the say in French policy to the south, towards Italy and Spain, not entirely dissimilar was the way in which Conti brooded from high level over French policy to the east, in regard to those German and Polish affairs which Stainville had studiously avoided. Only, whereas Conti conducted the King's Secret behind the back of the foreign minister, Noailles acted as the recognized overseer of his adherent, the Marquis de Saint-Contest. Furthermore both these grandees overtopping ministers were considerably active in internal affairs, in that parliamentary dispute of religious derivation which then beset the government of the distant Louis XV and was now to condition the diplomacy of the thrusting Count de Stainville.

On 27 July 1752 Stainville had written to Bernstorff: 'Our only news is the war between the parliament and the clergy. It is still very

[1] Pope Benedict XIV to Cardinal de Tencin, Rome, 20 Feb. 1754: Benoît-Tencin, ii. 322.

lively, with the parliament not sparing its adversaries. I do not know how it will end. So far the parish priests are the victims.'[2]

France, under strong influences both catholic and intellectual, has almost traditionally been excessively embroiled in internal issues between clericals and their opponents. The eighteenth-century version was now in the latest phase of that long antagonism between leading factions of the law and the church which was to climax in the revolution. After the strife of Machault's clerical twentieth, of the affair of the General Hospital, there had swiftly ensued the graver conflict of the Billets de Confession.

The drive against latter-day Jansenists, 'refractories against the bull Unigenitus'[3] of 1713, by the Molinist clergy had lately been pressed home under the tactless Archbishop Christophe de Beaumont. As the future Choiseul was to recall:

The Archbishop of Paris had bethought him to ordain that the viaticum should be given only to those who presented to their priest a certificate of confession [by a priest obedient to Unigenitus]. This ordinance on his part had two motives: first to prevent priests not approved by him from giving confession in his diocese; secondly, to have absolution refused by approved priests to Jansenists, for then infinitely more Jansenists were obscure [rather than] known. The archbishop ... made of this rebellion [against Unigenitus] a special case which he reserved to himself alone.

If a priest gave absolution to a non-certificated patient 'the archbishop at once withdrew that priest's authority; if he refused it him, he died without receiving the viaticum, which is a harsh extremity for a poor Jansenist. By this conduct the archbishop thought that he had found the real way to persecute Jansenism. I even believe that he had obtained the verbal approval of the king, who had not understood and is not in case to understand the consequence of such a project. The royal family, without understanding it any better, incited by Jesuit confessors to a horror of Jansenism, had exalted the views of such a brave and holy prelate.'

'It was not long', continued Stainville, 'before the archbishop perceived that his project would meet with difficulties ... His system of oppression and inquisition was divulged and contested by the secular tribunals.' The procedure of the so-called Billets de Confession was treated by militant Jansenists as an act of defamation calling for legal redress, notably from the sympathetic Parliament of Paris as the constitutional guardian of civil order. Here the parliament had twice run up against Brother Bouettin, Curé of Saint-Étienne-du-Mont, before the case of Lemaire flared up in March 1752.

[2] Count de Stainville to Baron von Bernstorff, Paris, 27 July 1752: *Bernstorffske Papirer*, ii. 645.
[3] Choiseul, *Mémoires*, pp. 110–11 for the following.

Lemaire, an adherent of the pious Duke of Orleans, was an old Jansenist priest in trouble with his bladder and going gangrenous. The zealous Bouettin refused him the sacraments and he died without them on 28 March. Popular indignation against the treatment of Lemaire produced a demonstration by ten thousand at his funeral. The Parliament of Paris presented a powerful remonstrance to the king and by July, when Stainville wrote, it was ordering the arrest of Brother Bouettin, who fled.

At the end of August 1752 Stainville added to Bernstorff: 'I am not speaking to you of the affairs of the parliament and the clergy, which constitute the general news and which have risen to the highest degree of vivacity. I am afraid that the details of this business would not be approved by the court',[4] inspiring caution in young Stainville through fear of the postal censorship of the Cabinet Noir. In governmental circles Rouillé, of parliamentary origin, was in fact working through President Ogier to moot a mediatory declaration in concert with Joly de Fleury who, observed the elder Stainville, 'passes for the most enlightened magistrate of the century'.[5] Joly de Fleury, along with Trudaine and some others, had recently been appointed to a bipartisan commission to study the question of Billets de Confession under Cardinal de La Rochefoucald. The latter was, for the then Count de Stainville, 'a mild man, noble, simple, a real gentleman'.[6] More sympathetic to Archbishop Beaumont than was wholly helpful, however, was the disappointing Chancellor Lamoignon, who produced a redraft of Rouillé's declaration wherewith the balancing Marshal de Noailles was also concerned.[7] None of this came to much under a king reluctant to give a lead. Meanwhile both sides were mobilizing reinforcements, the Parliament of Paris other parliaments, the Archbishop of Paris other prelates.

Beaumont, remarked the then Stainville, 'believed himself supported by the Court. He maintained his resolve with fierce obstinacy. They set for him snares into which he fell, as will a stubborn man who has not enough intelligence to suit his conduct to circumstances. He refused to give the sacraments. Parliament had them given on its own authority . . . Things became extremely confused',[8] while 'friends

---

[4] Count de Stainville to Baron von Bernstorff, Paris, 29 Aug. 1752: *Bernstorffske Papirer*, ii. 647.

[5] Marquis de Stainville to Emperor Francis I, Paris, 4 June 1752: Esteri del Granducato di Toscana, vol. 2296/1287, no. 94.

[6] Choiseul, *Mémoires*, p. 113.

[7] For particulars of the parliamentary crisis given here and elsewhere I am indebted to the study by J. M. J. Rogister, 'Conflict and Harmony in Eighteenth-Century France: reappraisal of the nature of relations between the Crown and the Parliaments under Louis XV (1730–1771)', *passim*.

[8] Choiseul, *Mémoires*, pp. 111–12 for the following.

of truth' like Stainville's old opponent, the President de Meinières, breached their obligation of discretion by leaking parliamentary proceedings to Jansenist sectaries.

The future Choiseul continued his balanced evaluation of the crisis by criticizing the archbishop for taking such vehement issue 'upon a point of controversy rather than of doctrine, which had already caused infinite trouble in France and upon which there was no hope of winning back' the Jansenists:

> The archbishop should have seen what good society in the kingdom saw, that there would no longer be Jansenists when the Molinists stopped talking about them, and when the bishops, like the government, preserved a contemptuous silence upon the questions of grace, which are a mystery for humanity, and upon the bull Unigenitus, an old product of intrigue and bad faith. Upon its side parliament, where there was a Jansenist party, behaved in the way which the spirit of party always induces when it takes hold of a body. Instead of infusing its deliberations with wisdom, prudence and good example to the people, qualities so worthy of the old magistracy, it injected an indecent precipitancy; it cited, banished vicars and priests ... and seemed to have no more measure in its conduct than the archbishop had had in his. If the confusion between the spiritual and the temporal had occurred two centuries earlier, it could have caused blood to flow.

This cool contempt reflected both the percipience of the author and the triviality, often, of the dispute in its expression, as in a pother of December 1752 over a Jansenist community of Saint Agatha, while in essence it tapped deep and radical currents of opinion. The opening of 1753 found the Parliament of Paris drafting sweeping remonstrances which, thought the Marquis d'Argenson, would prove to be 'a veritable tocsin against the government and a call for the states-general'.[9] After a sight of the document he described it as 'beginning with the definition of authority, liberty and legislation'.[10]

Even the middle years of the reign of Louis XV were richer in constitutional history than is sometimes supposed. Louis XV was aware of this. During the affair of the General Hospital he had nonplussed Chancellor Lamoignon by asking him what were the fundamental laws of the kingdom. When people begin discussing politics in terms of first principles it is time for rulers to watch out.

One day Louis broke out to Madame de Pompadour: 'These [legal] Long Gowns and the clergy are still at daggers drawn. They drive me to despair with their quarrels, but I detest the Long Gowns much the most. My clergy, at bottom, is attached and faithful to me; the others want to put me in tutelage ... The Regent made a big mistake in restoring to them [the parliaments] their right to make remonstrance; they will end by destroying the state.'[11] When Gontaut, who

---

[9] D'Argenson, vii. 379.   [10] Ibid., p. 394.

[11] Madame du Hausset, *Mémoires de Mme du Hausset*, ed. H. Fournier, pp. 36–7 for the following.

had entered, interjected that such 'little shysters' could not do that, the king replied: 'You do not know what they are doing and what they are thinking: it is an assembly of republicans. Still, that is enough of that. Things as they are will last as long as I shall.'

Clear-sighted is what Louis XV regularly was, constructive as regularly not. The ironic comment of the future Choiseul was characteristic. In suggesting that two centuries earlier there would have been bloodshed, he remarked that 'while this idea makes one shiver, we should be sensible of our good fortune in that, being governed by a prince of the tenth century, his enlightenment preserves us from fear of such ills'.[12] The tenth century in France had mainly been one of decadent confusion under the Carolingian epigoni terminating with Louis V, Louis le Fainéant, the do-nothing king. But now Louis XV did do something.

II

From March 1752 to May 1753 the Parliament of Paris was seized of twenty-two major cases involving Jansenism and the clergy of six dioceses, latterly Orleans. The king's growing impatience was liable to reinforce in his council such rigorists as the Count d'Argenson against the moderates in matters parliamentary, Rouillé, Machault, Noailles.

Authority confronted by revolt as often as not finds itself deploying tactically against a strategic onset. On 22 February 1753 Louis XV issued letters-patent evoking from the parliament to the royal council all matters concerning the sacramental dispute. Renewed protests by parliament culminated in its assertion on 5 May that those were precisely the only matters it would deal with while going on strike from its regular duties as courts of law. Next day Noailles himself wrote to the king that in the darkest days under Louis XIV 'I did not see such critical times ... People no longer recognize the rules of propriety and subordination... Everybody is aiming at independence ... Things have reached such a point that it is absolutely necessary to apply the promptest remedies ... Nothing, Sire, is impossible to you when you will it, and will it effectively.'[13]

On the night of 8–9 May 1753 musketeers packed four constitutional ringleaders off to remote fortresses – the Abbé Chauvelin to Mont-Saint-Michel, only his weak chest earned him a typically considerate switch to Caen. Seven chambers of the parliament, nearly

---

[12] Choiseul, *Mémoires*, pp. 112–13.
[13] Marshal de Noailles to King Louis XV, 6 May 1753: Abbé Millot, *Mémoires politiques et militaires*, vi. 317–21.

two hundred lawyers, were exiled in different directions, leaving only the senior Grand' Chambre. In the government some expected that the First President of the parliament, Maupeou the elder, would take the opportunity to offer to conciliate. Instead, that smallminded spokesman told the Grand' Chambre that he regarded its exemption from the unfrightening punishment 'as an insult to our zeal'.[14] This was repaired on 10 May by its relegation to Pontoise, back to the days of the mistaken Regent Orleans.

The Marquis d'Argenson had been making out that the Parliament of Paris 'has won the support of the peers by inviting them to its deliberations. People like Richelieu, the Duke d'Ayen, the Marshal de Noailles ... are today speaking up in favour of the parliament.'[15] If that now applied to Noailles with appreciable reservations, Richelieu, conceivably in concert with Machault, had just forewarned Maupeou of the imminent exile of the Grand' Chambre. Richelieu had become intermediary between Maupeou and the king, partly at least via Madame de Pompadour. Louis, however, scouted these approaches through distrusted Richelieu, and when Maupeou thereafter did submit a plan for a new law of appeasement the king wrote curtly to the duke on 30 May 1753: 'The draft declaration of the first president is worth nothing at all.'[16]

The exile of the Parliament of Paris left about a third of France without its higher court of law and appellate jurisdiction. Clear enough by now was the gravity in that crisis of the issues religious and constitutional, of parliamentary disobedience to the king and of his failure to find an acceptable mean through legislation which might, in particular, assuage the frustration of magistrates by royal letters-patent. All was compounded, too, by bad luck from a combination of personal limitations: Archbishop Beaumont with his crass tactics, Chancellor Lamoignon not the man that his predecessor was, chequered in his earlier career in parliament and often at odds with opinion there, President Maupeou, disingenuously inadequate, tending to sulk at having been overtaken by Lamoignon in the succession to d'Aguessau, at not having been taken earlier into the confidence of the king, himself under some personal handicap.

As the future Choiseul implied, Louis XV was too weak, or wise, to cow the nation by stern repression. Nor, though, was he the man to give his people a ringing call and try to channel new aspirations

---

[14] Cited by Marquis de Stainville to Emperor Francis I, Paris, 13 May 1753: Esteri del Granducato di Toscana, vol. 2296/1287, no. 121.

[15] D'Argenson, viii. 11.

[16] King Louis XV to Duke de Richelieu, 30 May 1753: J. L. G. Soulavie, *Mémoires du Maréchal de Richelieu pour servir à l'histoire de Louis XIV, de la Régence, de Louis XV et des quatorze premières années du règne de Louis XVI* (London etc., 1790–3), viii. 289–90. For acceptance of the authenticity of this letter see J. M. J. Rogister, op. cit., p. 147 and appendix B.

into a happier reconciliation of crown and constitution – that residual constitution of royal France which lawyers were then reviving in men's minds. Instead, the king gave limited expression to his understandable displeasure and, in his elevated way, hoped that the legal troublemakers could be brought to see sense. Both for good and for ill Louis XV rode trouble with slackened rein, though that was hardly the immediate impression since parliament after all remained in exile.

Provincial exile was, like all travel then, expensive but the magistrates soon ensconced themselves snugly enough, the chief Zélés in their cause at Bourges. There the sympathetic Intendant Dodart urged the influential President de Meinières to relax his righteous indignation in a social round wherein the richer entertained the poorer to repasts of a lavishness that passed into local legend. The chief sufferers were the litigants and dealers left in Paris without the necessary framework for their affairs. In places, though, the capital was spattered with leaflets proclaiming 'Long live the parliament! Death to the king and bishops.'[17] The Marquis d'Argenson observed that 'people look upon the disgrace of the parliament as the last bludgeon-blow against the little national liberty which remained'. In a premonitory phrase he described the exiled magistrates as 'the senators of France'.[18]

By 22 June 1753, however, the Count de Stainville was writing with characteristic optimism: 'They say that the business of the parliament will be accommodated a week hence. It is the Prince de Conti who is at the head of the negotiation.'[19] Some days earlier the writer's father had specified that 'the Prince de Conti being the sole intermediary between the king and his parliament, even the ministers are no longer taking a hand in it'.[20] Though Conti had conferred with most of them earlier that month, and probably kept in touch with some.

The Count de Stainville's old patron was, like many intelligent princes, keen to do something or other striking to benefit king and country and his standing with them both. At the beginning of that year Conti had already weighed in and involved Rouillé in a sensible but premature proposal for a law of silence to blanket the bother. This proposal Conti now sought to revive in pourparlers with Maupeou whom he had gone to meet while still on the way to

[17] D'Argenson, viii. 35, and for the following.
[18] Ibid., p. 81.
[19] Count de Stainville to Baron von Bernstorff, Paris, 22 June 1753: *Bernstorffske Papirer*, ii. 650.
[20] Marquis de Stainville to Emperor Francis I, Paris, 17 June 1753: Esteri del Granducato di Toscana, vol. 2296/1287, no. 125.

Pontoise, where the president lodged in Conti's Maison de Saint-Martin. They would put their heads together on Conti's estate at Vauréal down river from Pontoise, not far from l'Isle-Adam. The prince was said to be still under the influence of Stainville's old detractor, the Jesuit Father Latour, though some made out that this busy priest was actually tacking against the Molinists. On the other side Maupeou could call upon his slim son, that legal Maupeou who was to become a prime antagonist of the future Choiseul. The elder Maupeou seems to have impressed Conti unfavourably by the unhelpful attitude which he maintained in solidarity still with the hard-liners at Bourges, with whom Conti was also in uncertain touch through the Joly de Fleurys. By mid-July young Stainville was writing again: 'There is hardly any talk still of the parliament. The business is lasting too long for it to be capable of occupying the public. I believe however that it is ready to finish.'[21] It did not.

The Prince de Conti continued through that hot summer to be parliamentarily active by stops and starts against a background of shooting with Maupeou at l'Isle-Adam, of river-parties with the ladies and fireworks at Vauréal. Nothing came of Conti's contacts with the unpopular President Chauvelin who concerted with his uncle, the ever-exiled erstwhile foreign minister, nor of consultations with another protege of Machault, also of Madame de Pompadour, Counsellor Louis Salabéry. A main factor, as so often, in keeping things in suspense was probably the indecision of the king himself. On 1 August 1753 he sent the Marshal de Noailles a questionary as to the likely value of a law of silence, and modalities for applying it. Even in midsummer the highest nobility of France might then have other employment than idling around at court. This is also worth contrasting with the course of French history just a century earlier.

The summer of 1653 had been the first in the aftermath of the Fronde, the beginning of the long stretch towards the personal autocracy of King Louis XIV in his resolve henceforth to scale down his frivolously factious nobility. If the First Fronde had been unleashed by Mazarin's imprisonment of Broussel, worthy protagonist of the Parliament of Paris in the constitutional conflict whereof the issue now of the Billets de Confession was but the latest phase, the Second Fronde had sprung from Mazarin's imprisonment of Conti's forbears, the great Condé and his brother Conti. They had led the nobility of the sword, in flimsy alliance with the nobility of the robe and the future Cardinal de Retz, upon the rampage against the royal authority: whereas Condé's lesser descendant was now laboriously if

[21] Count de Stainville to Baron von Bernstorff, Paris, 16 July 1753: u.s. p. 652.

vainly trying to assuage both parliament and church beneath the French crown.

In this larger view even the form of the crisis of 1753 registered a notable advance in France of the royal authority, as in the sidelong admission of the future Choiseul in relegating the danger now of wars of religion. If Louis XIV had learnt his constitutional lesson under the regency of Anne of Austria, Louis XV had learnt his under the regency of the Duke of Orleans. This time, though, they were largely negative lessons for a negative monarch, almost suggesting that soon his continued success in weaning the nobility away from popular Paris to royal Versailles might be becoming too complete, a negative success. Such were the slow and subtle dangers already menacing the throne of Louis XV. Nor did they escape that historically perceptive prince.

III

An immediate danger in that summer of 1753 was that the dispersed Parliament of Paris would radiate sparks throughout the kingdom, as it had indeed begun to do. The turbulent parliament of Rennes had needed little prompting to follow Parisian fashion over a refusal of sacraments to a Jansenist in the diocese of Nantes. The parliaments at Bordeaux and at Toulouse likewise took issue with priests while that of Aix ran up against the Bishop of Sisteron. At Rouen the parliament was actually trying to fine the Bishop of Evreux six thousand livres for insisting upon Billets de Confession. The parliament defiantly sought to distrain on the bishop till a royal commissioner constrained the first president to knuckle under while local opinion was duly outraged. It was really rather an enjoyable commotion. By 19 August 1753 the Count de Stainville could succinctly inform Baron von Bernstorff: 'There is no more talk of the Parliament of Paris; that of Rouen has resumed its functions.'[22]

A settlement might have been expected by 7 September, failing which the Parliament of Paris was liable to break up for its two-month vacation without appointing the usual Chambre des Vacations to carry on current business. Somewhat to the surprise of parliamentarians they were allowed to do just that. The king then appointed a special commission of lawyers to act in the stead of a vacational chamber. This produced a fresh crop of wearisome legalisms in dispute with the lower instance of Parisian jurisdiction, the still

[22] Count de Stainville to Baron von Bernstorff, Paris, 19 Aug. 1753: *Bernstorffske Papirer*, ii. 653.

functioning Châtelet. At the end of the vacation the recalcitrant Grand' Chambre under Maupeou was further exiled to Soissons and ceased all its functions. The crisis deepened. On 11 November 1753 Louis in turn replaced the parliament by a special court, the Chambre Royale comprising eighteen counsellors of state and twice as many Maîtres des Requêtes. A month later Pope Benedict XIV was writing to the Cardinal de Tencin: 'We cannot find words enough to extol the great stroke which His Most Christian Majesty has effected in establishing a Royal Chamber to dispense justice to those who need it ... His Majesty's letters patent ... should indeed make the [parliamentary] rebels blush if they have an ounce of shame in their hearts.'[23]

Such was the tension of constitutional conflict which was to condition the embassy to Rome of the newly appointed Count de Stainville. The crisis, it is now clear, had been notably involving three of his chief protectors, past or present, Conti, Noailles, Madame de Pompadour herself, not to mention Rouillé, soon the foreign minister instructing Stainville for Rome, and the latter's legal acquaintances such as the controversial Abbé de Chauvelin and the count's friend and foe from his wife's lawsuit, respectively the presidents Ogier and de Meinières. Of these figures in Stainville's circle those who were not committed to parliamentary pretensions against the government were yet liable to take a comparatively balanced view of them in general keeping with the fairly evenhanded disdain with which he was subsequently to describe the crisis. Contemporary allusions to it in Stainville's correspondence were usually brief and cheerfully noncommittal – something in itself from the person who from the ecclesiastical end, rather than Conti from the parliamentary, was now to play a leading part in eliminating the Billets de Confession from that parliamentary and religious strife whose later crosscurrents were yet to influence importantly the administration of the future Duke de Choiseul.

IV

The preparation of the Count de Stainville for his embassy to Rome transcended the run of practical arrangements and diplomatic questions owing to the domestic crisis which then gripped France. The exile of the Parliament of Paris arising from the controversy over Billets de Confession involved issues that were not only legal,

[23] Pope Benedict XIV to Cardinal de Tencin, Rome, 12 Dec. 1753: Benoît-Tencin, ii. 309.

constitutional but also religious, ideological. The latter especially
were revealing of Stainville's outlook even though there was yet far
to go before ideological implications for politics were projected to, or
beyond, their term by such as Jean-Jacques Rousseau in his *Contrat
social*. The Marquis d'Argenson, indeed, had already written two
years earlier: 'A philosophic wind of free and antimonarchical
government is blowing over to us from England. It enters people's
minds and one knows how opinion rules the world . . . Every class is
discontented at once.'[24] For the present, however, Rousseau was
perhaps to exaggerate rather less than might be supposed in claiming
that in the parliamentary confrontation at the end of 1753 he had
possibly prevented a revolution by diverting public attention into the
frivolous furore over his *Lettre sur la musique française* – another topic
of special interest to the Count de Stainville.

Rousseau's untutored genius embraced music more than is always
remembered. He had failed to win over the French Academy of
Science, so early as 1742, to his new system of musical notation by
figure; but he copied music for a living and had scored a notable
success with his artless opera, *Le Devin du village,* performed at
Fontainebleau in 1752. This did not prevent Rousseau now from
savaging all French music in an onslaught which, following his often
unattractive motivation, largely derived from the feud that he was
pursuing against Rameau with the venom of a disciple scorned by his
master. The immediate context was the Guerre des Buffons bubbling
up from the limpid lightness of Italian music as recently revealed to
Paris in Pergolesi's *La Serva Padrona* and other Opera Buffa
performed by Manelli's visiting troupe. It provoked vehement attack
by adherents of more traditional French modulations so as to bring
what Stainville had termed 'the sect of the old Lullists' together, even,
with the rival Ramoneurs.

Counterattacking with typical exaggeration, Rousseau in his *Lettre
sur la musique française* pronounced that 'the French have no music
and can have none',[25] their singing a continual barking, their
orchestras too loud, their ballets conventional. There was, however,
a smack of truth in his plea for a more modern and less artificial
lyricism following through from Rousseau's earlier attack in his
Discours sur les sciences et les arts against their corrupting influence in
promoting high civilization. 'The taste for display is hardly to be
associated in the same souls with that for honesty. No, it is not
possible that spirits degraded by a multitude of futile cares can ever

[24] D'Argenson, vi. 464.
[25] J.-J. Rousseau, *Lettre sur la musique française* cited in this translation by S. Baud-Bovy,
'Rousseau as a musician' in *The Times Literary Supplement,* no. 3724, p. 830.

rise to anything great; and if they should have the strength to do it, their courage would fail them.'[26] Such, perhaps, was rather the inward challenge of that society to the Count de Stainville.

Four years before Rousseau's musical polemic Stainville, ever in the van artistically and otherwise, had, as noticed, registered that Italian music was daily gaining ground in Paris and had boldly suggested that *Linus* be set to music in Rome if one could not get admired Rameau. For the present the count may well have been laughing along with his father's diplomatic associate, Mareschal, over Rousseau's stoking of the furore over the 'question of either sending the Italian Buffons away or renewing their expired contract. The Duke de Gesvres and the Prévôt des Marchands do not dare to take either course on their own account. The matter will be debated in the Royal Council and decided by His Majesty.'[27] Even moderate opinion in Paris, explained Mareschal's musical bulletin, was 'vexed that there is no rational reply to this letter, [so that they] blame its author for delivering them from an error which they cherished, and say that he is an outrageous cynic, a misanthrope who ought to be banished from society. In short nothing is more laughable than everything one hears said about it, and with all that perhaps he will be a divine, adorable, charming man, etcetera, if the Buffons stay in Paris.' They did not, though.

If the Count de Stainville, set for Rome, was heading into the musical swim, intellectually the eternal city was already becoming a citadel under siege.

Since the coincidental Peace of Aix-la-Chapelle and *L'Esprit des lois*, opinion in France had been working up a new intensity of criticism against the government in an aftermath of economic distress, against the king in his expensive love of Madame de Pompadour, against the church in its fiscal privilege and factional strife of the Billets de Confession.

If *L'Esprit des lois* was anything but revolutionary, behind it lurked *Les lettres persanes* mocking the order which the Great Monarch had exalted. Young Montesquieu had preached the eighteenth-century creed of sociability, of that brand of benevolent activity (*bienfaisance*) minted by the Abbé de Saint-Pierre on behalf of another exciting new word, of humanity itself. This new order of human solidarity was ominously liable to turn established values topsy-turvy with speculation upon divorce and the marriage of priests, with 'valets

---

[26] J.-J. Rousseau, *Discours sur les sciences et les arts: Œuvres complètes de Jean-Jacques Rousseau*, ed. Bernard Gagnebin and Marcel Raymond (Paris, 1966–9), iii. 20.
[27] Mareschal to Count Kaunitz, Paris, 2 Dec. 1753: O.S./H.H.S., Frankreich/Berichte (1753), docket 141, and for the following.

being served by their comrades, and tomorrow perhaps by their masters'.[28]

Now, more soberly in *L'Esprit des lois*, the admirer of the Countess de Stainville looked across to the republican virtues of antiquity, the idealized merits of the English constitution in his sweep of geographical and historical relativity. Institutions and the laws which governed them were to be judged by utilitarian standards of adequacy and success in relation to their several environments and climates of opinion. That called for rational evaluation. This was the built-in challenge of Montesquieu against the Ancien Régime, still resting upon the prescribed absolutes of authority, both monarchical and, behind that again, ecclesiastical, the imposed authority of an irrational faith, of catholicism, of christianity itself.

V

In 1751 the new challenge had become more articulate in the publication of the first volume of the great Encyclopedia edited by leading philosophs of the enlightenment, Diderot and d'Alembert. Once again the challenge was veiled in forms of outward respect. In this significantly subtitled 'dictionnaire raisonné' the respect, though, was ironically inflected, the veil sometimes twitched aside a moment in some disturbing entry, Agnus scytichus, Aigle, Amentès, Bramines.

The battle for the minds of men in France was now engaged even if, tactically, the rationalist assailants still had to resort to what d'Alembert called 'semi-attacks, this kind of underhand war'.[29] For the next twenty years, the remainder of the active career of the then Count de Stainville, volume after volume of the Encyclopedia would be driving home its challenge to the old order in France, in Europe, authoritative, catholic, obedient to church and king, in favour of the new and seemingly sunnier creed of rationalism, free thought and toleration under the sign of the supposed perfectibility of man. Such was the developing and optimistic background of ideas to the political emergence of the Duke de Choiseul. Only, none could tell where it would all end. Because only expediency, not logic, could set a term to the human questioning of established authority. In this sense the enlightenment formed a sequel to the reformation such that the events of 1517 were to find their projection in those of 1789.

Another French publication in 1751, less remembered if hardly

---

[28] Montesquieu, *Les Lettres persanes*, p. 279 in *Œuvres complètes de Montesquieu*, ed. A. Masson, vol. i.

[29] Cited, Daniel Mornet, *Les Origines intellectuelles de la Révolution française* (4th ed. Paris, 1947), p. 78.

less indicative, was the considerably successful *Considérations sur les moeurs de ce siècle* by Duclos, now the historiographer royal, later the detractor of the Count de Stainville's youth. The author may have sensed that the count's admiration was modified. Stainville's reading was characteristically up to date. On 7 March 1751 he had written to Nivernais in Rome:

Duclos will doubtless have sent you his book. It seems to me that there is plenty of intelligence in it and a very laudable morality, but it does not make me fond of it. I find the work very dry and heavy going. It does not address the heart. I find its discussion so abstract, so devoid of charm. Its tone is so dogmatic, so trenchant that I confess that I was very glad when I had finished it. It could be my fault or that of my vapourish condition, but it stretched my mind more than it enlightened it. I applauded very nice distinctions but nothing has stayed with me, and I do not find myself rewarded for the pains I took to understand it.[30]

The *Considérations sur les moeurs de ce siècle* began: 'Before speaking of morals, let us begin by determining the different ideas that are attached to this term; for far from having synonyms it allows of several senses.'[31] And so it went on from there. Dry and epigrammatic is what Charles Duclos was, drawing such nice distinctions as: 'Policed peoples are worth more than polite peoples'[32] – typical of contemporary enthusiasm for civilized curbing of old violence – or, more suggestively, 'religion is the perfection and not the basis of morality'.[33]

Such now was the suave if minatory progression, in a work dedicated to Louis XV ('the hero and pacificator of Europe'),[34] from cartesian sapping of the achievement of Louis XIV, the Sun King who had almost given a new inflection to the renaissance formula of *cujus regio ejus religio,* in the sense not merely of the religion which the prince professed, but that which he personified. Whereas Descartes had provided an intellectual alternative to religious orthodoxy, logically sanctioning appeals against traditional faith and authority to the dread tribunal of reason, there in the thinking of a mere individual. If in the seventeenth century the freethinking school of the Libertines had often turned more to seductive instinct than to rigid intellect, they could look back to still earlier sceptics from the renaissance such as Rabelais and Montaigne. Their disciples were La Fare with his sensual *Béatitudes de ce monde,* Chaulieu, the epicurean Saint-Évremond, witty opponent of hypocrisy and advocate of toleration. Toleration and freedom, of thought at all events,

[30] Count de Stainville to Duke de Nivernais, 7 Mar. 1751: W.N.A., docket V/1, fo. 51.
[31] C. P. Duclos, *Considérations sur les moeurs de ce siècle* in *Œuvres complètes de Duclos* (Paris, 1806), i. 66.
[32] Ibid., p. 70.   [33] Ibid., p. 109.   [34] Ibid., p. 61.

had been central for Pierre Bayle with his protestant background. He relentlessly applied cartesian method if not theory in his appeal to rational observation, daring to subject faith to cool appraisal and sly comparison, shewing the philosophs the way to undermine the establishment. Bayle's formidable hodgepodge of 1697, the *Diction-naire historique et critique*, had led towards the Encyclopedia of 1751.

Cartesian also was the other leading popularizer of rationalism in France, the sprightlier Fontenelle, then over ninety. Furthering the good work of religious emancipation, he had also led the attack upon dry-as-dust history and stepped ahead from the renaissance revival of classicism, still preponderant in the eighteenth century, towards philosophic modernism. In proclaiming that time was on the side of the angels, tilting the balance in favour of the higher development of modern man, Fontenelle had helped launch the eighteenth century upon its master-themes of human progress and perfectibility. No longer was man to bow down to the wisdom of the ages. Secularized, he should brace himself in optimistic endeavour towards a kinder and more rational future. By 1751 the critical Count de Stainville was reading Duclos's pronouncement on men: 'To render them better, they only need to be enlightened: crime is always a wrong judgement. That is the whole science of morality.'[35] If only it were.

One of Fontenelle's modernist arguments had been drawn from the uniformity of nature, asking whether the trees of antiquity were larger than those of today, already preparing the way for a philosophy of materialism. Fontenelle, inciting scientific curiosity, had speeded the intellectual advance in France from Descartes to Newton in that debate between about 1715 and 1740 wherein Voltaire had notably contributed to the belated victory of gravitation over vortices. If Fontenelle had rather balanced between them he rejoiced that Newton had 'overturned that immense celestial edifice which we might have thought immovable'.[36] Thus did Fontenelle, the early author of the allegorical *Relation de l'île de Bornéo* in comparative religion, span three of the main directions in which the French enlightenment reached out towards new frontiers of thought – to protestant England, out again overseas to realms of the noble savage and wise aborigines, and on ahead to new worlds of science. All three directions were, in more political and practical contexts, to engage the particular concern of the future Choiseul.

The headstrong English were for contemporaries exemplars of unrest, what with their reformation in the sixteenth century, and in

[35] Ibid., p. 69.
[36] Fontenelle, cited in this translation, Kingsley Martin, *French Liberal Thought in the Eighteenth Century* (2nd ed. London, 1954), p. 45.

the seventeenth that Great Rebellion which had succeeded where the Fronde had failed. The essentials of the Great Rebellion had been largely clinched in the Glorious Revolution of 1688, itself matched by the liberal philosophy of John Locke. His *Essay concerning Human Understanding* (1690) provided the enlightenment with its psychological credo. A human inheritance of innate ideas and religious guilt was rejected in favour of the data of sensory experience, of environmental factors organized through the principle of association. This psychology of human rationalism offered a scientific basis under natural law for individual responsibility and democratic government by parliamentary consent, for liberal toleration and reasonable christianity. Divine revelation only had to be hollowed out and the way lay open for the deism of Tindal or Toland, the natural religion of Clarke whose *Discourse concerning the Being and Attributes of God* was translated into French in 1727, the year after the translation of Wollaston's *Religion of Nature*. Locke's own treatise on *Civil Government* had been done into French in 1724 and he was soon to be available to Madame de Graffigny even out at Demange.

Soon, indeed, French authors were surpassing moderate deism from pragmatic England, and so early as 1722–3 the fierce testament of Curé Meslier had begun to take shape. In his grim materialism man was already a human machine and his God 'a monster of unreason, injustice, malice and atrocity'.[37] Meslier wanted all ruling tyrants to be 'hung by the guts of priests'.[38] In that dark heart revolution had already arrived. This shocking stuff circulated only in manuscript, though Voltaire claimed to have seen over a hundred copies and it sold for stiff prices up to ten louis each. Much more to popular taste of the time was the remote radicalism of the successors since the last quarter of the seventeenth century to that Utopia bred of the renaissance. By 1732 there had been five editions of Gabriel de Foigny's *La Terre australe connue*, whose Australians practised primitive communism. Fontenelle had already made his philosophic excursion to Borneo and Montesquieu had swung the indirect critique nearer home in the *Lettres persanes*, precursors of so many, including the *Lettres péruviennes* and, more popular and influential, those of the Marquis d'Argens, churning out his *Lettres juives*, *Lettres cabalistiques*, *Lettres chinoises*, and the programmatic *Philosophie du bon sens*.

Cosmopolitanism proclaimed the enlightenment. Since the Abbé de Saint-Pierre, international peace to promote the arts and bourgeois prosperity was increasingly becoming the ideal in place of the noble

[37] Cited, Alfred Cobban, *A History of Modern France* (3rd ed. London, 1963), i. 85.
[38] Cited, D. Mornet, op. cit., p. 28.

elevation of war and the happy warrior, still exalted however by such a rare spirit as Vauvenargues. If cosmopolitanism connoted a certain shallowness, rather few of the philosophs were strictly philosophers. Mostly they were literary intellectuals eagerly disseminating a rational outlook on society, a framework of reference increasingly human rather than divine. They indulged in a luxury of criticism which came to carry a suggestion that in politics it was almost more blessed to argue than to obey. Yet was it in more senses than one that the philosophs sought to transform western society from being theocentric into one that was geocentric. They were helping to give that society a new setting not only in extent, culturally, but also in depth, scientifically. Montesquieu himself had by 1720 read papers to the Academy of Bordeaux on echo, transparency, flux.

In the eighteenth century scientific knowledge advanced along with geographical exploration, and for French science it was a time of burgeoning. The age which found the terrestial sphere flattened by Maupertuis saw Clairaut thrusting out in geometry, Romé de Lisle in crystallography, with Peyssonel discovering the animal nature of coral in 1723, in 1750 the Abbé Lacaille down at the Cape of Good Hope mapping the heavens of the southern hemisphere. Seven years earlier d'Alembert had initiated a general theory of mechanics in his *Traité de dynamique*, while the natural sciences blossomed with great names, Réaumur, Buffon. This scientific achievement of, largely, the French bourgeoisie is less often recalled than its economic and political ascent. Yet this exciting expansion of knowledge made new the world of the philosophs in a literal as well as a literary sense.

The second quarter of the eighteenth century had multiplied learned academies across the provinces of France upon the models of Bordeaux and Rouen, from Orleans in 1725 to Clermont-Ferrand in 1747 and thenceforth with gathering impetus, also with increasing shift of emphasis from literary to scientific subjects. This shift aroused protest from classicists in the Académie des Belles Lettres in 1751 and some regret in Voltaire. Science, however, came to include the human sciences, leading through to 'natural philosophy' under the sign of Buffon's *Histoire naturelle de l'homme*, the landmark from 1749.

Buffon, botanist to Louis XV, was not merely typed as a philosoph. Like Montesquieu, that other special intelligence, Buffon was something more in the expanding effect of his comparative method. For him the earth was to be studied in the vaster context of the universe, man in that of all animal creation and in novel perspective natural to one for whom, already almost, the medium was the message (*'le style est l'homme même'*). With 'Wild Animals' as the heading Buffon turned round to observe that 'in countrysides where men have spread, terror seems to dwell with them; there is no more society among the animals, all industry ceases, all art is stifled'.[39] This striking inversion of the strict subordination of animals to man in most catholic thinking came from one reaching out towards the transformation of species. Man was already being brought closer to the apes than to angels. The seeming contradiction of the book of Genesis scandalized the Sorbonne. In 1751 Buffon published a declaration of respect for Holy Writ and the Sorbonne, and of course the latter was always right about the former. Only he did not actually alter anything. It was a gently ominous intimation of a growing separation of powers no less important than that preached by Montesquieu. Even in catholic lands the church would increasingly have to learn not only to render unto Caesar as politically appropriate but also to acknowledge the claims of science in an expanding sphere.

In the *Lettre sur les aveugles,* published in the same year as the first volume of the *Histoire naturelle,* Diderot won towards a theory of evolution by way of natural selection. It cost him three months in prison. This great assimilator also pushed out beyond Buffon in the direction of a mechanistic determination of the world and La Mettrie's *L'Homme machine* (1748) as a combination of particles, with thought as a kind of molecular motion, merely a modification of matter, with ideas deriving from the senses. Out ahead again lay the materialism of Helvétius and, still more, Holbach.

The new religion would be as natural, and as rational, as thought itself. Gluttonous La Mettrie's manifesto had crudely preached pleasure as the object of human existence, while subtler epicureans looked to natural law, originally of stoic inspiration. Since the days of Newton and Locke natural law had become truly scientific, the rational rock of truth 'upon which', explained Voltaire, 'all religion is founded'.[40] The seminal year of 1748 had further produced one of the most popular of all expositions of 'natural religion' in the second-rate *Moeurs* by Diderot's friend, F. V. Toussaint. This apostle of humane happiness wanted his teaching to be as relevant for a Mahometan as for a Christian. The horrid book was solemnly burnt by order of the Parliament of Paris, was of course what everyone wanted to read. It was hostile to religious humility, penance, mortification, celibacy, indissoluble marriage, eternal damnation, nay, even judicial execution. The place of christianity in a happier world here below was

[39] Buffon, *Histoire naturelle de l'homme,* 'Des Animaux sauvages': cited, Philippe Sagnac, *La Formation de la société française moderne* (Paris, 1945–6), ii. 81.

[40] Voltaire, trans. in Carl L. Becker, *The Heavenly City of the Eighteenth-Century Philosophers* (New Haven, 1932), p. 52.

becoming questionable indeed. As Diderot gloated, bombs were beginning to rain down upon the house of the Lord.

Such was the apt spread in France of an epicurean philosophy behind the delicious facade of the age of the rococo. Mostly, though, this did represent some advance from pure hedonism in the renaissance. That of the rococo was, ideally at least, epicurean not only in pleasure but also in virtue: as exemplified in the great Encyclopedia, in the article *Bonheur*, again suggesting the overlap between the contrasting schools of old, bowing towards the stoic spirit of Vauvenargues, of those Stoics themselves whom Montesquieu praised: 'born for society, they all believed that their destiny was to work for it.'[41] And the Count de Stainville was to read in his other literary acquaintance, Duclos, that men should be educated 'for one another ... so that they are accustomed to seek their personal advantage upon the level of the general good'[42] – the platonic ideal refurbished.

VI

By the time that the Count de Stainville was preparing his mission to the Roman citadel of catholic faith most leading intellectuals in France were deists or atheists. Already, too, some progression from one to the other was beginning to modify the movement of the enlightenment. Deists looking to natural law were liable to be overtaken by atheist champions of utility.[43] The Abbé de Saint-Pierre himself had been an early utilitarian for ever thinking up eudemonic projects of practical advantage, for a patent armchair, 'for making roads passable in winter', and then his prime wheeze 'for making peace perpetual in Europe'.[44] But if the early enlightenment in the first half of the century had been mainly a moral movement in terms of religion, against revealed christianity, the political implications were as yet barely emergent. Philosophs might be heading towards a modern paganism but they remained monarchists and, at that, mainly in favour of authoritative monarchy on the French model of benevolent despotism rather than of any full development of parliamentary government. If Montesquieu defended parliaments against the king, Voltaire was to come to do the opposite.

The regency had indeed revived the constitutional pretensions of peers and parliaments, and Mably's *Parallèle des Romains et des*

41 Montesquieu, *L'Esprit des lois*, ii. 90 in *Œuvres complètes de Montesquieu*, vol. i.
42 C. P. Duclos, op. cit., p. 78.
43 Cf. Peter Gay, *The Enlightenment: An Interpretation: The Rise of Modern Paganism* (English ed. London, 1967), p. 18.
44 Cf. trans. in C. L. Becker, op. cit., pp. 39–40.

Français of 1740 had trimmed monarchical positions in conformity with 'fundamental laws'. But if Mably could be considered a precursor of socialism and Morelly's *Basiliade* of 1753 preached nothing less than communism, nobody then really took it very seriously. Next year the Abbé Barral in his *Manuel des Souverains* warned against 'the despotism of the multitude' even if he did also proclaim that 'the tyrannical despotism of sovereigns is an infringement of the rights of human fraternity'.[45] Such high-flown phrases might wing their way into the future but their context as yet was not that of comprehensive programmes for political reform but rather a vague aspiration towards the millennium of happy humanity, towards perfecting the improved present into a golden future for that shining concept of the enlightenment, for posterity regenerate. The philosphs brought the golden age up to date, transposing it from the past into the future.

The philosophic emphasis upon the future was critical in more senses than one. It often happens in a creed that its central tenets are precisely pointers to its cental flaw. In the splendid achievement of the enlightenment there were mainly two.

The enlightenment was in its very name an optimistic movement of thought. In the earlier part of the eighteenth century, certainly, optimism was primed by a glad sense of rational release from an oppressively theological outlook which, in the sign of human inadequacy and imperfection, despite Jesuit pliancy and ornamentation, had been rendered, where not forbidding, then largely melancholic. Deism renewed hope. Leibniz and Wolff gave philosophic form to the trust of Fénelon and of Pope that whatever is, is right, all somehow for the best. This providentialism easily degenerated into the vapid lore of Nieuwentyt or Pluche, making tides exist in order to bring ships into harbour, and suchlike facile comfortings.[46] Voltaire, while retaining a basic optimism, came to react against its simplified creed, notably in his classic take-off of human nature in *Candide*, grim and gay. Within a few years now *Candide*, for all its lasting sparkle, was to reveal the central flaw in that philosophic school of thought which led out towards democracy and so much else besides. While the new faith in the perfectibility of man may have redressed the previous balance of religion to a desirable extent, the question remained, just to what extent. If optimism about human nature was indeed correct, it was yet precariously so. If original sin could be rationally washed out, yet something very like it, that old Adam in man was not so easily got rid of. That was what Rousseau uneasily sensed, so that his prescriptions for democracy were to acquire an ominously authoritarian ring. Another looming figure in

[45] Cited, D. Mornet, op. cit., p. 115.   [46] Cf. ibid., p. 30.

his own way would be the Marquis de Sade. In him the French eighteenth century itself exemplified the darker forces of nature in newly conscious and sophisticated forms. Such forces did not escape the Count de Stainville and were indeed to distance him from his king. As the later Choiseul was to put it concisely to Voltaire: 'Terror is a horrible pleasure.'[47] And, as Hume came to confess, the age-old problem of evil in this world remained unsubdued by the enlightenment.

The philosophs were increasingly led to thin out their optimism from the present into the future. Complacency in that largely static society was to give way to a gathering urge for change. The perfectibility of human nature presented a challenge in terms of education for progress, the master-theme for democrats ever since. The millennium for posterity became the lay goal over the horizon. As Diderot was to put it, 'posterity for the philosopher is what the other world is for a religious man.'[48] Only, that was to reintroduce faith by the back door, or rather by the front door on to the future. This was the second critical flaw in the philosophic movement, following on from the first.

The strictly scientific rationalization of human nature upon principles of Newtonian certainty was somehow not quite working out. And as the intellectual hold threatened to become more precarious, that of the emotions tightened. If religious feeling was fading, and it was so only partially, the void swiftly began to fill with a lay sentimentality. It has been suggested[49] that by about 1750 in France the man of sense was becoming the man of sentiment – considerably true of the Count de Stainville. On the philanthropic side masonic lodges had been mushrooming in France since the seventeen-thirties. In literature delicate Marivaux, the Abbé Prévost and Marquis de Vauvenargues, for whom nature had a single soul to inspire social responsibility, led on towards Rousseau, the apostle of the general will and emotional sensibility.

The sentimental strain did sweeten life in France as elsewhere, tending to make educated men and women somewhat kinder and gentler than their forbears. Emotion, though, exacts its price. A repetition of its cycle within the catholic church was already threatening outside it. Among the exciting and admirable discoveries of the enlightenment that of toleration had been the cental stab at the catholic church whose traditional authoritarianism and intolerence

---

[47] Duke de Choiseul to Voltaire, Versailles, 11 Apr, 1762: P. Calmettes, *Choiseul et Voltaire*, p. 147.
[48] Diderot to Falconet, Feb. 1766: *Œuvres complètes de Diderot*, ed. J. Assézat and Maurice Tourneux (Paris, 1875–7), xviii. 101.
[49] Cf. C. L. Becker, op. cit., p. 41.

had so largely overlaid the consoling beauties of christianity and subjected them to rationalist counter-attack. Yet the philosophs were anything but dispassionate philosophers. Their contempt for metaphysics usually matched their respect for science. They were crusaders against the crusades of yore, propagandists to twist religion inside out in favour of the new enthusiasm. Certain that they were right and – so exciting – on the winning side, the philosophs soon set up a howl of righteous indignation against anyone daring to stand out against them, against Palissot and above all Fréron, the impressively independent editor of *L'Année littéraire*. He was to ask: 'Is not the fanaticism of your irreligion more absurd and more dangerous that the fanaticism of superstition? Begin, then, yourselves by tolerating the faith of your fathers. You talk of nothing but tolerance, and never was a sect more intolerant.'[50]

The reaction against the philosophs, such as it was, mostly, however, lay a little ahead, along with the patronage of Palissot by the future Choiseul and his mistress, the Princess de Robecq. Choiseul too was to defend against the venom of Voltaire his erstwhile schoolmate, Fréron, who proclaimed: 'As for me, I belong to no cabal of wits, to no party unless it be that of religion, of morals, and of honesty.'[51] Such an attitude of fearless criticism, far from coldhearted yet confidently aloof, hence potentially unpopular, was largely that of the then Count de Stainville himself. This was already discernible in his critique of Voltaire's *Siècle de Louis XIV*.

VII

Soft and sentimental ideologies of humanitarian intent tend to appeal in epochs of weakness and decline. The flaws of the enlightenment were embedded in the circumstance that while the philosophs were doing their best to render the reign of Louis XV unlike that of Louis XIV, yet for so many contemporaries the age of the great-grandson represented a sad decline, psychologically if not economically, from the great days of the Great Monarch. The optimistic thrust of the enlightenment in France was in part a reassurance and reaction against this prevalent sense of loss and declension. A number, indeed, pushed this loss further back, to Charlemagne in the case of Mably. According to him France had somehow let slip the admirable constitution which she had then enjoyed.

---

[50] Fréron, Paris, 3 Jan. 1768: *L'Année littéraire: année MDCCLXVIII* (Amsterdam, 1768), i. 19.

[51] Fréron, cited, Kingsly Martin, op. cit., p. 96.

The old order of the greatest Louis of France had been new enough in its day, a fact of long significance for the eighteenth century. It is arguable that the two chief introducers and interpreters of the magnification of monarchy under the Sun King had been Bossuet, the catholic apologist of absolute monarchy for whom the king was a very god, and Colbert who had imposed a modern administration upon a feudal framework. In both instances the new achievement was, or threatened to be, at the expense of gallican liberties of old. The gradual failures of the achievements both of Boussuet and of Colbert were the warp and woof of the internal history of eighteenth-century France.

If in France the enlightenment had been eating away the concept of theocentric government and its relegation of political or social amelioration within a prescribed vale of tears, the very efficiency of the great administrative achievement since Colbert carried its own subtle dangers. Even a modern authority, critical of Colbert's reforms and especially of his promotion of the financial sway of the controller-general at the expense of the legal one of the chancellor, has deduced from the reign of Louis XV that the administrative monarchy killed the monarchy.[52] Nor was it only the king who stood to lose, as contemporaries appreciated. There in Duclos's *Considérations sur les moeurs de ce siècle* it was already written for the Count de Stainville to read in 1751: '*Grand Seigneur* is a word whereof the reality no longer exists except in history'[53] – and again: 'The credit of the greatest lord is a long way from that of the least minister, often even of a chief clerk.' That was one aspect of the challenge to young Stainville, already something of a great nobleman in his own estimation at least, and setting out to become a great minister.

A year after the appearance of Duclos's book Voltaire's *Siècle de Louis XIV* was published in Berlin. Quick as usual on to anything new, the Count de Stainville, in writing to Bernstorff of the Duchess de Luxembourg, had remarked so early as 20 March 1752: 'I have read Voltaire's book with her ... There are only four copies of it [here]; it is Madame de Pompadour's one that I have been reading with Madame de Luxembourg; so the present which he had made you is the more flattering in that it is so rare.'[54] Voltaire had sent the *Siècle de Louis XIV* to Bernstorff 'not only as to a judge of style and taste, but as to the best judge of all the matters which this book contains ... The two copies, indeed, which you will find in this

[52] Cf. Michel Antoine, *Le Conseil du Roi sous le règne de Louis XV* (Geneva, 1970), p. 634.
[53] Duclos, op. cit., i. 145–9 for the following.
[54] Count de Stainville to Baron von Bernstorff, Paris, 20 Mar. 1752: *Bernstorffske Papirer*, ii. 642–3.

packet are corrected by hand, and thereby they are becoming rare pieces in libraries.'[55] Bernstorff duly remitted one copy to the King of Denmark and replied to Voltaire: 'It falls to you alone to give us so just and brilliant a picture of the most memorable reign whereof history makes mention, and to paint for us with so much truth, delicacy and taste an age for whose short duration you are our only consolation.'[56] One sees why the elegant baron had hit it off in French society.

The readers of Madame de Pompadour's copy, who did not have to thank the author, reacted otherwise. The Duchess de Luxembourg, wrote Stainville, 'has not approved it, and I think that she has judged it a little lightly'.[57] His measured critique of her criticism was justified. Voltaire's ambivalent attitude towards the age of Louis XIV had produced a study which, despite its defects, remained seminal, exerting its influence upon the greatest historian of that century, Edward Gibbon.

'It is not the intention to write only the life of Louis XIV ... but [of] the spirit of men in the most enlightened age that ever was.'[58] The challenging start of Voltaire's history was programmatic against traditional forms of heroic biography, of patriotic chronicles of tedious wars and confused diplomacy. His late mistress at Cirey had asked: 'What does it matter to me, a Frenchwoman living on my estate, to know that Egil succeeded Haquin in Sweden, and that Ottoman was the son of Ortogrul? ... I have never yet been able to finish any long history of our modern nations.'[59] To satisfy her Voltaire in his *Essai sur les moeurs* had already struck out towards a 'philosophy of history'. Now he carried ahead with novel emphasis upon culture and society, upon intellectual currents as evaluated by an engaged and keenly critical intellect; although, in seeking to dig below the episodic surface of events, Voltaire not infrequently scratched it only superficially. As though to clinch his journalistic approach to historical writing, Voltaire gave his *Siècle de Louis XIV* a new look painful to one staid critic in its 'two very puerile affectations'.[60] These were a modernized spelling which was to set a new standard for the French language and, less successful, an almost total abandonment of capitals, even for Louis XIV.

Even analytical historians are apt to find themselves tiresomely

[55] Voltaire to Baron von Bernstorff, Berlin, 8 Feb. 1752: ibid., ii. 706.

[56] Baron von Bernstorff to Voltaire, Copenhagen, 4 Mar. 1752: ibid., ii. 707.

[57] Count de Stainville to Baron von Bernstorff, Paris, 20 Mar. 1752: ibid., ii. 642.

[58] Voltaire, *Siècle de Louis XIV: Œuvres complètes de Voltaire*, ed. L. Moland, xiv. 155.

[59] Marquise du Châtelet cited in this translation by John Morley, *Voltaire* (London, 1886), pp. 297–8.

[60] Earl of Chesterfield to Philip Stanhope, London, 13 April (O.S.) 1752: *The Letters of Philip Dormer Stanhope, 4th Earl of Chesterfield*, ed. B. Dobrée, v. 1860.

tied down to untidy facts in a temporal succession. While the second volume of the *Siècle de Louis XIV* opened out into functional chapters on the court and government, arts and religion, the first had to enliven what it still could not avoid, the interminable cycle under the Roi Soleil of alliances, war, peace, alliances, more wars in succession to the cruellest one, that Thirty Years War into which, suggested Voltaire, France had been plunged by Cardinal de Richelieu in order 'to make himself necessary.'[61] If the age of Louis XIV had in many ways already become another land, it loomed up from nine centuries wherein 'the French genius had been nearly always cramped beneath a gothic government'.[62]

The ignorant misery of man's past was confidently put in its place by the historiography of the enlightenment. But, in writing history, to dismiss the procedures of the past as stupid is so often to stamp the verdict as superficial. It is difficult for a confidently clever and conceited person to be a great historian. Few modern historians would turn for a sure source to Voltaire's remarkable rendering of the age of Louis XIV.

The Count de Stainville had a modern cast of mind. After questioning the Duchess de Luxembourg's too sweeping condemnation of the *Siècle de Louis XIV*, he yet proceeded: 'The first volume is but agreeable and should be read as a pretty romance. The beginning of the 2nd is pitiable, except however for the picture of the court of Louis XIV. But there is a piece on Calvinism, quietism, and especially on Jansenism which seemed to me sublime.'[63]

Stainville's terse vehemence in both criticism and praise was characteristic. What he was apparently saying in so few words was that neither the political narrative nor the subsequent treatment of French police, commerce, finance, army, and marine really stood up. Such was the reaction of the future minister of Louis XV to the political history of Louis XIV. The heavy themes apart, Stainville allowed Voltaire his court anecdotes and eagerly responded to the newest, most controversial treatment of religion, which significantly came as the climax. This response is the more striking since Stainville had the reputation about then of living 'in society without any relations with these [Jesuit] fathers, still less with the Jansenists'.[64]

In the *Siècle de Louis XIV* Voltaire was as yet advancing his critique of christianity from the high ground of an elevated and tolerant humanism. If he led in with an idealized contrast between

---

[61] Voltaire, *Siècle de Louis XIV, u.s.*, xiv. 177.
[62] Ibid., xiv. 158.
[63] Count de Stainville to Baron von Bernstorff, Paris, 20 Mar. 1752: *Bernstorffske Papirer*, ii. 642.
[64] Baron de Besenval, *Mémoires de M. le baron de Besenval*, i. 363.

pagan innocence and the bloody registers of christianity, yet he allowed for instance that Pascal's *Lettres provinciales*, hailed as a masterpiece, had been unfair to the Jesuit order, here acquitted by Voltaire of having deliberately plotted to corrupt human morals. His warmly humane denunciation of the revocation of the Edict of Nantes, with its miserable cruelties and economic loss, could be set against his gentle deflation of Arnauld of *La Fréquente Communion*, the pugnacious Jansenist controversialist of the seventeenth century. His approach, remarked Voltaire, 'seemed too much in accordance with pure Calvinism. This was precisely the grounds of the dispute between the Gomarists and the Arminians. It divided Holland as Jansenism divided France.'[65] Voltaire's wry account of the origins of the cult of Cornelius Jansen (1585-1638), Bishop of Ypres, after the Jesuits had in 1641 secured papal condemnation of his study of Saint Augustine, characteristically observed: 'It would not seem that there is much to be gained from thinking with Jansen that God commands things that are impossible. That is neither philosophic nor consoling; but the secret pleasure of belonging to a party, the hatred which the Jesuits attracted, the desire to distinguish oneself and restlessness of spirit combined to form a sect.'[66]

Voltaire's blandly ironical estimation of the sectaries doing battle over Jansenism pointed the way for Gibbon's treatment of their theological precursors back in the decline of the Roman empire. 'The labyrinth of fatality and of liberty wherein all antiquity went astray'[67] was how Voltaire described the coil in which old Baius of Louvain had entangled himself in the middle of the sixteenth century in starting it all by his learned propositions on grace and on predestination, the grim theme of the Calvinists that salvation was reserved to God's elect. By the time of Jansen, denounced as a horrid restorer of Baius, the Jesuits had captured the field of catholic orthodoxy for the suave and subtle doctrine of their champion, Molina: that the efficiency of grace could under divine providence subsume human freewill. This Molinist doctrine of congruism came to terms with the world and with destiny, human and divine, more agreeably than the stern creed of ascetic Jansenists such as Arnauld. That was their aggravating or attractive quality, whichever way you looked at it across that lasting divide in society between those mainly wishing to live and let live and those with an itch to improve it in ways usually uncomfortable for others better off and conveniently deemed unworthy according to some fashionable canon of the time.

Such, in extreme compression, were the doctrinal intricacies behind that conflict between Molinists and Jansenists which was

---

[65] Voltaire, op. cit., xv. 44.   [66] Ibid., p. 42.   [67] Ibid., pp. 39–44 for the following.

being fought out in eighteenth-century France, usually in much different terms, more bluntly actual and political. Of course Voltaire and his disciples laughed at such doctrinal contortions, echoing the mockery of the Jesuit-Jansenist strife already launched by Crébillion in 1734 in his story of *Tansai et Néadarmé*, of how the grand sacrificer had to lick the skimmer in order to be nominated patriarch. On a higher level Voltaire used the religious strife as a text from which to preach that philosophic toleration which is 'the resource of the wise who govern, against the passing enthusiasm of those who argue'. If the Count de Stainville thought Voltaire's treatment of Jansenism sublime, that was a passage which the future Duke de Choiseul was largely to exemplify in his years of power, perhaps not least in his dealings with Voltaire.

Voltaire, always one for a belittling perspective, brought his chapter on Jansenism to a moving close in the context of world-history: 'One sees the small figure cut upon earth by a Molinist and a Jansenist. One blushes, then, for the frenzy displayed on behalf of a party which is lost in the multitude and the immensity of things.'[68]

That was the perspective of lofty tolerance which had captivated the new ambassador of France to Rome.

VIII

A 'little intestine war'[69] between rival sectaries of the catholic church was how Voltaire had featured the Jansenist controversy. So indeed it was in its immediate aspect. This led not only Voltaire, in his inevitably close-up appreciation, but also other historians, not least protestant ones, to underestimate the Jansenist issue as a catholic wrangle of no lasting consequence. Whereas at the juncture of 1754, when Stainville was poised for Rome, Jansenism posed a more immediate and serious challenge to French church and state than all the writings of the philosophs put together. Not only that in terms of practical politics, but upon a broader and more philosophic plane, Voltaire's own, it can be argued that his view of Jansenism as insignificant in the face of world-history, was, as not infrequently, superficial.

The tides of human thought and awareness, being human, have both an intellectual and an emotional aspect. The renaissance of learning, from the blossoming of the Italian mind in particular, largely coincided with the reformation of religion, though not in Italy. The extension of the renaissance into the enlightenment, this

[68] Ibid., p. 63.   [69] Ibid., p. 49.

time mainly in France, was also matched by a more emotional current of development which, for want of a more accepted title, could be termed the enthusiasm.

Carrying through from the reformation, the enthusiasm in its original expression renewed the religious theme of a more intellectually individual and direct implication in a christian faith of purified austerity. In its Jansenist form, with its affinities to Calvinism, this renewal ran counter to the counter-reformation of the Jesuits. That France was largely caught on this Jansenist rebound, whereas Italy and Spain were not, is of wide significance – wider than is always made clear – for an understanding of modern catholicism.

Jansenism, however, was but one modulation of a religious trend that was more than merely French. Jansen's treatise was condemned by Rome just as English puritans were preparing to fight it out against the background of the greater and grimmer war of religion in Germany. And if, as Voltaire indicated, Jansenist currents in France could be correlated with others in Holland, which acquired its Old Catholic Church, the very heart of the movement lay in between in the catholic Netherlands intellectually centred upon the famous university of Louvain, the spiritual home both of Baius and of Jansen. Nor was this true only of the origins.

Events in what had become the Austrian Netherlands were prefigurative for France. The Jesuits, going to the source, made the catholic Netherlands their proving-ground against the Jansenists. Thomas de Chimay, Archbishop of Mechlin from 1716 to 1759, was the spirtiual precursor of Christophe de Beaumont in Paris. In alliance with Cardinal de Bissy, the doughty Archbishop of Mechlin hammered the Jansenists decade after decade: yet another suggestion that religious apathy was far from general in the eighteenth century. It did not apply in the case of Doctor van Espen, the ornament of Louvain, hounded out at the age of eighty-two to go to die among the schismatics in Holland. At Louvain the celebrated faculty of theology was secured against the Jansenists fifteen years earlier than the Sorbonne. Priority too was won by the archdiocese of Mechlin in denying sacraments and burial to Jansenists. So early as 1721 the Emperor Charles VI was trying to allay the strife by prescribing in regard to the Bull Unigenitus what he termed indifference, a generation earlier that that silence which King Louis XV was now to seek to impose.

To the east of the Austrian Netherlands thousands of German protestants fared forth to seek a kinder future as the so-called Pennsylvania Dutch. From further east again the Moravian Brethren helped to kindle the new enthusiasm of Wesleyan

Methodism in England and in New England. This new low-church movement among the protestants was at times to promote ecstatic eccentricities of enthusiasm comparable to those of the Jansenist Convulsionists in the low-church movement among the catholics. More importantly, methodism was to be among the first of all creeds to grip the approaching industrial revolution.

The industrial revolution and the French one were respectively to be the great economic and great political outcome of the scientific spirit of the enlightenment. If they lay in the future as yet, so did the great cultural outcome of the accompanying enthusiasm, namely the romantic movement. The way in which the emotional drive of Jansenism quickly petered out in the later decades of the eighteenth century was to signal the lay victory, in France in particular, of the rationalism of the enlightenment. The emotional vacuum was promptly filled by the lay religiosity and sentimental enthusiasm of Rousseau and so many others heading into the romantic movement. And if that, in the international pull of ideas, was to come to owe even more to Germany than to France, the enlightenment was similarly endebted for its very name, acknowledging the *Aufklärung*. If Germany had largely inspired the reformation also, the enthusiasm now was to rend apart not just catholicism but christianity itself. Yet this larger context of continuity permits a truer estimation of the significance in France, in particular, of the Jansenist movement during the first half of the eighteenth century.

IX

France seemed clinched for the counter-reformation by the revocation of the Edict of Nantes. Historians have understandably treated it as a turning-point and, not least with protestant writers, as a deplorable one in terms of religious toleration and of economic loss to France, already rubbed in by Voltaire. The revocation was, however, widely approved by Frenchmen of the day, even among the best of them. After the wartime rising in the Cevennes had been put down, the success of the persecution of the protestants under Louis XIV was confirmed. Thereafter only occasional tidying up seemed necessary. The Duke de Bourbon's edict of 1724 against the protestants was indeed more severe on paper than the revocation itself. But a more humane and settled age could afford to restrict its rigours to occasional instances: in 1749 in Bordeaux forty-six persons were commanded to separate for concubinage in protestant marriages, their children disinherited as illegitimate; three years later at

Montpellier a protestant preacher was hanged.[70] As for the economic loss which the expulsion of Huguenots certainly entailed, still, France in the eighteenth century contrived on the whole to do pretty well for herself commercially.

It is arguable that, internally at least, the revocation of the Edict of Nantes by King Louis XIV was a less grievous error in terms of political realism than his imposition of the Constitution Unigenitus a generation later. This time, in the words of Fleury, 'a hundred thousand voices were promptly raised from every quarter'[71] in a protest which was to distract France off and on for the next forty years and more. More than a generation after this imposition it was still for a Jansenist sectary the event wherein 'God had allowed Satan to prevail'.[72] Since this Jansenist clamour occurred within the catholic context, did not provoke an actual war of religion, its significance seems faded. So indeed it is by comparison with the later incidence of free thought, lastingly dividing French society into two, catholic and anticlerical. Yet the Bull Unigenitus of 1713 had promoted a schism in the French church and, nearly, state. For the first time since the Fronde the Parliament of Paris had in 1714 objected to registering a royal edict, that imposing the bull. The parliament was constrained, but this resistance to the Great Monarch himself pointed ahead, towards the constitutional turmoil which had set in by 1754.

The Unigenitus bull had been craftily promoted in concert with Rome by Le Tellier, Jesuit confessor to Louis XIV. Already some days before the king died, according to Saint-Simon, the Duke de Noailles, in touch with the Parliament of Paris, had been contemplating the expulsion of the Jesuits from France. That was to take more than half a century yet, but the regency of Orleans soon excluded them from the confessional and the pulpit. The revocation of this prohibition in 1729 had been sad amends by the dying Cardinal de Noailles, formerly leader of the recusants against Unigenitus. The Regent Orleans before him had swung similarly. So had slim Fleury. A French pamphlet denouncing the Society of Jesus to the plenipotentiaries at the Congress of Soissons (an early if futile attempt at publicity through an international assembly) had been publicly burnt. Parliamentary Jansenism, cowed by Fleury after the Council of Embrun and the promulgation of the Constitution Unigenitus as a law of the realm in 1730, had lost impetus after the

[70] Cf. A. Cobban, op. cit., i. 62.
[71] Bishop of Fréjus, charge of 9 May 1714: F. Rocquain, *L'Esprit révolutionnaire avant la révolution*, p. 4, n. 3.
[72] *Nouvelles écclesiastiques*, 1747: cited, ibid., p. 120.

excesses of the Convulsionists and under the impact of the War of the Austrian Succession. The acceptants of the bull increasingly became the party of the increasingly aristocratic French episcopal establishment. The unpopularity of the Jesuits began to rub off on to bishops tending to figure also as ultramontanes rather than as the gallican champions of Bossuet's day. For if the king chose the bishops in France, it was still in Rome that cardinals were created. This careerist dualism in the upper church supplies the key to much ecclesiastical manoeuvring in eighteenth-century France.

The doctrinal content of Jansenism was becoming somewhat overlaid, the movement increasingly factorized in terms of two others, Gallicanism and Richerism. If the church in England had become anglican from the initial impetus of Henry VIII, the church in France had become increasingly gallican from the time of Henry IV and, for instance, of the dispute of 1682 between Louis XIV and the papacy concerning the royal prerogative of choosing bishops, when Bossuet had mobilized them. Implicit in the gallican liberties of old was a denial of papal infallibility, an issue revived by the condemnation under Unigenitus of the propositions of Quesnel. Ten years later the diarist Marais glumly observed: 'Rome is dominating us more than ever. Our liberties are going, and we are going to fall into infallibility'[73] – theologically justified, sure enough, next year (1724), by an obliging Benedictine, Father Petit-Didier. By 1753 the Parliament of Paris was enjoining all French universities to teach the four propositions of the church assembly of 1682, in the good old days when bishops still were gallicans. Such an intrusion by the constitutional lawyers of the parliament suggests in itself how political Jansenism in its gallican aspect had become by the middle of the eighteenth century. And gallicanism under Bossuet had itself looked back to Richer whose synodal assertion against the swells of the church carried protestant overtones with long reverberation among the Jansenist lower clergy in France, sounding towards new forms of popular radicalism.

The ecclesiastical stay of the French throne, the Gallican Church, was rent by internal conflict just when it needed to gather up its forces to resist the philosophic onslaught. Moreover, while the government had but recently lost in its trial of strength against the Molinist episcopacy over Machault's Vingtième, Jansenist militancy had found dangerous expression through the parliaments in their own challenge to the government, nourished by the kind of historical constitutionalism popularized by Mably. The parliaments surpassed

---

[73] Marais, 22 June 1723: *Journal et mémoires de Mathieu Marais*, ii. 469.

the nobility in prolonging and extending the revival of their political influence under the Regency. In ominous inversion of Bossuet's distinction, the French monarchy was becoming more arbitrary than absolute. The government of the old regime was caught in a crossfire of conservative opposition from the parliaments and liberal opposition from the philosophs. And there was a forbidding convergence between them in that realm of natural law and moral contract which could only too quickly take on a popular slant.

Already in 1751 the young Abbé de Loménie de Brienne, of whom more would be heard, had been suggesting that the authority of princes derived not only from the ordering of God but also from the consent of the people. France was facing a theoretical transition from the divine right of kings to popular sovereignty, and beyond. It was actually the Jansenists who pointed out that it was all very well for Loménie de Brienne to try to hedge his theory against its logical consequence of the popular right to depose a monarch. One might almost as well say by now that it was all very well for the Parliament of Paris and its country cousins to try to keep its constitutional opposition upon a conservative basis. As the religious disputes had earlier ventilated ecclesiastical issues among the public, so now was political strife promoting constitutional debate.[74] In the month in which the Count de Stainville was appointed to Rome the Marquis d'Argenson remarked that parliamentary doctrines were suggesting *that the nation is above kings,* as the universal church is above the Pope. Imagine what changes can issue thence in all governments.'[75]

Such was the implicit challenge to church and state now besetting the young envoy to the papacy in his endeavour for France to heal her catholic rift at a turning-point of the enlightenment.

---

[74] Cf. J. M. J. Rogister, op. cit., p. 177.
[75] D'Argenson, viii. 153.

CHAPTER XI

DEPARTURE

I

THE future Choiseul wrote:

Everybody knows that the function of an ambassador consists of two points: first, to carry out the desires of his court and make them succeed; secondly, to inform the court of everything which could interest it in the projects and deliberations of the prince and the council of the court at which he is residing. I make bold to believe that these two essential points are to be certainly and easily secured only by bowing with natural grace to the character either of the prince or of the ministers who have most influence, and by setting oneself to study the means of capturing their fancy and consequently their confidence.

It is against nature that a man who does not for a moment lose sight of the object of his mission, and who manages to inspire liking in him with whom he is dealing, should not sooner or later win his confidence to the point of knowing the secrets which will be of interest to him. I think that this method, when one has it in oneself to make it successful, is better than that of espionage, all the more so in that it does not prevent one from using that means as well. I am so persuaded that the success of an ambassador, if it is to be sure, depends upon the plus or minus of flexibility in his character and upon his capacity to please, in nearly all courts at least, that, if I were sent to a court to declare war upon it, not precisely as a herald but so that I should sojourn there for some time before the declaration, then right up to that moment I should study how to deserve the friendship and confidence of those to whom I should have to say that my master was going to make war on them, and I should do this with the same care which I should employ if I had to enlist them in a common war along with my own court. In politics one cannot change facts; but there is great advantage to be drawn from forms, and above all from those of seduction, in order to attain the object which one sets oneself. When I speak of seduction, you must not misunderstand me. I do not mean duplicity. To my mind nothing is more harmful than duplicity in business. True finesse is the truth spoken sometimes with force and always with grace.[1]

Those are words of wisdom, and of experience of the world. They remain one of the best guides to the true practice of diplomacy, and to the character of the future Duke de Choiseul. No wonder he was apt to be so successful in his dealings with all kinds and conditions of men, and women, from his servants to his king, from his mistresses to the pope himself.

Certainly, the Count de Stainville started under handicap with

[1] Choiseul, *Mémoires*, pp. 106–7.

Benedict XIV but lost little time in putting into action his philosophy of diplomacy. Early in the new year of 1754 the pope resumed to Cardinal de Tencin on Stainville's appointment: 'We were afflicted by it, for we have no need here of an increase in libertinage in action and in manner of thinking. You much console us in assuring us that the marquis [*sic*] is quite resolved to change, and we will tell you that the same thing was written to us by Count Durini, who is filling the place [in Paris] of the nuncio, his uncle [Cardinal Durini], or rather of his successor, the new nuncio, M. Gaultieri',[2] Luigi Gualterio.

There was a significant suggestion that the papal score against Stainville was not only moral but also intellectual. Still, a pope who had read Voltaire's *Mohamet* 'with the greatest pleasure'[3] might be less severe than some upon the kind of latitudinarianism evident in the count's response to the religious relativity of the *Siècle de Louis XIV,* in his aloof moderation towards the ecclesiastical issues deepening the constitutional crisis in France.

As the hard winter wore on into 1754 the Parliament of Paris, upheld by public sympathy, remained obdurate in exile under its tricky First President. Maupeou made no démarche which the government could construe as an act of submission towards ending the exile. If the boredom of Soissons did begin to whittle resistance, in Paris the distrusted Chambre Royale found itself almost equally idle, an object of derision. The king and his government also appeared passive, lost face, to the consternation of the pope, anguished by the constitutional drift of the religious struggle in France. By the beginning of 1754 even the kindly Benedict XIV was preaching 'courses of severity to reduce the rebels to the obedience which they owe to their sovereign'.[4]

In the previous year the pope had suggested to Louis XV that the gallican movement might reproduce the anglican schism. Already in 1751 such a French observer as Barbier had expressed fears of a protestant revolution against a background of renewed unrest in the Cevennes and another, minor, wave of Huguenot emigration. French political circles feared that England might repay in kind their own support of the Jacobites, by fomenting and subsidizing an unrest in France that also had both religious and constitutional aspects. By February 1754 the Marquis d'Argenson was suggesting to a French minister that in place of the existing 'little parliament of bourgeois pettifoggers' the nation might come to impose upon the king 'one that was more serious and more nearly approaching the English one'.[5]

[2] Pope Benedict XIV to Cardinal de Tencin, 16 Jan. 1754: Benoît-Tencin, ii. 316.
[3] Pope Benedict XIV to Voltaire, Rome, 19 Sept. 1745: *Œuvres complètes de Voltaire,* iv. 102.
[4] Pope Benedict XIV to Cardinal de Tencin, 9 Jan. 1754: Benoît-Tencin, ii. 315.
[5] D'Argenson, viii. 222.

It was already occurring, however, to thoughtful Frenchmen like the Marquis d'Argenson that their reformation might exceed that of English or German protestantism. Three months later, on 9 May 1754, he wrote in his diary: 'One is assured that everything in France is getting ready for a great reformation in religion and that it will be something very different from that crude reformation, compounded of superstition and of liberty, which reached us from Germany in the sixteenth century ... Since our nation and our century are much more enlightened than those of Luther, we shall go as far as one should go: banished will be every priest, every sacerdotal function, all revelation, all mysteries.'[6] And again, 'people have never been so well informed as they are today regarding the rights of the nation and of liberty.'[7] Liberty, Justice, Law figured in French prints as allegorical ladies, later to win a revolutionary popularity.

The rule of King Louis XV was weakened. Yet on 20 June 1754 the Marquis d'Argenson was writing further: 'In this business people have not got in it for the king but more and more for royalty, and a revolution is more to be feared than ever. It is asserted that if it is to come in Paris, it will be through some priests in the streets, or even the archbishop of Paris, being torn to pieces ... since the populace regard these ministers [of religion] as the true authors of our ills.'[8] If d'Argenson was habitually full of dire forebodings, pragmatic Barbier, who lived in Paris, had concluded some months earlier: 'The spirit of disobedience is general.'[9] The expectant year of 1754 represented a revolutionary extreme in the cleavage of the French eighteenth century down the middle in politics and in the ideas which nourished them.

Pope Benedict XIV, gazing from afar towards the French capital, wrote that May: 'We seem to behold a great fire where there is no water to extinguish it.'[10] Such was the baleful background to the preparations of the Count de Stainville setting forth in an attempt to subdue the conflagration.

II

Diplomacy, like other high avocations, calls for logistical underpinning. Stephen de Stainville, already familiar with military problems of planning and staff, now had to organize his embassy based upon the Palace Cesarini near the baroque dome of Sant' Andrea della

---

[6] Ibid., pp. 289–90. [7] Ibid., p. 315.
[8] Ibid., p. 309. [9] Barbier, v. 443.
[10] Pope Benedict XIV to Cardinal de Tencin, 8 May 1754: Benoît-Tencin, ii. 338.

Valle in the loop of the Tiber before the Vatican. The Duke de Nivernais's predecessor in Rome, the Cardinal de La Rochefoucauld, had admitted of the French embassy that 'there could be objections to it because externally it is not of a fine appearance, but . . .'[11] there had been nothing else suitable to rent. And it was really roomy with two suites of eight apartments apiece and a large garden.

It was recognized, however, that the Cesarini Palace was inadequate as a focus for France in the Eternal City in the way in which the Piazza d'Espagna had become one for the other Bourbon hegemony. When in 1751 Nivernais had given a large celebration of the birth of the Duke of Burgundy he had had to hire the Farnese palace. For the best part of ten years, on and off, French representatives in Rome had been angling for the Palazzo Madama belonging to the Emperor Francis as the heir to the Medici. The idea had been to buy this Tuscan property in the name of Pâris-Monmartel. Nivernais had hoped to secure it for 100,000 Roman crowns, had all but got it down to 80,000 when this secret negotiation had leaked to the Austrian minister, who stepped in to stop it. It was to be just on fifty years yet before the French government did acquire the Palazzo Madama, later known as the Villa Medici.

For the present Stainville asked Saint-Contest whether he should start looking again. He does not seem to have waited unduly upon the answer. By 10 July 1754 the pope was writing to Tencin: 'We are told that the staff of the new French ambassador are not satisfied with the Cesarini palace where the Duke of Nivernais used to live, and they think that it would suit their master better to take the palace d'Altemps at the Apollinaris which you inhabited and which Cardinal Cavalchini is leaving to go to live in the palace d'Aste on the Piazzo San Marco. The Marquis de Stainville must be proposing to cut a big figure here. Forty-seven persons of his household have already arrived, among them a large number of cooks, orderlies and several seamstresses.'[12]

If the Count de Stainville was to have to resign himself to the Palace Cesarini, he was determined to measure up to his first assignment of official representation. Nivernais could be relied on to do the decent thing in making over the embassy furnishings, still basically those contrived nearly a decade ago by the Cardinal de La Rochefoucauld, very handsomely, he thought: Venetian chandeliers in all the reception-rooms and Venetian velvet to upholster the fauteuils and settees in a crimson floral pattern on a gold ground,

---

[11] Cardinal de La Rochefoucauld to Duke de Nivernais, Rome, Dec. 1747: Lucien Perey, *Un Petit-Neveu de Mazarin*, p. 62.

[12] Pope Benedict XIV to Cardinal de Tencin, 10 July 1754: Benoît-Tencin, ii. 351.

with curtains in 'a strong silken stuff which I had specially made to go with the fauteuils'.[13] Stainville, though, was not one to take another's taste on trust. Whereas Nivernais in like case had largely left such practicalities to those on the spot, La Rochefoucauld and the sybaritic Abbé Count de Canillac, Auditor of the Rota, a judicial functionary whose gallic aspersions upon the Roman ways he knew so well helped to frustrate his longing for a cardinal's hat. Upon arrival Nivernais had found the embassy in some confusion with some of the cardinal's old servants doing well out of it and Canillac presenting implausible accounts: not the kind of thing to wash with the Count de Stainville, laying down the line in advance.

Early in 1754 the count, in preparation for his embassy, was sorting through samples of table-linen from Dresden, to be returned via Strasburg, those selected being stamped with his seal.[14] He personally signed an order that February for some twenty tablecloths of various patterns, at least half a dozen of which were to seat fifty people, and over sixty-two dozen matching napkins, even though he considered some to be on the wide side, others dreadfully overpriced. Stainville enjoined that all should carrry the initials C and S. The whole order was reckoned to cost rather over eleven thousand livres including an estimated 280 for carriage from Dresden to Rome. If letters of credit to cover this should prove insufficient Sieur Petit, the steward of Stainville's house in the Rue de Richelieu, was to settle any balance presented on the authority of the Count de Broglie, French ambassador at Dresden, supervising the Saxon end of this transaction for his former schoolmate and future rival.

It may seem doubtful whether Broglie himself could easily have afforded such an order – a little angle perhaps upon relations between the two counts. Stainville, incidentally, was further grumbling that samples for bed-sheets were missing, but if they arrived within a month that should be time enough. Another personal angle here is total silence as to the Countess de Stainville. One can only say that despite her husband's habit of personal control, not least in matters of taste, she may in fact have had some say in choosing her own linen.

That the Countess de Stainville, recovering from her malady, was already capable of placing her own orders, if upon a smaller scale, appears from the registers of Lazare Duvaux, that Parisian purveyor of objects of art in the age of Madame de Pompadour. In August 1753 Madame de Stainville had bought of him two paperweights in

---

[13] Cardinal de La Rochefoucauld to Duke de Nivernais, Rome, 1747: *u.s.*, p. 63.
[14] Cf. former collection of Sir Thomas Phillipps/22927, *apud: Bibliotheca Phillippica, New Series: Sixteenth Part: Catalogue of French, Spanish, Greek and Serbo-Croat Manuscripts with a few Slavonic and Portuguese*, Sotheby catalogue (London, 1976).

Dresden china 'mounted on gilt terraces of ormolu'.[15] That December she further acquired 'two cups of Vincennes [china], jonquil and blue' with matching teapot and little tray for ninety-six livres the set. At the beginning of that month over eight hundred tradesmen in Paris were reported to have declared themselves bankrupt. At the end of it the Count de Stainville bought 'a round Vincennes chamberpot in sky-blue with cartouches of flowers, 168 l[ivres]. – Another oval one, same kind, 144 l.' These purchases of 30 December 1753 might have been teasing gifts for the new year.

More serious, doubtless, was the provision of china for the embassy at Rome, not to mention such staples of good living as wine and silver. Sent on ahead were quantities of plate, which the Stainville staff in Rome put on show to give the locals a foretaste of the elegant luxury of the new ambassador and ambassadress. Such ostentation had not been the style of the Duke de Nivernais.

The Count de Stainville's table-linen alone cost him the best part of half a year's salary as ambassador. His basic pay was of the order of 24,000 livres. One sees how useful the countess was likely to be, if not always in choosing their equipment then in paying for it. Her fortune, however, rendered her husband no less keen to extract whatever he could from his own estate, whose accounts for 1753 he had signed off in Paris four days after ordering that linen.

The glittering prospect of Rome prompted a special scrabble for cash back at Stainville. Brigeat was selling off for his master some furniture which had apparently come to him from Couvonges. The agent was also trying to lay hands on 3,000 livres which had been owing to the Count de Stainville for ten years. The same amount was due to him on the more recent account of his emolument for the last six months as governor of Mirecourt; Brigeat was trying to overcome the usual kind of parsimonious difficulties raised by the treasury at Nancy.

The beginning of 1754 found Brigeat also going through the papers of Lescaille, the late demesne provost, to extract anything useful for the Count de Stainville's archives. Brigeat recommended a certain Thouvenot to succeed Lescaille but Aubry, the count's lawyer at Bar-le-Duc, chipped in in favour of his own brother-in-law. In the event the count appointed a certain Charles Lefebvre to be demesne provost of Stainville. The appointment was unlikely to be wholly congenial to Brigeat since a couple of years earlier Lefebvre had pipped another of Brigeat's nephews, called Gerard, for the lesser post of demesne provost of Beurey and Mussey. This now produced

[15] Lazare Duvaux, *Livre-Journal de Lazare Duvaux*, ed. Louis Courajod (Paris, 1873), ii. 165–86 for the following.

a screed from Brigeat pleading that his nephew should at least succeed Lefebvre at Beurey. The letter incurred the bleak endorsement 'Nihil'.[16] Three years later a legal document about the endless woodland disputes with the abbey of Jovilliers was to feature Lefebvre as provost, with Brigeat and Gerard signing for the Stainville team, whereas a mention of 'the procurator-fiscal of the marquisate of Stainville'[17] was immediately followed by a blank, as though for a name.

The vacancy arose from Carré's implication in the diplomatic fortunes of his master. During the absence in Rome perhaps a new procurator-fiscal was judged unnecessary. Brigeat at all events regarded himself as taking on the count's 'procuration' [18] and was moving in on the Stainville estate more closely than before. There was a question now of furnishing a bedroom and study for him in the château, still the administrative citadel of the marquisate. Carré's wife was to be left behind there as concierge, and he was keen to get her a certificate to that effect from the Count de Stainville 'in order to exempt her from *tailles* during my absence'.[19] For his part of the caretaking Brigeat promised that 'nobody shall damage your property by hunting over it. I will take care to preserve it well.'[20] Making doubly sure as usual, the Count de Stainville proceeded to injure Brigeat's feelings by writing direct to his head keeper, Maiziert, and giving him instructions which apparently did not except Brigeat himself, who protested that he was not 'a hunter nor a fisherman'.[21]

Not in Lorraine alone was the Count de Stainville seeking then to increase his fortune while characteristically advancing the fortunes of other Lorrainers. In Paris, according to one likely story,[22] Stainville, who had taken over the running of the Crozat property in the Rue de Richelieu, then had in prospect an advantageous sale of the outlying kitchen-garden. Immediately beyond it in the Grange-Batelière a magnificent mansion had been built by Etienne Bouret, perhaps the greatest of the farmers-general, a favourite with Madame de Pompadour, with the king himself. The constricted site of this 'palace' would be nicely eased by that kitchen-garden, said to be worth thirty to forty thousand livres. Stainville entrusted the matter

[16] Endorsement on Brigeat to Count de Stainville, Ligny, 21 May 1754: Arch. Meuse, J 18[11], docket II.

[17] Procès-verbal between marquisate of Stainville and abbey of Jovilliers, 4 Nov. 1757: Arch. Meuse, J 18[9] (Gruerie de Stainville. Juridiction. Bois. Arpentages. 1618-An VIII), docket IV (Bois du Petitval), no. 184.

[18] Brigeat to Count de Stainville, Ligny, 17 Feb. 1754: Arch. Meuse, J 18[11], docket II.

[19] Carré to Count de Stainville, Stainville, 18 Dec. 1753: ibid.

[20] Brigeat to Count de Stainville, Ligny, 22 Jan. 1754: ibid.

[21] Ibid., 17 Feb. 1754.

[22] Cf. anonymous French newsletter of 2 Mar. 1755: Bibliothèque municipale de Rouen; Collection Leber 5830, no. 1, fo. 116: by courtesy of Dr. J. M. J. Rogister.

to the family friend in that financial class, Pâris-Monmartel, who raised Bouret to the sum of 190 thousand livres. Furthermore Stainville, before leaving for Rome, persuaded Bouret to give some more or less secretarial employment to a literary youth from Lorraine called Charles Palissot. Such, in part, is the indication that the future Choiseul was already protecting the future goad of the philosophs.

If Palissot was fitted up in Paris, other Lorrainers were headed for Rome. A French ambassador in the eighteenth century was still likely to proceed upon his mission as a proper nobleman with an almost feudal retinue. Nivernais in Rome had had a male staff of some 145 including a theologian from the Sorbonne, two French secretaries and two Italian, eleven gentlemen of the chamber, a surgeon, sixty-two valets and lackeys of various kinds, four trumpeters, a French chef and his minions plus coachmen, postilions and pages. Stainville had to scratch around to measure up, though his tenantry were evidently keen to proffer their sons as pages. A Lescaille boy seems to have been among those in the market, and the beginning of 1754 found Brigeat advising the count: 'Do not refuse the son of M. de Longeau. He is the prettiest child that I have seen among all those who are offering themselves ... The son of M. Mayeur would also suit you very well. He is very pretty. I am not saying the same of the son of M. Dalys, who seemed to me very heavy.'[23] The Count de Stainville duly made his pick of the pretty boys, and Brigeat was to inform their parents of the proposed arrangements. Presumably Stainville, like Nivernais, would employ 'a governor of the pages'.[24] On occasions, at least, even a country lad from the lesser middle-class might be presented with early opportunity for foreign travel. Stainville did take with him his father's valet's son, Hubert Robert, whose artistic bent he was already encouraging.

III

It was natural to the working of the old system on most levels that some of the success of a principal should rub off upon his dependants, his family not least. Brigeat – and he does not seem untypical – had the makings of a champion nepotist, almost on principle as it were since he did not restrict his solicitude to his own family. In a letter of 15 February 1754 he started strikingly to the Count de Stainville:

Sir, I much wish that you could answer for it that the Abbé, your brother, is nominated to the bishopric of Toul, which brings in fifty thousand livres a year. If

---

[23] Brigeat to Count de Stainville, Ligny, 1 Jan. 1754: *u.s.*
[24] 'État de la maison de l'Ambassadeur de France à Rome': L. Perey, op. cit., appendix V, pp. 559–60

the king does not do him the justice to give it him, at least arrange for him to obtain the abbey of Vaux which produces 12 to 14,000 livres, which adjoins Demange. This arrangement would obviate many cases which have long subsisted with your subjects in the said Demange and with your father as its lord.[25]

It was not only nations in those days which sought to round off their territorial sway by dynastic policies of neighbouring alliance. It was almost expected of Stainville that he would employ his new influence for the good of his clan. Perhaps it was mainly in modes of expression that the workings of English party-politics were then so very different. In general the pattern is a persistent and respectable one in less advanced societies. However, Leopold Charles de Choiseul-Stainville had to wait for a bishopric beyond the term of his brother's embassy to Rome. Still, things were looking up and it would not be so long now before the third brother Jacques became an intimate also of Madame de Pompadour, even while he was yet in Austrian military service wherein he was advancing to command the Löwenstein light horse and figure as a chamberlain to the emperor.

In the French diplomatic postings in Italy the honorific consolation of Rome hardly compared with the political plums secured by Ossun and Chauvelin. Only, France was then politically quiescent in Italy. Noailles had told the thrusting Chauvelin not to try to precipitate anything at Turin – 'the juncture is not favourable and the moment has not yet come'.[26] Whereas religiously things were anything but quiescent for France. It was Stainville after all who was to have the greatest diplomatic opportinity. Significant here was a staff-posting from the French embassy in Turin.

The Chevalier de Chauvelin was writing from Turin to the Marshal de Noailles on 16 February 1754:

At this present moment there is no overture, either direct or indirect, to be made. We must wait upon events . . . Allow me, Sir, to profit from this opportunity to ask your protection for Monsieur Boyer. It was rather from zeal than from necessity that he entered upon a political career and decided to accompany the Marquis des Issarts to Saxony. He remained there for two years as His Majesty's Chargé d'Affaires and earned commendations during that space. When I arrived at Turin he had been performing the same functions there for nine months with universal approbation. Very upright, he also possesses capacity, application and a very gentle character which makes him liked by everybody who knows him.[27]

[25] Brigeat to Count de Stainville, Ligny, 15 Feb. 1754: Arch. Meuse, J 18[11], docket II.
[26] Marshal de Noailles to Chevalier de Chauvelin, Versailles, 15 Sept. 1753: B. N., MS. fr. no. 10661: Du Perron de Castéra, 'Correspondance diplomatique', vol. 3, fo. 67. (Cf. Arch. Aff. Étr., Mémoires et Documents: France, vol. 534, fos. 269–79.)
[27] Chevalier de Chauvelin to Marshal de Noailles, Turin, 16 Feb. 1754: Arch. Aff. Étr., Mémoires et Documents: France, vol. 534, fos. 116–17.

This warm recommendation for further employment was remitted to Noailles by Boyer himself, whose time at Turin was now up. The marshal assured Chauvelin that he 'was already predisposed in ... favour'[28] of Boyer and would bear him in mind. Perhaps, though, Noailles scarcely needed to nudge the Count de Stainville. He was already acquainted with the promising young diplomatist, a year or two younger than himself, whom he now appointed his diplomatic secretary.

This was the beginning of the collaboration and lifelong friendship between the future Choiseul and Joseph Roch Boyer de Fonscolombe, where he had been born of an old family of Provence. His father, Honoré Boyer, had become a royal secretary, one elder brother was an agronomic counsellor in the Parliament of Provence and another, Jean-Baptiste, an infantry officer who painted attractive miniatures. Such was the cultivated background of Joseph Boyer de Fonscolombe, who now arranged the first meeting between his new master and his southern compatriot and close friend, the Abbé Barthélemy.

Jean-Jacques Barthélemy had been born in 1716 at the little port of Cassis near Marseilles. This sprightly Provençal became a formidable scholar and linguist, stretching out from Latin and Greek to Hebrew and Arabic. Arrived in Paris in 1744 to seek his fortune, he secured the protection of Boze, the neat and prudent keeper of the king's medals and sometime secretary to the Academy of Inscriptions, to which Barthélemy was soon elected. At Boze's weekly dinners the young Abbé met such as Réaumur, the connoisseur Count de Caylus, and Stainville's inimical acquaintance, the historian Duclos. Barthélemy worked under Boze and became his obvious successor as keeper of the magnificent medals – 1,800 of them in gold – ranged upon marble tables, with another gallery full of antiques including what passed for the shields of Scipio and Hannibal and the treasure from the tomb of Childeric unearthed a century earlier at Tournay. When Boze died in 1753, however, Barthélemy's succession was hotly contested. He was supported by Malesherbes, the liberal director of the censorship, and by Caylus, the friend of the Crozats. They in turn mobilized the two Crozat sons-in-law at court and, now, intimates of Madame de Pompadour, the Marquis de Gontaut and the Count de Stainville. The latter was not then personally acquainted with the Abbé Barthélemy. He got the job.

Barthélemy was now able to thank Stainville when Boyer de Fonscolombe introduced them in the spring of 1754. In this connexion another friend, Nivernais, was to write of Stainville:

---

[28] Marshal de Noailles to Chevalier de Chauvelin, Paris, 1 Mar. 1754: ibid., fo. 281.

A connoisseur of men and of talent, he allied to his natural generosity a design which all statesman should have: that of favouring, helping and being beforehand with persons distinguished by recognized merit. He proposed to the young scholar that he should make the journey to Italy under his [Stainville's] auspices and with his assistance ... Monsieur and Madame de Stainville obligingly offered to take Barthélemy to Rome in their coach.[29]

It was a wonderful offer. Stainville too stood to gain. He was not one to neglect the enlightened tradition whereby an eighteenth-century French ambassador appointed to a cultural capital would include in his suite one or two savants capable of enriching the royal collections or, at least, French scholarship. To take the Abbé Barthélemy to Rome would be in line with the way in which the Marquis de Villeneuve had adorned his classic mission to Constantinople with the Abbés Sevin and Fourmont, also of the Academy of Inscriptions. Their special assignment had been to penetrate the Sultan's library to locate manuscripts. Barthélemy's would be to make studies and acquisitions to enrich the royal collections of medals and antiquities. Such was the ambassador's enthusiastic initiative in the cultural project that Barthélemy described it, in relation to his patron, as 'a journey for which he had first had the idea'.[30] Within two days Stainville secured official approval through the Count d'Argenson.

For the Stainvilles this was the beginning of a lifelong friendship closer even than that with Boyer. If the count was a connoisseur of men, certainly Barthélemy was another of his intimates who was a good and upright man, like Bernstorff, like Nivernais himself. Stainville, however, liked merit to be laced with wit, and that the Abbé could supply. Another trait liable to be sympathetic to Stainville was Barthélemy's tolerance towards Jansenism and reservations in regard to the Jesuits, who had partly taught him in Marseilles under the rule of Bishop Belzunce. The Abbé recalled how one Jesuit teacher 'for three whole years, and for two hours every day, used to foam and gesticulate like one possessed to prove to us that the five [heretical] propositions were in Jansen. I had fortunately formed for myself a plan of study which rendered me indifferent to the stupidities and furies of my new masters.'[31] The plan included 'the system of Descartes, which was highly disagreeable to the Jesuits'. Belzunce, recalled Barthélemy, got to know, at least, 'that I had read Saint Paul and the Jansenist fathers of the early church, such as Saint Augustine

[29] Duc de Nivernais, *Essai sur la vie de J. J. Barthélemy* (Paris, 1795), pp. 26–7.
[30] Abbé Barthélemy, 'Mémoire sur les anciens monuments de Rome' in *Voyage en Italie de M. l'Abbé Barthélemy*, ed. A. Sérieys (Paris, 1801), p. 361.
[31] Abbé Barthélemy, 'Mémoires sur la vie et sur quelques uns des ouvrages de J. J. Barthélemy écrits par lui-même en 1792 et 1793' in *Voyage du jeune Anarcharsis en Grèce* (Paris, 1838 ed.), i. v–xx. for the following.

and Saint Prosper. He also knew that I seldom saw two Jesuits by whom he was flanked': the main one's 'antechamber, always full of curés and vicars, resembled that of a minister or a lieutenant of police'.

Thus, Barthélemy recollected, 'I finished my seminary, and, although imbued with religious feeling, perhaps even because I was imbued with it, I had not the slightest idea of entering the ecclesiastical ministry.' Such a spirit was congenial to the Count de Stainville, to the countess too.

That Stainville, just off to Rome in the thick of the Jansenist controversy, should have taken up Barthélemy was suggestive. As for the Abbé, more than a generation later he was to evoke that year when 'M. de Stainville was destined for the embassy at Rome. It is with extreme pleasure that I recall this date, because it was the time of my fortune and, what is worth still more, that of my happiness.'

Realization of that happiness had to be deferred after all. Barthélemy, instead of accompanying his new friends in their coach, conscientiously found that his superintendence of the king's medals would not allow him to leave so soon. Without an assistant yet, he was keen to improve the public utility of the collection, arranging appointments to view, answering learned correspondents, recataloguing and sifting fakes, an area in which Boze's caution had tended to mislead. If Barthélemy's association with Stainville's embassy was thus postponed, it provided plenty of immediate work for his friend Boyer.

While Boyer was preparing in Paris, in Rome the diplomatic interim since Nivernais's departure was being filled by his secretary, Stainville's Little Man. La Bruère, disgruntled at not receiving formal letters of credence, had, related the pope, 'left the palace of the Duke de Nivernais and has taken a house. He is a very gentlemanly person, amiable and liked by everybody'[32] – well, by most people, anyway. In the new year of 1754 La Bruère had handed Benedict the habitual letter of good wishes from Noailles who this time, the pope noticed, 'does not fail to draw attention to the merits of the Abbé de Canillac, doubtless in order to reproach us for not having just made him a cardinal or to urge us to make him one in another promotion'.[33] Benedict sent Noailles a reply which 'may perhaps not have pleased him'.[34]

The prickly Abbé de Canillac was approached with circumspection by the Count de Stainville, himself indebted to the Marshal de Noailles. Stainville had heard that Nivernais had fallen out with

[32] Pope Benedict XIV to Cardinal de Tencin, 9 Jan. 1754: Benoît-Tencin, ii. 315.
[33] Ibid., 16 Jan. 1754, p. 316.   [34] Ibid., 20 Feb. 1754, p. 322.

Canillac over the annual accounts of the French foundation of Saint-
Louis in Rome. Stainville noticed that, whereas they had been
rendered by Cardinal de La Rochefoucauld when ambassador, they
did not figure in the dispatches of Nivernais. The new ambassador
asked the foreign minister in advance to be excused from rendering
them since he wished to afford no pretext for a difference 'with the
Abbé de Canillac, who deserves all kinds of consideration on my
part':[35] an estimate to be confirmed in an instruction that the Auditor
of the Rota 'could be a great resource to the Count de Stainville
especially at the beginning of his embassy'[36] when finding his way
around Roman society. This was one little instance of the way in
which, as the later Choiseul explained, 'I employed this year in
preparations for the embassy. I did everything that was in my power
to acquire information which could render my sojourn at Rome
useful.'[37]

IV

The Count de Stainville, ever one for making the most of anything,
did so in the French tradition that an ambassador-designate should
do his homework on the dispatches of his predecessor and from
earlier still. He plunged back towards the beginning of the century in
what was possibly the most concentrated course of reading that he
ever undertook. It may help to explain the interest which that
ebullient aristocrat took thereafter in questions concerning official
archives. Meanwhile he was beginning to plumb European diplomacy
in depth. The breadth he could more easily supply.

For diplomatists policy is conditioned by practicalities often
presented as protocol. Stainville unearthed an outward dispatch of
28 July 1745 giving contingent instructions upon the status to be
accorded to the representative in Rome of the Knights of Malta.
Nivernais had informed the Bailli de Solar that his own distinguished
treatment of him was no precedent if Austria and Spain did not
subsequently conform. Had they done so, asked Stainville. What was
the present position? Nobody, perhaps, really knew or cared very
much, apart from Nivernais. Talks with him doubtless helped in
sifting out from Stainville's reading the questions and requests with

---

[35] Count de Stainville, memorandum of the earlier part of 1754: 'Demandes du Comte de
Stainville, Ambassador Extraordinaire à Rome, à Monsieur le Marquis de St. Contest, 1754':
Arch. Aff. Étr. C.P., Rome, vol. 816, fo. 83.
[36] Mémoire pour servir d'instruction au Sieur Comte de Choiseul-Stainville, Versailles, 22
Sept. 1754: Arch. Aff. Étr. C.P., Rome, vol. 815, fos. 341f.: Recueil des instructions, xx (Rome),
323.
[37] Choiseul, Mémoires, p. 94.

which he peppered the failing foreign minister. The present example strikes one because the Bailli de Solar was to become perhaps the closest friend and confidant of the Count de Stainville in Rome, almost a successor to Bernstorff.

An older, larger issue was the presentation by the French ambassador in Rome of letters of credence not to the pontiff alone but to each cardinal. Since the Prince of Monaco had last observed this tiresome punctilio in 1690 the French government had been vainly trying to consign it to oblivion. Its omission by Nivernais had evoked complaint from Benedict XIV in his liberal concern for the collegiality of the governance of the Church of Rome. 'We have', he wrote, 'always done and always shall do everything we can for the Sacred College'[38] on whose behalf he had extracted a French assurance of observance next time, now. The pope told Tencin that the suspect Stainville could not 'do anything better, to render his arrival agreeable, than to come here with letters of credence for each cardinal'.[39]

The Count de Stainville, as an advocate of diplomacy by ingratiation, threw himself into this papal cause with his habitual vivacity and drive, prodding the Marquis de Saint-Contest with a characteristic reflection: 'The cardinals are very jealous of their prerogatives and spend their lives, as it has seemed to me from what I have read, in thinking only of their personal interests.'[40] The new ambassador, supported possibly by Nivernais and others, had wheedled the French government into preliminary agreement to accede in fact, though not in principle, to papal pressure to appease the princes of the church. Actually to extract the letters of credence was another matter, and Stainville saw to it that his efforts should be appreciated by the nuncio in Paris and so by the pope. Shortly before Stainville set out, Benedict was to write to his crony of the envoy's grapple with French officialdom over the letters: 'They told him that they would send them to him, but he replied that he did not wish to leave without them. They are looking for the draft of the letter which was remitted to the Prince of Monaco . . . If God so wills it the Sacred College and we ourselves will be under a great obligation to the new ambassador, and we shall be content. For we ought no longer to think of acquiring [advantages], being very happy to preserve those at least which we already hold.'[41] The church militant, fashionably philo-

[38] Pope Benedict XIV to Cardinal de Tencin, 23 Jan. 1754: Benoît-Tencin, ii. 318.
[39] Ibid., 20 Feb. 1754, p. 322.
[40] Count de Stainville, 'Demandes du comte de Stainville, Ambassadeur Extraordinaire à Rome, à Monsieur le Marquis de St. Contest, 1754': u.s., fo. 82.
[41] Pope Benedict XIV to Cardinal de Tencin, 11 Sept. 1754: u.s., ii. 359.

sophic, had become a satisfied power. The new ambassador to Rome, before ever arriving there, was notching up personal success.

Stainville was not one to be fobbed off by the argument, accurate enough, that the precious letters would only be presented at formal visits paid to the cardinals directly after the ambassador's ceremonial entry into Rome, not to take place for the best part of two years yet. He achieved his diplomatic lead-in to his diplomatic mission. His final instructions specified that the letters to the cardinals 'from His Majesty dispatched in secretariat of state'[42] were duly appended.

Stainville was adept at sifting essentials. In contrast to his pliancy over formalities stood his request that his instructions should include a provision that all approaches by the French clergy for favours from Rome should be centralized through himself rather than routed via, say, the influential Tencin. The count, incidentally, had not failed to notice that that cardinal retained the rights and emoluments of 'the protectorate of France' at Rome so that it was only by Tencin's concession that the Spanish Cardinal Porto Carrero now preconized French episcopal appointments. Another ecclesiastical concern for Stainville was the doctrinal question of the canonization of Bellarmine.

The venerable theologian, Cardinal Bellarmine (1542–1621), was a Jesuit controversialist whose ultramontane championship had incurred hostility even in retrospect from the gallican church, and not only there. The process of canonization was then stalled by opposition within the Vatican itself, notably, recalled the instructions to Stainville, 'by the prayer or vote of Cardinal Passionei, which constitutes a volume of three hundred pages in folio and in which this cardinal brings out in the clearest light all the reasons which ought to exclude Cardinal Bellarmine from the altars. If in the course of the embassy of Messire the Count de Stainville an attempt be made to revive this same matter, he will be at pains to represent to the ministers of His Holiness that it would be prudent of the court of Rome not to pursue an objective which would be criticized equally in countries catholic and protestant, and that such a canonization would certainly never be recognized in France.'[43] The reference to protestant opinion makes one wonder whether Stainville, like so many ambassadors, may have had a hand in drafting his own instructions. Their stiffness on a strictly religious issue came to the knowledge of Pope Benedict XIV even before the new ambassador reached Rome.

[42] 'Mémoire pour servir d'instruction au Sieur Comte de Choiseul-Stainville', Versailles, 22 Sept. 1754: *Recueil des Instructions*, xx. 319.
[43] Ibid., xx. 315.

The niceties of canonization did not monopolize the intellectual curiosity of the Count de Stainville, also involved that summer in a mathematical controversy over squaring the circle. This was provoked by Colonel de Mauléon de Causans who had in the previous year claimed in a *Prospectus apologétique* to have solved the problem. An excellent fellow apart from his monomania, Causans was leaning towards that mercenery charlatanism which affected society then in its sometimes rickety emergence from the closed reaches of faith into the taxing age of reason. The colonel was apt to urge fashionable doubters 'to lay money ... Monsieur de Stainville was of this number and found himself pledged, pretty much in spite of himself, to part of a bet of 100,000 livres. Solicitors were appointed and gave their specific recognizance that, after the verdict of the Academy of Sciences'[44] due on 25 June 1754, they would settle strictly.

At 'the fatal term', however, the academy withdrew behind the loftly explanation that it judged problems not lawsuits. One was indeed brought against Causans, who claimed that he had really won, by a mathematical young lady. In this agreeable rumpus the king as usual had to intervene. The bets were quashed. The academy, though, was finally badgered into pronouncing that the Causans proof did not hold water. The mathematician only went on to maintain that it did, however, hold the secret of original sin and of the trinity. Less rarified were the religious issues over which the Count de Stainville co-operated with the papal envoy in Paris, Count Durini, and, now that June, the new nuncio, Gualterio, nephew of a cardinal who had himself been nuncio there.

Papal policies included those disputes with Venice which had already been attracting Stainville's notice four years earlier. If the aftermath of papal discord with Venice was to linger throughout Stainville's embassy to Rome, he was to be spared the unpleasantness with the emperor over Carpegna, where Francis was at last climbing down. Towards the end of June 1754 Benedict was rejoicing to his confidant in Lyons: 'We still have good news to give you about Carpegna. The Austrian troops have left it ... But since the boat of Saint Peter is forever to be tossed by tempests although, by divine protection, without ever foundering, a terrible squall is blowing up in Prussia. The Marquis of Brandenburg wants to disgrace the Bishop of Breslau.'[45] The bishop, hitherto the papacy's main link with predominantly protestant Prussia, was having a difficult time of it in the aftermath of her Silesian grab and now took refuge in the

---

[44] Luynes, xiii. 294 for the following.
[45] Pope Benedict XIV to Cardinal de Tencin, 26 June 1754: Benoît-Tencin, ii. 346.

fragment of his diocese remaining to catholic Austria. This religious aspect of Frederick's political coup has figured less in history than it did for contemporaries.

The King of Prussia was aiming at running down catholic foundations in Silesia by cutting off their recruitment from Austria. He had already had a passage with the Bishop of Breslau over a young Abbé de Prades, another advanced French thinker who had sought refuge with Frederick as the champion of the philosophs against catholic authority. A thesis sustained by Prades at the Sorbonne had in 1752 been condemned by Benedict himself, notably for casting doubt upon the healing miracles of Christ. The catholic establishment rallied against this thesis to counter-attack the ideas being propagated in the Encyclopedia of Diderot, with whom Prades was identified; but the Bishop of Breslau, acting as mediator, had clinched the public repentance of the Abbé to the joy of the good pope. Soon, though, his communications with the bishop were interrupted, the more ominously since Frederick was off on another tack, trying to come it over the Elector Palatine in the guise of protestant champion in the duchies of Berg and Jülich where, explained the pope, catholics were mixed up 'pell-mell with Lutherans'.[46] Benedict wondered whether perhaps, through the intermediary of Louis XV, one could represent to Frederick II 'that it is not reasonable to reach for one's sword over every complaint which the heretics prefer against the catholics'. Even in the age of reason the embers of religious strife flickered on in Germany, of imperial ambition in Italy, as over the Genoese fiefs of Campo Freddo and San Remo, foci of concern that summmer for Stainville and his mentor, Noailles.

V

A protégé of Madame de Pompadour was hardly one for whom bookwork would imply any neglect of personal contacts. The Count de Stainville came in at the top level of those two French overlords of a decade earlier who still largely held the balance in his present sphere in the form of a tug between the Cardinal de Tencin, the erstwhile hammer of the Jansenists, and Marshal de Noailles, more equivocal, more moderate, more influential, one suspects, with Stainville.

Noailles, presiding over policy to the south, was in direct and more

[46] Ibid., 23 Oct. 1754, ii. 367 for the following.

or less regular correspondence with the French ambassadors there who had got in ahead of Stainville. The marshal prodded the inadequate Duras who, when setting out earlier for Madrid, had, so unlike Stainville now, betrayed to Noailles a certain negativism towards delicate negotiation. The other Bourbon court of Naples was better served by the Marquis d'Ossun, the protege of Noailles, who kept an eye on his family and sent him friendly criticism, as over certain Neapolitan overtures: 'Since the court of Naples is little pleased with the last treaty concluded at Aranjuez and is anxious and jealous of the King of Sardinia ... one might perhaps have wished that you had replied to these overtures with a little more unction and warmth of heart.'[47] Though, at the same time, such was the constricted posture now of France in the Italian peninsula that Noailles considered that 'a new definitive treaty between the King [of France] and the King of the Two Sicilies would acquire them no new ally, would put Spain out and would not reconcile the King of Sardinia'.[48]

A striking conspectus of French policy in Italy in the aftermath of the formative Treaty of Aranjuez distinguished the correspondence between Noailles and Chauvelin in Turin. Before proceeding thither Chauvelin had on 14 July 1753 sent Noailles a 'Memorandum on the present situation in Italy', and how France should exploit it. The ambassador-designate proposed a forward policy towards the King of Sardinia, strengthened now by his pact with Austria and Spain. Whereas, argued Chauvelin, it was essential to swing 'this naturally irresolute prince'[49] into alliance with France. A French subsidy should if necessary be dangled before Charles Emmanuel but chiefly should he be constrained by the French formation of an Italic league of Naples, Parma, Genoa, and Modena. Nor need France shrink from military threat since, maintained Chauvelin, the Sardinian government had pondered that campaign which had featured the Count de Stainville in 1744 and had proved 'that the passage of the Alps could be forced by a number of troops roughly equal to those ... defending its extent, and that a French army could in three months' campaigning be introduced into Piedmont and there constitute the seige of Coni'.

If Chauvelin's reading of Conti's alpine campaign breathed an optimism simpler than Stainville's, their patron in a long reply two months later told Chauvelin that he disagreed with his analysis upon

[47] Marshal de Noailles to Marquis d'Ossun, Versailles, 16 Jan. 1753: Arch. Aff. Étr., Mémoires et Documents: France, vol. 534, fos. 295–6.

[48] Ibid., fos. 297–8.

[49] Chevalier de Chauvelin, 'Mémoire sur la situation actuelle de l'Italie' enclosed in letter to Marshal de Noailles, Paris, 14 July 1753: ibid., fos. 104–6 for the following.

almost every point. Experienced Noailles knew Charles Emmanuel better than to suppose him merely irresolute; and he was against trying to bribe him with 'useless subsidies in time of peace because that is to deprive oneself of the means of giving useful and necessary ones in time of war.'[50] As for Chauvelin's Italic league, neither Spain nor Naples would be likely to join, the Duke of Modena was already making up to Austria, and Genoa was unlikely to be keen on risking further fearful perils. Even if such a league did materialize:

I believe in the first place, Sir, that the only effect would be to bind the King of Sardinia more closely to the Queen of Hungary and to England . . . Fear is always a very dangerous means to employ. Far from attracting, it repels, and even when it does attract it gives birth to the desire to break away so soon as a favourable opportunity shall arise.

As for military lessons from the Italian campaigns of the War of the Austrian Succession, for Noailles they were nearly opposite to Chauvelin's. With Piedmont hostile, argued the marshal, a French army 'in the centre of Italy without other communications with the Kingdom [of France] that that by sea would appear in the eyes of every really military man to be an army compromised, which would never allow us to dispense with having another one to cover our own country. I am persuaded and convinced that if one gave the King a contrary opinion one would be giving him pernicious and fatal advice.' Noailles summed up: no French campaigning nor any league in Italy without Sardinian support; and 'far from the aggrandizement of the King of Sardinia being adverse to us, I think that it could be very useful to us from the fear and jealousy which it would necessarily cause our true enemies.'

For France a reversal of antagonism, if not of alliance, from the preceding war was already under way in Italy, the setting of Stainville's first mission. The cool reasoning of the Marshal de Noailles, for once approximating to the emotional Marquis d'Argenson over Sardinia, contained a germ of peace. Soon now Italy at least would find shelter this time from the seven-year spread of war.

This stiff but friendly argument between Noailles and Chauvelin on high policy in the Italian peninsula is one of the most instructive dialogues on French foreign policy in the middle of the eighteenth century. Though it was rather one way, with Chauvelin, setting out for Turin, asking Noailles when he 'could come again to receive from

---

[50] Marshal de Noailles to Chevalier de Chauvelin, Versailles, 15 Sept. 1753: B. N., MS. fr. no. 10661: Du Perron de Castéra, 'Correspondance diplomatique', vol. 3, fos. 64–8 for the following. (Cf. Arch. Aff. Étr., Mémoires et Documents: France, vol. 534, fos. 269–79.)

you one of those lessons to which I attach such price'.[51] If Chauvelin received lessons on Italy so, most probably, did Stainville. And his mentor was perhaps France's shrewdest and most experienced statesman in a season of small men.

The workload of old Marshal de Noailles had been increasing as he irritably found himself standing in for the fiftythree-year-old Marquis de Saint-Contest. The foreign minister had for some time been gravely ill, coughing continually, frequently bled: too many prostitutes in youth, they said: a weak chest inherited, they said, from his father, formerly intendant of Metz and a French plenipotentiary at the peace of Baden in 1714, at the congress of Cambrai a decade later. On 24 July 1754 the foreign minister died.

Noailles was thought to favour the succession of the Marquis de Silhouette. Saint-Séverin and Conti himself were always hovering in the wings. Also mentioned were two of Noailles's Italian team, Ossun and Chauvelin. On the latter Noailles likely had something to say; but then Chauvelin was on friendly terms with the power-centre of the government, the Keeper of the Seals and Controller-General, Machault, then well in with Noailles. Machault himself, however, was to be involved in the surprising outcome. As the then Count de Stainville was to recall:

M. de Saint-Contest ... was replaced by M. Rouillé. The former was absolutely devoid of talents for the ministry, but he had been brought up by his father, who had some political knowledge. He had wanted to learn; at any rate, when one spoke to him, he used to give an indication of having some ideas. As for M. Rouillé, he had not any in this department. He was too old to acquire any and, although I was very fond of him personally, I must admit that it was in the last degree absurd and grossly ridiculous to have made him Minister for Foreign Affairs.[52]

Always one for the larger view, the mordant Stainville added:

There is a providence which watches over the affairs of princes, but for which they would not be despatched. For, during the reign of the king whom we have, the choices have nearly always been made by him without paying the smallest attention to furthering the conduct of business. On this occasion M. Rouillé, who had [earlier] been chosen, I know not how, to replace M. de Maurepas at the Ministry of Marine, and who had displayed in this ministry the mediocrity of his talents, was chosen for a ministry which demands much more talent than that of the Marine: because M. de Machault, who had influence with Madame de Pompadour, was bored with being controller-general and wanted the Marine, which he regarded as a more stable position.

[51] Chevalier de Chauvelin to Marshal de Noailles, Paris, 19 Nov. 1753: Arch. Aff. Étr., Mémoires et Documents: France, vol. 534, fo. 112.
[52] Choiseul, Mémoires, pp. 94–6 for the following.

The future Choiseul was to write in the plenitude of power to Voltaire: 'It is of small importance for a kingdom and its history that Peter or Paul be ministers, and Joan or Margaret the mistress.'[53] That most human of statesmen had a vivid sense of the insignificance of human beings in the long swing of events. And yet the present ministerial switch could conceivably have had a deeper significance than that suggested by Choiseul, and this precisely in regard to interests submerged in that other field of political influence for Noailles, the internal one of the continuing struggle with the parliaments which was to condition the diplomatic mission of the Count de Stainville.

VI

Young Stainville was linked with Rouillé when foreign minister in a garbled story evidently deriving from the preceding lent when the French court had been agog with the temerarious sermons of the Jesuit Father Laugier. The handsome preacher had laid about him, sparing not the king, sparing less the parliament, 'asking that it be dismissed, dissipated and annihilated as impious and destructive of religion'.[54] One is told that one evening after supper with Rouillé 'the Count de Stainville, bored by the importance ascribed to this business, said that the Jesuit should be expelled from Versailles, with no more talk of sermons and Jansenists'.[55] This private utterance was said to have reached the Jesuits and to have earned him entry in their black books. One can only say that such a remark would have been in keeping with Stainville's attitude of disinterest, in keeping too with the king's subsequent imposition of silence. Meantime, despite some possible royal reluctance, Father Laugier had been relegated from court by the beginning of May 1754.

A shared interest in the Count de Stainville may have contributed something about then to the good standing of the Marshal de Noailles with the Marquise de Pompadour. It was more suggestive, however, that those prime protectors of the count shared some discreet sympathy with the parliamentary cause. As the stalemate of Soissons carried over into the spring of 1754 Noailles had at the beginning of March apparently opposed, unsuccessfully, in the royal council its annulment of sentences pronounced by several provincial parliaments in the spread of the conflict over Billets de Confession.[56]

[53] Duke de Choiseul to Voltaire, Versailles, 13 July 1760: P. Calmettes, *Choiseul et Voltaire*, p. 108.   [54] D'Argenson, viii. 278.
[55] Baron de Besenval, *Mémoires de M. le baron de Besenval*, i. 364.
[56] Cf. J. M. J. Rogister, op. cit., p. 176 *et passim* for other particulars here adduced.

Noailles had been supported by Rouillé, often in the thick of parliamentaty affairs as a moderate like Machault. The controller-general, however, had lately seemed to be out of patience with Maupeou, and to be taking soundings in some contact with the Duke de Richelieu, also dabbling in those troubled waters before leaving to preside over the estates of Languedoc. By 18 May, however, Noailles was being sent to tell the obdurate Archbishop of Paris from the king that he could no longer reckon upon the issue of royal decrees in the form of Arrêts du Conseil to quash parliamentary judgements or evoke awkward cases. On 3 June Louis took a critical initiative, summoning Maupeou from Soissons to Versailles next day. They conferred in secret for an hour and a quarter, a signal honour and success for Maupeou, who had recently been strengthened by the death of President Chauvelin, the friend of Machault. Now rumours promptly spread that the Jesuits were to be expelled and parliament recalled to Paris. The rumours were wishful, exaggerated, premature, in their general bearing accurate.

The break-through may have been the king's own though the Prince de Conti was said to be behind it. Thereafter certainly Conti resumed a leading role: back in February the procurator-general, Joly de Fleury, had imparted a warning in the direction of Machault and Richelieu that Conti was capable of queering the initiatives of others. It looks as though it was now Joly de Fleury who enabled Conti to stymie Machault in his apparent desire, reasonable enough but characteristically rigid, to link the return of the Parliament of Paris with a law forbidding cessation of parliamentary service.[57] Whereas Conti had always looked to the imposition of a law of silence upon the whole dispute over Billets de Confession, in effect favourable to parliament beneath a mantle of aloof impartiality liable to appeal to Louis XV. Machault smarted under his rebuff but the king now seems to have excluded his ministers from the parliamentary negotiations, entrusted primarily to Conti. Once again the shrouded and influential role of aristocratic grandees on a level higher than ministers suggests some corrective to the usual estimates of the extent to which the government of eighteenth-century France was in the hands of the lesser noblesse de robe.

After the royal impulsion at the beginning of June 1754 things seemed superficially to settle back in a rather obscure lull. But it did lessen any impression of royal action under pressure. The king particularly consulted the moderate and respected Cardinal de La Rochefoucauld, a friend of Maupeou. One stumbling-block to

[57] Cf. ibid., p. 180.

accommodation was overcome by the physical decline of rigid old Boyer, former archbishop of Mirepoix, so long and so unfortunately in charge of French ecclesiastical appointments. The Marshal de Belle-Isle also seems to have lent a hand, possibly in connection with a second secret conversation between the king and Maupeou in the middle of July. When Louis saw Conti a week later the prince appeared agitated and as though suggesting that fresh impediments were preventing the recall of parliament. Then three days later the death of Saint-Contest loosened the ministerial fabric. Three days later again, on 27 July 1754, Louis XV at last ordered the return of the exiled parliament to Paris for 1 September. Only a day or two after that did the public learn of the ministerial reshuffle centred upon Machault.

In a rare tribute to a ministerial predecessor the then Count de Stainville later described Machault as 'a man of much merit, very able in finance, with a mind as cultivated as it was just and profound, and worthy of all the confidence which Madame de Pompadour bestowed upon him . . . He was disgusted with the office of controller-general. He saw that the king was unwilling to reduce expenditure so as to be able to make good the deficit and from that moment he had formed the design of leaving the controllership-general at the first opportunity. He succeeded, at the Marine, to M. de Rouillé, who took the place of M. de Saint-Contest ... M. de Machault was then replaced as controller-general by M. Moreau de Séchelles, an upright man well viewed by the public',[58] and by the king, said to have intended him to succeed Saint-Contest: and that not so much under the influence of Séchelles's particular friend, the Count d'Argenson, as of the Prince de Soubise, the intimate of Madame de Pompadour. Yet there was also a story that Madame de Pompadour and Machault had persuaded Louis to appoint Rouillé and switch Séchelles to finance, so relieving Machault.

Machault was the rigid minister who had failed to impose his taxation upon the French clergy while ensuring their resentment. Upon the other hand this lawyer, who retained his other office of keeper of the seals, had now fallen out also with the leading lawyer of the exiled parliament, Maupeou, and seemingly, to some extent at least, with the Prince de Conti, the leading mediator in that stalled crisis. Though the upright Machault retained the confidence of the king and his mistress, he had become something of a double liability. His relegation to the Marine was neatly calculated to be welcome to both of the opposing parties as a gesture of conciliation. And Louis,

[58] Choiseul, 'Mémoires inédits', 2/16/8/497/2.

despite the later disparagement of Choiseul, was not a stupid monarch.

There is no proof that the royal recall of the Parliament of Paris was connected with the ministerial changes. But the dates and the circumstances seem suggestive. If in that constitutional crisis of the Ancien Régime there was for once something approaching a cabinet reconstruction under a parliamentary system, the pressures towards it were, here too, in their own way parliamentary. If in this French instance the precise significance and sequence of events remain obscure, they ran true to the court of Louis XV. At the beginning of that year the Marquis d'Argenson had been writing darkly: 'The king likes mystery and deepness without seeking in them justice or just plans. Everything is conducted by the idea of shadows and loses substance.'[59] Not the secrecy but the indeterminacy was antipathetic to the Count de Stainville.

As Stainville indicated, Machault may well have felt financial disillusion. That and political rebuff could indeed have inclined him towards prudential retreat. Retreat once begun, though, is difficult to halt. Coincidence or not, within less than three years Machault would be finally dismissed. For the present in any case, retaining favour as he did behind the bland secretiveness of government, Machault would naturally assure Stainville or others, as Louis assured Noailles, that the change of office was at his own request.

Stainville for all his rising favour was hardly likely as yet to be initiated into the penetralia of a government jealously monarchical and aristocratic at the highest level. He had indeed secured an entree through the Marquise de Pompadour but her graceful touch concealed, more than is always recognized, a deep and comparted discretion. Her rift with Conti dating from the days of Saxe may by no means have excluded her now from all influence; nor was Stainville, with his special relations with both, one to miss any opportunity for mutually advantageous intervention. In any case the closely affected ambassador-designate to Rome, with his penchant for gathering intelligence, stood to gain significantly from those relations.

Soon after the change in ministry the Prince de Conti was drafting the critical letters-patent to impose a formula of silence to loosen the constitutional knot threatening to strangle French government. He is said to have put his head together over it with Joly de Fleury and with 'Sieur Pothouin, a famous lawyer and a great Jansenist'.[60] Hence, perhaps an apparent inclination by the king to criticize

[59] D'Argenson, viii. 209.
[60] Luynes, xiii. 444.

Conti's draft for seeking, fairly enough, to conciliate parliamentary opinion but without a sufficiently balanced regard for that of the clergy. Thereafter Louis wrote to Conti from Bellevue on 9 August 1754: 'I have told you what troubled me in the draft of letters-patent. I am returning them to you with some notes which I have made. I am also sending you another one, very imperfect, but it will prove to you that my head is busy. I had gathered fragments right and left, and they are very badly stitched. Make your observations and give them me in writing, for long audiences with you make too much stir, and I confess that it never stays in my head as does what I read and think over either by day or by night when I do not sleep.'[61]

This rare self-revelation by Louis XV of himself as a painstaking and rather diffident worker, with some suggestion of insomnia, carries the suggestion also that the decisive pronouncement may have been quite largely of his own devising. His chancellor and ministers seem to have had little or no hand in it, though they would likely have been consulted in council before the decree was promulgated to the Parliament of Paris, returned on 31 August and 1 September 1754 from exile to the capital, to bonfires of welcome and popular jubilation. On 2 September the king at Versailles signed the still unpublished letters-patent.

At eight o'clock on the morning of Wednesday, 4 September, the dignitaries of the parliament came driving up in their coaches to the Palais. As each arrived cheers went up from the crowd jamming the forecourts and entrances, crying *Vive le Roi! Vive le Parlement!* in an emotional reconciliation between king and capital. The cheering reached crescendo with the advent of the first president, Maupeou, probably the only parliamentarian to have had much advance intimation of what was now in store for them.

A briefly moving allocution from d'Ormesson, acting as first advocate-general, introduced the reading of the royal declaration with a view to its registration. After a preamble censuring the insubordination of parliament in abandoning its routine functions the year before, and justifying its exile, the declaration summoned it to resume its duties and for the future imposed upon all parties a respectful silence in the religious controversy in the interests of concord and appeasement. Judicial proceedings that had been taken were to be suspended and, with some exceptions, delivered judgements would be without effect.

Even now an aftermath of parliamentary resistance to registration flickered up disconcertingly. More than seventy Zélés, injured

[61] King Louis XV to Prince de Conti, Bellevue, 9 Aug. 1754: cited, J. M. J. Rogister, op. cit., p. 184.

especially by the preamble of the royal declaration, favoured its outright rejection, It was debated dingdong for two days, on the second with only a break for 'a snack in the refreshment-rooms of the chambers'.[62] Maupeou mobilized the waverers to such effect that the final count on 5 September in favour of registration, subject to some face-saving glosses, was ninety-two against seventy-two. Next day only three votes defeated a motion by the intransigent Durey de Meinières, Stainville's old opponent, that the officers of the Châtelet be summoned to report upon past proceedings in the absence of parliament. The settlement just escaped wreck. On 7 September the Parliament of Paris adjourned for the vacation. The French crisis of 1754 was at an end.

Popular government was alien to the old regime. Yet that critically close debate in the Parliament of Paris suggests the way in which the lawyers at their level, like the peasants of Stainville at theirs in their village assemblies, could already bring sections of public opinion to bear with telling effect upon the conduct of affairs by authorities whose powers were in practice a good deal short of absolute. The lesson that parliament could hardly be replaced by procedures of authority was to condition the long administration of the future Choiseul until his protege and then antagonist, the son of President Maupeou, steered Louis XV back in his last years to a constitutional imposition of dangerous and disputable success.

As can happen in stubborn disputes, the precarious solution painfully achieved in 1754 was in fact rather more solid than might appear. For all the spirited show of last-minute resistance, many members of the Parliament of Paris had learnt a lesson from their long exile at Soissons. Upon the other hand, as Barbier shrewdly observed, the judicious balance of the royal declaration, while avoiding any suggestion of capitulation, in practice meant that 'parliament is tacitly obtaining everything that it has always claimed; for by imposing this silence and forbidding all fresh initiative the king is forbidding Billets de Confession, refusal of sacraments, questions upon the Constitution [Unigenitus]. And he not only allows but enjoins parliament to take proceedings against contravening ecclesiastics. The Archbishop of Paris and the clergy are not pleased with this declaration.'

Louis XV had sought to mollify his clergy in an audience at Choisy on 3 September which he had granted to the cardinals de la Rochefoucauld and de Soubise along with his archbishops of Paris and of Narbonne. The king could explain that his declaration did not impair the legal position of the Constitution Unigenitus or of the

---

[62] Barbier, vi. 54–5 for the following.

ecclesiastical courts. The months ahead were, however, to yield the Molinists small comfort, as the pope foresaw with consternation. Benedict XIV commented to Cardinal de Tencin upon the declaration of 2 September 1754: 'The king drily imposes silence upon both the good and the bad . . . To have imposed silence without any kind of preparation favourable to the church is to leave things in the same disorder [as before] and to render the good guilty if they complain of the wrong done to the church. As to the registration [with parliamentary riders], it is very scandalous. They dare to protest clearly and without disguise that thereby it is not intended to introduce any innovation in the administration of the sacraments, thus giving it to be understood that the parliaments, which have meddled in this administration, will be continuing their encroachments and taking proceedings against those who resist their violence.'[63]

The Jansenist conflict arising from the Billets de Confession was certainly not over. The French government, however, was easing its general support of the Molinist hierarchy in a neutral direction, which in practice must mean towards the parliaments, a critical shift of emphasis. This shift was in the direction of the liberal attitude, already just adumbrated, of the future Choiseul in regard to the parliaments and the issue of the Jesuit order. In the immediate event it may have been in the nick of time that the French court finally assessed the extent of the constitutional danger threatening from the religious issue. It had been touch and go that summer. There may quite possibly be something in the suggestion that one false move then by the government in trying to impose its authority might have touched off, already, a revolution, which it in fact defused by delicate manoeuvring towards the declaration of 2 September 1754. Carrying on from there, it has even been suggested from hindsight[64] that the forestalling of a revolution then could in the long run be regarded as regrettable since such a constitutional revolution might well have forestalled a more violent and extreme one a generation later.

Even governments, peer ahead as they may, can rarely predict the future with long-term accuracy. What is only too well known to nearly every government is that if it takes strong action it is almost certain to be accused of heavy-handed oppression, if conciliatory action, of craven weakness, if a careful blend of both, then it is most likely to get the worst of both worlds. Of few governments was this truer than of that of Louis XV. In the present instance it has received scant credit for what might appear a masterly tack in beginning to

[63] Pope Benedict XIV to Cardinal de Tencin, 2 Oct. 1754: Benoît-Tencin, ii. 363.
[64] Cf. F. Rocquain, op. cit., pp. 180–1.

ease the nation away from a whirlpool. The credit accrued considerably to the king himself, whose reign of forty years already would now be fairly peaceably prolonged for another twenty. At the crux that summer he had perhaps come closest to action as his own first minister; but that, characteristically, while relegating his ministers in the royal council, where the royal presence tended to be equivocally ineffective, and while working as a secret solitary in touch, however, with that princely confidant also at the centre of the personal foreign policy of the King's Secret.

The constructive influence in 1754 of French magnates standing higher than ministers was likely fortified by that of the declared favourite. The Marquise de Pompadour, personally devoted to the king as few others were, yet possessed a liberal intelligence generally in some sympathy with the outlook if not the performance of both philosophs and parliaments. Distant as she may have remained from the Prince de Conti, it was noticed that they were both supping in intimacy with the king on 9 July 1754; a month earlier it had happened that the marriage-contract of a court factotum was witnessed by Madame de Pompadour and her brother Marigny along with Machault and, more interesting, Joly de Fleury and a clutch of Condés, the senior branch to the Contis. Such straws are of no proven significance. A year later, though, the inimical Marquis d'Argenson rounded off one of his diatribes against Madame de Pompadour's extravagance with the concession: 'Some good things are the doing of the favourite. She softens the despotic strokes of the ministers; it is through her that the king has made it up with the parliament.'[65] It was precisely in July 1754 that Luynes described her as 'more powerful than ever'.[66] And a prime proof of the power of the 'little minx (péronnelle) of a favourite'[67] was the ambassador-designate to the key-posting, now, of Rome.

It was with considerable ingratitude, one feels, that the later Duke de Choiseul explained: 'Since the king is not susceptible of the sentiment of loving, he has no greater strength to maintain his sentiment of aversion. A little while after the return from Fontaine-bleau [in the winter of 1753] he admitted me into his intimacy. He had the air of forgetting the reasons for displeasure which he thought he had had against me, and he treated me in a way that astonished me until I left for Rome, which was roughly a year after my nomination.'[68] Louis was soon speaking genially to Madame de Pompadour of 'this rascal Stainville',[69] as she informed that young envoy, whom she was

[65] D'Argenson, ix. 109.   [66] Luynes, xiii. 436.   [67] D'Argenson, viii. 286.
[68] Choiseul, Mémoires, p. 94.
[69] Marquise de Pompadour to Count de Stainville, 1755: Général de Piépape, u.s., p. 14.

proudly to call, with coy possessiveness, 'my ambassador':[70] that is, when she did not address him as her 'little monkey'.

VII

The successes of Louis XV and of the Marquise de Pompadour were set in a society long conditioned to conspicuous expenditure but increasingly critical of its exaggeration at the top. From the French court Count Kaunitz had reported extravagances 'which would seem incredible anywhere else':[71] two thousand three hundred horses in the royal stables compared with six hundred under Louis XIV, new napkins at every meal, a public provision of coffee costing more than a hundred thousand francs per annum. In May 1754 the Marquis d'Argenson noted:

The king has just given a pension of 5,000 livres to the widow of the Marquis de Lambert who ... died worth four millions ... The finances are being squandered as in the time of Charles VI or Henry III ... They are persuading the king to govern always of his own, *so as to grant favours*, they say; but these favours done to individuals are dagger-thrusts against the state.[72]

The financial indolence of Louis XV figured prominently in the picture of his court at about that period which was later drawn by Choiseul. In his critique, long shrouded, the king 'no longer wanted to work regularly or upon difficult subjects' such as finance:

He made the excuse that work on accounts gave him a headache and he no longer required anything of his controller-general except that there should always be money at his disposal. Madame de Pompadour, who suffered from seeing Louis XV debase himself to this extent, resolved to draw him out of his shameful inactivity by going for his self-esteem, which is extreme. It was effort wasted. But Madame de Pompadour wanted the king at least to be able to pronounce in the council an opinion which would appear to be his own. In consequence she had the courage to take a part in business matters and was soon up in them because she had a lively and accurate mind. She gave the king advice and it was rare that it was not judicious. Louis XV acquired the habit of letting himself be guided by her advice, and she became the arbitress of the destinies of the kingdom. It is a role of which she had scarcely dreamt and which she was obliged to assume in spite of herself. It has been the cause of unworthy calumnies and of terrible vexations which poisoned the rest of her life, and for which the king felt no gratitude towards her, because egotism is the basis of his nature and the cause of all the stupidities which he commits.'[73]

If Choiseul should seem unfairly dismissive of his elusive king's political capacity, suggested by the constitutional crisis, yet such

[70] Marquise de Pompadour to Count de Stainville, Jan. 1756: ibid.
[71] Kaunitz/Mémoire, p. 841.   [72] D'Argenson, viii. 296–8.
[73] Choiseul, 'Mémoires inédits', 2/16/8/497/3.

criticism was matched remarkably by another statesman of calibre. Kaunitz reported of Louis XV in his council: 'Malice asserts that he is bored to death there, that he yawns a lot, and that by dint of curtailing business, in order to pay him court, it is commonly strangled there. Incapable of application, dividing his time between hunting and pleasure, he has no idea of what is called government.'[74] Whereas the Marquise de Pompadour with 'excellent qualities of heart... governs despotically. The ministers inform her of everything that they have to say to the King. It is he himself who requires it. The least evasion and they would be lost. She has one quality which renders her very fit for great affairs, which is that of impenetrable secrecy. That is how she has captured the King's confidence.'

Madame de Pompadour's failing, Kaunitz had continued, was 'an insatiable desire to amass' treasures, reputedly worth more than thirty millions. In any case 'what is certain is that she has a share in all the tax-farms, that the ministers hand over to her the nomination to offices and that she divides the rake-offs (*pots de vin*) with them. Malice asserts that it is to these arrangements that the Controller General [Machault] owes his elevation.' If, by comparison, the royal mistress was to be spared by Choiseul, the royal princes were not. The future arbiter of the French court continued his indictment of it:

The princes of the blood had attained a degree of debauchery and brutishness almost equal to that of the king. I have never known a man more prodigal of his substance than the Prince de Conti, who ruined himself with girls, among others with the Durancy girl. He had so many debts that one of his former mistresses, Madame d'Astic, felt obliged to give him money so that he should have something to live on. His wife, whose profligacy is known to everybody, used to go to ask for money from the king, who bestowed it from vanity, not wishing that a prince of the blood should live in a style inferior to that of his courtiers. The Prince de Conti had the good fortune, despite the bad state of his affairs, to marry his daughter to the Duke de Chartres, grandson of the regent.[75]

After recalling this young couple's initial demonstrations of conjugal excess, Choiseul proceeded: 'However the Duchess de Chartres, become in 1752 the Duchess of Orleans, did not always content herself with the caresses of her husband. She had, like her mother, abundant health and taste for pleasure. To this she added a very spiteful tongue which made her detested by the whole court. The king could not stand her. Her profligacy was public and her husband had the weakness to be jealous. She pushed her effrontery

[74] Kaunitz/Mémoire, pp. 446–9 for the following.
[75] Choiseul, 'Mémoires inédits', loc. cit, and for the following.

so far as to go to try her luck outside her own home', as in a suggestive encounter one evening in the garden of the Palais-Royal with a well set up young Dutchman.

'I have not yet', continued the formidable chronicler, 'said anything of the Dauphin. Such a personage, however, certainly deserves attention.' After describing his early progression from sensuality to religiosity, Choiseul remarked that the Dauphin 'specially detested Voltaire, whom he regarded as the leader of the ungodly and the introducer of many fatal ideas. The Dauphin's opinions frightened sensible people, who foresaw great misfortunes under his reign ... But that is enough said of the court.'

The contemptuous flick of dismissal was all Choiseul. And once again, so far from things being what they might seem in the light age of Madame de Pompadour, the revulsion of the loose-living Count de Stainville against the licentious court may well have brought him closer to her, surpassed now in her original achievement, as just recently by little Morfi, O'Murphy, Murphy. The British ambassador in Paris began a dispatch on 8 May 1754:

Sir, Mlle. Murphy was brought to bed of a Boy last Sunday, at the Castle of Versailles, in an Apartment which Madame de Mailly formerly occupied, and to which Mlle. Murphy was removed, from the little House belonging to the French King, in the Park of Versailles, in which she lived before: it is kept private as yet, and only whispered in Confidence ... Whether this will occasion a Revolution with respect to the *Reigning Favourite,* will be known in a little time. In my own Opinion, His Most Christian Majesty's present liking to Mlle. Murphy is no more than a *fantaisie passagère* that will not hold long.[76]

Lord Albemarle was right. Rumour had it that while the Irish beauty was out of action Louis was bedded down with another, with 'several little bits at the same time'.[77] The royal reputation was running downhill, into the private brothel of the Parc aux Cerfs.

If sex and religion are poles of human existence, their forces then at Versailles fretted into a classic pattern of conflict at court between the king's mistress and his confessor, between the Pompadour and the Jesuits. Such was the religious importance, still, of that order, and such the high influences behind the mounting enmity that was soon, now, to overwhelm it. This most intimate aspect of the French court at that time could have influenced the appointment to Rome of the Count de Stainville at the behest of Madame de Pompadour, liable to profit from his advocacy there. The penetralia of Versailles were indeed to be authoritatively illuminated some five years later by the

---

[76] Earl of Albemarle to Sir Thomas Robinson, Paris, 8 May 1754: P.R.O./S.P.F. 78, France, vol. 249.   [77] D'Argenson, viii. 274.

then Duke de Choiseul writing for papal benefit in the name of Madame de Pompadour herself. This is how he rendered her pathetic little story in her subsequent instructions for a negotiation at Rome for the restitution of sacraments to the king:

At the beginning of 1752 being impelled, by motives which it is unnecessary to explain, to preserve for the King only feelings of gratitude and of attachment of the purest kind, I so informed His Majesty, begging him to have the doctors of the Sorbonne consulted and to write to his confessor for him to consult others in order to find means of leaving me near his person, since he desired it, without being exposed to the suspicion of a weakness which I no longer entertained. The King, knowing my character, perceived that there was no hope of my changing my mind, and lent himself to what I wished. He had the doctors consulted. He wrote to Father Pérusseau, who demanded of him a total separation. The King answered him that he was in no way minded to consent to it; ... that I was necessary to the happiness of his life, to the good of his affairs; that I was the only one who dared to tell him the truth so useful to kings, etc. The good Father hoped at this moment to make himself master of the king's mind, and he ever repeated the same thing. The doctors [of the Sorbonne] gave answers upon which it would have been possible to come to an arrangement if the Jesuit had consented to it. I spoke at this time to people who desired the good of the King and of Religion. I assured them that if Father Pérusseau did not chain the king with the sacraments, he would give himself over to a manner of living which would offend everybody. I did not persuade them and in a little while they saw that I had not been mistaken.[78]

If this suavely elegiac plea could be seasoned with a pinch of salt, yet it was true enough that, apart from the irreducible exception of her reformed self, the mistress and the confessor now shared the same interest against further royal amours. Only, an experienced woman knows well enough that a pliant morality can be the most tactful, and the most efficient. As it was, from now on, the Marquise de Pompadour had only the wan comfort of being proved right, had to accommodate herself as best she might, passively or actively, to royal promiscuity.

The king's old pander, his valet Bachelier, died in May 1754. The previous month had carried off another intimate, the Marquis de Meuse. His cousin Stainville by now had influential friends enough: a week later the Duke de La Vallière was noted by the Marquis d'Argenson with subversive animus as 'one of the favourites of the private apartments; he is stealing what he can ... and is devouring his substance in frivolous luxuries or follies ... Our Luculluses are quickly becoming Catalines.'[79] La Vallière was later to let delicious Champs to Madame de Pompadour in a scrape-round for cash in the

[78] 'Instructions rédigées au nom de Mme de Pompadour et relatives à la négociation entamée en cour de Rome pour vaincre l'opposition des confesseurs qui refusent de laisser approcher Louis XV des sacrements tant qu'il gardera près de lui Mme de Pompadour', 1759: Choiseul, *Mémoires*, appendix V, pp. 376–7.   [79] D'Argenson, viii. 275.

interests, it was then said, of costly building at another property at
Montrouge, where the king supped with him after shooting that
September, shortly before Stainville left for Rome.

It was a time of severance in the aftermath of a winter long and
bitterly cold. That March the Prince de Craon had been taken in the
presence of his son, Stainville's old friend, the Prince de Beauvau.
Ten other children survived together with their mother, the ever
beloved Princess de Craon. Crueller is the cutting off of youth. On 15
June 1754 Madame de Pompadour's only child, her much loved
Alexandrine, turning ten, died, probably of appendicitis. The royal
favourite had lost her surest achievement, was left lonely and exposed:
'Sad news, but not for the public',[80] commented Barbier. Afflicted,
however, was the child's grandfather, François Poisson. He died ten
days later. It was a grim month for Madame de Pompadour.

The king himself had on 22 February 1754 lost a grandson, the
Dauphin's second boy, the months-old Duke of Aquitaine. Counter-
balancing, however, was the birth of the Duke of Berry on 23 August,
the week before parliament returned to the capital where he would be
executed as King Louis XVI.

VIII

A month after the return of the Parliament of Paris the Count de
Stainville was at last to leave for Rome. The timing is suggestive even
though he was not required at present to take up there the all too
delicate issues of French church and state. The French government
probably hoped devoutly that the silence which it had just imposed
at home would extend to the Holy See. In this connection the parting
instructions to Stainville blandly observed: 'There is cause to hope
that the submission will soon be general and invariable; but if,
contrary to all expectation, the enemies of subordination should
attempt to rekindle the flame of discord, the Pope can rely upon His
Majesty to be careful to adopt the measures of prudence and firmness
which he shall judge most appropriate to secure a return to the
bounds of their duty.'[81] As to that, time would show, through
measures which were to involve both the pope and the new
ambassador much more actively than then seemed likely, and were
to bestow upon the embassy of the Count de Stainville to the Roman
backwater a long importance for the ecclesiastical affairs of France.

The initial instructions to a departing ambassador in that age of

---

[80] Barbier, vi. 36.
[81] Mémoire pour servir d'instruction au Sieur Comte de Choiseul-Stainville, Versailles, 22
Sept. 1754: *Receuil des instructions*, xx. 309.

slow communications could importantly lay down guide-lines for his whole mission. Such briefs were drafted with special care and usually, as for Stainville, at considerable length. Looking back to that period of bureaucratic preparation the then Stainville recalled:

Monsieur de Saint-Contest had as his chief clerk a Monsieur de La Chapelle, who was a fool, as lazy as his minister so that the policy of the office was to do nothing. Monsieur Rouillé on arrival took back as clerk the Abbé de la Ville who only knows how to write commonplaces so that the king's political ministry was infinitely less likely to come to harm when it was directed by Monsieur de Saint-Contest, who used to do nothing, than when the minister was Monsieur Rouillé, who did want to do things.[82]

Here again Stainville's judgements were confirmed, less crisply, by others, by the Marquis d'Argenson and the then Abbé de Bernis. It looks as though it was not till the end of 1754 that Rouillé formally squeezed out the 'very mediocre and very lazy'[83] La Chapelle, on two small pensions, to reinstate the much more considerable Abbé de La Ville, an erstwhile Jesuit already noticed as French envoy at the Hague and chief clerk in the foreign ministry. It could well have been, however, that La Ville was already active again in the late summer of 1754, as Stainville implied in his account of his take-off for Rome. As for La Ville's commonplace style, his address on reception into the French Academy in 1747 has been assessed as a piece of discouraging banality.[84]

La Ville, who was in fact to toil on throughout the ministry of Choiseul, could indeed, on style, have had a hand in the helpful opening to his present directive: 'Religion has at all times constituted the basis of empires, the security of sovereigns, the felicity of peoples. The founders of Rome, plunged in the darkness of idolatry, thought that they should invent a system of religion . . .'[85] and on and on, with philosophic and gallican overtones, to the renaissance and the reformation when resistance had developed to wrongful papal pretensions to a jurisdiction which properly 'cannot be extended over the authority which sovereigns derive from God alone and from the form of the government of each nation'. Thus:

There has thus been an endeavour as though in concert in nearly all the states of Europe for nearly the last three hundred years to confine the power of Rome within its just bounds and this has met with perfect success. The court of Rome has lost the influence which it had for several centuries in the general affairs of Europe. It is no

---

[82] Choiseul, *Mémoires*, pp. 95–6.   [83] Bernis, i. 172.

[84] Cf. Camille Piccioni, *Les Premiers Commis des affaires étrangères au XVII et au XVIII siècles* (Paris, 1928), p. 225.

[85] 'Mémoire pour servir d'instruction au Sieur Comte de Choiseul-Stainville', Versailles, 22 Sept. 1754: *Receuil des instructions*, xx. 306–7 for the following.

longer as formerly the centre of the principal negotiations. One no longer sees there a concourse of ministers of the first rank on behalf of the different powers.

If it would be wrong to read that as an almost insulting insinuation against the Count de Stainville, yet the concluding passage had been subtly stiffened as compared with the corresponding one in the model instructions to his nobler predecessor, the Duke de Nivernais. So, too, had the compensating assurance to Nivernais that nevertheless King Louis XV had consistently taken pains to send to Rome 'ministers equally distinguished by their birth, by their dignities and by their talents':[86] become, for Stainville, 'ministers equally recommendable by their birth and by their talents'.[87] Such nuances were rarely lost upon the Count de Stainville, still without the blue ribbon of the Saint-Esprit.

In place, however, of a brief allusion to the value of Nivernais's Italian connections, it was warmly observed in the case of Stainville:

The sagacity of his mind will make him seize all the interesting points of observation. The employment which he will make of the knowledge which he will have acquired in his researches will render them useful to the royal service. He will know how to profit from the talents which he has received from nature in order to render himself agreeable in his place of destination, a very important object for every ambassador of the king and particularly for him whose place of residence is, so to say, the rendezvous of all the nations.

Those were not just standard encomiums; though he might himself have angled this glimpse of his assessment at the court of Louis XV, primarily in terms of his probing industry and his winning personality, a precious combination for any diplomatist. The instructions continued:

Messire the Count de Stainville has too much perspicacity and knowledge not to know the distinctions which it is very important to draw between the church and the court of Rome, between the Pope considered as the common father of the faithful and the Pope considered as a temporal prince having under his domination territories which give him some influence in Italian affairs.

Such was the papal issue, still, of church and state. From the French end the instructions paid respect to the 'liberties of the Gallican Church' and stressed:

His Majesty will never suffer the Court of Rome to form any enterprise which may be contrary to them. This is a point to which the Count de Stainville should pay particular attention ... For the rest the King, while opposing the exaggerated opinions or perchance the unjust pretensions of the ultramontanes, will always

---

[86] 'Mémoire pour servir d'instruction au Sieur Duc de Nivernais', Fontainebleau, 10 Nov. 1748: op. cit., xx. 261.
[87] 'Mémoire pour servir d'instruction au Sieur Comte de Choiseul-Stainville', Versailles, 22 Sept. 1754: op. cit., xx. 307f. for the following.

prevent his subjects from departing from the respect which is due to the Holy See, and His Majesty, in maintaining the salutary practice of ecclesiastical appeals against abuse of authority, will never permit that these appeals should themselves become abuses to the prejudice of the just rights of the Church.

Fear of ultramontane designs still prompted the French government, as yet, to strive to stave off any papal intervention in the Jansenist conflict. In this situation the instructions to Stainville in regard of questions of high policy came disappointingly close to nothing. In his first audience of Benedict XIV 'the Count de Stainville will declare that the King has given him no more express order than to employ his mission to maintain and strengthen more and more the good intelligence which happily subsists between the Holy See and France, and which is in all respects appropriate'.

This left a welter of lesser matters wherewith to pad the long instructions, that question of canonizing Bellarmine, or the appropriate relations to maintain with the Old Pretender and Cardinal York: they should now be prudently infrequent so as not to 'excite the anxiety or at least the complaints of the court of London'. (This represented an appreciable cooling off from Nivernais's instructions of 1748.) Stainville was of course to protect French ecclesiastics in Rome, while keeping a sharp eye out in order to report any personal correspondence or contacts between clergy in France and the Holy See. On the personal side he was also set a task well suited to a Méchant: to prepare a study of all the cardinals and other papal possibles in the light of the fact that 'the great age of the pope does not allow one to hope that he will live as long as one could wish'. Benedict XIV, then in his eightieth year, was a martyr to gout – it suggested to him a characteristic gloss upon psalm 90 as to the strength of octogenarians: 'they cannot avoid being like horses, subject to ailments in the legs.'[88]

Stainville's instructions were rounded off with the usual prescriptions regarding couriers, cyphers, archives, and the prevention of abuse of diplomatic privilege. The massive brief, in substance appreciably pallid and jejune in the image of the foreign minister who issued it, was dismissed by its recipient thus: 'I cultivated the friendship of Monsieur Rouillé and neglected his instructions; and I judged that it would be better to draw upon the information which I should acquire in Rome and upon circumstances in order to afford my minister enlightenment, rather than to expect any from him.'[89]

The written instructions to the Count de Stainville understandably enough did not cover one matter of particular delicacy, arising from

[88] Pope Benedict XIV to Cardinal de Tencin, 27 Mar. 1754: Benoît-Tencin, ii. 329.
[89] Choiseul, Mémoires, p. 96.

yet another death earlier that year. On 30 April 1754 there had died after childbirth the gentle Maria Theresa d'Este, a princess of Modena, grand-daughter of Duke Leopold of Lorraine, mother of the Prince de Lamballe, wife in nearly ten years of happy marriage, devoted and devout, to a prince of the blood from the influential stock of Toulouse, the twentyeight-year-old Louis-Jean-Marie de Bourbon, Duke de Penthièvre, Grand Admiral of France. The bereaved duke was cast into grief and seclusion. He withdrew to an isolated house of his near Fontainebleau. There he ate his meals almost in silence and went nearly every day for long walks and drives alone in the forest, only occasionally permitting the company of some special friend like the Bailli de Froulay. At first he did not even see his three surviving children.

When August came, however, Penthièvre briefly reappeared at court and changed his handsome apartment at Versailles, now too full of memories. In the middle of September 1754 the young widower, trying to forget, left for the south to inspect his naval establishments at Marseilles and Toulon, and then on to Italy, in fact to Rome. There could however have been an inwardness in the journey. It was whispered that the grief-stricken Duke de Penthièvre was actually contemplating a second marriage, one which would require papal dispensation and of which the king did not approve. On the morrow of his bereavement Penthièvre had been assured by Louis XV that he was 'always disposed to be favourable to you in everything that I can ... and to do my best to comfort you in your afflictions'.[90] Now the nuncio informed the pope that the Count de Stainville was specially instructed to make representations against the grant of a dispensation for this mysteriously mooted marriage.

Also in the middle of that September, on Sunday the 15th, the Countess de Stainville preceded her husband in taking formal leave of the court at Versailles. Next day the long instructions drafted for Stainville were read over to Louis XV and approved by him for issue. The ambassador, one week later than his wife, had his farewell audience of the king on 22 September 1754. That was the date given to the general instructions for the embassy of the Count de Stainville and to the accompanying letters wherein Louis now asked each cardinal, his 'cousin', to 'accord entire faith' to the assurances which Stainville was ordered to give him of 'my esteem and affection'.[91]

[90] King Louis XV to Duke de Penthièvre, Versailles, 1 May 1754: Maison Charavay, *Lettres autographes et documents historiques,* no. 758 (Paris, 1976), p. 35.
[91] King Louis XV to Cardinal Imperiali, Versailles, 22 Sept. 1754: 'Papers of Card[nl]. Liugi Gualterio. Letters from various French writers', vol. ii; British Library, Add. MSS. 20,671, fo. 157.

These documents were formally communicated to the ambassador that day, at the equinox. He would not have learnt by then that his departure had suddenly been rendered the more urgent by an event four days earlier in Rome.

Benedict XIV had written to Cardinal de Tencin on 18 September:

La Bruère who, as you know, is at present conducting the affairs of France, has been attacked by smallpox at the age of 38 [*sic*]. He first of all asked for the sacraments which he received with the most exemplary edification. He was in great peril, but he is rather better. He is an amiable man, prudent, of good intelligence, aiming at good and at peace. The whole town has always been and is still fond of him. We are close to the equinox ... P.S. – They tell us this moment that M. La Bruère ... has died this night.[92]

Stainville had lost his Little Man, no longer capable of exercising him over a libretto for Rameau, or of helping to initiate him into diplomatic life in Rome. His own secretary, Boyer de Fonscolombe, was to leave ahead of the ambassador and be his harbinger. For the present there were still last-minute arrangements to be made. On 25 September Stainville picked up some supplementary papers from the foreign ministry. One was a note from Rouillé explaining the annual douceurs which the French government paid secretly to adherents in Rome. The Abbés Rossi and Rota rated 2,000 Roman crowns apiece while 600 went to a Neapolitan prelate, de l'Erma, to compensate him for the fact that his French sympathies had earned him 'enemies who have injured his advancement'.[93] Unmentioned in this note, and upon rather another level, was the time-honoured principle of subsidizing the press, to the tune then of an annual sixteen or seventeen thousand francs to intelligencers in Rome, the Abbé Dari, one Joseph Reffini, and a clerk in the papal secretariat of state. In due course Stainville was to have something to say about these little arrangements.

Another document collected by Stainville that Wednesday was a special memorandum on the disputes over Campo Freddo and San Remo between the republic of Genoa and the Holy Roman Empire. Stainville's main memorandum of instruction had referred generally to French inclination to defend the papal states against aggression, and had added:

The enemy the most to be feared by the popes in this respect is the Emperor of Germany [*sic*] who, especially since the imperial crown has gone to the house of Austria, has never ceased to profit from every opportunity of establishing his authority in all Italy, basing himself upon the ancient titles of sovereignty which the

[92] Pope Benedict XIV to Cardinal de Tencin, 18 Sept. 1754: Benoît-Tencin, ii. 361.
[93] Rouillé to Count de Stainville, Versailles, 25 Sept. 1754: Arch. Aff. Étr. C.P., Rome, vol. 816, fo. 35: *Receuil des instructions*, xx. 325, n. 1.

emperors and the empire once exercised in this part of Europe and even in the very city of Rome. One knows that the maxim of the Germanic body and above all that of the court of Vienna is to think or at least to try to persuade people that the rights of the Empire suffer no prescription, a dangerous maxim which serves even today as the basis or rather the pretext of the vexations which the Republic of Genoa is experiencing from the court of Vienna in regard to the fiefs of Campo Freddo and of San Remo. The protection which the King has generously granted to the Republic of Genoa is a sure guarantee of the particular attention which the King will always devote to everything which could concern the rights of sovereignty of the princes of Italy.[94]

Such was the long stretch from the middle ages of the empire and the papacy, their conflict now in transition towards a modern modification with France supporting Italian resistance to the heavy incidence of Austria in the peninsula. There the Austrian base was still Lombardy. The Count de Stainville was instructed to do anything he could to unravel and neutralize the activities of Count Cristiani, Grand Chancellor of Milan, who had lately 'traversed all the countries of Italy, and laboured to set against France all the princes of this part of Europe by dint of false and artful insinuations.'[95] On the Tuscan side of the Austrian spread in Italy it was prescribed that if Stainville journeyed via Florence he should not take the initiative in calling upon the head of the regency of Tuscany, no other than the Count de Richecourt, the old rival of the Count de Stainville's father, eclipsed there as in the higher reaches of European diplomacy, and in the testimony of his greater son.

The subdued diplomacy of the Marquis de Stainville, however, can now be seen to supply a wry introduction to the contribution of the future Duke de Choiseul towards overpassing centuries of hostility between France and Austria. More broadly again, he was to set the reversal of alliances within the eighteenth-century transition from the age of dynasties in Europe to the era of commerce across the world. Choiseul was to stretch out his statecraft against England to embrace the new continents beyond the oceans. The future, though, expands the past.

The travelling-coach carrying the Count and Countess de Stainville drove out from Paris at the close of September 1754 in the direction which he had mainly favoured, towards the sun and the south, along the road to Lyons, Turin, all the way to Rome, and then on from there maybe to, who knew, what heights. This beneficent and fallible man of exceptional potential in his penetrating relegation of the subordinate in enterprise, in the arts and in the reaches of the heart, now found himself upon his way.

The military and social apprenticeship of the youthful Count de Stainville was at an end. The diplomatic and political career of the future Duke de Choiseul had begun.

ABBREVIATED SOURCES AND AUTHORITIES

Arch. Aff. Étr. C.P.	Archives des Affaires Étrangères, Correspondance Politique. Paris.
Arch. Guerre C.	Archives de la Guerre, Archives Historiques, Correspondance. Paris.
Arch. M-et-M/Vienne	Archives départementales de Meurthe-et-Moselle, Fonds de Vienne. Nancy.
Arch. Meuse	Archives départementales de la Meuse. Bar-le-Duc.
Arch. Nat.	Archives Nationales. Paris.
Arch. Vosges	Archives départementales des Vosges. Épinal.
Arneth	Alfred Ritter von Arneth, *Geschichte Maria Theresia's* (Vienna, 1863–79: vols. i–iii printed as *Maria Theresia's erste Regierungsjahre*). 10 vols.
Barbier	Barbier, *Chronique de la Régence et du règne de Louis XV (1718–1763): ou Journal de Barbier* (Paris, 1857). 8 vols.
Benedetto-Tencin	*Le Lettere di Benedetto XIV al Card. de Tencin.* ed. Emilia Morelli (Rome, 1955f.). 2 vols.
Benoît-Tencin	*Correspondance de Benoît XIV,* ed. Émile de Heeckeren (Paris, 1912). 2 vols.
Bernis	*Mémoires et lettres de François-Joachim de Pierre, Cardinal de Bernis (1715–1758),* ed. Frédéric Masson (Paris, 1878). 2 vols.
Bernstorffske Papirer	Aage Friis, *Bernstorffske Papirer. Udvalgte Breve og Optegnelser vedrørende Familien Bernstorff i Tiden fra 1732 til 1835.* (Copenhagen, 1904–13). 3 vols.
Besenval	*Mémoires de M. le baron de Besenval* (Paris, 1805–6). 4 vols.
B.N., MS. fr.	Bibliothèque Nationale, Manuscrits français. Paris.
Braubach	Max Braubach, *Versailles und Wien von Ludwig XIV bis Kaunitz* (Bonn, 1952).

Broglie/Alliance	Duc de Broglie, *L'Alliance Autrichienne* (Paris, 1895).
Broglie/Fréd-LXV	Duc de Broglie, *Frédéric II et Louis XV* (Paris, 1885). 2 vols.
Broglie/Fréd-MT	Duc de Broglie, *Frédéric II et Marie-Thérèse* (Paris, 1883). 2 vols.
Broglie/Impératrice	Duc de Broglie, *Marie-Thérèse Impératrice* (Paris, 1888). 2 vols.
Broglie/Paix	Duc de Broglie, *La Paix d'Aix-la-Chapelle* (Paris, 1892).
Broglie/Saxe	Duc de Broglie, *Maurice de Saxe et le Marquis d'Argenson* (Paris, 1891). 2 vols.
Campagne	*Campagne de Messieurs les Maréchaux de Broglie et de Belle-Isle en Bohème et en Bavière* [ed. P. F. Du Moulin] (Amsterdam, 1772–3: printed as vols. ii–ix to vol. i, *Campagne de Monsieur le Maréchal de Maillebois en Westphalie l'an MDCCXLI & II*). 9 vols.
Campagne/43	*Campagne de Monsieur le Maréchal Duc de Noailles en Allemagne l'an MDCCXLIII* [ed. P. F. Du Moulin] (Amsterdam, 1760–1). 2 vols.
Carré/Lavisse	H. Carré, *Le Règne de Louis XV (1715–1774)*; part ii of vol. viii of Ernest Lavisse, *Histoire de France depuis les origines jusqu'à la Révolution* (Paris, 1900–11). 9 vols.
Choiseul, *Mémoires*	*Mémoires du duc de Choiseul 1719–1785*, ed. Fernand Calmettes (Paris, 1904).
Choiseul, 'Mémoires de la main'	'Mémoires de la main d'Étienne François de Choiseul-Stainville, Duc de Choiseul. Écrits dans sa retraite de Chanteloup, après son Ministère' (i.e. manuscript of Choiseul, *Mémoires*): Bibliothèque de Versailles, MS. F.850.
Choiseul, 'Mémoires inédits'	'Mémoires inédits du duc de Choiseul.'
D'Argenson	*Journal et mémoires du marquis d'Argenson*, ed. E. J. B. Rathery (Paris, 1859–67). 9 vols.

Droysen

Joh. Gust. Droysen, *Die Geschichte der preussischen Politik* (Leipzig, 1868–86). 5 parts.

Du Deffand/Lescure

Correspondance complète de la marquise du Deffand avec ses amis, ed. de Lescure (Paris, 1865). 2 vols.

Du Deffand/Ste-Aulaire

Correspondance complète de Mme du Deffand avec la duchesse de Choiseul, l'abbé Barthélemy et M. Craufurt, ed. Marquis de Sainte-Aulaire (3rd ed. Paris, 1877). 3 vols.

Erbfolge-Krieg

Oesterreichischer Erbfolge-Krieg 1740–1748 (K. und K. Kriegs-Archivs. Vienna, 1896–1914). 9 vols.

Essai/Arsenal 5808

'Essay sur la vie de M. le duc de Choiseul': Bibliothèque de l'Arsenal, MS. 5808. Paris.

Esteri del Granducato di Toscana

Archivio di Stato di Firenze: Segreteria degli Esteri del Granducato di Toscana. Florence.

Frederick

Œuvres de Frédéric le Grand (Berlin, 1846–57). 30 vols. and catalogue vol.

Gleichen

Baron von Gleichen, *Denkwürdigkeiten des Barons Carl Heinrich von Gleichen* (Leipzig, 1847).

Guerres des Alpes

Les Guerres des Alpes: Guerre de la succession d'Autriche (1742–1748): Mémoire de la correspondance de la cour et des généraux, par F.-E. de Vault, ed. P. Arvers (Paris and Nancy, 1892). 2 vols.

Hénault

Mémoires du Président Hénault, ed. Baron de Vigan (Paris, 1855).

Kaunitz/Koch

Correspondance secrète entre le comte A. W. Kaunitz-Rietberg, ambassadeur impérial à Paris, et le baron Ignaz de Koch, secrétaire de l'impératrice Marie-Thérèse—1750–1752, ed. Hanns Schlitter (Paris, 1899).

Kaunitz/Mémoire

Count Kaunitz-Rietberg, 'Mémoire sur la cour de France' (1752), ed. Vicomte du Dresnay in *La Revue de Paris* (11ième année. Paris, 1904), vol. iv.

ABBREVIATED SOURCES AND AUTHORITIES 1083

Lodge	Sir Richard Lodge, *Studies in Eighteenth-Century Diplomacy 1740–1748* (London, 1930).
Luynes	Duc de Luynes, *Mémoires du duc de Luynes sur la cour de Louis XV*, ed. L. Dussieux and E. Soulié (Paris, 1860–5). 17 vols.
Ö.S/H.H.S.	Österreichisches Staatsarchiv: Haus-, Hof- und Staatsarchiv. Vienna.
Pajol	Comte Pajol, *Les Guerres sous Louis XV.* (Paris, 1881–91). 7 vols.
Politische Correspondenz	*Politische Correspondenz Friedreich's des Grossen*, ed. J. G. Droysen, M. Duncker, H. von Sybel (Berlin, 1879–1925). 1st series. 39 vols.
P.R.O/S.P.F.	Public Record Office; State Papers, Foreign. London.
Recueil des instructions	*Recueil des instructions données aux ambassadeurs et ministres de France depuis les traités de Westphalie jusqu'à la révolution française* (Paris, 1884f.). 29 vols.
Rigsarkiv/T.K.U.A.	Danish State Archives. Rigsarkiv, Tyske Kancelli: Udenrigsministeriet Arkiv. Copenhagen.
Rousset	Camille Rousset, *Correspondance de Louis XV et du maréchal de Noailles* (Paris, 1865). 2 vols.
Sautai/Débuts	Maurice Sautai, *Les Débuts de la Guerre de la Succession d'Autriche* (Paris, 1909).
Sautai/Préliminaires	Maurice Sautai, *Les Préliminaires de la Guerre de la Succession d'Autriche* (Paris, 1907).
Vitzthum/Saxe	Comte C.-F. Vitzthum d'Eckstaedt, *Maurice Comte de Saxe et Marie-Josèphe de Saxe, Dauphine de France* (Leipzig, 1867).
Walpole Correspondence	*The Yale Edition of Horace Walpole's Correspondence*, ed. W. S. Lewis (London, 1937f.). 39 vols.
W.N.A.	White Notley Archives. White Notley Hall, Essex.

Yale/Beinecke: Phillipps/Graffigny 23900   Yale University Library (Beinecke Rare Book and Manuscript Library), former collection of Sir Thomas Phillipps/Graffigny 23900.

Zévort   Edgar Zévort, *Le marquis d'Argenson et le Ministère des Affaires Étrangères du 18 novembre 1744 au 10 janvier 1747* (Paris, 1880).

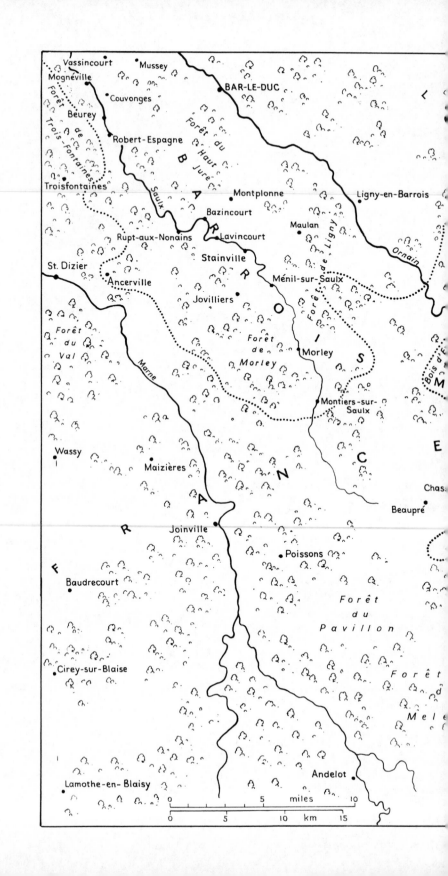

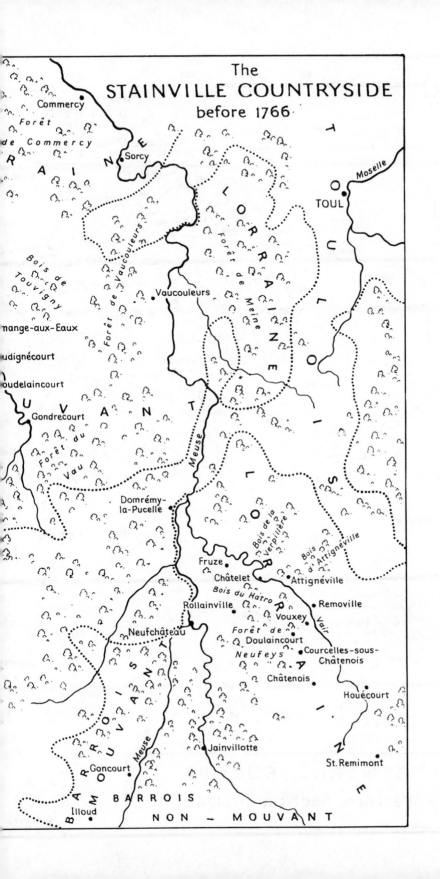

The
STAINVILLE COUNTRYSIDE
before 1766

Commercy

Forêt
de Commercy

Sorcy

LORRAINE

Moselle

TOUL

Bois de
Touvigny

Forêt de Vaucouleurs

Forêt de Meine

mange-aux-Eaux

udignécourt

oudelaincourt

Vaucouleurs

TOULOIS

Gondrecourt

VAUVANT

Forêt du Vau

Meuse

Domrémy-
la-Pucelle

LOR

Bois de la
Verpillière

Bois d'Attignéville

Fruze

Châtelet

Attignéville

Bois du Hatro

Rollainville

Vouxey

Removille

Neufchâteau

Forêt de
Doulaincourt

Neufeys

Courcelles-sous-
Châtenois

Vair

Châtenois

RAIZE

Houécourt

BARROUVISANT

Meuse

Jainvillotte

St. Remimont

Goncourt

BARROIS

Illoud

NON — MOUVANT

CENTRAL EUROPE

Western Section in 1740

CENTRAL EUROPE
Eastern Section after 1742

P O L A N D

•Lissa

L

Upper
Lusatia

P
R
U
S
S
I
A

•Wohlau

Liegnitz
×

Breslau•

Oder

S I L E

Brieg

S
I
A

N Y

× Hohenfriedberg

Mollwitz
××

Neisse

Oppeln•

rna

itz

A

Leitmeritz

Budin•

Sudeten

N

Soor
×

Mtns.

Glatz

Neisse•

Klein Schnell-
endorf•

AUST. SILESIA

Jägerndorf•

Brandeis•

Elbe

Prelauc•

Chotusitz
××

Troppau•

akonitz

Prague•
•Tachlowitz

Czaslau

Chrudim

•Beraun

Zebrak•

E

I

•Moldau

M I A

•Beneschau

R

Goltzjenikau•

•Deutsch Brod

A

Olmütz•

E

M O R A V I A

•Tabor

Iglau•

Brünn•

Pisek•

konitz

Protiwin•

Sahay ×
•

Budweis•

•Wesely

•Neuhaus

Frauenberg•

Znaim•

H
U
N
G
A
R
Y

A R C H D U C H Y

Stockerau•

Danube

O F

Vienna•

Pressburg•

SSAU

Linz•

St. Polten•

auth

USTRIA

A U S T R I A

AUSTRIA

Enns

LOWER

R

0   50   miles   100

0   50   100   150 km

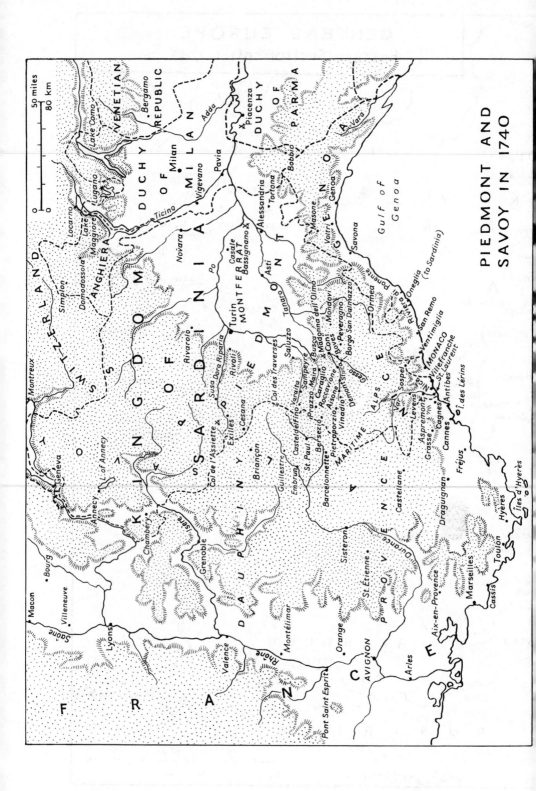

PIEDMONT AND SAVOY IN 1740

INDEX